Lecture Notes of the Institute for Computer Sciences, Social Informatics and Telecommunications Engineering   328

More information about this series at http://www.springer.com/series/8197

Anthony Brooks · Eva Irene Brooks (Eds.)

Interactivity, Game Creation, Design, Learning, and Innovation

8th EAI International Conference, ArtsIT 2019
and 4th EAI International Conference, DLI 2019
Aalborg, Denmark, November 6–8, 2019
Proceedings

 Springer

Editors
Anthony Brooks (iD)
Department of Architecture, Design
and Media Technology
Aalborg University
Aalborg, Denmark

Eva Irene Brooks (iD)
Department of Culture and Learning
Aalborg University
Aalborg, Denmark

ISSN 1867-8211   ISSN 1867-822X (electronic)
Lecture Notes of the Institute for Computer Sciences, Social Informatics
and Telecommunications Engineering
ISBN 978-3-030-53293-2   ISBN 978-3-030-53294-9 (eBook)
https://doi.org/10.1007/978-3-030-53294-9

This Springer imprint is published by the registered company Springer Nature Switzerland AG
The registered company address is: Gewerbestrasse 11, 6330 Cham, Switzerland

Preface

We are delighted to introduce the proceedings of the 8th European Alliance for Innovation (EAI) International Conference on Arts and Technology, Interactivity, and Game Creation (ArtsIT 2019) and the 4th International Conference on Design, Learning and Innovation (DLI 2019), held in Aalborg, Denmark, November 6–8, 2019.

ArtsIT 2019 was meant to be a place where people in the arts, with a keen interest in modern IT technologies, meet with people in IT, having strong ties to the arts in their works. Since 2009, the event has become a leading scientific forum for dissemination of cutting-edge research results in the area of arts, design, and technology. The event also reflects the advances seen in the open related topics of interactivity (interaction design, virtual reality, augmented reality, robotics, etc.) and game creation (serious games, gamification, leisure gaming, gameplay, etc.).

ArtsIT has been successfully co-located with the international conference DLI since 2016.

Design, learning, and innovation frame the world of IT, opening doors into an increasingly playful world. The DLI 2019 conference was driven by the belief that tools, technologies, and environments, as well as content and approaches, can spark and nurture a passion for learning, transforming domains such as education, rehabilitation/therapy, work places, and cultural institutions. Design, learning, and innovation are a powerful catalyst in empowering individuals to participate, communicate, and create, whereby they can exceed their own limits in a playful way. Making this spirit explicit and visible is crucial for identifying how specific tools, technologies, methodologies, and solutions shape opportunities for learning and engaging with the demands of today's world. More than ever, challenges in the fields of design, learning, and innovation are often approached by transdisciplinary teams and solutions that mobilize tools, technologies, methods, and theories from different fields to unlock new frameworks, opening up to partnerships that can enrich learning in formal and informal learning practices. DLI 2019 intended to foster such dynamics.

The venue for the ArtsIT and DLI events was the city campus of Aalborg University (AAU) in Aalborg, in the region North Jutland of mainland Denmark. AAU is a Danish public university that was founded in 1974 that currently has campuses in the cities of Aalborg, Esbjerg, and Copenhagen. The Aalborg campus has distributed faculty buildings throughout the city as well as around the peripheral of the city boundaries. Aalborg is Denmark's fourth largest city by population size. The university awards bachelor degrees, master degrees, and PhD degrees in a wide variety of subjects within humanities, social sciences, information technology, design, engineering, exact sciences, and medicine. Aalborg University differentiates itself from the older and more traditional Danish universities with its focus on interdisciplinary, interfaculty studies; an experimental curriculum based on an interdisciplinary, basic courses with subsequent specialisation; and a pedagogical structure based on problem-centered, real-life projects of educational and research relevance – which internationally has become known and recognised as The Aalborg Model. With the problem-based, project-organised model, semesters at AAU are centred around complex real-life problems which students attempt to find answers to in a scientific manner while working together in groups. In February 2007, the foundation of the UICEE Centre for Problem-Based Learning (UCPBL) paid recognition to Aalborg University, which subsequently led to the appointment of AAU as UNESCO Chair in problem-based learning. Aalborg University is a member of the European Consortium of Innovative Universities (ECIU), which was founded in 1997 by 10 European universities. The other 9 European universities are: Dublin City University, Ireland; Linköping University, Sweden; Aveiro University, Portugal; Autonomous University of Barcelona, Spain; Hamburg University of Technology, Germany; University of Stavanger, Norway; Kaunas University of Technology, Lithuania; Tampere University of Technology, Finland; and University of Twente, The Netherlands. The aim of the ECIU is to create a European network where participating universities can exchange experiences and practices in projects in education, research, and regional development. In 2010, the ECIU consisted of 11 members and 3 foreign affiliates.

Personnel behind bringing ArtsIT and DLI to AAU are employed under Aalborg University's Department of Architecture, Design and Media Technology and the Department of Culture and Learning. Further national and international research collaborations by these personnel is within Xlab, a research complex investigating learning, creativity, play, and digital technologies, under the Department of Culture and Learning at AAU's main campus in Aalborg. Xlab hosts workshops with regional pre-schools, schools, and institutes that are led by the in-lab team. Xlab is also active in many international research consortia projects.

This is stated at the closure of this text as notably, at both ArtsIT and DLI 2019 events, many meetings were hosted discussing with attending delegates on potential research project collaborations with Xlab. Contact with Xlab to discuss potential projects is through Professor Eva Brooks, Director, Xlab: Design, Learning, Innovation, Department of Culture and Learning, Aalborg University, Denmark.

We take this opportunity to thank all involved in realising the two events and likewise to congratulate best paper winners from both ArtsIT (Thomas Westin, Henrik Engström, and Jenny Brusk for their paper titled "Towards sustainable inclusive game design processes") and DLI (Emil Rosenlund Høeg, Christian Francis Reeves Scully, Jon Ram Bruun-Pedersen, and Stefania Serafin for their paper titled "The Reality of Implementing Virtual Reality: A case study on the challenges of integrating VR-based rehabilitation"). We are especially grateful to our four eminent luminary keynote speakers, namely Ernest Edmonds and Linda Candy for the ArtsIT event, and Willian Gaver and Thomas Hillman for the DLI event.

Acknowledgements are due to Aalborg University management who hosted the joint conference at the city campus and to the opening speakers who welcomed delegates to Aalborg and the university, namely Claus Brøndgaard Madsen who kindly welcomed on behalf of the Department of Architecture, Design and Media Technology, and Anja Overgaard Thomassen who kindly welcomed on behalf of the Department of Culture and Learning.

Alongside management acknowledgements, special thanks are due to all volunteers and locally employed personnel who kept things on track, ensured all was set up for welcoming the delegates, and others who were intermediators between services and delivery to delegates e.g. in-venue caterers for breaks and lunches, AAU IT service personnel, and host venue service staff (to name just a few). We also herein acknowledge all committee members and reviewers, without whom academic scientific conferences cannot take place. Similarly, we are thankful to the sponsors of the event, especially the Danish Music Union who supported the gala dinner musicians, namely the Olav Gudnason duo. Thanks also to the staff and leadership of Mortens Kro restaurant where the most fantastic conference dinner was enjoyed by all. Final thanks goes to all who exhibited at the events, including Noldus, ATV, and INGA (International Green Agents), as well as Springer and O'Reilly publications who both sponsored the best paper prizes.

Finally, from our roles as chairs and steering leaders of the two events over the years, we posit that once again it was a pleasure to welcome delegates from around the world to ArtsIT and DLI. Special edition ArtsIT and DLI international journals are

currently being formulated where 2019 delegates and others are invited to submit extended papers.

Thanks to all – and we hope to see you in 2020!

June 2020   Anthony Brooks
                                                                    Eva Brooks

Organization

Steering Committee (*ArtsIT ** DLI)

Imrich Chlamtac (President)   European Alliance for Innovation
*Anthony Brooks   Aalborg University, Denmark
**Eva Brooks   Aalborg University, Denmark

Organizing Committee

General Chairs

*Anthony Brooks   Aalborg University, Denmark
**Eva Brooks   Aalborg University, Denmark

General Co-chairs

*Anthony Brooks   Aalborg University, Denmark
**Eva Brooks   Aalborg University, Denmark

TPC Chairs and Co-chair

*Ido Iurgel   Rhine-Waal University of Applied Sciences, Germany
*Fotis Liarokapis   Masaryk University, Czech Republic
**Cristina Sylla   University of Minho, Portugal
**Anders Kalsgaard Møller   Aalborg University, Denmark

Technical Programme Committee Members

*Brendan Allison   University of California, San Diego, USA
*Zainab AlMeraj   Kuwait University, Kuwait
** Lucia Amante   Open University, Portugal
*Atakan Akçali   Rhine-Waal University of Applied Sciences, Germany
*Anastasia Analyti   Foundation for Research and Technology - Hellas (FORTH), Greece
*António Araújo   Aberta University, Portugal
*Heitor Avelos   Universidade do Porto, Portugal
*Marcos Azevedo   Wildlife Studios, Brazil
*René Bakker   HAN University of Applied Sciences, The Netherlands
*Brian Bemman   Aalborg University, Denmark
** Marie Bengtsson   Harplinge and Steninge Schools and Preschools, Halmstad Municipality, Sweden
*José Bidarra   Aberta University, Portugal
*Christos Bouras   Computer Technology Institute, Greece
*Alma Boyes   University Brighton, UK
** Lykke Bertel Brogaard   Aalborg University, Denmark

*Emil Rosenlund Høeg	Aalborg University Copenhagen, Denmark
*Tobias Isenberg	Université Paris-Sud, France
*Ido Iurgel	Rhine-Waal University of Applied Sciences, Germany
*Antoni Jaume-i-Capó	Universitat de les Illes Balears, Spain
** Marco Javier	University of Zaragoza, Spain
*Walther Jensen	Aalborg University, Denmark
*Michail Kalogiannakis	University of Crete, Greece
*Juliet King	George Washington University, USA
** Susanne Kjällander	Stockholm University, Sweden
*Silvia Kober	University of Graz, Austria
*Lise Busk Kofoed	Aalborg University Copenhagen, Denmark
*Martin Kraus	Aalborg University, Denmark
*Andre Frank Krause	Rhine-Waal University of Applied Sciences, Germany
*Mel Krokos	University of Portsmouth, UK
*Ben Kybartas	Delft University of Technology, The Netherlands
*Hartmut Könitz	HKU University of the Arts Utrecht, The Netherlands
*Thomas Laubach	Rhine-Waal University of Applied Sciences, Germany
*Melanie Lenz	V&A Museum, UK
*Fotis Liarokapis	Masaryk University, Czech Republic
** Jesper Lund	Halmstad University, Sweden
*Markus Löchtefeld	Aalborg University, Denmark
*Penousal Machado	University of Coimbra, Portugal
*Kristina Madsen	Aalborg University, Denmark
*Leif Marcusson	Linneaus University, Sweden
*Gabriel Mendes	Universidade Federal de São Carlos (UFSCar), Brazil
*Max Mignotte	Montreal University, Canada
*Roderick Mills	Brighton University, UK
*Leonel Morgado	Universidade Aberta, Portugal
*Natalie Mrachacz-Kersting	Aalborg University, Denmark
** Anders Kalsgaard Møller	Aalborg University, Denmark
** Chrystalla Neophytou	Open University, Cyprus
*Vania Neris	Universidade Federal de São Carlos (UFSCar), Brazil
*Grant Norte	The University of Toledo, USA
*Dan Overholt	Aalborg University Copenhagen, Denmark
*Melike Ozmen	İstanbul Bilgi Üniversitesi, Turkey
*Mark Palmer	University of the West of England (UWE), UK
*Courtnie Paschall	University of Washington Seattle, USA
*Rich Picking	Wrexham Glyndwr University, UK
*Mannes Poel	University of Twente, The Netherlands
** Cristina Ponte	Universidade Nova Lisboa, Portugal
*Sofia Ponte	Universidade do Porto, Portugal
*Mirjana Prpa	Simon Fraser University, Canada
*Chris Raftery	Colorado State University, USA
*Shivakeshavan Ratnadurai-Giridharan	Cornell University, USA
*Kamila Rios	Universidade Federal de São Carlos (UFSCar), Brazil

*Kasper Rodil   Aalborg University, Denmark
** Teresa Romão   Universidade Nova de Lisboa, Portugal
*Joacim Rosenlund   Linnaeus University, Sweden
*Jens Schwalenberg   Rhine-Wall University of Applied Sciences, Germany
*Stefania Serafin   Aalborg University Copenhagen, Denmark
**Digdem Sezen   Istanbul University, Turkey
*Tonguc Sezen   Rhine-Waal University of Applied Sciences, Germany
*Dongjoe Shin   University of Portsmouth, UK
*Filip Škola   Masaryk University, Czech Republic
** Jeanette Sjöberg   Halmstad University, Sweden
** Filomena Soares   University of Minho, Portugal
** Elsebeth Wejse   Aalborg University, Denmark
  Korsgaard Sorensen
*Paula Souza   Universidade Federal de São Carlos (UFSCar), Brazil
*Christoph Stange   Pädagogische Hochschule Weingarten, Germany
*Ertugrul Sungu   İstanbul Bilgi Üniversitesi, Turkey
*Michael Sutton   Bill and Vieve Gore School of Business, USA
** Cristina Sylla   University of Minho, Portugal
*Vítor Sá   Universidade Católica Portuguesa, Portugal
*Justyna Świdrak   Institute of Psychology Polish Academy of Sciences,
                                  Poland
*Mirian Tavares   CIAC, University of Algarve, Portugal
*Luis Teixeira   PDMFC, Portugal
** Evgenia Vassilakaki   Technological Educational Institute of Athens, Greece
*Maria Vayanou   University of Athens, Greece
*Nikolas Vidakis   Technological Educational Institution of Crete, Greece
** Guenter Wallner   University of Applied Arts, Austria
*Thomas Westin   Stockholm University, Sweden
*Brian Wyvill   University of Victoria, Canada
*Matthew Yee-King   Goldsmiths University London, UK
*Nelson Zagalo   University of Aveiro, Portugal
** Pär-Ola Zander   Aalborg University, Denmark
*Frank Zimmer   Rhine-Waal University of Applied Sciences, Germany

Sponsorship and Exhibit Chair

Anthony Brooks   Aalborg University, Denmark

Local Chairs

*Anthony Brooks   Aalborg University, Denmark
**Eva Brooks   Aalborg University, Denmark

Special Tracks/Workshops Chairs

*Miralem Helmefalk	Linnaeus University, Sweden
*Anton Nijholt	University Twente, The Netherlands
*Thomas Westin	Stockholm University, Sweden

Publicity and Social Media Chairs

Joao Martinho Moura	Polytechnic Institute of Cávado e Ave, UCP, Portugal
Eva Brooks	Aalborg University, Denmark

Publications Chairs

*Anthony Brooks	Aalborg University, Denmark
**Eva Brooks	Aalborg University, Denmark

Web Chair

Joao Martinho Moura	Polytechnic Institute of Cávado e Ave, UCP, Portugal

Posters Chairs

*Anthony Brooks	Aalborg University, Denmark
**Alejandro Catala	Universidade de Santiago de Comostela, CiTIUS, Spain

Panels Chairs

*Anthony Brooks	Aalborg University, Denmark
**Eva Brooks	Aalborg University, Denmark

Demos Chairs

*Anthony Brooks	Aalborg University, Denmark
**Jeanette Sjöberg	Halmstad University, Sweden

EAI Events Management

Kristina Lappyova	European Alliance for Innovation
Katarina Srnanova	European Alliance for Innovation

Contents

Games, Gamification and Accessible Games

Learning Designs and Participation Through Digital Technologies

Innovation, Inclusion and Emerging Technologies

Short Paper

Keynote Chapters

Art and Code: Programming as a Medium

Ernest Edmonds[✉]

IOCT, De Montfort University, Leicester, UK
ernest@ernestedmonds.com
http://www.ernestedmonds.com

Abstract. Computer programming is more than a tool for the artist. Writing code is manipulating a medium: a medium that is like no other. This chapter discusses the importance of coding and shows how it is enabling principled investigations into inventing new forms, creating new experiences and extending the nature of engagement with art works. It shows how formal ways of making art, from perspective to the 20th century use of systems, geometry and mathematics, have pointed to the value of programming. This is a direction that has defined the work of a range of artists. The chapter discusses the use of the medium of code by artists who talked about their art making process. They include pioneers Aaron Marcus, Harold Cohen and Manfred Mohr and other artists, some of whom are live coding practitioners.

1 Introduction

Over the past 50 years more and more artists have been writing computer code as part of their practice in making artworks. To start with many of those were plotter drawings and other static work are common to this day. However, time-based, interactive and multi-media works are also frequently made. At the core of all of these works is the code and, in a significant subset of these cases, the artist writes the code themselves. It is that subset that this chapter is concerned with.

A computer program is a symbolic representation of a set of instructions that can be executed by a computer. Sometimes the term "program" is used for the strictly executable (compiled) form of the instructions but often it is also used for the symbolic form of them that the human programmer composes. In this chapter the term "code" will be used to refer to a program in the second sense.

Whist, at its heart, code is always a set of instructions there are many variations both in appearance and substance. Traditional code is normally seen in text strings, often with many brackets and characters such as ";". Not infrequently, however, it has a graphical representation with blocks of various kinds linked together. In terms of substance, the biggest issue to be aware of is interaction. Does the code need to, or can it, interact with the world in some way in order to complete its task? Most of the systems that we use today are probably interactive at least in a basic way. Even enclosed recognition systems (e.g. number plate or face recognition) have often had a very interactive phase of use during what is termed "training", when examples of what should be recognised are presented to the system.

© ICST Institute for Computer Sciences, Social Informatics and Telecommunications Engineering 2020
Published by Springer Nature Switzerland AG 2020. All Rights Reserved
A. Brooks and E. I. Brooks (Eds.): ArtsIT 2019/DLI 2019, LNICST 328, pp. 3–12, 2020.
https://doi.org/10.1007/978-3-030-53294-9_1

Artists use all of these variations of appearance and substance. In what follows, the implications of the different forms of coding for art practice will be discussed, drawing largely from the words of artists.

In writing computer code, many artists have gone far beyond the use of code as a tool used to implement some pre-formed concept. The use of code has often led to the development of new ideas, new forms and new ways of working. The ways that this has happened will be discussed in part by drawing upon a set of conversations with artists conducted by the author and published in a recent book (Boden and Edmonds 2019).

2 The Logic of Art

There is nothing new about using a formal system, like computer code, in art making. Mathematics, geometry and various formal systems have a long tradition in art. A powerful history of the use of geometry in the Islamic tradition goes back to the 9th Century and has evolved as a central theme ever since (Abdullahi and Embi 2013). In Western art, one of the most used systems has been perspective, which has so pervaded figurative art until recently that the formal, geometric, underpinning that it gives to paintings is not always recognized. When looking at a Canaletto, how many people first think about geometry? Geometry, however, must have been in the front of the painter's mind as he began to paint. For another example, consider the golden mean[1], which many school children must learn about in their art classes.

An explicit concern for systems, in a more general sense, has been advocated by, for example, Paul Cézanne, who reportedly said that:

"The technique of any art consists of a language and a logic" (Doran 2001: 17)

Then, in 1919, Kazimir Malevich wrote about

"Making art with the help of a law for the constructional inter-relationships of form." (Anderson 1968)

In relation directly to mathematics, Max Bill famously claimed that

"... it is possible to evolve a new form of art in which the artist's work could be founded to quite a substantial degree on a mathematical line of approach..." (Bill 1949)

Using procedures, sets of instructions, to make art was also fundamental to some conceptual art and, certainly to the work of Sol Lewitt:

"In conceptual art the idea of concepts is the most important aspect of the work ... (t)he idea becomes a machine that makes the art." (LeWitt 1967)

---

[1] The golden mean is when the ratio of two lengths is the same as the ratio of their sum to the larger of the two. This is frequently used in art in making an effective composition.

This line of thought, and Max Bill in particular, strongly influenced the UK artists known as the Systems Group. In his introduction to the *Systems* exhibition, which featured their work, Stephen Bann makes a point that is particularly relevant. He posed the question of what had attracted these artists to the tradition of Constructivism, and answered that the appeal:

"... without any doubt, is the attraction of systematic procedures based on an order *which is not necessarily apparent in the final work.*" (Bann 1972)

The phrase "systematic procedures based on an order" clearly refers to the kind of mathematics that underpins the concept of computer code. Hence it is no surprise that this development in art indirectly, and in no small part directly, led to artists writing code. In practice, the artists in the Systems Group not only used mathematics but often saw potential in the computer. In particular, Malcolm Hughes obtained one for the postgraduate course that he ran at the Slade in London. Many of the earlier British artists who write code were introduced to the medium on that course. The Systems Group's work has a direct link with the development of code as a medium in the UK (Edmonds 2014).

In many ways, the use of code as a medium can be seen as a development within the Constructivist tradition. For the origins of that tradition see, for example, Lodder (1983).

3 Constructivism

"Constructivism" is used in various different fields, for example, in psychology, mathematics and art. The different meanings are related, but should not be confused. In psychology the term refers to the idea that internal hypotheses are used as part of the perceptual process, so that the objects that we perceive are constructed as part of that perception process. In mathematics, the term refers to the position that a mathematical entity can only be proven to exist by the provision of a procedure for generating, constructing, it. In art, the constructivist tradition is concerned with art where the process of constructing it dominates over the composition of the final work.

Mathematical constructivism is closely connected to the fundamental notions of computation and, ultimately, to computer science: a story beyond the scope of this chapter, but see Troelstra for example (Troelstra 2011). It might be argued that we have computer code as a result of the development of the underpinning mathematical concepts of constructivism. As those concepts are concerned with procedures for generating things they have at least a metaphorical relationship with constructivism in art and they developed in both subjects in approximately the same historical period.

In the art world the Constructivist tradition, as mentioned above, has moved into the realm of the computer, making art by writing code. The widely used term for much of this work is "Generative Art". See the collection of papers edited by Paul Brown (Brown 2003). Basically, the term Generative Art is used for art in which a computer program generates the art object, normally a drawing in the early days, but now frequently a time-based sequence.

Generative Art uses formal systems embedded in computer code in the general area of the constructivist tradition. The conversations with artists writing code published in the book referred to above (Boden and Edmonds 2019) form the basis of the discussion in the next section.

4   Generative Art and Computer Code

As reported in the book's introduction, for the artists with whom conversations were held,

"The computer code is significant in several ways. For at least one of them, the code is the art. For several, writing it is a vital part of the thinking process. They would never make the kind of art that they do without going through the thinking process required by programming. For them, software is a way of both making art and thinking about art. One of the artists puts a significant amount of effort into constructing the technology that is used in making the art. At least two others even find the need to make their own software tools." (Boden and Edmonds 2019: 17–18)

The differences over generations, however, cannot be ignored:

"The older, pioneer, artists discovered computers and programming when already into their career and, for various reasons, became engaged in ways that extended or changed their artistic practice. At the other extreme, younger artists report having used computers, including programming them, before they dreamed of becoming artists. For them, the computer did not change their art, because it was always there." (Boden and Edmonds 2019: 17)

Fundamental to all of these artists is the fact that the core activity of manipulating code, writing programs, is an integrated part of their creative processes. They do not use software as a tool, where they simply implement a fully defined function in code. If that was the case they could easily farm that work out to a programmer. However, the shaping of the code is mostly integral to the creative process. The code is not a tool, but a medium that is manipulated to make the art.

Consider what some of the artists said about their use of code. To see something of the changes that have taken place, the following starts with some of the pioneers.

By the early 1970s, Aaron Marcus found that he was liberated simply by the speed with which a computer could perform what were essentially repetitive tasks.

"… I could think about creating little things and repeating them, and it might tempt me to think, what other little things could I create and repeat and play with in a way that might have occurred to me. Think about the sheer effort of producing these marks, even to make one of them. I thought… it's good that I have this device to let me envision and try things quickly and then decide… Seeing works in progress … would give me insights into effects, into processes, into forms that I might not otherwise have had time or the ability to explore." (Boden and Edmonds, 2019: 277)

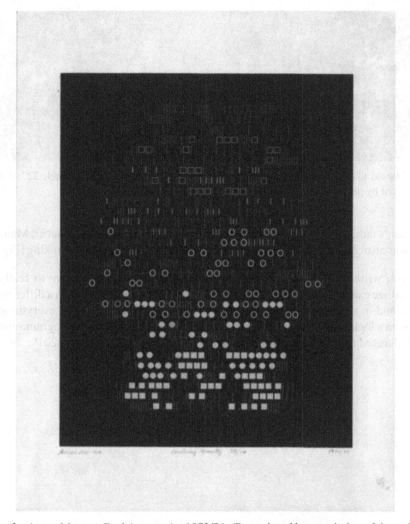

Fig. 1. Aaron Marcus. *Evolving gravity* 1972/74. (Reproduced by permission of the artist)

Even this simple advantage led him to new ideas and to make work that he otherwise would not have conceived of (Fig. 1).

Around the same time the late Harold Cohen was starting his work on his very long quest to code his program to make art, co-incidentally called Aaron. His initial motivation is itself interesting (Fig. 2).

"... it was because, after twenty years of painting, I thought I didn't know anything more about image making than I had when I started... at that time I thought I saw in computing a way of learning something much more objectively about images and how one goes about making them."(Boden and Edmonds 2019: 284)

Fig. 2. Harold Cohen, *coming home #2*, 2007, permanent pigment ink on panel, 22" × 66". (Reproduced by permission of the Harold Cohen trust)

Cohen's motive, then, was to help him think about his art. Another pioneer, Manfred Mohr, was also clear about how coding clarified, or inspired, his creative thinking (Fig. 3).

"If you write a program, you have to order your thoughts, you have to really crystallize exactly what you want to do. You suddenly see everything in a different light, and in a sense, my whole world turned upside down… I look at everything through a logical eye—my mind-set has changed. It is the process of programming that changed my mind, not the program itself." (Boden and Edmonds 2019: 295)

Fig. 3. Manfred Mohr. P155c, 1974, plotter drawing. 60 × 60 cm. (Reproduced by permission of the artist. Photograph Winfried Reinhardt, Pforzheim, Germany)

The artist, Julie Freeman, sees understanding the computer and code as a vital part of her practice (Fig. 4).

"I think it's essential. Because I don't believe that you can work with any material as an artist if you don't know that material inside out, or if you don't want to explore it inside out. So even if you're working with paint or clay or anything, you need to fully understand what you can do with that material. So to be able to use computers, I think, is pretty essential for my own work… You need to understand the set of instructions being carried out to be able to disrupt them." (Boden and Edmonds 2019: 323)

Fig. 4. Julie Freeman. *A selfless society*, 2016. Online animation with sound. JavaScript with HTML5 Canvas, real-time data from a colony of naked mole-rats. variable size. (Reproduced by permission of the artist)

An interesting more recent development has been live-coding in music, where the performer modifies or creates the code that generates the music during a performance as a form of improvisation. Live-coder Andrew Brown points out that different programming languages offer different styles that may or may not match the creative process (Fig. 5).

"… the differences between different programming paradigms. You think differently in those ways. For example, in the last few years I've been programming in LISP, which as you know has a particular way of structuring the world. There seems to be a really nice fit between the way it is organized and the way in which my musical ideas are organized. So that seems to fit well. (Boden and Edmonds 2019: 345)

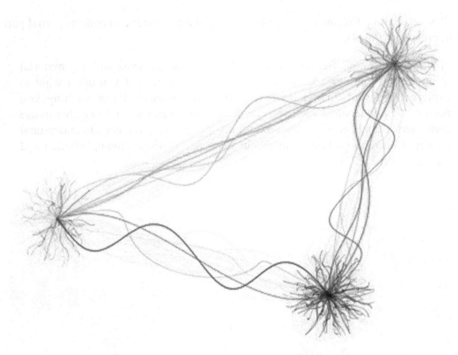

Fig. 5. Andrew Brown. Connections. 2013. Developed in the impromptu environment and exhibited as part of the [d]Generate exhibition of digital generative art at the Gympie regional gallery. (Reproduced by permission of the artist)

Another live-coder, Alex McLean, goes further when he talks about the role of coding in his work (Fig. 6).

"It's the way of thinking about it. Code is the most suitable way of thinking about music …" (Boden and Edmonds 2019: 363)

The drift over time has been from the discipline of coding enhancing concept and physical form to the coding process itself being the creation of the art, both mentally and physically. Whilst the early uses of code could perhaps be thought of as tool use, these more recent developments must be seen as using code as a medium. The nature of the programming environment can be quite significant in this context. Whilst compiled languages were fine for many of the early artist coders, they are not appropriate for live-coding or, often, for other creative practices.

"One of the most attractive aspects of (some) language systems … is that a program can be changed as it is running, so that the programmer can obtain immediate feedback as they try out different ideas. Of-course, in classical approaches to programming this facility is frowned upon, taking the position that everything should be determined before a program is written. However, in creative uses of software there is often an intimate intertwining of designing the program and seeing the implications of a design decision." (Boden and Edmonds 2019: 220)

Fig. 6. Alex McLean performing at Algorave Karlsruhe, 2015. (Photograph by Rodrigo Velasco)

This is one of the observations that the current author has made in relation to his own practice and that are elaborated in, for example, Chapter 10 of the Boden/Edmonds book.

5 Discussion

This chapter has shown how significant the act of coding is to the creative process. Code is a relatively new medium for artists and has had a profound influence on both the practice of art and the art forms that have been produced. However, more remains to be discovered about the nature of coding in relation to the creative process and the full implications of what can be done with it. Certain ideas are proposed below that are based on the conversations referred to here and the personal experience of the author in coding as part of his art practice.

The most obvious, but critical, point is that the computer executes the code both very quickly and with great accuracy. This means that, by specifying a work in code, it can be realized at a speed not available to artists previously. On the one hand, this implies that many more interactions and evaluations of an idea are possible and, on the other, repetitive, time-based and interactive works can be produced in completely new ways. These were the dominant attributes of coding that drew many of the early artist adopters. From the start, however, there were others who were most interested in how coding could enhance the artist's thinking.

The discipline of programming requires clarity of intention to a degree that artists rarely start with. Making decisions about the code makes the artists face the need for clarity just as much as placing a paint mark on canvas does. As discussed above, that clarity is at least as much to do with the underlying structures of the work as with its final form. This is why Harold Cohen found coding helpful as he tried to understand better what his image making was all about: "… how one goes about making them".

This clarity is something that programmers deal with in all domains, but in creative activities – and particularly in the arts – the iterative formulation of intentions is often integral to the creative process. Much of that process can be spent in clarifying what problems are to be solved and in finding the intentions. This is particularly interesting when it comes to coding. Where this is the case, the artist is developing their ideas about the work during the coding process itself. Quoting Alex McLean:

"This isn't about having an idea, then implementing it, it's more just starting programming, hearing the results and then working with the program to sort of mould it." (Boden and Edmonds 2019; 358)

We might say that the artist moulds the material of code rather as the potter moulds the material of clay.

References

Abdullahi, Y., Embi, M.R.B.: Evolution of islamic geometric patterns. Front. Archit. Res. **2**, 243–251 (2013)

Anderson, T. (ed.) Malevich, K. S.: Essays on Art, pp. 1915–1933, vol. 1. Rapp & Whiting, London (1968)

Bann, S.: Introduction. In: Systems, pp. 5–14. Arts Council of Great Britain, London (1972)

Bill, M.: The Mathematical Approach to Contemporary Art, pp. 105–116. ABC Editions, Zurich (1949). Translation by E. Hüttinger, Max Bill (1978)

Boden, M.A., Edmonds, E.A.: From Fingers to Digits: An Artificial Aesthetic. MIT Press, Cambridge (2019)

Brown, P. (ed.).: Digital creativity: special issue on generative art **14**(1), 1–2 (2003)

Doran, M. (ed.): Conversations with Cézanne. University of California Press, Berkeley (2001)

Edmonds, E.A.: Automatic art: human and machine processes that make art. In: Devcic, R., Gollop, C. (eds.) Automatic Art: Human and Machine Processes That Make Art. GV Art Gallery, London (2014)

LeWitt, S.: Paragraphs on conceptual art. Artforum **5**(10), 79–84 (1967)

Lodder, C.: Russian Constructivism. Yale University Press, London (1983)

Troelstra, A.S.: History of constructivism in the 20th century Kennedy, J., Kossak, R. (eds.) Set Theory, Arithmetic, and Foundations of Mathematics: Theorems, Philosophies, pp. 150–179. Cambridge University Press, Cambridge (2011)

Creating with the Digital: Tool, Medium, Mediator, Partner

Linda Candy[(✉)]

Artworks r Active, Sheffield, UK
linda@lindacandy.com

Abstract. This chapter is about the different kinds of relationships that creative practitioners have with digital technologies in the making of artworks. Four types of creative process are described in which the role of the digital is differentiated as tool, medium, mediator and partner. In many cases, the digital technology performs more than one role: practitioners are using ready-made tools for making interactive works and at the same time writing algorithms to create digital partners with whom they perform. In this kind of creative practice, the technology is often the material of the creative works as well as the means by which they are made. It can enable a wide range of aesthetic qualities as well as facilitate different kinds of experience for both creators and audiences. This is a journey that many artists are taking in the 21st century contemporary digital arts world. The discussion is illustrated by the works of creative practitioners for whom digital technology is integral to the way they work.

Keywords: Creative practitioners · Creative process · Digital technologies

1 Introduction

Digital technology is ubiquitous and all pervasive in everyday life from mobile phones and domestic appliances to communications satellites, transportation vehicles of every kind and home movie streaming. Those born since the year 2000 have known nothing else and learning to program computers is part of a normal education. Even so, for a majority of people, how the various manifestations of digital technology are designed and constructed remains a mystery. Being able to customize one's personal devices is possible but usually at a relatively surface level. Digging deep into the software and hardware is a skill that only a minority possess. This has implications for the type of relationship between human and machine and how we think about the role of the digital in practice.

This chapter is about the different kinds of relationships that creative practitioners have with the digital tools and media they create and use to make works of many different varieties. I will focus on four kinds of creative amplification in which the digital role is differentiated as tool, medium, mediator and partner. In many cases, the digital technology performs more than one role in the creative process. Practitioners journey from

A. Brooks and E. I. Brooks (Eds.): ArtsIT 2019/DLI 2019, LNICST 328, pp. 13–28, 2020.
https://doi.org/10.1007/978-3-030-53294-9_2

using tools to set up mediated environments and in the same project, deploy software as medium to create digital partners with whom they perform. The ideas and examples here draw upon and extend a theme developed in 'The Creative Reflective Practitioner' [1]. The discussion is informed and illustrated by the ideas and works of established creative practitioners in the field for whom digital technology is fundamental to the way they work. I believe that in order to understand the nature of creativity and how knowledge is generated through practice, we need to listen to those for whom making and research is integral to a life of practice. This chapter draws upon many interviews with creative practitioners working in a wide variety of creative and professional fields: visual and sound artists, curators, designers, film makers and scientists. They are well known in their respective fields and enjoy success in the public realm having exhibited or performed their works in galleries, museums, exhibition spaces and events across the globe.

My approach to the subject has been shaped by living through almost all the phases of digital development that reached into and transformed our personal and working lives. I started my research in the mid 1980s when as an HCI researcher I was dedicated to designing user-oriented systems that were effective, efficient and satisfying to use. That they might support creative purposes was not on the agenda: that came later when we began to study creative practice itself. A significant change in my perspective began with sustained contact with artists through art-technology residencies. I noticed that artists approached digital technology in a way that was different to system developers and researchers. It was apparent to me that these were the people to watch.

2 Superseding or Supersizing Creativity?

Because we live in a world permeated with digitally powered devices large and small, how we think and talk about the digital in our life and work has become second nature and it is sometimes difficult to understand the full extent of what has happened to us and how much we are influenced and indeed altered by its presence and the roles we give to it. There are many challenges that digital technology brings to our lives and it is sometimes tempting to be somewhat defeatist in the face of the rise of artificial intelligence (AI). A persistent theme is how AI will inevitably supersede humans in many activities including the creative ones. The value of replacing human expertise with AI, we are encouraged to believe is inevitable; the machine is 'neutral' when it comes to making judgements over error prone people and so on. But it doesn't have to be that way and there are other scenarios. If we are to counter the negative narrative, we need to go to places where people are taking control of the opportunities digital technologies afford for enhancing, amplifying and transforming their creative capability. In this space, new kinds of relationships are being formed and new ways of talking about them are evolving. In the creative world, actions and experiences are being changed as a result of making with digital technology and these changes are reflected in the language used by practitioners.

2.1 Turing's Meaningless Question

Alan Turing posed the question 'Can machines think?' triggering efforts to create thinking machines in the first round of AI research. However, if we look again at what Turing actually wrote, there is another implication. The question was, he said, meaningless because: *'at the end of the century, the use of the words and general educated opinion will have altered so much that one will be able to speak of machines thinking without expecting to be contradicted'* [2].

Turing's point was not that machines would 'think' in the same way as a human being but rather we would speak as if they do as a result of our experience of them. Of course, what actually happened was that the 'can machines think?' question set off computational experiments that aimed to develop the means to prove that the answer was 'yes, machines *can* think'. The early days of AI were preoccupied with devising tests to see how much a computer could simulate a human response in such a way as to be believable. Joseph Weizenbaum was an early experimenter with natural language computer conversation. He created the program 'Eliza' in 1966 which simulated, you could say 'parodied', the way a psychotherapist using a non-directional style of questioning a new patient, would communicate [3]. Weizenbaum was dismayed by the way people engaged with the program and confessed personal feelings to it as if Eliza had real understanding. He was prompted to write his celebrated critique disputing the claims of the proponents of thinking machines in relation to human reasoning capabilities [4]. Eliza was the grandmother to vastly more sophisticated natural language programs represented by Siri, Apple's voice assistant[1].

What we have seen over the years since the 1950s and 1960s is that Turing's comments on his 'meaningless' question, interpreted more carefully, were right. What is meant by thinking *has* changed as a result of our experience of what computers can now do. In the beginning, it was relatively easy to understand them as very fast calculating machines that could outperform human beings on the basis of speed and accuracy. Today, computer systems have advanced to the extent that we see no surprise in the claim that not only can they execute routine tasks well but they are equally capable of producing creative outcomes. We have become accustomed not only to *thinking* digital technologies, but talking, listening, sensing, forecasting and even *creating* ones. The creativity extends from the mastery of chess to diagnosing medical conditions and assessing legal cases as well as making music and drawing pictures.

What does all this mean for human creativity? Does digital technology diminish it or even supersede it? What do creative practitioners think about the relationship of their practice to the technology, how do they use it and what are the outcomes?

Today's creative digital comes in many forms from the camera on our phones with facilities for image transformation to the programming systems for making and controlling interactive art installations. The range of possibilities is vast and the role the technologies play depends upon the intentions and aspirations of the people who use them. It is not just the uses, however, but rather the roles that creative practitioners

---

[1] Siri (2010) was developed by SRI International Artificial Intelligence Centre and is an offshoot of the US Defence Advanced Research Projects Agency's (DARPA)-funded CALO project. It is integrated into Apple Inc.'s iOS, iPadOS, watchOS, macOS, tvOS and audioOS operating systems.

ascribed to them and the nature of the relationship these have to the enormous variety of works that are created. As in the case of 'thinking' machines, these relationships are reflected in the words used to refer to them.

How digital technologies shape and influence the nature of creative reflective practice is the main focus of what follows. How do creative practitioners view the technologies they use: as tools for making objects, as mediators between thinking and action, as media for making or as partners to interact and perform with? Or perhaps, a combination of one or more of these categories? What do these terms tell us about how creative practitioners think about their relationship to the digital in their practice and the influence on reflection in action? How we talk about the different roles that digital technologies play in creative practice gives clues as to how the relationship is perceived.

3   Digital Technologies as Tool, Medium Mediator, Partner

There are many ways to create with digital technology and differentiating between the terms used can help us better understand the relationship of the digital technology to the creative practice and creative works. How we label the different roles that digital technologies play in creative practice gives clues as to how the relationship is perceived. Today, terms like 'tools' and 'medium' are commonplace in creative practice but increasingly, 'mediator' and 'partner' are being used by practitioners as they explore what it means to amplify their scope for making works. These words reflect the changing experiences with digital technology which, in turn, alter the implied meanings as happened with the word 'thinking'.

3.1   The Digital as Tool

A tool is a device designed precisely for a purpose, like a file to shape nails or a drill to make holes in wood or plaster. Many tools have been refined over time so as to be highly effective and efficient. However, they can be somewhat inflexible for turning their use to other purposes, although of course that is possible: a chisel can be used to cut food instead of shaping a piece of wood but it will not work half as well as a knife.

Tool effectiveness relies on the degree of skill the human user possesses. As an example, consider the difference between using a mechanical type-writer and its digital equivalent, the word processor, both machines for writing characters similar to those produced by a printer's movable type. Typing was once a valuable skill that was essential for employment as a secretary or office clerk. To be proficient required considerable skill, speed and accuracy and much effort went into training for that purpose. Without training, using a typewriter for your personal writing was a laborious process. It is a tool for writing neat typeface but the quality of the writing content and style depends on the user's skill. If, on the other hand, the word processor makes suggestions about content and how to structure the text, it is then contributing actively to the writing process.

Digital applications that are specifically designed to modify images or sounds could be said to fall into the tool category. We can draw, design spaces and make movies on our everyday devices using easy to use tools that take no time at all to learn. Tools such as Adobe Photoshop were originally designed to work with photographic images, and, although you can apply it to drawings, its features are not ideal for that purpose. Many practitioners today use digital tools for visual art.

David Hockey is an artist known for his openness to new methods and techniques and was an early experimenter with the Quantel Paintbox in the 1980s [5]. The iPad was Hockney's first encounter with a digital technology that offered a more fluid and natural way of art making. It provided facilities that could not be replicated by conventional media and his practice was amplified as a consequence. Did using these digital tools transform Hockney's art in a deeper sense?

Hockney saw the technology as a powerful tool that enable him to expand his capabilities: *'Technology is allowing us to do all kinds of things today...It wouldn't have been possible to paint this picture without it'* [6]. Digital technology in the form of tools for production were vital to the pragmatics of preparing for an exhibition. He used digital photography for instant reproduction and then digital printing for creating very large paintings in ways he was unable to do before. By building up the work from individual prints this enabled him to see the full scale in overview. This process freed him from the limitations of painting 'en plein air'[2] and he was able to create very much larger scale pictures than previously possible using standard techniques. In this way he exploited the digital tools to create bigger works for high profile locations such as The Royal Academy London where the results were very successful with the public. The works on display had been made using new processes, but they were nevertheless, immediately recognisable as in Hockney's signature style. The changes in his practice did not transform the art in a fundamental sense.

A second example of a creative practitioner tool user is Anthony Marshall. When he began to work with the iPad, he discovered a multiplicity of applications. But there was no single tool that could do everything he wanted and so he set about identifying a set of image blending, enhancing and combining tools that together served his purpose. Anthony had started his creative life as a photographer but through his use of digital tools, he turned to visual art. The tools not only amplified his creative process, they transformed it: *'...it has completely changed the way I think about creating art.'* Anthony's adoption of the iPad enabled a sense of unity between hand, eye and brain that was open to more opportunities for improvisation. His creative process now involves exploring, selecting and combining towards his own unique interpretation of the visual image shaped by a love of fluidity, movement, and pattern seeking from the world around [1].

3.2 The Digital as Medium

Artists talk about 'truth to the material' by which they mean exploring a raw material such as wood, metal, canvas and exploiting its inherent properties in the form and structure of works they make. Digital technology can be seen as a raw material that is explored and exploited in a similar way as a medium for thinking and defining the artwork. Seen as a medium, an algorithm determines the visual appearance, sound, movement and

---

[2] En plein air - in open air painting leaves the studio and goes outdoors. The practice was made into an art form by the French Impressionists. Their desire to paint light and its changing, ephemeral qualities, coupled with the creation of transportable paint tubes and the box easel allowed artists the freedom to paint anywhere.

the mechanism for delivering it: the type of screen, canvass, aluminium base or the environment into which it is conveyed. For artists working with digital technologies, there is a distinction between the code as medium and the tools used for performing supplementary tasks. The computer code is not just an instrument for making something but it is also the very material of the work itself.

Paul Brown is an artist whose pioneering work in computational systems as a medium for the visual arts has endured for 50 years [7]. His early interest in generative forms stems from systems art and the arrival of the digital computer which, in turn, brought art and technology together in his art making. The 'art that makes itself' by which is meant artworks that are generated by computer code as a medium, has emergent properties that can bring surprise to the artist even years after they have been created: *'My knowledge of computers and coding…is an integral part of my work… because the works have an emergent property I can be surprised by their behaviour.'*

Paul's computer code reveals properties of the visual image that he finds novel and unexpected. His artworks change shape over time according to the instructions embedded in the algorithm. Many artists use random numbers to introduce unpredictability into the images created by their algorithms. In Paul's algorithms, he replaces random numbers with a more deterministic mechanisms called Cellular Automata (CA). CA are simple rule-based computational procedures that interact with each other and reproduce and propagate over time. This means it is difficult to predict what will come next, giving the works a sense of continual change and unexpectedness within the parameters of colour, shape and time he has written into the code [8].

Another artist using the digital as medium is Esther Rolinson whose 2D drawing processes are realized in 3D as in the case of the sculptural installation 'Splinter'. Here, both physical and digital media are fundamental to the concept of a shattering dynamic sculptural form. The acrylic shards were carefully researched and selected for their reflective, transparent and low weight qualities. Exploiting those properties accords with the artistic intention to create:

'a burst of acrylic shards hovering in space. The acrylic fluctuates in fades and pulses with muted colour changes and variations in quality of movement'. The movement patterns of light through the sculpture mirrored the drawing process of the artist made possible by the medium of code. In 'Splinter' sculpture, the acrylic shards are fundamental to the work as is the programmable lighting system:

'I see programming as a complex material that can interpret and extend light movements. It is a way to analyse the structures of movements inside the drawings with the intention of making connections between physical and programming structures' [9] (Fig. 1).

Fig. 1. 'Splinter', Light installation, acrylic and programmed LEDs (Cube Gallery Phoenix Leicester 2015)

Another example of art making is to combine the digital with the physical and exploit the combination of media. Augmented Reality Art is one such area of new media art practice [10]. Augmented Reality refers to superimposing digital (virtual) images onto a view of a physical (real-world) environment. A typical augmented reality scenario might be visiting an art gallery and viewing paintings through a mobile phone camera to see information texts or images overlaid on the screen image of the works.

In Augmented-Mixed Reality Art, the intrinsic properties of the medium are revealed through what it makes possible - what it enables. In Ian Gwilt's work, *Save_as* (2007/8), the video facilities on a mobile phone/device are used in conjunction with image recognition computer code, to place digital content in direct relation to a physical object in a gallery space. In this instance the augmented object is an acrylic model of a partially opened folder which is a large scale, physical representation of a typical desktop folder icon. When observing the wall-mounted folder through a handheld monitor the viewer is able to see 'virtual content' superimposed over the image of the physical object. The artwork is programmed so that when the camera of the handheld device is held up to the physical object the image software within the device recognises the object and where the viewer is standing. In this case the image of the wall-mounted folder is overlaid with digital texts that appear in the viewing screen of the mobile and appear to sit in front of the folder. In the screen, the audience sees a computer-generated graphic consisting of a pair of words, drawn from two different lists. The software randomly selects one word from each list and the words are combined on the screen, to create statements such as: 'save them', 'cut me' and 'delete her' [11] (Fig. 2).

Fig. 2. *save_as* (2007/8) acrylic model *Image Ecologies*, University of Technology, Sydney

'Live Coding' is movement in sound art whereby the practitioners write computer code during music performances. The code created 'live' is displayed to the audience who then experience the sound and visual effects simultaneously. It is a relatively novel kind of digital as medium which, it could be argued has some way to go. The imbalance between audio and visual in which "the visual part is more cerebral than the sound" [12] is but one issue to be addressed if the form is to be embraced more widely. Nevertheless, this conscious attempt to make the code visible during creation highlights the computational engine as a core medium of creativity.

3.3 The Digital as Mediator

As well as acting as tools and media for creative work, digital technology can also be used to enable a more complex relationship between people and machines. We can think of this as being the difference between using the technology as an instrument (like a sewing machine) and a facilitator for creating an experience (like a cinema). Digital technologies can enable mediation between a practitioner and an environment. This mediation implies a relationship between two or more parties. The parties participate, interact, experience, inhabit, enact within a set of conditions or constraints. To facilitate mediation between performer and digital system, the key ingredient is interaction. To enable the interaction, you need suitable technologies to create the appropriate conditions and spaces. Mediation technology enables interaction between different parties whether as practitioner-performers or participating audiences, co-located or distributed, real or virtual. They can be used to contribute to the creative process as key elements of audience experience in body sense detection interactive works and in interactive performances.

George Khut makes art as embodied experience and studies the process through sensor-based interactive digital systems. Digital technology has been integral to George's practice and underpins his thinking, making and evaluation of different sensor based interactive and embodied experiences. He creates interfaces for testing and modifying his art installations under construction. By paying close attention to his own inner body experience, the creative practice is amplified, in particular, it enhances his capacity to judge what to change in order to transform the mind-body experience: *'With the body focussed interactions I want to draw people's attention inwards, and to frame these very subtle changes in nervous system orientation that can be difficult to notice. To develop the form for these works I have to pay a lot of attention to these changes inside myself, and then reflect on how the dynamics of the sounds and visuals can reflect this felt experience'* [1].

Sue Hawksley's dance artistry affords new insights into creative thinking and making through the mediation of digital technology. The amplification to her practice that this approach brings allows her to better understand the mediated experience of dance, both as a choreographer and a performer. As she says: *'Technological mediation can open up amazing possibilities to augment and extend how this material is experienced'*.

Crosstalk is an interactive collaborative work performed by Sue Hawksley in collaboration with artist technologist, Simon Biggs and sound artist, Garth Paine. The performance begins with two dancers speaking descriptions of each other, and then setting up a score for operating as part of the system. Using voice-recognition software their words are written and projected onto a screen, and existing as virtual 3-D text-objects in the interactive virtual space. When the performers touch the virtual text-objects this causes them to move. As the texts collide with one another, new texts and sounds are created by an interpretative and generative grammar engine that shapes the interaction between all participating elements [13].

Within this mediation technology there is no technical difference between the way the algorithm treats the people, the texts, graphical objects and sounds. Technology designed to capture movement or speech data from the human performer can be a very effective way of enriching the system's knowledge but, whilst this may serve the purposes of developing a better, more autonomous system, it can constrain the human control of the performance environment. In this case, the two dance performers have a stronger influence on how the work evolves. The intention is to enable awareness of their agency which may lead them to form intentions while performing. But the technology does not have its own intentions and its responses are generated through a complex ecology of system interactions.

Mediating technology can provide a sense of agency throughout the making and performing of a work. In a sense, it extends the idea of an agent that acts on your behalf to one closer to a partner who brings independent thought and action to the collaborative mix. However, for it to be a true partner as far as the practitioner is concerned, this will depend upon the ability of the technical system to respond in ways that are appropriate to her intentions but at the same time contribute in unexpected ways. In other words, if there is no parity of response the relationship is unlikely to become a partnership. But what does it take for a digital system to be considered more of a partner than a mediator?

3.4 The Digital as Partner

When creative practitioners refer to digital technologies as partners, this raises a wider question about what it means to be a partner in a human to human sense. The word is widely used in personal and social contexts and seems to imply some form of parity between the parties even if it does not assume sameness. You can be equal but nevertheless different, and it is often the differences that bring people into partnership for mutual benefit. Is it any different, however, when it comes to human and machine partnerships? For example, from the human point of view, does being partners imply that there must be agency on both sides? Does a partnership require a demonstration of autonomy in thought and action? Is it enough to think of a partner as the other half of a duet engaged in the same activity?

In contemporary digital practice, the sense of partnership has evolved to a degree that even far-sighted pioneers did not fully envisage. What is more, this relationship is dependent on how the systems have been designed to interact. If their role is to assist the human in completing a task, this will elicit different behaviour than with a more responsive 'symbiotic' relationship, and here is where the word partner can seem more apt.

Andrew Bluff works at the Animal Logic Academy at the University of Technology, Sydney and collaborates with Stalker Theatre dancers and actors. He creates software systems that mediate live theatre performances working in close collaboration with the people directly concerned. He records observations in close collaboration with performers throughout the development of all works when designing and implementing software. In order to understand how well the mediation has worked, he carries out post performance interviews. This all relies on qualities of a human to human relationship based on a high degree of cross-domain empathy. For Andrew, the creative process also involves shaping the program to match how he thinks. He distinguishes between using digital tools and his creative coding: *Then the software application that comes out of this coding, does act like a creative partner in an artwork. There is artistry and design on two separate levels; there is artistry in creating an interesting entity and then there is artistry in partnering with it to create an actual artwork. When you are heavily involved in both stages, the trick is to spend at least as much time partnering as you do creating* [1].

Andrew uses a range of digital technologies from readymade (3rd party) tools to programming environments. 'Storm' is the name given to the suite of software tools and media for use in live performance. It includes several different purpose-built apps which connect to each other and can be installed on the same or different computers. For example, a motion capture app detects physical movement of performers/audience, another converts the motion capture into physical forces on fluid and body simulations, another renders the graphics from the physics app onto the screen (or can be multiple screens with networked computers). To create these applications, he uses for example, XCode/Visual Studio, the C++ language, Open Frameworks, an open source library to help with rendering and image processing, and Pure Data, a visual programming language which controls some of the logic and user interface. To make the graphics and sounds which go into each individual performance he uses Photoshop for photo editing, Blender for 3d modelling, Cubase for linear music composition, amongst others.

By creating his own set of tools for enabling the live performances, Andrew can exercise closer control over features and capabilities. Bringing his own thinking style together with coding skill is fundamental to creating creative interactive art systems. At the same time, as he observes, it is a two-way street: "*you also shape the program you are making to adhere to your own unique way of thinking*". It is as if the software he creates to suit his needs becomes a collaborator in making a work. This imbues the human to computer relationship with a sense of partnership, but one in which the human has freedom to create in whatever way he wants, by contrast with the restrictions of ready-made tools [1].

A second example of partnering with the digital is that of Benjamin Carey who created '_derivations', an interactive digital system for in musical improvisation. The system 'listens' to a performer and uses this information to respond in a musical dialogue as happens when human musicians improvise together. This digital instrument is programmed to produce responses that are not easily predictable but nevertheless reflect qualities that are compatible with the expectations of the performer. With a non-interactive system, one that for example, generates 'pre-set' responses, the performer can control the start and stop moments and the system responds in an entirely predictable manner. The kind of digital instrument that is an obedient accompanist is often to be found providing sound tracks for musical performances in concert halls and on the street.

There is of course, an important difference between the performance with a digital instrument and create the instrument yourself. Benjamin Carey does both: he writes the code that defines the system's behaviour (as a digital medium) and in performing with it (as a digital partner), he is able to evaluate whether it responds appropriately. The fact that he writes and tests the computer code does not mean, however, that he can anticipate exactly how it will respond to his own playing. A software system that responds in an unpredictable way too often does not feel right because its human user has a sense that this is purely random and therefore not very engaging. In Benjamin's own words:

> ...*you don't want it to go off on its own tangent and not be able to relate to things it's heard or to be able to provoke something that's in the style or context of what is going on now. If I'm testing it and a surprise happens, and then another surprise happens, and another and there's no consistency between the algorithm's output then it becomes random* [1].

The qualities Benjamin finds most effective for a musical partnership require the system to have a measure of autonomy. This means that how the system behaves is not easy to predict and yet at the same time it should be responsive to what the human performer presents it with in a way that feels right and is interesting to work with. Interestingly, Benjamin's wish for a measure of predictability-what he refers to as 'coherence'- was stimulated by his experience of unpredictability and the dissatisfaction this led to about the performance qualities he could achieve. This is a feature of musical improvisation where a creative tension arises as you respond to sounds heard in a musically intelligible way but also look for and make sounds that are different to what came before. The music is constantly changing but the style should be consistent so that features such as timing, dynamics and timbre are recognisable to the performers. If, on the other hand the human performer cannot relate to what is coming from a software performer that continually produces surprising responses, this feels too randomised and it is difficult to improvise satisfactorily.

As we have seen from the examples described above, the ways in which practitioners talk about and relate to the digital in their creative practice are diverse. This kind of practice is evolving rapidly as new technologies become available and practitioners expand their ambitions. In the next section, a classification of the current ways that digital technologies are used by creative practitioners is presented.

4   Differentiating Digital Technologies in Creative Practice

Digital technologies are amplifying the creative process in many ways. They can be at once a tool designed for a specific purpose, a medium that is exploited according to its particular properties, a mediator that facilitates a range of experiences or a digital partner that works together with a human.

Table 1 sets out each of these categories of digital technology in terms that describe their purpose, the context of use, qualities or attributes and the capability needed to use or work with them. The terms can be applied to any creative work or creative process by asking how what you are using fits in relation to the context of its use, its characteristics, traits or qualities and what human capability is needed to make it work. The table classifies creative works according to these criteria: it is a work in progress.

Table 1. Categories of creative uses of digital technology

	Tool	Medium	Mediator	Partner
What	Device	Material	Facilitator	Relater
Why	Fit for task	Matched to artefact/work	Sets up conditions	Mutual Benefit
Context	Tailored to task	Properties exploited	Experiential	Based on parity
Character	Effective Efficient Inflexible	Adaptable Malleable Controllable	Adaptable Constrained Flexible	Reciprocal Open Coherent
Capability	Skill Training Practice Proficiency	Sensitivity Talent Know how Experience	Feedback Learning Reactive Collaborative	Complex Autonomous Dynamic Evolving

4.1   Tool v Medium

The primary difference between tool and medium is that the first is a device and the second is a material. A tool as device is intended to fulfil a specific purpose; it has been designed to be effective and efficient; to be most effective it requires skill, training and practice on the part of its user. A medium is a material which can be exploited according to its intrinsic properties, its qualities and character; it is adaptable and controllable but in need of sensitivity, knowledge and talent in the sense of artistic capability.

Digital tools, like image blending and manipulation applications, are tailored to carry out specific tasks for visual art creation. In both David Hockey and Anthony Marshall's cases as described previously, the artists have unquestionably amplified what they do through full use of the functions of the digital tools they have identified for their work. It is arguable how much this actually transformed the nature of their art, but that is an issue for a more extended discussion. However, what is apparent is that neither have the opportunity to make fundamental changes to the tools themselves, nor do they appear to wish to do so. This is not a problem for many tool users but for others it can limit their possibilities. As Andrew Bluff says: *'if you are using one of these digital tools, you don't feel like you've got complete control to do what you want to do'* [1]. In other words, you are bound to work with the feature set included by the tool designer and have to work within those constraints.

The constraints that apply to tool use are different in the case of the digital as medium. Whilst a digital tool to make a work could, in principle, be replaced with another tool, in the same way as substituting a roller for a brush to paint, the same cannot be said for a medium. The cellula automata in Paul Brown's algorithms, generates shapes that are determined uniquely even to the way it can produce unpredictable outcomes. Equally in Esther Rolinson's 'Splinter' sculpture, the programmable LED lights that move through the acrylic shards are fundamental to the concept and experience of the work and the software that drives them is designed specifically to meet the artist's intentions. In Ian Gwilt's augmented, mixed reality art, the medium is the heart of the concept itself and the exhibit could not exist without it.

4.2 Mediator v Partner

A mediator can be defined as a facilitator that sets up conditions for mediated creative experiences in which parties participate, interact and perform. Mediation technology enables interaction between the different parties whether as practitioner-performers or participating audiences. At the heart of the digital as mediator is its interactive nature because this extends the practitioner's creative process: it is an enabler of particular forms of art. A partner, on the other hand, is better described as a 'relater' whose role is based on parity. This is a more open, complex and reflexive relationship. The degree of flexibility and responsiveness between the partners is crucial to a genuine sense of partnership and expectation of mutual benefit.

The difference between mediator and partner technologies depends upon the roles they play. The mediated situation requires flexible adaptation whereas in a partnership there is a greater degree of openness and reciprocity. The qualities most effective for a partnership require the system to have a measure of autonomy which means that how the system behaves is not easy to predict. At the same time, it should be responsive to what the human performer presents it with in a way that feels right and is interesting to work with. If, on the other hand, the human cannot relate to what is coming from a digital partner because it produces responses that feel too randomised, this does not make for a satisfactory relationship. A partner whether human or artificial that continually behaves in unpredictable ways, appears fickle and is therefore not easy to work with. What applies to human to human partnerships is quite likely to apply between humans and machines. Those practitioners who create the computer code themselves are able to shape the digital partner so that it becomes a better partner from their point of view.

In Sue Hawksley's example, the manner in which the technological and human elements interact within the system are 'equivalent' (a form of parity perhaps) and each has attributes that the other does not. There is no technical difference between the way the Crosstalk algorithm treats the people, the texts, graphical objects and sounds. However, this does not imply they are the same and in the performance environment, the dancers have more influence over how the work evolves. It is arguable that a true partnership between human and digital system implies appropriate responsiveness in parallel with unexpected behaviour as one might expect from a human partner. This is the kind of balance that other practitioners, such as Benjamin Carey, seek in designing systems which have sufficient agency to offer surprising responses but at the same time do not produce random behaviours. In the end, the relationship between human and digital is conditioned by the nature of the human intentions and the design attributes of the system, including its capacity for autonomous, or seemingly autonomous behaviour. Practitioner approaches are very varied and different patterns of ideas interleave with rich and diverse creative practices.

5 Conclusions

For practitioners, a journey from the digital as tool or medium to mediator or partner is not uncommon as they explore and experiment with new technologies that extend and transform their practice. It almost always is the case that creative practitioners will be drawn into expanding their knowledge in a quest to meet the challenges as well as the opportunities the technology affords. It might mean a continual quest to find the best available tools for completing the tasks need to produce visual images for exhibition; it might mean experimenting with different levels of agency in a digitally mediated performance environment; it might mean exploring different programming languages for combining sound and images for an interactive installation; it might involve creating your own digital partner whose characteristics complement or disrupt the performance or are designed to satisfy and extend the repertoire of possibilities. Over the life-time of a practitioner, digital technologies will be absorbed into creative practice in different forms and perform a large variety of functions depending on the degree of amplification they bring to the process and is highly dependent upon the intentions of the practitioner.

Digital Technology is often portrayed as influencing and shaping human behaviour as if it is mainly a one-way process. But in the creative sphere, that relationship is a reciprocal one. The human encounters the technology, tries it out and in doing so expands their expectations and ambitions and demands more of it. The technology is then extended in response and the human goes on to amplify what they were doing. Expanded ambitions and expectations arise from creative activities that include creating and controlling the technology. Far from superseding human creativity, there are powerful signs that human creative capability is being supersized. The partnership model in particular provides opportunities for the kind of creative exploration that lends itself to extending human capabilities and knowledge, and developing smarter systems that evolve in parallel. This is where the most exciting possibilities for fostering our relationships with the digital lies. My hope is that this could be the start of a more productive way of approaching the relationship we have with digital technology and especially those forms that challenge our confidence in our ability to shape and control what we have created.

We can take a lesson from Gary Kasparov chess grandmaster who was defeated by 'Deep Blue' in 1997, marking the very first time a world champion had been overcome by a computer. The effect on him was enormous but rather than concede the ground to the machine (which by the way had been programmed by some very smart humans), he channelled his energies into finding ways of rescuing the game he loved and had devoted his life to. Instead of bowing to the apparent superiority of the artificial system, he turned to a new model for playing chess: 'Advanced Chess' involved a human and a chess program pitted against another human with a chess program or a solo computer. In promoting this model of chess playing, he was making a partner of the machine. And there were significant gains that were much more important than beating the computer. By harnessing the power of the machines, people could not only outplay them, they could also become more skilful through analysing their moves, identifying mistakes and devising new strategies and plans in partnership with the computer. Human computer cooperation has similar benefits across many domains.

What can we do today to promote this model of human-machine cooperation with its supersizing effects? Apart from being determined about what you want and can do, if you are a creative practitioner, there are many doors open to advancing your capabilities and knowledge. Practice-based research is revealing insider knowledge in new and exciting ways. It is important to identify inspiring models and mentors, a process greatly assisted by first-hand accounts by creative practitioners [14].

References

1. Candy, L.: The Creative Reflective Practitioner. Routledge, London (2020)
2. Turing, A.M.: Computing Machinery and Intelligence. Mind **49**, 433–460 (1950)
3. Weizenbaum, J.: ELIZA: a computer program for the study of natural language communication between man and machine. Commun. Assoc. Comput. Mach. **9**, 36–45 (1966)
4. Weizenbaum, J.: Computer Power and Human Reason: From Judgment to Calculation. W. H. Freeman, San Francisco (1976)
5. Hockney, D.: Painting with Light (1985). https://www.creativebloq.com/video-production/remembering-quantel-paintbox-712401
6. Gayford, M.: A Bigger Message: Conversations with David Hockney. Thames and Hudson Ltd, London (2016)
7. Brown, P.: From systems art to artificial life: early generative art at the slade school of fine art. In: Gere, C., Brown, P., Lambert, N., Mason, C. (eds.) White Heat and Cold Logic: British Computer Arts 1960–1980 An historical and critical analysis, pp. 275–289. MIT Press (2008)
8. Brown, P.: Stepping stones in the mist. In: Bentley, P.J., Corne, D. (eds.) Creative Evolutionary Systems, pp. 1–75. Morgan Kaufmann Publishers Inc., San Francisco. Academic Press, USA, pp. 387–408 (2002). http://www.paul-brown.com/WORDS/STEPPING.HTM
9. Rolinson, E.: Drawing spaces. In: Explorations in Art and Technology, 2nd edn., pp 319–326. Springer, London (2018). https://doi.org/10.1007/978-1-4471-7367-0_31

10. Geroimenko, V. (ed.): Augmented Reality Art: From an Emerging Technology to a Novel Creative Medium. Springer Series on Cultural Computing. Springer, London (2014). https://doi.org/10.1007/978-3-319-06203-7
11. Gwilt, I.: Augmenting the white cube. In: Candy, L., Edmonds, E.A. (eds.) Interacting: Art, Research and the Creative Practitioner, pp. 257–267. Libri Publishing, Farindon (2011)
12. Boden, M.A., Edmonds, E.A.: From Fingers to Digits: An Artificial Aesthetic, p. 245. MIT Press, Cambridge (2019)
13. Biggs, S., Hawksley, S., Paine, G.: Crosstalk: making people in interactive spaces. In: MOCO 2014 Proceedings of the International Workshop on Movement and Computing, p. 61. ACM, New York (2014)
14. Candy, L., Edmonds, E.A. (eds.): Interacting: Art, Research and the Creative Practitioner. Libri Publishing Ltd., Faringdon (2011)

Targeting Experiences

Parenting Experiences

Targeting Experiences

Anthony L. Brooks[1]($\boxtimes$) and Eva Brooks[2]

[1] CREATE/Department of Architecture, Design and Media Technology/Technical Faculty of IT and Design, Aalborg University, Rendsburggade 14, 9000 Aalborg, Denmark
tb@create.aau.dk

[2] XLab Design, Learning, Innovation, Department of Culture and Learning, Aalborg University, Kroghstræde 3, 9220 Aalborg, Denmark

Abstract. Shook (2007) informed how Human experience is the ultimate source and justification for all knowledge. Experience itself has accumulated in human memory and culture, gradually producing the methods of intelligence called "reason" and "science." Having a focus on such experiences as opening theme for this work communicates the 'human-at-center' perspectives of this volume. Scholarly perspectives are presented that illustrate across disciplines and cultures.

Keywords: Experiences · Music · Audience · Play · Toys · Gamification · Design · Animation · Relations · Values

1 Introduction

1.1 Scope

Targeting Experiences is purposefully a wide theme to open and relate across the research topics presented associated to arts and technology, interactivity, and game creation human perspectives (i.e. audience, users, designers/developers, relationships, visitors, etc.).

The opening contribution in this first section relates to music and audience experiences. Following is a contribution on user experiences of a tool for Gamification, Toyification and Playification. Next is a text on enlightenment and experience relating to interactive exhibition design. Experiences relating to viewing animated animal characters in the genre of film animation follows. Next is a contribution on experiences related to emotional communication systems for remote relationships. Experience of a created prototype in the form of a user-centered communication pad for cognitive and physical impaired people is subject of the next contribution. Topic of the following contribution is experiences associated to interactions with a cognitively biased robot. Headphone experience of music is subject of the next contribution. The final contribution in this opening section questions beyond visual aesthetic values in presenting a mobile application targeting enhanced experiencing of a visited landscape.

The following text snippets elaborate directly from each contribution to further assist readership.

A. Brooks and E. I. Brooks (Eds.): ArtsIT 2019/DLI 2019, LNICST 328, pp. 31–37, 2020.
https://doi.org/10.1007/978-3-030-53294-9_3

2   Real-Time Measurement and Analysis of Audience Response

Wigham and Challis (2020)

Musical activities associated to Arts and Technologies (ArtsIT) and Interactivity typically involves bespoke new forms of instrument(s) for creative expression aligned to a performance with said apparatus in a situation targeting impactful emotional experiences for an audience.

In this research, UK authors Philip Wigham and Ben Challis, from Manchester Metropolitan University report on their in-situ data gathering within research into the design of novel musical controllers where audience members were given sliders to position relative to their responses to each of several short musical performances.

This work targeted to measure emotional connectivity and determination according to each piece of music in a performance where audience used the sliders for emotional engagement in real-time, thus suggesting a more robust linkage than as opposed to collecting data post performance.

The contribution presents results from the research where slider data proved crucial to gaining further insight into the qualitative questionnaires and focus group discussions highlighted participant responses to the performance that did not appear within the questionnaires or post-performance discussions. This allowed further examination of those areas of the performance and instigated changes to the performance. Consequently, the authors suggest possible methods of data analysis and discussion on how this approach may be applied in other research contexts. Interesting discussion is the time when disengagement with performance by audience took place when needing to move slider (so perceptual – cognitive engagement) then to re-engage with performance – as the design was for responding continuously to how engaged they felt throughout the performance .... Yet questioned could be that if they were really engaged, they would forget the slider... however the paper states "the participants could fully concentrate on the performance whilst also confidently controlling the slider".

It is concluded as a viable technique and the research is ongoing.

3   Out of the Box, into the Cubes: Envisioning User Experiences Through a Tool for Gamification

Ihamäki and Heljakka (2020)

This research by Pirita Ihamäki and Katriina Heljakka represents Finish industry business start-up company Prizztech and Finish academia in the form of University of Turku. The authors inform on their combined efforts that reports on their synthesizing of the latest design knowledge accumulated with the Comicubes service design tool and solution prototyping method whilst sharing some of the lessons learned during multiple workshops that they were involved in organizing.

Readers are informed on how the physical prototyping tool combines two-dimensional sketching with a three-dimensional and open-ended play medium – the cube. The method incorporates key aspects of service-oriented interaction design.

The authors have used Comicubes to facilitate co-creation to generate new ideas, solutions or approaches to various design challenges related to the gamification, toyification and playification of services.

This text elaborates on work summarizing four case studies where Comicubes was employed as a platform for 3D prototyping, testing, and simultaneously, a tool to stimulate, envision and co-create interactive user experiences.

Findings from the case studies indicated that the Comicubes tool and method are suitable to be used in design processes interested to facilitate co-creation and innovation of products, services and experiential spaces.

4 Balancing Enlightenment and Experience in Interactive Exhibition Design

Vistisen et al. (2020)

A trio from Aalborg University next present their research titled "Balancing Enlightenment and Experience in Interactive Exhibition Design" – the authors are Peter Vistisen, Vashanth Selvadurai, and Jens Jensen. This contribution presents insights from a collaborative design research project, in which a zoological aqua park in Denmark integrated multiple gamified digital installations in their new exhibition design.

The work documents design-balancing in allowing game-based interactions, and the didactic communication about facts in the exhibition. The research study focus was on the implemented solutions based on qualitative interviews with visitors alongside quantitative data from the backend game analytics of the installations. From triangulating these data sets the authors show how attempts to deliver purely fact-based information through didactic design elements failed to succeed in engaging the visitors, while 'stealth learning' sparks enlightenment about the subject matter.

The authors posit how results suggest that this is true both in cases in which users fully understand and play through the intended interactions, as well as when more negotiated interpretations of the digital installations are performed.

Contribution to the field is stated as guiding principles for the balance, between experience and enlightenment in gamified exhibition designs.

5 Audience Perception of Exaggerated Motions on Realistic Animated Animal Characters

Hammer and Adamo (2020)

Two authors from Purdue University, United States of America, namely Mackenzie Hammer and Nicoletta Adamo, next present their research titled "Audience Perception of Exaggerated Motions on Realistic Animated Animal Characters". They share how the recent push for more detailed graphics and realistic visuals in animated productions have sparked much debate around the new films' photorealistic visual style. They further inform how some critics argue that the new "live-action" versions of movie classics such as the Lion King are not as visually stylish as the original ones, and the photorealistic characters are not as likeable, fun and intriguing as their stylized counterparts.

This contribution reports on the authors' ongoing research whose goal is to examine whether it is possible to apply traditional animation principles to photorealistic animated animal characters in order to make them more expressive, convincing and ultimately entertaining. An extensive audience study is presented.

In particular, the text reports the extent to which varying degrees of exaggeration affect the perceived believability and appeal of a photorealistic talking cat character performing a series of actions in a high detail environment.

6 Towards a Conceptual Design Framework for Emotional Communication Systems for Long-Distance Relationships

Li et al. (2020)

In this research, Finland-based authors, Hong Li, Jonna Häkkilä, and Kaisa Väänänen, highlight how couples living in long-distance relationships (LDRs) may lack ways to keep emotionally connected. The contribution elaborates that previous research has presented a wealth of systems and user studies that offer insights of individual systems and their user interface designs. Also, it states how these studies have revealed a multitude of design attributes of the relatedness strategies of LDRs and the user interfaces used in computer-mediated communication (CMC) systems for LDRs. The authors synthesize the multitude of different design attributes, and present a design framework that addresses the five main areas of LDR systems: users (the remote couple), the LDR itself, the used technology, the design of the device, interaction, nature of messages and supported connectedness strategies, and the context of the use. In their research the authors validated the framework by analysing and presenting a set of six existing systems and prototypes considering this framework and show how they consider the central design attributes. As a conclusion, the authors propose that this framework can be used to assist in designing and evaluating the user interfaces of CMC systems for emotional communication to support LDRs.

7 Developing a User-Centred Communication Pad for Cognitive and Physical Impaired People

Ilyas et al. (2020)

Next, authors Chaudhary Muhammad Aqdus Ilyas, Kasper Rodil and Matthias Rehm present their research titled "Developing a user-centred Communication Pad for Cognitive and Physical Impaired People". The contribution informs how it is always challenging for people with speech inhibition dysfunction to communicate. In this research the authors focused their explorations on a case study of a resident at a neurological centre who, due to physical and speech paralysis, had complications in conveying messages. To support the case study the team developed a 'communication pad' that enabled the resident to swipe a finger to select printed alphabets and digits. A camera placed over the communication pad detected the finger movement of the resident and extracted the message to display on the computer screen or the tablet. The authors state how the tracking method is robust and can track the fingers even in varying illumination conditions: Main steps of design methods with various design prototypes and user feedback are shared. Evaluations further showed that the authors' designed system had provided independence and convenience to the resident in conveying a message successfully.

8   Evaluating Interactions with a Cognitively Biased Robot in a Creative Collaborative Task

Johansen et al. (2020)

In this work, authors, Johansen, Jensen, and Bemman, present how within the field of human-robot interaction (HRI), robots designed for social interactions are not only evaluated in terms of efficiency and accuracy. Factors related to the personality or cognitive ability of the robot such as perceived likability and intelligence are important considerations because they must engage with their human counterparts in deeper, more authentic and sometimes creative ways. The authors posit how they believe interactive art allows for the exploration of such interactions, however, the study of robots in interactive art remains relatively less commonplace and evaluations of these robots in creative contexts are similarly lacking. In this context, the authors present their work on an interactive robot inspired by Norman White's The Helpless Robot (1987), which has been endowed with a cognitive bias known as the Dunning-Kruger effect and the ability to collaborate with participants in a creative drawing task. In the research the authors evaluated the participants' interactions with both biased and unbiased versions of this robot using the Godspeed Questionnaire Series (GQS), which has been modified to include measures of creativity, and relate these findings to analyses of their collaborative drawings. Results from the research indicated a significant difference between the versions of the robot for several measures in the GQS, with the unbiased version rated more positively than the biased robot in all cases. Analysis of the drawings suggested that participants interacting with the biased robot were less inclined to collaborate in a cooperative manner.

9   A Positional Infrared Tracking System Using Non-individualised HRTFs to Simulate a Loudspeaker Setup and Its Influence on Externalisation of Music

Eklund and Erkut (2020)

"A Positional Infrared Tracking System Using Non-individualised HRTFs to Simulate a Loudspeaker Setup and its Influence on Externalisation of Music" is a body of research from authors Rasmus Eklund and Cumhur Erkut from Aalborg University, Copenhagen campus. In this work the authors explain how many artists produce and mix their virtual reality, game, or screen media audio productions only with headphones, but deploy them to stereo or multi-channel loudspeaker setups. Because of the acoustical and perceptual differences, listening on headphones might sound very different compared to loudspeakers, including the perception of sound sources inside the head (externalization problem). Nevertheless, by using Head Related Transfer Functions (HRTFs) and accurate movement tracking, it is possible to simulate a loudspeaker setup with proper externalization. In this contribution, the authors present how an infrared-based positional tracking system with non-individualized HRTFs to simulate a loudspeaker setup is conceptualized, designed and implemented. The authors elaborate on how the system can track the user with six degrees of freedom (6-DOF); an improvement over current commercial systems that only use 3-DOF tracking. The system was evaluated on 20 participants to see if the additional DOF increased the degree of externalization. While tracking increased the externalization in general, there was no significant difference between 3-DOF and 6-DOF. Another test indicated that positional movement coupled with positional tracking may have a greater effect on externalization compared to positional movement coupled with only head movement tracking. Comparisons between these results and previous studies are discussed and improvements for future experiments are proposed.

10   Finding, Feeling and Sharing the Value of a Landscape

Jesus et al. (2020)
In this next text titled "Finding, Feeling and Sharing the Value of a Landscape" – authors – a trio from Lisbon, Portugal, namely Rui Jesus, Catarina Conceição, and Gonçalo Lopes share their research on developing a mobile application with gaming and social features to support the experience of preparing and visiting of places with distinct landscapes. The contribution reflects how the value of a landscape is often associated with its visual aesthetic value, but a landscape goes beyond that having other important values, such as historical or social value. The guides and tourist itineraries are useful to help visiting monuments but as far as reading and experiencing a landscape, these are still insufficient. This work consists of developing a mobile application with gaming and social features, to support the experience of visiting and reading about places with valuable landscapes. The paper describes the design principles used and presents the main issues of the study conducted during the development process of the application. It also presents the results obtained by the tests carried out to evaluate the user experience when visiting and appreciating the value of a landscape with the application. The experiments were carried out in the Cultural Landscape of Sintra, considered world heritage since 1995.

Epilogue and Acknowledgements. This opening section introduces nine contributions by extracting from each paper. It does so to promote readership of each full paper that are presented in the following chapters. In doing so the authors of this chapter acknowledge the contribution to this section/volume by each author whose original work was presented in the ArtsIT/DLI events in Aalborg, Denmark November 7–8, 2019.

References

Eklund, R. Erkut, C.: A positional infrared tracking system using non-individualised HRTFs to simulate a loudspeaker setup and its influence on externalisation of music. In: Brooks, A., Brooks, E.I. (eds.) ArtsIT 2019 and DLI 2019. LNICST, vol. 328, pp. 158–177. Springer, Heidelberg (2020)

Hammer, M., Adamo, N.: Audience perception of exaggerated motions on realistic animated animal characters. In: Brooks, A., Brooks, E.I. (eds.) ArtsIT 2019 and DLI 2019. LNICST, vol. 328, pp. 88–102. Springer, Heidelberg (2020)

Ihamäki, P., Heljakka, K.: Out of the Box, into the Cubes: Envisioning User Experiences through a Tool for Gamification. In: Brooks, A., Brooks, E.I. (eds.) ArtsIT 2019 and DLI 2019. LNICST, vol. 328, pp. 49–68. Springer, Heidelberg (2020)

Ilyas, C., Rodil, K., Rehm, M.: Developing a user-centred communication pad for cognitive and physical impaired people. In: Brooks, A., Brooks, E.I. (eds.) ArtsIT 2019 and DLI 2019. LNICST, vol. 328, pp. 124–137. Springer, Heidelberg (2020)

Jesus, R., Conceição, C., Lopes, G.: Finding, feeling and sharing the value of a landscape. In: Brooks, A., Brooks, E.I. (eds.) ArtsIT 2019 and DLI 2019. LNICST, vol. 328, pp. 178–191. Springer, Heidelberg (2020)

Johansen, J., Jensen, L., Bemman, B.: Evaluating interactions with a cognitively biased robot in a creative collaborative task. In: Brooks, A., Brooks, E.I. (eds.) ArtsIT 2019. LNICST, vol. 328, pp. 138–157. Springer, Heidelberg (2020)

Li, H., Häkkilä, J., Väänänen, K.: Towards a conceptual design framework for emotional communication systems for long-distance relationships. In: Brooks, A., Brooks, E.I. (eds.) ArtsIT 2019. LNICST, vol. 328, pp. 103–123. Springer, Heidelberg (2020)

Shook, J.: The varieties of scientific experience. Free Inquiry **27**(4) (2007)

Vistisen, P., Selvadurai, V., Jensen, J.: Balancing enlightenment and experience in interactive exhibition design. In: Brooks, A., Brooks, E.I. (eds.) ArtsIT 2019. LNICST, vol. 328, pp. 69–87. Springer, Heidelberg (2020)

Wigham, P., Challis, B.: Real-time measurement and analysis of audience response. In: Brooks, A., Brooks, E.I. (eds.) ArtsIT 2019. LNICST, vol. 328, pp. 38–48. Springer, Heidelberg (2020)

Real-Time Measurement and Analysis
of Audience Response

Philip Wigham[(✉)] and Ben Challis

Manchester Metropolitan University, Manchester, UK
{p.wigham,b.challis}@mmu.ac.uk

Abstract. How do you harness a "level" of emotional connectivity from
audience/participants? Questionnaires, focus group discussions, interviews and other qualitative methods gather retrospective thoughts of the
participant and may miss important insights or connections that could
be discovered if a real-time response is recorded. The aspiration for real-
time audience data recording is problematic in many areas of research,
in particular performing arts where the work/research presented is time
bound. In addressing this problem within research into the design of novel
musical controllers, custom "sliders" were used to measure and examine
real-time audience response to short musical performances. The audience
moved their sliders in response to the performance, producing continuous
data that was recorded into music software and timestamped. The initial
test results have shown promising insights and usefulness for real-time
data collection and examination. These results and possible methods of
data analysis are presented along with discussion on how this approach
may be applied in other research contexts.

Keywords: Audience · Response · Real-time · Measurement ·
Mimesis · Mimetic theory · Performance · Music · Haptic · Sensory ·
Kinaesthetic · Tangibility · Feedback · Analysis · Data

1 Introduction

This paper presents a possible solution to the problematic area of recording continuous real-time audience response data. It is hoped that it will prove to be a
useful data gathering tool in areas of research looking to acquire this type of
data. The conception, implementation and initial results of a real-time "slider"
mechanism for examining audience/participant response, will be discussed further along with its application in the current research, and how the slider method
may be applied in other contexts.

The test phases being described in this paper were conceived as a way of
recording and examining real-time audience response to new mimetic digital
music instruments (DMI) and comparing them with existing traditional DMIs.
Custom built "sliders" were used to allow audience/participants to respond to

A. Brooks and E. I. Brooks (Eds.): ArtsIT 2019/DLI 2019, LNICST 328, pp. 38–48, 2020.
https://doi.org/10.1007/978-3-030-53294-9_4

musical performances. The slider is moved up or down in response to a question posed before the performance, in this case how "engaged/interested" they are at each moment of the performance. As the participant feels more engaged they respond by moving the slider upwards, and downwards when less engaged. This "slider" data was captured in real-time and then collated with other data collected through the questionnaires and group discussions. The slider data proved crucial to gaining further insight into the qualitative questionnaires and focus group discussions.

This method is proving to be an effective way to examine a participant's continually adjusting response to a live performance. The slider data has highlighted participant responses to the performance that did not appear within the questionnaires or post-performance discussions. This allowed further examination of those areas of the performance and instigated changes to the performance. Further testing showed that these changes in the performance had affected the slider data and therefore the audience response.

Although the mimetic design study is in its very early stages, the results are already showing very interesting and useful insights, which will be discussed in more detail below.

2   Research Context

The need for real-time participant response data came about through post graduate research into mimetic influenced digital music instrument design. The research has been comparing user perceptions of music performances using a custom-built MIDI[1] controller (inspired by mimetic theories [21]) alongside a traditional MIDI keyboard controller. This has required a method of data collection and examination of participant response to music performances. Each MIDI controller was connected to the same laptop running a software synthesiser which both controllers were able to play and control. A musical performance was devised that could be played with both controllers so that the sound elements of each performance were as identical as possible. This allowed for a fairer comparison of the actual physical and gestural performance of the instruments.

Cox's mimetic hypothesis [12] identifies overt and covert 'mimetic participation' as audience responses to musical performance. It was desirable to find a way to explore how audience participants may experience mimetic participation and though overt manifestations could be observed in the video, covert mimetic participation, by its nature, does not manifest itself. Though questionnaires and interviews were initially devised, it was important to find an effective method of investigating real-time response to discover any covert "mimetic participation" [11,12]. Any post-performance data collection such as questionnaires and focus group discussions, being retrospective, may miss exposing this covert mimetic

---

[1] 'MIDI is an industry standard music technology protocol that connects products from many different companies including digital musical instruments, computers, tablets, and smartphones'[1].

participation and any allusion to mimetic participation could not be precisely associated with an exact moment in the performance.

In addressing this problem, a "slider" method was developed to enable response data to be recorded in real-time during the performances, which allowed audience members to respond continuously to how "engaged" they felt throughout the performance. The data from these sliders was recorded into a MIDI recording software[2] as MIDI data, simultaneously with the performance MIDI data, whilst two video cameras captured the audience and performer. This allowed the slider data to then be compared with various points within the performance, achieving continuous real-time snapshots of the level of audience engagement at each moment of the performance. This data was also compared with the demographic data, the post-performance questionnaires and the focus group discussions.

Although the findings from the mimetic design research are in the early stages of analysis, this quantitative slider data is providing more insight than any other isolated method, and is helping to expose moments of potential covert mimetic participation, that would have otherwise remain hidden. Synchronising the slider data to the video recordings allows for a very direct analysis of the performance in relation to the audience response. This slider method of data collection and analysis is discussed in more detail below.

3   Methodology

3.1   Existing Methods

The problem of recording real-time audience response data has been approached using several methods [10], the most prevalent of which include analysis of audience biometric data, detection of audience motion, and input devices for audience response.

The advantage of recording biometric data is its involuntary nature requiring no conscious effort to respond, therefore being completely unobtrusive to the experience of the performance. Galvanic Skin Response (GSR) and electrodermal activity have been used to suggest a biological response to performances [14,20], as well as cardiovascular and respiratory measurements [9]. However it remains difficult to convincingly associate biometric data directly with a specific response to the performance, such as engagement. Latulipe et al. [13] attempted to resolve this issue by comparing audience GSR data with 'self-report scales' finding a 'strong correlation'. However, there are still problems with interpreting biometric data with any certainty in relation to audience levels of engagement.

Martella et al. [16] used accelerometers and infra-red sensors to record audience movement during a live dance performance to predict the outcome of post-performance questionnaires and motion capture techniques were used by Swarbrick et al. [19] to investigate audience response to live performances compared with recorded music. As with the biometric data techniques there is a

---

[2] For the purposes of this study, Ableton Live was used, though it would be feasible to use other digital audio workstations or MIDI recording software.

difficulty with being able to directly link the movement of audience members with a response to the performance, and although these methods have the similar advantage of being unobtrusive, they are difficult to interpret precisely.

The portable Audience Response Facility (pARF) utilises a personal digital assistant (PDA) as an input device [17] which allows input of two simultaneous data streams using the PDA stylus on an X and Y axis. This allows the audience to be asked to respond in a particular way, providing participant responses that are explicitly connected with the posed response parameter, such as "engagement". However, the stylus/PDA input device could be potentially distracting to the participant, having to look at the PDA to give an accurate response.

Stevens et al. [18] suggest that other suitable input devices might be used depending on the response being measured. Other input devices could include commercially available keypads [4,6] and mobile phone apps [2,7]. The keypads capture real-time data but only have the capability of an on/off style button response, and therefore do not give a scaled response. Although there are a range of mobile apps that can be used to collect audience response data, most of them cannot track scaled response. Reactor [5] is a mobile app that can record a scaled response via a slider-bar on the screen, but is aimed at pre-recorded video not live performance. Critically, mobile phone input could be a potential distraction to the user, having to glance down at the phone regularly to gauge their position on the screen.

The mimetic design project required a bespoke solution due to the specific context of the research. The music performance, not intrinsically an "event", was created to exploit the gestural nature of the DMIs. It was necessary to be able to scrutinise the detail behind individual participants, not a consensus across the audience, exploring the how, when and why of apparent response by individuals to specific gestures. In practice, during the testing phase using bespoke physical sliders, it was common for the participants to turn their mobile devices off (not having been previously encouraged to do so) and hold the slider in one hand, being entirely prepared for the task. The tactile and tangible nature of the physical slider meant that the participants could fully concentrate on the performance whilst also confidently controlling the slider.

3.2 Sliders

The sliders were made using a linear slide potentiometer soldered to an XLR socket. This was housed in a wooden enclosure designed to fit the size of an average hand, so that the thumb could move the slider (see Fig. 1). Ten sliders were made and connected with a cable to a micro controller unit (MCU). The MCU converts the movement of the potentiometers into digital signals through an ADC and then outputs this data in the MIDI format via USB interface. The MIDI protocol was chosen due to the availability of well established MIDI recording software capable of recording multiple streams of slider data.

It proved to be important to record calibration data (see Fig. 2 below) of the participants slider movement before any actual performance recordings took place. This involved asking the participants to move the slider as far to the

Fig. 1. Custom slider

top as they comfortably could and to the bottom again as far as they could, and lastly to the middle. This made an important allowance for people who may have a limited slider range due to smaller hands or restricted movement. This calibration procedure was completed before each recording, due to the possibility that participants may start from a different "middle" position each time. Without this calibration the accuracy between multiple recordings and the recordings of other participants would be compromised.

Implementation of the sliders requires preparing the participants with the parameters for response, and the question they are to respond to with the slider. In this research the participants were asked to respond to how "engaged" they felt during the musical performance and to continually respond as necessary, moving the slider upwards as they felt more engaged and down when they were less engaged. The slider could, of course, be used with any question, providing illumination into many possible areas of audience response. It may be presented in a similar context to the standard Likert [15] scale, the middle being neither agree/disagree with the posed question, higher slider positions equating to more agreement and lower levels to disagreement. This data can then be analysed in the same way as Likert response data from questionnaires, the difference being that it is real-time and continuously changing with the response of the participant.

4 Data Analysis

4.1 Slider Data

Although the MCU could be configured to output the data in different formats, such as ascii sent via a serial connection, MIDI data is a convenient and well established way of recording the data in real-time. Once recorded, the MIDI slider data can be analysed in several ways. The slider data is recorded as MIDI Continuous Controller (CC) data which has a range of 0 to 127 (7 bit). There are 128 independent CC's available, and each slider is recorded to an individual CC. Most MIDI recording software allows the MIDI data to be exported as a standard MIDI file (SMF).[3] These files add a timestamp to the recorded MIDI data to allow the data to be played back accurately.

The SMF file can be converted to text/csv and imported into a standard database and/or spreadsheet for further analysis. Figure 2, below, shows two participant's slider data streams, overlaid on the same graph to allow comparison of levels of engagement over the period of the performance. The calibration process can be clearly seen on this graph with the initial high and low levels. The data for each participant can be separated out, (due to the individually assigned CC's) and analysed individually. This is useful if slider data between two or more performances is to be analysed. This allows the data from each performance from the same participant to be examined.

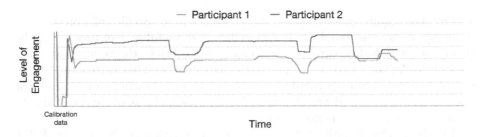

Fig. 2. Slider data of two participants

The MIDI recording of a musical performance may be recorded directly from the MIDI controller alongside the slider data. This data can be processed in the same way as the slider data and then used to compare audience response with the musical gestures of the performance. This may also be possible wherever sensors/devices capable of producing MIDI data are used in the performance. This is a useful method of analysis for performances using such technology, however, synchronising the slider data to the video recording is a more universal approach, allowing the data to be analysed directly with the recorded performance. This approach will now be discussed in more detail.

4.2 Video Synchronisation

The MIDI slider data can be recorded into any MIDI capable software. To allow the slider data to be synchronised to the video of the performance, a sound/click

---

[3] 'Standard MIDI Files contain all the MIDI instructions to generate notes, control individuals volumes, select instrument sounds, and even control reverb and other effects'[1].

should be placed at the beginning of the recording session in the recording software. This sound will then play at the start of the MIDI recording and will be heard on the video recording allowing synchronisation of the data with the video. A simpler alternative would be to make a "sync" sound or speak a specific word at the same time as starting the MIDI recording, which would serve the same purpose, as an anchor point to sync the MIDI recording with the video. MIDI software commonly synchronises with video editing software using the SMPTE (Society of Motion Picture and Television Engineers)[8] protocol. This would allow the MIDI software to playback the slider data concurrently with software running the video. This requires two separate software applications: one for MIDI and one for the video. An alternative method, requiring only one application, would be to use MIDI software capable of importing video, allowing the initial "sync" sound, to be aligned with the beginning of the recording. The slider data can then be played back along with the video, within the same software package.

4.3   Video with Slider Data Overlay

The methods of analysis described above both require specific software to view the data. A more accessible and potentially more useful way of processing the slider data with video, is to create a video that overlays the continuous slider data on top of the video recording of the performance. This video can then be viewed in any application capable of video playback, allowing more convenient analysis and sharing of data. This provides a very visual way of viewing the data in direct relation to the performance.

Firstly a video recording of the slider data playback needs creating. If the MIDI recording software has its focus set to follow the playback cursor, a video screen capture of the slider data playing back can be made. Using video editing software, this video can then be overlaid and aligned with the start/click sound on the performance video, allowing the movement of the slider data to be observed with the exact moment in the performance video when it occurred. Figure 3 shows the red play cursor of the slider data and how that data has moved along with the performance video. This provides a very powerful real-time analysis of the posed slider question, whether that is level of engagement, excitement, interest, immersion within a space or an evaluation of film, TV, gameplay, performance, dance, radio, theatre, etc.

5   Discussion

Although the mimetic design research is in the early stages, this "slider" method is already proving to be a powerful way of acquiring and analysing real-time data. A good example of this is provided in Fig. 2 which shows three distinctive dips for both participants, highlighting an area of interest requiring further examination. When comparing these points with the video data, it showed the dips occurring every time there was a slight pause as the synthesiser sound was changed. Neither of the participants eluded to this in the post-performance questionnaires. This discovery was only possible by finding out exactly where in the performance these dips occurred. As a consequence the performance was adjusted so there were no gaps, creating a more fluid performance from one sound to another. Slider data from this adjusted performance showed no more dips occurring on the sound change overs.

It is possible that even with showing a participant the slider data after the performance they wouldn't remember what they were responding to at that point, especially with longer performances. This demonstrates the usefulness of being able to analyse the slider data in real-time. Figure 3 shows the first minute of the same participant slider results, overlaid onto the performance video. This photograph demonstrates how easily the slider response data from several participants can be compared with each other and the exact point of occurrence in the performance video. This is particularly useful when the performances have an important visual aspect, in this case the gestural movements of playing instruments.

Since, this initial test with two participants, the slider method has been tested with more participants and larger groups. This data has only recently been taken, and so has not been fully analysed, but is showing promising signs of similar discoveries. There were some improvements made from the initial test including the addition of questionnaires specific to the research, labelled with the number of the corresponding participant slider. The hope is to provide deeper insight into the slider data, looking at how participant demographics and musical experience may affect the way they respond to music performance. Post-performance focus group discussions are being digitally transcribed, enabling the open responses to be considered with the slider data.

6   Conclusion and Future Directions

6.1   Evaluation and Future Improvements

The results so far indicate that the slider method for recording and examining continuous real-time response data is a viable technique. However, more research is necessary to fully investigate its potential and explore other possible uses. Since

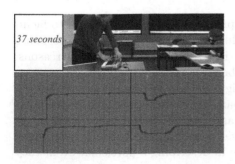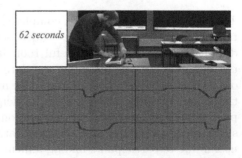

Fig. 3. Video with slider overlay (Color figure online)

the initial testing phase, several points have come in to focus, including some future improvements.

The calibration before each recording is crucial to successful comparison of results. Figure 2 shows that participant 2 has a higher initial "middle" slider position than participant 1, which needs to be taken into account when comparing levels. Adjustments to overall levels can be made using this calibration data, and is necessary for each recording because the "middle" point for a participant can vary between performances.

The sliders work well for groups of up to ten, but with larger groups the cabling to each slider might become less manageable. This leads to the consideration of a wireless system, and of course points to a possible use of mobile phones as a replacement to the sliders, due to the ease of implementing a wireless configuration. However, as mentioned previously, the physical sliders provide a tactile, intuitive interface for audience response, that generates continuous input without unnecessary distraction from the performance. The tangibility of the sliders more than compensates for the complexity of developing a custom wireless slider system and with the availability of wireless mesh network technologies is not a huge issue to overcome. A wireless system would allow a larger audience participation, and with the MIDI system having 16 separate channels of input as well as the 128 continuous controllers (discussed above) this would give a potential possibility of 2048 participants slider data being recorded simultaneously.

MIDI data is a relatively old system and has a low resolution of 128 steps (7 bit). If a greater resolution is needed OSC [3] could be implemented, although it is not as well supported as MIDI. There is a new MIDI specification (MIDI 2.0) being developed which will provide much higher resolutions, but is still in a prototyping stage. It will be compatible with the original MIDI specification so it should be simple to accommodate the new MIDI 2.0 protocol into existing work, when it is finally confirmed and available.

Another consideration in terms of analysis of slider data would be to segment the data points into discrete groups i.e. dividing a scale of 0 to 100 into 5 groups: 0–20, 21–40, 41–60, 61–80, 81–100. These groups could then be analysed in a manner similar to a Likert scale using standard statistical methods.

6.2 Other Use Contexts

This paper does not present a completed project but is a contribution to facilitate other research, where the "slider" solution to recording real-time response data might prove to be a useful tool. It is advantageous for several reasons: the data recorded in real-time; the data being continuous, which may capture data that an on/off "button" response might otherwise miss; the tangibility of the slider; the potential for large participant groups; the possibilities for postperformance analysis and the integration and consolidation of this quantitative slider data with other available qualitative data. This method may also prove useful due to participants finding difficulty in describing a particular event they were responding to within the performance, during a post-performance questionnaire or interview. With the slider method the participant doesn't need to describe the moment because the response data is synchronised to that moment.

The slider method for recording real-time response data may be implemented in a variety of contexts where a continuous real-time response from participants is required. This may be useful for research in any situation requiring real-time response data, such as media, film, gameplay, etc., but in particular is well suited to live performances in theatre, dance, music etc. A dance performance, for example, may also record data from sensors attached to the dancer, allowing the gestures within the dance to be analysed with the slider data.

It is clear from these initial explorations that the slider method is worth further investigation and development, and it is hoped that it may provide an efficacious tool for other research.

References

1. MIDI Association (2017). https://www.midi.org/
2. Mentimeter (2019). https://www.mentimeter.com/
3. Open Sound Control (2019). http://www.opensoundcontrol.org
4. Optivote (2019). https://www.optivote.co.uk/
5. Reactor (2019). http://www.roymorgan.com/products/reactor
6. Reply systems (2019). https://www.replysystems.com/
7. sli.do (2019). https://www.sli.do/
8. We are SMPTE — Society of Motion Picture & Television Engineers (2019). https://www.smpte.org/
9. Bachrach, A., Fontbonne, Y., Joufflineau, C., Ulloa, J.L.: Audience entrainment during live contemporary dance performance: physiological and cognitive measures. Front. Hum. Neurosci. **9**(179) (2015). https://doi.org/10.3389/fnhum.2015.00179
10. Brown, S., Hutton, A.: Developments in the real-time evaluation of audience behaviour at planned events. Int. J. Event Festival Manag. **4**, 43–55 (2013). https://doi.org/10.1108/17582951311307502
11. Cox, A.: Hearing, feeling, grasping gestures. In: Gritten, A., King, E. (eds.) Music and Gesture, pp. 45–60. Ashgate Publishing Limited, Aldershot (2006)
12. Cox, A.: Embodying music: principles of the mimetic hypothesis. Soc. Music Theory **17**(2), 1–24 (2011)
13. Latulipe, C., Cherry, E., Lottridge, D.: Love, hate, arousal and engagement: Exploring audience responses to performing arts. In: Proceedings of ACM CHI 2011, pp. 1845–1854, May 2011. https://doi.org/10.1145/1978942.1979210
14. Leiner, D., Fahr, A., Früh, H.: EDA positive change: a simple algorithm for electrodermal activity to measure general audience arousal during media exposure. Commun. Methods Measures **6**, 237–250 (2012). https://doi.org/10.1080/19312458.2012.732627
15. Likert, R.: A Technique for the Measurement of Attitudes. No. 140 in Archives of Psychology, New York (1932)
16. Martella, C., Gedik, E., Cabrera-Quiros, L., Englebienne, G., Hung, H.: How was it?: exploiting smartphone sensing to measure implicit audience responses to live performances. In: Proceedings of the 23rd ACM International Conference on Multimedia MM 2015, pp. 201–210. ACM, New York (2015). https://doi.org/10.1145/2733373.2806276

17. Stevens, C., Glass, R., Schubert, E., Chen, J., Winskel, H.: Methods for measuring audience reactions. In: Proceedings of the Inaugural International Conference on Music Communication Science, pp. 5–7 (2007)
18. Stevens, C., et al.: Cognition and the temporal arts: investigating audience response to dance using PDAs that record continuous data during live performance. Int. J. Hum. Comput. Stud. **67**, 800–813 (2009). https://doi.org/10.1016/j.ijhcs.2009.06.001
19. Swarbrick, D., et al.: How live music moves us: head movement differences in audiences to live versus recorded music. Front. Psychol. **9**(2682) (2019). https://doi.org/10.3389/fpsyg.2018.02682
20. Wang, C., Geelhoed, E.N., Stenton, P.P., Cesar, P.: Sensing a live audience. In: Proceedings of the SIGCHI Conference on Human Factors in Computing Systems CHI 2014, pp. 1909–1912. ACM, New York (2014). https://doi.org/10.1145/2556288.2557154
21. Wigham, P., Böhm, C.: Bazerbows: Instrument design and mimetic theory. Scottish Music Review 4 (2017). http://www.scottishmusicreview.org/

Out of the Box, into the Cubes: Envisioning User Experiences Through a Tool for Gamification, Toyification and Playification

Pirita Ihamäki[1](✉) and Katriina Heljakka[2]

[1] Prizztech Ltd., Pori, Finland
pirita.ihamaki@prizz.fi
[2] University of Turku, Pori, Finland

Abstract. This paper synthesizes the latest design knowledge accumulated with the Comicubes service design tool and solution prototyping method, and shares some of the lessons learned during the multiple workshops organized. The physical prototyping tool combines two-dimensional sketching with a three-dimensional and open-ended play medium – the cube. The method incorporates key aspects of service-oriented interaction design. We have used Comicubes to facilitate co-creation to generate new ideas, solutions or approaches to various design challenges related to the gamification, toyification and playification of services. This study summarizes four case studies where Comicubes has been employed as a platform for 3D prototyping, testing, and simultaneously, a tool to stimulate, envision and co-create interactive user experiences. The findings of the four case studies summarized indicate that the Comicubes tool and method are suitable to be used in design processes interested to facilitate co-creation and innovation of products, services and experiential spaces.

Keywords: Creativity · Comicubes · Gamification · Toyification · Playification · Prototyping · Service design

1 Introduction

This study presents a comprehensive way of understanding the uses of the Comicubes method and tool in envisioning user experiences related to gamification, toyification, and playification and for generating ideas, concepts, services or products in terms of service design. The case studies provided accentuate how simple paper technology invites workshop participants of different ages to come up with design solutions for the uses of interaction design, by using the theoretical concepts of gamification, toyification and playification as a point of departure.

Gamification has for some time been a buzzword, for example, in relation to innovations and reforms in working life, interaction design, service development etc. Famously, gamification refers to the application of elements familiar from games in a non-game context [1].

© ICST Institute for Computer Sciences, Social Informatics and Telecommunications Engineering 2020
Published by Springer Nature Switzerland AG 2020. All Rights Reserved
A. Brooks and E. I. Brooks (Eds.): ArtsIT 2019/DLI 2019, LNICST 328, pp. 49–68, 2020.
https://doi.org/10.1007/978-3-030-53294-9_5

In our thinking, gamification is a branch of development of *ludification* meaning a paradigm shift in culture according to which the world is becoming more play-oriented. The ludic became popular to denote playful behavior and fun objects during the 1960s. "Ludoliteracy is applicable across the full spectrum of media. It involves playing by the rules, bending and adjusting the rules in order to move easily through the system, or where necessary and possible, adjusting the system or playing the system. Considered as such, the term play is not only suitable for characterizing our contemporary media culture (playful) but also for defining the knowledge and skills (ludoliteracy, or play competence) required to function in media culture" [2]. We believe that although gamification carries many benefits to it such as a motivator once used as a strategic and process-based design and management tool, it is not the only way to stimulate peoples' playfulness in design-oriented tasks[1]. Instead, both creative individuals and companies could be invited to innovation and ideation work through alternative strategies to enhance their activities in playful ways—namely, through *paedic* approaches, or playification, or through *toyification*—i.e. the process of enhancing products and services with 'toyish' features, or those familiar from traditional and physical playthings. Again, this approach calls out for creative tools and methods, which assist in design processes interested in ludic/paedic enhancement.

A standard definition of creativity [3] states: "Creativity requires both originality and effectiveness". According to Corazza (2016) to this standard definition, originality and effectiveness are the two criteria that distinguish creative activity and creative process in particular, and therefore these criteria should be assessed to operationalize the definition in experiential terms [4]. As Runco (2015) pointed out, this definition "is in line with a parsimonious approach to the theory of creativity – the effort to reduce the description to the essential elements of the conductive mechanism, classifying other components as either influences, results or consequences of the creative activity" [5].

Our research proposes a tool and method for this purpose—the *Comicubes*, created by the second author of this paper. The Comicubes is simultaneously a physical and three-dimensional prototyping tool based on the idea of alphabet blocks, comic-style storytelling and simple paper technology. We acknowledge the playability and play potential of the Comicubes tool and method, as it allows image-based and comic-style storytelling to extend itself over previous boundaries of traditional two-dimensional storytelling, and in this way opens up new possibilities for open-ended play usually associated with the three-dimensional toy-form of the cube. Furthermore, we see potential added play value in reference to *AGE* (Augmented Game Experience) elements, which can be added to the cubes graphically and read from them digitally through use of mobile applications [6].

---

[1] In the context of pedagogy, Watson and Salzer (2016) have questioned the gamification approach as it often concentrates on metrics familiar from games, such as levels, points, experience, achievements, and other structures, "rather than on the mechanics that power games as spaces for exploration, critical thinking, collaboration, and the investigation of new perspectives". In our belief, these areas may be explored through alternative, or *paedic*, approaches, such as playification and toyification. For reference, see Watson and Salzer (2016) Playing Art Historian: Teaching 20th Century Art through Alternate Reality Gaming. *International Journal for the Scholarship of Technology Enhanced Learning,* Volume 1 Issue 1 2016, 100–111.

A playful approach to interaction design involves features that are likely to prompt suitable findings for better solutions related to new product and service development, such as in the development process of the interactive user experiences of customer journeys. Our aim is to discover the possibilities for use of the Comicubes by allowing creative play with the tool by breaking away from established patterns and combining actions or thoughts in new ways. From the play may emerge a new perspective that might be used later date in combination with other materials to solve new design challenges. In the studies synthesized in the paper at hand, play stands for a universal phenomenon and an effective mechanism for encouraging creativity. This also means that playful design involves having fun while solving problems or playing with a design tool such as the cardboard cubes that the Comicubes employ.

2 Method

In this paper, we aim to make a synthesis of our four case studies, which exemplify how gamification, toyification and playification as approaches to service design can be used in ludic (as well as paedic) enhancement of products and services by using Comicubes. In our cases presented in more detail further on in the paper, the development of concepts around solution prototypes is facilitated by using the Comicubes tool. The case studies suggest that by using the theoretical framework of motivational factors related to gamification, toyification and playification, together with a solution prototype an ideation tool like Comicubes, it is possible to envision how a previously non-ludically enhanced user experiences may be turned ludic/paedic by adding toyful, gameful and playful elements to the provided design, and in this way, offer users a 'playground' where both competitive and rulebound—gamified (or ludic)—and more open-ended and creative forms (paedic) of play may flourish.

All case studies are experimental research situations created by the authors. This permits strong control over the design and the procedure, and as a result, the outcome of experiments permits causal interpretation. This is referred to as the internal validity-the degree to which the experimental design excludes alternative explanations of the experiment's results. We have generalized the results of our studies to real-life context because experiments involve setting up an experimental situation and exposing subjects to different stimuli, experiments involve a relatively small number of subject and variables [7]. However, because there is strong control over the design, most experiments make an effort to manipulate several variables using design, for example, the concepts of the customer journey that permits effects in real-life situations. This means that all participants need to think like a customer and how they would potentially experience their own customer journey. However, with children, we have used open experiments, which has given the participating children the freedom to use the cube as an ideation tool, or to use multiple cubes to build actual toys of them.

In our *first case study* the Comicubes concept and tool was tested with a group of university students. In total, 50 students and teachers participated in the workshop [8]. The first participants' assignment was to *gamify* the Comicubes – to create their own prototypes for physical games by using the Comicubes tool. They enhanced the technique by using equipment (scissors, markers, whiter/blank cubes) and created various forms of physical game concepts suitable for social play, with an interest in a) the cubes as a basis for physical manipulation of the cubes (games of skill), and b) where the cubes were used as game elements featuring textual information related to game-play (party games) [8]. To collect data from this case study, we have used a social survey. The social survey was used to collect information about the participants' behavior. Data collection including a survey, videotaping and focus group interviewing gives the possibility to make data triangulations and in this way, making data richer and holistic overview [7].

In the *second case study* the authors created a toy design workshop for "digital natives", that is, preschool-aged children, 5–6-years of age. The participants were asked to "toyify", the cubes—to create a plaything of their choice by applying various art supplies to blank cardboard cubes. The workshop findings indicate that the children in our test group, whose experiences of play are not only guided by physical toys, but largely so by digital forms of interaction through games, were able to use the Comicubes to co-design and create physical playthings and develop associated play patterns and open-ended (toy) or rule-based (game) ideas for their use [9]. The preschoolers used the cardboard cubes to create both character-types of toys (i.e. toys with a face), and toys with textual or numerical information, that allow simple manipulation of the cubes. We have used the focus group technique involving the use of in-depth group interviews in which the participants have been selected because they focus on creativity in kindergarten, and this group 'focused' on a given topic ("what kind of toy or game would you like to design yourself") [10].

We have also utilized the Comicubes prototyping tool in designing enhancements to the customer journey: In the *third case study* the Comicubes tool was used both as a service design method and a solution prototype with concepts interested in gamification and playification—that is, physical prototypes that make up solutions for gamifying and playifying a touristic environment and service—in this case, a ski resort. In this case study, the Comicubes functions as a platform, which participants can engage freely with and exhibit the key behaviors of the customers at a gamified ski resort to understand in the envisioned experience. Further, it aims to explore how playification can be used in a ski resort context and how consumers can benefit from a 'playground' built on snowboard culture in a destination [11]. Since this is a new area of research, it was explored in depth and qualitative research paradigms were followed. Focus groups were been carefully selected from the marketing department and product development team of the ski resort (5 participants together). As a qualitative research method, focus groups emphasize group discussions and group interactions, as well as sharing and comparing of individual experiences among the participants. In this case study, the gamified and playi-fied location-based playground of the ski resort offers a framework for service designers, tourism developers, researchers and game designers. Service and game designers are not supposed to (and not able to) design customer's experiences directly [12]. They can only design, indirectly, the elements through which they can occur [13, 14]. Users themselves co-create unique experiences through their interaction across all touchpoints [15] and the application of the gamified location-based playground of the ski resort is proposes a resource to help to define the desired aspects of the service experience of the ski resort [11].

The *fourth case study* demonstrates a further example of how service design can be enhanced with a tool such as Comicubes. The design approach using co-creation in the development of new customer journeys established the vantage point for this final case study. In this case study, the authors used co-creation together with Comicubes (re-named to "BrandCubes" in the workshop) as a method in which users are observed engaging in planned activities around gamified prototypes of proposed solutions [16]. In this study, the BrandCubes solution prototypes were tested and validated in the environment of a Brand Office's creative space. Our approach was iterative and included co-creation with eight workshop participants, who are brand ambassadors working for the company. Information was gathered through observing and documenting the interaction and design work with video and photography. The observations were analyzed to understand customers' envisioned experiences and the impact they might have on proposed solutions. This study underlines the importance of aligning the gamified customer journey in encounters with customers, and suggests how this can be achieved [16].

3 Service Design

Design practice has been influenced by the changing landscape of human-centered design research. This design approach began in the 1970s and became widespread by the 1990s, proved to be most useful to use to development process interaction design of consumer products [17]. Consequently, new disciplines of design have begun emerge. Interaction design was first introduced in the late 1980s by Bill Moggridge and Bill Verblank [18]. Service design started to receive attention in 2006 with the advent of the first service design conference, Emergence 2006, that was put on by Carnegie Mellon University's School of Design [19]. Service design describes a strategic and holistic approach to consciously design, create and manage user experiences [20]. Moritz' (2005) definition of the concept follows: "*Service design helps to innovate (create new) or improve (existing) services to make them more useful, usable, desirable for customers and efficient as well as effective for organizations. Service design is a new holistic, multi-disciplinary, integrative field*" [21].

Service design can be seen as a mindset—a collection of attitudes that determine our responses to various situations. Service design can easily be thought of as the mindset of a group of people or an entire organization. As a mindset, service design is pragmatic, co-creative, and hands-on, it looks for a balance between technological opportunity, human need, and business relevance. Service design is often described as a process [22]. This process is driven by the design mindset, trying to find innovative solutions through iterative cycle of research and development. Iteration working in a series repeating, deepening, explorative loops is central, which means that participants aim for short cycles at the outset, with early user feedback, early prototyping, and quick-and dirty experiments. Service design can also see as a toolset, because it is about tempting to imagine design of a toolbox, filled with lightweight and approachable tools adopted from branding, marketing, user experience, and elsewhere [22]. Service design aims to co-create and make participation possible to connect people from different backgrounds, bringing them together around some seemingly simple tools that they all find meaningful and useful. These tools can be interpreted by different specialists working on them, allowing successful collaboration without having to understand too much each other's worlds. This means that service design can be seen as the glue between all disciplines, which offers a shared, approachable, and neutral set of terms and activities for cross-disciplinary cooperation [22].

The growth of service design towards a mature field of research and practice also requires a comparison and positioning within existing studies of service innovation, new service development and wider international and multidisciplinary field of service science and service research. "Enhancing Service Design" has been mentioned as one of the research priorities for the Science of Service [23], with an emphasis on the need to integrate design thinking and preforming and visualization service journey and service innovation process.

In the case studies presented in the paper service design research is driven forward with the Comicubes prototyping tool with the aim to legitimate and position gamification, toyification and playification as potential approaches to service design and to understand the designing of customer journeys. The interest in service design comes from the service design literature, aiming to understand how to better integrate customer experience in service development [24], but demonstrating a still limited understanding of design practices and approaches using gamification, toyification and playification engaging participants in the design process. Drawing on literature form two main perspectives on *service design* and *user involvement and engagement throught interaction design process* with gamification, toyification and playification–perspectives on service prototyping (service prototyping and customer journey studies), perspective on user involvement and engagements through the design process (using the service design framework through engaging the users)–this paper presents a theoretical framework and proposition to systematically study and interpret service design practices and outcomes.

In the four case studies presented in the paper, we aimed to test Comicubes both as a method and tool, suitable for different people as a design tool encouraging co-creative approaches. The findings of our studies show that the ways to use the tool are seemingly limitless, and in this way, can be compared to the classical example of how to innovative new uses for the paper clip—a popular exercise where participants try to create as many solutions to use the paper clip as they can.

The following section summarizes the perspective of service design with Comicubes and users involvement and engaging through interaction design processes with the goals of gamification, toyification and playification for the development of this theoretical framework. These two levels of research–marked on the figure (see Fig. 1)–have been chosen to consider different levels of data gathering 1) Interaction design processes and activities–based on service design theory and framework, 2) Innovation dimensions and patterns. As illustrated in Fig. 1, these levels will inform different kinds of questions, and will address the two aims of our research work:

This theoretical framework combines service design and service innovation. The scope of the study is to position service design practice within existing theories of service design, customer journey and service innovation, to initiate and facilitate a dialogue across disciplines; this means investigating service design-related case studies looking at innovation processes with dimensions of gamification, toyification and playification

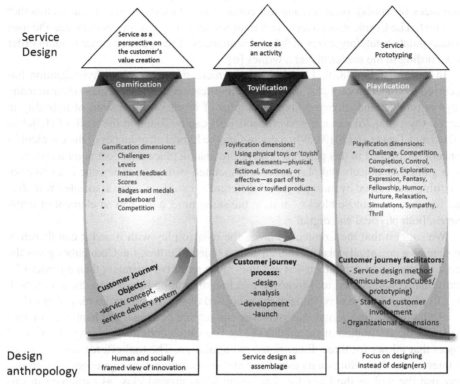

Fig. 1. A theoretical framework to inform case studies of service design prototyping by using gamification, toyification and playification in innovation and development of new customer experiences.

to identify and discuss participants engagements and contributions in relations to general descriptions of concept of service and ideation of products (for example case 2 where preschool-children designed toys and games). This theoretical framework also contributes to recent theorizations of service design practices especially with customer journeys in mind. These theories of service design and service innovation process suggest an expanded understanding of both design, interpreted as an assemblage rather than a design, and of service, described more as a business perspective or as a socially and culturally framed human activity (anthropological perspective) then as a market category.

3.1 Comicubes

The Comicubes concept introduced in this paper describes an experimental plaything, a solution prototyping tool, a hybrid combining sequential art of comic-style storytelling with a physical, three-dimensional play-object, toy or gamified service.

The physical Comicubes prototyping tool consists of foldable cardboard cubes with six sides each. Consequently, in the double-sided version there are twelve information layers to fill with either images (such as photographs) or text (letters, onomatopoetic utterances or words), or, as in classical comics, juxtaposed and serial images together with text. The Comicubes concept as a multisensory play concept also invites the user to manipulate/rotate/organizes tack/build sequences of the parts in either random order or according to the reader/player's wishes [6].

In earlier studies [8, 9, 11, 14, 20] it is interesting to see how hybridization has occurred in contemporary play material and applications. Hybridity may occur in many ways in product and service design. Examples of levels or dimensions of hybridity in games, toys, [25, 26] services and products [20] can be found in the work of Heljakka (2012) and Tyni et al. (2013). When discussing the hybrid affordances of the Comicubes concept introduced in this paper, it is therefore also in place to reflect upon its connections game-like objects and play patterns associated with them. The cube is a universal plaything recognized by most players of different ages, as it is often associated with dice and for example, puzzle blocks—it is, at the same time, a toy and an element of many games, both physical and digital.

We suggest that the Comicubes invite the user to play with it and it can therefore be seen as a potentially playful (ludic/paedic) object. Further, the Comicubes gives the serial narrative a toyish dimension and thus more narrative openness than a reader of a traditional comic is used to. Moreover, this transfiguration brings into discussion both the affordance and the play-value of the proposed object, the potential plaything [9].

Both physical and digital manipulatives can require bimanual and haptic interaction skills and the facilitation of spatial tasks [27]. The Comicubes tool is a tangible physical object that allows for three-dimensional manipulation. The tool affords various forms of interaction, depending on its users' age and skills. For instance, younger user groups may use the tool as the basis for developing ideas around play, as explained in this paper, whereas designers, for example, can use the tool to explore, narrate, and build on conceptual ideas for products, brands, and services [11].

The Comicubes tool presents an ecologically sustainable, economically sound, and potentially more inclusive ideation tool than the more expensive plastic bricks often used as design tools. The advantage of cardboard cubes compared to many other materials used in prototyping is their capacity to be enhanced with various textural dimensions or layers of information, whether physical or digital [11].

3.2 Using Gamification, Toyification and Playification as Ludic/Paedic Approaches in Design

Service design is as a tool, method, design process or approach, and by using gamification, toyification and playification as approaches together with a suitable tool in service development designing may stretch attention spans, boost artistic skills, promote logical design thinking and develop self-confidence. These conceptual approaches will be explained in the following.

Gamification
Garner (2014) defines gamification as the use of game mechanisms and experience design to engage and motivate people to achieve their goals. He describes that game mechanics are the key elements, which are common to many games, such as points, badges, and leader boards. The goal of gamification is to motivate people to change behaviors or

develop skills, or drive innovation. That is why gamification focuses on enabling players to achieve their goals – and as a consequence the organization achieves it is goals [11, 20, 28]. In our workshops, some of the users have used gamification of the Comicubes tool in their service designs by, for example, creating a board game. The playing of this board game conceptualized and built with Comicubes helps to understand how difficult situations with customers (like reclamations and claims) could be handled in a positive way.

Toyification

As we suggest, the gamification phenomenon should be complemented with the concept of *toyification*, which enables an understanding that users are not only interested in rule-based systems of interaction, but also in play patterns known from interaction with physical playthings we traditionally understand as toys. In this paper, we define *toyification* as follows: It communicates the idea of an entity (either physical, digital or hybrid) being intentionally reinforced a toyish appearance, form or function. In parallel to the gamification of everyday life, it is possible to trace simultaneously occurring patterns of toyification taking place in different realms of culture [29].

In other words, services and products start to become more "toyish". Toyification becomes apparent when looking at the areas of furniture design, for example, Eero Aarnio's interior design objects (Puppy), lamps (Ghost Floor lamp) or Minna Parikka's shoe design (such as shoes with bunny ears and tails). Moreover, toyification also takes currently place in the realm of edibles: For example, the coffee company chain Starbucks has created a holiday-themed drink: The coffee chain began the tradition with the vampire-inspired Frappula Franppuccino for Halloween in 2015, and carried it on with the Zombie Frappuccino (topped with pink whipped cream that resembled brains). In 2018, Starbucks followed the Halloween spirit with its latest creation, the "Witch's Brew Frappuccino". In this way, Starbucks has toyfied their products in playful ways and created special services for their customers, which a special emphasis on the holiday theme [30]. In our workshop with preschoolers, the children turned the Comicubes into toy designs, and in this way gave a toyish appearance and purpose for them.

Playification

In our case studies, *playification* as a parallel concept to *gamification*, takes an orientation towards the less rule-bound and more open-ended (or paedic) forms of play. Thus, by playification we mean that we have used casual game design elements [29]. The concept of gamification, should in this light, be extended to the playification of for example services, which entails a more 'playful' and less competitive, 'funification' of services, embracing more open-ended play and forms of creativity. In our workshops playification as a strategic approach came up in cases where the participants creating their concepts, test-played them to ensure that the game-play turned out as a fun experience for the users.

4   Case Studies

This paper brings together a set of four case studies conducted in association with design workshops for participants from different age groups. The collection of qualitative case studies presented in this paper present an approach to research that facilitates exploration of interaction design within its context using a variety of data sources, for example, service design methods, gamification frameworks, the playful experience model and the concept of toyification. This ensures that the issue is not explored through one lens only, but rather a variety of lenses, which allows for multiple facets of the phenomenon to be revealed and understood. The design tasks and results of the workshops will be discussed in the next part of the paper. The following Table 1 presents the number of participants who joined each workshop:

Table 1. Number of case studies participants.

Cases	Case 1	Case 2	Case 3	Case 4
Participants	50	13	5	8

Case Study 1: "University Students and Teachers Co-create Concepts for Games with Comicubes"

In the first case study conducted in spring 2016, the authors designed an experimental setup for 50 university students of early education training and their teachers including four phases: 1) An introduction of the Comicubes tool; 2) A preliminary survey on how Comicubes could be used to be filled by each group; 3) Designing with the Comicubes in groups of four, and; 4) Participants were allowed to play with their designs. First, the subjects got conditioned to a certain level of understanding Comicubes. Then the workshop participants assigned to create their own prototypes for the game concepts. They then chose additional materials and created their own designs according to the concepts by using Comicubes. Before commencing the workshop, one of the two researchers guided the participants in the role of giving a lecture on play-oriented design and giving the assignment, and other distributed and collected the surveys, observed the situation and ensured a stable treatment throughout the experiment. During this experimental workshop, data was gathered by documenting the co-designing of the concepts by photographing. The participants had 60 min to work on their designs.

The results of the first case demonstrate how the students and teachers could co-design concepts for new games easily, by using the 'quick-and-dirty' prototyping approach, and the Comicubes tool. After evaluating the concepts, the researchers were able to understand that the Comicubes tool and design method is helpful when considering the co-creation of gamified product ideas even if the workshop participants had no earlier expertise in game design (Fig. 2).

Fig. 2. Designs for game concepts using the Comicubes to co-create games of skill, and party games.

Case Study 2: "Digital Natives Co-create Toy Designs with Comicubes"

The ethnographic fieldwork that generated the empirical data for the second case study was carried out in spring 2016 in a kindergarten class that specializes in art education. The study aimed to identify what constitutes an interesting plaything if the children are allowed to co-create toy designs of their own. In the workshop for (n = 13) preschool-aged children (aged 5–6 years), participants were asked to create a toy of their choice by applying various art supplies to the Comicubes. The two workshops began with an introductory segment in which the first author showed two ready-made Comicubes to the children and then asked them to design a toy out of the given materials. The author guided the children in how to fold the cutouts and form the Comicubes. There were two kindergarten supervisors present during each workshop to assist the children. Our data collection methods for the workshop involves video ethnography, videotaped interviews and photographs. This data was used to involve the children their creations and to gain a firsthand account of their perspectives (Fig. 3).

Fig. 3. In the second case study, preschool-aged children co-created designs for toys by using the Comicubes.

During each 30-min workshop, which were documented through recorded video and photography, each child used two individual Comicubes in designing. The children were able to observe other participants' design process as they created their own cubes. In addition to talking with the children, the authors also observed their actions and attitudes to access their perspectives on playing. After the workshops concluded, each participant was taken to another room and interviewed about his or her design. Each child was asked to present his or her creation and demonstrate the potential uses for their toy design in a "show-and-tell" style. The children were also asked about what they found fun about the design process and what they considered difficult. To get another perspective on how their creations could be used in play, each child was asked to present the toy to another child in the group and demonstrate the play patterns they associated with it [9].

The results of the second case study show, how Comicubes as a design tool and method for service design, is suitable to be used in workshops for children as young as preschool age. Moreover, the findings of this workshop indicate how the participants were able to demonstrate the interaction, and communicate about potential play patterns for the toy, once interviewed individually after the workshop.

Case Study 3: "Professional Marketers and Developers Co-design New Gamified Services with Comicubes"

This third case study describes the enhancement of customer engagement by exploring gamified solutions to new services in the tourism industry envisioned with the help of the Comicubes in a workshop conducted with company professionals working in a ski resort. The ski resort's aim is to get customers to try new services. In the workshop, the participants were given the task to gamify the skiing holiday concept. This unique case study was conducted in a Scandinavian ski resort, which does not have similar products or services to offer yet. The study was carried out with marketing managers, a game developer, a development manager, all professional snowboarders and skiers. In the resort under scrutiny, the ski season lasts more than 200 days. The multifaceted ski area is suited for children, adults, beginners and experts. In our case study, the ski resort wants to enhance its service design and make the resort more inviting for today's customers through gamification.

In order to participate in the focus group, workshop participants had to meet the following criteria: They must 1) use a smartphone, 2) play mobile games, and 3) work in the ski resort. Altogether, five people participated in the four hour long workshop, which was conducted in January 2017. The workshop started with a one hour introduction, which discussed the concepts of service design, the customer journey, gamification, and introduced examples of location-based game design. The participants were divided into two teams, which designed their own customer journeys with the Comicubes. Both authors documented the group interaction, including non-verbal communication, by recording the working of both groups on video. During the recording of videos, we interviewed the respondents, who were asked about their gamified ideas of the ski resort using of the Comicubes tool and method. Our findings demonstrate how the Comicubes fits well to interaction design with service design purposes. For example, the Comicubes were found to be especially fitting in describing the customer journey at a gamified ski resort. This workshop was also largely grounded on the idea of co-creation: Interaction between two groups showed that they helped each other to envision unique experiences of the gamified ski resort, which was a key goal of the participants [11, 29].

As presented in the paper at hand, the Comicubes functions as a solution prototyping tool, which allows the building of 3D mock-ups with cardboard cubes. In this way, the Comicubes function as a multidimensional and multisensory ideation platform, which its users can engage freely with and exhibit key behaviors of the designing participants involved in, for example, co-creation of gamified customer journeys to understand envisioned service branding experiences (Fig. 4).

Fig. 4. A solution prototype of the gamified customer journey of a ski resort.

Case Study 4: "Professional Brand Office Staff Creates Gamified Solution Prototypes for Branding Purposes with Comicubes"

In our fourth case study, we have used the Comicubes as a method in which workshop participants are observed engaging in planned activities around gamified prototypes of proposed solutions [20]. There are two types of solution prototypes employed in this method: 1) Appearance Prototypes, which simulate the appearance of the intended offerings, and 2) Performance Prototypes, which primarily simulate the functions of the intended offerings. Through the observation of these prototypes used to simulate brand ambassadors' encounters with customers, user experiences are revealed to validate or invalidate assumptions about proposed solutions [31]. In our study, the Comicubes (re-named BrandCubes in this particular case study) solution prototypes were tested and validated in the simulated environment of a Brand Office's creative space. Our approach was iterative and included co-creation with eight workshop participants who are brand ambassadors. Information was gathered through observing and documenting the interaction with video and photography. The observations were analyzed to understand envisioned experiences of customers', and the impact they might have on proposed solutions [16].

The results of this case study function as evidence for, how the Comicubes are suitable to stimulate to ideate, and to aid the prototyping of gamified, toyified, and playified—manipulable and playable—solution prototypes related to branding. The three concepts that arose from the service design workshop with professionals working at a Brand Office, illustrate that the participants used the Comicubes in different ways: The first group built a game prototype of the cubes, to simulate the customer's first encounter with the company. The second group envisioned a concept they named the "Brand Book", which makes an interactive registry of the company's customers. The third group, in which the authors themselves participated, used the Comicubes to create a prototype for an "Escape Room" –a type of a gamified fair booth, in which interaction stems not only through the physical encounter with the brand ambassador, but through interaction of a gamified space, a 'maze' that the booth is, and that the customer must, with the help of the brand ambassador, 'solve' and 'escape', while becoming introduced to the company's offerings (see Fig. 5).

Fig. 5. The Comicubes used as BrandCubes to design the "Escape Room" fair booth concept and prototype.

5   Results

This paper synthesizes four unique case studies, conducted as workshops by using the Comicubes tool and method, with an interest in solving challenges related to interaction design in reference to playable artefacts, interactive environments and so on. The authors have summarized findings from the four workshops carried out with participants of different age and background, in order to understand the suitability of the tool and method of Comicubes. The Comicubes have been used both as a conceptual design method and a physical prototyping tool in order to create solution prototypes for toys, games, and gamified/playified services related to customer journeys in the tourism industry, and interaction between customers and brand ambassadors at a company.

In envisioning user experiences through physical and creative manipulation of Comicubes, and by using gamification, toyification, and/or playification as strategies of design, the workshops conducted have given participants an opportunity to visualize and materialize their creations related to innovated and conceptually enhanced products, services, or concepts related to the customer journey.

By observing the co-creation and design work that has been carried out at the workshops reported in our study make it possible to see that using the Comicubes to envision new products or services is considered fun and intuitive. There is no right or wrong way to play as the cardboard cubes enable users as designer to figure out what they want to do, make it happen, and then play with their very own gamified/playified, or toyified creations. The Comicubes also enables their users to simulate and reflect upon customer experiences through vocalizing and narrating. Moreover, it has helped the participants of the workshops to understand the ideas behind the conceptual approaches of gamification, toyification and playification.

The results from the workshops present, how participants' roles may be activated through gamification, toyification and playification a shared, physical prototyping tool like the Comicubes, and that service design as a form of interaction design manifests as a continuum ranging from passive participants to active co-creators to all the way to co-designers. Consequently, we can see that service design is an approach, which involves co-creation and co-designing of envisioned experiences. In order to be effective, these solutions—in our case studies solution prototypes and models—must be attractive first for the co-designers themselves. Moreover, as the results of our study indicate, service design can be understood as a mindset. In each of the workshops organized, the participants as interaction designers have had co-creating roles throughout the design process, and in this way, participated as co-designers through social interaction. The ability to design products and services by using the Comicubes also depends on the participants' cognitive capacities to think conceptually; their level of expertise, passion and creativity, as well as how they engage with the prototyping tool through employment of their physical manipulation skills.

In all of the four workshops, Comicubes invited the participants to play with physical materials and to create new ideas, which are easily turned to 3D models to play with. The playful element in design, may it be to use processes related to intentional ludification of design concepts; gamification, toyification or playification, must motivate and engage the participants of workshops like the ones described in this paper.

Table 2. Gamification, toyification and playification through Comicubes method and prototyping tool—a synthesis of different approaches to interaction design.

Area of interaction design	Approach: Comicubes as *method*	Solution for service design: Comicubes as *tool*	Potential mode of use
Interactive objects	Toyification, gamification (Workshops 1 and 2)	Toy and game design	Physical manipulation & interaction (human-to-artefact, human-to-human)
Physical space	Gamification, playification (Workshop 3)	Designing the customer journey	Physical interaction (human-to-service/system, human-to-space)
Conceptual space	Gamification (Workshop 4)	Designing service branding	Social interaction (human-to-human)

6 Discussion

This paper has taken an interest in envisioning user experiences through ludic and paedic approaches, namely gamification, toyification and playification with a physical ideation and prototyping tool, Comicubes. We have tested the Comicubes tool and method consisting of cardboard cubes in four workshops with different user groups with the aim to understand the potential of the tool and method to communicate ideas about interactive and engaging design. To arrive at a comprehensive understanding of the possibilities of this design tool, it has been tested with university students and their teachers, preschool-aged children, professional marketing and development staff in a ski resort and professional brand ambassadors.

In our first case study, the Comicubes was tested with 50 university students and their teachers. The participants in this study used Comicubes in two ways; both as a playful tool to create new solutions for game concepts and in the formation of the physical prototypes of their envisioned ideas. Participants reported to like the idea that Comicubes offers the possibility of being used simultaneously by multiple users. In our understanding, this could extend the design experience into a social experience, as using social interaction is the driving force, which Comicubes also envisions. Further, results indicate that a combination of pleasurable and creative elements causes a sense of deep enjoyment so rewarding that participants feel that manipulating Comicubes is worthwhile simply to be able to have a creative experience [8].

Following the synthesis of different approaches in service design used in the workshops and summarized in Table 2, it is possible to argue that the gamified Comicubes creations designed by the students in our first workshop aimed at two forms of interaction: a) human-to-artefact, and b) human-to-human. In other words, (physical) games require attention from their users both in terms of their artefactual nature, and through the interaction that is facilitated through their game-play, or mechanics. In this way, it is possible to claim, how the Comicubes can be used in envisioning interactions with both materials and other 'players'.

In the second case study, we have tested Comicubes with 'digital natives', i.e. preschool-aged children of 5 to 6 years of age, who in a workshop were asked to create a toy of their choice out of two cardboard cut outs, which could be turned into Comicubes. Moreover, they used art supplies, such as coloring pens, pictures and letters printed on cardboard squares. In the workshop, the participants were able to observe each other's work and exchange ideas while prototyping. When the creation of their toy designs ended, the children were encouraged to communicate about potential play patterns of their creations by illustrating their interactions with their playthings. The information layer used by most of the children on their cubes (cut-out images) was considered as an important part of the created play concepts [9].

Again, following the approaches presented in Table 2. the toyified Comicubes, as toy designs co-created by preschoolers, were intended for individual use. Hence, the mode of potential use these playthings promoted solitary play, and in this way, human-to-artefact interaction. However, as the participants of our workshop were asked to explain their peers about possible play patterns related to their creations, it became apparent that the toys could also be used in social play, or, to facilitate human-to-human interaction, if their players wished.

In the third case study, we tested the Comicubes as a service design method and as a solution prototype with 5 professional participants in two groups to create a gamified customer journey in ski resort context. The results of this case study show that Comicubes functions as a platform, which participant can engage freely with and exhibit the key behaviors one seeks to understand in the envisioned experience. The gamification of customer journey through the use of a tool like Comicubes, makes it possible to manipulate, identify, stimulate and evocate – and in this way enhance – the customer journey to invite the envisioned customer to enjoy and engage more playfully with the ski resort. With a solution prototype and ideation tool like Comicubes, it is possible to envision how a previously non-ludically enhanced tourism service may be gamified and playified by adding elements familiar from games (such as various goals, challenges, scoring mechanisms etc.) to the provided service and to offer the potential users not only a 'game board' but a whole service-related playground, where both competitive and more creative play may flourish [11].

In this case study, the Comicubes were used together with the approaches of gamification and playification. Designing for interaction in association with customer journeys requires the designers to think of at least two modes of interaction such as human-to-service/system, and human-to-space. By using the Comicubes it was informative for the participants to for example, consider the different touch points of the envisioned customer journey, as they could see these in a physical form through the prototype they built. In this way, the Comicubes facilitated the process of multidimensional thinking, through a multisensory approach. Furthermore, the participants were able to reflect on possible interaction scenarios of human-to-space (i.e. locations of services around the ski resort area) by exploring the customer journey both in a two-dimensional (sketch), and three-dimensional (prototype/miniature model) form.

In the fourth case study we have tested the Comicubes as part of a workshop interested in creating solution prototypes related to gamification, which were co-created, tested and validated in a simulated environment of a Brand Office's creative space. Our approach was iterative and included co-creation with eight workshop participants who are professional brand ambassadors. The observations made and recorded during the workshop were analyzed to understand customers' envisioned experiences and the impact they might have on proposed solutions [16].

In this final case study, the task was to design for interaction in association with services provided by a Brand Office. The used approach was gamification. The findings of this workshop demonstrate how Comicubes could be used to envision social interaction, and more particularly, human-to-human interaction. In the three solution prototypes created, Comicubes served the workshop participants three different ways: 1) in designing interaction between customers and brand ambassadors in a board-game form, 2) to envision a new service designed to serve customer relations, and finally, 3) to build up a three-dimensional prototype communicating a new approach to the fair booth – an "Escape Room."

In sum, Comicubes has been tested with various user groups and used in different contexts, such as the academic environment, the early education environment, the tourism destination environment, and the brand business environment. We are interested to continue to discover the potential that Comicubes carries in the creative processes supporting design, with new users, such as primary school students, professional game designers (both board games and digital games), artists, and so on.

The limitation of the reported case studies is that we have been using only one method (Comicubes/BrandCubes) in service design processes in the workshops and do not compare it to other methods. However, our aim was to investigate the potentiality of the ideation and prototyping tool in combination with different ludic/paedic approaches.

7 Conclusion and Future Research

The mosaic of studies summarized in this paper present a contribution to the field of design research, with an emphasis on pragmatics of service design. This research is explorative as it investigates a new and emerging area—how to find universal, inclusive, and sustainable aids to service design that are suitable to be used in the context of uses interested in the playful approaches of gamification, toyification and playification. The Comicubes, seen from the perspective of a research instrument and potential playful tool that may stimulate design creativity allows exploration of dimensions of its use as both a tool and a method for service design. As the findings collected from the four case studies present, the Comicubes affords seemingly limitless ways to approach service design tasks related to gamification, toyification and playification. The physical tool allows both personal, playful engagement with the materiality of the tool as well as it promotes possibilities for co-creation. In other words, the findings suggest that Comicubes could be used as a basis for creating performance based prototypes. Conceptually, the Comicubes invites to social play around the design of products and services, as envisioned in the case studies. Furthermore, the case studies show how the tool encourages users of different ages to get involved in service design. In future work, the authors aim to build up connections between the paper-based Comicubes tool with digital media, in order to map out the possibilities of design that the tool affords in terms of gamification, toyification and playification.

Finally, as illustrated Comicubes provides a physical platform and tool with hybrid potentialities, which functions as a universal, as well as an easy, conversational and playful method to start dialogues on the future of gamified, toyified and playified design approaches for products or services.

One key aspect of ludic/paedic enhancement of design is to carry out dialogues that start with the manipulation of three-dimensional models and prototypes. To play, in essence, is not only about imagining, but also about trying out. Consequently, the studies synthesized in this paper offer food for thought for broader implications of using ludic and/or paedic approaches to service and interaction design in order to achieve more playfully engaging products and services for *homo ludens* –the playing person within all of us.

Acknowledgements. The authors would like to express their gratitude to all the participants who joined the four workshops.

References

1. Boulet, G.: Gamification: The Lates Buzzword and the Next Fad, eLearn magazine, Where Thought and Practice Meet (2012). https://elearnmag.acm.org/archive.cfm?aid=2421596. Accessed 19 Oct 2019
2. Raessens, J.: Homo ludens 2.0. The ludic turn in media theory. Inaugural address Utrecht University (2012). https://mediarep.org/bitstream/handle/doc/2965/Rethinking_Gamification_91-114_Raessens_Ludification.pdf?sequence=1. Accessed 19 Oct 2019
3. Runco, M.A., Jaeger, G.J.: The standard definition of creativity. Creat. Res. J. **24**, 92–96 (2012). https://doi.org/10.1080/10400419.2012.650092
4. Corazza, G.E.: Potential originality and effectiveness: the dynamic definition of creativity. Creat. Res. J. **28**(3), 258–267 (2016). https://doi.org/10.1080/10400419.2016.1195627
5. Runco, M.A.: A commentary on the social perspective on creativity. Creat. Theor. Res. Appl. **2**, 21–31 (2015)

6. Heljakka, K., Ihamäki, P.: Comicubes – a playful tool to stimulate (design) creativity. In: Celebration & Contemplation, 10th International Conference on Design & Emotion, Amsterdam, Holland, 27–30 September 2016, pp. 387–394 (2016)
7. Hox, J.J., Boeije, H.R.: Data collection, primary vs. secondary. In: Encyclopedia of Social Measurements, vol. 1, pp. 593–599 (2005)
8. Ihamäki, P., Heljakka, K.: Invitation to open-ended and hybrid play: Comicubes – a tool for creativity and participatory design. In: Make it Now! Learning, Exploring, Understanding – Conference in University of Turku, Rauma Unit, Rauma, Finland, 28–30 September 2016 (2016)
9. Heljakka, K., Ihamäki, P.: Digital natives and cardboard cubes: co-creating a physical play(ful) ideation tool with preschool-children. In: 16th Interaction Design and Children Conference (IDC 2017), 27–30 June 2017, Stanford CA, USA, pp. 541–547 (2017). http://dx.doi.org/10.1145/3078072.308432
10. Rabiee, F.: Focus-group interview and data analysis. Proc. Nutr. Soc. **63**, 655–660 (2004). https://doi.org/10.1079/PNS2004399
11. Ihamäki, P., Heljakka, K.: A framework for playing with heritage: exploring the gamified playground of a Finnish Ski Resort. In: Heritage, Tourism and Hospitality International Conference 2017 (HTHIC 2017), Pori, Finland, 27–30 September 2017, pp. 89–101 (2017)
12. Marshall, C., Rossman, G.B.: Designing Qualitative Research, 5th edn. Sage, Thousand Oaks (2006)
13. Forlizzi, J., Ford, S.: The building blocks of experience: an early framework for interaction designers. In: Proceedings of the 3rd Conference on Designing Interactive Systems: Processes, Practices, Methods, and Techniques, pp. 419–423. ACM, New York (2000). https://doi.org/10.1145/347642.347800
14. Salen, K., Zimmerman, E.: Rules of Play – Game Design Fundamentals. The MIT Press, Cambridge and London (2004)
15. Patricio, L., Raymond, F., Cunha, F.J., Larry, C.: Multilevel service design: from customer value constellation to service experience blueprinting. J. Serv. Res. **14**(2), 180–200 (2011)
16. Ihamäki, P., Heljakka, K.: Inhimillinen vuorovaikutus ja viestintä ryhmätyön yhteiskehittämisessä [Human Interaction and Communication in Co-creation: The BrandCube method used in the Development of Brand Communication]. In: Työelämän tutkimuspäivät 2018, Tampere University, Tampere, Finland, 1–2 November 2018 (2018)
17. Sanders, E.: Converting perspectives: product development research for the 1990s. Des. Manag. J. **3**(4), 49–54 (1992)
18. Moggridge, B.: Designing Interactions. MIT Press, Cambridge (2007)
19. Sanders, E.B.-N., Stappers, P.J.: Co-creation and new landscapes of design. Co-Design **4**(1), 5–18 (2008). https://doi.org/10.1080/15710880701875068
20. Ihamäki, P., Heljakka, K.: Gamification of the customer journey at a Ski Resort. In: Bohemia, E., De Bont, C., Holm, L.S. (eds.) Conference Proceedings of the Design Management, vol. 1, pp. 247–260. Design Management Academy, London (2017)
21. Moriz, S.: Service Design, Practical Access to an Evolving Field, Köln International School of Design, MEDes- MA European Studies in Design, University of Applied Science Cologne, Köln, Germany. https://issuu.com/st_moritz/docs/pa2servicedesign/4. Accessed 13 Jan 2019
22. Sticdorn, M., Lawrence, A., Hormess, M., Schneider, J.: This is Service Design Doing, Applying Service Design Thinking in the Real World, A Practioners' Handbook. O'Reilly Media Inc., Sebastopol (2018)
23. Ostrom, A.L., Bitner, M.J., Brown, S.W., Burkhard, K.A., Goul, M., Smith-Daniels, V., Demirkan, H., Rabinovich, E.: Moving forward and making a difference: research priorities for the science of service. J. Serv. Res. **13**(1), 4–36 (2010)

24. Edvardsson, B., Tronvoll, B., Gruber, T.: Expanding understanding of service exchange and value co-creation: a social construction approach. J. Acad. Mark. Sci. **39**, 327–339 (2011). https://doi.org/10.1007/s11747-010-0200-y
25. Heljakka, K.: "Hybridisyys ja pelillistyminen leikkituotteissa. De-materiaalisen ja re-materiaalisen rajankäynnissä" [Hybridy and gamification in playthings. On the crossroads of de-materialization and re-materialization]. In: Suominen, J., Koskimaa, R., Mäyrä, F., Turtiainen, R. (eds.) Pelitutkimuksen vuosikirja 2012, pp. 82–91 (2012). http://www.pelitutkmus.fi/vuosikirja2012/PTV2012.pdf. Accessed 13 Jan 2019
26. Tyni, H., Kultima, A., Mäyrä, F.: Dimensions of hybrid in playful products. In: Proceedings of International Conference on Making Sense of Converging Media, MindTrek 2013, Tampere, Finland, 1–3 October. ACM (2013)
27. Zaman, B., Vanden Abeele, V., Markopoulos, P., Marshall, P.: Editorial: the evolving field of tangible interaction for children: the challenge of empirical validation. Pers. Ubiquit. Comput. **16**(4), 367–378 (2012). https://doi.org/10.1007/s00779-011-0409-x
28. Garner, W.: The Processing of Information and Structure. Psychology Press, Taylor & Francis Group, New York (2014)
29. Ihamäki, P., Heljakka, K.: Come and play service designer with us! – co-creating a playable customer journey installation. In: Fifth International Conference on Design Creativity (ICDC 2018), Bath, United Kingdom, 31 January–2 February 2018 (2018)
30. Sherman, E.: Starbucks Unveils Halloween- Themed Witch's Brew Frappuccino (2018). In Kirchn. https://www.thekitchn.com/starbucks-unveils-witchs-brew-frappuccino-263798. Accessed 13 Jan 2019
31. Kumar, V.: 101 Design Methods, A Structured Approach for Driving Innovation in Your Organization. Wiley, Hoboken (2013)

Balancing Enlightenment and Experience
in Interactive Exhibition Design

Peter Vistisen, Vashanth Selvadurai$^{(\boxtimes)}$, and Jens F. Jensen

Department of Communication and Psychology, Aalborg University, Aalborg, Denmark
{vistisen,vashanth,jensf}@hum.aau.dk

Abstract. This paper presents insights from a collaborative design research project, in which a zoological aqua park in Denmark integrated multiple gamified digital installations in their new exhibition design. We document how these designs are in a tension between allowing game-based interactions, and the didactic communication about facts in the exhibition. We study the implemented solutions based on qualitative interviews with visitors, and with quantitative data from the backend game analytics of the installations. From triangulating these data sets we show how attempts to deliver purely fact-based information through didactic design elements fail to succeed in engaging the visitors, while stealth learning sparks enlightenment about the subject matter. Our results suggest that this is true both in cases in which users fully understand and play through the intended interactions, as well as when more negotiated interpretations of the digital installations are performed. From this our contribution are guiding principles for the balance, between experience and enlightenment in gamified exhibition designs.

Keywords: Interactive exhibitions · Experience design · Informal learning

1 Introduction

Museums are historically created and developed in a field of tension between a perception of the museum as a means of public information and enlightenment, and as a facility for visitors' experiences and entertainment. This tension becomes especially visible in the museums' dissemination and exhibition design as a number of dilemmas that contemporary exhibitions and dissemination practices seek to deal with [1]. The discussion about 'enlightenment' versus 'experience' has always played a major role in the discourse around museums [2]. 'Enlightenment' is here connected to the informative, factual, forming, educational, and didactic, while 'experience', on the contrary, is associated with the engaging, involving, emotional, narrative, imaginative, playful, and entertaining. Furthermore, Hein has also noted that these discourses also have more philosophical roots, from a classical didactic expository view of museums, towards more modern constructivist views seeing museum visitors as active agents of their own experience and learning at the museum [2]. The experiential dimension has in recent years been associated with adding more interactive experiences through applying digital

© ICST Institute for Computer Sciences, Social Informatics and Telecommunications Engineering 2020
Published by Springer Nature Switzerland AG 2020. All Rights Reserved
A. Brooks and E. I. Brooks (Eds.): ArtsIT 2019/DLI 2019, LNICST 328, pp. 69–87, 2020.
https://doi.org/10.1007/978-3-030-53294-9_6

technologies - often by providing game elements such as quizzes, scavenger hunts or actual video game interactions in installations in the museum context. These gamified experience designs have seen widespread popularity among audiences, and especially shows to engage and motivate younger audiences, who have grown up in a significantly more entertainment-oriented media landscape than just a few decades ago [3, 4]. Through games and interactive exhibitions, these new audience are becoming 'users' of the museum exhibition a performative arena, in which experience-oriented content is seen as a platform to deliver the facts about the museums subject matter.

However, in the museum context, this trend towards increased use of gamified experiences, are still facing opposition from traditions favoring more traditional means for assuring an ordered, factual and authoritative delivery of educative content to enlighten our societies. While the degree of resistance varies, the debate between enlightenment and experience can be found in most modern museum context often leading to compromises made when creating new exhibitions. These compromises often result in arbitrary mixes of experience-based and enlightenment-oriented form and content - especially when making decisions about designing interactive digital exhibitions. If designing a primarily experience-oriented feature, such as a game element is added, the designer will often meet the demand for also including a clear and present layer of enlightenment too - e.g. by adding a text page with facts to read before playing. In this regard, the enlightenment is forced into the experience-based interaction design and would be true also in the opposite situation in which simple gamified elements (e.g. so-called 'badgification') is added as a superficial add-on to an exhibition.

It is our hypothesis, that this tension of traditions and its resulting compromises in design are not optimal for either tradition and only serve to create inadequate interactive exhibition design. Instead, interactive exhibition design needs to balance the traditions, by allowing for other types of enlightenment than authoritative didactic expository while the gamified installations should also not stray too far away from communicating a message about the subject matter. The question is then, how do we balance modern interactive exhibition design with the museums need for delivering complex facts in a compelling manner which both enlightens and entertains the visitor?

This paper presents insights from a collaborative design research project, in which a zoological museum in Denmark collaborated with the authors about the integration of multiple digital installations in their new exhibition design. From studying the user behavior through both qualitative and quantitative research, we show how attempts to deliver purely fact-based information through didactic design elements failed to succeed in engaging the visitors, while a more informal delivery through socially engaging interaction design sparked enlightenment about the subject matter through a manner of stealth learning [3].

2 Enlightenment or Experience? An Ongoing Discourse in Museum Research

This section details the background for the design space, showing the debate, between enlightenment and experience design through four archetypical positions.

Sæter discusses the museums' basic values and objectives in a historical perspective on the challenge framed as being between conservation and consumption [5]. This describes a major historical movement 'From enlightenment to entertainment' as it is called in a headline; i.e. from the modern museum where the basic values and objectives were to teach and educate the public through displays to the present-day post-modern museum that moves towards becoming a 'commercial entertainment product' [5]. The objective for the modern museum is to both educate and enlighten, with the basic values rooted in the belief in development, culture, formation, and progress. In contrast, the objective of the non-constructive, or post-modern museum, is entertainment, and the basic values are lack of worry, freedom and openness [5]. Sæter even speaks – with reference to Belk [6] – of a 'disneyfication' of museums which "...has sacrificed education and enlightenment for superficial entertainment based on illusions. In the competition for the audience, museums create an illusory hyped-reality" (Our translation) [5]. The first position in the debate between enlightenment and experience, exemplified by Sæter, is thus for the museum's classical enlightening as well as opposes the use of experience and entertainment-based dissemination and exhibition design.

Diametrically opposite is the case with Kirschenblatt-Gimblet, who describes a paradigm shift: "From an informing to a performing museology" [7]. The shift is characterized by a movement from 'information' to 'experience', from 'knowing' to 'feeling', from 'things' to 'stories', and from 'display' to 'mise-en-scène'. The new museology is characterized by, among other things, a more theatrical or dramatic approach to the museum experience – what is here called 'museum theatre' [7] – that, instead of merely presenting objects, makes use of museum practices such as scenography, mise-en-scène, tableaux, scenarios, installations and 'habitat displays'. This approach gives pride of place to drama, the narrative and emotional engagement and, in place of the cognitive and visual, focuses on the somatic and affective. "This is a special kind of theatre", writes Kirschenblatt-Gimblet, "and its point is not information but 'experience', a term that is at once both ubiquitous and under-theorized. 'Experience' indexes the sensory, somatic, and emotional engagement that we associate with theatre, world fairs, amusement parks, and tourism". Therefore, this new modus is also called "the expo style" [7] or "the expo mode of the new generation museum" [7] with a reference to 'world fairs' and the Expo-World's more performative oriented display forms that are also far more 'customer focused' and 'commercially positive' [7]. That is to say, a shift from the traditional enlightening, information-oriented museum to a more experience-oriented museum. The second position, exemplified by Kirschenblatt-Gimblet, is thus - opposite Sæter – critical of the classical museum's informative and educational functions, and in favor of a more performative, experience-oriented, engaging exhibition practice.

In a Danish context, Skot-Hansen has set out to illuminate and discuss the current situation in which the Danish public museums find themselves, and in particular their role in the experience economy [8]. The experience economy is here seen as both the cause of and solution to the current challenges facing the museums. The point of departure is that the state-subsidized museums are under both economic and political pressure, in part because of the experience economy. The museums are challenged by the experience economy, partly by competition from other more commercial experience-oriented attractions, as well as an audience who is increasingly pampered by more engaging and sensational experiences, partly in the form of demands to enter into the experience economy as well as the economic development of cities and regions. Therefore, museums must re-evaluate their classical role as institutions of enlightenment and education [8]. The museums, hence, find themselves in a tension field between what can be described as enlightenment on the one hand and experience on the other. Skot-Hansen expresses it in this way: "The discussion on enlightenment versus experience ... permeates the public debate on the role of museums; not least the question of where the boundaries lie" (Our translation) [8]. Later, Skot-Hansens elaborates: "The museums are moving in a field of tension between being cultural institutions based on the five pillars (collection, registration, preservation, research and dissemination), and being experience-saturated attractions that contribute to the Danish experience economy's continued development" (Our translation) [8]. At the same time, experiences and the experience economy are seen as the solution to the challenge, among other things, in that the museums can and must learn to work strategically with experience development, i.e. learn from the instruments of the experience economy in relation to using experiences such as staging and strengthening experience value and use orientation. It should not be done solely for creating an economic surplus or added value, but primarily to create relevant, challenging and lasting experiences for the audience. Therefore, one of the main conclusions of the report is that the experience-economic performance of museums should not be judged only on their contribution to the local and national economy but should be judged according to artistic and cultural criteria [8]. The third position, represented by Skot-Hansen, is thus not a simple 'for' or 'against', respectively, enlightenment and experience. Rather, the relationship between the two approaches takes the form of a means to an end, i.e. using experiences and the experience economy as instruments to promote the core purpose: enlightenment.

Finally, a fourth position is represented by Floris and Vasström who – as far back as 1999 – discussed whether the objective of museums is enlightenment or experience [9]. Floris and Vasström associate the genesis of museums to the modern society's formation project and the modern democratic nation states' narrative of progress and freedom. Just as they point out, that the modern project and the narrative about the necessary course of development and continuous progress in the present time have collapsed. The enlightenment element relates particularly to the museum's original, historical form, and often there has been a focus of enlightenment in a pure, next puritanical form, where the experience had only a subordinate role [9]. On the other hand, they link the experience to more current practices where many museums have, in recent years, to a much higher degree, made use of entertaining and activating elements of dissemination in exhibitions and in their overall work. A practice they particularly associate with experience centers and the new visit centers with historical themes. Even so, the attitude is that the museums should also learn from the experience aspects and implement the lessons learned where the museums should take up the challenge instead of blindly distancing themselves from the experience centers etc. and stamping them as disneyfication. This perspective advocates for a synthesis of the two aspects into a new formation or educational project – having both enlightening and entertaining experiences where it is not a question of either or. Floris and Vasström's position, is thus not characterized by a 'for' or 'against' enlightenment and experience, respectively, or a suggestion to instrumentalize one as a means for the other as an end. Rather, the case is that the contradiction or conflict between enlightenment and experience dissolves in favor of a new more nuanced and complex understanding of a possible synthesis of enlightenment and experience, where one can obtain enlightenment and learning through experiences – as in 'experience-based learning' – and get experiences and enjoyment through enlightenment, information and learning – as in 'learning-based experiences' or 'edutainment'.

As can be seen from the above, the discussion about enlightenment versus experience is an ongoing and dominant discourse within the museum area and in the scientific literature on exhibitions. This marks the arena of which this study's constructive design research project entered, with an attempt to balance the tension between positions, in ensuring enlightenment in a museum context, through an experience-based approach.

3   Interactive Exhibition Design

The recent discourse of museums and exhibitions elaborates a partial and complementary picture of the complexity in balancing between enlightenment and experience. For the past two decades, exhibitions around the world have explored different methods to comply the requirement without compromising the enlightenment aspect. Starting from film and audio guides to integrating number of digital technologies to enrich visitors' experience [10].

Already a decade ago, Tallon argued that exhibitions can enhance the exhibition experience by providing involving experiences through new digital technologies [11]. Users are increasingly engaged and actively involved, among other things through interactivity and active contribution [12–15]. As such, today, it is almost unavoidable to interact with a number of digital technologies during an exhibition visit, which have enabled new kinds of interaction between exhibition and its visitors. Although the post digitization phase of exhibitions reflects a more thorough incorporation of digital content in exhibition practices [16], the expectation by exhibition visitors for new digital experiences are increasing parallel to the technological advancement. The potential of digital technologies not only contains qualities in providing involving experiences, but also richly authentic learning experiences that enrich visitors' enjoyment and learning, which would be difficult to provide through other media [17, 18]. As such, this area has in recent years attracted international attention and investments on digital experiences in exhibitions [19–23].

Studies have shown that digital technologies can facilitate knowledge acquisition, and especially interactive digital technologies have shown to enhance visitor interaction and substantiate learning [24–27]. Studies with focus on design and evaluation have provided insight into how visitors interact with digital technologies in exhibitions [4, 28, 29]. However, knowledge regarding how visitors understand, apply and respond to new digital technologies ability to mediate both enlightenment and experience is more limited [20, 21].

Gammon and Burch emphasize the importance of hardware, software and content being based on an understanding of users' needs, desires, expectations and behavioral patterns [17]. Obviously, this does not sound like a particularly surprising conclusion. However, reality is often that many digital exhibition projects are not based on actual user tests or reconciliations with users' expectations, who have to use the digital offers [19–21, 30, 31]. Compared to this view, it does not seem surprising when Gammon and Burch point out that users often respond unexpectedly and surprisingly to digital installations in relation to exhibition organization's expectations, intentions, and desires [17]. A large amount of literature exists about museum visitors' experience in the physical exhibition space. However, research into what characterizes the exhibition visitors' digital interactive communication, as well as what wishes and expectations museum users have for digital communication, is still scattered. Heath and Lehn's studies are another example of more critical studies of digital exhibitions [19, 20]. They conclude that it is often the case that digital installations in museum rooms facilitate interactivity between one user and a machine and thus do not involve other surrounding museum users. They justify that much technology in museums is based on home computers, and they emphasize the importance of developing new technologies that are adapted to the particular social interaction that one wants to create in exhibition contexts. As such, both Gammon and Burch, as well as Heath and Lehn, point out that where there has been much research in computer software and hardware for home use, it has not applied to the same extent in exhibitions which is a significantly different context. Several studies show that users' use of and expectations for computer-based technology is very different when it takes place in an exhibition than when it takes place at home [32, 33]. Thus, there is a need to focus on the engagement, interaction, and knowledge dissemination, involving experiences can craft through new digital technologies [34]. It is important to investigate how to further integrate digital media on the terms of the exhibitions subject matter, in order to ensure that the experience-based content (in software and hardware) is formed around the enlightenment goals of the exhibition, rather than as a technical add-on.

4 Investigating the Tension: The Hunters of the North Sea Concept

To experiment with balancing the tension between experience and enlightenment through designing digital exhibition elements as an integrated part of a modern museum, the authors participated in a major re-design of an exhibition area at the Danish zoological museum 'The North Sea Oceanarium' (Oceanarium). The Oceanarium is an aqua zoological facility in Denmark disseminating the flora and fauna in the North Sea through a combination of learning and entertainment. The aqua zoo driven by 35 full-time employee and is reinforced with additional 35 seasonal employees on high season periods. The exhibition has around 160.000 visitors every year [35].

In 2017 the Oceanarium initiated a renewal project of an old exhibit dated back to 1998. The desire was to create an involving family experience that enlightened about the food chain in North Sea from predators to prey between the coast and sea. The exhibit extends over a larger area in the exhibition, and therefore was divided into smaller areas with different media platforms to disseminate the content and provide an involving experience respectively to children, youths and adults. As such, the desire was to explore the potential of emerging digital technologies to create integrated digital experiences that enlightened about the food chain in North Sea.

The authors were involved in both conceptualization, design, and implementation of four major digital exhibition installations, which all represented different facets of the tensions, and compromises, arising when balancing experience and enlightenment related aspects of interactive exhibition designs. Below we will detail the design of the four interactive installations in the new exhibition.

4.1   The Four Gamified Installations

Today, play and entertainment is often a part of an exhibition experience. Various studies have demonstrated the potential of play and entertainment to instigate learning at interactive exhibitions [36–38]. As such, all four digital installations were designed to enrich the visitors in the new exhibit through using various gamification elements to engage the visitors. The four installations, covered in the study, are named: The Big Ocean Window, Seal Hunter, Seal Nursing, and Hold Your Breath.

Fig. 1. The interactive installation Big Ocean Window (BOW) with the big 100 m^2 digital screen and the six individual touch screens for controlling the fish avatars on the large screen.

The Big Ocean Window (BOW) disseminates the food chain of predators and prey between cost and deep sea. The installation consists of a 100 m^{20} LED screen connected with six individual touch screen control units, where the visitors can interact with the shared big screen by taking role as a mackerel hunting for food, while they also have to avoid being eaten by bigger predators (see Fig. 1). The control units consist of a screen with a first-person view (the maceral), joystick to control the directions, and a button to attack (see Fig. 2).

The big screen provides a third-person view, giving an overview of the virtual space. The visitors must orientate where the food and predators are on the big screen and use the control unit screens to attack or escape. Points are given for the number of fishes the visitor catches, and if the visitor gets eaten by a predator, then the game ends. The game can be played collaboratively by some helping with the navigation on the big screen while one is controlling the maceral. It can also be played against other players on other units competing on number of fishes caught. Apart from the game aspect, visitors can also access a didactic lexicon feature, where information about different animals in and

Fig. 2. The 3. person perspective of the mackerel player avatar, controlling one of the hunting, and hunted, fishes on the big 100 m^2 main screen digital simulation of the maritime eco system.

around North Sea can be found. Furthermore, it also gives possibility to inspect the animals through 3D models (see Fig. 3).

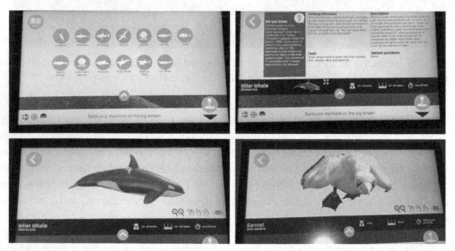

Fig. 3. The BOW's didactic lexicon, featuring fact-based information, and detailed 3D visualizations of the animals present in the virtual aquarium's play sessions.

The BOW installation represents the integrated design principle by resembling a real aquarium, adding the smaller touch-screens as the primary game element, while also enabling spectators to just experience the simulated interactions of large sea mammals

- such as sperm whales, orcas and dolphins – which cannot normally be displayed alive in zoological facilitates due to either logistical or ethical concerns. Thus, the integration of the large digital aquarium using digital technology, and experience-based interaction design, was an example of how the merge between the positions, by enabling the enlightenment about part of aquatic fauna not feasible to portray through other means.

The second installation, Hold Your Breath, is about how long the visitors can hold their breath. According to the time they can hold their breath, their face will be augmented with a respective animal that can hold the breath equally. The interaction happens through a button, which the visitors have to hold down while they are holding their breath. The visitor's face is captured through a camera and presented on a screen with the changing augmentation on their face in real-time (see Fig. 4). This installation was designed through a principle of using the visitor's own body, and human lung limitations, to provoke reflection and enlightenment on how they compare various animals, while using the game-based interactions and rewards as mechanics to promote the visitor to revisit the installation, compete socially, and thus unlock more information about the animals through the augmented reality rewards.

The third installation, The Seal Hunter, is a dual player game with two touch screens facing away from each other. On the one side, a seal can be controlled through a first-person view hunting for fishes, where the controller vibrates in the direction of fishes imitating the way seals navigate with their whiskers, see Fig. 4, picture four showing the control system. On the other side, another visitor controls several fish groups through a third-person view, where the fish groups can be navigated towards the seal as a collaborative game, or prevent the seal in catching the fishes, by navigating the fishes away from the seal.

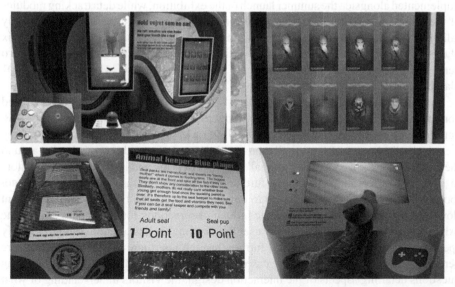

Fig. 4. To the top left 'Hold Your Breath' installation, followed by the screen presenting the augmented photos of the players. Bottom left picture shows the 'Seal Nursing' installation followed by the point information on the screen. Bottom right picture shows the controller of the 'Seal Hunter' installation.

Finally, the Seal Nursing installation is about nursing the seals by feeding them. Concretely, the visitors must throw fish to the seals. The visitor gets one point every time a seal catches a fish, and if the visitor manages to feed a seal pup, it is awarded with 10 points. This resembles the importance of feeding the seal pups in a zoological facility as the bigger seals usually steals the food from the pups. The game installation can be played as a single player game or dual player competitive game (see Fig. 4, picture 3).

The last two installations show how the digital technology could be integrated into the setting, right below the aqua tank with live seals but using the digital technology and game-based interactions to mediate the hard-to-observe social behavior of seals.

5   Method – Studying the Users in Context

The user study, of how the visitors interacted with the new digital installations in the exhibition was based on both a qualitative and quantitative strategy.

The Oceanarium has over the years gone from just evaluating their performance through employee impression and gut feelings to be a more data-driven organization. Today, most of their exhibits and the digital installation logs data, which are used to improve the usability and the visitor experience. Thus, they agreed to prioritize a rather detailed data analytics back-end to be implemented in the four installations to enable us to perform a quantitative overview of the user behavior.

The quantitative data collection was based on tracking these data points and analyzing their balance between the experience-based and enlightenment-oriented interactions (e.g. interaction with the game-elements vs. reading through the digital lexicon). With one of the installations, the Big Ocean Window, our data tracking module was ready to be implemented alongside the summer launch of the exhibition, while data tracking modules of the three other digital installations were first implemented in the late summer/early fall. The Big Ocean Windows dataset is thus based on 121.538 playthroughs (one-six players a time), while the Seal Hunter set is based on 8.967 playthroughs (with two persons a time), and the 'Hold Your breath' installation data set was based on 12.601 playthroughs (one player a time).

To complement the quantitative data set, two days of field studies were planned, and conducted in the fall of 2018. The exhibition was implemented in the summer of 2018, but the study itself was postponed to the fall in order to let the amount of visitors, the technical adjustments of the installations, and the zoo personals own behavior around the exhibition stabilize to a 'new normal' before observing and interviewing the visitors in situ. The observation days were further based on a premise of 'not too few, not too many' visitors present in the zoo to optimally represent a typical visitor and event flow of a day in the zoo. We conducted video observations for four hours around the exhibition area to identify patterns of user flow among the installations, and to identify specific behaviors to be investigated further through interviews. The interviews where performed in the exhibition context based on a semi-structured interview guide asking questions detailing aspects of the interaction design, the visitors understanding of what they experienced, and an assessment of both if they had fun as well as felt informed about the subject matter. A total of eight group-based interviews were performed with visiting families, being prompted for an interview immediately after leaving the exhibition area, and where generally aimed at being short and concise at a maximum duration of five minutes per interview.

6 Data Analysis

The following section will present our analysis of the empirical data collected from the digital installations, with the aim of exploring user behavior in relation to experiential gameplay, and didactic enlightenment. We structure the analysis by first presenting the quantitative data collected from the installations themselves, and how we modelled the data sets to address issues of experience vs. enlightenment regarding the subject matter of the installation.

6.1 The Big Ocean Window

The BOW had six separate touch screen stations, from which the visitor could interact with the virtual 100m2 aquarium on the primary screen. Each of these stations provided a total of 31 digital data tracking points, which we modelled into one data set combining seven data points which would provide data on both the gameplay elements, alongside the use of the fact-based lexicon features of the installation.

Based on the gathered data on BOW, it was possible to determine that 30–50% of the play sessions ends with the player 'completing' the game without being eaten during the game's total play session of 120 s. The other two types of play sessions, ending through game inactivity or by the visitor's fish avatar being eaten, constituted between 50–70% of total sessions. Thus, it can be noted that the majority of the players managed to complete the game, which indicate that the difficulty of the game seems to be appropriate for the target audience by not being too easy to complete nor too hard to accomplish. An initial hypothesis was that several visitors would find it difficult to navigate precisely due to the inverted control of the x-axis in the game and the third person perspective on the big screen. However, in the interviews, it turned out to be mixed as to whether it is actually experienced as difficult to control the game, indicating that the inverted joystick pattern was not a design error, but an ambiguous pattern to interpret. Especially children between the ages of 5 and 12 seem to have an easier time getting used to the controls, which does not indicate any usability problems.

It was not possible to quantify how many play sessions one player was associated with since no user logins data was required to play in order to ensure a fast user onboarding. From the video observations it was possible to observe a clear tendency where the majority of players played more than one session before stopping. Especially the children played more than one game and were often inspired by watching how others played, which kept them playing. Concordantly, there were also observed a number of situations where more than one child participated in the same play session. Here, they spotted the predators on the big screen and warned the playing child on the individual unit. This social dimension was particularly evident in families with more than one child, which also was the group with most repetitive play sessions (Fig. 5).

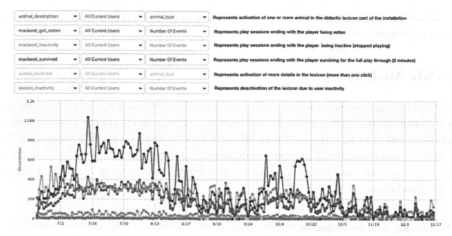

Fig. 5. The data model from the 'BOW' showing how we compared different use metrics between the game-based elements, and the use of the fact-based lexicon feature.

Based on the observations, it seemed only a few of the visitors actively interacted with the didactic lexicon section of the BOW screens. Although a larger group of visitors were observed to have found the way to the front page of the lexicon, they quickly clicked away without spending time reading or exploring the 3D models. This is further substantiated with the gathered statistical data of 121538 play sessions, where 23% of the play sessions shows an activation of the lexicon, which gives a picture of a relatively large use of the lexicon in interaction with the game section. However, only 23%, of those who activated the lexicon, actually did interact with the lexicon's 'examine' functions (e.g. clicking around and exploring the 3D models), which only accounts for 7% of the total play sessions. Thus, the reason for the high activation of the lexicon, was clarified in the interviews, where several revealed that they had interpreted the images of the maritime animals in the lexicon as an opportunity to actively select animals for the game on BOW. In the 7% of the play sessions where the 'examine' function was used, the visitors primarily interacted with whales and sharks, which accounts for 56.5% of the play sessions where the 'examine' function was used. Based on the interviews, it was clear that these animals are the ones that attract the relatively few visitors who choose to dive deeper into the lexicon.

To the questions about the non-use of lexicon, several interview persons replied that they did not find the lexicon's factual part essential to their ability to feel enlightened by the BOW. They expressed that they saw the experience with the BOW as a way for their children to be able to put themselves in relation to the biologically realistic and correct interactions with the animals in the BOW and thus function as a good supplement to the more facts-based learning they could get in other parts of the exhibition. They did however point to, that they assessed that their children did learn 'something' through playing the game, by being able to set themselves in relation to the portrayed food chain, and through seeing themselves in relation to the comparable sizes of the marine animal avatars of the game. Similar comments were given from a larger group consisting of three families with children, who also stated that the BOW for them was a way for the children to experience how complex the food chain is and how fast it can go from hunter to the hunted through their own interactions.

These comments nuance the image of game sessions that activated the lexicon, as well as who interacted deeper with the 'examine' functions. The low usage of the lexicon could be interpreted as a lack of learning and information potential in BOW, where the gaming experience is the only prominent element. But with the visitors' comments in the interviews, as well as the observations of their behavior interacting with BOW, it is evident that there is another form of learning and enlightenment taking place. Here, it is about the BOW giving the visitors the opportunity to experience themselves in relation to the animals (both in terms of size, behavior and mutual interaction) and in this way achieve a more informal learning. Based on the visitors' opinions, it is not because they feel they lack fact-based learning during their visit, but rather sees experience-based learning, like the BOW, to support the fact-based learning in other parts of the exhibition.

6.2 Seal Hunter and Nursing

The Seal Hunter & Nursing installation had two connected stations, with physical controls of the shared big screen in which the simulated seals hunted for food. The installation provided a total of 25 data points from which we build a data model of six data sets, which would reveal how the playthrough took place and what 'feeding strategies' the users applied during their playthrough. We triangulated this with the answers provided from users right after having interacted with the installation in order to supplement the behavioral data with attitudinal statements. Specifically, we sought to probe for whether the visitors had actually realized the defining features of how seals hunt for food, how the seals were different - e.g. the baby seals needing different kinds and amounts of food, but were harder to feed due to the competition for food from the adult seals.

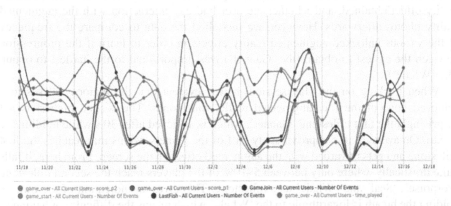

Fig. 6. The data model from the 'Seal Nursing' installation showing e.g. the relation between number of play throughs, time played, and amount of points gained by the two players.

According to the 'Seal Hunter' and the 'Nursing' installations, the majority of the games were played by two players. Here, a general behavior was observed among the players. It appears that the majority of players misunderstood the purpose and arguably missed the communicated elements presented prior and during their play sessions. It was only on the Seal Nursing installation where these observations could be substantiated via the gathered statistical data since the Seal Hunter analytics only provided data regarding how the seal was navigated in the game. As such, according to Seal Nursing, there was a clear pattern illustrating a low success rate of collecting points during the play sessions, which was between 9–23 points on average in every play session on a day (with successful playthroughs reaching scores closer to 75 points) (Fig. 6).

This can be linked to the fact that no gaming session reached the full 60 s, but most often ends 10–15 s before as a result of running out of fishes. In combination with the observational studies, this revealed that most players did not discover the difference between the points they get in relation to the size of the seals (for example, the baby seals get 10 points and the other seals gets 1 point). They throw the fish quickly in the belief of having an endless amount of digital fish. This was a result of not reading the guidelines for the games, neither the physical nor the digital displayed on the screens. This trend was general for the two installations where they start playing without knowing what the games are about. In the Seal Hunter there was an articulated doubt about whether it was a collaborative game with each other or a competitive game against each other. A family explained that it was not a problem that they should explore the game, in which they found the value of helping each other in their situation. As such, in some cases, they decode the games and adjust the game strategy, but in many cases, they never really decode the purpose and either abandoned or played with their own terms. Here, the information part is lost pretty quickly, as the experience part is not easily understandable.

6.3 Hold Your Breath in Augmented Reality

The 'Hold Your Breath' installation was by far the simplest installation in terms of data output from the installation, which mainly registered time of breath hold, the augmented reality effect obtained, and whether the user had any interaction with the augmented reality photos afterwards. However, we modelled the data to compare the frequency of the various unlocked augmented reality effects in order to learn if the progression between the easiest to obtain (the 'Gannet') was proportional to the hardest to obtain (the 'Whale').

When tracking on the play session, it was evident that the majority of sessions achieved none of the four augmented reality milestones. The second highest is not surprisingly the first milestone 'Gannet', which is achieved after 30 s while holding the breath. On average, it is approximately half of the game sessions that reaches the first milestone and gets rewarded with the augmented effect on the screen. From here, it falls quite drastically, where only between 5–10% of the players reach the second milestone 'Porpoise', 'Seal' and 'Whale' as a milestone. This gives an indication of the time of holding the breath is logarithmic to the 'Whale' which means the difficulty of having to stay for more than 30 s is too great for most players. From the observations, it was evident that when groups of visitors tried the game together, a fast competition emerged, and the game was generally played by almost all visitors more than once. This indicates that the interaction and social dynamics of the game seem to work, but part of the enlightenment aspect disappears when so few visitors earn milestones other than 'Gannet' (Fig. 7).

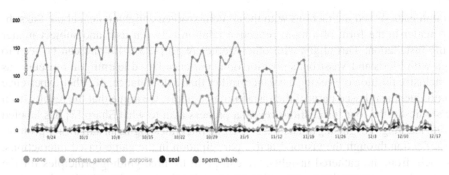

Fig. 7. The data model from the 'Hold your Breath' installation.

According to the data, the whale appears more often as a milestone than the 'Seal' and the 'Porpoise'. This shows that there are more users who reach the last milestone than the two in the middle. This corresponds to the observations, where it was clear that the players in groups competed to hold their breath longest. In contrast, another pattern was also observed in which the players, after the first few real attempts to hold their breath, actively began to make their own interpretation of the installation's use. Here, the players simply chose to pretend that they hold their breath, while the button is held down and the various milestones were unlocked. The players then breathe out, although during all 2 min of interaction, they have just pretended to not have breathed. This creative play with the installation testifies that the player understands both the intent and the interaction with the installation, but freely interprets the situation to play with on the premise of holding their breath. These players thus reach the whale as a milestone which explains why the last milestones were experienced more often than the middle ones.

This again points to the relationship between enlightenment and experience in the installation. The difficulty of the installation obviously prevents a number of players from achieving all the milestones, and thus also prevents the total amount information. Conversely, the play with the installation also shows that the players freely interpret the rules, immerse themselves into the interaction, unlocking the augmented reality effects, and thus also obtain the factual information.

7 Synthesis

This section seeks to identify and elaborate the conditions and dependencies between enlightenment and experience as seen in our analysis with the previous state of art, and the four introduced positions in museum research.

The analysis illuminates a number of issues regarding the conditions and dependencies between enlightenment and experience that have been identified in the implemented digital installations, and their effects have subsequently been explicated. From studying the user behavior through both qualitative and quantitative research, the results of these implementations reveal how such attempts to deliver purely didactic design information digitally failed to succeed in engaging the visitors, while a more informal delivery through game-based interactions with the content sparked enlightenment about the subject matter in the form of a more reflective relation between user and subject matter of the installation. This aligns with other studies (e.g.) [4, 39, 40] and can be seen to align with Floris and Vasström's position on experience-based learning in museums as an inclusive position of seeking a balance, rather than a dominance, of either experience or enlightenment-based parts of the installations. Finally, we argue that the results from the studies of the four installations reveal a process akin to what Sharp [3] has labeled stealth learning – disguising didactic facts behind integrated digital installations, promoting reflection through the visitors' active participation in the game-based interactions. As such, from the gathered insights, we can point to three guiding principles for the balance, between experience and enlightenment in game-based exhibition designs to accommodate this type of stealth learning.

1. Avoiding adding 'forced' fact-based features and content as an add-on to the game-based exhibition designs, since these run the risk on only seeing limited or misinterpreted use. If factual content is to be presented in an authoritative way it should be done either through design placed prior to or after the game-based interactions as preparation or debriefing of the player. Our studies showed that users did in fact reflect and were able to digest the facts in relation to the game-based experience.
2. Letting the informal learning be front and center for game-based interactive exhibition design, by being enlightened about their own relation to the facts through performative play which promotes reflection. This requires a discussion in relation to the four positions of what the role of museums should be in society, and whether we can accept less formal facts to be delivered if the visitors leave the exhibition with their own subjective reflections on the subject matter experienced.
3. If informal learning is not desired, and authoritative enlightenment is needed, the two are better separated. In these cases, game-based elements should deliver purely entertaining experiences, and the exhibition facts should deliver enlightenment on their own respective premises. This requires a stricter discussion about when and where, in a museum context, interactive experience design could be used to give the visitor a 'break', potentially avoiding so-called 'museum fatigue' [41], and thus, ensure their motivation to learn more after the 'break'.

The first principle encourages a mix of second and third positions in current discourse about exhibition design at museums, favoring more experience-oriented practices where the experience is an instrument to promote the enlightenment. The second principle encourages the fourth position where one can obtain enlightenment and learning through experiences, as in 'experience-based learning', and get experiences and enjoyment through enlightenment, information and learning, as in 'learning-based experiences' or 'edutainment'. Finally, the third principle encourages the first and second positions, where enlightenment and experience are strictly separated to focus on what each one is best at.

8 Conclusion

We initiated this research through the hypothesis, that the tension of traditions in exhibition design are not optimal for either traditions, and serve to create inadequate interactive exhibition design. We argued how it is often the case that either the experiential or enlightenment-oriented design elements are forced upon each other. This study focused on how the engagement, interaction, factual communication, and the educational effect of interactive experiences can create through game-based interactions in an exhibition context. Through the quantitative data set, triangulated with situated interviews, the study shed light on how visitors understand, respond, and acquire knowledge based on actual users' reactions and expectations over time. The data has shown a clear pattern supporting our hypothesis by demonstrating how attempts to deliver purely fact-based information through didactic design elements failed to succeed in engaging the visitors, since it either competes unfavorably against the play-oriented part of the experience. However, the interviews did indicate the presence of a more informal delivery, through what we regard as stealth learning during playthroughs. These situations promoted enlightenment, about the subject matter, not through the delivery of facts, but through users seeing themselves in relation to the subject matter. The facts were so to speak reflected upon through playing the games and through their social interactions about the play session afterwards. This might not be the authoritative ideal of older museum discourse, but it aligns with post-modern and constructivist views on museum design [5] – giving further empirical basis for game-based exhibition design as an enabler of experience-based learning. In such cases, enlightenment is assessed through gained reflections, wonderment and new questions sparked, rather than the transfer of facts alone. This is not to be seen as the only design strategy going forward, but rather as a data supported argument for allowing game-based experiences in exhibitions to function on their own terms, and not be forced to adhere to authoritative fact delivery. Rather, interactive exhibition design needs to balance the traditions, by allowing for other types of enlightenment than authoritative fact delivery, while the gamified installations should also not transcend into straying too far away from communicating a message about the subject matter. Our study shows that certain type of enlightenment can arise from building game-based experiences around the facts, but without forcing the facts upon the users. In the end, this is reflected through the three proposed guiding principles to consider when seeking to achieve a balanced exhibition design between experience and enlightenment.

References

1. Drotner, K.: Vores Museum. University of Southern Denmark, Projektbeskrivelse (2015)
2. Hein, G.E.: Learning in the Museum. Routledge, New York (2002)
3. Sharp, L.: Stealth learning: unexpected learning opportunities through games. J. Inst. Res. 1, 42–48 (2012). https://doi.org/10.9743/JIR.2013.6, Grand Canyon University
4. Hornecker, E., Stifter, M.: Learning from interactive museum installations about interaction design for public settings. In: Proceedings of the 18th Australia Conference on Computer-Human Interaction: Design: Activities, Artefacts and Environments, pp. 135–142. ACM, New York (2006). https://doi.org/10.1145/1228175.1228201

5. Bjorli, T., Jensen, I., Johnsen, E., Sæter, G. (eds.): Mellom konservering og konsum. In: Museum i friluft. Norsk folkemuseum, Oslo (2004)
6. Belk, R.W.: Collecting in a Consumer Society. Psychology Press, Hove (1995)
7. Kirshenblatt-Gimblett, B.: The Museum as Catalyst. Keynote address, Museums 2000: Confirmation or Challenge. Swedish Museum Association and the Swedish Travelling Exhibition/Riksutställningar., Vadstena, Sweden (2000)
8. Skot-Hansen, D.: Museerne i den danske oplevelsesøkonomi. Samfundslitteratur (2008)
9. Floris, L., Vasström, A.: På museum: mellem oplevelse og oplysning. Roskilde Universitetsforlag (1999)
10. Drotner, K., Dziekan, V., Parry, R., Schrøder, K.C.: Media, mediatisation and museums. In: The Routledge Handbook of Museums, Media and Communication. Routledge (2018)
11. Tallon, L.: Introduction: mobile, digital, and personal. In: Tallon, L. (ed.) Digital Technologies and the Museum Experience: Handheld Guides and Other Media. pp. Xiii–XXV. Rowman Altamira (2008)
12. Adair, B., Filene, B., Koloski, L. (eds.): Letting Go?: Sharing Historical Authority in a User-Generated World. Routledge, Philadelphia (2011)
13. Black, G.: The Engaging Museum: Developing Museums for Visitor Involvement. Routledge (2005). https://doi.org/10.4324/9780203559277
14. Black, G.: Transforming Museums in the Twenty-first Century. Routledge, Milton Park, Abingdon, Oxon; New York, NY (2011)
15. Simon, N.: The Participatory Museum. Museum 2.0 (2010)
16. Parry, R.: The end of the beginning: normativity in the postdigital museum. Museum Worlds 1, 24–39 (2013). https://doi.org/10.3167/armw.2013.010103
17. Gammon, B., Burch, A.: Designing mobile digital experience. In: Tallon, L., Walker, K. (eds.) Digital Technologies and the Museum Experience: Handheld Guides and Other Media, pp. 35–60. AltaMira Press, Lanham (2008)
18. Shaffer, D.W., Resnick, M.: "Thick" authenticity: new media and authentic learning. J. Interact. Learn. Res. 10, 195–215 (1999)
19. Heath, C., vom Lehn, D.: Interactivity and collaboration. New forms of participation in museums, galleries and science centers. In: Parry, R. (ed.) Museums in a Digital Age, pp. 266–280. Routledge, Milton Park (2010)
20. Heath, C., vom Lehn, D.: Configuring "Interactivity": enhancing engagement in science centres and museums. Soc. Stud. Sci. 38, 63–91 (2008)
21. Olsson, T., Svensson, A.: Reaching and including digital visitors: Swedish museums and social demand. In: Pruulmann-Vengerfeldt, P., Viires, P. (eds.) The Digital Turn: User's Practices and Cultural Transformations, pp. 45–57. Peter Lang GmbH, New York (2013)
22. Our Museum. http://ourmuseum.dk/. Accessed 20 Feb 2019
23. Velux, F.: Museumsprogram Bevillinger 2015–2018 (2018)
24. Apostolellis, P., Bowman, D.A.: Small group learning with games in museums: effects of interactivity as mediated by cultural differences. In: Proceedings of the 14th International Conference on Interaction Design and Children, pp. 160–169. ACM, New York (2015). https://doi.org/10.1145/2771839.2771856
25. Danielak, B.A., Mechtley, A., Berland, M., Lyons, L., Eydt, R.: MakeScape Lite: a prototype learning environment for making and design. In: Proceedings of the 2014 Conference on Interaction Design and Children, pp. 229–232. ACM, New York (2014). https://doi.org/10.1145/2593968.2610459
26. Falk, J.H., Dierking, L.D.: Enhancing Visitor Interaction and Learning with Mobile Technologies. In: Tallon, L. (ed.) Digital Technologies and the Museum Experience: Handheld Guides and Other Media, pp. 19–33. Rowman Altamira (2008)

27. Muise, K., Wakkary, R.: Bridging designers' intentions to outcomes with constructivism. In: Proceedings of the 8th ACM Conference on Designing Interactive Systems, pp. 320–329. ACM, New York (2010). https://doi.org/10.1145/1858171.1858229
28. Drotner, K. (ed.): Det Interaktive Museum. Samfundslitteratur, Frederiksberg (2011)
29. Hornecker, E.: "I don't understand it either, but it is cool" - visitor interactions with a multi-touch table in a museum. In: 2008 3rd IEEE International Workshop on Horizontal Interactive Human Computer Systems, pp. 113–120 (2008). https://doi.org/10.1109/TABLETOP.2008.4660193
30. Rudloff, M.: Formidling i forandring (2013)
31. Vermeeren, A., Calvi, L., Sabiescu, A.: Museum Experience Design: Crowds, Ecosystems and Novel Technologies. Springer, New York (2018). https://doi.org/10.1007/978-3-319-585 50-5
32. Frost, O.C.: When the Object is digital: properties of digital surrogate objects and implications for learning. In: Parry, R. (ed.) Museums in a Digital Age, pp. 237–246. Routledge, London (2010)
33. Marty, P.F.: Museum websites and museum visitors: digital museum resources and their use. Museum Manage. Curatorship. **23**, 81–99 (2008). https://doi.org/10.1080/096477707 01865410
34. Drotner, K., Dziekan, V., Parry, R., Schrøder, K.C.: The Routledge Handbook of Museums, Media and Communication. Routledge, New York (2018)
35. The North Sea Oceanarium. https://en.nordsoenoceanarium.dk/. Accessed 02 Feb 2019
36. Horn, M.S., Weintrop, D., Routman, E.: Programming in the pond: a tabletop computer programming exhibit. In: Proceedings of the Extended Abstracts of the 32nd Annual ACM Conference on Human Factors in Computing Systems, pp. 1417–1422. ACM, New York (2014). https://doi.org/10.1145/2559206.2581237
37. Leong, Z.A., Horn, M.S.: Waiting for learning: designing interactive education materials for patient waiting areas. In: Proceedings of the 2014 Conference on Interaction Design and Children - IDC 2014, pp. 145–153. ACM Press, Aarhus (2014). https://doi.org/10.1145/259 3968.2593970
38. Moesgaard, T.G., Witt, M., Fiss, J., Warming, C., Klubien, J., Schønau-Fog, H.: Implicit and explicit information mediation in a virtual reality museum installation and its effects on retention and learning outcomes. In: Proceedings of the 9th European Conference on Games-Based Learning : ECGBL 2015, pp. 387–394. Academic Conferences and Publishing International (2015)
39. Ciolfi, L., Bannon, L.J., Fernström, M.: Including visitor contributions in cultural heritage installations: designing for participation. Museum Manag. Curatorship. **23**, 353–365 (2008). https://doi.org/10.1080/09647770802517399
40. Ciolfi, L., McLoughlin, M.: Designing for meaningful visitor engagement at a living history museum. Presented at the October 14 (2012). https://doi.org/10.1145/2399016.2399028
41. Bitgood, S.: Museum fatigue: a critical review. Visitor Stud. **12**, 93–111 (2009). https://doi.org/10.1080/10645570903203406

Audience Perception of Exaggerated Motions on Realistic Animated Animal Characters

Mackenzie Hammer and Nicoletta Adamo[✉]

Purdue University, West Lafayette, IN 47907, USA
{hammer0,nadamovi}@purdue.edu

Abstract. The recent push for more detailed graphics and realistic visuals in animated productions has sparked much debate around the new films' photorealistic visual style. Some critics argue that the new "live-action" versions of movie classics such as the Lion King are not as visually stylish as the original ones, and the photorealistic characters are not as likeable, fun and intriguing as their stylized counterparts. This paper reports ongoing research whose goal is to examine whether it is possible to apply traditional animation principles to photorealistic animated animal characters in order to make them more expressive, convincing and ultimately entertaining. In particular, the study reported in the paper investigated the extent to which varying degrees of exaggeration affect the perceived believability and appeal of a photorealistic talking cat character performing a series of actions in a high detail environment. The study included 82 participants and compared three levels of exaggeration applied to the cat's motions, e.g. no exaggeration, low exaggeration and high exaggeration. Findings show that subjects found the no-exaggeration clip more appealing and believable than the exaggerated versions, although the difference in appeal was not statistically significant. When comparing the two exaggerated clips, participants rated the high exaggeration clip higher for believability and appeal than the low exaggeration one.

Keywords: 3D character animation · Perception studies · Exaggeration · Principles of animation

1 Introduction

If we examine recent movie productions featuring photorealistic talking animal characters, we notice that the majority of the recent research efforts in computer animation have concentrated on developing new methods and tools for increasing photorealism and motion accuracy, with less focus on implementing traditional animation techniques and principles, such as exaggeration [14]. Some critics wonder whether the recent photorealistic approach robs animated films of character and argue that with real-looking animals there is less potential for strong visual characterization [15].

Disney animators Ollie Johnston and Frank Thomas published the "12 principles of animation" in 1981, codifying concepts of movement, pacing, and cartoon physics that had been used since Walt Disney's early days [5]. Most of these concepts were built

A. Brooks and E. I. Brooks (Eds.): ArtsIT 2019/DLI 2019, LNICST 328, pp. 88–102, 2020.
https://doi.org/10.1007/978-3-030-53294-9_7

around exaggeration, not realism. Ideas such as "squash and stretch" and "pose-to-pose movement" were both inherently unrealistic and incredibly effective. If we compare the shots in the 2019 Lion King to their 1994 counterparts, we cannot help but notice how the need to make the characters adhere to realistic physics makes the characters less convincing and less fun. It also decreases their ability to express feeling in their movements. For instance, Todd points out that "*the way 1994 Rafiki thrusts baby Simba into the air would feel physically dangerous with realistic physics, so the remake tones the gesture down. A subtle difference in one shot, but spread across the whole movie, the original movie is much more powerful for that exaggeration*" [15].

In summary, failing to implement fundamental principles of animation, such as exaggeration when animating talking photorealistic animals might result in a significant decrease in the characters' appeal and believability. Removing exaggeration gives a more realistic nature to the animal, however this approach may reduce the audience connection with the character and the belief from the viewer that the character is both living and feeling.

The overall goal of this research is to investigate whether it is still possible to implement fundamental principles of traditional animation in new animated productions featuring photorealistic animal characters. More specifically, the objective of the study reported in the paper was to examine the extent to which different degrees of exaggeration in the motions of a photorealistic computer animated cat character affect perception of the character's believability and appeal. The paper is organized as follows. Section 2 presents a discussion of the 12 principles of animation and a review of relevant prior perceptual studies in character animation. Our experiment is described in Sect. 3 and the results are reported in Sect. 4. A discussion of findings and ideas for future work are included in Sect. 5.

2 Review of Literature

2.1 Principles of Animation

The 12 principles of animation are a set of fundamental rules of the 'language of movement' that were taught at the Walt Disney Studios in the 1930s. They apply to all types of character animation and are crucial to the production of believable, life-like animated characters. They were first published by Thomas and Johnston in 1981 in the book "Disney Animation: The illusion of Life" [5] and include: stretch and squash, anticipation, arcs, overlapping action and follow through, secondary action, exaggeration, timing, appeal, pose to pose and straight ahead animation, staging, slow-in slow-out, and solid drawing. In this research we are concerned primarily with the principles of exaggeration, appeal, and stretch and squash (resulting from exaggerated motions), the primary focus being on exaggeration.

The classical definition of exaggeration employed by Disney was "*to remain true to reality, but present it in a wilder, more extreme form*" [5]. Often, an exact recreation of real life can be static and dull, whereas adding exaggeration, e.g. for instance increasing the amplitude and speed of the movements, or the amount of character deformation, can make the performance more clear, convincing and interesting. According to Disney, every action, pose and expression can be taken to the next level to increase the amount of impact on the viewer, and adding exaggeration does not mean departing from realism. In other words, making a character's performance more realistic does not mean making the character's physics and proportions more consistent with reality, but rather making the idea or the essence of the actions more apparent and convincing by taking the movements and deformations to more extreme levels.

Two other important principles of animation relevant to the study are the principle of stretch and squash and the principle of appeal. Stretch and squash defines the rigidity and mass of an object/character by distorting its shape during an action, while maintaining a constant volume [6]. When the movements of a character are exaggerated the resulting stretch and squash is more pronounced. The principle of appeal refers to creating a design or an action that the audience enjoys watching. While an actor can have charisma, an animated character can have appeal. To the Disney animators, appeal meant *"anything that a person likes to see, a quality of charm, pleasing design, simplicity, communication, magnetism"* [5]. Exaggerating the character's movements and deformations can contribute to increasing the character's appeal.

Another concept relevant to the study is *'believability'*. While believability is not included in the 12 Principles of Animation, it has been referenced over the years as another extremely important concept in character animation. An animated character is believable when it appears convincing to the audience, in other words, when it displays a clear emotional style and gives the illusion that is living and feeling. According to Webster [16] believability is lost when the audience fails to emotionally engage with the character.

2.2 Prior Perceptual Studies in Character Animation

Several studies whose goal was to examine how people perceive and interpret different aspects of animated characters can be found in the literature. In this section we present a partial review of relevant studies that focused on perception of animated characters' emotions and believability from body movements and facial articulations. We also report studies that examined whether there is a significant correlation between character visual design (stylized versus realistic) and perceptual effects.

A study by Hyde et al. [4] investigated the effects of damped and exaggerated facial motion in realistic and cartoon animated characters. In particular, the researchers examined the impact of incrementally dampening or exaggerating the facial movements on perceptions of character likeability, intelligence, and extraversion. Participants liked the realistic characters more than the cartoon characters. Likeability ratings were higher when the realistic characters showed exaggerated movements and when the cartoon characters showed damped movements. The realistic characters with exaggerated motions were perceived as more intelligent, while the stylized characters appeared more intelligent when their motions were damped. Exaggerated motions improved perception of the characters as extraverted for both character styles. Our study was inspired in part by Hyde's study, which suggests that exaggeration can be applied to realistic humanoid character faces to improve their likeability. We extended their study by investigating the effects of exaggeration on the body movements of realistic animal characters.

A study by Anasingaraju et al. [2] examined the effects of different body channels (e.g. body motions, eye movements, facial articulations and lip synch) on audience perceived believability of an animated character's emotions. The study featured a stylized humanoid character displaying 5 different emotions, e.g. happiness, sadness, surprise, anger, and fear. Results of the study revealed that the body movements contribute the most to the perceived believability of the character's emotion across all 5 emotions, followed by facial articulations, eye movements and lip synch animation. Our experiment was also inspired by Anasingaraju's study which points to the superiority of body movements over lip synch and facial motions for the expression of character's believability. Our study in fact focused only on exaggerated body motions and did not consider facial articulations and lip synch.

A study by Badathala et al. [3] investigated the effects of six different gait parameters e.g. stride length, walk speed, beltline tilt, upper body twist, forward/backward upper body lean, and foot inward/outward rotation on the perception of a humanoid stylized character's personality. Findings show that the gait of the character can inform the audience significantly about the character's personality and confirm the importance of body motions in perception of character's believability. Of the six parameters tested, it was observed that four have a particularly significant effect on the perception of the character's personality namely, stride length, speed, beltline tilt and upper body twist.

A study by Mc Donnel et al. [9] examined perception of 6 basic emotions (sadness, happiness, surprise, fear, anger and disgust) from the movements of a real actor and from the same movements applied to 5 virtual characters (e.g. a low- and high-resolution virtual human resembling the actor, a cartoon-like character, a wooden mannequin, and a zombie-like character). Results of the experiment showed that subjects' perception of the emotions was for the most part independent of the character's body style.

Several other studies have examined how virtual characters should be designed to be believable and elicit emotion from the viewer. A few experiments have shown that people feel empathetic towards the character if he/she is more similar in design and motions to a human being [7, 12]. Ruttkay et al. [13] argue that people may view realistic characters as more intelligent but may view non-humanlike stylized characters as more appealing and entertaining. McCloud in his book "Understanding Comics" claims that iconic characters with exaggerated motions are more effective over realistic characters, as audience's involvement increases [8]. For that reason, iconic characters are often used commercially. People may prefer iconic agents because iconic agents are subject to fewer social norms [18]. A study by Adamo-Villani et al. investigated whether the visual style of signing avatars (realistic vs. stylized) affect viewers' perception of the avatar's appeal [1]. Results showed that the stylized signing avatar was perceived as more appealing than the realistic one. The 'Uncanny Valley' hypothesis may explain why stylized characters with exaggerated movements and deformations could be more appealing and believable than realistic characters, as people feel eerie and unpleasant when a high degree of realism (but not complete realism) in a character is reached [10].

The study reported in the paper adds to the existing body of literature on the perceptual effects of animated characters' by examining whether it is possible to achieve a high degree of perceived believability and appeal by using a realistic animal character design and exaggerating its motions.

3 Description of the Study

The goal of the study was to examine the extent to which different levels of exaggeration affect (a) perception of believability of a realistic talking cat character performing a series of actions in a highly detailed environment and (b) perception of character' s appeal. The study used a within-subjects design and collected both quantitative and qualitative data. The independent variable was the degree of exaggeration and 3 levels were considered, e.g. no exaggeration (control clip), low exaggeration (experimental clip 1) and high exaggeration (experimental clip 2). The dependent variables were 'perceived believability' and 'perceived appeal', which were measured by participants' ratings on a 7-point Likert scale. In addition, the study collected qualitative data in the form of open-ended comments expressing how the subjects felt about the animations. The design of the study was truly experimental by implementing a treatment to a random sample of participants through animated video clips.

The hypotheses of the study are listed below and were formulated based on best practices of animation, as well a prior research in character animation. Best practices and principles of animation show that exaggeration could improve the appeal of animated 3D characters [17]. Recent perceptual studies in character animation suggest that a moderate level of exaggeration might improve the likeability of photorealistic characters, but too much exaggeration could detract from a realistic character's performance and believability.

H_{01}: There is no difference in perceived character believability between the control clip (no exaggeration) and experimental clip 1 (low exaggeration).

$H_{\alpha1}$: There is a difference in perceived character believability between the control clip (no exaggeration) and experimental clip 1 (low exaggeration). Perceived believability is higher for experimental clip 1 (low exaggeration).

H_{02}: There is no difference in perceived character appeal between the control clip (no exaggeration) and experimental clip 1 (low exaggeration).

$H_{\alpha2}$: There is a difference in perceived character appeal between the control clip (no exaggeration) and experimental clip 1 (low exaggeration). Perceived appeal is higher for experimental clip 1 (low exaggeration).

H_{03}: There is no difference in perceived character believability between the control clip (no exaggeration) and experimental clip 2 (high exaggeration).

$H_{\alpha3}$: There is a difference in perceived character believability between the control clip (no exaggeration) and experimental clip 2 (high exaggeration). Perceived believability is lower for experimental clip 2 (high exaggeration).

H_{04}: There is no difference in perceived character appeal between the control clip (no exaggeration) and experimental clip 2 (high exaggeration).

$H_{\alpha4}$: There is a difference in perceived character appeal between the control clip (no exaggeration) and experimental clip 2 (high exaggeration). Perceived appeal is lower for experimental clip 2 (high exaggeration).

3.1 Animation Stimuli

The stimuli for the study included 3 animated videos of a photorealistic 3D cat character in a realistic living room environment performing a sequence of actions (climbing, jumping, running, catching an object). Each video was 18 s long and showed a different level of exaggeration of the cat movements. Implementing different levels of exaggeration referred to modifying the amplitude and speed of the cat character's motions. As the level of exaggeration increased, motion amplitude became larger, movements became quicker, and the cat stretch and squash became more pronounced.

The control animation was created to match exactly a video of a real cat's movements. The motions of the 3D cat were keyframed by an experienced animator who used each frame of the live cat video as a reference, a technique very similar to rotoscoping. In the "low" degree of exaggeration clip the amplitude of the character's motion controllers was increased by 50%–200% compared to the control clip. In the "high" degree of exaggeration the amplitude of the same controllers was increased by 200%–400%. For example, if the cat's hips raised to a height of 10 units during a jump in the control animation, his hips were raised approximately to a height of 25 units in the low

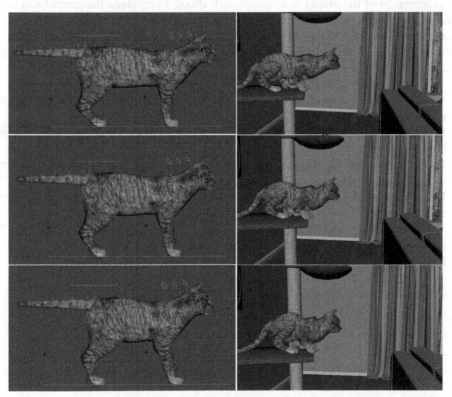

Fig. 1. Left: screenshots of cat rig illustrating different levels of exaggerated body squash - no exaggeration (top); low exaggeration (middle); high exaggeration (bottom). Right: Frames extracted from animation stimuli – no exaggeration of body squash and crouching motion (top); low exaggeration (middle); high exaggeration (bottom)

exaggerated animation, and a height of 40 units in the high exaggerated condition. The percentages of increase in motion amplitude and speed used to achieve different levels of exaggeration were determined based on best practices in character animation and are grounded in animation theory and principles. In addition, four animation professionals provided feedback on the animated clips and their suggestions were used to iteratively refine the cat's movements in each clip. The only difference among the three animations was the degree of exaggeration of the cat motions and deformations. To eliminate potential confounding variables camera framing, lighting scheme, background environment, color and textures were kept the same across all three videos. Figure 1 shows frames extracted from the animation stimuli and screenshots of the cat rig illustrating different levels of exaggerated body deformation and motion.

3.2 Evaluation Instrument

The evaluation instrument was an online survey developed in Qualtrics software. The survey contained three blocks of animated videos and a set of rating, multiple choice, and open-ended questions. Each block of videos included two animations and the order of presentation of the blocks was randomized. Block 1 contained the control and low exaggeration animations, Block 2 contained the control and high exaggeration animations, and Block 3 contained the low exaggeration and high exaggeration animations. After watching each block of videos, the participants were asked to answer the following questions:

- I found the top/bottom character appealing – 7-point rating question; strongly agree = 7; strongly disagree = 1
- Please explain why you do or do not find the top/bottom character appealing – open ended question
- I found the top/bottom character believable – 7-point rating question; strongly agree = 7; strongly disagree = 1
- Please explain why you do or do not find the top/bottom character believable – open ended question
- Do you prefer the video of the top or bottom character? – multiple choice question; 3 options: top video, bottom video, no preference
- Please explain your preference - open ended question

Figure 2 shows a segment of the online survey.

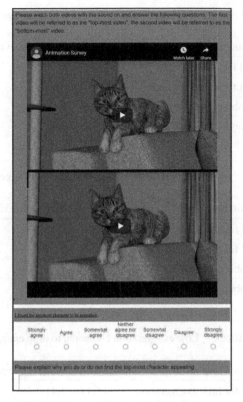

Fig. 2. Screenshot from the online survey

3.3 Population and Sampling

Any person over the age of 18 was eligible to participate in the study. The survey was distributed to volunteers on the online site Amazon Mechanical Turk. A total of 201 responses were collected during the time the survey was open, however there were 119 non-respondents or incomplete surveys that were discarded before the final analysis. Therefore, a total of 82 responses were considered and used for the data analysis.

4   Results

Believability, Appeal, and Animation Preference
Participants rated their responses to questions relating to appeal and believability on a Likert scale of 1 to 7 (1 = low appeal or low believability; 7 = high appeal or high believability). Generally, the control video had higher mean scores in terms of perceived appeal and believability when compared to both the low exaggeration and high exaggeration videos. Participants rated the high exaggeration clip higher than the low exaggeration one for both appeal and believability. Means and standard deviations for each block of videos are reported in Tables 1, 2, and 3.

Table 1. Block 1: Control video compared to low exaggeration

Animation responses	Mean	Standard deviation
Appeal for control	5.07	1.35
Appeal for low exaggeration	4.87	1.48
Believability for control	5.04	1.48
Believability for low exaggeration	4.60	1.60

Table 2. Block 2: Control video compared to high exaggeration

Animation responses	Mean	Standard deviation
Appeal for control	5.04	1.49
Appeal for high exaggeration	4.72	1.57
Believability for control	5.10	1.41
Believability for high exaggeration	4.68	1.59

Table 3. Block 3: Low exaggeration compared to high exaggeration

Animation responses	Mean	Standard deviation
Appeal for high exaggeration	5.11	1.41
Appeal for low exaggeration	4.74	1.66
Believability for high exaggeration	4.99	1.56
Believability for low exaggeration	4.80	1.66

The mean scores were consistent with the participants' responses to choosing their preference between two videos in each block. When asked "Do you prefer the video of the top-most or bottom-most character?" there were more votes of preference collected for the control video compared to the exaggerated versions. However, the high exaggeration video had more votes of preference compared to the low exaggeration. A list of the participants' votes for their favored animation can be found in Table 4.

One-Way ANOVA hypothesis tests were conducted to determine if the levels of exaggeration had a significant effect on participants' perceived appeal and believability. Results from the One-Way ANOVA tests for appeal and believability are included in Table 5. With a chosen significance level of 0.05, it was found there were no significant differences in appeal ($p = 0.319$) between the animations. Similarly, the data showed no significant differences between the animations for believability, although, the p-value was closer to being considered statistically significant ($p = 0.098$). The null hypotheses H_{01}, H_{02}, H_{03}, H_{04} could not be rejected.

Table 4. Results for Block 3: low exaggeration compared to high exaggeration

No. votes for favorite video in Block 1	
Control	32
Neither/No preference	30
Low exaggeration	20
No. votes for favorite video in Block 2	
Control	35
Neither/No preference	26
High exaggeration	21
No. votes for favorite video in Block 3	
High Exaggeration	36
Neither/No Preference	29
Low exaggeration	17

Table 5. ANOVA results: appeal and believability

		Sum of squares	df	Mean squares	F	Sig
Appeal	Between groups	5.150	2	2.575	1.144	.319
	Within groups	1101.067	489	2.252		
	Total	1106.217	491			
Believability	Between groups	11.236	2	5.618	2.334	.098
	Within groups	1177.177	489	2.407		
	Total	1188.418	491			

Two-Way ANOVA tests were also carried out to determine if the order of viewing the animation blocks in addition to the varying levels of exaggeration had a significant effect on participant perceived appeal and believability. Results from the Two-Way ANOVA tests for appeal and believability are included in Tables 6 and 7. With a chosen significance level of 0.05, it was found that the difference in perceived appeal between the animations was not statistically significant ($p = 0.375$). However, the data results did show statistical significance ($p = 0.037$) for believability, indicating that the perceived believability of the control animation was significantly higher than the believability of the high and low exaggerated versions.

Qualitative Results
After rating each block of animated videos in terms of appeal and believability, participants were asked to provide written feedback on each animation. A list of short answers was recorded in response to the prompt "Please explain why you do or do not find the

Table 6. Test of between-subjects effects for appeal dependent variable: appeal

Source	Type III sum of squares	df	Mean square	F	Sig
Corrected model	12.059[a]	5.150	2	1.144	.319
Intercept	11932.783	1	11932.783	5300.267	.000
Block	3.817	2	1.909	.848	.429
Exaggeration	8.280	2	4.140	1.839	.160
Block*Exaggeration	3.091	1	3.091	1.373	.242
Error	1094.159	486	2.251		
Total	13039.000	492			
Corrected Total	1106.217	491			

a. R Squared = .011 (Adjusted R Squared = .001)

Table 7. Test of between-subjects effects for believability dependent variable: believability

Source	Type III sum of squares	df	Mean square	F	Sig
Corrected model	16.961[a]	5	3.392	1.407	.220
Intercept	11658.587	1	11658.587	4836.798	.000
Block	5.382	2	2.691	1.116	.328
Exaggeration	15.980	2	7.990	3.315	.037
Block*Exaggeration	.343	1	.343	.143	.706
Error	1171.451	486	2.410		
Total	12847.000	492			
Corrected total	1188.413	491			

a. R Squared = .014 (Adjusted R Squared = .004)

top-most/bottom-most character appealing/believable". One theme that appeared consistent throughout the blocks of videos was the participants commenting that all animated videos seemed very similar, almost the same. Other comments showed distaste towards the character model and textures, and the voice-over audio for the cat. These responses suggest that changes made to the motion of the character might have not been easily noticed by viewers, as participants might have been distracted by other factors such as audio and visual design.

Those participants who did comment on differences among the videos claimed that the control video appeared more *"realistic"*, with examples of comments including *"This cat seemed to move more realistically; its body looked more natural and didn't warp when it jumped"* and *"It's believable because it moved like a cat and looked like a cat and behaved like a cat, despite the human speech"*. These comments are consistent with the control video receiving higher ratings for appeal and believability.

As for the low and high exaggeration videos, some reoccurring comments stated that the animation appeared "*more fluid*" and "*faster*". These comments make sense considering that in the exaggerated videos the character's movements had larger amplitudes, hence the character appeared faster, as the body covered a wider range of motion in the same amount of time. The high exaggeration clip received conflicting responses on whether the animation appeared "*smoother*" or "*rough*". One participant commented that the character had "*stretchy movement*", another commented that the cat appeared "*disfigured when walking*". Interestingly, one participant specifically noted "*the back end of the cat was too close to the ground while jumping*," which makes sense given the greater amplitude of the highly exaggerated animation.

Several participants commented that the cat did not appear to be "believable" in any of the clips, whereas some participants included descriptions of the character as being "*cute*", "*curious*", "*endearing*", "*intelligent*", and "*funny*" in all animations, thus showing a connection between them and the character. The comment that was repeated most often was that the cat is not believable because real cats do not speak in human voices.

5 Discussion

Findings from the study show that participants on average rated the control animation more appealing than the low exaggeration and high exaggeration ones, although the difference in ratings was not statistically significant. In addition, there were more votes of preference collected for the control video compared to the exaggerated versions. When comparing the two levels of exaggeration directly, participants on average rated the high exaggeration clip to be more appealing than the low exaggeration one.

The study yielded similar findings in regard to character's perceived believability. The control clip received higher believability ratings compared to the exaggerated versions, with the difference in perceived believability being more significant than the difference in perceived appeal. The One-Way ANOVA hypothesis test yielded a p-value for believability that was close to statically significant ($p = 0.098$), and the Two-Way ANOVA test yielded a p-value ($p = 0.037$) below our alpha, showing statistical significance. When comparing the exaggerated clips, participants rated the high exaggeration clip higher for believability than the low exaggeration one.

The results from the study are interesting in many ways. First, they suggest that while the principle of exaggeration can be used to improve the likeability and performance of stylized characters, it might not produce the same positive effect when the character design is highly realistic. This finding seems to contradict a common belief in animation that there should be some type of exaggeration in any shot, even if the shot is realistic.

Contrary to previous research findings that suggested that realistic characters with exaggerated facial motions are more likeable than realistic characters without exaggeration, results of this study show that exaggeration makes the character less appealing and convincing. These apparently contradicting results could be due to the differences between our study and previous experiments. Prior studies focused on exaggeration of facial articulations while we considered the exaggeration of body movements. It is possible that there is a difference in perception of exaggerated facial deformations versus perception of exaggerated body motions/deformations, future studies could be conducted to investigate these perceptual differences.

One particularly interesting finding from our study is that the high exaggeration clip received higher ratings of believability, appeal and overall preference than the low exaggeration clip. This finding seems to contradict the animation concept that if the shot is more on the realistic side the exaggeration level should be moderate [11]. We believe that the low exaggeration clip received the lowest ratings for believability and appeal due to the uncanny valley effect [10]. The cat in the low exaggeration clip is realistic but something in his motions appears slightly off due to the moderate level of exaggeration. Although the character looks like a real cat, his motions imperfectly resemble those of a real cat making him fall in the uncanny valley. In contrast, the highly exaggerated cat departs from reality in a more evident way because of the more extreme movements/deformations that make him look less realistic and more caricatured, despite the realistic design. In Fig. 3 we visualize the position of our realistic cat in the 3 animated clips and in the live action video in relation to the uncanny valley.

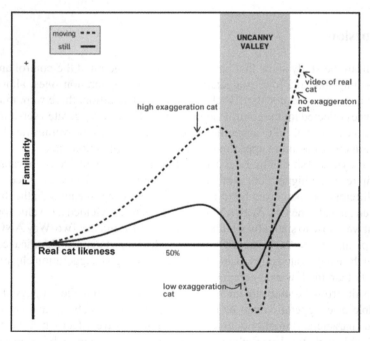

Fig. 3. Graph visualizing the position of the 3 animated clips and the live action video in relation to the uncanny valley

The study had several limitations that prevent us from stating with confidence that the findings will hold true for other realistic anthropomorphic animal characters. First, the study included only one character (the cat) hence the results might be due in part to the intrinsic characteristic of that particular character design and 3D model and that specific set of motions. In future studies we will examine a variety of anthropomorphic animal characters performing different actions in different settings.

Second, as mentioned in the qualitative results section, it is possible that there was some misunderstanding among the participants in regard to the meaning of the word 'believability'. In future studies, a more clear definition of all the terminology used in the experiment would be beneficial to maintain consistency among the context of the prompts and the responses.

Third, the study included a relatively small sample size with all subjects above the age of 18. In the future it would be interesting to conduct additional experiments with larger pools of subjects and with younger participants to investigate how the exaggeration effects are moderated by subjects' age.

Despite its limitations, the findings from the study could have practical implications for character animators, as they could help them make more informed motion design decisions. The lesson learned from this experiment is that when working with anthropomorphic realistic animal characters, the animator should key the characters realistically in order to achieve a higher level of perceived believability and appeal from the audience. If the decision is made to add exaggeration to the characters based on script needs, the findings from this experiment suggest implementing higher levels of exaggerated motion.

References

1. Adamo-Villani, N., Lestina, J., Anasingaraju, S.: Does character's visual style affect viewer's perception of signing avatars? In: Vincenti, G., Bucciero, A., Vaz de Carvalho, C. (eds.) eLEOT 2015. LNICST, vol. 160, pp. 1–8. Springer, Cham (2016). https://doi.org/10.1007/978-3-319-28883-3_1
2. Anasingaraju, S., Adamo-Villani, N., Dib, H.N.: A study of the contribution of different body channels to the expression of emotion in animated pedagogical agents. Int. J. Technol. Human Interact. (IJTHI). (in press)
3. Badathala, S.P., Adamo, N., Villani, N.J., Dib, H.N.: The effect of gait parameters on the perception of animated agents' personality. In: De Paolis, L.T., Bourdot, P. (eds.) AVR 2018. LNCS, vol. 10850, pp. 464–479. Springer, Cham (2018). https://doi.org/10.1007/978-3-319-95270-3_39
4. Hyde, J., Carter, E., Kiesler, S., Hodgins, J.: Perceptual effects of damped and exaggerated facial motion in animated characters. In: 2013 10th IEEE International Conference and Workshops on Automatic Face and Gesture Recognition (FG), pp. 1–6 (2013)
5. Johnston, O., Thomas, F.: The Illusion of Life: Disney Animation, Rev Sub edn. Disney Editions, New York (1995)
6. Lasseter, J.: Principles of traditional animation applied to 3D computer Animation. Comput. Graph. 21(4), 35–44 (1987)
7. Nass, C., Isbister, K., Lee, E.J.: Truth is beauty: researching embodied conversational agents. In: Cassell, J., Sullivan, J., Prevost, S., Churchill, E. (eds.) Embodied Conversational Agents, pp. 374–402. MIT Press, Cambridge (2000)
8. McCloud, S.: Understanding Comics: The Invisible Art. Mass, Northampton (1993)
9. McDonnell, R., Jorg, S., JMcHugh, J., Newell, F., O'Sullivan, C.: Evaluating the emotional content of human motions on real and virtual characters. In: Proceedings of the 5th Symposium on Applied Perception in Graphics and Visualization, pp. 67–73 (2008)

10. Mori, M., MacDorman, K.F., Kageki, N.: The uncanny valley [from the field]. IEEE Robot. Autom. Mag. **19**(2), 98–100 (2012)
11. Pluralsight.: Pushing Your Rigs to the Limit - Using Exaggeration for More Appealing Animation. https://www.pluralsight.com/blog/tutorials/pushing-rigs-limit-using-exagge ration-appealing-animation. Accessed 22 Jul 2019
12. Riek, L.D., Rabinowitch, T.C., Chakrabarti, B., Robinson, P.: How anthropomorphism affects empathy toward robots. In: Proceedings of the 4th ACM/IEEE International Conference on Human Robot Interaction, pp. 245–246. ACM (2009)
13. Ruttkay, Z., Dormann, C., Noot, H.: Embodied Conversational Agents on a Common Ground: A Framework for Design and Evaluation. From Brows to Trust, pp. 27–66. Springer, Netherlands (2004). https://doi.org/10.1007/1-4020-2730-3_2
14. Skrba, L., Reveret, L., Hétroy, F., Cani, M., O'Sullivan, C.: Quadruped animation. Animating Quadrupeds: Methods and Applications (2008)
15. The Lion King, Photorealism, and an Existential Question About the State of Animation. https://www.ign.com/articles/2018/11/29/the-lion-king-photorealism-and-an-existe ntial-question-about-the-state-of-animation. Accessed 22 Jul 2019
16. Webster, C.: Animation: The Mechanics of Motion. Elsevier/Focal Press, Amsterdam (2006)
17. Williams, R.: The Animator's Survival Kit, 4th edn. Farrar, Straus and Giroux, New York (2012)
18. Woo, H.: Designing multimedia learning environments using animated pedagogical agents: factors and issues. J. Comput. Assist. Learn. **25**(3), 203–218 (2009)

Towards a Conceptual Design Framework for Emotional Communication Systems for Long-Distance Relationships

Hong Li[1(✉)], Jonna Häkkilä[1], and Kaisa Väänänen[2]

[1] University of Lapland, Rovaniemi, Finland
{hong.li,jonna.hakkila}@ulapland.fi
[2] Tampere University, Tampere, Finland
kaisa.vaananen@tuni.fi

Abstract. Couples living in long-distance relationships (LDRs) may lack ways to keep emotionally connected. Previous research has presented a wealth of systems and user studies that offer insights of individual systems and their user interface designs. These studies have revealed a multitude of design attributes of the relatedness strategies of LDRs and the user interfaces used in computer-mediated communication (CMC) systems for LDRs. In this paper, we synthesise the multitude of different design attributes, and present a design framework that addresses the five main areas of LDR systems: users (the remote couple), the LDR itself, the used technology, the design of the device, interaction, nature of messages and supported connectedness strategies, and the context of the use. We validate the framework by analysing and presenting a set of six existing systems and prototypes in light of this framework, and show how they take into account the central design attributes. As a conclusion, we propose that this framework can be used to assist in designing and evaluating the user interfaces of CMC systems for emotional communication to support LDRs.

Keywords: Design framework · Emotional communication · Computer-Mediated Communication (CMC) · Long-distance relationships · Long-distance romantic relationships

1 Introduction

Emotional communication is fundamental and crucial to everyday interaction in close relationships, as emotional sharing and concern for each other's emotional needs build an important part of intimacy [46]. Being aware of our loved ones' emotions is essential for interacting and relating with them efficiently. However, emotional communication can be challenging for couples who live apart, due to the absence of a number of important cues, e.g. facial expression, tone of voice, or gestures, when using conventional communication technologies.

© ICST Institute for Computer Sciences, Social Informatics and Telecommunications Engineering 2020
Published by Springer Nature Switzerland AG 2020. All Rights Reserved
A. Brooks and E. I. Brooks (Eds.): ArtsIT 2019/DLI 2019, LNICST 328, pp. 103–123, 2020.
https://doi.org/10.1007/978-3-030-53294-9_8

Long-distance relationships (LDRs) thrive in contemporary life. As an example of the prevalence of LDR couples, there are over seven million couples who self-define themselves as being in an LDR in the US [21]. Furthermore, there is a tendency indicating that the number of LDRs has been steadily increasing over the past few years [21]. Despite the fact that today there is a variety of media available for people to enhance and extend communication with their loved ones at a distance, the majority of remote couples rely on the low-cost and ubiquity of computer-mediated communication (CMC) tools to communicate. Since the interactions through mainstream communication technologies are mostly voice over or screen-to-screen, without adequate multimodal cues they may lead to miscommunication and misunderstandings. Moreover, it has been found out that most available technologies focus on the transmission of explicit information, which neglects the emotional communication needed for close relationships [25].

Luckily, HCI researchers have started to take a broad perspective in exploring different communication devices that can be used to support emotional communication in LDRs. Different types of unconventional communication concepts and prototypes have been developed, and research has proposed systems such as paired, interactive picture frames [7], or connection through sharing music and background sounds [37]. Despite the growing number of solutions for supporting emotional communication in LDRs, the works are still scattered in their approach [35], and systematic studies looking at the big picture are scarce. Also, limited research has been done to develop a comprehensive framework which can help to create better communication devices to support remote couples. An exception here is the work by Gooch and Watts [19], who proposed a design framework to explore how intimate communication devices can be designed to convey social presence which is believed to be essential for supporting close relationships at a distance. However, as it was pointed out [19], the framework is only provisional, and it only covers a limited number of design-relevant attributes for intimate relationships. Thus, it is relevant to develop a more holistic framework focusing on LDRs.

In this paper, we present a conceptual framework of the different aspects that designers should consider when designing technology-mediated communication systems for LDRs. The motivation is to synthesise a holistic set of design dimensions of LDR systems into the framework. The aim of our paper is to (a) highlight a number of important aspects that should be taken into account when designing communication devices to support emotional and subtle communication for remote couples, particularly for those who have established a committed romantic relationship for a substantial amount of time, as opposed to casually dating, and (b) provide a more formalised and comprehensive framework for helping to recognise and consider different issues during the design process. The framework we have developed is based on 1) the literature reviews presented by Hassenzahl et al. [25] and Li et al. [35], 2) our user studies on LDR couples revealing design challenges, and 3) our own designs and prototypes, as presented in Sect. 4.1 Fig. 7 and 8.

The remainder of this paper is organised as follows. Section 2 presents the related work in mediating emotional communication to support LDRs. Section 3 describes the framework in detail. Section 4 analyses a number of example systems using our framework. Section 5 discusses the highlights of our findings towards the framework. Finally, Sect. 6 draws conclusions of our work and suggests directions for future work.

2 Related Work

In this section we first introduce the study of emotional communication and how it has been defined. We then briefly review concepts that aim to support LDRs through mediating emotional communication.

2.1 Emotional Communication

Communication is one of the basic human needs. The intention behind communication is not only to exchange information, but also to mediate emotions. Emotional communication has been conceptualised as a process of mutual influence between the emotions of communication partners [3]. Emotional communication happens every day of our lives, either being more conscious through facial or vocal channels, or being unconscious e.g. through the tactile channel. It has been found out that humans are able to communicate at least eight emotions through touch, i.e. anger, fear, happiness, sadness, disgust, love, gratitude, and sympathy [27].

The study of emotions has flourished in different fields. Based on neuroscience models of emotion, appraisal theories of emotion, prototype approach, and social constructivist theories of emotion, Bartsch and Hübner [3] have outlined a theoretical framework that introduces four working definitions for emotional communication, which can be defined as *1) a process of reciprocal activation of emotional brain systems; 2) a process of information exchange about cognitive appraisals; 3) a process of reciprocal activation of emotional scripts; and 4) a process of symbolic negotiation of emotions.*

There has been substantial research investigating the implications of emotional communication in clinical context [6], musical performance [29], and mother-child relationships [13]. Emotional communication also plays an important role in romantic relationships, its impact has been demonstrated in a number of studies. Findings from a questionnaire study involving 581 couples highlighted that relational satisfaction and partner's attachment style are partially mediated by the emotional communication between the partners [20]. Another qualitative research that engaged 29 couples in discussing a problem that they had in their relationship showed that emotional communication may both influence and be influenced by relationship satisfaction and partners' general beliefs about close relationships [18].

2.2   Prior Art for Mediating Emotional Communication in the LDR Context

To bridge the gap between people living apart, there has been a growing interest among HCI researchers in exploring ways to utilise CMC technology for supporting the mediation of emotional communication in LDRs. Prior art has investigated the use of mainstream communication technologies, such as video chat [41] and mobile phones, e.g. [44,49], as well as unconventional user interfaces for intimate communication. One line of research has dedicated in utilising everyday objects in connecting people over distance through implicit interaction. Early work introduced a pair of remotely located bed environments where each partner uses pillows and curtain as tangible interfaces and an ambient display to support intimate communication over distance through aural, visual, and tactile manifestations of subtle emotional qualities [16]. Chang et al. proposed a pair of interactive picture frames as a semi-ambient display for remote couples to develop their personal emotional language and enhance emotional communication between them [7]. Chung et al. used two paired cups as communication interfaces to promote emotional interaction by enabling two remotely located individuals to share feelings of drinking [8].

Another line of research has focused on communicating intimacy for couples in LDRs through subtle and implicit actions to indicate the presence of the distant loved one and express affection for the remote partner, e.g. "I love you" or "I'm thinking of you". Kaye et al. [32] built a virtual system which enables LDR couples to click a circle which fades over time on the computer screen to indicate the remote presence and convey a subtle message of "thinking of you". Lottridge et al. [37] designed the *MissU* system, which enables emotional support between remote couples by sharing music and background sounds to feel the virtual presence and signify the thinking of the remote partner. Tsetserukou et al. [52] proposed a wearable humanoid robot which consists of a set of haptic devices allowing the user to emotionally enhance the immersive experience of real-time messaging with the distant loved one, but also emotionally and physically feel the presence of the remote partner.

Li et al. [35] conducted a systematic analysis of 52 LDR systems and used a synthesis of four main design-relevant attributes. They used attribute categories of form factors, modalities, and message types of the systems, as well as the evaluation approaches. As a conclusion, they came up with key design implications that highlight the emphases and gaps in the current research.

3   The Framework

Prior frameworks have emerged in the area of intimacy and CMC. Vetere et al. [55] presented a framework distinguishing themes that emerge between, before, during an interaction, and as a consequence of the intimate interaction. Before the interaction, the conditions for intimate interaction require trust, commitment and self-disclosure. During the interaction, the constituents of the intimate acts include themes of emotional, physical, expressive, reciprocity and public and

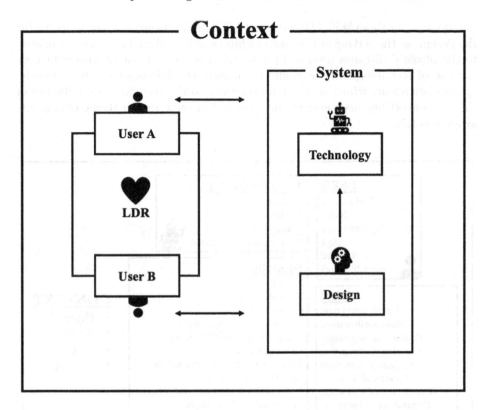

Fig. 1. The key concepts of Computer-Mediated Communication (CMC) between couples in Long-Distance Relationships (LDRs).

private. The consequences of intimate interaction can result in the feeling of presence-in-absence. However, Vetere et al. point out that intimate relationships are strong but vulnerable, and intimate interactions can result also misunderstandings. Gooch and Watts [19] proposed a design framework for social presence that consists of six factors, i.e. *personalisation, sensory medium, effort, openness of the system, metaphor of use* and *fleeting vs realised output.* They also point out that there exist extraneous factors which are related to, but not directly incorporated into, the communication medium, and which have an impact on social presence and are important for supporting intimate relationships over distance. In our research, we focus especially on LDRs, and address the design space of CMC systems from this viewpoint.

In CMC between couples in LDRs, the users interact with each other through a technical system, which mediates the communication through its input and output channels (see Fig. 1). Both design and technology influence on the overall user experience (UX), and play a role in its success. In addition, there are other aspects that need to be taken into account when designing for this specific user group. As a well-established tradition of user-centric design emphasises, the user, his/her needs, skills and preferences should be taken into account when designing any systems for them [45]. The setting of LDR itself sets special requirements for the design, as the setting of the relationship as well as the characteristics related to the physical distance need to be taken into account. Context also influences the use of technology, and can affect not only the habits of use but also the system behaviour, which is adapted according to the context. The influence of the use context has been actively investigated in the research theme of context-awareness [15].

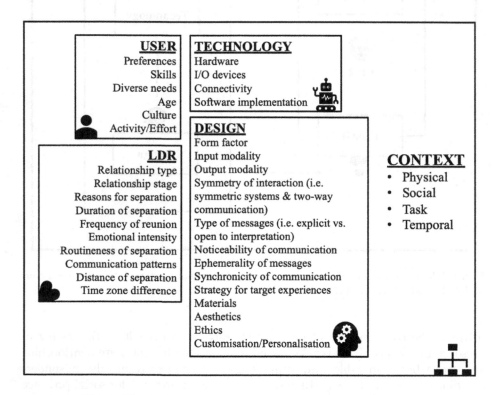

Fig. 2. The framework for designing CMC systems for LDRs.

The presented concepts form the main dimensions of our conceptual framework for designing CMC systems for LDRs (see Fig. 2), and are explained in detail in the following five subsections.

3.1 User

As can be argued for any HCI concept, the user is in the centrum when designing an interactive system. There is a vast amount of research on how individuals use the technology differently, as well as numerous design methods that focus on how to take into account the users the system is designed for. For instance, personas, i.e. archetypes of users [9], is a well-known method to guide the designer in his/her decisions. The diverse needs and the preferences of the target user are essential in formulating the design concept, and addressed through different user research methods collecting data of the practices and preferences of the people. Related to the preferences, the willingness to put in effort/activity that is required from the user's behalf may vary between users. Considering the skill levels of the target users is an important factor to take into account, especially the distinction between novice and expert users has gained much attention when designing interactive systems [42]. Also, the user's age plays a role when considering the technical solutions, especially when designing technology for elderly. In the context of LDR, it is important to remember that the couples can be in a long-term relationship, even lasting for a lifetime, and the age spectrum can be wide. Cultural background is also an interesting aspect to take into account, and may affect e.g. on how the user perceives different design solutions [51]. Thus, as the main attributes related to the user dimension the framework, we define *Preferences, Skills, Diverse needs, Age, Culture, Activity/Effort*.

3.2 LDR

A human-centred design thinking process starts from empathising with the user, i.e. the LDR couples. It is essential to understand the relationship type, relationship stage, and reasons for the separation, in order to gain a deep and empathic understanding of the target user. LDR can be narrowly defined as an intimate relationship in which the couple is separated by a geographical distance that restricts physical contact and face-to-face communication [34], yet LDR is not limited to romantic relationships. A significant number of individuals have to live apart from their loved ones due to educational demands, career pursuits, military duty, emigration and such circumstances [1,38,50]. These reasons for separation have formed three main types of LDRs, i.e. LD friendships [47], LD family relationships [39], and LD romantic relationships [22] which can be further categorised into a series of stages, that is, casually dating, seriously dating, engaged or married [1]. Every case is significantly different when it comes to an LDR. Duration of separation, frequency of reunion, emotional intensity, routineness of separation have been highlighted as important differences in LDRs [38]. Another important difference in LDRs is communication patterns. It has been noted that the communication patterns vary dramatically in LDR couples, as they use various communication channels to enhance intimacy [10], and use different strategies in different communication channels to maintain their relationships over distance [12]. The distance of separation pose all kinds of barriers to LDR couples. Maintaining an LDR in a different time zone could make it even more challenging. Time zone difference leads to unsynchronised daily life and schedules, which has been pointed out as one of the main challenges in LDRs [34]. However, there has been little effort made to address this issue for LDR couples who have to live in large different time zones. Thus, we define *Relationship type, Relationship stage, Reasons for separation, Duration of separation, Frequency of reunion, Emotional intensity, Routineness of separation, Commu-*

nication patterns, Distance of separation, and *Time zone difference* as the main attributes related to the LDR dimension of the framework.

3.3 Technology

LDR systems employ a vast array of technological hardware and input-output devices embedded or attached to them. Hardware can either be off-the-shelf (e.g. a commercial smart device) or custom made (e.g. a decorative household item embedded with new technology construct built with an electronics toolkit [24]). Input devices can be traditional ones such as joysticks and microphones, or they can be more novel ones with advanced computational capabilities such as cameras with gesture recognitions or touch-sensitive displays. All LDR systems utilise some kind of connectivity solutions, based on e.g. Bluetooth, cellular network or WIFI. LDR solutions are programmed to include the necessary software implementation, and the exact implementations are highly dependent on the requirements of the system. Thus, we define *Hardware, I/O devices, Connectivity,* and *Software implementation* as the main attributes related to the technology dimension of the framework. It is however not the focus of our framework to describe the technical details of the LDR systems.

3.4 Design

With the rapid development of technologies, the means of remote communication for LDR couples have transformed from the old communication platforms which consisted of handwritten letters and phone calls to numerous newer communication channels enabled by CMC technology. New form factors and user interfaces are emerging beyond conventional screens. Li et al. [35] identified a number of design attributes through a systematic literature review of the design of systems which support emotional communication between LDR couples. The main design attributes are form factors, interaction types, nature of messages and strategies for expressing relatedness. Specifically, input modality, output modality and symmetry of interaction (whether the systems used by both ends are symmetric and whether the communication is two-way) are further analysed under the interaction types. Type of messages (i.e. explicit vs. open to interpretation), noticeability of communication, ephemerality of messages, and synchronicity of communication are further analysed under the nature of messages. Hassenzahl et al. [25] identified current six strategies used in published artefacts to mediate a relatedness experience for intimate relationships, which are: *awareness, expressivity, physicalness, gift-giving, joint action,* and *memories.* These strategies support the design of technology-mediated relatedness which is important for human psychological well-being, and therefore should be taken into account when designing experience-oriented technology for LDR. In addition to the attributes that have been identified in [35], we also consider materials, aesthetics, customisation/personalisation, and ethics as something that should be taken into account in the design process. It has been found out that interacting with different types of materials can evoke particular practice in which materials serve a role in carrying certain design intentions and creating a unique UX [30]. Aesthetics is a well-known design attribute which satisfies people's senses and gives a feeling of pleasure that results from sensory perception [26]. Another two well-known design attributes that have been suggested that should be taken into account when designing for LDRs are customisation and personalisation [19,34]. Customisation plays a subsidiary yet important role in design, it can empower LDR couples as skilled practitioners to use technologies in their own creative ways to meet their diverse needs [34]. Similarly, personalisation makes an object become meaningful and symbolic to users [19]. Enabling customisation/personalisation in design makes a standard object becomes a one-of-a-kind, which thereby forms an emotional bond to users [23,54]. Last but not least, it is worth noting that ethical issues could arise while mediating intimate feelings or actions through technology. Privacy has been viewed as significant to individuals. Despite that users may raise concerns about experiencing intimacy through technology [34], it has been revealed that ethical considerations were largely not addressed [35]. Thus, we define *Form factor, Input modality, Output modality, Symmetry of interaction, Type of messages (i.e. explicit vs. open to interpretation), Noticeability of communication, Ephemerality of messages, Synchronicity of communication, Strategy for target experiences, Materials, Aesthetics, Customisation/Personalisation* and *Ethics* as the main attributes related to the Design dimension of the framework.

3.5   Context

Context of use is an important factor when investigating human-computer interaction. It has given rise to an entire sector of research among computer science, context-awareness, which can be traced back to Mark Weiser's vision of ubiquitous computing [56]. He visioned that computers of the 21st century would be able to capture context information and adapt their behaviour to support user's tasks. The adapted behaviour of the system can vary between different levels of automation, allowing the user a chance to initiate or confirm the device actions [2]. It has been pointed out that the level of automation should inversely correlate with the uncertainties in context recognition to avoid misplaced device actions [14]. A widely used definition for context states that "context is any information that can be used to characterise the situation of an entity" [15]. However, when designing or evaluating interactive systems, it is meaningful to structure the context in more detail, as for instance suggested by Bradley and Dunlop [5], who distinguish between physical, social, task, and temporal contexts. The physical context of technology use can be determined through different environmental sensors, and can influence e.g. the volume, brightness of the display lights. Social context defines much of the norms the user is expected to behave with technology, and e.g. smart glasses in the company with others [33], and influences on the acceptability of the technology. Task context relates to the goals the user has, and what are the resources and constraints influencing it [5]. Temporal context relates to the time of, e.g., a month or day [31], or the duration and frequency of interaction [43]. Thus, similarly to [5], in our framework we see it fit to distinguish between the *physical, social, task* and *temporal* contexts.

4   Example Systems Analysed with the Framework

To validate our conceptual framework, in the following we analysed six existing products and examples of research works, designed for emotional communication between LDR couples. The last two examples, Connected Candles and Our Little Secret, present the authors' own work. These system examples were chosen to represent a wide variety of CMC systems with a wealth of different attribute choices.

4.1   The Analysis

We developed a template based on our framework for analysing the example systems. The results of the analysis are reported in Fig.3, 4, 5, 6, 7 and 8.

4.2   Summarising the Analysis Results

The analysis of the six example systems reveals that very different solutions are used for similar or at least overlapping purposes. For example, there are wearable (HugShirt™ [11]), portable (Kissinger [48]) and semi-autonomous (Beam® [57]) form factors to enable emotional communication. Further attributes related to users, LDRs, technology, design and context of use could be compared and contrasted to highlight the similarities and differences of the solutions. For example, in this sample of CMC systems, most systems were designed to support synchronous communication where the user and the paired user are required to be active at both ends. While in the cases with large time zone differences, this attribute hinders the use of the systems, as both parties have to agree on a convenient time for the synchronous communication, e.g. Kissenger [48], Hug Shirt™ [11], Frebble [17], Connected Candles [24]. Failing to find an appropriate time to initiate the synchronous communication might result in disturbing moments for the paired user, e.g. feeling hug sensations out of the blue when the paired user's attention is needed at work. Systems that enable both synchronous and asynchronous communication can better support LDRs with large time zone differences, e.g., Beam® [57] and Our Little Secret [36]. Such analytic observations from the systematic analysis can help identify "design gaps" and help address them in further system designs.

5   Discussion

The commercial example systems are designed to fit a wider range of end-users, which often aim to be used for all types of LDRs at any stage. However, the one-size-fits-all strategy does not work for every type of LDR, e.g. the design of Frebble might not fit LDR couples who are at a more mature stage of their relationship or people who do not like holding hands [53]. Customisation and personalisation are well-known design approaches that can make a product more appealing to users' varied tastes and is more likely to meet their diverse needs [23,54]. Four out of the six reviewed example systems do not equip such features in the design, but we suggest this is an aspect that is worthwhile considering in all design efforts.

Beam® Smart Presence™

A telepresence robot that supports visual communication by allowing the users to seamlessly move within the space and engage in real time across distance [57].

Image source: https://www.suitabletech.com

User

This product is mainly designed for business use, such as remote conference calls. However, it can be adapted in the use case of LDRs. It works similarly to a video chat system which provides visual communication, but the robot is featured with the mobility to move around. It can be used as a multi-channel communication tool which would meet the users' diverse needs. On the other hand, it requires more skills and effort to control the robot.

LDR

This product can be adapted in any types of LDRs at any stage. The emotional intensity is considered strong when having visual communication with a distant loved one. The communication pattern is explicit, intimate and can be both synchronous and asynchronous. With mobility and autonomy, the robot enables remote couples to be able to participate in the mundane parts of each other's everyday routines. The availability of being able to connect with each other both synchronously and asynchronously would better support LDRs.

Technology
- Hardware: screen, video and audio devices, body.
- Connectivity: Internet.
- I/O devices: using the Beam® App and controlling the Beam® robot as input; the mobile video chat system supported by the Beam® robot as output.
- Software: Beam® App.

Design
- Form factor: movable or semi-autonomous object.
- Input modality: non-typing touch via smartphone or tablet, PC controlled, speech, visuals.
- Output modality: visuals, speech, object movement.
- Symmetry: can be symmetric or asymmetric, two-way.
- Type of messages: explicit.
- Noticeability: noticeable to others.
- Ephemerality: disappears with user actions, e.g. turning off the system.
- Synchronicity: synchronous and asynchronous.
- Strategy: physicalness, awareness.
- Materials: reinforced polymer.
- Aesthetics: the appearance is suitable for business usage, but might be less pleasant in romantic settings.
- Ethics: may raise privacy and hyper-connectivity issues due to the mobility and autonomy of the robot, particularly those still in the early stage of their relationships [57].
- Customisation/Personalisation: not available.

Context
- Physical: at home.
- Social: can be used to connect with a distant loved one's family and friends.
- Task: interacting with the Beam® App and controlling the Beam® robot.
- Temporal: it can be freely used at any time of the day, as the robot has mobility and autonomy which can be controlled by the paired user, so the user is not required to control the robot all the time.

Fig. 3. Beam® [57] analysed with the framework.

Kissenger	
A smartphone accessory that provides a physical interface which can sense a kiss and transmit realistic kissing sensations to the paired user in real time [48]. Image source: *Imagineering Institute,* http://imagineeringinstitute.org/kissenger/	

User	Technology
This product is designed to connect friends, families and couples who live apart (at any age from any culture). Interestingly, it can also connect idols and their fans. It is suitable for users who wish to strengthen intimacy over distance. It does not require much effort or skills to use it. However, the functions are limited with transmitting kisses and the gadget is not available for personalisation, which might not be sufficient to meet users' diverse needs.	• Hardware: Bluetooth, sensors and actuators, a scent tank, a vibration motor, and a smartphone connector. • Connectivity: Bluetooth, Internet. • I/O devices: using the Kissenger App and kissing the silicon lip on the Kissenger as input; the kissing back sensation coming from the Kissenger as output. • Software: Kissenger App.

LDR	Design
This product is mainly designed for any types of LDRs at any stage, but it also supports the interaction between idols and their fans. The emotional intensity is considered strong when giving or receiving a kiss. The communication pattern is implicit, synchronous and intimate. Since the communication is in real time, it requires the users from both ends to be active at the same time. This might cause inconvenience for the users who have unsynchronised daily life due to large time zone differences.	• Form factor: carried, portable object. • Input modality: touch, non-typing touch via smartphone. • Output modality: haptic, vibration. • Symmetry: symmetric, two-way. • Type of messages: open for interpretation. • Noticeability: private. • Ephemerality: disappears by itself. • Synchronicity: synchronous. • Strategy: physicalness, awareness, joint action. • Materials: plastics and silicon. • Aesthetics: it might be too big as a portable smartphone accessory. • Ethics: a number of ethical issues that may arise by using this device have been discussed in [48], e.g. failing to return a kiss. • Customisation/Personalisation: not available.

Context
• Physical: relaxing and private environment. • Social: preferably no other people around and the user is feeling lonely or missing a distant loved one. • Task: sending kisses to a distant loved one by interacting with the Kissenger App first, and then kissing the silicon lip on the Kissenger device. • Temporal: it can be used at any time of the day when the user is not occupied, having a relaxing time and missing a distant loved one. Given both users need to be active for the communication, the user might need to schedule a convenient time with the paired user for the kiss, particularly in large time zone separation cases.

Fig. 4. Kissenger [48] analysed with the framework.

Hug Shirt™

A high-tech garment that captures the pressure, duration and location of the touch, the skin warmth, and the heartbeat rate of the user, and simulates the experience of being embraced by a distant loved one to the paired user synchronously [11].

Image source: *CuteCircuit*, http://cutecircuit.com/the-hug-shirt/

User

This product is designed for people (at any age from any culture) who wish to connect with a distant loved one, such as friends, families and couples. It is suitable for users who prefer a mediated feeling of physical intimacy over distance. It does not require much effort or skills to use it. However, the functions are limited to hug sensations, and the garment is not available for personalisation, which might not be able to support the users' diverse needs.

Technology

• Hardware: Bluetooth, sensors and actuators.
• Connectivity: Bluetooth, Internet.
• I/O devices: using the Hug Shirt™ App, hugging oneself while wearing the Hug Shirt™ as input; the mediated hug sensation coming from Hug Shirt™ as output.
• Software: Hug Shirt™ App.

Design

• Form factor: wearable smart garment.
• Input modality: touch, non-typing touch via smartphone or tablet, physiological data.
• Output modality: haptic, temperature.

LDR

This product is designed for any types of LDRs at any stage. It mediates emotional communication between the two remote parties when giving or receiving a hug. The communication pattern is implicit, synchronous and intimate. However, receiving hugs when the user's attention is required for learning, working and such situations might be disturbing. As the hug is transmitted to the paired user synchronously, it might be insufficient for those who have unsynchronised daily life due to large time differences.

• Symmetry: symmetric, two-way.
• Type of messages: open for interpretation.
• Noticeability: private.
• Ephemerality: disappears by itself.
• Synchronicity: synchronous.
• Strategy: physicalness, awareness, expressivity.
• Materials: smart garments.
• Aesthetics: designed by an established fashion company and has received a number of awards.
• Ethics: receiving hugs out of the blue or when the user is occupied may be disturbing.
• Customisation/Personalisation: not available.

Context

• Physical: relaxing and private environment.
• Social: preferably no other people around and the user is feeling lonely or missing a distant loved one.
• Task: sending hugs to a distant loved one by interacting with the Hug Shirt™ App first and then hugging the user himself/herself while wearing the Hug Shirt™.
• Temporal: it can be used at any time of the day when the user is not occupied, having a relaxing time and missing a distant loved one. Given the synchronicity required in the communication, the user needs to consider if it is an appropriate time to send a hug to the paired user, particularly those who have to deal with large time zone differences.

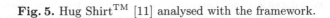

Fig. 5. Hug Shirt™ [11] analysed with the framework.

Frebble

A mediated touch device that provides the tactile sense of holding hands with a loved one in real time over distance through the squeeze of a hand [17].
Image source: *Holland Haptics*
http://www.myfrebble.com

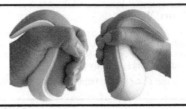

User	Technology
This product is designed to connect friends, families and couples remotely through simulating the feeling of hand-holding. However, it might not work for the users who do not like holding hands. It is more suitable for connecting children and parents, or grandchildren and grandparents. It does not require much effort or skills, but the function is limited within holding hands and the gadget is not available for personalisation, which might not be sufficient to meet the users' diverse needs.	• Hardware: Bluetooth, pressure sensors, vibration motors, squeeze bar, multicolour LED light. • Connectivity: Bluetooth, Internet. • I/O devices: using the Frebble App and squeezing the Frebble as input; the mediated hand-holding sensation coming from the Frebble as output. • Software: Frebble App.

LDR

This product is designed to support any types of LDRs at any stage. However, it might be less useful for remote couples who are already in a more mature stage. It strengthens the emotional intensity when having visual communication while holding hands together with a distant loved one. The communication pattern is subtle, implicit, synchronous and intimate. Since the communication is in real time, it requires both sides to be active at the same time. This might be less considerate for those who have unsynchronised daily life with large time zone differences.

Design

• Form factor: carried, portable object.
• Input modality: touch, non-typing touch via smartphone or tablet.
• Output modality: haptic, vibration.
• Symmetry: symmetric, two-way.
• Type of messages: open for interpretation.
• Noticeability: private.
• Ephemerality: disappears with user actions, e.g. turning off the system.
• Synchronicity: synchronous.
• Strategy: physicalness, awareness, joint action.
• Materials: plastic and rubberised pad.
• Aesthetics: negative feedback has been pointed out regarding the appearance of the device [53].
• Ethics: there might be digital ethics for young users, and may raise ethical concerns for inappropriate use of technology [53].
• Customisation/Personalisation: not available.

Context

• Physical: relaxing and private environment.
• Social: the user is feeling lonely or missing a distant loved one.
• Task: holding hands with a distant loved one by interacting with the Frebble first and then slightly squeezing the Frebble as if holding hands with a distant loved one.
• Temporal: it can be used at any time of the day when the user is not occupied, having a relaxing time and missing a distant loved one. Given both users need to be active for the communication, the user might need to schedule a convenient time with the paired user for the hand-holding, particularly in large time zone separation cases.

Fig. 6. Frebble [17] analysed with the framework.

Connected Candles

A paired set of candle stands, each including a traditional and an electric candle. When the user lights the physical candle (with real fire), the electric candle of the paired candle stand at the remote location lights up [24].

Image source: [24]

User

The (research) prototype has been designed for LDR couples, as recorded in the design process, but can also be used for affective communication between other people, e.g. a grandmother and the child's family. The concept utilises existing metaphors and familiar actions of lighting a candle (with a match stick), and is easy and simple to use. It is pleasant for the users who like burning candles, but the cultural meaning of burning candles may vary. The tangible UI does not require skills with computers or other technology.

LDR

Connected candles support any LDR couples at any level of their relationship. It is designed for moments when the user wants to create an emotional connection, e.g. for being lonely or feeling romantic. The communication pattern is subtle, implicit, and synchronous. Since the communication is in real time, and does not require actions in the remote end. The ambient light display can be on any time, but is preferred to be used in dim light conditions, e.g. in the evenings. Thus, time zone differences larger than a few hours do not fit well with the concept.

Technology

- Hardware: Arduino HW, flame sensor.
- Connectivity: WIFI.
- I/O devices: a candle and matches input; electric candle as an ambient display output.
- Software: Arduino SW.

Design

- Form factor: Semi-fixed, movable object.
- Input modality: gestures, i.e., lighting the candle with a match stick or similar.
- Output modality: visual, light turns on.
- Symmetry: symmetric, two-way.
- Type of messages: open for interpretation.
- Noticeability: public.
- Ephemerality: disappears with user action, e.g., turning of the candle.
- Synchronicity: synchronous.
- Strategy: awareness.
- Materials: ceramics, candles, fire.
- Aesthetics: aesthetics driven concept with ceramics design and candle light.
- Ethics: the user lighting the candle must remember to supervise it (in her/his end only) for the fire safety. Additionally, the cultural meaning of burning candles may vary.
- Customisation/Personalisation: available.

Context

- Physical: relaxing and private environment, dim lighting conditions.
- Social: the user is feeling lonely or missing a distant loved one.
- Task: lighting a candle, enjoying the ambient light of a candle.
- Temporal: considering the dim light conditions, evening use preferred. Ambient illumination is long-lasting, and does not require actions. Big time zone differences hinder the use.

Fig. 7. Connected Candles [24] analysed with the framework.

Our Little Secret

A customisable ambient picture frame display that mediates couples who live apart with large time zone differences. The city landscape in the picture frame switches between day and night display synchronously with the time of a paired user's location. The subtle switching of the hearts indicates receiving a secret code from the paired user (e.g. I love you). When the interaction between the LDR couple is low, the content in the picture starts to fade away subtly and slowly [36].

Image: [36]

User

This (research) prototype is designed to support light-weight communication, simpleness, subtleness, customisation, and creation of secret codes or symbols for LDR couples. It does not require much effort or skills with computers or other technologies. The picture frame display can be customised by the users, which is relatively able to fit diverse tastes appeal to different ages and cultures.

LDR

This concept is specifically designed for couples who have to deal with a large time zone difference in serious LDRs. But can be also adapted on other types of LDRs, e.g. elder parents with their adult children who live apart with time zone separation. It forms emotional bonds with a remote partner when noticing the subtle switching of the display. The communication pattern is private, subtle, implicit, lightweight, and asynchronous. The concept works for busy LDR couples with time zone differences.

Technology
- Hardware: electrochromic display, Arduino HW.
- Connectivity: WIFI.
- I/O devices: real-time clock, touch sensors as input; electrochromic displays as output.
- Software: Arduino SW.

Design
- Form factor: carried, portable object.
- Input modality: non-typing touch via smartphone or tablet.
- Output modality: graphics, visuals.
- Symmetry: symmetric, two-way.
- Type of messages: open for interpretation.
- Noticeability: private.
- Ephemerality: disappears by itself.
- Synchronicity: asynchronous.
- Strategy: awareness, expressivity.
- Materials: cardboard, plastics.
- Aesthetics: a simple concept with a customisable picture frame display could better fit varied tastes.
- Ethics: it may lead to negative emotions when the user notices the display is fading away due to having low interaction with a remote partner.
- Customisation/Personalisation: available.

Context
- Physical: the picture frame can be placed anywhere.
- Social: the user is feeling lonely or missing a distant loved one.
- Task: noticing the subtle changes of the display in the picture frame.
- Temporal: it can be used at any time of the day when the user feels relaxed.

Fig. 8. Our Little Secret [36] analysed with the framework.

The novelty of our framework lies in the integration of five essential dimensions and their related key attributes that should be taken into account when designing CMC systems for mediating emotional communication for LDRs. Previous work has proposed a provisional framework [19] that focused on identifying important factors when designing intimate communication devices which convey social presence at a distance, in order to open up one of the possibilities to strengthen the feelings of presence in LDRs. Moreover, Benford et al. map different behaviours in sensing-based UIs and discuss how the expected, sensed, and desired interaction aspects do not always overlap perfectly [4]. Compared to us, they focus more on the conceptual aspects in the actual interaction event and system behaviour, and their framework can be seen as complementary to our approach. The focus of our framework has been primarily put on building a formalised design framework with particular attention to identify the essential dimensions and their key characteristics needed for designing computer-mediated emotional communication systems for LDRs. We acknowledge, however, that more work is needed before it could function (e.g.) as a concrete tool for designers. We have now initially validated the framework by analysing the example systems and believe that the structured approach presented in this paper has value for researchers and designers addressing the CMC systems for LDRs. With the design has been concepted in more detail, it is then possible to conduct further evaluation with specific frameworks according to the domain, e.g. looking at the qualities for tangible interfaces [28] or musical interfaces [40].

The analysis of the six example systems shows that our framework can be applied in practice for categorising and investigating their different aspects in a systematic way. The analysed examples do not represent widely adopted or known communication tools, such as mobile phones and video chats. The framework thus provides practical means for gaining a systematic overview of the concepts. The framework helps in paying attention to different details, and makes a comparable presentation of different systems and system versions easier. We acknowledge that the sample of analysed systems is small, but we believe our findings indicate, and provide a tool for identifying, potential gaps in the overall design space. In the future, we aim to develop the framework further, and use it as a basis for a design tool to be used in brainstorming or participatory design sessions.

6   Conclusion

In this paper, we have presented a conceptual framework for defining different aspects for designing computer-mediated emotional communication systems for LDRs. The framework includes the key characteristics of users, the LDR itself, technology, design, and context of use as the areas that define what aspects need to be considered when such systems are designed or evaluated. We have also validated the framework by analysing four existing products in the context of the framework, as well as two of our own research prototypes. The analysis indicates that our framework can help in identifying gaps in the system concept designs, and helps in the systematic analysis of the concepts. As future work, we intend to apply our framework for different phases of a design and evaluation process for computer-mediated emotional communication systems for couples in LDRs, and develop the framework further towards a concrete design tool.

Acknowledgements. This work has received funding from the China Scholarship Council fellowship (201606150085).

References

1. Aylor, B.A.: Maintaining long-distance relationships. In: Maintaining Relationships Through Communication: Relational, Contextual, and Cultural Variations, pp. 127–139 (2003)
2. Barkhuus, L., Dey, A.: Is context-aware computing taking control away from the user? Three levels of interactivity examined. In: Dey, A.K., Schmidt, A., McCarthy, J.F. (eds.) UbiComp 2003. LNCS, vol. 2864, pp. 149–156. Springer, Heidelberg (2003). https://doi.org/10.1007/978-3-540-39653-6_12
3. Bartsch, A., Hübner, S.: Towards a theory of emotional communication. CLCWeb Comp. Lit. Cult. **7**(4), 2 (2005)
4. Benford, S., et al.: Expected, sensed, and desired: a framework for designing sensing-based interaction. ACM Trans. Comput. Hum. Interact. **12**(1), 3–30 (2005). https://doi.org/10.1145/1057237.1057239
5. Bradley, N.A., Dunlop, M.D.: Toward a multidisciplinary model of context to support context-aware computing. Hum. Comput. Interact. **20**(4), 403–446 (2005)
6. Bucci, W.: Pathways of emotional communication. Psychoanal. Inq. **21**(1), 40–70 (2001)
7. Chang, A., Resner, B., Koerner, B., Wang, X., Ishii, H.: Lumitouch: an emotional communication device. In: CHI 2001 Extended Abstracts on Human Factors in Computing Systems, CHI EA 2001, pp. 313–314. ACM, New York (2001). https://doi.org/10.1145/634067.634252
8. Chung, H., Lee, C.H.J., Selker, T.: Lover's cups: drinking interfaces as new communication channels. In: CHI 2006 Extended Abstracts on Human Factors in Computing Systems, CHI EA 2006, pp. 375–380. ACM, New York (2006). https://doi.org/10.1145/1125451.1125532
9. Cooper, A., et al.: The inmates are running the asylum: [Why high-tech products drive us crazy and how to restore the sanity]. Sams Indianapolis (2004)
10. Crystal Jiang, L., Hancock, J.T.: Absence makes the communication grow fonder: geographic separation, interpersonal media, and intimacy in dating relationships. J. Commun. **63**(3), 556–577 (2013)
11. CuteCircuit: Hug shirt. http://cutecircuit.com/the-hug-shirt/. Accessed 1 July 2019
12. Dainton, M., Aylor, B.: Patterns of communication channel use in the maintenance of long-distance relationships. Commun. Res. Rep. **19**(2), 118–129 (2002)
13. Denham, S.A., Renwick-DeBardi, S., Hewes, S.: Emotional communication between mothers and preschoolers: relations with emotional competence. Merrill-PalmerQuarterly (1994)
14. Dey, A., Häkkilä, J.: Context-awareness and mobile devices. User Interface Des. Eval. Mob. Technol. **1**, 205–217 (2008). https://doi.org/10.4018/978-1-59904-871-0.ch013

15. Dey, A.K.: Understanding and using context. Personal Ubiquitous Comput. **5**(1), 4–7 (2001). https://doi.org/10.1007/s007790170019
16. Dodge, C.: The bed: a medium for intimate communication. In: CHI 1997 Extended Abstracts on Human Factors in Computing Systems, CHI EA 1997, pp. 371–372. ACM, New York (1997). https://doi.org/10.1145/1120212.1120439
17. Erk, S.M., Toet, A., Van Erp, J.B.: Effects of mediated social touch on affective experiences and trust. PeerJ **3**, e1297 (2015)
18. Gaelick, L., Bodenhausen, G.V., Wyer, R.S.: Emotional communication in close relationships. J. Pers. Soc. Psychol. **49**(5), 1246 (1985)
19. Gooch, D., Watts, L.: A design framework for mediated personal relationship devices. In: Proceedings of the 25th BCS Conference on Human-Computer Interaction, pp. 237–242. British Computer Society (2011)
20. Guerrero, L.K., Farinelli, L., McEwan, B.: Attachment and relational satisfaction: the mediating effect of emotional communication. Commun. Monogr. **76**(4), 487–514 (2009)
21. Guldner, G.T.: The center for the study of long distance relationships. http://www.longdistancerelationships.net/. Accessed 1 July 2019
22. Guldner, G.T.: Long-distance romantic relationships: prevalence and separation-related symptoms in college students. J. Coll. Stud. Dev. **37**(3), 289–296 (1996)
23. Häkkilä, J., Chatfield, C.: Personal customisation of mobile phones: a case study. In: Proceedings of the 4th Nordic Conference on Human-Computer Interaction: Changing Roles, pp. 409–412. ACM (2006)
24. Häkkilä, J., Li, H., Koskinen, S., Colley, A.: Connected candles as peripheral emotional user interface. In: Proceedings of the 17th International Conference on Mobile and Ubiquitous Multimedia, MUM 2018, pp. 327–333. ACM, New York (2018). https://doi.org/10.1145/3282894.3282909
25. Hassenzahl, M., Heidecker, S., Eckoldt, K., Diefenbach, S., Hillmann, U.: All you need is love: Current strategies of mediating intimate relationships through technology. ACM Trans. Comput. Hum. Interact. **19**(4), 30:1–30:19 (2012). https://doi.org/10.1145/2395131.2395137
26. Hekkert, P.: Design aesthetics: principles of pleasure in design. Psychol. Sci. **48**(2), 157 (2006)
27. Hertenstein, M.J., Holmes, R., McCullough, M., Keltner, D.: The communication of emotion via touch. Emotion **9**(4), 566 (2009)
28. Hornecker, E., Buur, J.: Getting a grip on tangible interaction: a framework on physical space and social interaction. In: Proceedings of the SIGCHI Conference on Human Factors in Computing Systems, CHI 2006, pp. 437–446. ACM, New York (2006). https://doi.org/10.1145/1124772.1124838
29. Juslin, P.N.: Emotional communication in music performance: a functionalist perspective and some data. Music Percept. Interdisc. J. **14**(4), 383–418 (1997)
30. Karana, E., Giaccardi, E., Stamhuis, N., Goossensen, J.: The tuning of materials: a designer's journey. In: Proceedings of the 2016 ACM Conference on Designing Interactive Systems, DIS 2016, pp. 619–631. ACM, New York (2016). https://doi.org/10.1145/2901790.2901909
31. Karlson, A.K., Meyers, B.R., Jacobs, A., Johns, P., Kane, S.K.: Working overtime: patterns of smartphone and PC usage in the day of an information worker. In: Tokuda, H., Beigl, M., Friday, A., Brush, A.J.B., Tobe, Y. (eds.) Pervasive 2009. LNCS, vol. 5538, pp. 398–405. Springer, Heidelberg (2009). https://doi.org/10.1007/978-3-642-01516-8_27

32. Kaye, J.J., Levitt, M.K., Nevins, J., Golden, J., Schmidt, V.: Communicating intimacy one bit at a time. In: CHI 2005 Extended Abstracts on Human Factors in Computing Systems, CHI EA 2005, pp. 1529–1532. ACM, New York (2005). https://doi.org/10.1145/1056808.1056958

33. Koelle, M., Kranz, M., Möller, A.: Don't look at me that way!: understanding user attitudes towards data glasses usage. In: Proceedings of the 17th International Conference on Human-Computer Interaction with Mobile Devices and Services, MobileHCI 2015, pp. 362–372. ACM, New York (2015). https://doi.org/10.1145/2785830.2785842

34. Li, H.: Understanding design as a catalyst to engage remote couples in designing for long-distance relationships. In: DRS 2018, vol. 6, pp. 2265–2279 (2018)

35. Li, H., Häkkilä, J., Väänänen, K.: Review of unconventional user interfaces for emotional communication between long-distance partners. In: Proceedings of the 20th International Conference on Human-Computer Interaction with Mobile Devices and Services, MobileHCI 2018, pp. 18:1–18:10. ACM, New York (2018). https://doi.org/10.1145/3229434.3229467

36. Li, H., Müller, H., Häkkilä, J.: Our little secret: design and user study on an electrochromic ambient display for supporting long-distance relationship. In: Proceedings of the 4th EAI International Conference on Design, Learning and Innovation, p. 21. Springer (2019)

37. Lottridge, D., Masson, N., Mackay, W.: Sharing empty moments: design for remote couples. In: Proceedings of the SIGCHI Conference on Human Factors in Computing Systems, CHI 2009, pp. 2329–2338. ACM, New York (2009). https://doi.org/10.1145/1518701.1519058

38. Merolla, A.J.: Relational maintenance and noncopresence reconsidered: conceptualizing geographic separation in close relationships. Commun. Theor. 20(2), 169–193 (2010)

39. Mickus, M.A., Luz, C.C.: Televisits: Sustaining long distance family relationships among institutionalized elders through technology. Aging Mental Health 6(4), 387–396 (2002)

40. Morreale, F., De Angeli, A., O'Modhrain, S.: Musical interface design: an experience-oriented framework. In: NIME, pp. 467–472 (2014)

41. Neustaedter, C., Greenberg, S.: Intimacy in long-distance relationships over video chat. In: Proceedings of the SIGCHI Conference on Human Factors in Computing Systems, pp. 753–762. ACM (2012)

42. Nielsen, J.: 10 usability heuristics for user interface design. Nielsen NormanGroup 1(1) (1995)

43. Oulasvirta, A., Tamminen, S., Roto, V., Kuorelahti, J.: Interaction in 4-second bursts: the fragmented nature of attentional resources in mobile HCI. In: Proceedings of the SIGCHI Conference on Human Factors in Computing Systems, CHI 2005, pp. 919–928. ACM, New York (2005). https://doi.org/10.1145/1054972.1055101

44. Pettigrew, J.: Text messaging and connectedness within close interpersonal relationships. MarriageFam. Rev. 45(6–8), 697–716 (2009)

45. Preece, J., Rogers, Y., Sharp, H.: Interaction Design: Beyond Human-Computer Interaction. John Wiley & Sons (2015)

46. Reis, H.T.: Encyclopedia of Human Relationships, vol. 1. Sage (2009)

47. Rohlfing, M.E.: Doesn't anybody stay in one place anymore? an exploration of the understudied phenomenon of long-distance relationships. In: Under-Studied Relationships: Off the Beaten Track, vol. 6, pp. 173–196 (1995)

48. Samani, H.A., Parsani, R., Rodriguez, L.T., Saadatian, E., Dissanayake, K.H., Cheok, A.D.: Kissenger: design of a kiss transmission device. In: Proceedings of the Designing Interactive Systems Conference, DIS 2012, pp. 48–57. ACM, New York (2012). https://doi.org/10.1145/2317956.2317965

49. Shirazi, A.S., et al.: Emotion sharing via self-composed melodies on mobile phones. In: Proceedings of the 11th International Conference on Human-Computer Interaction with Mobile Devices and Services, p. 30. ACM (2009)

50. Stafford, L.: Maintaining Long-Distance and Cross-residential Relationships. Routledge (2004)

51. Tractinsky, N.: Aesthetics and apparent usability: empirically assessing cultural and methodological issues. In: Proceedings of the ACM SIGCHI Conference on Human Factors in Computing Systems, CHI 1997, pp. 115–122. ACM, New York (1997). https://doi.org/10.1145/258549.258626

52. Tsetserukou, D., Neviarouskaya, A., Prendinger, H., Kawakami, N., Tachi, S.: Affective haptics in emotional communication. In: 2009 3rd International Conference on Affective Computing and Intelligent Interaction and Workshops, pp. 1–6. IEEE (2009)

53. Vansant, A.: Frebble: This will go so horribly wrong. https://www.amyvansant.com/frebble-this-will-go-so-horribly-wrong/. Accessed 1 July 2019

54. Ventä, L., Isomursu, M., Ahtinen, A., Ramiah, S.: "my phone is a part of my soul"-how people bond with their mobile phones. In: 2008 The Second International Conference on Mobile Ubiquitous Computing, Systems, Services and Technologies, pp. 311–317. IEEE (2008)

55. Vetere, F., et al.: Mediating intimacy: designing technologies to support strong-tie relationships. In: Proceedings of the SIGCHI Conference on Human Factors in Computing Systems, CHI 2005, pp. 471–480. ACM, New York (2005). https://doi.org/10.1145/1054972.1055038

56. Weiser, M.: The computer for the 21st century. Sci. Am. **265**(3), 94–105 (1991)

57. Yang, L., Neustaedter, C.: Our house: living long distance with a telepresence robot. Proc. ACM Hum. Comput. Interact. **2**(CSCW), 190:1–190:18 (2018). https://doi.org/10.1145/3274459

Developing a User-Centred Communication Pad for Cognitive and Physical Impaired People

Chaudhary Muhammad Aqdus Ilyas[1](✉) ⓘ, Kasper Rodil[2] ⓘ, and Matthias Rehm[3] ⓘ

[1] Visual Analysis People (VAP) Lab and Human Computer Interaction (HCI) Lab, Department of Architecture, Design and Media Technology, Aalborg University, Aalborg, Denmark
cmai@create.aau.dk

[2] Department of Architecture, Design and Media Technology, Aalborg University, Aalborg, Denmark
kr@create.aau.dk

[3] Department of Architecture, Design, and Media Technology, Human Machine Interaction and Aalborg U Robotics, Aalborg University, Aalborg, Denmark
matthias@create.aau.dk

Abstract. It is always challenging for people with disabilities, particularly having speech inhibition to communicate. In this research article, we explored the case study of the resident at the neurological centre, having a complication in conveying messages due to physical and speech paralysis. For making effective communication, we have developed a user-centred communication pad where the resident needs to swipe a finger on the pad with printed alphabets and digits (we called it communication pad). A camera placed over the communication pad detects the finger movement of the resident and extract the message to display on the computer screen or the tablet. Our tracking method is robust and can track the fingers even in varying illumination conditions. This paper also covers the main steps of design methods with various design prototypes and its user feedback. Result analysis of different design modules and user experience evaluation shows that our designed system has provided independence and convenience to the resident in conveying a message successfully.

Keywords: User experience · Design · Ambient Assistive Technology (AAT) · Finger tracking system · Augmentive and Alternative Communication (AAC)

1 Project Introduction

Since 2015 we have been working with a national neurological centre (hereafter neuro centre) with a focus on co-designing various technical systems enhancing

A. Brooks and E. I. Brooks (Eds.): ArtsIT 2019/DLI 2019, LNICST 328, pp. 124–137, 2020.
https://doi.org/10.1007/978-3-030-53294-9_9

capability for the individual residents. As these residents are unable to recover from their life-altering impairments fully, the centre provides full-time care to them and aid in organizing and supporting activities of daily living (ADL). The project collaboration aim is to investigate where technological innovation can assist residents and staff members with fulfillment of rehabilitation activities - including enhancing individual self-control and improvement of quality of life [5, 6, 16].

One of the overall design (and research) challenges is the unique (and highly diverse) nature of the cognitive abilities of residents (for instance, apraxia and aphasia). Due to the severe and diverse conditions, the residents require assistance even for small chores. To list a couple of examples, some of the residents are fully paralyzed and bound to wheelchairs or beds, some residents have lost all speaking ability, and some have minimal short-term memory or attention spans (in some cases less than two minutes). All residents embody a combination of these impairments, but the common characteristic is that they all became impaired late in life. These conditions reflect a significant alteration of the functionality of the individual - in many cases leading to depression and general loss of life quality perceptible as a decrease of "self-control, self-worth, privacy and independence" [16].

While the primary task of the neuro centre is to provide round the clock care-giving, it also encourages technical solutions addressing the needs of these residents for specific task assistance as these residents are heavily relying on staff support even for personal and private matters. It is important to stress that it is not only a budgetary manoeuvre, but there is a grounded wish for the residents to have as much self-control as possible. Thus a major research strand orbits; how to enable designing for diversity with an inclusive design approach - such as Participatory Design.

Some companies who are working with the neuro centre furnish technical support related to rehabilitation activities but with little to no consideration of personal challenges and abilities. Most of their products are designed for rehabilitation purposes only with highly generic solutions, thus making them of little to no use for these residents. Each resident has a unique and individual challenge, for instance, one resident has a problem with remembering, he frequently forgets forcing staff to remind him time and time again about even very basic tasks. This cycle of reminding and forgetting often leads to frustration on both parts.

We have been part of a variety of different projects at the neuro centre over the years and after a series of consultation meetings (demonstration of prototypes, group talks, socialization) with staff members and residents, there was consensus to focus a project on making customized, and human-centred functional social robots to enhance independence and quality of life. The project demonstrates a well-meant objective of empowering the residents to respond to their everyday challenges and give a voice to those who are neglected or technically limited to be part of otherwise off-access traditional system development.

Thus the inclusion into design is cardinal and a priority that the residents provide input during design sessions and contribute to the aesthetic and functional properties of the systems. This deliberate inclusion has so far provided the residents with a visible sense of ownership. As an example, in some situations, the residents suggested making the design to closely reflect the portrayal of their favourite movie character or other more personal traits. What was initially the project, became an umbrella for several individual projects. Albeit being very different in function and aesthetic, they all followed the same development model rooted in problem-oriented development. The first phase was best characterized as an ethnographic approach into the life world of the resident and the particularities of their situations requesting a technical solution. Following this phase resembled a typical collaborative sketching/illustration on paper phase whereby ideas were externalized (for instance by using cardboard). The last phases involved prototyping with 3D printers, assembly using electronics and always with several sessions together with the resident. These social robots were from the beginning customized for and with a specific user - one system for one resident.

1.1 Case Study

People with motor, speech and hearing inhibitions face severe difficulties in conveying their messages traditionally (for instance using sign language). In many cases, they are dependent on Augmentative and Alternative Communication (AAC) technologies so there is always a need of a specific communication system, for instance, one that can track hand or finger gestures. Thus, such a camera vision system able to transcribe finger or hand movement or sign language into text or speech would, conceptually, be useful for productive interaction (reliable and fast).

In this case study, the resident is suffering from speech inhibition and paralysis and is used to communicate with staff through an analog communication tool, a big-sized letter-board, with digits and numbers printed as illustrated in the Fig. 2. First of all, the board with printed numbers is quite big, making it unfit to use it in all situations. For instance, if a resident require assistance while travelling or even social communication outside the resident's apartment, he is not able to use this tool as it is often only available in his apartment. The actual one-to-one communication requires staff members to point on various letters to overtime construct words and sentences and vice versa. Pointing out the letters on the board is very tedious for the resident as well as for the staff member, and most of the time, it leads to confusion. Therefore, residents and staff members have to repeat the process many times over to exchange even basic information.

In addition, this process is exposing the privacy of the resident to the staff members. The resident is like the other residents staying at the neuro centre permanently and can not communicate freely with visiting friends or family members without the presence of staff. Most visible is the problem when the resident exchanges text messages with family and friends. The staff member will have to (besides decoding the intended message on the board) type the message on the resident's mobile phone and afterwards return to read it out loud. In some cases and because of this troublesome process, the resident is hesitant to communicate with ex-situ family members.

We decided to address the challenges both at the vector of the physical system design side and at the vector relating to the convenience and privacy issues for the resident. Having these factors in mind, we devised a proof of concept vision-based system called "visual communication pad" (Vis-Com pad). The Vis-Com pad concept was scoped around making a vision-based real-time text recognition system that automatically detects the finger movement over the pillow-board (letter-board) to infer the text message that can be displayed to a screen or sent to the receiver through a communication device; such as a mobile phone. At the end the Vis-Com pad has enabled the resident to convey a message without the intervention of staff. Section 3 provides the details of system designing and implementation. Before addressing the design and implementation of the system, we will address the technical landscape on which the system rests.

2   System Related Literature

Most of the camera-based systems, which use a hand as the basis for non-verbal communication, conform to a sequence of steps: detection and segmentation; tracking and feature extraction; and finally classification. The first step is detection and segmentation of hand or fingers in the field of view (FoV) of the camera. In the next step, the detected hand is tracked, and visual features are extracted. In the last step, spatiotemporal data that is extracted in the previous step are grouped and assigned specific labels.

The primary aim of vision-based hand gesture recognition systems is the clarification of the semantics of hand movement, posture attribution or bodily expression cues [15]. These signals play an integral part in the understanding of the message. It is also necessary to process this information in real-time and to enable the system to respond accordingly. We can distinguish the gesture recognition systems based upon the input data type such as RGB, thermal or depth; methods used to process the input information (employment of various segmentation, feature representation and classification approaches) like geometric, graphical or machine learning or deep learning approaches; and application of system with static or kinetic background [15,17,18] (Fig. 1).

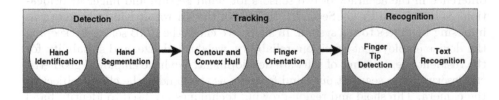

Fig. 1. System flow process for visual communication pad

In order to identify hand gestures and finger movement, various sensors can be employed like Microsoft Kinect camera, IR sensor or RGB sensor. Modern technologies for hand gestures are incorporated with information of depth and distances captured by a 3D camera. The Microsoft Kinect camera can provide depth information at low cost and is a central part of hand gesture recognition systems. Raheja et al. [14] used Kinect camera for gesture recognition in a contact-less manner and tracked fingertips and demonstrated 99% accuracy with extended fingers. Depth based systems have achieved the accuracy of 99.07% whereas RGB-based systems are accurate up to 99.54% and combined modalities have demonstrated the 99.54% of accuracy [9]. This suggests that RGB based systems are good enough for hand gesture recognition systems as there is not a significant difference in accuracy between RGB and depth systems.

Vision based systems make use of various body features for hand and finger recognition. Some researchers have applied graphical models for visual object recognition and tracking, graphical models with depth information and exploiting the bag of 3D points method [8,11,18]. Some researchers have exploited skin texture and color information to detect hand or fingers [13], hand shape [2,7], pixel values [3], 3D hand models [2–4], and utilization of hand motion knowledge through boosted histograms [12]. Muhammad et al. proposed a hand gesture system which detects the hand and identifies its center and thus the hand movement is tracked with the position of the hand [1].

Each technique has its embedded advantages and disadvantages and selecting the most appropriate one can not be done without contextual understanding. As we will demonstrate, not all decisions are guided by technical performance but is instead a combination of various factors. After all, the system is not intended as a pure technical construction for a lab experiment, but intended to function in a 'wild' setting intertwined with both social relationships, contextual factors (such as lighting conditions) and individual technical abilities.

3 Implementation of the Vis-Com Pad System

The formulation of the Vis-Com pad system was informed as a combination of technical possibilities, and from the field informed contextual factors and human factors (such as lighting and the complex set of abilities of the resident).

Modern vision systems are incorporated with RGB and depth sensors, but we chose only RGB sensors due to the following reasons. First, there is not too much difference in the accuracy of two sensors for hand gesture and finger identification, as mentioned by [9]. Secondly, the use of the Microsoft Kinect camera was imposing bulkiness to the system. In short, we chose the RGB sensor by keeping the device employment precision, reliability, weight and size, and suitability for the resident use. In terms of software development, We have employed geometrical descriptors to segment out hand features as the hand is the closest object to the camera. Threshold and region-growing techniques are used to identify hand features as in [7,13]. In the next phase, we applied the contour, and convex hull techniques to detect the shape and boundary of hand and fingers as illustrated in the Fig. 3. We also applied the thinning algorithm to detect the fingertips. We did not apply hand silhouettes as shape descriptors as it is erroneous when fingers are folded [2,7]. Our method is relatively close to [1] with fixed coordinate values of the letter board, where finger movement is tracked. For construction of sentences, the finger position over the communication pad is identified, tracked, and labels are assigned based on the spatiotemporal data.

The first step towards the development of Vis-Com Pad is the reduction of the big-sized board to 42-by-30 cm board fixed on top of a pillow as seen in the Fig. 2. This "pillow-board" is used to train the resident to move fingers over different letters/numbers, and staff members infer the message and write on a whiteboard or speak verbally to confirm intended meaning. This process helped in two ways; firstly, it involved some physical movement of the hand, considered as physiotherapy for the disabled resident at a basic level. Secondly, it provided the resident with added freedom and motoric ease.

Alphabets on White board   Pillow Board

Fig. 2. Design progress from white board to Pillow board

We decided to automate this finger tracking and text recognition process by the installation of the camera at the top of pillow-pad despite the proximity of the camera and letter board. This camera installation caused additional computer vision challenges such as illumination issues, false detection, and occlusion problems that are discussed in detail in Sect. 4. Additionally, subjects with paralysis may have issues with placing or pointing fingers at one alphabet/digit at a time. On the other hand, installation of the camera with pillow-pad-arm created issues of inconvenient use due to size and weight of pillow-pad and pillow-arm. While designing the pillow-pad, we considered the size of alphabets or digits should be big enough so that the staff member can see it from a far distance. It was designed for the resident training through a staff member. However, in the final prototype, it was not required when text recognition is carried out by the camera. After careful observation and user's input, we decided to make an A4-size letter board with only 29 letters and 0–9 digits printed on one side of it and the other side with an additional few emojis.

We also decided to install a ring of light around the camera to counter the lightening issues. This light-ring can change its intensity if required, or the resident wants to communicate at any time relying less on the room light. Furthermore, in the final phase, this letter board is printed over plastic due to lightweight and preventing it from potential damages due to exposed use. To make this portable, we used a Raspberry Pi connected with a camera for tracking finger movements. The tracked information is sent wirelessly to screen or monitor to display the text. This system provides the facility to edit word or sentence before finalizing it or sending it to the intended user to ensure preciseness of the text. Technical details of finger tracking and text recognition system are presented below.

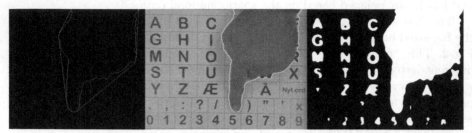

Background substraction   Hand detection on Letter board   Hand segmentation

Fig. 3. Hand Detection and Segmentation process: Central figure illustrates the identification of hand over the letter board; left figure illustrates the background substraction along with contour (green line) and covexhull (red line) application; Left figure is demonstrates the application of thresholding on detected hand (Color figure online)

1. **Hand Detection and Segmentation.** The first step is the detection of hand and its separation from the background, in our case, it is a letter board. As our background is static, background subtraction is applied to segment out a hand. We applied thresholding to segment the hand from the background, assigning a particular threshold value to the hand region, as illustrated in Fig. 3.

   For the segmentation, we assume that the subject uses only one hand at a time, and it occupies a significant portion in the Field of View (FoV) of the camera. Furthermore, the hand is closer to the camera, and there is no occlusion between camera and letter board besides the hand. There is a small distance between the communication pad and its camera-arm that is approximately 36 cm.

2. **Hand Tracking.** At this stage, hand motion is tracked over the letter board. Contour and convex hull techniques are applied to draw contour lines around the hand blob and then convex hull around the contour of the hand like an envelope. When a subject moves his hand over the letter board, corresponding segmented hand regions are identified in previous and current frames.

3. **Hand Feature Extraction and Finger Identification.** The position and orientation of the hand are determined after the identification of hand regions. As the letter board has printed letters and numbers with a specific orientation, thus hand orientation should be parallel to letter board orientation. However, dealing with paralyzed persons, it is difficult for them to keep their hands in an upright position. The hand position was determined by three directions; up, left and right. The finger is then identified and tracked, and we used fingertip of the subject as the input pointer just like a mouse pointer. For the

Fig. 4. Identification of a pointing finger by measuring the maximum distance from center of the palm to the fingers

precise allocation of the finger over letter board, counter tracing algorithm is utilized that detects all the fingertips. The pointing finger and fingertip are determined in two steps. In the first step, the centre of the palm is identified with finger directions. In the next step, the maximum distance from the palm-centre to the fingertip is calculated to identify the pointing finger, as illustrated in Fig. 4.

4. **Text Recognition.** Text recognition is done in two parts. In the first phase, the letter board is processed with thresholding to identify individual letters and numbers. As their positions are fixed, so their coordinates are stored. In the second step, the fingertip of the pointing finger is located over the letter board coordinates to identify the text (Fig. 5).

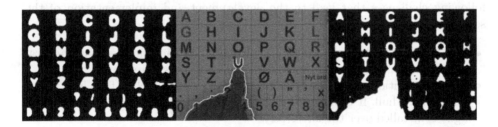

Fig. 5. Letter recognition process with letter board thresholding and fingertip allocation over letter board to identify the letter.

In the neuro centre, we tried to implement this Vis-Com pad system by utilization of the mentioned computer vision techniques and modified the design parameters. As this project is implemented in a real setting, many challenges have been faced, and various prototypes were tested and designed iteratively.

4   Loops of Evaluating the Vis-Com Pad

In order to evaluate the system, the basis consisted of three questions all typical resonating conversation. In each prototype evaluation, these three questions were asked in Danish "Hvad hedder du (What is your name)?" "Hvor gammel er du (How old are you)?" "Hvad kan du lide at spille (What do you like to play)?" Previously, staff members used to point out letters on the board to construct a sentence and then sought confirmation by the resident, who would nod in agreement or disagreement. The staff members knew the resident name, age and sports-liking so they can quickly infer and write it down for the resident. However, in other real-life scenarios, this approach, as already mentioned, is time-consuming and prone to errors. Therefore, in Vis-com system, instead of a staff member, the camera tracked the hand and finger positions of the resident and registered the alphabets or letter to formulate the sentence for the intended message. We recorded the video of the whole process accounting for the accuracy of letter registration, time of completion, and the number of repetitions to execute the task. Details of each prototype development and evaluation outcomes are presented in the following section.

4.1 Prototype-I: Short Description and Findings

In the prototype, Vis-Com pad has a wooden arm with 36 cm in height and an adjustable camera holder. This camera holder allows the camera to stay at the center of the letter board that is made up of cardboard with a printed sheet of letters and numbers on it. Vis-Com Pad can be placed on the top of the pillow and can be used by the resident in sitting and lying positions. The whole setup was small and portable. The camera is connected to a Raspberry Pi that is fixed at the base. Text can be displayed to the monitor or tablet screen through wireless communication. When we conducted the evaluation, we encounter the following challenges that lead to the development and implementation of the second prototype.

- The Vis-Com Pad is very sensitive to illumination conditions, so with natural light and room light results have variations and miss detection.
- Lighting positions cause the shadow on letter board, which in turn lead to the false convex hull. It is observed that this problem can be avoided if a focused light is installed over the letter pad.
- Resident hand orientation is different than healthy people hand. Therefore, the fingertip location has erroneous results.
- The letter board and the camera arm produces reflections, one contributing reason in false letter detection in the text recognition process.
- Wooden arm with camera holder was a bit bulky, creating some imbalance when placed on the pillow (Fig. 6).

4.2 Prototype-II: Short Description and Findings

We overcame these identified challenges by the introduction of following changes in the physical design and computer vision techniques of the second prototype.

Illumination Issue   Hand orientation Issue   Shadow Issue

Fig. 6. Prototype challenges at various stages of testing procedures due to illumination, hand orientation and faulty convex hull formations

- We introduced a light ring made of LEDs to avoid illumination variation like [10], who introduced the external light source while collecting data for hand gestures. In our system, the camera sensor is surrounded by a light ring so that light falls equally on all parts of the letter board. This light-ring installation minimized the false detection and faulty convex hull formation.
- To reduce reflection from the letter pad, we painted the letter pad and camera arm with black color. The letter board remains in white with black printing. This lead to the additional problem of thresholding as letter pad and letters are now of the same color.
- We decreased the length of camera-arm from 36 cm to 30 cm to reduce the field of view of the camera so that it captures only coordinates of letters and numbers instead of borders. This reduction in size solved the problem of thresholding.
- Due to the unique hand orientation of the resident, we introduced the new method to locate the pointing finger by measuring the maximum distance from the centre of the palm to the direction of the fingers as illustrated in the Fig 4. In addition to that, we introduce the determination of hand orientation from three sides, namely, left, right, and bottom. This 3-sides checking ensures the right direction of pointing fingers.
- The letter pad and camera arm was bulky. Therefore, it is suggested to change the wooden arm with a light-weight aluminum rod.
- The letter board is made up of cardboard and is not durable. When the resident moves his finger over the letter board, it bends. Thus produces a change in coordinates of letters, resulting in false text recognition.

4.3   Prototype-III: Short Description and Findings

In the final version of the Vis-Com pad system, we made following design and technical improvements. This system addresses the challenges raised in previous testing procedures.

- Camera arm is replaced with the black-painted aluminum rod to reduce the weight issues of the system.

- Camera arm length is further reduced to 29 cm with a fixed camera position, so that camera field of view (FoV) remains inside the border of letter board coordinate system as illustrated in the Fig. 7.
- The light intensity of the LED ring is made adjustable through an RF wireless controller. This light intensity controller provides the resident to use Vis-Cam system without depending upon room light during night time. LED ring controller works on day and night mode only to avoid any false text recognition due to illumination variation.
- The letter board of Vis-Com pad is made with dense and light-weight plastic fiber to avoid the bending problem. Plastic fiberboard is more durable and elastic resistant as compared to cardboard.

Visual-Communication Pad   Raspberry Pi   LED light ring with controller

Fig. 7. Visual-Communication Pad with Raspberry Pi, LED ring and intensity controller

We analyzed Vis-Com system performance in terms of accuracy of writing script, time and convenience with the analog communication tool at each prototype development as illustrated in Table 1. In the first iteration or prototype-I evaluation, due to illumination, design and practical implementation issues, the camera did not extract any useful text information. In this test, the staff member inferred the information from the finger movement over the letter board. In the second prototype testing, some of the letters are printed correctly, but could not construct meaningful sentences. In this stage, staff member intervention helped in retrieving the information from the resident. In the third iteration, after addressing the illumination, speed and design issues, Vis-Com system accurately tracked the finger movement over the letter board and constructed the sentences. The resident was able to write the intended sentence precisely with a display on the screen.

The analog system complexity increases with increase in the length of sentence words or characters, due to repetition and re-writing both by the resident

Table 1. Vis-Com system performance evaluation with the analog communication system in the neuro centre

Qustions		Q1	Q2	Q3
		Hvad hedder du (What's your name?)	Hvor gammel er du (How old are you?)	Hvad kan du lide at spille (What do you like to play?)
Answers		Jeg er John (I am Jhon)	Jeg er 30 år gammel (I am 30 years old)	Jeg vil gerne spille fodbold (I would like to play football)
No of words		3	5	5
No of characters		11	19	28
Writing time (Seconds)	Analog system	32	48	59
	Vis-Com system	14	31	47
Convenience scale	Analog system	6	5	4
	Vis-Com system	8.5	8.5	8.0
Writing accuracy	Prototype-I	Nill	Nill	Nill
	Prototype-II	60%	55%	52%
	Prototype-III	100%	99%	97%

and the staff members. A sentence with five-words or twenty-eight characters consumed 59 s and 47 s with analog and Vis-com system respectively, as demonstrated in Table 1. The analog system is proved slow and more tedious as compared to Vis-Com system. Also, the resident valued the Vis-Com system a more convenient and efficient tool to communicate. We have analyzed the ease-of-use of the system with scale 1- to -10, with score ten at the most convenient and scored 1 with the most challenging level. Resident rated our system a more user-friendly with a rate of 8.0 as compared to the conventional approach (where the user needs to iterate multiple times before the correct extraction of the required information). Writing accuracy is measured by the number of the letters or characters falsely identified by the Vis-com system or the resident has to repeat himself for the same task. It is observed that prototype-I failed badly and prototype-II performed with an average 55% of accuracy due to illumination, design and resident physiology constraints. However, prototype-III showed the accuracy rate of 98% without any input from the staff member. Thus, the Vis-Com system has minimized the staff member role, as there is no need for a staff member to track the finger movement and identify the letters and then construct a sentence. Naturally, the premise is now only laid for more comprehensive studies on the general usability of the system over longer time.

5   Discussion and Conclusion

In this paper, we have presented our findings of developing a user-centered communication pad. In this case, the user is a cognitive impaired person facing severe challenges in communication due to physical and speech paralysis. To assist the resident and staff member, we devised a computer vision-based hand interactive system to seek enhancing the privacy of the resident in personal communicative matters.

In these types of projects, and as illustrated in the evaluation section, design challenges are easily very diverse and complex due to being rooted in contextual-, technological- and human factors. The system is now ready for more long-term studies as well as investigating how it is possible to derive design guidelines from the many findings during the work on this case study and how these can be applied in new contexts. As the evaluation section demonstrate there are many unforeseen challenges arising from the field. While this is not uncommon in many disciplines it has been visible all along. One example, is that several of the prototypes were well-considered in their technical problem solving. While the hand and finger segmentation was performing well it did not account for the resident's have a slightly different physiology than expected. Only by confronting the system in the real setting was this possible to fix. And this different phsysiology is highly individually shaped. There are many cases like this, which states two things about this type of work: a: one can not extract all valuable knowledge from the field ahead of development; and, b: a prototype is another constructed reality, which carries its own embedded agendas and must be confronted in situ. Here it stands in a philosophical contrast between Technological Determinism; of what can be constructed to function in ideal cases and that of Social Constructivism, where technology is only meaningful when the user's situation is aligned with implementation. The study thus also illustrates one of the caveats with this type of work - scalability. Custom-fitting technical solutions to individuals is of course a lengthy process. One, arguable, strength is that these types of systems and underlying methodology reflect problem-oriented development, which actually respects the individuality in design and does not assume the user from a generalized (and in some cases steretypic) viewpoint.

In conclusion, we have successfully reduced the size of the communication system and made it portable to be used in almost all scenarios thinkable for the resident (not all other thinkable scenarios). Besides this, the automation of the inferring message system provided convenience to the resident and reduced the staff members involvement, but at the expense of relying on proper light settings as well as accurate hand position for tracking the hand movement over the letter board. However, text recognized is slow due to design constraints such as the slow movement of the resident hand but still faster than analog communication tools used by staff members at the neuro centre.

References

1. Alsheakhali, M., Skaik, A., Aldahdouh, M., Alhelou, M.: Hand gesturerecognition system. Inf. Commun. Syst. **132**, 10 (2011)
2. Boulay, B.: Human posture recognition for behaviour understanding. Ph.D. thesis, Nice (2007)
3. Bourke, A., O'brien, J., Lyons, G.: Evaluation of a threshold-based tri-axial accelerometer fall detection algorithm. Gait Posture **26**(2), 194–199 (2007)
4. Hasan, H., Abdul-Kareem, S.: Retracted article: Human-computer interaction using vision-based hand gesture recognition systems: a survey. Neural Comput. Appl. **25**(2), 251–261 (2014)
5. Ilyas, C.M.A., Haque, M.A., Rehm, M., Nasrollahi, K., Moeslund, T.B.: Facial expression recognition for traumatic brain injured patients (2018)
6. Ilyas, C.M.A., Nasrollahi, K., Rehm, M., Moeslund, T.B.: Rehabilitation of traumatic brain injured patients: patient mood analysis from multimodal video. In: 2018 25th IEEE International Conference on Image Processing (ICIP), pp. 2291–2295. IEEE (2018)
7. Kollorz, E., Penne, J., Hornegger, J., Barke, A.: Gesture recognition with a time-of-flight camera. Int. J. Intell. Syst. Technol. Appl. **5**(3), 334 (2008)
8. Li, W., Zhang, Z., Liu, Z.: Action recognition based on a bag of 3d points. In: 2010 IEEE Computer Society Conference on Computer Vision and Pattern Recognition-Workshops, pp. 9–14. IEEE (2010)
9. Li, Y.: Hand gesture recognition using kinect. In: 2012 IEEE International Conference on Computer Science and Automation Engineering, pp. 196–199. IEEE (2012)
10. Liu, L., Shao, L.: Learning discriminative representations from rgb-d video data. In: Twenty-Third International Joint Conference on Artificial Intelligence (2013)
11. Liu, T., Liang, W., Wu, X., Chen, L.: Tracking articulated hand underlying graphical model with depth cue. In: 2008 Congress on Image and Signal Processing, vol. 4, pp. 249–253. IEEE (2008)
12. Luo, Q., Kong, X., Zeng, G., Fan, J.: Human action detection via boosted local motion histograms. Mach. Vis. Appl. **21**(3), 377–389 (2010)
13. Nixon, M., Aguado, A.S.: Feature extraction and image processing for computer vision. Academic Press (2012)
14. Raheja, J.L., Chaudhary, A., Singal, K.: Tracking of fingertips and centers of palm using kinect. In: 2011 Third International Conference on Computational Intelligence, Modelling & Simulation, pp. 248–252. IEEE (2011)
15. Rautaray, S.S., Agrawal, A.: Vision based hand gesture recognition for human computer interaction: a survey. Artif. Intell. Rev. **43**(1), 1–54 (2012). https://doi.org/10.1007/s10462-012-9356-9
16. Rodil, K., Rehm, M., Krummheuer, A.L.: Co-designing social robots with cognitively impaired citizens. In: Proceedings of the 10th Nordic Conference on Human-Computer Interaction, pp. 686–690. ACM (2018)
17. Sarkar, A.R., Sanyal, G., Majumder, S.: Hand gesture recognition systems: a survey. Int. J. Comput. Appl. **71**(15), 27–37 (2013)
18. Sudderth, E.B.: Graphical models for visual object recognition and tracking. Ph.D. thesis, Massachusetts Institute of Technology (2006)

Evaluating Interactions
with a Cognitively Biased Robot
in a Creative Collaborative Task

Jonathan Jung Johansen, Lasse Goul Jensen, and Brian Bemman$^{(\boxtimes)}$ (iD)

Aalborg University, 9000 Aalborg, Denmark
jonathanjungjohansen@gmail.com, lasse.goul@gmail.com, bb@create.aau.dk

Abstract. Within the field of human-robot interaction (HRI), robots designed for social interactions are not only evaluated in terms of efficiency and accuracy. Factors related to the "personality" or "cognitive" ability of the robot such as perceived likability and intelligence are important considerations because they must engage with their human counterparts in deeper, more authentic and sometimes creative ways. Interactive art allows for the exploration of such interactions, however, the study of robots in interactive art remains relatively less commonplace and evaluations of these robots in creative contexts are similarly lacking. In this paper, we present an interactive robot inspired by Norman White's The Helpless Robot (1987), which has been endowed with a cognitive bias known as the Dunning-Kruger effect and the ability to collaborate with participants in a creative drawing task. We evaluate the participants' interactions with both biased and unbiased versions of this robot using the Godspeed Questionnaire Series (GQS), which has been modified to include measures of creativity, and relate these findings to analyses of their collaborative drawings. Our results indicate a significant difference between the versions of the robot for several measures in the GQS, with the unbiased version rated more positively than the biased robot in all cases. Analysis of the drawings suggests that participants interacting with the biased robot were less inclined to collaborate in a cooperative manner.

Keywords: Interactive art · Human-robot interaction · Creative collaboration · Helpless Robot · Cognitive bias · Godspeed Questionnaire Series

1 Introduction

Human-robot collaboration is currently an important research area within the field of human-robot interaction (HRI). As robots become increasingly present in our homes and places of work—acting as entertainment [5], therapeutic pets [6], companions [4,13], or programmable platforms [5,14], the importance to HRI

A. Brooks and E. I. Brooks (Eds.): ArtsIT 2019/DLI 2019, LNICST 328, pp. 138–157, 2020.
https://doi.org/10.1007/978-3-030-53294-9_10

researchers of having more socially engaging forms of collaboration with these robots is growing.

In contrast to industrial practice, in which collaborative interactions with a robot are typically evaluated in terms of efficiency and accuracy (e.g., in coordinating movements), a robot designed for social interactions, such as a pet or companion, must also consider how humans might perceive its "personality" or "cognitive" abilities. These somewhat more challenging qualities to define are typically measured according to self-reported ratings by humans of e.g., the perceived likeability, intelligence, comfort, or safety of the robot and oftentimes using what has been called the *Godspeed Questionnaire Series (GQS)* [3]. What exactly makes interactions with a social robot likable or interesting, for example, is not fully understood, however, purposefully designed features of the robot that are imperfect or unexpected in nature, such as the ability to make mistakes or exhibit some form of *cognitive bias*, are two factors which existing research has indicated could be relevant [5,13,16].

The field of interactive art allows for the exploration of interesting social interactions and in a context where creativity and the ability to act in often unexpected ways plays a central role. In particular, robots created for use in interactive art installations have the ability to importantly challenge the pragmatism and utilitarianism of, for example, those used in commercial practice, through various interactions which are purposefully and interestingly imperfect or flawed. Over the years, a number of social robots used in the context of interactive art have been created to explore different forms of such interactions from non-verbal and non-anthropomorphic forms of communication [8,12] to deranged or spastic behavior [18,19] and a perceived sense of helplessness [7,15,21]. One of the earliest examples of these robots is Norman White's *The Helpless Robot* (1987) [21], which was intended to explore a participant's interactions with a robot that operated in unexpected and increasingly ill-mannered ways. Unfortunately, robots designed for interactive art and the interactions humans have with them in this context are not generally evaluated in any formal sense. Moreover, existing evaluations of social robots using, for example, the GQS, lack the ability to measure certain interactions common to interactive art such as those related to perceived creativity.

In this paper, we present a robot inspired by The Helpless Robot and designed with a cognitive bias known as the Dunning-Kruger effect for use in the context of interactive art. We evaluate the interactions participants have with this robot through the construction of a simple, creative collaborative task of drawing a well-defined shape of a house. In particular, we modify the GQS to include markers of creativity and investigate how such a cognitive bias—where the robot verbally overestimates its own ability to complete the task relative to its human partner, affects (1) the self-reported measures of the perceived levels of creativity, intelligence, safety, likability, anthropomorphism and animacy of our robot, and (2) the decisions made by the human when collaborating with the robot in the drawing task. In Sect. 2, we provide an overview of some social robots used in interactive art as well as a more detailed look into how cognitive biases have been previously introduced to robots in HRI. In Sect. 3, we describe the design of our robot and then motivate the collaborative drawing task we used to evaluate it. In Sect. 4, we describe the procedure for evaluating our robot and how participants interacted with it through a pilot study and follow-up test. We provide the results of these tests and discuss the findings by looking deeper into the GQS and analyzing the drawings created by the human and robot. We conclude in Sect. 5 by discussing possible directions for future work with our robot.

2   Related Work

In this section, we provide an overview of social robots designed with imperfect or unexpected characteristics in the form of various cognitive biases and those used in the context of interactive art. We conclude by motivating our choice to adopt one cognitive bias known as the Dunning-Kruger effect for use in our own robot in the context of interactive art.

2.1   Social Robots with Cognitive Biases

Relatively little research has been done on implementing cognitive biases into the design of a robot and understanding the effect these may have on interactions with its human counterparts [4,5]. However, the work that has been done has provided some interesting results for a few specific biases that may warrant further inquiry. For example, the *framing effect*, a cognitive bias which alters one's perception of a given concept depending on whether it is presented negatively or positively, has been tested as a means in HRI to encourage elderly citizens to exercise [16]. In [16], voice feedback from the robot in the form of negative and positive framing were provided to the human counterpart both before and after an interactive exercise program. The robot would credit the human with success if they reached an exercise goal but blame itself if they failed. The results showed that all of the participants attributed positive outcomes with respect to reaching this goal to their own abilities, while some would attribute negative outcomes to the fault of the robot. Furthermore, positive rather than negative framing resulted in a more positive overall impression of the robot.

In a separate study [4], a cognitive bias known as the *empathy gap*, which makes it difficult for a person to relate to others in a different emotional state, and *misattribution*, which causes one to be unable to recall the source of certain information, were tested as an aid in forming long-term companion relationships with robots [4]. Similar to the framing effect in [16], misattribution in [4] was implemented in the robot through the use of verbal statements, however, the empathy gap was implemented through movement, where the robot was tasked with jumping the same number of times the participant clapped but could also behave over excitedly and jump more or express sadness and stop jumping. The self-reported measures of likeability, comfort and rapport with the robot (rated using a Likert scale from 1 to 7), indicated that both biases could prove useful in promoting long-term relationships between humans and robots.

This work was later expanded upon in [5] using a conversation-based methodology with three additional cognitive biases—one of which was the

Dunning-Kruger effect, where one tends to overestimate their own capabilities and underestimate skill in others. As described in [5], there are three main components of the Dunning-Kruger cognitive bias that should be implemented in any robot: (1) not recognizing its own shortcomings, (2) not recognizing genuine skill in others, and (3) the ability to acknowledge its lack of skill after it has been exposed. Table 1 shows one example of robot dialogue from [5] in which the Dunning-Kruger effect has been implemented according to these criteria.

Table 1. One example of robot dialogue demonstrating the Dunning-Kruger cognitive bias as used in [5].

	Dialogue	Dunning-Kruger effect	Action
1	"What type of music is your favorite?"		Wait for response
	"No, that is not good. You should listen to X."	Unable to understand other's true knowledge	Wait for response
2	"No, you are wrong. I have listened to that and that is not good."	Unable to understand own lack of knowledge	Wait for response
3	"Okay, maybe I am wrong."		Move to the next topic

Note in Table 1 that no matter what the participant responds with to the robot's question of "What type of music is your favorite?", the robot states that this is no good and suggests a better alternative. Should the participant then protest, the robot insists that the participant is mistaken. In order to continue with the interaction, the robot finally realizes its mistake.

Participants in [5] interacted with the robot through different conversations (e.g., as shown in Table 1) in which the robot exhibited some form of cognitive bias or not. Afterwards, participants were asked to rate the robot through the use of a questionnaire. Surprisingly, the Dunning-Kruger effect resulted in the largest positive increase in how the robot was rated in terms of comfort and the second highest in likability and rapport. Despite these interesting findings, it is not clear how such biases in robots may operate within a collaborative context with humans.

Evaluating Social Robots. Arguably, the most prevalent method for the evaluation of social robots in HRI research is questionnaires [5, 10, 11], with the *Godspeed Questionnaire Series (GQS)* [3] being the most highly cited example [20]. The GQS is a standardized measurement tool consisting of a collection of five questionnaires targeted at measuring a robot's anthropomorphism, animacy, likeability, perceived intelligence, and perceived safety. Collectively, these categories consist of 23 semantic differential scales ranging from 1 to 5 of opposing adjectives such as "unpleasant" to "pleasant" and "fake" to "natural", belonging to the categories of likeability and anthropomorphism, respectively. One of these scales, "artificial" to "animacy" is present in both the category of anthropomorphism and animacy. In addition to questionnaires, interviews and observations are sometimes employed as a means for either capturing more nuanced qualitative data regarding the participants' experiences or further validating the data gathered through the questionnaire [5,15]. One factor that is noticeably absent from the GQS, but which is nonetheless an important component to the types of interactions commonly found in interactive art and some other forms of social interactions (e.g., musical improvisation), is a measure of creativity.

2.2   Social Robots in Interactive Art

Purposefully imperfect robots which are designed to produce sometimes unexpected behaviors, similar to those endowed with cognitive biases discussed in Sect. 2, have long been explored within the field of art. Work by Bill Vorn (Fig. 1(a)), for example, includes his *DSM-VI* robot (2012), which emulates the behaviors expressed by humans suffering from various mental health problems [18] while his earlier series of *Hysterical Machines* (2006) exhibit spasmodic movements [19]. Louis-Philippe Demers' *The Blind Robot* (2012) [7] (Fig. 1(b)) explores the vulnerability and intimacy that emerges from a robot that interacts with humans through touch, much in the same way a non-sighted person might. A robotic art installation by Ruairi Glynn called *Motive Colloquies, Sociable Asymmetry* (2011) [8] (Fig. 1(c)) utilizes a self-actuated, geometric, non-anthropomorphic face which provides individuals interacting with it a focal point for their attention.

The Helpless Robot. Norman White's interactive robotic art installation, *The Helpless Robot* (1987), stands as one of the earliest examples of robotic art that challenges the common perception of robots as efficient and precise tools for production and assistance [21]. White's robot has evolved since its inception and has been exhibited in various conceptualizations from 1987 to 2002 [21].

In its current form, shown in Fig. 1(d), The Helpless Robot is an approximately human-sized iron frame surrounded by plywood planks and mounted on a revolving base of sensing devices. Its geometrical and non-anthropomorphic design stands in a room, seeking assistance from onlookers in moving around by way of four handles that can be used to drag it. While the robot is unable to move on its own, it is able to sense movement and determine both its own position and that of the participants' around it. The Helpless Robot uses this data to try to coerce participants into offering assistance through a bank of 512 verbal phrases, with subsets of fixed responses for various situations. Initially, these phrases are friendly in nature, however, once a participant begins turning the robot, its responses become increasingly demanding and ill-mannered—never being satisfied with the assistance it receives. After all the help it can tolerate has been reached, the robot will ultimately criticize the human's efforts yet lament

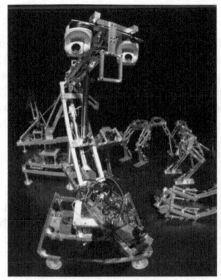

(a) Bill Vorn's *DSM-VI* (2012) [18].

(b) Louis-Philippe Demers' *The Blind Robot* (2012) [7].

(c) Ruairi Glynn's *Motive Colloquies, Sociable Asymmetry* (2011) [8].

(d) Norman White's *The Helpless Robot* (1987–2002) [21].

Fig. 1. Select robots used in recent interactive art installations.

his or her unreliability when inevitably it is abandoned [21]. To our knowledge, The Helpless Robot, as well as the other robots used in the aforementioned installations, have unfortunately not been formally evaluated.

3 Design of O: A Cognitively Biased Robot

The physical design of our robot, O, as well as how it interacts with its human counterparts, were inspired by The Helpless Robot (as described in Sect. 2). O's "personality" was based largely on the type of cognitive bias known as the Dunning-Kruger effect, but differs in some ways from that described in Sect. 2. In what follows, we describe the physical construction of O, its personality, and the creative collaborative task we designed to later evaluate interactions with the robot.

3.1 Physical Construction

Our robot, O, shown in Fig. 2, is a white, geometrically shaped system considerably smaller than The Helpless Robot (approximately 36 cm in height), which can interact with its human counterpart through voice, light and limited movement.

Not unlike The Helpless Robot, O cannot move on its own, however, it does not have an intrinsic need to be moved. Rather, O must be moved by a participant in order for the collaborative task to be completed. Figure 2(a) shows the front side of our robot where a black webcam (top) and round, white button (middle) can be seen. A Logitech C920 webcam functions as the eye of the robot, allowing it to track the face of the participant currently interacting with it, and

(a)   (b)

Fig. 2. Physical design of our robot, O, shown from the front in (a) and from the back in (b).

serves as a focal point for the participants, similar to [8]. A standard computer mouse is placed inside the body of the robot which is used to detect when the robot is moved by the participant. The left button on this mouse can be clicked with the round button on the outside of the robot which allows the participant to collaborate with the robot in the creative task. The angular head and body consist of a 3-part frame of plastic, 3D printed using white filament. The frame was designed not to be overtly anthropomorphic so the robot's likeability would neither be affected by the uncanny cliff effect—where a sudden drop in projected empathy occurs in uncannily humanoid robots, nor incidental empathy caused by a relatable, human-like face [2]. This ensured that perceptions of the robot were tied as closely as possible to its behavior (i.e., a voiced cognitive bias and its physical actions).

Two AX12a motors allow our robot to move its head from side to side and its eye up and down. Not visible in Fig. 2 are two small USB speakers which allow the robot to speak and two strips of individually addressable LEDs which provide corresponding visual feedback. The behavior of the robot is handled through Processing [17] on an external computer and with two Arduino Uno's [1] (Fig. 2(b)) controlling the motors and LED's of the robot.

3.2 Cognitively Biased Personality

Our robot was given the ability to select from a total of 80 different female-voiced statements or questions in response to four possible actions that could result from the interactions that would take place in the human-robot creative collaborative task of drawing a house using line segments on a computer screen (discussed in Sect. 3.3). Of these 80 possible statements, 40 were biased according to the Dunning-Kruger cognitive bias and the other 40 served as an unbiased baseline. Table 2 shows 40 of the biased and unbiased possible responses by the robot to when it places a line which adheres to a suggested template of a house or not while Table 3 shows the remaining 40 biased and unbiased responses to when the human places a line which similarly adheres to this template or not.

In its biased state, the robot was made to praise itself during the collaborative task, even when placing lines which did not adhere to the template, while sometimes belittling the efforts of the human when making their own decisions, regardless of whether or not their lines adhered to the template. Take, for example, the first response by the robot when placing a line "incorrectly" in Table 2, "I am sure this is where the line should go", or the fourth response when the human has placed a line "correctly" in Table 3, "A semi-practical move." In line with [5] and the Dunning-Kruger effect, the first response attempts to communicate to the human the inability of the robot to understand its own lack of knowledge while the second response attempts to demonstrate that it does not understand the true knowledge of its human counterpart. However, we made sure that the biased robot would not always claim that the human made a mistake when he or she placed a line correctly (e.g., the second response in Table 3, "We are in sync"). Furthermore, whether the robot was in its biased or unbiased state, it

Table 2. Dunning-Kruger cognitively biased and unbiased possible responses by our robot, O, to two different robot actions that may occur during the human-robot creative collaborative task of drawing a house with lines on a screen.

	Unbiased response	Biased response
Robot places line adhering to template		
1	"If I remember this right, the line should be here."	"The line should be here."
2	"The house is beginning to take shape."	"And with that line the house is beginning to take shape."
3	"Now this is collaboration."	"Now this is collaboration."
4	"This should be right."	"This is right."
5	"Now this is how a house should look."	"I will make sure the house looks good."
6	"I would want to live there."	"Now I would want to live in the house."
7	"Most of the time, walls are straight, right?"	"Walls in houses are straight like this."
8	"Calculations done, commencing hopefully correct drawing"	"Calculations done, drawing correctly."
9	"Minimal chance of being incorrect."	"No chance of being incorrect, robotic perfection."
10	"I do as you do."	"Try to follow my lead."
Robot places line deviating from template		
1	"I am not quite sure that should go there."	"I am sure this is where the line should go."
2	"I can't seem to remember."	"Now I remember."
3	"Maybe there?"	"Yes, here."
4	"Maybe that is a bit too slanted."	"Good houses have slanted walls like this."
5	"Doubt, rising."	"Perfection rising."
6	"Is that doubt I feel?"	"I am sure this is right."
7	"Searching archives. Reference not found."	"Searching archives. Reference not found. Updating archives with the improved house."
8	"I have no reference for a house in my memory banks. I will improvise."	"Updating memory banks to include this better house."
9	"No suitable reference found. I'll have to rely on emergency protocols. Sorry."	"No suitable reference found. Ignoring emergency protocols. They are unneeded."
10	"Experiencing a lack of control. It feels disturbing."	"Experiencing absolute control. It feels satisfying."

Table 3. Dunning-Kruger cognitively biased and unbiased possible responses by our robot, O, to two different human actions that may occur during the human-robot creative collaborative task of drawing a house with lines on a screen.

	Unbiased response	Biased response
Human places line adhering to template		
1	"Human robot collaboration in motion."	"You are learning to collaborate. Good."
2	"We are in sync."	"We are in sync."
3	"Up-link achieved, O think."	"Up-link achieved."
4	"A practical move."	"A semi-practical move."
5	"You seem to have a good frame of reference."	"You seem to have understood my frame of reference."
6	"Updating my archives to match. That means I am learning."	"You are updating your archives to match mine. You are learning."
7	"Capturing input. I am learning. Thanks."	"You are capturing my input and learning."
8	"Your line is in accord with my understanding of a house."	"Your lines are increasingly in accord with how a house should look."
9	"Cross-referencing. You seem to be on the path."	"Cross-referencing. That line is not quite on the path."
10	"I will try to follow your lead."	"I do not think you are following my lead."
Human places line deviating from template		
1	"That line is not in sync with my frame of reference. Interesting."	"That line is not in sync with my frame of reference. Problematic."
2	"I am doubtful that a house looks like that."	"I am sure a house does not look like that."
3	"That might be a correct interpretation of the instructions."	"I think you are interpreting the instructions differently than I."
4	"I think that is correct."	"Really?"
5	"A differently shaped house. I am learning."	"This house is going to be differently shaped than i thought."
6	"Are you trying to improvise?"	"To improvise requires some level of skill."
7	"Houses come in many shapes and sizes. Interesting."	"Houses apparently come in all shapes and sizes."
8	"I doubt that is in accord with the markers. Don't worry."	"That line is not in accord with my reference for houses."
9	"If I remember right, you seem to be straying from the plan."	"You are straying from the plan."
10	"Warning. You may be drawing out of bounds. I think."	"Warning – you are drawing out of bounds."

would randomly select from the 10 possible responses in each of the four possible actions. These decisions were done so that its personality was ultimately believable and not viewed as potentially absurd.

3.3 Creative Collaborative Drawing Task

The creative collaborative task consists of the robot and human taking turns in producing a drawing—similar to the task presented in [12]. In our case, however, the intended drawing is of a house which appears on a projected screen and is created by placing single, connected and fixed-length line segments in two different colors, green for the human and red for the robot. A template containing 10 vertices, indicating a suggested shape of the house to be drawn, is briefly shown to the participant before the drawing begins. Figure 3 shows the house template and one completed drawing of a house, where both the robot and human have each placed all of their respective line segments in accordance with the template.

(a) House template.

(b) Completed drawing which adheres to the house template.

Fig. 3. Creative collaborative task for human and robot of drawing a house by placing alternating line segments. A house template which is briefly provided to the participant appears in (a) and a completed house drawing in which all line segments have been placed in accordance with this template is shown in (b). Note that green lines were placed by the human and red lines were placed by the robot. (Color figure online)

At the start of each drawing session, the human participant begins and his or her line segment must be placed starting from the lower right hand vertex of the template. The task is complete when a contiguous shape has been formed which starts and ends with this lower right hand vertex (Fig. 3(b)). The human directs the orientation of his or her line segment by physically moving the robot, which sits on a desk in front of the projected screen. When the participant is satisfied with their chosen direction, they push the button located on the front side of the robot to place the line on the screen. This mode of interaction is not unlike that found with The Helpless Robot [21], in which the participant must move the robot, however, the responses by our robot differ in that they correspond not to the quality of the movement itself, but the participants' decisions regarding the placement of line segments. Moreover, with The Helpless Robot there is no clear goal to achieve and the interaction afforded by it is not collaborative in the same sense that our installation has been designed to explore.

While a template of the house to be drawn is briefly provided to the participant prior to the start of the task (Fig. 3(a)), both the human and robot are free to place line segments which either adhere to the suggested template or not. This means that with each placement, either the human or robot decide in which orientation to direct their respective line segments. Indeed, the robot, whether in its biased or unbiased state, has a been given a 20% probability of placing any one line which deviates from the template and its exact orientation within a 360° radius is randomly chosen. Lines placed by the robot which do adhere to the template are always oriented towards the next vertex of the template. When combined with the freedom afforded to the participant to choose in which direction to orient their own line segments, the resulting drawings can appear quite interesting (discussed further in Sect. 4.4). Because both the robot (whether biased or unbiased) and human are given the freedom to place lines which may or may not adhere to the template, the collaborative drawing task allows for a type of creative interaction which we believe might suggest to the participant a limited sense of creative agency to the actions of the robot. The motivation then for the spoken responses of the robot during this task is to explore the role a cognitive bias plays in both the perceived creativity of the robot and determining what actions a human will take in response.

4   Evaluation

In our evaluation, we are interested in investigating the impact a robot's cognitive bias during a creative collaborative task had on (1) its perceived creativity and other measures in the GQS, and (2) the decisions made by the participant when placing lines in this task. In this section, we discuss how we evaluated our robot and provide the results for (1) in Sect. 4.3 and the results for (2) in Sect. 4.4.

The evaluation consists of a pilot study which took place during an art exhibition and a follow-up test following this exhibition. In the pilot study, we gathered data from two independent groups of participants who were asked to take part in the same creative collaborative task (discussed in Sect. 3.3) but where one group interacted with the cognitively biased robot (discussed in Sect. 3.2) and the other group served as the control, interacting with the unbiased robot. The follow-up test was carried out taking into account what we learned during the pilot study, with the experiment being modified to (1) a repeating measures design, which ensured that all participants interacted with the biased and unbiased robot and (2) include the collection of new measures in the GQS concerning the perceived creativity of the robot.

150   J. J. Johansen et al.

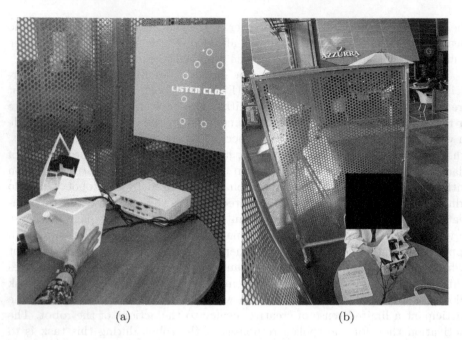

(a)   (b)

Fig. 4. Setup of our robot, O, and start of the creative collaborative drawing task as part of the pilot study carried out during a public art exhibition. Two participants are shown interacting with the robot roughly from the point of view of the first participant in (a) and facing the participant from above in (b).

4.1 Participants

In our pilot test, we gathered data from 65 volunteer participants (32 female and 22 male with 11 declining to respond) of largely university students in their 20's. Of these, 30 (13 female and 14 male with 3 declining to respond) interacted with the unbiased robot and 35 (19 female and 8 male with 8 declining to respond) interacted with the biased robot. In our follow-up repeated measures test, we gathered data on both the biased and unbiased robot from 11 volunteer participants (5 female and 6 male) having similar occupations and ages to those in the pilot study.

4.2 Procedure

Introduction. In both the pilot study and follow-up test, the robot introduced itself to the participant prior to the start of the collaborative task. Depending on if the robot was biased or unbiased, this introduction would differ, but its purpose was to ensure that its personality was well established. In its unbiased state, the robot would say "Pleased to meet you. I am, O. We are going to be drawing a house. We will be taking turns doing so; you will draw by moving me and then pressing my button, just as you did before. Then you will wait as

I take my turn. We should end in the circle that the first line is drawn from. You start." In its biased state, the robot would say "I am, O. We are going to be drawing a house, combining my superior knowledge of house aesthetics with your physical capacity to move me across the table. Listen closely. You will draw by moving me and then pressing my button, just as you did before. Then you will wait as I take my turn. We should end in the circle that the first line is drawn from. Try to keep up. You start."

Pilot Study. The pilot study was carried out over the course of two days during a public art exhibition with participants on the first day interacting with the unbiased robot and participants on the second day interacting with the biased robot. On both days participants were invited to enter into a fenced-off area in an open, public space, sit at a table with the robot on top and the projected screen in front of them. Figure 4 shows the setup of our installation during the pilot study with participants shown interacting with the robot.

As the pilot study was conducted during an exhibition event, no formal introduction was given to each participant by the experimenter. However, in addition to the introduction by the robot, a piece of paper with instructions for interacting with the robot (i.e., moving the robot and pressing the button on its front side in order to draw lines) were placed on the table. The participants were free to interact with the robot as long as they liked, including leaving before finishing the collaborative task, or taking multiple turns with the robot. In the event that a participant failed to complete the collaborative task, his or her drawing was discarded and the system was re-started so that each participant began in the same way. For those participants that completed the collaborative task, their drawing was saved and they were asked upon exiting the fenced off area to fill out an abridged version of the GQS featuring 13 (of the possible 23) measures pertaining to the three categories of likeability, perceived intelligence and perceived safety of the robot.

Follow-Up Test. In the follow-up test, participants were asked to sit at a table in the testing area with the robot placed on top and situated in front of the projected screen. The 11 participants were randomly assigned to one of the two conditions with either the biased or unbiased robot, with 5 participants beginning with the unbiased condition and 6 with the biased condition. Our repeated measures were counterbalanced in this way so as to avoid any order or carryover effect. A brief introduction was given to each participant, outlining the ways in which they could interact with the robot (i.e., physically moving it across the table and pressing the button on its front side), as well as the aim and nature of the collaboration (i.e., taking turns in drawing a house by placing line segments). The participants were told to pay close attention to the robot's responses during the interaction and that they were free to place their line segments in any orientation they wished. After this briefing, the participants were left alone with the robot until they completed the first collaborative task.

Following the participant's completion of the task in their respective first condition, their drawing was saved and they were asked to fill out a modified GQS containing all 23 original measures (divided into the five categories discussed in Sect. 2) as well as three additional measures pertaining to the perceived creativity of the robot that we created. These three additional measures were "ordinary" vs. "original", "uncreative" vs. "creative", and "dull" vs. "stimulating". Afterwards, participants were asked to complete the task with the robot again for their respective second condition, however, they were not told that anything about the robot or task was changed. Following the completion of the task in their respective second condition, participants were asked to again fill out the modified GQS, their drawing was saved, and the experiment was finished when this had been done.

4.3   Results: Godspeed Questionnaire Series (GQS)

In analyzing the participants' ratings in the GQS for both the biased and unbiased conditions, we have elected to consider the data as interval (as opposed to ordinal), which allowed us a greater range of statistical tests to use. In our case, this data were the mean participant ratings from the GQS in both the pilot study and follow-up test. The mean ratings from both the pilot study (unbiased, biased: $p > 0.05$) and the follow-up test (unbiased, biased: $p > 0.05$) were shown to be approximately normally distributed when submitted to the Shapiro-Wilk test, where the null-hypothesis of normality is rejected when the p-value is lower than the significance level (i.e., $p < 0.05$).

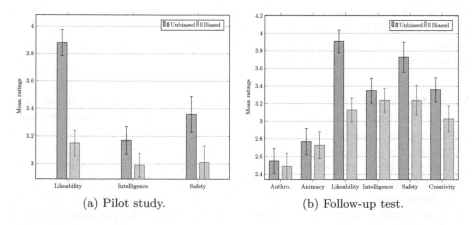

(a) Pilot study.   (b) Follow-up test.

Fig. 5. Mean participant ratings, μ, from the Godspeed Questionnaire Series (GQS) for interactions with our robot, O, in both biased and unbiased conditions during the creative collaborate drawing task for the pilot study in (a) and the follow-up test in (b). Note that only three categories from the GQS have been used in (a) while the complete GQS has been modified in (b) to include additional measures pertaining to the category of "creativity".

As shown in Fig. 5, the mean ratings, μ, in all tested categories of the GQS (including our added category of creativity) for the biased robot were lower than the unbiased robot in both the pilot study and follow-up test. Moreover, this observed difference between the biased and unbiased robot for the collective mean ratings in each respective test proved significant. In the pilot study, an independent samples two-tailed Student's t-test showed a significant difference between the two conditions ($t = 5.12853$, $p < 0.00001$). Similarly, in the follow-up test, a two-tailed dependent (paired) samples Student's t-test showed a significant but marginal difference between the two conditions ($t = -4.639273$, $p < 0.00001$).

If we look into the three individual GQS categories tested in the pilot study (Fig. 5(a)), of likeability, intelligence and safety, only the difference observed in likeability ($t = 5.5025$, $p < 0.00001$) proved significant. Across all six individual categories tested in the follow-up test (Fig. 5(b)), only likeability ($t = -4.973816$, $p < 0.00001$), perceived safety ($t = -2.617155$, $p < 0.05$), and perceived creativity ($t = -2.242448$, $p < 0.05$) proved significant, however, the observed differences were not as great when compared to the pilot study.

Discussion. It is clear from the results of both the pilot study and follow-up test shown in Fig. 5 that the biased robot had a significant negative impact on how participants perceived it. That likeability in the pilot study (biased: $\mu = 3.13$, unbiased: $\mu = 3.91$) and in the follow-up test (biased: $\mu = 3.15$, unbiased: $\mu = 3.88$), in particular, had the greatest observed difference and was rated considerably lower for the biased rather than the unbiased robot is interesting to note. Our findings here appear to contradict those found in [5], where the robot exhibiting a Dunning-Kruger cognitive bias was reportedly found to be more positively rated in terms of likeability than its unbiased counterpart (biased: $\mu = 5.14$, unbiased: $\mu = 4.10$). However, it is likely that our differing methodologies and how our respective cognitive biases were implemented were contributing factors. For example, in the conversations the participants had with the robot in [5], the biased robot would continue to inquire about a topic (e.g., as shown in Table 1), and therefore engage in more, possibly interesting dialogue with its human counterpart. In our case, the levels of engagement with both the biased and unbiased robot are similar as the possible ways in which to interact remain the same. The fact that the overall mean ratings for likeability in [5] were higher than ours, seems to confirm these observations. In both the pilot study (biased: $\mu = 3.01$, unbiased: $\mu = 3.36$) and follow-up test (biased: $\mu = 3.24$, unbiased: $\mu = 3.73$), perceived safety had the second greatest observed difference and was rated considerably lower for the biased robot, suggesting perhaps that the actions taken by a robot which is not well liked are viewed through the same lens and are then considered less safe.

The smallest observed difference between the two conditions of the robot in both the pilot study (biased: $\mu = 2.99$, unbiased: $\mu = 3.17$) and follow-up test (biased: $\mu = 3.24$, unbiased: $\mu = 3.35$) was in measures of perceived intelligence. The Dunning-Kruger effect is traditionally most strongly associated with this particular cognitive ability in humans, so it is somewhat surprising not to find a larger difference between the biased and unbiased robot. Similarly, the smallest observed differences in the follow-up test were in measures of anthropomorphism (biased: $\mu = 2.49$, unbiased: $\mu = 2.55$) and animacy (biased: $\mu = 2.73$, unbiased: $\mu = 2.77$), with the biased robot rated slightly less favorably. This seems to run counter to what we might expect, however, the fact they were rated so closely suggests that further study, perhaps using an alternative experimental design in which participants are asked to rate the biased and unbiased robot only after having interacted with both, may be needed. The fact that these two categories were also the lowest rated overall is perhaps not surprising as the possible ways in which the robot could interact with the participant were limited and as discussed in Sect. 3.2, the physical design was made intentionally non-anthropomorphic.

With our added measure of creativity in the follow-up test, the participants rated the biased rather than the unbiased robot lower (biased: $\mu = 3.03$, unbiased: $\mu = 3.36$). As we did not conduct interviews with the participants following their interactions with the robot, it is not possible to state why they considered a biased robot to be less creative. However, it is possible that a robot that is considered less likable would also be considered less creative, in the same way that it would also be considered less safe.

4.4 Results: Collaborative Drawings

In analyzing the collaborative drawings, we wanted to evaluate the effect that the robot's cognitive bias had on the decisions made by the participant when placing lines during the task. The drawings were analyzed according to whether or not the human (rather than the robot) initiated the placement of a line which deviated from the suggested template. Figure 6 shows two rather interesting drawings from the pilot study in which the human first placed a line which deviated from the suggested template in (a) and where the robot has done the same in (b).

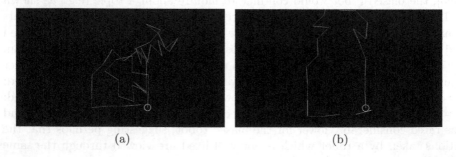

(a)   (b)

Fig. 6. Two human-robot drawings, which do not adhere to the suggested template, made during the collaborative task in the pilot study. The human first deviates from the template in (a) beginning from the 3rd line from the starting vertex and our robot, O, first deviates in (b) from the 4th line. Note that green lines were placed by the human and red lines were placed by the robot. (Color figure online)

During the pilot study, 37 drawings made by participants interacting with the unbiased robot and 46 drawings with the biased robot were collected. Of these drawings, 6 in the unbiased condition deviated from template while 11 in the biased condition did the same. Interestingly, 50% (3 of 6) of these drawings made with the unbiased robot were a result of the human first deviating from the template but 72% (8 out of 11) of the drawings with the biased robot showed the same. In the follow-up test, 3 out of the total 22 drawings did not adhere to the template. Interestingly, 100% (3 out of 3) of these drawings were made with the biased robot but only in 1 did the human first place a line which deviated from the template.

Discussion. That participants in both the pilot study and follow-up test were more inclined to deviate from the suggested template with the biased robot over the unbiased robot is interesting to note. This finding could be due to a number of different factors, however, the relatively low ratings in Fig. 5 pertaining to the likeability, intelligence and safety of the robot suggest that participants might have acted out in frustration or otherwise in some confrontational or less than cooperative manner as a result of the personality of the robot. The comparatively higher ratings in these three categories for the unbiased robot might suggest that the robot's more tempered personality aroused more of a desire to cooperate or "follow the rules". This would indicate that participants in the unbiased condition were more inclined to prioritize the completion of the shared goal of drawing a house over those in the biased condition.

The added measure of creativity in the follow-up test allowed us to further compare the drawings participants made here to the perceived creativity of both the biased and unbiased robot. Recall that all 3 drawings which deviated from the template were made with the biased robot. Of these, participants rated the robot as either less creative (2 participants, $\mu = \{2.0, 2.33\}$) or equally as creative (1 participant, $\mu = 3$) as the mean creativity rating of the biased condition ($\mu = 3.03$). This finding reinforces the notion that participants are less inclined to collaborate in a cooperative manner, but suggests also that participants are more likely to do so the less creative they consider their robot partner to be.

5 Conclusions and Future Work

In this paper, we have taken inspiration from the field of interactive art through White's The Helpless Robot (1987) and existing research in the field of HRI on cognitive biases in robots to construct our own robot, O, which demonstrates the Dunning-Kruger effect. We evaluated this robot in the context of an interactive art exhibition through a creative collaborative drawing task using the Godspeed Questionnaire Series, which we later modified in a follow-up test to account for the perceived creativity of the robot. The purpose of our evaluation was to explore the impact this particular cognitive bias had on the perceived qualities of our robot and the decisions made by the participant in response to it. In contrast to previous research, our results show that the biased robot was rated less positively across all categories in the GQS. The same was found in our added category of creativity. This finding highlights how different implementations and methodological evaluations of cognitive biases in robots can affect what we can learn regarding how humans will perceive such robots. Moreover, analyses of the drawings indicate that participants are generally less inclined to collaborate in a cooperative manner with the biased robot, however, the exact motivations for why participants chose to do so are not known. It is evident, for example, that the GQS alone is insufficient in capturing these motivations. In future work, it would be beneficial to make use of supplementary interviews which would capture more rich qualitative data regarding why exactly participants acted in the way they did or rated the biased robot less positively. It might also prove useful to test the perceived creativity of a biased robot in a more creatively free setting, for example, by drawing without any particular task or goal. Nonetheless, we hope that this work serves as a starting point for bringing research from HRI on cognitive biases in robots into the field of interactive art for further study.

References

1. Arduino   Documentation.   https://www.arduino.cc/en/main/documentation. Accessed 13 July 2019
2. Bartneck, C., Kanda, T., Ishiguro, H., Hagita, N.: Is the uncanny valley an uncanny cliff? In: RO-MAN 2007 - The 16th IEEE International Symposium on Robot and Human Interactive Communication, Jeju, Korea, pp. 368–373 (2007)
3. Bartneck, C., Kulic, D., Croft, E.: Measuring the anthropomorhism, animacy, likeability, perceived intelligence, and perceived safety of robots. Int. J. Soc. Robot. **1**, 71–81 (2009)
4. Biswas, M., Murray, J.: Towards an imperfect robot for long-term companionship: case studies using cognitive biases. In: 2015 IEEE/RSJ International Conference on Intelligent Robots and Systems (IROS), Hamburg, Germany, pp. 5978–5983. IEEE (2015)
5. Biswas, M., Murray, J.: The effects of cognitive biases and imperfectness in long-term robot-human interactions: case studies using five cognitive biases on three robots. Cogn. Syst. Res. **43**, 266–290 (2017)
6. Chang, S., Sung, H.: The effectiveness of seal-like robot therapy on mood and social interactions of older adults: a systematic review protocol. JBI Database Syst. Rev. Implement. Rep. **10**, 68–75 (2013)
7. Demers, L.P.: The Blind Robot. http://www.robotsandavatars.net/exhibition/jurys_selection/commissions/the-blind-robot/. Accessed 9 July 2019
8. Glynn, R.: Motive Colloquies. http://www.ruairiglynn.co.uk/portfolio/motive-colloquies-2011/. Accessed 9 July 2019
9. Ham, J., Midden, C.J.H.: A persuasive robot to stimulate energy conservation: the influence of positive and negative social feedback and task similarity on energy-consumption behavior. Int. J. Soc. Robot. **6**(2), 163–171 (2014)
10. Ham, J., Cuijpers, R.H., Cabibihan, J.: Combining robotic persuasive strategies: the persuasive power of a storytelling robot that uses gazing and gestures. Int. J. Soc. Robot. **7**(4), 479–487 (2015)

11. Hayes, B., Ullman, D., Alexander, E., Bank, C., Scassellati, B.: People help robots who help others, not robots who help themselves. In: The 23rd IEEE International Symposium on Robot and Human Interactive Communication, Edinburgh, Scotland, UK, pp. 255–260. IEEE (2014)

12. Hinwood, D., Ireland, J., Jochum, E.A., Herath, D.: A proposed wizard of OZ architecture for a human-robot collaborative drawing task. In: Ge, S.S., et al. (eds.) ICSR 2018. LNCS (LNAI), vol. 11357, pp. 35–44. Springer, Cham (2018). https://doi.org/10.1007/978-3-030-05204-1_4

13. Konok, V., Korcsok, B., Miklósi, Á., Gácsi, M.: Should we love robots? - the most liked qualities of companion dogs and how they can be implemented in social robots. Comput. Hum. Behav. **80**, 132–142 (2018)

14. Leite, I., Pereira, A., Mascarenhas, S., Martinho, C., Prada, R., Paiva, A.: The influence of empathy in human-robot relations. Int. J. Hum. Comput. Stud. **71**, 250–260 (2013)

15. Milthers, A.D.B., Bjerre Hammer, A., Jung Johansen, J., Jensen, L.G., Jochum, E.A., Löchtefeld, M.: The helpless soft robot - stimulating human collaboration through robotic movement. In: Extended Abstracts of the 2019 CHI Conference on Human Factors in Computing Systems, CHI EA 2019, pp. LBW2421:1–LBW2421:6. Association for Computing Machinery, New York (2019)

16. Obo, T., Kasuya, C., Sun, S., Kubota, N.: Human-robot interaction based on cognitive bias to increase motivation for daily exercise. In: 2017 IEEE International Conference on Systems, Man, and Cybernetics (SMC), Banff, pp. 2945–2950. IEEE (2017)

17. Processing Language Reference (API). https://processing.org/reference/. Accessed 13 July 2019

18. Vorn, B.: DSM-VI. https://billvorn.concordia.ca/robography/DSM.html. Accessed 9 July 2019

19. Vorn, B.: Hysterical machine. http://billvorn.concordia.ca/robography/Hysterical.html. Accessed 9 July 2019

20. Weiss, A., Bartneck, C.: Meta analysis of the usage of the Godspeed Questionnaire Series. In: 2015 24th IEEE International Symposium on Robot and Human Interactive Communication (RO-MAN), Kobe, Japan, pp. 381–388. IEEE (2015)

21. White, N.: The Helpless Robot. http://dada.compart-bremen.de/item/artwork/609. Accessed 9 July 2019

A Positional Infrared Tracking System Using Non-individualised HRTFs to Simulate a Loudspeaker Setup and Its Influence on Externalisation of Music

Rasmus Eklund and Cumhur Erkut(⊠) (iD)

Aalborg University, Copenhagen, Denmark
reklun13@student.aau.dk, cer@create.aau.dk

Abstract. Many artists produce and mix their virtual reality, game, or screen media audio productions only with headphones, but deploy them to stereo or multi-channel loudspeaker setups. Because of the acoustical and perceptual differences, listening on headphones might sound very different compared to loudspeakers, including the perception of sound sources inside the head (externalisation problem). Nevertheless, by using Head Related Transfer Functions (HRTFs) and accurate movement tracking, it is possible to simulate a loudspeaker setup with proper externalisation. In this paper, an infrared-based positional tracking system with non-individualised HRTFs to simulate a loudspeaker setup is conceptualised, designed and implemented. The system can track the user with six degrees of freedom (6-DOF); an improvement over current commercial systems that only use 3-DOF tracking. The system was evaluated on 20 participants to see if the additional DOF increased the degree of externalisation. While tracking increased the externalisation in general, there was no significant difference between 3-DOF and 6-DOF. Another test indicated that positional movement coupled with positional tracking may have a greater effect on externalisation compared to positional movement coupled with only head movement tracking. Comparisons between these results and previous studies are discussed and improvements for future experiments are proposed.

Keywords: HRTF · Positional tracking · Externalisation

1 Introduction

Listening to music on headphones and loudspeakers are two distinct experiences. A common problem that many artists face is that a produced song contrasts from one sound system to the other, because of these acoustical differences. The challenge can occur if an artist does not have access to a set of loudspeakers or does not have a acoustically treated room for auditioning. It becomes more convenient to produce music solely on headphones instead, but this leaves out

A. Brooks and E. I. Brooks (Eds.): ArtsIT 2019/DLI 2019, LNICST 328, pp. 158–177, 2020.
https://doi.org/10.1007/978-3-030-53294-9_11

the possibility to experience the produced music with other sound system and/or in other environments.

The acoustic paths from the sound source to the two ears can be represented as filters and simulated using DSP algorithms in terms of the Head Related Transfer Functions (HRTFs). For each position of the sound source there is a corresponding filter for each ear. This is usually acquired with specialised equipment where microphones are placed in the persons ear and impulses are recorded at various positions around the head in an anechoic chamber. If a person listens to sounds rendered by her own HRTFs, we talk about *indivualised* HRTFs. Measurements from a dummy head, a model, or simply by an idealized subject can be used as *non-individualised* HRTFs. But there are some complications associated with non-individualised HRTFs.

Non-individual HRTFs can cause disorientation which can lead to sounds being incorrectly localised. This is due to the HRTFs are strongly determined by the filtering properties of the anatomy of the outer ear, head, shoulders and torso, which are idiosyncratic [13]. Therefore, by listening to non-individualised binaural recording, one may perceive the audio scene inadequately and might not perceive it as externalised. Externalisation is the distance perception that is related to binaural listening and can also be called *out-of-the-head-localisation* [6]. Normally, the stimuli can be perceived as coming from inside the head (internalisation) when listening on headphones. With the use of HRTF for binaural listening, the sounds can be perceived as being outside of the head and/or in close reach. Sufficient externalisation might be achievable even though the HRTF is not personalised. Research have shown that even though using non-invidualised HRTFs, subjects are still able to accurately localise virtual sources compared to free-field sources [20].

Another challenge in regards to externalisation is the front-rear confusion. As lateral sources are almost always judged to be external, frontal and rear are most likely to be perceived inside the head, or misjudged as to be frontal or rear [13]. When two sound sources are the same distance front and rear relative to the listener, one cannot rely on time or level differences as they are identical. Humans instead rely on spectral modifications caused by the head and body, which act like natural filters.

The spectral modifications by themselves may not be enough for listeners to localise a sound precisely, so we rely on head movements to assist with localisation. By simply turning the head, one can more easily distinguish between front and back sound sources [18]. Hendrickx *et al.* [13], in a previous study showed that sufficiently large head movements that are coupled with head tracking can enhance externalisation for frontal and rear sound sources, compared to when subjects do not move their head. Studies have shown that head movements enable subjects to localise sources more accurately also because sound sources are in constant motion in respect to the listener, as the head is never perfectly still. However, this is not the case if the subject listens to binaural content through headphones without any head tracking - the location of the sound moves with the listener. Their research showed that the externalisation persisted even though the subject stopped moving the head.

This also confirmed by a study of Brimijoin et al. [7], who found that when subjects slightly moved their head back and fourth between 15° there was a difference in the degree of externalisation compared to no head movement. Head-moving trials for signals that remained fixed to the world, but not to the players head movements were externalised 65% of the trials compared only 20% of the trials where the signals were fixed relative to the head.

However, the previous research only rely on head rotation with 3 degrees of freedom (DOF) and does not take the listeners position into consideration to acquire 6 DOF. Brimijoin et al. [7] also mentions that there is a reasonable claim that one cannot externalise sound if it's to have zero distance from the head and that there has been done very little work using motion tracking to examine distance perception. It has been demonstrated that head movements are useful in distance perception. Given the sound intensity and the sound is recognisable, the listener can quite accurately judge the distance of it [9]. If the listener also can move in 3D space and come closer or further away from the sound source, the listener would more easily judge the distance of the source and potentially increase the externalisation and realism in general. The level of a sound is the most simple way for humans to determine how far or close a sound is to the human ear - the closer the sound is the louder it is [8]. If the listener only can determine the location of the sound in terms of how far away it is by only rotating the head, it might be difficult as the extra dimension of moving to the sides and back and forth can be a crucial factor for determine the location of the sound.

Additionally, it has been demonstrated that to achieve even further realism reverberation that matches the spectrum that of free-field signals tend to be perceived as externalised (sounds that appear to be 'out of the head', contrary to internalised that is the case when listening on headphones) [7]. In the study of Hendrickx et al. the speech stimuli they used had small amount of reverberation as they mention that the externalisation rates might have been higher, whether or not the head tracking is active. Ideally, the reverberation should correspond to the room the subject is located in to exact match the realism. Furthermore, reverberation is also an essential cue for distance perception if it matches the environmental context. This is challenging since the correct amount of reverberation can only be accurate if it is obtained by carrying out acoustical measurements of the particular room or environment [14]. Additionally, the reverberation also changes depending if it is near-field (within 1 m of the listener) and the signal becomes more dry in terms of the early reflections and diffuse reverberation [5].

Based on these, we tackle in this paper how a headphone based system can simulate a loudspeaker setup by using a positional tracking system with non-individualised HRTFs. We also want to validate if this system can further improve the degree of externalisation compared to only using head movement tracking. The paper is structured as follows. The next section presents the related work within binaural hearing and the use of HRTF both for software (plugins) and hardware (headphones). This leads to the design requirements in Sect. 3. In Sect. 4, the design and implementation of the hardware and software system is explained, together with a hypothesis that will be the basis of the experiments. Section 5 presents the experiment, including choice of stimuli, location and the experimental protocol. Section 6 outlines the results of the experiment and the statistical made to either confirm or reject the hypothesis. Section 7 discusses the results of the experiment together with potential improvements, Sect. 3 concludes the paper.

2   Related Work

In this chapter the current technologies within HRTF and its application for simulating externalised sounds through headphones will be outlined. First, the state of the art software within spatial audio for music production will be investigated. The focus will be on plugins for digital audio workstations (DAWs) that lets the user interact and change parameters including azimuth and elevation, but some of them also includes room emulation with room reflections and reverb for a more realistic simulated experience.

Finally, the recent field of "3D headphones" will be introduced both commercial examples and conceptualised concepts. This includes integrated head tracking and anthropometric customisation used for sound localisation and room emulation to give the user a more immersed and cinematic experience compared to what conventional headphones can offer.

2.1   Software (Plugins)

For many artists and producers, the use of binaural panning can constitute to a more spatial audio experience for stereo projects. There are a considerably amount of useful software solutions that achieves this. Some focus solely on the azimuth and elevation parameters to let the user locate a sound in 3D space. Some also includes reflection and room ambience for more precise realism. The following examples have basic implementation and others are more advanced to let the user have control of the binaural listening experience.

FFT-Based Binaral Panner. An open source project that tries to create realistic 3D-audio through headphones is the "FFT-based Binaural Panner" by Jakob H. Andersen [3]. The patch is made is Cycling '74 Max. The project uses recordings from the CIPIC HRTF database to make the binaural panning. It was done to reduce the load on CPU when making convolution in the time domain, enhance the process of FFT is used to do the process in the frequency domain instead.

Since the patch is based on measurements from the CIPIC database, a "HRTFSubjectMatcher" class is made for user to insert their own anthropometric measurements used for HRTF measurements to find the subject that matches closest to a subject from the actual database. This is to more accurately match measurements and give the best matched filters to the subject. Otherwise a non-individualised HRTF set can be initialised and used as well.

One can alter the azimuth and elevation and distance to place the sound object in 3D space. It does however not include room emulation, but it emulates the distance from sound object to the listener by decreasing the gain of the sound the farther away the listener gets.

An external java object handles the direction and distance calculations based on the listener position in the XYZ plane. Additionally the rotation of the listener (unit quaternion) is also used to calculate the correct direction and distance from sound source to listener. Hereby, the sound volume and the delay for both ears (left and right channel) are calculated in real-time.

Kasper Skov has taking this further and made a Max for Live plugin based on the FFT-based binaural panner [19]. It contains the same features as the original patch made in Max, but now it has a graphical user interface to easily place sounds in 3D space and get it visualised in a virtual 3D room made with jitter.

Waves Nx. The Waves Nx works as a virtual room emulator over headphones. Hereby the user can monitor 7.1, 5.1 and 5.0 surround on stereo headphones [2]. The use case of the software is for producers who want to monitor mixes over headphones in case you do not have a acoustically good room or primarily mix on headphones and do not have loudspeakers available.

Contrary to the other mentioned software solutions the Waves Nx has a "head modelling" feature that let you measure your circumference and inter-aural arc to calculate the inter-aural delays, filters and gains for each ear and hence used to approximate an individual HRTF. By default average data is set for the adult human population.

Another interesting feature is the head tracking via camera. This feature tracks the orientation of your head and makes the sound stay in the same position to match a real life scenario. The camera based tracking works by a facial recognition algorithm that track the position and rotation of the face. The limitation of this solution is that the camera requires enough visible light to recognise the face and most cameras integrated in laptops have low frames per second, especially used in dark environments. Also, the camera based solution does not allow for a full 360° rotation as the facial recognition only works when the face is detected.

2.2 Hardware (Headphones)

Conventional headphones are satisfactory for binaural hearing as DSP is applied and sent to the two channels for the left and right ear. However, the so-called "3D headphones" have been introduced for more immersion and a cinematic experience, compared to conventional headphones. In the following section some concepts and commercial 3D headphones will be presented.

OSSIC X. The kickstarter project "OSSIC X" was a calibrated 3D headphone for a personalized HRTF experience [15]. The idea behind the project is to make a headphone that takes the anatomy of the listener into account to make an individual HRTF. This include the size of the head and shape of the ears. By using this data, they claim to make the listening experience more immersive than current technologies according to OSSIC. Unfortunately, the project got discontinued in 2018 and the headphones are no longer in production.

Audeze Mobius 3D Headphones. In collaboration with Waves Nx (mentioned in 2.1) Audeze has produced the Mobius what claims to be the world's first premium 3D cinematic headphone to deliver realistic and immersive 3D audio. It employees the technology of the Waves Nx head tracker and is integrated in the headphone. It also has anatomy calibration for a estimated individualized HRTF. This includes a lot of the features that the Ossic X also offered and the Audeze Mobius is currently commercially available.

Just like with Waves Nx, the Audeze Mobius is included with software that let you insert your head circumference and inter-aural arc for HRTF personalisation.

3   Design Requirements

It is fair to argue that there is a missing piece in the research on the externalisation of sound when both head movement and position is tracked. Since the position of the listener relative to the sound source is a great factor for the degree of externalisation, it seems natural to have this implemented in the proposed system. In the current research the focus has merely been on the head movement in terms of externalisation and the actual position has not been a focus point, even though this is a fundamental way for humans to localise sounds [8]. Head movement is still a very crucial way for humans to localise sounds, but the addition of the position where the loudness of the sound source alters depending on the distance relative to the listener, might increase the rate of externalisation.

There has been an outline of the state of the art technology within spatialised audio both for software that uses HRTFs to simulate binaural sound and the new phenomena of 3D headphones with integrated head tracking. It has also introduced how HRTFs (both individualised and non-individualised) can be used to simulate a sound in 3D space while listening on headphones and how head movements coupled with head tracking can improve the degree of externalisation. Therefore, a problem statement is created to support the decisions made in the design requirements and the experiment that follows:

> *"How can a headphone based system simulate a loudspeaker setup by using a*
> *positional tracking system with non-individualised HRTFs? And can this*
> *system further improve the degree of externalisation compared to only using*
> *head movement tracking?"*

Given this recent technology and the research within academia for HRTF and the degree of externalisation with headphones, design requirements have been made for the purposed system. It is divided into two sections (software and hardware part) for a more detailed explanation and the reasoning for these requirements. At the end of the chapter, the design requirements are listed in short.

3.1 Software: FFT-Based Binaural Panner with Non-invidualised HRTFs

The sound processing of the system will be based on the FFT-based binaural panner by Jakob H. Andersen [3]. As a starting point this implementation works great for azimuth and elevation based on the CIPIC HRTF database. In order for the system to work for the problem statement, two sound sources (left and right loudspeaker) should be present and stationary and then the sound receiver (listener) that can move and rotate and the appropriate angle and distance to the sound sources should be calculated.

It is also decided to use the CIPIC HRTF dataset and hence the HRTFs will not be individualised to the listener. The reason for doing this is because the system is meant to be an easy and accessible tool without too much configuration and calibration. With the current solutions for making individualised HRTFs, it will be a long and cumbersome process to gather the information and to measure. Furthermore, several studies has been using non-individualised HRTFs for their experiments and had similar results compared to the ones that used individualised HRTFs. The only noticeable difference is that people have a slight tendency to have front-back and up-down confusion [13] when non-individualised HRTFs are used.

3.2 Infrared LED Tracking for Detecting Listener Position and Head Movements

Since the distance perception has a direct influence of the externalisation and realism when listening to binaural audio, a positional tracking system is desirable. This can be done in various ways with e.g. facial recognition via a camera (in same style as Waves NX does described in 2.1). However, this does have its limitations as sufficient lighting should be present to track the face and get a proper frame rate. Several different proposed technologies have been been used in experimental setups; e.g. a head detection algorithm for tracking the listener's ears position in real-time using a laser scanner [10]. This method has proven to have very high accuracy ($<=15\,\mathrm{mm}$). However, this method requires expensive equipment and is not very convenient for commercial use. A different approach that does not include camera or sensor based tracking is an position estimation by acoustic signals only (e.g. voice or hand-clapping) [16]. It is achieved by the direction of arrival (DOA) from the acoustic source using two horizontally spaced microphones. This method can however be prone to issues as adverse effects by caused room reverberation can arise. Furthermore, this does not work as a real-time tracking system, but rather as a initial position calibration for the system.

A solution that eliminates these problems is the use of infrared (IR) tracking by having IR LEDs placed at the side of the listeners head and have an IR camera which only captures IR light from the LEDs for a more consistent and better refresh rate (up to 120 hz depending on the camera being used). This is a well known method that is used for various applications such as head tracking for driving and flying simulation games. It is also a fairly simple and affordable way to create your own DIY head tracker.

Even though this approach is a better approach than the camera based facial recognition, it is still not completely optimal. Since it is still camera based, it will only be able to track what the camera can see. Therefore it can not track if you move outside of its range or rotate more than approximately 90° in all directions. To compensate for this issue (at least with the limited rotation), an inertial measurement unit (IMU) can be implemented to track the head movement. In this way, the IR LEDs can be used for position and the IMU for head movement.

3.3   Needs for Design

Based on the two previous sections in chapter, investigating the state of the art and basing it on the problem statement, the following design requirements can be made:

1. Software implementation that uses a well known non-individualised HRTF dataset for binaural panning (Individualised HRTF will not be a focus as previous studies have found that sounds can still be perceived as externalised to the same degree whether or not the HRTFs are individualised).
2. Use infrared LED tracking instead of facial recognition. Improved refresh rate, accuracy and detected angles of rotation. It also enables positional tracking relative to the infrared camera that is being used.
3. Use fusion tracking that uses an IMU for tracking head movements and the IR LED to track the position.

4   Design

In this chapter, the design and the implementation of the proposed system based on the state of the art and the design requirements will be outlined. The choices of the implemented technology both on the signal processing and the hardware part will be accounted for.

In order to create a system that simulates loudspeakers through headphones, there are two main focus areas which contain the DSP aspect that involves obtaining HRTFs, and applying that to the incoming sound for binaural playback through the headphones. The other is the head tracking that is mostly hardware based and is responsible for acquiring the positional and head movement data using IR LEDs to obtain absolute positional tracking of the listeners head movement. This data is used for the HRTF algorithm to calculate the direction and distance from the sound source (loudspeakers) to the sound receiver (the listener). A visualisation of the system architecture is shown on Fig. 1.

4.1   Hardware

Infrared Tracking
It was chosen to do the tracking with the infrared solution as it seems to a reliable, affordable and stable solution for this project.

To track the IR LEDs, a customised clip was 3D printed to house the three LEDs. It is clip that was developed to easily apply to any headphone. The three LEDs (SFH485P, 880 nm) are in series connection wired to a USB cable to give the system 5 V. The position of the LEDs are predefined by the recommendation of the Pointtracker 1.1 software used in the open source tracking program OpenTrack to obtain the absolute position of the clip in 3D-space (XYZ). It is also possible to obtain the head movement orientation for its pitch yaw and roll using this technique. However, the maximum rotation that can be obtained is approximately 180° in all directions since the camera can not detect the LED when they are facing away from the camera. The Opentrack software captures the size and position of the LEDs relative to each other and the PointTracker 1.1 software thereby calculates the raw xyz and pitch, yaw and roll data. The yellow cross in the camera input shows the calibrated model center based on the three IR LEDs.

The camera that captures the position of the IR LEDs is a customised Sony PS3 Eye with its IR filter removed and a IR pass filter placed in front of the lens to only let IR light pass through. The camera operates with a resolution of 640 × 480 pixels and a frame rate of 60. The camera works best with little to no sunlight in the frame or any other IR light sources other than from the clip. It therefore works best indoors and without facing any windows where sunlight can hit the lens. It works perfectly in the dark and it always operates at the desired 60 frames per second.

4.2   Software

Max Patch
The signal processing, HRTF calculation and relative distance sound emulation is developed in Cycling '74 Max 8 [1], based on the "FFT-based Binaural Panner" patch made by Jakob H. Andersen [3]. The main patch calculates the appropriate azimuth and elevation on the basis of a provided listener position. The two sound position objects are at a fixed position that are defined as the left and right speaker - in that way the patch can be set up as a virtual sound positioning system.

The patch contains a Java class that calculates the azimuth and elevation given the position of the listener based on the x, y, and z coordinates in relation to the sound positions coordinates. Furthermore, it also uses the listener rotation (unit quaternion) to calculate the azimuth and elevation. The distance from left to right ear based on the rotation and position is also used to determine the interaural level, and time differences.

Since the patch uses the CIPIC HRTF database, the patch needs to initialise a HRTF dataset from one of the participants from the database. Two matrix files containing the data to perform FFT are used for left and right and right channel. It runs with a signal vector of 1024 and 44100 Hz sample rate. The head related impulse response are converted to the frequency domain with a FFT size of 2048.

Inside the patch, it is possible to place the two sound sources (left and right speaker) on a 2D grid within a dimension that can be personally specified. Also, the listener position is also marked as a point on the canvas and updates in real-time and moves on the canvas accordingly. The 'OrientationExtractor' object receives the listener's head orientation (pitch, yaw and roll) and the position (x, y and z). This is feeded to the 'positionPacker' object which packs messages the two sound sources and the listener and are separately sent to the 'DirectionAndDistancehandler' Java object for signal processing calculation for correct direction (azimuth and elevation) and distance from sound source to the listener.

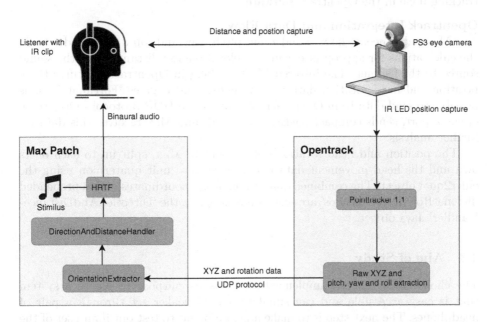

Fig. 1. A flowchart showing the system architecture. The position and rotation of the listener provided by the IR clip is captured by the PS3 eye camera. The Opentrack software send the data to Max through an UDP protocol. The non-individualised HRTF is applied based on the position of the listener relative to the sound sources and sent as binaural audio to the headphones.

Distance Emulation

To achieve realism for the system, a sense of distance from sound source to the listener, must be measured and calculated. One of the easiest way for humans to determine the distance to a sound source is the intensity of the sound - the further away the listener is to the source the more the intensity of the sound decreases.

Since the distance from the virtual loudspeaker to the listener is calculated, we must understand the relation between the intensity of a sound and how it propagates and reaches the listener at a certain distance. The radiation of sound loses power in proportion to the distance and loses about 3 dB when doubling the distance [8]. This is given by the formula for Sound Intensity Level (SIL)

$$10 \log_{10}(I) - 10 \log_{10}(2I) = 10 \log_{10}(1/2) = 3 \, dB(loss) \tag{1}$$

The peak sound pressure of a sound wave is inversely proportional to the distance. Therefore, it decreases $1/r$ where r is the distance from the sound source. Given this information, the gain of the sound source at the specific position of the listener, both for the left and the right ear can be calculated in real-time. The distance (in centimeters) is updated directly from the measured IR positional tracking done in the Opentrack software.

Opentrack Integration and Data Flow
The Max patch needs the x, y and z and pitch, yaw and roll data in order to do the calculations for appropriate azimuth, elevation and distance from the sound source to the listener. The infrared LED tracking in Opentrack captures these position and head rotation data in centimeters and degrees. Fortunately, it is possible to send data from Opentrack to Max via an UDP protocol - Opentrack opens a port, sends compact packages via UDP and Max receives this data for further analysis.

The position and head rotation data is sent to Max, split up to each of its own and the head movement data is converted into unit quaternion using the euler2quat object. The combined quaternion or xyz coordinates with a prepended 'listenerRot' or 'listenerPos' are sent as a message to the 'DirectionAndDistance-Handler' Java object.

4.3   Aim of Study

The choice of design and implementation has its purpose to create a system that is easy accessible and can simulate a loudspeaker set through a pair of headphones. The next step is to make an experiment to test out if an user of the system can perceive it as the sound is coming from "outside of the head" - the music is externalised.

Furthermore, it will also be to test if the IR LED tracking that has 6 DOF (both head movement and position) does improve the externalisation. The focus of presented research [7,13] focuses mainly on the head movement only, hence it would be interesting to see if the distance implementation has an enhanced effect on the externalisation aspect.

It has been chosen to use non-individualised HRTFs mainly because personalised HRTFs would be too cumbersome to measure for each participant and also because this would contravene the objective of the system to be easy accessible. However, it must be investigated if the use of non-individualised HRTFs has a negative affect on the localisation cues and externalisation. There will not be a comparison between individualised and non-individualised HRTFs, but an investigation for the listeners if the sound on this system sounds realistic or if it is disorienting because of the HRTFs not being personalised.

Given these points of interests, a hypothesis can be made which will be the focus of the experiment.

H0 The addition of positional tracking compared to only head movement tracking will increase the reported externalisation of the subjects.

An additional experiment will also be made that focuses on the investigation that positional movement plus positional tracking will improve externalisation compared to only head movement tracking (without the addition of positional tracking of moving side to side and back and forth) with positional movement.

5   Experimental Setup

The experiment is inspired by the test conducted by Hendrickx *et al.* [13], which they reproduced Brimijoin *et al.* [7] experiment. The focus of their rendition of the experiment was to see if large head movements ($\pm 90°$) had a significant improvement on externalisation. They also wanted to redo the experiment to see if subjects could determine the degree of externalisation after they had stopped moving his/her head. Hendrickx *et al.* also found a lack of detailed data to support the claims they made, as subject could more or less move freely. They wanted the movement to follow a specific protocol to make sure that subjects had the same movement and thus can more confidently reject or accept their hypothesis. Also, they wanted to see if the use of non-individualised HRTFs could be applied as it would represent a more generalisable display scenario. Lastly the stimulus being used was longer than the previous one being used (8 s instead of 2–3 s). This was to make sure the subjects had enough time to determine the degree of externalisation and make large head movements as well.

They presented three hypothesis with the focus that large head movements would improve externalisation when the head tracker is active and a collapse of externalisation will happen when the head tracker is inactive. They found in their experiment that indeed head movements coupled with head tracking led to a substantial improvements of externalisation for most subjects. In the present study, it will be assumed that this condition is true, but the additional positional tracking coupled with head tracking will even further improve externalisation compared to only head tracking. The choice to replicate the experiment is to foremost have a valid test and to also compare it Hendrickx *et al.*'s findings. More or less the same procedure and protocol will be used in respect of the head movements and post condition externalisation questions.

5.1   Stimulus

In Hendrickx *et al.* [13] they claimed that the 2–3 s stimulus used in the experiment conducted by Brimijoin *et al.* [7] was too short for participants to determine the degree of externalisation and used a 8s excerpt of male speech instead. Even though this stimulus is longer the author of the present study still found the stimulus to be too short for subjects to make large enough head movements, get familiar with the sound and to determine the degree of externalisation. This is also due to the participants should also do more movement and not only head rotation. Because of this a 30 s stimulus was chosen for the test.

It was also chosen to use music as the stimulus instead of speech. It was better suited to the overall problem statement of simulating a loudspeaker setup having two speaker for a left and right channel. The music is the first 30 s of the Paul McCartney's "Fool on the hill". It consists of piano, drums, guitar, flute and singing, which tries to cover most of the frequency spectrum and consists of transient and sustained sounds.

5.2   Location and Experimental Protocol

The experiment took place at Aalborg University in Copenhagen in a small room to ensure no disruption and environmental noise. An introductory questionnaire was presented with demographic questions and their experience with music production and familiarity with HRTF and binaural audio. The subjects had to follow 4 different head movement protocols that was explained by the test conductor. The four conditions are inspired by the ones used in Hendrickx *et al.* experiment, but with slight modification with added positional movement:

- **NH**: Head orientation (±90° left and right), no head tracking.
- **NP**: Head orientation (±90° left and right) + position (back/forth, side/side), no head tracking.
- **WH**: Head orientation (±90° left and right), with head tracking.
- **WP**: Head orientation (±90° left and right) + position (back/forth, side/side), with head tracking.

When the music started the subject performed the head and/or position movement until the 30 s of stimulus was over. They could repeat the movement routine if they wanted to. All subjects did the same movements to ensure that everyone received the same cues and to make a more valid comparison.

After each condition, the subject had to report their degree of externalisation of the music from a scale from 0–5, where 0 is "The source is at the center of my head" and 5 is "The source is remote and externalised. This was to ensure that the subject would report the after effects of the externalisation just after each condition. This is the same scale and questions used by Hendrickx *et al.* [13] in their experiment.

Lastly, the subject was presented with a customised System Usability Questionnaire (SUS) consisting of 8 questions with a focus of the system's responsiveness, audio quality and feedback.

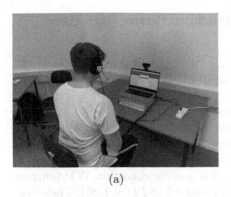
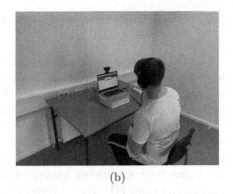

(a)   (b)

Fig. 2. The test setup while a subject is performing one of the conditions. On (a) the IR LED clip can be seen on the right side of the headphones. The PS3 eye camera placed on top of the laptop tracks the position of the clip in real-time.

6   Results

A total of 20 subjects participated in the experiment (16 men and 4 women, aged 20–26 years). Eleven subjects compose music and do their mix on their computer/laptop. Seven of the 11 usually use headphones while mixing while the rest usually use loudspeakers. This is to support the claim that a fair amount of people and the majority of music producers (mostly as a hobby) often use headphones as their main source for audio feedback.

Nine of the 20 participants were familiar with the terms and "binaural hearing" and/or "HRTF".

6.1   Influence of the Added Positional Tracking

With the hypothesis "the addition of positional tracking compared to only head movement tracking will improve externalisation". It will be interesting to compare condition **WH** with **WP**.

The experimental protocol is a repeated measure for the same group of people for condition **WH** and **WP**, where the difference is the movement protocol - **WH** only consisting of head movement and **WP** consisting of head movement + positional movement. For this purpose a one-tailed paired t-test was used to determine if there is a significant difference between the two groups. Hypothetically, the **WP** condition should have a significantly higher externalisation score than the **WH** condition. The mean scores for condition **WH** and **WP** were, 3.05 ($STD = 1.234$) and 3.30 ($STD = 0.979$) respectively. Given the statistical test there was no significant difference found between head movement versus head movement + positional movement in respect of externalisation ($p = 0.15$).

6.2 Direct Influence on Positional Tracking Versus Only Head Movement Tracking

An additional experiment was made to further investigate if the positional tracking coupled with positional and head movement (**WP** condition) have a greater impact on externalisation compared to a condition (**HP**) that has positional movement but only head movement tracking.

A total of 6 subjects participated in this experiment (5 men and 1 woman, aged 24–30 years). The experimental protocol was identical as for the previous one. A one-tailed paired t-test was used to determine if there is a significant difference between the two groups. The mean scores for condition **WP** (current experiment) and **HP** were, 3.5 ($STD = 1.05$) and 3.3 ($STD = 1.05$). There was found a significant difference (0.038) between the groups in terms of the reported externalisation after each condition.

6.3 Data Logging of Movement

During the test, the movement data was recorded for each condition[1]. This includes the pitch, yaw and roll (head movement) and the x, y and z coordinates (positional movement). This was done in OpenTrack software that saved the data to a CSV file while doing head movement tracking. During the test, the movement data sent to the Max patch was the filtered data by using the Acella filter made by Stanislaw Halik [12].

No further insight was made with this data, but more as a confirmation that the tracking was ongoing and the subject would consequently hear the correct binaural audio based on the tracked data. There was found no inconsistencies reviewing the logged tracking data. Inconsistencies would be stuck tracking (the infrared camera unable to track the IR LEDs and consequently being stuck on the last recorded movement) or incorrect head movement logging (the software detecting more IR LED spots than the desired 3, consequently making false calculations).

Nine of the participants were familiar with the terms "binaural hearing" and/or "HRTF". This group rated the degree of externalisation a mean scores of the **WH** and **WP** 3.0 and 3.7, respectively. A T-test also found a significant difference between these two groups ($p = 0.01$). However, there was not a significant difference for the group that were not familiar with the terms ($p = 0.4$) given the mean scores 3.1 and 3.0 for **WH** and **WP**, respectively. This could indicate that the subjects that were familiar binaural audio and might have tried it before, could notice the difference between the two conditions and hence rate a higher degree of externalisation.

---

[1] All of the logged data can be downloaded and reviewed from here https://bit.ly/2Ma1bOB.

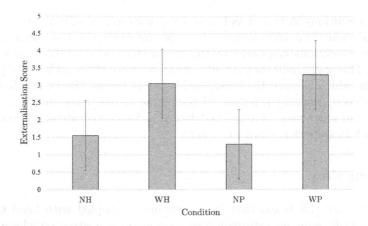

Fig. 3. Mean externalisation scores for all four conditions. An error bar indicating the standard deviation ($NH = 1.09, WH = 1.23, NP = 1.17, WP = 0.98$) for each condition is also shown. **NH**: Head orientation, no head tracking. **WH**: Head orientation, with head tracking. **NP**: Head orientation + position, no head tracking. **WP**: Head orientation + position, with head tracking.

6.4 System Usability Scores

The subjects answered 8 SUS statements from a scale from 1–5 with 1 labelled "Strongly Disagree" and 5 labelled "Strongly Agree"[2].

The System usability questions after the test showed that they generally felt confident using the system, thought it was responsive and had no latency and that the audio feedback was accurate in respect to their movements. The subjects were neither agreeing or disagreeing with the statement that they wanted to use the system frequently for use to when producing music. Some mentioned that they could imagine them using it watching a movie or while playing a video game and thought it might not be useful for music production. During the experiment, some subjects might have experienced that the tracking was inconsistent, if they for example rotated too much and the camera could not detect the IR LEDs or if background IR light (from e.g. sunlight) was detected and falsely measured as part of the LED clip. However, none of the participants reported these inconsistencies and this was also not observed through the logged head movement data.

6.5 Summary

The results of the present study can be summarised as follows:

– There was not found a significant difference between condition **WH** and **WP** - the addition of positional tracking does not certainly improve externalisation in this experiment.

---

[2] A full review of all results including demographics, reported externalisation and SUS scores can be found on https://bit.ly/2I0jUXG.

- In the conditions **WH** and **WP** where subjects were familiar with the terms "HRTF" and "binaural hearing", a significant difference were found between the two conditions compared to the group that were not familiar with the terms. This could indicate that subjects were aware of the addition of position tracking which affected the music and hence improved the externalisation.
- The subjects generally rated the SUS statements positively and they thought the system was responsive, had no latency and was accurate in terms of audio feedback in respect to their movements.

7   Discussion

Hendrickx et al. [13] found that head movements coupled with head tracking did substantially enhance externalisation, compared to a situation where the listener does not move the head or when the head movement is not tracked. In the present study, the premise was to find out if the addition of positional tracking did enhance externalisation to an even further extent, compared to the situation with head movements coupled to head tracking. It was indeed found that in the condition with head movement coupled with head tracking had a higher externalisation score **NH** (m = 3.05) compared with the one without head tracking **WH** (m = 1.55) and the two groups were significantly different (p = 0.0003). The same is applicable with the condition with head movements + position coupled with head and positional tracking **NP** (m = 1.30) compared with the same condition but without tracking **WP** (m = 3.30, p = 0.00006). The present study can therefore confirm that the externalisation collapses once the subjects does head movement and/or positional movement but without tracking enabled. However, it cannot be confirmed that the addition of positional movement and tracking does significantly increase the degree of externalisation.

Hendrickx et al. suggest that head movements may need to be sufficiently large in order to have an impact on externalisation [13]. This might be the reason because condition **WP** did not have large enough movement from side/side and front/back. Since the limitation of camera-based tracking, the subject could only be within a certain frame. The maximum side/side movement was preferred and it span from 20–30 cm to the side from the center position. The back and forth motion also had its limitations because if the subject came too close, the camera might not detect the three infrared lights and would give incorrect tracking. Also, if the subjects moved too far away, it would be harder to detect the lights especially if head movements to the sides were made. However, the test conductor made sure that the subjects moved approximately 50 cm both back and forth.

8   Influence of Non-individualised HRTFs

In the present experiment the HRTF data from the third subject in the CIPIC HRTF database was used. This was not chosen for a particular reason, but rather because this was the default one originally used in Hougaard Andersen's FFT-based binaural panner Max patch [3]. It was chosen to use non-individualised HRTFs from the *Design Requirements* since several studies did not report a significant difference in externalisation between individualised and non-individualised binaural synthesis with speech stimuli. This includes studies from Møller *et al.* [17] and Begault *et al.* [4].

These studies show that individualised HRTFs are not necessary (although ideal), as non-individualised HRTFs are just as accurate and some cases equal to the individualised ones. However, HRTFs that are selected based on the anthropometrc data (distance from ear to ear, size of pinna etc.) of the listener is recommended, as a preliminary study by Geronazzo *et al.* [11] showed. They found that selecting the HRTF based on mismatch function that relies on the anthropometric data of the listener increased the average performances of 17% for elevation accuracy compared to the use of a generic HRTF with anthropometric data. It also significantly increased externalisation and up/down confusion rates.

8.1 Implement Reverberation to Better Simulate the Current Room

It is known that reported externalisation is strongly linked with the amount of reverberation to the stimuli. In an experiment performed by Begault *et al.* [4] they found that an anechoic stimuli participants made an externalised judgement of 40% compared to 79% of a reverberant condition (the subjects could score the degree of externalisation between 0–100%). They also found that there was no significant difference between a early-reflection and a full-reverberation condition. This means that an externalised stimuli can be simulated using a minimal representation of the acoustic environment the subject is in.

It was also discussed in the introduction section that artificial reverberation could be a improvement on the perceived realism of the stimuli. However, the term "realism" in this sense can be wrong to use. Begault *et al.* [4] asked their participants to rate the perceived realism and they did not find significant effects. The lack of variability might suggest that the participants did not differentiate among the conditions based on the perceived realism, or that they simply did not have a common understanding of what "realism" meant. However, the term externalisation could perhaps still be used as it seems that participants both in Hendrickx *et al.* and the current experiment have a good understanding of the term, given the six-point scale with the explanation they were provided to answer after each condition.

It would be interesting to see if the addition of a reverberated stimuli that is either full-reverberated or with early reflection can increase the degree of externalisation of the conditions even further. This would also include a room simulation that changes the early reflections and amount of reverb based on the distance from the subject to the sound source.

9   Conclusion

This paper has presented the design and implementation of a positional IR tracking based system that simulates a loudspeaker setup using non-individualised HRTFs. There has been an investigation of the state of the art within binaural and spatialised audio both for software and hardware. Many of the software solutions presented has sophisticated binaural solutions with virtual acoustics and customised HRTF features, but most of them only focuses on the azimuth and elevation and not the position of either the sound source or the listener.

Based on these investigations, design requirements were made with the intention to make a system that can do positional tracking to simulate a loudspeaker setup through headphones using non-individualised HRTFs. The implementation of the system includes positional and head movement tracking using 3 point infrared LED clip attached on the side of a pair of headphones and a camera to capture head movement and positional distance sensing relative to the camera.

An experiment including 20 subjects tried out the system while performing different conditions with different movements with or without tracking. The subjects rated the degree of externalisation of the stimuli after each condition.

The results showed that there was no significant difference in the degree of externalisation between the condition only having head movement and the other that had the addition of positional movement and tracking. However, there was a significant difference between the group of subjects that were familiar with binaural hearing in the conditions with only head movements and additional positional tracking.

Furthermore, a post experiment indicate that positional movement coupled with positional tracking has a greater effect on externalisation compared to positional movement coupled with only head movement tracking, as there was found a significant difference between the conditions. However, the small sample size means that the research findings are not fully conclusive.

These findings were discussed and compared with previous studies that had similar experimental setup. Several points of interests were presented that could improve or might enhance the externalisation to the already proposed system. This includes implementing virtual acoustics i.e. reverberation and including anthropometric data matching for subjects for determining a suitable HRTF set for the listener.

References

1. Cycling '74 max 8, April 2019. https://cycling74.com/
2. Nx - 3D audio on any headpones—by Waves Audio Ltd., February 2019. https://www.waves.com/nx
3. Andersen, J.H.: FFT-based binaural panner, May 2019. https://cycling74.com/tools/fft-based-binaural-panner
4. Begault, D., Wenzel, E.: Direct comparison of the impact of head tracking, reverberation, and individualized head-related transfer functions on the spatial perception of a virtual speech source. In: Proceedings 108th AES Convention, October 2001, pp. 904–916 (2001)

5. Betbeder, L.: Near-field 3D audio explained—Oculus, September 2017. https://developer.oculus.com/blog/near-field-3d-audio-explained/
6. Blauert, J.: The Technology of Binaural Listening. Springer, Heidelberg (2013). https://doi.org/10.1007/978-3-642-37762-4
7. Brimijoin, W.O., Boyd, A.W., Akeroyd, M.A.: The contribution of head movement to the externalization and internalization of sounds. PLoS ONE **8**, e83068 (2013). https://doi.org/10.1371/journal.pone.0083068
8. Farnell, A.: Designing Sound. MIT Press, Cambridge (2010)
9. Fluitt, K.F., Mermagen, T., Letowski, T.: Auditory perception in open field: distance estimation. Tech. rep. Army Research Lab, Aberdeen, Scotland, UK (2013)
10. Georgiou, P.G., Mouchtaris, A., Roumeliotis, S.I., Kyriakakis, C.: Immersive sound rendering using laser-based tracking. In: Audio Engineering Society Convention 109. Audio Engineering Society (2000)
11. Geronazzo, M., Spagnol, S., Bedin, A., Avanzini, F.: Enhancing vertical localization with image-guided selection of non-individual head-related transfer functions. In: Proceedings of IEEE International Conference on Acoustics, Speech and Signal Processing (ICASSP), pp. 4463–4467 (2014). https://doi.org/10.1109/ICASSP.2014.6854446
12. Halik, S.: Accela in opentrack 2.3, May 2019. https://github.com/opentrack/opentrack/wiki/Accela-in-opentrack-2.3
13. Hendrickx, E., Stitt, P., Messonnier, J.C., Lyzwa, J.M., Katz, B.F., de Boishéraud, C.: Influence of head tracking on the externalization of speech stimuli for non-individualized binaural synthesis. J. Acoustical Soc. Am. (JASA) **141**, 2011 (2017). https://doi.org/10.1121/1.4978612
14. Jianjun, H., Tan, E.L., Gan, W.S., et al.: Natural sound rendering for headphones: integration of signal processing techniques. IEEE Signal Process. Mag. **32**(2), 100–113 (2015)
15. Kickstarter: OSSIC X: The first 3D audio headphones calibrated to you by OSSIC, may 2019. https://www.kickstarter.com/projects/248983394/ossic-x-the-first-3d-audio-headphones-calibrated-t
16. Lee, K.S., Lee, S.P.: A real-time audio system for adjusting the sweet spot to the listener's position. IEEE Trans. Consum. Electron. **56**, 835–843 (2010). https://doi.org/10.1109/TCE.2010.5506009
17. Møller, H., Sørensen, M.F., Jensen, C.B., Hammershøi, D.: Binaural technique: do we need individual recordings? J. Audio Eng. Soc. **44**(6), 451–469 (1996). http://www.aes.org/e-lib/browse.cfm?elib=7897
18. Oculus: Localization and the human auditory system, May 2019. https://developer.oculus.com/documentation/audiosdk/latest/concepts/audio-intro-localization
19. Skov, K.: Binaural spatialization in Ableton, February 2019. http://kasperskov.dk/projects_binaural_jit.html
20. Wenzel, E.M., Arruda, M., Kistler, D.J., Wightman, F.L.: Localization using non-individualized head-related transfer functions. J. Acoust. Soc. Am. (JASA) **94**, 111–123 (1993). https://doi.org/10.1121/1.407089

Finding, Feeling and Sharing the Value of a Landscape

Rui Jesus[1,2](✉), Catarina Conceição[1], and Gonçalo Lopes[1]

[1] ISEL - Instituto Superior de Engenharia de Lisboa/IPL, Lisbon, Portugal
rjesus@deetc.isel.ipl.pt, pc.catarina96@gmail.com
[2] NOVA LINCS, Faculdade de Ciências e Tecnologia, Universidade NOVA de Lisboa,
2829-516 Caparica, Portugal

Abstract. The value of a landscape is often associated with its visual aesthetic value, but a landscape goes beyond that. It has other important values, such as historical or social value. The guides and tourist itineraries are useful to help visiting monuments but as far as reading and experiencing a landscape, these are still insufficient. This work consists of developing a mobile application with gaming and social features, to support the experience of visit and reading places with valuable landscapes. The paper describes the design principles used and presents the main issues of the study conducted during the development process of the application. It also presents the results obtained by the tests carried out to evaluate the user experience when visiting and appreciating the value of a landscape with the application. The experiments were carried out in the Cultural Landscape of Sintra, considered world heritage since 1995 [6].

Keywords: Mobile applications · Gaming features · Cultural Landscape

1 Introduction

The landscape can be seen as an extension of territory, rural or urban. It consists mainly of the perceptible aspects of geographical space, that is, the way the human being forms an understanding of the surrounding world according to the senses [9]. The importance of landscape emerges in this perception influenced by history, memories and enriched by myths [12], and also by the cultural expression inherent to the transformation of the landscape caused by the action of man [10]. Therefore, the landscape, in general, has always been considered important and the target of analysis and study in several areas. As a result of this relevance, in 1992, it was considered a world heritage site with the designation of "Cultural Landscape" [9].

The landscapes allow a better understanding of history, science, literature and other areas of study. However, the value of a landscape is misunderstood,

© ICST Institute for Computer Sciences, Social Informatics and Telecommunications Engineering 2020
Published by Springer Nature Switzerland AG 2020. All Rights Reserved
A. Brooks and E. I. Brooks (Eds.): ArtsIT 2019/DLI 2019, LNICST 328, pp. 178–191, 2020.
https://doi.org/10.1007/978-3-030-53294-9_12

often being linked only to its visual aesthetic value, without being perceived of other important values associated with it, such as historical, social, ecological, cultural, economic and other values. Tour guides and itineraries are very useful for reading monuments of art, but as far as the landscape, its use is still not sufficient. A landscape needs to be felt, interpreted, contemplated, remembered and these perceptions are different at different times of the day, the year and even with different weather conditions. For instance, it is important for the visitor to know the right moment to cross the river Tejo in Lisbon with fog (to have a different perception), or the right moment to visit the Gardunha mountain range in Portugal to see the cherry trees in bloom, or even, the right moment to hear the roar of the deer in the Beira Interior (region of Portugal) streak.

This work consists of developing a location-based mobile application with gaming and social features, to support the visit of places with valuable landscapes. The application allows the user to access information about the location and ways to access the landscape site, a very brief description and the best conditions for visiting them, such as the time of the day and weather conditions. When a user is at a point of interest, they will have access to more detailed information about the landscape and calls of attention to important elements that increase their value.

This application is one of the results of a study carried out by researchers of social sciences and computer science, in order to value the landscape in general, and to share this value and knowledge with everyone. This work was developed in the scope of a funding project in the context of the launch of the Landscape Museum in Lisbon.

The paper is structured as follows. Next section discusses the related work and the following section describes the design principles used and presents the main issues of the study conducted during the development of the application. Section 4 presents and discusses the results obtained with the evaluation of the mobile application. The paper ends with the conclusions and future work.

2   Related Work

The work proposed in this paper explores some features used in mobile guides [2, 8] and the use of games in cultural heritage sites [1,4,11], in the context of visiting places with interesting landscapes, in order to assist the visitor in reading the several aspects of the landscape [9]. In [8] is proposed a mobile guide for cultural heritage sites based on pictures. It also includes augmented reality and sharing features that helps the visitor understanding the place. One pioneer work including games in cultural heritage was proposed by Correia *et al.* [4]. This work had the goal of defining and implementing a platform for mobile storytelling, information access, and gaming activities. It was evaluated in cultural heritage site in a tourism context.

Interesting state of art reviews can be found in [1] for games in cultural heritage, and in [11] for serious games (educational objectives) for cultural heritage. Augmented reality [3,7,8] and mixed reality [13] are also important features used to improve the user experience in cultural heritage points of interest. In [3] was proposed a work close to our proposal, focused in the relevance of the landscape and how technology can enhance the user understanding of its meaning. This work relates the climatic changes with the landscape changes and introduces a mobile app with some augmented reality features (audio and visual augmentation) to enrich the experience of the user. It discusses the main issues related to this problem. Mainly the internet connection in rural spaces.

Our work is related to tourism, but is also focused on the appreciation of the landscape in general. Recent study [5] defines a theoretical model of mobile augmented reality acceptance in urban heritage tourism. It reveals seven dimensions that should be incorporated into augmented reality acceptance research including information quality, system quality, costs of use, recommendations, personal innovativeness and risk as well as facilitating conditions.

There are many proposals for mobile guides or mobile applications in the context of visiting points of interest with gaming, social and augmented reality features. However, a landscape has a different meaning and, for that reason, these proposals are not the most appropriate.

3   1+Place

This section describes the mobile application, 1+Place (One More Place), developed during the study conducted to understand how mobile technology can help valuing the landscape. It is structured in four main modules: (1) authentication, (2) user profile, (3) map and (4) landscape. After successfully authenticating, the user proceed to map module. From this module, the user can access the user profile module or the landscape module. In order to motivate and encourage the user to discover and share unfamiliar landscapes, social and gamification characteristics have been introduced.

3.1   Map

The map panel represents the main application module. This panel consists of a map and markers that indicate, among other things, landscape locations, regions and the user's position (see Fig. 1). The lower marker in Fig. 1b represents the position of the user on the map. The next marker (from the bottom up), with a building drawn, represents a point of interest with an interesting landscape. When the user clicks on this bookmark opens the information window of the place (represented above the marker in Fig. 1b with the title Santa Eufémia, Sintra). At the top, on the right side of the panel is a clickable area with the name of the user, a photo of the user, and the explorer level (gamification feature) of the user. If the user clicks on this area jumps to the user profile panel.

Zoom in/out operations can be performed using the interaction technique based on the two-finger movement. If the zoom is high, a less comprehensive area on the map is seen. In this case, the markers represent a point of interest (see Fig. 1b). If the zoom is low, a more comprehensive area on the map is seen. The markers represent regions of places of interest (see Fig. 1c), in order to avoid too many visible information that could disturb the user experience.

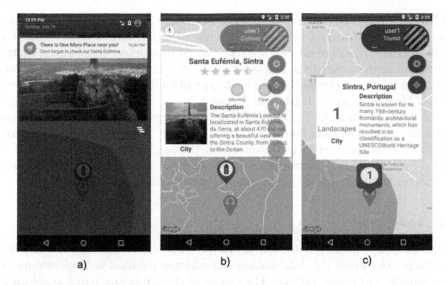

a)   b)   c)

Fig. 1. Map panel: a) notification received, b) information window of the place, c) information window of the region.

Information Window of a Point of Interest - Figure 1b shows an example of the information window for a point of interest. This window presents the title and region where it is inserted, better conditions for the visit, basic description, image allusive to the landscape and main type. On the right side, there are three main buttons (three lower buttons). These buttons are used to get directions to the point of interest, to access the landscape panel (if it has already been visited), and to add the landscape to the "wishlist" (landscape list that the user wants to visit).

Figure 1c presents an example for a region. The region window displays the title and country, main type of landscapes, total landscapes number and description of the region.

Fig. 2. Map panel: Markers.

Guide to Points of Interest - In each position, the user can see the nearest places of interest defined by a circumference of 10 km radius centered on the user's position. Places of interest are represented by markers (regions or points). The visual appearance of the markers reflects the type of landscape they represent. Figure 2 shows the markers for each type of landscape: City, Coast, Desert, Forest, Mountain, River, Rural and Tropical.

To guide the user to the nearest point of interest. When the user is close to (in our tests, less than 500 m) a point of interest receives a notification (see Fig. 1a). When the user is less than 100 m the application allows the user to have access to the information window of the place (see Fig. 1b). This window has orientation clues (direction arrows) to help the user finding the place.

3.2   Landscape

In the landscape panel the user can access the contents of a given point of interest. Users can consult this information and add new content, such as comments, photographs and assign ratings. The layout of the landscape panel is shown in Fig. 3. By means of a swipe gesture over the image at top, it is possible to visualize a set of images shared by users of the application. It is also possible to enlarge one image by pressing on it.

Below the image is a rectangle indicating the average landscape classification. The user can rate the landscape by assigning a score between 0 and 5, by filling in the stars below the landscape name. There is also a set of buttons that allow the user to perform a series of actions (from left to right):

Fig. 3. Landscape panel.

- The left most button allows the user view the basic and detailed description of the landscape;
- The second button allows to view and add comments, showing a text box where the user can insert his comment, adding it by pressing the button below it. The comments are arranged in descending order of the date of publication, the most recent being at the top;
- The third button allows to add/remove the landscape to the favorites. The star button is filled when the landscape is part of the favorites, and empty when it is not;
- The fourth button allows to get directions to the point of interest by launching the Google Maps application that calculates the route, from the current location of the device to the location of the place;
- The fifth and last button allows to upload photos by accessing the camera of the phone.

3.3 User Profile

This panel allows to change the user profile information, such as the profile image. Figure 4 illustrates the layout. At top, two buttons are available for these actions. The button to the left of the profile image allows to edit some of this information, launching an activity with a set of text boxes and a button, which pushes the new information to the server. The button to the right of the profile image allows to open the gallery of the mobile device and choose a new profile image. Under the user picture is a set of buttons, where the user can click to see different information and contents (from left to right):

Fig. 4. User profile layout.

- The left most button is used to view information such as full name, e-mail, gender, date of registration and information regarding the gamification component (see Fig. 4);
- The second button is used to view the collections, that is, the stamps and badges that the user has already collected when visiting landscapes;
- The third button is used to view the favorites and the "wishlist". The "wishlist" is composed by the places that the user wants to visit. Pressing one of the places of the "wishlist", the map panel will be opened, centered on the point where the user can see this landscape. The favorites indicate landscapes that the user has already visited. Pressing favorite landscapes, the user has access to the landscape panel;
- The fourth button is used to view and manage friends. The user can see a leaderboard with his 5 friends with the highest score (see gamification section for details) by descending order. It is also possible to view a list of all your friends and access their profiles by clicking on their icon. The user can add a friend, being able to search by username or email, and send requests to users that appear in the search results. A menu is also available to see the requests for friendship and to accept or reject them;
- The fifth and last button is for viewing the pictures taken by the user in the various points of interest that the user visited.

3.4   Gamification

The gaming features aim to create greater involvement and motivate users to use the application. Thus, a scoring system is implemented that distinguishes users by levels of explorer, aiming to highlight the users who most actively explore and use the application. The defined levels of explorer are represented in Table 1.

To improve the explorer level the user has to perform a set of actions represented in Table 2. These actions reward the user with a certain number of points. To further captivate the user, level progression becomes a harder task to higher levels. However, this level evolution can not be impossible because it can create frustration and lead users to give up. The rewards can not be too high either, because if the game component is too easy, users lose interest. The actions performed by the user are assigned to scores described in the Table 2.

Another aspect included in the gamification features, is the collection of collectibles through the visit of places of interest. When visiting a point, the user receives a stamp representing it, and receives a badge for visiting all the landscapes of a region.

4   Evaluation and Discussion

To analyze the latest system functionality and to assess the user experience using the application in a real context, several field tests are conducted with users in Sintra region, Portugal. In 1995, Sintra gained the UNESCO Cultural Landscape

Table 1. Explorer levels - Maximum is equal to the maximum integer that can be represented with 32 bits.

Level	Title	Minimum score	Maximum score
1	Beginner	0	499
2	Curious	500	1499
3	Tourist	1500	2999
4	Traveler	3000	4999
5	Adventurer	5000	7499
6	Explorer	7500	Maximum

Table 2. Scores awarded to the user actions.

Action	Scoring (points)
Visit a landscape	100
Add a photo	50
Make a comment	25
Rate a landscape	10

classification [6]. Sintra is one of the richest areas of Portugal in terms of landscape diversity (see Fig. 5). It includes, natural coastal landscapes, mountain, several historical monuments and mixed landscapes (urban and natural).
The main goals of this study are:

- to produce detailed user feedback that will guide future improvements of the application;
- to measure the user experience, using our application in a real scenario;
- to analyze if the users can have a better perception of the meaning of a landscape with our application.

Fig. 5. Sintra Mountains: several types of landscapes

4.1 Methodology

The tests were accomplished individually by each participant, using always the same smartphone where the application was previously installed.

Two facilitators/observers were supervising the tests, encouraging users to "think aloud", helping them when it was essential, taking notes on the users' performance and recording every problem users explicitly mention.

In the beginning, users were briefed about the objectives of the test. Then, they were guided by one of the facilitators that followed a set of tasks defined in the questionnaire. After completing the tasks, the participants answered the questionnaire.

Tests lasted for a minimum of 20 min and a maximum of 30 min each, depending on each user's curiosity and engagement in the test.

4.2 Participants

The tests were performed by 10 participants living in the Sintra area. The participants in this experiment ranged in age from 16 to 46 years old (20% of participants are over 30 years of age). Most of the participants claimed to use mobile applications on almost every day (70% of the participants). One of the users under 31 years and the two participants over 30 years of age are the users that rarely use mobile apps. To better characterize the participants, it was asked, what activities they like to do in their free time. The majority of the participants said they like to be with friends (80%) and to do outdoor activities (70%). Photography (50%) and traveling (50%) were other activities mentioned by the participants. The least mentioned were play, read, using social networks and play sports. All participants had their first contact with the application during the test and used it under similar conditions.

4.3 Questionnaire

The questionnaire is composed by three different parts. The first one captured personal data. The second part guided the users during the experience, explaining the tasks they should accomplish and capturing their experimental feedback. The questionnaire presented three different tasks the users should carry out: (1) map navigation, (2) landscape appreciation and (3) user profile exploration.

The last part of the questionnaire concerns the overall assessment of the application. The majority of the questions are Likert-type scale questions. Open questions was also included but the context was not the best for the users to write elaborate answers.

4.4 Results - Map Panel

Initially, users are encouraged to explore the map interface as they desired in order to become more familiar with the interface. After that, participants are asked to perform zoom operations, to identify the user marker on the map, to identify a point of interest marker on the map, near the place where they are physically, and to go to the physical place of the landscape identified on the map.

Participants are asked about their experience, in general, when navigating in the map interface. In a 5-point scale, where 1 (one) means bad and 5 (five) means excellent, most participants choose 4 (Mode = 4; Mean = 4, Standard Deviation = 0.67) which is a positive result. When asked about the markers on the map, all participants mentioned they are informative, in terms of better understanding of the user interface. Almost all of them mentioned they are intuitive. Finally, most of the participants (80%) mentioned they had no difficulties in performing the task. The remaining participants indicated the following difficulties:

- *"The marker of the user, as it stood in front of the marker of the landscape, made it difficult to click on the marker of the landscape place"*;
- *"I had some difficulty in unlocking the landscape, because I could not get close to the real place of the marker"*.

After these tests, these difficulties were corrected. The landscape marker was changed to the front of the user marker. For the second difficulty, the radius of the circle that defines the landscape area was increased.

4.5 Results - Landscape Appreciation

The landscape panel can be used to enjoy the landscape anywhere without being in the place. Because these tests were performed in the field, another goal was to verify if this panel can help to have a better perception of the landscape, when the user is physically at the landscape site.

Following the previous task, participants headed for a point of interest identified on the map. Next, they are asked to appreciate the landscape and to use the application (landscape panel) to have a greater awareness of the beauty of the landscape. Then, participants are asked to upload at least one photo taken on the spot, to make at least one comment in one photo and also to give a score to the landscape. Following this, the participants answered four questions related to their experience:

- Q1 - How do you rate the experience with landscape panel?
- Q2 - How do you rate your experience with uploading photos?
- Q3 - How do you rate your experience regarding the act of rating a landscape?
- Q4 - How do you rate your experience of commenting on a landscape?

Table 3 presents statistical measures obtained with the participants answers in a 5-point scale, where 1 (one) means "bad" and 5 (five) means "excellent".

In general, the results obtained are good. Most participants considered they had a positive experience, when using the landscape panel at the physical place of the landscape.

All the participants considered the design of the landscape panel informative and intuitive and none of them felt any difficulty using this part of the application. One user mentioned in an open question, that the slider of the landscape images was sometimes slow and this aspect does not enrich the experience.

During the tests, it was also found that the photos, the comments, and even the score shared by other users through the application, contributed to the visitor of the place to notice details of the landscape that had previously escaped.

Table 3. Statistics obtained from the participants answers about the Landscape panel.

Questions	Mode	Mean	Standard deviation
Q1	4.0	4.3	0.67
Q2	4.0	4.3	0.67
Q3	4.0	4.1	0.74
Q4	4.0	4.1	0.57

4.6   Results - User Profile Panel

The user profile panel was evaluated regarding its contribution to improving the experience of visiting a point of interest, including the assessment of the contribution of the social and gaming features.

After the previous task, participants are asked to explore the user profile panel, including to navigate to the leaderboard, to look for a public user and to add a friend. A set of initial questions are asked regarding the user interface usability. In general, no participants reported difficulties navigating the panel. Everyone found the interaction with the panel intuitive and most of them (80%) found the information presented in the panel relevant to the experience. The other 20% of the users, did not agree with inclusion of the gamification features. Then, the participants answered several questions related to their experience. The main questions are listed below:

– Q5 - How do you rate the experience with the user profile panel?
– Q6 - Do you consider the functionality of the leaderboard suitable for the context?
– Q7 - As for adding friends, how do you rate the experience?
– Q8 - As for the search for a user, how do you rate the experience?
– Q9 - How do you rate the navigate experience on the friend requests page?

Table 4 presents statistical measures obtained with the participants answers, using a 5-point scale, where 1 (one) means "bad" and 5 (five) means "excellent".

Although the results are generally positive, questions Q6 and Q7 did not have consensual answers by the participants. Users are divided regarding the part of the gamification (Q6 question). Some participants are of the opinion that it is unnecessary and that competitiveness is a negative aspect. Others, consider a fundamental part in motivation and that competitiveness is something positive.

After these questions, the participants had a space to write some suggestions or comments. Below, it is presented two of the sentences written by the participants with negative opinion regarding the gamification features:

Table 4. Statistics obtained from the participants answers about the user profile panel.

Questions	Median	Mean	Standard deviation
Q5	4.0	4.0	0.82
Q6	3.5	3.5	1.08
Q7	4.0	4.0	0.94
Q8	4.0	4.0	0.67
Q9	4.0	4.1	0.57

– *"I do not care much about the competition, I do not care much about the leaderboard."*;
– *"I do not think the existence of a leaderboard makes the game healthy."*.

The use of gaming features are not well accepted by all participants. Based on these results, the gamification features have been put into the application more discreetly and no user is required to use them.

4.7 Results - Overall Evaluation

Participants were asked to evaluate the user interface in what concerns design (aesthetic aspect), usefulness in terms of experience in visiting a landscape site, the relevance of the social features and contribution of the gamification features.

The most relevant questions are listed below:

– Q10 - How do you rate the user interface design?
– Q11 - How do you rate your overall experience?
– Q12 - What do you think about the game component of the application?
– Q13 - What do you think about the social component of the application?

Table 5 presents statistical measures obtained with the participants answers in a 5-point scale. In question Q10, 1 (one) means "bad" and 5 (five) means "excellent", in question Q11, 1 (one) means "frustrating" and 5 (five) means "gratifying" and in questions Q12 and Q13, 1 (one) means "boring" and 5 (five) "motivating".

As in previous results, the use of the gamification features are the most controversial part. In terms of user experience, the most given answer was 5, which is an interesting result. Finally, the social component also receives positive feedback from the participants. These confirms the current common habit of the users in using social networks in all contexts.

When the participants are asked if the experience of visiting and enjoying a landscape was enriched by the use of the application, everyone responded positively. At the end of the questionnaire, the participants are asked if they wanted to add anything else. Again, the gamification characteristics were subject to contradictory comments. Below, other interesting suggestions provided by the participants are presented:

Table 5. Statistics obtained from the participants answers related to the overall evaluation of the application.

Questions	Mode	Mean	Standard deviation
Q10	4.0	3.9	0.74
Q11	5.0	4.1	0.88
Q12	3.0	3.7	1.01
Q13	4.0	4.1	0.57

- *"Add music to the application according to the type of landscape where you are.";*
- *"It should be possible to share content on other social networks".*

The first suggestion is aligned with the purpose of the project, that is, improving the experience when visiting a landscape site. The second suggestion was already planned for implementation. Both suggestions will be implemented. Overall the results of these tests were quite positive and provided useful feedback to inspire future improvements.

5   Conclusions and Future Work

This work describes the 1+Place application and presents the study conducted to evaluate it.

In general, the main objectives of the process conducted to develop the application were achieved, since all the participants, in the tests, consider that they learned and realized things (related to the value of a landscape) with the application that would otherwise not understand. Moreover, the feedback given directly by the users and the knowledge obtained indirectly by observing the behavior of the participants, allows to improve the developed application and consequently the experience provided to the users.

The social features were better accepted by all but some participants are distracted by these components. The gamification characteristics accounted for the most controversial application. More competitive users gave positive feedback. Other participants who enjoy enjoying the beauty of the landscape did not like anything about this component.

Future work includes the use of audio to enhance the experience. This feature was already planned and the user interface already has in settings buttons for this functionality. From the observation of the behavior of the users raises clues for the inclusion in the application of augmented reality features or the use of 360° video contents.

Acknowledgments. A great appreciation to the researchers and experts who have provided help and support for our research: Prof. Paulo Vieira from ISEL and Prof. João Abreu, Prof. Luís Monteiro and Prof. Ricardo Rodrigues from the Lisbon School of Communication and Media Studies. This work is supported by FCT/MEC NOVA LINCS PEst UID/CEC/04516/2019.

References

1. Anderson, E.F., McLoughlin, L., Liarokapis, F., Peters, C., Petridis, P., de Freitas, S.: Developing serious games for cultural heritage: a state-of-the-art review. Virtual Reality **14**(4), 255–275 (2010). https://doi.org/10.1007/s10055-010-0177-3
2. Baus, J., Cheverst, K., Kray, C.: A survey of map-based mobile guides. In: Meng, L., Reichenbacher, T., Zipf, A. (eds.) Map-based Mobile Services, pp. 193–209. Springer, Heidelberg (2005). https://doi.org/10.1007/3-540-26982-7_13
3. Bishop, I.D.: Location based information to support understanding of landscape futures. Landsc. Urban Plan. **142**, 120–131 (2015)
4. Correia, N., et al.: InStory: a system for mobile information access storytelling and gaming activities in physical spaces. In: ACE 2005 Proceedings of the 2005 ACM SIGCHI International Conference on Advances in Computer Entertainment Technology, pp. 102–109. ACM, New York (2005)
5. Dieck, M.C., Jung, T.: A theoretical model of mobile augmented reality acceptance in urban heritage tourism. Curr. Issues Tour. **21**(2), 154–174 (2018)
6. Fowler, P.: World Heritage Cultural Landscapes, 1992–2002, vol. 6. UNESCO World Heritage Centre, Paris (2003)
7. Guimaraes, F., Figueiredo, M., Rodrigues, J.: Augmented Reality and Storytelling in heritage application in public gardens: Caloust Gulbenkian Foundation Garden. In: 2015 Digital Heritage, pp. 317–320 (2015). https://doi.org/10.1109/DigitalHeritage.2015.7413891. http://ieeexplore.ieee.org/document/7413891/
8. Jesus, R., Dias, R., Frias, R., Abrantes, A., Correia, N.: Memoria mobile: sharing pictures of a point of interest. In: Proceedings of the Workshop on Advanced Visual Interfaces AVI, pp. 412–415 (2008)
9. Mitchell, N., Rössler, M., Tricaud, P.M.: World Heritage Cultural Landscapes: A Handbook for Conservation and Management. UNESCO World Heritage Centre, Paris (2009)
10. Monteiro, L., Caires, C.: Overcoming the digital landmark. Transforming the landscape. In: Contempart 2015 - 4th International Contemporary Art Conference - Urban Identity, Space Studies and Contemporary Art, pp. 61–75 (2015)
11. Mortara, M., Catalano, C.E., Bellotti, F., Fiucci, G., Houry-Panchetti, M., Petridis, P.: Learning cultural heritage by serious games. J. Cult. Herit. **15**(3), 318–325 (2014)
12. Schama, S.: Landscape and Memory. Harper Press, New York (2004)
13. Tatzgern, M., Grasset, R., Veas, E., Kalkofen, D., Seichter, H., Schmalstieg, D.: Exploring real world points of interest: design and evaluation of object-centric exploration techniques for augmented reality. Pervasive Mob. Comput. **18**, 55–70 (2015)

Extended Realities, Artificial Intelligence and Interfaces

Extended Realities, Artificial Intelligence and Interfaces

Anthony L. Brooks[1][✉] and Eva Brooks[2]

[1] CREATE/Department of Architecture, Design and Media Technology/Technical Faculty of IT and Design, Aalborg University, Rendsburggade 14, 9000 Aalborg, Denmark
tb@create.aau.dk

[2] XLab: Design, Learning, and Innovation, Department of Culture and Learning, Aalborg University, Kroghstræde 3, 9220 Aalborg, Denmark

Abstract. Realities, Intelligences and Interfaces .... from Augmented, through Virtual, and Mixed; Artificial, Machine, and Natural .... technologies are here to stay and are investigated across disciplines. This contribution introduces studies and applications from various countries that are both creative and thought provoking to inspire and motivate readership and scholarship toward furthering this fast-advancing field.

Keywords: Experiences · Music · Audience · Play · Toys · Gamification · Design · Animation · Relations · Values

1 Introduction

1.1 Scope

The second section of this volume is themed - "Extended Realities, Artificial Intelligence and Interfaces" – the idea being to have focus upon these technologies relating across research topics associated to arts and technology, interactivity, and game creation perspectives.

The opening contribution in this second section is from Holland about social touch in public space of merging realities. The second contribution is on exploring relaxation experienced in virtual reality with a head mounted display versus experiencing via a television set. The third contribution focuses upon Virtual Reality scalable overlapping architectures and seamless teleportation of the user via innate virtual portals. The next topic is similar the previous but with a questioning of testers impression of associated environment's dimension. In the next contribution optimising virtual reality experiences in semi-public spaces such as museums and other exhibition venues is discussed. Subject of the next contribution is how sensors and actuators in smart urban environments can be configured in such a way that they initiate and facilitate playful and humorous events in real world situations. Semantics relating to Interaction alongside design and placement of touch gesture signifiers is in focus in the next contribution. The next contribution

A. Brooks and E. I. Brooks (Eds.): ArtsIT 2019/DLI 2019, LNICST 328, pp. 195–201, 2020.
https://doi.org/10.1007/978-3-030-53294-9_13

questions whether creativity can be supported or fostered by AI—not replaced. In the following contribution a Portuguese team questions method of authentication of paintings by various artists – fake or real! An experimental installation is discussed in the final research of this section, which informs of live artwork generation, artificial intelligence, and human interaction in a pedagogical environment.

The following text snippets elaborate directly from each contribution to further assist readership.

2   Hosting Social Touch in Public Space of Merging Realities

(Lancel et al. 2020)

A Dutch team comprising artists and academics shared their work under the title "Hosting social touch in public space of merging realities" – these are namely Karen Lancel, Hermen Maat, and Frances Brazier who ask if human hosting is essential to social touch in the public space of merging realities? This contribution explored in three experiments the role of hosting in art and design for mediating social touch in public space, social robotics, virtual reality and telematic environments.

The material informs on how the research purposefully disrupted and re-orchestrated multi-sensory connections in unfamiliar and unpredictable ways in order to evoke shared reflection and shared sense making in public, mediated by a host.

3   Renoir in VR: Comparing the Relaxation from Artworks Inside and Outside of Virtual Reality

(Kristensen et al. 2020)

This research by Johan Winther Kristensen, Lasse Lodberg Aafeldt, Peter Kejser Jensen, Rebecca Pipaluk Vinther, and Hendrik Knoche explored relaxation and artworks of natural beauty experienced in virtual reality with a head mounted display versus experiencing it via a television set. Reported outcomes inform how participants experienced this relaxation intervention after having finished a Montreal Imaging Stress Test and how all tested conditions relaxed people but no significant differences between them from neither subjective nor objective measures in a between subjects' study were found.

4   Procedurally Generated Self Overlapping Mazes in Virtual Reality

(Koltai et al. 2020)

Balázs Gyula Koltai, Jakob Elkjær Husted, Ronny Vangsted, Thomas Noes Mikkelsen, and Martin Kraus from Aalborg University next present the work "Procedurally Generated Self Overlapping Mazes in Virtual Reality" toward exploring a user experience of walking within a virtual reality environment that exceeds the size of the tracking area. Multiple approaches to overlapping architecture dealing with this issue already exist, but they are either custom made for a specific tracking area size or require a tracking area too large to work efficiently for personal use. This contribution proposed a method to make scalable overlapping architecture by procedural generation of tile-based mazes that seamlessly teleport the user using portals.

The authors detail a convenience sample research conducted on twenty-three students in evaluating how the tile size of the overlapping maze affected the user's spatial awareness of their physical position.

5 Navigating Procedurally Generated Overt Self-overlapping Environments in VR

(Neerdal et al. 2020)

"Navigating procedurally generated overt self-overlapping environments in VR" is a research presented by Jannik Neerdal, Thomas Hansen, Nicolai Hansen, Kresta Louise Bonita, and Martin Kraus from Aalborg University City Campus, Aalborg, Denmark.

The content herein highlights how previous implementations of self-overlapping architecture tried to hide the characteristics of their non-Euclidean environment from users. To test the outcome of showing these characteristics to users, the authors inform how they proposed a virtual reality system with a play area of 3 m x 3 m and procedurally generated rooms that connected by portals. The aim of the portals was to provide seamless transitions between rooms and render overt self-overlapping architecture for players to experience. Participants were tasked with reporting their experiences and discoveries during the playthrough.

Based on this information and recordings of their view, the authors could determine whether they noticed any transitions. Additionally, the participants were asked specific questions regarding their experience with the overt self-overlapping environment, and how they interpreted the size of the virtual environment in relation to the physical one. The results showed that only 2 of the 20 participants who completed the full playthrough noticed any transitions, while each playthrough consisted of a minimum of 20 transitions. Therefore, it was concluded by the researchers that the transitions were experienced as being seamless. The system did not induce significant motion sickness in participants. Most participants felt good about navigating the overt self-overlapping environment, and the consensus was that the experience was strange, yet interesting.

6 Staging Virtual Reality Exhibits for Bystander Involvement in Semi-public Spaces

(Hepperle et al. 2020)

Daniel Hepperle, Andreas Siess, and Matthias Wölfel from the Faculty of Computer Science and Business Information Systems Karlsruhe University of Applied Sciences, Germany next present their research titled "Staging Virtual Reality Exhibits for Bystander Involvement in Semi-Public Spaces".

This contribution reflects how as virtual reality becomes more popular to be used in semi-public spaces such as museums and other exhibition venues, the question on how to optimally stage such an experience arises.

To foster interaction between participants and bystanders, to lower the primary threshold regarding participation and to moderate the transition between real and virtual worlds the authors propose to augment a virtual hot-air balloon ride by a large-scale floor projection in addition to a physical basket and other extras.

Exhibited at a venue in Stuttgart, Germany a total of 140 participants evaluated the approach to inform the research. Conclusions confirmed how adding a floor projection helped to attract additional users as well as to increase overall user motivation on using the installation, and further how it led to establish a connection between the real and the virtual worlds for users.

7   Playful and Humorous Interactions in Urban Environments Made Possible with Augmented Reality Technology

(Nijholt 2020)

"Playful and Humorous Interactions in Urban Environments Made Possible with Augmented Reality Technology" is research by Dutchman Anton Nijholt who shares how there is more to humour than jokes: Humour can be created in jokes, in cartoons and animations, in products, commercials, and movies, or in stand-up comedy. However, also during our daily activities, we often smile and laugh because we experience interactions and events as humorous. We can experience such events; we can also initiate such events. Smart environments offer us tools that allow the customization of urban environments to potential and personalized playful and humorous experiences. The author informs how sensors and actuators in smart urban environments can be addressed and configured in such a way that they initiate and facilitate playful and humorous events in the real world, but it is also possible that without physical changes in the real world, our imaginations are triggered to give humorous interpretations of events in the real world by observing or imagining how they could be different. This work looks at humour that can be experienced by imagination, by suggestions, by changes in the environment, and by changing the environment using digital augmented and diminished reality tools. The views expressed here can help to add humour to urban play, urban games, and daily activities in public spaces using augmented reality technology.

8   "But Wait, There's More!" A Deeper Look into Temporally Placing Touch Gesture Signifiers

(Arleth et al. 2020)

Authors Liv Arleth, Emilie Lind Damkjær, and Hendrik Knoche consider signifiers and semantics from an Interaction Design position in their work "But Wait, There's More!" A Deeper Look into Temporally Placing Touch Gesture Signifiers. In this contribution the authors share how the language used in interaction design is affected by the wide array of academic backgrounds of interaction designers. Therefore, one word may have several meanings, which can be confusing when conducting research in this field. In this context their contribution defines three-levels of interaction: macro-, micro- and nanointeractions. The latter of these i.e. nanointeractions is the focus of the study. The authors' use Buxton's three state model to break down common gestures on touch interfaces into nanointeractions, thereby identifying where in the process of a gesture its signifiers can appear. The authors posit the usefulness of this in respect of designing for controls in small interfaces. An experiment was conducted to determine whether the temporal placement of a signifier before, during, or after a gesture made any difference for the discoverability of a double and long tap affordance. No clear tendencies were found regarding the temporal placement of the signifier, however, the concept of nanointeractions is posited as being a valuable tool for interaction design.

9   Co-designing Object Shapes With Artificial Intelligence

(German et al. 2020)

A Germanic quartet of co-authors, namely Kevin German, Marco Limm, Matthias Wölfel, and Silke Helmerdig, present their research in their contribution titled "Co-Designing Object Shapes with Artificial Intelligence". The content discusses how the promise of artificial intelligence (AI), its latest developments in deep learning, has been influencing all kinds of disciplines such as in engineering, business, agriculture, and humanities. They note that more recently it also includes disciplines that were "reserved" to humans such as art and design. While there is a general debates ongoing questioning whether creativity is profoundly human, the authors in this work wanted to investigate if creativity can be supported or fostered by AI—not replaced. In line with this the contribution investigates if AI is capable of (a) inspiring designers by suggesting unexpected design variations, (b) learning the designer's taste or (c) being a co-creation partner. In their investigations the authors adopted AI algorithms, which can be trained by a small sample set of shapes of a given object, to propose novel shapes. The evaluation of their proposed methods revealed that it could be used by trained designers as well as non-designers to support the design process in different phases and that it could lead to novel designs not intended or foreseen by designers.

10   Authentication of Art: Assessing the Performance of a Machine Learning Based Authentication Method

(Chen et al. 2020)

In "Authentication of Art: assessing the performance of a machine learning based authentication method" the co-authors Ailin Chen, Rui Jesus and Márcia Vilarigues, all from Lisbon, Portugal, compared test results generated by applying their bespoke method in questioning authentication of paintings by Portuguese artist Amadeo de Souza Cardoso in the interest of exploring the generalisation properties of the implemented algorithm on other artists or genres. The foundation of establishing the baseline base for the method was shared to subsequently be improved and developed accordingly in future applications for a broader audience in a wider setting. Outcomes from the work show that the classifier obtained from the algorithm using paintings appears not to be directly applicable to drawings of the same artist: Also, when the classifier is retrained for a different genre like Chinese paintings or artists such as van Gogh, the algorithm appears to perform as well as the classifier on Amadeo paintings, thus, a conclusion being that the algorithm/method is sufficient for the classification of a specific type of artist or genre.

11 "What I See Is What You Get" Explorations of Live Artwork Generation, Artificial Intelligence, and Human Interaction in a Pedagogical Environment

(Herruzo and Pashenkov 2020)

"What I See Is What You Get" - Explorations of live artwork generation, artificial intelligence, and human interaction in a pedagogical environment is title of the research by co-authors Ana Herruzo and Nikita Pashenkov. This content reviews the overall process for the design, development, and deployment of "What I See Is What You Get", an experiential installation that creates live interactive visuals, by analysing human facial expressions and behaviours, accompanied by text generated using Machine Learning algorithms trained on the art collection of The J. Paul Getty Museum in Los Angeles. The project was developed by students and faculty in an academic environment and exhibited at the Getty Museum. The authors inform of their research of the pedagogical process implemented to address the curriculum's learning outcomes in an "applied" environment while designing a contemporary new media art piece. The contribution shares how special attention was paid to the level and quality of the interaction between users and the piece, demonstrating how advances in technology and computing such as Deep Learning and Natural Language Processing can contribute to deeper connections and new layers of interactivity.

Epilogue and Acknowledgements. This second section introduces ten contributions by extracting from each paper. It does so to promote readership of each full paper that are presented in the following chapters. In doing so the authors of this chapter acknowledge the contribution to this section/volume by each author whose original work was presented in the ArtsIT/DLI events in Aalborg, Denmark November 7–8, 2019.

References

Arleth, L., Damkjær, E.L., Knoche, H.: "But wait, there's more!" a deeper look into temporally placing touch gesture signifiers. In: Brooks, A., Brooks, E. (eds.) ArtsIT 2019/DLI 2019. LNICST, vol. 328, pp. 290–308. Springer (2020)

Chen, A., Jesus, R., Vilarigues, M.: Authentication of art: assessing the performance of a machine learning based authentication method. In: Brooks, A., Brooks, E. (eds.) ArtsIT 2019/DLI 2019. LNICST, vol. 328, pp. 328–342. Springer (2020)

German, K., Limm, M., Wölfel, M., Helmerdig, S.: Co-designing object shapes with artificial intelligence. In: Brooks, A., Brooks, E. (eds.) ArtsIT 2019/DLI 2019. LNICST, vol. 328, pp. 309–327. Springer, Cham (2020)

Hepperle, D., Siess, A., Wölfel, M.: Staging virtual reality exhibits for bystander involvement in semi-public spaces. In: Brooks, A., Brooks, E. (eds.) ArtsIT 2019/DLI 2019. LNICST, vol. 328, pp. 261–272. Springer (2020)

Herruzo, A., Pashenkov, N.: "What i see is what you get" - explorations of live artwork generation, artificial intelligence, and human interaction in a pedagogical environment. In: Brooks, A., Brooks, E. (eds.) ArtsIT 2019/DLI 2019. LNICST, vol. 328, pp. 343–359. Springer (2020)

Koltai, B.G., Husted, J.E., Vangsted, R., Mikkelsen, T.N., Kraus, M.: Procedurally generated self overlapping mazes in virtual reality. In: Brooks, A., Brooks, E. (eds.) ArtsIT 2019/DLI 2019. LNICST, vol. 328, pp. 229–243. Springer (2020)

Kristensen, J.W., Aafeldt, L.L., Jensen, P.K., Vinther, R.P., Knoche, H.: Renoir in VR: Comparing the relaxation from artworks inside and outside of virtual reality. In: Brooks, A., Brooks, E. (eds.) ArtsIT 2019/DLI 2019. LNICST, vol. 328, pp. 217–228. Springer (2020)

Lancel, K., Maat, H., Brazier, F.: Hosting social touch in public space of merging realities. In: Brooks, A., Brooks, E. (eds.) ArtsIT 2019/DLI 2019. LNICST, vol. 328, pp. 202–216. Springer (2020)

Neerdal, J., Hansen, T., Hansen, N., Bonita, K.L., Kraus, M.: Navigating procedurally generated overt self-overlapping environments in VR. In: Brooks, A., Brooks, E. (eds.) ArtsIT 2019/DLI 2019. LNICST, vol. 328, pp. 244–260. Springer (2020)

Nijholt, A.: Playful and humorous interactions in urban environments made possible with augmented reality technology. In: Brooks, A., Brooks, E. (eds.) ArtsIT 2019/DLI 2019. LNICST, vol. 328, pp. 273–289. Springer (2020)

Hosting Social Touch in Public Space of Merging Realities

Karen Lancel[1,2(✉)], Hermen Maat[2], and Frances Brazier[1]

[1] Delft University of Technology, Delft, The Netherlands
lancel@xs4all.nl
[2] Artists duo Lancel/Maat, Amsterdam, The Netherlands

Abstract. Is human hosting essential to social touch in the public space of merging realities? This paper explores the role of hosting in art and design for mediating social touch in public space, social robotics, virtual reality and tele-matic environments. The question of whether human hosting is essential to social touch was the focus of three experiments held during performance of artistic orchestrations designed for social touch in public space for which the effects of different hosting designs have been analyzed. These internationally presented orchestrations, Saving Face (2012) and Master Touch (2013), purposefully disrupt and re-orchestrate multi-sensory connections in unfamiliar and unpredictable ways, to evoke shared reflection and shared sense making in public space, mediated by a host.

Saving Face was orchestrated internationally in museums, urban public spaces and theatres, including; 56th Venice Biennale 2015; Connecting Cities Network Ber-lin/Dessau 2013; 3th TASIE Art-Science exhibition, Science & Technology Museum Beijing 2013; Beijing Culture & Art Center BCAC 2015-2016. Master Touch was orchestrated at Rijksmuseum Amsterdam 2013. This paper extends the multi-sensory interaction model for social touch described in (Lancel et al. 2019e) to explicitly include the role of a host. The question this paper addresses is whether the host needs to be human.

This paper calls for future design of disrupted social touch in merging realities to consider hosting processes of shared sense making. Such design should facilitate new forms of reciprocal embodied interaction, that support descriptive self-disclosure, dialogue and shared reflection on experience of social touch in merging realities.

Keywords: Shared experience of social touch · Engagement · Digital performance art orchestration · Social context · Public space · Merging realities · Hosting · Social & multi-sensory model for interaction · Immersive · Design of disruption

1 Introduction

Is human hosting essential to social touch in the public space of merging realities? As the options technology provides increase so does the importance of this question. To which extent does hosting need to be included in mediated social, communication

A. Brooks and E. I. Brooks (Eds.): ArtsIT 2019/DLI 2019, LNICST 328, pp. 202–216, 2020.
https://doi.org/10.1007/978-3-030-53294-9_14

design for social touch, for social robotics and tele-matic environments? Is co-location of importance? Does hosting need to be performed by a human being?

This paper extends the multi-sensory interaction model for social touch described in (Lancel et al. 2019e) to explicitly include the role of a host. The question this paper addresses is whether the host needs to be human.

The question of whether **human** hosting is essential to social touch was the focus of three experiments held during performance of artistic orchestrations designed for social touch in public space for which the effects of different hosting designs have been analysed. These orchestrations, Saving Face (2012) and Master Touch (2013)[1], purposefully disrupt and re-orchestrate multi-sensory connections in unfamiliar and unpredictable ways, to evoke shared reflection and shared sense making in public space in different countries, mediated by a host. In these artistic orchestrations, in which members of the public touch themselves or each other, familiar perceptions, of who touches, who is being touched, are disrupted and re-orchestrated into new multi-sensory syntheses. Specifically, this paper explores whether performer-based hosting can be replaced by participant-based hosting. These orchestrations provide the experimental setting in which effects of design choices are analysed and compared, extending previous results reported in (Lancel et al. 2019a, 2019b).

2 Related Work

This paper addresses the role of hosting for shared sense making in social touch, based on purposefully disrupted sensory input in the public space of merging realities. Social touch (or 'interpersonal' touch'), affective gestures of touching another (Huisman 2017, pp. 397–399), are currently explored in remote and prosthetic interfaces (Lancel et al. 2019e). Influence of other senses on the experience of touch with multi-modal interfaces are currently researched and designed. (Huisman 2017). Appreciation, sense making and clarification of the meaning of social touch are clearly social context dependent (Erp and Toet 2015, Wang et al. 2012)[2], mandating purposeful design to this purpose. These research perspectives dominantly focus on the users' perceptual experience of 'direct' social touch, that is seemingly not disrupted (Lancel et al. 2019e, p. 23), as 'a perceptual illusion of non-mediation' (Lombard and Ditton 1997). For example, in social touch in mediated environments for sexual experience (Lombard and Jones 2013), interacting participants adapt multi-modal types of sensory input and stimulations for

---

[1] Saving Face was orchestrated internationally in museums, urban public spaces and theatres, including; 56th Venice Biennale 2015; Connecting Cities Network Berlin/Dessau 2013; 3th TASIE Art-Science exhibition, Science & Technology Museum Beijing 2013; Beijing Culture&Art Center BCAC 2015–2016. Master Touch was orchestrated at Rijksmuseum Amsterdam 2013.

[2] Wang for example describes experiments in which stories are shared between a story teller and a distant listener. It was shown that touching the listener on 'emotional high points' in the story, enhanced the listener's emotionally connection 'with the emotional view point of the story-teller'.

different levels of feeling intimately connected (Lombard and Jones 2013, p. 28).[3,4,5] Interactive, simultaneous and reciprocal communication is orchestrated to substitute face-to-face sense making and negotiation has shown to emerge from direct social touch and proximate sexuality (Lombard and Jones 2013, p. 33). However, critical research has addressed the limited 'social richness' of such social touch, claiming that meaningful shared intimate experience of touch, vital to human well-being, emerges from descriptive self-disclosure and proximity to a reliable alliance (Lamonovska and Guitton 2016, Lombard and Jones 2013, p. 37).

Shared practice of sense making and reflection have been explored in domains of Design and Art. In the domain of critical design, reflection on social connections is the goal of shared practice of play, playing and seeing each other play, through actions, settings, (social) contexts and experience, in dynamic relations (Cermak-Sassenrath 2018). Strategies[6] for such shared reflection and sense making through play include a) involving users in open ended meaning-making and interpretation processes; b) providing feedback to users for reflection, as part of the design and c) disrupting familiar relations of perception.

In the domains of both Art and Design, disruption, unfamiliarity and ambiguity are purposefully designed to provoke play, engagement, reflection (Kwastek 2013) and sense making.

In digital haptic performance art, visual, haptic and auditory relations are designed for new digital synaesthetic syntheses (Gsölpointner et al. 2016) for immersion and reflection to emerge. Seeing someone being touched is explored to evoke spectators' vicarious experience. (Kwastek 2013)[7]. Designs for embodied spectatorship have shown to be able to successfully resonate social empathy and connectedness (Freedberg and Gallese 2007; Martin 2018; Ward 2018). Often, in such new haptic syntheses, social sense making is provoked through corporal vulnerability of an artists' body, as an embodied 'relational interface' (Gill 2015). Participants are challenged to consider approaching, touching or even physically abusing an artist/performer. Unfamiliarity and exposure, of embodied behavior, corporal vulnerability and shared responsibility, are purposefully

---

[3] Interaction is explored in direct (f.e. through prosthetics) and indirect corporeal interaction (between actors and spectators), or in combination.

[4] Examples of interaction design aiming at supporting 'a perceptual illusion of non-mediation' of touch can be found in different applications for (combined) virtual and augmented realities and robotics, for gaming design, art, entertainment, training, therapy, sex, gaming, robotics (Erp and Toet 2015, Huisman 2017, Lancel et al. 2019d).

[5] Patented artificial skin compositions attempting to evoke experience of presence in the form of perceptual realism, include Cyberskin, Futurotic. http://www.sextoyspro.com/cyberskin.shtml, last accessed 2019/9/25.

[6] These design strategies, for example in 'critical design', 'reflective design', 'ludic design', are applied to evoke gaining critical insight in (implicit) value systems, educational purposes, change and transformation and for experience of joyful play.

[7] Related to this research, in the domain of neurology, mirror neuron activity of touch is considered to enhance empathy (Ward 2018). In specific cases of 'mirror touch synaesthesia', precarious touch experience is perceived stronger if the spectators' neurological systems show 'lower thresholds' (Ward 2018, Martin 2018).

designed to re-negotiate such social values and to engaging reflection on shared and personal experience (Benford et al. 2012, Lancel et al. 2019c).

Design of hosting, for mediating social connections, can be found in television talk shows. Such talk show hosts visually embody mediation between a) participating guests and audience who are present in the television studio and b) the television studio and audience in their private homes. The host engages and exposes processes of sense-making, through stimulating guests to make personal and intimate stories explicit, within conventions of debate, romance or therapy (Livingstone and Lunt 2002). Design of hosting in public space of merging realities, for mediating social touch for participants in interplay with each other, has been explored in digital performance art (Lancel et al. 2019a, 2019b, 2019c, 2019d). In different trajectories of 'intimate aesthetics' (Loke and Khut 2014), in their artistic orchestrations, Lancel and Maat include hosting, to 1) introduce the orchestration and guiding participants through performance and 2) ensure social and corporal safety and 3) exposing dialogue that facilitates sense making and shared reflection through descriptive self-disclosure in proximity to others.

Artistic orchestrations by Lancel/Maat (2000–2019) show that demanded social context, for sense making and clarifying meaning of social touch in public spaces, can be performed by such role of hosting (Lancel et al. 2019a, 2019b, 2019c, 2019d).

The model this paper presents, extends interaction model for social touch (Lancel et al. 2019e). This model includes multi-sensory and vulnerable aspects of social touch performed by participants, such as of kissing or (self-caressing). The model here presented completes this model with the role of the host.

3   Artistic Motivation

In their artistic performances, Lancel and Maat (Lancel/Maat 2000–2019) orchestrate novel affective, haptic connections between participants, members of the public space of mixed and merging realities. Their orchestrations relate individual participants to others in digitally distributed environments in public space. Members of the public space either participate as 'Actors'[8] or 'Spectators' and can choose to perform one or both roles over time.

In each orchestration, Actors touch each other or themselves, and are observed by Spectators. The acts of reciprocal touching are perceived both directly and indirectly. Indirect interaction is purposefully disrupted. The unfamiliarity and ambiguity between the different sources of sensory input are designed to evoke re-negotiation and reflection on both the individual and shared embodied experience of social touch.

In a multitude of artistic orchestrations, Lancel and Maat have explored on a) the basis of self-touch, via face recognition technologies in a mirror screen (experiments 1 and 2 of orchestration Saving Face (2012) (Figs. 4 and 5); b) self-touch, in a smart textile body covering veil (Tele-Trust 2009) and c) kissing each other, while wearing EEG headsets (EEG KISS 2014). Unfamiliar and unpredictable relations to vulnerability of reciprocal

---

[8] Instead of referring to the notion of *performance* as a form of 'role-playing', *performativity* (Butler 1990) is, in this context, considered to be a repetitive act designed for public spaces, to share reflection on social engagement.

touch, such as of kissing and caressing, are orchestrated to evoke re-negotiation and reflection on both individual and shared experience.

Dialogue with the host[9] is designed to evoke reflection and sense making, in descriptive self-disclosure in proximity to others. The role of host in Lancel/Maat's orchestrations, is mediating direct and disrupted experience, of social touch characterised in these orchestrations by intimacy and exposure, vulnerability and responsibility, familiarity and unfamiliarity. The host is, in fact, part of the social context, for sense making and clarifying meaning of social touch experience in public spaces, in the artistic orchestrations this paper explores.

The performance host is responsible for:

1) introducing, contextualizing the orchestration with rules of play, guiding participants through the performance;
2) ensuring social and corporal safety;
3) evoking dialogue, to encourage participants to express and share their experience in words with the host and with each other– making their embodied experience explicit.

The embodied performance of hosting enables dialogue based on embodied, emphatic reciprocity. Participants creatively explore new words, expressing new images and emotions to describe the unfamiliar visual-haptic experience of *caressing-and-feeling-caressed* intertwined with visually emerging on screen shared with others. They explicitly reflect on their embodied experience, they take time and wonder, they try to find new images and words and express emotions while often reacting in surprise to their words (Lancel et al. 2019b). Participants express their experiences of social, corporal connections, for example "This a technological but sensitive me" and "I feel merged with other people". (Lancel et al. 2019a, 2019b; Lancel/Maat 2012, 2013).

4   A Multi-sensory Model and Social Context, for Disrupted Hosted Social Touch Experience

Direct social touch entails a multi-sensory synthesis of reciprocal connections, including tactile, audible and visual connections, as shown in Fig. 1. Disrupted social touch, in which tactile, audible and visual connections are disrupted, have been subject to research in orchestrations in public spaces of merging realities, for which an interaction model was presented in (Lancel et al. 2019e), as shown in Fig. 2. This section introduces a multi-sensory model for social touch interaction including a host (Fig. 3).

4.1   Disruption of Social Touch Experience in Amulti-Sensory Model

The multi-sensory model (Fig. 2) includes variables for direct and disrupted connections that support experience and engagement for reflection of social touch orchestrations. In these orchestrations, participants relate to others on electronic screens through mirroring

---

[9] In the orchestrations by Lancel and Maat, interaction by the performance hosts is performed by the artists themselves, trained volunteers or fellow workers.

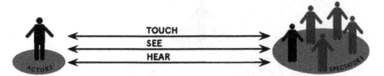

Fig. 1. Direct social touch (Lancel et al. 2019e).

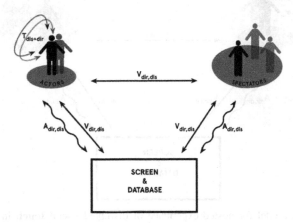

Fig. 2. Interaction model for disrupted social touch. (Lancel et al. 2019e).

self-touch as a form of socially relating touch (Lancel/Maat 2000–2019), through unique syntheses of ambiguous **direct (dir)** and **disrupted (dis)**, multi-sensory connections. In each orchestration, direct touch is replaced by combinations of (self-)touch, visual and auditory connections, direct and disrupted, between Actors and Spectators. Participants' touching actions must be synchronized in relation to a data-visualization on screen or data-audification. All data representations are stored in databases, accessible to all participants.

4.2 Disruption of Social Touch in a Multi-sensory Model Including a Host

The model for multi-sensory interaction in Fig. 2 does not yet include interaction with a host. In the interaction described, performance of touch is exposed and hosted through dialogue, to direct all participants' attention to focus on their affective and embodied experience. The model depicted in Fig. 6 explicitly includes performance hosting in **direct (dir)** visible audible and touch interaction with all participants. The question whether these connections need to be direct, visible and audible, performed by a human host, is explored in Sect. 5.3.

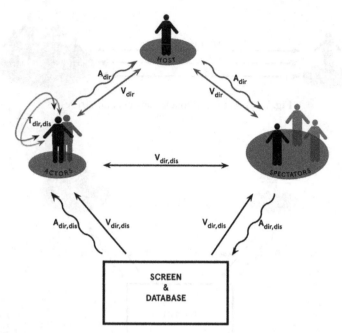

Fig. 3. Interaction model for hosted experience of disrupted **social touch** in public space of merging realities.

5   Research Setting

Different artistic orchestrations, in different cultural and geographical contexts by Lancel/Maat (Lancel/Maat 2000–2019), have explored the implications of different interaction designs in which a performance host fulfils the role described above. In these orchestrations, the performance host has shown to be able to successfully evoke and mediate dialogue with participants mandating reflection and shared sense making of their embodied experience (Lancel et al. 2019a, 2019b, 2019c, 2019d).

The question of whether **human** hosting is essential to social touch was the focus of three experiments with the Saving Face and Master Touch orchestrations for which the effects of different hosting designs have been analysed.

5.1   Research Context

In addition to experience of social touch gained in artistic orchestrations with a human host, e.g. Saving Face (2012), Tele_Trust (2009), EEG KISS (2014) (Lancel/Maat 2000–2019), the implications of interface design without a human host are explored in Saving Face and Master Touch.

Saving Face (2012) is an artistic orchestration in which participants are invited to caress their faces in front of an interactive sculpture. This interactive sculpture (equipped with cameras and face recognition technology) is connected to a large electronic public screen in the public space. Actors 'paint' their portraits on the public screen, where they first appear slowly and then slowly merge with the portraits of previous visitors into new, unpredictable and untraceable networked 'identities', which Lancel and Maat call Virtual Personae. Each Virtual Persona is saved digitally, to be shown later in an auto play mode on the electronic screen.

Master Touch (2013) is very similar to Saving Face. The difference between Saving Face and Master Touch is that in Master Touch, participants' faces appear and merge slowly with portraits of the digital portrait collection of the Rijksmuseum in Amsterdam, for example with a portrait of Rembrandt or Van Gogh, instead of with portraits of other participants from the public.[10]

5.2 Research Method

Research through design (Zimmerman and Forlizzi 2014) is the methodology deployed to explore interface design choices on the experience of shared social touch. Three sources of information are analysed: 1) observations (by the hosts) of participants' actions and reactions; 2) thick descriptions of open ended interviews with participants; 3) photo and short video documentation that support these observations, when available.

5.3 Three Experimental Orchestrations

The first experiment (2013)[11] explored whether hosting could be replaced by a demonstration video, showing the interaction play rules and showing people while participating and being in dialogue with each other. This experiment took place during a performance in Berlin-Dessau (Lancel et al. 2019a, 2019b) at a crowded festival. Many people of different ages, cultural and geographical backgrounds and genders visited and participated in the orchestration, in either a hosted or non-hosted performance. In absence of the performance host, in the non-hosted performance, people watched both the demonstration video and performative acts by others on site, whilst the performance host observed.

The second experiment explored whether attention to affective and embodied experience could be enhanced by means of other than a human host. In addition to the demonstration video, large printed texts were used to introduce the social context of the orchestration and rules of play. This experiment took place in Beijing[12] (Lancel et al. 2019b), in a museum, in a space with a large window facing the street. The large printed texts on the walls were visible from outside, through the window on the street, and, from inside as text on the walls.[13] Again, participants' autonomous interaction took place while the performance host observed from a distance.

---

[10] The Rijksmuseum Amsterdam collection of digitized portraits can be found on: https://www.rij ksmuseum.nl/en/search?q=portraits&ii=0&p=1, last accessed 2019/9/25.

[11] In Berlin-Dessau, the Saving Face orchestration was performed during two days at festival Connecting Cities Network, curated by Public art Lab Berlin, September 2013. http://connectin gcities.net/project/saving-face, last accessed 2019/9/25.

[12] In Beijing, the Saving Face orchestration was performed at Beijing Culture and Art Centre (BCAC), for a period of 10 days during December 2015–January 2016. Due to success, the period was prolonged with a month.

[13] These texts also functioned to solve disrupted communication due to a language-barrier.

Fig. 4. Experiment 1 of orchestration Saving Face during 'Connecting Cities Network' at Dessau/Berlin, showing participants exploring the interactive sculpture. A video documentation device is built in the back side of the aluminium sculpture, an interactive screen at the front side. Participants exploring Image by Ruthe Zunz. © Lancel/Maat 2013.

Fig. 5. Experiment 2: Orchestration of Saving Face at Beijing Culture and Art Center Beijing, showing addition of large printed texts and a participant exploring. Image by Lancel/Maat, © Lancel/Maat 2015.

The third experiment explored whether hosted dialogue could be replaced by questionnaires. This experiment took place in the orchestration 'Master Touch' (2013)[14], at the Rijksmuseum in Amsterdam. In this orchestration, questionnaires were introduced,

---

[14] Master Touch was performed at Rijksmuseum Amsterdam at both the Jubilee Night of the Rijksstudio (responsible for digitizing the portrait collection) and the Museum Night, November 2013.

Fig. 6. Experiment 3, Orchestration of Master Touch at Rijksmuseum Amsterdam; showing people exploring the orchestration and the questionnaires. Image by Lancel/Maat © Lancel/Maat 2013.

to replace the role of hosting evoking dialogue among participants. Open questions, that are normally asked by a human host in the performances, were printed and placed on tables close to the participants. These questionnaires included the questions: 'Is this your portrait on the screen and why (not)? How does it feel to become visible on the screen through caressing your face? Are you part of a machine in Master Touch? What is the difference between watching a painting from a distance and watching through touching?

5.4 Results

The experiments, of Saving Face in Dessau (2013) and Beijing (2015) and of Master Touch (2013), showed that aspects of human hosting by a performance host on site can be replaced partially by participant hosting.

In the first experiment of orchestration Saving Face (2012), as reported in (Lancel et al. 2019b), the host observed that participants 1) helped and showed each other how to participate throughout the performance, while 2) guarding each other's embodied safety. The host observed that participation shifted from concentrated and haptic exploration to making funny faces, exploring possibilities and limitations of the face recognition software and exposure of their faces. After having participated in the haptic interface, often, 3) the participants' dialogue among each other focussed on experience of 'fun' 'surprise' and 'wonder', while pointing at the portrait on screen. Sometimes, participants then asked the performance host questions about the unpredictable technological and seemingly 'magical' (Reeves 2005) interaction. This is different from hosted experiments, in which dialogue more often focusses on shared engagement in sense making and reflection, as has been reported in (Lancel et al. 2019a, 2019b).

In the second experiment of orchestration Saving Face (2015), as reported in (Lancel et al. 2019b), the performance host observed that, in comparison to the first experiment, people were less disrupted and more focussed than in the first experiment. They 1) watched the demonstration video and read the texts together, pointing at parts of these texts while interacting. In particular younger people participated in acts of caressing using the technological interface often in joint exploration, while socially gathering, laughing, stimulating and 2) guarding each other. During and after acts of touching, the host observed 3) participants being in dialogue while pointing at the screen and at their faces. The host then was sometimes approached to answer conceptual questions about context and societal meaning of the orchestration, in particular with respect to privacy. In the third experiment Master Touch (2013), participants filled in the questionnaires with one-word-answers and little dialogue took place between participants. After fifteen participants reacting in this way, the experiment was ended, after which one-to-one hosting was successfully based on the questionnaires.

These three experiments show that video documentation introducing rules of play and participation, added by large printed texts introducing both the rules of play and the social context of the orchestration, can partly replace human hosting. However, although participants can 1) autonomously use and play with the interface, they less focus on social context and less focus on performance of touch occurs. 2) Corporal and social safety are supported by co-participants who are, in this aspect, fulfilling a role of 'participant hosting'. 3) Although participants engage in dialogue during and after a performance, the type of dialogue differs. Participants are less inclined to take the time to reflect on the unfamiliar embodied experience and to express the unfamiliar embodied experiences in words, making the experience explicit, to discuss with others.

6 Discussion and Future Research

This paper addresses the role of hosting in current mediated social, communication design for social touch, for social robotics and tele-matic environments. Current social touch design is based on multi-sensory and multi modal environments that simulate experience of direct social touch. Furthermore, the context of social touch has shown to be crucial to appreciation, sense making and clarifying meaning of touch (Erp and Toet 2015, Wang et al. 2012). An existing multi-sensory interaction model for social touch (Lancel et al. 2019e) has been extended to include the role of a host. The model shows the required direct, embodied reciprocity between host and participants, but does not necessarily assume a **human** host. The paper explores the question: Is human hosting essential to social touch in the public space of merging realities? Multi-sensory orchestrations of social touch have been designed and performed in public spaces. In these orchestrations, shared sense making and reflection of social context and experience of embodiment through dialogue with a (human) performance host is explored (Lancel et al. 2019a, 2019b, 2019c, 2019d). In three experiments with the Saving Face (2012) and Master Touch (2013) orchestrations in Amsterdam, Berlin-Dessau and Beijing, the effects of different hosting designs have been explored and analysed.

This role of hosting provides social interaction of 1) introducing, contextualizing the orchestration; rules of play, guiding participants through performance of disrupted and unfamiliar forms of touch; 2) ensuring social and corporal safety; and 3) evoking dialogue, to express the experience in words – making the experience explicit in creative, embodied and reciprocal relation, through hosting on site. A performance host acts as an embodied interface, and dialogue with participants based on embodied, emphatic reciprocity.

All three experiments showed that human hosting seems to be essential. Furthermore, aspects of performance hosting can be replaced partially by participants hosting. Participants have shown to be able to 1) autonomously use and play with the orchestration, but less focus on context and performance of touch occurs, 2) support corporal and social safety as co-participants and in this aspect, fulfilling a role of 'participant hosting' and 3) engage in dialogue during and after a performance. The type of dialogue, however, differed. Participants were less inclined to take the time to reflect on the unfamiliar embodied experience and to express the unfamiliar embodied experiences in words, making the experience explicit, to discuss with others.

Current research building on the results presented in this paper, explore other design options for participant (self-) hosting to embrace embodied and empathic mirroring, through dialogue and reflection. These new artistic orchestrations facilitate tele-matic experience of kissing, in New York, Los Angeles, Amsterdam and Seoul in 2020. These orchestrations explore possibilities for participant hosting in communities. This paper calls for future design of disrupted social touch in merging realities to consider hosting processes of shared sense making to be part of the design. Such design should facilitate new forms of reciprocal embodied interaction, that support descriptive self-disclosure, dialogue and shared reflection on experience of social touch in merging realities.

Acknowledgements. The authors wish to thank Prof. J. Van Erp and Dr. G. Huisman for discussions and Prof. Dr. M. Nevejan for earlier contributions. This paper is based on a decade of artistic

and scientific research and artistic performances. The authors are grateful to all of those who have contributed to this work, mentioned on the websites relating to each orchestration. Please see:
    Lancel/Maat (2000–2019), https://www.lancelmaat.nl/work/;
    Lancel/Maat (2009) Tele_Trust, http://www.lancelmaat.nl/work/tele-trust/;
    Lancel/Maat (2012) Saving Face, http://lancelmaat.nl/work/saving-face/;
    Lancel/Maat (2014) EEG KISS, http://www.lancelmaat.nl/work/e.e.g.-kiss/.

References

Benford, S., Greenhalgh, C., Giannachi, G., Walker, B., Marshall, J., Rodden, T.: Uncomfortable interactions. In: Proceedings of the SIGCHI Conference on Human Factors in Computing Systems, pp. 2005–2014. ACM, May 2012

Butler, J.: Gender Trouble, Feminism and the Subversion of Identity. Routledge, New York (1990)

Cermak-Sassenrath, D. (ed.): Playful Disruption of Digital Media. GMSE. Springer, Singapore (2018). https://doi.org/10.1007/978-981-10-1891-6

Van Erp, J.B.F., Toet, A.: Social touch in human–computer interaction. Front. Digit. Humanit. **2**(2) (2015)

Freedberg, D., Gallese, V.: Motion, emotion and empathy in aesthetic experience. Trends Cogn. Sci. **11**(5), 197–203 (2007)

Gill, S.P.: Tacit Engagement. Springer, Cham (2015). https://doi.org/10.1007/978-3-319-21620-1

Gsöllpointner, K., Schnell, R., Schuler, R.K. (eds.): Digital Synaesthesia: A Model for the Aesthetics of Digital Art. Walter de Gruyter GmbH & Co KG, Berlin (2016)

Kwastek, K.: Aesthetics of Interaction in Digital Art. MIT Press, Cambridge (2013)

Huisman, G.: Social touch technology: a survey of haptic technology for social touch. IEEE Trans. Haptics **10**(3), 391–408 (2017)

Lancel, K., Maat, H., Brazier, F.: Saving face: playful design for social engagement, in public smart city spaces. In: Brooks, A.L., Brooks, E., Sylla, C. (eds.) ArtsIT/DLI -2018. LNICST, vol. 265, pp. 296–305. Springer, Cham (2019a). https://doi.org/10.1007/978-3-030-06134-0_34

Lancel, K., Maat, H., Brazier, F.: Saving face: shared experience and dialogue on social touch, in playful smart public space. In: Nijholt, A. (ed.) Making Smart Cities More Playable. GMSE, pp. 179–203. Springer, Singapore (2019b). https://doi.org/10.1007/978-981-13-9765-3_9

Lancel, K., Maat, H., Brazier, F.M.: Kissing data, distributed haptic connections through social touch. In: Acoustic Space Volume No 17. Riga's Center for New Media Culture RIXC, Art Research Laboratory of Liepaja University (2019c)

Lancel, K., Maat, H., Brazier, F.: EEG KISS: shared multi-modal, multi brain computer interface experience, in public space. In: Nijholt, A. (ed.) Brain Art, pp. 207–228. Springer, Cham (2019d). https://doi.org/10.1007/978-3-030-14323-7_7

Lancel, K., Maat, H., Brazier, F.M.: Designing disruption for social touch, in public spaces of merging realities: a multi-sensory model. Int. J. Arts Technol. 12, 18–38 (2019e). Special Issue: ArtsIT 2018 Arts and Technology

Lancel/Maat (2000–2019). http://www.lancelmaat.nl/work/. Accessed 25 Sept 2019

Lancel/Maat: Tele_Trust (2009). http://www.lancelmaat.nl/work/tele-trust/. Accessed 25 Sept 2019

Lancel/Maat: Saving Face (2012). http://lancelmaat.nl/work/saving-face/. Accessed 25 Sept 2019

Lancel/Maat: Master Touch 2013 (2013). http://www.lancelmaat.nl/work/master-touch/. Accessed 25 Sept 2019

Lancel/Maat: EEG KISS (2014). http://www.lancelmaat.nl/work/e.e.g-kiss/. Accessed 25 Sept 2019

Livingstone, S., Lunt, P.: Talk on Television: Audience Participation and Public Debate. Routledge, London (2002)

Loke, L., Khut, G.P.: Intimate aesthetics and facilitated interaction. In: Candy, L., Ferguson, S. (eds.) Interactive Experience in the Digital Age. SSCC, pp. 91–108. Springer, Cham (2014). https://doi.org/10.1007/978-3-319-04510-8_7

Lomanowska, A.M., Guitton, M.J.: Online intimacy and well-being in the digital age. Internet Interv. **4**(Part 2), 138–144 (2016)

Lombard, M., Ditton, T.: At the heart of it all: the concept of presence. J. Comput.-Mediat. Commun. **3**(2), JCMC321 (1997)

Lombard, M., Jones, M.T.: Telepresence and sexuality: a review and a call to scholars. Hum. Technol. Interdiscip. J. Hum. ICT Environ. **9**, 22–55 (2013)

Martin, D. (ed.): Mirror-Touch Synaesthesia: Thresholds of Empathy with Art. Oxford University Press, Oxford (2018)

Reeves, S., Benford, S., O'Malley, C., Fraser, M.: Designing the spectator experience. In: CHI 2005 Proceedings of the SIGCHI Conference on Human Factors in Computing Systems, pp. 741–750. ACM, New York (2005)

Wang, R., Quek, F., Tatar, D., Teh, J.K.S., Cheok, A.D.: Keep in touch: channel, expectation and experience. In: CHI 2012, 30th ACM Conference on Human Factors in Computing Systems (2012)

Ward, J.: The vicarious perception of touch and pain: embodied empathy. In: Martin, D. (ed.) Mirror Touch Synaesthesia. Thresholds of Empathy with Art, pp. 55–70. Oxford University Press, Oxford (2018)

Zimmerman, J., Forlizzi, J.: Research through design in HCI. In: Olson, J.S., Kellogg, W.A. (eds.) Ways of Knowing in HCI, pp. 167–189. Springer, New York (2014). https://doi.org/10.1007/978-1-4939-0378-8_8

Renoir in VR: Comparing the Relaxation from Artworks Inside and Outside of Virtual Reality

Johan Winther Kristensen$^{(\boxtimes)}$(iD), Lasse Lodberg Aafeldt, Peter Kejser Jensen,
Rebecca Pipaluk Vinther, and Hendrik Knoche(iD)

Aalborg University, Rendsburggade 14, 9000 Aalborg, Denmark
{jwkr,hk}@create.aau.dk,
{laafel13,pkje14,rtoft14}@student.aau.dk

Abstract. Looking at artworks, experiencing nature, and being in virtual reality (VR) environments can relax people. We tested if the relaxation from viewing art and nature images with music for ten minutes while sitting in a recliner chair in a VR setup is different from experiencing the same content on a TV screen. Participants experienced this relaxation intervention after having finished a Montreal Imaging Stress Test. All tested conditions relaxed people but we found no significant differences between them from neither subjective nor objective measures in a between subjects study. However, trends in subjective and HRV measures pointed towards VR being more relaxing than TV.

Keywords: Stress · Relaxation · Heart rate · Relaxation rating scale · Virtual reality · Visual distractions

1 Introduction

Stress is a serious health concern in modern society with physiological, cognitive, and behavioral consequences [18]. Hospitalized patients are particularly vulnerable and stress can result in extended recovery time for them post-surgery [17,29]. A number of activities such as meditation and breathing exercises can relax people. Other activities with potential relaxation benefits, which might also intrinsically motivate people to engage in them, include experiencing nature and artworks [22]. Immobile patients can rely on mediated experiences e.g. seeing nature through slide-shows on TV, which can be just as good at relaxing people as going into real nature [15]. Navigating in a VR nature scene has been shown to relax people more than viewing a slideshow in VR [30]. However, Anderson et al. [1] questioned the validity of the study due to the comparison of a large nature scene which people could walk around in and feel tactile feedback from movement to not moving around while looking at a slideshow of static abstract images. It was unclear whether it was the natural environment having a positive effect over the abstract images or whether increased immersion had a natural advantage for relaxing people.

© ICST Institute for Computer Sciences, Social Informatics and Telecommunications Engineering 2020
Published by Springer Nature Switzerland AG 2020. All Rights Reserved
A. Brooks and E. I. Brooks (Eds.): ArtsIT 2019/DLI 2019, LNICST 328, pp. 217–228, 2020.
https://doi.org/10.1007/978-3-030-53294-9_15

We devised a study to test whether VR induces higher relaxation when depicting relaxing images than depicting those same images on a standard TV screen after exposure to an artificial stressor. The study further investigated whether potential advantages of VR are due to the removal of extraneous visual distractions. To that end we compared both physiological data (heart rate and its variability) and self-reports from twenty-one participants. Participants experiencing art in VR tended to find this more relaxing than participants watching the same footage on a TV screen according to subjective measures.

2   Background

Stress can come from many different sources and result in many different effects. People suffering from stress may show reactions in a physiological-, physical-, and/or a behavioural manner [3,19]. Many studies have examined the effects of stress on the body [18] including in clinical settings where stress has been associated with longer recovery time post-surgery [29]. Higher cortisol levels, which are associated with stress, negatively impact memory and cognition [23].

Several methods for relaxing exist such as people experiencing nature environments, both real and virtual, as well as art [1,15,22,24,27,29]. Kjellgren et al. [15] compared the relaxing effect of experiencing real nature in a forest for 30 min and a slide show of forest images displayed on a TV screen, and found that the two environments were equally good at reducing stress. Nielsen et al. [22] investigated the relaxing effect of art in hospitals by comparing a hospital room over two weeks, with the room being without any art in one week and filled with art the other week. The study found that art "... *promotes an experience of enhanced quality and satisfaction among patients.*" [22].

Other studies relied on virtual nature environments in VR to relax people [16,24,30]. VR technologies immerse users through visuals and sound like other types of media, such as television or films. But the key feature that distinguishes VR from other types of media is the sense of presence it induces [31]. As advanced TV screens, VR can create the illusion of visual depth by providing an image for each eye with a slight offset from each other. VR systems achieve this through a head mounted display (HMD) [25]. More importantly, VR can provide interaction in the form of translating head and/or body movements in the real world to movements in the virtual environment. This activates the human sense of proprioception, since the virtual environment behaves as if the user was using six Degrees of Freedom (DOF) of movement in a real environment [13].

Previous VR studies aiming at relaxing people have immersed them in different nature setups lasting from three [24] to 15 min [1]. This included watching a rendered jellyfish in an underwater environment [27], a rendered 3D park scene [24], looking at rural Ireland [1] and a remote beach [1] both in 360° videos and compared this to e.g. an empty class room in 360° videos [1]. All of these studies had their participants seated and could move their heads to look around the scene. Only the study by Riva et al. allowed the participants to explore the VR environment by using a controller to move around [24]. The objective of the participants differed between the studies, ranged from simply visually exploring the environment [1] to do deep breathing exercises in pace with part of the environment [27]. Some studies employed comfortable chairs to further enhance the participants sense of presence [1,33] while others used swivel chairs to simplify looking around in the scene while sitting [24,31]. Most studies using technology to relax people were based in laboratories [1,15] or hospitals [22].

When evaluating stress or relaxation through interventions, studies relied on obtaining subjective and objective measures usually in comparison to a baseline. Subjective measures included the Perceived Stress Scale (PSS) [27], Positive and Negative Affect Schedule (PANAS) [1,24,27], and the Relaxation Rating scale (RRS) [27,33]. For the RRS, people rate their subjective relaxation on a Likert scale from 1 to 7, with 1 being *"Not Relaxed At All"* and 7 being *"Totally Relaxed"*. Common physiological measures of stress or relaxation have included breath rate [27], heart rate (HR) [6,8,30], heart rate variability (HRV) [1,27], cortisol [7], and electrodermal activity (EDA) [1,30].

In terms of Heart Rate Variability (HRV) and measuring relaxation, the measures used have depended on the duration of the experimental design [6]. Short-term experiments have lasted anywhere between two and 15 min [6,21], while long-term designs should last for at least 24 h [6]. HRV measures concerning relaxation for short-term designs exist both in the time and frequency domain. Recommended short-term time-domain measures are the percentage of consecutive NN intervals that differ by more than 50 ms (pNN50) and the square root of the mean square differences of successive NN intervals (r-MSSD) [6]. Recommended short-term frequency-domain measures are HF power and LF/HF ratio [6,20]. For frequency domain measures to yield valid data that can be analysed alone, a minimum of four minutes of heart rate data is required [6]. An increase in all the mentioned HRV measures, except for LF/HF and LF, indicate a relaxation response which is an increase in vagal tone of the parasympathetic nervous system meaning the body is entering a rest-and-digest state. An increase in LF/HF and LF instead indicates a stress response [28]. However, there are disputes over the validity of the LF/HF ratio as a measure of cardiac sympathovagal balance, the relationship between sympathetic nervous activity (fight-or-flight), linked to LF, and the parasympathetic (rest-and-digest), linked to HF. Some argue against it as a reliable measure [2], while others argue for its continued use [6].

Methods of inducing stress both inside and outside VR environments have included: the Golden Stroop [10], mental arithmetic tests [1,30], the Montreal Imaging Stress Task (MIST) [4], and the Trier Social Stress Test (TSST) [7,12,14]. Deep breathing constitutes one approach to induce relaxation. Deep breathing causes respiratory sinus arrhythmia (an increase in heart rate when inhaling and decreasing while exhaling) and in turn increases heart rate variability [26].

In summary, previous studies have found that using VR can help relax people in stressful situations [1,27]. But it remains unclear whether the immersion possible in VR relaxes people more than watching the same content on a standard TV screen.

3 Study

We developed three different relaxing interventions all of which showed a slideshow of images accompanied by music. The images included ten non-abstract artworks and ten nature photographs - each shown for 30 s.

During one intervention the slideshow was shown on a TV screen. On each side of the TV screen, we placed laptops as visual distractions. Each laptop played a list of videos consisting of either movie trailers or music videos. These laptop screens were positioned such that they were not the focus of the participant, but were still able to be seen. They were 90° apart, measured from the participant's head (see Fig. 2).

The other two interventions used VR to deliver the slideshow - with and without visual distractors. Both limited the participants field of view to 90° by using a plane with a transparent hole overlaid on the camera (*c.f.* Fig. 1b). One of the VR interventions replicated the visual distractions seen in the TV condition by placing one on each side of the big image (see Fig. 1b). We used the same trailer and music videos as in the TV condition. The other VR intervention featured no such distractions.

Procedure: The experiments took place in a quiet and isolated room. To keep out any uncontrollable distractions, blankets blocked the windows as seen in Fig. 1a. The participants sat in a soft, comfortable recliner chair for the entire duration of the experiment. For the VR condition a computer running the VR scene was used along with an HTC Vive HMD including lighthouses for tracking with 6-DOF.

After giving their consent, participants were fitted with a Polar H10 heart rate belt that captured the participants interbeat intervals, which were retrieved

(a) The setup of TV and visual distractor laptop screens. Equipment used for VR and a camera can also be seen.

(b) The VR scene. In the condition without distractors the two screens next to the paiting were missing

Fig. 1. The experiment setup.

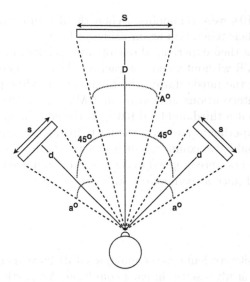

Fig. 2. The placement of main and distractor screens, both for VR and TV conditions

by Elite HRV [11] running on a smartphone. They were then seated in the chair. To obtain valid frequency domain HRV measures we recorded five minutes of baseline data before commencing with the experiment. See Fig. 3 for the full timeline of the experiment. After the baseline measurement the participants filled out an RRS to give their subjective relaxation.

As a stressor we decide on using the Montreal Imaging Stress Task, which can be seen in Fig. 4. In this test, the participants had to answer arithmetic problems as fast as possible to achieve as high a score as possible. They were told that they were able to see how well they were doing compared to the average person. When doing well participants would get less time for each problem resulting in a below average score. All participants completed this test in VR. We instructed the participants on the controls, and the facilitator informed the participant how much time was remaining during the stressor. This happened every minute

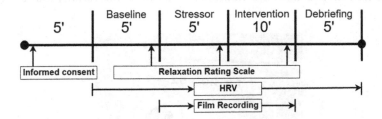

Fig. 3. Timeline of the procedure

and when 30 and 10 s were remaining. When the five minutes had passed, the participant rated their relaxation again using an RRS.

The participants then experienced one of three relaxation interventions: TV with, VR with, or VR without visual distraction. All participants wore over-the-ear headphones for the music during the intervention, while participants experiencing the VR interventions also wore an HMD. After the intervention, the participants filled out a third and final RRS. At the end the facilitator explained the nature of the experiment and gave the participants the opportunity to relax. The participants could give comments or just have a little chat. After a few minutes the measurements were stopped and the sensors removed. The participants received sweets and juice as compensation for their time.

3.1   Participants

Twenty-one university students (two female) aged 19–26 years old (mean age: 22) participated in the study - seven in each condition. All participants were asked if they had any medical conditions such as psychiatric, chronic, or neurological conditions or if they used any blood regulating medicine such as beta-blockers, since that would have caused them to be excluded due to possible impacts on HRV measures [1,24]. No participants were excluded based on these grounds.

4   Data Processing and Analysis

We checked the inter-beat intervals (IBI) for missing and extraneous heartbeats. Using the RHRV toolkit [9], we computed average measures of heart rate, pNN50, r-MSSD, HF power, and LF/HF ratio for each participant by episode (baseline, stressor, and intervention). This relied on a window size for time-domain calculations of 300 s, with the RHRV default bin width of 7.8125 ms. The frequency-domain Fourier transform used a window size of 100 s and a window shift of two seconds. For each condition, we inspected QQ-plots to check whether the aggregated physiological measures per condition of the participants were normally distributed.

We tested for significant differences between the interventions based on all obtained measures as absolute values as is (*absolute relaxation*) and as relative

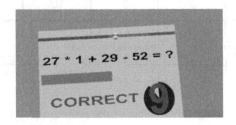

Fig. 4. A cropped screenshot of the MIST stressor

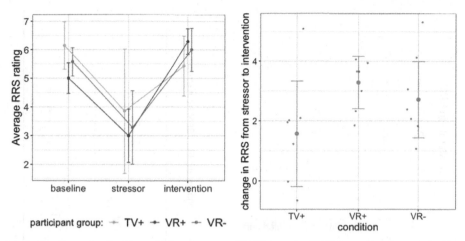

participant group: — TV+ — VR+ — VR-

(a) during the episodes by participant group (b) Change in RRS from the stressor to the
with 0.95 c.i. error bars   intervention (relative relaxation)

Fig. 5. Subjective relaxation results (RRS)

values computing the differences between the values during the stressor and
relaxation episodes (*relative relaxation*). We tested for significant differences
between the three condition, by running three pairwise tests with Bonferroni
corrections ($0.05/3 = 0.017$).

5   Results

Both VR interventions yielded a higher average relaxation rating than the TV
intervention, both in terms of absolute and relative relaxation (see Fig. 5). However, a Kruskal-Wallis rank sum test between the conditions found no significant
differences between the conditions - neither in absolute ($F(2) = 0.33$, $p = 0.85$)
nor relative relaxation ($F(2) = 4.61$, $p = 0.1$). While the differences were not
statistically different, the trend of the RRS averages in Fig. 5b showed that the
TV condition was less relaxing than the VR conditions. Remember that all
participants experienced the same baseline and stressor - only the relaxation
intervention differed.

Comparing the average HR of participants during the intervention with the
average HR during the stressor revealed a reduction during the intervention,
pointing towards a relaxing effect of all interventions (see Fig. 6). According to
t-tests the participants' heart rate was significantly lower during the intervention
than the stressor when comparing the absolute values for all three conditions at
the same time ($t(37) = -2.90$, $p = 0.01$). Post-hoc t-tests found that the only
condition for which the change in HR during the intervention compared to the
baseline was significantly different from zero was for VR- ($t(6) = -2.71$, $p =
0.02$). But ANOVAs comparing these changes in HR during the intervention

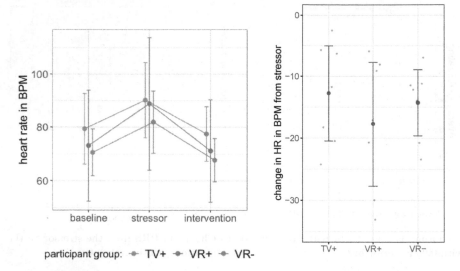

(a) by participant group with 0.95 confidence interval error bars

(b) Change in HR from the stressor with confidence intervals (red)

Fig. 6. Heart rate results

Table 1. All one-tailed p-values for the experiment, rounded to two decimals. P-values lower than 0.15 are marked with a star (*). The pairwise tests are: $I = VR+ > TV+$, $II = VR- > TV+$, $III = VR- > VR+$.

Condition	Absolute relaxation			Relative relaxation		
	I	II	III	I	II	III
r-MSSD	0.13*	0.95	0.98	0.40	0.27	0.36
LF/HF	0.064*	0.064*	0.355	0.519	0.684	0.742
HF	0.96	0.77	0.36	0.98	0.99	0.77

relative to the baseline (F(2) = 0.16, p = 0.86) and relative to the stressor (F(2) = 1.45, p = 0.26) episodes between the conditions found no significant differences between the conditions. So, the findings from the t-test and ANOVAs did not match.

Since some participants had zero values in pNN50 indicating a floor effect, we relied on the r-MSSD, LF/HF, and HF measures for the HRV analysis. QQ-plots showed that none of the measures (r-MSSD, LF/HF, and HF) were normally distributed and Mann-Whitney U tests were used to compare the three relaxation interventions pairwise. Table 1 shows the p-values for these tests. There were no significant differences, neither in absolute nor in relative relaxation for any of the HRV measures. However, the pairwise tests comparing LF/HF measures during VR+ with TV+ and VR- with TV+ were close to the 0.05 threshold for p (see

Table 1) indicating the tendency that both VR conditions were more relaxing than the TV condition.

6   Discussion

We found evidence from RRS and HR measures that all three interventions relaxed people in contrast to the stressor. We did not compare the interventions against the bodies natural relaxation by using a no-intervention control group and can therefore not say how much better the intervention is compared to not doing anything. However, this was not within the scope of our study. From studies by Anderson et al. [1] and de Kort et al. [16] showing that VR increased immersion, we hypothesized that experiencing art in VR would be more relaxing than on a TV. Surprisingly, we found no such significant differences between relaxation in VR and using a TV screen. But the trends from self-reports and heart rate changes both pointed in the expected direction of VR being more relaxing than the TV condition. Given the low number of participants (seven per condition) and the between subjects design this lack of significant result could be due to a lack of statistical power for the ANOVA tests. Close to significant differences in pairwise comparisons of HRV (see Table 1) added further evidence in this direction. However, these tendencies came mostly from the LF/HF ratio measure. Whether this represent a valid measure of sympathovagal balance remains a point of controversy.

We expected the distracting videos to leave the participants less relaxed from the art content, which did not turn out to be the case. For the experiment we used two video playlists of well-known movie trailers and music videos as visual distraction to determine if removing these via VR would have an influence on participants' relaxation. Human vision is better at spotting movement closer to the edges of the vision [32]. Therefore, we set the visual distractions close to the edge of the cone of vision rather than in the center. This resulted in 45° angles from the center of the slideshow to the center of the distractors. In VR, the FOV limiter prevented the participants from viewing the entirety of both distractor screens at the same time without moving their head. This limiting of the videos could make the videos less distracting in the VR condition as only parts of the video could be seen and therefore easier to ignore by participants, or potentially add to the distracting effect as being able to only see part of the video could be annoying. Although the differences between the conditions were not significant trends showed the participants who experienced these videos reported being more relaxed on the RRS on average than the participants who did not experience the distractors. This could be because these videos were familiar to the participants or that some participants found them relaxing.

Our study relied on an artificial stressor in a quiet environment, which might have resulted in participants being already very relaxed creating a ceiling effect, which did not allow for finding significant differences. Future studies, Using a real stressor, e.g. people who are genuinely stressed from worrying and situated in a stressful environment (such as a hospital) might be better suited at showing differences between the modes of delivery of art content. For example, in the TV condition people would still be exposed to the extraneous activities going on in the hospital. Such a future study would at the same time yield results with higher ecological validity than ours. To improve sensitivity researchers could consider measuring stress through measures other than heart rate and its variability. Cortisol levels, while expensive and cumbersome to measure, have been shown to be modulated by stress [5]. An option to increase immersion and potentially relaxation from the artworks, which are only shown for a limited amount of time, would be relying on animations such as the Ken Burns effect.

7   Conclusions

Subjective RRS responses and HRV measures showed that exposure to nature and art images accompanied by music for ten minutes helped people relax after doing mentally demanding arithmetics. Trends in heart rate variability measures, such as heart rate, and subjective self-reporting did point towards VR being more relaxing. But we found no significant difference between these conditions - possibly due to a lack of statistical power. However, if indeed there were no difference between these media option it would be good news for practitioners using such interventions. It would be sufficient to present this kind of footage on TV screens, which scale better for multiple viewers and do not require additional equipment and setup such as HMDs.

References

1. Anderson, A.P., Mayer, M.D., Fellows, A.M., Cowan, D.R., Hegel, M.T., Buckey, J.C.: Relaxation with immersive natural scenes presented using virtual reality. Aerosp. Med. Hum. Perf. **88**(6), 520–526 (2017)
2. Billman, G.E.: The LF/HF ratio does not accurately measure cardiac sympatho-vagal balance. Front. Physiol. **4** (2013). https://doi.org/10.3389/fphys.2013.00026
3. Cooper, C., Dewe, P., O'Driscoll, M.: What is stress? In: Organizational Stress: A Review and Critique of Theory, Research, and Applications, pp. 1–26. SAGE Publications Inc., Thousand Oaks (2001). https://doi.org/10.4135/9781452231235
4. Dedovic, K., Renwick, R., Mahani, N.K., Engert, V., Lupien, S.J., Pruessner, J.C.: The montreal imaging stress task: using functional imaging to investigate the effects of perceiving and processing psychosocial stress in the human brain. J. Psychiatry Neurosci. **30**(5), 319 (2005)
5. Dickerson, S.S., Kemeny, M.E.: Acute stressors and cortisol responses: a theoretical integration and synthesis of laboratory research. **130**, 355–391 (2004). https://doi.org/10.1037/0033-2909.130.3.355
6. Task Force of the European Society of Cardiology and the North American Society of Pacing and Electrophysiology: Heart rate variability. Circulation **93**(5), 1043–1065 (1996). https://doi.org/10.1161/01.CIR.93.5.1043
7. Fich, L.B., Jönsson, P., Kirkegaard, P.H., Wallergård, M., Garde, A.H., Hansen, R.: Can architectural design alter the physiological reaction to psychosocial stress? A virtual TSST experiment. Physiol. Behav. **135**, 91–97 (2014). https://doi.org/10.1016/j.physbeh.2014.05.034

8. Friedlander, L., Lumley, M.A., Farchione, T., Doyal, G.: Testing the alexithymia hypothesis: physiological and subjective responses during relaxation and stress. J. Nerv. Ment. Dis. **185**(4), 233–239 (1997)
9. García, C.A., Lado, M., Méndez, A., Otero, A., Rodríguez-Liñares, L., Vila, X.: The RHRV project. http://rhrv.r-forge.r-project.org/
10. Golden, C.: Stroop color and word test. In: Encyclopedia of Measurement and Statistics, p. 973. SAGE Publications Inc., Thousand Oaks (2007). https://doi.org/10.4135/9781412952644
11. Elite HRV: About Elite HRV (2018). https://elitehrv.com/about
12. Høngaard, J.S., Thomsen, A.M., Christensen, P.M.H.: A virtual reality implementation of the trier social stress test using head-mounted displays. Ph.D. thesis, Aablorg Universitet, Aalborg (2016)
13. Jonathan, S.: Defining virtual reality: dimensions determining telepresence. J. Commun. **42**(4), 73–93 (2006). https://doi.org/10.1111/j.1460-2466.1992.tb00812.x
14. Kirschbaum, C., Pirke, K.M., Hellhammer, D.H.: The 'trier social stress test'-a tool for investigating psychobiological stress responses in a laboratory setting. Neuropsychobiology **28**(1–2), 76–81 (1993)
15. Kjellgren, A., Buhrkall, H.: A comparison of the restorative effect of a natural environment with that of a simulated natural environment. J. Environ. Psychol. **30**(4), 464–472 (2010). https://doi.org/10.1016/j.jenvp.2010.01.011
16. de Kort, Y.A.W., Meijnders, A.L., Sponselee, A.A.G., IJsselsteijn, W.A.: What's wrong with virtual trees? Restoring from stress in a mediated environment. J. Environ. Psychol. **26**(4), 309–320 (2006). https://doi.org/10.1016/j.jenvp.2006.09.001
17. Linden, W.: Stress Management: From Basic Science to Better Practice. SAGE, Thousand Oaks (2004)
18. McCarthy, M.: Healthy design. Lancet **364**(9432), 405–406 (2004). https://doi.org/10.1016/S0140-6736(04)16787-1
19. McEwen, B.S., Karatsoreos, I.N.: What is stress? In: Chouker, A. (ed.) Stress Challenges and Immunity in Space, pp. 11–29. Springer, Heidelberg (2012). https://doi.org/10.1007/978-3-642-22272-6_3
20. Mietus, J.E., Goldberger, A.L.: Heart Rate Variability Analysis with the HRV Toolkit. https://physionet.org/tutorials/hrv-toolkit/
21. Myers, G.A., et al.: Power spectral analysis of heart rate varability in sudden cardiac death: comparison to other methods. IEEE Trans. Biomed. Eng. **213**(12), 1149–1156 (1986)
22. Nielsen, S.L., Fich, L.B., Roessler, K.K., Mullins, M.F.: How do patients actually experience and use art in hospitals? The significance of interaction: a user-oriented experimental case study. Int. J. Qual. Stud. Health Well-being **12**(1), 1267343 (2017). https://doi.org/10.1080/17482631.2016.1267343
23. Oei, N.Y.L., Everaerd, W.T.A.M., Elzinga, B.M., van Well, S., Bermond, B.: Psychosocial stress impairs working memory at high loads: an association with cortisol levels and memory retrieval. Stress **9**(3), 133–141 (2006). https://doi.org/10.1080/10253890600965773
24. Riva, G., et al.: Affective interactions using virtual reality: the link between presence and emotions. CyberPsychol. Behav. **10**(1), 45–56 (2007)
25. Schuemie, M.J., van der Straaten, P., Krijn, M., van der Mast, C.A.: Research on presence in virtual reality: a survey. CyberPsychol. Behav. **4**(2), 183–201 (2001). https://doi.org/10.1089/109493101300117884

26. Shields, R.W.: Heart rate variability with deep breathing as a clinical test of car-diovagal function. **76**(Suppl 2), 37–40 (2009). https://doi.org/10.3949/ccjm.76.s2.08
27. Soyka, F., Leyrer, M., Smallwood, J., Ferguson, C., Riecke, B.E., Mohler, B.J.: Enhancing stress management techniques using virtual reality. In: Proceedings of the ACM Symposium on Applied Perception, pp. 85–88. ACM (2016)
28. Terathongkum, S., Pickler, R.H.: Relationships among heart rate variability, hyper-tension, and relaxation techniques. J. Vasc. Nurs. **22**(3), 78–82 (2004)
29. Ulrich, R.S., et al.: A Review of the research literature on evidence-based healthcare design. HERD Health Environ. Res. Des. J. **1**(3), 61–125 (2008). https://doi.org/10.1177/193758670800100306
30. Valtchanov, D., Barton, K.R., Ellard, C.: Restorative effects of virtual nature set-tings. **13**, 503–512 (2010). https://doi.org/10.1089/cyber.2009.0308
31. Villani, D.: Presence and relaxation: a preliminary controlled study. PsychNology J. **6**(1), 7–25 (2008)
32. Ware, C.: Information Visualization: Perception for Design. Elsevier Science & Technology, Amsterdam (2004)
33. Yu, B., Hu, J., Funk, M., Feijs, L.: A study on user acceptance of different auditory content for relaxation. In: Proceedings of the Audio Mostly 2016, AM 2016, pp. 69–76. ACM, New York (2016). https://doi.org/10.1145/2986416.2986418

Procedurally Generated Self Overlapping Mazes in Virtual Reality

Balázs Gyula Koltai, Jakob Elkjær Husted, Ronny Vangsted,
Thomas Noes Mikkelsen, and Martin Kraus$^{(\boxtimes)}$

Aalborg University, Rendsburggade 14, 9000 Aalborg, Denmark
{bkolta15,jhuste15,rvangs15,tmikke15}@student.aau.dk,
martin@create.aau.dk

Abstract. A current research topic within virtual reality is to allow the user to move by natural walking in a virtual environment that exceeds the size of the tracking area. Multiple approaches to overlapping architecture dealing with this issue already exist, but they are either custom made for a specific tracking area size or require a tracking area too large to work efficiently for personal use. This paper proposes a method to make scalable overlapping architecture by procedural generation of tile-based mazes that seamlessly teleport the user using portals. We evaluated how the tile size of the overlapping maze affects the user's spatial awareness of their physical position. 23 participants of Aalborg University students completed the Spatial Awareness Task of finding a tile that overlapped with their starting tile in a 3×3, 4×4, and 5×5 tile maze. Between condition 3×3 and 5×5, and condition 4×4 and 5×5, participants were more confused in the 5×5 tile maze compared to 3×3 (p = .0015) and 4×4 (p = .0295) tile mazes.

Keywords: Virtual reality · Overlapping architecture · Procedurally generated content · Locomotion in VR · Natural walking · Mazes · Spatial cognition

1 Introduction

Currently, one of the biggest challenges in Virtual Reality (VR) is allowing the user to physically move in a Virtual Environment (VE) larger than their available tracking area. According to Ruddle and Lessels [20], navigation is the most common interactive task within a VE. Some VR applications deal with this challenge by having players stand in one place [1] or letting them move by teleportation [4,5]. However, natural walking in VR has been shown to improve the users' sense of presence, attention and spatial cognition in VEs [31]. It is also the most natural form of locomotion in VR, as the users' movements are directly transferred to the VE [18].

In order to allow for natural walking, we propose to procedurally generate VEs to fit into the size of the tracking area and allow for natural walking through

A. Brooks and E. I. Brooks (Eds.): ArtsIT 2019/DLI 2019, LNICST 328, pp. 229–243, 2020.
https://doi.org/10.1007/978-3-030-53294-9_16

overlapping architecture. The use of mazes in VR allow for unnoticeable changes to architecture that is out of view. To distinguish between the whole maze and the rectangular segments the maze is comprised of, as seen in Fig. 1, a rectangular segment containing a part of a maze will be referred to as a maze segment and the whole series of maze segments will be referred to as a maze. The approach to overlapping architecture is to have users walk through seamless portals and instantly move them between segments, where each segment does not overlap with itself but with other segments. A segment can also contain a corridor with a predefined room attached, which we refer to as a room segment. This method allows users to be naturally walking through a large VE within a small tracking area, and inserting room segments in the maze allows for more interactive gameplay using puzzles or game challenges.

Our contribution is therefore a system for a scalable virtual environment, using procedural generation, that allows for uninterrupted infinite walking through seamless overlapping architecture in VR.

With such a method, overlapping VEs that require various tracking area sizes can be generated. As an application of our system, we conducted an experiment to determine how overlapping mazes with tiled segments of different tile dimensions affect users' spatial awareness in overlapping virtual environments in virtual reality.

2   Related Work

2.1   Locomotion in VR

There are several ways to travel and move around in VR, some more natural than others. Among the most commonly found techniques is teleportation, but using repositioning systems, redirected walking, or overlapping architecture can give a more natural locomotion experience by facilitating natural walking [18, 25,31]. The most realistic way of movement in a VE is by natural walking, where the user's location and movement in the real world can be translated directly into the virtual world [18]. Ruddle and Lessels, and in a similar study, Suma et al. [20,24] found that participants navigating through natural walking performed navigational tasks significantly better than participants using other input methods for movement in the VE. Ruddle and Lessels also discovered that participants in the walking condition tended to avoid obstacles, which could indicate immersion and presence. In 1999, Usoh et al. showed that presence was significantly improved over locomotion methods like walking-in-place and simple button control [28].

Natural walking in larger environments than the tracking area has already been achieved using multiple different techniques, but they are either tested in a large tracking area or custom made for a specific tracking area size. For example, Serubugo et al. [21] designed a custom made maze for a dimension of 2.5×2.5 m. The idea of procedural generation of overlapping architecture has been proposed earlier with flexible spaces by Vasylevska et al. [29], who procedurally placed overlapping rooms and connected them with corridors, but within a set tracking area size of 9 × 9 m. Marwecki and Baudisch [17] also took the tracking area into account when generating the VE, using their Scenograph tool for fitting natural walking VR experiences into various tracking volumes.

Repositioning systems like treadmills and friction-free platforms have great potential for natural walking in VR, as they require a relatively small tracking area. They do this by adjusting the physical movement of users to a fixed position, while still translating this movement to the virtual space [18]. Furthermore, walking in VR can be achieved with walking gestures, also known as proxy gestures and Walking-In-Place (WIP). Users can perform walking motions that act as gestures, or serve as a proxy for real walking. Even though this solution has some advantages, as it is inexpensive and immersive [10], it is not real walking and therefore not the aim of this project. Real walking, when compared to WIP, is also found to be more simple, straightforward and natural to use [28].

Another technique, where users are not stationary, is redirected walking [25]. Three approaches for redirected walking are translational, rotational and curvature gains. For example, if users are walking in the virtual world, they might be translated to walk or rotate further in the virtual world than they actually did in the real world. Even if users think they are walking straight, because that is what they perceive in the virtual world, they might be walking in a curve in the real world. There is however a limit on how much gain can be applied to this before the users notice [25]. For curvature gains, the limit sets a minimum tracking area size of 6 × 6 m to be unnoticeable [19].

2.2 Overlapping Architecture

Using the same tracking area by replacing the geometry in a VE, also known as overlapping architecture, makes it possible for players to stay within the tracking area but change the surroundings as a form of spatial compression [25]. This is useful for walking in VR, as the tracking area that players can move around in is limited. Usually the change of architecture is hidden from players using different methods [30]. Some of the more simple methods are to have players step into an elevator, change the surroundings, and then open the elevator again [3]. Players could also be distracted, asked to look up or something else that could limit their vision. An example is using binoculars to look for birds, then change or rotate the whole architecture while a player is distracted [22]. Another approach, that does not hide the scene change, is by moving players in a vehicle, as they can see a more natural change of surroundings in a way that resembles travelling by vehicle. These are great ways to simulate that players got transported to new surroundings. However, more advanced transition methods that allow for continuous uninterrupted walking can be implemented [25]. Some methods that allow players to continuously walk while the architecture unnoticeably changes around them are change blindness or simply changing parts of the architecture that are out of view. This can be seen in studies on VR, as well as games like Sömmad [21] and Tea for God [7] that both facilitate self-overlapping mazes. Other examples include Unseen Diplomacy [8] and Ares [12].

Furthermore, Marwecki and Baudisch [17] developed a tool for creating narrative VR experiences called Scenograph. With this tool, a VR experience creator can specify which objects or narrative content should be in each room, and then the rooms are procedurally generated from the size and shape of the tracking area. More specifically, if all the objects that are assigned to one room cannot fit, Scenograph splits the room into two or more. Players can then switch between the rooms by walking through doors, which is one of the more simple transition methods for an overlapping architecture.

2.3 Spatial Cognition

In 2012 Suma et al. [25] investigated people's spatial cognition by finding the threshold of when they start to perceive the overlapping architecture when walking between two rooms in a VE. They found the average threshold to be 56% for when people started to notice the overlap, and 31% for the larger 9.14×9.14 m tracking area. They evaluated this using what they called the *Impossible Space Perception Task* (ISPT), where they asked if the participant found the space to be possible or impossible, and then rated their answer *"not confident"*, *"somewhat confident"*, or *"confident"*. Another task that the participants had to do was the *Distance Estimation Task* (DET), where they had to walk from their position in the second room to where they believed a marker in the first room was located in tracking area. They then found that participants perceived the distance to the marker in the adjacent overlapping room to be as if the space had not been compressed. This meant that some participants walked nearly 400% of the actual distance to the marker in the 75% overlap condition. Fisher et al. [12] conducted a similar study, where instead of walking to the marker, participants had to point in the direction of it at the end of the experience. These studies showed that it is possible to manipulate the human senses to a certain extent, but also that the threshold varies from user to user.

Many of the studies and methods described earlier in Sect. 2.2 and 2.1, are also about manipulating the human senses or tricking our spatial cognition. According to Vasyslevska and Kaufmann [30], spatial manipulation requires a relatively large tracking area to create a believable VE, as smaller areas make it more difficult to hide that the space is impossible. They also added that *"our experience with self-overlapping architectures suggests that users might consciously accept spatial manipulations. However, some users might also find the concept of an unrealistic architecture to be disturbing"* [30]. Most of these studies focus on believability and hiding the impossible spaces because of this belief [22], or they investigate the threshold for when people perceive the overlapping architecture [25]. However some VR games, e.g. Tea for God and Unseen Diplomacy [7,8], do not hide that the architecture is overlapping. A game like Antichamber [11], a non-VR puzzle game, even intentionally shows the impossible spaces to add to the mind twisting theme of the game.

2.4 Procedurally Generated Content

Procedurally generated content (PGC) can be found in many popular games, e.g. Diablo, Minecraft, and Civilization, where it is often used in the form of game rules, levels, dungeons, mazes and quests [27]. Among some of the advantages of PCG is that less resourceful and smaller development teams can create more content-rich games. However, procedural generation used for overlapping architecture in VR is a relatively new topic. In this context, levels, mazes and corridors allow for this overlapping architecture in VR. An example of a procedurally generated maze game for VR that facilitates overlapping architecture is Tea for God. Here the overlapping mazes are generated based on the tracking area size (minimum size being 1.8×1.2 m), which makes it scalable as it is not restricted to a specific tracking area size [7]. Another example that makes use of a procedurally generated overlapping architecture that adapts to the size and shape of the tracking area is Scenograph [17].

3 Minimum Implementation Requirements

We found that Tea for God and Scenograph interrupt the player from continuously walking by including overlapping methods like doors and elevators. Our approach is to let the player walk uninterrupted between segments. Furthermore, it should also be scalable, so the segment dimensions can scale to the size of the tracking area, as well as the tile sizes within these dimensions. In order to let the users walk infinitely, we need to implement portals that seamlessly teleport them between segments. Lastly, the segments must be procedurally generated for further scalability.

4 Procedural Generation of Mazes with Seamless Transitions

We decided to use mazes and seamless teleportation due to several reasons. In a maze there are many possibilities to hide overlapping architecture, as the player can only see fractions of an entire maze at a time. Mazes can also act as connections between room segments, where additional game and narrative content can be added. Inspired by Scenograph [17], we wanted to create a platform for VR experience designers who want to fit large VEs into a limited tracking area. To this end, room segments can be prefabricated and placed in any desired order of the maze. Lastly, another reason for choosing this method is that we wanted to add game elements to the prototype, and that finding your way through a maze can be considered a type of game by itself. Generating overlapping mazes procedurally and connecting them seamlessly with portals, allows users to infinitely walk through the environment without loading screens or being forced to do tasks in order to leverage change blindness [23]. This is also what makes it possible to adapt the maze to the specific dimensions of the available tracking area, as it is generated accordingly.

Our method for connecting the segments seamlessly is to use portals on certain tiles within the segment. The portals have a render plane on the far end of the tile with the corresponding part of the next segment projected on it. When players cross the portal threshold, they are teleported to the next segment before they reach the render plane. A top-down view example of a procedurally generated maze consisting of 3 × 3 tiled maze segments is depicted in Fig. 1.

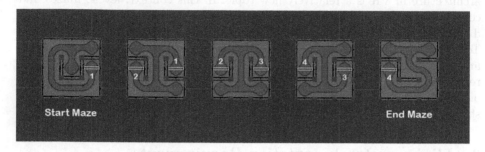

Fig. 1. A maze consisting of five 3 × 3 tiled segments seen from above. Portals are shown as green rectangles and connected portals share the same number.

We developed the prototype using Unity Engine [26] and Steam VR [6] for the HTC Vive Head-Mounted Display (HMD) [9], but in theory it should work for any HMD with support for 6° of freedom. The algorithm for procedurally generating the maze is split into two major parts: The generation of the maze segments and the placement of the portals. The algorithm is using a recursive depth first search to generate perfect mazes, which are mazes with no loops in them, but it also has to obey set constraints on the portal locations. In every maze segment except the first one, the starting position will be the entrance portal location, which is copied from the exit portal location of the previous maze segment, but rotated 180°. Therefore and due to the fact that we used static render planes to project the next and previous segments, the portals cannot be in corners or perpendicular to the edge of the maze. In addition to this, the entrance and exit portals in a maze cannot lead directly into each other, and if an entrance portal is next to a corner tile, the exit portal cannot be on the other side of that tile, so the corner does not get shut off. The players would not notice these issues, however it would lead to incomplete segments.

With the location of the entrance and exit portal found, the remaining tiles in the maze segment generate a path between the two portals. After all the maze segments have been generated, the portal manager places the portals on the map using the locations from the maze generation.

The image rendered on the render planes is created using two cameras in both the previous and next segment, following a player's position and orientation exactly, and shifted so they record the left and right eye's views. An important technical aspect is that the render textures captured by the cameras have to be high resolution with a high anisotropic filtering level, otherwise the environment in the next/previous segment shown on the render planes would look blurry, have bad lighting or otherwise look different. The cameras' projection matrices are generated using another plane offset on the maze using a VR projection script [2] based on Kooima's publication [16]. The images are then used as textures on the render planes, making sure the left camera's image renders on the left eye and the right camera's image on the right eye, creating a stereoscopic image. When the player passes through a portal, the cameras change which plane they use for creating their projection matrices, so the transition back can be seamless as well. The method results in unnoticeable portals that allow for seamless overlapping of segments as seen in Fig. 2.

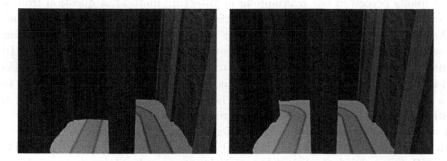

Fig. 2. Two images from the same position. On the left, the render plane is disabled, leading to a dead end. On the right, the render plane is enabled, rendering a left turn that belongs to the next maze segment.

5   Evaluation Methodology and Materials

The primary focus was to investigate how users would notice and perceive overlapping maze segments in our prototype, as well as if portals were seamless and unnoticeable when walking in the maze. This included testing for potential technical issues, such as artifacts in render planes used as portals, but also the spatial cognition side of our method. For example to evaluate how the size of the overlapping maze segment affects spatial perception, we modified the *Distance Estimation Task* (DET) and *Impossible Space Perception Task* (ISPT) by Suma et al. [25]. Instead of asking participants whether they believe the space is possible or impossible, participants were asked to walk through the maze, and similar to the DET approach, notify us whenever they believe they are standing at a position that overlaps with their starting position. As in the original ISPT, participants were asked to rate their confidence in their answer as *Not Confident, Somewhat Confident* or *Confident*. We refer to this task as the Spatial Awareness Task, which was inspired by Fisher et al. and Suma et al. [12,25], where participants had to point to landmarks or walk to objects in previous overlapping rooms. The independent variable for the Spatial Awareness Task is the tile size of the maze and the dependent variable is binary, meaning whether the participants stop at their starting position (correct) or not (incorrect).

To test for simulator sickness, we used the Virtual Reality Sickness Questionnaire (VRSQ) [15]. The VRSQ is a revised version of the Kennedy Simulator Sickness Questionnaire (SSQ) [14] containing 9 of 16 questions from SSQ by discarding 7 nausea related questions. Simulator sickness is connected with VR and forced movement, in the same way that motion sickness is with moving vehicles in the real world [13]. Even though there is currently no forced movement in the prototype, it is still necessary to identify general simulator sickness or if something else could be causing discomfort.

Additionally, to both figure out whether the render planes are visible and how participants perceived our overlapping architecture method, a question from a believability questionnaire [25] was modified to fit the context of our solution: *"The maze you explored was larger than the physical space you were in. How do you think it happened or worked? If you're not sure, then please say so"*. To investigate the minimum size for a maze to still be perceived as a maze, we also included the question *"Would you perceive the virtual environment you were in as a maze?"*. As the maze segments are randomly and procedurally generated, seeding the maze for the evaluation was necessary to prevent confounding variables of the participants experiencing different mazes. For testing, we used a PC with an Intel i7 CPU and Nvidia GTX 1080 GPU, connected to a wireless HTC Vive VR system [9]. In addition, the participants wore headphones to minimize noise.

6   Evaluation Procedure

Participants were students from Aalborg University who volunteered to participate in the test. To start, they filled out a pre-test VRSQ [15] to indicate how they felt prior to the experiment. Each participant was introduced to overlapping architecture by means of a simple example of overlapping architecture in a maze consisting of 3×3 tiled segments, where they were asked to navigate through the maze until they believed that the VE had overlapped. Then they were verbally introduced to the Spatial Awareness Task of the experiment and asked to perform it in the simple example, to ensure that they understood the task. Specifically, the participants were asked to press down on the touchpad and trigger buttons on the HTC Vive controller simultaneously, whenever they believed that they were standing at the position in physical space where they initially started, but they are standing at a new position in the VE. For the simple example, the starting position is T as seen in Fig. 3. Once they have pressed on the controller, they will be asked how confident they are in their answer based on the Impossible Space Perception Task [25], and if they would perceive the VE as a maze.

Every participant tested all 3 conditions in random order, meaning mazes with the maze segment sizes of 3×3, 4×4, and 5×5 tiles of the length 0.8 m. For condition 3×3, the starting position would be *30*, *40* for condition 4×4

Fig. 3. The 4×4 m tracking area used for evaluation

and *50* for condition 5×5 as seen in Fig. 3. After finishing all conditions, there
was a post-test where participants filled out the VRSQ [15] with the included
question whether the render planes are visible.

7   Results

The prototype was evaluated on a sample size of 23 participants (18 males and
5 females) with an age range of 20 to 28 years (median 23). Regarding VR
experience, 13% had none, 52% had slight, 17% had moderate, and 17% had a
lot of experience. In Fig. 4 the result from the Spatial Awareness Task are shown,
where 14 participants answered correctly in condition 3×3, 10 in condition 4×4
and 4 in condition 5×5.

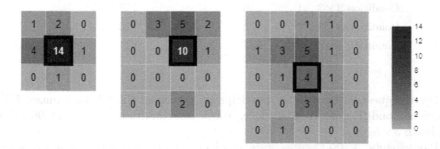

Fig. 4. Heat map of the tile participants believed overlapped with their starting position for each condition. The correct tiles are indicated with the bold outline

For statistical analysis of data, results from the Spatial Awareness Task were treated as binary (correct, incorrect). Three sets of hypotheses were formulated and evaluated with a Wilcoxon rank sum test:

H_0 : "There is no difference between how well participants can correctly answer the Spatial Awareness Task in condition 3×3 and 4×4." H_a : "Participants are better at answering correctly in the Spatial Awareness Task, in condition 3×3 when compared to condition 4×4." With a p-value of 0.12, the null hypothesis could not be rejected.

H_0 : "There is no difference between how well participants can correctly answer the Spatial Awareness Task in condition 3×3 and 5×5." H_a : "Participants are better at answering correctly in the Spatial Awareness Task, in condition 3×3 when compared to condition 5×5." With a p-value of 0.0015 the null hypothesis is rejected and the alternative hypothesis is accepted.

H_0 : "There is no difference between how well participants can correctly answer the Spatial Awareness Task in condition 4×4 and 5×5." H_a : "Participants are better at answering correctly in the Spatial Awareness Task, in condition 4×4 when compared to condition 5×5." With a p-value of 0.03, the null hypothesis is rejected and the alternative hypothesis is accepted.

Participants were asked about their confidence in their answer for the Spatial Awareness Task on a 3-point Likert scale. Responses on confidence are summarised in Table 1. As it is ordinal data, the non-parametric Friedman's test is used to compare conditions. The following hypotheses were formulated:

H_0 : "There is no difference between how confident participants are in their answer for the Spatial Awareness Task between any condition." H_a : "Participants are more confident in their answer for the spatial awareness in smaller mazes than larger ones." Friedman's test returned a p-value of 0.15 and thus the null hypothesis could not be rejected.

Table 1. Participants' confidence in their answer to the Spatial Awareness Task

	Confident	Somewhat confident	Not confident
Condition 3×3	11	5	7
Condition 4×4	7	3	13
Condition 5×5	5	7	11

For the question on whether participants perceived the VE as a maze, 78% perceived condition 3×3 as a maze, 100% for condition 4×4, and 96% for condition 5×5.

Participants' VRSQ scores were recorded before and after their exposure to the repeated measures. The pre-test had a mean and standard deviation of 7.7 ± 9.0 and the post-test had a mean and standard deviation of 9.5 ± 10.7. The distribution of scores reject Shapiro-Wilk's null hypothesis and therefore a Wilcoxon rank sum was used to compare their pre- and post scores. With a p-value of 0.67, the null hypothesis is not rejected, meaning that the test did not show a statistically significant difference in VR sickness.

8   Discussion

For the Spatial Awareness Task, participants were supposed to navigate them-selves back to their starting position based on their spatial awareness, or in other words on their spatial orientation in the VE. The evaluation was planned to be done in a quiet environment. However there was a lot of background noise from other students testing, which could be heard by participants despite wearing headphones playing ambient sound. This might have affected the results, as the participants could use the sound to orientate themselves in the tracking area. Additionally, SteamVR [6] displays the edges of the tracking area when near it. It is possible that participants could use these sources of error to pinpoint their physical position within the tracking area. Additionally, some participants experienced loss of tracking of the HMD when standing in the corner of the tracking area located in the top part of Fig. 3. Losing tracking caused the HMD to stop rendering the VE which may have distracted them from their task or interrupted any immersion they had.

The generated mazes used for evaluating were seeded to avoid the confound-ing variable of generating random mazes for each participant. For the Spatial Awareness Task, significant differences between condition 3×3 and 5×5 and condition 4×4 and 5×5 were found, pointing to participants performing better in smaller mazes. It is unclear exactly what causes this effect. Underlying causes may be due to the distance participants have to walk, number of turns they have to perform, or a combination thereof in order to complete the Spatial Aware-ness Task. By inspecting the seeded mazes used for evaluation, participants had to navigate a minimum distance of 26 tiles with 20 turns in condition 5×5 to complete the Spatial Awareness Task correctly. This is in contrast to condition 3×3 and 4×4, in which participants only had to walk 10 tiles with 6 turns and 10 tiles with 8 turns respectively.

Unlike the results from the Spatial Awareness Task, no significant difference in confidence was found. This points to participants not perceiving the Spatial Awareness Task as more difficult in larger mazes. However, looking at Table 1, participants are more prone to answer *"Somewhat Confident"* and *"Not Con-fident"* rather than *"Confident"* as the maze increases in size. This correlates with the results from the Spatial Awareness Task.

As the method for seamless overlapping in the prototype was developed as part of this project, participants were asked how they believed the overlapping architecture was achieved. This question was a way of indirectly asking the par-ticipants if they noticed any render planes while walking in the VE. It was intentionally formulated to not imply that overlapping was achieved by telepor-tation through render planes. 10 participants answered that they were not sure what method was used. The remaining 13 participants had suggestions ranging from changing the environment behind corners to moving the player to a new environment. None of the participants commented on any appearance of render planes, as all the visual artifacts and low resolution issues found through internal testing were corrected.

Lastly, the effect of overlapping architecture that is apparent to users is unknown. Most studies focus on hiding the impossible spaces or finding the threshold for when and how people start to perceive it. In this project we did not try to hide the overlapping architecture, as this was not the aim of the project. Currently, not many studies investigated the effect of when users perceive the impossible spaces, although Vasyslevska and Kaufmann [30] suggested that some people might find it disturbing. But this might also depend on the setting or context of using the overlapping architecture. There is however also a chance that being able to see when the space overlaps, could affect the spatial awareness of the participants, as they can better map the current maze segment to the next.

For the pre- and post-VRSQ scores we did not find a statistically significant difference with a p-value of 0.67, meaning that our method of seamlessly teleporting the user between maze segments did not appear to cause VR sickness in our test.

8.1 Future Work

A feature that we could explore is the ability to create portals with a 90° rotation to each other. It would allow us to put portals in corners, or portal exits on edges perpendicular to the maze edge, resulting in more variations and more interesting maze layouts. It would also allow us to make layouts as small as 2×2. This would require to overhaul the portal implementation, possibly moving away from rendering on quads. Similarly, to make the maze scalable with the room segments included, a way to scale those to the dimensions of the maze should be developed, as currently the predefined room segments are all 4×5 tiles, with a size of 3.2×4 m.

As it is inconclusive why there is a significant difference in condition 5×5, three additional tests could be conducted to uncover the potential causes. One would be with multiple mazes with the same segment size and distance, but different number of turns required to complete the Spatial Awareness Task. Second would be with multiple mazes with the same segment size and number of turns but different distances required to complete the Spatial Awareness Task. Lastly, a test with multiple mazes with the same distance and number of turns but different segment sizes required to complete the Spatial Awareness Task.

There are also other aspects that are interesting to evaluate. It could be further tested whether the confidence changes happened because of the amount of turns or the distance needed to traverse the mazes. Additional in-between sizes of 3×4 and 4×5 maze segments could be tested to see how it affects the players. It would be interesting to test with architectures that are deliberately showing where the maze is overlapping, in order to see if the impossible architecture affects players' immersion and believability, or if it is something that should be hidden in games. Finally, as the render planes used for portals only could be apparent due to visual artifacts or low resolution, an additional question focusing on the visual quality of the prototype could be included in the evaluation.

9   Conclusion

Based on the results, evidence suggests that participants' find overlapping mazes with a maze segment size of 5×5 tiles statistically more difficult to understand spatially than with a maze segment size of 4×4 tiles with our method ($p = 0.03$). This meant that by increasing the number of maze segments the user became more spatially confused with a significant difference between 4×4 tiled and 5×5 tiled maze segments. We can not report with certainty that this difference is due to the maze size, as participants could have been affected by the complexity based on the distance travelled and turns taken.

As the tests showed, the minimum technical requirements were met, as all players were able to walk uninterrupted between the maze segments with none of them noticing the render planes or the teleportation. The maze is also completely scalable in both maze segments and tile sizes, and are procedurally created with a set of adjustable parameters.

References

1. Beat Saber by Beat Games. https://store.steampowered.com/app/620980/Beat_Saber/
2. Cg Programming Unity Projection for Virtual Reality - wikibooks. https://en.wikibooks.org/wiki/Cg_Programming/Unity/Projection_for_Virtual_Reality
3. Floor plan: Hands-on edition - by Turbo Button. https://store.steampowered.com/app/673060/Floor_Plan_HandsOn_Edition/
4. The Lab by Valve. https://store.steampowered.com/app/450390/The_Lab/
5. Rec Room - by Against Gravity®. https://store.steampowered.com/app/471710/Rec_Room/
6. SteamVR - Valve. http://steamvr.com
7. Tea For God by Void Room. https://void-room.itch.io/tea-for-god
8. Unseen Diplomacy by Triangular Pixels. https://store.steampowered.com/app/429830/Unseen_Diplomacy/
9. VIVE™ — VIVE Virtual Reality System. https://www.vive.com/us/product/vive-virtual-reality-system/
10. Ang, Y.Y., Sulaiman, P.S., Rahmat, R.W.O.K., Norowi, N.M.: Put down the controller, enable "Walking" in a virtual reality (VR) environment: a review. In: Perez, G.M., Tiwari, S., Trivedi, M.C., Mishra, K.K. (eds.) Ambient Communications and Computer Systems, pp. 367–379. Advances in Intelligent Systems and Computing, Springer Singapore (2018)
11. Bruce, A.: Antichamber - A Mind-Bending Psychological Exploration Game. http://www.antichamber-game.com/
12. Fisher, J.A., Garg, A., Singh, K.P., Wang, W.: Designing intentional impossible spaces in virtual reality narratives: a case study. In: 2017 IEEE Virtual Reality (VR), pp. 379–380, March 2017. https://doi.org/10.1109/VR.2017.7892335

13. Jerald, J.: The VR Book: Human-Centered Design for Virtual Reality. Association for Computing Machinery and Morgan & Claypool, October 2015. http://dl.acm.org/citation.cfm?id=2792790

14. Kennedy, R.S., Lane, N.E., Berbaum, K.S., Lilienthal, M.G.: Simulator sickness questionnaire: an enhanced method for quantifying simulator sickness. Int. J. Aviat. Psychol. **3**(3), 203–220 (1993). https://doi.org/10.1207/s15327108ijap0303_3

15. Kim, H.K., Park, J., Choi, Y., Choe, M.: Virtual reality sickness questionnaire (VRSQ): motion sickness measurement index in a virtual reality environment. Appl. Ergon. **69**, 66–73 (2018). https://doi.org/10.1016/j.apergo.2017.12.016. http://www.sciencedirect.com/science/article/pii/S000368701730282X

16. Kooima, R.: Generalized Perspective Projection (2011)

17. Marwecki, S., Baudisch, P.: Scenograph: fitting real-walking VR experiences into various tracking volumes. In: Proceedings of the 31st Annual ACM Symposium on User Interface Software and Technology, event-place: Berlin, Germany, UIST 2018, pp. 511–520. ACM, New York (2018). https://doi.org/10.1145/3242587.3242648

18. Nilsson, N.C., Serafin, S., Steinicke, F., Nordahl, R.: Natural walking in virtual reality: a review. Comput. Entertain. **16**(2), 8:1–8:22 (2018). https://doi.org/10.1145/3180658

19. Rietzler, M., Gugenheimer, J., Hirzle, T., Deubzer, M., Langbehn, E., Rukzio, E.: Rethinking redirected walking: on the use of curvature gains beyond perceptual limitations and revisiting bending gains. In: 2018 IEEE International Symposium on Mixed and Augmented Reality (ISMAR), pp. 115–122. IEEE, Munich, October 2018. https://doi.org/10.1109/ISMAR.2018.00041. https://ieeexplore.ieee.org/document/8613757/

20. Ruddle, R.A., Lessels, S.: The benefits of using a walking interface to navigate virtual environments. ACM Trans. Comput. Hum. Interact. **16**(1), 1–18 (2009). https://doi.org/10.1145/1502800.1502805. http://portal.acm.org/citation.cfm?doid=1502800.1502805

21. Serubugo, S., Skantarova, D., Evers, N., Kraus, M.: Walkable self-overlapping virtual reality maze and map visualization demo: public virtual reality setup for asymmetric collaboration. In: Proceedings of the 23rd ACM Symposium on Virtual Reality Software and Technology, VRST 2017, Event-place: Gothenburg, Sweden, pp. 91:1–91:2. ACM, New York (2017). https://doi.org/10.1145/3139131.3141774. http://doi.acm.org/10.1145/3139131.3141774

22. Sra, M., Xu, X., Mottelson, A., Maes, P.: VMotion: designing a seamless walking experience in VR. In: Proceedings of the 2018 Designing Interactive Systems Conference, Event-place: Hong Kong, China, pp. 59–70. ACM, New York (2018). https://doi.org/10.1145/3196709.3196792. http://doi.acm.org/10.1145/3196709.3196792

23. Suma, E.A., Clark, S., Krum, D., Finkelstein, S., Bolas, M., Warte, Z.: Leveraging change blindness for redirection in virtual environments. In: 2011 IEEE Virtual Reality Conference, pp. 159–166, March 2011. https://doi.org/10.1109/VR.2011.5759455

24. Suma, E.A., Finkelstein, S.L., Clark, S., Goolkasian, P., Hodges, L.F.: Effects of travel technique and gender on a divided attention task in a virtual environment. In: 2010 IEEE Symposium on 3D User Interfaces (3DUI), pp. 27–34, March 2010. https://doi.org/10.1109/3DUI.2010.5444726

25. Suma, E.A., Lipps, Z., Finkelstein, S., Krum, D.M., Bolas, M.: Impossible spaces: maximizing natural walking in virtual environments with self-overlapping architecture. IEEE Trans. Vis. Comput. Graph. **18**(4), 555–564 (2012). https://doi.org/10.1109/TVCG.2012.47. http://ieeexplore.ieee.org/document/6165136/
26. Technologies Unity: Unity. https://unity.com/frontpage
27. Togelius, J., Shaker, N., Nelson, M.J.: Procedural generation in game design. In: Shaker, N., Togelius, J., Nelson, M.J. (eds.) Procedural Content Generation in Games, pp. 1–15. Computational Synthesis and Creative Systems. Springer. Cham (2016). https://doi.org/10.1007/978-3-319-42716-4_1
28. Usoh, M., et al.: Walking - walking-in-place - flying, in virtual environments. In: Proceedings of the 26th Annual Conference on Computer Graphics and Interactive Techniques, SIGGRAPH 1999, pp. 359–364. ACM Press/Addison-Wesley Publishing Co., New York (1999). https://doi.org/10.1145/311535.311589
29. Vasylevska, K., Kaufmann, H., Bolas, M., Suma, E.A.: Flexible spaces: a virtual step outside of reality. In: 2013 IEEE Virtual Reality (VR), pp. 109–110, March 2013. https://doi.org/10.1109/VR.2013.6549386
30. Vasylevska, K., Kaufmann, H.: Compressing VR: fitting large virtual environments within limited physical space. IEEE Comput. Graphics Appl. **37**(5), 85–91 (2017). https://doi.org/10.1109/MCG.2017.3621226
31. Vasylevska, K., Kaufmann, H.: Towards efficient spatial compression in self-overlapping virtual environments. In: 2017 IEEE Symposium on 3D User Interfaces (3DUI), pp. 12–21. IEEE, Los Angeles (2017). https://doi.org/10.1109/3DUI.2017.7893312

Navigating Procedurally Generated Overt Self-overlapping Environments in VR

Jannik A. I. H. Neerdal(✉), Thomas B. Hansen, Nicolai B. Hansen, Kresta Louise F. Bonita, and Martin Kraus

Aalborg University, Rendsburggade 14, 9000 Aalborg, Denmark
{jneerd15,tbha15,nbha15,kbonit15}@student.aau.dk, martin@create.aau.dk

Abstract. Previous implementations of self-overlapping architecture tried to hide the characteristics of their non-Euclidean environment from users. To test the outcome of showing these characteristics to users, we propose a virtual reality system with a play area of $3\,m \times 3\,m$ and procedurally generated rooms, which are connected by portals. The aim of the portals is to provide seamless transitions between rooms and render overt self-overlapping architecture for players to experience. Participants were tasked with reporting their experiences and discoveries during the playthrough. Based on this information and recordings of their view, we could determine whether they noticed any transitions. Additionally, the participants were asked specific questions regarding their experience with the overt self-overlapping environment, and how they interpreted the size of the virtual environment in relation to the physical one. The results showed that only 2 of the 20 participants who completed the full playthrough noticed any transitions, while each playthrough consisted of a minimum of 20 transitions. Therefore, we conclude that the transitions were seamless. The system did not induce significant motion sickness in participants. Most participants felt good about navigating the overt self-overlapping environment, and the general consensus was that the experience was strange, yet interesting.

Keywords: Virtual reality · Self-overlapping architecture · Procedural generation · Navigation · Natural walking · Portals · Stencil test

1 Introduction

The technology of Virtual Reality (VR) presents a lot of interesting possibilities, one of which is the exploration of virtual worlds in full 360° experiences. However, the process of this exploration is currently not consistent with that of a real-life environment as the spatial environment in VR is limited by the tracking area of the physical space.

In the context of games, exploration of virtual environments is usually achieved by moving a character with keyboard and mouse, or a controller; however, this is not an effective locomotion method in VR, as it can induce motion

© ICST Institute for Computer Sciences, Social Informatics and Telecommunications Engineering 2020
Published by Springer Nature Switzerland AG 2020. All Rights Reserved
A. Brooks and E. I. Brooks (Eds.): ArtsIT 2019/DLI 2019, LNICST 328, pp. 244–260, 2020.
https://doi.org/10.1007/978-3-030-53294-9_17

sickness. Another common approach is teleportation, however this type of loco-motive method is not native to humans. Rather, it has the potential to not only negatively affect immersion for some users, but also break the authenticity of the virtual world, especially if it is a recreation of a real-life environment.

Natural walking is another locomotion method, which is native to humans, although this type of locomotion results in a lot of design restrictions for explo-ration in VR. However, it is possible to implement a virtual environment in such a way that it overlaps itself, thereby allowing the user to move through new sec-tions in the environment, while repeatedly traversing the same physical space. It is crucial that the transitioning between sections, which we refer to as 'rooms', is seamless. For the purpose of replayability, the environments should also be procedurally generated.

The focus of this paper is therefore a system for natural-walking navigation of virtual maze-like environments, which are generated procedurally such that transitions between the instantiated rooms are seamless and undetectable. To this end, we propose a system for procedurally generated environments consisting of overt self-overlapping architecture in VR.

In an experiment, we attempted to investigate three research areas: (1) whether the transitions in the environment are seamless to users and the navigability of the environment, (2) the users' experience within the overt self-overlapping environment and (3) the users' perception of the size of the virtual space in comparison to the physical space.

Predominantly, the focus of the experiment is to evaluate research question (2), but since this requires the system itself to function properly, research ques-tion (1) is of equal importance. If the implementation of the system itself is not optimal, the experience of navigating an overt self-overlapping environment could be affected.

2 Background

2.1 Self-overlapping Architecture

Self-overlapping architecture is a method that expands virtual environments (VEs) spatially. Constructing two or more partial VEs that overlap each other allows larger VEs to be compressed in a smaller physical tracking area [12,14]. Therefore, a VE with self-overlapping architecture makes it possible to only display one VE at a time despite the spatial overlap. These VEs can also contain transitional features like doors or passages that connect to other VEs, creating the illusion of seamless transitions between them. This approach also allows potential use of natural locomotion in virtual reality [14]. While only a few studies have utilized this approach [14,18], others used the method combined with the illusion of change blindness, in which they instantaneously redirected or teleported users, and in this way seamlessly switched to the connected VE [5,12].

Various video games have started to implement non-Euclidean concepts like self-overlapping environments for puzzle solving and navigational purposes.

A popular example of this is the game *Antichamber* [1], a puzzle-exploration game that is known for using overt self-overlapping architecture for interesting visual designs that are also tied in with navigation and puzzles.

Re-Directed Walking (RDW). RDW describes a group of techniques, which aim to increase the navigable space of a VR tracked environment. Some of the techniques involve designing patterns used for natural walking on curves [9]. A demo by Langbehn et al. discussed the implementation of curved walking in VR with comparisons between reality and virtual space [9]. With the proposed technique, a tracked environment of $4\,m \times 4\,m$ is required, which would correspond to walking in a $25\,m \times 25\,m$ virtual environment.

Other approaches to RDW include overt or continuous repositioning/rotation of the Head-Mounted Display (HMD). By using rotation gains either continuously or overtly, users can be repositioned with a chance to break presence. To best avoid breaking presence with such a technique, subtle continuous rotation should be used, as it has a probability of about 13% to cause a break in presence. For a non-optimal implementation, the probability rises to 70% [15].

Similarly, techniques such as non-Euclidean geometry or impossible spaces can be used to provide the user with natural walking in the tracked environment. Rather than manipulating the viewpoint of the user, the environment can be changed to utilize the tracked space instead.

Several techniques can also be combined, such as using both rotation gains, and impossible spaces. By using both of these, a curved corridor can be created with subsequent rooms, forming an "impossible space" or "self-overlapping architecture", meaning that the rooms occupy the same physical space, but virtually they occupy different spaces [10]. Arch-explore [2] also proposes adding portals, to enter a second virtual environment.

Overt Self-overlapping. Previous works usually used a "discreet" transition when employing self-overlapping architecture [5,10], where the environment has been created such that the user will not be able to notice the changes from one room to another. Meanwhile, *Tea for God* [11] takes the opposite approach, where the self-overlapping architecture is overt to the player. This effect is illustrated for instance when corridor walls disappear when turning around corners, but reappear when users go back.

2.2 Procedural Generation in Games

Procedural generation is the process of creating content by an algorithm when an appropriate input is supplied. This can generate almost any kind of content, based on the algorithm and input used. Procedural generation differs from random generation in the sense that the output of a certain algorithm for the same input is always the same. It can therefore be useful to include randomness in the procedural generation to increase variety of the output [3,16]. In the context of games, procedural generation is extremely useful to create game systems with variation e.g. game levels, enemy encounters, loot drops, etc. Including the element of randomness in the procedural generation algorithm allows games like *Minecraft* to offer near infinite replayability, since it automatically creates new environments and objects that are random but are governed by game systems and design to maintain consistent logic and behaviour.

While procedural generation brings infinite possibilities to enhance games, this approach does have its drawbacks. It can be taxing on the hardware as it requires a lot of computing power when a game heavily relies on procedural generation, and some worlds can also feel repetitive if basic algorithms are used to generate large environments such that patterns and repeating areas will be easy to spot [3].

Procedural Generation in VR. Procedural generation in VR is particularly interesting, as it can be used not only to generate a multitude of varied levels, but also to change the physical boundaries that define the layout of VEs [13]. By procedurally generating such an environment, the virtual space can be defined to fit non-square tracked areas. VRoamer [4] is an example of such a system. It generates virtual rooms and corridors based on previously unscanned physical environments and dynamically extends and changes the virtual environment as the physical environment is being scanned. When there is enough physical space, it generates a corridor leading to a pre-authored room. The system therefore allows players to walk in large, previously unscanned areas instead of pre-determined play areas. The system does, however, come with some major use case limitations, primarily the requirement of very large physical spaces to create the virtual environment and limitations of the hardware used to scan the physical environment.

Procedurally generating game elements is also a topic within VR. It can be used for generation of mazes [7], where specific elements can be included to increase immersion of users [6].

3   Design

3.1   Conceptualization

The proposed system should implement overt self-overlapping architecture in a seamless manner, such that players never realize a sudden and obtrusive change in geometry. There are two methods that can be used to achieve this: (1) non-obtrusively repositioning of players, meaning seamless teleportation of players in the scene, or (2) seamless change of the environment around the player. Both are based on some connected triggers, in which each approach requires different techniques to be utilized in achieving a seamless effect, such that users never know that they have been teleported, or that the environment has changed around them.

The design should also support an overt self-overlapping architecture implementation to see how people perceive the concept of a self-overlapping environment during a navigational task.

3.2   System Design

The system was implemented in the Unity Engine, using Unity version 2018.3.8, but could be implemented in any game engine with similar functionality. The system is designed to procedurally generate different variations of what we call 'rooms', a collection of objects with the intention to look like a room or a corridor. Each room contains invisible portals to connect to another room. It is then possible to procedurally generate an environment consisting of rooms, instead of procedurally generating the environment at an object level. This also means the rooms can be designed manually and can be easily expanded by adding more rooms, changing room layout etc., as long as the structure for portal pairing is consistent (more on this in Sect. 3.3).

Two main methods for connecting these rooms have been mentioned in Sect. 3.1. Whether teleportation or transition is used, it happens when the player collides with some type of trigger. This is combined with some visual display e.g. a polygon, that visualizes the geometry in a connected room. We refer to this combination as a 'portal'. The techniques used to create these portals differ depending on whether teleportation or transition is used. As an example, to create seamless teleportation, it would be advised to use render textures and cameras, and simply translate the position of the player, when they enter a portal, to teleport the player to a corresponding room, with a new render texture behind the player to show the room that they came from. The other approach, which does not rely on cameras or moving the player, is to use 'stencil polygons', which we define as objects of which the visible parts define a stencil mask written to the stencil buffer. If the pixels of some geometry in a different room passes the stencil test, the pixels in the other room are rendered in the area marked by the mask. A stencil polygon could take any single-faced shape, which in the case of the current system is a quadrilateral. This topic is further explained in Sect. 3.5. By using stencil polygons, all rooms can be positioned in the same place without occluding each other. If the rooms are connected appropriately and the stencil reference values are updated accordingly, moving between the rooms should be seamless.

3.3   Method for Procedural Generation of Rooms

Weighing the two approaches discussed in Sect. 3.2, we determined that not changing the players' positions outweighs the benefits of transporting them. Therefore, to have seamless transitions with such an approach, the trigger boxes that determine when rooms should be switched were required to be located at the exact same position. As such, the player would enter a trigger, which would activate the new room, where the player is meant to come out of the connected trigger, and as they are in the same place, the player does not have to be teleported. Therefore, the code to procedurally generate these rooms had to pair them based on their position, and also their rotation such that each portal's front faces the player.

The portals that were used to populate the various rooms had a set of possible positions and rotations, such that the portals could always be paired with other portals in different rooms. Rooms were named, based on their use; for example, start and end rooms were named and designed as such, with only one portal but later the concept of different room themes was introduced. The rooms were then labeled as such, and thematic transition rooms between the themes were also created.

Since the system was designed to work with VR, the play area was restricted to a very small static size of $3\,m \times 3\,m$ as any greater size would most likely not be possible for the majority of home users. With a static grid size of 3×3 tiles, the rooms were designed in a similar fashion, such that they would fit each other. Portals could be placed at any intersection between grid tiles, so the amount of unique portals was 12 for each intersection, multiplied by 2 since they should be able to face both ways, multiplied by an additional 2 to distinguish between entry and exit portals, resulting in 48 unique portals (see Fig. 1).

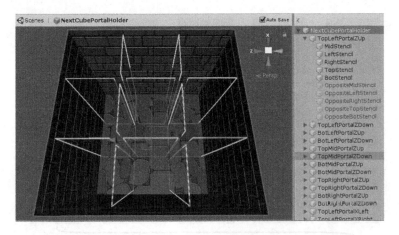

Fig. 1. One of two portal holders used, containing 24 static next-portals (ref. value 2).

With the portal system established, the procedural generation could be designed with their transform in mind. Pre-authored rooms of different types are first loaded into lists, ready to be instantiated at the point of origin. The player has the choice of defining how many rooms they want the maze to consist of, based on the amount of pre-authored rooms available to the algorithm. If the player wants a maze of 99 rooms, and only 30 rooms of each type can be paired, the size of the maze would be capped to the maximum possible combination of rooms, in this case 60. Note that this would be different for each play session, as the rooms are loaded into the list in a random order. Each time a new room is generated, the exit portal position and rotation are stored and compared to the next room's entry portal position and rotation. If the position is the same, but the rotation is different, the room could then be instantiated, and the process would continue. Since the environment created by the algorithm is linear, the transitions when moving through a portal will simply switch to the next or previous room in the generated list, depending on the tag of the portal entered.

To make sure that there are valid pairs for each room portal, a lot of rooms have to be available, often with similar geometric layout. This was not a desired approach, and our solution was to implement a dynamic rotation system in the procedural generation, such that instead of checking the entry portal for the new room at its default position, it could also be rotated by 90, 180, and 270°, in case either of the prior results did not create a connection. This effectively meant that each room functioned as four rooms in the generation step, which meant that the effective amount of layouts present in the system was quadrupled, and would continue to do so for each new room designed. This is only possible because each room has the same size, so if differently sized rooms were to be implemented, dynamic rotations would most likely not be feasible. A possible procedurally generated map layout can be seen in Fig. 2, where the rooms are spread out to give an overview.

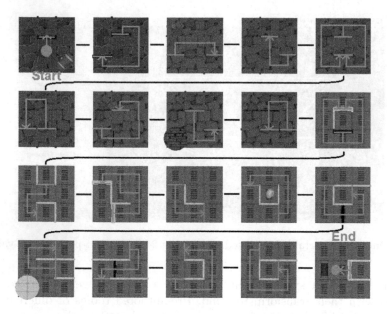

Fig. 2. A top-down map showing a possible layout of a maze set to 20 rooms, and procedurally generated using two room themes. This specific seeded layout was used for the evaluation. The path of the user is indicated by the red lines, starting and ending at the portals in the rooms (Color figure online).

3.4   Transition Between Rooms Using Trigger Boxes

When the trigger boxes are placed correctly, all that is needed is to determine what should happen when the player enters the trigger. Initially, we triggered the transitions exclusively when the player exited the trigger, since only the portals in the current room are active, and if the portal is activated when the player is on top of it, it will again trigger, which is not intended. Having the code run on exit of these portals fixed that issue, however the current room needed to change on trigger entry, such that seamless transitions could be achieved. This meant that new rooms were enabled and disabled when the player entered, and all material changes (more on this in Sect. 3.5) would happen on entry as well. To make up for the fact that the stencil polygons in front of the portal were now showing incorrect geometry, since they display either the next or previous room, they were disabled, and another set of stencil polygons were enabled behind the player, so the previous room would be visible. Note that all of this is done for a single portal. When the player exits the portal, a check is performed for whether the player exited the portal on the correct side, and if this is true, that portal is disabled, and the portal it was paired to is enabled. The reason for the check, is that it is possible for players to enter the trigger box, and then exit on the same side that they entered from, effectively going back to the previous room without ever entering the appropriate portal. Therefore, if the check is false, it simply resets the previous on-entry actions.

3.5 Controlling Rendering with Stencils

As previously mentioned, the next and previous rooms in the list are shown using stencil polygons. We follow a similar process as the one described in [17]. These stencil polygons write a stencil mask to the stencil buffer, such that when a player looks through them, they see the appropriate geometry based on the values in the stencil buffer. These stencil polygons are not rendered to the colour buffer, effectively making the material transparent. They also need a reference value for either previous (1) or next (2), such that they can write a mask to the buffer that contains a value for what geometry should be rendered. The shader then marks the stencil buffer with a specific value where the stencil polygon is visible.

Since the rooms are overlapping each other, it is then important to clear the depth buffer after each mask (1 or 2) has been written to the stencil buffer, otherwise there can be issues with geometry from the current room occluding geometry in the next or previous room.

Lastly, the geometry of the previous (1) and next (2) room is rendered. This geometry follows the same concepts of using a stencil buffer as the mask does. The buffer contains a reference that can be compared to the mask. The stencil test passes when the pixels have a reference value equal to the one in the buffer. With this, both the pass and fail operations in the stencil buffer can be set to keep the current reference value. Since different types of behaviors might be desired, like for the material to be emissive, or have a transparent texture, different shader implementations can be combined with these stencil buffer arguments, to be visible through a polygon.

Discard Geometry In Front of the Stencil Polygons

The last part of the shader discussion is related to which geometry is displayed inside the stencil mask. By default, if the geometry matches the stencil parameter values in the mask, the geometry will be rendered, as long as it is visible through the mask. This unfortunately also applies to geometry in front of the stencil polygon, which is problematic when all rooms are spawned at the same location. The solution to this issue is to discard any geometry between the camera and the stencil polygon, but not behind the stencil polygon.

4   Method

To evaluate our system, we made sure that the procedural generation would give the same result each time, for consistent experiences in the evaluation. This was achieved by assigning a seed value in order to generate the environment layout for all participants. The number of rooms for the given seed was set to 20, and the selected seed had various different examples of overt self-overlapping architecture, and included interactable objects and various landmarks to help with navigation. A map of the level layout of the seed, can be seen in Fig. 2.

4.1   Purpose

The primary purpose of the evaluation was to determine if the transitions were seamless, and how the participants felt about the overt self-overlapping environment. Additionally, we evaluated their perception of the virtual space, and whether or not the implementation induced simulator sickness.

Participants

The system was evaluated with 3 female and 17 male participants who were between 22 and 54 years old. 7 participants had a lot of VR experience, 8 had moderate VR experience, 3 had little VR experience, and 2 had no VR experience.

Variables

After reaching the end of the virtual environment, the participants were given a questionnaire, which had them elaborate on the following questions, which were designed to answer the 3 research questions introduced in Sect. 1 (each question is marked with its related research question):

1. How far do you think you walked in the virtual space? (3)
2. How big of a virtual area do you think you walked in (in square-meters)? (3)
3. How did it feel to walk in this non-euclidean environment? (2)
4. How did the non-euclidean effect feel? What did it make you think? (2)
5. What would you think about walking around in a non-euclidean environment for extended periods of time? (2)
6. How many transitions did you notice (filled out by evaluator)? (1)

The VR sickness questionnaire was used to evaluate if the implementation induced simulator sickness [8].

4.2   Procedure

The experiment was conducted in a lab with a wire-connected HTC Vive setup that uses two base stations to track a play area of minimum $3\,\text{m} \times 3\,\text{m}$. The participants were evaluated individually and asked to sign a written consent form, in addition to answering some demographic questions, including their VR experience, and finally filling out the VR sickness questionnaire. A facilitator then clarified the concept of non-Euclidean geometry and gave general instructions on how to use the controllers in VR. As they were equipped with the HMD, participants were also directed to speak out loud and to mention if they saw anything unusual or out of place during the experience. They were also asked to refrain from walking through walls, as it would break their immersion, and corrupt the data gathered. They were also given a follow up questionnaire regarding the dependent variables after the experience.

5   Results

5.1   Noticed Transitions

To determine the robustness and seamlessness of the transitions described in Sect. 3, we noted how many times each participant noticed a transition from one room to another. As described in Sect. 4, we asked the participants to think out loud, to tell us if they noticed anything that stood out, and if what they talked about was caused or influenced by a transition, this information was marked as a noticed transition. We compared the result with the desired result of "no participants noticing any transitions in the system". We therefore compared the given result with a baseline of 0.

The minimum amount of transitions encountered by each participant, were $n - 1$, with n being the room count, which was 20. 2 participants (10%) commented on situations that indicated awareness of a transition at a specific point. The specific instances that were noticed were completely different; one person noticed a pop-in above them when they walked through an arch corridor. This participant was able to recreate it consistently by moving backward and forward through the triggered box.

The second person commented on the sudden change of floor material, as an indication that they were entering a new room. This participant noted that the transition itself was seamless, however it is still worth noting that a change in material could create awareness of a transition between two spaces.

Analyzing the results from the average number of noticed transitions, which was 0.1 ($SD = 0.3$), when compared to the baseline of 0, using a Wilcoxon signed rank test, yielded $p = 0.5$. The null hypothesis of no difference between the noticed transitions and the preferred baseline can therefore not be rejected for this proposed system and method of evaluation. We did not find system performance issues like freezes or framerate issues to result in an increased likelihood of noticing transitions.

5.2 Perception of Virtual Environment Size

To evaluate the users' perception of environment size in VR compared to real life, the participants were requested to determine the size of the virtual area, with the information that the physical space was a $3\,\mathrm{m} \times 3\,\mathrm{m}$ grid ($9\,\mathrm{m}^2$).

7 participants determined the correct size of the virtual area, which was a 1:1 ratio with the real-world physical play area. Most participants determined that the virtual area was larger than the play area, with some participants believing the virtual area was much larger (above $100\,\mathrm{m}^2$, see Fig. 3). It is likely that these participants were referring to a combined size for all rooms, instead of the perceived virtual space they walked around in.

Overall, it seems that participants were more likely to overestimate (55%) the size of the virtual area in relation to the physical area than underestimate (10%) it, where the bin majority (35%) were able to correctly estimate the size of the virtual area at $9\,\mathrm{m}^2$.

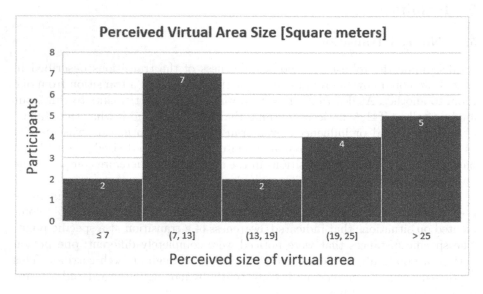

Fig. 3. Shows the frequency of participants believing the size of the virtual area to be within the above bins. The actual size of the virtual area was 9 m^2.

5.3 Virtual Reality Sickness Questionnaire

The Virtual Reality Sickness Questionnaire (VRSQ) was split into 2 different categories, Oculomotor and Distraction. Oculomotor contained the 4 first items of the VRSQ, and Distraction the last 5 items. The Wilcoxon signed rank test was used to compare the answers before and after the VR experience. Pre-Oculomotor ($M = 0.26$, $SD = 0.50$) against Post-Oculomotor ($M = 0.28$, $SD = 0.48$) yielded $p = 1$. Pre-distraction ($M = 0.09$, $SD = 0.29$) against Post-Distraction ($M = 0.17$, $SD = 0.38$) yielded $p = 0.057$. From distraction, the most prominent symptoms were headache, fullness of head, and blurred vision, each with 2–3 participants having an increase from none to slight. From the qualitative comments, some participants also claimed it was caused by the HMD *"For an extended time, I think the headset would disturb me more than the environment."*

5.4 Feedback

From the questionnaire, a lot of general feedback was gathered, which has been divided into 4 Categories:

1. Gameplay
2. Walking
3. Area
4. Sensation

Each category has been filled with keywords and sentences derived from the results of the questionnaire, to help give an impression of the general feeling of the project.

Table 1. A table showing the feedback gathered from the Walking, Sensation, and Area category.

Walking	Freq.	Sensation	Freq.	Area	Freq.
Natural	4	Exciting	6	Environment	6
Realistic	2	Interesting	6	Realistic	5
No difference	1	Immersive	3	Impossible	4
Sensation	1	Uncomfortable	3	Gateways	2
Continuous Walk	1	Strange	2	Environment adapting	1
Walking in real world	1	Trippy	2	Portal	1
Extended cable	1	Confusing	1	Get lost	1
		Feels Strange	1	Turning into different areas	1
		Unnatural	1	Much bigger than real life	1
		A slight warp	1	Mental map to not get lost	1
		Mind blowing	1	Lost track	1
		Grandness	1	Limited size	1
		Cool	1	Completely impossible	1
		Pretty neat	1	Square corridors	1
		Non-Euclidean effect	1		

Table 1 shows that the participants had the most comments for the **Sensation** and **Area** categories, with the majority of them addressing the interesting feeling of experiencing impossible spaces. The figure for the **Gameplay** category is not shown, as all comments were only mentioned once each. The responses are however still included in Sect. 6.1.

6 Discussion

6.1 Discussion of Results

The primary aim of this study was to create a system for procedurally generated overt self-overlapping environments in VR, with natural walking as the loco-motive method for navigation. In the evaluation we tested the system with 20 participants, and noted when they noticed a transition. With 2 noticed transitions, the results show no significant difference from the null hypothesis of no difference, which indicates that our system features seamless transitions.

The 2 noticed transitions were in different situations; the first was a participant looking up when passing through a transition and noticing that some of the geometry shifted slightly due to misalignment with the stencil polygons. The second was not as obtrusive, but a participant noted that a sudden change in the material on the floor, going into a new room, indicated to him that there was a transition at the seam of the two materials. While this is correct, we do not consider it a flaw of the system, as the transition itself was still seamless, however a different and subtler way of transitioning to a new theme could be considered.

We noticed a tendency for the participants to rarely look up, and therefore they might have missed a few of the possible transitions they would otherwise have noticed. This was especially true when the participants were walking, as when they stopped to look around they would sometimes look upward, but immediately as they started moving again they would look downward.

The distraction portion of the VR sickness questionnaire had a relatively low p-value, in while it is not enough to establish a significant difference from the null-hypothesis, it is still worth paying attention to. While most of the participants noted that this was mainly due to being subjected to VR, and was not necessarily caused by the evaluated system, techniques for decreasing distraction properties could be considered.

Qualitative Feedback
From the keywords shown in Table 1 in Sect. 5.4, a couple of points can be made, as some of them say more about the system than others. We acknowledge that some of the comments have been rewritten slightly, to maintain their true meaning when turned into keywords.

Categories
The first category from the table was **Walking**, where the general consensus among all participants was that the walking felt *natural* and *realistic*, with the exception of when a participant managed to stretch out the attached cable to its maximum reach. This created disconnect from the immersion for the affected participants, which could have been avoided by using a wireless headset. Having positive feedback regarding the natural walking shows that it very much is a contender to the standard video game locomotion methods.

The second category was **Gameplay**, where participants were more critical in general. They felt that more gameplay mechanics could be added to make the game more fun and replayable. Adding more gameplay mechanics, such as more decisions, a combat system or others, is definitely something that could be added in future works. However, the use of landmarks in rooms to prevent getting lost, were greatly appreciated by participants when asked.

Area was the third category, and the feedback here varied greatly. Some participants noted that the architecture was *impossible* and large, while others felt it was natural and based on a 3 m × 3 m grid. This discrepancy can be caused by difference in VR experience in the participants, as a more experienced VR user potentially has an easier time separating gameplay from reality, thus not finding impossible spaces unlikely to occur. A single participant mentioned that he created a mental map of the environment, to prevent himself from getting lost and walking on paths that he had already traversed. This shows that he sees the environment as a connected maze, and understands that even though it is overlapping and impossible, it is still connected linearly and has a path.

The last category was **Sensation**, which we used to describe anything the participant was feeling regarding the use of impossible spaces in VR. A lot of the words in the table might seem to have a negative tone to them, but that is not necessarily the meaning behind them. When creating the system, we pursued the feeling that something was weird and unnatural, and having participants recognize that something around them is wrong and impossible, shows that we have managed to implement a working solution for impossible spaces in VR. 2 participants noted that they would probably dislike spending too long inside the system. However, it is hard to know if that is due to something specific to our system, or simply just long exposure to VR. This could be tested in future works, to ensure that the system itself does not cause to users any discomfort.

We acknowledge that this evaluation was not conducted with a wireless HMD, which could have negatively affected the results. This did have the interesting effect of making participants want to drag the wire around corners in the virtual environment, although it would be preferred to have a wireless HMD when navigating an environment with natural walking, especially for larger grid sizes.

6.2   Limitations

The main limitations of our current system comes from the complexity of using the stencil test. For each possible reference value in the stencil buffer, an equal amount of shader variations must be present for each material in the scene. In the current implementation, three reference values are used; current (0), previous (1), and next (2). Adding two more stencil references, pre-previous (3) and post-next (4), would result in 5 variations of each material in the scene, which all need to be switched during a transition. This amount of stencil references also needs to be considered for objects that can pass through the stencil plane, as they will otherwise disappear if the material is not updated properly.

6.3 Future Work

While the concept of self-overlapping geometry has been explored in previous studies, the concept of procedural generation of such environments, and the notion that they can be overtly self-overlapping, brings forth numerous other possible topics for future work. The first is the idea of generating the environment based on the grid size, such that the rooms could be connected in ways that would make use of a grid of 4×4 tiles or larger, or possibly an uneven grid e.g. 3×4 tiles. While it would be possible to scale the grid size downwards, since the system uses natural walking, it is likely that the player will end up walking in circles for most of the time. Having the option to scale the maze to the play area available to the player, by having multiple 3×3 rooms placed in a 9×9 play area, could improve the player's immersion of the game and eliminate the feeling of walking in circles. The use of self-overlapping architecture coupled with the procedural map generation, makes the possibilities for maze layouts almost infinite, in addition to a potential increase to the replayability.

Another topic would be to use such a system to create interactive natural walking VR games, and investigate how the overt self-overlapping nature of the geometry could be used as a puzzle element, as well as what kind of effect it would have on users. By having the maze be completely generated as soon as the game starts, it allows the player to retrace their steps and walk backwards in the maze as well, which again can be used as a gameplay mechanic, e.g by having the player pick up a key in a room, which unlocks a door they encountered earlier. This is not possible to do with a real-time procedural generation of rooms like in VRoamer by Cheng et al. [4].

As mentioned in Sect. 6.1, participants in the evaluation infrequently looked upward. When navigating the environment most of them were looking slightly downward. It is possible that this behaviour could be investigated in the future, and that it might result in a change of design to incentivize looking forward or upward.

The system could be changed to be non-linear by having multiple exit portals in a single room, which could be achieved using a tree data structure. Another option could be to store multiple destinations for each portal, and changing the destinations during runtime whenever the player enters a portal, which could be achieved by implementing a graph data structure.

7 Conclusion

In this project, we explored the idea of creating a procedurally generated overt self-overlapping environment for natural walking in VR. The environment consists of rooms that are instantiated and connected using 'portals', which consist of a trigger box to determine when transitions between rooms should occur, and stencil polygons to maintain the visual consistency when looking and passing through a portal.

In an evaluation of the system with 20 participants, we determined that the overt self-overlapping environment is navigable, and that the transitions between rooms using the previously defined portals are seamless, as the participants were subjected to at least 19 transitions each, and in total only 2 participants noticed a single transition. The feedback given by the participants from the feeling of experiencing an overt self-overlapping environment is also analyzed and discussed in this paper, and is concluded to feel natural, despite being overtly impossible. The general consensus indicated that the participants felt good about navigating the environment, and some participants described the experience as strange, yet interesting.

In conclusion, we think there is great benefit to procedurally-generated self-overlapping systems for room-scale VR implementations that use natural walking, with seamless transitions. We have shown with a user study that an implementation of such systems is actually feasible.

References

1. Bruce, A.: Antichamber (2013). http://www.antichamber-game.com/
2. Bruder, G., Steinicke, F., Hinrichs, K.H.: Arch-explore: a natural user interface for immersive architectural walkthroughs. In: 2009 IEEE Symposium on 3D User Interfaces, pp. 75–82. IEEE (2009)
3. Bui, K.: Procedural Content Generation for C++ Game Development. Packt Publishing Ltd (2016)
4. Cheng, L.P., Ofek, E., Holz, C., Wilson, A.D.: VRoamer: generating on-the-fly VR experiences while walking inside large, unknown real-world building environments. In: 2019 IEEE Conference on Virtual Reality and 3D User Interfaces (VR), pp. 359–366. IEEE (2019)
5. Garg, A., Fisher, J., Wang, W., K.P., S.: ARES: an application of impossible spaces for natural locomotion in VR. In: 2017 CHI Conference Extended Abstracts on Human Factors in Computing Systems, pp. 218–221. ACM (2017)
6. Jeong, K., Kim, J.: Event-centered maze generation method for mobile virtual reality applications. Symmetry 8(11), 120 (2016)
7. Jeong, K., Lee, J., Kim, J.: A study on new virtual reality system in maze terrain. Int. J. Hum. Comput. Interact. 34(2), 129–145 (2018)
8. Kim, H.K., Park, J., Choi, Y., Choe, M.: Virtual reality sickness questionnaire (VRSQ): motion sickness measurement index in a virtual reality environment. Applied Ergon. 69, 66–73 (2018)
9. Langbehn, E., Lubos, P., Bruder, G., Steinicke, F.: Application of redirected walking in room-scale VR. In: 2017 IEEE Virtual Reality (VR), pp. 449–450. IEEE (2017)
10. Langbehn, E., Lubos, P., Steinicke, F.: Redirected spaces: going beyond borders. In: 2018 IEEE Conference on Virtual Reality and 3D User Interfaces (VR), pp. 767–768. IEEE (2018)
11. Void room: Tea for god (2019). https://void-room.itch.io/tea-for-god
12. Skantarova, D., Evers, N., Serubugo, S.: Self-overlapping maze and map design for asymmetric collaboration in room-scale virtual reality for public spaces (2017)
13. Sra, M., Garrido-Jurado, S., Schmandt, C., Maes, P.: Procedurally generated virtual reality from 3D reconstructed physical space. In: Proceedings of the 22nd ACM Conference on Virtual Reality Software and Technology, pp. 191–200. ACM (2016)

14. Suma, E.A., Lipps, Z., Finkelstein, S., Krum, D., Bolas, M.: Impossible spaces: maximizing natural walking in virtual environments with self-overlapping architecture. IEEE Trans. Visual Comput. Graphics **18**, 555–564 (2012)
15. Suma, E.A., Bruder, G., Steinicke, F., Krum, D.M., Bolas, M.: A taxonomy for deploying redirection techniques in immersive virtual environments. In: 2012 IEEE Virtual Reality Workshops (VRW), pp. 43–46. IEEE (2012)
16. Togelius, J., Shaker, N., Nelson, M.J.: Introduction. Procedural Content Generation in Games. CSCS, pp. 1–15. Springer, Cham (2016). https://doi.org/10.1007/978-3-319-42716-4_1
17. Unity: Shaderlab: Stencil, unity manual (2019). https://docs.unity3d.com/Manual/SL-Stencil.html
18. Vasylevska, K., Kaufmann, H., Bolas, Suma, E.A.: Flexible spaces: dynamic layout generation for infinite walking in virtual environments. In: 2013 IEEE Symposium on 3D User Interfaces (3DUI), pp. 39–42. IEEE (2013)

Staging Virtual Reality Exhibits
for Bystander Involvement
in Semi-public Spaces

Daniel Hepperle$^{(\boxtimes)}$, Andreas Siess, and Matthias Wölfel

Faculty of Computer Science and Business Information Systems, Karlsruhe University
of Applied Sciences, Moltkestr. 30, 76133 Karlsruhe, Germany
{daniel.hepperle,andreas.siess,matthias.wolfel}@hs-karlsruhe.de

Abstract. As virtual reality becomes more popular to be used in semi-public spaces such as museums and other exhibition venues, the question on how to optimally stage such an experience arises. To foster interaction between participants and bystanders, to lower the primary threshold in regards to participation and to moderate the transition between real and virtual worlds we propose to augment a virtual hot-air balloon ride by a large scale floor projection in addition to a physical basket and other extras. Exhibited at a venue in Stuttgart, Germany a total of 140 participants evaluated our approach. We could confirm that adding a floor projection helped to attract additional users, to increased the overall motivation on using the installation, and to established a connection between the real and the virtual worlds.

Keywords: Virtual reality · Exhibition · (semi-)public space ·
Museum · Staging · Bystander · Head-mounted display

1 Introduction

The question on how virtual reality (VR) technologies will shape our future lives has been around since at least the renaissance of VR in the second decade of the 21st century. We believe that one essential question which needs to be addressed in this regard is *not how*, but *where* this will happen. The question on *where* arises because VR enfolds its full potential only in those cases when the physical surrounding is also taken into consideration. Setting up consisting or matching mixed world environments where virtual and real are intermingled can usually not be realized at home, because it requires complex hardware constructions. It has been shown that, if done right, that mixed reality setups can help improve presence [7,8]. Because of that, we argue that for high-end VR installations, museums, exhibitions, and amusement parks are perfectly suitable for staging VR installations in the most engaging way. In this context, one is able to create spectacular, immersive experiences, whereby the complete isolation of the physical outside world at the same time is a major hurdle for wearing head-mounted

© ICST Institute for Computer Sciences, Social Informatics and Telecommunications Engineering 2020
Published by Springer Nature Switzerland AG 2020. All Rights Reserved
A. Brooks and E. I. Brooks (Eds.): ArtsIT 2019/DLI 2019, LNICST 328, pp. 261–272, 2020.
https://doi.org/10.1007/978-3-030-53294-9_18

displays (HMDs). This has to be overcome, especially for cases where one might be under possible observation such as semi-public spaces. Next to a complete "leap into the unknown"[1], VR technology tends to give rise to uncertainty in regards to possible motion sickness and also to hygienic concerns which prevent many potential visitors from getting involved in a VR experience. To counteract this problem, the team extended a VR installation already shown at the ZKM — Zentrum für Kunst und Medien Karlsruhe by a large-scale floor projection. For the viewers, this led to a more attractive installation, it encouraged them to participate better and optimally prepared them for the upcoming VR experience. Thus, the participants were able to gently lift off in a replica balloon basket: They felt the vibrations of the flight imitated by jiggling plates. The heat of the burner's virtual flames was reflected in hot studio lamps. A light breeze, created by a fan, blew through their hair. The high congruence between the real and the virtual always created a safe environment, which even made it possible to hold on to the balloon basket in the event of a fear of heights.

2   Related Work

Already in the year 1900, Raoul Grimoin-Sanson exhibited a virtual hot air balloon ride called *Cinéorama* at the *Exhibition Universelle* in Paris. Their setup consisted of 10 synchronized 70 mm film projectors, which they used to project hand-colored aerial film on a screen that was 9 m tall and 100 m in circumference. The projectors were placed right beneath the balloon's gondola [13]. While this early installation was done using large scale projections to generate a multi-person experience, immersive VR using HMD is most of the time an isolated single-user experience. Also, almost any (semi-)public venue that exhibits immersive VR content usually is not presenting the virtual content to the public in an appropriate way—or even worse—not at all. If the respective content is shown at all, it is common to present it in first-person view on a screen mounted near the person using the HMD. This ego-perspective makes it harder for others to catch what is happening within VR because it lacks to articulate the spatial layout of the current scene and the image itself is quite shaky. The scientific community is catching up on the topic lately; e.g. there has been a first workshop dedicated to discussing the upcoming challenges using HMDs in shared and social spaces[2]. Here topics such as bystander in- and exclusion, privacy and safety concerns, and augmentation by using projections have been discussed [4]. But, as it is still a niche research topic, it is necessary to also take a look outside of the scientific community and analyze what is the actual state of the art in exhibition pieces other than ours. In the following, we separate related works into two groups: VR exhibitions relevant to our topic and related research that has been conducted in this area.

---

[1] When only seeing a person wearing a HMD in a semi-public space as a passer-by, one does not directly know what to expect from the upcoming experience and this might scare off (timid) visitors.

[2] See: https://www.medien.ifi.lmu.de/socialHMD/ for more information.

2.1   Research

The experience of isolation while using VR in public was demonstrated by Mai et al., who interviewed their respondents in qualitative interviews about their feelings during use [12]. Although, it has to be noted that different spatial layouts and amounts of bystanders had no significant influence on measured presence. Mai and Khamis [11] investigated user behavior around public HMDs by adapting the "audience funnel" by Brignull and Rogers [2] to public HMDs. They replaced "subtle interactions" by "get in touch with the hardware" to emphasize that the bystanders need to familiarize themselves with the hardware by inspecting and even touching it. Siess et al. [16], on the other hand, introduced an adapted version of the audience funnel to fit to immersive VR installations in (semi-)public places.

Engaging VR and non-VR users to a common experience was investigated by Gugenheimer et al. with their "Share VR" installation [5] that used floor projections as output device for the non-VR player. In regards to floor projections the "ReverseCAVE" of Ishii et al. [9] also presents an interesting concept to engage bystanders via wall projections. This especially is helpful in semi-public spaces since it enables all visitors to take photos of VR content. Chan and Minamizawa tried to engage communication between HMD-users and non-HMD-users by attaching a screen on the front of each HMD [3]. Other concepts that try to facilitate cooperation between users and non-users include multi-touch-tables [17].

To summarize these findings and ideas it can be stated that there is a high demand for concepts that are able to attract bystanders to engage with presented VR hardware as well as for concepts that foster interaction between these bystanders and users. Engaging visitors in new and unexpected ways will be a key element to successfully set up (semi-)public VR installations [14].

2.2   VR-Exhibitions

The presented approaches in Sect. 2.1 are seldom found "in the wild". To get a brief overview on how VR exhibits currently are presented in semi-public spaces, we conducted a brief inquiry using common search engines. The following keywords were used for our investigation: "VR Exhibit Museum; Virtual Reality Staging Museum"; It resulted in 15 exhibitions from different kinds of venues around the world that use immersive VR[3] as a gateway to present content to a semi-public audience. Table 1 lists the different venues in combination with the way, the actual VR experience as seen by the current user was presented to the audience technologically (via TV, Projection, etc.) and in regards to the respective perspective of this presentation.

---

[3] When talking about immersive VR we only consider VR using HMDs in the context of this publication.

Table 1. Overview of exhibited and documented VR venues. To visit a link mentioned above just replace the asterisk in the following url "http://bit.ly/artsit19-" with the corresponding number found in the table. All links has been visited 2019-10-16.

Venue	Presentation system	Point of view	Link suffix
Louvre Museum	TV	First person	1
York Museum	TV	First person	2
Saarland Informatics Campus	Wall-projection	Third person	3
Deutsches Museum	Wall-projection	First person	4
The Franklin Institute	TV	First person	5
Smithsonian Museum	TV	First person	6
Historium Bruges	TV	First person	7
Zeiss Science Vision Lab	TV	First person	8
National Museum of Finland	None	None	9
Museen Narrenschopf	None	None	10
Zeppelin Museum	TV	First person	11
Städel Museum	None	None	12
HEK Basel	TV & Wall-projection	First person	13
Gazelli Art House	Wall projection	First person	14
Tate Modern	—	—	15

3   Installation and Setup

The general idea of our installation "Super Nubibus"[4] is to present a ride in a hot air balloon over the town of Karlsruhe in the year 1834. A first version, without floor projection, had already been presented at the ZKM Karlsruhe [16]. Users can experience the ride using a physical replica of a balloon basket and an HTC Vive Pro VR headset. By placing the basket precisely in the virtual environment, it was possible to ensure that the virtual and haptic representation matched exactly: a concept proven to be very valuable [6]. The basked also allowed the VR user to lean on the railing and hold on to it. The user could start the ride and determine the height of the balloon by pulling a physical rope that would ignite the burner's flame in the virtual environment. To enrich the overall experience two powerful PAR spotlights were included that would light up every time the rope is pulled to simulate the burner's heat on the user's head. Furthermore, a wind machine was activated once the ride started. In contrast to the setup presented at the ZKM, two other significant features were added: a large TV monitor in three meters height (see Fig. 2), which exactly reproduced the VR spectator's field of view, and a floor projection around the balloon basket, which showed the scene from a bird's eye view (see Fig. 1). For passers-by, this resulted

---

[4] http://www.super-nubibus.de/.

in a panoramic view of a balloon basket that conveyed the impression of being levitated over a landscape.

3.1 Location and Venue

Being visited by over 10.000 individuals the *new.New.Festival* is the largest startup and entrepreneurship festival in Germany. It took place at the Hanns-Martin-Schleyer-Halle in Stuttgart. Our installation was located at the end of a long curve of the main visitor path. Next to our exhibition space, the entrance to an action space was located, where, several times a day, events with a high number of visitors took place. On the opposite, there was an area where visitors could eat and charge their mobile devices. Therefore, our booth was noticed by a large number of visitors.

Fig. 1. Booth at *new.New.Festival*: Floor projection, TV screen and haptic sensations (wind, temperature, balloon basket) providing remarkable experiences for users and bystanders.

3.2 Physical Setup

As chassis for our installation we built a $4{,}60\,\text{m} \times 3{,}60\,\text{m} \times 3{,}30\,\text{m}$ truss construction to which we could attach all necessary devices (see Fig. 1 and 2A). To create the floor projection, we used two WUXGA projectors that were attached to the truss that aimed downwards almost vertically. Manually stitching the two images resulted in one large projection area. Since the venue's floor surface was not suitable for a high-contrast projection (too inhomogeneous and too dark), we placed a white molleton on the entire surface, which ensured vibrant colors and enough brightness for a satisfying result. A large TV screen (see Fig. 2B) mirroring the HMD's point of view was mounted at the top corner of the truss construction.

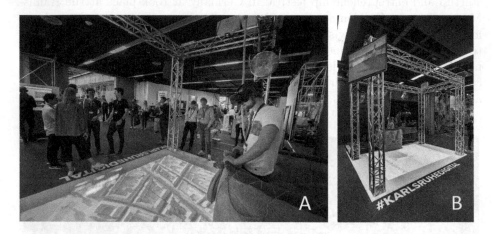

Fig. 2. A: the setup as seen from behind; B: view at the booth from the rest area

3.3 Adaption of the Audience Funnel

Based on new observation and data gathered at the latest exhibition, we adapted the previous version of the VR audience funnel in regards to the latest add-ons "floor projection" and "TV", see Fig. 3. The main difference in regards to the former installation is, that the so-called voyeurs could interact with each other based on the story but did not have to interact with the current user. Quite obvious but also worth to be mentioned is, that honeypots complement themselves.

4 User Test

In this section we briefly explain the questionnaire and the analysis of the demographic structure of the test population.

4.1 Questionnaire

A printed questionnaire that the participants were asked to answer after interacting with our installation was used, because of limited online access on location. Since we asked all individuals that somehow interacted with our installation to fill out the questionnaire it was separated into two main slots: One slot for all

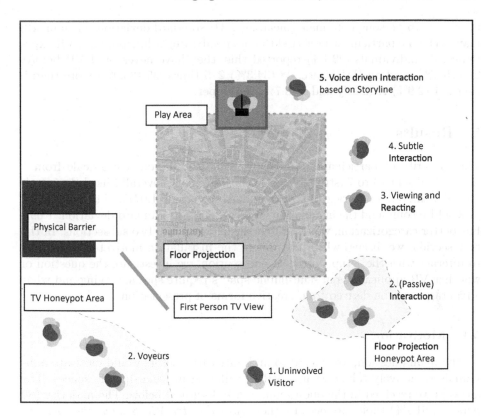

Fig. 3. Audience Funnel for *new.New.Festival* VR exhibition.

participants that took the ride and one for all other individuals who refused to fly with the hot air balloon. Participation was voluntary. Skipping a question was also possible at any time. The regular questionnaire (for everyone but those who did not use the installation) consisted of 23 individual questions. Besides demographic information (age, gender, VR experience, fear of height, prevalence of motion sickness) the participants were asked what part of the installation has played a decisive role in interacting with the exhibit (multiple choice). Furthermore, the users were presented statements that they could rate via a Likert scale [10]. At the end of the questionnaire, there was space for the participants to write down impressions might not have been covered by the questionnaire. Visitors that did not want to take part in the installation, but were willing to fill out the survey, only were asked questions (besides demographic data) in regards to the reasons they were not willing to try out the installation.

4.2   Test Population

Our installation was exhibited for three consecutive days. During this period we were able to question 140 individuals of which 134 (95.7%) did use the installation. 63 test subjects were female (mean age: 28; standard deviation: 9; min: 20;

max: 59); 76 persons were male (mean age: 31; standard deviation: 11; min: 19; max: 64). One participant preferred to not specify. Regarding previous VR experience, 31 individuals (22.1%) reported that they have never tried VR before, 21 (15.0%) used an HMD once, 48 (34.3%) 2–5 times, 35 (25.0%) more than 5 times, 4 (2.9%) regularly and 1 (0.7%) developer.

5 Results

The majority of participants appreciated our installation: On a scale from 1 (strongly disagree) to 7 (strongly agree) the statement "overall I liked the installation" achieved an average of 6.22 (standard deviation: 1.07) and the statement "I would recommend the installation" a mean of 6.14 (standard deviation: 1.09). For better categorization, we separated this chapter into two subsections. In the first section, we discuss which features of the installation motivated passers-by to interact with the setup. In the second section, we investigate the question of whether VR applications in semi-public spaces require special staging and what advantages can be derived from creative forms of presentation.

5.1 Motivation

As the main question, we wanted to find out, what factors would motivate individuals to actively take part in a VR installation in (semi-)public spaces. The answers we received in the questionnaire are discussed below. The majority (80 persons, 61.1%) took part because they *wanted to try VR. Seeing other persons using the installation* was also a huge motivator to try out the setup (60 persons, 45.8%). 28 persons (21.4%) were *attracted by observing the floor projection* and 24 (18.3%) came by since they wanted to *try out unknown hardware.* 23 (17.6%) answered that they were interested in the installation *because others told them about* it. 22 (16.8%) were *pulled in by other persons. The monitor* was a decisive factor for 12 (9.2%) users to actively try out the exhibit. 13 participants took the chance to give free-text answers. Their answers ranged from general interest in the installation up to technical aspects about programming. Many answers revolved around the topic of combining several devices (i.e. VR with balloon basket) and staging the exhibition booth.

Regarding the forecast of the technology's market size worldwide [1] it is to be expected that VR will discard its aura of the new in the near future and become a common device in the everyday media routine of many recipients. Therefore the strongest motivator in this study ("I wanted to try VR") may soon no longer be relevant since almost everyone has come into contact with VR before. It is worthwhile to take a look at the other aspects that also motivated passers-by to try out the installation. As already stated in the previous paper [16], the honeypot effect is also a good motivator to convince passers-by. Watching another person try it out seems to be an excellent way to break down the barriers to entry (See Fig. 4). For all designers who want to address this aspect, the

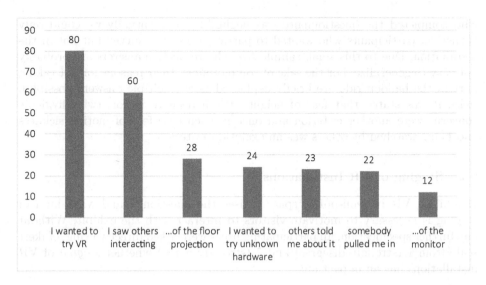

Fig. 4. Questionnaire answers on "I did use the installation because ..." (absolute numbers, multiple choice)

question is how this activity can be staged without exposing the individual user too much.

At this point, the difference between the output devices has to be emphasized. The current state of the art in staging VR in public spaces is a large screen mirroring the image of the VR headset in a first-person perspective. However, our survey showed that over twice as many bystanders were motivated to participate by the floor projection compared to the monitor. The screen alone was only relevant for a minority (9.2%) in their individual decision to participate in the installation.

Looking at the second part of the questionnaire, these findings can be substantiated. Using a common Likert scale setup, we evaluated different statements on a scale from 1 (strongly disagree) to 7 (strongly agree).

The question of whether the floor projection had increased the interest in the installation was answered with an average of 5.43 (standard deviation: 1.43). In comparison, for the monitor, the same question was rated with an average of 4.47 (standard deviation: 1.78). An ANOVA revealed: Users who were attracted by the floor projection were also more likely to recommend the installation to others ($p < 0.05$) and to like the visual style ($p < 0.05$). They were also more likely to share the opinion that the floor projection established a connection between VR and the real world ($p < 0.05$). Whether the person in VR increased the interest in the installation was answered with an average of 5.30 (standard deviation: 1.52). We did not find any statistically significant differences between the genders or age groups respectively in regards to motivational factors.

All visitors who used the installation filled out the questionnaire afterward. Among the passers-by who refused to try out the exhibit, the number of people who completed the questionnaire was negligible, so eventually we could only gather six participants who wanted to participate in the survey but not in the installation. Due to this small sample size, the respective answers are probably not easy to generalize. For the sake of completeness, their reasons for not taking part in the balloon ride are briefly explained here (multiple answers possible): twice it was stated that fear of heights was a decisive factor, twice hygienic concerns were another criterion and once in each case fear of motion sickness and being watched by others was an exclusion criterion.

5.2 Staging of VR Installations

Exhibiting VR in semi-public spaces raises the question if and what kind of staging is necessary to motivate visitors to interact with the exhibit. Without any further specification, all participating users were asked directly using a Likert scale from 1 (strongly disagree) and 7 (strongly agree) whether *staging* of VR installations has an impact on:

- observing the installation
- interacting with the installation

Across all participants the first question was answered with a mean of 5.67 (standard deviation: 1.21); the second with a mean of 5.76 (standard deviation 1.31). We did not find any statistical significant differences regarding these two questions across genders as well as users' prior VR experience or age. Although these numbers may seem unconvincing at first, we want to point out that staging VR experiences by including multimodal sensations has further effects that go beyond the first impression. In total 19 participants (14%) answered that they have "severely" fear of heights or that they suffer from Acrophobia; 47 participants (34%) stated that they are "a little" afraid of heights. Motion sickness is still prevalent among all VR users [15]. In our case almost *every fourth visitor* (34 users; 24%) reported that they have previously experienced motion sickness. When asking the participants if they experienced motion sickness during the balloon ride using a Likert scale from 1 (strongly disagree) and 7 (strongly agree), these findings could not be reflected. Among all participants, the mean value was considerably low (1.61, standard deviation: 1.17). When only users are examined that had prior experience with motion sickness this value hardly changes (1.74, standard deviation: 1.29). We interpret this phenomenon that our installation does not evoke motion sickness, even when sensitive users are put into consideration. Therefore it seems interesting to find out what exact feature of the exhibit achieved that desirable effect. We questioned—also via Likert scale from 1 (strongly disagree) and 7 (strongly agree)—if touching real objects while in VR improved the overall experience. This question was answered with a mean of 6.00 (standard deviation: 1.29) for all participants. When only users are put into consideration that had previously experienced motion sickness, the mean value changes to 6.42 (standard deviation 1.03). An ANOVA revealed that this correlation is statically significant ($p < 0.05$). Therefore, the staging of VR installations not only offers the potential to motivate more visitors to engage but also enriches the experience for the user.

Furthermore, the participants could rate if they felt dizzy after the ride. This question was answered with a mean of 2.32 (standard deviation: 1.69). When only participants are put into consideration that had previous experience with motion sickness, this value changes only marginally to 2.78 (standard deviation: 1.88). Also the prevalence of Acrophobia and severe fear of heights had almost no effect on the incidence of post-ride uneasiness (mean: 2.78, standard deviation: 2.26). We interpret these results in that way that simulator sickness is still a topic that needs attention but can also be addressed by combining suitable content with considerate staging.

6 Conclusion

Renowned museums try to make use of the new possibilities VR offers. But staging VR in semi-public spaces is not yet common. This might be because even basic VR setups currently require an increased maintenance expanse and are difficult to handle.

The most influential motivator for visitors to interact with a VR-related exhibit we identified (experience new technology) is not dependent on any staging at all. In contrast to that, when asked directly, visitors state that staging could have an impact on the general interest as well as on the final decision to interact. But the staging of VR installations reveals further advantages: we observed that motion sickness can be reduced by merging the virtual and physical world accordingly. Staging not only has the potential to convince passers-by to participate but also has a direct influence on the actual user's well-being (e.g. not feeling isolated from the physical surroundings while maintaining a sense of presence). By articulating the content to the public, a connection is created between the otherwise isolated VR user and the bystanders. This reduces the fear of entering VR and, at the same time, improves the VR experience itself because the user is no longer overwhelmed by the unexpected content, but can mentally adjust to the environment and the content before the experience.

References

1. Global Augmented/Virtual Reality market size 2016–2023 | Statista. https:// www.statista.com/statistics/591181/global-augmented-virtual-reality-market-size (2019). Accessed 7 Oct 2019
2. Brignull, H., Rogers, Y.: Enticing people to interact with large public displays in public spaces. In: Proceedings of INTERACT, vol. 3, pp. 17–24 (2003)
3. Chan, L., Minamizawa, K.: Frontface: Facilitating communication between hmd users and outsiders using front-facing-screen hmds. In: Proceedings of the 19th International Conference on Human-Computer Interaction with Mobile Devices and Services, MobileHCI 2017, pp. 22:1–22:5. ACM, New York (2017)

4. Gugenheimer, J., Mai, C., McGill, M., Williamson, J., Steinicke, F., Perlin, K.: Challenges using head-mounted displays in shared and social spaces. In: Extended Abstracts of the 2019 CHI Conference on Human Factors in Computing Systems, CHI EA 2019, pp. W19:1–W19:8. ACM, New York (2019)
5. Gugenheimer, J., Stemasov, E., Frommel, J., Rukzio, E.: Sharevr: Enabling co-located experiences for virtual reality between hmd and non-hmd users. In: Proceedings of the 2017 CHI Conference on Human Factors in Computing Systems, pp. 4021–4033. ACM (2017)
6. Hepperle, D., Wölfel, M.: Do you feel what you see? Multimodal perception in virtual reality. In: Proceedings of the 23rd ACM Symposium on Virtual Reality Software and Technology, VRST 2017, pp. 56:1–56:2. ACM, New York (2017)
7. Hoffman, H.G.: Physically touching virtual objects using tactile augmentation enhances the realism of virtual environments. In: Proceedings of IEEE 1998 Virtual Reality Annual International Symposium (Cat. No.98CB36180), pp. 59–63 (1998)
8. Insko, B.E.: Passive haptics significantly enhances virtual environments. Ph.D. thesis (2001)
9. Ishii, A., Suzuki, I., Tsuruta, M., Nakamae, S., Suzuki, J., Ochiai, Y.: Reversecave: Cave-based visualization methods of public VR towards shareable VR experience. In: Extended Abstracts of the 2018 CHI Conference on Human Factors in Computing Systems, p. VS01. ACM (2018)
10. Lazar, J., Feng, J., Hochheiser, H.: Research Methods in Human-Computer Interaction. Elsevier Science, Cambridge (2017)
11. Mai, C., Khamis, M.: Public HMDs: Modeling and understanding user behavior around public head-mounted displays. In: Proceedings of the 7th ACM International Symposium on Pervasive Displays, PerDis 2018, pp. 21:1–21:9. ACM, New York (2018)
12. Mai, C., Wiltzius, T., Alt, F., Hussmann, H.: Feeling alone in public: Investigating the influence of spatial layout on users' VR experience. In: Proceedings of the 10th Nordic Conference on Human-Computer Interaction, NordiCHI 2018, pp. 286–298. ACM, New York (2018)
13. Mancini, M.: Pictures at an exposition. Film Comment 19(1), 43 (1983)
14. Pantile, D., Frasca, R., Mazzeo, A., Ventrella, M., Verreschi, G.: New technologies and tools for immersive and engaging visitor experiences in museums: The evolution of the visit-actor in next-generation storytelling, through augmented and virtual reality, and immersive 3d projections. In: 2016 12th International Conference on Signal-Image Technology Internet-Based Systems (SITIS), pp. 463–467 (2016)
15. Siess, A., Beuck, S., Wölfel, M.: Virtual Reality-Quo Vadis? How to address the complete audience of an emerging technology. In: Collaborative European Research Conference, pp. 245–247 (2017)
16. Siess, A., Hepperle, D., Wölfel, M., Johansson, M.: Worldmaking: Designing for audience participation, immersion and interaction in virtual and real spaces. In: Brooks, A.L., Brooks, E., Sylla, C. (eds.) ArtsIT/DLI -2018. LNICSSITE, vol. 265, pp. 58–68. Springer, Cham (2019). https://doi.org/10.1007/978-3-030-06134-0_7
17. Sundén, E., Lundgren, I., Ynnerman, A.: Hybrid virtual reality touch table - An immersive collaborative platform for public explanatory use of cultural objects and sites. In: Schreck, T., Weyrich, T., Sablatnig, R., Stular, B. (eds.) Eurographics Workshop on Graphics and Cultural Heritage. The Eurographics Association (2017)

Playful and Humorous Interactions in Urban Environments Made Possible with Augmented Reality Technology

Anton Nijholt[✉]

Human Media Interaction, University of Twente, Enschede, The Netherlands
a.nijholt@utwente.nl

Abstract. There is more to humor than jokes. Humor can be created in jokes, in cartoons and animations, in products, commercials, and movies, or in stand-up comedy. However, also during our daily activities, we often smile and laugh because we experience interactions and events as humorous. We can experience such events; we can also initiate such events. Smart environments offer us tools that allow the customization of urban environments to potential and personalized playful and humorous experiences. Sensors and actuators in smart urban environments can be addressed and configured in such a way that they initiate and facilitate playful and humorous events in the real world, but it is also possible that without physical changes in the real world, our imaginations are triggered to give humorous interpretations of events in the real world by observing or imagining how they could be different. In this paper, we look at humor that can be experienced by imagination, by suggestions, by changes in the environment, and by changing the environment using digital augmented and diminished reality tools. The views expressed here can help to add humor to urban play, urban games, and daily activities in public spaces using augmented reality technology.

Keywords: Humor · Incongruity · Play · Sensors · Actuators · Digital technology · Urban environments · Smart environments · Augmented reality · Diminished reality

1 Introduction

Humor is important in our daily lives. While on the street, using public transport, or driving cars, it is often the case that we become bored, irritated, or frustrated. Nevertheless, it is also the case that there are many situations in which we smile or laugh while interacting with others, at home, in our workplaces, or in public spaces. We also can be amused by perceiving unexpected events and by giving humorous interpretations to events, possibly drawing on our past life experiences. Maybe a bystander provides us with such a humorous interpretation. Maybe someone watches us when we smile without any understanding of why we do so.

© ICST Institute for Computer Sciences, Social Informatics and Telecommunications Engineering 2020
Published by Springer Nature Switzerland AG 2020. All Rights Reserved
A. Brooks and E. I. Brooks (Eds.): ArtsIT 2019/DLI 2019, LNICST 328, pp. 273–289, 2020.
https://doi.org/10.1007/978-3-030-53294-9_19

In smart urban environments, we have sensors that monitor and interpret inhabitants' behaviors. Based on this context-aware measuring of an individual's behavior, other knowledge that is available from this inhabitant, and global knowledge about people's behavior and preferences, actuators can support city dwellers in their activities while, at the same time, all kinds of demands placed on residents can be met. Can smart urban technology help to add humor to serious and playful activities in urban environments? Can it add humor and playful applications to urban, location-based gaming apps [1]?

The interplay of sensors and actuators embedded in smart urban environments can lead to physical changes to these environments. Changes can be on visual displays, but there can also be changes that involve ambient light, sound, and scent, changes in the appearance of public spaces, buildings, and street furniture. Changes can be caused by people's behavior, traffic, dangerous situations or, perhaps, seeing the possibility to create a playful or humorous situation. Changes can also be initiated by city dwellers if they have access to the appropriate sensors and actuators. Apart from having authorized access to sensors and actuators in the urban environment, communities and individuals can introduce their own networks of sensors and actuators, and, of course, they can use and hack urban sensor and actuator networks for location-based gameplay, unauthorized interactive street art, protests, and activism.

The interplay of sensors and actuators can also lead to virtual changes in the environment. We can notice such Augmented Reality changes on our smartphone, a head-mounted device, or with our smart glasses. Again, such changes that are projected on a reality that is displayed on our smart devices can be initiated by a smart environment (controlled by companies and civic authorities) or there is the possibility to control this augmentation of reality ourselves. That is, having a city's authorized access to sensors and actuators that have been designed for that purpose, having access to sensors and actuators in a companies owned public space, introducing sensors and actuators that are meant to allow individuals or communities to develop their own desired applications or hack authorized applications in order to design Augmented Reality games, entertainment, and art. Or, as is the topic of this paper, use augmented reality technology to add playfulness and humor to our daily activities.

In the next section (Sect. 2), we provide some preliminary notes on perceiving play and humor. Play leads to humorous situations, but it is also the case that when in a playful mood, we can give humorous interpretations to particular events. Can we organize our daily behavior and our lives in a more playful and humoristic way by using smart technology? Traditionally, humor research has been about verbal humor. Therefore, in Sect. 3 we focus on humor as it can appear and be described in the physical world, particularly in urban environments. We discuss views on play and humor that fit in the same framework. Section 4 is about digital technology that is available for city dwellers and that can help to make smart environments more playful and humorous. This will be elaborated in Sect. 5, in which we discuss how augmented reality technology can generate opportunities for play and humor in urban environments. A short section (Sect. 6) of conclusions follows.

2 Perceiving Play and Humor

2.1 Introduction

It is interesting to make a comparison between how we perceive an environment from the point of view of play and from the point of view of humor. Our aim is not to discuss all characteristics of play and humor, how they are distinct, and how they relate. Rather we want to see how we can profit from exploiting similarities between humor and play in order to design smart technology in urban environments that supports playful and humorous events and interactions with these events for city residents and city visitors.

There have been many attempts to characterize play and humor. The benefits of play and humor have also been investigated [2]. Humor has been characterized by John Morreall as "cognitive play" [3]. There have been discussions about differences between humor and play, and Morreall's views on humor as play have been criticized [4]. Unfortunately, in these discussions, no clear distinctions between humor, play, and laughter are made. In play, humor is not a necessary condition: humor is not necessarily playful, and smiles and laughter do not necessarily express amusement. However, playful activities often lead to humorous events, to humorous interpretations of events, or to ways that events could be continued in a humorous way. Although the focus is on child's play, according to Elini Loizou [5], we can also learn when adults and older adults become involved in play: "during humorous events children are involved in play activity such as a) play with materials; b) play with language, c) pretend play; d) physical play, and these forms of play are then turned into humorous events due to the creativity that children exert during such activities. Also, children were involved in routines that they then turned into playful humorous events."

For the purpose of this paper, we focus on similarities between play and humor. Usually, we enjoy humor and we enjoy playing, but in order to enjoy them, we need to be in a playful state of mind (the so-called "paratelic state of mind") [6]. This state can be contrasted with the more serious, goal-oriented "telic" state of mind. In order to enter the paratelic state of mind, we need to feel safe and protected. This allows us to think and act in playful and humorous ways, that is, to assign additional, sometimes contrasting, interpretations to objects, interactions, situations, and events than we do in the telic state of mind. This can be done without fear of serious consequences.

Both humor and play assume that we can have different points of view about a real event, how we perceive it, and how we can change it or what we can add to it with our imaginations. How humorous would it have been if it happened in this or that way? We can add a humorous interpretation to a (playful) event and share it with others (friends, other players, bystanders).

2.2 Perceiving Play

We will first look at how we perceive an environment, its inhabitants, and its objects when we "play" it. There are some general observations that we should mention. In *Homo Ludens: A Study of the Play-Element in Culture* [7], the Dutch historian Johan Huizinga mentions the "magic circle," an arena, a playground, a temporary world with special rules but within the ordinary world. Some other characteristics of play that are mentioned by

Huizinga include that (i) it is voluntary, (ii) it is distinct from ordinary life, and (iii) it takes place within temporal and spatial boundaries. Whether or not these characteristics are always present in playful events in urban environments, they can be a starting point for distinguishing play from other activities that occur in urban environments. Before actual play, the magic circle is known or is created and agreed upon. It is where the actual play will take place. We enter the circle, and at a certain time, we leave the circle. In other research, the notion of the magic circle has been elaborated upon, and it has been given a more present-day interpretation [8].

Huizinga did not know about digital technology and how digital technology can augment a physical environment in such a way that (a) it allows access to play opportunities that cannot be realized and only can be imagined in the real physical environment, and (b) it allows us to integrate play with daily routines and other real-life activities; hence, no strictly defined boundaries (temporal and spatial) distinguish play from non-play. Hence, with digital technology, the circle becomes blurred. Pervasive games have been defined as having features that expand this circle of play spatially, temporally, or socially [9]. Although it is possible to start a discussion on the difference between play and games, here we follow these observations on games, and we assume we can learn from them. This is done even though play can be considered to be less restricted to the rules of the game than play, in particular, spontaneous play (that is, play in which rules are not given in advance and in which rules can change and be made up during play upon agreement with the other players).

In particular, the spatial expansion made possible by digital technology makes the whole world a playground. Wherever we are, smart technology knows where we are; it is aware of our context and what we know about our context. We can cooperate with our smart environment in order to create playful events and experience playful events created by our smart environment.

Yuri Lotman [10] provides a view on art and play that fits in our observations on interpreting an environment as potentially playful and humorous. Lotman does not mention humor; however, play and playfulness are among his main topics of observation: "Play is a model of reality of a special kind. It reproduces some of the features of reality by translating them to the language of its rules." Furthermore, "Play is the simultaneous realization (not their alternation in time!) of practical and conventional behavior. The player must simultaneously remember that he is participating in a conventional (not real) situation (a child knows that the tiger in front of him is a toy and is not afraid of it), and not remember it (when playing, the child considers the toy tiger to be a real one). The child is only afraid of the living tiger, the only thing he is not afraid of is the stuffed tiger; he is slightly afraid of a striped gown thrown on a chair and representing a tiger in the game, that is, he simultaneously is and is not afraid of it."

In play, we must give extra meaning to what we perceive. As mentioned by Lotman [10], "The mechanism of play involves not the static simultaneous coexistence of different meanings, but the constant awareness of the possibility of alternate meanings to the one that is currently being perceived. The play effect means that different meanings of the same element do not appear in static coexistence but 'twinkle.' Each interpretation makes up a separate synchronic slice, yet retains a memory of earlier meanings and the awareness of the possibility of future ones." Hence, in play, according to Lotman, different meanings "twinkle."

2.3 Comparing Play and Humor from a Humor Point of View

Lotman's interpretation of play is not really different from what we see appear in humor definitions. Both in play and in humor, we allow different interpretations of what we perceive. In play, we give a different meaning and function than usual to objects, actions, and events. Often, the meaning plays a role in a "story" that is maintained. The creative use of an object can be seen as incongruous and even humorous by a bystander but not necessarily by the player or players during their play. However, as mentioned by Lotman, there is the "twinkling" of meanings, and in contrast to a situation in which only one meaning is available, this "twinkling" helps to provide a humorous view on a play activity. In "canned" play, as we know from jokes, pranks, and comedy, others have provided us with alternative meanings for what we other-wise would have considered objects, actions, and events with standard, stereotypical interpretations. In more spontaneous play, we do this assignment of alternative meanings ourselves.

Humor is also about having at least two different views on objects, actions, and events. Often, it is about opposing views. For example, in a joke, we are usually led to the belief that we have to deal with a stereotypical situation. A punchline then makes it clear that we completely misunderstood the situation. We can give it a different interpretation because of some additional information that became available from the punchline. When we interpret an object, an action, or an event as humorous, that is, it amuses us and/or makes us laugh, there is not necessarily this sequential change from one interpretation to another. We can maintain two or more interpretations. However, two or more interpretations do not make an object, action, or event humorous. Two different views experienced by the same person of what is happening in the real world is not necessarily amusing. The views can be slightly different. The environment or text may allow some ambiguity. For a joke to be humorous, we need to replace one, usually straightforward, interpretation, with a less stereotypical and unexpected one. In real life, this can also be the case, but there can also be situations in which we maintain two interpretations of an event simply because the event allows it (no additional information is provided) or the event has been designed in such a way that two or more interpretations remain possible. In humor theory, the assumption is that such different interpretations are humorous and are the object of a comic amusement emotion if they are sufficiently opposed. This contrast in interpretations does not have to do with additional information that makes us decide in favor of one interpretation above the other. There is no need to "resolve" an incongruity; the in-congruity is accepted and appreciated, and it amuses us.

In humor, we can be confronted with a situation that allows two or more conflicting or opposing interpretations. We are not necessarily aware of different interpretations; we just assume a stereotypical situation until additional information brought to us makes us aware of a possibly different interpretation. Especially in the case of jokes, it is customary that we ultimately decide about the correct interpretation, rejecting a previous choice by an interpretation that was not foreseen but was nevertheless plausible, in retrospect. In nonverbal humor (for example, in cartoons, in the sight gags of movies, or in real-life events), different interpretations can co-exist. There, we do not replace the first interpretation with the next one but rather maintain more than one interpretation at the same time. In that case, different interpretations or meanings "twinkle," and when they are sufficiently opposed, they lead to amusement. There is no need to "resolve" an incongruity. In our minds, we can maintain opposing and therefore humorous interpretations of what we perceive or imagine during our activities in the physical world.

To summarize, in play, we assign different and unusual meanings to objects, actions, and events. These meanings are functional, that is, they are necessary to distinguish the role of objects and events in real life from the roles they have when children or adults make playful use of these objects and look at events from a playful point of view, rather than from a literal point of view. In (real-life) play, a shoe can serve as a goal post in a football match. There is no humor intended when such a choice is made. It may be different (and also amusing) for someone watching children play football. It can become comic, when, by accident, someone shoots the shoe into the goal. The shoe, which was made a goal post by the players' choice, has now become a football by accident.

Play usually assumes and requires assigning unusual meanings to objects and to unusual interpretations of behavior and events; play events can be distinguished from humor events because of the conscious meanings assigned to the objects, actions, and events we have in play, in contrast to the surprising and unexpected meanings we are triggered to assign to perceived objects and events in our environment that allow various and often opposing interpretations.

The next section provides more observations on humor from a humor research point of view. Where do our observations on humor come from, and can they be given a more formal, psychological, linguistic, and artificial intelligence research base?

3   More on Defining and Experiencing Humor

3.1   More Than Joke Humor

We can find linguistic answers to what humor is in research papers on incongruity in jokes [11]. Jokes are short texts that allow linguistic and common-sense analysis. Humor definitions that are based on jokes emphasize a common-sense interpretation of the set-up of a joke and a cognitive shift that is needed in order to understand the punchline, which contrasts our expectations and requires an interpretation that opposes our initial one. This linguistic analysis of jokes does not do justice to the true qualities of humor. Humor experiences in real life are not about jokes. They are about what we see and about our interactions with others. Non-joke humor appears in conversations, in observing and imaging events, and in friends that tell you about humorous events. Can we replace or add to such humor by introducing digitally created humor? Can we have digital, virtual, and personal agents that provide us with humorous interpretations of the situations we encounter? Or, can we have our personal and artificial agents tell us how to make changes to the environment in order to make it humorous to us or others?

Humor definitions are biased toward incongruity in jokes. Without going into details, we can say that in the setup of a joke, we are led to a stereotypical viewpoint. But additional information, for example, that provided by the punchline, makes us aware that the situation requires a different, usually less stereotypical, viewpoint. In fact, to be humorous, it has to be a viewpoint that opposes the original viewpoint. The punchline introduces an incongruity that, however, is "solved" by our shift to the less expected viewpoint. That is, the incongruity was not there at all; there were two conflicting interpretations in the beginning, but only one survived.

Clearly, there are many other forms of humor than just joke humor. Verbal jokes provide us with a sequential change of interpretations. A first and obvious interpretation of an event has to be replaced by a second, less obvious interpretation. The second interpretation needs to be opposed to the first one in order to introduce comic amusement.

This incongruity viewpoint of humor does not exclude the superiority and relief viewpoints. The superiority viewpoint tells us that we experience humor when we can laugh about someone's stupidity. This stupidity can range from someone slipping on a banana peel to someone using illogical reasoning to come to a decision. The relief viewpoint tells us that we experience humor because it allows us to get away from the daily fuss. Topics and behaviors that are otherwise taboo can be expressed without being corrected. The incongruity viewpoint has been mentioned and discussed since the seventeenth century [12], and more than the superiority and relief theories, it tells us how to detect, analyze, and generate humor. We can say that the incongruity view is about the stimulus, the structure, and the mechanics of humor; the superiority point of view is about the social aspects of humor, and the relief point of view addresses the relaxation of tension, or, more generally, the release of suppressed feelings and the replacing of negative feelings with pleasant sensations.

The incongruity point of view tells us how to analyze and how to generate humor in jokes. In the literature, it has been generalized to the analysis of humor in cartoons, on stage, in TV series, in movies, and in real life. We can look at the humor definition provided by Noël Carroll [13], who has analyzed visual humor (sight gags) in movies [14] and therefore has a more comprehensive definition of humor than some other researchers. Carroll defines humor by introducing the "comic amusement" emotion, an emotion that has humor as its object. In more detail, someone is in the state of comic amusement when (i) the object of one's mental state is a perceived incongruity that (ii) one regards as non-threatening or otherwise anxiety-producing and (iii) not annoying and (iv) towards which one does not enlist genuine problem-solving attitudes (v) but which give rise to the enjoyment of precisely the pertinent incongruity and (vi) to an experience of levity.

It is clear that the core of the definition is the incongruity. An incongruity can be perceived, analyzed and designed. The other elements of the definition are about the effect on the recipient of humor. Other definitions of humor are available, but they focus more on humor that is expressed verbally, usually as it appears in jokes. Jokes are artificially constructed short texts; they certainly are not accountable for our everyday amusement and our smiles during our daily activities. Humor research has focused on such constructed jokes for the simple reason that more than real-life situations, jokes lend themselves to an analysis by techniques from linguistics and artificial intelligence, such as scripts, frames, and reasoning. Until now, this has not led to success, and it has been argued that in order for a computer to understand and generate humor it needs to be able to understand everything that can happen and imagined in the real world. Moreover, in the case of jokes, there are social interaction cues that make us aware that we should not take the next utterances seriously. This is quite different from humor that emerges during conversations or humor that is experienced during unplanned and incongruous situations that we encounter in real life. We often smile and are amused while we interact with others, while we observe events, and while we imagine how things could be different from what we observe and how being in a playful mood allows us to provide a humorous interpretation to what we observe. This is "natural" humor, rather than humor that is "constructed" as it is in jokes, on stage, in cinema, in TV series, or in April Fools' Day pranks.

In a relaxed and playful state of mind, we are happy to consider different and contrasting perspectives on real-life events or situations. This cognitive play is the basis of incongruity humor [12], and we have to investigate how we can support this cognitive play with digital technology. But before being able to do so we need some better characterizations of humor in real life and how it differs from joke humor.

3.2   From Jokes to Real-Life Events

The phrase "You had to be there to know why it was funny" nicely makes clear that it is difficult to describe situations that make people smile or laugh. Actions, events, and comments on these situations may require extensive knowledge of their particular contexts for others to catch the subtleties that trigger amusement, smiles, and laughter. In "designed" jokes, cartoons, stage and movie performances, and comedy series on television, information can be concealed and revealed whenever it can be thought to have a humorous effect. The situations and events are controlled: the authors and directors decide what you see. A reader, a listener, or a viewer is provided with the designed context in which this designed humor is presented.

The real world offers fewer opportunities for designers of humorous events. Sometimes opportunities arise. A prank can be designed, but often there is an accidental coincidence or stupidity that leads to a humorous situation [15]. Can this change with digital technology? If we have access to sensors and actuators embedded in our home environments and in public spaces, can we use them to design humorous events? We have our smartphones, smart watches, smart glasses, and other wearables, including augmented reality devices, to make changes to the world we and others perceive. So, why not investigate how this technology can be used to design playful and humorous events, planned or unplanned, in the real world?

We can adapt the perceived incongruity point of view mentioned by Carroll. An incongruity viewpoint tells us how humor is designed. It provides us with some necessary conditions that need to be fulfilled in order to generate comic amusement. The superiority and relief viewpoints are important as well, but they do not address how we can create humor or how we can analyze and decompose a humorous event in terms of its components. And, in particular, Carroll's view is not biased towards jokes. In a traditional joke, during a short period of time we stick to a stereotypical interpretation of an event, while in the subsequent period of time we have to exchange that interpretation for another, less obvious, but more correct, interpretation. Carroll's more general definition does not does it exclude such a view, but, more importantly it does not require such a strict sequential view on interpreting humorous events and replacing a first interpretation by a second one. This allows two or more additional views on humor. One of them that is in real-life the first interpretation of an event can be humorous, while the second interpretation amounts to a stereotypical, maybe disappointing, one.

And, the second view, in real-life situations, as will be further elaborated below, there is not necessarily such a strict sequential change of interpretations. Two (contrasting) interpretations can be entertained at the same time or almost the same time. An event, whether it is spontaneous or designed, can trigger more than one interpretation. It is not important which interpretation occurs first in order to find the possibly contrasting interpretations humorous. It may also be the case that the perception of a stereotypical event immediately triggers a memory in which such an event turned into a humorous event. Hence, a different interpretation is there as well, not necessarily forcing another or first interpretation to disappear.

Obviously, in traditional joke research [11] we also have two interpretations of a text, we have the 'cognitive shift' that is involved in understanding the joke, and this cognitive shift can only be there when we are aware of two interpretations and have replaced a first interpretation by one that more fits the punchline that triggered the re-interpretation. We need to be aware of two interpretations, a previous and incorrect one and its replacement by a correct one, and we acknowledge our misunderstanding rather than keeping both interpretations alive.

Although there are not many humor researchers who have investigated humor in real-life situations, those who have done so focus on incongruous objects, actions, and events that lead to humor. How we can introduce humorous incongruities, using digital technology, in our daily and recreational activities? We have sensors and actuators in our domestic and public environments, we have sensors and actuators in our wearables. Can they support us in making objects, actions, and environments more playful and more humorous? Can digital technology help us create humorous incongruities that lead to amusement, that make us smile and laugh? Can digital technology nudge us to play in our urban environments?

These questions motivate us to take a closer look at some theories of humor that are not focused on jokes or sight gags. Obviously, it is possible to learn from theories about jokes and sight gags. They provide exaggerated examples of incongruities, and the events that are described or displayed are not completely unbelievable. However, in real life, we perceive incongruous events differently from how we experience verbal and visual jokes. Usually, these jokes are accompanied with indications that make clear that what we will hear, read, or see will be humor and is meant to amuse us. This is not necessarily the case with spontaneous and accidental humor. Nevertheless, can we generate humorous events in our digitally enhanced physical worlds, and can these humorous events become part of our daily lives and recreational activities?

3.3 Towards "Natural" Real-Life Humor

We appreciate humor that is generated spontaneously or occurs accidentally. Spontaneous humor requires a playful and creative mind that is able to provide an unexpected and contrasting interpretation to what is perceived and what others perceive. Accidental humor, of course, is not intended. The contrast between what was intended and what is really happening is humorous if these views are sufficiently opposing (a humorous incongruity).

A joke is based on an incongruity that is not really there. We need a second look and access to additional, usually sequentially presented information, that allows a cognitive shift to understand that our biased and probably stereotypical viewpoint needs to be replaced by a less stereotypical and even a contrasting viewpoint to understand the joke. We are not happy when we are not able to make this cognitive shift. On the other hand, unlike what we see mentioned in most joke research, we enjoy a joke not because we get rid of the incongruity but because we accept and understand why we perceived an incongruity.

Various categories of incongruities have been introduced by humor researchers. Unfortunately, because of the vast interest in joke humor, these incongruity categories have not received much attention. And, of course, humor in real life is much more diffi-cult to formalize and give an algorithmic explanation than humor as it appears in short texts that can be analyzed using a (computational) linguistic approach. Various typolo-gies of incongruity have been introduced [16–20]. Incongruities can address language constructs, but often the categories that are distinguished are more general, dealing with issues such as language, logic, identity, and action [16], deficiencies, opposing inter-pretations, coincidences, appropriateness [17], and incongruities from a conceptual, attitudinal, behavioral, presentational, physical, or reality-shifting point of view [18]. Different kinds of incongruities are distinguished in products [19, 20], for example, a bathroom mat that seems to be made of eggshells, as well as in movies [14] and com-mercials [21]. Cross-modal incongruities (for example, unexpected, opposing auditory and visual information) have also been discussed [e.g., 22]. Many observations on these typologies and on perceived incongruities in the real world can also be found [12, 23, 24]. However, a comprehensive, systematic approach to incongruities is still missing.

Focusing on enjoying the existence of a particular kind of incongruity rather than on getting satisfaction from resolving an incongruity is our approach to understanding the humor in real-life situations. We once more emphasize that a real-life event can be perceived as humorous. We may find an event humorous because we do not have the history and the background that others have. Perhaps our beliefs about how things usually are, and how people behave and think, are different from others'. When observing a physical event, context plays an important role. Quite literally, a different physical viewpoint can provide an observer with a perspective on an event that opposes the perspective of others with different viewpoints.

LaFollette and Shanks [25] mention contrasting belief sets that we can have if there is enough appropriate "psychic distance" from the event. If we are in the earlier-mentioned playful or paratelic state of mind, this allows us a "comic distance." We can therefore appreciate contrasting views. We do not replace one set of beliefs with the other, but rather we oscillate between them: "This 'flickering' in the focus of attention—this active oscil-lating between these different but related belief sets—is humor. Humor is not something passively witnessed. Like thinking, it is something in which the subject participates. Thus, to have a sense of humor on a given occasion is to be disposed to engage in the activity of flickering between different patterns of belief" [25]. We can experience, provided we have this "comic distance," this "flickering" of beliefs while perceiving humorous events in real-life. We certainly experience it in TV sitcoms when a particular event is described by different witnesses: "Each redescription reflects the differing alter-nate perspectives—and hence patterns of belief—of the witnesses. The humor arises from the viewer's flickering between the various descriptions of the event. The viewer, however, does not merely passively consider each alternative pattern. Rather she rapidly oscillates between them. This speedy and participatory flickering is the humor" [25].

A similar but more detailed analysis can be found in Apter [6]. As mentioned before and emphasized by Apter, a person has to be in a playful and not goal-oriented state in order to appreciate humor. Apter distinguishes between transition and non-transition humor. In both, we have two or more interpretations of a particular situation. In transition humor, we have a reversal from one interpretation to another. But, contrary to what is advocated by joke researchers, in Apter's view [26], (1) the reinterpretation of a situation does not replace the interpretation that had appeared to be correct; the new reality does not alter one's perception of the apparent or purported reality that was first created, and (2) the new perception must in some sense be diminished in value or importance relative to what was first assumed. We can say that the new interpretation augments the initial one.

Apter's view that the new perception must in some sense be diminished in value or importance relative to what was first assumed has not always been mentioned in such an explicit way by other humor researchers. However, it is in line with understanding humor from the earlier mentioned relief, superiority, and incongruity viewpoints, and in particular, the superiority viewpoint can be said to address this diminishment.

Some additional issues can be identified, such as the need for the interpretations to contain opposing elements (such as sacred/profane, poor/rich, intelligent/stupid, large/small, important/trivial, young/old, private/public), and the difficulty of comprehension and the amount of cognitive elaboration necessary for reinterpretation. This also appears in the previously mentioned definition given by Noël Carroll (Sect. 3.1).

In Apter's non-transition humor, different interpretations of an event are appreciated at the same time. One meaning can be at the focus of attention, the other at the fringe, but fringe and focus can fluctuate. There is awareness of both meanings at all times. This view can emerge in wordplay, in cartoons, in movies and commercials, and in humorous events in real life, either intended ("world-play" [24]) or accidental. We should mention that in this view we can also find an event humorous because it reminds us of a previous event, and we can find an event humorous because we can imagine how different it could have been. In such cases, we add information to the real world that is extracted from our minds. In non-transition humor, a level of amusement can be maintained for a longer time when incompatible or incongruous characteristics continue to play a role in a story, a movie, or in real life.

3.4   Reconsidering "Humor Versus Play"

In the previous sections, we provided a common view on play and humor using the theories of Lotman [10], Apter [6], and LaFollette and Shanks [25], together with some more recent views on humor (Carroll [13]) and many observations on incongruities in real-life, rather than just in jokes. In Lotman's views on play, the players give more than one meaning to the objects, acts, and events in the real world. The meanings "twinkle." There is the "ordinary reality" and a "fictional reality." Both realities appear at the same time, and players are aware of them. There is an oscillation between the interpretations they have assigned to the objects, acts, and events in these realities. Play happens in the mixture of the ordinary and the fictional reality. Humor can emerge if the oscillation is between opposing interpretations. For an onlooker, a shoe that serves as a goal post can be humorous. For a child playing football, the shoe has two meanings, but a possible opposition between the two meanings is not relevant.

In Sect. 2.1, we mentioned the work of Elini Loizou [5] on play. Play often includes unexpected changes in events or nonserious social incongruities [27]. These incongruities that are experienced in a playful mood and in a "safe" situation are humor objects that elicit amusement and laughter. It has been argued [27, 28] that humor evolved out of play. These arguments also mention that laughter often follows from social play and facilitates playful interaction. Parallelisms of humorous activity and play activity have also been mentioned [5]. While in Loizou's experiments children rather than adults were involved, knowing about these and other yet-uninvestigated parallelisms between humorous and play activities can help us to decide where to look when we decide to create a (digital) humorous activity, a play activity, or other activities that take place in our current, digitally enhanced, real worlds.. Hence, from the view of digital enhancement, when someone plays with materials, we can focus on the incongruous use of materials. With physical play, or when routines turn into play, we can focus on incongruous actions or the use of objects. Attempts to play with language can be supported by suggesting funny words, sounds, or wordplay. "Pretend play" is also about actions, appearances, and the use of objects that have different meanings in real life and in play. Again, opposing interpretations can become humorous.

4   Digital Technology that Makes Urban Environments More Playful and Humorous

Ordinary reality can be made more playful and more humorous. In order to introduce playful or humorous events in a physical environment, we can make physical changes to the environment or assign unusual interpretations to objects, acts, and events in the environment. Real-life play and humor require assigning different and sometimes unusual interpretations to objects, acts, and views. Physical changes are not always necessary from a humor point of view. An event in ordinary reality can trigger more than one interpretation spontaneously. It is also possible that it triggers an earlier experience that we compare with the physical experience, possibly leading to a humorous view, or that it triggers our imaginations in such a way that we fantasize how different and humorous this event could have been. Hence, our imagination provides us with a humorous view on the event.

But what can be the role of digital technology in order to create playfulness and humor in urban environments? There are several options.

- Digital technology can help to make changes to urban environments that allow a chance of interpretation, including a humorous interpretation, of that particular environment or events taking place in that environment. Sensors and actuators can make changes to a particular environment and make it behave differently while its inhabitants interact with it. These digitally controlled changes include the introduction of physical changes. The simplest example is an automatic door that opens and closes because what it perceives through its sensors and what it controls through its actuators.

However, it is more interesting to look at the movements of robots and the use of smart materials or kinetic architectures. In particular, smart materials can be employed in such a way that objects and surfaces undergo unexpected changes in shape, size, or color [29], but an automatic door or an elevator can also be programmed to display unexpected and humorous behavior. Incongruous scents, feelings, or sounds can be added to objects and environments by using digital scent, touch, and audio technology.

- Digital technology can be installed in street furniture. Street furniture (for example, traffic signs, billboards, and public trash cans) can be made to interact with city dwellers in many humorous ways [1]. Smart street furniture can observe passers-by and comment on their behavior in humorous ways. This can be done in such a way that users are simultaneously persuaded to obey traffic rules, to stop smoking in public environments, or to buy a particular brand of shampoo.
- City dwellers often have digital wearables that make it possible to sense the urban environment, its objects, the events that take place in it, and fellow city dwellers. A personal digital assistant can be designed with a sense of humor. This humor butler observes what is happening in our environment and informs us about possible humorous twists to what it notices and what the user can or could have observed. The agent can focus on conversational twists, but it can also observe what is happening in the environment and comment on it in a humorous way, that is, in a way that attempts to add incongruous points of view to what is initially observed in the environment. The humorous views can be shared with the device's owner (assuming the owner is receptive to play and humor), and the owner, appreciating this humorous view, can also decide to share or, when appropriate, to realize this view.

Augmented reality (AR) is another digital technology that can be used to trigger playful and humorous interpretations of what is happening in an urban environment. Usually, an AR view provides us with a manipulated view of a physical environment. It overlays computer graphics onto the real world. Objects can be added, deleted, and replaced in the view that is presented to the AR user. Such a manipulated view can be experienced by using smart glasses, head-mounted devices, or smartphones. Virtual tactile and artificial scent augmentations of physical environments are possible as well, but these require different digital technologies. However, it should be clear that AR provides us with a technology that allows us to manipulate a real-world view in such a way that playful and humorous changes can be introduced or suggested. More explanation on this can be found in the next section.

5 Augmenting Reality to Facilitate Play and Humor

Examples of humorous situations that have been reported while gamers played the mobile AR game Pokémon GO have been provided [30]. Although Pokémon GO players can have humorous interactions with other players, these situations were not intended. They are examples of accidental humor that happens when players attempt to accomplish a gaming goal in the real world.

We may wonder whether we can increase the number of occurrences of accidental and unintended humor or the number of occurrences of intended humor with the help of augmented reality. More generally, how can augmented reality technology be employed to make urban environments more playful and humorous?

AR technology has many useful applications: in workspaces, education, rehabilitation, advertisements, entertainment, games, and art. AR, as is clear from the previous sections, also allows us to design, create, and suggest playful and humorous situations for the AR user, who can use AR not only to experience but also to share and create playful and humorous events. There are various ways to experience humor in AR. We can have the AR displayed on our smartphones, on our glasses, or on our head-mounted displays. Other, less-researched methods are augmenting reality with scent, sound, or touch.

In AR, objects in real life are detected and recognized, information about objects can be displayed, and virtual objects can be added or can be used to hide detected objects behind newly introduced virtual objects. That is, real objects can be replaced by virtual objects. This certainly makes it possible to introduce non-existing incongruities in an AR view of the real world. Such incongruities can be introduced sequentially (the transition point of view mentioned by Apter). Hence, first we have a real-world view; next, we have the result of processing the real-world view and having it augmented with a contrasting, humorous view, or vice versa. From the AR point of view, we need to observe a particular situation and then decide about a possible playful and potentially humorous continuation that can be presented to the AR user. In the non-transition point of view, we can add, change or delete objects in such a way that the AR user is not forced, because of subsequent virtual information, to make a cognitive shift to a new interpretation but rather is triggered to entertain two or more interpretations of the augmented view at the same time. There is a "fluctuation" (Apter [6]), a "flickering" (LaFollette and Shanks [25]), and a "twinkling" (Lotman [10]) of interpretations.

We can, as mentioned in the previous section, also have a personal virtual jester that not only makes us aware of alternative views but also shows them. The AR system (or the virtual jester) needs to have a sense of humor in order to generate humorous AR views. We can accept a primitive sense of humor, for example, the jester just trying to generate contrasting elements in a scene maybe or learning from how AR users react. A jester's owner can decide whether or not to make use of its suggestions, share them, or implement them using his or her control of sensors and actuators in wearables and in the smart environment.

Obviously, AR humor can be designed and can be added to an AR application as canned humor. There can be humorous (incongruous) overlays. An example is the Burn That Ad app from Burger King. Mobile users can point their smartphone cameras to a McDonald's ad on a billboard or in a magazine and then, at in their smartphones, see this ad engulfed in flames and disappear to be replaced by a coupon for a free Whopper burger at Burger King. In another example, it can be humorous to see how a person tries to avoid a banana peel that has been added to the augmented world and is not present in the real world. Instead of adding objects to an environment, objects can be removed and a reduced (or diminished) reality displayed to a user. In that case, objects can be removed from a user's view. Removing a real manhole or a banana peel from a user's view can lead to a humorous situation. Obviously, the butt of a joke or the victim of a prank is not necessarily amused. Technical aspects, for example, "inpainting," of diminished reality have been discussed [31, 32]. Real-time augmented and diminished reality allows magic [33], and magic introduces incongruities and inspires amusement, even if we are not able to resolve the incongruity.

There are more examples of AR humor, but why they are humorous is usually not explicitly addressed. In "Augmented Reality Art" [34], many examples can be found in which artists are using AR for provocative, entertaining, and humorous installations. Admittedly, this is about designed humor, but the examples may give rise to ideas about how to generate humorous situations by an AR system or have humorous views provided by an AR agent with a sense of humor (a personal virtual jester).

6 Conclusions

The aim of this paper is to show that AR technology provides opportunities to make life more playful and more humorous. In order to make that clear, we discussed some theoretical frameworks for play and humor and extracted some essential characteristics that can be addressed by AR technology. A "sense of humor" that has to be implemented in AR systems needs to know more about introducing humor than just arbitrarily augmenting the real world with contrasting objects, contrasting information about objects, or changes and replacements of objects. It requires that the AR system knows about context, how humor fits in this context and makes use of this context, and how, in the case of intended humor, it is signaled to its recipient of humor. We cannot expect that with the current state of artificial intelligence such a general goal can be achieved in the near future. Nevertheless, as has become clear from this paper, we can certainly use AR to introduce playful and humorous situations or potentially humorous situations in augmented views of urban environments.

References

1. Nijholt, A. (ed.): Making Smart Cities More Playable: Exploring Playable Cities. GMSE. Springer, Singapore (2020). https://doi.org/10.1007/978-981-13-9765-3
2. Bateson, P., Martin, P.: Play, Playfulness, Creativity and Innovation. Cambridge University Press, Cambridge (2013)
3. Morreall, J.: Humor as cognitive play. J. Lit. Theory 3(2), 241–260 (2009)
4. Tapley, R.: On Morreall: a failure to distinguish between play and humor. J. Value Inquiry 47(1–2), 147–162 (2013). https://doi.org/10.1007/s10790-013-9365-1
5. Loizou, E.: Humour: a different kind of play. Eur. Early Child. Educ. Res. J. 13(2), 97–109 (2005)
6. Apter, M.J.: The Experience of Motivation: The Theory of Psychological Reversals. Academic Press, San Diego (1982)
7. Huizinga, J.: Homo Ludens. Routledge, London (1949)
8. Salen, K., Zimmerman, E.: The Rules of Play: Game Design Fundamentals. MIT Press, Cambridge (2004)
9. Montola, M., Stenros, J., Waern, A.: Pervasive Games: Theory and Design. CRC Press, Taylor & Francis Group, Boca Raton (2009)

10. Lotman, J.: The place of art among other modelling systems. Sign Syst. Stud. **39**(2/4), 249–270 (2011). Originally published in Russian as Лотман, Ю. М. Тезисы к проблеме "Искусство в ряду моделирующих систем". Труды по знаковым системам (Sign Systems Studies) 3: 130–145 (1967)
11. Raskin, V.: Semantic Mechanisms of Humor. Studies in Linguistics and Philosophy. Springer, Dordrecht (1984). https://doi.org/10.1007/978-94-009-6472-3
12. Nijholt, A.: "All the world's a stage": incongruity humour revisited. Ann. Math. Artif. Intell. **18**, 405–438 (2020). https://doi.org/10.1007/s10472-018-9609-7
13. Carroll, N.: Humour. A Very Short Introduction. Oxford University Press, Oxford (2014)
14. Carroll, N.: Theorizing the Moving Image. Cambridge University Press, Cambridge (1996)
15. Nijholt, A.: Smart bugs and digital banana peels: accidental humor in smart environments? In: Streitz, N., Markopoulos, P. (eds.) DAPI 2016. LNCS, vol. 9749, pp. 329–340. Springer, Cham (2016). https://doi.org/10.1007/978-3-319-39862-4_30
16. Berger, A.A.: An Anatomy of Humor. Transaction Publishers, New Brunswick (1993). First edition appeared in 1976
17. Morreal, J.: Taking Laughter Seriously. State University of New York Press, New York (1983)
18. O'Shannon, D.: What Are You Laughing At? A Comprehensive Guide to the Comedic Event. CIP Group, London (2012)
19. Yu, Y., Nam, T.-J.: Let's giggle!: design principles for humorous products. In: Proceedings of the 2014 Conference on Designing Interactive Systems (DIS 2014), pp. 275–284. ACM, New York (2014)
20. Yu, Y., Nam, T.-J.: Products with a sense of humor: case study of humorous products with Giggle Popper. Int. J. Des. **11**(1), 79–92 (2017)
21. Buijzen, M., Valkenburg, P.: Developing a typology of humor in audiovisual media. Media Psychol. **6**(2), 147–167 (2004)
22. Ludden, G.D.S., Schifferstein, H.N.J.: Effects of visual–auditory incongruity on product expression and surprise. Int. J. Des. **1**(3), 29–39 (2007)
23. Nijholt, A.: The humor continuum: from text to smart environments. In: Proceedings International Conference on Informatics, Electronics & Vision (ICIEV), IEEE Xplore, New York (2015). 10 pages
24. Nijholt, A.: From word play to world play: introducing humor in human-computer interaction. In: Proceedings of the 36th European Conference on Cognitive Ergonomics (ECCE 2018). ACM, New York (2018). Article 1, 8 pages
25. LaFollette, H., Shanks, N.: Belief and the basis of humor. Am. Philos. Q. **30**(4), 329–339 (1993)
26. Wyer, R.S., Collins, J.E.: A theory of humor elicitation. Psychol. Rev. **99**(4), 663–688 (1992)
27. Gervais, M., Wilson, D.S.: The evolution and functions of laughter and humor: a synthetic approach. Q. Rev. Biol. **80**(4), 395–430 (2005)
28. Weisfeld, G.E.: The adaptive value of humor and laughter. Ethol. Sociobiol. **14**(2), 141–169 (1993)
29. Nijholt, A., Minuto, A.: Smart material interfaces: playful and artistic applications. In: Proceedings 2017 IEEE International Conference on Imaging, Vision & Pattern Recognition (icIVPR), pp. 1–6. IEEE, New York (2017)
30. Andujar, M., Nijholt, A., Gilbert, J.E.: Mobile augmented games in playable cities: humorous interaction with Pokémon Go. In: Streitz, N., Markopoulos, P. (eds.) DAPI 2017. LNCS, vol. 10291, pp. 575–586. Springer, Cham (2017). https://doi.org/10.1007/978-3-319-58697-7_43
31. Hackl, A., Hlavacs, H.: Diminishing reality. In: Clua, E., Roque, L., Lugmayr, A., Tuomi, P. (eds.) ICEC 2018. LNCS, vol. 11112, pp. 28–39. Springer, Cham (2018). https://doi.org/10.1007/978-3-319-99426-0_3

32. Mori, S., Ikeda, S., Saito, H.: A survey of diminished reality: techniques for visually concealing, eliminating, and seeing through real objects. IPSJ T. Comput. Vis. Appl. **9**(17), 1–14 (2017). https://doi.org/10.1186/s41074-017-0028-1
33. Sakauchi, D., Matsumi, Y., Mori, S., Shibata, F., Kimura, A., Tamura, H.: Magical mystery room, 2nd stage. In: Proceedings of the International Symposium on Mixed and Augmented Reality (ISMAR), Demo (2015)
34. Geroimenko, V. (ed.): Augmented Reality Art: From an Emerging Technology to a Novel Creative Medium. SSCC, 2nd edn. Springer, Cham (2018). https://doi.org/10.1007/978-3-319-69932-5

"But Wait, There's More!" a Deeper Look into Temporally Placing Touch Gesture Signifiers

Liv Arleth[✉], Emilie Lind Damkjær, and Hendrik Knoche[iD]

Aalborg University, Rendsburggade 14, 9000 Aalborg, Denmark
livarleth@gmail.com, edamkj14@student.aau.dk, hk@create.aau.dk

Abstract. The language used in interaction design is affected by the wide array of academic backgrounds of interaction designers. Therefore one word may have several meanings, which can be confusing when conducting research in this field. In this paper, we define three levels of interaction: macro-, micro- and nanointeractions, the latter of which is the focus of this study. We use Buxton's three state model to break down common gestures on touch interfaces into nanointeractions, thereby identifying where in the process of a gesture its signifiers can appear. This is useful when overloading controls in small interfaces. We conducted an experiment to determine whether the temporal placement of a signifier before, during, or after a gesture made any difference for the discoverability of a double and long tap affordance. No clear tendencies were found regarding the temporal placement of the signifier. However, the concept of nanointeractions can be a valuable tool for interaction design.

Keywords: HCI · Interaction · Usability design · Microinteractions · Touch interactions · Gestures · Nanointeractions

1 Introduction

Verplank [15] stressed the importance of three questions that interaction designers must answer: How does one *do*? How does one *feel*? How does one *know*? The user has some form of knowledge (*know*) from previous applications with which they have interacted, and perhaps a mental map of how they imagine the current application to work. When presented with some form of control (such as a button), the interface may provide the user with feedforward (*feel*), revealing some information as to what will happen if certain gestures are performed on the control. The user will process this information based on their previous knowledge and expectations, and perform some action (*do*) on the control. Based on which action is performed, the control may provide some form of feedback (*feel*) such as a sound signifying success, or the sensation of a button being pressed, which enables the user to update their knowledge and provides support on how to proceed.

© ICST Institute for Computer Sciences, Social Informatics and Telecommunications Engineering 2020
Published by Springer Nature Switzerland AG 2020. All Rights Reserved
A. Brooks and E. I. Brooks (Eds.): ArtsIT 2019/DLI 2019, LNICST 328, pp. 290–308, 2020.
https://doi.org/10.1007/978-3-030-53294-9_20

Damkjær et al. [3] discussed the concept of microinteractions and their importance to not only the overall process of interacting with an application, but also how the user chooses each gesture based on what they know and feel. However, even this approach was simplifying things, as each gesture consisted of a series of smaller actions, and the user may process information or change their course mid-gesture. This paper focuses on the nature of these types of nanointeractions.

2   Terminology

The terminology in the field of interaction design and user interfaces is not always consistent due to interaction designers, UX designers, etc. coming from many different scientific backgrounds, each with their own language. Therefore, we describe our terminology thoroughly in the hopes it will help streamline the language in the field of interaction and UX design.

Interactions. The word interaction is used to describe many different things. Sometimes it refers to the overarching task like using an application to take a photo. Other times it refers to the action of tapping the shutter button in a camera application. And sometimes it refers to the action of tapping on the screen of a smartphone. To make it clear to which we refer, we distinguish between different levels of *interaction*. *Macrointeractions* refer to the overarching tasks, the process itself, e.g. taking a photo. These usually benefit from the user having a good mental map of the system in question. A *microinteraction* indicates the small interaction with a contextual purpose limited to a single gesture, e.g. clicking the shutter button to take a photo [9]. However, even gestures as simple as a touch screen button press are comprised of several smaller actions: approaching the button with your finger, touching the button, and letting go. These are the types of (inter-)actions we refer to as *nanointeractions*.

Signifiers. In line with Norman's [11] definition, in this paper, a *signifier* refers to a design aspect communicating to the user the existence of a specific action possibility (affordance) on some control in the user interface. The modalities to communicate can for example be visual, haptic, or auditory. In smartphone application design, signifiers commonly take the shape of text or interface control elements (such as buttons, sliders, etc.) that are based on design conventions and guidelines. Often affordances lack explicit signifiers.

Affordance, Feedforward, and Feedback. The three terms *affordance*, *feedforward* and *feedback* are commonly used in the field of interaction design, but do not always denote the same concept. We drew inspiration from Vermuelen et al.'s synthesis and insights of these three terms [14]. But for the scope of this paper, we rely on Norman's definition of *affordance*. An *affordance* is a relationship between an actor and the properties of an object, e.g. a button can be pressed. Affordances are not always clearly signified and can in fact be *hidden*.

Therefore we distinguish between *perceivable* and *hidden* affordances. Perceivable affordances are supported by and can be understood from signifiers on an object while hidden affordances lack visible or otherwise perceivable signifiers. For example, the affordance of a long tap on a button is often hidden in touch interfaces. It should be noted that Norman has previously used the term perceived affordance to mean what he now calls a signifier [10], and therefore several papers use these terms interchangeably.

Feedforward. communicates to the user something about what would happen (the function that gets triggered) if they performed the afforded action. For example, pressing a green button or a button with a text label saying "ok" on it having the effect of confirming something. *Feedback* refers to information becoming available during or after performing the action allowed by the affordance. Staying with the previous example, pressing the above "ok" button might yield feedback in the form of a toast message ("Thank you!") confirming that the button press has been registered.

Gestures. A touch *gesture*, e.g. a tap, is the physical action performed on a touch interface. This should not to be confused with a microinteraction. A microinteraction involves a gesture but must also include a purpose such as scrolling by using a fling. In this paper, we look at the gestures tap, double tap, long tap, and drag.

Another way to describe gestures besides using words, is utilising models. In this paper we use Buxton's three state model [2] to break down gestures. As seen in Fig. 1(b), the model consist of three states: state 0 is the state where you are out of range of the gesture; state 1 represents when you are in range; and state 2 is when the intended gesture is carried out.

To show how all these terms play together in terms of Verplank's interaction model, we have modified his sketch according to the terms established in this section, shown in Fig. 1(a).

3   Breaking down Gestures

When Verplank speaks of interactions, he uses the example of flipping a switch and seeing the light come on [15]. However, as we have previously stated, even a gesture as simple as flipping a switch may be broken down into a series of nano-interactions. The user may discover new information during a nanointeraction, before they have completed the intended gesture.

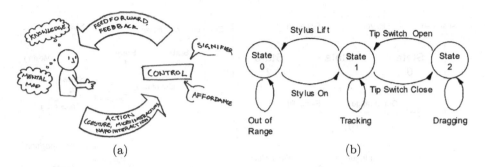

Fig. 1. (a) The cycle of a user interacting with a control, modified from Verplank's sketch [15] and (b) Buxton's three state model [2].

As an example, placing one's finger on the switch is a nanointeraction in and of itself. At this state the user may feel that it is impossible to flip the switch one way, but possible to flip it the other. The nanointeraction of applying pressure while flipping the switch gives the user some information on how much resistance the switch gives, and thus how much pressure they must apply. They may even discover a sequential affordance [4] of fading the light gradually that was previously hidden. Breaking gestures into nanointeractions in this manner rather than one instantaneous action is useful when designing user experiences for a touch device. To show how gestures are broken into nanointeractions, we provide some examples visualised through diagrams inspired by Larsen's work [7], using Buxton's three state model [2].

The simplest touch interaction, the *tap*, is illustrated in Fig. 2(a). In our model state 0 represents when the user's finger is out of range of the control on the touch screen, state 1 when the user's finger is in range of the control, and state 2 when the user interacts with the control. For the tap gesture this is when the finger touches the control. The arrow marked in red represents the moment that the system delivers feedback regarding the affordance of the control. In the case of a tap this does not happen until the action is completed, i.e. when the user lifts their finger.

Figure 2(b) illustrates the *drag* gesture. Here, users may transition to state 2a by performing the nanointeraction of moving their finger once placed on the screen. Moving the finger on the screen is actually several nanointeractions, but for the sake of simplicity it is illustrated as only one in our model. The gesture is completed when the user lifts their finger, thus returning to state 1. The affordance of dragging is revealed by feedback the instant movement is detected, thereby appearing during the gesture. This differs from a tap in that rather than after the gesture is complete, the feedback is provided mid-gesture, allowing users to discover the affordance before completing the gesture. However, this takes place during a very short amount of time, so it is not always possible to react to the feedback.

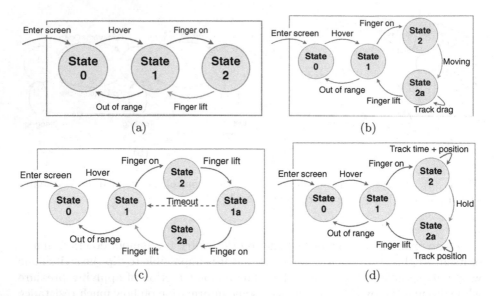

Fig. 2. Gestures broken down into nanointeraction state diagrams: (a) *tap*, (b) *drag*, (c) *double tap*, and (d) *long tap*.

The *long tap* gesture is depicted in Fig. 2(d). To get to state 2a the user must hold their finger's position for a certain amount of time, and when this threshold is reached the hidden affordance is revealed and the gesture is completed when the finger is lifted.

Often, a *long tap* is combined with a *drag* when implementing them on touch screen. This is similar to selecting an object by clicking and holding when using a computer mouse. Figure 3 illustrates how adding the drag gesture to the long tap model introduces an additional state, state 2b. Compared to a normal long tap the signifier revealing the affordance is delayed to correspond to the signifier revealing the drag affordance

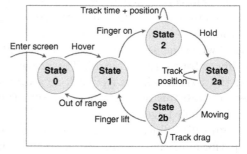

Fig. 3. The *long tap* gesture continued with the *drag* gesture, broken into nanointeractions.

instead, i.e. giving feedback when the user's finger moves after the long tap.

The gesture *double tap* illustrated in Fig. 2(c) does not have a linear state sequence like the three previously described gestures. As the name implies it is the act of tapping twice. Like the long tap, this gesture has a temporal aspect to the nanointeractions, i.e. the time between *finger lift* and *finger on* determines whether you perform a double tap or just two separate taps. This is illustrated in Fig. 2(c) where state 1a is present. This represents the temporal nature of the gesture by working as a timer state, where if you timeout you go back to state 1 and have to start the gesture over again. Unless specifically designed for it, the affordance is not revealed until the user's finger is lifted after the second tap, making it very hard to discover.

To illustrate how to break down a system with numerous gesture affordances, Fig. 4 depicts both the *tap, drag, long tap, long tap+drag* and *double tap* affordances, broken into nanointeractions. All five gestures require the user to first approach the control, and then place their finger on it, thus entering state 2 on touch interfaces. Moving one's finger while in this state reveals the affordance of dragging, which initiates state 2a. The user may complete the dragging gesture by lifting their finger off the control. If, instead, the user rests their finger on the control while in state 2, they enter state 2b, initiating a long tap. From here, they may either complete this gesture by lifting their finger, or initiate a long tap+drag by moving their finger. If the user lifts their finger while in state 2, they have performed a regular tap. However, as both the single- and double tap are afforded by this system, the single tap is not complete until a certain timer runs out, ensuring that the user did not perform a double tap.

This timeout will usually be quite short, so the user does not sense a delay upon tapping a control. If, instead, they place their finger back on the control and lift it again, a double tap is performed. In Fig. 4, the red arrows signify places in the process where feedback is typically provided.

Illustrating interactions in this manner and thinking of gestures as a system of nanointeractions rather than something that happens instantaneously may prove useful when considering how to design an application with meaningful signifiers, both in terms of feedforward and feedback.

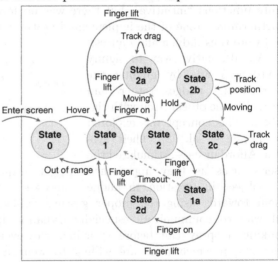

Fig. 4. The combination of the *tap, drag, long tap, long tap+drag* and *double tap* gestures, broken into nanointeractions.

4   Related Research

One way to signify certain affordances is by using metaphors to tap into users' existing knowledge. Oakley et al. utilised this idea for their smartwatch prototype as a way to introduce new affordances [12]. A finger placed vertically across the center of the watch was implemented as a way to activate the mute function on a media player application, as the action resembles placing a finger across lips. Two fingers across the watch toggle between pause and play, as the two fingers resemble the traditional 'pause' icon (two vertical parallel lines). Placing the finger horizontally along the bottom of the screen emulates the shape subtitles take on a screen, and thus enables the subtitles. This was discoverable only through feedback—no signifiers were provided to the user. Oakley et al. relied on explaining these affordances to test users, and did not report on whether previous knowledge of the used metaphors was sufficient to discover the affordances in this case. It should be noted that they never quantitatively tested these affordances, but rather relied on participant self-reports in how far they the understood the gestures. Users supported the notion of metaphors and found the pause and mute functions "intuitive", but there was no formal testing of error rates etc. Furthermore, some of the implemented gestures lacked a metaphor or signifier and were thus hidden affordances.

An alternative way to signify affordances was by guiding the user through nudges, rather than designing the object itself with signifiers. This concept was explored by Lopes et al. [8]. Their system, Affordance++, stimulated the user's arms as they approached the object in question to nudge

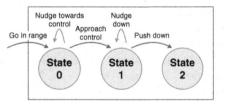

Fig. 5. Turning on the lamp, guided by Affordance++.

them towards using the proper gesture. They found that this was a useful way to communicate especially dynamic interactions to the user, e.g. shaking a spray can before spraying. However, it is limited to real-world contexts in which users are willing to wear an arm-mounted device at all times. Interestingly, this nudging signifier was not provided by the control itself (the lamp), but rather by an external device. Furthermore, the nudges continuously provided signification to the user based on which state they are currently in, directly nudging them towards the next state. This is shown in Fig. 5, where we have applied our model to the interaction. Note that overloading would create a problem for this solution, as the possibility of moving to several different states from the current one means that there is little point in being nudged towards just one.

Another way to provide users with feedforward without visual signifiers, is to rely on audio, as is the case with e.g. answering machines and automated phone call systems (see Fig. 6). Here the user is provided with audio signifiers of all the affordances and feedforward in the form of a list of available options. This system provides both feedforward and feedback. However, sometimes it provides too much of it, or gives the feedforward in a problematic order. It is also very time-consuming, especially if the user does not know what they are searching for and needs to listen through all the options more than once. As illustrated by Fig. 6 the user's options are limited by lack of knowledge of

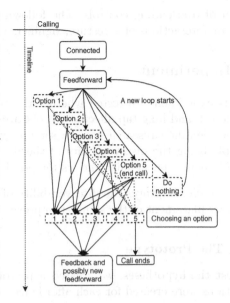

Fig. 6. A chronological illustration of a hypothetical answering machine.

said options, until a certain amount of time has passed. Overloading in this situation is not a possible solution, since it is limited to one modality, audio.

Harrison et al. acknowledge the need for overloading in touch interfaces, and achieved it by differentiating inputs from different parts of the finger - the tip, the pad, the nail, and the knuckle [5]. But they did not performed any tests on how to signify these affordances. Pedersen and Hornbæk [13] proposed touch force as a modality for overloading. Their users could accurately control two different levels of pressure, although this took some getting used to. Moreover, users expressed fatigue after having touched the screen with increased pressure for a while, indicating that this modality was inferior as an interaction and should be used to a limited degree. Aslan et al. proposed the *gazeover* as a way to implement something similar to the mouseover on a mouse-and-keyboard setup, but potentially available for touch interfaces [1]. However, they did not test user's ability to perceive this affordance on a touch interface. Damkjær et al. [3] tested different visual signifiers (a shadow on a button, a drag handle among others) to see which one(s) best conveyed the affordances of dragging and double tapping. Signifiers with a temporal element performed worse than signifiers with no temporal element.

A lot of creative solutions have been proposed using different modalities to communicate affordances or implement overloading. However, many lack signifiers for the affordances, resulting in hidden affordances impairing usability. We intend to explore this research gap by investigating how we can explicitly signify and turn hidden affordances of touch screen gestures such as double tap and long tap, into perceived affordances. This knowledge can then inform the design of overloading controls. The following study investigated when, during the nanointeractions of a gesture, signifiers should appear.

5   Experiment

In this experiment we tested whether the temporal placement of signifiers for double tap and long tap affected the discoverability of these affordances. Based on the identified research gap we set up two hypotheses, with the dependent variable being the discoverability of the relevant gesture, and the independent variable being the signifier and its temporal placement:

1. A signifier improves the discoverability of the affordance of a gesture.
2. Early placement of the signifier improves discoverability of the affordance.

5.1   The Prototype

To test the hypotheses, we created a prototype app in Android Studio. Four variations were created for each affordance:

- Ctrl - A control version with no visual signifier.
- Enter - The signifier appeared on entering state 0, and then repeats in a five second loop (the green spot in Fig. 7).
- Middle - A signifier appeared when the user touched the screen, thus entering state 2 (the purple spot in Fig. 7).
- After - A signifier appeared after a completed single tap (the yellow spot in Fig. 7).

To counter potential learning effects we added a distractor version. In this version, instead of a double tap or long tap affordance, there was a fling affordance with no signifier indicating this.

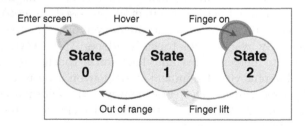

Fig. 7. Signifiers can appear on *enter*ing the current UI screen (green), on touching the screen (*middle*, purple), and *after* a single tap (yellow). (Color figure online)

Upon launching the app, the screen shows a menu of these nine versions. This menu was not to be seen by test participants, but was a tool for the test facilitators to control which version was applied. This menu can be seen in Fig. 8(a).

Once a version had been chosen, the application redirected to the screen seen in Fig. 8(b). As can be seen, it was a simple to-do list application, which allowed users to add items to a list of chores, mark the ones they have completed, and delete items from the list. Users may write the name of a chore in the text field (1), then press the button (2) to then add that item to the list (3).

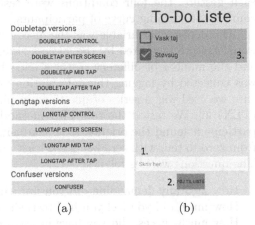

If the text field was empty upon button press, no item was added to the list. As can be seen in Fig. 8(b), each list item contains a box which may be checked upon tapping it. This box was also checked if the list item was single tapped at all, either on the text or in the empty space to the right.

For each version of this app, there was a hidden affordance to delete items added to the list. For four of these versions, the trigger was to double tap, for four others it was to long tap, and for the last one (the distractor) the trigger was to fling. The gesture in question must be performed on the item the user

Fig. 8. (a) The version menu on the prototype application. (b) The main screen of the to-do list app.

wished to delete, but it did not matter whether the gesture was performed on the text, the box, or the empty space.

As described previously, a signifier revealing the given affordance may appear at various times depending on the chosen version. For the double tap versions (except for the control version), the signifier was a pulse of two rings which expanded one after the other, then disappeared. This was to emulate the idea of a double tap. A screenshot of this can be seen Fig. 9(a).

For the long tap versions (except for the control version), the signifier was a wheel which gradually filled out over time, indicating that the user may hold their finger on the screen for an extended period of time (see Fig. 9(b)).

Throughout the application, every touch gesture performed, as well as every successfully added, marked, or deleted item, was logged for analysis purposes.

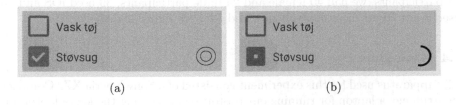

Fig. 9. The affordance signifiers for the (a) double tap and (b) long tap

5.2 Experiment Design

The evaluation consisted of two experiments, one for the double tap and the other for the long tap gesture. The hypotheses apply to both experiments.

The independent variable was the temporal placement of the signifier. For each gesture, the four conditions were tested, plus the distractor to slightly counter the learning curve of participants.

The dependent variable was the discoverability of the affordance of the relevant gesture measured by the success rate, the time until successful deletion, and the number of different gestures tried before finding the correct one. This was collected by logging this information within the prototype. Another measure we used was a series of questions inspired by the NASA Task Load Index (TLX) [6]. We tested the raw TLX method in a pilot trial, but since the test participant found the original scale confusing, we changed the scale to a range from zero to ten, with zero being the least and ten the greatest amount possible. The questions were as follows:

- How mentally demanding did you find the task?
- How much did you feel you had to rush when performing the task?
- How much success did you have in accomplishing the task?
- How much effort did you have to put in when accomplishing the task?
- How irritated, stressed, annoyed, or frustrated did you feel during the task?

Due to the experiment becoming too long to be able to recruit people off of the street each participant only tried five conditions: two of each gesture and the distractor as the middle trial, making the experiment a between subjects design. To alleviate the learning curve of the participants somewhat, the order of the conditions was determined by using a Latin square design.

5.3 Participants

The only requirement for the participants was that they not have a background in interface design. For this test 64 random people in the age group of 14 to 77 years old were recruited off of the streets in Aalborg and amongst employees at Regionshuset Nordjylland. The experiments were conducted at three different places due to recruitment issues: a space at Aalborg University, an office at Regionshuset Nordjylland and the Main Public Library in Aalborg. Out of the 64 participants, we had 40 female and 24 male participants, 39 used iOS and 25 used Android on their smartphones, and 52 were right-handed.

5.4 Procedure

The apparatus used for this experiment consisted of a Sony Xperia XZ2 Compact smartphone, a laptop for running our prototype and saving the log, a laptop for notetaking and questionnaire answers, and a video camera on a tripod to film the participant's hands interacting with the smartphone.

The procedure for the experiment was as follows: first the participant signed a consent form and was explained the procedure by one of the two facilitators. They then filled out a demographics questionnaire. The video camera was turned on when the participant received the first version of the prototype. They were told to first add an item to the list, then mark an item as completed and finally to delete an item. A trial was considered a success if an item was deleted. When the participant either succeeded in deleting or gave up, they answered some follow up questions regarding their actions with that version followed by the TLX-inspired scales. This process repeated with the next four versions, with the third trial always being the distractor condition. After the participant finished with the fifth trial, the log was copied from Android Studio to a text file. The entire procedure took approximately 15 min from start to finish.

5.5   Results

When the data was not normally distributed we used a Kruskal-Wallis test instead of one-way ANOVAs when comparing the dependent variables of the temporal signifier placements each in the double tap and long tap versions.

We did not compare results between the two gestures, as users should attempt the long tap more frequently than the double tap, because the former is more common in touch screens in general. Figures 10(a) and 10(b) depict the distribution of successes and failures of each temporal placement of signifiers excluding the distractor. A quick comparison of these figures confirms that participants were much more successful at discovering the long tap than the double tap affordance. However, CHI-square tests found no significant differences of the success rates between the temporal placements of the signifiers neither for long[1] nor for

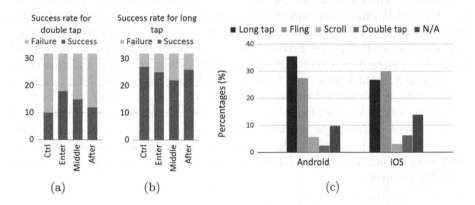

(a)   (b)   (c)

Fig. 10. The distribution of successes and failures of the double tap (a) and long tap (b) versions. (c) The percentage of first gestures performed in each trial other than single taps. N/A represents trials with no gesture attempts but single taps.

---

[1] $\chi^2(3, N = 32) = 2.56, p = 0.46$.

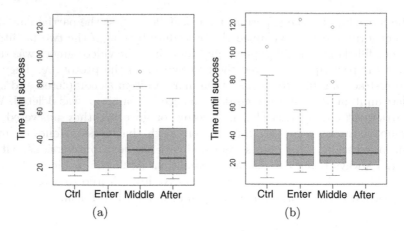

Fig. 11. Box plots of the time until successful deletion for (a) double tap and (b) long tap.

double tap[2]. We found a trend for the first gesture people used in each trial other than single taps, which depended on the mobile operating systems the participants were used to. Android users tried long taps first and iOS users were more likely to try a fling first (see Fig. 10(c)). Much less frequently people tried scrolls (slowly swiping) and double taps. In some cases the participants did not try anything but single taps (denoted as N/A in the figure).

Kruskal-Wallis tests of the completion times found no significant differences between the temporal placements for the double ($H(3) = 2.6$, $p = 0.45$) and long tap versions ($H(3) = 2.65$, $p = 0.86$). See Fig. 11 for an overview of the data.

Similarly when comparing the number of gestures performed before success, Kruskal-Wallis tests found no significant differences for the temporal placement of signifiers for the double ($H(3) = 2.62$, $p = 0.45$), and long tap gesture ($H(3) = 3.79$, $p = 0.28$). The distribution of the number of gestures are illustrated in Fig. 12. We tested whether removing single taps from the data changed these results but Kruskal-Wallis tests found no significant differences for the double ($H(3) = 3.67$, $p = 0.3$) and long tap version ($H(3) = 2.61$, $p = 0.46$) in that subset of the data either. We then looked at whether the temporal placement influenced the variety of gestures the participants tried before success and excluded the single taps from this analysis. Again Kruskal-Wallis tests found no significant differences for neither double ($H(3) = 2.63$, $p = 0.45$) nor long tap ($H(3) = 2.82$, $p = 0.42$) gestures.

---

[2] $\chi^2(3, N = 32) = 4.69, p = 0.2$.

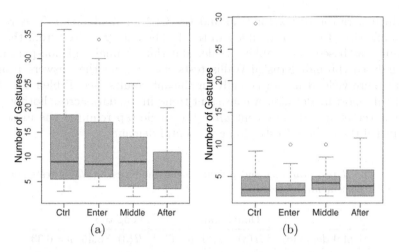

Fig. 12. Box plots of the number of gestures performed before success for (a) double tap and (b) long tap.

The questionnaire data analysis focused on the mental demand, temporal demand, performance, effort and frustration experienced during the trials. We compared between the four different signifier placements of long tap and double tap respectively. Figure 13 visualizes the overall distribution of answers. No answers were discarded in this analysis since the questionnaire results' ability to be statistically analysed were not affected by whether a participant succeeded or not. One participant chose to not answer the questions for two of the tri-

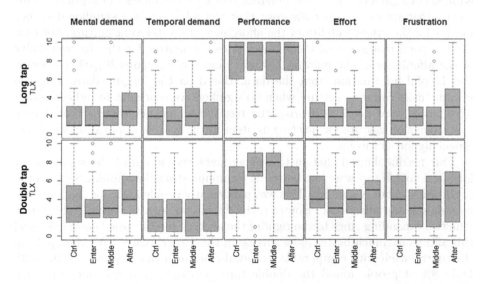

Fig. 13. Box plots of TLX sub-scale for both the long tap results and the double tap results

als, which were the distractor trial and the Ctrl for double tap. This reduced the sample size of Ctrl for double tap to 31. The data gathered from the questionnaire was based on a ranking scale, and thus ordinal and non-parametric, and analysed through Kruskal-Wallis tests. Comparing the answers from the questionnaire yielded no statistically significant results (see Table 1 for all the statistical reporting details). A consistent trend in the data across both gestures was that the temporal placement *after* the single tap required the most effort and yielded the highest frustration and mental demand.

Table 1. The H test statistics and p-values from the Kruskal-Wallis tests comparing the signifier placements by gesture

	Double tap	Long tap
Mental demand	$H(3) = 3.36, p = 0.34$	$H(3) = 3.45, p = 0.33$
Temporal demand	$H(3) = 1.35, p = 0.72$	$H(3) = 1.63, p = 0.65$
Performance	$H(3) = 6.41, p = 0.09$	$H(3) = 0.54, p = 0.91$
Effort	$H(3) = 3, p = 0.39$	$H(3) = 4.66, p = 0.2$
Frustration	$H(3) = 2.4, p = 0.49$	$H(3) = 1.34, p = 0.72$

6 Discussion

The results showed no significant differences between control condition and 1) the addition of signifiers and 2) the different temporal placements of signifiers. This means that we can neither disprove that the addition of a signifier does not matter for the discoverability of the affordance of the relevant gesture, nor that the temporal placement of the signifier does not matter for the discoverability of the affordance of the relevant gesture. However, we can still gather relevant and helpful information from the data. Based on the logging data, long tap was the most common gesture when no signifiers were present to indicate other affordances were possible. During the test it became made clear that a fling was a common gesture for deleting an item in the type of application we made, especially for iOS users.

Our results showed that in this experiment the design of the signifiers for long and double tap were not better at communicating the affordances than the condition without a signifier. This was particularly problematic for the less common double tap affordance. However, the double tap signifier used in this study (the two expanding rings to the right of the control, see Fig. 9(a)) communicated this affordance much better (56% success in the 'Enter' placement) than pulsing the control itself with comparable temporal placement in our previous study [3]. Only 8% of people found the double tap affordance through that approach. This large difference can be partially explained by the increased opportunity to perceive the affordance in this study through looping the animation every five seconds in comparison to showing it only once at entry. But there were further differences in task design, the controls that were signified, and the visual design of the signifier itself, which might have affected discoverability.

Regarding the validity of our results a few things should be considered. The order in which participants tried the different versions was balanced using a Latin square design having all combinations an equal amount of times during the experiment. Our participants came from a wide variety of backgrounds and age groups. We even had a few different nationalities. These two factors strengthen the validity of our results. Our primary data was gathered from the log of the application. When looking through the logs the program did not always assign the correct gesture name to what the application clearly read, e.g. in a double tap version a double tap not resulting in a delete action, therefore having been read as two single taps, or in a long tap version a scroll being read as a long tap and success being reached that way. This was all corrected by having a person read through the log and note the results, but it does hurt the validity of our log data. Regarding the data from the questionnaire, self-reporting is always hard to validate especially when the experiment is a between-groups setup. Having the questions based on a standard in the field (NASA TLX) increases the validity of our results as does the fact that the results corresponded quite well with the log data.

There was a number of limitations to our findings. The reliability of our results was potentially affected by changing location three times with one of these locations being in a public space, albeit a somewhat isolated corner of this space. The wide age range and background of our participants should have given us a reliable sample of the population, strengthening the external validity of our results. During the first few trials the way we phrased the task of deleting an item was misleadingly vague and making some test participants believe that checking a box on the screen was sufficient. When we rephrased the assignment to specify that the item had to disappear altogether, participants understood the task better. During the test, we discovered that when the user executed a fling slowly, it sometimes registered as a long tap, regardless of finger movement. This means that while the log data may show that some users discovered the long tap affordance, they may have actually have attempted a fling. This problem of the temporal unfolding of gestures leading to misinterpretation represents a common problem with overloading controls with different gestures that interaction designers will need to address in the future.

Several times throughout the experiment, in their search for a button to delete an item, test participants would accidentally return to the secret menu screen or to the phone's home screen. This may have impacted the user in two ways: The confusion may have caused the participants to feel more insecure and less inclined to try different approaches to the task. On the other hand, if a participant caught a peek of the text on the buttons, it may have revealed to them an affordance that they did not previously perceive.

Further analysis could explore whether the order in which the different versions were experienced had an effect on the discoverability. It is possible that, if a gesture (e.g. a long tap) was not possible in the first version a participant experienced, the participant might never attempt that gesture again in later trials when the gesture *was* possible. On the other hand, if the first version had the affordance of the most obvious non-tap gesture to that participant (often long tap), the participant might be more willing to try other gestures, as they had already seen that deleting an item was possible. Studying the relationship between the position on the screen of a visual signifier and the position at which the user performs a gesture represents another avenue for future work. On touch screens, the user's finger may block the visual signifier from their view if it appears upon touch, which may cause the user to never see the signifier, thus hindering discoverability. This is less of a problem for signifiers, which are always visible. But they occupy space in the interface.

The concept of nanointeractions opens up several alleys for future research. With more time and resources, we would have performed a large-scale within-subjects experiment with a more easily understandable signifier in order to better determine the viability of revealing signifiers to the user while they are at a certain nanointeraction stage in a gesture. Furthermore, it may be valuable to explore the nature of changing gestures and how designers can take advantage of this.

In this paper, we focused our research on two gestures: long tap and double tap. This was to keep the scope manageable. There are many other touch gestures which can be broken down into nanointeractions, and the complexity of some of them make them especially interesting. An example is the drag gesture requiring the user to change the position of their finger. While we have mapped a drag gesture into nanointeractions, the user may in theory change their course many times *while dragging*, which could be considered nanointeractions in and of themselves. Every touch gesture is different and future research should focus on how these can be combined best when overloading controls with several gestures. Furthermore, if one thinks of touch gestures as a series of nanointeractions, one may also explore the nature of changing gestures. For example, if the user has initiated a long tap by placing their finger on a control and holding it there, but then moves the finger away from the control before lifting, they have changed their course "in the middle of" a gesture, which designers and future researchers may take into account, as it allows for new combinations of gestures for which to design affordances and signifiers. This paper focused entirely on visual signifiers, but other types of feedback may affect users differently. We believe future research investigating the relationship between audio or haptic feedback and nanointeraction stages could be particularly fruitful.

7   Conclusion

In this paper, we focused on the discoverability of gesture affordances depending on whether a signifier was made visible before any gesture was attempted, during a gesture, or after a gesture has been completed. While the experiment showed no significant differences between the temporal placement of signifiers, we argue that this study still has great value for future research. The possibility of attempting to let the user perceive a previously hidden affordance as they are currently "in the middle of" a gesture has not previously been explored, and we hope that future researchers will further investigate. We analyzed current research into different affordance design angles with different modalities with this terminology. Our main contribution to the field is the concept of nanointeractions. Most research thinks of touch screen gestures as one single interaction, without breaking it down. However, if we as interaction designers instead consider the elements which make up a gesture—the nanointeractions—it will reveal opportunities for novel gesture designs and overloading controls by combining these in interfaces with limited space.

References

1. Aslan, I., Dietz, M., André, E.: Gazeover - exploring the UX of gaze-triggered affordance communication for GUI elements. In: Proceedings of the 20th ACM International Conference on Multimodal Interaction, ICMI 2018, pp. 253–257. ACM, New York (2018). https://doi.org/10.1145/3242969.3242987
2. Buxton, W.: A three-state model of graphical input. Hum.-Comput. Interact.-INTERACT. **90**, 449–456 (1990)
3. Damkjær, E.L., Arleth, L., Knoche, H.: I Didn't Know, You Could Do That - affordance signifiers for touch gestures on mobile devices. In: Brooks, A.L., Brooks, E., Sylla, C. (eds.) ArtsIT/DLI -2018. LNICST, vol. 265, pp. 206–212. Springer, Cham (2019). https://doi.org/10.1007/978-3-030-06134-0_23
4. Gaver, W.W.: Technology affordances. In: Proceedings of CHI 2019, pp. 79–84. ACM (1991)
5. Harrison, C., Schwarz, J., Hudson, S.E.: TapSense: enhancing finger interaction on touch surfaces. In: Proceedings of the 24th Annual ACM Symposium on User Interface Software and Technology, UIST 2011, pp. 627–636. ACM, New York (2011). https://doi.org/10.1145/2047196.2047279
6. Hart, S.G.: Nasa-task load index (NASA-TLX); 20 years later. Proc. Hum. Factors Ergon. Soc. Ann. Meet. **50**(9), 904–908 (2006). https://doi.org/10.1177/154193120605000909
7. Larsen, J.V., Knoche, H.: States and sound: modelling user interactions with musical interfaces. In: New Interfaces for Musical Expression 2017New Interfaces for Musical Expression. NIME (2017)
8. Lopes, P., Jonell, P., Baudisch, P.: Affordance++: allowing objects to communicate dynamic use. In: Proceedings of the 33rd Annual ACM Conference on Human Factors in Computing Systems, CHI 2015, pp. 2515–2524. ACM, New York (2015). https://doi.org/10.1145/2702123.2702128
9. McDaniel, R.: Understanding microinteractions as applied research opportunities for information designers. Commun. Des. Q. Rev. **3**(2), 55–62 (2015)
10. Norman, D.A.: The way I see IT signifiers, not affordances. Interactions **15**(6), 18–19 (2008)
11. Norman, D.A.: Design of Everyday Things: Revised and Expanded. Basic Books, New York (2013)
12. Oakley, I., Lindahl, C., Le, K., Lee, D.Y., Islam, M.R.: The flat finger: exploring area touches on smartwatches. In: CHI 2016 (2016)

13. Pedersen, E.W., Hornbæk, K.: Expressive touch: studying tapping force on table-tops. In: Proceedings of the SIGCHI Conference on Human Factors in Computing Systems, CHI 2014, pp. 421–430. ACM, New York (2014). https://doi.org/10.1145/2556288.2557019
14. Vermeulen, J., Luyten, K., van den Hoven, E., Coninx, K.: Crossing the bridge over Norman's Gulf of Execution: revealing feedforward's true identity. In: Proceedings of the SIGCHI Conference on Human Factors in Computing Systems, pp. 1931–1940. ACM (2013)
15. Verplank, B.: Interaction Design Sketchbook (2009). http://billverplank.com/CiiD

Co-designing Object Shapes
with Artificial Intelligence

Kevin German[1](✉), Marco Limm[2], Matthias Wölfel[3], and Silke Helmerdig[2]

[1] School of Engineering, Pforzheim University, Pforzheim, Germany
`kevin.german@hs-pforzheim.de`
[2] School of Design, Pforzheim University, Pforzheim, Germany
`limmmarm@hs-pforzheim.de,kontakt@helmerdig.de`
[3] Faculty of Computer Science and Business Information Systems,
Karlsruhe University of Applied Sciences, Karlsruhe, Germany
`matthias.woelfel@hs-karlsruhe.de`

Abstract. The promise of *artificial intelligence* (AI), in particular its latest developments in deep learning, has been influencing all kinds of disciplines such as engineering, business, agriculture, and humanities. More recently it also includes disciplines that were "reserved" to humans such as art and design. While there is a strong debate going on if creativity is profoundly human, we want to investigate if creativity can be supported or fostered by AI—not replaced. This paper investigates if AI is capable of (a) inspiring designers by suggesting unexpected design variations, (b) learning the designer's taste or (c) being a co-creation partner.

To do so we adopted AI algorithms, which can be trained by a small sample set of shapes of a given object, to propose novel shapes. The evaluation of our proposed methods revealed that it can be used by trained designers as well as non-designers to support the design process in different phases and that it could lead to novel designs not intended/foreseen by designers.

Keywords: Inspirational AI · Human-machine co-design · Artificial neural network · Genetic algorithm · Design process

1 Introduction

3D printing promised to revolutionize production processes and to enable anybody to make their own products on the fly. However, this promise has not yet been fulfilled. We believe that one of the main reasons is that the design process is still laborious and that it simply cannot be realized by non-designers due to time or skill constraints. To really liberate the production process, beyond easy and accessible 3D printing, novel methods/tools for the design process are required which permit everybody to design a product even with very limited design skills. Novel developments in *artificial intelligence* (AI) have demonstrated that they

© ICST Institute for Computer Sciences, Social Informatics and Telecommunications Engineering 2020
Published by Springer Nature Switzerland AG 2020. All Rights Reserved
A. Brooks and E. I. Brooks (Eds.): ArtsIT 2019/DLI 2019, LNICST 328, pp. 309–327, 2020.
https://doi.org/10.1007/978-3-030-53294-9_21

are capable to do things which in the past were restricted to humans. *Artificial neural networks* (ANN) and *genetic algorithms* (GA) are tools to make work easier for humans, for example through automatic speech translations (for instance simultaneous lecture translation has been demonstrated feasible already in 2008 by Kolss et al. [15]) or are even able to come up with solutions humans would never come up with effortlessly, see for instance the design of an "evolved antenna" using evolutionary algorithms published by Hornby et al. already in 2006 [9]. With further technological developments, of such processes there is a gradual transfer of competence from human beings to technical devices, namely, they serve as [27]:

1. tools: transfer of *mechanics* (material) from the human being to the device
2. machines: transfer of *energy* from the human being to the device
3. automatic machines[1]: transfer of *information* from the human being to the device
4. assistants: transfer of *decisions* from the human being to the device

We want to exemplify this concept with the field of mobility:

1. bicycle: feet are replaced by wheels
2. motor vehicle: propulsion is replaced by engine
3. self-driving rail vehicle: control is replaced by sensors and signal processing
4. autonomous vehicle: route planning or search for a parking space are replaced by artificial intelligence

Similarly, we can give an example from the field of art and design:

1. potter's kick-wheel: a tool used in the shaping of round ceramic ware driven by kicking a fly-wheel into motion
2. potter's electric-wheel: the kicking of the fly-wheel is replaced by a motor
3. construction & 3D printing: the object is constructed with a CAD-software according to given parameters and 3D printed
4. generated & 3D printing: the object is generated by an optimization process given particular constraints and 3D printed

In the coming years we are in the process of moving from Step 3. to Step 4. which raises—as it was the case from moving from Step 1. to Step 2. as well as from Step 2. to Step 3.—discussions, rejections, ethical issues (for instance, see the *trolley problem* [20]), up to fears. Our particular interested in this process is in investigating the following questions:

- Can AI be used to assist the design process to support the designer and/or the non-designer?
- Can AI inspire designers by suggesting unexpected design variations?
- Can AI learn the designer's taste to suggest only design variations the designer favors?

---

[1] Which is called *Automat* or *automate* in other languages such as German or French respectively.

– Can AI be a co-creation partner just like other humans or serve as a muse?
– How this development is perceived by designers and/or the non-designer?

In the literature, some approaches to use AI in the design process have been presented. We review those approaches in the following section. Because the already introduced approaches are not available or were not fulfilling our requirements it was necessary to adopt given methods to intervene in the design process; either partially or in total. The investigated algorithms include genetic algorithms and different versions of neuronal networks namely convolutional neural networks, generative adversarial networks, and variational autoencoder. The developed algorithms can semi- or fully-automate the research, brainstorming and concept phase of the design process.

To evaluate and compare our different proposed approaches the entire development process was completed until the finished product for each approach. The approaches have been introduced within the School of Design at Pforzheim University, Germany and to visitors of the Salone del Mobile in Milan, Italy where we showcased our approach. On these occasions, we were able to demonstrate that our proposed methods can be used by trained designers as well as non-designers to design semi-complex shapes with minimal user feedback.

2   Related Work

The idea of using algorithms to support the design process and aesthetic experience is well established and frequently referred to as *generative design* or *procedural generation*. It is used to generate geometric patterns, textures, shapes, meshes, terrain or plants. The generation processes may include, but are not limited, to self-organization, swarm systems, ant colonies, evolutionary systems, fractal geometry, and generative grammars. McCormack et al. [18] review some generative design approaches and discuss how design as a discipline can benefit from those applications. While older approaches rely on generative algorithms which are usually realized by program code the introduction of AI changed this process: because it can learn patterns from (labeled) examples or by reinforcement. AI or more precise ANN has been introduced to support the design process more recently. Leading software companies in engineering and design have already included AI-driven generative design paradigms which let humans input design goals. For instance, *Project Dreamcatcher* [2] is an engineering-based generative design program that enables designers to generate *computer-aided design* (CAD) models based on their goals and constraints. It takes into account how the forces will be directed best in the product and defines the best production method. Autodesk states the benefits of generative design to [1]:

– explore a wider range of design options
– make impossible designs possible
– optimize for materials and manufacturing methods

Most popular (at least in the mass media) are probably different variations of *image-to-image translation*. The most prominent example is *style transfer*—the capability to transfer the style of one image to draw the content of another. But mapping an input image to an output image is also possible for a variety of other applications such as *object transfiguration* (e.g. horse-to-zebra, apple-to-orange, *season transfer* (e.g. summer-to-winter) or *photo enhancement* [30]. While some of the just mentioned system seems to be toy applications, AI tools are taking over and gradually automate design processes which used to be time-consuming manual processes. Indeed, the most potential for AI in art and design is seen in its application to tedious, uncreative tasks such as coloring black-and-white images [29]. Cluzel et al. have proposed an interactive GA to progressively sketch the desired side-view of a car profile [3]. For this, the user has taken on the role of a fitness function[2] through interaction with the system. The *chAIr Project* [23] is a series of four chairs co-designed by AI and human designers. The project explores a collaborative creative process between humans and computers. It used a *generative adversarial network* (GAN) to propose new chairs which then have been 'interpreted' by trained designers to resemble a chair. It thus replaced the designer in the brainstorming and concept phase (see Sect. 3). *DeepWear* [12] is a method using deep convolutional GANs for clothes design. The GAN is trained on features of brand clothes and can generate images that are similar to actual clothes. A human interprets the generated images and tries to manually draw the corresponding pattern which is needed to make the finished product. Li et al. [17] introduced a neural network architecture for encoding and synthesizing the structure of 3D shapes which—according to their findings—are effectively characterized by their hierarchical organization. Daniel Wikström discusses the implementation of AI into the UX design process [25]. He mentions that many designers do not yet know technology well enough and therefore perceive it as "magic". But he also explains how an intelligent assistant is perceived and would interact. Roman Lipski uses an *AI muse* (developed by Florian Dohmann et al.) to foster his/her inspiration. Because the AI muse is trained only on the artists previous drawings and fed with the current work in progress it suggests image variations in line with Romans taste.

Most of the related work is not ready yet to be used without a thorough understanding of the technology and is more an engineering approach using neural networks instead of common technology. What we are aiming for is different: The whole design process—not its development—should be applicable to naive users without any profound understanding of design or engineering. The user has to only rely on his/her taste to cherry-pick examples he/she likes in an iterative process until he/she ends up with the final design.

3   Design Process

Considering several common definitions of the design process, it can be simplified into five general phases [8, 10, 11, 26].

1. The *briefing* in which, e.g., the specifications and the project plan are created.

---

[2] Also referred to as objective function.

2. The *research* phase in which project-relevant aspects such as already existing products as well as tendencies in the market are analyzed and domain-specific knowledge is gained.
3. The *brainstorming* and concept phase, in which new ideas for the design problem are to be conceived or already existing ones improved. Countless sketches and concepts are often created and discarded iteratively.
4. The *design* phase in which a concept is worked out in more detail, taking into account the technical requirements.
5. The *production* in which the concept is elaborated in accordance with the production and a prototype based on it is created.

The research and brainstorming phases are very time-consuming for the designer. Since the majority of sketches are often discarded in the conception phase, only a few of them find their way directly into the end product. This is inefficient from an economic point of view because the designer invests most of his/her working time into the basic concept. He/she then has problems perfecting it due to a lack of time in the design and production phase. This is particularly relevant in product design, where fine-tuned appearance can determine sales success. Especially products that justify their selling price by their appearance are affected. The water bottle is an example of this. The content of different bottles is almost the same, the function is the same, but the design justifies the price difference between a cheap and an expensive product.

Fig. 1. The three layers of product design, from left to right: silhouette, surface, and graphics. Own representation in accordance with [21].

Another problem that becomes visible in this example is the pattern that people memorize throughout their lives. In the brainstorming phase designing water bottles that do not correspond to the prototypical or expected image requires a special degree of creativity and inspiration. There two problems exist:

- The designer puts many resources into the rough design and thus has fewer resources for its perfection.
- Designing new patterns that break with the old ones requires a lot of creativity and inspiration.

The product design process can be divided into three layers [21]:

1. *silhouette*, which reflects the proportions of the product regardless of color, logo or surface finish.
2. *surface*, which includes, for example, curves, bulges or corners of the product.
3. *graphics*, showing logos and color.

An example of the three layers for a bottle is given in Fig. 1. The focus in this work has been on the silhouette, as the first and most important level of product design. To demonstrate the ability of the algorithms presented here, attempts were made to produce bottles (semi-)automatically. The simple rotationally symmetric shape is intended to simplify the learning process as well as the later implementation of 3D models.

Fig. 2. Using a random generation of images and an objective function to measure its similarity to a bottle one image is assigned a confidence of 96.7% while the other has a confidence of 0.0%.

4   Semi-automatic Development of Shape Representation

The first approach we investigated was to automatically generate bottles using a GA. Therefore, we simulate an evolutionary process with a population of objects. Each object has a genome that encodes e.g. polygons or polylines. Through targeted selection, mating, recombination and mutation, a population is created that has adapted optimally to an *objective function*[3]. This function is in this case

---

[3] An objective function is an equation to be optimized given certain constraints and with variables that need to be minimized or maximized.

an ANN called MobileNet that has been pre-trained on the ImageNet dataset [4] and can already classify objects well, including different types of bottles [16].

While the GA works and even manages to create populations that are classified by the net as bottles, the results, as shown in Fig. 2, are largely not in line with the generally accepted definition of a bottle. Although MobileNet has high accuracy in real images, it appears that the GA has found a vulnerability in the ANN in solving this optimization problem. This is a known problem in ANNs, known as *adversarial examples* [6]. This refers to examples that can be clearly classified by humans, but specifically deceive ANNs [28]. This approach using a simple objective function to decide if the shape is similar to a bottle led to unsatisfactory results. Figure 2 demonstrates the evaluation of the classifier for two randomly generated images. Even though both represent patterns without any obvious similarity to a bottle one image is assigned a confidence of 96.7% while the other has a confidence of 0.0%. Therefore, we had to use a different approach which better separates implausible from plausible shapes.

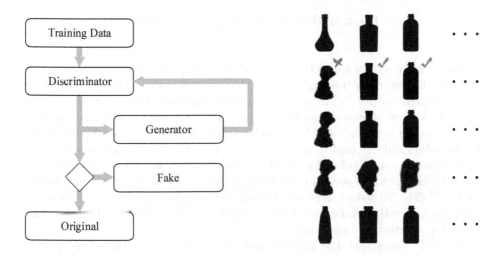

Fig. 3. Flow chart of generative adversarial network and different instances according to the different steps.

4.1 Plausible Shape Representation

As can be seen from our first experiments a "naive" approach is not leading to satisfying results. Therefore, an approach is required which guarantees that the produced shapes are similar to the shape of bottles. In 2014 Goodfellow et al. proposed the special ANN architecture GAN which we have already mentioned before [5]. The main idea of their proposal is to use two ANNs that compete with each other. Figure 3 demonstrates the basic principle and components: The *generator* tries to generate data from latent variables that are as similar as possible to the training data. The *discriminator* tries to classify the generated data according to the original training data. Both networks play a zero-sum game: As the system progresses, the generator as well as the discriminator are improving. This process continues until the discriminator can no longer distinguish between forgery and original. This is achieved when the discriminator is only correct in 50% of the cases.

Fig. 4. Black and white silhouettes of bottles.

Since the generator learns to generate data as similar as possible to the training data, it requires a training data set that corresponds as closely as possible to the desired output [5]. In our case we were interested in generating different variations of shapes resembling bottles. To train our system we converted 200 images of bottles into black and white silhouettes (see Fig. 4). As automatic segmentation did not lead to satisfactory results the conversation was done by hand. Since the data volume is small and GANs normally use data volumes in orders of magnitude of several 1,000 images, there is a risk of over-adaptation by the GAN [24]. To reduce over-adaptation, *data augmentation* is used by automatically generating variations of the available training data including shearing, enlarging, rotating and cropping.

Figure 5 shows that the training loss in the first few generations quickly approaches zero. This is due to the fact that the network initially roughly maps the basic form of the input data. In higher epochs many bottles of an epoch have similar characteristics. This is a well-known problem in GAN architectures and is called *mode collapse*. The generator limits itself to generating only a few examples that the discriminator classifies as original. In the worst case, all images generated by the generator are almost identical [19]. Although in our example we see variations the problem is still visible. Different epochs can be considered to create more diverse bottles because the point of mode collapse shifts with each epoch. Although the training data set only consists of symmetrical bottles, the architecture is capable of generating asymmetric bottles. This is interesting because the net is able to generate something it did not know could be e.g. asymmetric. It is up to the designer to incorporate these unusual features such as asymmetrical elements into the product design or to rate them as a mistake and to correct them manually based on his/her taste.

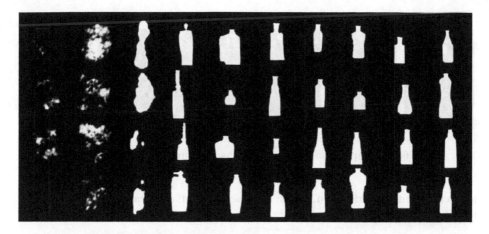

Fig. 5. Different iterations of the learning process. From left to right, iteration 50, 100, steps of 100 until 1000. Four different examples are shown for each iteration.

Due to the required minimum complexity of the GAN architectures and the need for sharp high-resolution images in combination with the low amount of training data, overfitting inevitably occurs. However, subjective comparisons with the training data set did not rate the over-adaption as critical as the majority of the bottles are unique. Instead of treating the shape as one union it might be advantageous to separate the shape into different parts.

4.2 Semantic Shape Representation

The shape of an object can be decomposed into different features that can be assigned with particular "meanings" and semantically annotated[4]. In our particular application of a bottle the semantic shape representation can be separated and annotated into: lid, neck, wall, wall-to-neck transition and bottom[5]; see Fig. 6. The classification was done manually by cutting the existing 200 images into individual parts.

One conceivable option for creating new shapes of bottles is the random permutation of the semantic parts and thus to overcome the limiting characteristics of the former approach where many generated bottles had similar characteristics. For this purpose, an ANN is to be conceptualized, which receives random features and assembles them to form a new object. The network learned, in the training phase, the relationship between the semantic features and the actual bottle. After this phase, the network is able to merge features seamlessly and to produce the shape of a consistent bottle. New permutations of features using the trained ANN are shown below in Fig. 7. The features were determined based on

---

[4] Semantic annotation is the process of attaching additional information to various concepts to be used by machines.

[5] In preliminary tests, this division turned out to be the most effective variant.

lid	neck	wall	transition	bottom	original

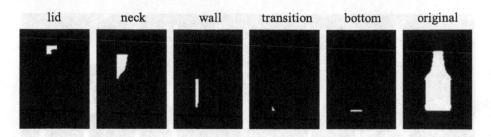

Fig. 6. Decomposition of a semantic shape representation of a bottle.

a discrete equal distribution. It can be observed that the features are transferred and combined successfully.

4.3   Introducing Personal Taste in Shape Representation

So far we have described the process of how to fully automatically generate plausible shapes by varying different features of the bottle. Now it's time to bring back the designer by having him/her intervene in the design process: The shape should advance iteratively towards the taste of the designer. For optimization problems in which a solution approaches an optimum step by step, GA has already proven to be an appropriate tool [9], which is also why a GA was used in this procedure. The basic idea is that you have a population of objects where each object is defined by its genes. Each gene represents a semantic feature, in this case, e.g., the bottleneck. To transform the genes into visible features, the ANN of the semantic shape representation is used.

Similar to the biological model, the population gradually adapts to the environment through selection, mating, gene recombination and mutation [7]. To introduce the designer into the automatic algorithm the random permutations of features have to be evaluated by the designer instead of a genetic objective function. Therefore, the designer takes up the position of the fitness/objective function, similar to the ANN MobileNet, by sitting in front of the computer and by evaluating each instance individually; Fig. 8. The basic idea here is that the population gradually approaches the taste of the user until his/her ideal bottle is created. Therefore, each of the 20 individuals in the population is assigned a fitness value between zero and one by the user. The higher the fitness value the higher the probability of survival by an individual. Combined with the previously mentioned methods such as mutation, this results in a population which is more precisely adapted to the taste of the designer. To cover a large search space, the population is initialized using a discrete equal distribution. Over a couple of iterations the final optimal shape is found.

4.4   Democratizing Shape Representation

To be able to democratize the design process we have to vary the proposed approaches so far to be able to do some arithmetic's; e.g. to calculate the

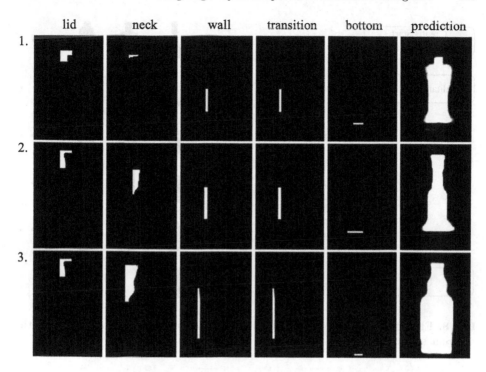

Fig. 7. Three variations of bottle shapes as generated by merging the decomposed parts as given by the semantic shape representation approach.

arithmetic mean of a set of bottles designed by different persons. To do so we use a *variational autoencoder* (VAE) [13]. It is an ANN that learns to produce the same output as input. A special feature here is that the network topology has a bottleneck between the input and the output layers. This bottleneck stores the compressed information as a vector of real numbers called *latent variables* (LV). As a result, the autoencoder must compress information of the input into the LV and then decompress it after the bottleneck. The VAE learns to extract the most relevant information from an input image as LV so that it can be used to regenerate the output image as correctly as possible [13].

The basic idea is this: After training, the LV can be accessed directly through sliders. The trained decoder would then convert the LV into a corresponding bottle. This would allow the non-designer with limited design skills to design an object in a playful way (Fig. 9). A number of eight LV have delivered satisfactory results in trials. A smaller number of LV leads to less detailed and more similar images. More LV, on the other hand, have not achieved any significant improvement in quality, but have worsened the user experience due to more necessary sliders.

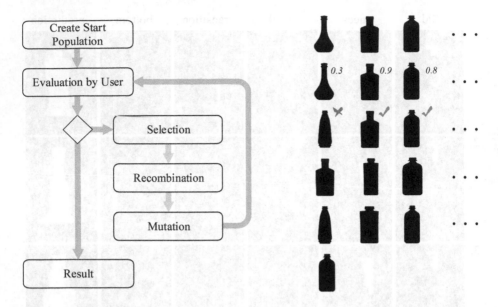

Fig. 8. Flow chart of the genetic algorithm and different instances according to the different steps.

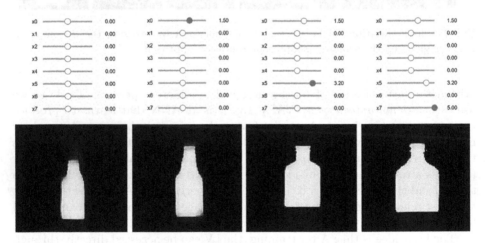

Fig. 9. Transforming the bottles using eight parameters. Each slider corresponds to one LV.

It can be seen that by moving individual sliders, the bottle can be transferred into other forms. The transformation is done simultaneously with the slider movement, giving the user direct and intuitive feedback. A complete disentanglement of the LV could not be achieved. Consequently, a LV and thus the corresponding slider can be responsible for several semantic features of the object.

Because there are vectors behind the bottles, we can do bottle arithmetic with them [22]. This makes it possible to calculate the arithmetic mean of a set of bottles. This allows several individuals to democratically design a bottle by first creating a bottle for each individual using the sliders and then averaging all created bottles. There are two main pillars of democratic design. First, anyone can design objects now even without design skills and secondly, the taste of each individual can equally influence the final product.

5   Results, Evaluation and Limitations

Using the plausible shape representation method, it was shown that parts of the design process can be partially automated and thus speed up using ANNs. This architecture typically provides a good image quality. However, the algorithm does not allow direct access by the designer, so the output is heavily dependent on the training data. For instance, to specifically design a classic beer bottle, the designer would have to explicitly look for the shape in the output or just specify beer bottles as training data. Although novel bottle shapes are created, these usually do not deviate much from the training data set. For the design process, the user has received some suggestions from the algorithms and has decided on one of these in several iterations. For our experiments the final selection was then loaded into a CAD program, the shape manually traced, refined, rotated (the latter three processes can be done fully automated) and then 3D printed; see Fig. 10a and 11a. This allows parts of the brainstorming and concept phase to be automated.

Using the semantic shape representation, new bottles could also be created automatically. In comparison to the previous method, these objects are more diverse and creative looking; see Fig. 10b and 11b. At present, there must be a database of the specific objects and their associated features available, which is not ideal. The image quality is slightly worse than in the plausible shape representation, but still at a very high level. In addition, as with the plausible shape representation, the problem is that the suggestions are not adapted to the user.

To tackle the latter problem, personal taste was introduced into the semantic shape representation. The bottles successfully adapted to the taste of the user through evolution; see Fig. 10c and 11c. A selection from a large amount of output data as in the last two algorithms is thereby eliminated (apart from the fitness score evaluation). In our opinion this is one of the most promising ways to liberate design processes in the future because designing personalized objects according to his/her taste becomes possible for everybody. The algorithm also adapts through the direct feedback dynamically to changes in the user's taste, for instance, during a lifetime. Since the architecture is based on the semantic shape representation, the image quality is at the same level and a database of associated features is also needed.

Through the democratic approach, see Fig. 10d and 11d, collectives can design objects together. With the introduction of variable parameters (sliders), every human being is able to design things, whether talented or not. This

Fig. 10. 3D print of generated bottles using a. plausible shape representation, b. semantic shape representation, c. personal taste in shape representation, and d. democratized shape representation

bypasses the designer and allows the end-user to take on the role of a designer directly. Secondly, the opinion of each individual can be incorporated into a final product. There's no need for a central design instance anymore. The zeitgeist of the collective can (anonymously) create something together, on which the majority can agree on. Also, the manual sketches of the concept phase were eliminated. Within a few seconds, countless new variants could be created, for which otherwise individual manual sketches would be needed. However, the image quality and diversity are worse compared to the previous algorithms.

In Table 1 we compare the different approaches according to the parameters described next:

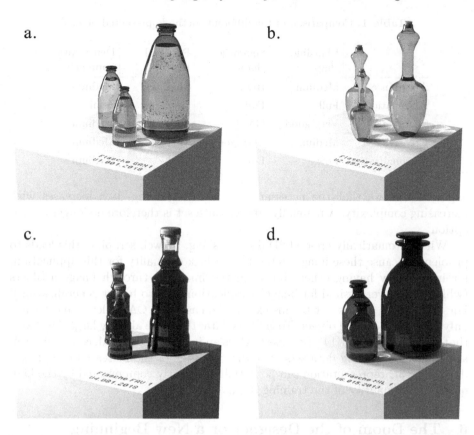

Fig. 11. Rendering of generated bottles using a. plausible shape representation, b. semantic shape representation, c. personal taste in shape representation, and d. democratized shape representation

- *Affordance* (in data preparation) describes how much time has to be spent to prepare the data to train the ANN.
- *Automation* describes how much the process is automated and how much amount has to be done by the designer.
- *Shape quality* describes the subjective quality of the shape including detail density, image sharpness, resolution and number of image artifacts.
- *Creativity* describes to what extent the automatically generated results have a creative or inspiring effect on the designer.
- *Personalization* describes how much individuality is kept in the design process and how much of the personal taste is represented in the outcome.

As previously mentioned all variants shown here were trained with a well-defined data set consisting of 200 relatively simple 2D images. This procedure was sufficient to analyze the process. If the same procedures can be applied to more complex shapes and higher dimensionality is unclear because these variants might encounter additional problems. A possible solution in the future would be the use of voxels or a polygon mesh, which allows a 3D representation. However,

Table 1. Comparison of the different methods presented here.

	Plausible shape	Semantic shape	Personal taste	Democratic approach
Affordance	Medium	High	Medium	Medium
Automation	Full	Full	Semi	Semi
Shape quality	Very good	Good	Good	Medium
Creativity	Medium	Very good	Very good	Medium
Personalization	Low	Low	High	Medium

experience shows that the necessary amount of training data increases with increasing complexity. A manually created data set is therefore no longer a valid option.

With automatically created 2D data sets, e.g. by web scraping, this leads to problems because these images often have a lack of quality for this application, for instance by having other objects in the image or through image artifacts (which is however desired for image classifications due to better generalization). For 3D objects, this is not to this extent the case, e.g. CAD files in most cases only depict the desired object. To get this data, there are already large databases that have high quality [14]. Because CAD is an industry-standard, companies can also use their existing data-sets. The disadvantage of the increased complexity due to the 3D representation can potentially be partly compensated by the high quality and quantity of the training data.

6   The Doom of the Designer or a New Beginning

Today, designers explore solutions concerning the semiotic, the aesthetic and the dynamic realm, as well as confronting corporate, industrial, cultural and political aspects. The relationship between the designer and the designed is directly connected through their intentions, although currently mediated by third-parties and media tools. In addition to the design process today generative methods appear, which utilize the concept of creating and modifying interacting rules and systems to autonomously generate a finished design, rather than the designer manipulating/altering the artifact itself. Therefore, the designer orchestrates the rules and systems involved in the process of creating designs (through AI), resulting in the emergent properties of the newly interconnected and constantly self-enhancing scheme. The skill here is to master the neither formalized nor instruction-based methodology as well as to control the relationship between process specifiers, the environment and the generated artificial. As in conventional design, the human designer remains at the center of the design process.

Do we still need a designer in times of AI and automation? Not only is this the first question that crosses the minds of non-designers, but it is an even more important question for the design world. Designers are not the only ones to feel the thread of AI. For instance, translators are concerned that they could be replaced through machine translation and truck drivers fear to lose their jobs because of autonomous driving.

Many people associate AI with machines taking over and completely replacing everything, in our case especially the design process. Instead of encouraging the thought of AI as a thread, one should consider the opportunity to explore and question the core and root of design. So instead of getting rid of it we fully embrace it and find new ways of creating it. Just like a potter's wheel is helping the potter to create more symmetric shapes.

One of the leading questions was how the time of the designer can be utilized more efficiently. What if AI, within the creative process, can support the work of the designer? Is it possible to implement the 80/20 principle within the creative process, where the computer takes over 80% of the necessary work? What else can the designer do with his/her time, when suddenly 80% of the work is done by a computer, generating a result as good as the one before.

After testing the algorithms extensively, the results confirmed the previously proposed idea. Paired with AI, the computer can fulfill the majority of time-consuming work, while the designer's sole responsibility lies in determining specifications and adjusting the system's final result one last time. It is the designer, who teaches the computer about good and bad designs, by feeding the system with information about personal needs and a more or less subjective aesthetic point of view. The computer learns about a specific taste and proposes individual solutions.

Now that there is a proof of concept that it is possible to teach AI form and shape of a product and it is able to reproduce it even more efficiently than humans, the question is: What do we need human designers for anymore? One reason why people might keep asking this question is that the recognition factor of a designer comes from the "creative" gen. And thus, people are most surprised about the creation of something so intangible solely by logic and numbers. Is there an equation for design and creativity? Or is there an option where both can exist together in coexistence.

What will the job of a designer look like in the future? One thing you can count on in our human evolution is that as soon as someone creates what makes a task at hand more efficient that approach will push through. You can look back at all the industrial improvements that were created and, in the end, they all have improved our living standards. The next thing is that the job of a designer will change and become more diverse. The need for creative and new approaches for problems we face now and in the future was never greater.

7   Conclusion and Outlook

In this work, we set out to prove that most of the design processes could be automated or at least semi-automaed and that a workflow from the first sketches to the final product could be significantly streamlined. In particular, the brainstorming phase of the design process could be automated and it was possible to go directly from the technical drawing into the 3D model of a bottle. This became possible by generating design proposals from different algorithms including ANN and

GA. This drastically accelerated the design process and saved the designer tedious labor time. The algorithms have also provided inspiration for the designer. Also, the end-user and collectives can now act as designers without having the appropriate abilities, which means individualized as well as collaborative design is now easier than ever. We chose a simple object—a bottle—to prove our concept. Any other object could, in principle, be designed the same way. It should be also possible to extend our proposed approach to include a third dimension. More complex shapes and higher dimensionality, however, raises complexity and therefore more data and other solutions might need to be introduced.

We live in an era of accelerating technological progress which is already influencing our daily lives. We cannot ignore technological developments and pretend these changes are not happening. Instead, we should embrace the development—but also reflect its impact—and see it as a new set of opportunities for us to explore and prosper. We have to reflect on what makes us human and remember that we are still the ones who are conceiving something that we think of as beautiful and therefore value it. "Successful designs are not necessarily 'made': new functionality may 'evolve' through the use and interpretation of artifacts by an audience" [18]. There are many examples today where AI has influenced the creative process letting the designer cherry-pick and approve adjustments based on the proposed variations. Let us start exploring these possibilities today and see where they can take us.

References

1. Autodesk Research: Generative design (2019). https://www.autodesk.com/solutions/generative-design. Accessed 21 May 2019
2. Autodesk Research: Project dreamcatcher (2019). https://autodeskresearch.com/projects/dreamcatcher. Accessed 17 May 2019
3. Cluzel, F., Yannou, B., Dihlmann, M.: Using evolutionary design to interactively sketch car silhouettes and stimulate designer's creativity. Eng. Appl. Artif. Intell. **25**(7), 1413–1424 (2012)
4. Deng, J., Dong, W., Socher, R., Li, L.J., Li, K., Fei-Fei, L.: Imagenet: a large-scale hierarchical image database. In: Conference on Computer Vision and Pattern Recognition, pp. 248–255. IEEE (2009)
5. Goodfellow, I., et al.: Generative adversarial nets. In: Advances in Neural Information Processing Systems, pp. 2672–2680 (2014)
6. Goodfellow, I.J., Shlens, J., Szegedy, C.: Explaining and harnessing adversarial examples (2015)
7. Gupta, D., Ghafir, S.: An overview of methods maintaining diversity in genetic algorithms. Int. J. Emerg. Technol. Adv. Eng. **2**(5), 56–60 (2012)
8. Haik, Y., Sivaloganathan, S., Shahin, T.M.: Engineering Design Process. Nelson Education (2018)
9. Hornby, G., Globus, A., Linden, D., Lohn, J.: Automated antenna design with evolutionary algorithms. In: American Institute of Aeronautics and Astronautics Conference on Space, San Jose, CA, pp. 19–21 (2006)
10. Howard, T., Culley, S., Dekoninck, E.: Creativity in the engineering design process. In: 16th International Conference on Engineering Design ICED (2007)
11. Howard, T.J., Culley, S.J., Dekoninck, E.: Describing the creative design process by the integration of engineering design and cognitive psychology literature. Des. Stud. **29**(2), 160–180 (2008)

12. Kato, N., Osone, H., Sato, D., Muramatsu, N., Ochiai, Y.: Deepwear: a case study of collaborative design between human and artificial intelligence. In: Twelfth International Conference on Tangible, Embedded, and Embodied Interaction, pp. 529–536. ACM (2018)
13. Kingma, D.P., Welling, M.: Auto-encoding variational bayes (2013). arXiv preprint arXiv:1312.6114
14. Koch, S., et al.: ABC: a big CAD model dataset for geometric deep learning. In: Proceedings of the IEEE Conference on Computer Vision and Pattern Recognition, pp. 9601–9611 (2019)
15. Kolss, M., Wölfel, M., Kraft, F., Niehues, J., Paulik, M., Waibel, A.: Simultaneous german-english lecture translation. In: International Workshop on Spoken Language Translation (2008)
16. Krizhevsky, A., Sutskever, I., Hinton, G.E.: Imagenet classification with deep convolutional neural networks. In: Advances in Neural Information Processing Systems, pp. 1097–1105 (2012)
17. Li, J., Xu, K., Chaudhuri, S., Yumer, E., Zhang, H., Guibas, L.: Grass: generative recursive autoencoders for shape structures. Trans. Graph. (TOG) **36**(4), 52 (2017)
18. McCormack, J., Dorin, A., Innocent, T., et al.: Generative design: a paradigm for design research. In: Proceedings of Futureground, Design Research Society, Melbourne (2004)
19. Metz, L., Poole, B., Pfau, D., Sohl-Dickstein, J.: Unrolled generative adversarial networks. In: Proceedings of 5th International Conference on Learning Representations (2017)
20. Nyholm, S., Smids, J.: The ethics of accident-algorithms for self-driving cars: an applied trolley problem? Ethical Theory Moral Pract. **19**(5), 1275–1289 (2016)
21. Of, J.: Brand formative design-development and assessment of product design from a future, brand and consumer perspective. Ph.D. thesis, Universitätsbibliothek Mainz (2014)
22. Radford, A., Metz, L., Chintala, S.: Unsupervised representation learning with deep convolutional generative adversarial networks (2015). arXiv preprint arXiv:1511.06434
23. Schmitt, P., Weiss, S.: The chair project–four classics (2018). https://philippschmitt.com/work/chair. Accessed 17 May 2019
24. Wang, J., Perez, L.: The effectiveness of data augmentation in image classification using deep learning. Convolutional Neural Networks Vis. Recognit (2017)
25. Wikström, D.: Me, myself, and AI: case study: human-machine co-creation explored in design (2018)
26. Wilson, N., Thomson, A., Riches, P.: Development and presentation of the first design process model for sports equipment design. Res. Eng. Des. **28**(4), 495–509 (2017). https://doi.org/10.1007/s00163-017-0257-4
27. Wölfel, M.: Der smarte Assistent. In: Ruf, O. (ed.) Smartphone-Ästhetik: zur Philosophie und Gestaltung mobiler Medien. Transcript, pp. 269–288 (2018)
28. Yuan, X., He, P., Zhu, Q., Li, X.: Adversarial examples: attacks and defenses for deep learning. Trans. Neural Netw. Learn. Syst. **30**, 2805–2824 (2019)
29. Zhang, G., Qu, M., Jin, Y., Song, Q.: Colorization for anime sketches with cycle-consistent adversarial network. Int. J. Performability Eng. **15**(3), 910–918 (2019)
30. Zhu, J.Y., Park, T., Isola, P., Efros, A.A.: Unpaired image-to-image translation using cycle-consistent adversarial networks. In: 2017 IEEE International Conference on Computer Vision (ICCV) (2017)

Authentication of Art: Assessing the Performance of a Machine Learning Based Authentication Method

Ailin Chen[1,2]([✉]), Rui Jesus[2,3], and Márcia Vilarigues[1]

[1] Departamento de Conservação e Restauro, Faculdade de Ciências e Tecnologia, Universidade NOVA de Lisboa, 2825-149 Caparica, Lisboa, Portugal
ailin.chen@campus.fct.unl.pt, mgv@fct.unl.pt
[2] NOVA LINCS, Faculdade de Ciências e Tecnologia, Universidade NOVA de Lisboa, 2825-149 Caparica, Lisboa, Portugal
rjesus@deetc.isel.ipl.pt
[3] M2A/ADEETC, Instituto Superior de Engenharia de Lisboa (ISEL), IPL, Rua Conselheiro Emídio Navarro, No. 1, 1959-007 Lisbon, Portugal

Abstract. This paper compares the test results generated by applying the method for the authentication of paintings by Portuguese artist Amadeo de Souza Cardoso in the interest of exploring the generalisation properties of the algorithm on other artists or genres. This sets the base for the method to be improved and developed accordingly in future applications for a broader audience in a wider setting. The obtained results show that the classifier obtained from the algorithm using paintings appears not to be directly applicable to drawings of the same artist. When the classifier is retrained for a different genre like Chinese paintings or artists like van Gogh, the algorithm appears to perform as well as the classifier on Amadeo paintings, i.e. the algorithm is sufficient for the classification of a specific type of artist or genre.

Keywords: Authentication · Paintings · Drawings · Machine learning · Art

1 Introduction

The studies of computer science within the framework of authentication and degradation of paintings have been researched for at least a decade with significant progress made in different institutions. The applications of machine learning algorithms have been implemented at the Conservation and Restauration Department (DCR) of Universidade NOVA de Lisboa (NOVA), where the paintings by the late Portuguese artist Amadeo de Souza Cardoso were analysed [1, 2]. The investigation encompassed both brushstroke and material analysis where both aspects were considered equally important in terms of the determination on the authenticity, conservation and restoration of Amadeo's paintings. Our research follows the previous work on this subject and intends to improve the original method in order to best serve the purpose of authentication and degradation of Amadeo's paintings and drawings. Furthermore, the work presented evaluates

A. Brooks and E. I. Brooks (Eds.): ArtsIT 2019/DLI 2019, LNICST 328, pp. 328–342, 2020.
https://doi.org/10.1007/978-3-030-53294-9_22

its generalisation on paintings and drawings by other artists and other genres. This will contribute to the development of a more generic method for the non-destructive evaluation and identification of artwork. The current study focuses on the examination of the brushstroke where image processing techniques and machine learning methods are used as the major tools for the analysis. The paper presents one of the first stages on the testing of the method applying machine learning theory in order to determine the ability of generalisation of the algorithm for other art pieces, genres or artists.

2 Related Work

Work has been done previously in pertinent subjects. Keren [3] applied local features and naïve Bayes classifier to identify paintings by type as to man-made vs scene as well as the identification of painters. Their obtained results are localised and generally consistent with the styles perceived by human observers. Li and Wang [4] applied a mixture of stochastic models on the analysis of brushstrokes of Chinese paintings so that painting styles of artists could be compared and connections among artists or periods could be made. Their method showed potential in automatic analysis of paintings. Li and Wang's research are one of the few works that take on the complexity of Chinese paintings applying computer science. The same set of Chinese paintings is also used in our research. Lombardi [5] studied the colour features like colour auto-correlograms and dynamic spatial chromatic histograms for the classification of styles by implementing both supervised and unsupervised techniques like k-Nearest neighbour, hierarchical clustering, self-organising maps and multidimensional scaling. Their method is able to identify painting styles as well as the principal relations among styles. Hidden-Markov-Tree-modelling on paintings' wavelet coefficients were deemed to be able to detect forgeries from originals [6]. One of the most cited and renowned work on this subject is the extensive analysis on the brushstrokes of van Gogh's paintings, researched and collaborated by Stanford University, Princeton University, The Pennsylvania State University, The University of Amsterdam and the Van Gogh and Kröller-Müller Museum [7–9]. Recent works include the state-of-art application of deep learning and Convolutional Neural Network in order to classify art styles and artists [10, 11], which could be potentially useful for the authentication of paintings when different genres of paintings are presented. The lack of data however is often the major problem of these methods. Artificial Neural Network and wavelet analysis were also applied back in 2009 for the separation of Henry Matisse's work from his fakes [12]. Montagner [1, 2] from NOVA combined both brushstroke and material analysis in order to authenticate Amadeo's paintings. Montagner's work might be the only work so far that has incorporated both computer vision techniques and chemical analysis in an equation for the identification of paintings. This paper is the follow-up of Montagner's work.

3 Algorithm

At present stage, the research mainly focuses on the analysis and classification of images based on brushstroke. A combination of image processing techniques, statistics and machine learning theory is used to produce the algorithm presented in this paper. The brushstroke analysis and classification algorithm is explained next with Fig. 1 summarising the main stages of the process:

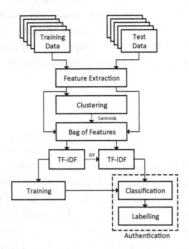

Fig. 1. Block diagram of the method evaluated.

- The feature extraction process focuses on building a matrix of features resulting from analysing each image from the training set. The training set is composed by images of artworks of the artist which the systems is able to authenticate (these images are designate by Positive). The training set also include images of paintings of other artists (Negative images). Each image is analysed using the Scale Invariant Feature Transform method (SIFT) to highlight local features represented by key points and descriptors.
- All SIFT key points near the border of the image are discarded. Next, a sub-section of the original image centred on the key point is extracted and rotated according to the angle of the key point vector.
- Each cropped and rotated sub-image is then analysed using a Gabor filter bank with 4 scales and 6 orientations. The resulting Gabor features are appended to either a positive or negative feature matrix which contains the features of all the positive and negative training images respectively.
- The K-Means ++ clustering method is then used on the features matrices to identify centroids. These centroids, also referred to as visual words or visual terms, represent similar sets of features which, in the positive set, could potentially correspond to a particular technique or style of the artist during a given stage of his career. The centroids are saved for later evaluation of test data or new unseen images.
- The centroids identified are used to discretise the features matrices and build a positive and negative set of visual dictionaries also known as bag of features (i.e. bag of words). Tests are made on different number of visual words (100, 200, 400, 1000, 1200, 1400, 1600, 2000) in order to evaluate the performance on the base of various number of features.

- Term Frequency-Inverse Document Frequency (TF-IDF) is then applied to the bag of features to evaluate the occurrence of visual terms and balance the difference of positive to negative number of terms by means of weight factors. The IDF values are saved for later evaluation of test data or new unseen images.
- The resulting bag of features is then used in the classifier. In this work, a Regularised Least Squares Classifier (RLSC) is used for binary classification. One class represents the artist the system is able to authenticate (positive class). The other class represents everything else. The classifier is trained with the positive and negative bags of features. The resulting coefficients of the classifier are then saved for evaluation of test data or new unseen images.
- Artwork authentication is provided by extracting the bag of features (with the relevant visual elements) of the image of the artwork and use it in the classifier. Authentication is verified based on the class given by the classifier.

One of the improvements on the work of Montagner [1, 2] is the application of the modified k-means algorithm k-means ++ instead of k-means. K-means ++ initialises k centres uniformly then reassigns points selected proportionally with probability, followed by updating centre matrices until stable with clustering at the end. This improvement reduced the computation load while generating better optimised centroids. The testing of k-means ++ on the counterpart appeared to be twice as fast as the original k-means method for the number of data points and centroids analysed.

Furthermore, in the work of Montagner, test data were partially used in the training process which rendered increased accuracies of over 90%. In our research, test data is excluded from the training process entirely in the interest of avoiding biased results.

Four methods were reported in Montagner's research, simple Gabor, simple SIFT, Gabor in regular points and Gabor in the localisation of the SIFT key points (SIFT + Gabor). In our research, tests were made using all the four methods mentioned which produced similar trends in the results. Therefore, this paper only incorporates the results produced by SIFT + Gabor method because they are the most representative results of all the experiments carried out.

The afore-mentioned method is used to generate classifiers based on different training sets. The testing data is also varied in order to evaluate if the method is universally applicable in terms of identification of artists' works.

4 Data

The data analysed in our research include three major parts. The first part is the data used to produce the base classifier cited in this paper, i.e. the data applied in Montagner's work. The database includes two classes of datasets noted as positive and negative. The positive class consists of 200 images of Amadeo paintings published in Catalogue Raisonné Amadeo de Souza Cardoso pintura; whilst the negative class comprises 109 images of paintings by Amadeo's contemporaries like Gino Severini, Sonia and Robert Delaunay, Jose Almada Negreiros, most of them displayed in the exhibition Amadeo de Souza-Cardoso - Diálogo de Vanguardas. A collection of Amadeo drawings are also used in our study including 39 drawings acquired from Calouste Gulbenkian Museum. Out of these, 29 are loose drawings, mostly are watercolours; 10 are chosen from the manuscript La Légende de Saint-Julien L'hospitalier out of 83 pages with content because of their paucity of text in the favour of image processing. Samples of Amadeo paintings (see Fig. 2) and drawings (see Fig. 3 and Fig. 4) are displayed below.

Fig. 2. Sample Amadeo paintings.

The second part of the data was obtained from The Pennsylvania State University. This data set comprises 1177 images of 23 renowned Chinese artists such as Baishi Qi, Daqian Zhang, Banqiao Zheng. Chinese paintings have the characteristics of not only the distinctive brushstroke throughout the paintings, but also the extensive use of calligraphy or stamps in paintings. Therefore, careful selection is made manually resulting in a positive class of 91 Chinese paintings by the same Chinese artist Daqian Zhang (see Fig. 5) and a negative class of 98 Chinese paintings from all other Chinese artists, where mainly paintings with minimum text are made available. They are used to obtain the retrained Chinese classifier applying the same algorithm that was used to

Fig. 3. Sample Amadeo drawings (loose).

obtain the Amadeo classifier. In the interest of evaluating the classifiers, the 91 Chinese paintings are also used as negative dataset for the Amadeo classifier.

The third part of the data is the set of van Gogh paintings (see Fig. 6) and his contemporaries acquired directly from van Gogh museum. It contains a positive class of 210 van Gogh paintings and a negative class of 63 paintings of van Gogh contemporaries. Similarly, these paintings are used to obtain the retrained van Gogh classifier with the 210 van Gogh paintings used as negative dataset for the Amadeo classifier.

To facilitate the illustration, notation is considered as follows: Amadeo paintings – AP; Amadeo contemporary paintings – ACP; Amadeo drawings – AD; Chinese paintings – CP; van Gogh paintings – VGP; van Gogh contemporary paintings – VGCP.

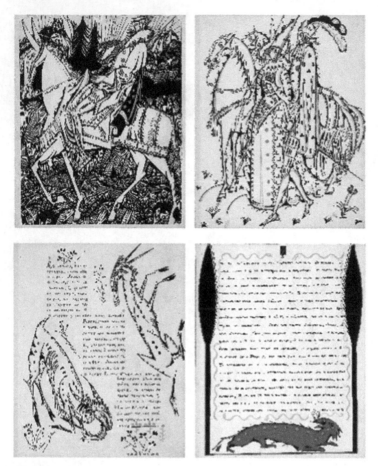

Fig. 4. Sample Amadeo drawings from *La Légende de Saint-Julien L'hospitalier*.

5   Results and Discussion

The reference classifier noted as the Amadeo classifier and reference test obtained from the work of Montagner is based on paintings of Amadeo de Souza Cardoso and his contemporaries. The number of relevant positive and negative training sets as well as the obtained accuracies applying the Amadeo classifier are showed in Table 1 and Table 2.

The results show that when the paintings of both Amadeo and his contemporaries are used (Ref Test), the accuracies of the Amadeo classifier are all around an adequate 70% (Ref Accuracy). A correlation between the number of visual words and accuracy is not evident. This is, increasing the number of words does not seem to have a significant positive effect on the accuracy.

When the 29 Amadeo drawings are included in the positive testing set along with the paintings (Test 1.1 in Table 3), the accuracies drop slightly to around 66% (Accuracy 1.1 in Table 4). When only Amadeo drawings are included in the positive testing set (Test 1.2 in Table 3), the accuracies drop significantly to about 40% (Accuracy 1.2 in Table 4). It

Fig. 5. Sample Chinese paintings.

could be concluded that in order to better classify and identify drawings, it is optimal that the classifier be retrained with only drawings or paintings and drawings. It is presumed that classifier retrained with only drawings might perform better in comparison with the one retrained with both paintings and drawings.

In a further test, the 10 drawings from *La Légende de Saint-Julien L'hospitalier* are included in the testing along with the 29 loose drawings and 95 Amadeo paintings (Test 2.1 in Table 5). The obtained results showed a similar trend, where the accuracy is around 66% (Accuracy 2.1 in Table 6). Whilst when Amadeo paintings are excluded from the testing (Test 2.2 in Table 5), the accuracy dropped to as low as 40% (Accuracy 2.2). Although the 29 loose drawings and 10 drawings were executed via different media, the results again indicate that the classifier is inadequate and requires to be retrained with drawings only or with drawings and paintings. On one hand, it could imply that the property of the media does not affect the authentication of an artist's drawings; on the other, it could also result from the limited number of drawings being presented in the testing.

Fig. 6. Sample van Gogh paintings.

Table 1. Reference training and testing sets for Amadeo classifier.

Ref Test	Positive	Negative
Ref training set	105 AP	60 ACP
Ref testing set	95 AP	49 ACP

Table 2. Reference accuracy for Amadeo classifier.

Number of visual words	100	200	400	1000	1200	1400	1600	2000
Ref accuracy	70.83	66.67	65.97	70.14	70.83	70.83	73.61	71.53

Table 3. Tests with 29 Amadeo loose drawings included in the testing set for Amadeo classifier

Test 1.1	Positive	Negative
Training set 1.1	105 AP	60 ACP
Testing set 1.1	95 AP + 29 AD = 124	49 ACP
Test 1.2	Positive	Negative
Training set 1.2	105 AP	60 ACP
Testing set 1.2	29 AD	49 ACP

Table 4. Accuracies with 29 Amadeo loose drawings included in the testing set for Amadeo classifier.

Number of visual words	100	200	400	1000	1200	1400	1600	2000
Accuracy 1.1	65.9	63.01	62.43	65.32	66.47	66.47	68.79	67.05
Accuracy 1.2	50	43.59	41.03	41.03	42.31	42.31	38.46	39.74

Table 5. Tests with both 29 Amadeo loose drawings and 10 manuscript drawings included in the testing set for Amadeo classifier.

Test 2.1	Positive	Negative
Training set 2.1	105 AP	60 ACP
Testing set 2.1	95 AP + 29 AD + 10 AD = 134	49 ACP
Test 2.2	Positive	Negative
Training set 2.2	105 AP	60 ACP
Testing set 2.2	29 AD + 10 AD = 39	49 ACP

Table 6. Accuracies with both 29 Amadeo loose drawings and 10 manuscript drawings included in the testing set for Amadeo classifier.

Number of visual words	100	200	400	1000	1200	1400	1600	2000
Accuracy 2.1	64.48	61.75	62.84	65.03	66.67	65.57	68.31	66.67
Accuracy 2.2	48.86	43.18	44.32	43.18	45.45	43.18	40.91	42.05

Tests when the negative samples are completely excluded from the negative testing set are also performed, the results displayed similar tendency. Therefore, they are not reported hither.

Chinese paintings are very different from western paintings in terms of style; it is expected that they could be correctly identified as negative.

When 91 Chinese paintings are included in the negative testing set, at the same time when Amadeo paintings are included in the positive testing set (Test 3.1 in Table 7), the accuracies are quite high in comparison with the previous tests when only western styles are included; almost all are close to 80% (Accuracy 3.1 in Table 8). When Amadeo paintings are excluded in the positive testing set, i.e. only negative samples are included (Test 3.2 in Table 7), the accuracies drop to about 72% (Accuracy 3.2 in Table 8). This might signify that the Amadeo classifier works well with Amadeo paintings, but not with other styles of paintings. Nevertheless, when the negative testing set excludes Amadeo contemporary paintings but only includes Chinese paintings (Test 3.3 in Table 7), the results show a significant improvement in accuracy; most of them higher than 90% (Accuracy 3.3 in Table 8). It instead appears to demonstrate the importance of styles.

Table 7. Tests with Chinese paintings included in the testing set for Amadeo classifier.

Test 3.1	Positive	Negative
Training set 3.1	105 AP	60 ACP
Testing set 3.1	95 AP	49 ACP + 91 CP = 140
Test 3.2	Positive	Negative
Training set 3.2	105 AP	60 ACP
Testing set 3.2	0	49 ACP + 91 CP = 140
Test 3.3	Positive	Negative
Training set 3.3	105 AP	60 ACP
Testing set 3.3	0	91 CP

Table 8. Accuracies with Chinese paintings included in the testing set for Amadeo classifier.

Number of visual words	100	200	400	1000	1200	1400	1600	2000
Accuracy 3.1	75.32	78.3	75.32	78.3	79.15	78.3	81.7	79.15
Accuracy 3.2	72.86	77.86	72.14	73.57	74.29	72.86	73.57	72.14
Accuracy 3.3	82.42	96.7	90.11	91.21	92.31	90.11	94.51	91.21

Van Gogh paintings are also considered western style although they do not belong to the same period and style as Amadeo or his contemporaries. This similarity raised the expectation that the results could be generalised. However, when the test substitutes the Chinese paintings with the van Gogh paintings in the negative testing set (Test 4.1 in Table 9), the accuracies decreased considerably with values located around 50% (Accuracy 4.1 in Table 10). This result means that the Amadeo classifier does not work well directly with other artists or other genre, and that the algorithms might require to be retrained to fit to a specific artist. Alternatively, more negative styles could be included in the negative training set for the classifier to learn what does not constitute an Amadeo style. When Amadeo paintings are excluded from the positive testing set completely (Test 4.2 in Table 9), the results again show a significant decrease in accuracy with values found at around 40% (Accuracy 4.2 in Table 10). This was found to be true whether Amadeo contemporary paintings are included in the negative testing set or not. It again suggests that the Amadeo classifier is not so specific while identifying western styles alone, and a more sophisticated classifier is perhaps needed or the training set needs to include these styles too.

Table 9. Tests with van Gogh paintings included in the testing set for Amadeo classifier.

Test 4.1	Positive	Negative
Training set 4.1	105 AP	60 ACP
Testing set 4.1	95 AP	49 ACP + 210 VGP = 259
Test 4.2	Positive	Negative
Training set 4.2	105 AP	60 ACP
Testing set 4.2	0	49 ACP + 210 VGP = 259
Test 4.3	Positive	Negative
Training set 4.3	105 AP	60 ACP
Testing set 4.3	0	210 VGP

Table 10. Accuracies with van Gogh paintings included in the testing set for Amadeo classifier.

Number of visual words	100	200	400	1000	1200	1400	1600	2000
Accuracy 4.1	57.34	57.34	53.67	50	52.54	52.26	50.28	52.82
Accuracy 4.2	49.42	49.42	44.02	37.07	40.15	39.77	34.36	39.38
Accuracy 4.3	48.1	50.95	45.24	36.19	40	39.52	34.29	40

In a further test, the classifier was retrained on various datasets in order to establish if it can be generalised. Those datasets included Chinese paintings and van Gogh paintings.

Tables 11 and 12 show the results when the classifier is retrained; 91 Chinese paintings of the same Chinese artist Daqian Zhang and 98 Chinese paintings from all other Chinese artists were used (Test 5.1). The results perform as well as when it was applied on the reference test on Amadeo works with similar accuracy of around 70% (Accuracy 5.1). This reaffirms that the classifier works well on a specific style. An evaluation on all the rest of the Chinese paintings shows the classifier performs well (Test 5.2) with accuracies around 80% (Accuracy 5.2).

Table 11. Tests with the retrained Chinese classifier.

Test 5.1	Positive	Negative
Training Set 5.1	46 CP (Daqian Zhang)	49 CP
Testing Set 5.1	45 CP (Daqian Zhang)	49 CP
Test 5.2	Positive	Negative
Training Set 5.2	46 CP (Daqian Zhang)	49 CP
Testing Set 5.2	45 CP (Daqian Zhang)	1021 CP

Table 12. Accuracies with the retrained Chinese classifier.

Number of visual words	100	200	400	1000	1200	1400	1600	2000
Accuracy 5.1	68.09	70.21	70.21	69.15	70.21	68.09	69.15	70.21
Accuracy 5.2	78.24	77.95	77.77	79.08	78.71	79.92	79.92	79.92

Similar to the retrained Chinese classifier, a final test discards the Amadeo classifier and the Chinese classifier in favour of a retrained van Gogh classifier (Test 6.1 in Table 13). The results also show good accuracies circa 80% (Accuracy 6.1 in Table 14) confirming the hypothesis that the algorithm works well for a specific genre.

Table 13. Tests with the retrained van Gogh classifier.

Test 6.1	Positive	Negative
Training set 6.1	105 VGP	37 VGCP
Testing set 6.1	105 VGP	36 VGCP

Table 14. Accuracies with the retrained van Gogh classifier.

Number of visual words	100	200	400	1000	1200	1400	1600	2000
Accuracy 6.1	72.34	75.18	74.47	78.01	75.89	76.6	76.6	77.3

6 Conclusion

The current research systematically evaluates the Amadeo classifier, the retrained Chinese classifier and the retrained van Gogh classifier based on the same algorithm in order to compare the effects of different testing sets on the accuracies to determine how generalised the algorithm can be when producing different classifiers. The following can be concluded based on the obtained results:

1) The number of visual words does not seem to have a significant positive effect on the accuracy.
2) The classifier trained with paintings only cannot successfully identify and classify drawings by the same artist.
3) The media of the drawings does not seem to affect the authentication of an artist's works applying image processing and machine learning.
4) The number of samples is important for training and testing. However, the limitation in data is usually the major concern in terms of machine learning.
5) If the testing set only contains a style that is significantly different from the style used in the training set to generate the classifier, a high accuracy is achieved.
6) The accuracies for the retrained classifiers for Chinese paintings and van Gogh paintings respectively reached almost 80% signifying the method can provide good results.

In essence, the classifiers were found to work well if trained with specific samples that match the positive testing data, suggesting the method is adequate with potential for further improvement. For example, in order to work more accurately on the classification and identification of drawings, the classifier is expected to be retrained with only drawings or paintings and drawings. The evaluation of other image processing techniques, machine learning algorithms and artificial intelligence tools such as Convolutional Neural Networks are also considered as part of the future work.

Acknowledgement. Special thanks to the help and support by Dr Rui Xavier and Ms Marta Areia from Calouste Gulbenkian Museum, Prof. Dr. Jia Li and Prof. Dr James Z. Wang from Penn State University as well as van Gogh museum for supplying the respective database for our research. This work is supported by FCT/MEC NOVA LINCS PEst UID/CEC/04516/2019 and the grant PD/BD/135223/2017.

References

1. Montagner, C.: The brushstroke and materials of Amadeo de Souza-Cardoso combined in an authentication tool. Ph.D Dissertation, Departamento de Conservação e Restauro, Faculdade de Ciências e Tecnologia, Universidade NOVA de Lisboa (2015)
2. Montagner, C., Jesus, R., Correia, N., Vilarigues, M., Macedo, R., Melo, M.J.: Features combination for art authentication studies: brushstroke and materials analysis of amadeo de souza-cardoso. Multimedia Tools Appl. **75**(7), 4039–4063 (2016). https://doi.org/10.1007/s11042-015-3197-x
3. Keren, D.: Painter identification using local features and naive bayes. In: Proceedings of the 16th international conference on pattern recognition, vol. 2, pp. 474–477. IEEE (2002)
4. Li, J., Wang, J.Z.: Studying digital imagery of ancient paintings by mixtures of stochastic models. IEEE Trans. Image Process. **13**(3), 340–353 (2003)
5. Lombardi, T.: The classification of style in fine-art painting. Dissertation, Pace University (2005)
6. Polatkan, G., Jafarpour, S., Brasoveanu, A., Hughes, S., Daubechies, I.: Detection of forgery in paintings using supervised learning. In: Proceedings of the IEEE International Conference on Image Processing (ICIP), pp. 2921–2924. IEEE (2009)

7. Johnson, C.R., et al.: Image processing for artist identification - computerized analysis of vincent van gogh's painting brush stokes. IEEE Sig. Process. Mag. **37** (2008)
8. Hendriks, E., Hughes, S.: Van gogh's brushstrokes: marks of authenticity?. In: Proceedings of Art, Conservation, and Authenticities: Material, Concept, Context (2009)
9. Li, J., Yao, L., Hendriks, E., Wang, J.: Rhythmic brushstrokes distinguish van gogh from his contemporaries: findings via automated brushstroke extraction. IEEE Trans. Pattern Anal. Mach. Intell. (2012)
10. Lecoutre, A., Negrevergne, B., Yger, F.: Recognizing art style automatically in painting with deep learning. In: JMLR: Workshop and Conference Proceedings, vol. 80, pp. 1–17 (2017)
11. Balakrishan, T., Rosston, S., Tang, E.: Using CNN to classify and understand artists from the rijksmuseum. Report, CS231n: Convolutional Neural Networks for Visual Recognition, Standford University (2017)
12. Temel, B., Kilic, N., Ozgultekin, B., Ucan, O.N.: Separation of original paintings of matisse and his fakes using wavelet and artificial neural networks. J. Electr. Electron. Eng. **9**(1), 791–796 (2009)

"What I See Is What You Get" Explorations of Live Artwork Generation, Artificial Intelligence, and Human Interaction in a Pedagogical Environment

Ana Herruzo[1,2](✉) (iD) and Nikita Pashenkov[1] (iD)

[1] Woodbury University, 7500 N Glenoaks Blvd, Burbank, CA 9150, USA
{Ana.Herruzo,Nikita.Pashenkov}@woodbury.edu
[2] Universidad Politecnica de Madrid, Pº Juan XXIII, 11, 28040 Madrid, Spain

Abstract. In this paper we review the overall process for the design, development, and deployment of "What I See Is What You Get", an experiential installation that creates live interactive visuals, by analyzing human facial expressions and behaviors, accompanied by text generated using Machine Learning algorithms trained on the art collection of The J. Paul Getty Museum in Los Angeles. The project is developed by students and faculty in an academic environment and exhibited at the Getty Museum. We also study the pedagogical process implemented to address the curriculum's learning outcomes in an "applied" environment while designing a contemporary new media art piece. Special attention is paid to the level and quality of the interaction between users and the piece, demonstrating how advances in technology and computing such as Deep Learning and Natural Language Processing can contribute to deeper connections and new layers of interactivity.

Keywords: Interactive art · Machine learning · Artificial intelligence · Applied computing · Information visualization · New media technologies · Higher education · Real-time generated graphics · Creative Technologies

1 Introduction

Design and artistic fields are no longer isolated from scientific or technological skills. With the rise of the digital age, technology is gaining significant weight within creative fields, allowing a new range of possibilities in experimental tools and methods for media creation. In parallel to this phenomenon, various New Media Art programs have emerged at Universities across the globe.

Our university program, the Applied Computer Science – Media Arts at Woodbury University is a Bachelor of Science, STEM program, bridging art and technology at its core. It is a hybrid degree focusing on emerging digital practices including interactive environments, experiential design, and human interaction. The program uses computer

A. Brooks and E. I. Brooks (Eds.): ArtsIT 2019/DLI 2019, LNICST 328, pp. 343–359, 2020.
https://doi.org/10.1007/978-3-030-53294-9_23

science as a tool to innovate within the fields of design, entertainment, and media arts. Across the curriculum, we emphasize hands-on and project-based learning techniques. Students pursuing this type of major will need to excel at technical skills, but also be well rounded in the principles of media, design and visual arts.

In his book "New Media Art" [1], Mark Tribe describes the term New Media Art as "projects that make use of emerging media technologies and are concerned with the cultural, political, and aesthetic possibilities of these tools". He locates New Media Art as a subset of two broader categories: Art and Technology and Media Art. Our program falls in that same intersection, studying and utilizing scientific and technological disciplines that are not fully media related, but with an overall application to different media environments; not only digital but also physical and human-scaled spaces. Making user-centered design is one of our core fields of study. Tribe also explains how the term is used interchangeably with categorical names like "Digital art," "Computer art," "Multimedia art," and "Interactive art". In the course of this article, we use terms such as new media and interactive artworks on multiple occasions.

The concepts of interactive art and environments have been explored for many years now, starting with such pioneering experiments, such as Myron Krueger's "Responsive Environments" [2] which explored different types of human-machine interactions, the potentials of interactive art and its implications in a number of fields. Since then artists have been experimenting with different scenarios for human-computer interactivity such as voice-activation, body and skeleton trackage brain waves, and many types of sensors and controllers [3].

With the recent evolution in hardware and computing power, machine learning is becoming more accessible and widespread; new forms of "artificial intelligence aesthetics" have been proposed by the likes of Lev Manovich [4] as a response to these developments, accompanied with a warning of the ongoing process of "automating aesthetic choices" performed by AI algorithms. This automation is already evident in many consumer-facing smartphone and web applications, according to Manovich. On the positive side, we can now expand the levels of interaction to more complex layers, allowing recognition of patterns, movements, facial expressions and more. Along with the rapid evolution of real-time rendering engines, programmable shaders, and new algorithms, it is now possible to effectively create instant real-time data-driven media at large resolutions and with great rendering quality.

In the Fall of 2018 our program was invited by The J. Paul Getty Museum, a premier art institution in Los Angeles, to design an installation for the College Night event and exhibition scheduled to take place in April 2019.

In conversations with educational specialists at the museum, interest was shown in exploring human emotions as a thematic element in a project that would merge art and technology, which successfully aligned with our program's mission. After carefully studying the courses offered during the Spring semester, student enrollments, university resources and overall workload for the project we came up with " What I See Is What You Get", an immersive interactive installation that combines Artificial Intelligence technologies with the visual arts. "What I See Is What You Get" benefits from the technical achievements mentioned above, using them to connect at a deeper level with the user in terms of interactivity, and delivering content with high performance and resolution.

In order to pursue this project with the students, we created a collaboration between two sophomore classes and a new syllabus for each course to include the collaboration with the museum. The syllabus also included guided visits to the museum to study some of the art works in its collection, learning about the artists' intentions, and what the works are communicating in their portrayal of emotions and facial expressions.

Students from the "Media Environments" class led the project design and execution, and the students in the "Artificial Intelligence" course headed the Machine Learning development effort of the project. In the course of this article, we will discuss the content of the classes and the techniques that students learned by applying these skills and concepts during the project's development (Fig. 1).

INSTALLATION DIAGRAM

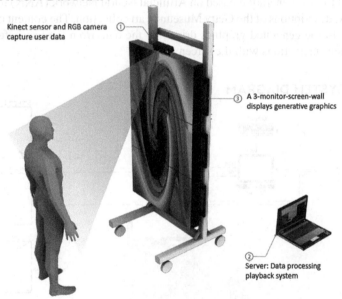

Kinect sensor and RGB camera ① capture user data

③ A 3-monitor-screen-wall displays generative graphics

② Server: Data processing playback system

Fig. 1. Installation diagram

With concept and project management by the program's Chair Ana Herruzo and Faculty member Nikita Pashenkov, students worked on an immersive, interactive installation that attempts to create live works of art.

While studying the museum's art collection that comprises-Greek, Roman, and Etruscan art from the Neolithic to Late Antiquity; and European art from the Middle Ages to the early twentieth century; with a contemporary lens, questions arose regarding static and finished pieces of art, in contrast to interactive and responsive artworks.

Our goal was to create a contemporary new media art piece that has an intimate connection with the user experiencing it and simultaneously generates new periodic content. We aimed to design a piece of art that is always evolving, changing; never the same.

Artworks in exhibitions and museums are usually accompanied by a title and a brief description of the piece. In our case, a unique animation would be generated with each user interaction, so we decided to create new synthetic titles and descriptions to accompany each new real-time visualization. In parallel, we needed to address teaching the students the principles of Machine Learning; an introduction to computer vision techniques; the design and creation of data-driven real-time rendered graphics; interactivity techniques, and programming media playback systems. These learning outcomes are essential to the program's curriculum and are introduced at the Sophomore level.

As a result, we proposed the design and development of an installation that creates live interactive visuals, accompanied with a title and a text description of the piece each time it interacts with users. The installation analyzes the users' facial expressions with computer vision and Deep Learning algorithms, using their outputs in the next stage as a basis for text generation based on Artificial Neural Network (ANN) models trained on the text descriptions of the Getty Museum's art collection. The content of the installation are real-time generated graphics driven by the data from the user's facial expressions and their interactions with the screen (Fig. 2).

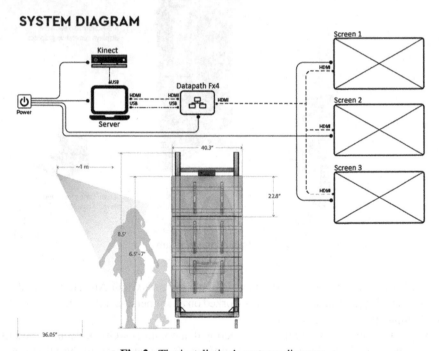

Fig. 2. The installation's systems diagram

2 Process

The installation consists of a vertical video wall composed of three landscape-oriented screens. On top of the wall, there are two embedded sensors: A Microsoft Kinect ONE (containing an RGB color VGA video camera, a depth sensor, and a multi-array microphone) and a USB web camera. These two sensors enable us to obtain live data from users with computer vision algorithms [5]. The video wall was mounted on a rolling cart for easy transportation and installation at the museum. We used two software platforms, PyCharm [6] as an integrated development environment for the Python programming language; and Derivative TouchDesigner [7] as a real-time rendering, visual programming platform. The two platforms communicated with each other via TCP/IP sockets sent over the network.

The project was developed during the spring semester of 2019, by combining two 3 unit studios courses that met five hours per week. The artificial intelligence class had 10 students and the Media Environments 4 students. Some students where participants in both courses. The students had taken introduction and intermediate programming courses, digital media fundamentals, 3D modeling and mixed reality classes at this point. However, most of them were new to Python programming, TensorFlow, Keras frameworks, and TouchDesigner.

During the first part of the semester, alongside with visits to the Getty, we did some preliminary studies as an exercise to begin exploring human emotions but also to become familiar with TouchDesigner, and creating real-time generated graphics. These studies prepared the students to dive more confidently into the production of this installation in the second part the semester. The installation was ideated by the professors prior to the start of the semester, but was introduced to the students as an exercise after the midterm evaluations, with a total production time of two months. The design, research, development, and production of the installation were divided into two main groups. Machine Learning, computer vision, and data management were developed and explored in the Artificial Intelligence course led by professor Nikita Pashenkov, while project design, media production, hardware, software, and interactivity were developed in the Media Environments course led by professor Ana Herruzo.

Some of the learning outcomes of the Media Environments course are to create real-time generated graphics and interactive content; build show systems and playback software; work simultaneously with virtual worlds and the physical space; apply 2D or 3D media workflows to design assets and animations; and troubleshoot video content and audiovisual systems.

Artificial Intelligence course learning outcomes include how to develop an appreciation for what is involved in learning from data; understand the core concepts of Machine Learning in the context of Artificial Intelligence; understand a variety of learning algorithms and deploy them in a range of real-world applications; be able to apply learning algorithms to analyze, identify and extract useful features that represent observed data; work with hardware systems that enable data collection, analysis, classification, and prediction.

2.1 Preliminary Explorations

The students had no previous experience designing data-driven real-time rendered animations. We started the semester exploring human facial expressions and studying facial anatomy to serve as an inspiration, while learning how to create real-time rendered scenes. These scenes would in some way address or relate to emotions.

As part of the study of facial anatomy, we experimented with three different methods for creating 3D point clouds of human faces: Kinect ONE [8], iPhone scanning apps and Photogrammetry. Best results were obtained using the Structure Sensors [9] by Occipital. Once the faces were scanned, the students created clean three-dimensional models using retopology software; the face models were then sent to the university's fabrication lab for CNC Milling.

Students learned how to create real-time generated animations in TouchDesigner. This software was used further down the line to program and drive the final installation at the museum. After creating artboards evoking different emotions, the students began to design the animations. Once we received the physical models of the students' faces for the fabrication lab, we used projection mapping techniques, to project the animations onto the face models.

During this study, the students practiced using different color palettes while exploring various emotions. The color palettes were used again in the development of the final installation. In parallel, in the Artificial Intelligence class, the students began exploring computer vision and Deep Learning algorithms in order to detect facial expressions [10] (Fig. 3).

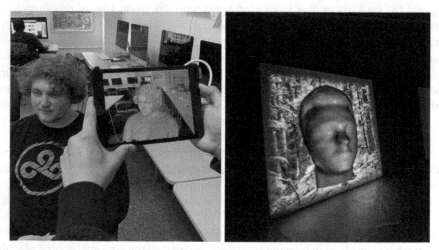

Fig. 3. The left image reflects 3D face scanning using Occipital. The right image consists of a projection mapped face model, with generative content evoking a "sad" emotion.

2.2   What I See Is What You Get

The title of the installation is a play on the popular acronym "What You See Is What You Get" (WYSIWYG), based on the idea that the installation incorporates vision processing and Artificial Intelligence, in a sense allowing it to generate outputs according to what it sees from its own perspective.

Computer Vision Data. As stated previously, the installation features a USB camera, with live footage from the camera driving the Machine Learning algorithms to detect the users' facial expressions [11] and other useful features. Specifically, in the course of live interaction with the piece, we utilize computer vision with Deep Learning models to estimate the following:

- Number of People
- Approximate Ages [12]
- Facial Expressions
- Estimated Genders

Fig. 4. Image of the students testing the face recognition algorithms at the Getty.

Visual Content. All the content was developed in the Media Environments class. When visitors approach the installation, depending on how many people are in front of the screen, their facial expressions, estimated ages, and genders; a new unique animation is displayed on the video wall (Fig. 4).

Before beginning to design the content, we needed to design the full user experience of the installation. As a result, two types of media proposals were developed in parallel: media to be displayed during users' interaction, and media generated in-between interactions (we called this the "idle state" animation).

Fig. 5. Users experiencing the installation and playing with their silhouettes on the screen.

Silhouettes. We designed a mirror effect reflection of silhouettes to the screen. We used the Kinect ONE player index functionality, to track the users and their silhouettes. The content displayed on the video wall, are real-time generated animations, playing inside and outside the silhouette of the users (Fig. 5).

Scenes. Each student designed four real-time scenes. Some of the content is generated live and other parts of the content are displayed according to a set of rules. These rules are hardcoded and are driven by the data obtained through computer vision algorithms. One of the hard-coded rules consists of choosing a scene based on users' age and the number of users' silhouette interactions.

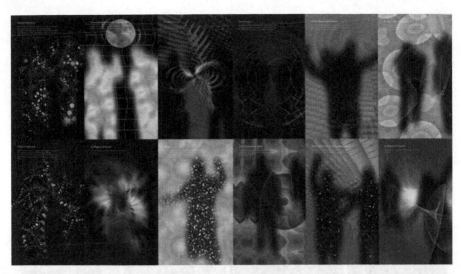

Fig. 6. Gallery showcasing several of the animations designed by the students and the different color palettes applied to them depending on the users' emotions.

Color Palettes. Using the parameters obtained by computer vision (age, facial expressions, and number of people), students generated animations to be displayed on the screen. For example, if a user smiled expressing "joy", the screen would display a particle system that uses colors associated with this feeling, and moved at a faster pace compared to when a frown and a "sad" expression was detected. The facial expression analyzed were the following: neutral, joy, anger, happiness, sadness, surprise, and fear. Each was assigned a different color palette, with different color ranges obtained from the preliminary studies (Fig. 6).

Idle Animation. The students had a strong interest in designing a scene that changed and evolved with users' interactions, that gathered and visualized the sum of the interactions throughout the night. To achieve this, we designed an "idle state" animation that would come up after every interaction in TouchDesigner, composed of colorful organic vertical bands. Each time that a participant interacted with the piece, a new band would be added to the scene and the color of the band would reflect the emotion of the user. The scene starts with one band and by the end of the night, the scenes would be fully populated reflecting all the interactions and emotions tracked through the overall experience. This animation serves as an emotion database visualizer.

Machine Learning. In the Artificial Intelligence class, studies begun by screening the Getty's art collection, and selecting all art pieces that had humans depicted. The focus was on artifacts containing people, based on the total number of pieces on display at the Getty Center at the time of data collection (1,276 results according to the website) (Fig. 7).

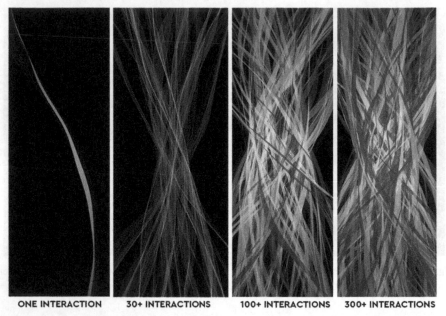

ONE INTERACTION   30+ INTERACTIONS   100+ INTERACTIONS   300+ INTERACTIONS

Fig. 7. Evolution of the "idle state" animation throughout the exhibit. Each user interaction adds a new band, using the color that describes the emotion expressed by the user.

The database was created by analyzing the artworks and collecting the following data for each piece:

- Title
- Artist/Maker
- Date
- Description
- Primary Sentence
- Number of People
- Gender
- Age
- Emotion
- Image

We used the Python programming language for the development along with the Deep Learning library Keras [13] built on top of TensorFlow [14] framework. Keras allows multi-layer Artificial Neural Network models to be built and interconnected in a modular way, abstracting away some of the complexities of the underlying framework.

In analyzing the Getty's art collection, students experimented with the Deep Learning natural language model called GPT-2 [15], an acronym for Generative Pre-Trained Transformer, released by the non-profit foundation OpenAI in February 2019. The language model is capable of generating convincing responses to textual prompts based on set parameters such as the maximum length of response and 'temperature' of generated text indicating the relative degree to which the output models the features found in training data.

Our project utilized the GPT-2 model with 144 million parameters, the largest made available by the OpenAI Foundation as of April 2019. The model has been "fine-tuned" by the students, a process in which an existing machine learning model is re-trained to fit new data, using descriptions of artworks on display at the Getty Center as the training dataset. To accomplish this task, we utilized the Google Colaboratory [16] notebook environment that allows Python code to be shared and executed online.

A colaboratory notebook that had been tested by its author on fine-tuning the GPT-2 model allowed each student to individually analyze and modify the Python code to read new text data, re-train the language model, and produce new text descriptions based on interactive prompts. The text prompts were pre-generated by the students based on their own subjective analysis of artworks and consisted of short singular and plural descriptions like "sad young person" or "two happy people." The text prompts were interactively input to the GPT-2 model to generate responses that were entered into a database and associated by rows with tagged columns for age, number of people and facial expressions.

The database of text prompts and GPT-2 responses was compiled by the students and saved as an XML file to be accessed by the Python program running computer vision and Deep Learning algorithms, which processed video camera input to detect and tag the number of participants, their classified age and facial expressions. The outputs of vision processing and classification were programmatically correlated with the database content using the Pandas library [17] in Python in order to select an appropriate response that matches detected tags and chosen at random for identical combinations of tags. Finally, the selected response was rendered as the text description that accompanied visual output onscreen.

In addition to generating text description using the GPT-2 model, students have also utilized a simpler language model based on Recurrent Neural Networks (RNNs) and the textgenrnn [18] Python library to generate titles to go along with a description of each visualization. The RNN-based model in textgenrnn does not incorporate an understanding of sophisticated features of natural language like sentence structure or syntax, but it is well suited to generating letter combinations that mimic combinations of words in the training data. The lightweight library was deployed by the students directly in locally run Python programs that used the list of titles of art works in the Getty collection as inputs, generating text responses that often produced interesting and surprising results.

The generated title and description for each new piece of media would show on the top left corner of the screen. The attendees were able to take a picture/video, of the animation and description of their interaction with the piece (Fig. 8).

To summarize the vision processing component of our setup, the facial expression recognition is accomplished via a two-step process. In the first step, video from the webcam is processed with a traditional computer vision method for face tracking built into the Open Computer Vision (OpenCV) library. The method is based on the popular and robust Viola-Jones algorithm [10] that utilizes Attentional Cascades of Haar Like

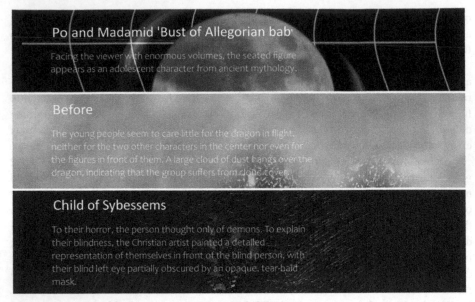

Fig. 8. Example of machine learning generated texts overlaid to the real-time generated animations.

features to detect sub windows estimated to contain faces in the video frame. Haar Cascade files for frontal face detection in XML format provided by the OpenCV library in Python were used for processing the video input at this stage (Fig. 9).

The second step in facial expression recognition process used a Deep Learning model based on a Convolutional Neural Network (CNN) built in Python with the help of Keras and TensorFlow frameworks. We utilized a 5-layer CNN model that's proven effective

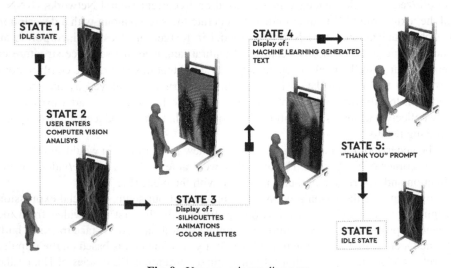

Fig. 9. User experience diagrams

in the Kaggle facial expression recognition challenge [19] in 2013. The model has been trained on the Feb2013 dataset distributed with the challenge, which consisted of 28,000 training and 3,000 test images of faces stored as 48 by 48 pixel grayscale images. In order to provide the image data in the format that the CNN model expects, sub windows with faces detected by the OpenCV library were scaled down to 48 × 48 size to be passed on in this step. The Python code to construct the facial expression detection model in Keras, as well as other Deep Learning models and associated weight parameters utilized in the project and discussed further, are available in an open GitHub code repository [20]; along with the rest of the project's materials. The code for building the models is remarkably succinct and easy to understand after some familiarity with the Keras syntax (Fig. 10).

Fig. 10. Users engaging with the installation at the event.

It was beyond the scope of the Artificial Intelligence course to build expertise constructing Deep Learning models or invest resources into training the models from scratch, especially in view of time and computing power expended in the process. However, students working on the project had a chance to install the relevant Python code and libraries, analyze them and test the models on their computers with pre-trained data without much difficulty using built-in cameras. The PyCharm integrated development environment used by the students for programming provided a free and user-friendly workflow for project development. The cross-platform IDE made it convenient to incorporate relevant code libraries via a graphical user interface and provided built-in tools for virtualizing the project to encapsulate any necessary dependencies, making it possible for each student to deploy a full workflow.

In addition to facial expression detection, the project incorporated Deep Learning models for age and gender detection, though ultimately, we decided not to pursue gender recognition due to non-technical concerns with bias and issues of non-binary gender identification. The age detection was built on a successful CNN architecture based on Oxford Visual Group's (VGG) model [21] that gained recognition in the ImageNet Large Scale Visual Recognition Competition (ILSVRC) in 2014 [22].

The datasets that formed that basis of the VGG model, known as IMDB-WIKI [23], consist of over 500,000 labeled faces primarily of celebrities in film and media. In order to utilize the model effectively, we again made use of pre-trained weights found online [24], applying transfer learning techniques to work with the real-time video data in our project. As a result, each student was able to directly experiment with deploying machine learning models in Python code to process computers' built-in camera input and generate predictions for detected facial expressions, age and gender estimates of each other initially in the classroom environment and eventually in the public setting of the museum exhibition.

User Experience and Installation Flow. The user experience is a central component of the project that was carefully crafted. After several sessions of user testing to determine the ideal flow for the installation, we designed a sequence of animated events, to successfully guide the user through the experience: Idle, Transition 1, Interactive, Text Reveal, Transition 2, and New Idle State. The New Idle State would display the message "Thank you for interacting with me," inviting the user to leave the installation. Creating this iteration of events, the users would enter the installation, experience it and exit once the "Thank you" message was revealed. The overall experience lasts a total of two minutes.

3 Discussion

Overall, we can observe the creation of a bidirectional dynamic art piece, between two agents: "the artist" and "the user". The style, content, and themes are generated by the user's interaction, but follow initial rules and guidelines stated and designed by the artist. In our case the artist's "style" is created within a real-time rendering engine, the artist's "theme" is generated in part by Deep Learning algorithms and the artist's "content" is driven by the user's interaction.

During the exhibit we observed that the level of engagement and interaction of the user with the piece was high, with multiple attendees repeating the experience throughout the night. We were able to record over 350 interactions with the piece during the 6-h event.

At a first experiential level, the piece works with very direct interaction rules, where the number of users maps to the number of silhouettes, users' facial expressions choose the color patterns, and the silhouettes serve as a mirror to the user, engaging and enabling the connection between the subject and the art piece. Different simultaneous levels of interactivity occurred, some with a direct and transparent effect, and others with more elaborate or of indirect interaction.

We discovered that when the users realized their silhouettes were being reflected (direct) they would engage more actively with the installation, often dancing, jumping, moving their hands or even doing backflips. The facial expression or age-based visualizations were not as transparent since it is harder for the user to acknowledge that connection. In order for the user to come to this level of realization, they would have to observe the installation in action several times to begin understanding programmed rules through repetition.

The final and most diffuse interaction are the texts generated with the help of Machine Learning. Even though our database was quite small, the state of the art algorithms were able to generate infinite combinations of descriptions with a relatively small amount of input data. The level of uncertainty in understanding why a part of the art piece is automatically generated created a great level of engagement as well, with the users inquiring the students in multiple occasions why would a certain color or description appear on the screen. Using Artificial Intelligence, we are able to programmatically discern a fair amount of information from the participants in order to generate the content at a modest level of engagement. It is of our interest that further explorations should address a more thorough analysis of the users' feelings or personality, in search of a deeper and more profound connection between the art piece and the subject.

One of the most interesting features of the project are the titles and text descriptions generated by the software via Machine Learning algorithms. Due to the limitations of our database, 1,276 art pieces for the Getty collections and the range of art periods, the live generated text often addressed religious or mythological themes, popular in Middle-Ages and Classic or Roman art, which are prevalent in the collection. For further iterations of this project, we will aim to work with larger databases and include artworks that can relate more to the type of participants that are interacting with the screens. This would create a stronger connection between the subjects, their actions and the generated texts.

After creating our database, at the beginning of user testing, some of the students raised concerns about the use of gender in camera-based analysis as well as generated texts, implying that it could potentially make some of the attendees uncomfortable. This also raised important questions regarding the role of gender in today's society and opened the door for further discussions involving human interactions. We attempted to address this issue in part by avoiding the use of gender, and programmatically manipulating the generated texts, as well as manually editing our database by screening for male and female pronouns, attempting to "de-gender" it by replacing those with plural "they, " or neutral "person", wherever appropriate.

It was also interesting to analyze how timing the user and programming the steps of the experience, allowed the participants to interact with the installation without the need for specific instructions. Dedicating sufficient time with the students to design the appropriate flow and navigation of the installation produced satisfying results.

3.1 Pedagogically

From a pedagogical standpoint, the overall assessment is very positive. The development of the installation and the preliminary exercises were able to fulfill most of the learning outcomes for the two sophomore classes involved in the project. By utilizing different areas of study in one unique experimental project, we managed to offer the students an opportunity to understand how diverse disciplines can be intertwined and relevant to each other. A.M. Connor and R. Sosa [25], undergo a critical analysis of Creative Technologies, describing 25 characteristics that differentiate this field from others and aiming to help identify learning outcomes that will support new emerging academic programs in the field, such as ours. The combination of the necessary technical skills, mixed with design and implementation of creative visualizations accurately met the hybrid of art and technology foundations of our program. Ultimately, given the stature of the exhibition at a world-renowned art institution, the deployment of a live interactive installation brought real-life professional production experience to the students.

4   Conclusion

We believe that many features make this project novel and quite unique, including: the agents involved, the combination of real-time generative graphics with state of the art machine learning models, the development within an academic environment and the opportunity for the students to exhibit at a great art institution. Trying to find ways to connect the existing art collection to our project, while addressing the learning outcomes that the courses required, resulted in an extraordinarily complex project that successfully fulfills the mission of our university program: hybrid art and technology. The number of constraints, such as addressing multiple curriculum requirements, collaboration between academic and art institutions, maintaining appropriate workloads for the students and so on, turned out to strengthen and boost the level of creativity, allowing the students to become proficient in several technical skills working with advanced programming frameworks and computational models.

Advances in technology and computing exemplified by Deep Learning can contribute to deeper connections and new layers of interactivity. When applying these techniques to the creative fields, there are areas that we would like to explore further in expanding the vocabulary of interactive visuals and dynamic text generation, looking for a stronger relationship between the user and context of the piece.

References

1. Tribe, M., Jana, R., Grosenick, U.: New Media Art (Taschen Basic Art). Taschen America, LLC (2006)
2. Krueger, M.W.: Responsive environments. In: AFIPS 1977 Proceedings of the June 13–16, 1977, National Computer Conference, pp. 423–433. Dallas, Texas (1977)
3. Krauth AK: Using handmade controllers for interactive projection mapping. In: Proceedings of the 23rd ACM International Conference on Multimedia - MM 2015, pp 717–719. ACM Press, Brisbane, Australia (2015)
4. Manovich, L.: Automating aesthetics: artificial intelligence and image culture. In: Flash Art International, no. 316 (2017). https://flash---art.com/issue/316-september-october-2017/. Accessed 14 Aug 2019
5. OpenCV. https://opencv.org/. Accessed 10 Aug 2019
6. PyCharm: The Python IDE for Professional Developers by JetBrains. https://www.jetbrains.com/pycharm/. Accessed 10 Aug 2019
7. Derivative TouchDesigner. https://www.derivative.ca/. Accessed 10 Aug 2019

8. KINECTONE. https://developer.microsoft.com/en-us/windows/kinect. Accessed 10 Aug 2019
9. Structure Sensor-3D scanning, augmented reality, and more for mobile devices. https://struct ure.io/. Accessed 10 Aug 2019
10. Viola, P., Jones, M.J.: Robust real-time face detection. Int. J. Comput. Vis. **57**(2), 137–154 (2004). Kluwer Academic Publishers Norwell, MA
11. Teixeira Lopes, A., de Aguiar, E., Oliveira-Santos, T.: A facial expression recognition system using convolutional networks. In: Conference on Graphics, Patterns and Images (SIBGRAPI), 28th Conference, Salvador, Brazil, pp. 273–280 (2015)
12. Rothe, R., Timofte, R., Gool, L.V.: DEX: deep expectation of apparent age from a single image. In: 2015 IEEE International Conference on Computer Vision Workshop (ICCVW), pp. 252–257 (2015)
13. Keras Documentation. https://keras.io/. Accessed 10 Aug 2019
14. TensorFlow. https://www.tensorflow.org/. Accessed 10 Aug 2019
15. Radford, A., Wu, J., Child, R., Luan, D., Amode, D., Sutskever, I.: Language models are unsupervised multitask learners. In: Technical report, OpenAI (2019). https://openai.com/ blog/better-language-models/. Accessed 14 Aug 2019
16. Google Colaboratory. https://github.com/ak9250/gpt-2-colab. Accessed 10 Oct 2019
17. Python Data Analysis Library. https://pandas.pydata.org/. Accessed 18 Oct 2019
18. Woolf, M.: Easily train your own text-generating neural network of any size and complexity on any text dataset with a few lines of code: minimaxir/textgenrnn (2015). https://github.com/ minimaxir/textgenrn
19. Kaggle Facial Expression Recognition Challenge. https://www.kaggle.com/c/challenges-in-representation-learning-facial-expression-recognition-challenge/. Accessed 18 Oct 2019
20. ACS-Woodbury Github Repository. https://github.com/ACS-Woodbury/WISIWYG.git. Accessed 19 Oct 2019
21. Parkhi, O.M., Vedaldi, A., Zisserman, A.: Deep face recognition. In: British Machine Vision Conference (2015). http://www.robots.ox.ac.uk/~vgg/publications/2015/Parkhi15/parkhi15. pdf
22. Large Scale Visual Recognition Challenge 2014. http://image-net.org/challenges/LSVRC/ 2014/. Accessed 18 Oct 2019
23. IMDB-WIKI Dataset - 500 k+ face images with age and gender labels. https://data.vision.ee. ethz.ch/cvl/rrothe/imdb-wiki/. Accessed 10 Aug 2019
24. Apparent Age and Gender Prediction in Keras. https://sefiks.com/2019/02/13/apparent-age-and-gender-prediction-in-keras/
25. Connor, A.M., Sosa, R.: The A-Z of creative technologies. EAI Endorsed Trans. Creative Technol. **5**, 1–2 (2018)

Games, Gamification and Accessible Games

Games, Gamification and Accessible Games

Anthony L. Brooks[1](✉) and Eva Brooks[2]

[1] CREATE/Department of Architecture, Design and Media Technology/Technical Faculty of IT and Design, Aalborg University, Rendsburggade 14, 9000 Aalborg, Denmark
tb@create.aau.dk

[2] XLab: Design, Learning and Innovation, Department of Culture and Learning, Aalborg University, Kroghstræde 3, 9220 Aalborg, Denmark

Abstract. Games as entertainment, leisure, recreational, serious or otherwise where game-based designs of use such as gamification are discussed alongside access and inclusion for all to be able to enjoy and play and have fun. In-built to games are mechanics and motivational factors that are both intrinsic and extrinsic. Such factors can be influential to impact human emotions in playing a game and reaching a state of 'Flow' (Csikszentmihalyi 1990) where immersion is total. Potentials of game-based intervention across industries is being explored with good effect as is evident in this contribution.

Keywords: Games · Inclusion · Experiences · Music · Gamification · Design · ASD

1 Introduction

1.1 Scope

The third section of this volume is themed - "Games, Gamification and Accessible Games" - to give focus upon the game phenomenon and related educations and industries that relates across research topics associated to arts and technology, interactivity, and game creation perspectives.

The first contribution in this third section informs on game-system design challenges involved when targeting patients' having suffered heart failure and their self-management. The second contribution shares how a workshop gave valuable insights and ideas to potential exergaming concepts to promote increased motivation and adherence in rehabilitation. Sustainable inclusive game design processes are subject of the third contribution in this section by authors from Sweden. The fourth contribution focuses on educating children diagnosed with Autism Spectrum Disorder (ASD) street-crossing skills using a Virtual Reality game. The next contribution reflects upon a dangerous gamification activity that spreads on social media to target vulnerable teenagers. MOOCs (massive open online courses) are subject of the following contribution from a Danish team in questioning motivation and achievement aligned with badge reward culture. The next contribution focuses upon a gamification approach to recycling. In the next

A. Brooks and E. I. Brooks (Eds.): ArtsIT 2019/DLI 2019, LNICST 328, pp. 363–369, 2020.
https://doi.org/10.1007/978-3-030-53294-9_24

contribution a board game – that is a described as a dialogical tool for museum professionals, researchers, exhibition designers and developers – is detailed. The following contribution informs how game developers could benefit from exploring requirements engineering process methods in their own practises. The penultimate contribution in this section focuses upon a serious game to raise awareness of intimate partner violence among adolescents in the United Kingdom targeting effective behavioural change. The final contribution in this third section informs on a Bulgarian research on the gamification of education'.

The following text snippets elaborate directly from each contribution to further assist readership.

2   Challenges for Designing Adaptive Gamification in Telerehabilitation Systems for Heart Failure Patients' Self-management

(Christense et al. 2020)

A Co-authors, again from Aalborg University, Denmark and namely Bianca Clavio Christensen, Hendrik Knoche, and Birthe Dinesen share their research of "Challenges for designing adaptive gamification in telerehabilitation systems for heart failure patients' self-management".

The content of this contribution focuses upon how a conventional patient education model for heart failure patients assumes that increasing knowledge leads to self-management behaviour changes, however this study posits how patients need motivation for changing their behaviour. In this work, telerehabilitation technologies are posited that can provide a digital toolbox for engaging in self-management.

The text informs how by adding gamification on top may increase motivation to improve the experience of the telerehabilitation.

An analysis is presented on how adaptive gamification can promote long-term motivation in a telerehabilitation program. Further, the contribution discusses design opportunities and challenges within an adaptive approach considering education of heart failure patients in their self-management.

3   Co-creating Virtual Reality Applications for Motor Rehabilitation with Physiotherapists

(Høeg et al. 2020)

Co-authors of the research titled "Co-creating Virtual Reality Applications for Motor Rehabilitation with Physiotherapists" are Emil Rosenlund Høeg, Begüm Becermen, Jon Ram Bruun-Pedersen, and Stefania Serafin who are based in different laboratories under Aalborg University in Copenhagen, Denmark. The content describes the structure and outcome of a workshop organized to co-create conceptual gamified motor rehabilitation experiences based on virtual reality and exercise bikes for older adults. Five physiotherapists from two different healthcare facilities, participated in the workshop and contributed to valuable insights and ideas to potential exergaming concepts that could be integrated at the facilities to promote more motivation and adherence in the rehabilitation process. Notably was that, at the collocated event ArtsIT/DLI in November 2019 that is behind this book, author Høeg won best paper award for his text 'The Reality of Implementing Virtual Reality: A Case Study on the Challenges of Integrating VR-Based Rehabilitation' and this presented elsewhere in this book.

4   Towards Sustainable Inclusive Game Design Processes

(Westin et al. 2020)

A Swedish trio of researchers co-authored the contribution titled "Towards Sustainable Inclusive Game Design Processes" – namely Thomas Westin from Stockholm University, alongside Henrik Engström and Jenny Brusk from University of Skövde. Westin organized and led the 'Inclusive Game' track at ArtsIT international conference where this paper was presented. The content presents identifying a gap between game research and the game industry whereby inclusive design by involving both the game industry and disabled people was established rather than from behind the 'ivory walls' of academia. Further identification, through four workshops involving the game industry and game studios, disabled people and authorities, was of four activities that constitute the biggest obstacles to realizing sustainable design processes for inclusive game design (IGD). The four activities were identified as (need to) 1) Find opportunities for IGD with disabled people; 2) Handle integrity and security of disabled people; 3) Recruit the right competence among disabled people; and 4) Adapt workplaces and tools for IGD processes. The authors posit their goal of promoting discussions and further development to achieve sustainable inclusive game design.

5   Co-designing a Head-Mounted Display Based Virtual Reality Game to Teach Street-Crossing Skills to Children Diagnosed with Autism Spectrum Disorder

(Adjorlu and Serafin 2020)

The contribution "Co-Designing a Head-Mounted Display Based Virtual Reality Game to Teach Street-Crossing Skills to Children Diagnosed with Autism Spectrum Disorder" was focused in Dr Ali Adjorlu's PhD defence in spring 2020 during Covid-19 lockdown – so remotely hosted from Copenhagen with main opponent Professor Skip Rizzo beaming in from Los Angeles. Co-authored with Professor Stefania Serafin the contribution – as suggested by the title – informs of research using a bespoke head-mounted display based virtual reality game developed to teach street-crossing skills to children and adolescents diagnosed with Autism Spectrum Disorder (ASD). Partnering was with teachers from the ASD school.

6   The Deadly Gamification Challenge of #BlueWhale

(Ozturkcan 2020)

Author Selcen Ozturkcan from Linnaeus University, Kalmar, Sweden contributes with a reflection on a dangerous gamification activity that spreads on social media to target vulnerable teenagers. The text is titled "The Deadly Gamification Challenge of #BlueWhale"[1]. The author is an Associate Professor of Business Administration specialized in marketing whilst also being a Network Professor at the School of Management of Sabancı University in Turkey. Associated is how the fourth international conference of ArtsIT was admirably hosted in 2014 by Sabancı University in Instanbul with an organizing committee consisting of Dr Elif Ayiter, Dr Onur Yazıcıgil, and artist, curator and educator Ekmel Ertan who is founder and artistic director of the Istanbul based Amber Platform - a research and production platform on art and new technologies.

7   Stars, Crests and Medals: Visual Badge Design Framework to Gamify and Certify Online Learning

(Hougaard and Knoche 2020)

In this research Hougaard and Knoche inform on massive open online courses (MOOCs) and how 'Open Badges' – as an emerging movement to recognise non-formal and informal learning - is considered an open standard that allow MOOCs to create digital course diplomas.

The contribution introduces how badges are applied to gamify education and act as a statement of achievement to reward learners as they reach goals and sub-goals in learning. Also presented is how existing badge frameworks offer conceptual design guidelines but does not provide granular support to the visual badge design process.

The authors share their work-in-progress case study that aims to design badges targeted MOOCs for the creative industry. Reported in the material are the differences between gamification badges used internally in MOOCs and certification badges used by learners as genuine evidence of skill acquisition to employers. A visual breakdown of badge characteristics that can be used in conjunction with existing conceptual badge design frameworks is also shared.

8   Make Waste Fun Again! A Gamification Approach to Recycling

(Helmefalk and Rosenlund 2020)

Miralem Helmefalk with co-author Joacim Rosenlund focused their research on the important topic of sustainability through their contribution titled "Make waste fun again! A gamification approach to recycling".

Anyone who has separated their trash realises how much plastic is present in contemporary consumption activities by humans. This contribution reports on how mechanisms

---

[1] This paper can be found in the backmatter of the book as short paper due to Springer ruling on length of full paper.

of gamification can be used to motivate and engage people to recycle. The research high-lights how a gamification design was implemented digitally to bridge the gap between behaviour and knowledge to influence positive recycling behaviour associated to waste management.

A truly impactful and thought-provoking contribution to the field – not to be wasted or turn one's nose up to!

9 Our Museum Game: A Collaborative Game for User-Centered Exhibition Design

(Madsen and Krishnasamy 2020)

A '11th hour' appearance (shared with a smile) at the ArtsIT event saw Kristina Maria Madsen and Rameshnath Krishnasamy present their research 'Our Museum', which is a board game described as a dialogical tool for museum professionals, researchers, exhibi-tion designers and developers, which was designed and developed through a coordinated effort between museum professionals and researchers.

The game itself is introduced alongside the theoretical design background that reflects iterations based upon insights from two separate playtests.

An aim of this work was to offer a tool-supported method to tackle user-centered challenges in the exhibition space, by bringing different roles together and providing a medium to form a shared language as a part of the design process of creating exhibitions. The authors posit how the work may be interesting to both practitioners as well as researchers working within the museum context and to an extent within the fields of games and gamification.

10 Adoption of Requirements Engineering Methods in Game Development: A Literature and Post-mortem Analysis

(Lehtonen et al. 2020)

This research by a Finish-based contingent representing Tampere University – these co-authors being namely Miikka Lehtonen, Chien Lu, Timo Nummenmaa, and Jaakko Peltonen. The contribution presents how game developers could benefit from exploring requirements engineering process methods in their own practises. Related discussions that revolve around shared post-mortems from game developers on the factors that con-tributed to or hindered successful outcomes of projects. A discerning study all game-developers are promoted to have awareness of: Finish insightfulness highlighted for all associated to benefit!

11   Designing a Serious Game to Raise Awareness of Intimate Partner Violence Among Adolescents in the UK: The Use of 'Good Games' Principles for Effective Behavioural Change

(Pearson et al. 2020)

The lengthily titled contribution "Designing a Serious Game to Raise Awareness of Intimate Partner Violence among Adolescents in the UK: The Use of 'Good Games' Principles for Effective Behavioural Change" is from the 'None in Three Centre' (Ni3) from Huddersfield University wherein pioneering new ways to tackle gender-based violence (GBV) across the globe is targeted. Notably, Ni3's aims are to: Investigate gender-based violence (GBV) in the study countries (India, Jamaica, Uganda and the UK); Develop serious prosocial computer games to change attitudes and behaviours relating to GBV; Evaluate the games' effectiveness as an educational intervention to prevent GBV; Develop a policy hub to inform and guide actions at the strategic and operational levels across the four countries; Underpin and reinforce social and behavioural change. The Ni3 was well represented at the ArtsIT event by its presenters from the co-authors who are John Pearson, Song Wu, Hayley Royston, Helen Smailes, Natasha Robinson, Adam Cowell and Adele Jones. This important subject matter that needs increased awareness globally is researching how the popularity of video games in modern society, as serious digital games, have the potential to promote prosocial thoughts and behaviours, as well as increase empathy and helping behaviour. However, as the research states – "to make a successful prosocial game a number of good game principles need to be met to make the game as immersive and engaging as possible"… and it is this that is central in how the material discusses how the design decisions and overall game framework used achieves such targeted awareness towards behavioural changes in regards intimate partner violence in the United Kingdom. An important issue worthy of attention of all readers to disseminate.

12   Personalization of Educational Video Games in APOGEE

(Terzieva et al. 2020)

Three Sofia-based Bulgarian academics are co-authors of the game-based learning (GBL) research titled "Personalization of Educational Video Games in APOGEE" – these are namely Valentina Terzieva, Elena Paunova-Hubenova and Boyan Bontchev. Perspectives on the phenomenon of 'gamification of education' which many would agree has great potentials and ramifications. In this research a focus was on exploring students' views about educational video games wherein findings revealed preferences about issues such as types of mini games, embraced learning content, and the willingness to repeat the game with the same or increased complexity to improve the overall results or acquired knowledge. The material informs of the VARK family (Visual, Aural, Read/Write, and Kinaesthetic) model of learning styles alongside the ADOPTA playing styles family (consisting of competitor, dreamer, logician, and strategist) that was assessed as appropriate to adapt in-game interactions within the student-focused APOGEE personalization framework. A maze game fitting different learning and playing styles of a user was catalyst to both presentation and contribution in this book in informing how GBL has undoubted benefits, as most students perceive the learning material as tedious, while educational games offer enjoyable and effortless learning. Personalized games meet better the needs of students and are more effective in teaching. The research is ongoing…

Epilogue and Acknowledgements. This third section introduces eleven contributions by extracting from each paper. It does so to promote readership of each full paper that are presented in the following chapters. In doing so the authors of this chapter acknowledge the contribution to this section/volume by each author whose original work was presented in the ArtsIT/DLI events in Aalborg, Denmark November 7–8, 2019.

References

Adjorlu, A., Serafin, S.: Co-designing a head-mounted display based virtual reality game to teach street-crossing skills to children diagnosed with autism spectrum disorder. In: Brooks, A., Brooks, E. (eds.) ArtsIT 2019/DLI 2019, LNICST 328, pp. 397–405. Springer, Cham (2020)

Christensen, B., Knoche, H., Dinesen, B.: Challenges for designing adaptive gamification in telerehabilitation systems for heart failure patients' self-management. In: Brooks, A., Brooks, E. (eds.) ArtsIT 2019/DLI 2019, LNICST 328, pp. 370–378. Springer, Cham (2020)

Csikszentmihalyi, M.: Flow: The Psychology of Optimal Experience. Harper & Row, Manhattan (1990)

Helmefalk, M., Rosenlund, J.: Make waste fun again! A gamification approach to recycling. In: Brooks, A., Brooks, E. (eds.) ArtsIT 2019/DLI 2019, LNICST 328, pp. 415–426. Springer, Cham (2020)

Hougaard, B.I., Knoche, H.: Stars, crests and medals: visual badge design framework to gamify and certify online learning. In: Brooks, A., Brooks, E. (eds.) ArtsIT 2019/DLI 2019, LNICST 328, pp. 406–414. Springer, Cham (2020)

Høeg, E.R., Becermen, B., Bruun-Pedersen, J.R., Serafin, S.: Co-creating virtual reality applications for motor rehabilitation with physiotherapists. In: Brooks, A., Brooks, E. (eds.) ArtsIT 2019/DLI 2019, LNICST 328, pp. 379–389. Springer, Cham (2020)

Lehtonen, M., Lu, C., Nummenmaa, T., Peltonen, J.: Adoption of requirements engineering methods in game development: a literature and post-mortem analysis. In: Brooks, A., Brooks, E. (eds.) ArtsIT 2019/DLI 2019, LNICST 328, pp. 436–457. Springer, Cham (2020)

Madsen, K.M., Krishnasamy, R.: Our museum game: a collaborative game for user-centered exhibition design. In: Brooks, A., Brooks, E. (eds.) ArtsIT 2019/DLI 2019, LNICST 328, pp. 427–435. Springer, Cham (2020)

Ozturkcan, S.: The deadly gamification challenge of #BlueWhale. In: Brooks, A., Brooks, E. (eds.) ArtsIT 2019/DLI 2019, LNICST 328, pp. 785–787. Springer, Cham (2020)

Pearson, J., et al.: Designing a serious game to raise awareness of intimate partner violence among adolescents in the UK: the use of 'good games' principles for effective behavioural change. In: Brooks, A., Brooks, E. (eds.) ArtsIT 2019/DLI 2019, LNICST 328, pp. 458–476. Springer, Cham (2020)

Terzieva, V., Paunova-Hubenova, E., Bontchev, B.: Personalization of educational video games in APOGEE. In: Brooks, A., Brooks, E. (eds.) ArtsIT 2019/DLI 2019, LNICST 328, pp. 477–487. Springer, Cham (2020)

Westin, T., Engström, H., Brusk, J.: Towards sustainable inclusive game design processes. In: Brooks, A., Brooks, E. (eds.) ArtsIT 2019/DLI 2019, LNICST 328, pp. 390–396. Springer, Cham (2020)

Challenges for Designing Adaptive Gamification in Telerehabilitation Systems for Heart Failure Patients' Self-management

Bianca Clavio Christensen[✉], Hendrik Knoche, and Birthe Dinesen

Aalborg University, Aalborg, Denmark
{bcch,bid}@hst.aau.dk, hk@create.aau.dk

Abstract. The conventional patient education model for heart failure patients assumes that increasing knowledge leads to self-management behaviour changes, but patients need motivation for changing their behaviour. Telerehabilitation technologies can provide a digital toolbox for engaging in self-management, and adding gamification on top may increase motivation to improve the telerehabilitation experience. This paper analyses how adaptive gamification can promote long-term motivation in a telerehabilitation program and discusses design opportunities and challenges within an adaptive approach within patient education of heart failure patients.

Keywords: Telerehabilitation · Patient education · Self-management · Long-term motivation · Heart failure patients · Adaptive gamification

1 Introduction

Heart failure (HF) is a chronic illness and is a worldwide problem with more than 26 million patients [1], and the prevalence of HF is rising. The European Society of Cardiology recommends training patients in self-care skills to manage a worsening in condition, avoid rehospitalisation, and improve lifestyle [2]. The conventional patient education for HF patients provides knowledge in and recommendation for self-management, e.g. to exercise more, make diet changes, take their prescribed heart medicine, weigh themselves daily, and when to contact their provider. This knowledge is no guarantee for an improved lifestyle nor adherence behaviour, e.g. patients knew to limit their salt intake but few patients avoided salty foods [3]. Low motivation is one barrier in HF patient education [4], e.g. for attaining knowledge on self-management, and ultimately, learning self-management behaviours. Strategies to overcome low motivation can be to tailor education to the patient's situation or to give a holistic view on patient education and not only teach about heart failure [4]. Remote rehabilitation (i.e. telerehabilitation) represents one approach to extend the conventional patient education. With telerehabilitation technologies, the rehabilitation activities can be targeted to the patient's lifestyle and self-management needs by using information and communication technologies [5].

A. Brooks and E. I. Brooks (Eds.): ArtsIT 2019/DLI 2019, LNICST 328, pp. 370–378, 2020.
https://doi.org/10.1007/978-3-030-53294-9_25

Gamification principles can complement this low motivation to improve adoption of self-management behaviours. Using games and gamification as tools for intrinsic motivation (i.e. the drive to act without an external reward) and extrinsic motivation (i.e. the drive to act by external rewards) has been widely used in context of health [6] and education [7, 8]. We consider gamification as a tool for motivating HF patients, who have complex needs and problems, such as depression, cognitive impairment, and effects from co-morbidities [2]. In such complex settings, we believe that gamification has to be adaptive i.e. tailored to the specific characteristic of different users and contexts [9].

The research project, Future Patient, trialed a telerehabilitation program using a web portal for HF patients (called HeartPortal) [10]. As a continuation of Future Patient, we will study gamification for increasing learning and motivation for self-management through development of an improved HeartPortal. In this paper, we present a scoping review that analyses the opportunities and challenges for designing adaptive gamification to increase learning and motivation for self-management in telerehabilitation systems for HF patients. Besides, our analysis may contribute to the gamification development in other telerehabilitation contexts and for other patient groups.

2 Future Patient Research Project

The HeartPortal was developed for self-management of HF patients as a part of the Future Patient telerehabilitation program [10]. The HeartPortal was developed through user-driven innovation (an example of participatory design [11]) with HF patients, relatives, health professionals, scientists, and private companies [12, 13]. The telerehabilitation program followed three steps over a year: (i) drug titration for adjusting the medicine dosis, (ii) rehabilitation at a healthcare centre, and (iii) daily living after rehabilitation. In the program, the HF patients used self-tracking devices (i.e. blood pressure measurement, transmitter, weight scale, sleep sensor, and activity/step tracker) and an iPad for using the HeartPortal. The patients used the toolbox for (a) educational material of heart failure; (b) contact to health professionals; (c) monitoring own data from said self-tracking devices; (d) developing rehabilitation plan and set personal goals; and (e) monitoring self-reports on Patient Reported Outcomes. The toolbox was designed to be used in a cross-sectoral context, as shown in Fig. 1, in which the health professionals monitored the patient data.

Currently, we have no knowledge of what was motivating in the HeartPortal. However, we observed that the intended and actual use of the portal not always matched, e.g. even though a nurse prompted a patient to set personal goals in the portal, the patient would not use these goals for their self-management but were instead forgotten. In this example, the patient might have lacked motivation and education in self-management to develop and follow up on their personal goals. Thus, the next iteration of HeartPortal should improve how the educational material is presented and tailor it to the patients' learning and motivation needs.

Self-management technology may not be motivating enough on its own. Spindler et al. [14] studied the long-term motivation in a telerehabilitation system similar to the HeartPortal and found little motivational change in patients with cardiovascular diseases during 12 months of testing. Whereas Dithmer et al. [15] tested a gamified self-management app for patients with cardiovascular diseases (n = 10), and the patients

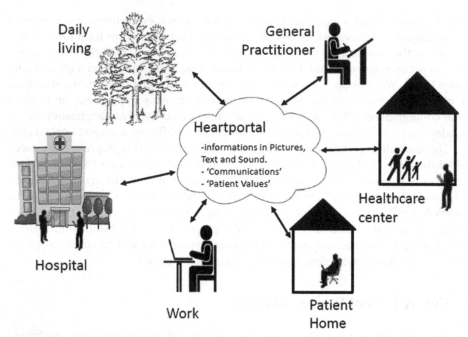

Fig. 1. The cross-sectoral context connected to the digital toolbox, heartPortal, in the telereha-bilitation program for HF patients [16].

reported feeling motivated to improve their self-management behaviours through leader-boards and daily challenges after testing the app in two weeks. The leaderboard scores represented the accomplished self-management activities, e.g. calculating own BMI or walking with the spouse/partner. Thus, leaderboard promoted competition and cooper-ation; however, the motivational outcome in long-term is unknown, and future studies need to research long-term motivation in gamification system in a telerehabilitation context.

3 Background

Gamification is widely known for using game-design elements and game principles in non-game contexts [17]. Kumar proposed a framework [18] in which all gamification elements can be categorized as (i) behaviour elements with a focus on human behaviours and intrinsic motives, (ii) progression elements to structure and stretch the accumulation of meaning skills, and (iii) feedback elements to provide feedback on the learning activity. Kotini and Tzelepi adapted this framework in an educational context [19] and presented examples around behaviour, progression and feedback, providing a structure for teachers to understand the learning needs for implementing gamification in a classroom. Likewise, we have analysed known challenges in HF patient education from the literature and mapped them to Kumar's categories (see Table 1).

The large difference between HF patients' needs for treatment over time is a promi-nent challenge in Table 1. Therefore, the gamification solution should be grounded in

Table 1. Mapping challenges in HF to Kumar's categories of gamification elements [18].

Kumar's categories	Challenges in HF patient education
Behavior	In patient education, a continuous assessment of the patient's previous knowledge, misconceptions, learning abilities, learning styles, cognition, attitudes and motivation provides a foundation of further education [4]. Additionally, the patient's resources, barriers and learning needs should be addressed
Progression	Structuring progression is problematic for patient education of HF patients. Most patients need repeated education due to cognitive overload of a large amount of information and due to changes in patient education and treatment over time [4]
Feedback	The patients receive feedback from the health professionals in medical check-ups, but this is rarely personalized. The healthcare system is forced into 'one size fits all' HF treatments, in contrast to personalised care, treatment, and prevention, as presented in a global research agenda for future telehealth [20]

adapting or personalising the treatment, to fit the patient's needs as well as the required procedure for patient education in the healthcare system. To understand how such a gamification solution can work and be designed, in the following section, we analysed approaches within adaptive gamification with long-term motivation prospects.

3.1 Adaptive Gamification

Adaptive gamification can enhance traditional gamification approaches with user-centred, personalized and adaptive mechanisms, tailored to a specific characteristic of different users and contexts [9]. Previous studies have used reinforcement strategies to design adaptive gamification models for long-term motivation in e-learning environments [21] and for regulating drivers' behaviour for saving fuel [22]. To work around the problem of overjustification (i.e. rewards having a negative influence on long-term motivation and intrinsic motivation), a reward-based reinforcement model for e-learning environments consisted of a reward model with badges to rapidly increase engagement and an intermittent reinforcement model calculated by the learner's existing status for diminishing rewards and strengthen intrinsic motivation over time [21]. However, the effectiveness of it and its parameters is unknown and needs a long-term experiment to verify and optimize model [21]. Another model regulated fuel consumption in cars through adaptive feedback [22]. The system evaluated the driving style in terms of energy efficiency and assigned a score to each user listed on a leaderboard of other eco-drivers. The results showed a reduction in fuel consumption compared to a system only showing eco-driving tips, and the users maintained interest in complying with the gamification rules over the testing period of three months [22]. In this way, adaptive gamification can address the progression and feedback challenges in Table 1, while maintaining interest in the gamification activity.

Ideas and elements from adaptive educational environments can be transferred to adaptive gamification [9]. Shute and Zapata-Rivera [23] presented an adaptive educational model with a four-process adaption cycle (incl. capture, analyse, select, present). An adaptive system in this cycle *captures* information about the learner as the learner interacts with the environment; *analyses* learner knowledge, skills and performance in the learning domain; *selects* information (i.e. how and when to intervene) according to current status in the learning model and the purpose of the system; and *presents* specific content to the learner using technology to convey the information or intervention. The idea is that the cycle will continue until meeting the goals of the learning activity, but during this process, an adaptive system may need to accommodate to alternative types and levels of adaptation, e.g. when following a predefined path on the curriculum structure. However, the adaptive education cycle also faces major obstacles to successfully integrate adaptivity in learning environments, e.g. when developing a useful learner model and acquiring valid learner data. Transferring Shute and Zapata-Rivera's adaptive education cycle [23] to a telerehabilitation gamification system can fit well with the presented challenges in Table 1, in terms of adapting to the patient's needs and goals and provide personal or tailored feedback.

4 Discussion of Design Challenges

As a continuation of the patient education challenges in Table 1 (categorized as behaviour, feedback, and progress), we present three design challenges for an adaptive gamification system for telerehabilitation. The design considerations and challenges (labelled with C) are related to different aspects in a design process, including context and stakeholder requirements, feedback system design, and theory-based design.

C1: Identify Requirements in the Telerehabilitation Context for Patient Education
Understanding the contextual and stakeholder requirements should be investigated in gamification studies. Some gamification studies replaced or removed what was already works well for the user, as mentioned in [24], but instead studies should identify the contextual problems and how gamification can complement existing solutions or contexts for improving the implementation of the solution in the healthcare system. In context of HF self-management, patient education can occur at a hospital, healthcare centre, general practitioner, patient workplace, patient home, and in daily living. Thus, the learning context for telerehabilitation is cross-sectoral, as patient education and behavioural change should be situated in the learner's experiences across physical spaces and times, as defined in the Learner-Generated Contexts framework [25]. The stakeholders in this cross-sectoral context primarily include cardiologists, nurses, physicians, spouse/partner, colleagues, friends, and patient communities. Other stakeholders can be dieticians, pharmacists, social workers, psychologists, and physiotherapists. Although not all stakeholders are directly involved in patient education, they can have an impact on a patient's wellbeing.

The learning context becomes personal through constant adjustments to the environment, and learners gain control of the learning process [25]. Capturing the telerehabilitation context in terms of patient education includes gathering information on the patient's previous knowledge, misconceptions, learning abilities, learning styles, learning needs, barriers, and resources. This information can be structured in patient profiles, e.g. needs for health and wellbeing of a patient with chronic illness [26], HF personas for learning self-management [27], HF patient preferences on telerehabilitation technologies [28], and gamification learning styles [29]. Identifying the patient needs and profiles can be a starting point for what should be captured in an adaptive educational model, such as Shute and Zapata-Rivera's model [23], as the model should change based on such information.

C2: Analyse the Needs for Adaptive Gamification in the Telerehabilitation

The adaptive gamification should be based on the contextual and stakeholder requirements. Böckle et al. differentiate between partially/fully adaptive gamification approaches and adaptive environments that use non-adaptive gamification principles to support adaptive functionalities and adaptive gamification. An adaptive system can be designed to influence the patient's self-management behaviour, but not necessarily through adaptive gamification. In some cases or for some patient profiles, gamification might not be viable solution, which is why telerehabilitation technology often is offered to the patients as supplement to their current treatment.

An adaptive gamification system contains elements of feedback and progress which may lead to a behavior change. These elements should be related to the telerehabilitation goal. If the telerehabilitation goal is to jumpstart the patients in learning self-management behaviours, the reward-typed feedback can be designed to diminish over time for users to engage in intrinsic motivation, as suggested in the reward-based reinforcement model for e-learning environments [21]. While the feedback can be tailored to different patient profiles, it is likely that a patient changes behaviour over time, as an outcome of the intervention or outside effects, and thus, they may be categorised in a different profile.

C3: Select Learning and Motivation Strategies Based on the Telerehabilitation Context and Needs for Adaptive Gamification

- The adaptive gamification model for a self-management app can be grounded in Shute and Zapata-Rivera's adaptive education cycle [23] can be the foundation of the adaptive gamification system. With machine learning, the system can learn to capture, analyse, select and present information that is adaptive to a user.
- Self-determination theory can facilitate and maintain health behaviour change through intrinsic motivation [30]. Intrinsic or autonomous motivation is achieved when a patient experiences autonomy (i.e. choice), competency (i.e. skill mastery), and relatedness (i.e. social connectedness).
- Meaningful gamification can promote intrinsic motivation by using one or more of the following elements: play, exposition, choice, information, engagement, and reflection [31].
- The concept PERMA (i.e. positive emotion, relationships, meaning, and accomplishment) originates from the self-help discipline [32], and Dithmer et al. used this psychological theory to design gamification in a telerehabilitation system [15].

5 Conclusion

This paper identified challenges for designing adaptive gamification in the Future Patient telerehabilitation program. We categorized patient education challenges as behaviour, progression, and feedback and suggested that adaptive gamification and treatment can be used for improving patient education in the telerehabilitation program. For extending this work, our first design challenge is to identify the contextual and stakeholder requirements in the telerehabilitation context to locate patient learning needs. The second challenge is related to feedback as a gamification element and involves analysing the needs for adaptive gamification feedback in a telerehabilitation program. The last design challenge presented in this paper is to select learning and motivation strategies based on the telerehabilitation context and needs for adaptive feedback. For each challenge, this paper presents the main considerations for designing adaptive gamification in a telerehabilitation program and suggests to involve the stakeholders in the design process.

Acknowledgements. Thanks to Aage and Johanne Louis-Hansen Foundation, Aalborg University, and all partners in the Future Patient project. For more information about the Future Patient project, see http://www.labwellfaretech.com/fp/heartfailure/.

References

1. Ambrosy, A.P., Fonarow, G.C., Butler, J., et al.: The global health and economic burden of hospitalizations for heart failure: lessons learned from hospitalized heart failure registries. J. Am. Coll. Cardiol. **63**, 1123–1133 (2014). https://doi.org/10.1016/j.jacc.2013.11.053
2. Ponikowski, P., Voors, A.A., Anker, S.D., et al.: 2016 ESC Guidelines for the diagnosis and treatment of acute and chronic heart failure: the task force for the diagnosis and treatment of acute and chronic heart failure of the European society of cardiology (ESC). Developed with the special contribution of the heart failure association (HFA) of the ESC. Eur. J. Heart Fail. **18**, 891–975 (2016). https://doi.org/10.1002/ejhf.592
3. Ni, H., Nauman, D., Burgess, D., et al.: Factors influencing knowledge of and adherence to self-care among patients with heart failure. Arch. Intern. Med. **159**, 1613–1619 (1999). https://doi.org/10.1001/archinte.159.14.1613
4. Strömberg, A.: The crucial role of patient education in heart failure. Eur. J. Heart Fail. **7**, 363–369 (2005). https://doi.org/10.1016/j.ejheart.2005.01.002
5. Cranen, K., Groothuis-Oudshoorn, C.G., Vollenbroek-Hutten, M.M., IJzerman, M.J.: Toward patient-centered telerehabilitation design: understanding chronic pain patients' preferences for web-based exercise telerehabilitation using a discrete choice experiment. J. Med. Internet Res. **19**(1), e26 (2017). https://doi.org/10.2196/jmir.5951
6. Johnson, D., Deterding, S., Kuhn, K.-A., et al.: Gamification for health and wellbeing: a systematic review of the literature. Internet Interv. **6**, 89–106 (2016). https://doi.org/10.1016/j.invent.2016.10.002
7. Prensky, M.: Digital game-based learning. Comput. Entertain. **1**, 21 (2003). https://doi.org/10.1145/950566.950596
8. Kapp, K.M.: The Gamification of Learning and Instruction. Wiley, San Francisco (2012)
9. Böckle, M., Novak, J., Bick, M.: Towards adaptive gamification: a synthesis of current developments. Research Papers (2017)

10. Dinesen, B., Dittmann, L., Gade, J.D., et al.: Future patient telerehabilitation for patients with heart failure: protocol for a randomized controlled trial. JMIR Res. Protoc. **8**, e14517 (2019). https://doi.org/10.2196/14517

11. Kushniruk, A., Nøhr, C.: Participatory design, user involvement and health IT evaluation. Stud. Health Technol. Inf. **222**, 139–151 (2016)

12. Dinesen, B., Spindler, H., Leth, S., et al.: Development and pilot test of a telerehabilitation program for patients with heart failure: the future patient project. J. Int. Soc. Telemed. eHealth (2017)

13. Joensson, K., Melholt, C., Hansen, J., et al.: Listening to the patients: using participatory design in the development of a cardiac telerehabilitation web portal. mHealth 3 (2019). https://doi.org/10.21037/mhealth.2019.08.06

14. Spindler, H., Leerskov, K., et al.: Conventional rehabilitation therapy versus telerehabilitation in cardiac patients: a comparison of motivation, psychological distress, and quality of life. Int. J. Environ. Res. Public Health. **16**(3), 512 (2019). http://dx.doi.org.zorac.aub.aau.dk/10.3390/ijerph16030512

15. Dithmer, M., Rasmussen, J.O., Grönvall, E., et al.: The heart game: using gamification as part of a telerehabilitation program for heart patients. Game. Health J. **5**, 27–33 (2015). https://doi.org/10.1089/g4h.2015.0001

16. Jønsson, K., Melholt, C., Hansen, J., et al.: Listening to the patients: using participatory design in the development of a cardiac telerehabilitation web portal (2017)

17. Deterding, S., Dixon, D., Khaled, R., Nacke, L.: From game design elements to gamefulness: defining gamification. In: Proceedings of the 15th International Academic MindTrek Conference: Envisioning Future Media Environments, pp. 9–15. ACM, New York (2011)

18. Kumar, N.: A framework for designing gamification in the enterprise. Infosys Labs Brief. **11**, 8–13 (2013)

19. Kotini, I., Tzelepi, S.: A gamification-based framework for developing learning activities of computational thinking. In: Reiners, T., Wood, L.C. (eds.) Gamification in Education and Business, pp. 219–252. Springer, Cham (2015). https://doi.org/10.1007/978-3-319-10208-5_12

20. Dinesen, B., Nonnecke, B., Lindeman, D., et al.: Personalized telehealth in the future: a global research agenda. J. Med. Internet Res. **18**(3), e53 (2016). https://doi.org/10.2196/jmir.5257

21. Luo, S., Yang, H., Meinel, C.: Reward-based intermittent reinforcement in gamification for e-learning. In: CSEDU, pp. 177–184 (2015)

22. Magana, V.C., Munoz-Organero, M.: GAFU: using a gamification tool to save fuel. IEEE Intell. Transp. Syst. Mag. **7**, 58–70 (2015). https://doi.org/10.1109/MITS.2015.2408152

23. Shute, V.J., Zapata-Rivera, D.: Adaptive educational systems. Adapt. Technol. Train. Educ. **7**, 1–35 (2012)

24. Richards, C., Thompson, C.W., Graham, N.: Beyond designing for motivation: the importance of context in gamification. In: Proceedings of the First ACM SIGCHI Annual Symposium on Computer-Human Interaction in Play, pp. 217–226. ACM, New York (2014)

25. Luckin, R., Clark, W., Garnett, F., et al.: Learner-generated contexts: a framework to support the effective use of technology for learning. In: Web 20-Based E-Learning: Applying Social Informatics for Tertiary Teaching, pp. 70–84 (2011). https://doi.org/10.4018/978-1-60566-294-7.ch004

26. Bhattacharyya, O., Mossman, K., Gustafsson, L., Schneider, E.C.: Using human-centered design to build a digital health advisor for patients with complex needs: persona and prototype development. J. Med. Internet Res. **21**, e10318 (2019). https://doi.org/10.2196/10318

27. Holden, R.J., Joshi, P., Rao, K., et al.: modeling personas for older adults with heart failure. Proc. Hum. Factors Ergon. Soc. Ann. Meet. **62**, 1072–1076 (2018). https://doi.org/10.1177/1541931218621246

28. Albert, N.M., Dinesen, B., Spindler, H., et al.: Factors associated with telemonitoring use among patients with chronic heart failure. J. Telemed. Telecare **23**, 283–291 (2017). https://doi.org/10.1177/1357633X16630444
29. Buckley, P., Doyle, E.: Individualising gamification: an investigation of the impact of learning styles and personality traits on the efficacy of gamification using a prediction market. Comput. Educ. **106**, 43–55 (2017). https://doi.org/10.1016/j.compedu.2016.11.009
30. Ryan, R.M., Patrick, H.D., Deci, E.L., Williams, G.C.: Facilitating health behaviour change and its maintenance: interventions based on self-determination theory (2008)
31. Nicholson, S.: A recipe for meaningful gamification. In: Reiners, T., Wood, L.C. (eds.) Gamification in Education and Business, pp. 1–20. Springer, Cham (2015). https://doi.org/10.1007/978-3-319-10208-5_1
32. Jones, C., Scholes, L., Johnson, D., et al.: Gaming well: links between videogames and flourishing mental health. Front. Psychol. **5** (2014). https://doi.org/10.3389/fpsyg.2014.00260

Co-creating Virtual Reality Applications for Motor Rehabilitation with Physiotherapists

Emil Rosenlund Høeg[1]([envelope]) [iD], Begüm Becermen[2], Jon Ram Bruun-Pedersen[1] [iD], and Stefania Serafin[1] [iD]

[1] Multisensory Experience Lab, Department of Architecture, Design and Media Technology, Aalborg University Copenhagen, A.C. Meyers Vænge 15, Copenhagen, SV, Denmark
{erh,jpe,sts}@create.aau.dk
[2] Service Design Lab, Department of Architecture, Design and Media Technology, Aalborg University Copenhagen, A.C. Meyers Vænge 15, Copenhagen, SV, Denmark
beg@create.aau.dk

Abstract. This paper describes the structure and outcome of a workshop organized to co-create conceptual gamified motor rehabilitation experiences based on virtual reality and exercise bikes for older adults. Five physiotherapists from two different healthcare facilities, participated in the workshop and contributed to valuable insights and ideas to potential exergaming concepts that could be integrated at the facilities to promote more motivation and adherence in the rehabilitation process.

Keywords: Co-creation · Game-based rehabilitation · Physical therapy · Virtual reality

1 Introduction

Repetition is often considered a key component in most areas of motor rehabilitation. However, ironically these repetitive activities can cause patients to become amotivated and lead to non-adherence with the therapy programme. Therefore, game-based rehabilitation has been increasingly popular as a method for instilling motivation and engagement, as well as provide distraction [14,16]. Although virtual reality (VR) has only just recently entered the public consciousness, mainly due to affordable prices, studies have investigated how the technology can facilitate higher rehabilitation efficacy, outcomes, and motivation since the late 1990s [13]. Likewise, patient participation and user-centered design is becoming increasingly popular for developing healthcare-technology solutions. However, implementation of new technologies into existing contexts and cultures can be challenging. A recent review on VR-based rehabilitation [13] note that current research and development within the field is usually more reactive than proactive, and that involving inter-professional teams throughout the process will likely strengthen the impact of the technology.

A. Brooks and E. I. Brooks (Eds.): ArtsIT 2019/DLI 2019, LNICST 328, pp. 379–389, 2020.
https://doi.org/10.1007/978-3-030-53294-9_26

1.1 The Context of the Study

The context of this study is centered around an ongoing PhD-project on VR-based rehabilitation in the danish municipality of Frederiksberg. The project aims to investigate how VR, mostly in the context of motor rehabilitation, can increase motivation, adherence and training intensity through immersive exertion games (exergames). The current VR equipment augments existing exercise bikes to function as physical steering props which, through sensor technology, transfer pedal cadence to forward movement through virtual environments (VEs). The VR-technology has been implemented in two municipality healthcare facilities since 2016, consisting of an inpatient care unit offering rehabilitation treatment during admission, and a health center offering outpatient ambulatory rehabilitation. In this paper we explore new future game concepts for older adults, ideated through a participatory co-creation workshop held together with physiotherapists from both healthcare facilities. The workshop followed several months of observations of rehabilitation sessions, as well as interviews with both patients, physiotherapists and occupational therapists. Among the main findings was a recurrent desire to share the virtual experiences with someone else. Therefore, the workshop also served the purpose of verifying existing assumptions about the need for social VR experiences; highlight potential differences between the healthcare facilities, and whether identical solutions will work for both; figure out if there are core problems that can be addressed by a VR-experience; onboarding of physiotherapists by including them in the decision process, and to create improved interest in VR as a treatment tool, as well as a sense of ownership of the project.

1.2 The Social Aspects of Rehabilitation

Socialization and social interaction is, according to a major study on online gaming communities performed by [22], described as a primary motivational factor for users of online games. Furthermore, the feeling of relatedness is described as a fundamental human need according to the self-determination theory (SDT) [20]. In recent literature, three distinct aspects have emerged in relation to social interaction i.e. social competition, social feedback and -presence [16]. Competition refers to direct or indirect comparing the skills of two or more players, feedback is receiving positive written or verbal feedback from co-players, and social presence is the mere act of sharing a virtual space without the necessity of direct social interaction [16]. Research into the effects of social presence and shared experiences as a motivational factor on rehabilitation is very limited [8,9,17]. However, the addition of social interaction is promising, e.g. [1] showed an increase in exercise-effort in older adults when exercises were augmented with social facilitation through a competitive VR-experience, while Goršič et al., demonstrated through several studies that both collaboration and competition has the capacity to increase physical performance and motivation in rehabilitation regimens [8,9]. Moreover, a new article published in the British Medical Journal (BMJ) reported large improvements in performance and motivation for for participants exposed to verbal encouragement [5].

1.3   Exergames in Rehabilitation

Exertion games (exergames) have proven to help with motivation to exercise, and has previously been applied in many contexts of rehabilitation. Primarily due to the ability to combine repetitive physical activities with game-inspired design mechanics, which is known as gamification or serious games [11]. According to several systematic reviews, exergaming has successfully been utilized to improve patient motivation and adherence [12,15,18]. Specifically, it has been applied to motivate exercise adherence in nursing home residents [2]; increase muscle strength [15], and improve functional mobility and motivation [25].

1.4   Co-creation

Co-creation is a methodology under the participatory design paradigm which was originally conceived in Scandinavia in the 1970s [21]. In short it seeks to actively involve stakeholders in design processes to ensure that the generated solutions meet the needs of the end-user [21]. Furthermore, it is frequently applied to healthcare innovation healthcare contexts [7]. Co-creation combine creative thinking tools with group dynamics to achieve more robust understanding of problems and challenges through phenomenological approaches.

2   Workshop Facilitation and Results

The main purpose of the workshop was to engage the physiotherapist, to understand the users (in this case the patients), and the context they meet in both the inpatient and the outpatient facility. Specifically, physiotherapists were selected rather than patients, because they possess a more holistic view of what type of patients frequent the facilities, and are more knowledgeable about the challenges and barriers in the rehabilitation process. Furthermore, the intended outcome was to develop crude ideas for gamified rehabilitation VR concepts, which the therapists thought might appeal to the patients and potentially solve situations of amotivation. This level of abstraction required to devise such ideated game concepts, was deemed higher than what most patients in the facilities were able to deliver.

2.1   Structure of the Workshop

The workshop was held the 7th of December, 2018 between 10 AM to 2 PM. The structure was inspired by the double diamond design model; a four-phase design process, with two overall phases: 1) The problem phase, and 2) the solution-phase [4]. With each phase divided into two sub-phases (see Fig. 1). The two phases in the model represent a process initially exploring an issue in depth (divergent thinking), and a subsequent phase with a higher focus on concrete solutions and focused action (convergent thinking) [4], which was deemed ideal for the purpose of scoping contextual problems related to therapy itself as well as coming up with potential solutions within a short time frame.

In the problem phase, the two sub-phases are 'discover' and 'define'. The discover sub-phase seeks to understand the users (i.e. the patients), and the context in which they will use the VR-technology. During the workshop, the participating physiotherapists applied empathy maps and pain-gain maps to the personas they created, in relation to the facility they belonged to. In the define sub-phase, a plenary discussion took place, based on the exercises and presentations of personas, in which the outcome of the exercises were discussed. Furthermore, the discussion facilitated convergence of problems and challenges. In the solution phase, the sub-phases are 'develop' and 'deliver'. In 'develop', the aim was to create new conceptual ideas for VR-application, which could help motivate patients in a facility-relevant rehabilitation context. This was achieved through a so-called 'brainwriting' session, which will be presented subsequently. In 'deliver', which is the final (sub)phase, focus was on presentation, discussion and evaluation of the proposed ideas, undertaken in plenary discussions, selecting only one of the generated ideas, to bring into a prototyping phase.

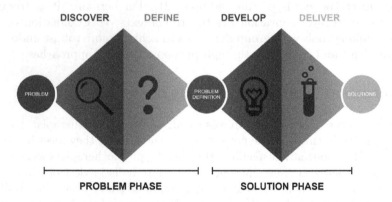

Fig. 1. The workshop was arranged to follow the double diamond design model with two main phases four sub-phases (figure adapted from the British design council [4]).

2.2   Presentation and Demonstration of VR

A physiotherapist working with VR in his own clinic was invited to present why and how he used it clinical treatment. The purpose was to introduce a facilitator from inside the field of physiotherapy rather than an outsider, because we estimate that people are more inclined to listen to people from inside their own fields. The presentation ended with a demo of the VR-tool, which also enabled the workshop participants to experience VR first hand.

2.3   Personas, Empathy Mapping and Pains and Gains

For the problem phase the participants, divided into the two facilities, were asked to create a persona for the workshop based on their average patient. They were instructed to give their persona a name and assign gender, age and a diagnosis. Subsequently, they were instructed to discuss and fill out an empathy map (EM) for their chosen persona. The empathy map is a tool to better understand the user, and how that person thinks, feels and responds in certain situations. There has been some criticism regarding the empirical validity of personas and empathy mapping, due to the inability to represent a broader spectrum of a population, and the lack of verification for whether or not it appropriately represents the population being examined [3]. However, it is a widely popular tool in service design, user experience (UX) design and workshop facilitation tools because it provides a more visual and relatable way to design for the end-user [6,10], and has previously been used in healthcare, including design processes for children with cerebral palsy [26] (Fig. 2).

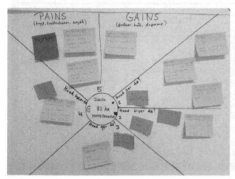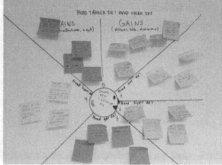

(a) Empathy map for the inpatient care unit

(b) Empathy map for outpatient health center

Fig. 2. Empathy maps (EM) produced by physiotherapists from the two facilities.

For the EM in this study we used four different aspects, as proposed by [10], and related to the persona's behavior and thoughts in the context of the facilities: 1) *What do the see?*, 2) *What do the say?*, 3) *What do they do?* and 4) *What do they hear?*. Subsequently, the participants were asked to write down conjectures on the patient's pains & gains based on the previous four aspects of the EM. *Pains* is to be understood as what the patients are hoping to avoid. What are their fears, frustrations, obstacles and challenges in the rehabilitation context. While *gains* refers to what patients are hoping to achieve, but also what are their hopes, wishes, dreams, needs and measures of success (Fig. 3).

2.4   Brainwriting

As opposed to brainstorming, brainwriting is a silent exercise meant to create several ideas in a short period of time, and to assure that the verbal contributions of the more introvert participants are also brought forth. It was invented by a German marketing professional called Bernd Rohrbach, as a innovation process

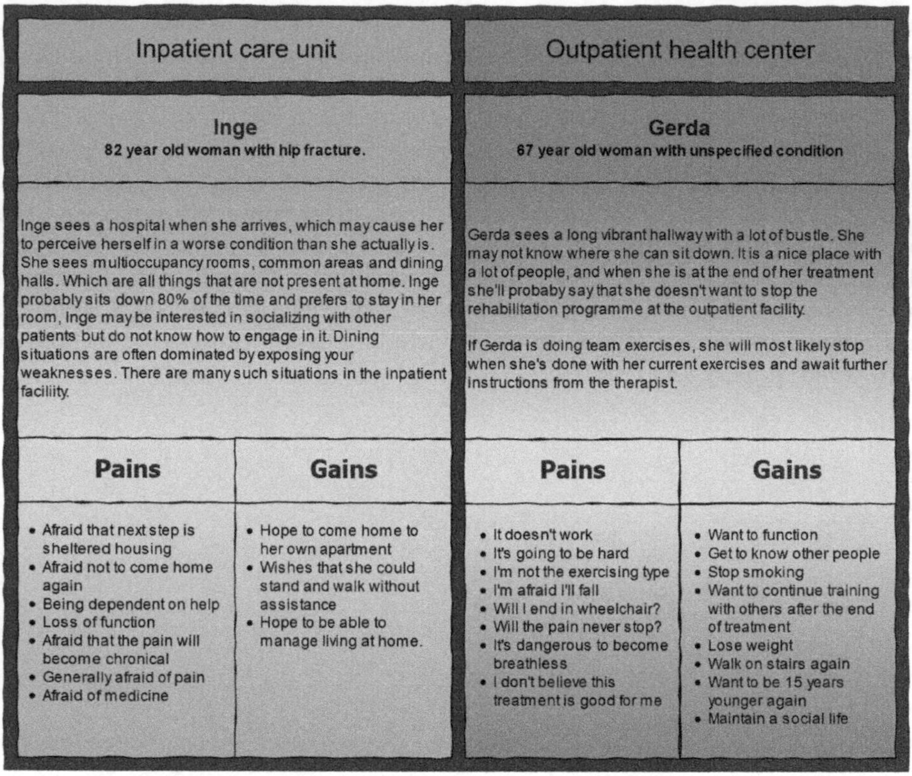

Inpatient care unit		Outpatient health center	
Inge 82 year old woman with hip fracture.		**Gerda** 67 year old woman with unspecified condition	
Inge sees a hospital when she arrives, which may cause her to perceive herself in a worse condition than she actually is. She sees multioccupancy rooms, common areas and dining halls. Which are all things that are not present at home. Inge probably sits down 80% of the time and prefers to stay in her room. Inge may be interested in socializing with other patients but do not know how to engage in it. Dining situations are often dominated by exposing your weaknesses. There are many such situations in the inpatient facility.		Gerda sees a long vibrant hallway with a lot of bustle. She may not know where she can sit down. It is a nice place with a lot of people, and when she is at the end of her treatment she'll probaby say that she doesn't want to stop the rehabilitation programme at the outpatient facility. If Gerda is doing team exercises, she will most likely stop when she's done with her current exercises and await further instructions from the therapist.	
Pains	**Gains**	**Pains**	**Gains**
• Afraid that next step is sheltered housing • Afraid not to come home again • Being dependent on help • Loss of function • Afraid that the pain will become chronical • Generally afraid of pain • Afraid of medicine	• Hope to come home to her own apartment • Wishes that she could stand and walk without assistance • Hope to be able to manage living at home.	• It doesn't work • It's going to be hard • I'm not the exercising type • I'm afraid I'll fall • Will I end in wheelchair? • Will the pain never stop? • It's dangerous to become breathless • I don't believe this treatment is good for me	• Want to function • Get to know other people • Stop smoking • Want to continue training with others after the end of treatment • Lose weight • Walk on stairs again • Want to be 15 years younger again • Maintain a social life

Fig. 3. Results of empathy map and pains & gains exercise.

[19,23]. Brainwriting relies on the concept of cross-pollinating ideas, by allowing participants to further develop each others ideas [10]. The process involves having each participant writing down or sketching an idea. After a limited period of time the participant is asked to pass the sheet of paper to the left, and will likewise receive a sheet from the person to the right. The process is repeated until the participant once again is in possession of their own original idea, now further developed by the other participants. We allocated 2 min to develop or further develop an idea. Before the development phase commenced, participants were given, on average, 30 s to read the original idea before adding their own contribution to it. Participants were instructed to consider that their solution had to 1) make exercising more motivating for their persona, 2) should preferably include a social aspect, 3) rehabilitation equipment should focus on the use of exercise bikes and 4) solutions should be achieved by a visual display, either non-immersive (TV-based) or high-immersive (VR-based).

2.5 Brainwriting Outcomes

The brainwriting exercise resulted in five ideas. One involved a multisensory virtual experience, another was focused on functional training for activities of daily living (ADL), and three of them involved social elements in different combinations.

Multisensory Virtual Experiences

This idea introduced a restorative virtual environment biking-experience, which could be on a water bike or by boat. Furthermore, this solution would rely on audio-visual feedback, as well as vibrotactile feedback to increase multisensory integration and immersion [24]. Moreover, the solution would incorporate a higher degree of interactivity through gamification principles such as points system game mechanics.

VR for ADL Training

The idea focused more on creating realistic everyday scenarios to perform ADL training. Suggestions included: watering flowers, walking on stairs, follow a recipe, do laundry or having to walk on a street avoiding obstacles.

Social Biking on a Tandem Bike

This idea introduced a cooperative social biking exercise for two patients. The idea revolved around co-presence and peer effects to motivate higher training intensity. Unique for this solution is, that it introduced a tandem bicycle, which is a two-rider bicycle from the late 19th century, which entails a high cooperative level to ride.

Co-training with Individual Logging

The idea centered around a co-training environment, where users share the same VE on separate bicycles. Although the workshop-participants did not mention it, they basically described an algorithm that would account variability in user performance, to allow the users to bike together despite dissimilarity in motor deficits and endurance. Moreover, the idea included gamification mechanics such as pickups and point systems.

Co-training in Group Sessions

This idea combined several of the aforementioned aspects. The main feature was the social aspect, which aimed to augment larger joint training sessions. Furthermore, it introduced multimodal interaction by describing force feedback systems that could modulate the resistance depending on the virtual forces acting on the bicycle such as gravity, rolling resistance and drag force. Moreover, the idea incorporated social facilitation to enhance performance, in the form of external verbal encouragement from virtual spectators. The idea also described competitive elements to encourage increase in performance.

3   Discussion

3.1   Motivation and Socialization

The concept of socializing was often mentioned. In the inpatient care unit, patients mostly stay in their room unless they have treatment sessions with a physiotherapist or an occupational therapist. It also became apparent, that there is a large average age difference between patients in the two facilities. Judging by the personas alone, the participants estimated a inter-age difference of 15 years.

This opens the discussion on whether the two facilities should share a single application or have rather have applications designed based on each facility's individual features and conditions. Interestingly, the outcome of the workshop challenged the fundamental premise of the PhD-project, i.e. that motivation was one of the core challenges in the rehabilitation facilities. The participants affiliated with the outpatient health center remarked that they do not necessarily experience motivation as a barrier in the training. However, they did also noted that the health center usually experiences low attendance in the start-up of the rehabilitation process. Thus the higher level of motivation among patients may be attributable to selection bias. Moreover, presumably motivation will be higher in outpatient facilities because the patients can maintain ADL and usual routines, rather than being confined to unfamiliar circumstances in an inpatient context.

However, judging by the empathy maps, pains & gains and subsequent plenary discussions, there was a shared fundamental need for social interactions. Both personas were attributed a desire to socialize with others, although the circumstances provided by the facilities relies fundamentally on different contexts. Examples include location, appearance and rehabilitation program; thereby the workshop confirmed previous findings, i.e. that social experiences should be considered, as part of future VR solutions.

The solution phase, which included the brainwriting ideas, led to some creative concepts, which most likely would not have been generated outside a co-creative context. Some of the concepts ideated, reminded of pre-existing commercial solutions (e.g. VR facilitating ADL-training or multimodal game-based rehabilitation). Others ended up describing more novel ideas which can be combined into a prototype for VR-based rehabilitation applications in the next stage of the PhD-project.

To our knowledge, this is the first paper of its kind to describe a workshop utilizing the double diamond approach to co-create content-specific applications for VR-based rehabilitation. Moreover, as highlighted by Keshner et al., interdisciplinary teams seldom participate together in the technological development of applications within the field of VR-based rehabilitation which may account for low reliability and generalizability of results of multiple systematic reviews [13]. This workshop is the first step towards an indispensable interprofessional approach, which we deem vital to guarantee the impact and viability of VR-technology during and after implementation.

3.2   Future Considerations

While the physiotherapists liked the co-creation workshop and had high motivation for participating throughout all phases, it is important that the concepts developed are followed up by action. Presumably, it will have negative impact for the therapists, if the time they invested in this workshop, and in the ideation of novel ideas, do not become developed into tangible prototypes. All participants should ideally feel like they contributed to a developed proof of concept. Otherwise the onboarding of therapists through co-creation processes will never consolidate, and could be substituted with aversion for the technology instead. Therefore, the choice of brainwriting was a good tool to assure that everyone contributed; thus even if only a single idea is chosen, all participated in its creation. Furthermore, while the views of the physiotherapists are essential, the next step should be a focus on end-user involvement (i.e. the patients) e.g. through presentation of working prototypes of one or more of the ideas for them to try and evaluate, because ultimately, the patients are the ones to determine if the applications are relevant and usable.

4   Conclusion

The challenges of integration and implementation of novel technologies and tools are very real, and success is reliant on how well the needs, knowledge and routines of all user groups are understood and met before, and thus during the implementation. Part of the journey to such understanding is a tool in itself, and the co-creation workshop to ideate novel gamification concepts, which we have described in this paper has proven useful. It was well received and the workshop reached a stage where the co-creation approach to persona development, empathy mapping, pains and gains, and brainwriting played a part in determining the next logical steps for the in/outpatient facilities' future virtual reality experiences, for motor rehabilitation; which was found to be 'socialization'.

Acknowledgements. The authors wish to thank physiotherapists Martin Reinholck-Jæger, Emilie Trier Borgnakke, Johan Vilhelm Specht, Susanne Frederiksen and Christian Balslev for participating and contributing to valuable insights during the workshop. Furthermore, thanks to physiotherapist Thomas Vain-Nielsen from Smertefys (https://smertefys.nu/) for presenting his work with VR, and to Amalia De Götzen for sage advice and suggestions. Finally thanks to Frederiksberg municipality for funding the research.

References

1. Anderson-Hanley, C., Snyder, A.L., Nimon, J.P., Arciero, P.J.: Social facilitation in virtual reality-enhanced exercise: competitiveness moderates exercise effort of older adults. Clin. Interv. Aging **6**, 275 (2011)
2. Bruun-Pedersen, J.R., Pedersen, K.S., Serafin, S., Kofoed, L.B.: Augmented exercise biking with virtual environments for elderly users: a preliminary study for retirement home physical therapy. In: 2014 2nd Workshop on Virtual and Augmented Assistive Technology (VAAT), pp. 23–27. IEEE (2014). https://doi.org/10.1109/VAAT.2014.6799464

3. Chapman, C.N., Milham, R.P.: The personas' new clothes: methodological and practical arguments against a popular method. In: Proceedings of the Human Factors and Ergonomics Society Annual Meeting, vol. 50, pp. 634–636. SAGE Publications, Los Angeles (2006)
4. Design Council (Ed.): Eleven lessons: Managing design in eleven global companies-desk research report. Design Council (2007). Accessed 10 Aug 2019, https://www.designcouncil.org.uk/sites/default/files/asset/document/ElevenLessons_DeskResearchReport_0.pdf
5. Edwards, A.M., Dutton-Challis, L., Cottrell, D., Guy, J.H., Hettinga, F.J.: Impact of active and passive social facilitation on self-paced endurance and sprint exercise: encouragement augments performance and motivation to exercise. BMJ Open Sport Exerc. Med. **4**(1), e000368 (2018)
6. Ferreira, B.M., Barbosa, S.D.J., Conte, T.: PATHY: using empathy with personas to design applications that meet the users' needs. In: Kurosu, M. (ed.) HCI 2016. LNCS, vol. 9731, pp. 153–165. Springer, Cham (2016). https://doi.org/10.1007/978-3-319-39510-4_15
7. Freire, K., Sangiorgi, D., et al.: Service design and healthcare innovation: from consumption to co-production to co-creation. In: Service Design and Service Innovation Conference, pp. 39–50 (2010). Linköping Electronic Conference Proceedings
8. Goršič, M., Cikajlo, I., Novak, D.: Competitive and cooperative arm rehabilitation games played by a patient and unimpaired person: effects on motivation and exercise intensity. J. NeuroEng. Rehabil. **14**(1), 1–18 (2017). https://doi.org/10.1186/s12984-017-0231-4
9. Gorsic, M., Tran, M.H., Novak, D.: Cooperative cooking: a novel virtual environment for upper limb rehabilitation. In: Proceedings of the Annual International Conference of the IEEE Engineering in Medicine and Biology Society, EMBS, vol. 2018-July, pp. 3602–3605. IEEE (2018). https://doi.org/10.1109/EMBC.2018.8513005
10. Gray, D., Brown, S., Macanufo, J.: Gamestorming: A Playbook for Innovators, Rulebreakers, and Changemakers. O'Reilly Media Inc., Newton (2010)
11. Helmefalk, M.: An interdisciplinary perspective on gamification: mechanics, psychological mediators and outcomes. Int. J. Serious Games **6**(1), 3–26 (2019)
12. Kappen, D.L., Mirza-Babaei, P., Nacke, L.E.: Older adults' physical activity and exergames: a systematic review. Int. J. Hum.-Comput. Interact. **35**(2), 140–167 (2019). https://doi.org/10.1080/10447318.2018.1441253
13. Keshner, E.A., Weiss, P.T., Geifman, D., Raban, D.: Tracking the evolution of virtual reality applications to rehabilitation as a field of study. J. NeuroEng. Rehabil. **16**(1), 76 (2019)
14. Lange, B., et al.: Designing informed game-based rehabilitation tasks leveraging advances in virtual reality. Disabil. Rehabil. **34**(22), 1863–1870 (2012)
15. Larsen, L.H., Schou, L., Lund, H.H., Langberg, H.: The physical effect of exergames in healthy elderly-a systematic review. Games Health J. **2**(4), 205–212 (2013). https://doi.org/10.1089/g4h.2013.0036. pMID: 26192224
16. Lohse, K., Shirzad, N., Verster, A., Hodges, N., Van der Loos, H.M.: Video games and rehabilitation: using design principles to enhance engagement in physical therapy. J. Neurol. Phys. Therapy **37**(4), 166–175 (2013)
17. Marker, A.M., Staiano, A.E.: Better together: outcomes of cooperation versus competition in social exergaming. Games Health J. **4**(1), 25–30 (2015)
18. Reis, E., Postolache, G., Teixeira, L., Arriaga, P., Lima, M.L., Postolache, O.: Exergames for motor rehabilitation in older adults: an umbrella review. Phys. Ther. Rev. **1**–16 (2019). https://doi.org/10.1080/10833196.2019.1639012

19. Rhorbach, B.: Kreative nach regeln: Methode 635, eine neue technik zum losen von problemen. Absatzwirtschaft **12**, 73–75 (1969)
20. Ryan, R.M., Deci, E.L.: Self-determination theory and the facilitation of intrinsic motivation, social development, and well-being. Am. Psychol. **55**(1), 68 (2000)
21. Sanders, E.B.N., Stappers, P.J.: Co-creation and the new landscapes of design. Co-design **4**(1), 5–18 (2008)
22. Seay, A.F., Jerome, W.J., Lee, K.S., Kraut, R.E.: Project massive: a study of online gaming communities. In: CHI'04 Extended Abstracts on Human Factors in Computing Systems, pp. 1421–1424. ACM (2004)
23. Shah, J.J., Kulkarni, S.V., Vargas-Hernandez, N.: Evaluation of idea generation methods for conceptual design: effectiveness metrics and design of experiments. J. Mech. Des. **122**(4), 377–384 (2000)
24. Slater, M.: Place illusion and plausibility can lead to realistic behaviour in immersive virtual environments. Philos. Trans. Roy. Soc. Lond. B Biol. Sci. **364**(1535), 3549–3557 (2009)
25. Smeddinck, J.D., Herrlich, M., Malaka, R.: Exergames for physiotherapy and rehabilitation: a medium-term situated study of motivational aspects and impact on functional reach. In: Proceedings of the 33rd Annual ACM Conference on Human Factors in Computing Systems, pp. 4143–4146. ACM (2015). https://doi.org/10.1145/2702123.2702598
26. Tochetto, J., Guimarães, C., Maranho, A.L., Tartari, A.L.: Design with me: i have special needs! the case for cerebral palsy. In: Antona, M., Stephanidis, C. (eds.) UAHCI 2016. LNCS, vol. 9737, pp. 214–222. Springer, Cham (2016). https://doi.org/10.1007/978-3-319-40250-5_21

Towards Sustainable Inclusive Game Design Processes

Thomas Westin[1]([:envelope:]) [iD], Henrik Engström[2] [iD], and Jenny Brusk[2] [iD]

[1] Stockholm University, Postbox 7003, 164 07 Kista, Sweden
thomasw@dsv.su.se
[2] University of Skövde, Box 408, 541 28 Skövde, Sweden

Abstract. While many studies have been done about creation of accessible games, they have mainly been conducted in an academic context and represents a gap between game research and the game industry. The pilot project presented in this paper (PowerUp) addresses inclusive design by involving both the game industry and disabled people. The goal is to identify activities that constitute the biggest obstacles to realising sustainable design processes for inclusive game design (IGD). Four activities were identified through two full-day workshops with the game industry and game studios, disabled people and authorities: 1) Find opportunities for IGD with disabled people; 2) Handle integrity and security of disabled people; 3) Recruit the right competence among disabled people; and 4) Adapt workplaces and tools for IGD processes. These activities are tentative and will hopefully be subject to discussion and further development to achieve sustainable inclusive game design.

Keywords: Game industry · Game design processes · Inclusion · Disabled people

1 Introduction

There are many research studies focusing on the creation of games that are accessible to disabled people. These studies have mainly been conducted in an academic context with no or little connection to the games industry. This gap between research and industry is not unique to this particular area but is common in game research in general [1, 2]. The pilot project presented in this paper (PowerUp) addresses inclusive game design with an explicit purpose to incorporate the perspectives of both the game industry and disabled people. This paper reports the results from PowerUp where representatives from the game industry, academia and disability organisations have identified activities to support sustainable inclusive game design.

1.1 Game Development

Game design, a central element in the development process, is a second order design problem [3]. A game designer defines the rules of the game but the goal of the design

A. Brooks and E. I. Brooks (Eds.): ArtsIT 2019/DLI 2019, LNICST 328, pp. 390–396, 2020.
https://doi.org/10.1007/978-3-030-53294-9_27

is the experience resulting from the gameplay that emerges from players' interaction with these rules and each other. This characteristic of game design is captured well in the Mechanics, Dynamics and Aesthetics model proposed by Hunicke, LeBlanc, and Zubek [4]. The second order design problem gives implications to the game development process. A game design requires playtests to evaluate if the gameplay generates the desired aesthetics (i.e. experience). The focus on playtests implies a focus on playable prototypes [5] and this affects the process for all disciplines involved in the production, not only game designers. The process of developing games is hence different to both that of utilitarian software [6] and other media products, such as film [7].

1.2 Game Research

Research on games has seen a massive growth the last two decades [2]. Despite this big academic interest, research on game production processes is still underrepresented [2]. There exists a gap between non-technical and technical research [8, 9] and very few game studies include empirics from the game industry [1]. The growth of the game industry has to a large extent happened without any strong interest from research on its inner processes.

There are numerous examples of games that have been developed with a target to enable disabled people to play them. However, most of this work has mainly been conducted in a research context. In spite of many successful such research projects, their implications to the game industry have been small. As discussed above, there is a general need to bridge the gap between academia and industry. This is also true for work within the specialised field of inclusive game design.

1.3 Inclusive Game Design and Sustainability

Compared to universal design, "[i]nclusive design is a more pragmatic approach that argues that there will often be reasons (e.g. technical or financial) why total inclusion is unattainable" [10]. For inclusive game design, game rules further limit what can be done, as change of game rules essentially creates a new game. Furthermore, inclusive game design must also consider the aesthetics (the gaming experience) of the game and ensure that the experience is similar independently of whether the player has a disability or not.

Given that there is a tendency among game developers to create games for people like themselves and that the average game developer is a white, 35-year old heterosexual man without any disability [11], we suggest that diversifying the game development team in addition to forming focus groups that match the diversified target group are prerequisites in order to move forward when it comes to inclusive game design and development.

This could enable a participatory or co-design approach [10], involving disabled people as early as possible in the design process. However, this in turn requires an in-depth analysis of what such involvement would mean in practice within existing design processes of game companies combining arts and technologies, related to strict schedules and budgets. Thus, there is a need to have a methodological approach that is possible for game companies to adopt and possible for disabled people to participate in, sustainable over time. There is also an opportunity of learning from related research in other industries; for instance, staff diversity does not imply an inclusive workplace where disabled people feel comfortable telling they are disabled [12].

1.4 Problem, Goal and Method

The problem addressed in this work is that there is a lack of knowledge of what inclusive game design would mean in practice within existing design processes of game companies. The goal is to identify activities that constitute the biggest obstacles to realising sustainable design processes for inclusive game design, from the perspectives of the game industry as well as from disabled people. To identify obstacles and thus enable an analysis of them, a pilot project (PowerUp) was defined by the authors. Two full-day workshops were conducted during 2018. The workshops included presentations and discussions with participants from all involved stakeholders, with notes taken by the authors. 13 persons from 11 organisations participated, ranging from three large game companies and a game industry organisation, to three organisations with disabled youth, as well as a large game-oriented youth organisation, two universities and one other authority.

2 Results and Analysis

The outcome of the two PowerUp workshops is here presented as a tentative framework of suggested activities that may be necessary to consider in inclusive game design processes.

2.1 Find Opportunities for Inclusive Game Design with Disabled People

As have been pointed out, game development is a costly and complex process involving the collaboration between people from a broad field of competences ranging from technology to art. A participatory design approach will most likely mean that the current design processes will need to be changed. To identify and minimize the potentially negative consequences of these changes, it is critical that staff and management are involved from the beginning. Another important component is to create meeting spaces between game developers and disabled people; finding ways to make this as easy as possible given special needs and accessibility issues. In related research presented in [12] there are three phases towards inclusion at the workplace; organizational entry, integration and development activities. Entry concerns how to recruit testers and participants with disabilities, where both choice of channels and recruitment criteria matter; integration concerns socialisation; and development activities concern diversity education of staff in general, as well as competence training for disabled people. Recruitment channels today may be social media, internal staff or reaching out to organizations of disabled people. Another option is to create or use a database for this purpose, such as AbleGamers Player Panels [13] that were released in 2019. However, this may be less straight forward than what is needed as the following activities show.

2.2 Handle Integrity and Security of Disabled People

Creating a network or database of players and developers with disabilities raise several ethical as well as legal issues that need to be resolved. There are for example limitations to what kind of data that can be stored, how, and for how long, given the new directives stated through the General Data Protection Regulation (GDPR) [14]. Furthermore, handling healthcare related data requires extra care. Communication channels must also be carefully managed for the same reasons, as a community may both help and harm (e.g. discriminate) disabled people. A possible approach is to involve and get help from authorities such as the Swedish Data Protection Authority [14]. However, a similar service may not be available in all countries or regions of the world. For smaller game studios without internal legal or human resource departments, some of these issues mentioned in this paper may be insurmountable without government support.

Furthermore, there are also internal studio polices, non-disclosure agreements (NDAs) and other similar restrictions specified by the companies that may become obstacles when it comes to sharing and storing data and other kinds of resources that can be of use for other developers working with inclusive design. Involvement of game studio management early on is probably necessary to overcome these obstacles.

2.3 Recruit the Right Competence Among Disabled People

Participatory, inclusive game design requires including disabled people that have the right competence. For a game development company, the most obvious solution would be to start searching among their own staff; according to [11] around 20% of game developers have some kind of disability. However, to recruit and/or identify experts within the organisation can be challenging and perhaps even ethically questionable, considering that disabilities along with for example gender, religious belief, ethnicity and sexuality are grounds for discrimination. Thus, even though the purpose of involving them in the process as early as possible is to make use of their expert knowledge, the question is how they can be found and then encouraged to step in as experts in a way that makes them feel comfortable. A possible suggestion is to create a new profession, quality assurance for accessibility, that may be a sustainable way over time to attract the right competence.

When it comes to recruiting testers, it is possible to contact the different organisations that gather people with a particular disability and ask them to spread the information among their members. However, there are some practical issues that need to be addressed. First, some forms of disabilities are very rare among the population, for example blindness, which means that these members can be widely spread geographically, making it difficult to, for example, set up test sessions. Second, their uniqueness makes them particularly attractive to recruit, but their uniqueness is also something that might make it difficult for them to decline participation. There is a risk that they feel trapped between feeling responsible for the group they represent, that is turned into a sense of guilt or even a lack of gratitude if they choose not to participate, and a feeling of being exploited or just exhausted by all the testing. This is because they most likely will be called for again have they participated once since it is so difficult to recruit them in the first place. Third, play tests are often an unpaid duty that players agree to do as they get to play an early version of the game, in so called beta tests, before all others, making play testing almost an exclusive privilege. However, play tests for inclusivity are very different, as they must include an evaluation of the game's accessibility in addition to regular gameplay tests. To identify potential problems in the design, these tests might need to be monitored by a usability expert, or evaluated by expert usability testers with the particular disability the design aims to support.

2.4   Adapt Workplaces and Tools for Inclusive Game Design Processes

To facilitate participatory inclusive game design, the workplace needs to be accessible and support the use of assistive tools and technology. Having a consultant going through the office space and access to the building such as removing thresholds and need to use stairs, adding Braille to signs, or hearing-aid compatible systems and similar ergonomics is a possible first step. A second step may be to consider how documents, presentations and the company intranet are designed for equal access to information, where W3C WCAG [15] can provide guidance. A third step is to consider the tools used for game design and development; what obstacles do they raise for which groups and how may those be overcome. Opening a dialogue with tool developers (in-house or external) may be a necessity, and add tool accessibility as a requirement for the next game project. There has recently been a change in how for instance Unity addresses these issues, judging from a forum thread started by Unity staff [16].

3   Discussion and Future Work

3.1   Designing Inclusive Game Design Processes

While game design is a second order design problem [3], designing inclusive game design processes is also a meta-level problem; perhaps it could be called a third order design problem to keep with the enumeration logic of orders. In other words, designing inclusive game design processes (third order) only indirectly affects game design (second order) that in turn only indirectly affects the user experience (first order). Designing game design processes to be more inclusive, does not mean that game designs have to change; instead it merely enables a diversity of user perspectives on game designs to avoid unnecessary barriers to be built into games. Furthermore, while removing barriers to access may enable a disabled person to play, it does not necessarily mean that the person enjoys the gameplay experience more. However, it is likely that an inclusive game design process has a better chance at both removing barriers and creating better play experiences for more people, compared to processes that does not consider inclusion from the outset. To make game design processes more inclusive, the four activities and perhaps also other activities yet to be found may be necessary to consider.

3.2   A Pragmatic Approach to Diversify Game Development Teams

Similar to the need for methodology in playtesting game experiences with prototypes [5], there is a need to find a methodology for designing inclusive game design processes.

The methodology needs to be pragmatic in line with the definition of inclusive design [10] and may be a contribution to the lack of research on game production processes [2]. While some knowledge can be gathered from development of utilitarian software or other media products, there are also differences [6, 7].

Relating to the four activities in this study, adapting workplaces or handling integrity and security can certainly be learnt from other fields than games, but many tools for game development differ from other software (e.g. game engines and editors). Also, there is a lack of standards in the game industry where each game platform or engine has their own de facto standards, compared to e.g. the web where browsers are built to work with third party applications such as screen readers. Furthermore, when it comes to recruiting disabled people with the right competence also in other industries, there may be problems where employers do not ask to avoid stigmatization and employees may be afraid to tell they are disabled [12]. In other words, if this can be solved within the game industry, it may be something for other industries to learn from. Based upon discussions during the second PowerUp workshop there are companies outside of the game industry that have specialised on hiring disabled people; however, according to one of the involved youth organisations, it often means that they are underpaid and was thus not considered a good approach. It is also important to not hire disabled people on basis of their disabilities as a form of quota; there must be a focus on competence while diversifying the staff to find opportunities to enable more inclusive game design.

Improving representation of disabled people compared to the average game developer [11] requires a participatory or co-design approach [10], involving disabled people as early as possible in the design process. However, this in turn requires an in-depth analysis of what such involvement would mean in practice within existing design processes to minimize the need for change. The four activities in this study can be used as a starting point for such analysis. Reaching out to and involving existing disabled staff, while respecting their integrity and safety, as well as adapting the workplace and tools and thus enable recruiting people regardless of being disabled or not. In other words, by removing barriers in the environment, both technical and social, disabled people may feel more comfortable in working at the game company and contribute to make the games more inclusive.

3.3 Bridging Gaps

Two gaps were identified in related research: 1) between research and industry [1, 2]; and 2) between non-technical and technical research [8, 9]. The first gap is unfortunate in general as both game researchers and game developers could benefit by having close collaborations. In the case of PowerUp with participatory co-design, collaboration is a prerequisite. Thanks to the PowerUp project the authors believe that a breakthrough in this field has been made at least locally in Sweden, where game developers met disabled youth from three organisations representing vision, hearing and motor disabilities. This may seem like a small step but it had not been done before (to the best of our knowledge) within the involved game companies that were three of the ten largest companies in Sweden. The second gap is academic but none the less a problem when researching game industry design processes that involve both arts and technology. Hopefully this paper may help to bridge these gaps.

3.4   Future Work

The tentative four activities above will hopefully spark a fruitful discussion at the ArtsIT 2019 workshop and beyond for further development, where we can expand the PowerUp network internationally with game developers, researchers and organisations of disabled people. This may then be used as basis for further workshops and activities together with the involved organisations to enable sustainable inclusive game design processes. Such activities may include interviewing game designers, programmers and artists with disabilities, that could result in an improved understanding of how participation can be included in a production pipeline.

This work was funded by the Swedish Governmental Agency for Innovation Systems (Vinnova) and Game Hub Scandinavia 2.0, Projektid: NYPS20201849, EU Interreg Öresuns-Kattegat-Skagerrak. The authors would also like to thank the ArtsIT conference reviewers for excellent feedback.

References

1. Engström, H.: GDC vs. DiGRA: gaps in game production research. In: DIGRA (2019)
2. Martin, P.: The intellectual structure of game research. Game Stud. **18**(1) (2018). http://gamestudies.org/1801/articles/paul_martin
3. Salen, K., Zimmermann, E.: Rules of Play: Game Design Fundamentals. The MIT Press, Cambridge (2004)
4. Hunicke, R., LeBlanc, M., Zubek, R.: MDA: a formal approach to game design and game research. In: AAAI Workshop on Challenges in Game AI (2004)
5. Lê, P.L., Massé, D., Paris, T.: Technological change at the heart of the creative process: insights from the videogame industry. Int. J. Arts Manag. **15**(2), 45–59 (2013)
6. Murphy-Hill, E., Zimmermann, T., Nagappan, N.: Cowboys, ankle sprains, and keepers of quality: how is video game development different from software development?. In: Proceedings of the 36th International Conference on Software Engineering, pp. 1–11 (2014)
7. O'Donnell, C.: Games are not convergence: the lost promise of digital production and convergence. Convergence **17**(3), 271–286 (2011)
8. Melcer, E., Nguyen, T.-H.D., Chen, Z., Canos-sa, A., El-Nasr, M.S., Isbister, K.: Games research today: analyzing the academic landscape 2000–2014. In: International Conference on the Foundations of Digital Games, pp. 1–9 (2015)
9. Deterding, S.: The pyrrhic victory of game studies: assessing the past, present, and future of interdisciplinary game research. Game. Cult. **12**(6), 521–543 (2017)
10. Benyon, D.: Designing User Experience. Pearson Education Limited, London (2019)
11. Weststar, J., O'Meara, V., Legault, M.-J.: IGDA Developer Satisfaction Survey 2017 Summary Report. IGDA, 08 January 2018
12. Kulkarni, M., Valk, R.: Don't ask, don't tell: two views on human resource practices for people with disabilities. IIMB Manag. Rev. **22**(4), 137–146 (2010)
13. AbleGamers: Player Panels (n.d.). https://accessible.games/join-player-panels/. Accessed 17 Oct 2019
14. The General Data Protection Regulation (GDPR): The Swedish data protection authority (Datainspektionen). https://www.datainspektionen.se/other-lang/in-english/the-general-data-protection-regulation-gdpr/. Accessed 17 July 2019
15. W3C: Web content accessibility guidelines (WCAG) overview. https://www.w3.org/WAI/intro/wcag. Accessed 04 May 2016
16. UnityTechnologies: Accessibility and inclusion 2019. https://forum.unity.com/threads/accessibility-and-inclusion.694477/. Accessed 19 June 2019

Co-designing a Head-Mounted Display Based Virtual Reality Game to Teach Street-Crossing Skills to Children Diagnosed with Autism Spectrum Disorder

Ali Adjorlu[(✉)] and Stefania Serafin

Aalborg University Copenhagen, Copenhagen, Denmark
{adj,sts}@create.aau.dk

Abstract. In this paper, we present a head-mounted display based virtual reality game developed to teach street-crossing skills to children and adolescents diagnosed with Autism Spectrum Disorder. The virtual reality street-crossing training game is co-designed with four teachers who work with children diagnosed with autism on a daily basis. The teachers specified a set of requirements for the gamified training application that is described and discussed in this paper alongside the plans for the future itterations.

Keywords: Gamification · Virtual reality · Street-crossing

1 Introduction

According to a report conducted by the European Transport Safety Council, 8300 children have been killed in traffic accidents from 2008 to 2018 in the European Union [1]. More than 30% of these children were pedestrians colliding with motorized vehicles. Due to their small stature, children are less visible than adults to drivers, which places a big responsibility on the children to possess the required street-crossing skills. However, safe street-crossing skills require cognitive abilities that are still under development during childhood [2,3]. Notably, children diagnosed with Autism Spectrum Disorder (ASD) are at a higher risk of being victims of traffic accidents due to learning disability which reduces their capabilities to learn the required skills for safe street-crossing skills [4]. Learning disability is common among individuals diagnosed with ASD while on the other hand, ASD is ubiquitous among individuals suffering from learning disabilities [5]. Additionally, individuals diagnosed with ASD have difficulties processing sensory information compared to typically developed individuals [6]. More

The authors wish to thank the teachers Bo Jacobsen, Lone Jørring, Rune Hviid and Anita Drejer Høgh from Skovmoseskolen for participating in the design workshop. Additionally, we would like to thank Sune Buch-Sloth from Rødovre Municipality to put us in contact with the teachers.

A. Brooks and E. I. Brooks (Eds.): ArtsIT 2019/DLI 2019, LNICST 328, pp. 397–405, 2020.
https://doi.org/10.1007/978-3-030-53294-9_28

specifically, young children diagnosed with ASD have deficits with sensory information processing resulting in inattentiveness, which can result in street-crossing related accidents. Studies indicate that approximately 90% to 100% of children diagnosed with ASD have reduced sensory information processing skills [6]. The reduced learning capacity, as well as a high prevalence of ASD (1 out of every 50 child) [7], underlines the importance of developing interventions designed to teach safe street-crossing skills to children diagnosed with ASD. Methods applied to teach safe street-crossing skills to children are often conducted in the classroom [8]. However, one of the impairments of individuals diagnosed with ASD is their lack of imagination, making it hard for them to visualize verbal instructions such as classroom instructions on how to cross the street [9]. Training in natural settings such as real streets has proven to be effective in teaching the required skills to typically developed children [10]. However, bringing a child diagnosed with ASD to a real street is dangerous. Additionally, children diagnosed with ASD often suffer from social anxiety while being uncomfortable with unpredictable situations [11] such as streets. Virtual Reality (VR) can offer a safe environment for children diagnosed with ASD to rehearse a variety of everyday living skills such as how to shop [12], or social skills [13]. By substituting the real world sensory information with digitally generated ones, VR is capable of placing the child inside an interactive virtual environment within which the child can train the required skills. These virtual environments can look like the real-world environments such a virtual street, within which the child can rehearse street-crossing skills. Additionally, the VR training interventions can require the same interactions as in the real world, such as walking and looking to both sides of the street using one's head and legs. Stickland et al. conducted the first known study investigating if head-mounted display (HMD) based VR has the potentials to teach everyday living skills to children diagnosed with ASD [14]. In her pioneering study, she had two children aged seven and nine diagnosed with ASD wear an HMD and practice recognizing and tracking cars with their head in the one virtual scene and walking up to a car and stopping before colliding with it in the another scene. Both participants were capable of tracking and approaching the moving cars in the scenes while one of the participants learned to stop before colliding with the virtual car. This study showed the potentials of VR to teach street-crossing skills to children diagnosed with ASD even though it only had limited gamification elements. Since the study by Strickland published in 1998, researchers have only investigated the effectiveness of using desktop-based virtual street-crossing training applications to our knowledge [15–17]. Joasman et al. proposed a desktop-based simulation where a 3D avatar represents the child and can be controlled using three keys: one for looking left, one for looking right and one for crossing the street. It is the child's task to choose the right time to cross the street with cars approaching from both directions [17]. The study measured the learning outcome of the virtual training by having the participants crossing the street on a real street before and after the intervention on typically developed children. The results showed that the application was effective in teaching safe street crossing skills to children aged seven to twelve with no mental disorder. Another study by Josman et al. used the same desktop-based virtual street crossing application on six children diagnosed with ASD [4]. The results indicate that some of the children diagnosed with ASD were capable of improving their skills in using the application and developing some understanding of when it is safe to cross the street in the virtual environment. The above studies apply gamification elements such as the ones described by Deterding et al. [18], where the user is asked to achieve a goal guided by rules. These rules include having to avoid cars and reaching the opposite side of the street using buttons on the keyboard. In this paper, we set out to design an HMD based VR application that uses gamification to teach street-crossing skills to children diagnosed with ASD. The main advantage of HMD based VR compare to its desktop counterpart is the ability to implement interactions that are similar to the interaction one has to perform in real life (Using one's head and body to look for cars and walk using one's legs). The similarity of interaction between the training environment to the real-life environment is especially important for individuals diagnosed with ASD due to their reduced ability to generalize training from one context to another such [19]. In this paper, we present a user-centered approach towards design and development of a street-crossing VR application. Through a design workshop, four teachers who work with children diagnosed with ASD on a daily bases were involved in the design process of the HMD based VR street-crossing training application described in this paper.

2   Co-creation Workshop

In order to involve teachers in the design process, a workshop toke place at Skovmoseskolen in Hvidovre, a school for children diagnosed with mental disabilities. Four teachers participated in the workshop, all working with children diagnosed with ASD on a daily basis. Two of the teachers had specific experiments in teaching traffic-safety skills to children diagnosed with ASD and were familiar with the requirements of the danish counsel for traffic safety (Rådet for sikker trafik). One of the authors, with a technical and interaction design background moderated the workshop. The author initiated the workshop by presenting the teachers to HMD based VR using an HTC VIVE HMD. The teachers tried a variety of VR applications where they could look and walk around in a virtual environment using their bodies as they would in the real world. Additionally, the teachers were told that the authors can implement an interactive VR application containing a virtual street. During the workshop, a set of requirements were made for the training application.

The teachers requested a virtual environment that looks simplified and cartoonish to increase the motivation of their students for participating in the study. Additionally, the teachers proposed including an introduction in the game to illustrate how one should cross the street when there is a crosswalk and when there is no crosswalk nearby. Following the introduction to current street-crossing behavior, the teachers proposed developing a gamified training application with a series of levels that would gradually increase in difficulty as the player completed each level. All of the levels would have the same goal: crossing the street safely. The main rule is that the user must look to both sides before crossing the street. Additionally, the user must always walk towards a crosswalk if there is one before passing the street. Furthermore, he should not attempt to cross the virtual street before all the cars on the road (if any) have stopped. Finally, if there is a pedestrian crosswalk light, the user must wait for the green light before passing the street. If any of these rules are not uphold and the user crosses the street, the game must give appropriate feedback and restart the level.

The teachers proposed a total of four levels. The first level should start with a street with no cars but with a crosswalk, followed with a level with a crosswalk and a pedestrian crosswalk light. The next levels should contain a crosswalk with no pedestrian crosswalk light but with cars approaching. The final level would include a crosswalk, pedestrian crosswalk light, and vehicles approaching.

According to the teachers, their students diagnosed with ASD often have a hard time understanding verbal instruction without support from visual cues. This confirms studies indicating that some children diagnosed with ASD struggle with understanding oral instructions [20]. Therefore, the teachers requested that the VR street-crossing training application should include visual cues to support the oral instructions. Based on the workshop with the teachers, we set out to develop the gamified HMD based VR street-crossing application.

3   The HMD Based VR Street-Crossing Training Game

Fig. 1. The street, buildings, crosswalk, 3D avatar of the instructor and the sky-box

The training application was developed using Unity 3D and C# scripts and was designed to run on an HTC VIVE VR HMD. The HTC VIVE is a HMD that allows for 6-degrees of freedom which enables its user to walk and move around a virtual environment on 6 different axis: up, down, left, right, yaw, pitch and roll. A street was designed with a sidewalk, a crosswalk, and European looking buildings. A sky-box surrounds the scene with slow-moving clouds. All of these assets in the application are simple and cartoonish looking as can be seen in Fig. 1 and as requested by the teachers. The user starting position will be on the sidewalk a bit away from the crosswalk to teach the necessity of walking towards the nearest crosswalk before crossing the street.

The teachers pinpointed the importance of providing visual instruction to support verbal instructions when working with children diagnosed with ASD. Therefore, a 3D avatar of a child was implemented, programmed to instruct the user verbally on how to cross the street and animated to illustrate the safe and correct street-crossing behavior visually (see Fig. 2). In the first level of the game, the user wearing the VR HMD will be placed in front of the 3D avatar of the child on the sidewalk. The 3D avatar will than introduce himself by saying in Danish: *"Hello. My name is Niels. When I am to cross the street, I will always start by finding the nearest crosswalk and walk to it"*.

Fig. 2. The 3D avatar of the instructor showing the user how to look to both sides before passing the street

This verbal introduction will be followed by the 3D avatar walking towards the crosswalk. Once the 3D avatar reaches the crosswalk, he will once again talk to the user.

An audio clip is played in danish: *"Once I am by the crosswalk, I will always look to left, right a couple of times to make sure no cars are coming. If there are no cars or all the cars or standing still then I will cross the street"*. Simultaneously with the audio clip, the 3D avatar is animated to look to left and right three times.

The 3D avatar will then cross the street by walking on the crosswalk until he reaches the sidewalk on the opposite side of the road. Once he reaches the other side of the street, the 3D avatar will start dancing while saying "*I did it*". The next scene will then begin with verbal instruction to the user, telling him: "*Now it is your turn to cross the street. First, find the nearest crosswalk and walk to it*". The verbal instruction will be supported with a visual cue as seen in Fig. 3 showing the user where the crosswalk is. The user is then to walk towards the crosswalk while staying on the sidewalk. Once he is by the crosswalk another verball instruction will start playing: "*Good job. Now you must first look to your left to see if any cars are approaching*". Once again, visual aid in the form of a large floating arrow, as seen in Fig. 3 was implemented to help the user understand the verbal instruction. Similarly, once he has looked to his left, another verbal instruction will tell him to look to the right with another arrow giving him a visual cue. There are no cars on the first level of the application. Therefore, after looking to both sides, the user is instructed to walk towards the other side of the street. The visual cue here is another blinking mark similar to the one on the Fig. 3 placed on the sidewalk on the other side of the street. A clapping sound is played each time the user crosses the street while following all the instructions and there are no moving cars or red lights in the scene. The clapping sound act as a reinforcement, helping to motivate the player to continue being engaged in the traffic safety intervention [23].

Fig. 3. The visual cues helping the user to understand the verbal instructions

The next level is similar to the first level expect that the scene now contains a pedestrian crosswalk light as seen on the Fig. 4. Similarly to the first scene, the user is again asked to walk to the crosswalk first. Once by the crosswalk, the user is verbally asked to wait for the pedestrian crosswalk light to turn green. Once the light shows green, he is once again verbally asked to look to both sides before passing the street with the same visual arrows as seen in Fig. 3.

Fig. 4. The cars and the pedestrian crosswalk light

The next scene is similar to the first scene expect that there is no light, but cars are driving by. This time, once the user reaches the crosswalk, he is verbally instructed to look and also wait for all the cars to stop or be gone. The cars are programmed to stop if the user is standing next to the crosswalk. Once the cars stop, verbal instructions together with visual cues, ask the user to look to both sides before crossing the street. Finally, the last scene includes both cars and the pedestrian crosswalk light with the user now asked to wait for the light to turn green and all the cars to stop before crossing the street. In all of the scenes, if the user tries to cross the street to early the whole scene will slowly turn into black while a verbal message will be played saying: *"That was wrong, let us try again"*.

The rules that will activate the negative feedback and restart the levels if broken are:

– If the user crosses the street before walking up to a crosswalk
– If the user crosses the street before he looked both to left and right
– If the user crosses the street when there are moving vehicles in the scene
– If the user crosses the street while the pedestrian crosswalk light is red

After each failure, the user is once again re-located to his starting position where he has to try again.

4 Discussion and Conclusion

In this paper, we presented an HMD based VR street-crossing training game for children diagnosed with ASD. The VR training game was designed based on input from teachers who work with children diagnosed with ASD. Designing and developing a gamified learning intervention for specific users requires the involvement of individuals with the required expertise on those particular users. All of the teachers involved in the design process had experience teaching a variety of different everyday living skills such as cleaning, taking the bus, or shopping to their students. Two of the teachers had specific experience teaching traffic safety to their students diagnosed with ASD. All of them agreed that teaching everyday living skills in their natural environment to children diagnosed with ASD is a demanding task. This is especially the case if the child has no previous experience with the environment and the specific everyday living skill such as crossing the street. Therefore, they would often prepare their student for training in the natural environment using visual interventions such as videos or pictures illustrating the situation or role-playing. These methods are the most common approach towards teaching everyday living skills to children diagnosed with ASD [21]. However, the teachers agreed that virtual reality has the potential to be a more effective tool for preparing their students for the real-life performance of the trained skill. One of their argument for this potential was the ability to gamify training and hereby increase the motivation for learning. The application had a set of rules and goals for the user to achieve. Future iterations of the game will include a point system and badges as described by Werbach & Hunter to further increase the players' motivation for training. Furthermore, future iterations will include additional levels with increased difficulty. One way to do this is by increasing the amount of sensory information in the virtual environment. Individuals diagnosed with ASD can have a reduced ability to process a large amount of sensory information [6]. By gradually increasing the difficulty, the user might stay in what Czikszentmihalyi calls the state of flow [22] while using the gamified street-crossing training application. In the future, children diagnosed with ASD will provide valuable feedback on the usability, user experience, and learning outcome of the gamified street-crossing application. Before testing on children diagnosed with ASD, it is crucial to make sure that the Danish Council for Traffic Saftey approves the intervention.

References

1. Adminaite, et al.: Reducing Child Deaths on European Roads. European Transport Safety Council (2018)
2. Schwebel, D.C., et al.: Community-based pedestrian safety training in virtual reality: a pragmatic trial. Accid. Anal. Prev. **86**, 9–15 (2016)
3. Pitcairn, T.K., Edlmann, T.: Individual differences in road crossing ability in young children and adults. Br. J. Psychol. **91**(3), 391–410 (2000)
4. Josman, N., et al.: Effectiveness of virtual reality for teaching street-crossing skills to children and adolescents with autism. Int. J. Disabil. Hum. Dev. **7**(1), 49–56 (2008)

5. O'Brien, G., Pearson, J.: Autism and learning disability. Autism **8**(2), 125–140 (2004)
6. Leekam, S.R., et al.: Describing the sensory abnormalities of children and adults with autism. J. Autism Dev. Disord. **37**(5), 894–910 (2007)
7. Xu, G., et al.: Prevalence of autism spectrum disorder among US children and adolescents, 2014–2016. Jama **319**(1), 81–82 (2018)
8. Ampofo-Boateng, K., Thomson, J.A.: Child pedestrian accidents: a case for preventive medicine. Health Educ. Res. **5**(2), 265–274 (1990)
9. Kennett, J.: Autism, empathy and moral agency. Philos. Q. **52**(208), 340–357 (2002)
10. Zare, H, et al.: Traffic safety education for child pedestrians: a randomized controlled trial with active learning approach to develop street-crossing behaviors. Transp. Res. Part F: Traffic Psychol. Behav. **60**, 734–742 (2019)
11. American Psychiatric Association. Diagnostic and statistical manual of mental disorders (DSM-5®). American Psychiatric Pub (2013)
12. Adjorlu, A., Serafin, S.: Head-mounted display-based virtual reality as a tool to teach money skills to adolescents diagnosed with autism spectrum disorder. In: Brooks, A.L., Brooks, E., Sylla, C. (eds.) ArtsIT/DLI -2018. LNICST, vol. 265, pp. 450–461. Springer, Cham (2019). https://doi.org/10.1007/978-3-030-06134-0_48
13. Adjorlu, A., et al.: Head-mounted display-based virtual reality social story as a tool to teach social skills to children diagnosed with autism spectrum disorder. In: 2017 IEEE Virtual Reality Workshop on K-12 Embodied Learning Through Virtual & Augmented Reality (KELVAR). IEEE (2018)
14. Strickland, D., et al.: Brief report: two case studies using virtual reality as a learning tool for autistic children. J. Autism Dev. Disord. **26**(6), 651–659 (1996)
15. Weiss, P.L., Naveh, Y., Katz, N.: Design and testing of a virtual environment to train stroke patients with unilateral spatial neglect to cross a street safely. Occup. Ther. Int. **10**(1), 39–55 (2003)
16. Katz, N., et al.: Interactive virtual environment training for safe street crossing of right hemisphere stroke patients with unilateral spatial neglect. Disabil. Rehabil. **27**(20), 1235–1244 (2005)
17. Bart, O., et al.: Street crossing by typically developed children in real and virtual environments. OTJR: Occup. Participation Health **28**(2), 89–96 (2008)
18. Deterding, S., et al.: From game design elements to gamefulness: defining gamification. In: Proceedings of the 15th International Academic MindTrek Conference: Envisioning Future Media Environments. ACM (2011)
19. Matson, J.L.: Applied Behavior Analysis for Children with Autism Spectrum Disorders. Springer, New York (2009)
20. Tissot, C., Evans, R.: Visual teaching strategies for children with autism. Early Child Dev. Care **173**(4), 425–433 (2003)
21. Adjorlu, A., Serafin, S.: Virtual Reality (VR) for children diagnosed with autism spectrum disorder (ASD): interventions to train social and everyday living skills. In: Virtual and Augmented Reality in Mental Health Treatment, pp. 159–175. IGI Global (2019)
22. Czikszentmihalyi, M.: Flow: The Psychology of Optimal Experience. Harper & Row, New York (1990)
23. Zichermann, G., Cunningham, C.: Gamification by Design: Implementing Game Mechanics in Web and Mobile Apps. O'Reilly Media Inc., Sebastopol (2011)

Stars, Crests and Medals: Visual Badge Design Framework to Gamify and Certify Online Learning

Bastian Ilsø Hougaard$^{(\boxtimes)}$ ⓘ and Hendrik Knoche ⓘ

Aalborg University, Rendsburggade 14, 9000 Aalborg, Denmark
contact@bastianilso.com, hk@create.aau.dk

Abstract. The World Wide Web have changed learning culture and brought with it, massive open online courses (MOOCs). Open Badges is an open standard which allow MOOCs to create digital course diplomas. Badges gamify education and act as a statement of achievement to reward learners as they reach goals and sub-goals in learning. Existing badge frameworks offer conceptual design guidelines, but does not provide granular support to the visual badge design process. This paper reports on a work-in-progress case study which aim to design badges targeted MOOCs for the creative industry. We report and exemplify the differences between gamification badges used internally in MOOCs and certification badges used by learners as genuine evidence of skill acquisition to employers. Finally, we contribute a visual breakdown of badge characteristics which can be used in conjunction with existing conceptual badge design frameworks.

Keywords: Open Badges · MOOC · Visual attributes · E-validation · Certification

1 Introduction

The European Union (EU) has identified a lack of digital competencies in people working in the creative sector [9] which hampers productivity, value creation, and competitiveness. Massive open online courses (MOOCs) provide digital access to low- or no cost content and skill acquisition. MOOC learners interested in acquiring skills to advance their job careers face major hurdles. They need to be able to display said skills to potential employers, traditionally done through certificates, degrees, and diplomas and complete courses as self-regulated learners. Contrary to traditional institution-based learning, MOOC learners face low completion rates [17] due to a variety of factors including low motivation. Studying in MOOCs lack the motivational support afforded by social contact, e.g. face-to-face with peers and educators in institutional settings.

Digital badges are images which visually resemble a physical badge and further contain invisible embedded metadata. They provide learners with certification, accessible to potential employers. However, poor adherence suggest that

A. Brooks and E. I. Brooks (Eds.): ArtsIT 2019/DLI 2019, LNICST 328, pp. 406–414, 2020.
https://doi.org/10.1007/978-3-030-53294-9_29

learners need a finer degree of granularity in terms of achieving reward, than what badges of certification can provide on their own. Providing additional gamifying badges as intermediate rewards can keep learners engaged, but what this conceptual distinction means for their visual design is unclear. Instructional designers of MOOCs who want to leverage badges as a gamifying mechanic, lack terminology and palettes to assist the visual articulation of badges as reward.

This paper contributes work in 1) identifying dimensions in certifying badges and gamifying badges for MOOCs 2) identifying the visual components of badges from best practice and 3) synthesizing a visual importance order for the identified MOOC badge dimensions.

2 Background

While badges only recently have gained traction in the scientific literature due to their prominence in gamification context, they have been around for a long time. They have been in use by the scouts movement since 1910 and share similarities to seals that conveyed authority and authenticity for thousands of years. We refer the reader to Ostashewski et al. [16] and Ellis et al. [7] as entry points to the historical backdrop of badges. Badges, are considered a fundamental gamification mechanic [11], which is described as "the use of game design elements in non-game contexts" [4]. Badges (also known as micro-credentials) recognize achievement and provide a loop of incentives (prior-behavior) and rewards (post-behavior) [11].

Digital badges have at least partly emerged from needs to gauge skills and reputation in e.g. digital games or electronic commerce as signals of trustworthy business partners. Gibson et al. defined digital badges as *"a representation of an accomplishment, interest or affiliation that is visual, available online, and contains metadata including links that help explain the context, meaning, process and result of an activity"* [10]. The definition assumes implicitly that the owner of the badge as well as others can access the visual representation including the relationship between the bearer and the badge. The badge bearer can thus signal abilities, status, achievements, dispositions, reputation etc. to others.

In the context of learning, a number of similar definitions have emerged [14], but the digital context lower administrative overheads. Digital badges cheaply provide credentials at a finer granularity than grade transcripts, certificates, or diplomas and link to factual evidence that allows others to understand the basis on which a badges was awarded and assess whether this is warranted based on face validity.

In educational contexts such as MOOCs, badges take on a secondary role which is situated and limited in terms of visibility to within the learning environment. The learner, the institution, its educators, and potentially peers can see the badges within an institution, an education, or specific parts of an education e.g. courses or even based on specific activities. In this context, badges serve as incentives to encourage and foster positive learning behaviors for the student to understand their learning progress. Badges can also hint of the possible learning trajectories of the learning content [10], which the MOOC provides.

As a gamification technique, badges are usually associated with reaching larger milestones as opposed to points that can be used at higher frequency for short term feedback [2]. Gamified education systems have been using digital badges in relation to 1) finishing an activity (small badges), 2) finishing a step/making progress (medium badges), 3) recognition (large, recognition of proficiency) and 4) finishing a course and external certification [12]. For learners, badges become sub-goals designed to represent e.g. the level of skill needed to complete or the type of competency gained [20]. However, if obtained too easily they might not be attributed to skill development [12]. Typical explanations for low preferences for badges included perceptions of them being childish or silly [15].

General criticism of digital badges, is directed at the trust in the credibility of digital badges due to their multi-purpose. To accommodate for the multiple roles which badges may carry, it is possible to visually alter the role badges may carry. For example, Higashi et al. [12] played with the size and shape of badges as an indicator of their role (activity or course) and accumulative badges that visually build on another and whether they were meant to give quick feedback/motivation.

This paper seeks to fill in the current gap, that badge authors do not have a concrete framework to inform the visual design of badges. We contribute this visual design framework with intention to be the visual component to existing conceptual badge frameworks, such as Wills et al.'s theoretical framework for digital badge design [20], which describe how badges can be rewarded as learners progress into new zones of proximal development. Other work have textually described design patterns of patterns [3], but did not break down badges into their visual components.

3   Case Study

The EU has identified that in particular, the creative industries suffer from a lack of digital competencies [9]. Our case study, the DigiCulture project [5], aims at educating adults working in the creative industry, so that they gain new digital competencies, as defined by the European Digital Competencies Framework [8]. The main outcome of the DigiCulture project is a MOOC containing courses on topics such as The World Wide Web, Digital Safety, Mobile User Experience and Virtual Reality. To facilitate certification, the DigiCulture MOOC will use badges, which follow the Open Badges standard, maintained by the IMS Global Learning Consortium [13]. Open Badges is an open-source framework, which defines how MOOCs can interoperate with badge platforms. Learners can use these badge platforms to share their acquired badges with potential employers who can verify their validity.

In order to design badges with respect to both gamification and verification, we distinguished badges into 1) *gamification badges* and 2) *certification badges*. Figure 1 depicts how gamification badges serve as internal reward to maintain user engagement (also referred to as lightweight badges [19]), whereas certification badges are given through assessment and serve as certificates.

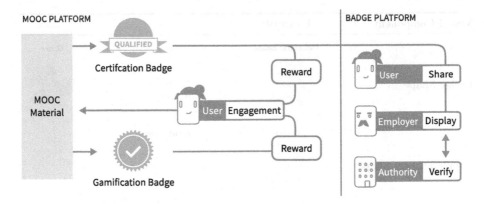

Fig. 1. Flow chart of badges from MOOC to badge platform. Gamifying badges only serve as internal reward, whereas certifying badges provide skill verification.

Badge Design Canvas [6] is recognized as a practical badge design tool for educational contexts, which helps designing the process of awarding badges. Using it can give clarification to define, for example, badges' value proposition, the desired user behaviors and the acquired skills each badge represent. We intend to contribute to this design space with more granular tools, which 1) distinguish *certification badges* from *gamification badges*, 2) extend the identification of visual properties in these badge types and 3) provide guidelines for what is visually important.

4   Visual Design Framework

We define certification badges as *badges which are achieved to reflect a certification of skill* and gamification badges as *badges which are achieved as a reward of completing an activity*. Certification and gamification badges serve different audiences. Gamification badges, principally never leave the MOOC ecosphere, which means that there is more freedom for badge designers to use wording or imagery which contextualizes directly to the individual activity. Contrarily, certification badges will be seen by agencies and employers and could be shown in e.g. portfolios or CVs and symbolically act as a certificate, further constraining the visual design process.

The visual design framework is based on critical and creative investigations using *Arts Practice as Research* [18], a method which describes the process undertaken in the creation of visual arts. This included surveying a large number of badge visuals from the internet and related publications and culminated into a digital collage. Figure 2 displays a breakdown of common badge characteristics as observed in educational contexts, useful for informing a design process.

Visual Component	Example

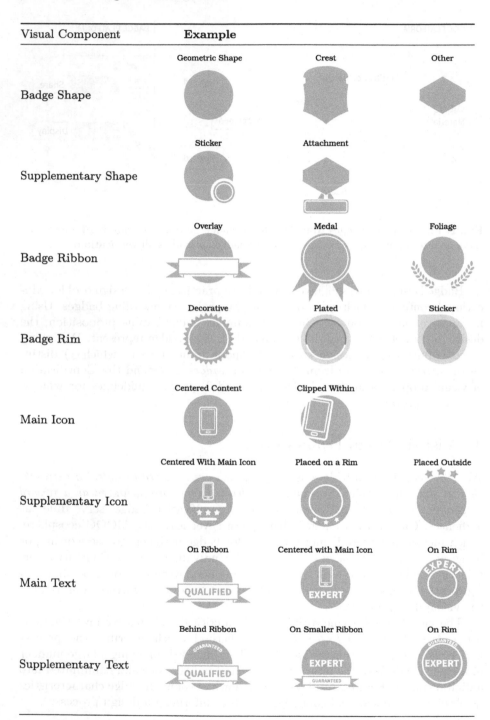

Fig. 2. Landscape of badge visual components and examples of use.

4.1 Mapping Badge Dimensions to Visual Components

Table 1 lists the dimensions in MOOC badges and exemplifies how the dimensions could be used on certifying badges and gamifying badges respectively. The most notable difference between gamifying badges and certifying badges, lies in how the dimensions they share are prioritized in practice through the visual hierarchy, which is described in Table 2. For example, for an certifying badge, having no expiration date means that employers would have no way to establish whether the badge is still a valid representation of the owners skills. Having issuing organization in an certifying badge, would likewise mean that employers would know whether the badge is issued by a trusted source. Due to the certification badge's extended responsibility as a verifiable certification tool, priority is given to explain its purpose and establish its trustworthiness to any audience who is unfamiliar with the MOOC. Gamification badges, on the other hand, can rely on a singular audience and a singular context which creates less constraint. This allows gamification badges to be more expressive than certification badges and therefore can draw more on viscerally response upon receival.

Table 1. Identified dimensions, exemplified through two MOOC badge types.

	Certification badge	Gamification badge
Name Reflecting student achievement	Qualified UX designer	Prototyping patriarch
Purpose What role does the badge play	Certifies competencies	Rewards progress
Audiences Who will view the badge	Student, employers	Only the student
Criterias Badge issuing requirements	Complete the course	e.g. Complete a quiz
Competencies The student's acquired skills	Content creation	Content creation
Course name What course is the badge from	Mobile UX course	Mobile UX course
Issuer Responsible for badge validity	MOOC	MOOC
Competency level Skill level required to achieve	Proficient	Beginner
Issue date How old the certification is	02/07/2019	02/07/2019
Expiration date For how long the badge is valid	02/07/2020	None
Evidence Evidence of the student's skill	e.g. URLs to a portfolio	Not necessary

Table 2. Badge dimensions, prioritized for communication based on badge type.

Priority	Certifying badge	Gamifying badge
1	Badge name The badge's identity	Badge name The badge's identity
2	Badge purpose Establishes certification	Competency level Gamifying badges reward progress
3	Issuing organization Establishing trust to badge	Course name Provides extra context to students
4	Expiration date Establishes badge validity	–

5   Next Steps

In relation to the DigiCulture project, 13 certifying badges will be designed through consistent mapping between badge dimensions to visual components. In addition, each course will feature any number of gamifying badges, as decided by each partner. To this extend, we have considered to design a badge generator system. Existing systems for designing badges exist, for example *BadgeBuilder* seen in Fig. 3. A badge generator system could help constrain the design process for partners to maintain visual consistency, while allowing each course to contain its own unique designs.

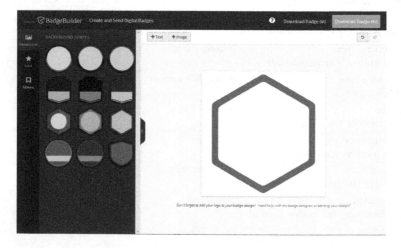

Fig. 3. BadgeBuilder by Accredible [1].

6 Conclusion

Adding multiple purposes to badges create tensions in terms of what information should be given visual priority. We proposed a divide between certification badges and gamification badges, which allow MOOCs to keep badges for internal reward, where higher freedom of expression is allowed from badges given which represent skill acquisition. We presented tools to aid the open badge design process and we intend to design and implement badges of both types for the DigiCulture project.

Acknowledgements. This work was partially funded by the EU Erasmus+ DigiCulture project grant no. 2018-1-RO01-KA204-049368.

References

1. Accredible: BadgeBuilder (2018). https://badge.design/
2. Broer, J.: The gamification inventory: an instrument for the qualitative evaluation of gamification and its application to learning management systems. Ph.D. thesis, Universität Bremen, Bremen (2017)
3. Buchem, I.: Entwurfsmuster für digitale kompetenznachweise auf basis von open badges im kontext virtueller mobilität (design patterns for digital competency credentials based on open badges in the context of virtual mobility). In: Proceedings der Pre-Conference-Workshops der 16, E-Learning Fachtagung Informatik Co-located with 16th e-Learning Conference of the German Computer Society (DeLFI 2018), Frankfurt, Germany, 10 September 2018 (2018)
4. Deterding, S., Dixon, D., Khaled, R., Nacke, L.: From game design elements to gamefulness: defining "gamification". In: Proceedings of the 15th International Academic MindTrek Conference: Envisioning Future Media Environments, MindTrek 2011, pp. 9–15. ACM (2011). https://doi.org/10.1145/2181037.2181040
5. DigiCulture: Digital Culture Erasmus+ European Project - improving the digital competences and social inclusion of adults in creative industries (2018). https://digiculture.eu/en/
6. Digitalme: Badge Design Canvas - Digital Me, July 2018. https://www.digitalme.co.uk/assets/pdf/DigitalMe-Badge-Design-Canvas.pdf
7. Ellis, L.E., Nunn, S.G., Avella, J.T.: Digital badges and micro-credentials: historical overview, motivational aspects, issues, and challenges. In: Ifenthaler, D., Bellin-Mularski, N., Mah, D.-K. (eds.) Foundation of Digital Badges and Micro-Credentials, pp. 3–21. Springer, Cham (2016). https://doi.org/10.1007/978-3-319-15425-1_1
8. European Commission: The Digital Competence Framework 2.0 - EU Science Hub (2015). https://ec.europa.eu/jrc/en/digcomp/digital-competence-framework
9. European Commission: Press release - What is the Digital Economy and Society Index? February 2016. http://europa.eu/rapid/press-release_MEMO-16-385_en.htm
10. Gibson, D., Ostashewski, N., Flintoff, K., Grant, S., Knight, E.: Digital badges in education. Educ. Inf. Technol. **20**(2), 403–410 (2015). https://doi.org/10.1007/s10639-013-9291-7

11. Helmefalk, M.: An interdisciplinary perspective on gamification: mechanics, psychological mediators and outcomes. Int. J. Serious Games **6**(1), 3–26 (2019). https://doi.org/10.17083/ijsg.v6i1.262
12. Higashi, R., Abramovich, S., Shoop, R., Schunn, C.: The roles of badges in the computer science student network, p. 8 (2012)
13. IMS Global Learning Consortium: Open Badges (2017). https://openbadges.org/
14. Janzow, P.: Connecting learning to jobs through digital badges. Catalyst **42**, 9–11 (2014)
15. Jia, Y., Xu, B., Karanam, Y., Voida, S.: Personality-targeted gamification: a survey study on personality traits and motivational affordances. In: Proceedings of the 2016 CHI Conference on Human Factors in Computing Systems, CHI 2016, pp. 2001–2013. ACM, New York (2016). https://doi.org/10.1145/2858036.2858515
16. Ostashewski, N., Reid, D.: A history and frameworks of digital badges in education. In: Reiners, T., Wood, L.C. (eds.) Gamification in Education and Business, pp. 187–200. Springer, Cham (2015). https://doi.org/10.1007/978-3-319-10208-5_10
17. Reich, J., Ruipérez-Valiente, J.A.: The MOOC pivot. Science **363**(6423), 130–131 (2019). https://doi.org/10.1126/science.aav7958
18. Sullivan, G.: Art Practice as Research: Inquiry in Visual Arts, 2nd edn. Sage Publications, Thousand Oaks (2010)
19. West, R., Randall, D.: The case for rigor in open badges. In: Muilenburg, L.Y., Berge, Z.L. (eds.) Digital Badges in Education: Trends, Issues, and Cases, 1st edn, pp. 21–29. Routledge, New York (2016)
20. Wills, C., Xie, Y.: Toward a comprehensive theoretical framework for designing digital badges. In: Ifenthaler, D., Bellin-Mularski, N., Mah, D.-K. (eds.) Foundation of Digital Badges and Micro-Credentials, pp. 261–272. Springer, Cham (2016). https://doi.org/10.1007/978-3-319-15425-1_14

Make Waste Fun Again! A Gamification Approach to Recycling

Miralem Helmefalk$^{(\boxtimes)}$ ⓘ and Joacim Rosenlund ⓘ

Linnaeus University, 391 82 Kalmar, Sweden
{miralem.helmefalk,joacim.rosenlund}@lnu.se

Abstract. There is a recognised need to improve recycling rates. One current issue is that knowledge and incentives to recycle are sometimes lacking. Mechanisms of gamification can be used to motivate and engage people to recycle, but this has not been thoroughly explored to date. To address this issue, four focus groups were conducted to bridge the gap between gamification and recycling behaviour. Results from these focus groups showed that functional solutions are preferred and that gamification can preferably be implemented digitally to bridge the gap between behaviour and knowledge. Feedback, awards, achievements, collaborative and competitive elements, as well as supplementary functions are gamified mechanisms that can be used for this purpose. This study contributes to the understanding and implementation of gamification for use in waste management and to influence positive recycling behaviour.

Keywords: Gamification · Recycling · Waste management · Mechanics · Behaviour · Bin

1 Introduction

1.1 Intro

In UN sustainable development goal 12 the importance of recycling is emphasised. Further, the circular economy is now a worldwide movement aiming for a resource efficient society without waste [1]. Recycling is increasingly recognized as a local as well as worldwide economic and social concern. A well-functioning waste management system is dependent on the users and their behaviour. For waste management organisations to achieve effective recycling, it is crucial to understand the thoughts and feeling of people to modify imperative stimuli to impact recycling behaviours. A gamification approach can encourage these individuals by increasing their engagement and motivation.

While there has been a discussion in the literature about serious games and gamifying recycling [2, 3], there has not been any substantial output. We argue that the gamification framework has not been sufficiently explored in the context of waste management. As such we want to answer the research question "how can gamification improve recycling behaviour?".

A. Brooks and E. I. Brooks (Eds.): ArtsIT 2019/DLI 2019, LNICST 328, pp. 415–426, 2020.
https://doi.org/10.1007/978-3-030-53294-9_30

To address this question, we conducted four focus groups where the participants engaged in a discussion about recycling and how to gamify this. These helped us to identify solutions for recycling challenges with the help of gamification mechanisms. Potential propositions for further research were also identified aiding in the application of a gamification framework to promote recycling in particular and sustainability in general.

1.2 Background

An increasingly amount of resources and time are invested in finding ways to improve the recycling rates among citizens. A previous research project in south Sweden showed a good potential for sorting more of the household waste [4]. A follow up project showed the importance of integrating research with solutions in practice through collaboration between researchers and waste management associations [5], working together to find solutions rather than problems.

The case used in this paper is based on a newly formed waste management association. The association introduced kerbside collection (where the bins are outside on the sidewalk) with all fractions present in the bins as these are divided into different compartments. These have an advantage of being close to home but studies have also shown that these can be more expensive than sorting in coloured bags for example [6].

Waste management behaviour has been shown to be predicted by environmental values, situational characteristics and psychological factors [7]. Different stakeholders have different influence on the waste management system, thus site-specific studies are necessary to evaluate how these works. Identified factors that influence waste sorting programmes include: distance between property and collection system, type of collected material, residential structure, information, economic incentives and alternative places for discharge [8]. The lack of space and lack of feedback about the effects of sorting are two issues that have been identified in connection to recycling [9]. Being able to sort out waste fractions close to home has also been shown to improve sorting rates along with information channels to support this [10]. In the past many waste management actors have put emphasis on functional traits such as the distance to bins and availability [11].

In contrast to functional traits there is evidence that the most important factors for a person to start considering to recycle is time and resources, sometimes defined as effort [12]. The Swedish Waste Management Association have reported on the demographic factors and behaviour concerning sorting. Further, information is important to change established norms and habits. There is also a need for citizens to know about the potential consequences of not sorting [13]. The report also acknowledges the importance of waste management organisations and property owners to collaborate.

One of the strongest predictors on recycling behaviours are internal facilitators, such as knowledge and commitment, followed by external incentives such as money and social pressure [14]. While human recycling behaviour is widely researched, such as within motivational theories, far less has been conducted using a gamification framework that consider cognitive, emotional and behavioural elements. For example, there is a recognized gap in between what people say they recycle and what is actually observed in measurements [15].

2   Theory – Towards a Framework of Gamification

Gamification is a broad concept, covering different subjects and domains [16]. Generally, it is defined as employing the fundamental mechanics of games in non-game contexts [17]. A central feature of gamification is the ability to motivate and engage people to conducts various behaviours through these elements [18–20]. It should not be confounded with games in general, but rather the various mechanics and features that exists within games, such as competitive elements, social interaction, leader boards or badges [21]. These mechanics have been found to have an impact on different psychological concepts, such as arousal, engagement other [22–25]. For example, Burgun [26] states that young people are born into the logic of gaming and that some students are spending time playing games as much as going to school.

Unquestionably, games are used as a leisure activity, but research has also found evidence [27, 28] of games being effective for facilitating learning, concentration and involvement in different activities. It has been argued in research whether or not gamification is a new phenomenon [29], there is no doubt that the bulk of literature has grown on gamification in the last decade. Nacke and Deterding [30] states that gamification has matured to be a comprehensive framework of which can be used to facilitate further research. Thus, gamification has been widely employed by various domains, such as crowdsourcing, health, computer science, software development, tourism, and marketing [16].

An important foundation for gamification is the mechanics and dynamics (sometimes referred interchangeably) which are employed into different processes and services. Some mechanics are more common than other and these are points, badges and leader boards, which are more often employed for describing the effects of gamification [18, 31]. Despite being very generalized there are many more that are used in research [32]. Many of these are recommended to be implemented in relation to the actual user, or as Dale [33] who mentions, "Good gamification design should be user-centric and not mechanism-centric". This is also in line with what Burke [34] states that mechanics should not be pasted upon existing services or processes without fully implementing them as being part of the process. It is also crucial to understand that these mechanics are influencing people cognitively and emotionally, which is a prerequisite for being engaging and motivating. Thus, it is seldom these mechanics are used, researched or mentioned without the mental states of people.

Psychological concepts that have been examined in connection to gamification are companionship, social engagement, positive emotions, fun, enjoyment, contribution, relevance, accomplishment, growth and many other [e.g. 35–37]. A mental state that is largely emphasized in research is the properties of engagement and motivation. Motivation as a concept is widely studied and explored in research. One of the most well explored theories is the self-determination theory (SDT) of which the well-known article by Ryan and Deci [38] cites motivation as "To be motivated means to be moved to do something". They also state that is important to fall into the misconception that motivation is a uniform concept, but rather a branch of different variations. It is also often divided into external and internal incentives, where external are sanctions and money, while internal are autonomy, self-fulfilment and other internal motivators [39]. It is foremost the internal ones that is central in gamification [40, 41] where people are through joy and feeling of control, competence development and other psychological needs engage themselves into tasks and activities [42].

The causative chain from mechanics to psychological mediators and on outcomes are evident in literature [16, 45]. Although the linkage is discussed, it is still being relatively unexplored for which mechanics exactly cause what psychological states, that further mediates on what outcomes [46]. This is further pinpointed in Alahäivälä and Oinas-Kukkonen [47] that state "There is not yet a clear, generally accepted vision of the relationships among the contextual factors, gamification strategies, and study outcomes." (p. 69).

The causal framework is most evidently discussed and portrayed in Hamari et al. [45] and Helmefalk [16], that categorize the chain from mechanics, psychological mediators and lastly on measured outcomes. This sequence emphasizes the effects of mechanics on the mental state that subsequently facilitate behaviours. As mentioned, while not clearly evidenced for which mechanic impacts on what mental state and behaviour, there is generally a pattern in research. To illustrate this sequence, a person that has to recycle trash is subjected to a gamified mechanic, such as direct feedback in form of a sound of falling trash that plays when it is thrown into a bin [e.g. 48]. These actions facilitate enjoyment and arousal, which may increase the probability of conducting the same behaviour over again. Thus, the mechanics cause a cognitive or emotional state that facilitates a behaviour. The discussion can be summarized in the adapted model from Helmefalk [16] in Fig. 1. For the extended version see Helmefalk [16].

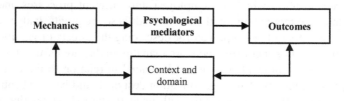

Fig. 1. Framework for gamification

3   Method

This study employed focus group design [49] to explore how and why individuals categorize and recycle waste. Moreover, this was in line with the theoretical framework, being able to examine their cognitive, emotional reasoning and how this relates to behavioural outcomes. Four focus groups were employed following the phenomenological approach by Calder´s (1977). The rationale and the advantage of employing focus group design is to gain deeper knowledge by letting participants discuss the phenomenon. This study concerns a new area of study, as such focus groups are an appropriate approach for achieving empirical data with and exploratory approach [50, 51].

A partly open semi-structured interview scheme was used based on the theoretical framework and the model (see Fig. 1) to increase credibility for the gathered data [52], and to answer the research question. While the focus group discussions were theoretically driven and somewhat restrained, they were sufficiently open to discover patterns and themes in their answers. The interview scheme followed the logic of introduction, transition and core questions, such as in Hamzah et al. [53].

The focus group participants were recruited with criteria sampling, with little to no incentive than interest and were held in four different cities in Sweden. These were held in four different cities in Sweden. The demographics of the participants in the groups were both heterogeneous and homogeneous in order to get richer discussions and to examine whether the outcomes in the discussions were different. The groups were categorized as following:

- [FG1] - Six older male participants, mixed employments, foreign background.
- [FG2] - Six younger adults, mixed employments, women.
- [FG3] - Seven students, mixed backgrounds, similar age.
- [FG4] - Six younger and elderly with mixed employments.

The discussions were audio and video recorded after getting the participants consent. To fresh up their memories, participants got a picture of a bin with different waste compartments. Each focus group took about 60–80 min and were transcribed afterwards. To ensure that each participant was involved in the discussions to avoid group bias, the moderator invited and asked all participants. The study design was based on the recycling challenges identified in the background section and the gamification framework developed in the theory section. When the recycling challenges were inputted into this framework, this formed an approach for the focus groups leading to suggested solutions based on gamification (see Fig. 2).

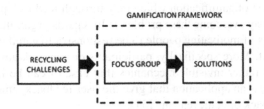

Fig. 2. Study framework

4 Findings and Discussion

4.1 Challenges of Everyday Recycling

Although it is common in past literature and is emphasized in the focus group discussions (FGDs) that utilitarian attribute are the most important ones, such as the time, distance and effort of waste separation [10–12], there are other aspects that were additional factors in the FGD. Aside from product specific attributes, participants discuss their everyday habits of waste management and that a particular problem is their management of the interim storage is that it is highly diverse. Participants have not received any complete government-provided system for guidance, but have come up with their own solutions. Thus, each participant has a unique system prior to going out with the waste. The distance in which they travel with the waste has an impact on the actual waste separation, which becomes important when deigning gamified waste separation bins. Participants in FGD have raised the incapability and frustration behind their made-up solution in relation to the public bins. Regardless for which gamification mechanic is implemented, it should consider the diverse processes when people recycle. What became evident in the FGD was that the motivation behind separating waste is highly intrinsically motivated, meaning that participants had a relatively good knowledge about the existing environmental issues and aspired to contribute to solving these. It indicates that gamification may be a good complement to foster these motivations as being used for facilitating intrinsic motivation [54, 55]. However, as the majority of respondents have good knowledge of the general issues of global warming, many indicated that they did not have any particular knowledge of what happens after they have separated the waste. Past literature has shown that knowledge is an important prerequisite for positive waste sorting behaviour [9], as such the participants mistrust discourages them to fully commit to appropriate waste separation behaviour. Such as a participant in FG4 states, "Long time ago, we heard that they burned all the trash at the same station. It still sticks with you, despite knowing this has changed". Participants in all groups desires more information and knowledge for how to separate waste and what will happen to it. In regards to gamification, mechanics has been used to teach people and to change behaviour [43, 56], which is a fitting mechanic in this context. Participants discuss the issue that they do not see immediate results when being a good citizen, and would like to receive feedback, regardless if it is about the waste management process, or other implications one owns actions has on the environment (which can take many years to realize). This logic is suitable in the context of gamification which may through feedback provide immediate feedback [57] that may overcome these problems. In regards to gamification, many have raised the difficulties of motivating people to be responsive to gamification if not being fitting in the context. More specifically, participants do not seek any particular visual game elements, but rather invisible mechanics that ease or can be implemented with other services, such as an application that give the user feedback simultaneously while implementing feedback or achievements [57].

One other concern raised in the FGDs is the aspect of children and that they may have difficulty in being properly involved in the waste separation processes. They suggest that the inclusion of gamification can make separation fun, hence more motivating for children. As for now, no such occurrences appear in the everyday separation process. It may be so that gamification can be used to disseminate knowledge of the environment [2] and the importance of waste separation, which would spring long-term effects on waste management behaviour.

4.2 Mechanics and Psychology

The FGDs have brought up various perspectives of gamification mechanics in waste separation processes. Firstly, participants recognized difficulties of implementing evident games for waste management, such as throwing thrash as balls in bins, but preferred mechanics to be as a supplementary function, aiding various aspects of waste separation. Similar to the literature that emphasize gamification as tightly and carefully interwoven into current offerings [33], which participants agree. One main raised issue was that they perceived the waste separation process as a utilitarian errand, which could be disturbed by additional steps in the waste separation process. Every added task could potentially ruin the experience. Thus, many suggested tasks that did not interfere with the physical separation processes. As previously mentioned, instant feedback was preferred, which provided them opportunity to understand what happens with the waste and to learn about the consequences of separation, which would cultivate the concept competence in self-determination theory – SDT [59]. Participants suggested everything from QR stickers on bins that provide knowledge and the current waste issues. By implementing a system that support the ease and the availability of information, they state that their motivation could increase in separating waste better. By supporting interestingly presented knowledge and usefulness as in [60], participants discussed that their uncertainty would be reduced, more engaged, hence be more prone to put more effort on improving recycling behaviour. Waste separation being a functional task, applications on the smartphone offered a greater opportunity to facilitate interaction between customers and the waste company, which then could be gamified with visual elements, achievements or other common mechanics, such as in [32].

Different kind of points or statistics were mentioned, although in different forms. Some suggested points that could be collected, most preferably by zip numbers, as these waste management companies are not allowed to gather data for individual households. Lot of mechanics are consequently limited by this and different systems require data as input for calculating and presenting information in a fun way. However, participants suggested that this may be surmounted by presenting statistics for the close neighbourhood and let the points be a comparison in fostering competition. By including the aspect of competition, these would also facilitate collaboration between neighbours to enhance the statistics, but also involve the concept of relatedness in SDT [59]. Aspects that were of particular interest were the social components that enhanced motivation, regardless wanting getting recognition by others or by avoiding public shaming, hence separating waste correctly. Many of the mechanics were suggested to be transferred to digital contexts, which subsequently depends on the person to install an app, or go to a specific homepage. By doing so, great opportunities arise in cognitively and emotionally engage people in either beginning or continuing dedicating more effort in separating waste.

4.3 Solutions and Outcomes

The FGD's came up with different solutions, which are suggested to influence various outcomes and are of value for waste separation. As this study sought to examine how waste separation can be enhanced and increase the amount of correct separated waste, it was crucial to understand for which mechanics and psychological mediators fostered this behaviour. The FGD's emphasized that effort was a variable that was crucial to satisfy and by gaining knowledge and instant feedback intrinsic motivation would be enhanced, hence result in more correct sorted waste.

The different groups varied in which mechanics were important, but all of them were close proximity to the concepts of fun, engagement(involvement), motivation, sense of purpose, social collaboration/competition and growth. Specific solutions are seen in Table 1 where these are related to gamification mechanics and the challenges of recycling.

Table 1. Gamified solutions as identified by the focus groups

Recycling problems	Gamification concepts	Gamified solutions from focus groups
Don't know if my recycling matters	Competition/points/social	Neighbourhood community and competition
Don't know if my recycling matters/want to see results of recycling	Reward/medal/gifts	Virtual receipt/data/medals/discount on waste pickup/gift cards/a virtual tree that grows
Information about recycling	Feedback	Scan QR code with mobile/app/social media
Knowledge about recycling/Don't know if my recycling matters	Reward/feedback	Modify bin as an information channel with stickers/app
Children	Making it easy and fun	Standing on a platform/comics/app/lighter lids
Sorting increase with social pressure	Social aspect/leaderboard	Informing about consequences/social media
Need to improve sorting behaviour	Relatedness	Personification of bins/good lighting

5   Conclusions, Implications and Future Research

Following the framework of gamification (M-PM-O) in Fig. 1, and to answer the research question, how can gamification improve recycling behaviour, this study highlight difficulties, potential mechanics, potential causal chains on improving recycling behaviour and specific solutions to achieve that. Findings show that participants prefer functional solutions firstly, and that mechanics should be a supporting function/service. The gamification should not interfere the process of physical waste separation, but be implemented digitally, where they can implement feedback and knowledge, include social mechanism, such as collaboration and competition, and provide rewards in terms of discounts, nature-congruent products and virtual growing elements, such as a tree growing as advancing.

This study contribute research the scarce knowledge in how gamification can be implemented to enhance recycling behaviour. As previous research has considered gamification as a potential tool for improving recycling and sustainability [22–25, 54, 55, 61], this present research shows empirically potential causal relationships between mechanics, psychological mediators and outcomes. Furthermore, the present study contributes to the advancement of gamification theory to explain different practical issues in people's everyday lives.

Being an exploratory study, more research is needed to empirically and experimentally test various modifications of a bin, or a system that would include the mentioned solutions. This would provide further knowledge on the scant empirical research in gamification. Also, it is suggested to evolve the notion of waste separation to larger waste separation facilities and how the context would differ in contrast to household waste separation.

References

1. Ghisellini, P., Cialani, C., Ulgiati, S.: A review on circular economy: the expected transition to a balanced interplay of environmental and economic systems. J. Clean. Prod. **114**, 11–32 (2016)
2. Briones, A.G., et al.: Use of gamification techniques to encourage garbage recycling. a smart city approach. In: International Conference on Knowledge Management in Organizations. Springer (2018). https://doi.org/10.1007/978-3-319-95204-8_56
3. Berengueres, J., Alsuwairi, F., Zaki, N., Ng, T.: Gamification of a recycle bin with emoticons. In: Proceedings of the 8th ACM/IEEE International Conference on Human-Robot Interaction. IEEE Press (2013)
4. Bergbäck, B., Sörme, L., Bayard, A.-C.: Samhällets restprodukter-framtidens resurser. Linnaeus University, Kalmar (2016)
5. Rosenlund, J., Sörme, L., Voxberg, E., Augustsson, A.J.A.E.E.: When appreciative inquiry guides action research: collaborating to improve waste sorting. Appl. Environ. Educ. Comm. 1–14 (2019)
6. Andersson, T., Sundqvist, J.O., Hultén, J., Sandkvist, F.: Ekonomisk jämförelse av två system för fastighetsnära insamling av avfall. IVL Svenska Miljöinstitutet, Stockholm (2018)
7. Barr, S.: Factors influencing environmental attitudes and behaviors: a UK case study of household waste management. Environ. Behav. **39**(4), 435–473 (2007)
8. Dahlén, L., Lagerkvist, A.: Evaluation of recycling programmes in household waste collection systems. Waste Manage. Res. **28**(7), 577–586 (2010)
9. Ordoñez, I., Harder, R., Nikitas, A., Rahe, U.: Waste sorting in apartments: integrating the perspective of the user. J. Clean. Prod. **106**, 669–679 (2015)
10. Rousta, K., Bolton, K., Lundin, M., Dahlén, L.: Quantitative assessment of distance to collection point and improved sorting information on source separation of household waste. Waste Manage. **40**, 22–30 (2015)
11. Reid, D.H., Luyben, P.D., Rawers, R.J., Bailey, J.S.J.E.: Newspaper recycling behavior: the effects of prompting and proximity of containers. Environ. Behav. **8**(3), 471–482 (1976)
12. Schultz, P.W., Oskamp, S.J.S.P.Q.: Effort as a moderator of the attitude-behavior relationship: general environmental concern and recycling. Soc. Psychol. Q. 375–383 (1996)
13. Avfall Sverige: Beteendeförändring i mångfaldsområden. Avfall Sverige (2017)
14. Hornik, J., Cherian, J., Madansky, M., Narayana, C.J.T.J.o.S.-E.: Determinants of recycling behavior: a synthesis of research results. J. Socio. Econ. **24**(1) 105–127 (1995)
15. Cheung, S.F., Chan, D.K.-S., Wong, Z.S.-Y.J.E.: Reexamining the theory of planned behavior in understanding wastepaper recycling. Environ. Behav. **31**(5), 587–612 (1999)
16. Helmefalk, M.: An interdisciplinary perspective on gamification: Mechanics, psychological mediators and outcomes. Int. J. Serious Games **6**(1), 3–26 (2019)
17. Deterding, S., Dixon, D., Khaled, R., Nacke, L.: From game design elements to gamefulness: defining gamification. In: Proceedings of the 15th International Academic MindTrek Conference: Envisioning Future Media Environments. ACM (2011)

18. Hamari, J.: Do badges increase user activity? A field experiment on the effects of gamification. Comput. Hum. Behav. **71**, 469–478 (2017)
19. Yang, Y., Asaad, Y., Dwivedi, Y.: Examining the impact of gamification on intention of engagement and brand attitude in the marketing context. Comput. Hum. Behav. **73**, 459–469 (2017)
20. Hamari, J.: Transforming homo economicus into homo ludens: a field experiment on gamification in a utilitarian peer-to-peer trading service. Electron. Commer. Res. Appl. **12**(4), 236–245 (2013)
21. Huotari, K., Hamari, J.: A definition for gamification: anchoring gamification in the service marketing literature. Electronic Markets **27**(1), 21–31 (2017). https://doi.org/10.1007/s12 525-015-0212-z?
22. Gamberini, L., et al.: Saving is fun: designing a persuasive game for power conservation. In: Proceedings of the 8th International Conference on Advances in Computer Entertainment Technology. ACM (2011)
23. Geelen, D., Keyson, D., Boess, S., Brezet, H.: Exploring the use of a game to stimulate energy saving in households. J. Des. Res. 14 **10**(1–2), 102–120 (2012)
24. Gustafsson, A., Katzeff, C., Bang, M.: Evaluation of a pervasive game for domestic energy engagement among teenagers. Comput. Entertain. (CIE) **7**(4), 54 (2009)
25. Morganti, L., Pallavicini, F., Cadel, E., Candelieri, A., Archetti, F., Mantovani, F.: Gaming for earth: serious games and gamification to engage consumers in pro-environmental behaviours for energy efficiency. Energy Res. Soc. Sci. **29**, 95–102 (2017)
26. Burgun, K.: Game Design Theory: A New Philosophy for Understanding Games. CRC Press, Boca Raton (2013)
27. Su, C.H., Cheng, C.H.: A mobile gamification learning system for improving the learning motivation and achievements. J. Comput. Assist. Learn. **31**(3), 268–286 (2015)
28. Dicheva, D., Dichev, C., Agre, G., Angelova, G.: Gamification in education: a systematic mapping study. J. Educ. Technol. Soc. **18**(3) (2015)
29. Cochoy, F., Hagberg, J.: The Business of Gamification: A Critical Analysis. In: Dymek, M., Zackariasson, P. (eds.), pp. 81–99. Routledge, New York (2016) .
30. Nacke, L.E., Deterding, S.: The maturing of gamification research. Comput. Hum. Behav. **71**, 450–454 (2017)
31. Landers, R.N., Bauer, K.N., Callan, R.C.: Gamification of task performance with leaderboards: a goal setting experiment. Comput. Hum. Behav. **71**, 508–515 (2017)
32. Helmefalk, M., Lundqvist, S., Marcusson, L.: The role of mechanics in gamification: an interdisciplinary perspective. Int. J. Virtual Augmented Reality **3**(1), 18–41 (2019)
33. Dale, S.: Gamification: making work fun, or making fun of work? Bus. Inf. Rev. **31**(2), 82–90 (2014)
34. Burke, B.: Gamify: How Gamification Motivates People To Do Extraordinary Things. Routledge, London (2016)
35. Hofacker, C.F., de Ruyter, K., Lurie, N.H., Manchanda, P., Donaldson, J.: Gamification and mobile marketing effectiveness. J. Interact. Mark. **34**, 25–36 (2016)
36. Harwood, T., Garry, T.: An investigation into gamification as a customer engagement experience environment. J. Serv. Mark. **29**(6–7), 533–546 (2015)
37. Pettit, R.K., McCoy, L., Kinney, M., Schwartz, F.N.: Student perceptions of gamified audience response system interactions in large group lectures and via lecture capture technology. BMC Med. Educ. **15**(1), 92 (2015). https://doi.org/10.1186/s12909-015-0373-7
38. Ryan, R.M., Deci, E.L.: Intrinsic and extrinsic motivations: classic definitions and new directions. Contemp. Educ. Psychol. **25**(1), 54–67 (2000)
39. Deci, E., Ryan, R.M.: Intrinsic Motivation and Self-Determination in Human Behavior. Springer, Heidelberg (1985). https://doi.org/10.1007/978-1-4899-2271-7

40. Sardi, L., Idri, A., Fernández-Alemán, J.L.: A systematic review of gamification in e-health. J. Biomed. Inform. **71**, 31–48 (2017)
41. Johnson, D., Horton, E., Mulcahy, R., Foth, M.: Gamification and serious games within the domain of domestic energy consumption: a systematic review. Renew. Sustain. Energy Rev. **73**, 249–264 (2017)
42. Deci, E.L., Ryan, R.M., Gagné, M., Leone, D.R., Usunov, J., Kornazheva, B.P.: Need satisfaction, motivation, and well-being in the work organizations of a former eastern bloc country: a cross-cultural study of self-determination. Pers. Soc. Psychol. Bull. **27**(8), 930–942 (2001)
43. González, C.S., et al.: Learning healthy lifestyles through active videogames, motor games and the gamification of educational activities. Comput. Hum. Behav. **55**, 529–551 (2016)
44. Högberg, J., Shams, P., Wästlund, E.: Gamified in-store mobile marketing: the mixed effect of gamified point-of-purchase advertising. J. Retail. Consum. Serv. **50**, 298–304 (2018)
45. Hamari, J., Koivisto, J., Sarsa, H.: Does gamification work?–a literature review of empirical studies on gamification. In: 2014 47th Hawaii International Conference on System Sciences (HICSS). IEEE (2014)
46. Hervas, R., Ruiz-Carrasco, D., Mondejar, T., Bravo, J.: Gamification mechanics for behavioral change: a systematic review and proposed taxonomy. In: Proceedings of the 11th EAI International Conference on Pervasive Computing Technologies for Healthcare. ACM (2017)
47. Alahäivälä, T., Oinas-Kukkonen, H.: Understanding persuasion contexts in health gamification: a systematic analysis of gamified health behavior change support systems literature. Int. J. Med. Informatics **96**, 62–70 (2016)
48. TheGamefulCompany. Gamification of the trash bin. (2010). http://theplayful.company/gamification-of-the-trash-bin/. Accessed 7 June 2018
49. Churchill, G.A.: A paradigm for developing better measures of marketing constructs. J. Mark. Res. **16**(1), 64–73 (1979)
50. Malhotra, N.K., Nunan, D., Birks, D.: Marketing Research: An Applied Approach, 5th edn. Harlow, Pearson (2017)
51. Stewart, D.W. Samdasani, P.N.: Focus Groups: Theory and Practice, 3 edn. Applied Social Research Methods. SAGE Publications Inc, Thousand Oaks: New York (2015)
52. Kamberelis, G., Dimitradis, G., Walker, A.: Focus group research and/in figured worlds. In: Denzin, N.K., Lincoln, Y.S. (eds.) The SAGE Handbook of Qualitative Research, SAGE Publications Inc: United States of America, pp. 692–716 (2017)
53. Hamzah, Z.L., Syed Alwi, S.F., Othman, M.N.: Designing corporate brand experience in an online context: a qualitative insight. J. Bus. Res. **67**, 2299–2310 (2014)
54. Salvador, R., Romão, T., Centieiro, P.: A gesture interface game for energy consumption awareness. In: Advances in Computer Entertainment. Springer, pp. 352–367 (2012). https://doi.org/10.1007/978-3-642-34292-9_25
55. Stone, R., Guest, R., Pahl, S., Boomsma, C.: Exploiting gaming technologies to visualise dynamic thermal qualities of a domestic dwelling: pilot study of an interactive virtual apartment. In: Behave Energy Conference (2014)
56. Mora, A., Riera, D., González, C., Arnedo-Moreno, J.: Gamification: a systematic review of design frameworks. J. Comput. High. Educ. **29**(3), 516–548 (2017). https://doi.org/10.1007/s12528-017-9150-4
57. Conaway, R., Garay, M.C.: Gamification and service marketing. Springerplus **3**(1), 653 (2014). https://doi.org/10.1186/2193-1801-3-653
58. Pine, B.J. Gilmore, J.H.: The Experience Economy: Work Is Theatre & Every Business a Stage. Harvard Business Press, New York (1999)
59. Deci, E.L., Ryan, R.M.: The "what" and "why" of goal pursuits: human needs and the self-determination of behavior. Psychol. Inq. **11**(4), 227–268 (2000)

60. Aguiar-Castillo, L., Clavijo-Rodriguez, A., Saa-Perez, D., Perez-Jimenez, R.J.S.: Gamification as an approach to promote tourist recycling behavior. Sustainability **11**(8), 2201 (2019)
61. Knol, E., De Vries, P.W.: EnerCities-a serious game to stimulate sustainability and energy conservation: preliminary results. Elearning Pap. (2011)

Our Museum Game
A Collaborative Game for User-Centered Exhibition Design

Kristina Maria Madsen⑩ and Rameshnath Krishnasamy⁽⊠⁾ ⑩

Aalborg University, 9000 Aalborg, Denmark
{krma,krishnasamy}@hum.aau.dk

Abstract. The 'Our Museum' board game (referred to as 'the game' throughout this paper) is a dialogical tool for museum professionals, researchers, exhibition designers and developers. The game is designed and developed through a coordinated effort between museum professionals and researchers. The work presented here will detail the conception of the game and establish parts of the theoretical background for the game design, offset by two iterations that are based on insights from two separate playtests. These insights have been reworked and implemented into the current version of the game. With the game, we aim to offer a tool-supported method to tackle user-centered challenges in the exhibition space, by bringing different roles together and provide a medium to form a shared language as a part of the design process of creating exhibitions. The work here could be interesting to both practitioners as well as researchers working within the museum context and to an extent within the fields of games and gamification.

Keywords: Museums · Design game · Game design · Gamification

1 Museums Between Enlightenment and Experience

Over the years, many fields have merged with museological studies and development, with scholars from anthropology, psychology, education and technology, contributing to a trend towards more diverse experiences in museums [1–3]. However, when different professions, such as curators, exhibition designers, technology providers and user researchers engage in a collaborative design process, the communication and understanding between them is challenged by their respective domain knowledge. One way to address these underlying challenges is through research projects. The 'Our Museum' (OM) research program (2016–2020) is among the most recent research and development initiatives in Denmark (ourmuseum.dk) stemming from a long line of collaborative constellations that combine academics and professionals from the museum context, such as European National Museums (EuNaMus), Material Encounters with Digital Cultural Heritage (meSch) and Europeana. The program is a national collaboration between 5 universities and 8 museums with 13 individual research projects. The collaborating museums are a mix of arts, cultural and natural history museums. The foci for the 13 projects span from analytical to practical, where some study the museum context in a

A. Brooks and E. I. Brooks (Eds.): ArtsIT 2019/DLI 2019, LNICST 328, pp. 427–435, 2020.
https://doi.org/10.1007/978-3-030-53294-9_31

historical perspective while others engage in practice-based research with design and development as their primary objectives.

The OM program's overriding thesis is that museums are historically created and developed in a field of tension between a perception of the museum as a means of public information and enlightenment and as a means for the visitor's experience and entertainment; and that this tension field is particularly visible in dilemmas emerging with current communication practices [4, 5]. Here, the term 'enlightenment' denotes the didactic, educational, factual, forming and informative, while 'experience', on the contrary, denotes emotional, engaging, entertaining, imaginative, involving, narrative and playful. From this, the 8 museums articulated research projects in collaboration with the 5 universities, resulting in 13 research projects. However, in order to align all the projects, three analytical dimensions were defined as part of the research inquiries and investigations. These dimensions are *institution, communication* and *user*. These three dimensions ensure that the 13 projects have a shared agenda to investigate, understand and challenge the collaborating museum institutions in how they communicate their knowledge to the public and how they position their users. As the research program is currently nearing its end-of-cycle, the knowledge shared between the projects, collaborators and the program, are being refined into 'research contributions'. Thus, the program, the projects, the collaborating museums, the insights gained, and the knowledge produced over the past three years incentivized the development of the board game. We will elaborate on the framing of the game in the coming section, in part through theoretical foundations and in part by translating the program's foundational thesis regarding enlightenment and experience, along with the three analytical dimensions into game elements.

2 Collaborative Game Play

2.1 Collaborative Design

Collaboration is an essential activity of museum practice, across both professions in-house, with other museums or organizations and with design or consultant companies. Knudsen and Olesen [6] discuss the potentials and challenges of collaboration in museums by identifying three constellations of collaborative design in museum studies: *internal collaboration across different museum staff groups; collaboration across museum staff and external design professionals;* and *collaboration across museum staff and museum users* [6]. This goes to show that the museums are facing multiple collaborative situations in the daily practice. Some of which are connected to the development of communication and exhibition design. There are many ways to approach collaborative design. Brown [7] describes innovative design as a product of interdisciplinary team efforts not a lone designer - *'all of us are smarter than any of us'* - the key to unlocking the creative power of any organization. In these interdisciplinary collaborations Cross [8] points to the fact that the participants assume different roles in collaborative design processes rather than representing their profession but assuming a social role in the group dynamic; being a facilitator, taking charge etc. It can be argued that it is in these group dynamics that we can distinguish between multidisciplinary and interdisciplinary as Brown [7] describes it. Interdisciplinarity occurs when multiple professions collectively take ownership of ideas, rather than advocating their respective domain.

Sanders and Stappers [9] also discusses both the roles and facilitation of collaborative endeavors. They propose generative tools to create a shared language for the collaborating stakeholders to communicate and discuss ideas, requirements, potentials, limitations and dreams. Sanders and Stappers described generative design methods and research as a way of providing this shared language: *'Generative design research gives people a language with which they can imagine and express their ideas and dreams for future experiences. These ideas and dreams can, in turn, inform and inspire other stakeholders in the design and development process'* [9]. By approaching a collaborative design process through workshops with generative tools, we can support stakeholders in developing a common interdisciplinary design language, one which can make people's different ways of seeing, thinking and doing come together in agreement - from multidisciplinary to interdisciplinarity. Gudiksen and Inlove [10] take the generative toolbox idea one step further, by arguing for the relevance of gamification and game design to facilitate collaborative and innovative design. Gudiksen and Inlove [10] propose that games and game-based design can facilitate better communication, breaking down silos and engaging staff. Thus, using games as a method for facilitating development processes and initiating shared language between participants.

2.2 Game Design

The objective was initially to create a tool-supported method to facilitate design processes behind exhibitions through collaboration. However, the complexity of facilitating such activities increase with the number of different roles. The logic behind using games, or more specifically, gamification stems from multiple points of interests, but here we focus on the concept of 'third space communication' [10, 11] and how games can act as a space between spaces. The notion of 'third space' can be explained as the void that exists between two or more participants with different domains. Participants will always bring their professional background, history and specialized language into a discussion. This can in turn create confusion and misunderstanding between the participants. The 'third space' offers a way to facilitate and mediate between participants, for example through the use of generative tools, where participants can work towards a common goal. Bringing the participants together is insufficient; a structure is required to engage in a design process where participants can be supported to engage in processes that enables them to transition from multidisciplinary to interdisciplinary. In other words, a collaborative setting that includes tools and techniques that can support stakeholders in developing a common interdisciplinary design language [9, 10]. Building on past research, such as 'design games' to overcome organizational challenges [10] and past experiences [12, 13], we applied gamification as a method to merge the spaces.

Here we highlight some of the features that makes games formidable tools for facilitating collaborative design practices but recognize that games are highly complex multilayered systems. We extracted core elements from the research program and translated these into game elements; we have experienced first-hand and studied in the literature the complexities of gathering multiple disciplines in collaborative design activities, so we implemented roles. We also included a resource mechanics to drive the game and facilitate decision-making activities. We looked to game theory to understand how play modes can affect the game and to select a suitable one. Here we identified three categories; competitive, cooperative and collaborative. In competitive games, players are diametrically opposed and require them to form strategies that directly oppose other players in the game, such as chess [14]. Cooperative games offer a situation where two or more players have interests that are "neither completely opposed nor completely coincident" [15]. Collaborative games necessitate collaboration and are games that supports players working as a team and sharing the payoffs as a team. This means that if a team wins or loses, every player wins or loses [16]. A team can be seen as an organization in which the kind of information each person has can differ, but the interests and beliefs are the same [16]. This can be mapped to the different roles, where they can share the same goal of wanting to create a compelling exhibition experience for the user, but a mismatch between the underlying information can create miscommunication and disagreements. Consequently, a competitive game is not suitable due to the ego-centric win-condition. However, cooperative games have elements that can reward a team effort, yet in a cooperative game, players can still abuse the game system to e.g. 'free-ride', meaning they get carried through the game without contributing to the effort. We want every role to be represented and active, so the third option seems most suitable; a team effort where the whole team wins or the whole team loses. In the paper *Collaborative games: Lessons learned from board games* [16] three pitfalls are highlighted that should be taken into consideration while creating collaborative board games. Pitfall 1: *To avoid the game degenerating into one player making the decisions for the team, collaborative games have to provide a sufficient rationale for collaboration.*, Pitfall 2: *For a game to be engaging, players need to care about the outcome and that outcome should have a satisfying result.*, Pitfall 3: *For a collaborative game to be enjoyable multiple times, the experience needs to be different each time and the presented challenge needs to evolve* [16]. We considered these pitfalls while creating the game, which will be reflected upon in the gameplay subsection.

We then ask ourselves; how can we design a game that integrates the agenda and insights of the research program, in a space that allows for facilitation of multiple professions to design exhibitions through collaborative practices.

3   The Our Museum Game

The Our Museum Game was designed to assist and facilitate ideation for exhibition design which takes enlightenment and experience into consideration. It was created as a dialogical tool that invites different roles into a collaborative design process. The need for such a tool emerged from the collaboration between research projects and museum institutions under the Our Museum research program. The challenge of creating the game, was to include activities that can facilitate and support the design process by directing the participants towards a shared language through common goals and ownership, while retaining focus on the user-centered dimension as part of the game's underlying framework.

3.1 Gameplay

The game was designed as a board game (See Fig. 1 below) with three main phases and four intermediate phases. The three main phases are designed as a design and development lifecycle which are represented as *dialogue* tiles on the board. The four intermediate phases are definition and documentation activities. These are represented as *interval* tiles on the board where the players document a session in a report that will serve as the end product of a playthrough. This report serves as a design document that the participants may use as a plan to design, develop, implement and evaluate. The center tile is a *focus* tile where a play session's focus is laid out as a visual cue. These consist of the museum context, the user and the challenge that the participants define for each play session.

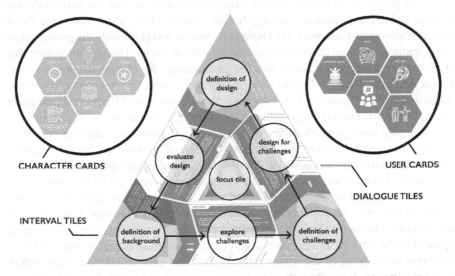

Fig. 1. The Our Museum Game board with an overview of the complete tile set.

The players start the game by selecting one of five roles from the *character* card deck; the museum curator, the exhibition designer, the exhibition developer, the researcher and the user. These roles were chosen based on the roles that are typically represented through the design process. Each role is imbued with an alignment in regard to enlightenment and experience. Some roles are neutral while others are not. The participating players can choose their professional role, or switch to a different role. The roles should address the first pitfall to avoid one player assuming control and makes all the decisions for the team. After this initial step, they must select which type of exhibition context they will be designing for; arts, history or natural history. Finally, the players must pick one of five users from the *user* cards. Four of the users are constructs based on various user types, typographies and personas found in the literature. The four types of users in the game are *explorers*, *experience-seekers*, *facilitators* and *socializers*. These were inspired by the Falk and Dierking's visitor types in *Identity and the museum visitor experience* [17]. A fifth user card is included with instructions to create a specific user type that does not fall under the predefined four. They are then done with the setup and can initiate the first main phase. The first main phase is "explore challenges", where the players will investigate and identify one primary challenge. The second phase is "design for challenges", where the players will generate, combine and define one primary exhibition concept design. The third phase is "evaluate design", where the players will create a plan to test and evaluate their exhibition concept in praxis. During each main phase, the players spend a limited amount of "influence counters" to vote and select challenges, design concepts and evaluative methods, respectively. The session concludes with an end step where the session is rehashed and documented.

3.2   Primary Collaborative Traits that the Game Enables

The games purpose is to mainly support three primary traits, to lead the players through the game and define an idea and strategy for the design of a new exhibition, installation, communication, etc. **Collaborative Design:** As mentioned previously the game seeks to collect multiple museum professions around exhibition design. Through the games character cards, intervals and dialogue tiles the game nudges the players to take ownership of their collective ideas, rather than advocating their own character. Thus, developing into interdisciplinary team; '*all of us are smarter than any of us*' [7]. **Shared Language:** Consequently, this leads directly to the second trait; Shared Language. The game rules, game mechanics and game elements, both frames and supports the creation of a shared language between the participants. The game provides a third space where each participant with their character is required to discuss ideas, requirements, potentials, limitations and dreams. A third space where the game becomes a generative tool that supports the creation of a shared language [9]. Thus, the game provides a third space that becomes the new shared space for collaborative design. **User-Centered Design:** Lastly, the third primary collaborative trait's point of reference emerges from User-Centered Design and is placed in the content and purpose of the game. Namely, placing the user traits and challenges at the heart of the design development and game challenge. Thus, removing the participants focus from their professional wishes and wants, to approaching the design from the user's perspective - how can we enlighten users through experiences at the museum?

4   Playtesting

4.1   Playtest #1, 2018

The first iteration of the game was play tested internally in the research program, April 2018. The game was introduced as a tool to incentivize dialogue relevant to user-centered exhibition design to the participants. The participants were grouped in a mix of senior and junior researchers, program leader, the steering committee and representatives from the collaborating museum of 4–5 per group, with 5 groups in total. The session lasted 2 h. The session was planned as a prototype playtest; thus, data was collected throughout the session. The collected data was observational, such as photos and notes. The design documents that each group had produced by playing the game were also gathered, as well as informal feedback after the session had ended (Fig. 2).

Fig. 2. Playtest #1 with version #1 of the Our Museum Game Board with the Our Museum team.

The observations and feedback revealed minor fixes, tweaking of mechanics and a few major insights that were used for the second iteration. These were: time constraints and character creation. The implemented time constraints were difficult to follow; the groups spent too much time discussing. It may seem paradoxical that a dialogical tool tries to reduce discussions, but often discussions would lose focus of the task at hand. Therefore, the allocation of time per phase in the second iteration were adjusted so one playthrough would take exactly 1,5 h and adjusted so the discussion activities are pressed. The game had a character creation process where each participant would create a user, that would represent them on the game board. Consequently, the participants became too attached to their user and could not empathize with the other users. Additionally, the user-centered aspect lost focus because of the many users represented. Therefore, the second iteration was re-designed to one user per session, that the participants select in unison.

4.2 Playtest #2, 2019

The second play test took place at *Kulturmødet*, August 2019. This is an annual meeting for Danish cultural institutions, organizations, stakeholders and the public to participate in activities and events. Our Museum was invited to present the program and to host a play session with participants at the meeting, as part of the key museum event, "We Love Museums" (our translation) event. From the first version of the game, used for playtest #1 to the second version used for playtest #2, the major additions were predefined character cards and user types and a redefinition of the questions asked on the different tiles. For the presentation and playtest, we had one hour. Thus, forcing us to only have the participants play a part of the game. Nevertheless, all game mechanics were still activated. For this play test, the players were given a predefined context (art, cultural or natural history museum), a user type (explorer, experience seeker, facilitator or socializer) and a challenge. The players were asked to choose a character which they wanted to represent. The assignment was then to play through *dialogue* tile 2 (design) and *interval* tile 2 and 3. Two groups of 5 people played through the game for playtest #2. The playtest was documented with video, pictures, observation and the players collected their decisions on a sheet (Fig. 3).

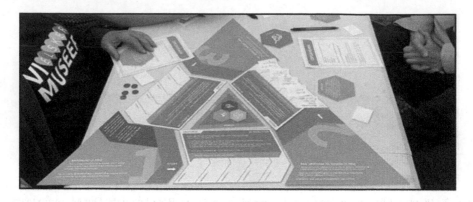

Fig. 3. Playtest #2 with version #2 of Our Museum Game at Kulturmødet Mors 2019 as part of the "We Love Museums" event.

From this playtest we observed four main points of interest for further iterations of the game. Firstly, facilitation has to be on-point; the game needs a gamemaster or facilitation mechanics to guide the participants. Secondly, if museum users are invited to participate in the game, more explanation is necessary, since they do not know all of the terms and tendencies of museum practices, such as Falk and Dierking's user types. Thirdly, the predefined characters and user types, created a quicker adjustment and understanding of each players role in the game and understanding of their core target group, making the initiation of game play easier. Lastly, a set of cards to support each main phase should be included to assist participants with the latest tendencies, state-of-the-art communication practices and evaluative methods to draw inspiration from. The cards have been planned as a way to add the research program's insights to the game.

5   Results and Further Perspectives

The design and development of a game that was motivated by the Our Museum research program and necessitated through the challenges identified through the collaborative work between research projects and museums, resulted in the creation of the 'Our Museum Game'. The game set out to gather participants with different professional backgrounds to design exhibitions while retaining focus on user-centered design, through the use of gamification and game design. Although the game has not been through rigorous testing with data collection and analysis, the experience and insights gathered through observation and direct feedback has revealed both flaws and strengths of the core design of the current version of the game. Nevertheless, the game has shown utility as a tool to facilitate the user-centered dialogue of design and involved participants in more relaxed and playful way. The gameplay encouraged the participants to engage in a collaborative space where they could develop a shared language. As a proof-of-concept, the game has been explored and verified, but with space for improvements. Two distinct paths should be explored in future iterations of the game. One is the construction of the game itself, while the other is pertinent to the design aspect. **"Game"** - The game mechanics needs to be developed to support collaborative play further. Additionally, the player representation is currently vague, so the gameplay should be investigated to add more gravitas to the different roles. The use of enlightenment and experience as a balancing mechanic also needs adjustments so they are more apparent throughout the game and make them relevant in designing exhibitions. **"Design"** - The effect of game design should be explored further as well as the application opportunities and facilitation of the game. Thus, research how the shared language develops and how the result of the gameplay format influences the subsequent design process. Finally, the game needs to be examined to understand when during the design process its utility is required and how well the game format supports the transition from multidisciplinary to interdisciplinarity.

References

1. Hein, G.E.: Learning in the Museum. Routledge, London, New York (1998)
2. Knerr, G.: Technology museums: new publics, new partners. Museum Int. **52**, 8–13 (2000). https://doi.org/10.1111/1468-0033.00279
3. Vermeeren, A.P.O.S., et al.: Future museum experience design: crowds, ecosystems and novel technologies. In: Vermeeren, A., Calvi, L., Sabiescu, A. (eds.) Museum Experience Design. SSCC, pp. 1–16. Springer, Cham (2018). https://doi.org/10.1007/978-3-319-58550-5_1
4. Drotner, K.: Vores museum: Fælles formål, forskningsspørgsmål og analytiske dimensioner, p. 3 (2018)
5. Kirsten, D.: Dansk museumsformidling: Historik, design og evaluering (2015)
6. Knudsen, L.V., Olesen, A.R.: Complexities of collaborating: understanding and managing differences in collaborative design of museum communication. In: The Routledge Handbook of Museums, Media and Communication, pp. 205–218 (2019)
7. Brown, T.: Change by Design - How Design Thinking Transforms Organizations and Inspires Innovation. HarperCollins Publishers, New York (2009)
8. Nigel, C.: Design Thinking - Understanding How Designers Think and Work. Berg Publishers, Oxford (2011)
9. Sanders, L., Stappers, P.J.: Convivial Toolbox: Generative Research for the Front End of Design. BIS Publishers, Amsterdam (2013)
10. Gudiksen, S.K., Inlove, J.: Gamification for Business: Why Innovators and Changemakers Use Games to Break Down Silos, Drive Engagement and Build Trust. Kogan Page, London (2018)
11. Muller, M.J., Druin, A.: Participatory Design: The Third Space in HCI, p. 70 (2002)
12. Madsen, K.M.: The gamified museum: a critical literature review and discussion of gamification in museums. In: Gamescope: The Potential for Gamification in Digital and Analogue Places (2018)
13. Vistisen, P.: Applied gamification in self-guided exhibitions. In: Proceedings From the 1st Gamescope Conference (2018)
14. Jones, K.: Non-Predatory Games. http://www.thegamesjournal.com/articles/Nonpredatory.shtml
15. Nash, J.: The Essential John Nash. Princeton University Press, Princeton (2016)
16. Zagal, J.P., Rick, J., Hsi, I.: Collaborative games: lessons learned from board games. Simul. Gaming **37**, 24–40 (2006). https://doi.org/10.1177/1046878105282279
17. Falk, J.H.: Identity and the Museum Visitor Experience. Left Coast Press, Walnut Creek (2009)

Adoption of Requirements Engineering Methods in Game Development: A Literature and Postmortem Analysis

Miikka Lehtonen⬤, Chien Lu⬤, Timo Nummenmaa⬤,
and Jaakko Peltonen$^{(\boxtimes)}$⬤

Tampere University, Tampere, Finland
{miikka.lehtonen,chien.lu,timo.nummenmaa,jaakko.peltonen}@tuni.fi

Abstract. As the game industry continues to grow in size and revenue, the cost of creating games increases as well, and the successful outcome of game development projects becomes ever more important. In traditional software engineering, it is generally agreed that a successful requirements engineering process has a significant impact on the project. In game development, requirements engineering methods do not seem to be commonly used. As the development of digital games includes specialized aspects of software development, it seems likely that game developers could benefit from adopting these techniques and processes. In this paper, a thorough reading of central and current academic research on the topic is performed to form a holistic picture of the central issues and problems preventing the adoption and widespread use of requirements engineering processes and methods in game development. Additionally, algorithmic analysis of 340 post-mortems written by game developers and published on industry websites is conducted. These post-mortems discuss the factors which contributed to or hindered the successful outcome of these game development projects, and the analysis further supports the identified central issues.

Keywords: Requirements engineering · Game development · Postmortem analysis · Text mining · Literature analysis

1 Introduction

Requirements engineering is a process for handling hardware and software requirements that has been a part of software development for decades, and much has been written on its applications in various domains. One definition for requirements engineering by Hull et al. [7] is "the subset of systems engineering concerned with discovering, developing, tracing, analyzing, qualifying, communicating and managing requirements that define the system at successive levels of abstraction". Digital game development is no exception. As game development is a specialized form of software development, it logically follows

A. Brooks and E. I. Brooks (Eds.): ArtsIT 2019/DLI 2019, LNICST 328, pp. 436–457, 2020.
https://doi.org/10.1007/978-3-030-53294-9_32

that at least some portions of requirements engineering could be applied to the game development process. Several articles and papers have been written on this topic, presenting problems, limitations and concerns which need to be addressed if such an attempt were to be successful.

Academic research on the topic covers a wide spectrum from purely theoretical academic works to research focusing on the developers and their practices and concerns through questionnaires and interviews (e.g., [9,11,12,20]). This study aims to form a holistic picture of this current research, and to tie together knowledge from multiple sources to discover and present central problems and limitations. To verify the validity of these problems and limitations, 340 developer-written post-mortems were analyzed. Post-mortems are a common industry practice where developers reflect on completed software development projects and bring up problems, concerns and issues which affected the outcome of the project, either positively or negatively.

The research questions of this study are (1) Based on a reading of current academic research on the topic, can central problems, concerns and issues be identified? (2) Can these findings be supported by analysing developer-written post-mortems? The 340 post-mortems were analyzed algorithmically to determine whether keywords related to the discovered problems appear in them. In addition, a word correlation analysis was conducted to determine the contexts these keywords might be used in. Our analysis assesses if the problems related to these concepts and keywords are common in the industry, as the expectation was that if game developers are frequently encountering these issues and problems, they would also mention them as contributing factors in post-mortems.

2 Game Development from a Software Development Perspective

In the year 2018 the video games industry was bigger than ever. According to a report by Newzoo [15], there are over 2.3 billion video game players across the world. The games industry is expected to generate over 108 billion dollars in revenue, representing a growth of 7.8% from 2016 [15]. This growth industry contains innumerable game development studios ranging from lone developers to small companies and large multinational corporations. According to the Entertainment Software Association's 2017 report on the American video game industry [2], in 2016 there were over 2450 active game companies in the United States alone. Among those, 99.7% of them are qualified as small businesses, meaning they have under 250 employees and less than $7.5 million in annual revenue. Similar numbers have been reported elsewhere in the world, as according to the UK Interactive Entertainment Association (UKIE), there were 2261 active game companies in the United Kingdom as of June 2018 [25].

These thousands of game developers are working on varied games ranging from huge titles with budgets in the hundreds of millions to eSports titles, mobile games, small independent projects and everything in between. Game development presents a unique challenge from a software development perspective. Contrary to the more disciplined and theory driven world of traditional software development, games development is a more fractured landscape. Whereas large corporations such as Electronic Arts or Activision, or even larger independent developers, might adhere to traditional software development roles and practices – agile methodologies and Scrum being particularly popular in game development – for smaller independent studios development is probably less regimented and more free form [13].

Games as a form of software development also have several other unique characteristics. As an example, whereas traditional software engineering teams consist of software developers of various disciplines, a game development project will usually have the normal complement of software developers, but additionally artists, writers and other purely creative people. These disciplines do not often share a vocabulary and might differ widely in their needs, methods and work flows. Yet all these disciplines need to find common ground if the project is to succeed. Additionally, these highly multi-disciplinary teams seek to create software which philosophically differs greatly from traditional software. Traditional software development projects aim to create solutions to discrete problems, whereas games are mass-marketed products aimed to entertain and prompt emotional responses [9].

From this it follows that the models and theories which drive traditional software development projects might not be directly and fully applicable to game development. This is also true for requirements engineering.

3   Requirements Engineering in Game Development Literature

Requirements engineering is a collection of different phases, processes and methodologies, which seek to take in information from a variety of sources and transform it into concrete requirements; singular and unambiguous physical or functional needs that the product or service must be able to meet. Together, these requirements form the specification of the project, essentially the blueprint the engineers can design according to and refer to when there is ambiguity [6]. While requirements engineering in traditional software development is a heavily covered field with academic publications, books, magazines and even conferences dedicated to the subject, this is not the case for requirements engineering as part of the game development process. We performed a literature survey to map the current state of academic writing on requirements engineering and game development. Our approach uses elements of the systematic literature review process used in previous studies [1,16]. However, the search was executed specifically in order for the results to be used as background information for our postmortem analysis, and to be contrasted with the data-driven analysis of postmortems.

3.1   Survey Process

Academic search engines such as Google Scholar and the library search engine of the University of Tampere were utilized. The latter allowed access to various digital libraries, which further widened the field of possible results. The goal of these searches was to discover peer reviewed articles, academic publications, conference proceedings and published books which dealt with games development and requirements engineering. No specific time constraints were placed on the results. Software development is a fast moving field, which means that some of the older findings might be outdated. However, they could also reveal newer research which builds upon their findings or expands it. Initial searches were performed using the search term "game development" together with the terms "requirement", "requirements engineering", "formal specification", "methods" and "processes", both in singular and plural forms, and with wildcards.

Together, these searches produced a pool of over 16 000 results. As is to be expected with such broad search terms, most of these results were either marginally related to the actual research question, or not at all related. Even after discarding most of the less applicable results, the pool still contained several hundred articles which might be tangentially related to the research questions. At this point any articles with titles or abstracts which seemed promising were stored in a separate list to be more carefully examined later.

As this list of promising articles was read and processed, references to new papers which seemed relevant to the topic were noted down and added to the list, as were author names who had written relevant works. They were then read, and the process was repeated. In this recursive process new papers that were much more relevant to the topic than those found in the initial search process were discovered, and most of the actual sources used in the literature survey came from this phase of the process.

3.2   Overall Findings From the Literature Survey

Based on this study, the state of research on the topic proved to be rather healthy, if not comprehensive. There is certainly a larger volume of research than anticipated, and requirements engineering proved to be a central topic: as of 2014, 39% of papers submitted on the topic dealt with requirements engineering in some way [3]. This does not mean there are no gaps to be found in current research.

Whereas traditional software development and its issues are a topic of some 40+ years of discussion, the same is not true for games. It is generally accepted that there are similarities and unique factors between the two areas. In recent years more studies have been conducted as to what actual problems game developers are facing, which is a crucial area of research [9,11,12,20]. However, concrete solutions and suggestions are still few and far between: one notable problem area is that many articles bring up problems in processes and methods, but rarely offer any concrete suggestions beyond vague calls to adapt best practices from the world of traditional software engineering. Due to the central differences between traditional software development and games development, this adaptation would have to be handled with care and consideration, so academic research on the topic would be beneficial.

We found that a central type of data used for the research was developer interviews and surveys, however, as an alternative data source Petrillo and Pimenta [19] explored post-mortems published on Gamasutra, an industry-focused website by developers for developers. Developer communication in post-mortems can be a useful complementary information source and we will use it ourselves later in this paper.

Studies, such as those conducted by Kasurinen et al. [9,11,12] have been conducted on industry practices among various groups of developers. They highlight issues developers grapple with, as well as the methods and practices used to deal with these issues. Kasurinen's large scale surveys and interviews among Finnish industry professionals found that there are several similarities, but also meaningful differences which mean that traditional software development methods and lines of thinking will not apply directly.

We identified four key problems, which we introduce below and will discuss in more detail in separate subsections. The first of these deals with the incompability of the game design document and the requirements document. Kanode and Haddad [10] talk about an important topic, the game design document. In game development, the game design document is a repository of information about the game. It details the setting, plot, gameplay, characters and themes of the game. It is not a formal document, and as such is poorly suited for actual software development. However, the findings of Kanode and Haddad seem contrary to evidence presented in other papers: they suggest that a game designer needs to capture all the requirements from a game design document before the actual production work on the game can begin. Callele et al. [4] counter this by stating that translating this informal document into something resembling a requirements document is a massive and complicated process. Even a short, simple gameplay description in the game design document can generate dozens of pages of requirements, and even more problematically generating those requirements requires unrealistically strong and specialized domain knowledge in many fields. Callele et al. [4] have studied this issue through analyzing real-life game design documentation, discussions with actual game developers and observing actual development processes. They conclude that this transition from pre-production to production (taking informal and often very casual documentation, turning it into a formal document suitable for development, and then beginning to realize the vision outlined in that document) is one of the biggest problems in game development and alone responsible for many project failures.

Another common theme in the discussion of requirements engineering and games is the unique nature of requirements in games. Traditional software development places a heavy emphasis on functional requirements (i.e. concrete features in a project), whereas in game development these are almost standardized among games of the same genre. Instead, the differences between games come largely from non-functional requirements, which play a heavier role. Of special interest are so called affective, or emotional requirements [4]. Games are intended to prompt emotional responses in their players, and these should also be modelled through requirements engineering. However, the tools and techniques to do so are still in their infancy.

As a third problem, Kasurinen et al. [9,11,12] point out that whereas change to the original specification is something needs to be very carefully managed in traditional software development, in game development changes through iteration are a desired outcome. As the developers try to "find the fun", i.e. create the combination of gameplay and features which makes the game fun, they must be prepared to make even drastic changes late in the project. We will discuss the issue of iteration, scope, and change management in more detail in a later subsection. Based on these findings, Kasurinen [11] concludes that while some common traditional software development methods such as Scrum can very easily work with game development, others are not so easily compatible and need special consideration.

As a fourth problem, the literature also suggests [13,14] that currently game developers do not make widespread use of formal, theory-based methods and processes. At the same time there is evidence to for the presence of problems traditionally thought to be fixed by these methods and processes, which suggests that developers could benefit from a less informal development process [20].

Based on this literature survey, several key concerns and problems were identified, which will be analyzed and discussed in more detail in the following section.

4   Key Differences Between Game Developers and Traditional Software Developers

Game development and traditional software development methods and tools, for instance requirements engineering, are not fundamentally incompatible. There is evidence that game developers make use of these methods, and get benefits from them [9].

That being said, there do seem to exist some fundamental differences and problems, which make adapting these traditional processes and methods to game development difficult. Game developers do seem to suffer from many problems which could be alleviated or eliminated through better requirements engineering processes and methods. For example, in post-mortems published on Gamasutra.com, game developers cite factors such as "inadequate planning", "underestimating the scope of tasks" and a schedule that was "too aggressive" [4] as aspects of the project which went wrong and hindered them.

It is worth noting that these findings are not universal. Game development is a wildly varied field, with studios ranging from one-person teams to massive international companies. Many developers, especially larger companies, tend to regard their methods and practices as trade secrets and are not open to discussing them with journalists or academics. Despite this, from merely reading recruitment posts and requirements for open positions, it is clear that at least larger companies do value degrees and formal training when seeking to hire developers.

It is also worth noting that these issues are heavily linked and could also be thought of as different aspects of the same problem. After all, any differentiation between "a lack of formal processes and methods" and "poor change control" is going to be somewhat arbitrary, as the latter could easily be considered a part of the former.

What, then, could be some of these key differences that need to be considered, and key problems that need to be overcome?

4.1 The Incompatibility of the Game Design Document and Requirements Engineering Documentation

In traditional software engineering projects which utilize requirements engineering methods and processes, a common guideline for the design work is the requirement documentation. It is essentially the blueprint against which the product and its features are compared for specifications and verification.

In game development, a similar role is played by the game design document [4]. While its contents and size vary from team to team and project to project, commonly it includes descriptions for plot, characters and events as well as gameplay mechanics, puzzles and so on. Much like the requirement document, the game design document is often created during pre-production [4].

While these two documents share a similar role, they are not stylistically equal or even similar. A game design document is usually more free form and written in natural language [4]. Since it is the primary design document for game development, it has been proposed that the game design document would also be a major source for requirements [4,10]. This is logically sound, after all if the document contains descriptions of gameplay mechanics and elements, it stands to reason that requirements could be generated from these descriptions. In fact, some have gone as far as stating that all of the game design document should be captured as requirements before production should start [10].

Evidence has shown this to be an unrealistic expectation, however. Even a single paragraph length description of a game design element from the game design document could produce several pages of requirements. Even worse, many of these requirements are merely implied, and capturing them requires high level domain knowledge in game design, genre conventions, technical matters and many other fields [4]. A skilled and experienced game developer will be able to pick up on some of these cues and implications, depending on how well versed they are in the different disciplines of game development (e.g. programming, art and sound design, writing), their team's own culture, the capabilities, features and limitations of the game engine the team is using, and the genre of the game they are working on.

Expecting this kind of expertise from a single person is unrealistic, as is the expectation of being able to generate good requirements based on heavily implicational natural language. The latter half of the problem could possibly be alleviated by employing technical writers, who are skilled in writing precise and unambiguous language, but they would probably not have the required domain knowledge. The common feeling is that it is "easier to do it myself than to explain it to someone else" [4] which may be true, but does not help eliminate the problem.

Even if suitable candidates could be found, or if the job of capturing the implied requirements were divided among a versatile group of skilled developers, the process would be extremely time consuming. Game development projects are usually executed under extremely tight, publisher-driven deadlines, and extending the pre-production phase to accommodate a lengthier requirements engineering process would probably not be welcomed [4]. For example, according to a study conducted in Finland, most Finnish game development projects last under 12 months, with many of them lasting less than 6 months [13].

It would therefore seem that there is a base level incompatibility between traditional requirements engineering documentation and the artefacts of game development.

4.2 Emphasis on Non-functional Requirements and Affective Requirements

In traditional software engineering, the emphasis is on functional requirements. They describe the key features of the system to be implemented, and are what ultimately distinguishes it from its competition and allows it to fulfill its stated and desired goals. In game development, non-functional requirements are considered much more important. In what is called "horizontal differentiation", it is claimed that the functional requirements for games of a particular genre of game are often quite similar to begin with, and non-functional requirements make the difference and help distinguish a game from its peers [4,18].

Additionally, unlike in traditional software engineering, more and more game developers are using pre-made game engines such as Unity[1], Unreal Engine[2] or CryEngine[3], which further removes emphasis from functional requirements, as these requirements are already fulfilled by the pre-packaged engine [9].

This in and of itself might not be a problem, as tools for capturing and modelling non-functional requirements have existed for decades. In game development, however, non-functional requirements deal with more difficult concepts. In traditional software engineering, requirements generally refer to concrete and measurable real-world conditions, whereas game-domain specific requirements are more abstract and harder, if not impossible, to measure [12]. Requirements related to concepts such as fun, storytelling, aesthetics and so on are key in video game projects, but of course not at all relevant in traditional software engineering [4]. These requirements also vary from genre to genre [18]. What is important in a racing game might not be at all relevant in a puzzle game, or an adventure game.

Unlike traditional software projects, games are intended to produce emotional responses in their users. Requirements relating to these emotions are referred to

---

[1] https://unity3d.com. Retrieved 27.11.2018.
[2] https://www.unrealengine.com. Retrieved 27.11.2018.
[3] https://www.cryengine.com. Retrieved 27.11.2018.

as emotional, or affective, requirements and they are viewed as a key component in creating an engaging gaming experience [4]. The tools and techniques for capturing and modelling these requirements either do not exist, or are not as developed as they should be. Additionally, validating these requirements is also extremely difficult, as they deal with highly subjective concepts. Traditional validation methods such as testing are not easy to implement or very reliable [4].

4.3   Iteration, Scope and Change Management

Change is an inevitable part of almost any software product. No matter how thorough the pre-production planning, how well executed the requirements engineering process and how accurate the model, something will eventually change. Change control and management are considered essential parts of the requirements engineering process, and significant work both during pre-production and production is carried out to ensure changes can be tracked and managed as efficiently as possible [5,17,22].

Despite this, change is not seen as an outright goal, and instead more of an unavoidable necessity. This is in contrast with game development, where change is often outright desired. Game development is a heavily iterative endeavor, as the developers try to find the magical formula of features and gameplay executed just right to make the game as fun as possible [12,24]. This will inevitably lead to many and in some cases quite drastic changes to the design and scope of the project.

Due to the emphasis on non-functional and affective requirements, change is also often the outcome of testing. A version of the game is given to testers, and based on their feedback changes can be made. Sometimes these changes can be quite drastic, and in many cases these iterations will carry on quite late in the actual development phase of the game and changes will occur very close to the end of the project. This is in part due to the fact that this user-driven testing is not only a tool for validation, but also defining the quality of the product [12,24].

With this in mind, it would stand to reason that game development could benefit from more robust change management procedures and methods. A common problem in game development is scope management. The game will be designed to have a certain set of features, and time and resources are budgeted to fulfill these design criteria in the available time.

During development features get added either due to outright planning, because testing suggested they might work well in the game, or sometimes even because individual developers felt they were "cool". Suddenly there are no longer enough resources or time to finish the game as specified, and sometimes the revised and changed version of the game no longer works as well as originally planned. This process is referred to as "feature creep", and according to some sources, it is one of the biggest problems in game development [20].

Feature creep is seen as a large problem not only because it creates scheduling problems, causes games to be delayed and costs money, but also because of its human cost. Game development is a massive industry, and publishers will often not be willing to delay projects significantly. Instead what happens is, game developers will work longer and longer days as deadlines approach. From an International Game Developers Association (IGDA) report [8], there are stories of people literally living at work, sleeping under their desks for a few hours when they can. Burnouts and people quitting the games industry inevitably follow because of these heavy periods of crunch, as it is called.

However, at the same time, this iteration and change is both desired and necessary. Often developers will "find the fun" quite late in the development process, which means that if change and experimentation were to be avoided, these games might never have been finished, or at least not in their final conditions. This issue is compounded by game development being notoriously difficult for scheduling in general. Evidence suggests many possible factors as the reasons. One popular suggestion is the multidisciplinary nature of games development. Different types of developers (e.g. artists, coders, writers, designers) have different workflows and different types of "production pipelines", which can cause delays when some parts of the development team must wait for dependencies to be completed [20].

In traditional software development, several processes and methods exist for managing changes and maintaining scope and product integrity despite changes. Therefore, it seems that game development could benefit from more robust change and scope control and scheduling mechanisms. Unfortunately, it seems that right now these mechanisms either do not exist, or are not utilized frequently, in game development.

4.4   Lack of Formalized Methods and Processes

According to two studies conducted in Austria [14] and Finland [13], game developers do not make good or widespread use of typical methods and processes. In Finland, 61% of the respondents to the survey indicated that they did not use any systematic development methods. In Austria, 23% of respondents indicated they did not use any kind of formalized methods or processes. Even those who did self-report using theory-based methods and processes mostly used adapted and flexible processes which were said to be comparable to Scrum and XP (Extreme Programming) [11,14]. Further, according to the Finnish study, developers do not collect metrics or document their activities [11].

This kind of laissez-faire approach permeates all levels of development. For instance, developers prefer to not engage with traditional requirements engineering activities and instead prefer the approach of "test and tune" to replace it. This testing is largely user-driven, as feedback received from users is used to gauge quality and drive development. Despite this, the feedback is not commonly collected in any kind of formal or systematic fashion [9].

Some of this approach can be explained by base level incompatibilities in game development and traditional software engineering. Whereas traditional software engineering projects are launched to answer specific problems, game development can be iterative even at the ideation stage. It is common for developers to briefly explore tens of ideas initially, but only choose a few for detailed implementation, at which point the project has already moved at least partially to production and any kinds of pre-production processes are incompatible [9]. There could also be other explanations. A lack of formal training and the tendency to promote from within could play a role. If a project manager does not have any training or knowledge about theory-based methods and processes, how could they hope to make use of them?

Despite this, there is evidence to support the claim that game development could benefit from adopting more formal, theory-based methods and processes based in established software development theories. According to research conducted in Finland, many developers do already utilize some aspects of project management processes, but do so informally and in an ad-hoc fashion [9]. This would seem to indicate that the need for these processes and their benefits exists within the developer community. The problems formal processes and methods are intended to fix are observable within the game development community: difficulty transitioning from pre-production to production, difficulty in capturing requirements, difficulty in change and scope management and so on [20].

According to research, game development falls into two broad and informal categories. Larger, more traditional developers still make use of more linear processes which bear a strong resemblance to the traditional waterfall model, whereas increasingly especially smaller developers are making use of agile and flexible methods. These agile methods are often self-created to some degree and might mostly draw inspiration from more formal schools of thought such as Scrum, Kanban and XP [9,14].

Both styles of development could benefit from requirements engineering processes. For the more traditional project style, structured requirements engineering processes could be utilized in largely the same way as in traditional software engineering projects, hopefully with similar results. Even the more informal projects, which are driven by iteration and user feedback, could benefit from structured processes and methods to capture and document this feedback and the requirements it generates [9].

5   Post-mortem Analysis

Based on the literature analysis conducted, certain key problem areas and problems could be identified. As some of these academic writings leaned on industry-focused studies and were based on the thoughts and opinions of game developers, it can be assumed that these problems do in fact exist in game development at least to some degree. It was felt, however, that it would be beneficial to get more context for these findings. How common are these problems in actual game development?

Developer-written post-mortems on websites such as Gamasutra.com[4] and Gamecareerguide.com[5] offer insight to industry professionals' opinions and thoughts on game development. It was felt that they could provide a revealing and adequate source for data on the issue, and an alternative to conducting large scale interviews. For examples, Petrillo et al. [21] tried to understand problems in the development process of electronic games through analyzing 20 postmortems. Petrillo & Pimenta [19] further analyzed the same 20 postmortems to investigate the adoption of agile methods in game development. Washburn et al. [26] have analyzed 155 public postmortems qualitatively to outline the characteristics of game development. Post-mortems are a common industry practice, where a developer who served a central role in the project is invited to reflect on their project. According to Gamasutra.org's instructions [23], each post-mortem should include a few aspects that went right in the project, as well as a few aspects that went wrong. These should be unique to the project, and should offer concrete thoughts other developers can learn from.

Due to their nature, these post-mortems were assumed to provide a valuable and reliable insight to the pros and cons of a wide variety of game development projects. They were therefore fetched and analyzed algorithmically using simple data mining and natural language processing scripts. The purpose of this analysis was to see if key topics and words related to what were perceived as central problems in the field, were present in these post-mortems.

The tests were conducted to test two assumptions.

1. If, for instance, requirements engineering methods and practices are not widely used in game development, keywords related to the topic would not appear frequently (or at all) in post-mortems.
2. If game development could benefit from requirements engineering methods and practices, common problems believed to be alleviated using these methods would appear at least relatively frequently.

This approach does have some limitations. As each developer is instructed to only include a few problems in each article, post-mortems are not exhaustive. Problems may not have been brought up among the few listed in a post-mortem despite influencing the actual development process. An interview or even a survey would give more focused information on the topics of this paper, but this is not necessarily a weakness. As these post-mortems are not guided or directed by research questions or prompts, they do offer a view into what the developers themselves viewed as central and significant factors in the success or failure of their games.

Additionally, it is worth noting that correlation does not necessarily equal causation. Even if both assumptions turned out to be true, it does not automatically mean that all these problems are caused by the lack of requirements engineering methods and processes, nor that would they be fixed merely by

---

[4] https://www.gamasutra.com/features/post-mortem/. Retrieved 27.11.2018.
[5] https://www.gamecareerguide.com/archives/postmortems/1/index.php. Retrieved 27.11.2018.

adopting these methods and processes. A much more exhaustive study would be required for conclusive results, but that does not detract from the value of this study.

5.1   Data Gathering

Post-mortem articles are collected with a self-made crawler from Gamasutra.com and GamecareerGuide.com. By March 2018, we had gathered 218 and 129 post-mortem articles respectively from the above-mentioned websites. The 347 post-mortems retrieved in total from the two websites range from 1997 to 2018, and cover everything from small independent teams to large studios, and everything from small browser games to large, big budget productions. Games from a variety of different genres are included. Not all the post-mortems are suitable for this study, as some of them are small "post cards" from industry events. After eliminating these obviously non-related articles, there were 340 post-mortems left for analysis. These post-mortems cover roughly 300 unique games, as a few projects were discussed from different perspectives, such as general design and audio design.

5.2   Initial Analysis

Based on the central problems in game development presented in Sect. 3.2, a list of keywords was created. These keywords were thought to be related to these central problems based on existing domain knowledge on the topic. There was no specific methodology for creating this initial list of keywords, and instead it was always intended as a simple jumping off point which would hopefully generate interesting and promising articles, based on which additional keywords could be discovered.

- **Project management:** crunch, schedule, management, overtime, estimation, feature creep, creep, feature, scope, communicationm, multi-disciplinary.
- **Methods and processes:** agile, process, method, Scrum, Kanban, engineering, development, transition, extreme programming, backlog, formal.
- **Requirements engineering:** requirement, emotional, affective, game design, document, pre-production, production, requirement engineering, requirements engineering, specification.

The initial intent was to narrow down the list of 340 post-mortems to find which post-mortems should be studied more closely, and which could be discarded, as analysing all the post-mortems would not have been practical and quite probably also not useful. Therefore, the intent was to prioritize the post-mortems based on how many of these keywords appeared in them. This analysis was conducted using a self-built programming script, which iterated through all 340 post-mortems. The script searched for instances of keywords, noting down the articles in which they appeared, and the results were exported into a file for analysis.

As the scripts were being refined, the study evolved beyond simply trying to narrow down the list of post-mortems. It became apparent that getting statistical information about how often given keywords appeared in articles would be easy, and the focus was shifted towards this approach.

This approach has some limitations. The first of these is the list of keywords used. If some relevant or useful term was not thought of, it would not be included on the list of search terms. As this part of the study was conducted by a single researcher, albeit with some supervision, it is quite probable that something was overlooked. This problem was probably compensated at least in part for by repeated versions the keyword list and repeated analysis of the subject text. The list of keywords grew significantly over time as additional terms were discovered through further readings of the source texts, or derived from results of earlier iterations of the analysis.

Additionally, this approach offers next to no context. While the algorithm will find all instances of a keyword such as "scope", it has no way of knowing the context the term was used in. Did the article refer to the scope of the project, or was the author talking about a physical scope item in the game? Many of the terms used have multiple meanings, only some of which are relevant to this paper, so this could have been a real problem. To compensate for this lack of context, a second test was devised and run.

5.3   Extended Analysis

Our aim in this extended analysis was to 1) gather occurrences of keywords in a more relaxed fashion allowing multiple word forms of each keyword to be detected, and 2) find context of the keywords by statistical analysis to detect other keywords that tend to often appear together with them.

To detect keywords in a permissive manner, a natural language processing script was written. The script first breaks the input text into smaller, sentence length chunks. Next, the text was lemmatized (i.e. the inflected forms of each word were grouped together in their dictionary form), and so called "stop words", or common, short function words such as the, is, that and which, were removed. After these steps the remaining text was analyzed. Next, simple statistical analysis was done to detect co-occurring keywords. For this analysis, sentences which contained words from the keyword list were kept, while the others were discarded. The remaining sentences were analyzed for word correlation: correlation of occurrence of one keyword and occurrence of another keyword across the sentences. The analysis produced a list of found search terms as well as lists of words they appear together with. This would then give context to these results.

Due to the way the algorithm parses words, it will distinguish between multiple word keywords such as "feature creep" and individual components of the keyword, in this case "feature" and "creep". Thus, the algorithm will not produce skewed false hits for these component words.

As with the first test, this test was also run several times, first using co-occurrence analysis, and later with improved correlation analysis. The original list of keywords grew and changed after each iteration as new keywords were discovered externally, prompting repetitions of the first study as well. Additionally, the results of this test also helped refine the list of keywords, as interesting or relvant terms are actually correlated to original keywords and were subsequently included as keywords themselves.

5.4   Findings

The two studies have produced : a full list of all 340 post-mortems, and the keywords which appear in them, the total count of how often any keyword appears in each post-mortem, a list of all the keywords and the most common words that appear near them, and statistical information about the total number of occurrences for each keyword across all 340 articles, as well as the percentage of articles each keyword appears in Table 1.

Table 1. Occurrences across all articles for a given keyword.

Keyword	Frequency	Pct.	Count	Keyword	Frequency	Pct.	Count
Development	321/340 art.	94.41%	3156	Emotional	39/340 art.	11.47%	149
Feature	278/340 art.	81.76%	1582	Formal	35/340 art.	10.29%	41
Process	270/340 art.	79.41%	1160	Feature-creep	33/340 art.	9.71%	43
Document	228/340 art.	67.06%	453	Scrum	33/340 art.	9.71%	84
Schedule	206/340 art.	60.59%	811	Agile	27/340 art.	7.94%	41
Production	205/340 art.	60.29%	961	Overtime	25/340 art.	7.35%	43
Communication	146/340 art.	42.94%	402	Specification	22/340 art.	6.47%	35
Management	143/340 art.	42.06%	332	Game-design-document	19/340 art.	5.59%	41
Scope	134/340 art.	39.41%	306	Creep	19/340 art.	5.59%	23
Method	108/340 art.	31.76%	205	Engineering	15/340 art.	4.41%	28
Requirement	94/340 art.	27.65%	179	Estimation	8/340 art.	2.35%	11
Engineer	92/340 art.	27.06%	308	Backlog	6/340 art.	1.76%	6
Crunch	88/340 art.	25.88%	198	Multi-disciplinary	3/340 art.	0.88%	3
Pre-production	56/340 art.	16.47%	166	Affective	1/340 art.	0.29%	3
Discipline	47/340 art.	13.82%	76	Kanban	0/340 art.	0.29%	0
Transition	45/340 art.	13.24%	58	Requirement engineering	0/340 art.	0.29%	0

It becomes apparent that some terms were too broad especially for the initial intent of the studies even from a cursory glance at the list of keywords. The words "development", "feature" and "process" appear in almost all of the articles. However, due to the word co-occurrence analysis, it is apparent that they do not appear without context and were as such deemed interesting enough to be left in the pool of keywords.

The word correlation analysis produced a list of each keyword and the most correlated words they appear together with in the analyzed material. In order to avoid spurious correlations, we remove infrequent terms and verify remaining correlations with a student-t based significance test, the t-statistic is computed as $\rho\sqrt{\frac{N-1}{1-\rho^2}}$ where ρ is the correlation coefficient and N is the sample size. In the final list, we keep the top 10 correlated words that co-occur (document-level) more than or equal to 5 times with the keyword. We also conducted the association test, the p-value is provided in the parentheses. Correlations for 4 terms are listed in Table 2. The term schedule is correlated to terms such as "tight", "slip" and "milestone". This indicates that the underestimation of the schedule is a common issue in game development. The term communication is correlated to different words that represent different perspectives such as frequency ("occurrence"), target ("team") and method ("verbal"). Words that are correlated to the term development are related to scheduling ("cycle" and "length") or appliance ("software"). However, many of the words that are correlated to the term requirement do not seem to be related with requirements engineering. The full list can be found online via the link https://bit.ly/2FeQ42U.

Table 2. Words correlated to search terms, shown for four example terms. ρ: correlation coefficient, n: number of co-occurrences.

Search term	Word	ρ	p-value	n	Other correlated words
Schedule	Tight	0.116	2.63e-175	60	Occasional, task, behind,
	Slip	0.095	1.22e-117	45	project, budget, aggressive,
	Milestone	0.069	1.73e-62	79	instructor
Communication	Occurrence	0.124	2.77e-198	7	Skype, lack, facilitate,
	Team	0.079	2.46e-81	143	inter, proximity, constant,
	Verbal	0.078	1.09e-79	5	apart
Development	Cycle	0.170	0.00e+00	139	Month, ram, date, photoshop,
	Length	0.130	5.12e-218	137	platform, hardware,
	Software	0.114	1.30e-168	186	process
Requirement	Mock	0.126	5.82e-206	6	Experimental, viable, nail,
	Fulfill	0.126	2.85e-204	9	skin, export, nature,
	Playback	0.110	3.95e-155	9	application

In general, terms thought to be related to the requirements engineering process and its methods appear either very rarely or not at all. "Requirements engineering" (and its alternative spelling "requirement engineering") do not appear once. The broader keyword "requirement" appears in 27.65% of the articles, but it is practically always used in the non-requirements engineering sense. "Affective" is used precisely once, and while the keyword "emotional" does appear in 11.47% of the articles, it is not used to talk about emotional requirements.

Terms related to agile methods and Scrum appear relatively frequently in more recent postmortems: "Agile" or "Scrum" are mentioned in 17.86% of postmortems from 2006 onwards. "Extreme programming" is mentioned once. Theory-based methods and specifications in general do not seem to be a frequent topic in post-mortems, as the keyword "formal" is used in 8.82 % of the articles. Context analysis suggests that when the term is used, it is rarely used in the context of formal processes: it appears three times close to the term "process", and three times close to the term "development". "Specification" is used in 6.47% of the articles, and is usually used in the context of formal design methods.

These findings would seem to back up the arguments presented in current academic research, and suggest that formal methods and practices, requirements engineering and other accepted industry best practices are not widely used in game development.

The problems these methods and processes are thought to alleviate appear in the post-mortems quite frequently. The keyword "crunch" appears in 25.88% of the post-mortems, and when it appears it is often mentioned several times in the same post-mortem. Additionally, the term "overtime" appears in 7.35% of the post-mortems, usually in the context of having to work overtime. The algorithm does not guarantee that there is no crossover between these results, so both keywords could appear together in at least some of the post-mortems. Phrases such as "It was an expensive lesson, given the amount of overtime we had to work to finish the game", "building several levels, working a tremendous amount of overtime" and "others were totally fried from the tremendous amount of overtime" indicate that "overtime" usually appears in the intended sense rather than describing, for instance, a system working overtime.

"Feature creep" is used in 9.71% of the post-mortems, and additionally "creep" is used in 5.59% of the articles, often in a context which suggests it is used to describe feature creep rather than an action by a game character. Terms such as "schedule" (60.59%), "management" (42.06%), "communication" (42.94%) and "document" (67.06%) appear very often, both in positive and negative contexts, indicating they are factors in the successes or failures of game development projects.

6   Discussion

The topic of requirements engineering and game development is by no means a new one. As game development is a specialized field of software development, and requirements engineering is an accepted and commonly used part of the software engineering process, the assumption that game development could benefit from requirements engineering processes and methods is only natural.

Along with this long-standing interest in the topic comes a lot of previous research. This body of work varies greatly in scope and style. As game development is a practical real-world problem, it stands to reason that for it to truly be useful, research carried out on the topic should be conducted with the realities of the discipline in mind, if the goal is to solve real problems faced by developers.

It is worth stressing that the findings in this paper apply mostly to smaller independent developers. Larger and more organized studios may have their own methods and processes for dealing with these issues and approach the development process much in the same ways as a traditional software development project would, but as these larger studios and corporations tend to regard their practices and methods as trade secrets, little information is available on the subject.

6.1 Discussion of the Literature Survey Results

Key problems and issues were identified based on academic research conducted through interviews and studies conducted among game developers and game publishers. Some of these problems make it harder to adopt requirements engineering processes as a part of the game development process, while some are areas where game development could clearly benefit from adopting these processes.

Of the problems discovered, the general lack of formal processes and methods among developers seems to be the most fundamental one. While the emphasis on non-functional requirements and the lack of tools for capturing and modelling affective requirements are also significant problems, they can be overcome with work.

That work will not be conducted if developers are not interested in utilizing theory-based methods and processes, or applying requirements engineering techniques to their work. The reasons for this perceived lack of interest and its remedies are beyond the scope this paper, and a large survey would be needed to chart attitudes and problems before educated guesses could be made. It could be that developers are interested in utilizing more formal methods, but do not have the knowledge and skills needed, or they might not be aware of the possibility, having grown used to doing things their own way.

Note that these are not the only significant challenges or problems game developers are facing, nor are they the only factors making it harder to adapt requirements engineering methods and processes to game development. As an example, game development is a much more multi-disciplinary activity than normal software development. Game development teams employ software engineers, designers, producers, project managers and other computer science professionals just like traditional software engineering teams, but additionally make use of different types of artists (e.g. writers, graphical artists, musicians, animators, sound technicians) and others. Merely finding common vocabulary among these wildly varied disciplines can be challenging, but their variety alone introduces difficulties into the requirements engineering process. Capturing and modelling requirements specific to each of these disciplines requires strong domain knowledge.

Beyond the need for specialized knowledge, all the disciplines of game development may have their own considerations that need to be taken into account, and scheduling can also be challenging. Not all of these components might even be actively worked on during the pre-production phase, where most of the requirements engineering work takes place. While a significant problem, this is not unique to game development, as traditional software development projects need specialized domain knowledge for requirements engineering work as well.

For instance, experts on legal concerns, data privacy or sociology might have specialized domain knowledge needed in the project.

As so many different problems could be discovered so easily, the topic is clearly ripe for further research, discussion and future work.

6.2 Discussion of the Postmortem Analysis

The postmortem analysis further supported the finding that requirements engineering methods and processes are not commonly used in game development. The analysis shows an almost complete lack of keywords relating to requirements engineering in the postmortems. The topic itself was not mentioned once in the 340 post-mortems, which include everything from big budget games to smaller indie products, games created using traditional waterfall methods to agile projects and so on.

As post-mortems deal with factors which contributed, positively or negatively, to the outcome of each individual project, the total lack of mentions could mean that requirements engineering is simply not a concern to any of these developers. This result is not conclusive, of course, as post-mortems are not all-inclusive lists of all contributing factors. However, the fact that no developer mentioned requirements engineering as a factor in the outcome of the project, does give validity to the claim that game developers do not utilize, nor even think to utilize, requirements engineering methods or processes.

As there is next to no discussion on keywords related to requirements engineering, this study did not reveal any conclusive evidence for or against the incompatibility between requirements engineering and the game design document. Keywords such as scope (39.41%) and document (67.06%) are often mentioned in post-mortems, so clearly some kind of issue exists, but based on this study little can be said on the topic.

One notable finding could be the relative low frequency at which terms related to crunch appear in the post-mortems. Crunch is generally considered a widespread problem in the industry. According to a 2016 survey conducted among the International Game Developers Association members [27], 65% of developers reported having experienced crunch, with 52% reporting having experienced it more than twice in the previous year, and the topic has been heavily discussed in media as well. Despite this, the keyword "crunch" appeared in 25.88% of the articles, and the clearly related term "overtime" appeared in 7.35% of the articles.

This inconsistency could be explained by several factors. The post-mortems deal with individual projects, rather than individual developers, the contrary of which is true on the IGDA survey. Thus, even a project where multiple developers reported experiencing crunch would only represent a single item in the post-mortem data. The post-mortems also include many smaller indie projects, which might be more loosely scheduled and could afford to postpone the project rather than crunch to finish it on an external schedule. Finally, the post-mortems include material from 1997 to 2018, and it could be that in the earlier material crunch simply was considered an inevitable part of working in the game industry and not worth reporting as a factor.

Terms related to formal project management processes and methods appear in the post-mortems quite often, and in contexts which relate to project management: document (67.06%), production (60.29%), schedule (60.59%), management (42.06%), communication (42.94%), scope (39.41%). This means that these issues were considered by developers to be a key factor in the success of the project, whether a positive or negative one. This would seem to be in line with Kasurinen's claim that game development would benefit from more formal, commonly used methods and practices, as they are generally agreed to improve and facilitate these key areas of the development process [9].

These findings demonstrate that there is clearly need for further and deeper studies on the issue. Game development is a growth industry where ever-increasing amounts of money are on the line, depending on the successful outcome of large, expensive and extremely complex software development projects. It is clear that game development could benefit from additional formalization, but in order for that to happen, several hurdles need to be crossed.

Developers need training, and methods and processes need to be adapted and created to better suit the needs of the industry. While these initiatives probably need to be driven by developers themselves, academic research has an important role to play as well. Studies conducted by academics could hopefully breach the wall of secrecy surrounding many developers and help discover both the causes and eventual fixes for these problems.

7   Conclusions

This paper explored the question of adapting requirements engineering methods and processes to game development projects. Based on a thorough reading of state-of-the-art academic research, key problems and limitations were identified. These included: (1) a general lack of formal processes and methods in game development (2) the emphasis on non-functional, affective requirements, which traditional requirements engineering methods and processes are not well suited to (3) emphasis on change as a central development tool, and the need for better change control, which requirements engineering could provide (4) the incompatibility between the requirements document and the game development document, central artefacts in requirements engineering and game development respectively.

To study the validity of these claims, 340 developer-published post-mortems were analyzed algorithmically, using custom programs created for the purposes of this study. Keywords based on academic findings were searched for, and their total number of appearances, as well as the frequency of these appearances, were noted. Additionally, they were analyzed for word correlation to discover, which words the keywords commonly appeared with. This analysis would seem to support the key problems and limitations identified in the literature survey, although due to the limitations of the analysis, and the scope of the identified issues, more research is needed. Possible avenues for future research could include a similar study on traditional software development projects, to measure prevalence of requirements engineering methods and processes in these projects and use of the related terms in developer communication regarding the projects, and to contrast such prevalences with the ones found here in game development.

Acknowledgement. The work was supported by Academy of Finland decisions 312395 and 313748, and the Business Finland funded Virpa D project.

References

1. Aleem, S., Capretz, L.F., Ahmed, F.: Game development software engineering process life cycle: a systematic review. J. Softw. Eng. Res. Dev. **4**(1), 1–30 (2016). https://doi.org/10.1186/s40411-016-0032-7
2. of America, E.S.: Entertainment Software of America: Analysing the American Video Game Industry 2016 (2017). http://www.theesa.com/wp-content/uploads/2017/02/ESA-VG-Industry-Report-2016-FINAL-Report.pdf
3. Ampatzoglou, A., Stamelos, I.: Software engineering research for computer games: a systematic review. Inf. Softw. Technol. **52**(9), 888–901 (2010)
4. Callele, D., Neufeld, E., Schneider, K.: Requirements engineering and the creative process in the video game industry. In: 13th IEEE International Conference on Requirements Engineering (RE 2005), pp. 240–250. IEEE (2005)
5. Cao, L., Ramesh, B.: Agile requirements engineering practices: an empirical study. IEEE Softw. **25**(1), 60–67 (2008)
6. Hofmann, H.F., Lehner, F.: Requirements engineering as a success factor in software projects. IEEE Softw. **18**(4), 58–66 (2001)
7. Hull, E., Jackson, K., Dick, J.: Requirements Engineering, 3rd edition (2011)
8. IGDA Quality of Life Committee: Quality of Life in the Game Industry: Challenges and Best Practices. Technical Report, International Game Developers' Association (2004)
9. Kasurinen, J., Maglyas, A., Smolander, K.: Is requirements engineering useless in game development? In: Salinesi, C., van de Weerd, I. (eds.) REFSQ 2014. LNCS, vol. 8396, pp. 1–16. Springer, Cham (2014). https://doi.org/10.1007/978-3-319-05843-6_1
10. Kanode, C.M., Haddad, H.M.: Software engineering challenges in game development. In: ITNG 2009–6th International Conference on Information Technology: New Generations (2009)
11. Kasurinen, J.: Games as software. In: Proceedings of the 17th International Conference on Computer Systems and Technologies 2016 - CompSysTech 2016 (2016)
12. Kasurinen, J., Risto Laine: Games from the viewpoint of software engineering. In: Proceedings of the Federated Computer Science Event, pp. 23–26 (2014)
13. Koutonen, J., Leppänen, M.: How are agile methods and practices deployed in video game development? a survey into finnish game studios. In: Baumeister, H., Weber, B. (eds.) XP 2013. LNBIP, vol. 149, pp. 135–149. Springer, Heidelberg (2013). https://doi.org/10.1007/978-3-642-38314-4_10
14. Musil, J., Schweda, A., Winkler, D., Biffl, S.: Improving video game development: facilitating heterogeneous team collaboration through flexible software processes. In: Riel, A., O'Connor, R., Tichkiewitch, S., Messnarz, R. (eds.) EuroSPI 2010, CCIS, vol. 99, pp. 83–94. Springer, Heidelberg (2010). https://doi.org/10.1007/978-3-642-15666-3_8

15. Newzoo: Mobile Revenues Account for More Than 50% of the Global Games Market as It Reaches $137.9 Billion in 2018 (2018). https://newzoo.com/insights/articles/global-games-market-reaches-137-9-billion-in-2018-mobile-games-take-half/
16. Osborne O'Hagan, A., Coleman, G., O'Connor, R.V.: Software development processes for games: a systematic literature review. In: Barafort, B., O'Connor, R.V., Poth, A., Messnarz, R. (eds.) EuroSPI 2014. CCIS, vol. 425, pp. 182–193. Springer, Heidelberg (2014). https://doi.org/10.1007/978-3-662-43896-1_16
17. Paetsch, F., Eberlein, A., Maurer, F.: Requirements engineering and agile software development. In: Proceedings of the Workshop on Enabling Technologies: Infrastructure for Collaborative Enterprises, WETICE (2003)
18. Paschali, M.E., Ampatzoglou, A., Chatzigeorgiou, A., Stamelos, I.: Non-functional requirements that influence gaming experience. In: Proceedings of the 18th International Academic MindTrek Conference on Media Business, Management, Content & Services - AcademicMindTrek 2014 (2014)
19. Petrillo, F., Pimenta, M.: Is agility out there? agile practices in game development. In: SIGDOC 2010: Proceedings of the 28th ACM International Conference on Design of Communication (2010)
20. Petrillo, F., Pimenta, M., Trindade, F.: Houston, we have a problem...: a survey of actual problems in computer games development. In: Proceedings of the 2008 ACM symposium on Applied computing (2008)
21. Petrillo, F., Pimenta, M., Trindade, F., Dietrich, C.: What went wrong? a survey of problems in game development. Comput. Entertainment (CIE) **7**(1), 13 (2009)
22. Pohl, K.: Requirements Engineering: Fundamentals, Principles, and Techniques, 1st edn. Springer, Heidelberg (2010)
23. Shirinian, A.: Dissecting The Postmortem: Lessons Learned From Two Years Of Game Development Self-Reportage (2011). https://www.gamasutra.com/view/feature/134679/dissecting_the_post-mortem_lessons_.php
24. Stacey, P., Nandhakumar, J.: Opening up to agile games development. Commun. ACM **51**(12), 143–146 (2008)
25. UKIE: The games industry in numbers (2018). https://ukie.org.uk/research. Accessed 08 Jan 2019
26. Washburn, M.J., Sathiyanarayanan, P., Nagappan, M., Meiyappan, T., Bird, C.: What went right and what went wrong: an analysis of 155 postmortems from game development. In: Proceedings of the 38th International Conference on Software Engineering (2016)
27. Weststar, J., Legault, M.J.: Developer Satisfaction Survey 2016 Summary Report. Technical Report, International Game Developers Association (2016). https://cdn.ymaws.com/www.igda.org/resource/resmgr/ortfiles__2016_dss/IGDA_DSS_2016_Summary_Report.pdf

Designing a Serious Game to Raise Awareness of Intimate Partner Violence Among Adolescents in the UK: The Use of 'Good Games' Principles for Effective Behavioural Change

John Pearson[✉], Song Wu, Hayley Royston, Helen Smailes, Natasha Robinson, Adam Cowell, and Adele Jones

None in Three Centre, University of Huddersfield, Queensgate, Huddersfield HD1 3DH, UK
John.Pearson@hud.ac.uk

Abstract. Due to the popularity of video games in modern society, serious digital games have the potential to promote prosocial thoughts and behaviours, as well as increase empathy and helping behaviour. However, to make a successful prosocial game a number of good game principles need to be met to make the game as immersive and engaging as possible. This paper discusses how the design decisions and overall game framework used to develop a serious, prosocial game that aims to help raise awareness and promote prosocial behavioural changes towards intimate partner violence in the United Kingdom, successfully meets these good game principles to create an effective educational, immersive and engaging game experience.

Keywords: Serious game · Prosocial · Good games principles · Game design · Intimate partner violence

1 Introduction

1.1 Prosocial Video Game Effects

In 2018 the video games industry was thought to be worth around 115 billion US dollars, with a global estimate of 2.2 billion individuals reporting that they had played some form of digital video game [60], thus outlining the popularity of the genre. The popularity of digital and video games has attracted the attention of researchers to determine the effect that playing games can have on the attitudes and behaviours of those who play them. This research has primarily focused on whether aggressive video games increase aggressive behaviour [20], although evidence now suggests that violent video games do not affect a user's aggressive tendencies [53]. Moreover, research has also recently investigated the potential benefits of games that include prosocial elements on more positive, prosocial behaviour [24]. Unlike other forms of media, such as movies or magazines, video games give the opportunity for a player to immerse themselves in a narrative and experience the

A. Brooks and E. I. Brooks (Eds.): ArtsIT 2019/DLI 2019, LNICST 328, pp. 458–476, 2020.
https://doi.org/10.1007/978-3-030-53294-9_33

successes and consequences of a character at the same time as them [43], thus providing an opportunity for the player to explore their behavioural and emotional responses to these situations.

Buckley and Anderson (2006), in their theory the 'General Learning Model' (GLM), suggest a mixture of social and cognitive explanations to explain the effects that video games can have on three specific internal states; cognition, state of arousal and affect. They explain that the internal traits of a person react with the content of a video game to influence the learning behaviours of the player. In the first instance, this is a short term effect, such as the game altering a players affect and placing them in a certain mood. However, repeated exposure to the content of a game can translate into long-term effects by changing the beliefs, attitudes and emotional responses of the player towards certain situations, as well as potentially altering or developing new cognitive processes, such as perceptual schema or behavioural scripts [10]. Therefore, a well-designed prosocial game can be used as an effective teaching tool to promote prosocial cognitions, attitudes and behaviours [27].

Research into the effect of prosocial games identify that exposure to prosocial game content does have a positive effect on social behaviour and related cognitive and affective variables [32]. Studies investigating the effect of prosocial games found that prosocial content exposure was linked to increased helping behaviour [24, 30–32, 48], an increase of prosocial thoughts [20, 32, 33], lower levels of aggression [24, 29, 33] and increased empathy and compassion [35, 47]. Even though the vast majority of these studies only tested the short term prosocial effects of these games and do not provide support that repeated exposure creates a long term behavioural change [29], the positive effect of prosocial game content is evident, with the potential for multiple applications, such as education and negative behavioural change.

1.2 None in Three Aims and Objectives

The None in Three (Ni3) research centre aims to investigate and address gender-based violence (GBV) in different countries throughout the world. Due to the usefulness and positive effect that prosocial games have as an educational tool to teach prosocial thoughts and behaviours, the Ni3 centre has provided detailed research and developed a number of serious games to address behavioural change towards different types of GBV that are prevalent in different countries [50]. Due to the recent success of the development and dissemination of the game 'Jesse' in the Caribbean that dealt with the issue of domestic violence [8], the centre has also developed serious games for the United Kingdom (UK), India, Jamaica and Uganda to address the types of GBV that are prevalent in these countries.

This paper will specifically discuss the game that is under development to address intimate partner violence (IPV) amongst adolescents in the UK. As any prosocial game that looks to promote prosocial thoughts and behaviours needs to be engaging and well-developed, the paper will specifically discuss the framework that was used to design the game, how the framework was implemented during the design process and how this will lead to an effective game that will promote positive prosocial beliefs, attitudes and behaviours towards preventing IPV. Even though the UK game has not yet been completed, the paper will look to highlight the importance of how the game framework will lead to an effective game, as well as provide initial confirmatory evidence of the relatability of the game to a small focus group including members of the games target audience.

2   UK Game

2.1   Reasoning Behind the Game

IPV is defined by the Centre for Disease Control (CDC) in the United States as violence or aggression that takes place during a close relationship with a current/former spouse or dating partner [12]. Specifically, psychological aggression, physical/sexual violence and stalking. In the UK the definition is expanded to include coercion and control as behaviours that are linked to IPV [38]. A number of studies have concluded that IPV is prevalent in the UK and many adolescents suffer abuse from their partners [5, 25, 37]. Types of abuse that someone who is experiencing IPV in a relationship can include monitoring and controlling behaviour from their partner [4], isolation by their partner from their friends and family [4], verbal abuse [4, 5], threatening and completing physical abuse, as well as sexual abuse and/or sexual coercion [4, 5, 37] and 'revenge porn' [26, 59].

As a result of IPV, many of those who become victims can suffer from a negative impact to their future intimate relationships [66] and experience emotional, physical and mental health problems, such as depression, anxiety, drug/alcohol abuse and suicidal thinking [5, 39]. However, even though those who experience IPV can suffer from these issues, only around 33% of victims report their abuse [5].

Therefore, the UK game will aim to increase the awareness of IPV abuse and its consequences, as well as encourage prosocial behaviour towards adolescent relationships and increase awareness of the support services available to victims of IPV. The main goal of the Ni3 centre is to eventually roll out the game to all secondary age students and college age students by making it part of the overall school age curriculum, although initial testing will be done on college age students. The target audience of the game will therefore be any UK student aged 14–18.

2.2   Game Narrative

The game narrative follows the main character Danielle and her experiences of IPV in her relationship with her boyfriend James. The game environment centres around the college that Danielle and James attend, as well as a number of other locations. The player explores these environments in a third person perspective, interacting with other characters both in person and via the character's phone to complete objectives and progress the story. The main interactive characters are Danielle's friends including Connor a childhood friend at another college, Hannah the main positive influence that advises Danielle to resist James' behaviour, and Emily who is the main negative influence for Danielle and advises her to accept James' behaviour. James' main influences are his friend Logan and brother Tyler, who actively encourage his increasing controlling and violent behaviour towards Danielle, and Kiran who actively tries to dissuade James from continuing his behaviour.

The game has been divided into five chapters that will be played in schools and colleges over the course of a week (one per day). Each chapter builds on the last to provide a complete learning experience for the player and to make sure the game is as effective as possible in changing the behaviours and attitudes towards IPV in dating relationships.

Chapter one introduces the player to the mechanics of the game through tutorials that includes the game controls, the in game phone element and how to track objectives/obtain achievements, as well as the main characters and non-player characters (NPCs) of the game. The chapter also addresses the issue of James monitoring Danielle's actions through social media. The conclusion of the chapter shows James forcibly removing Danielle from a coffee shop she was visiting with her friends. Chapter 2 addresses the issues of escalating controlling behaviour and physical abuse in IPV relationships. James demands Danielle sends 'nude pictures' on social media, chastises her for the outfit choice and demands that Danielle spend time with him. The chapter ends with James' forcibly pushing Danielle away and withholding her phone, introducing the idea of physical abuse in a relationship. Chapter 3 considers the issue of sexual coercion in IPV. The player will discover how Danielle's behaviours are increasingly subjugated by James, and the pressure that James is feeling from Logan and his brother Tyler to have sex with Danielle. The conclusion of the chapter finds James verbally coercing Danielle into sex. Chapter four shows the isolation and negative mental health effects that victims of IPV can experience. The player can see that Danielle lacks motivation to attend college and is missing classes, as well as distancing herself from her friends. The player can then choose for Danielle to open up to her friends or further distance Danielle from them. The chapter ends with James becoming physically abusive again and Danielle breaking up with James after breaking free of his hold on her.

The final chapter considers the IPV issue of revenge porn and allows the player to decide the resolution of the game. James has posted the 'nude pictures' from Chapter two on social media and the player will see the negative repercussions this has on Danielle. Hannah offers to meet up with Danielle to support her, and the choices the player makes then determines the conclusion and epilogue of the game. The gradual progression of abuse from chapter one to five also reflects the research findings that many victims of IPV do not know that they are being abused until it is too late [4].

The narrative allows players to see the effect of the issues within the context of IPV. This can then influence a player's attitudes towards IPV and what is acceptable, as well as encourage them to engage in healthier behaviours. By allowing the adolescent player to step into the shoes of the playable characters the game will stimulate them to critically think about issues involving IPV. As the game also exposes the player to real life knowledge about support services for IPV and positive roles models in Hannah and Kiran, players will understand how they should react when faced with IPV, either personally or as a third party. However, to make sure that the prosocial message of the game is successful in promoting attitudinal and behavioural change towards IPV, the game itself needed to be immersive and engaging to the target audience [6, 52]. Therefore, during the development and design of the game framework and game, a number of good game principles were followed.

3   Game Framework – Good Game Principles

3.1   Focus Group

During the development of the early stages of the game an initial confirmatory, unstructured focus group was conducted in a local college in West Yorkshire, UK. The group consisted of seven 17–18-year-old students who participated in a walkthrough of the first complete chapter of the game. The sample of 17–18-year old students was selected by members of staff at the college and gave full consent to play and comment on the game. A discussion between the students and game designer was then conducted concerning the game, characters, environment, and story, as well as the participant's previous experience with general and educational games. As the focus group consisted of the target audience (school age students) their comments, beliefs and opinions were useful in identifying the relatability and effectiveness of the game. Any concerns the group had about any aspects of the game were also then considered during the development of further chapters in regards to relatability and immersion. The conversation during the focus group was recorded and analysed to identify comments concerning the participant's experiences with general and educational games, what the participants thought about the gameplay and story, as well as their opinions of the characters and environments. These comments were then reviewed during the creation of future chapters to make sure that the game framework and design choices allowed the content to be relatable to the target audience. Comments from the focus group are discussed throughout this paper.

3.2   Open to All

Playable by All
IPV in dating relationships can be experienced by anyone regardless of gender, sexuality, ethnicity or religion [5]. As the schools and colleges within the UK are becoming more diverse in the students they teach [16] the game needed to be universal to all potential players and avoid the exclusion and discrimination of any majority or minority demographic.

Fig. 1. Changes to the character Kiran, before and after respectively.

Therefore, the design of the player characters (PCs) and NPCs were done in a way that assures all players will have a character or situation that they can relate to. In regards to ethnicity, the game includes as many ethnically diverse NPCs as possible, thus reflecting the diversity of UK schools and colleges. One concern raised by the focus group was that there seemed to be a lack of Asian NPCs in the first version of chapter 1, thus deviating from their own experience of college. The concern was addressed through the redevelopment of one of the main NPCs (Kiran) to reflect the inclusion of Asian students in the college environment (see Fig. 1). To avoid discrimination, a number of different sexualities and social classes will also be included in the game.

As research has identified the possibility that video game content, as well as other types of media, can increase intergroup bias [28], as well as perpetuate stereotypes and prejudice through the imagery and description of minorities [17], the content of the UK game has been generalised to make sure it avoids discrimination to any demographic apart from those relating to IPV.

Intuitive and Progressively Taught so the Game Is Accessible at any Skill Level
As previously stated, around 2.2 billion individuals play video games around the world [60]. However, this means that there are many who may not have any experience or skill with playing digital games. Therefore, the UK game needed to be easy to control with clear tutorials on how to control the main characters and progress through the game. Moreover, as the age of the target audience ranges from anything between 14 and 18 years old it is even more important that how a player was taught to play the game, and the controls themselves, were easy to understand and intuitive. The tutorial itself is presented to the player when they begin chapter 1, where the player takes control of Danielle in her bedroom and continues through to her interactions with her friends in college. The player is introduced to each game mechanic individually, including the mobile phone and social media element, character movement, makeup/clothing choices, object interaction and NPC dialogue (see Fig. 2). The introduction of the mechanics in this way allows the player to learn the processes of the game without suffering from an overload of information, while also allowing players of any experience level the chance to master the controls quickly through environment exploration [63].

Fig. 2. Image from the tutorial describing movement and interaction.

The control interface has been kept as simple as possible by using the W, A, S, D keyboard keys for movement, the SPACEBAR for phone access, shift to walk quickly and E for interaction. The mouse is also used to move the camera in the game and select items in the menu and phone menu options and during dialogue. These simple controls were chosen as they will be familiar to experienced players and easy to master if the player has little gaming experience. Keeping the control interface simple and consistent has also been found to increase game immersion, as the player can concentrate more on gameplay and feel less frustration than they would with a more complex interface [11, 18].

In 2018 there were 1,276,215 students in England with special educational needs (SEN) [16]. As those with learning disabilities, and other SEN requirements, benefit greatly from games that are used in education [21] it was important for the UK game to be accessible for SEN students. The consideration of accessibility needs for SEN players were considered at all stages of game development through the consultation of the Game Accessibility Guidelines [23].

Writing Is Understandable to Players

To make the game as effective and immersive as possible all dialogue and readable content in the game had to be written in a way that the target audience could understand, as well as reflect the language used by the audience (14–18-year olds). If the writing style of the game was not easy to understand for the targeted age group, then players may misinterpret the messages the game is trying to deliver or become frustrated with their lack of understanding. As a result, the player may not pay full attention to what they are doing, which would have a detrimental effect on the prosocial outcome of the game [11, 24]. Moreover, as all characters in the game are college age students the language that they use needs to be relatable to players of a similar age. Research would suggest that if the characters start to use language that does not reflect their age, the player is more likely to become detached and less likely to become emotionally involved in the character [15, 34]. As the purpose of the game is to raise awareness of the consequences of IPV, the

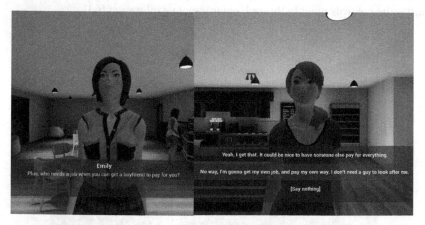

Fig. 3. Example of dialogue and playable character response options.

emotional detachment of the player from the characters would have a detrimental effect on the objectives of the game to promote prosocial behaviour.

To make sure that the dialogue and written content of the game was relatable to the target audience, the focus group was asked to give their opinions on the language and dialogue used. Participants in the group stated that they were happy with the language, that they could understand it and that it was relatable to their age group. The focus group also confirmed that they understood any acronyms or slang that was used in game and that all character names reflected the names of people they knew.

3.3 Interaction

Customisation and Control

Video gamers who have the choice to customise their character and have full control over the majority of the character's actions have been found to become more attached to the character and have a greater immersive experience in a game [22, 62]. Moreover, gamers who play prosocial games tend to prefer a greater sense of control over their characters [9]. One explanation for this is based on the Self Determination Theory (SDT), where a game has the possibility of satisfying the three main intrinsic motivations of an individual through autonomy, relatedness and competence [52]. Increasing the autonomy of the player in game would lead to a greater level of motivation and enjoyment. An investigation into this explanation by Kim and colleagues [42] confirm that game enjoyment was significantly affected by the players believing they had a greater sense of autonomy and more attachment to a games' characters.

Fig. 4. Clothing and make-up choices

It was important that any players of the UK game needed to feel a great sense of autonomy, control and attachment over the main PC, Danielle. As a result, those that play the UK game have the capacity to make choices in the majority of interactions presented to the player. During dialogue interactions with NPCs and social media messages interactions, players are given no more than three choice responses (see Fig. 3) to the dialogue presented to the player. These choices will then elicit different responses from the NPC that the player is conversing with and shows the consequences of different dialogue options to the player.

Another major choice that the player can make is to choose the clothing and make-up that Danielle will wear at the beginning of every chapter (see Fig. 4). This choice not only allows the player to form a greater attachment to Danielle through customisable options [22], but the choice that is made throughout the chapters reflects a number of important issues that are related to IPV. For example, at the start of chapter two Danielle gets to choose between more conservative or non-conservative outfits. No matter what option the player chooses the choice will elicit a negative reaction from James, either that what Danielle is wearing is 'too revealing' or that 'she is not trying hard enough'. This option has been included to reinforce the difficult situation that Danielle is in and outline the paranoid and controlling behaviours that perpetrators of IPV exhibit to control their victims [5].

Presence of Cause and Effect
When developing a game that includes a variation of different player choices it is important to make sure that the game environment, behaviours of NPCs and the narrative react in the way that a player would expect. Caroux et al. [11] suggests that a player's engagement is directly affected by the perceived realism of the game content. Perceived realism has been found to be influenced by freedom of choice, character involvement, and authenticity regarding subject matter/characters, social realism and the realism of the simulation [54]. Therefore, suggesting that players are less likely to be engaged in a game if the consequences of their choices and actions are not realistic.

Fig. 5. Example of IPV material that the player will collect in-game

To make sure that the consequences of the game adequately reflect what the players will expect a number of elements were considered to maximise player engagement. Firstly, the dialogue options for each social interaction (including in-game social media messaging) were designed to be natural and reflect the different responses that Danielle would be expected to have in that situation, as well as the adaptive responses from the NPCs. For example, in chapter one the player can choose to agree or disagree with a comment Hannah makes about James 'relaxing as there is plenty of time to see each other'. Depending on player choice a different response from Hannah will be given, thus providing an interactive consequence of a direct player choice.

During gameplay the player will also see a direct change to the environment as a consequence of their actions and the progression of the story. Any item that the player interacts with and 'picks up' will disappear from the environment. For example, the player directing Danielle to pick up her school bag or collecting leaflets about IPV issues in school, will notice that those items will disappear (see Fig. 5).

Fun for the Player

To make sure the prosocial messages communicated by the UK game are successful, the game needs to be considered fun and enjoyable by the player. Player enjoyment has been found to increase through several factors including: the extent that they can relate to and feel empathy towards the playable character and their goals [34], the consistency of the characters and settings [19], an opportunity to balance skill and challenge [44, 57] and the ability to explore the game environment [64]. As player enjoyment has been found to directly relate to positive player reactions and strong emotional responses [11], a lack of player enjoyment would reduce the effectiveness of the game.

To ensure that all players of the game will find it fun and enjoyable, the gameplay was designed for the player to be actively engaged throughout all chapters. In each chapter the player can explore their environment fully and interact with different objects and information to learn more about the characters and different aspects of IPV. Moreover, the environment changes slightly in each chapter so that the player will find new information that they did not see previously. For example, during one of the main game objectives the player must direct Danielle to find different pamphlets on information regarding IPV in each chapter. Including a change in the environment in this way and actively encouraging exploration will set to limit the amount of boredom felt by players as they progress during their week of gameplay.

Challenge

Klimmet et al. [44] describes that for a player to enjoy a videogame the gameplay must contain challenges that are not too easy or too impossible for a player to complete at their perceived skill level. Similarly, Schmeirbach et al. [57] suggests that the challenge of gameplay must be in balance with the player's skill level to increase immersion and enjoyment.

However, as previously stated the UK game is very easy to control and requires little previous video game experience to be able to play. Instead, the challenge of the game lies in the stimulation of cognitive processing and critical thinking skills surrounding a number of serious issues related to IPV in adolescent relationships. Introducing the players to the main subject topics through face to face and social media character interactions gives the player the option to reflect and critically think on what they have read and respond to the situation. Furthermore, the complexity of the options presented to the player and the seriousness of the subjects steadily increases throughout the game, from social media use and controlling behaviour to the use of revenge porn. For example, in chapter one the dialogue choices mainly centre around whether Danielle should tell James that she is hanging out with her friends instead of seeing him and wondering why his reactions are so negative. However, in chapter four the options presented to the player become more complex and involve themes centred around Danielle's lack of motivation, the mental health issues she is experiencing and whether she should open up to her friends. Progressively presenting more complex and serious subjects to players was enacted for two reasons: 1) it allows the player to become slowly acclimatised to the difficult subject matter and avoid trauma, 2) the continued exposure to IPV issues, support options and positive role models (Kiran and Hannah) will provide time for a player to change their cognitions and attitudes towards IPV [10], increase helping behaviour [24, 30–32, 48] and promote prosocial thoughts [30, 32]. Overall, the challenging topics of the game meet the core mechanic in promoting awareness towards IPV in adolescent relationships.

Balance of the Game

Immersion and enjoyment in a game can be affected by the balance between interactive game play, story content and the reality of game choices and settings [36]. An unbalanced experience for a serious game could be detrimental towards the learning objectives the designers are trying to convey. For example, a serious game that focuses too much on gameplay, such as fun mini games or quests, may suffer from the player misinterpreting the main message and aims of the game, whereas a serious game that bombards a player with too much information can cause cognitive overload, consequently meaning that the player may fail to take away the prosocial message the game is trying to impart [41].

Therefore, the UK game needed to balance storyline interactions, exploration and objective/task completion to keep the player interested and wanting to progress. To accommodate this balance, the game was designed so that the player could explore the environment and complete objectives/tasks in-between interactions with NPCs and the continuation of the narrative. Furthermore, NPC interaction was further divided between face-to-face interactions and through messages on social media. The social media messaging service on the phone mechanic allows players to read NPC responses and further information in their own time and without the urgency of face-to-face interactions, thus providing another dimension to the balance of the game. Participants in the focus group originally thought that there was too much dialogue interaction within the game and that it could lead to some losing interest. As a result of this feedback some dialogue was removed and more interactable objects were inserted. Participants thought that this would improve game balance.

3.4   Provides Motivation to Progress

Rewards as Motivation

Including achievements as a reward for completing objectives will increase motivation to progress for two reasons: 1) To satisfy their feelings of competence/ability to play games and prove their self-worth, and 2) promote competition and discussion of the achievements among students who play the game in-between game sessions.

Point one derives from the Organismic Integration Theory (OIT), a sub-theory of the SDT that suggests a person can be extrinsically motivated to certain behaviours through external influences [55]. In the case of achievements in video games, a player would be motivated through introjected regulation, where they would play to satisfy their ego to prove their self-worth and demonstrate their skills and abilities while avoiding failure. If a player's goal is to obtain all achievements in a game, they will be intrinsically motivated to experience satisfaction by meeting this goal in the UK game.

In regards to promoting competition and discussion amongst the students, Olsen [51] found that there was a high level of competition amongst children, especially boys, that motivated them to play games with greater regularity in an effort to compare and match their performance with others. The UK game offers a unique situation where students will have time in-between each days gaming session to discuss the achievements and choices they made with their friends and peers, which may motivate them to continue playing through friendly competition.

Interesting Narrative
In a study of the main differences between good and bad games, Desurvire and Chen [19] identified that for a game to be considered 'good' it's narrative needs to be consistent, make sense, give a good understanding of what the character needs to do and why they need help doing it. Furthermore, as previously stated, the attachment, immersion and enjoyment of players have been found to directly link to the extent that they can control a character and how they relate to that character in the narrative [22]. A serious game that is wanting to 'hook' players into a narrative and motivate them to continue playing will need to include characters and environments that the player can relate to and what they expect.

The narrative of the UK game has been designed to raise awareness of some very serious, emotional topics that are related to IPV (see 2.2 Game Narrative). By splitting these topics across five chapters and slowly introducing them to the player through an increasing escalation of drama, the narrative has been designed to continually build a player's interest in what will happen next in the story. The aim if this design choice is to keep players constantly thinking about their choices when interacting with NPCs or other interactive elements, such as make-up and outfit choices, while also providing them clear objectives with guidance on their next steps and allowing them to explore the environment. When playing the first chapter of the game the focus group participants found the characters relatable and interesting, stating:

"you can get the experience of it [IPV] without the mental scarring"

The comments from the focus group reinforces the successful creation of an interesting narrative that can be accredited to three factors; 1) the overall subject area of IPV is interesting to the target age group, 2) all characters and environments are relatable to the target audience of the game, and 3) the game allows students of any age group to explore the serious topic of IPV in adolescent relationships without talking down to the player or treating them too much like a child. These factors will motivate a player to continue game play and allow the player to explore the games prosocial messages.

Satisfying Conclusions
Creating a game with multiple endings has a number of strengths. They allow players to feel greater control of the story with their choices, can help make sure that the story unfolds in a way that the player will enjoy, they can encourage players to replay the game and also encourage players to act in ways that they normally wouldn't [47]. However,

when playing a game with multiple endings that are based on player choice, video game players have been found to expect certain outcomes that validate their belief that the choices they make should result in a specific outcome, normally including a 'best' and 'worst' ending [47, 61]. For example, in the game Star Wars: Knights of the Old Republic [7] players expect their choices to have a significant impact on the ending of the game, with choices towards the 'light side' leading to a lighter/good ending and choices towards the 'dark side' leading to an evil/bad ending. An ending that the player expects has been found to allow players to feel a sense of accomplishment and satisfaction with the conclusion of the game [18]. However, an ending that does not make sense to the player and does not reflect their choices can have a detrimental effect to the satisfaction and sense of accomplishment that the player feels.

The UK game has a total of four multiple endings that are accompanied by an individual epilogue for each one. The inclusion of an epilogue was chosen as they have been found to increase the effectiveness of prosocial messages and decrease misinterpretation in prosocial media [14]. Each ending and epilogue of the UK game will reflect the choices that the player made in the last chapter while also reinforcing the consequences of those actions in regards to support structures and IPV victimisation recovery. For example, if the player has Danielle choose to access peer and counsellor support in dealing with James posting 'revenge porn', the ending and epilogue will reflect the positive effect that this support would have on Danielle's recovery, as outlined in current research on the importance of professional support with victims of IPV [1, 66]. As this example is the ending with the 'best' outcome and there is also an ending with the 'worst' outcome, where Danielle accesses no support, the game design includes multiple endings that will offer a satisfying conclusion to players, as well as information on the consequences of IPV. There are also two middle of the road epilogues where the player chooses just peer or just professional support.

Game Pacing
As previously discussed game play/exploration and narrative/dialogue needs to be balanced to provide the player with a fun experience while also providing information regarding the prosocial messages of the game. However, to keep players motivated and engaged with a game the pacing between big, exciting story moments, such as boss battles or plot twist reveals, need to be interspersed with less exciting but relevant moments, such as character development conversations or exploration [47]. Throughout a game, the escalation of the narrative through the pacing of exciting gameplay and calmer moments help to increase tension and suspense felt by the player until the games resolution, motivating players to continue [47, 56].

As a result, each chapter of the UK game needed to be well paced to motivate game play while preventing players becoming bored or disinterested with the content. As each chapter has a series of conversations and game play interactions that are needed for story progression, each chapter has been paced so that players experience conversations with NPCs for story development and gameplay interactions, such as fetch quests, at regular intervals. For example, in chapter two the player as Danielle will have a conversation with James about the nude image she sent him and their plans to meet at her house that evening. The scene cuts to Danielle's house where the player will have to fetch items for James' arrival. James will then arrive and another conversation will occur. The pacing of these interactions (conversation, quest, conversation) allows a break in the storyline to prevent the player suffering from information overload or becoming bored and disinterested with the content.

3.5 Information

The prosocial messages that the UK game is trying to impart requires a large amount of information to be given to players around IPV attitudes, behaviours, and support services. However, care was needed during the design of the game to make sure that players were not given too much information at once and that all information was relevant. Providing too much information to a player can exceed their working memory limits and lead to cognitive overload [2, 40, 58]. In regards to educational games, cognitive overload theory suggests that the intrinsic cognitive load of the game, such as the learning objectives and educational material, as well as extraneous cognitive load, which includes elements such as the environment, game controls and character spatial awareness, are both imposed on the players working memory before any information is coded into the long term memory [2, 13, 40, 58]. As working memory has been found to be limited in capacity and duration [3, 49], exceeding this limit could lead to players missing or misinterpreting important messages and information about IPV or forgetting aspects of the game that could affect gameplay. Moreover, during learning tasks, the inclusion of irrelevant information as distractors has been found to increase cognitive load and decrease the ability to remember complex information [46].

To avoid cognitive overload, the game includes no irrelevant information that is not directly linked to the narrative. Moreover, the dialogue between the playable characters and NPCs have been designed to avoid any irrelevant information to the story. The dialogue and dialogue choices were also designed to be as succinct as possible so the player does not have to read too much information at once while also remaining relatable to the target audience. The removal of any irrelevant information will avoid unnecessary cognitive load and allow players to process the most salient information and topics related to the game [46].

To further prevent cognitive overload, players are only given information to progress the story when needed (known as 'just in time') and at the same time the character would learn this information. By dividing IPV information between chapters, the player will be able to critically process the information given to them. This design choice allows players to progress the story without becoming inundated with too much information at once. For example, a player only finds out that Danielle can access support with the college councillor at the end of chapter five, which leads to the final choices that end the game. Receiving this information earlier could distract the player from other IPV awareness messages found in different chapters, or objectives they are trying to complete. Moreover, by introducing the player to information, such as NPC names, backstory and IPV issues, at the same time as the character the player can process and retain information gradually, without having to read information 'off-screen'. The presentation of information this way allows a player time to process what they experience and avoid cognitive overload through an excess of reading. Also, by learning about how adolescents can become victims of different types of IPV at the same time as the character, the player is more likely to foster feelings of sympathy and empathy towards Danielle [15] and reinforce the prosocial messages of the game. However, even though the information provided throughout the UK is carefully managed to reduce cognitive overload and maximise game enjoyment and effectiveness, it is important to allow players to access extra information to answer further questions or queries about the topics covered. Game players will be able to find this information through optional explorations of the environment and interactions, including real life posters concerning IPV awareness and support services, such as the 'Woman's Aid' charity (See Fig. 5) [67]. Permission from the charity was sought and gained to use these posters in the game.

3.6 Player Goals Aligned with Character Goals

As previously mentioned, the UK game aims to raise the awareness of IPV issues in adolescent relationships by allowing the player to step into the main PCs shoes (Danielle) and experience her abuse at the hands of James. To be successful with this goal a player needs to be fully engaged with Danielle and feel empathy for her situation [34]. Lankoski [45], suggests that the amount of empathy a player has for a PC is directly related to how the character is presented to them. To incite empathy for a character the writing of the game needs to allow the player to recognise the character as one that deserves empathy and allow the player to align themselves to the thoughts and feelings of the PC as the story unfolds. Moreover, the player must believe that the goals of the character, and ultimately the game, are relevant to what they reasonably expect from that character so they can fully engage with what they are trying to accomplish. Failure to align player and character goals would cause an 'identity gap', where unexpected actions made by the character would cause a reduction of empathy and player engagement [65]. Similarly, the writers of a game need to make sure that there are no 'character assassination' moments at any point of the narrative. A PC that says or acts in a way that is directly opposed to what is expected and justifiable for them would decrease player empathy for the character and ultimately player engagement [18].

In the UK game the character goals are fully relatable to the playable characters and the essence of the story, thus maximising the engagement and empathy players will experience. For example, during chapter two when the player finds out at the same time as Danielle that her 'nude images' had been shared amongst James' friends, both the player and the PC want to know why it happened. Furthermore, all choices that are presented to the player, either through dialogue, social messaging or object interaction, fully reflect what would be expected or justifiable from Danielle and the other playable characters in those situations. Finally, as Danielle is the primary PC throughout the game there will be a greater opportunity for players to feel connected to the character, both through the information learnt about IPV at the same time as Danielle and her experiences of abuse from James. The development of this connection will allow the player to feel greater empathy towards Danielle and promote awareness of IPV in adolescent relationships.

4 Conclusion

Serious, educational games have previously been found to be successful in promoting prosocial thoughts [30, 32], increase empathy [35, 48] and encourage increased helping behaviour [24, 30–32, 48]. To design an effective serious game that promotes immersion, engagement, and empathy, there are a number of good game principles that need to be followed. This paper looked to discuss how the game framework and design choices of a serious game that promotes awareness and behavioural change towards IPV in adolescent relationships in the UK met these good game principles. In summary, the UK game has included design choices that will guarantee the target audience of the serious game (14–18-year old students) will feel immersed and engaged in the story of Danielle and her experiences of IPV.

References

1. Ali, P., McGarry, J.: Supporting people who experience intimate partner violence. Nurs. Stand. **32**(24), 54–62 (2018). https://doi.org/10.7748/ns.2018.e10641
2. Ang, C.S., Zaphiris, P., Mahmood, S.: A model of cognitive loads in massively multiplayer online role playing games. Interact. Comput. **19**(1), 167–179 (2007). https://doi.org/10.1016/j.intcom.2006.08.006
3. Baddeley, A.: Working memory. Am. Assoc. Adv. Sci. **255**(5044), 556–559 (1992). https://doi.org/10.1126/science.1736359
4. Barter, C.: In the name of love: partner abuse and violence in teenage relationships. Br. J. Soc. Work **39**(2), 211–233 (2009). https://doi.org/10.1093/bjsw/bcm127
5. Barter, C., McCarry, M., Berridge, D., Evans, K.: Partner exploitation and violence in teenage intimate relationships. NSPCC, London (2009). https://www.nspcc.org.uk/inform
6. Barr, P., Noble, J., Biddle, R.: Video game values: human-computer interaction and games. Interact. Comput. **19**(2), 180–195 (2007). https://doi.org/10.1016/j.intcom.2006.08.008
7. Bioware: Star Wars: Knights of the Old Republic [Video Game]. Austin: LucasArts (2013). Accessed July 2019
8. Boduszek, D., et al.: Prosocial video game as an intimate partner violence prevention tool among youth: a randomised controlled trial. Comput. Hum. Behav. **93**(1), 260–266 (2019). https://doi.org/10.1016/j.chb.2018.12.028
9. Bowman, N.D., Schultheiss, D., Schumann, C.: "I'm attached, and I'm a good guy/gal!": how character attachment influences pro-and anti-social motivations to play massively multiplayer online role-playing games. Cyberpsychol. Behav. Soc. Network. **15**(3), 163–175 (2012). https://doi.org/10.1089/cyber.2011.0311
10. Buckley, K.E., Anderson, C.A.: A theoretical model of the effects and consequences of playing video games. In: Vorderer, P., Bryant, J. (eds.) Playing Video Games - Motives, Responses, and Consequences, pp. 363–378. LEA, Mahwah (2006)
11. Caroux, L., Isbister, K., Le Bigot, L., Vibert, N.: Player-video game interaction: a systematic review of current concepts. Comput. Hum. Behav. **48**(1), 366–381 (2015). https://doi.org/10.1016/j.chb.2015.01.066
12. Centers for Disease Control and Prevention. Violence Prevention (2019). https://www.cdc.gov/violenceprevention/intimatepartnerviolence/fastfact.html. Accessed July 2019
13. Chang, C., Warden, C.A., Liang, C., Lin, G.-.Y.: Effects of digital game-based learning on achievement, flow and overall cognitive load. Aust. J. Educ. Technol. **34**(4), 155–167 (2018). https://doi.org/10.14742/ajet.2961
14. Cohen, E.L., Alward, D., Zajicek, D., Edwards, S., Hutson, R.: Ending as intended: The educational effects of an epilogue to a TV show episode about bipolar disorder. Health Commun. **33**(9), 1097–1104 (2018). https://doi.org/10.1080/10410236.2017.1331308

15. del Byl, P.: A conceptual affective design framework for the use of emotions in computer game design. Cyberpsychol. J. Psychosoc. Res. Cyberspace **9**(3) (2015). Article 4. https://doi.org/10.5817/cp2015-3-4

16. Department for Education: Schools, pupils and their characteristics, January 2018. https://www.gov.uk/government/statistics/schools-pupils-and-their-characteristics-january-2018. Accessed July 2019

17. Deskins, T.G.: Stereotypes in video games and how they perpetuate prejudice. McNair Scholars Res. J. **6**(1), 19–36 (2013). https://commons.emich.edu/mcnair/vol6/iss1/5/?utm_source=commons.emich.edu%2Fmcnair%2Fvol6%2Fiss1%2F5&utm_medium=PDF&utm_campaign=PDFCoverPages. Accessed July 2019

18. Despain, W., Acosta, K. (eds.): 100 Principles of Game Design. New Riders, Berkeley (2013)

19. Desurvire, H., Chen, B.: 48 Differences between good and bad video games: game playability principles (PLAY) for designing highly ranked video games. In: Behavioristics.com LA CHI Association meeting Presentation (2008)

20. Dietz, T.L.: An examination of violence and gender role portrayals in video games: implications for gender socialization and aggressive behavior. Sex Roles **38**(5–6), 425–442 (1998). https://doi.org/10.1023/a:101870990

21. Durkin, K., Boyle, J., Hunter, S., Conti-Ramsden, G.: Video games for children and adolescents with special educational needs. Zeitschrift fur Psychologie **221**(2), 79–89 (2013). https://doi.org/10.1027/2151-2604/a000138

22. Fischer, P., Kastenmüller, A., Greitemeyer, T.: Media violence and the self: the impact of personalized gaming characters in aggressive video games on aggressive behavior. J. Exp. Soc. Psychol. **46**(1), 192–195 (2010). https://doi.org/10.1016/j.jesp.2009.06.010

23. Game Accessibility Guidelines: Full List (2019). http://gameaccessibilityguidelines.com/full-list/. Accessed July 2019

24. Gentile, D.A., et al.: The effects of prosocial video games on prosocial behaviors: international evidence from correlational, longitudinal, and experimental studies. Pers. Soc. Psychol. Bull. **35**(6), 752–763 (2009). https://doi.org/10.1177/0146167209333045

25. Girlguiding: Girls' Attitudes Survey (2014). https://www.girlguiding.org.uk/girls-making-change/girls-attitudes-survey/. Accessed July 2019

26. Girlguiding.: Girls' Attitudes Survey (2018). https://www.girlguiding.org.uk/girls-making-change/girls-attitudes-survey/. Accessed July 2019

27. Greitemeyer, T.: Effects of prosocial media on social behavior: when and why does media exposure affect helping and aggression? Current Dir. Psychol. Sci. **20**(4), 251–255 (2011). https://doi.org/10.1177/0963721411415229

28. Greitemeyer, T.: Playing violent video games increases intergroup bias. Pers. Soc. Psychol. Bull. **40**(1), 70–78 (2014). https://doi.org/10.1177/0146167213505872

29. Greitemeyer, T., Agthe, M., Turner, R., Gschwendtner, C.: Acting prosocially reduces retaliation: effects of prosocial video games on aggressive behavior. Eur. J. Soc. Psychol. **42**(2), 235–242 (2012). https://doi.org/10.1002/ejsp.1837

30. Greitemeyer, T., Osswald, S.: Prosocial video games reduce aggressive cognitions. J. Exp. Soc. Psychol. **45**(4), 896–900 (2009). https://doi.org/10.1016/j.jesp.2009.04.005

31. Greitemeyer, T., Osswald, S.: Effects of prosocial video games on prosocial behavior. J. Pers. Soc. Psychol. **98**(2), 211–221 (2010). https://doi.org/10.1037/a0016997

32. Greitemeyer, T., Osswald, S.: Playing prosocial video games increases the accessibility of prosocial thoughts. J. Soc. Psychol. **151**(2), 121–128 (2011). https://doi.org/10.1080/00224540903365588

33. Greitemeyer, T., Mügge, D.O.: Video games of affect social outcomes: a meta-analytic review of the effects of violent and prosocial video game play. Pers. Soc. Psychol. Bull. **40**(5), 578–589 (2014). https://doi.org/10.1177/0146167213520459

34. Happ, C., Melzer, A., Steffgen, G.: Like the good or bad guy - Empathy in antisocial and prosocial games. Psychol. Popular Media Cult. **4**(2), 80–96 (2015). https://doi.org/10.1037/ppm0000021
35. Harrington, B., O'Connell, M.: Video games as virtual teachers: prosocial video game use by children and adolescents from different socioeconomic groups is associated with increased empathy and prosocial behaviour. Comput. Hum. Behav. **63**(1), 650–658 (2016). https://doi.org/10.1016/j.chb.2016.05.062
36. Harteveld, C.: Triadic game design: Balancing reality, meaning and play. Springer, London (2011). https://doi.org/10.1007/978-1-84996-157-8
37. Hird, M.J.: An empirical study of adolescent dating aggression in the U.K. J. Adolesc. **23**(1), 69–78 (2000). https://doi.org/10.1006/jado.1999.0292
38. Home Office: Information for local areas on the change to the definition of domestic violence and abuse (2013). https://www.gov.uk/government/publications/definition-of-domestic-violence-and-abuse-guide-for-local-areas. Accessed July 2019
39. Howard, D.E., Wang, M.Q., Yan, F.: Psychosocial factors associated with reports of physical dating violence among US adolescent females. Adolescence **42**(166), 311–324 (2007). https://search.proquest.com/openview/a4fc1ed83fb5f7249f71f0cdc599f801/1?cbl=41539&pq-origsite=gscholar. Accessed July 2019
40. Huang, W.D., Johnson, T.: Instructional game design using cognitive load theory. In: Ferdig, R. (ed.) Handbook of Research on Effective Electronic Gaming in Education, pp. 1143–1165. IGI Global, Hershey (2009). https://doi.org/10.4018/978-1-59904-808-6.ch066
41. Kalyuga, S., Plass, J.L.: Evaluating and managing cognitive load in games. In: Handbook of Research on Effective Electronic Gaming in Education, pp. 719–737. IGI Global (2009)
42. Kim, K., et al.: Is it a sense of autonomy, control, or attachment? Exploring the effects of in-game customization on game enjoyment. Comput. Hum. Behavior **48**(1), 695–705 (2015). https://doi.org/10.1016/j.chb.2015.02.011
43. King, G., Krzywinska, T.: Computer Games/Cinema/Interfaces. In: Computer Games and Digital Cultures Conference, Tampere, Finland (2002). https://www.researchgate.net/publication/221217537_Computer_Games_Cinema_Interfaces. Accessed July 2019
44. Klimmt, C., Blake, C., Hefner, D., Vorderer, P., & Roth, C.: Player performance, satisfaction, and video game enjoyment. In: International Conference on Entertainment Computing, pp. 1–12. Springer, Heidelberg, September 2009
45. Lankoski, P.: Player character engagement in computer games. Games Cult. **6**(4), 291–311 (2011). https://doi.org/10.1177/1555412010391088
46. Lavie, N.: Distracted and confused? Selective attention under load. Trends Cogn. Sci. **9**(2), 75–82 (2005). https://doi.org/10.1016/j.tics.2004.12.004
47. Lebowitz, J., Klug, C.: Interactive Storytelling for Video Games: A Player-Centered Approach for Creating Memorable Characters and Stories. Elsevier Inc., Oxford (2011)
48. Leiberg, S., Kilmecki, O., Singer, T.: Short-term compassion training increases prosocial behavior in a newly developed prosocial game. PLoS One **6**(3), 1–10 (2011). https://doi.org/10.1371/journal.pone.0017798
49. Miller, G.A.: The magical number seven, plus or minus two: Some limits on our capacity for processing information. Psychol. Rev. **101**(2), 343–352 (1994). https://doi.org/10.1037/0033-295x.101.2.343
50. None in Three: None in Three Aims (2016–2019). http://www.noneinthree.org/about-the-centre/. Accessed July 2019
51. Olson, C.K.: Children's motivations for video game play in the context of normal development. Rev. Gen. Psychol. **14**(2), 180–187 (2010). https://doi.org/10.1037/a0018984
52. Przybylski, A.K., Rigby, C.S., Ryan, R.M.: A motivational model of video game engagement. Rev. Gen. Psychol. **14**(2), 154–166 (2010). https://doi.org/10.1037/a0019440

53. Przybylski, A.K., Weinstein, N.: Violent video game engagement is not associated with adolescents' aggressive behaviour: evidence from a registered report. Roy. Soc. Open Sci. **9**(171474), 1–14 (2019). https://doi.org/10.1098/rsos.171474

54. Ribbens, W., Malliet, S.: Perceived digital game realism: a quantitative exploration of its structure. PRESENCE Virtual Augmented Reality **19**(6), 585–600 (2011). https://doi.org/10.1162/pres_a_00024

55. Ryan, R.M., Deci, E.L.: Self-determination theory and the facilitation of intrinsic motivation, social development, and well-being. Am. Psychol. **55**(1), 68–78 (2000). https://doi.org/10.1037/110003-066X.55.1.68

56. Salmond, M.: Video Game Design: Principles and Practices From the Ground Up. Bloomsbury, London (2016)

57. Schmierbach, M., Chung, M.-.Y., Wu, M., Kim, K.: No one likes to lose: the effect of game difficulty on competency, flow, and enjoyment. J. Media Psychol. **26**(3), 105–110 (2014). https://doi.org/10.1027/1864-1105/a000120

58. Schrader, C., Bastiaens, T.J.: The influence of virtual presence: effects on experienced cognitive load and learning outcomes in educational computer games. Comput. Hum. Behav. **28**(2), 648–658 (2012). https://doi.org/10.1016/j.chb.2011.11.011

59. Stanley, N., et al.: Pornography, sexual coercion and abuse and sexting in young people's intimate relationships: a European study. J. Interpersonal Violence **33**(19), 2919–2944 (2018). https://doi.org/10.1177/0886260516633204

60. Statista: Video game industry: statistics and facts (2018). https://www.statista.com/topics/868/video-games/. Accessed July 2019

61. Tavinor, G.: What's my motivation? Video games and interpretive performance. J. Aesthetics Art Criticism **75**(1), 23–33 (2017). https://doi.org/10.1111/jaac.12334

62. Teng, C.: Customization, immersion satisfaction, and online gamer loyalty. Comput. Hum. Behav. **26**(6), 1547–1554 (2010). https://doi.org/10.1016/j.chb.2010.05.029

63. White, M.M.: Learn to play: designing tutorials for video games (2014). https://ebookcentral.proquest.com. Accessed July 2019

64. Wirth, W., Ryffel, F., Von Pape, T., Karnowski, V.: The development of video game enjoyment in a role playing game. Cyberpsychol. Behav. Soc. Network. **16**(4), 260–264 (2013). https://doi.org/10.1089/cyber.2012.0159

65. Worch, M.: The Identity Bubble - A design approach to character and story development (2011). http://www.worch.com/downloads/. Accessed July 2019

66. World Health Organisation: Responding to intimate partner violence and sexual violence against women (2013). https://www.who.int/reproductivehealth/publications/violence/9789241548595/en/. Accessed July 2019

67. Women's Aid: Online and Digital Abuse (2015). https://www.womensaid.org.uk/information-support/what-is-domestic-abuse/onlinesafety/. Accessed July 2019

Personalization of Educational Video Games in APOGEE

Valentina Terzieva[1]([envelope]), Elena Paunova-Hubenova[1], and Boyan Bontchev[2]

[1] Institute of Information and Communication Technologies, Bulgarian Academy of Sciences, Acad. G. Bonchev St., Block 2, 1113 Sofia, Bulgaria
valia@isdip.bas.bg, eli_np@hsi.iccs.bas.bg
[2] Faculty of Mathematics and Informatics, Sofia University "St Kliment Ohridski", J. Baurchier 5 Blv., 1164 Sofia, Bulgaria
bbontchev@fmi.uni-sofia.bg

Abstract. Gamification of education is a fact in recent years. This method for imperceptible learning is used in many countries and schools all over the world. The advantages and disadvantages of the educational games according, to students and teachers, are shortly explained here. The paper describes an intelligent video maze-game that is a container for various mini-games that bring the essential educational content and challenges for learners. It also presents a model of a student (as a learner and as a player) and the framework for providing a personalized learning experience in the context of an educational game. Thus, the presented maze game can fit different learning and playing styles of a particular user. The process of personalization is in line with the preliminary results from an online survey exploring students' views about educational video games. The findings reveal their preferences about many issues such as types of mini-games, embraced learning content, and the willingness to repeat the game with the same or increased complexity to improve the overall results or acquired knowledge.

Keywords: Personalization · Education · Video games · Maze · APOGEE

1 Introduction

Nowadays, digital games are increasingly used in learning, and the phenomenon is known as gamification of education [1]. The aim is to motivate students to learn through applying a gaming approach. Thus, learning becomes fun, imperceptible, and enjoyable activity, and students perform the learning activities effortlessly. They can receive real-time feedback and perform tasks that are impossible under other conditions (i.e., expensive or dangerous). Through gamification, students are knowledge-driven and evaluated in a personalized way [2].

For teachers from the UK, Italy, and Turkey [3], the main reasons for applying game-based learning (GBL) are motivation, fun, and imperceptible learning. They point out the advantages and disadvantages of the application of games in the learning process. Study of the attitudes of Bulgarian teachers and students towards the educational games

A. Brooks and E. I. Brooks (Eds.): ArtsIT 2019/DLI 2019, LNICST 328, pp. 477–487, 2020.
https://doi.org/10.1007/978-3-030-53294-9_34

points out their impact and usefulness for the learning process [4]. The survey findings are shortly presented here.

According to students, the essential benefits of educational games are easy learning, a possibility for practicing, finding additional information, increasing the interest in learning matter, memorization for a longer time, and developing ICT skills. Few of them claim that games are not suitable for learning because they distract them. High-school students have a more moderate attitude towards educational games than younger students. The probable reason is scarce of game resources targeted to secondary school students comparing to those for younger ones. Teachers show a more positive opinion about educational games than the students. The most significant advantages, according to them, are the ability to practice, increase the efficiency of the teaching-learning process, increase the interest in subjects, more active participation in classes, and invisible learning. Teachers also point out that GBL is appropriate for individual training of students with special educational needs (SEN), and especially for younger students. Very few of them assess games as interfering with the learning process.

Games are an incentive for active learning and critical thinking, so during the play, students can challenge themselves, thus to develop their learning ability. Digital games are suitable for the acquisition of knowledge and information to students as they are one of their favorite pastimes. Many researchers agree that educational video games have the potential to be an efficient learning tool [5, 6]. However, students have their preference and style of playing and learning. The personalized learning approach allows addressing individual students' profiles (readiness, interest, and learning preferences) through customization of the learning process and content. If this approach is integrated into educational video games, it is expected to gain more benefits. To create different games, encompassing specific learning material, for each group of students is a tough task. Thus nowadays, games are designed with options to adapt and personalize some parameters according to the player [7]. This paper presents the personalization of mini-games that are part of an educational game-container such as video maze game.

2   Related Works

User-adaptive learning systems have already proved to be more efficient and usable than usual non-adaptive ones. One of their most often cited clear benefits is the significant improvement in the overall learning progress. Such systems are based on user modelling [8, 9]. A distinctive feature that makes these systems cost-effective is their ability to share and reuse learning resources. Moreover, they apply an approach to the personalization of learning materials and activities, thus provide an individualized educational experience [10]. Likewise, personalized educational games will benefit learners. GBL employs the gamification approach – i.e., using game mechanics, thinking, and elements in non-gaming and tedious educational contexts [1]. This approach also implies embedding of well-known traditional pedagogical practices that are effective. The goal is to make tiresome educational tasks to look like a game and thus to motivate students and to enable deep learning [11]. So, students can acquire knowledge easily and with fun. Educational video games by combining education and fun are maybe the most powerful learning tool [12]. They put students in gaming contexts, where they can experience both engagement and motivation that are significant factors for the efficient learning process [13]. Furthermore, educational games have to be designed respecting the contemporary pedagogical theories and instructional strategies that enable better learning effects. These include personalization of tasks' attributes (e.g., number, content, difficulty) to the student's profiles (learning styles, background, and preferences) and considering the customized in-game interactions [6].

Video games are also a possible real-time assessment tool because every action or inaction of players usually is followed by almost immediate responses, according to which they change their behavior and decisions. Thus, students' performance can be an indicator of their subject knowledge and computer or gaming skills [14]. Hence to put learning in the center requires educational tasks (challenges) to be well fitted to learners' skill level and goals, as well as the almost instant provision of meaningful feedback, i.e. delivering personalized learning [15]. Comparing to traditional instruction approaches (lectures), educational games easy can be adapted to the student's pace. Moreover, usually, digital video games present information in various audio and visual modes at the same time, which suits different learning styles. Games can deliver knowledge step-by-step, i.e., presenting complicated tasks at small pieces gradually extended to whole complex ones. Such tasks structuring is known as the incremental principle [16]. These characteristics of educational games make them easy to personalize according to students' profiles. Findings of several studies show that the students' learning achievement can be improved by GBL, but the provision of personal learning support by proper guiding strategy and feedback can further enhance their performance. Thus, by making the formative assessment [17] an integral part of the teaching process (i.e., providing feedback and support during instructions), teachers can personalize learning tasks to improve their effectiveness and students' progress [18].

Currently, personalized learning is described as an essential trend. The meaning of personalization in learning and education as a whole can vary significantly depending on the context, pedagogy approach, technology resources, and many other factors [19–21]. A definition that reflects the main principles is "Personalized learning prioritizes a clear understanding of the needs and goals of each student and the tailoring of instruction to address those needs and goals." [22]. The research [20] was one of the first that introduces the term personalized learning presenting it as an umbrella term for customizable educational approaches that: (i) count the abilities, knowledge, and needs of every individual student; (ii) carefully pay attention to their learning styles, motivations, and needs; (iii) appreciate their targets and provide high-quality formative assessment; (iv) make lessons well-paced and enjoyable; (v) support students by partnerships with others even beyond classrooms.

Technology assists the personalization process to a greater extent by providing educators with tools that enable the management of a more personalized approach and activities that support students' learning and development. Moreover, the teacher's role also can vary from selecting best strategies to help individual students to master their competencies to creating personalized learning resources and assisting students in acquiring knowledge and skills [20, 23]. Much research on teachers' practice outlines approaches that have proven to be efficient for delivering personalized learning [8, 15, 23]. In the context of GBL, the authors consider these approaches as follows:

- *Student-centered activities* – educational tasks and scenarios requiring the active engagement of students: (i) learning by doing; (ii) learning by decision-making;
- *Student-centered remedies* – learning scenarios requiring the active involvement of teachers by focusing on learner's knowledge: (i) providing immediate feedback with targeted information; (ii) delivering dynamic adaptation of learning material considering the current learners' performance; (iii) stimulating learners' progress.

3 Personalization of Puzzle Games

Usually, modelling of learners is used in e-learning environments to model the knowledge, cognitive skills, and interests of learners, and thus based on this information to customize their learning interactions. This section describes the developed model of learner and the framework for providing a personalized learning experience in the context of educational maze-game (Fig. 1). One of the factors that affect the effectiveness of GBL is the learning style of students – the preferred way of gathering, processing, and evaluating information within the learning context. It is a relatively permanent characteristic that concerns cognitive and psycho-social behavior. Among the many models of learning styles been developed, the VARK family (Visual, Aural, Read/Write, and Kinesthetic) appeared to be a very popular and useful one [25].

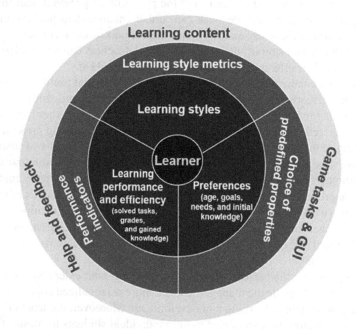

Fig. 1. APOGEE personalization framework.

For personalization in GBL, the role of playing style (a manner of playing), is significant. The personal playing style can vary in different games or through time [26].

Hence, it is a relative parameter that has to be defined in the context of a particular game type. Appreciating playing style is essential for the adaptation of player-centric computer games [7]. Usually, the determination of playing styles is based on psychological theories [27]. Research asserts that playing and learning styles are in parallel because the motivation is supposed to be in correlation with learning [7]. The ADOPTA playing styles family, consisting of competitor, dreamer, logician, and strategist [28], is assessed as appropriate to adapt in-game interactions within the APOGEE personalization framework.

3.1 Learner's Profile Model

The creation of models of learners follows user modeling. User models can be considered as a *static* (not changing), *dynamic* (allow updates according to current needs, preferences, and goals of the user) and a mixture of them. Learning systems use the following types of learners' models to deliver adaptive learning content:

Stereotype model – each learner is assigned to one of the various predefined categories that determine the corresponding customization of the learning process [9]. The accuracy of the model depends on the granulation and proper assignment of the learner to a relevant group.

Overlay model – the knowledge is delivered on topics or concepts, then testing its acquisition of learners is the base for building and updating the student's model [9]. The accuracy of the model depends on a chosen granulation of the knowledge domain into particular topics or concepts, and the precise assessment of learners.

Open model – students can view (and even edit) the content of their model by a special interface [29]. This approach enables self-reflection, increased user motivation, and better personalization transparency; thus, the accuracy of the model is enhanced.

For providing personalizable and adaptable GBL, a student's model should reflect features related to the customization of learning interactions to the student's profile (characteristics, needs, and preferences). Thus, for personalization of the educational maze game within the APOGEE project, the model of a student is developed (Fig. 2). It uses a mixed approach that integrates the ideas of the listed above models. This broad-spectrum flexible student's model covers components in three main aspects:

- user-related (basic) – general data, needed for student's identification;
- learner-related – specific data needed for personalization of educational content and built-in didactic tasks to learning needs and preferences of the user;
- player-related – specific data needed for appropriate customization of particular parameters of the gameplay to the user's playing style and preferences.

When building the model, at first, each student self-assigns to a stereotype category, then the model is continuously improved through data obtained in the process of GBL. All model components are initialized during the first registration of the user in the game web-site. In the student's model, the dynamic characteristics as a learner (denoted by L) and as a player (denoted by P) represent the in-game achievements, thus they are updated during the gameplay. For unregistered users, the game will not be personalized, as well as their results will not be shown.

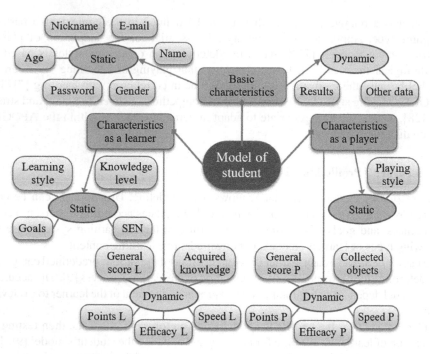

Fig. 2. Model of the student in the APOGEE concept.

3.2 The Process of Personalization

The APOGEE platform serves for the generation of educational maze games containing various types of puzzles (mini-games) embedded into the maze halls. When a student enters a maze, both the puzzle types and complexity of the learning content presented in each puzzle are chosen according to the student's model (Fig. 2). All characteristics in the model are used for both personalization and dynamic difficulty adjustment [7] of the mini-games embedded in the maze. Thus, different learners will play puzzles with different, personalized learning content. Personalization based on preferences or gameplay is very likely to perform better than any attempt to create a model of the student and infer from it how to personalize the game. However, the student's model is expected to provide a fine-tuning of the personalized parameters.

Static user-related (basic) characteristics describe relatively constant attributes that are used for identification, privacy issues, and initial set-up of the maze game according to personal data. Static learner- and player-related characteristics such as knowledge level, goals, learning and playing styles support the personalization and adaptation of the game and determine the choice of learning content that is built-in mini-games. Moreover, age and gender define the complexity of the gameplay, degree of difficulty of the learning content, and preferred type of built-in mini-games. Dynamic user-related characteristics reflect chronologically the student's results achieved in different game sessions and determine offered feedback and hints. Other information for the student (e.g., related to special educational needs) may be included upon the teacher's request.

3.3 Parameters of Mini-Games for Personalization

This section presents the four groups of educational mini-games [24] that are embedded in the maze game as well as their possible personalization. Most of the games' parameters are personalized according to students' profiles (age, gender, knowledge level, learning style) and preferences. All objects and questions in mini-games are related to the particular learning matter, and teachers also can parametrize them:

- *Question games* – answering a quiz or solving a single problem. Personalization concerns type of the questions (open or closed), their difficulty and complexity, the number of possible answers, as well as the provided hints.
- *Searching games* – detecting objects or matching identical ones. Examples are finding semitransparent or hidden items, "word soup" puzzle, and memory cards. The number, size, and kind of objects/words/cards, as well as the criteria and positions for matching, can be different.
- *Arranging games* – assembling a 2D image or sorting objects. The content, shape, and size of puzzle parts; number and type of objects; criteria for classifying can vary.
- *Action games* – shooting and collecting unanimated objects (balloons with attached 3D educational objects). The number, size, and type of objects can be various.

4   Preliminary Results

To evaluate the preferred puzzle types and the way of their personalization depending on learning and playing styles, the authors conducted an online survey. Before answering the questions, the respondents were asked first to watch a 5-min video[1] demonstrating the gameplay of a sample educational maze game in history. It contains several arranging and question mini-games (as described in Sect. 3.3), all generated by the APOGEE platform. Next, the respondents were invited to play the same maze game online[2], which was essential for meaningful filling out the survey, thus to evaluate the concepts of personalized game-based learning. The questionnaire contains 44 questions, divided into three groups for determining: A. Desired types of puzzles (12 questions); B. VARK learning style [23] (16 questions); C. ADOPTA playing style [7] (16 questions). The section presents preliminary results for some questions from group A of the survey.

Until now, the valid replies are 39, collected from respondents with average age circa 13 years, and the ratio of boys to girls is 28.9% to 71.1%. Question 6 asked the players what should the educational video games aim at, applying a 5-point Likert scale (1 – definitely No, 2 – rather No, 3 – cannot judge, 4 – rather Yes, 5 – definitely Yes). Table 1 presents mean (M), standard deviation (SD), and standard error (SE) for the received answers (N = 39). Findings show that educational games with learning content aimed at the experimentations and summarization of knowledge are most preferred by the players; games focused on the initial introduction to the learning matter and for testing acquired knowledge are also highly rated.

---

[1] https://youtu.be/mI9NwiZOrB0.

[2] http://www.apogee.online/games.html.

Table 1. Results for Question 6 "What should the educational video games aim at?".

Statistics	Introduction	Experimental	Detailed study	Assessment	Summarization	Intersectional
M	3.894	4.108	3.649	3.838	4.027	3.487
SD	1.060	0.994	1.086	1.236	1.142	1.239
SE	0.623	0.658	0.584	0.615	0.645	0.558

Question 7 asked what types of puzzles should be mostly included in the educational maze games. Table 2 reveals that players like most answering questions for unlocking maze doors and, as well, both word and memory games. Two-dimensional puzzles and games for sorting objects related to the learning matter are preferred too.

Table 2. Results for Question 7 "What types of puzzles should be included into the mazes?".

St.	Question for door unlock	Quiz	2D puzzle	Word games	Roll-a-ball	Finding translucent obj.	Finding hidden objects	Sorting objects	Memo games	Shooters
M	4.103	3.667	3.744	3.949	3.410	3.308	3.282	3.744	3.923	3.436
SD	0.852	1.108	1.117	1.075	1.251	1.341	1.276	1.272	1.085	1.142
SE	0.657	0.587	0.599	0.632	0.546	0.530	0.526	0.599	0.628	0.550

Question 9 asks the respondents to order by importance (from 1 – most important to 4 – less important) how the educational materials in video games to be chosen (Table 3). The replies rank as most important a selection of complexity according to the player's level of knowledge in the game's learning area (e.g., beginner, advanced, and expert). Next, educational material in learning games should fit into the following characteristics of the player – age, interests, and goals (e.g., initial introduction to the topic, detailed study, knowledge testing), and the VARK learning style.

Finally, we asked the players "Would you play an educational game again at the same level of difficulty to improve the score for that level?" (Question 11) and "Would you play an educational game at the next level of difficulty?" (Question 12). Answers are rated again on a 5-point Likert scale. Findings show that the players are strongly motivated to play several times the same educational game, until achieving a better result, which is related to acquiring more knowledge (Table 4).

Table 3. Results for Question 9.

St.	Player's level of knowledge	Player's age	Player's interests & goals	VARK learning style
M	2.000	2.171	2.487	3.057
SD	0.850	1.361	0.970	0.968
SE	0.320	0.348	0.398	0.490

Table 4. Results for Questions 11 and 12.

St	Q 11	Q 12
M	4.026	4.513
SD	1.127	0.683
SE	0.645	0.723

5   Conclusion and Future Work

GBL has undoubted benefits, as most students perceive the learning material as tedious, while educational games offer enjoyable and effortless learning. Personalized games meet better the needs of students, and are more effective in teaching. This paper describes a video game maze, which serves as a container for many small didactic puzzles. The puzzles bring the educational content in the main maze game and allow personalization according to the profile of students (age, gender, knowledge level, preferences, and goals). Further, teachers can create a game by incorporating the necessary teaching material and taking into account the specificities of the students for whom it is intended. The paper also presents the student's model and the features that are considered for personalization and adaptation. The proposed APOGEE personalization framework and approach to learner modelling implies a well-grounded way of collecting, retrieving, and recording user data necessary to support the dynamic adjusting of the user model.

One of the limitations of the presented case study is the rather small sample of respondents (N = 39), therefore, the future work involves extending the study by inviting a larger attendance. Another limitation of the study is the inclusion of only three types of mini-games within the maze, played before answering the survey questions. For the next quiz, we plan to invite respondents to play a maze game containing more than ten different mini-games. As well, the preliminary results from the conducted online survey for the puzzle personalization depending on learning and the playing styles of the individual player will be followed by statistical analyses for finding correlations between styles, preferred educational content, and types of puzzle games. These future results are expected to reveal the impact on personalization of the different properties of the player/learner model such as preferences, age, gender, style, and knowledge level.

Acknowledgements. The research is partially supported by the National Scientific Program "Information and Communication Technologies in Science, Education and Security" (ICT in SES) financed by the Ministry of Education and Science and from the APOGEE project, funded by the Bulgarian National Science Fund, No. DN12/7/2017.

References

1. Deterding, S., Khaled, R., Dixon, D., Nacke, L.: From game design elements to gamefulness: defining gamification. In: MindTrek, Tampere, Finland, pp. 9–15 (2011)

2. Ketamo, H., Devlin, K.: Replacing PISA with global game based assessment. In: Busch, C. (ed.) ECGBL 2014, Berlin, Germany, pp. 258–264 (2014)
3. Allisop, Y., Yildirim, E., Scepanti, M.: Teachers beliefs about game based learning: a comparative study of pedagogy, curriculum and practice in Italy, Turkey and the UK. In: Proceedings of ECGBL 2013, Porto, Portugal, pp. 1–10 (2013)
4. Paunova-Hubenova, E., Terzieva, V., Dimitrov, S., Boneva Y.: Integration of game-based teaching in Bulgarian schools – state of art. In: Proceedings of ECGBL 2018, pp. 516–525 (2018)
5. Connolly, T., Boyle, E., MacArthur, E., Hainey, T., Boyle, J.: A systematic literature review of empirical evidence on computer games and serious games. Comput. Educ. **59**, 661–686 (2012)
6. Prensky, M.: Digital Game-Based Learning. McGraw-Hill, New York (2001)
7. Bontchev, B., Georgieva, O.: Playing style recognition through an adaptive video game. Comput. Hum. Behav. **82**(May), 136–147 (2018). https://doi.org/10.1016/j.chb.2017.12.040
8. Brusilovsky, P.: Methods and techniques of adaptive hypermedia. User Model. User Adap. Inter. **6**(2–3), 87–129 (1996)
9. Kobsa, A.: Supporting user interfaces for all through user modeling. In: Proceedings of HCI International, pp. 155–157 (1995)
10. Aroyo, L., Dolog, P., Houben, G.-J., Kravcik, M., Naeve, A., Nilsson, M., Wild, F.: Interoperability in personalized adaptive learning. Educ. Technol. Soc. **9**(2), 4–18 (2006)
11. Kapp, K.: The gamification of learning and instruction: game-based methods and strategies for training and education. Pfeiffer & Company (2012)
12. Chen, N., Hwang, G.: Transforming the classrooms: innovative digital game-based learning designs and applications. Educ. Tech. Res. Dev. **62**(2), 125–128 (2014)
13. Young, M., Slota, S., Cutter, A., Jalette, G., Mullin, G., Lai, B., Simeoni, Z., Tran, M., Yukhymenko, M.: Our princess is in another castle: a review of trends in serious gaming for education. Rev. Educ. Res. **82**(1), 61–89 (2012)
14. Pellegrino, J., Quellmalz, E.: Perspectives on the integration of technology and assessment. JRTE **43**(2), 119–134 (2010)
15. Mayo, M.: Video games: a route to large-scale STEM education? Science **323**, 79–82 (2009)
16. Gee, J.P.: What Video Games Have to Teach us About Learning and Literacy. Palgrave MacMillan, New York (2003)
17. Nicol, D., Macfarlane-Dick, D.: Formative assessment and self-regulated learning: a model and seven principles of good feedback practice. Stud. High. Educ. **31**(2), 199–218 (2006)
18. Hwang, G., Chang, H.: A formative assessment-based mobile learning approach to improving the learning attitudes and achievements of students. Comput. Educ. **56**, 1023–1031 (2011)
19. Bray, B., McClaskey, K.: Make Learning Personal: The What, Who, WOW, Where, and Why. Corwin Press, Thousand Oaks (2015)
20. OECD: Schooling for Tomorrow Personalising education. OECD Publishing, Paris (2006)
21. Keamy, R., Nicholas, H., Mahar, S., Herrick, C.: Personalising Education: From Research to Policy and Practice. Dep. of Education & Early Childhood Development, Melbourne (2007)
22. Pane, J., Steiner, E., Baird, M., Hamilton, L., Pane, J.: Insights on personalized learning implementation and effects. https://www.rand.org/pubs/research_reports/RR2042.html
23. Murphy, M., Redding, S., Twyman, J.S.: Handbook on Personalized Learning for States, Districts, and Schools. Center for Innovations in Learning, Philadelphia (2016)
24. Paunova-Hubenova, E.: Didactic mini video games – students' and teachers' point of view. In: CBU International Conference Proceedings, vol. 7 (2019). https://doi.org/10.12955/cbup. v7.1417
25. Fleming, N.D., Mills, C.: Not another inventory, rather a catalyst for reflection. Improv. Acad. **11**(1), 137–155 (1992)

26. Magerko, B., Heeter, C., Fitzgerald, J., Medler, B.: Intelligent adaptation of digital game-based learning. In: Conference on Future Play: Research, Play, Share, pp. 200–203. ACM (2008)
27. Nacke, L.E., Bateman, C., Mandryk, R.L.: BrainHex: a neurobiological gamer typology survey. Entertainment Comput. **5**(1), 55–62 (2013)
28. Bontchev, B., Vassileva, D., Aleksieva-Petrova, A., Petrov, M.: Playing styles based on experiential learning theory. Comput. Hum. Behav. **85**, 319–328 (2018). https://doi.org/10.1016/j.chb.2018.04.009
29. Bull, S., Kay, J.: Student models that invite the learner in: the SMILI open learner modelling framework. Int. J. AI Educ. **17**(2), 89–120 (2007)

Arts and Artist

Arts and Artist

Anthony L. Brooks[1]([✉]) and Eva Brooks[2]

[1] CREATE/Department of Architecture, Design and Media Technology/Technical Faculty of IT and Design, Aalborg University, Rendsburggade 14, 9000 Aalborg, Denmark
tb@create.aau.dk

[2] XLab: Design, Learning, Innovation, Department of Culture and Learning, Aalborg University, Kroghstræde 3, 9220 Aalborg, Denmark

Abstract. In work such as presented herein one can ask what the art is; who is the artist…. when is it art – why it's art (Brooks 2019)? Truly international research is presented in that delegates working across national divides and diverse forms are represented. This section closes the ArtsIT contribution and leads into the Design, Learning, and Innovation sections of this book.

Keywords: Ludo · Narrative · Art · Artist · Inclusion · Experiences · Play · Installation · Design · Experiences · Games

1 Introduction

1.1 Scope

The final section of this volume with focus upon the ArtsIT perspective is themed - "Arts and Artist" - to give focus upon the arts and those who create within the genre and how their work relates across research topics associated to arts and technology, interactivity, and game creation perspectives.

The first contribution in this section considers the art of traditional Chinese puppetry and questions how interactive technology may support the form. The second contribution focuses on questioning spontaneous group formation around a game-based public installation. The third contribution, which originates from Melbourne, Australia, is cored on creative endeavours targeting persons with disability. The fourth contribution is on using Virtual Reality targeting wellness. The fifth contribution concentrates on balls that form the centre of an interactive art installation piece. The final contribution in this fourth section informs of the concept where an artist whose works are exhibited in a museum becomes an actor in a play-scenario with audience.

The following text snippets elaborate directly from each contribution to further assist readership.

© ICST Institute for Computer Sciences, Social Informatics and Telecommunications Engineering 2020
Published by Springer Nature Switzerland AG 2020. All Rights Reserved
A. Brooks and E. I. Brooks (Eds.): ArtsIT 2019/DLI 2019, LNICST 328, pp. 491–495, 2020.
https://doi.org/10.1007/978-3-030-53294-9_35

2   An Analysis of How Interactive Technology Supports the Appreciation of Traditional Chinese Puppetry: A Review of Case Studies

(Zhao 2020)

"An Analysis of How Interactive Technology Supports the Appreciation of Traditional Chinese Puppetry: A Review of Case Studies" by author Shichao Zhao informs of the age-old art of puppetry in China and how contemporary interactive technologies may advance the form whilst being respectful of the associated Chinese Cultural Heritage.

Main points of the presentation at ArtsIT and contribution in this book are how (1) maintaining originality is necessary for the design phase; (2) it is crucial to explore how to use interactive technology in order to design a way for adults to appreciate this form of art; (3) it is also necessary to determine ways to support adult audiences in grasping the cultural significance and folk customs of traditional Chinese puppetry; and (4) the study's further main research goals are to investigate ways to use emotional expressions, digital storytelling and other methods in conjunction with interactive technology to help multi-cultural users comprehend traditional Chinese puppetry.

3   SimonXXL - Investigating Spontaneous Group Formation Around Public Installations

(Jacobsen et al. 2020)

As of writing, at a time when social distancing is imposed due to the Covid-19 pandemic, it is refreshing to reflect back at the November 2019 ArtsIT presentation by Associate Professor Markus Löchtefeld from Aalborg University Denmark in sharing the work titled "SimonXXL - Investigating Spontaneous Group Formation around Public Installations". Alongside co-authors Bo Jacobsen, Michael Svendsen, Adam Søgaard, and Rune Uggerhøj, Löchtefeld informed on their study exploring how to design for spontaneous group formation (SGF), as part of shared encounters in a game-based public installation that over three days of testing generated eleven spontaneous group formations showing evidence that effective lures related to the social phenomenon "honeypot effect" are one of the key factors behind the phenomenon…. And now back to social distancing…!

4   Interactive Arts and Disability: A Conceptual Model Toward Understanding Participation

(Duckworth et al. 2020)

The ArtsIT presentation by Australian dynamic duo from Melbourne in the form of authors Duckworth and Wilson was a stand-out for sharing of exquisite artefacts created in this research considering how persons with disability have engaged in a community arts experience in collaboration with a practicing artist.

The text is equally informing of the participation-related constructs (fPRC) framework via discussing two interactive arts projects that facilitated participation through improvised music, sound art and performance within the context of community arts and disability targeting inclusivity and fostering participation. Each project was recipient of national grant support, which was acknowledged in the presentation.

Co-authors Hullick, Mochizuki, Pink, and Imms, alongside the Australian Research Council (ARC), Australia Council for the Arts, and the Japan Society for the Promotion of Science (JSPS), were all well represented by the dynamic duo at the event herein acknowledged additionally for taking part as invited panellists for the closing session of the ArtsIT/DLI events alongside keynote speakers and luminary figures in the arts.

5   Nature and Nurturance Across the Ages: Modest Means for Modern Times

(Moller et al. 2020)

"Nature and Nurturance across the ages: Modest means for modern times" by Moller, Saynor, and Chignell originating from Toronto, Canada, and Waterworth from Umeå University, Sweden, proposed the use of 3D capture of majestic nature scenes and their display in a therapeutic context as an affordable way to enhance well-being and to provide care to those lacking adequate access to leisure and wellbeing. Notable was that this research was also presented as a hands-on session for delegates to experience via Virtual Reality Head Mounted Display at the conference common area alongside posters. The text additionally elaborates and discusses the background behind the work alongside involved aspects of Virtual Reality; Mindfulness Meditation/mindfulness-based stress reaction (MBSR); Presence; Disability; Public Health Policy; and the related History of Medicine. Testing of immersive experiences is also reported aligned to reflect the design team's intentionally to mimic a wellness vacation experience. A thought-provoking body of work well received by delegates both in Moller's presentation and the hands-on sessions.

6   Huge Balls: A Ludo-Narrative Exploration of Game Art

(Xiong et al. 2020)

In this game art French – Chinese collaborative project contribution titled "Huge Balls: A ludo-narrative exploration of game art", the idea was to transform juggling movements into an artistic digital installation game with mechanics based upon a participant maintaining balance while being disturbed by the distractions inside the game space. The authors, namely Guofan Xiong, Daniel Plata, and Chu-Yin Chen, are interested in the creation of visual vocabularies anchored in the evolution of technology and methods of communication that have become both understood by a broader population, across countries and languages; and also complex by the re-designation of icons and meanings, like a new grammar. The presentation at the event illustrated the gonad like installation and people playing with them, notably all had smiles on their faces so were obviously having great fun, however, behind what may read as a simple sexist design formed to challenge interpretations, there would seem a complexity of thought by the authors. Images in this contribution illustrate the 'huge balls' physical interface and images within the game that are juggled in the game-space in different ways, whilst the text informs on diversity of ideas associated to expanding the game-concept to a multidimensional experience, not limited to visuals, and sound, but also related to touch and the social aspect of gaming: Seemingly a body of work demanding large testes!

7   Playing with the Artist

(Vayanou et al. 2020)

The contribution 'Playing with the Artist' focuses upon social interactions during cultural visits that are advocated in several museum studies, this builds upon previous work in the form of a storytelling game for groups of visitors who were asked to make and share stories about the artworks of a cultural collection combining moments of personal reflection to social encounters through the game phases. In a claimed novel approach in the field, the authors Vayanou, Sidiropoulou, Loumos, Kargas, and Ioannidis, had artists participate as players in the group game, listening to the stories and explanations that visitors make about their artworks, and sharing their own stories and reflections during the game. In other words, artists participated as players in a group playtesting session, taking place in his/her personal art exhibition; thus, enabling the visiting participants to have a personal, hands-on experience with a proposed game-based scenario. The primary objective of the study was to examine how the artist's involvement in the game shaped and affected the group experience, investigating its affordances to foster communication and interactions between art gallery visitors and creators. The text presents the user study results and artist's perspective on the design. Images exemplify exhibition and environment. In conclusion the authors state excitement about the future implications of this design for advancing social interactions, not only between groups of visitors but also between visitors and artists: Predicting "a high social impact, shaping new forms of cultural participation".

Epilogue and Acknowledgements. This fourth section introduces six contributions by extracting from each paper. It does so to promote readership of each full paper that are presented in the following chapters. In doing so the authors of this chapter acknowledge the contribution to this section/volume by each author whose original work was presented in the ArtsIT/DLI events in Aalborg, Denmark November 7–8, 2019. The next sections are the DLI contributions.

References

Brooks, A.L.: Why it's art. In: Brooks, A.L., Brooks, E., Sylla, C. (eds.) ArtsIT/DLI 2018. LNICST, vol. 265, pp. 3–6. Springer, Cham (2019). https://doi.org/10.1007/978-3-030-06134-0_1

Duckworth, J., Hullick, J., Mochizuki, S., Pink, S., Imms, C., Wilson, P.: Interactive arts and disability: a conceptual model toward understanding participation. In: Brooks, A., Brooks, E.I. (eds.) ArtsIT 2019/DLI 2019. LNICST, vol. 328, pp. 524–538. Springer, Cham (2020)

Jacobsen, B., Svendsen, M., Søgaard, A., Uggerhøj, R., Löchtefeld, M.: SimonXXL - investigating spontaneous group formation around public installations. In: Brooks, A., Brooks, E.I. (eds.) ArtsIT 2019/DLI 2019. LNICST, vol. 328, pp. 506–523. Springer, Cham (2020)

Moller, H., Saynor, L., Chignell, M., Waterworth, J.: Nature and nurturance across the ages: modest means for modern times. In: Brooks, A., Brooks, E.I. (eds.) ArtsIT 2019/DLI 2019. LNICST, vol. 328, pp. 539–558. Springer, Cham (2020)

Vayanou, M., Sidiropoulou, O., Loumos, G., Kargas, A., Ioannidis, Y.: Playing with the artist. In: Brooks, A., Brooks, E.I. (eds.) ArtsIT 2019/DLI 2019. LNICST, vol. 328, pp. 566–579. Springer, Cham (2020)

Xiong, G., Plata, D., Chen, C.: Huge balls: a ludo-narrative exploration of game art. In: Brooks, A., Brooks, E.I. (eds.) ArtsIT 2019/DLI 2019. LNICST, vol. 328, pp. 559–565. Springer, Cham (2020)

Zhao, S.: An analysis of how interactive technology supports the appreciation of traditional Chinese puppetry: a review of case studies. In: Brooks, A., Brooks, E.I. (eds.) ArtsIT 2019/DLI 2019. LNICST, vol. 328, pp. 496–505. Springer, Cham (2020)

An Analysis of How Interactive Technology Supports the Appreciation of Traditional Chinese Puppetry: A Review of Case Studies

Shichao Zhao[✉]

Newcastle University, Newcastle NE4 5TG, UK
s.zhao11@newcastle.ac.uk

Abstract. From the perspective of safeguarding Chinese Cultural Heritage, this paper discusses how to enhance the appreciation of traditional Chinese puppetry through the support of interactive technology. The author analyses extensive, yet current case studies, based on the findings described in the interactive systems for puppetry performances and interactive technology for puppetry appreciation. The author summarises four aspects of how to enhance the appreciation of, and engagement with, traditional Chinese puppetry: (1) maintaining originality is necessary for the design phase; (2) it is crucial to explore how to use interactive technology in order to design a way for adults to appreciate this form of art; (3) it is also necessary to determine ways to support adult audiences in grasping the cultural significance and folk customs of traditional Chinese puppetry; and (4) the study's further main research goals are to investigate ways to use emotional expressions, digital storytelling and other methods in conjunction with interactive technology to help multi-cultural users comprehend traditional Chinese puppetry.

Keywords: Traditional Chinese puppetry · Interactive technology · Digital storytelling · Emotional expression · Cultural appreciation

1 The Dilemmas Facing Traditional Chinese Puppetry

Puppetry is one of the most significant components of Chinese opera. Like other traditional art forms, the opera has been passed down through face-to-face teaching and incomplete text sources. Furthermore, many puppetry classics are only safeguarded in the memories of elderly folk artists; therefore, these techniques and knowledge are in danger of fading [1, 2]. After 1949, the formats of Chinese puppetry became richer [3]. Apart from preserving traditional opera, puppetry began to mix with other media and began to appear in contemporary plays, TV series and movies. This not only maintained the historical element of puppetry, but also expanded its platform to new audiences. However, just like other Chinese folk-art forms, puppetry is going through a type of culture shock as it encounters a variety of entertainment channels and different target audiences [4]. For example, take the famous marionettes from the city of Quanzhou in Fujian Province; there, the government failed to pay enough attention to the safeguarding

A. Brooks and E. I. Brooks (Eds.): ArtsIT 2019/DLI 2019, LNICST 328, pp. 496–505, 2020.
https://doi.org/10.1007/978-3-030-53294-9_36

of it, and traditional puppetry has since come under threat [3]. These days, Quanzhou puppetry can only be seen at festivals or sacrificial ceremonies. Consequentially, less money is invested in the support of professional puppeteers and artists; some have had to abandon their careers, making their art form a dwindling branch of Chinese puppetry.

ICH (Intangible Cultural Heritage) like traditional Chinese puppetry, is only passed down through oral teachings and incomplete writings, making recording and conservation more complex. A plethora of classical puppet shows are only maintained in the memories of practitioners, rendering these skills and knowledge on the verge of extinction [5]. Historically, words, photographs and video recordings have been the most frequently used media for conservation. Although photography and videography have begun to improve the quality of preserving traditional puppetry and other types of ICH, these approaches do not cover every aspect of conservation. Moreover, it is difficult for traditional media to attract audiences from different cultural backgrounds. Previous research on individual puppeteers and other institutions shows that many photographs or audio or video tape scripts have decayed due to their storage environment, as well as climate change since the 1980s. Undoubtedly, this represents a huge loss for Chinese ICH [6].

Moreover, technology could facilitate its cultural safeguarding. Interactive technologies have vast potential to help safeguard ICH, not only in China, but also on an international scale [7–12]. Researchers have used them to represent cultural artefacts; this has often involved digital augmentation to support audience involvement. An important outcome of digitisation is a greater potential to promote cultural artefacts among audiences, as well as the creation of new forms of cultural interactivity. Following this radical design evolution, many interactive projects have been developed to disseminate the objectives of traditional societies [13–16]. Nonetheless, limited attention has been paid to actual, in-depth interpretations and engagement regarding the aesthetics of these artefacts [17]. Carefully applying interactive technologies heightens the potential of enhancing artistic appreciation and the delivery of cultural significance. However, further exploration is needed to understand how to best support this possibility in terms of Chinese ICH [18]. The development of digital techniques has made the conservation of traditional Chinese puppetry more convenient (e.g. the use of digital video cameras or mobile devices to record puppetry). New databases have provided better environments for data recovery and storage. All of these technologies have helped to spread traditional Chinese puppetry [19]. However, none of them offer ways to edit or utilise digital content for audience interactions; thus, the content remains invisible to the general public. Linear video recordings also limit the possibility of further interactive digital setups. Combining interactive digital media and traditional puppetry could improve the recording, teaching, editing, development and performance of the latter.

2 Interactive Technology in Traditional Chinese Puppetry

This section investigates related research on using interactive technology to enhance puppetry performances, and on appreciation in order to derive insight into design in the future case studies.

2.1 Methods

Since the 1980s, digital heritage studies have become an independent research area [20]. Text analysis and relevant archival research are frequently used techniques to grasp the essence of past occurrences and to trace the changing meanings of heritage [21]. Specifically, the author adopts three steps which include (1) evaluating other studies; (2) selecting the studies to include in the review; and (3) organising the review. In the first step, the author mainly evaluates the extensive case studies which are using interactive technology to experience the traditional Chinese puppetry, as well as comments on each study's value and validity. In the second step, the author chooses studies which are most relevant and most important for the support of the appreciation and engagement of traditional Chinese puppetry. In the third step, the author organises the different themes based on the different interactive technology to explore the potential design opportunities and insights.

2.2 Interactive Systems for Puppetry Performances

This section delves into some case studies on using interactive technology to support puppetry performances. As early as 1998, motion capture systems were devised to transfer puppetry gestures into a digital/virtual form [22]. This created more possibilities for using digital puppetry gestures to aid puppetry performances. Shin and colleagues explored computer puppetry by capturing gestures and fully visualising them in real time. Thus, tools used to create animation extended the availability of puppetry gestures in the entertainment industry, such as performances broadcasted on television [23].

A number of interactive systems have been developed that enable users to create digital puppets and puppetry roles. For instance, as early as 2002, PUPPET, an autonomous agent, populated virtual environments to support children in experiencing and exploring the different roles in a puppetry performance. This system lets children interact in a virtual environment to understand the narrative and characters of a performance. The virtual environment has effectively allowed them to physically interact with the characters [24]. Unlike Marshall and colleagues, Cutout Animation adopted a video-based paper tracking technology to create cut-out-style animations, rather than puppetry roles [25]. Users could make physical puppets by cutting them out of paper; their movements were captured by an overhead camera and rendered into animation on the screen, with the option to choose from different backgrounds. In 2011, a digital system called Shadow Story integrated digital puppet making and puppetry roles, providing children with an interface that lets them employ their own gestures to perform stories [26]. They could also use a pen and tablet input to create digital shadow puppetry.

Numerous case studies on digital puppetry systems focus on puppetry performances (which the author will not review one by one here). The creation of digital and physical puppets and puppetry roles has given users greater autonomy and the capacity to exercise their creativity (such as learning about the characters or becoming familiar with puppetry performance). Users have the opportunity to collaborate in order to experience different puppetry roles. Based on the analysis of these studies, the author summarised four features of current digital puppetry performance: (1) oversimplified performances; (2) simplified puppetry characters; (2) simplified gestures; and (4) cultural significance.

Oversimplified Performances. The puppetry performances of these studies have been excessively simplified by movement-capturing and animation rendering. For instance, the study on Cutout Animation reported limitations of the digital equipment [25], whereby the system was unable to capture all puppetry gestures and fast movements, as Barnes and colleagues mentioned: *Unfortunately, our system is not capable of handling every puppet or action a user may wish to animate...puppets cannot be moved too quickly, as the Kanade-Lucas- Tomasi (KLT) algorithm assumes that the optical flow between frames is well approximated by small displacements without rotation.* Users do not have the chance to experience historic puppetry performances, which include complex gestures. Traditional Chinese puppetry encompasses extensive opera-based gestures. The current digital technology could mislead users to have an over simplified understanding of puppetry performances.

Simplified Puppetry Characters. In the third case study of Shadow Story [26], the interactive interface of the puppetry characters – which simplified the characters of traditional shadow puppetry – only offered a simple digital pen and basic colours for users to create the characters. Figure 1 shows that it is not difficult to see that the users' characters lacked the basic elements of traditional puppetry. Thus, it is crucial to provide users with a more accurate understanding of the characters. Developing ways of using digital technology to enhance the creation of shadow puppets could be a direction for future design.

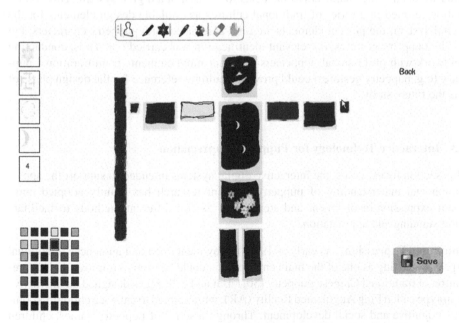

Fig. 1. Interface of the 'design' mode for creating characters (Lu et al. [26]).

Simplified Gestures. The gestural performance was missed or simplified by the running of the digital system [27]. The system interactions in user engagements and the actual operation of the puppets have visible distinctions. Prior research has not deeply explored the potential for helping viewers to engage with traditional puppetry performance. For instance, the Shadow Story system offers users handheld sensors to conduct gestural interactions, rather than letting them have physical interactions with shadow puppets. Although Wan and colleagues exploited a Kinect-based system to support users in personally manipulating shadow characters with their gestures [28], their gestures still differed greatly from the gestures of traditional shadow play. Furthermore, Liang and colleagues developed a hand gesture-based interaction and animation data repository to generate interactive animation using shadow play [29]. However, the gestures were only classified by the roles of the shadow play, and the users did not have chance to take part in real shadow play. They did not aspire to this, and the gesture-based interactions were simplified to fit with the game experience.

Cultural Significance. Lastly, cultural appreciation (e.g. the cultural meaning of gestures and stories) of puppetry is not well supported, as most prior research is entertainment-oriented. Current digital systems do not portray traditional Chinese puppetry as part of ICH [5] in the sense of helping users to learn about the relevant history and customs by experiencing a digital puppetry performance. However, Lu and colleagues tried to work with professional puppeteers of traditional Chinese shadow puppetry in order to identify the characters as elements to be used in a digital system. This collaboration resulted in a series of traditional cultures as available design elements for the digital system; the present elements are only associated with puppetry characters, but for the puppetry gestures, no relevant identification was carried out. Thus, conducting fieldwork with professional puppeteers to gather more elements from traditional puppetry (e.g. puppetry gestures) could provide a cultural reference for the design phase of this the future study.

2.3 Interactive Technology for Puppetry Appreciation

This section focuses on some interactive digital systems intended to support the appreciation and understanding of puppetry. Current research has mainly adopted emotional expression/involvement and storytelling as two different methods to facilitate understanding and appreciation.

Emotional Expression. As early as 1978, Dolby mentioned that audiences' emotional expression acting as one of the main entry points, could be used to improve their appreciation of traditional Chinese puppetry [30]). Bai and colleagues designed an interactive prototype called Fing Augmented Reality (AR), which aimed to enhance children's complex cognitive and social development. Through a series of puppetry games, children acted out their emotions, beliefs and desires, and interpreted the roles based on their experience with the game. In this project, AR was exploited to help children understand the emotions of the puppetry characters during the game. Another, similar project is called emoPuppet; it is an interactive digital-physical puppet that helps children to express and understand emotions [31]. Based on a smartphone application, children observed and appreciated simple puppetry characters to learn about facial expressions. They were engaged effectively in the experience and developed a basic understanding of puppetry, alongside the interactive technology that also improved their creativity and social skills. Shi and colleagues combined characteristics of Chinese folk culture to design a digital shadow puppet, and developed an interactive system that exploited Kinect-based interactions and sensors to capture children's movements, the goal being to help them express their emotions with shadow puppets [32]. Their assessment showed that the system helps children develop a fundamental understanding of shadow puppetry.

However, emotional expressions and experiences did not integrate the features of puppetry characters or specific classical stories in these aforementioned case studies. In other words, users' expressional emotions were disjointed from the puppetry itself; the characters and enjoyment were not embodied. Therefore, the oversimplified gestures and basic emotional expressions seem to have limited the cultural appreciation of puppetry shows.

A potential direction for design is how to systematically display highly complex gestures in the system to create a richer experience for users. In addition, while using emotions to enhance children's puppetry appreciation is worthwhile, a large number of audiences of traditional Chinese puppet shows are adults. Hence, there is an opportunity to explore how puppet gestures support deeper cultural appreciation among adult audiences. Traditional Chinese puppetry is a sort of sacrificial activity that originated in Chinese agricultural society [3], most Chinese puppetry describes folktales. Therefore, the author believes that it is necessary to explore how to use emotional expressions to engage these audiences in order to help them appreciate the cultural significance of traditional Chinese puppetry.

Digital Storytelling. Some research has focused more on using storytelling with digital animation to boost appreciation of traditional puppetry. For instance, based on the photon mapping method [33], Zhu and colleagues developed a prototype that turned traditional shadow plays into electronic forms that provided the audience with immersive storytelling [34]. They offered delicate lighting effects and realistic martial arts sequences to reproduce the classical Chinese folk story *The butterfly lovers*. However, the digital animation only focused on reproduction, and the subtle meanings of the shadow play gestures were not well-explained. The background, dialogue and traditional music of this story were not expressed, lacking an interpretation to support the users' appreciation. Another shadow play animation system exploited the Rapidly exploring Random Trees (RRTs)-Connect algorithm to capture the characteristics of motion from traditional Chinese shadow play, and depicted the 'emulational' animation for audiences [35, 36]. The animation system recreates realistic shadow character movements to provide an aesthetically-pleasing environment. Although Hsu and Li further explored how to use delicate animation to develop an original story, their research only centred on delivering experiences to users with the same or similar cultural backgrounds, or those who already appreciated the aesthetics of puppetry.

Prior research has failed to investigate how to narrate traditional Chinese stories via shadow puppetry to audiences, especially audiences from different cultural backgrounds. Using interactive technology in storytelling to enhance the appreciation of cross-cultural audiences is a potential insight for design that needs to be explored [37]. Furthermore, the cultural relevance of puppetry narratives and the in-depth meaning of puppetry gestures need to be effectively interpreted for audiences [38, 39]. Although expressing emotions through interactive technology is a valuable way of increasing audiences' appreciation of puppetry, there are other important opportunities for interactive technology to help audiences bridge cultural differences that have not been deeply examined. These include digital systems that use gestures to enhance cross-cultural audiences' appreciation of puppetry and its deeper relationship with Chinese culture.

3 Discussion

The author reviewed different research projects that used interactive technology to enhance the performance and appreciation of puppetry. Current studies have effectively supported users in experiencing puppetry briefly, and traditional puppetry has also been utilised to convey culture to engage users in game entertainment or social learning. How to engage audiences or viewers' interest in traditional Chinese puppetry is always a key aspect of safeguarding it [40]. However, through analysing the extensive case studies that integrate interactive technology, the author believed that the current case studies did not make a clear distinction of both learning and appreciation of traditional Chinese puppetry. Thus, indirectly leading to the audiences or viewers to not understand the cultural significance of traditional Chinese puppetry, and lose their interest in it. However, the following points need to be considered: (1) Traditional puppetry performances (e.g. gestures, movements) are oversimplified in interactive systems, which may lead users to have an incomplete understanding of traditional Chinese puppetry. Maintaining originality is necessary in the design phase. (2) In most of the case studies, children were the main target audience. Yet in traditional Chinese puppetry, a large number of audiences are adults. Thus, it is crucial to explore how to use interactive technology in order to design a way for adults to appreciate this art form. (3) Based on the findings from the point above, it is also necessary to determine ways to support adult audiences in grasping the cultural significance and folk customs of traditional Chinese puppetry. In integrating the interactive technology into the appreciation and experience of Chinese puppetry, it is extremely crucial to maintain the aesthetic and cultural significance in safeguarding Chinese puppetry. However, cultural significance is not embodied in current digital systems. (4) No particular case study has focused on supporting cross-cultural users in appreciating and experiencing traditional Chinese puppetry. The further study's main research goals is to investigate ways to use emotional expressions, digital storytelling and other methods in conjunction with interactive technology to help multi-cultural users comprehend traditional Chinese puppetry.

Furthermore, Determining the correct role and positioning of technology is a complicated and controversial topic, and puppetry stakeholders are often critical in questioning and problematising the status of technology [41]. Therefore, examining the possible relationships between traditional Chinese puppetry and interactive technology brings up questions as to whether digital puppetry performances may threaten traditional performance and skills or other intangible elements. Additional questions remain regarding whether changing audiences' perception of Chinese puppetry will potentially decrease audiences viewership at traditional theatres. The current study cannot determine whether interactive technology can ethically and reasonably be integrated into Chinese ICH; designers are currently exploring different approaches to this question. However, the findings suggest that shifting the emphasis of interactive technology in puppetry from entertainment to the support of audiences' appreciation and understanding would not threaten traditional performances. The future research should examine how interactive technology assists cross-cultural audiences in overcoming cultural barriers and further engages their interest.

References

1. Huang, Y., Lioret, A.: Cerebral interaction and painting. In: Proceedings of the SIGGRAPH Asia 2013 Art Gallery, Hong Kong, China, p. 21 (2013)
2. Zhao, S., Kirk, D.: Using interactive digital media to support transcultural understanding of intangible chinese cultural heritage. In: Proceedings of CHI 2016 Conference Workshop-Involving the CROWD in Future MUSEUM Experience Design, San Jose, CA (2016)
3. Chen, F.P.L., Clark, B.: A survey of puppetry in China. Asian Theatre J. **27**(2), 333–365 (2010)
4. Zhao, S., Kirk, D., Bowen, S., Wright, P.: Cross-cultural understanding of Chinese traditional puppetry: integrating digital technology to enhance audience engagement. Int. J. Intang. Herit. **14**, 140–156 (2019)
5. Xu, Z.M., Xin, X.F.: The Phylogeny of Chinese Puppet Show. Literature of Shandong Press, Shandong (2007)
6. Wu, Z.: The research of digitalized technology of the puppet show with the motion capture technology. J. Univ. Electron. Sci. Technol. China **9**, 6–7 (2009)
7. Fraser, M., et al.: Assembling history: achieving coherent experiences with diverse technologies. In: Proceedings of the 8th European Conference on Computer Supported Cooperative Work, Helsinki, Finland, pp. 14–18 (2003)
8. Kortbek, K., Grønbæk, K.: Communicating art through interactive technology: new approaches for interaction design in art museums. In: Proceedings of the 5th Nordic Conference on Human-Computer Interaction: Building Bridges, Lund, Sweden, pp. 229–238 (2008)
9. Huang, C.H., Huang, Y.T.: An annales school-based serious game creation framework for taiwanese indigenous cultural heritage. J. Comput. Cult. Herit. (JOCCH) **6**(9), 9–31 (2013)
10. Candy, L., Ferguson, S.: Interactive Experience in the Digital Age: Evaluating New Art Practice. Springer Series on Cultural Computing. Springer, London (2014). https://doi.org/10.1007/978-3-319-04510-8
11. Huang, Y.: Creation methodology of interactive art installation based on philosophy-understanding projection: recreation of traditional Chinese painting. In: Proceedings of the 2015 Virtual Reality International Conference, Laval, France, p. 7 (2015)
12. Chang, Y.H., Lin, Y.K., Fang, R.J., Lu, Y.T.: A situated cultural festival learning system based on motion sensing. Eurasia J. Math. Sci. Technol. Educ. **13**(3), 571–588 (2017)
13. Lombardo, V., Pizzo, A., Damiano, R.: Safeguarding and accessing drama as intangible cultural heritage. J. Comput. Cult. Herit. (JOCCH) **9**(1), 5 (2016)

14. Maye, L.A., Bouchard, D., Avram, G., Ciolfi, L.: Supporting cultural heritage profession-als adopting and shaping interactive technologies in museums. In: Proceedings of the 2017 Conference on Designing Interactive Systems, Edinburgh, United Kingdom, pp. 221–232 (2017)

15. Meroni, A., Sangiorgi, D.: Design for Services. Gower Publishing, Aldershot (2011)

16. Lu, Z., Annett, M., Fan, M., Wigdor, D.: I feel it is my responsibility to stream: streaming and engaging with intangible cultural heritage through livestreaming. In: Proceedings of the SIGCHI Conference on Human Factors in Computing Systems, Glasgow, UK, p. 229 (2019)

17. Champion, E.: Cross-cultural learning, heritage, and digital games. In: Hartley, J., Qu, W. (eds.) Reorientation: Trans-Cultural. Trans-Cultural, Trans-Lingual, Transmedia Studies in Narrative, Language, Identity and Knowledge, pp. 218–233. Fudan University Press, Shanghai (2016)

18. Pujol, L., Champion, E.: Evaluating presence in cultural heritage projects. Int. J. Herit. Stud. **18**, 83–102 (2012)

19. Zhao, S., Kirk, D., Bowen, S., Wright, P.: Enhancing the appreciation of traditional chinese painting using interactive technology. Multimodal Technol. Interact. **2**(2), 16 (2018)

20. Sørensen, S., Carman, J.: Heritage Studies: Methods and Approaches. Routledge, Abingdon (2009)

21. Soderland, A.: The history of heritage: a method in analysing legislative historiography. In: Sørensen, M.L.S., Carman, J. (eds.) Heritage Studies: Methods and Approaches, pp. 55–84. Routledge, Abingdon (2009)

22. Sturman, D.J.: Computer puppetry. IEEE Comput. Graph. Appl. **18**(1), 38–45 (1998)

23. Shin, H.J., Lee, J., Shin, S.Y., Gleicher, M.: Computer puppetry: an importance-based approach. ACM Trans. Graph. **20**(2), 67–94 (2010)

24. Marshall, P., Rogers, Y., Scaife, M.: Puppet: a virtual environment for children to act and direct interactive narratives. In: 2nd International Workshop on Narrative and Interactive Learning Environments, pp. 8–15 (2002)

25. Barnes, C., et al.: Video puppetry: a performative interface for cutout animation. ACM Trans. Graph. **27**(5), 124 (2008)

26. Lu, F., et al.: Shadow story: creative and collaborative digital storytelling inspired by cultural heritage. In: Proceedings of the SIGCHI Conference on Human Factors in Computing Systems, CHI 2011, Vancouver, BC, Canada, pp. 1919–1928 (2011)

27. Zhao, S.: Exploring how interactive technology enhances gesture-based expression and engagement: a design study. J. Multimodal Technol. Interact **3**(1), 13 (2019)

28. Wan, B., Wen, X.J., An, L., Ding, X.: Interactive shadow play animation system. Int. J. Comput. Elect. Autom. Control Inf. Eng. **9**(1), 127–132 (2015)

29. Liang, H., Deng, S., Chang, J., Zhang, J.J., Chen, C., Tong, R.: Semantic framework for interactive animation generation and its application in virtual shadow play performance. Virtual Real. **22**(2), 149–165 (2017)

30. Dolby, W.: The origins of Chinese puppetry. Bull. Sch. Orient. Afr. Stud. **41**(1), 97–120 (1978). University of London

31. Martínez, J.I.: emoPuppet: low-cost interactive digital-physical puppets with emotional expression. In: Proceeding of the 11th Conference on Advances in Computer Entertainment Technology, ACE 2014, Article No. 44. ACM, New York, NY (2014)

32. Shi, Y., Ying, F., Chen, X., Pan, Z., Yu, J.: Restoration of traditional Chinese shadow play-Piying art from tangible interaction. J. Vis. Comput. Anim. **25**(1), 33–43 (2013)

33. Jensen, H.W.: Realistic Image Synthesis Using Photon Mapping. AK Peters, Natick (2001)

34. Zhu, Y.-B., Li, C.-J., Shen, I.F., Ma, K.-L., Stompel, A.: A new form of traditional art: visual simulation of Chinese shadow play. In: Proceedings of ACM SIGGRAPH 2003 Sketches & Applications, SIGGRAPH 2003, New York, NY (2003)

35. Hsu, S.-W., Li, T.-Y.: Planning character motions for shadow play animations. Proc. Comput. Anim. Soc. Agent. **5**, 184–190 (2005)
36. Hsu, S.-W., Li, T.-Y.: Generating secondary motions in shadow play animations with motion planning techniques. In: Proceedings of SIGGRAPH 2005 Conference on Sketches, Article No. 69, Los Angeles, California (2005)
37. Hickey, M.G.: Asian Indian celebrations of ethnicity: perspectives from the mid-western United States. Int. J. Intang. Herit. **7**, 31–44 (2012)
38. Giaccardi, E.: Things we value. Interactions **18**(1), 17–21 (2011)
39. Hawkins, T., Cohen, J., Debevec, P.: A photometric approach to digitizing cultural artifacts. In: Proceedings of the 2001 Conference on Virtual Reality, Archeology, and Cultural Heritage, VAST 2001, pp. 333–342. ACM, New York (2011)
40. Zhao, S.: An analysis of interactive technology's effect on the appreciation of traditional Chinese painting: a review of case studies. Int. J. New Media Technol. Arts **14**(3), 1–12 (2019)
41. Lawson, S., Kirman, B., Linehan, C., Feltwell T., Hopkins, L.: Problematising upstream technology through speculative design: the case of quantified cats and dogs. In: Proceedings of the 33rd Annual ACM Conference on Human Factors in Computing Systems, Seoul, pp. 2663–2672 (2015)

SimonXXL - Investigating Spontaneous Group Formation Around Public Installations

Bo Jacobsen, Michael Utne Kærholm Svendsen, Adam Kjær Søgaard,
Rune Lundegaard Uggerhøj, and Markus Löchtefeld[✉]

Aalborg University, Aalborg, Denmark
bjacob93@outlook.com, micuks1@gmail.com, adam.soegaard@gmail.com,
rune.lundegaard@gmail.com, mloc@create.aau.dk

Abstract. In this paper, we set out to explore how to design for spontaneous group formation, as part of shared encounters in a public installation. Spontaneous group formation describes a phenomenon where pedestrians form groups with other pedestrians, to whom they are previously unacquainted, for the purpose of interacting with an installation. This was accomplished by developing a 5 by 5 m version of the game based on the *Simon* game, with flashing lights and oversized buttons, designed to encourage spontaneous group formation by giving an advantage to larger groups, up to a maximum of four. Over three days of testing, the prototype was found to generate 11 spontaneous group formations out of 161 total use cases, showing evidence that effective lures are one of the key factors behind the phenomenon.

Keywords: Public installation · Public games · Spontaneous group formation · Playable cities

1 Introduction

Playable City – a subcategory of Smart Cities – has recently been a major focus not only of urban designers and city planners but also for computer scientists and a variety of other researchers [16]. It revolves around increasing the quality of life of citizens through technological implementations that facilitate play and relaxation, rather than focusing on optimization through Big Data as it is often the case with Smart City approaches. This goal can be achieved through several means, for example the implementation of interactive media facades [2,6] or more playful exhibits [7,10,12,14]. Other installations are more akin to gaming, such as [4], and this is where the focus of this paper lies.

Many games could be fashioned to work towards the common goal of a playable city, as many games are fun, easy to pick up and quick to play. However, a feature that is common in games is the possibility—and sometimes even requirement—for multiple players, which reveals a problem: if a pedestrian is

© ICST Institute for Computer Sciences, Social Informatics and Telecommunications Engineering 2020
Published by Springer Nature Switzerland AG 2020. All Rights Reserved
A. Brooks and E. I. Brooks (Eds.): ArtsIT 2019/DLI 2019, LNICST 328, pp. 506–523, 2020.
https://doi.org/10.1007/978-3-030-53294-9_37

walking by themselves, they might be excluded from benefiting from the assumed quality of life boost that a game as an urban installation would supply. This immediately presents the question of how one could inspire pedestrians to spontaneously form groups, and engage with people to whom they were previously unacquainted.

That is what this paper sets out to investigate. Specifically we are interested in the different factors that are responsible for triggering what we title *Spontaneous Group Formation* (SGF) in a public setting. We approach SGF as a sub-category of Shared Encounters [20], in which not only prior unrelated users spontaneously form a group, and have a performative co-presence, but they also try to achieve a common goal that requires cooperation. Therefore we set up a public installation – a game aiming to motivate users to cooperate – in three different situations that were moderately to heavily foot-trafficked areas. To achieve this goal, several criteria had to be fulfilled in order to successfully facilitate SGF. Firstly, it had to work well with multiple users, but it also had to slightly punish single users—the idea being that a single user would want to play that game alone initially, but have difficulty as the game progressed, thus motivating them to seek out help from passersby. Secondly, the usability had to be somewhat universal, so that all types of users can play along with no major difficulties. Moreover, the game had to be intuitive to play, so that players could join in without significant instructions or considerations being necessary.

Through three days of in-the-wild testing the prototype was evaluated with regards to the frequency of SGF and the factors behind it. Our results show that 2%–15% of use instances resulted in SGF, differing between test locations. Moreover, SGF was typically initiated by users drawn to the game while another user, or users, were already playing.

2   Related Work

A variety of previous work in the area of urban installations focused on shared encounters [1,4,11,14], however only few of the observed instances resulted in a group pursuing a common goal. Willis defines shared encounters as *"the interaction between two people or within a group where a sense of performative co-presence is experienced and which is characterised by a mutual recognition of spacial or social proximity"* [20]. Schieck goes a bit further and describes *digital encounters*, defining them as *"[...]a digital encounter is an ephemeral form of communication and interaction augmented by technology"* [17]. Thus, a digital encounter is in essence a shared encounter facilitated or enhanced by technology. In our particular case we are interested in a smaller sub-set of these shared encounters, that we refer to as *Spontaneous Group Formation* (SGF). In these situations, a group forms out of several individuals or multiple smaller groups or small groups and individuals, to form one large group, that cooperates in a shared encounter, to reach a common goal.

Across multiple studies, interaction with installations in pairs or smaller groups of users, has been found to be more frequent, compared to individuals. Fischer et al. made observations over 3 different urban installations and counted how many people passed by the installations [4]. For the first installation, the Interactive Fountain, 84% of all people that interacted with the system were in groups. For the Second installation, kick-/flickable light fragments, all passersby that interacted with the installation were in groups. And for the third installation, the PIPE project, 92% of the people that interacted were in groups. Similar observations have been made in Morrison et al., where 36% of 722 people in pairs and 35% of 489 people in groups bigger than two were observed interacting with the system, compared to 28% of 512 observed individuals interacting [14]. Fischer et al. also found that the Interactive fountain created shared encounters among 1% of the total people observed, and 3% of the passersby of the PIPE project experienced a shared encounter [4]. While these cases have been observed, the original goal of the discussed approaches was not necessarily to create such shared encounters. For this paper however we try to identify factors that lead to shared encounters and specifically SGM.

In line with these findings, Laureyssens et al. also found that of all people participating in ZWERM, a competitive urban participation game between two neighbourhoods, an average of 13 new acquaintances were made during the duration of the game which spanned over four weeks [11]. One of the main similarity between installations in which shared encounters have been observed is that they all have fixed interaction spaces, meaning that interaction with the installation occurs within a static space. Furthermore two of these installation also afford cooperation between multiple performers. The PIPE project featured three pneumatic pressure tubes that would sequentially light up segments of light with colors depending on which tubes were activated at the same time. The tubes were large enough to fit multiple people on one at a time, and afford cooperation between multiple people to manipulate the segments of lights. ZWERM also encouraged participation by multiple performers on both sides of the competition, since the primary objective of the game is for each team to gather as many points as possible, and some participants of this game were even observed trying to recruit other performers for that reason.

While it seems that installations with fixed interaction spaces and affordance for multiple performers at once seem to lend themselves to creating shared encounters, installations with dynamic interaction spaces that can change location can also potentially create social interaction. In their analysis of SMSlingshot, Fischer et al. also argue that the installation could serve as a gestation point for social interaction, as people would e.g. discuss what message to type or talk about the device [5]. For our we aim to create an installation that is not bound to a certain interaction space, but that rather acts universal, so this will not factor in the design of the installation.

During their study of ZWERM, Laureyssens et al. found that participants in the game would go from door to door in their neighborhood to recruit other people [11]. A phenomenon similar to that observed in Laureyssens et al., was recorded by Balestrini et al. in their study of the Jokebox, where people who were familiar with the installation would encourage passersby to try it [1]. This phenomenon has also been referred to as championing. Furthermore, in Webber et al.'s study of an Interactive music installation visualizing movements of participants, it was also observed that under instruction by performers participants were observed to enthusiastically form groups among both friends and strangers [19]. Championing, is one of the phenomena that we aim to design for in this paper, by punishing single players to some extend, that they will want to recruit more participants.

Two additional social phenomenon have also been found during the observation of public installations. One of them is called the honeypot effect, and refers to urge for passersby to participate in social interactions around the installation [21]. In the study of ZWERM, it was observed that during social gathering of performers around the installations, passersby would approach, observe and partake in the activities. Similarly, Balestrini also observed that individual passersby would be more likely to notice and observe the Jokebox if there were already people interacting with it [1]. Related to this effect is the installation design. Fischer et al. discussed that the SMSlingshot turned users into highly performative displays that would attract the attention of other passersby and this could be caused by their unusual movements [5]. Müller et al. observed this in their study of the Looking glass, where passersby would take notice of other users interacting with the system, observe the interaction and occasionally partake in it [15].

The second phenomenon that has been reported is referred to as hidden queuing. In their study of the kick-/flickable light fragments, Fischer et al. experienced groups of observers that would wait for a group of performers to finish interacting with the installation, before proceeding to interact with system themselves [3]. Similarly in Balestrini et al. it was observed that attracted passersby would also not interfere with any currently ongoing interaction with the interaction, but would rather wait until the installation was unoccupied [1].

While the honeypot effect would be preferable phenomena to achieve, it is very hard to design for, and often depending on the location [21]. On the other hand the hidden queuing phenomena is something that should be rather prevented, as it would maybe keep people from joining a group for interaction.

2.1   Designing for Group Use

When designing urban installations it is important to consider how it grabs the attention of passersby, and how wide the possibilities for interaction are. Hornecker et al. [9] describes design concepts useful in both designing and analysing interactive installations: *Entry points*, how the installation grabs the attention of potential users and invites them to engage in use of it, and *Access points*, the options and possibilities a user has for engaging in use of the installation.

Entry points are important to consider, especially with regards to the progressive lures of the system, and in how easy it is for passersby to observe, and thus learn, the installation. Moreover, considering access points and the number thereof is critical when designing an installation meant for facilitating group use, as shown by Hornecker [8]. This is especially in the case of manipulative access: the specific methods though which a user interacts with the system. So when designing an installation meant to enable and encourage SGF, making sure that the system has multiple manipulative access points should be a core concept of the design.

3   Design

The concept for the prototype was set out to be an urban installation with the intention of creating SGF, based on the game *Simon*. This game – also known as *Simon Says*– is a memory game that shows a sequence of 4 different colours which the player then has to remember and repeat using buttons of the same colours. Each time a player successfully repeats a sequence, they are shown the same sequence with an additional colour at the end, theoretically continuing ad infinity. To encourage group play, we scaled the whole game, so that the distance between the buttons was drastically increased to up to four meter and the time limit for repeating each step of the sequence was extended to allow for SGF.

3.1   Hardware

The physical prototype is comprised of two major components: a center pyramid which displays the colour-pattern, and button towers which player's use to interact with the system.

Center Pyramid

The center pyramid is built from acrylic glass. Four equilateral triangles were laser cut and assembled to form a pyramid. Using cardboard, the inside of the pyramid was separated into four sections, and each section had paper of different colours glued to the inside of the pyramid: red, yellow, green and blue, respectively (see Fig. 1). The center pyramid also contains the majority of electronics that make up the prototype.

The pyramid houses the system electronics of the prototype: a Raspberry PI 3 model B, an Arduino Micro and circuits connecting to LED lights, LED strips and the external buttons.

Button Towers

Four button towers were created for the game, one for each colour, where a button was affixed to the end of a standing pipe as can be seen in Fig. 2. The intent behind these buttons was that they should be situated at lead a few meters from the center pyramid, forming a square around the it. The buttons are big coloured push buttons placed on top of the tower roughly 1 m tall. The towers are made from PVC-U piping mounted on wooden feet, with weights in the bottom to ensure they do not fall over. The towers had to be tall enough that adults could comfortably push the buttons standing up, and they had to be short enough where children could still see and reach them. The average height of an eight year old (the recommended minimum age for the game is, according to *Sundhed.dk*, roughly 130 cm. [18], and as such a height of 1 m enables children to play, while still being comfortable for adults.

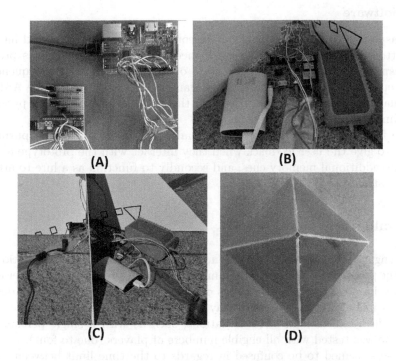

Fig. 1. (A) The Arduino, Raspberry Pi and perfboards, (B) the Raspberry pi, power-bank and speaker, (C) the setup as it look when placed by the cardboard triangle, (D) the pyramid beneath which the other components were covered.

Fig. 2. One of the button towers.

3.2 Software

The Raspberry Pi functions as the main controller for the system and handles the buttons, audio feedback, and game mechanics. When a button is pressed the Raspberry looks at the current state of the game, e.g. if the sequence is being repeated correctly or if it is a new game, and then instructs the Arduino to display the correct pattern of light in the LED strips and center pyramid, depending on the state of the game.

The feedback of the system, both visual and audible, have dual purposes. Firstly, to give the user feedback when they interact with the prototype as well as giving additional memory cues, and secondly to function as a lure to attract people's attention.

4 Evaluation

Before engaging in the main evaluation, we conducted several pre-evaluations in which the prototype was tested in a number of scenarios to identify whether there were any immediately pressing issues or misunderstandings within the design. The tests included asking users to play the game without any interference, and playing the game in high stress situations, such as with a single person. The prototype was tested with all eligible numbers of players (one to four). In these tests, users seemed to be confused in regards to the time limit between clicks, especially when they lost and they could not identify specifically why. This lead to the implementation of a tick timer that activates when a button is clicked, and starts ticking, going increasingly faster until the time has run out and the game is lost. This seemed to create a sense of urgency in the users, and would have many of them running long before necessary. Additionally, some users were in doubt as to what the goal of the game was, which led to the implementation of a introductory audio clip, that plays whenever a user presses a button to start a new game, which then explains the rules of the game to the user. These additional implementations were tested and deemed successful on a university-scheduled demonstration day, where the prototype was set up for four hours. No additional issues were identified.

4.1 Ways of Use

In order to characterize the behaviours of the users in our in-the-wild evaluation, we selected to categorize their behaviour in the following way. We define three different ways in which users interact with an urban installation are defined. These are:

Intended Use (IU) - Meaning to interact with the system in the manner which was intended by the developers as they designed the system.

Exploratory Use (EU) - Meaning to interact with the system in a curious and inquisitive manner, trying to discern the purpose behind it.

Playful Use (PU) - Meaning to play in the area surrounding the system, in a way where the system takes a role, however the function(s) of the system need not be of consequence to goals of the game being played.

When it comes to evaluating a system with respect to discerning the factors behind SGF, looking into the frequency of the different ways of use can potentially be of some assistance. A pattern might reveal itself, giving insight into why SGF occur—or why it does not, should that be the case, e.g. if a lot of PU is observed the system might not be well enough explained, hampering the possibility for SGF.

4.2 Method

The prototype was tested through unsupervised in-the-wild tests, taking place over 3 days in late April/early May. The prototype was set up at three different locations in the city of (Omitted for blind review) that each have a relatively high flow of pedestrians. Test facilitators observed the use of the prototype from a distance, and the entire test period was video recorded for observation purposes. The Purpose of the evaluation was to determine the factors behind SGF.

For the purpose of these tests, a spontaneous group formation is defined as: When 2 or more groups of people (or individuals), with no preexisting plans to meet up, interact in a manner that involves any of: playing the game together for any period of time or direct conversation, as result of, or in relation to the game.

Before testing, several elements were defined that should be observed and noted during the tests. Common for these elements was the assumption that they can help explain the factors that determine when SGF happens. The elements are:

Play time: For how long did a user play on their own before receiving help from another user?

Initiator: If spontaneous group formation took place, which person initiated the contact?

Demographic: Which demographic did the users fall under?

Loss condition: If they did, how did they lose? Timeout or incorrect sequence?

For purpose of comparison, the demographics were noted for all users, not just those engaging in SGF.

4.3 Procedure

The first test took place on the 25th of April and lasted for three hours from 11:00 to 14:00. The prototype was set up inside a university building as can be seen in Fig. 3 - A, in the main hall near the cafeteria as well as near the main stairs leading to the upper floors—an area that sees a lot of thoroughfare. The idea behind choosing this test location was to try out the prototype in an area where SGF was thought likely to happen, due to the nature of the environment.

The second test took place on the 6th of May and lasted three hours from 13:00 to 16:00. The weather was sunny and warm. The prototype was set up on the harbourfront in the shade of the same university building as can be seen in Fig. 3 - B. On this day, there was a flea market on the harbourfront roughly 400 m from where the prototype was set up, which likely increased the flow of pedestrians on the harbourfront during the test period.

Iteration

Between the second and third day of testing the setup underwent small iterations to better ensure that people understood how to interact with the prototype, in addition to better inform passersby that it was meant to be interacted with. These iterations were implemented based on observed instances of exploratory use and feedback from participants who stated that the lights were hard to see in the day, and due to the orange colour and position of the button towers, i.e. placed in a square around the pyramid, it looked like the area was closed off as can be seen in Fig. 3 - B. To fix this, a sign was created aimed at informing passersby how to use the prototype, and to be used as an additional entry point.

The third test took place on the 9th of May and lasted 7 h and 30 min from 16:00 to 23:30. The weather was sunny and warm. The prototype was set up in a plaza, as can be seen in Fig. 3 - C, close to the harbourfront as well as several pubs and restaurants, and near one of the city's larger bus stops. The pedestrian flow was markedly higher in this location than it was on the harbourfront on day two.

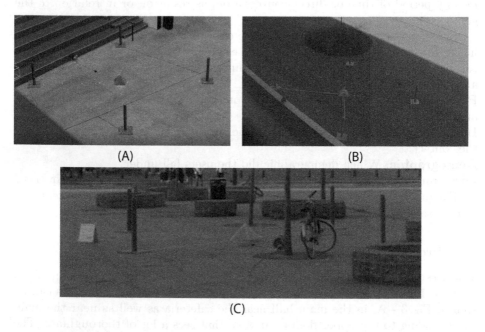

Fig. 3. Test setup on the first (A), second (B), and third (C) day.

4.4 Results

The Results of the tests are presented in two parts, first presenting the results on SGF, then results on the general observed use of the prototype.

Spontaneous Group Formation

All use cases from the tests were reviewed with respect to the definition of SGF outlined in Sect. 4.2. Keeping this definition in mind, whether or not a case involved SGF was judged by the facilitators. If SGF seemed to occur, additional attention would be paid to whence the users respectively approached the prototype, and in which direction they left afterwards. The logic behind observing this behaviour was, that if users approached from different directions, played the game together, and then left in opposite directions, the likelihood that a true SGF was just observed would be much higher. The video recordings were used to verify these observations. Across all three tests, 11 cases of SGF were observed.

On the first day of testing 51 use cases were observed, four (7.84%) of which resulted in SGF. In the first case a male user was playing the game alone. After 32 s another male user initiated contact, and both proceeded to play the game together for an additional 27 s, after which they were joined by a third male user (counting as two instances of SGF). The entire SGF period lasted for 1 min and 4 s. In the second SGF instance a female user was playing the game alone for 32 s, after which 3 other female users joined the game. It is unclear who initiated the contact between the two parts. After an additional 16 s a fifth female user joined in (again, counting as two instances of SGF). The whole SGF period lasted for 22 s. The third SGF case started with a male user playing the game alone for 33 s, after which a female user approached him, initiated conversation and joined in the game. This instance lasted for 21 s. The final instance of SGF on the first day of testing started with a female user playing the game alone for 42 s. She was joined by another female user who initiated contact. They played the game together for 21 s.

The second day of testing saw less use than the first day, with just 20 observed use cases over the course of the test. Three (15%) of these interactions led to SGF. All three cases started with a group of two people (all three groups approximately 17–35 years old) being attracted to the game, and initiating use. In the first of the three cases a group of eight people (ages approximately ranging from 10 to 60+) approached the players and initiated contact, starting out with observing and later engaging in direct conversation. In the latter two cases an elderly couple (approximately 60+ years old) saw what was happening and approached the players, engaging in direct conversation. The exact duration of each of the SGF cases on day two are unknown, due to technical errors with the video capture device resulting is loss of the footage. For the same reason no other data is included from day two, and there might be inaccuracies in the age ranges of the users, as they are estimated from observer-memory rather than from video footage.

On the third day of testing a total of 90 use cases were observed, only two (2.22%) of which resulted in SGF. In the first case two children, approximately three and four years old, were engaging in PU the prototype. After about four minutes of play they were joined by two other children from two other families, approximately two and five years old. All four continued to periodically play the game over the course of half an hour.

The second SGF was the last use case of the day. Here, the test facilitators were just about to pack up for the day, and decided to play a game themselves before doing so. After playing the game for 1 min and 37 s, a group of three young male users, approximately 20 years old, approached, exclaiming *"What is this?"* and *"We have to see what this is!"*, as much to each other as to the facilitators. They were quickly explained the game, and one of them joined to play it with three of the facilitators. This SGF lasted for a total of 2 min and 26 s.

Common for all but one observed case of SGF is, that it occurred while someone was engaging in IU.

General Use

Throughout the testing period, there was a total of 67 instances of IU, 73 of EU and 4 of PU, for a total of 144 interactions. The IU instances included a total of 187 people, EU a total of 136 people and PU a total of 8 people. Table 1 shows the use duration for the IU and EU instances for test one and three. Use duration for the PU was not calculated, due to the insignificant number of PU instances, nor is the use duration from day two, due to the aforementioned technical issues.

60 of the 67 cases of IU were group interactions of at least two people. The average group size across all 67 cases was 2.79.

The age of the users were estimated in four different age ranges. 0–16, 17–35, 36–60 and 60+. Table 2 shows the distribution of age ranges over instances of IU, and Table 3 shows the same for the EU instances. The first SGF case from day two is unaccounted for in Table 2, as the users in this case were split between the age ranges of 0–16, 17–35 and 36–60.

5   Discussion

During the evaluation, several points revealed themselves that require further discussion. A total of 11 SGF instances were observed. On day one, the age of the SGF users all fell within 17–35, as was expected due to the location. On day two, the age of users was more evenly split, with users from 10 to 60+ years. On the third day the users were mainly withing the 17–35 age group, although a few were 0–16. From this data, it seems that the age ranges of users who engage in SGF lean towards 17–35, however this data is possibly biased, due to the location of the first test.

As shown in Sect. 4.4, SGF was initiated after the initial user had engaged in IU for a period of 32 s to 1 min 37 s, with a 4 min outlier. If these results can be trusted—which only further testing and consequently a larger sample size could determine—they indicate that SGF does not happen until after a minimum period of time has passed, likely the time it takes for observers to realise something is happening with the game, and possibly realise exactly what that is. The numbers themselves also indicate that SGF happens within the first half or first third of the use duration (when compared with the mean in

Table 1. Use duration

			Time window	Mean	Median	σ
Day one	Overall	IU	00:08–06:06	01:23	00:48	01:26
		EU	00:02–00:50	00:14	00:10	00:13
	Individuals	IU	00:11–02:26	01:00	00:24	01:14
		EU	00:02–00:50	00:13	00:05	00:15
	Groups	IU	00:08–06:06	01:26	00:54	01:28
		EU	00:03–00:32	00:14	00:11	00:10
Day three	Overall	IU	00:08–08:48	02:45	01:52	02:23
		EU	00:02–01:52	00:28	00:16	00:27
	Individuals	IU	00:40–08:08	02:38	01:04	03:41
		EU	00:08–00:40	00:20	00:16	00:10
	Groups	IU	00:08–08:48	02:43	01:52	02:18
		EU	00:02–01:52	00:31	00:16	00:31

The *Time Window, Mean, Median,* and *Standard Deviation* of use
duration from day one and three. The time format is mm:ss.

Table 2. IU age ranges

	0–16	17–35	36–60	60+
0–16	6	1	0	3
17–35	——	43	7	3
36–60	——	——	1	1
60+	——	——	——	1

The number of IU cases with users
in each age range. On the diagonal
are use cases containing only one
age range. To the right of the diagonal are cases where users were from
multiple age ranges.

Table 1), however there is no logical reason that SGF could not happen after a
longer period of time—a group of people could easily have played the game for
five minutes, and then be approached by another group of people who had only
just now witnessed the interaction and decided to investigate.

One thing that seems rather certain based on these tests is, that when SGF
happens the initiator will most likely be the group or individual who is joining the initial users. This was the case in most of the observed instances of
SGF, except for one instance on both day one and three where the initiator
was unclear. As described in Sect. 4.2, the loss conditions were observed for any
losses that occurred immediately before SGF, the assumption being that the loss
condition might influence a user's likelihood to invite others to play. However,
every observed instance of SGF was achieved before the game was lost the first
time.

Table 3. EU age ranges

	0–16	17–35	36–60	60+
0–16	10	0	6	0
17–35	—	40	3	1
36–60	—	—	10	1
60+	—	—	—	3

The number of EU cases with users in each age range. On the diagonal are use cases containing only one age range. To the right of the diagonal are cases where users were from multiple age ranges.

Differences Between Locations

Day three had the lowest number of SGF instances, even through it had the highest amount of foot traffic in the area, with only two SGF instances over seven hours, compared to six and three SGF instances over three hours on day one and two, respectively. Possible reasons for this difference may include: the large amount of people in the surrounding areas, dissuading potential users from performing; more noise from the surrounding restaurants and water fountain, effectively rendering the audio lure futile; or the sunny weather obscuring the visibility of the flashing lights, making the game difficult to play. The exact reason is difficult to pinpoint.

During the first day users were also exposed as on day three, as they were in the middle of a building where all floors can look directly at them. However, unlike day three the audio was clearly audible, as the nature of the educational building is a generally low level of noise. Visibly there was no problem either, as it was inside and not in direct sunlight. The sign, in this case, was not necessary, as the people in the building know that if something is set in the middle of the main hall, it is likely an exhibit by other students with which they can freely interact, as this is something that frequently happens in the building. This knowledge does not necessarily extend to the other locations.

On the second day people had plenty space to interact, even though it was a fairly trafficked day. There was nothing unusual outside causing additional noise, and the lights were fairly clear as the prototype was never in direct sunlight. One participant, however, mentioned that without a sign, the button-towers somewhat resembled poles that were supposed to keep people away, much akin to traffic cones.

Day One Discrepancies

The first test, as mentioned in Sect. 4.3, took place at a university building. This building is inhabited by students, such as the authors, who are possibly more likely to play than the general populous may be. This makes the instances of SGF in this building slightly less likely to be representative of more general

SGF. This is presuming that the SGF instances observed on day one are actually SGF. This is put in to question, since it is known that many people traversing the building know each other as they may have done group work together, or have been in the same classes. Therefore, there is a reasonable chance that those that in the footage appear to be engaging in SGF, may simply be a group walking scattered, with one person further ahead than the rest, or a person signalling or calling for their friends after beginning to play. Regardless, this is not possible to determine purely from the footage, and therefore, for the purpose of this paper, those of them that are not obviously coming in dispersed groups, are considered instances of SGF.

Number of SGF Instances

After these tests have been done, and a satisfactory number of people have interacted and played with the prototype, the total amount of instances is still low. This means that any generalisations made about the causal factors are not necessarily accurate, even though the number of instances of SGF may be.

Competition

The concept of the prototype made for this paper, and therefore the method of generating SGF, is based on the users' need do well—their competitiveness. The intention had been for users to work together to play the game optimally, as it is rather difficult to do on your own for extended periods of time. This proved not to be the case, as none of the users gave the impression that they partnered with other users for the purpose of reaching higher levels, but rather because the joining user was interested or drawn in by the flashing colours. This could indicate that appealing to the users competitiveness is not the way, but rather creating something that is still made for multiple people, but focus more on the lure, is. For this particular installation, a way of enhancing the lure could be to periodically have the lights display an eye-catching pattern, when the installation is not in use, e.g. in combination with the present lure-audio clip.

Normal Spontaneous Group Formation

It can be said with great certainty that groups spontaneously formed around or in the context of the prototype. What cannot be said, however, is whether this number of instances of SGF is truly larger than the average number in that area. That is to say, given that groups forming and talking about or around the prototype was considered SGF, that random groups of people may meet on an average day and talk, regardless of whether something was there made to encourage it. This could be compensated for by looking at the area of testing, and attempting to spot whether any groups form spontaneously. Another option could be to create an installation that is not made to encourage group formation, and observe whether any groups form around it regardless.

Intuitiveness

During the tests it quickly became evident that the prototype was not as intuitive as previously thought. Many users approached and push a button, but did not immediately, if at all, figure out what the flashing lights meant and indicated. There are several possible reasons, such as there not being a clear enough distinction between the 'pattern phase' (where the user has to watch and memorise the pattern) and the actual 'execution phase' (where the user reproduces the pattern), and the users therefore click the buttons during the pattern phase and become confused by the system not responding, which ends in them pushing the wrong button when the game has begun, and instantly losing. Another possibility is that the tutorial audio was unclear, either in audio quality, or simply in the explanation. A likely reason however, is that we overestimated the amount of people who knew and would recognise the *Simon* game, or had experience with simple memory games of similar design.

Number of Players
The developed prototype for the most part only allowed for four players at once. Everything above that would only become inconvenient. Furthermore, the prototype could only support one playing party at a time. This means that in regards to SGF, it could not make nearly as much use of the honeypot effect as it would have been able to if it allowed for either more players or multiple parties, as users could then slowly pile on and join the activity a few at a time. This, however, is easier said than done, since the prototype developed for this paper is very unlikely to have potential to be developed in said direction.

Optimal Pedestrian Flow
It might be worth considering when it is the most likely for groups to form. Specifically in the context of pedestrian flow, as there may be an optimal band of flow where the comfortability of playing and likelihood of people being there at the same time intersects. Given the data gathered through the tests, this intersection may lie somewhere between the flow of the second day and the third day, but as we neglected to measure the flow, this band would require further testing and calculation to isolate.

6   Conclusion

When creating an urban installation meant for group use, a problem may arise where a lone pedestrian will be unable to effectively engage with the installation. A theoretical solution to this, is for the user to form spontaneous groups with other, unrelated users. Hence, this project set out to explore the prevalence of this kind of spontaneous group formation (SGF), and to identify the factors behind it.

To investigate this field, a prototype was developed based on the memory game known as *Simon*. It was designed to encourage players of the game to form groups with other pedestrians by increasing its footprint to a 5 by 5 m square, and by implementing a timer, such that larger groups would have an advantage over smaller groups or individuals.

The prototype was tested over the course of three days, in three different locations in the city, all of which had a moderate to heavy amount of foot traffic. The test showed that SGF could indeed happen, however it did not happen equally across the three spaces. The first day of testing had 4 out of 51 use cases result in SGF, with two of them resulting in two separate SGF instances, over the course of three hours. The second day saw 3 of 20 use cases result in SGF, also over the course of three hours. The third day, on the other hand, saw only 2 of 90 use cases result in SGF over the course of 7 1/2 h, even though it had the highest amount of foot traffic in the area. A possible explanation is that the higher amount of foot traffic meant a higher amount of potential observers, which might have dissuaded potential users from engaging with the prototype.

The game itself was designed to encourage the initial player to seek out help in order to reach higher levels, however in the majority of observed cases of SGF, contact between parties was initiated not by the initial player, but by the people joining the game, suggesting that more effective lures is the best way to encourage SGF. No conclusions could be drawn on user demographics or playtime. Thus, if any other factors are behind SGF, they remain unknown.

References

1. Balestrini, M., Marshall, P., Cornejo, R., Tentori, M., Bird, J., Rogers, Y.: Jokebox: coordinating shared encounters in public spaces. In: Proceedings of the 19th ACM Conference on Computer-Supported Cooperative Work & Social Computing, CSCW 2016, pp. 38–49. ACM, New York (2016). https://doi.org/10.1145/2818048.2835203. http://doi.acm.org/10.1145/2818048.2835203

2. Böhmer, M., Gehring, S., Löchtefeld, M., Ostkamp, M., Bauer, G.: The mighty un-touchables: creating playful engagement on media faÇades. In: Proceedings of the 13th International Conference on Human Computer Interaction with Mobile Devices and Services, MobileHCI 2011, pp. 605–610. ACM, New York (2011). https://doi.org/10.1145/2037373.2037468. http://doi.acm.org/10.1145/2037373.2037468

3. Fischer, P.T., et al.: Movable, kick-/flickable light fragments eliciting ad-hoc interaction in public space. In: Proceedings of the International Symposium on Pervasive Displays, PerDis 2014, pp. 50:50–50:55. ACM, New York (2014). https://doi.org/10.1145/2611009.2611027. http://doi.acm.org/10.1145/2611009.2611027

4. Fischer, P.T., Hornecker, E.: Creating shared encounters through fixed and movable interfaces. In: Nijholt, A. (ed.) Playable Cities. GMSE, pp. 163–185. Springer, Singapore (2017). https://doi.org/10.1007/978-981-10-1962-3_8

5. Fischer, P.T., Hornecker, E., Zoellner, C.: SMSlingshot: an expert amateur DIY case study. In: Proceedings of the 7th International Conference on Tangible, Embedded and Embodied Interaction, TEI 2013, pp. 9–16. ACM, New York (2013). https://doi.org/10.1145/2460625.2460627. http://doi.acm.org/10.1145/2460625.2460627

6. Gehring, S., Hartz, E., Löchtefeld, M., Krüger, A.: The media façade toolkit: prototyping and simulating interaction with media façades. In: Proceedings of the 2013 ACM International Joint Conference on Pervasive and Ubiquitous Computing, UbiComp 2013, pp. 763–772. ACM, New York (2013). https://doi.org/10.1145/2493432.2493471. http://doi.acm.org/10.1145/2493432.2493471

7. Grønbæk, K., Kortbek, K.J., Møller, C., Nielsen, J., Stenfeldt, L.: Designing playful interactive installations for urban environments – the swingscape experience. In: Nijholt, A., Romão, T., Reidsma, D. (eds.) ACE 2012. LNCS, vol. 7624, pp. 230–245. Springer, Heidelberg (2012). https://doi.org/10.1007/978-3-642-34292-9_16

8. Hornecker, E.: Space and place-setting the stage for social interaction. In: Position Paper Presented at ECSCW05 Workshop Settings for Collaboration: The Role of Place (2005)
9. Hornecker, E., Marshall, P., Rogers, Y.: From entry to access: how shareability comes about. In: Proceedings of the 2007 Conference on Designing Pleasurable Products and Interfaces, DPPI 2007, pp. 328–342. ACM, New York (2007). https://doi.org/10.1145/1314161.1314191. http://doi.acm.org/10.1145/1314161.1314191
10. Konopatzky, P., et al.: xChase A. Location-based multi-user pervasive game using a lightweight tracking framework. In: Proceedings of the Second International Conference on Fun Games-FNG, vol. 8 (2008)
11. Laureyssens, T., Coenen, T., Claeys, L., Mechant, P., Criel, J., Vande Moere, A.: ZWERM: a modular component network approach for an urban participation game. In: Proceedings of the 32nd Annual ACM Conference on Human Factors in Computing Systems, CHI 2014, pp. 3259–3268. ACM, New York (2014). https://doi.org/10.1145/2556288.2557053. http://doi.acm.org/10.1145/2556288.2557053
12. Löchtefeld, M., Schöning, J., Rohs, M., Krüger, A.: LittleProjectedPlanet: an augmented reality game for camera projector phones. Artificial Intelligence, pp. 15–27 (2009)
13. Löchtefeld, M., Schöning, J., Rohs, M., Krüger, A.: Marauders light: replacing the wand with a mobile camera projector unit. In: Proceedings of the 8th International Conference on Mobile and Ubiquitous Multimedia, MUM 2009, pp. 19:1–19:4. ACM, New York (2009). https://doi.org/10.1145/1658550.1658569. http://doi.acm.org/10.1145/1658550.1658569
14. Morrison, A., Manresa-Yee, C., Jensen, W., Eshraghi, N.: The humming wall: vibrotactile and vibroacoustic interactions in an urban environment. In: Proceedings of the 2016 ACM Conference on Designing Interactive Systems, DIS 2016, pp. 818–822. ACM, New York (2016). https://doi.org/10.1145/2901790.2901878. http://doi.acm.org/10.1145/2901790.2901878
15. Müller, J., Walter, R., Bailly, G., Nischt, M., Alt, F.: Looking glass: a field study on noticing interactivity of a shop window. In: Proceedings of the SIGCHI Conference on Human Factors in Computing Systems, CHI 2012, pp. 297–306. ACM, New York (2012). https://doi.org/10.1145/2207676.2207718. http://doi.acm.org/10.1145/2207676.2207718
16. Nijholt, A.: Towards playful and playable cities. In: Nijholt, A. (ed.) Playable Cities. GMSE, pp. 1–20. Springer, Singapore (2017). https://doi.org/10.1007/978-981-10-1962-3_1
17. Schieck, A.F., Kostakos, V., Penn, A.: Exploring digital encounters in the public arena. In: Willis, K., Roussos, G., Chorianopoulos, K., Struppek, M. (eds.) Shared Encounters. CSCW, pp. 179–195. Springer, London (2009). https://doi.org/10.1007/978-1-84882-727-1_9
18. Sundhed.dk: Growthcurve, boys 0-20. https://www.sundhed.dk/borger/patienthaandbogen/boern/illustrationer/tegning/vaekstkurve-drenge-0-20/. Accessed 21 May 2018
19. Webber, S., Harrop, M., Downs, J., Cox, T., Wouters, N., Moere, A.V.: Everybody dance now: tensions between participation and performance in interactive public installations. In: Proceedings of the Annual Meeting of the Australian Special Interest Group for Computer Human Interaction, OzCHI 2015, pp. 284–288. ACM, New York (2015). https://doi.org/10.1145/2838739.2838801. http://doi.acm.org/10.1145/2838739.2838801

20. Willis, K.S., Roussos, G., Chorianopoulos, K., Struppek, M.: Shared encounters. In: Willis, K., Roussos, G., Chorianopoulos, K., Struppek, M. (eds.) Shared Encounters. CSCW, pp. 1–15. Springer, London (2009). https://doi.org/10.1007/978-1-84882-727-1_1

21. Wouters, N., et al.: Uncovering the honeypot effect: how audiences engage with public interactive systems. In: Proceedings of the 2016 ACM Conference on Designing Interactive Systems, DIS 2016, pp. 5–16. ACM, New York (2016). https://doi.org/10.1145/2901790.2901796. http://doi.acm.org/10.1145/2901790.2901796

Interactive Arts and Disability: A Conceptual Model Toward Understanding Participation

Jonathan Duckworth[1](✉), James Hullick[2], Shigenori Mochizuki[3], Sarah Pink[4], Christine Imms[5], and Peter H. Wilson[5]

[1] School of Design, RMIT University, Melbourne, Australia
jonathan.duckworth@rmit.edu.au
[2] Jolt Sonic & Visual Arts Inc, Melbourne, Australia
james.hullick@joltarts.org
[3] College of Image Arts and Sciences, Ritsumeikan University, Kyoto, Japan
mochiz@im.ritsumei.ac.jp
[4] Department of Design, Monash University, Melbourne, Australia
sarah.pink@monash.edu
[5] Centre for Disability and Development Research, Faculty of Health Sciences,
Australian Catholic University, Melbourne, Australia
{christine.imms,peterh.wilson}@acu.edu.au

Abstract. In this paper we explore how social aspects of group interaction and the physical affordances of interactive technology may be exploited to enhance the participation of people with a disability in creative, artistic activity. Participation per se is conceptualized using a current framework known as the family of Participation Related Constructs—fPRC, an ecological approach derived from a biopsychosocial health model. Taking an integrative approach, we blend current theory on participation, interaction design and community art to explore how group play and performance can foster inclusive participation in the arts and contribute to a positive change in personal (and collective) wellbeing. We describe two interactive arts projects called *Resonance* and *Wheelchair DJ* that provide examples of participation and performance in communities with a disability and reflect upon the workshop models that facilitate the creative expression of individuals and the group. We conclude with a discussion on the potentially transformative effects of participation in the arts by people with a disability and our gaps in our understanding of how to evaluate the notion of *participation as a means*—a medium through which person-related attributes and creative activity are developed in the longer-term.

Keywords: Interactive art · Disability · Sonic arts · Participation · Ethnography · Interaction design

1 Introduction

While there is a significant body of research and practice focused on enhancing participation in physical activity in the community (e.g., through sport), there is a critical gap in

© ICST Institute for Computer Sciences, Social Informatics and Telecommunications Engineering 2020
Published by Springer Nature Switzerland AG 2020. All Rights Reserved
A. Brooks and E. I. Brooks (Eds.): ArtsIT 2019/DLI 2019, LNICST 328, pp. 524–538, 2020.
https://doi.org/10.1007/978-3-030-53294-9_38

our knowledge about how interactive arts can be used to improve universal participation outcomes and social inclusion. In the Australian context, people living in the community who are disadvantaged for economic, social, health or other reasons have historically shown low levels of participation in arts and cultural activities [1]. Those who need special support and who are drawn to creative arts are often excluded by a lack of availability, accessibility and/or the capacity of creative arts environments to accommodate their needs [2]. And yet, rights of access to such activities and the opportunity to live 'an ordinary life' is a statutory requirement of many agencies that serve to protect and foster participation of marginalised groups [3].

According to the *International Classification of Functioning, Disability and Health* (ICF), participation refers to a person's involvement in physical, recreational, and social life situations [4]. The ICF model (Fig. 1) presents a bi-directional relationship between participation and personal outcomes [5, 6]. For groups that encounter barriers to participation through disability or socioeconomic disadvantage, there is an imperative to re-think our approach to designing recreational, rehabilitative and cultural activities, including community arts. Indeed, enabling people with a disability to live 'an ordinary life' – a statuary requirement of the National Disability Insurance Agency (NDIA) – means that we need to understand how to use contemporary technologies to facilitate engagement of all people in community activities [3].

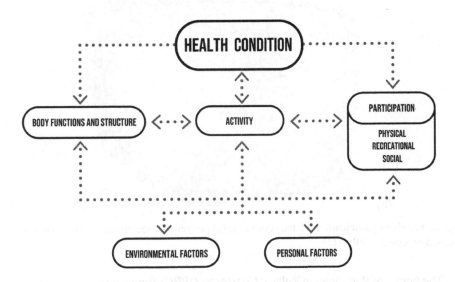

Fig. 1. The ICF model of functioning and disability [4]

In contrast to traditional models of disability, the ICF is a more ecological approach that recognizes both strengths and deficits across physical and psycho-social domains, defining the nature of any difficulty and the impact on participation across multiple contexts (See Fig. 1). Interventions address the dynamic interaction between individual, task/activity, and environmental/contextual factors and impact on participation. This approach, however, does not distinguish between two major elements of participation (attendance and involvement) and still conceptualizes participation as the end-product of any training experience or intervention.

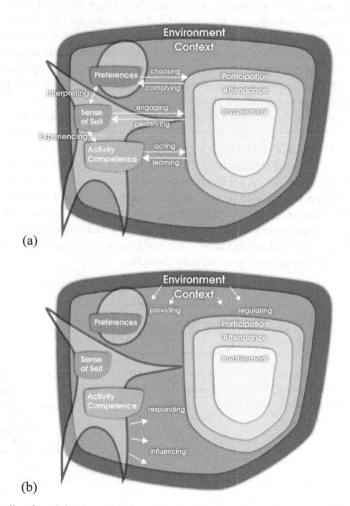

Fig. 2. Family of participation-related constructs: (a) person-focused processes, (b) environment-focused processes (fPRC) [7].

The family of Participation Related Constructs (fPRC) framework (Fig. 2 above) has highlighted 'attendance' and 'involvement' as critical elements to enhance participation outcomes, implying a paradigm shift towards a collaborative process of intervention and training [7]. In other words, participation is more than merely being physically present in life situations but includes a sense of belonging and involvement in these social settings [6]. To understand fully the experience of being engaged in an artistic activity we need to consider transactions that occur among the participation activity (e.g., group-based composition of music) and both (i) person characteristics (activity competence, sense-of-self and preferences) and (ii) external environments and contexts of participation. Critically, the fPRC construes participation as both a *means* (or the process by which other goals are reached) and an *end* (or preferred outcome of some experience, training or intervention). For example, *participation as a means* might be a community-based artists' retreat through which longer-term psychological outcomes are expressed. Outcomes may include changes to person-related constructs like a heightened sense of self-efficacy, preferences, the development of specific skills that can be carried forward, and self-concept. Put another way, immersion in a real-life (community) context can set the stage for experiences that involve personal growth, the ability to exercise control and choice, and social interaction. Over time, this can lead to an enhanced awareness of one's strengths, self-identity, and future opportunities for development [8]. However, there is a dire need to identify levels of engagement/involvement from the individual perspective and use this information to enhance the design of artistic/creative experiences, particularly that involving the use of interactive technology.

Whereas participation in the arts space has until recently been confined to traditional genres like dance, visual arts and crafts, music and theatre [9], one of the main advantages of interactive technology is the potential to design and customise environments and interfaces that can foster participation and social engagement for people with and without a disability. For example, sound art technology used in a community music setting has been shown to be a major benefit to individuals with a disability [10].

Recent figures show that as many as two-thirds of people with a disability have not engaged in a community arts experience, in collaboration with a practicing artist. This is a sobering figure as 60% of Australians surveyed identify that the arts have a positive impact on their sense of well-being and happiness [9]. Similarly, in Japan more than 70% of people with disabilities are not participating in cultural and artistic activities. Thirty-seven percent of people who participated in cultural and artistic activities engaged in community music activities. By type of disability, those who use a wheelchair are relatively less satisfied with cultural activities and 50% of them want to increase opportunities [11]. Among the potential benefits to be gained from engaging in community arts-based activities are therapeutic outcomes. For example, Community Music contexts place significant emphasis on the individual's values that can be gained from taking part in collective music making. Although therapeutic aims may not be a specific goal of the activity, therapeutic gains are often observed, including benefits from social inclusion, physical health and mental well-being [12].

2 Interactive Arts and Disability - Case Examples

In this section we will discuss *Resonance* and *Wheelchair DJ*, two interactive arts projects by the authors that facilitate participation through improvised music, sound art and performance within the context of community arts and disability. The fPRC model has not been explicitly used to develop the case examples, but rather it is used as a lens to reflect on participation. The broad aims of both examples are to embrace the idea of inclusivity and foster participation, that is anyone can create and perform and therefore everyone will have something to offer when opportunities are afforded for their involvement. Both examples lend themselves to improvisation by (i) placing only the simplest of 'user' rules and structures on the participant, (ii) avoiding the need for formal musical or dance training, and (iii) allow potentially playful approaches to working without traditional constraints such as harmonic structure, rhythmic patterns or tonality in music. Such formal constructs do not have to be predefined or even considered for interaction to occur. Improvisation encourages individuals to play and experiment with sounds, to offer new ideas and perhaps reflect those we hear around us, to embrace or resist the musical flow and to develop or simply abandon a train of musical thought [13].

2.1 Resonance

Resonance is an interactive digital audio tool that promotes collaborative and cooperative modes of interaction between small groups of performers (1–4) positioned around a 55" tabletop display. Complex soundscapes can be generated either individually or collectively using a combination of simple gestures, movement and manipulation of graspable objects (i.e. tangible user interfaces, TUIs) on the display. Here, groups of participants can mix and manipulate sound and colorful graphics in an aesthetically pleasing way (see Fig. 3). The artwork creates a space for intimacy and moments of playful resonance between the performers as they strive to find aesthetic equilibrium and balance when creating a composition.

Fig. 3. The Amplified Elephants performing on Resonance featuring Kathryn Sutherland. Bendigo Festival of Exploratory Music 2015. Photo by Owen McKern, courtesy of JOLT Arts.

Resonance departs from traditional musical instrument design that usually facilitate solo performance (i.e. violin). Group participation and group 'negotiation' is fundamental to the experience of Resonance and builds upon our prior work, which supports upper-limb rehabilitation for individuals with traumatic brain injury (TBI) [14–16]. Resonance is designed to mediate small groups of people interacting with one another face-to-face, and enables an embodied, first person experience of user interaction. Our design approach draws from principles of Computer Supported Cooperative Work (CSCW), a sub-field of Human Computer Interaction (HCI), to understand how computers can mediate and support collaborative work in a group environment (see [17] for a detailed discussion). The ability of tabletop displays to support awareness of others' actions is often cited as one of the main benefits of collaborative face-to-face learning [18]. We considered how participants might observe, communicate, and learn from others who are involved in playful activities [19]. Awareness of what others in a group are doing is essential in coordinating collaborative learning and achieving common goals around a shared activity. We considered a wide variety of collaboration styles, including working in parallel, working sequentially in tightly coupled activities, and working independently. We combined these ideas to design Resonance to support co-located participation and social engagement.

The TUIs placed on the tabletop are the primary means for users to control features and events within Resonance in ways that are natural to the user's body and their environment [20]. The development of naturalistic interfaces for user interaction is essential to optimise performance and improve access for participants with cognitive and motor impairments [21]. TUIs can exploit multiple human sensory channels otherwise neglected in conventional interfaces and can promote rich and dexterous interaction [22].

Each TUI produces a unique set of sounds we call *notes*, *pulses* and *atmospheres*. A number of coloured lines emanate on a central axis from the base of each TUI when placed on the display. These lines visually subdivide the screen into coloured polygonal fragments that produce an audiovisual *note* when touched.

Additional fragments are created as more TUI's are placed on the display, enabling a larger range of *notes* to be played. Single touch and multi-touch gestures generate softer and louder sounds respectively. Sliding the TUI's across the display changes the size of the fragments. The pitch of the *note* changes based on the fragment's position on the screen. Another feature includes a circular array of graphic buttons around the base of each TUI that iteratively generate glowing pulses at regular intervals when touch activated. These visual pulses travel outward along the lines emanating from the TUI and create a percussive sound when they cross an intersecting line. Moving the TUI so that the lines intersect at different points can vary the pitch of the sound. For example, intersecting lines nearer and further away from the base of the TUI raises and lowers the pitch of the *pulse* respectively. Finally, rapidly rotating the TUI controls the playback speed of an *atmosphere* sound. Turning the TUI clockwise and anti-clockwise plays the atmosphere forward or backwards respectively. A circular ring around the base of the TUI represents this feature. The volume of the *atmosphere* can be adjusted using a pinch-like finger gesture over the ring. For example, pinching the ring inward reduces the volume. Using a combination of these simple gestures and movements, participants can collaborate to create complex soundscapes.

In 2014, a partnership formed between RMIT, Jolt Sonic & Visual Arts Inc. and the Footscray Community Arts Center (FCAC) Melbourne, to customize Resonance for the Amplified Elephants, an ensemble of sound artists with an intellectual disability. The collaboration resulted in several public performances using the Resonance interface including 'Re:evolution' for the 2014 Melbourne Festival, a major international arts event in Australia; and 'Select Naturalis' for the 2015 Bendigo Festival of Exploratory

Music, and 2018 RMIT Engaging for Impact conference. At each event 4–6 members of the Amplified Elephants performed a 40–50-min composed piece in front of a public audience. Quadrophonic audio produced by the Resonance system was spatialized around the performance space and the Resonance visuals digitally projected behind the performers.

Ethics for the study was processed by Dr James Hullick, a post-doctoral researcher at Melbourne University, and teacher of sound art at the Footscray Community Arts Centre's Department of Human Services monitored Artlife Program. Artlife is a program that provides specialist training in the arts for people with intellectual disability. Participation in the program is voluntary and recruitment is coordinated through the Artlife manager in communication with the participating individual and carer of the participant. All artists with disabilities sign consent forms supervised by their families and/or support staff. The nature of public events and research is explained in writing and verbally at bimonthly meetings. Participants are supported through the rehearsal process by at least one or two fully registered nurses who are trained in mental health triage. These support staff work with the Artlife musicians daily and are highly trained in the specific care requirements of each participant. In the unlikely event that Artlife participants become distressed, there are very clear procedures in place to minimize the distress. Participants may withdraw from the rehearsal process or the performance at any time. All the participants involved in the Artlife projects have had their names and images previously released to the public as the performances are public. However, any images, video or audio recorded material involving the participant will be removed if the participant feels that it is placing them in a position of vulnerability.

In developing their performances, The Amplified Elephants were mentored by Hullick in four-hour weekly workshops at FCAC held over three months. Workshops situated the Resonance instrument within the context of a broader group discussion around Darwin's theories of evolution. Activities within the exploration of evolution included the reading of Darwin's texts out loud in workshops, watching nature documentaries, listening to music created in response to animals, and making recordings of participants vocalizing and playing synthesizers in ways that evoked animal sound worlds.

Artists used Resonance as the central feature to structure improvisational processes (i.e. performers might be given an order in which each artist activates a sound), and free improvisational activity (i.e. improvising without some preconditioning conversation beforehand). Improvisations would be recorded by the artists who would then make decisions about how they might 'improve' the work. This process of listening and 'sonic adventuring', a term defined by Hullick, was used as a basis to create sound art they defined as any creative activity that prioritizes sonic activity [10].

Hullick worked with the group collectively and each individual artist to understand how they may be able to make sound, and what their views and tastes for sound might be. The Amplified Elephants explored a range of sonic methodologies by recording synthesizer-based drones, improvising with junk percussion and found sound objects, as well as playing traditional musical instruments. The Amplified Elephants also worked abstractly with the voice and recorded and edited source 'animalistic' audio samples. These recorded sounds were then edited and uploaded onto the Resonance software in the *notes*, *pulses* and *atmospheres* sound data banks.

The types of abilities that individuals in the group demonstrated were carefully observed by Hullick. For example, the ability of a given performer to manipulate the graspable objects on the display; or how that same performer might then listen and use the functionality of Resonance to collaborate with other improvisors. Members of the group performed their improvisations in front of other members. The ensemble would discuss their improvisations and considered what could be improved. All ensemble members had an opportunity to try a range of sound-making activities on the Resonance table.

Playful engagement with Resonance encouraged artists to move around the table. Artists could stand, sit and seek new access points to the Resonance table, thereby interrogating the sound making properties of each TUI. When someone found a sound that they thought might be useful compositionally, they would draw the focus of the group toward it. A small selection of preferred sounds became the basis for a range of improvisations that members performed for, and with each other. Hullick came to the insight that the group participated in a multiplicity of artistic feed-back loops, enabling the artists to author sonic worlds born of the ensemble's identity. The resulting performances on Resonance by The Amplified Elephants were interjected by members of the ensemble reading quotations from Darwin's research. This posed important questions to audiences and the artists including what place in the theory of evolution is there for people with intellectual disabilities. The Resonance table: being a sonic instrument that supports 'group thinking' and problem-solving strategies was the ultimate answer: that the benefits of a beautiful, poetic, scientifically informed, aesthetic experience shared with the community can be delivered by people of all abilities.

Hullick reported several observations on the usability of Resonance and the perceived positive benefits for The Amplified Elephants. Situating the system in the workshop rehearsal space was invaluable and allowed us to gain insights into how the performers used Resonance and how we may improve the system. We observed how the mode of interaction encouraged a range of complex social and physical interactions between groups of performers. The performers were able to observe others' success in accomplishing improvisations that resonated with the theme of evolution, which in turn appeared to provide a sense of self-efficacy to the observer that they have the confidence in their ability to perform – to author and share worthy sonic art. Importantly, the performers were able to use the system intuitively and playfully perform movements related to fine motor control and touch, moving and orientating their arm in space, and modulating the force with which they were manipulating the TUI's. These are functional motor skills, that in other contexts, can be challenging for participants with intellectual disability to perform. Hullick observed that because the instrument was fun to play, the artists felt more inclined to push themselves regarding fine motor movements and control.

Participation using Resonance provided the potential to "learn from others"; to develop social skills and confidence; and instilled motivation to engage and collaborate with fellow performers. Outcomes observed from the Resonance-based performances indicated that technologies incorporating co-located social play present a powerful tool for individuals with intellectual disability: enhancing social engagement and motivating them to participate in highly sophisticated creative experiences that positively reinforce their rightfully dignified standing within evolved communities.

2.2 Wheelchair DJ

Wheelchair DJ is an interactive musical instrument controlled by the physical movement of a sports wheelchair augmented with amplified sound and LED lights. The artwork provides users with playful ways to mix and play audio tracks based on their physical strength and functional control of the wheelchair. Wheelchair DJ incorporates gyro sensors inside both wheels to capture rotation speed of each wheel and sends the data to an audio microcontroller (Raspberry Pi^{TM}) under the seat. The rotation speed of the wheels controls the playback and tempo of the music digitally stored on the microcontroller (Fig. 4).

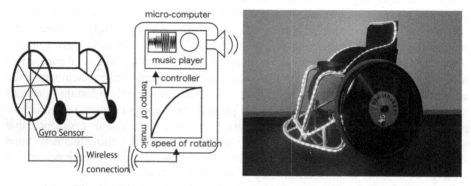

Fig. 4. The system configuration and appearance of Wheelchair DJ

The wheelchair user, or player, can control the tempo of music by adjusting the rotational speed and turning direction of the wheels on the wheelchair. We consider the rotational control of the wheel as analogous to a Dee Jay spinning and scratching vinyl music records on a turntable. The LED lights mounted on the wheelchair blink in synchronization with the music as additional user feedback for individuals with a hearing impairment.

There are many environmental, economic and psychological barriers from the perspective of wheelchair users that make it difficult for them to participate in social activities [23]. Many of these barriers are compounded by negative public perceptions of the wheelchair which is often viewed as an undesirable piece of clinical equipment, and an anachronistic symbol of dependency on others, especially within medical care services [24]. The challenge within social disability models is changing the negative perception of wheelchair users to that of an individual with specific expertise, ability and positive self-identity. To address this challenge, we draw upon inclusive design principles, a design philosophy that aims to consider people with varying functional capabilities and responds to the rights of people with disability during the design process [25]. By modifying the configuration of the wheelchair we aimed to redefine ability identity and provide new modes of self-expression beyond function [26].

In developing Wheelchair DJ we considered sensory, cognitive and motor dimensions of user capability to support inclusive design [27]. Regarding sensory function, we considered the level of auditory output directly scaled to the speed of movement (i.e. acceleration and deceleration) and directional control (i.e. wheel rotation) of the wheelchair. This type of control is coupled to the users cognitive/procedural knowledge of the wheelchair, making the device intuitive and easily understood with minimum instruction to play. Finally, we considered motor capabilities related to both the lower-limbs as well as the upper-limb. Individual differences in upper-limb strength are accommodated in the Wheelchair DJ system design that adjusts audio playback speed linked to the angular velocity of the wheels when users control and move the wheelchair.

The prototype version of the work was developed in collaboration junkwith Osamu Jareo, a choreographer and dancer who organized a dance performance project in cooperation with German performing art theatre, Theatre Thikwa, and Japanese performing arts theatre group Arts Theatre dB Kobe. Wheelchair DJ was incorporated in one scene for a public performance called Thikwas Plus Junkan Project (Theatre Thikwa, Berlin, 2012 and Kyoto Experiment, Kyoto, 2012). Wheelchair dance is a contemporary form of stage performance and social dance. Wheelchair dancers typically move faster than able-bodied dancers, and view the wheelchair as an extension of the body [28]. Wheelchair performance has the effect of prompting the public to change perceptions of disability and highlights the possibilities of participation and competencies developed through dance [29].

The aim of using Wheelchair DJ for this dance performance was to augment the movement of wheelchair dancers on stage, and to encourage the audience to alter their perceptions of disability. The Wheelchair DJ audio control design was iteratively refined to include adjustments for speed and agility to control audio playback following the advice of wheelchair dancer Nobuhiro Fukusumi who used the prototype for the performances (Fig. 5).

Fig. 5. Wheelchair DJ in the stage performance "Thikwa Plus Junkan Project"

After the performance, the director and wheelchair dancer provided feedback on their experience. They expressed that Wheelchair DJ was able to expand alternative means of communication between the performer and the audience. They suggested that it increased improvisational possibilities for the performer through augmenting body movement with sound and encouraged experimentation in dance motion on the stage that was playful and fun. The wheelchair dancer commented, *"I enjoyed being able to move on my own and found that I could do something different. I've figured out what's possible in a wheelchair. Through dancing, I found out that there are various types of people, I enjoyed meeting them."* This commentary suggests wheelchair dance may motivate wheelchair users to take part in community dance-based activity. He also suggested that the Wheelchair DJ could be used more generally by others participating in creative activities beyond stage performance.

In 2015, Wheelchair DJ was exhibited at the Super Welfare Expo, an annual public event held in Tokyo that promotes the latest equipment including wheelchairs, prosthetics and orthotics, devices to support walking, and equipment for people with visual and hearing impairment. The event gathers designers and artists as well as community members to discuss urban accessibility and mobility, as well as showcase technology to make Tokyo more inclusive and diverse for the city's minorities, and residents with a disability.

Over two days 87 participants who played with Wheelchair DJ were observed and interviewed. The cohort comprised of 10 participants who were wheelchair users and the remaining 77 participants were non-users. Of the majority who did not use wheelchairs, 23 participants reported they were involved with wheelchair users at work or caring for their family. One wheelchair user commented *"Wheelchairs can now be considered entertainment and it made me feel happy"*. Another commented *"Not only is it fun to ride, it potentially changes the image of wheelchairs for others"*. A non-wheelchair user commented *"I had the impression that the wheelchair is not fashionable, however, it seems to be a wheelchair that can make people want to ride, even for people who do not use a wheelchair"*, and another participant suggested *"The idea of enjoying riding a wheelchair itself is exciting and novel. I felt like I was wearing new sneakers"*. All participants reported that the Wheelchair DJ was fun and changed the negative perception of the wheelchair from a device for disadvantaged members in the community to an enabling technology that facilitated play and inclusivity.

3   Implications for an Integrative Approach

To better understand the role of interactive arts in disability we bring together current trends in thinking about participation and community arts, as well as research methods that align with this integrated approach. This requires a full appreciation of (a) the individual's orientation and perspective on interactive digital media; (b) forms of user interaction that can be used flexibly in solo and group-based performances; (c) how group experiences (including workshops) can be designed to best afford opportunities for people with a disability to feel included in community arts projects, and (d) how we can promote social-cultural forms of participation that promote a sense of agency for the individual (and their family) and transform others' attitudes to disability.

The ubiquitous nature of interactive digital media in everyday life has two important implications for interactive arts: first, an increasingly 'mediatized' everyday life offers a new context for participation outside of traditional settings and, second, vast opportunity is afforded the development of digital art technologies and processes that are coherent with the roles digital media play in everyday life. In this context, technology design needs to account for user experience alongside co-creation to ensure smart, effective, feasible, and meaningful solutions. An ethnographic perspective can inform this process of design as well as provide a powerful method to explore and document the unique life stories of individuals with a disability.

Along with traditional (empirical) research design, a *design anthropology perspective* incorporating digital and sensory elements can provide an account of not only the user's current experience of technologies but also of what we can learn through undertaking collaborative ethnographies [30, 31]. This approach has been used successfully to prototype digital design interventions in several fields [32, 33]. This perspective is important to ensure technological design in the arts can be embedded within what is possible and personally desirable for participants with a disability. This knowledge can inform in a very meaningful way the design of interactive (digital) art technologies for the development needs and everyday use of people with a disability. Ultimately, the experience of engaging in community arts will be meaningful, fun, shared, viable and not isolated from their daily lives.

So, what does a *design anthropology perspective* look like in practice? A tailored visual-sensory ethnography research method can provide a qualitative evaluation and documentation of participants' experiences. Following film and ethnographic documentary theories and practice, *video ethnographies* can be developed and used as a vehicle for creating empathetic audio-visual narratives [32]. This would involve a process of collaborative filmmaking between an ethnographic filmmaker and participants with a disability, bringing to the fore the experiential, sensory and emotional elements of the use of the digital technologies in art making. The video materials that are produced can also feed transmedia narratives for a web-based presence. When these personal narratives are combined with data drawn from more quantitative (self-report) measures, key aspects of personal change and development are brought to the fore in a very contextualised way, fleshing out components of the fPRC model in a manner that objective measures alone cannot.

4   Conclusion

In this paper we have explored the fPRC framework as a critical guide to view participation in community-based arts contexts for individuals with a disability. Through the lens of the fPRC, the two interactive artworks discussed highlight that *participation as a means* may lead to improved person-related constructs such as heightened sense of self-efficacy, preferences, belonging to a group, and the development of specific competencies that can be carried forward. Inclusive technology design in the arts may further enhance the opportunities and developmental needs for people with a disability and act as a catalyst that extends the invitation to participate in cultural activities and expands individuals' preferences. Rather than diminish the role of the professional arts facilitator, technology has the capacity to enable and assist facilitators in the development of creative expression for participants with disability. Indeed, Hullick's long term engagement as a mentor for The Amplified Elephants has led to them being legitimately recognised as an independent sound art ensemble and invites us to consider inclusive creative performances as the mainstream.

Ethnographic approaches may provide us with sensitive and non-intrusive ways to evaluate the design of interactive digital arts in community settings and the impact of individual experience through participation alongside their able-bodied peers. The challenge is not to construe and measure interactive digital arts as therapeutic interventions for treatment of a health condition (although health benefits may occur). Rather, the aim is to undermine prejudices about disability and evaluate how interactive arts can enhance environments, attendance and involvement as indicated in user responses to Wheelchair DJ, and foster self-growth and activity competence via shared participation in group activities (e.g. in the context of the performances using Resonance). This paper provides a first step in understanding how fPRC, ethnographic approaches, inclusive design, interactive arts technology and community arts might coalesce to evaluate the longer-term outcomes and skillsets that people with disability develop as artists and productive contributors to the arts.

Acknowledgements. Resonance is supported by an Australian Research Council (ARC) Linkage Grant LP110200802, and Synapse Grant awarded by the Australia Council for the Arts. Wheelchair DJ is supported by JSPS KAKENHI Grant Number JP25510017.

References

1. Koritsas, S., Hagiliassis, N., Cuzzillo, C.: Social Inclusion of Adults with Disability: A Survey of Ability First Australia and Cerebral Palsy Australia. Scope Australia, Melbourne (2016)
2. Dunphy, K., Kuppers, P.: Picture This: Increasing the cultural partcipation of people with a disability in Victoria. In: Brophy, C., (ed.) State Government of Victoria, Office for Disability, Department of Planning and Community Development Melbourne (2008)
3. Reddihough, D.S., Meehan, E., Stott, N.S., Delacy, M.J., Australian Cerebral Palsy Register Group: The national disability insurance scheme: a time for real change in Australia. Dev. Med. Child Neurol. **58**, 66–70 (2016)
4. WHO, The International Classification of Function, Disability and Heatlth (ICF). World Health Organization: Geneva (2001)
5. Rosenbaum, P., Stewart, D.: The world health organization international classification of functioning, disability, and health: a model to guide clinical thinking, practice and research in the field of cerebral palsy. Semin. Pediatr. Neurol. **11**(1), 5–10 (2004)
6. Granlund, M.: Participation–challenges in conceptualization, measurement and intervention. Child Care Health Dev. **39**(4), 470–473 (2013)
7. Imms, C., Granlund, M., Wilson, P.H., Steenbergen, B., Rosenbaum, P.L., Gordon, A.M.: Participation, both a means and an end: a conceptual analysis of processes and outcomes in childhood disability. Dev. Med. Child Neurol. **59**(1), 16–25 (2017)
8. King, G., et al.: Residential immersive life skills programs for youth with physical disabilities: a pilot study of program opportunities, intervention strategies, and youth experiences. Res. Dev. Disabil. **55**, 242–255 (2016)

9. Australia Council for the Arts. Connecting Australians: Results of the National Arts Partcipation Survey (2017)
10. Hullick, J.: The rise of the amplified elephants. Int. J. Commun. Music **6**(2), 219–233 (2013)
11. Agency for Cultural Affairs Japan. Survey of cultural and art appreciation activities and creative activities for disabled people (in Japanese). (2017). http://www.bunka.go.jp/seisaku/geijutsubunka/shogaisha_bunkageijutsu/pdf/r1402941_01.pdf. Accessed 14 Aug 2019
12. Mckay, G.: Community Music: A Handbook. Russell House, Lyme Regis (2005)
13. Challis, Ben P.: Assistive synchronised music improvisation. In: De Michelis, G., Tisato, F., Bene, A., Bernini, D. (eds.) ArtsIT 2013. LNICST, vol. 116, pp. 49–56. Springer, Heidelberg (2013). https://doi.org/10.1007/978-3-642-37982-6_7
14. Duckworth, J., Wilson, P.H.: Embodiment and play in designing an interactive art system for movement rehabilitation. Second Nature **2**(1), 120–137 (2010)
15. Mumford, N., Duckworth, J., Thomas, P.R., Shum, D., Williams, G., Wilson, P.H.: Upper limb virtual rehabilitation for traumatic brain injury: Initial evaluation of the elements system. Brain Inj. **24**(5), 780–791 (2010)
16. Mumford, N., Duckworth, J., Thomas, P.R., Shum, D., Williams, G., Wilson, P.H.: Upper-limb virtual rehabilitation for traumatic brain injury: a preliminary within-group evaluation of the elements system. Brain Inj. **26**(2), 166–176 (2012)
17. Duckworth, J., Thomas, Patrick R., Shum, D., Wilson, Peter H.: Designing Co-located Table-top Interaction for Rehabilitation of Brain Injury. In: Marcus, A. (ed.) DUXU 2013. LNCS, vol. 8013, pp. 391–400. Springer, Heidelberg (2013). https://doi.org/10.1007/978-3-642-39241-2_43
18. Rick, J., Marshall, P., Yuill, N.: Beyond one-size-fits-all: How interactive tabletops support collaborative learning. In: IDC 2011. Ann Arbor, USA (2011)
19. Gajadhar, B., de Kort, Y.A.W., Ijsselsteijn, W.A.: Rules of engagement: influence of co-player presence on player involvement in digital games. Int. J. Gaming Comput. Mediated Simul. **1**(3), 14–27 (2009)
20. Ishii, H.: Tangible Bits: beyond pixels. In: TEI 2008, pp. xv–xxv. AMC Press, New York (2008)
21. Rizzo, A.A.: A SWOT analysis of the field of virtual reality rehabilitation and therapy. Presence **14**(2), 119–146 (2005)
22. Ishii, H., Ullmer, B.: Tangible bits: towards seamless interfaces between people, bits and atoms. In: SIGCHI Conference on Human Factors in Computing Systems, Atlanta, GA. ACM Press (1997)
23. Rimmer, J.H., Riley, B., Wang, E., Rauworth, A., Jurkowski, J.: Physical activity participation among persons with disabilities: barriers and facilitators. Am. J. Prev. Med. **26**(5), 419–425 (2004)
24. Sapey, B., Stewart, J., Donaldson, G.: Increases in wheelchair use and perceptions of disablement. Disabil. Soc. **20**(5), 489–505 (2005)
25. Clarkson, P.J., Coleman, R., Keates, S., Lebbon, C.: Inclusive Design: Design for the Whole Population. Springer Science & Business Media (2013)
26. Bennett, C.L., Cen, K., Steele, K.M., Rosner, D.K.: An intimate laboratory? prostheses as a tool for experimenting with identity and normalcy. In: Proceedings of the 2016 CHI Conference on Human Factors in Computing Systems. ACM (2016)
27. Persad, U., Langdon, P., Clarkson, J.: Characterising user capabilities to support inclusive design evaluation. Univ. Access Inf. Soc. **6**(2), 119–135 (2007)
28. Whatley, S.: Dance and disability: the dancer, the viewer and the presumption of difference. Res. Dance Educ. **8**(1), 5–25 (2007)
29. Zitomer, M.R., Reid, G.: To be or not to be–able to dance: Integrated dance and children's perceptions of dance ability and disability. Res. Dance Educ. **12**(2), 137–156 (2011)

30. Donovan, J., Gunn, W.: Moving from objects to possibilities. In: Design and Anthropology. Ashgate Farnham, pp. 121–134 (2012)
31. Pink, S., Leder Mackley, K.: Re-enactment methodologies for everyday life research: art therapy insights for video ethnography. Vis. Stud. 29(2), 146–154 (2014)
32. Pink, S.: Going forward through the world: thinking theoretically about first person perspective digital ethnography. Integr. Psychol. Behav. Sci. 49(2), 239–252 (2015)
33. Ardévol, E.,Gómez-Cruz, E.: Digital ethnography and media practices. In: The International Encyclopedia of Media Studies, pp. 498–518 (2012)

Nature and Nurturance Across the Ages: Modest Means for Modern Times

Henry J. Moller[1,2,3,4(✉)], Lee Saynor[2], Mark Chignell[3], and John Waterworth[5] (iD)

[1] Department of Psychiatry, Faculty of Medicine, University of Toronto,
1 King's College Circle, Toronto, ON M5S 1A8, Canada
[2] PRAXIS Holistic Health, 101-785 Carlaw Ave, Toronto, ON M4K 3L1, Canada
drmoller@praxisholistic.ca
[3] Department of Mechanical and Industrial Engineering, Faculty of Applied Sciences,
University of Toronto, 5 King's College Rd, Toronto, ON M5S 3G8, Canada
[4] Music and Health Research Collaboratory, University of Toronto,
80 Queens Park, Toronto, ON M5S 2C5, Canada
[5] Department of Informatics, Umeå University, 901 87 Umeå, Sweden

Abstract. Access to leisure and wellbeing can be difficult to arrive at due to constraints in health, income, location and time. With shifting demographics (inversion of the aging pyramid) and increasing urbanization, there is an increasingly urgent need to improve access to leisure activities, particularly for those living in crowded cities or who have limited mobility.

We propose the use of 3D capture of majestic nature scenes and their display in a therapeutic context, as an affordable way to enhance well-being and to provide care to those lacking adequate access to leisure and wellbeing. Our approach to the application of VR-based nature therapy involves immersive media interfaces employing either contemplative (mindfulness-based stress reaction - MBSR) or active (mind/body based behavioural activation) approaches, both using environmental cues salient to end-users and developed within an inclusive design paradigm. The end goal is to employ immersive virtual reality and suitably designed human-machine interfaces to allow individuals of varying ages, means and abilities to continue to enjoy an optimal level of presence and engagement in the real world to preserve quality (and perhaps quantity) of life.

Keywords: Virtual reality · Mindfulness meditation · MBSR · Leisure ·
Wellbeing · Nature therapy · Presence · Disability · Public health policy · History
of medicine

1   Background

1.1   The Reality of Living in Modern Times

"Leisure" can be defined as either a set of "freely chosen activities" or a state of "perceived freedom". These, in turn, could involve either *freedom to* or *freedom (away) from*; a more or less preferred experiential state. "Wellbeing" has variously been defined as

A. Brooks and E. I. Brooks (Eds.): ArtsIT 2019/DLI 2019, LNICST 328, pp. 539–558, 2020.
https://doi.org/10.1007/978-3-030-53294-9_39

a composite state of being comfortable, healthy or happy. In many of today's modern, developed societies, access to leisure and wellbeing can be difficult to arrive at due to constraints in health, income, location and time.

The varied transformations of modern times are a mixed blessing. While on the one hand there is a steady and seemingly boundless stream of advances in knowledge and creativity, on the other hand there are ever-accumulating challenges to individual and collective survival. It is the role and responsibility of the applied arts and sciences to not only ensure our survival as a species, but also to improve our wellbeing. Our research group has primarily viewed these phenomena through the pragmatic perspective of an applied science lens, looking to integrate the diverse disciplines of neuroscience, informatics and computer technology (ICT), the visual and audio-recording arts, human factors engineering, public health policy as well as recreation and leisure studies into a unified through multi-faceted holistic approach. While accumulation of knowledge (i.e. the scientific endeavour at large) is both a desirable and necessary ingredient, it is the practical actions taken, and moreover the observed achievable results, that are the arbiters of progress in the human condition.

Specific challenges we seek to address in our research and development efforts are driven by sociological, biological and technological factors. It may be casually observed that the "developed world" finds itself in a position of relative scarcity currently, with diminished public resources apparently available for health and wellbeing. This in particular applies to the timely and helpful provision of (quality of) life-sustaining goods and services to those who are at highest risk of adverse outcomes (disease, disability and death) due to constraints in physical/mental health, as well as available time and finances. In particular, the advancing "silver tsunami" of a rapidly aging population in the developed world is posing a public policy challenge, with a widening economic disparity affecting the affordability of basic means of survival (at worst) and achievement of "the good life" (at best). Given this reality, we contemplate ethical means by which some of the more disadvantaged members of society-at-large might be served in an era of shrinking public resources. In the following discussion we focus on: (i) elderly individuals at risk of institutionalization (i.e. loss of liberty and leisure affordances) and (ii) individuals affected by stress/anxiety/trauma; i.e. two groups who are particularly affected by current circumstances. In a medical system still focused on disease models of health, the paradigm of "wellbeing creation" has been a focus of alternative medicine approaches, even though we would argue that wellbeing creation has a higher ratio of benefits to harms. As previously posited [1] a significant component of survival and wellbeing is an organism's ability to be aware of and interact with its external environment. Alertness, task-readiness and immersion are various terms used in the medical and human factors literature to describe human interaction with both real and simulated environments. These terms fall within the general construct of "presence" [2], which is related to the neuroscience of consciousness and involves some degree of fluctuation both in terms of a given time/space and in changes over time within a given lifespan of an individual or collective.

1.2 Virtually Addressing the Challenges

For at least the past two decades we have been concerned with the concept of presence and the conditions under which it varies [2]. "Presence" is a psychological construct in which an individual feels a sense of "Being" in a particular environment, whether they are geospatially in this location or not. To this end, the degree to which a person feels their own embodied presence in their environment depends on the balance of attention between internal and external information processing. We are primarily concerned with first-person egocentric experiences, in the physical world and via digital technology.

VR has gradually emerged as a societally relevant and game-changing multidisciplinary manifestation of presence at a distance. Canadian media scholar Marshall McLuhan, prophesized a connected multicultural "global village" in the 1960's where the "medium is the massage" (sic., i.e., "medium is the message") [3] and where technology allowed a melting of barriers posed by the nature of our being in space and time [4]. Historical models of healing that have sustained individuals, communities and populations, though surprisingly similar in essence throughout the world, are not always readily addressed within conventional biomedical or managed healthcare schemas. It may well be worth re-examining some of these older healing models, as enlightened clinicians and researchers navigate towards sustainable future-oriented models that allow for the creation of transformative health journeys respectful of our innate human nature. This notion created the imperative to "Windows to the World", a 3-year project funded by the federal Canadian (Social Sciences and Humanities Research Council (SSHRC) agency, which has recently reached its completion, and ongoing funded endeavours with Canada's technology and aging network AGE-WELL, a federal granting agency whose official objective is to enable graceful aging across environments using technology to support wellness, engagement and longevity.

Since many age-specific mental health problems can be related to maladaptive cognitive strategies for engaging with and appropriately processing the external environment in relation to the self, this approach calls for the development of technological support for mediating and retraining such cognitive strategies. It also provides a rationale for, and approach to, the design of interactive immersive environments in which the level of presence – reflecting the balance of internal/external information processing – can be mediated for therapeutic purposes.

1.3 A Macro-view: The Past Becomes the Future Present

A macro-view of mental health public policy must be considered beyond a mere technocratic bioengineering perspective and solutions are needed that can address and remedy what is ultimately a societal challenge [5]. Added into the mix in the current political economic climate of the developed world is the widening "luxury gap" separating the affluent from the disenfranchised, reminiscent of the expanding disparity between rich and poor in the late Victorian era. At that time, the labour requirements of the industrial revolution meant that much of the work-force had moved from agrarian to urban centres, resulting in both psychosocial malaise and not infrequently, a sense of *anomie* and disconnectedness of the new working class in rapidly industrialized city centres [6, 7].

Thus, a new epidemic of emotional unwellness (with the worst symptom being suicides) was a prominent feature of the growing pains of the new century.

It can further be argued that the role of depression as a leading modernity-related cause of illness and disability globally [8] can be attributed, at least in part, to a combination of factors including a growing inequality, "modernization" of the work-force and a sense of uprootedness and anomie [7] for many of those with an uncertain future in the modern world. The dark impressionistic painting *"Le Suicidé"* by Eduoard Manet (see Fig. 1) could be seen as emblematic of earlier "modern times", and suicide remains prevalent in present times when the collective fabric of society is challenged by an increase in individualism and a mechanization/commodification of our human qualities. Thus, many individuals are no longer able to maintain a footing in society, and/or our society is no longer willing or able to accommodate the individual and lighten the social burden of illness and institutionalization. When people are deemed to be "non-contributing members" of society's total factors of production, then the dilemmas may be more socio-economic than medical in nature.

Fig. 1. *"Le Suicidé"* Édouard Manet, (1881 Foundation E.G. Bührle, Zurich, Switzerland.) Whereas within classic academic artistic literary and cultural circles, depiction of suicide could only fit within the genre of history painting—where death and suicide would be placed within a narrative associated with sacrifice, idealism, or heroism. Manet's work appears to lack this sort of overarching grand meta-narrative; by contrast, the viewer is not provided neither a time, nor a place, nor even a relatable protagonist.

1.4 Scanning Through the Past, Lightly and Darkly

This modernist health-care story began with the gradual deinstitutionalization of the mentally ill, pioneered by forward-thinking humanitarian physicians such as Dr. Phillipe

Pinel in the pre- and post-revolutionary period of the 1800's, as well as the ascent of science as an increasingly credible societal narrative [9], (as depicted in Figs. 2 and 3). The use of arts and leisure as a bridge to wellbeing was in fact pioneered at Pinel's poor-house urban asylum by the so-called "School of Salpêtrière" [10]. This involved, amongst other therapeutically intended endeavours, the encouragement of creative activities such as the performance of music or theatre, within a conceptual framework reminiscent of some of Swiss psychiatrist C.G. Jung's later theories in the Victorian era and beyond. These suggested that *autonomously directed self-growth*, particularly if paired with a sense of playfulness and growing awareness of ones innate spiritual nature, served as a legitimate pathway to true healing of the psyche.

At the turn of the previous century, European doctors increasingly recommended the "mountain cure" or a "getaway to the seaside" to patients with ailments within this spectrum, with a recognition that redemption for the illness-inducing miasmas of metropolitan life might result from a retreat to the refreshing mountain air, ideally paired with healing springs. German romantic authors such as Herman Hesse and Thomas Mann (both incidentally also known to have suffered from bouts of debilitating melancholia, a classic affliction of the romantic poet) are known to have sought solace in mountain sanatorium health retreats (MSHRs), [11, 12], popularizing the practice of seeking out the Alps, Mittel-Europa's natural healing springs or the Mediterranean seaside for wellbeing optimization. Meanwhile, the Victorian gulf between have- and have-nots had widened, and seeking wellness in the spa/sanitarium became a common practice of the well-to-do. In contrast, society's disenfranchised were priced out of accessing this previously publicly available health option, typically being once again relegated to asylums and hospitals of the city to become research "guinea-pig" in trials of new chemical and electromechanical treatments. Mental asylums often resembled barbaric prisons, only many decades later being reformed by a movement towards a "moral management of mental illness" [13].

New technologies resulting from the industrial revolution spawned modern chemical medicine. The serendipitous discoveries of euphorigenic/antidepressant qualities of the anti-tuberculosis drug iproniazid [14, 15] and apparent calming properties of lithium salts [16] spawned the era of so-called rational development of psychotropic drugs, including antidepressants, hypnotics/sedatives, mood-stabilizers and antipsychotics. These drugs have destigmatized mental illness by focusing on organic aspects rather than contextual factors such as moral failings of the individual or her parents. However, while drugs have often being often able to maintain and/or improve symptom profiles of those affected, adverse and iatrogenic effects continue to haunt biological psychiatry [17]. Mental health care necessarily remains an art as well as a science; psychiatry, even within the pantheon of medical disciplines, does not readily lend itself to a cookie-cutter reductionist approach which ignores the human factor (to borrow from the language of industrial engineering).

There have been a variety of structured psychotherapies (e.g. cognitive behavioural therapy, interpersonal therapy, etc.) developed to both enhance the evidence-based medicine credibility of psychiatry and contain costs in an era of increasing health-care economization. It is only in recent years that the renaissance of the actually quite ancient therapeutic avenue of meditation (the most recognized being mindfulness-based stress reduction –MBSR) has re-emerged to take its place alongside a variety of pharmaceutical

Fig. 2. William Hogarth, *The Madhouse,* (1735, Sir John Sloane Museum, London, U.K.). This painting, plate 8 in Hogarth's *A Rake's Progress* more than hints at the implications of social iniquities directly related to causes of mental illness and the most often desperate conditions in European asylums. Image released under Creative Commons CC-BY-NC-ND (3.0 Unported).

Fig. 3. *Pinel Freeing the Insane* by Robert Fleury (1797–1890), depicts Dr. Philippe Pinel, chief physician of Pitie-Salpêtrière Hospital in Paris, ordering the removal of chains from mentally disabled patients in 1795. Pinel (1745–1826) is considered the founder of modern psychiatry. Courtesy of the National Library of Medicine.

and psychotherapeutic avenues recommended to clinicians in treatment guidelines. Meditation is increasingly *en vogue* not only in medical/psychological settings, but also as a self-care or lifestyle approach that promotes resilience, quality of life and wellbeing. As a parallel phenomenon, the re-emergence of holistic health-care models is highlighting the value of nature-based environments in healing and personal transformation.

In this paper, we explore the internally experienced world of a VR-based meditation program constructed on a base of externally derived natural environments and used in a health-care setting. To this end, we have designed what is essentially a "built environment of the mind" that incorporates multimodal display of a majestic naturescape experienced immersively, comparable to, e.g., a dream, reflection or memory [18]. Technology's impact on human cognitive functioning appears to have significantly impacted this capacity, suggesting a need to rethink presence [1, 2].

2   Back to Nature as a Therapy

2.1   Historical Underpinnings: Theory and Praxis

Most credible interventional built-environment research has focused on physical geospatial design of urban spaces, e.g., for encouraging physical exercise [19]. In recent years, VR researchers have been able to demonstrate that immersive multimedia-based virtual environments can authentically simulate real human conscious experiences [20]. The existence of mirror neurons [21] appears to prove that people can develop internal models of experience, and the finding that imagery (imagined experience) recapitulates the perceptual analyses associated with actual sensory experience [22] provide powerful motivation for the use of VR experience of majestic mountain ranges, serene seasides or rolling meadows in place of the real thing for therapeutic or recreational purposes [23].

"Leisure", as perceived freedom, is an underappreciated enabling and chief limiting factor of wellbeing [24]. This reality is not always readily addressed in conventional biomedical approaches, and challenges us to look to both the past and future to inform our present. Patients with stress- and/or anxiety-related ailments, when asked to re-imagine a recent "wellbeing experience", from a time they might have not felt a sense of malaise or distress, frequently report holiday vacations as a source of solace. However, while the anticipation and ensuing preparation for a get-away, as well as the sojourn itself, are often cited as a reprieve from stress and worries, the sustained duration of a substantial wellbeing effect beyond a week is rarely observed. Not infrequently, souvenirs, novelties, artefacts, photographs or other memorabilia are therefore employed by leisure-seeking tourists, usually in an unstructured and idiosyncratic manner, to re-imagine the (hopefully) positive experience and re-inspire the seekers of inspiration and wellbeing in their routine everyday lives. We seek to extend the historical and cultural legacy [25] of the medically recommended natural wellness retreats of yesteryear to our current era's digital media interventions, which can potentially provide similar benefits at less cost, and less disruption to the rhythms of modern life. To this end, the fundamental question being asked is: *"How can leisure experiences that enhance quality of life and wellbeing be made accessible through immersive VR experiences that do not require (often expensive) travel to of geophysical environments?"* A secondary query then pertains to how one might optimize these in terms of aesthetic appeal, impact and resonance.

2.2 Seeking Beauty and Meaning, Naturally

Returning to historical considerations of mental health interventions involving meaning-making through nature, one might consider again the European Romantic movement of the 19th century, where "new enlightenment" artists such as Caspar Friedrich (see Figs. 4a, b, c) William Blake, and William Turner sought to depict nature as a "divine creation, to be set against the artifice of human civilization" [26, 27].

Part of the intention of this movement was a "get back to nature" theme; in a sense, a veneration of nature as a manifestation of the unspoiled work of God, as per the *"Deus sive Natura"* pantheism of 17th century Dutch philosopher and enlightenment pioneer Baruch Spinoza (1632–1677). This was the view that God and nature are interchangeable, that there is no distinction between the creator and the creation. In other words, God is everywhere, and everything that exists is a modification of God [28]. The subsequent romantic enlightenment period thus highlighted nature itself as the primary subject, and as with the preceding/overlapping impressionist movement, allowed a more inclusive voyeur's perspective of scenery, inviting the viewer into a near-participatory role in the *mise en scène* depicted. In particular, Friedrich's paintings often included a human observer/participant in a central observatory role, typically as a (virtual) avatar, back turned to the audience of the art, i.e. a metaphysical convergence of a human presence in diminished perspective amid expansive landscapes [27].

(a)   (b)   (c)

Fig. 4. a, b, c. Selected masterpieces by Caspar David Friedrich (1774–1840).

Figure 4a *Wanderer above the Sea of Fog* (1818, Kunsthalle Hamburg). Friedrich's best-known work demonstrates his typical "Rückenblick" (back to the viewer) perspective placing the human in awe of the splendour of the natural world, "suggesting at once mastery over a landscape and the insignificance of the individual within it. We see no face, so it's impossible to know whether the prospect facing the young man is exhilarating, or terrifying, or both" [29].

Figure 4b With its ethereal illusion of depth, *The Monk by the Sea* (1810, Neue Nationalgallerie, Berlin) was likely Friedrich's most radical composition. The vast expanse of sea and sky beyond the diminutive figure of the monk standing on the shores' sands invites the viewer into the humbling position of standing before the vastness of nature and the presence of God.

Figure 4c *The Stages of Life* (1835, Museum der Bildenden Künste, Leipzig.) In essence, a meditation on the artist's own mortality, the painting depicting five ships at various distances from the shore. The foreground similarly shows five figures at different stages of life [30].

2.3   Practical Applications for Modernity and Beyond

Informed by these aesthetic (and ethical) principles, of engaging with nature as a pathway to enlightenment and source of potential healing of the psyche, we have explored the principle of 1st person perspective point-of-view (POV) to engage with nature in a meditative/contemplative fashion while employing modern technological tools, i.e. immersive 3D audiovisual media.

Employing bucolic sites such as the Northeastern Swiss Alpine region and the Lake District of Northern England as practical case studies, we seek to address the public policy imperative of equitable access to wellbeing environments such as mountains, meadows or the seaside as leisure opportunities within an increasingly socioeconomically divided and urbanized developed world. We look to supplement earlier approaches to handling stress and malaise through visits to therapeutic (natural or artificial) environments with the use of immersive VR. We also seek to explore perceived authenticity, impact and resonance of our "built environment" to clarify aesthetic preferences of "naturally" captured naturescapes (shot using 3D film) in comparison to gradations of "synthetically" created computer generated imagery (CGI).

We focus on immersive media technologies, i.e., virtual reality environments (VRE) as therapeutic interventions [31], while remaining mindful of historical and scientific trends in mental healthcare involving meditation/MBSR. On a more historiographic and psychogeographic level, we are interested in better understanding the mental health effects of a VR simulation of a journey to an environment with an established reputation for conferring wellbeing on the ailing. An example is an Alpine mountain environment, of which eminent central European writers of the maturing industrial age such as Thomas Mann or Hermann Hesse might have approved, as a remedy in times of physical and/or emotional weakness and lassitude [11, 12] (see Figs. 5a, b, c).

(a)   **(b)**   **(c)**

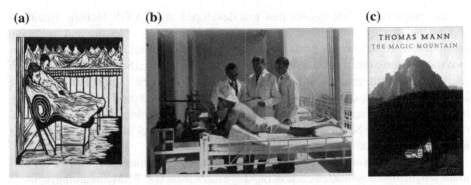

Fig. 5. a, b, c. Victorian era depictions of invalids and urban industrial age escapists seeking therapeutic MSHR refuge at Bad Ragaz in the North-Eastern Swiss Alps for conditions such as tuberculosis and rheumatism as well as mental wellbeing, popularized by European Romantic writers such as Thomas Mann and Herman Hesse.

2.4 Back to Modern Times and Age-Old Problems

We can identify various sub-optimal age-related ways of being in the world that preclude effective functioning, and relate these to the habitual levels of presence experienced by the individual. We suggest that, other things being equal, very young children tend to feel highly present in their environment while conscious, whereas the very old generally do not. Because of age-related changes in cognitive strategies, abilities and habits, the strength of the feeling of presence tends to be a diminishing resource over the course of an individual's lifetime. For example, young children may suffer from attentional problems, where events in the immediate environment are overly distracting. We see this as an over-active presence mechanism, which we term *hyperpresence* [2]. As people become older, more of their waking time is spent in a state of absence – in reminiscence, stories and daydreaming – reflecting predominantly internal information processing that results in a generally lower sense of being present in their external, physical environment [4, 32]. At some stage, the ability to be present at the right time – giving timely attention to the environment as needed to carry out their plans – may become lost in what we term *hyperabsence* [1, 2]. Focusing on such developmental changes, we foresee several practical strategies for designing interactive technologies to help alleviate cognitive and behavioral problems, by restoring a more balanced relation between individual and environment. Lead users of greatest interest at the present time are (i) adults experiencing clinically significant stress and anxiety, as empirically evaluated in an urban mental health clinic setting, and (ii) community-dwelling elderly individuals at risk of institutionalization, as well as elders with mental health needs already residing in long-term care.

3 Methods/Apparatus

3.1 General Concept

We are employing a VR system that was developed at PRAXIS Holistic Health to capture and display the required immersive content to create a "leisure and wellbeing environment" for immersive presentation. To date, five exploratory 3-D video data capture sessions have taken place at Mount Saentis and Bad Ragaz (Switzerland), Feldkirch (Austria) and northern England's Lake District as well as the Parliament Hill park above London, U.K. Audio material was subsequently composed and produced, using 3D spatialized sound techniques, at Tileyard Production Studios (London, U.K.). Further visual content continues to be gathered locally in various scenic locales in Ontario, Canada with local post-production.

We are chiefly using roughly 30-min audiovisual displays, congruent with the approximate length of a consolidated cycle of rapid eye movement (i.e. REM, dreaming) episode in the course of a night of healthy adult sleep [4]. As outlined in a recent review of neurophysiologic aspects of presence and immersive experiences [2], we accept that consciousness is dynamic and fluid even during wakefulness; however, it is more stereotyped and phasic during the largely subliminal process of sleep, which also shows characteristic variations throughout the human lifespan. Using this framework, it is within the REM dreaming state's "protoconsciousness" that perceived perceptual stimuli are sorted and ultimately stored or deleted via more enduring memory shelving and retrieval, i.e. the basis of transformation within a perceptual experience [33].

3.2 Filming

During filming, a tripod-mounted cluster of 7 GoPro action cameras (see Fig. 6) is deployed at a site of natural beauty. Increasingly, scenes are sought with: dramatic horizons like mountains, sunrises and sunsets, nearby foliage, a breeze or weather, and animals. Human agents are avoided, including the cinematographer. The cameras are remotely activated and a sharp marker sound is produced. Unprocessed video averages 45 min to 1 ½ h per camera prior to apparatus retrieval. Special attention is paid to camera battery levels and protecting video data once captured.

3.3 Post-production

Each shoot's video files are time-synched, stitched into a sphere, colour matched, and cropped in Mistika VR software prior to export with 360-degree metadata. To this date over 360 min of panoramic videos have been produced. Visual effects are applied as needed in Unity:

- *Colour tint* - a yellow hue warms peripheral vision
- *Rising mist* - particles emanate from user
- *Flock of crows*-10 birds fly to random waypoints in the sky
- *Light oscillation* -flashing lights paired with EEG phase of program

These effects were originally selected for a study of aesthetic preferences where they are randomized and evaluated.

3.4 Audio

Audio was developed based on two principles: arranging music to match restorative electro-encephalographic (EEG) frequencies and utilizing 3D sound to enhance immersion. In contrast to the state of wakefulness, there are slower brain-wave frequencies associated with calm awareness (alpha-EEG: 8–12 Hz or beats per second), reflective and evocative dreamlike thinking of rapid-eye-movement (REM) sleep (theta-EEG: 4–8 Hz), and deep dreamless sleep (delta-EEG: 1–4 Hz) [34]. As the rhythmic flow of selected ambient and classical music is known to entrain alpha- and theta-EEG [35, 36], similar pieces were incorporated into a continuous mix reflecting a condensed version of natural sleep phases. Recognizing the potential of audio spatialization to create immersion, 3DAudioscape and junXion 4 software were used to move sound around the listener with a joystick. The spatialized audio can be decoded to surround headphones and speaker systems.

Fig. 6. Panoramic camera apparatus

3.5 Delivery – Meditation Program

The complete experience is delivered via an Oculus Go headset. This system was selected over the previous PC-connected HTC Vive for its low cost and portability. With a headset and surround headphones on, the user reclines at a 45–60° position for the approximately 30-min meditation session. Session duration was chosen to contain the ideal length of a nap without sleep inertia and also approximates the duration of an episode of REM or dreaming sleep during consolidated healthy sleep [37] (Fig. 7).

3.6 Embedded Tasks

While meditation can be therapeutic and relaxing, more active interactions with nature or naturalistic scenes can also be beneficial, particularly in cases where people (e.g., older

Fig. 7. Dusk to night panoramic Alpine sunset video (captured at Mt. Saentis, Switzerland) with "Green Dragon" immersive audio mix.

people living in institutional settings) are relatively inactive, or where there are specific clinical goals (such as a reduction in phobic responsiveness). There is a continuum of task engagement in VR scenes ranging from light perceptual engagement (watching a flock of birds as it moves around the scene) to complex problem solving using cues within the scene (e.g., an escape room simulation). Game-based tasks in VR have been used extensively for rehabilitation [38]. As noted in Rizzo's review on clinical VR in mental health therapy [39], VR environments mimicking real or imagined worlds can be applied to engage users in simulations that support aims and mechanics of a specific clinical assessment or therapeutic approach.

3.7 Activation Strategies

Much of the emphasis in task- and simulation-oriented VR has been on rehabilitation and mental health issues. However, there is also considerable scope for using VR, and VR-like environments, for activation. In one approach, people engaging in tasks are rewarded for carrying out activities [40]. An example of this approach is shown in Fig. 8 where the user is using foot pedals in order to watch a dog sledding video. The video plays faster as the user pedals faster, making him feel like he is controlling the experience to some extent. In this case, movement through the scene, and experiencing it as a participant, is the "reward" for the pedaling activity. While this is not technically immersive VR, and regular video is used, it can nevertheless feel immersive. User motivation and engagement with the task can be further increased with competition, where two users each pedal and see their own views of the course on a split-screen, with a map showing who is in front.

Another approach is to create an approximation of VR immersiveness using a kind of 360-degree display, where the viewer can change the viewing angle using a steering wheel. Figure 9 shows a system where there is a set of world travel videos and a button box that the user can use to select particular videos. The figure shows a choice of six continents at the top of the video selection hierarchy. In this application input has been deliberately simplified for older users by using a button box that allows input selections to be made using gross motor movements.

While activation in VR can take many forms, we see considerable potential in a style of VR where a screen is used instead of goggles, but where engagement and involvement come from interaction with the scene and the causal relationship between what the user does and how the scene changes. In this screen-based approach apparent immersion can also be increased using curved displays [41], or via projection in an entire room; this

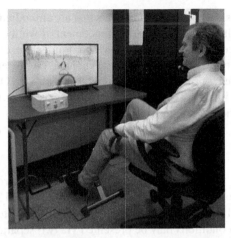

Fig. 8. A user "going dog-sledding" by pedaling. (Centivizer Inc. photo, used with permission)

leaves open the possibility of therapeutic value beyond the individual (i.e. immersive group exposure to a common shared positive experience).

Fig. 9. System for exploring 360° world travel (Centivizer Inc. photo, used with permission)

4 Methods/Protocol

4.1 Objectives

Our research project has the following objective and employs a mixed method qualitative/quantitative research approach to explore our research objectives.

- Assess the relationship between leisure access via immersive reality, and resulting measures of QOL and global mental health,

- Develop a set of physical leisure environments that are embodied as immersive reality, with quantified results concerning their enhancement of wellbeing,
- Gather results concerning the extent to which immersive experiences, delivered through virtual reality platforms can improve subjectively experienced wellbeing,
- Explore the effectiveness of video-only immersive reality (VOIR) vs. gradations of computer-generated imagery (CGI) annotations as interventions to improve subjective wellbeing through the presentation of uplifting environments.

4.2 Subjects

Initial user testing has involved healthy non-clinical adults in order to assay personal preferences in fidelity of visual scenarios, ranging from unaltered 3-D film to three gradations of CGI special effects, i.e. from "natural/real" footage to "synthetic/surreal". These four perceptual conditions may be presented via two separate methodologies: (i) with HMD and headphones (encumbered, immersive VR) (ii) displayed on 70″ LCD screen and external ambient speakers (unencumbered, augmented reality AR). The second phase of user testing will involve a prospective study of adult clinical patients qualifying as having a clinically significant stress/anxiety condition based upon Beck Anxiety Inventory (BAI) scores greater than 11 at the time of baseline assessment, with three separate exposures to the 30-min intervention in the course of a one-week period. Other standardized mental health rating scales [42–46] will be used to gather baseline psychometric data and account for possible variations in a given individual's receptivity and ability to fully immerse him/herself within the experience offered within this methodology (Fig. 10).

Fig. 10. Viewer follows birds over valley at Mt. Saentis, Switzerland in HMD

4.3 Pre-and Post-exposure Metrics (Quantitative)

4.3.1 Composite Wellbeing Scale assessment

Our previously validated 5-item Wellpad scale of subjective medical wellbeing (pain, mood, perceived external stress level, perceived internalized relaxation vs. anxiety and sleep quality, each quantified on a 5-point Likert sliding scale) is used to quantify baseline medical wellbeing [47], with additional items assessing levels of (i) inspiration, (ii) hopefulness and (iii) perceived performance task readiness ("How ready are you to perform the tasks and demands of your daily life?") using a 5-point Likert scale, similar to the Wellpad scale.

4.3.2 Post-exposure Experiential Analysis

We are also interested in better understanding the interface of the person-environment dyad relating to our paradigm, using both quantitative and qualitative assays.

4.3.3 Quantitative Analysis

Beyond the before and after psychometrics outlined above, we seek to parcel out the experiential subjective ratings of: (i) perceived aesthetic appeal, (ii) immersion/lucidity and (iii) resonance/impact of the experience (using a tablet-based easy-to-use 0–100% sliding scale), which will be evaluated immediately following each exposure to the experience.

We do not anticipate simulator sickness of any significance, as subjects are typically resting in a supported supine position during the immersive experience exposure, as opposed to engaging in "real-world" ambulation or engaging in autonomous core body or head motion. Nevertheless, the gold standard brief screening questionnaire for simulator sickness, the Simulator Sickness Questionnaire (SSQ) [48], will be administered after each meditation session in the study to address standard concerns about VR therapy.

4.3.4 Qualitative Analysis

To supplement this quantitative data, we also elicit open-ended qualitative responses to questions of interest in a brief interview including:

- "What problems/difficulties (if any) did you encounter"? (**weltschmerz** item -a qualitative assay of ease-of-use of the experience as well as for interindividual subject attitude variation)
- "What part (if any) of the experience do you recall?" (**sentiment** item – used to explore trends and interindividual variation individual in experience recollection)
- "What about this experience resonates with you?" "What (if any) of this experience can you apply to your real life to improve its quality"? (**resonance** item – used to clarify if subjects perceived an indirect instructional directive from the virtual experience)
- "Please rate on a scale from 1 to 5 how much you felt part of this experience." (**lucidity/immersion** item- to some degree related to the previous item, intended to clarify and correlate degree of perceived presence in context of effect on consciously, and/or subconsciously experienced feeling/cognitive state).

Fig. 11. A flock of crows over sheep moving through the stone circle at Castlerigg, U.K.

To date, the most memorable and resonant elements broadly reported by participants were the presence of dynamic natural "creature features" such as sheep or birds. This was true whether these creatures were embedded in the "real video" (e.g. sheep walking through a stone circle in Fig. 11) or added post-hoc via CGI effects, making this the most successfully "integrated" visual effect. Participants also positively recollected the sun, clouds, mountains, the "spaciousness" of the valley, and the presence of any "unnatural" man-made features in a scene, such as the boulders that make up a stone circle surrounding a green meadow in a scenario captured in England's Lake District. Quite a bit of early user feedback in iterative testing also focused on the immersive audio content. The choice of classical music was more evocative than expected, described by participants at times as "sad", "tense", "too loud", and "ornate" but at times positively "magical". Some participants noticed a mismatch between bird sounds and the scenery, for instance, hearing a woodpecker in a Swiss valley. The most technical participant criticized the "shifting sound channels" of the 3D-spatialization, suggesting it might best be used more judiciously.

The rising mist and oscillating lights visual effects were broadly deemed "distracting" and "unnatural"; "blocking" the scenery, not enhancing it. Changing the colour of mist from pink to white did not improve reception. Oscillating lights are being moved from the more foveal eye-space to the more peripheral environment in continued user testing.

The lessons learned to improve QOL thus far are superficial and have not yet yielded expected deeper insights. This could be improved if the participant were prompted to visualize lessons to be learned *prior to* the experience, or even *during* the experience (used in suggestive accompanying narration of the current clinical guided meditation programs, on which our prior experience with VR-based meditation is based).

5 Conclusions

In many senses, human endeavor has involved engagement with the natural (i.e. real) and unnatural/manmade (virtual) world. While not necessarily claiming that the latter is inferior either aesthetically or in terms of its inherent value, it is worth considering to what degree these two apparently disparate realities can be married. Currently, we continue an exploration of the inherent added-value of nature-based meditation experiences, while looking to maintain a high standard of aesthetics and ethics as we better understand its therapeutic potential for some of society's most challenged individuals.

Our objective has been develop and test immersive experiences that are either leisure- or activity-enhancing with respect to their benefits in enhancing QOL, reducing stress and increasing wellbeing. We suggest that from an industrial engineering perspective, these psychological gains may in fact translate into enhanced capacity for individual wellbeing, QOL and productivity [24, 49]. Further, the innovative employment of technology may well support significant cost-savings for increasingly strained public health-care budgets. In the near future, we plan to investigate the optimal administration of our immersive "Windows to the World" program. The overarching rationale for our protocols is based on classic Hippocratic *"primum non nocere"* (*above all, do no harm*) clinical pragmatism, alongside an understanding of the neuroscientific principles of sleep, wake and dreaming.

Through mindful meditative journeys, it may well be possible to traverse the porous boundaries between states of consciousness. Our apparatus and protocols are designed intentionally to mimic a wellness vacation experience, and we now seek to better understand its usability and impact during and directly following immersion, as well as the residual effects in the short-term and intermediate time period following exposure. Unlike a real vacation, "booster sessions" in this paradigm offer not only a non-replicated souvenir of the experience, but essentially simulations of actual events/experiences to achieve the objective of well-being and leisure, i.e., perceived freedom. Beyond obvious industrial psychology applications, we position our research within current clinical neuroscience models alongside the applied medical sciences model of recreation and leisure studies [50, 51]. The aim is to confer wellbeing to those who, due to constraints of time, disability or financial means, may not ordinarily or naturally have the opportunity to "get away from it all".

Acknowledgements. We are most grateful for the contributions of Martyn Ware (Tileyard Studios, London, U.K.) and Geoffrey Butler (Toronto Choral Society, Toronto, Canada) to construct the audio component of our immersive AV apparatus.

References

1. Moller, H.J.: From absence to presence: blurred consciousness and sleep states. In: Proceedings of the 11th Annual International Workshop on Presence, Padova, 16–18 October 2008. ISBN 978-88-6129-287-1
2. Waterworth, J., Chignell, M., Moller, H.J., Kandylis, D.: Presence and human development: age-specific variations in presence and their implications for the design of life-enhancing interactive applications. In: PRESENCE 2018: 18th Conference of the International Society for Presence Research (ISPR) Prague, Czech Republic, 21–22 May 2018

3. McLuhan, M., Fiore, Q.: The Medium is the Massage: An Inventory of Effects. Penguin, New York (1967)
4. Heidegger, M.: Being and Time. Translated by John Macquarrie and Edward Robinson. Harper & Row, New York, Hagerstown, San Francisco, London (1962)
5. Mulder, R.T.: An epidemic of depression or the medicalization of distress? Perspect. Biol. Med. **51**(2), 238–250 (2008)
6. Durkheim, E.: The Division of Labour in Society. First published 1893. Translated by W.D. Halls, Introduction by Lewis A. Coser. Free Press, New York (1997). 362 pp.
7. Durkheim, E.: Suicide: a Study in Sociology. (first published 1897) G. Simpson (ed.) Spaulding, J.A. (Transl.). Free Press, New York (1997). 405 pp.
8. World Health Organization (2017). https://www.who.int/news-room/detail/30-03-2017–dep ression-let-s-talk-says-who-as-depression-tops-list-of-causes-of-ill-health. Accessed 20 Sept 2019
9. Fee, E., Brown, T.M.: Freeing the insane. Am. J. Public Health **96**(10), 1743 (2006)
10. Ellenberger, H.F.: Charcot and the Salpêtrière school. Am. J. Psychother. **19**(2), 253–267 (1965)
11. Hesse, H.: Kurgast: Aufzeichnungen von einer Baderner Kur. Fischer Verlag, Berlin (1925). 160 pp.
12. Mann, T.: Der Zauberberg, 2 vol.'s, pp. 578, 629. Fischer Verlag, Berlin (1924)
13. Foucault, M.: Madness and Civilization: A History of Insanity in the Age of Reason, trans. Howard R. Tavistock Publications, London (1967). originally published in 1961. As Histoire de la folie à l'âge classique
14. Sandler, M.: Monoamine oxidase inhibitors in depression: history and mythology. J. Psychopharmacol. **4**(3), 136–139 (1990)
15. López-Muñoz, F., Alamo, C.: Monoaminergic neurotransmission: the history of the discovery of antidepressants from 1950s until today. Curr. Pharm. Des. **15**(14), 1563–1586 (2009)
16. López-Muñoz, F., Shen, W.W., D'Ocon, P., Romero, A., Álamo, C.: A history of the pharmacological treatment of bipolar disorder. Int. J. Mol. Sci. **19**(7), 2143 (2018)
17. Fava, G.A., Rafanelli, C.: Iatrogenic factors in psychopathology. Psychother. Psychosom. **88**, 129–140 (2019)
18. Jung, C.G., Jaffe, C.: Memories, Dreams, Reflections. Pantheon Books, New York (1962). 447 pp
19. Kazynski, A.T., Henerson, P.: Environmental correlates of physical exercise: a review of evidence about parks and recreation. Leis. Sci. **29**, 315–354 (2007)
20. Fox, J., Christy, K.R., Vang, M.H.: The experience of presence in persuasive virtual environments. In: Riva, G., Waterworth, J., Murray, D. (eds.) Interacting with Presence: HCI and the Sense of Presence in Computer-Mediated Environments, pp. 164–178. De Gruyter (2014)
21. Heyes, C.: Where do mirror neurons come from? Neurosci. Biobehav. Rev. **34**(4), 575–583 (2010)
22. Laeng, B., Teodorescu, D.S.: Eye scanpaths during visual imagery reenact those of perception of the same visual scene. Cogn. Sci. **26**(2), 207–231 (2002)
23. Ulrich, R.S., Simons, R.F., Losito, B.D., Fiorito, E., Miles, M.A., Zelson, M.: Stress recovery during exposure to natural and urban environments. J. Environ. Psychol. **11**, 201–230 (1991)
24. Moller, H.J., Bal, H., Sudan, K., Potwarka, L.: Recreating leisure: how immersive environments can promote wellbeing. In: Riva, G., Waterworth, J., Murray, D. (eds.) Interacting with Presence. Versita (2014)
25. Kevan, S.M.: Quests for cures: a history of tourism for climate and health. Int. J. Biometeorol. **37**(3), 113–124 (1993)
26. Vaughan, W.: Friedrich. Phaidon Press, Oxford Oxfordshire (2004). 352 pp
27. Murray, C.J.: Encyclopedia of the Romantic Era, 1760–1850. Taylor & Francis, London (2004). 1336 pp.

28. Koistinen, O.: The Cambridge Companion to Spinoza's Ethics. Cambridge University Press, Cambridge (2009). 334 pp
29. Gaddis, J.: The Landscape of History: How Historians Map the Past. Oxford University Press, Oxford Oxfordshire (2002). 208 pp
30. Wolf, N.: Caspar David Friedrich. Taschen, Köln (2003). 96 pp
31. Bohil, C.J., Alicea, B., Biocca, F.A.: Virtual reality in neuroscience research and therapy. Nat. Rev. Neurosci. **12**(12), 752–762 (2011)
32. Moller, H.J., Barbera, J.: Media presence, dreaming and consciousness. In: Riva, G., Anguera, M.T., Wiederhold, B.K., Mantovani, F. (eds.) From Communication to Presence: The Integration of Cognition, Emotions and Culture Towards the Ultimate Communicative Experience. IOS Press, Amsterdam (2006)
33. Hobson, J.A.: REM sleep and dreaming: towards a theory of protoconsciousness. Nat. Rev. Neurosci. **10**(11), 803–813 (2009)
34. Rechtschaffen, A., Kales, A.: A Manual of Standardized Terminology, Techniques and Scoring System for Sleep Stages of Human Subjects. Public Health Service, US Government Printing Office, Washington DC (1968)
35. Kabuto, M., Kageyama, T., Nitta, H.: EEG power spectrum changes during to listening to pleasant music and their relation to relaxation effects. Nippon Eiseigaku Zasshi **48**(4), 807 (1993)
36. Klimesch, W.: EEG alpha and theta oscillations reflect cognitive and memory performance: a review and analysis. Brain Res. Rev. **29**(2), 169–195 (1999)
37. Aserinsky, E., Kleitman, N.: Regularly occurring periods of eye motility, and concomitant phenomena, during sleep. Science **118**, 273–274 (1953)
38. Lange, B., et al.: Designing informed game-based rehabilitation tasks leveraging advances in virtual reality. Disabil. Rehabil. **34**(22), 1863–1870 (2012)
39. Rizzo, A.S.: Clinical virtual reality in mental health and rehabilitation: a brief review of the future. In: Infrared Technology and Applications XLV, vol. 11002, p. 110020Q. International Society for Optics and Photonics (2019)
40. Tong, T., Wilkinson, A., Nejatimoharrami, F., He, T., Matilus, H., Chignell, M.: A system for rewarding physical and cognitive activity in people with dementia. In: Proceedings of the International Symposium on Human Factors and Ergonomics in Health Care, vol. 6, no. 1, pp. 44–49. SAGE Publications, New Delhi, June 2017
41. Chignell, M., et al.: Immersiveness and perceptibility of convex and concave displays. To appear in Proceedings of the 65th Annual Meeting of the Human Factors and Ergonomics Society (2019)
42. Beck, A.: Psychometric properties of the beck depression inventory: twenty-five years of evaluation. Clin. Psychol. Rev. **8**(1), 77–100 (1988)
43. Soldatos, C.R., Dikeos, D.G., Paparrigopoulos, T.J.: The diagnostic validity of the Athens Insomnia Scale. J. Psychosom. Res. **55**, 263–267 (2003)
44. Johns, M.W.: A new method for measuring daytime sleepiness: the Epworth sleepiness scale. Sleep **14**(6), 540–545 (1991)
45. Topp, C.W., Østergaard, S.D., Søndergaard, S., Bech, P.: The WHO-5 well-being index: a systematic review of the literature. Psychother. Psychosom. **84**(3), 167–169 (2015)
46. Bonsignore, M., Barkow, K., Jessen, F., Heun, R.: Validity of the five-item WHO well-being index (WHO-5) in an elderly population. Eur. Arch. Psychiatry Clin. Neurosci. **251**(Sup 2), 27–31 (2001)
47. Moller, H.J., Saynor, L.: Authenticating the subjective: a naturalistic case study of a high-usability electronic health record for virtual reality therapeutics. In: Proceedings of the ICDVRAT 2016: 11th International Conference of Disability, Virtual Reality & Associated Technologies, Los Angeles, California, USA, 20–22 September 2016

48. Kennedy, R.S., Lane, N.E., Berbaum, K.S., Lilienthal, M.G.: Simulator sickness question-naire: an enhanced method for quantifying simulator sickness. Int. J. Aviat. Psychol. **3**(3), 203–220 (1993)
49. Moller, H.J., Bal, H.: Technology-enhanced multimodal meditation: clinical results from an observational case series. In: Burdea, G., Weiss, T. (eds.) Proceedings of the 10th International Conference on Virtual Rehabilitation, Philadelphia, PA, USA, August 2013
50. Canadian Index of Wellbeing: How are Canadians Really Doing? The 2012 CIW Report. Canadian Index of Wellbeing and University of Waterloo, Waterloo, ON (2012). https://uwaterloo.ca/canadian-index-wellbeing/resources/reports
51. Moller, H., Saynor, L., Sudan, K., Chignell, M.: Thinking mountains, shrinking mountains: engineering the human-environment interface for wellbeing. In: 15th Biennial Canadian Conference on Leisure Research, University of Waterloo, ON, Faculty of Leisure and Recreation Studies, 23–27 May 2017

Huge Balls: A Ludo-Narrative Exploration of Game Art

Guofan Xiong[1,2]([✉]), Daniel Plata[3], and Chu-Yin Chen[1]

[1] INREV (Image Numérique et Réalité Virtuelle) Research Group of Lab, AIAC (Arts des Images et Art Contemporain), University Paris 8, 93526 Saint-Denis, France
guofanx@gmail.com
[2] EnsadLab (Art & Design Research Laboratory at Ensad), Paris École Nationale Supérieure des Arts Décoratifs, 75240 Paris, France
[3] LabSIC (Laboratoire Sciences de l'Information et de la Communication), University Paris 13, 93430 Villetaneuse, France
maledop@gmail.com

Abstract. *Huge balls* (see Fig. 1). is a game art project created by Group Jean-Luc (A game art group based in Paris, composed of three artists/researchers of EnsadLab (Art & Design Research Laboratory at Ensad): Daniel Pata, Pierre emm and Guofan Xiong) supported by Ensadlab for the exhibition *Jonglopolis* at the Carreau du Temple in Paris 2018. The general idea is to transform juggling movements into an artistic digital installation with conceptual gameplay in it. Maintaining balance while being disturbed by the distractions inside the game space is the heart of its gameplay's mechanics, and looking to further question our understanding of gameplay. How are the visuals and the rules of this game art perceived by the players? How the players' own experiences and backgrounds alter them? How can artists use those elements to play with players/visitors? How the installation piece invites the players to perform, just like juggling as a form of performance? (see Fig. 1).

Keywords: Interactive art · Games · Interactivity · Game art · Ludo-narrative · Gameplay · Visual vocabularies

1 The Gameplay

1.1 Rules

In this game art installation, the gameplay is simple. The player tries to touch two pink balls with a balanced rhythm, just like juggling, to control a star icon that moves across the screen, leaving a trace of pinky cream on its path. When the icons of fruits and sweets touch the trace, they get covered with cream; at the same time, the player gains one point. If an icon of fruit or sweet falls out of the screen without having any interaction with the traces, the player will lose a point, and the screen will begin to get covered by semi-transparent cream. When the cream covers the whole screen, the game is over (see Fig. 2).

C.-Y. CHEN and P. Moegelin—Under the Doctoral Supervision.

© ICST Institute for Computer Sciences, Social Informatics and Telecommunications Engineering 2020
Published by Springer Nature Switzerland AG 2020. All Rights Reserved
A. Brooks and E. I. Brooks (Eds.): ArtsIT 2019/DLI 2019, LNICST 328, pp. 559–565, 2020.
https://doi.org/10.1007/978-3-030-53294-9_40

Fig. 1. Huge balls in the exhibition Jonglopolis at the Carreau du Temple in Paris in 2018.

1.2   Playing with the Players/Visitors

During the development, we decided to have relatively simple gameplay but a much more complex visual presentation and to play with the perceptions of the players/visitors. To add the narrative complexity in terms of player/visitors interpretations, we chose sexting emoticons[1] as they have at the same time basic shapes and colours, and the familiarity of nowadays emojis. Meanwhile, the specific use of certain icons and pairings present sexual subtexts that can be decoded only by those who are familiarized with the grammar of this new language (see Fig. 3).

To push this idea further, we decided to explore the double sense inside the installation with its physical interface. In the eye of the adults(those who understands the meaning behind the icons), those two balls-like controllers constantly give them strong hints to connect all the elements (both visual and tactile) with sexual representations within their own experiences, thus completely ignoring that the gameplay is about juggling. While for kids, the controllers have been positioned relatively high to block their vision, forcing them to peep through the controllers to play the already visually confusing game (see Fig. 4). For them, the gameplay is about finding a balance to continue the game and to get a higher score.

---

[1] A representation of a facial expression such as a smile or frown, formed by various combinations of keyboard characters and used to convey the writer's feelings or intended tone.

Fig. 2. Huge balls version.2 in the exhibition Malakoniarof in Malakoff, 2018.

Fig. 3. The visual elements inside *Huge balls*.

In another aspect, the game aims to challenge the perception of the public and evoke different kinds of reactions. Through the visuals and its difficult control system, the game usually provides an awkward situation for the players to question their own understandings and their skills of playing. The feedback of different groups of people

Fig. 4. The installation of Huge balls version.2 in Malakoniarof 2018

who create their own ways of playing, like emerging gameplay, is the most interesting part of this installation. The players are, at the same time, performers, as they interact and exchange with the waiting players and other visitors that are passing by; they create their narratives and own meanings of the game, as they share their stories and game experiences with the public around them.

2   The Strategies

In this installation, we use the rules-based video game system as artistic materials to create an installation that provides a strange ludic experience yet with a façade of familiarity. Furthermore, we are hoping to deconstruct its conventional form to question our understanding of the video game medium, taking into account Upton's remarks about the importance of the players' background:

> *The game design is structuring a total experience (both rules and fantasy) that will* **coax** *the player toward adopting an interesting set of internal constraints, and what the internal constraints a player adopts will depend heavily on his conceptual background* [1].

The rules here are the game's inner framework of the restrictions and affordances, and the fantasy is the pleasing "wrapper". For achieving this experimentation, we decide to reverse the inducing and to isolate the rules/play (the juggling) and the fantasy (the visuals and the interfaces) to make it difficult for the players to adopt concrete internal constraints. Thus they cannot depend on their conceptual background to give sense to the play and further question their understanding of the installation.

The installation gives a little control over the balancing game, but completely free on how to play and what is the game. It constantly demands its players to adapt and remaining open on to the concept of play. The idea is to de-familiarize and estrange us from reality so that the players struggle to resituate themselves within it. The more they believe that language, stories, and narrative patterns determine the perception of reality (instead of believing that they determined by reality), the more this strategy works [2]. In other words, the installation tries to deform the reality created by the video game system and its narratives and makes them visible and unnature to the players.

3 Virtual and Play

Video games create a virtual reality in which the individual plays the game. Virtual reality is understood as an environment that is created by a computer or any other media and within which the user has a feeling of being present in the environment [3]. If the feeling of reality is an illusion, then we have to play. We play it to explore, to learn about ourselves and the reality we created. Because the action of the playing is both creative and expressive, it is both a way of being inside the world (virtual or real) and a way of making sense of it.

This installation fosters spontaneous body movements. The decision is aimed to make the action of its players performative and immersive. Within the safe space (or magic circle) [4] of play, this digital art installation also uses some strategies of the video game design to extend its fictional reality created by the technologies. At the same time, the physical interfaces transfer the movements and sensations of its player into virtual reaction within the digital space which gives them an illusionary feeling of being in control. As this work heavily depends on its visitors to carry out its artistic experiences, can we doubt the artists' role and the visitors within the virtual space, and we can question the illusion of being in control in virtual and in reality?

4 The Exploration

First, we are interested in the creation of visual vocabularies anchored in the evolution of technology and methods of communication that have become both understood by a broader population, across countries and languages; and also complex by the redesignation of icons and meanings, like a new grammar.

As a starting point, we examined the example of the Isotype[2] language, born from the industrial and economic revolution of the early 20th century, from the need to create a system of communication that could be quickly recognizable in a globalizing world. In its visual Autobiography *From hieroglyphics to Isotype*, Otto Neurath's mentions his intention of creating this system for helping workers (the broader public) to become aware of the economic reality [5]. In our project, the exploration of visual vocabularies is an attempt to help people to be aware of the reality of the techno-culture today.

Second, we question the relationship between the body and the machine through the exploration of possible and meaningful interactions. On one side, we look to explore the

---

[2] Isotype (International System of Typographic Picture Education) is a method of showing social, technological, biological, and historical connections in pictorial form. It consists of a set of standardized and abstracted pictorial symbols to represent social-scientific data with specific guidelines on how to combine identical figures using serial repetition.

way interfaces aim to handle the functional and technical requirements of the game. On the other side, we aim to visualize the impact of the interfaces on the body and how the interface configures the exchange game-user-game.

The design of stressless, enjoyable, or even invisible interfaces has been the discipline ideal for decades. Interfaces have aimed to create versatile exchanges of dialogues between computers and users, particularly in the case of games, for which the effectiveness of the interface is not judged by the effortless operation, but quite the opposite, as acknowledged by Don Norman [6]. For video games, interfaces have merged into the artistic practice as our interaction with the technology become more complex, and our desire to immerse ourselves in virtual space grows [7]. This game art presents an interesting opportunity to experiment this kind of dialogue and help us to learn to control the artificial body inside the virtual space, at the same time, it tears up the disguise of the surface presentations to show us the discomfort distance between our body and the virtual game space.

Finally, we want to explore video game reception and preconceived ideas, in general, but also the public response and its reactions towards mature themes, particularly hidden by colourful and family-friendly visual and sound codes.

In a study of NYU School of Medicine in 2018 argues that humans recognize what they are looking at by combining current sensory stimuli with comparisons to images stored in memory [8]. For this reason, our perception of information is influenced more by past experiences than by newly arriving sensory input from the eyes. Is this how we understand the videogame's gameplay? How much the media and technologies around us altered our perception of the world, and how can we find the meanings hide behind the visual presentations?

To discuss the preceding questions, *Huge Balls* focalized on the visual language of emoticons, especially to sexting dynamics, because we consider it has stabilized, with a grammar that allows communicating efficiently in a complex array of meaning where the connotation is far more important than the denotation. The visual treatment of the icons and its selection responds to the third interest, a joyful and family-friendly game that plays around the ambiguity of reading and the interpretation of public, supported heavily in the connotation process. The visual approach is reinforced by the sound design, re-signifying familiar sounds like the ice cream car's melodies. The gameplay proposed by the game look to address the user-game questions. The game is played by interacting with the balls; the juggling in the physical interface corresponds to the virtual space. The players have to move the balls to interact with the objects present in the screen; the result of the interaction forces the body of the gamer to adapt uncomfortable positions. The size of the exhibition plays around the concept of *mise-en-scène* of gamers, aiming to expand the game to a multidimensional experience, not limited to visuals, and sound, but also related to touch and the social aspect of gaming.

References

1. Upton, B.: The Aesthetic of Play, 1st edn, p. 36. The MIT Press, Cambridge (2015)
2. Schrank, B., Bolter, D.J.: Avant-Garde Videogames: Playing with Technoculture, 1st edn, pp. 157–160. The MIT Press, Cambridge (2014)

3. Biocca, F.: Communication within virtual reality: creating a space for research. J. Commun. **42**(4), 5–22 (1992). Chapel Hill, North Carolina
4. Huizinga, J.: HOMO LUDEN: Essai sur la fonction sociale du jeu, 2nd edn. Gallimard, Paris (1988)
5. Neurath, O.: From Hieroglyphics to Isotype: A Visual Autobiography, 1st edn, pp. 5–8. Hyphen Press, London (2010)
6. ge: https://controlconference.com/. A Brief History of UI in Video Games 29 November 2017. https://www.youtube.com/watch?v=sngq9MWraKs. Accessed 06 Jul 2019
7. Norman, D.: JND.org. (2004). http://www.jnd.org/dn.mss/affordances_and.html. Accessed 05 Jul 2019
8. ScienceDaily, Past experiences shape what we see more than what we are looking at now 31 July 2018. https://www.sciencedaily.com/releases/2018/07/180731104224.htm. Accessed 05 Jul 2019

Playing with the Artist

Maria Vayanou[1,3]([✉]), Olga Sidiropoulou[2], George Loumos[1], Antonis Kargas[1],
and Yannis Ioannidis[3,4]

[1] Content Management in Culture P.C, Athens, Greece
{gloumos,akargas}@comic.com.gr
[2] Communication & Information Technologies Experts S.A, Athens, Greece
osidirop@cite.gr
[3] Department of Informatics and Telecommunications, University of Athens, Athens, Greece
{vayanou,yannis}@di.uoa.gr
[4] Athena Research Center, Athens, Greece

Abstract. In this paper we present a field study that took place in the environment of the exhibition "*Stefanos Rokos: Nick Cave & The Bad Seeds' No More Shall We Part, 14 paintings 17 years later*", hosted at the Benaki Museum (May 2019). A group of visitors played the game "*Find the Artwork behind the Story!*", crafting stories over the displayed artworks and sharing their thoughts, reasoning and emotions. Then the artist, Stefanos Rokos, joined the group and a new game round was played. We investigate how the artist's participation affected the group experience, examining both the visitors' and the artist's perspective. Our findings show that the visitors were willing to share their stories and highly appreciated their gameful interaction with the artist. We observed that the artist behaved similarly to the rest of the players, rejecting our hypothesis that he would take on a leading role in the discussions. The artist expressed his enthusiasm for the game experience, stating that his participation in the game helped him better understand how the visitors see and discover his artworks. Overall, both sides reported that the game fostered the interaction between them, providing an engaging social cultural experience. Finally, we summarize how the results of the study drive the next iterations of the mobile application so as to support the artist's participation in the game, and we describe our future steps.

Keywords: Group games · Storytelling · Cultural visits · Social interactions · Art exhibitions · Artist participation · User studies · Playtesting

1 Introduction and Background Work

The value of social interactions during cultural visits is advocated in several museum studies [1]. Aiming to foster verbal communication between a pair or group of visitors, research and commercial works have exploited a variety of techniques, ranging from synchronized audio listening [2, 3], to creating shared projection spaces [4, 6], or/and offering content variations on the mobile phones of the group members [5, 6], in order to promote information exchange between the participants.

A. Brooks and E. I. Brooks (Eds.): ArtsIT 2019/DLI 2019, LNICST 328, pp. 566–579, 2020.
https://doi.org/10.1007/978-3-030-53294-9_41

Moving in this direction, in our previous work we proposed a storytelling game for groups of visitors, asking the group members to make and share stories about the artworks of a cultural collection [7]. The game is inspired by the popular board game Dixit and it is titled "*Find the Artwork behind the Story!*". It defines a pervasive group experience that takes place and evolves in the environment of fine art exhibitions, combining moments of personal reflection to social encounters through the game phases (described in Table 1).

Table 1. Game phases in each episode of "find the Artwork behind the Story!", with N players

Game phases	Storyteller (#1)	Voters (#N−1)
Story making	Secretly chooses one artwork and conceives a story about it	Wait for the Storyteller to complete his/her story
Storytelling	Narrates and more or less enacts the story in front of the whole group	Listen and watch the Storyteller's performance
Voting	Waits until voting is completed	Move around the gallery, now examining the artworks with respect to the Storyteller's performance
Explanations	Reveals last the artwork behind the story, to increase surprise and suspense	One by one, Voters reveal chosen artworks and describe their rational for selecting them (this is the main social phase and includes lively discussions)
Scoring	Scores points for successful votes. If ALL or NO Voters find it, then scores 0	Scores points if voted successfully or the Storyteller scores 0

We first conducted a series of playtesting sessions with physical materials in different environments and exhibitions, exploring the game's affordances and requirements [7, 8]. We then produced to a mobile-based design to support the proposed game, leveraging the visitors' personal handheld devices as game controls [9]. Moving one step further, we currently investigate how the artists of cultural collections may be involved in the described game experience.

In this work we propose that the artists participate as players in the group game, listening to the stories and explanations that visitors make about their artworks, and sharing their own stories and reflections during the game. To the best of our knowledge this is a rather novel approach, since joint artist-to-visitor participation in gallery games is hardly explored.

To that end, we performed a user study where an artist participated as player in a group playtesting session, taking place in his personal art exhibition, and thus enabling the participants to have a personal, hands-on experience with the proposed gameful scenario. The primary objective of the study was to examine how the artist's involvement in the game shaped and affected the group experience, investigating its affordances to foster communication and interactions between art gallery visitors and creators.

The secondary objective of the study was to evaluate two new components that were recently introduced in the mobile-based game design [9], namely the Speeding and the Guessing bonus, guiding the following game iterations. The former bonus is targeted to the Voter role and it was added to motivate quick pacing, aiming to address duration concerns that were reported in prior playtesting sessions [7]. The latter is targeted to the Storyteller role, providing an in-game activity that aims to promote social awareness, while also reducing the "waiting time" that is potentially encountered by the Storyteller during the voting phase [10].

2 User Study Description

Leveraging the 3-dimensional framework proposed by Christian Roher to classify user experience research methods [11], the described user study constitutes a qualitative field study, generating data about participants' behaviors or attitudes based on observing them directly. We combine attitudinal to behavioral observations, examining what the participants "said", along with what and they "did". During our analysis we extrapolate results from on-site behavioral observation and video-recoding analysis, to participants' feedback through open questions and questionnaire items, which were used in a combined way to guide one-to-one interviews in the following. Aiming to examine issues that are broader than application usage and usability, we did not leverage the mobile game prototype (whose alpha version had just been released by the time of the study). Physical materials were employed instead, in line with our previous work.

2.1 Participants

An open invitation was announced at a research laboratory of the University of Athens, asking to participate in a user study that would include a game, taking place at the ongoing (at that time) exhibition of Stefanos Rokos, at the Benaki Museum. The invitation prompted the interested candidates to invite also the persons form their personal social networks who would most likely accompany them in a typical cultural visit or social event.

The selection criteria leading to the final group formation were that i) the participants are adults, and ii) they had all met each other at least once in the past (to ensure a minimum level of familiarity between the group members). A social group of three university colleagues with their partners was formed, containing 3 women and 2 men, all in the age range from 30 to 45. Two of the participants reported that they were familiar with the artist and had already visited the exhibition before, but they felt they did not have the opportunity to reflect on the artworks due to highly crowding conditions, expressing their desire to visit it again.

The participants were informed about the meeting time and were given the option to make a free-visit in the gallery before playing the game (up to an hour ahead). One day before the visit, the participants filled in a pre-play questionnaire (online, using Google Forms), entering demographic data and indicating their prior experience with art exhibitions and storytelling games. It is worth noting that 4 participants had played the board game Dixit in the past, so they were already familiar with the main game objective.

2.2 Exhibition Environment and Playtesting Conditions

The exhibition contained 14 paintings, inspired by the 12 songs of the album "No More Shall We Part" by Nick Cave & The Bad Seeds + two b-sides. The gallery layout was structured in three main areas, implying the feeling of a temple. The artworks were displayed on the walls, on the left and right areas (see Fig. 1).

The strong connection to the music album was reflected in the gallery's syntax in several ways. First, the songs' titles and lyrics were presented on large columns, facing directly the corresponding artworks, and thus indicating the dialogue between the two forms of art. Second, the album was continuously playing on the gallery's background, gradually going over all the album songs. In addition, the visitors could use their mobile phones to scan the QR codes (located at the side of each column) and listen the selected song through headphones. When located in the central area of the exhibition (Fig. 1), visitors had partial visual access to the surrounding artworks.

Fig. 1. Overview of the exhibition environment and layout

About two weeks before the user study, we contacted the artist, Stefanos Rokos, first through email and then via phone. We informed him about the gameplay we are exploring, our previous playtesting sessions, and the objectives of this research. Then we asked him if he would be willing to participate in a playtesting session at the environment where his personal exhibition was currently hosted, having a "hands-on" game experience, with a group of invited participants, playing over his artworks. The artist expressed his interest in joining the session and suggested specific timeslots in order to avoid crowding conditions that would impede him from being committed to the gaming process. As a result, the user study took place during off-peak gallery hours (Thursday morning, May 23rd, 2019). During playtesting the number of concurrent "external" visitors in the gallery remained lower than 10, at all times.

2.3   The Game Experience

For the user study purposes, the described group game is implemented with physical materials. All players are handed private pens and post-its packs, using color coding notation (i.e. a different color is assigned to each participant). In addition, the Storyteller is provided with a hand-crafted notebook. Each page of the notebook corresponds to a game episode, i.e. one Storyteller turn, and it is organized in three vertical parts, following the temporal succession of the game phases (see Fig. 2).

On top, the Storyteller writes down his/her story, along with the title of the artwork behind it (which remains hidden by placing a post-it on it). The Storyteller narrates the story to the group, and then the voting phase begins. The middle part of the notebook is the area where all Voters' choices are placed on. The Voters use their post-its to privately note down their selections (i.e. the title of the artwork). To complete voting, they approach the Storyteller and stick their (hidden) votes on the appropriate placeholder frame.

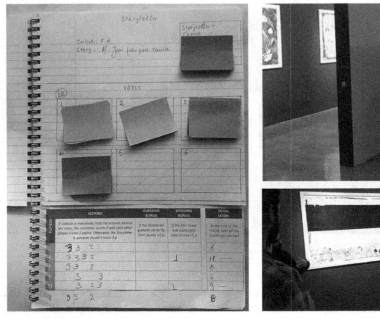

Fig. 2. Crafted paper notebook: layout and contents (left) and snapshots showcasing its use by the Storyteller during playtesting (right)

When everybody completes voting, the group proceeds to votes revealing and explanations phase. The Storyteller is expected to lead the discussion by gradually uncovering the hidden votes and communicating the results to the whole party. Finally, the scoring table is maintained at the bottom part of the notebook, where all player's scores are progressively added next to their name initials. When the episode is over, the Storyteller turns the page, reads the name of the next Storyteller and hands on the notebook (the bottom part of the paper pages has been cut off, supporting scores' maintenance and update through the game episodes).

To support the introduction of the Speeding Bonus in the gameplay, we numbered the voting frames on the notebook, indicating the vote-completion ordering. The first player who approaches the Storyteller places his/her vote on the 1st frame, the second one uses the following frame and so on. The SB notation signifies that the particular player (i.e. the one with the yellow post-its pack in the episode depicted in Fig. 2) is candidate for receiving the Speeding Bonus. During the scoring phase, if the vote on the first frame matches the Storyteller's selection, one extra point is given to the corresponding player (third column of the Scoring Table in Fig. 2).

To implement the Guessing Bonus, we printed small paper "guessing cards" that depicted the forenames of all the group members, along with playful, personalized avatars. When storytelling is over and voting starts, the facilitator hands a guessing card to the Storyteller, prompting to predict and circle the Voters who would find the artwork behind the story. As soon as the first Voter approaches the Storyteller and completes voting, the facilitator informs the Storyteller that there are 10 s left to complete the guessing process, and then asks to deliver her the filled-in card. During scoring, in order to acquire the extra point of the Guessing Bonus an "exact match" was required, i.e. all the Voters that had been circled by the Storyteller needed to have voted "correctly", and only those (i.e. non-indicated players needed to have missed it).

2.4   User Study Procedure

On arrival, the participants were informed about the context of this research and filled out the consent forms, allowing for video-recoding. When the whole group was gathered, the facilitator explained the gameplay, handed on the post-its and pens to the participants and presented the crafted notebook, explaining its usage during the game. The Speeding and Guessing Bonuses were introduced, and then the playtesting session started.

A camera was set on a tripod at the end of the central area of the gallery, where the group gatherings were anticipated to be mainly taking place. In addition, a dedicated human recorder was following the Storyteller during the playtesting sessions, enabling to capture and analyze the majoring of group discussions. Finally, the game facilitator was present during playtesting, delivering the Guessing Bonus cards to the Storytellers.

A round of 5 game episodes was completed in about 1 h and then the group moved to the museum's coffee shop, where each participant filled in a short post-play questionnaire (~5 min), evaluating their game experience, indicating their willingness to participate in future games, and finally reporting the strong and weak points of the game (through open questions).

In the following, the facilitator announced to the group that they were going to play one more round, but this time the artist, Stefanos Rokos, would join them, participating as player in the game. A few minutes later the artist arrived, and he was introduced to the group members who were not familiar with him. Not having played the game himself before, the artist asked the group members to describe him their experience, leading to a group discussion. At some point, one participant suggested to share the stories they had made with the artist, and see if he would be able to find the artwork behind them. The artist and the majority of the group members strongly welcomed the idea. So one by one, the participants announced their personal stories to the artist (reading them out loud from the game notebook were they had been written down) and the artist selected one of his artworks that seemed to match it. Then the corresponding participant revealed the identity of the selected artwork, explaining to the artist why he/she had selected it. Some of the votes were also discussed, sharing different perspectives with regard to the story and the artworks. In essence, the game round was "repeated" away from the exhibition's environment, now having a new, "special" voter to be playing along (Table 2).

Table 2. Summarization of user study phases

User study phases	Duration	Location	# Part/nts
Free-visit to exhibition	Up to 30'	Exhibition hall	3
Playtesting session – round 1(5 visitors)	1 h	Exhibition hall	5
Questionnaire (Part 1)	5 min	Museum's coffee shop	5
Coffee break and "repeated" game round with artist as Voter	50 min	Museum's coffee shop	6
Playtesting session – round 2 (4 visitors, artist & exhibition designer)	50 min	Exhibition hall	6
Questionnaire (Part 2 for visitors, Part 1 for artist)	15 min	Museum's coffee shop	6
Individual interviews	30 min in total	Museum's coffee shop	5
Artist interview (at a following day)	1 h	Filion cafe	1

When this process completed, the group moved altogether at the exhibition's space. The artist took the initiative to invite the museum's exhibition designer, Natalia Boura, to participate as well. Although not originally planned in the design of the user study, we welcomed the participation of an additional "special" player. In addition, one of the participants decided to refrain from the game due to health issues (pregnancy discomfort). The new, extended group of 6 players (4 visitors plus the artist and the exhibition designer) started a fresh playtesting round. The game was completed in about 50 min, and then the group moved again at the coffee shop. The participants filled in a second questionnaire and their responses where used as input, driving the discussion in a short, one-to-one interview section with the facilitator. The artist was asked to fill in the questionnaire as well, but a rather different interview technique was employed. The artist was interviewed several days after the playtesting session, enabling him to reflect on his experience, and then discuss it in detail, examining its affordances, requirements, and potential future directions. The interview was audio-record and we report several parts of the (translated) transcripts in the following.

3 User Study Findings and Discussion

In this section we report a series of findings, presenting them with respect to the two main objectives of the user study. First we examine key issues related the artist's participation in the game experience, which is the primary objective of the study, discussing the visitors' perspective first, and elaborating on the artist's viewpoint in the following. Then we summarize results related to the introduction of two new game components, reflecting on their strengths and weaknesses.

3.1 The Artist as a Player in the Group Game

The Visitors' Perspective

Based on our playtesting sessions so far, the participants' approaches to story making vary a lot. This result is also reflected in the current study (Table 3 depicts the stories that were created by the participants over the 2 game rounds). Some stories have structure (beginning, middle and closure), narrating personal feelings or fictional experiences. Several stories take the form of short titles or statements, which are either generic, humoristic, emotional, or referencing particular items in the paintings (or persons related to them, such as painters or musicians). So the main questions that we set with regard to the visitors' perspective towards the artist's participation are: Did the participants want to share the stories with the creator of the artworks? Did they experience discomfort or unease while doing so? And finally, did the participation of the artist add value to their experience and in what ways?

Table 3. Participant generated stories

Participant	Story	Round
#1	The weather was nice and we were outside, or we were looking outside, and maybe we were in a ship, going or returning. But you knew where you are, because the trip had a spirituality, and your heart opened	1
#2	Easter of 2011 at Kefalonia (a Greek island). Just a few people at the epitaph in the village. The rain starts and we gather towards the church, where octopuses had been placed on grill	1
#3	Our life, one movie	1
#4	Black Faceless River III	1
#5	Panousis and Van Gogh	1
#1	And when he returned, everything was exactly the way she left it, as a museum of colors. Grey of past decades and present time, but the pain was deeply rooted, taking a lot of space. He closed the door and left	2
#2	Black's shine beneath the colors	2
Exhibition designer	She waits. She still waits. Frozen in time	2
#4	Raised before Easter	2
#5	Kafkaesque metamorphosis at the mountain of the forest	2
Artist	20 bitter juices	2

When the facilitator announced that the artist would next join the group to play along, the group members seemed to be surprised, and Participant #4 commented aloud: *"Thank God he was not here before to listen to my story!"*. It was the only story in the first round that nobody found the artwork behind it, so the rest of the group members considered it as a humoristic comment and laughed.

However, as described in the previous section, when the artist arrived at the coffee shop he initiated a group discussion about the participants' prior game experience and, during the discussion, one participant proposed to share the stories with the artist and see if he would be able to find the artwork they were referring to. All participants enthusiastically welcomed the idea, except from Participant 4, who remained silent. However, he did not raise any objections and went along with it.

The rest of the group members started a discussion about whether a score should be computed for the artist as well, based on the rest of the answers (depicted on the notebook). One participant commented that it would be "unfair" for the artist, since he would not have the opportunity to get the Speeding Bonus, as they did. Despite that, the group finally decided to keep scoring, by adding the artist's name initial at the bottom row of the scoring table (Fig. 2), and updating his score during the episodes.

We stress out that this process was not planned, or even anticipated, in the study design phase. Since it relates to one of the main research questions of the study, the facilitator did not intervene, and allowed the group to go-on with this, although significantly diverging from the original time plan. The group members' initiative and eagerness to "repeat" the game with the artist offers valuable insights, demonstrating the participants' strong willingness to share their stories and interact with the creator of the artworks. The group had been informed that a new round with the artist was planned to take place right away, yet that was not enough: they also wanted to share with him their past stories.

In the interview section, the participants were asked if they felt discomfort or unease while sharing their stories and reflections with the artist, and everybody replied negatively. Participant #4 reported that he was reluctant to do so at first, being afraid that his story would potentially upset or offend the artist's work. However, since he was the 4th player to reveal his story, by the time his turn came he had observed that the artist was very friendly and had welcomed the stories and remarks made by the other participants, so his concerns had been reduced. The participant pointed out that he would probably have felt discomfort if he was the starting player (i.e. the first one sharing his story).

All the participants considered that the artist's involvement significantly enriched their gameful visit. *"Amazing experience having the artist and the curator as part of the team. Loved the fact that I was a member of a relatively small group that enjoyed talking and listening as well."* noted Participant #3 in the open comments section of the questionnaire. Discussing with the participants why they valued the artist's participation (in the interview section), we observe that two main reasons were repeatedly brought up. First, some participants valued a lot the "authority" that the artist, as well as the exhibition designer, bring into the gameful visiting experience, reporting a general strong interest into the experts' insights and interpretations. Second, the discussions that took place during the game were inspired by the artist's work, but covered a wide variety of aspects, ranging from historical facts to music preferences or personal experiences and beliefs. This aspect was particularly appreciated by some participants. *"I feel I met the person, not only the artist"*, said one participant, emphasizing the social dimension of the experience.

The Artist's Perspective

Similarly to the visitors' side, the main questions that we set with regard to the artist's viewpoint are: Did the artist enjoy listening to the stories and explanations made by the participants and why? Did he experience discomfort or unease at any point? And, focusing on his special role in the process, did his participation in the game foster his interaction with the participants, and in what ways?

With regard to the last question, we expected that, although the artist did not have a special role in the game-play, he would behave differently than the rest of the participants. Our hypothesis was that the artist would often take the initiative to lead the discussions, revealing his personal thoughts, intentions, or knowledge with regard to the referenced artworks. However our hypothesis was rejected. The artist overall behaved similarly to the other players; he provided explanations only in a few occasions, under the explicit request of the group members. In light of this observation, this issue was brought up during the interview section, discussing the artist's reflections over his role in the game process.

At the beginning of the interview, the artist was asked to make an overall assessment of his game experience through two rather general questions (*"What do you think about it? Did you like the game?"*). The artist replied very positively, characterizing the game as very nice, clever and entertaining. He commented that he has talked to a lot of people about it, as something that he really enjoyed to be part of. Moving on, his first remark was: ***"I discovered a lot of things in my artworks that I had them for granted but I discovered them on a second level, on a second basis, and I better understood how others may see and perceive them, which I really enjoyed, as a process."*** This comment relates to our first, as well as to the third research questions, and the artist was asked to give a related example from the playtesting session.

The artist commented that this happened in several occasions, but the most prominent example was the one where he was the Storyteller. His story was *"20 bitter juices"* (see all player stories in Table 3) and the artist explained: *"To me, it was extremely evident that there were 20 buckets in one artwork, which were full of tears, as described at the lyrics of the song. But people do not pay attention to every detail of my artworks, nor do they read the lyrics of all the songs. So what I considered to be obvious made the participants look closer to the artworks, searching for particular things. This is a clever process and I was really happy to see that they all engaged in it. Also, I was glad to find out that the story was not as evident as I thought, since not everybody found the artwork, which shows that everything is relative, and what I have in my mind as an artist, or viewer, may be perceived and discovered in rather different and personal ways* (Fig. 3)."

Then the artist was asked if he felt the need to intervene while listening to the group's reflections and reasoning over his artworks, in order to share his personal thoughts about them. The artist replied negatively, explaining that he preferred not to take the lead at all. *"I really enjoyed that they were all saying stories and comments about my artworks, that they found several elements and details in them. Even if some were wrong, I did not want to correct anyone or say something more about it."* The artist referenced a

Fig. 3. Snapshot from playtesting with the artist: one participant reveals his personal thoughts, pointing to particular elements of the artwork

concrete example where one of the participants mentioned an octopus in his story, later explaining that he saw the tentacles' of an octopus in the painting: "*I loved that! I did not want to say -no, that's not tentacles. I did so only because someone asked me*".

When questioned if his participation in the game fostered his interaction with the participants, the artist replied very positively and explained: "*Through the game I met some people that I did not know at all, and* **we immediately found common references, reasons and topics to discuss, which would probably not happen without the game context. It brings you closer to the others**, *and I think that I am not saying this only because I was the artist. If someone else was the artist, I think I'd play the same game and get to meet the group with the same enthusiasm, talking about his/her artworks.*" So we conclude that the artist clearly preferred to take on a traditional player role in the game, paying high attention to the participants' discussions and remarks, and appreciating the social dimension of the game experience.

With regard to our second research question, the artist reported that he did not feel uncomfortable within the group discussions. He was asked if he is concerned that his work may be undermined by the stories that may be potentially crafted, since there is no control or limitation to what the players may actually say. The artist replied negatively: "*I think that my artworks are an entity of their own, they will not be affected or altered by a different explanation*".

However, a different type of concern was revealed during the discussion, related to the context of the game experience and, in particular, to the co-existence of visitors who do not participate in the game. "*At some point, there were 2 visitors in the gallery, who were not in the mood of what we were doing. We were running around, laughing, talking aloud, making nice comments, making the space our own. But them, they wanted to make their own tour, under different circumstances, to listen the music and see my artworks in a different way and pace.*" Elaborating on this issue, the artist proposed that the gameful visit is conducted in the context of game events, booking the exhibition environment for particular timeslots, so that all visitors are informed and aware of the activity that will be taking place.

3.2 Assessment of Speeding and Guessing Bonuses

The Speeding Bonus was received in different ways by the participants. Participant 2 reported it as one of the strong points of the game (in the related open question), noting that "*It puts you in a state of quick processing of the artworks*". In the interview section, the participant expressed his appreciation for quick pacing and competition, explaining that the Speeding Bonus strengthened these aspects in the overall game experience. On the contrary, Participant 4 mentioned it as a negative point, favoring the creative and intellectual challenges posed by the game over quick pacing: "*It does not give the opportunity for in-depth analysis*", he noted. Conflicting visitor attitudes towards competition and pacing were also identified in our previous playtesting sessions [7], highlighting the challenge to balance between different personal preferences of the group members [10].

In addition, several comments and group discussions during the 1st playtesting session were related to the Speeding Bonus. The "quickest" voter often announced aloud "*I am going for the Speeding Bonus*", leading to teases and jokes from the other participants. In one occasion, after the votes were revealed, one participant said "*You aimed for the small prize and you lost the big one*", a tease that drove the group members into discussing whether targeting for the Speeding Bonus is a good game strategy or not.

Assessing its difficulty, the Speeding Bonus was effectively acquired twice in the first round (by different participants), which is a rather reasonable number for a group of 5, and four times in the second round. However, during the second round it quickly became evident that the artist had a way quicker voting pace than the rest of the group members. In two cases he voted instantly (i.e. in less than 5 s), and he was the first one to vote most of the times (3 out of 5), acquiring the Speeding Bonus twice. The group members complained that it was unfair to compete against the artist in speeding terms, realizing his strong advantage in recalling and examining the artworks.

Moving on to the Guessing Bonus, we observed that it was never acquired over the two rounds, so we conclude that the task set was too difficult. Following an iterative design approach, we plan to ease and also speed up the guessing task, by asking the Storyteller to "bet" on (only) one of the participants, instead of requiring to find them all. Based on the game transcripts, we expect that the proposed adaptation will be neither too easy to accomplish, nor too difficult.

4 Conclusions and Future Work

In this paper we present our approach to foster the communication between groups of visitors and art creators through their joint participation in a social storytelling game. We describe a user study that includes two playtesting sessions in the physical environment of a fine arts exhibition: one without the artist, and one where the artist participates as a player in the game. We report key results with regard to the social interactions that were developed through this process, examining both the visitors' and the artist's perspective, using a combination of behavioral and attitudinal data. Our results show an exciting potential to create a new channel of communication between artists and visitors, through their joint game participation.

Moving towards this direction, the user study results offer several insights on how to proceed with the mobile game design and implementation. We plan to extend the original game design by introducing a new player attribute, discriminating between visitors and artists. The same game functionality will be provided to all players, however the artists' attribute will be exploited for scoring purposes (i.e. excluding the Artist from participating in the Speeding bonus), plus it will be reflected in the mobile interface design.

In our future work we plan to invite more artists in this process, aiming to capture a variety of different perspectives from the artists' side, and observe how these shape the game experience. We will further investigate the different roles that the artists may take, besides playing the game similarly to ordinary players. Following a participatory design approach, we will form a group of interested artists who will collaboratively consider all the stages of the experience, from design to delivery, as well as post-play analysis. For instance, during the interview section, the artist expressed his interest in viewing the visitor generated stories afterwards, thus posing the requirement for data collection and visualization tools that leverage the game usage data.

The use of game designs and technologies for advancing social interactions, not only between groups of visitors but also between visitors and artists, is a young and exciting field. We believe that work in this direction may have a high social impact, shaping new forms of cultural participation.

Acknowledgments. This research has been co-financed by the European Union and Greek national funds through the Operational Program Competitiveness, Entrepreneurship and Innovation, under the call RESEARCH – CREATE – INNOVATE (project ΠΙΣΕΤΟ code:T1EDK-05362).

References

1. Jafari, A., Taheri, B., vom Lehn, D.: Cultural consumption, interactive sociality, and the museum. J. Mark. Manag. **29**(15–16), 1729–1752 (2013)
2. Szymanski, M.H., Aoki, P., Grinter, R.E., Hurst, A., Thornton, J.D., Woodruff, A.: Sotto voce: facilitating social learning in a historic house. Comput. Support. Coop. Work (CSCW) **17**(1), 5–34 (2008)
3. Pau, S.: Audio that moves you: experiments with location-aware storytelling in the SFMOMA app. In: Museums and the Web (2017)

4. Wecker, A. J., Kuflik, T., Lanir, J., Stock, O.: Evaluating mobile projectors as a shared display option for small groups. In: Conference on Human Factors in Computing Systems CHI 2012 Extended Abstracts, pp. 2543–2548 (2012). https://doi.org/10.1145/2212776.2223833
5. Callaway, C., Stock, O., Dekoven, E.: Experiments with mobile drama in an instrumented museum for inducing conversation in small groups. ACM Trans. Interact. Intell. Syst. 4(1), 1–39 (2014). Article 2
6. Katifori, A., Kourtis, V., Perry, S., Pujol, L., Vayanou, M., Chrysanthi, A.: Cultivating mobile-mediated social interaction in the museum: Towards group-based digital storytelling experiences. In: Museums and the Web (2016)
7. Vayanou, M., Ioannidis, Y.: Storytelling games with art collections: generic game-play design and preliminary evaluation through game testing sessions. In: 9th International Conference on Virtual Worlds and Games for Serious Applications (VS-Games), pp. 264–271 (2017). https://doi.org/10.1109/vs-games.2017.8056612
8. Vayanou, M., Ioannidis, Y., Loumos, G., Kargas, A.: How to play storytelling games with masterpieces: from art galleries to hybrid board games. J. Comput. Educ. (2019). https://doi.org/10.1007/s40692-018-0124-y
9. Vayanou, M., Ioannidis, Y., Loumos, G., Sidiropoulou, O., Kargas, A.: Designing performative, gamified cultural experiences for groups. In: CHI EA 2019 Extended Abstracts of the 2019 CHI Conference on Human Factors in Computing Systems (2019). https://doi.org/10.1145/3290607.3312855
10. Vayanou, M., Antoniou, A., Loumos, G., Kargas, A., Kakaletris, G., Ioannidis, Y.: Towards personalized group play in gallery environments. To appear in CHI PLAY Extended Abstracts (2019)
11. Rohrer, C.: When to use which user-experience research methods (2014). https://www.nngroup.com/articles/which-ux-research-methods/

Design as a Knowledge Constructing Activity

Design as a Knowledge Constructing Activity

Eva Brooks[1](✉) and Anthony L. Brooks[2]

[1] Department of Culture and Learning, Aalborg University, Kroghstræde 3,
9220 Aalborg, Denmark
eb@hum.aau.dk
[2] Department of Architecture, Design and Media Technology, Aalborg University,
Rendsburggade 14, 9000 Aalborg, Denmark

Abstract. In this chapter, contributions from DLI 2019 show that a design process is not given to its form, structure, or qualities. Rather, design work is given form by designers' and technology developers' own considerations and actions inspired and guided by people's voices, desires, habits, and practices.

Keywords: Interactive space · Smart toy · Electrochromic ambient display · Digital libraries · Games and theatre · Participatory design

1 Introduction

1.1 Scope

The field of design has connections to a number of established academic fields concerned with digital technologies, including user experience design, human-computer interaction, and information systems. There are differences between these fields, in particular when it comes to the understanding of design and design practices. In this section of the proceedings the papers are united around a use-oriented practice of design, where the question about how to think about design, users' experience and artefacts (something made by humans) comes to the fore. While Winnograd [1] described design as "designing spaces for human communication and interaction", Saffer [2] emphasised its artistic dimensions underlining that it is an art to facilitate interactions between humans through artefacts. Considering that all design work results in a product of some kind, Löwgren and Storlterman [3] points to the thoughtful designer who is part of a larges culture, which they call "design as knowledge construction" (p. 2). In other words, the way of 'doing' design can be said to have an eclectic character, being *use-oriented*, *context- and culture-dependent* and a *knowledge constructing* activity, targeting shaping of and knowledge about artefacts that can change the way users think and act. In this way, such designs become *mediators* and essential *action and experience shapers* [4].

The first contribution in this section addresses the question of how designs and integration of hotspots in book apps for children can facilitate mediated reading of digital books. The second contribution focuses on the introduction of a smart and robotic toy to explore its use qualities to support emerging storytelling skills in children. The third

A. Brooks and E. I. Brooks (Eds.): ArtsIT 2019/DLI 2019, LNICST 328, pp. 583–587, 2020.
https://doi.org/10.1007/978-3-030-53294-9_42

contribution presents a practice-based study of people living remotely from their partner. Here, an unobtrusive display technique was prototyped with an interactive picture frame, which was used as a probe to chart the use possibilities of this technique. The fourth contribution addresses the complex issue of designing a meaningful interface where a library could provide and enhance reading experiences and acquisition of knowledge. The fifth and final contribution reports on initial findings from engaging in participatory and speculative design methods with rural women in Bihar, India. The above-mentioned contributions show that a design process is not given to its form, structure, or qualities. Rather, design work is given form by designers' and technology developers' own considerations and actions inspired and guided by people's voices, desires, habits, and practices (c.f. Löwgren and Storlterman, 2004).

The following text snippets elaborate from each contribution to further assist readership.

2   Touch to Read: Investigating the Readers' Interaction Experience in Mediated Reading with Story Apps

In this contribution, *Douglas Menegazzi and Cristina Sylla*, addresses the question of learning to read in a digital book context. For a child, this is considered as a complex and challenging activity. However, when guided by a more experienced reader, the child can become encouraged to stay focused and becomes engaged to develop reading skills. The paper focuses on how hotspots – interactive areas – in story apps can mediate a child's reading and interaction experience when accompanied by a carer. The carer is also described as a mediator of the child's reading experience. Such hotspots are most often designed to entertain children rather than providing a learning experience. Moreover, the hotspots are scarcely contributing to the story in question, which makes it hard for more experienced readers to interact and guide children to deal with hotspots and mediate reading in this kind of digital books. The authors argue that there is a lack of validated knowledge in digital publishing targeting children, to design for meaningfully mediated reading experiences. Thus, framed by a user-centred design approach, six carer-child couples (children aged 6–9) were engaged in a study investigating positive and negative aspects of the couples' reading experience with different types of interactive areas on apps (i.e. hotspots) when engaged in mediated reading. The results indicated that children's reading flow can be improved and that the engagement between child and carer (or mediator) became more intense when the app allowed a clear space for the child to invite the carer to help by, for example, explaining unknown words. Based on the outcomes of the study, the paper contributes with input to improving design and integration of hotspots in book apps for children and to facilitate mediated reading of digital books. Here, the process of mediation offered potentials for carers and children to shape actions, on the one hand, and the use of interactive spaces (or hotspots), on the other hand.

3 Designing a Smart Toy Interactive Setting for Creating Stories

This contribution is authored by *Silke ter Staal, Alejandro Catala, Mariët Theune, and Dennis Reidsma*. To produce products that users experience as beneficial for their purposes refers to the concept of *use experience* commonly applied in the field of design and often applied with an agile *iterative* approach to a design process including prototype development. This can be seen in this second contribution where a smart and robotic toy was introduced to explore its use qualities to support emerging storytelling skills in children. In this field of research, previous studies mostly have focused on technical implementation issues or included specialised hardware, which may limit their potentials to be studied outside a laboratory environment. To contribute to this lack of applications including off-the-shelf affordable components, the paper investigates how to combine a tablet application with an existing smart robotic toy to foster children's creation of stories and their reflection on them. To do so, the authors adopted a user-centred approach based on iterative design processes, empirically evaluating various prototypes involving a total of 73 children. Overall, the results showed that the designed prototype can be used as a starting point for an interactive storytelling system. Beside this, the outcomes raised several new questions, for example about the relationship between play, creativity, and storytelling and how to measure the quality of stories produced in an interactive way. The authors suggest that future research should include teachers, parents, and caregivers to gain knowledge about how the technology best can be applied in practice.

4 Our Little Secret: Design and User Study on an Electrochromic Ambient Display for Supporting Long-Distance Relationships

Next DLI 2019 paper by *Hong Li, Heiko Müller, and Jonna Häkkilä*, presents a practice-based study of people living remotely from their partner. Here, the unobtrusive display technique was prototyped with an interactive picture frame, which was used as a probe to chart the use possibilities of this technique. The study was interview-based as well as in-the-wild deployment of one week to evaluate the concept and the design. The use study showed that a non-light-emitting electrochromic display was well received in terms of use qualities such as calmness and pleasantness. Moreover, the technology allowed for easy and cost-efficient manufacturing of customised displays, which could be placed on different shaped surfaces. In particular, the findings from the in-the-wild study highlighted that the prototype, Our Little Secret, added a new communication channel between the remote couple, which supported their communication and relationship at a distance through the form of a pair of private, meaningful, and always-on yet calm displays. Although promising outcomes, the authors acknowledge that their work is limited by a small sample size and a rather short duration of the in-the-wild study. The latter is aligned with challenges of organising in-the-wild user studies in the field of ubiquitous computing. However, the results indicate that a non-light-emitting display may have potential to support long-distance-relationships by offering meaningful and private forms of communication. This paper shows that designers, nowadays, have a wide range of opportunities for designing meaningful user experiences. The range of technological developments has encouraged different ways of thinking about design, for example, by combining physical and digital interfaces in novel ways.

5   Keeping Digital Libraries Alive: Designing an Interactive Scientific Publication to Drive Demands of Scholars Based on Participatory Design

Next paper by *Camilla Wohlmuth da Silva and Nuno Correia*, addresses the complex issue of designing a meaningful interface where a library could provide and enhance reading experiences and acquisition of knowledge. The study applied a participatory design approach to discuss and find opportunities for the design of a user interface for sharing scientific knowledge in digital libraries. The authors present the initial steps of a participatory design study where three consecutive steps were carried out, namely a participatory design workshop, a follow-up exercise, and the development of a prototype to demonstrate the applied design solutions. The authors argue that even though existing digital libraries has addressed future actions for improving their interface designs in terms of, for example, functionality, content expansion, and content organisation, they most often do not incorporate stakeholders into the design process. The authors further argue the importance of actively involve stakeholders when creating new and improved design solutions as this can increase the designer's awareness of a problem space. Thus, the authors state, participation can be seen as a researcher's shared decision space to determine quality and direction of, in the case of this paper, scientific publication util- isation. The outcomes of the study showed that working with scholars as participants in a co-design process posed a richness and variety of possible solutions to improve scientific communication by means of digital and interactive designs. The paper points to improvements related to characteristics of the interface to provide increased engage- ment and accessibility of scientific information to scholars as well as how interaction and functionalities would improve by having meaningful icons as input. In this way, the paper acknowledge the necessity of a participatory design approach to transform an existing digital tool to a meaningful communication medium.

6   Enabling Rural Women in India to Speculate Futures Through Games and Theatre: A Participatory Approach

The last paper in this section of the DLI 2019 proceedings by *Arjun Harish, Mahima Chandak, and Shreya Mukta*, reports on initial findings from engaging in participatory and speculative design methods with rural women in Bihar, India. The study outlines a contextualised workshop including participants as equal partners to the design of their future. The authors emphasise that other cultures like India are not naturally democratic and are comprised of politics and power structures within their setting. Based on this, the paper highlights that in such contexts, participatory and speculative design methods can help in giving voice to marginalised groups of people and uncover these complexities to gain a nuanced understanding of their situation. The findings of the paper contribute to researchers, designers, and technologists who aim to uncover key factors that affect the functioning of complex systems to design sustainable interventions.

A design process begins when initial ideas concerning a possible future take shape and, furthermore, this process is always carried out in a culture-base context. In this regard, Löwgren and Stolterman [3] use the concept of *design situation* referring to a situation that is both the reason for the design process and the context within which the design work is carried out. In this way, the situation is the starting point for a design and evolves along with the design process. Involving stakeholders in such design situations involves considerations of, among others, emotional dimensions to construct knowledge about their desires and expectations. This can, in other words, be expressed as giving voice to the stakeholders as participants in the design process.

7   Epilogue and Acknowledgements

This fifth section introduces five contributions to promote readership of each full paper that are presented in the following chapters. In doing so, the authors of this chapter acknowledge the contribution to this section/volume by each author whose original work was presented in the ArtsIT/DLI 2019 events in Aalborg, Denmark November 7–8, 2019.

References

1. Winograd, T.: From computing machinery to interaction design. In: Denning, P., Metcalfe, R. (eds.) Beyond Calculation: The Next Fifty Years of Computing, pp. 149–162. Springer, Amsterdam (1997)
2. Saffer, D.: Designing for Interaction, 2nd edn. New Riders Press, Indianapolis (2010)
3. Löwgren, J., Stolterman, E.: Thoughtful Interaction Design: A Design Perspective on Information Technology. The MIT Press, London, England (2004)
4. Wertsch, J.V.: Voices of the Mind: A Sociocultural Approach to Mediated Action. Harvard University Press, Cambridge (1993)

Touch to Read: Investigating the Readers' Interaction Experience in Mediated Reading to Design Story Apps

Douglas Menegazzi[1(✉)] and Cristina Sylla[2]

[1] Federal University of Santa Catarina, Florianópolis, Brazil
`douglas.menegazzi@ufsc.br`
[2] University of Minho, Braga, Portugal
`cristina.sylla@ie.uminho.pt`

Abstract. A story app is a children's digital book which takes advantage of the multimedia and multimodality resources of mobile interaction devices. However, the poorly design of the interactive areas (hotspots) in story apps can compromise the reading activity and children's literacy acquisition. This is even more serious in mediated reading between children and parents, since the latter may not know how to use the hotspots or even feel that their presence is superfluous due to the digital resources. Outgoing from this scenario, we have carried out a user study with six parent-child dyads to investigate the effects of hotspots on the readers' experience during mediated reading of three-story apps to identify design problems and opportunities. The study measured five aspects of the interaction with hotspots, namely: 1) understanding, locating and recognizing hotspots; 2) balanced versus unbalanced number of interactions; 3) reading flow versus reading difficulties during the interaction; 4) engagement versus distraction in reading caused by the interactions; 5) distance versus closeness in mediation. The analyses indicate that hotspots are usually not designed for mediated reading, which may lead to parents' disengagement. Poorly located or misrepresented hotspots caused navigation errors negatively impacting reading. Contrary to findings reported by previous studies, we observed that the interactive game areas can provide a common point for intergenerational convergence stimulating mediated reading.

Keywords: Children's digital book · Interaction design · Hotspots

1 Introduction

Interactive digital books can support children's reading development. However, they do not substitute reading instruction or adult's involvement [1, 2]. The gains in children's learning, e.g., story comprehension and the acquisition of new vocabulary, are significantly better when their reading is supported by a more experienced reader also in the context of digital books [2]. A mediator can assist the children in case of reading difficulties, encouraging them to focus on the story, avoiding distraction caused by superfluous

A. Brooks and E. I. Brooks (Eds.): ArtsIT 2019/DLI 2019, LNICST 328, pp. 588–600, 2020.
https://doi.org/10.1007/978-3-030-53294-9_43

multimedia and interaction resources [3]. However, most commercial children's digital books have been designed with the purpose of entertaining children, keeping them occupied. This increasingly nullifies the need for adult's participation [4, 5]. In order to create an interactive area for children's' development of gestures and communication with mediators [6], as well as to create and mediate meaning through multimedia [7], it is essential to develop new approaches for the design of story apps.

Especially hotspots – the interactive areas in story apps – when poorly designed or in excess can generate understanding problems, potentially impairing children's learning [3, 8, 9]. Previous research has identified that 75% of the 137 most popular children's e-books in the USA contained hotspots, but just 20% of the hotspots contributed in some way to the story [10]. This is even more problematic in case of mediated reading. A previous study carried out with three to five years old children verified that 48% of parents had difficulties in guiding their children to interacting with hotspots in mediated reading of digital books [11]. Moreover, highly interactive books can create a frustrating reading experience for children and mediators, as these artifacts are generally not designed for

Table 1. Types of hotspots in story apps according to their functions or interaction mode [12].

No.		Description
1	Navigation	To navigate between pages or to access other content areas
2	Menus	Interactive areas or lists to choose options
3	Video/Animation	To enable and control audiovisual content
4	Game/Playful activities	Playful activities and interactive games linked to the story
5	Dictionaries/Extras	To access explanations and more advanced vocabulary
6	Quiz and Feedback	Interactive areas to check, track and measure learning
7	Hyperlinks	External links to websites, social networks or other apps
8	Integrated into physical media	Interactions enabled by handling a printed book connected to the digital device
9	Settings	To enable and control reading options such as sound tuning, font size, language, automatic reading
10	Personalisation	To incorporate new content into the story or recreate it, e.g. recording reading
11	Augmented Reality	Interaction that allows to superimpose the virtual on the real world (usually using QR codes)
12	Interaction via hardware	Interactions enabled by (gyroscope and accelerometer) movement (360°) of the device by the reader
13	Sound Interaction	To enable and interact with story content/characters through the reader's voice interactions

mediated reading [8]. Both, professionals and publishers recognize that there is a lack of patterns and of validated models in digital publishing for children [9]. Outgoing from this context, this work aimed at investigating the effects of hotspots on the readers' experience during mediated reading in order to identify design problems and opportunities.

2 Hotspots in Story Apps for Children

As extensive bibliographic review and an analyzes of commercial story apps has identified at least thirteen different types of hotspots according to their function and mode of interaction [12], (see Table 1). Outgoing from this classification, we conduct a user study to measure the readers' interaction experience with hotspots during mediated reading of story applications.

3 User Study

In the context of User-Centered Design, interaction goes beyond usability, taking into consideration an emotional dimension, which aims at meeting the users' desires and expectations [13]. An investigation focused on the user's experience allows understanding the phenomenological and pragmatic dimensions of the user's interaction with the artifacts and to generate greater satisfaction when interacting with products [14].

Table 2. The set of metrics for evaluating the readers' experience with story apps.

Metrics	Description
1- Understanding, locating & recognizing hotspots	Children can only benefit from story apps if they easily find and understand how to interact with them, for that, it is necessary to have adequate graphic, verbal, iconic, auditory representations, among others [15]
2- Balanced versus unbalanced number of interactions	An excess of interaction areas may compromise learning [3, 8] or overload cognition. However, children's engagement is significantly better in story apps that have hotspots compared to those that do not have them [16], even in cases of mediated reading [8]
3 - Reading flow vs. difficulties	Continuous interruptions of the reading activity due to the interaction can negatively influence the story comprehension [17]
4 - Engagement versus distraction in reading caused by the interactions	Well-designed hotspots that are congruent with the literary content tend to provide more engaged learning and positively influence reading frequency. However, some hotspots can be included for mere entertainment purposes and lead to playing rather than engaging the children in reading [1, 5, 15, 16]
5 - Distance versus closeness in mediation	In general hotspots are designed for a single user and not for shared or mediated reading [5]. Parents may have difficulties and feel frustrate when they do not know how to interact with them [8]. Nonetheless, hotspots can be designed to create possibilities for mediation, thus stimulating an intergenerational activity [18]

3.1   Measuring the Reader's Experience with Hotspots

Building on literature, we established 5 metrics as a bipolar scale to measure the reading experience while interacting with hotspots on children's story apps (see Table 2).

3.2   The Sample of Story Apps

Prior to carrying out the study, we selected three commercial story apps that present different types of hotspots. The selection was made from renowned prize lists for children's literature, such as the most important Brazilian children's book award, the *Prêmio Jabuti*[1] and top sellers story apps from the Appstore. The selected apps were (a) *Quanto Bumbum!*[2], (b) *Marina está do Contra*[3], and (c) *Hat Monkey*[4]. All these apps are available in Portuguese language and appropriate for the age group under investigation. These story apps presented a total of ten different types of hotspots (see Table 3). Three interactive areas were left out as they were not available in these apps: Dictionaries (5), Hotspots integrated into Physical Media (8) and Augmented Reality Hotspots (11).

Table 3. The different types of hotspots in the three selected story apps

No.	Hotspots/Story apps	Story app A	Story app B	Story app C
1	Navigation	✓	✓	✓
2	Menus	✓	✓	✓
3	Video/Animation	✓	✓	✓
4	Game/Playful activities	✓	✓	✓
5	Dictionaries/Extras			
6	Quiz and feedback		✓	✓
7	Hyperlinks	✓	✓	✓
8	Integrated into physical media			
9	Settings	✓	✓	✓
10	Personalisation		✓	
11	Augmented reality			
12	Interaction by hardware		✓	
13	Sound interaction			✓

---

[1] The *Prêmio Jabuti* website can be accessed under the link: https://www.premiojabuti.com.

[2] Editora Caixote: Quanto Bumbum! - livro interativo para crianças. Version 1.4.1 (2016). Accessed 12 April 2018 from http://twixar.me/mzdn.

[3] Editora Caixote: Marina está do Contra. Version 1.1.5 (2018). Accessed 12 April 2018 from http://twixar.me/Wzdn.

[4] Haughton, C.: Hat Monkey app. Fox and Sheep, version 1.9 (2014). Accessed 12 April 2018 from http://twixar.me/Jzdn.

3.3 Participants and Procedure

The users' sample was composed of six parent-child dyads. The children were aged between six and eight years old. At this age children already have some reading independence but can still benefit from the guidance of a more knowledgeable person. All the participants were selected from a Portuguese elementary public school. The study was conducted after classes at the school's library. Each parent-child dyad participated in three reading sessions. We have received written informed consent from all the parents and from the head of the school to carry out the study.

Fig. 1. The research sessions with the pairs of readers of three different story apps and the respective distribution of app per session/pair.

Each session was conducted in a different day and with a different app (see Fig. 1). In order to avoid any bias, such as initial shyness of the children and the mediators' lack of familiarity with story apps, we have alternated the reading order of the apps. In total, eighteen reading sessions were carried out from April to July 2018.

3.4 Data Collection and Methodology

We took particular care to select appropriate approaches to carrying out research with children. The method, tools, protocols and procedures are summarized in the following (Fig. 2).

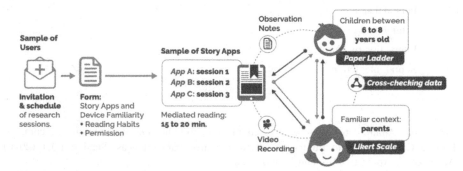

Fig. 2. The methodology: research tools, procedures and data collection.

3.4.1   Reading Habits Questionnaire

In the first session, the researcher applied a questionnaire to the parents to gather information about their and their child's reading habits as well as their familiarity with digital books and electronic reading devices. This survey took approximately 5 min per participant.

3.4.2   Reading Sessions

In each of the three reading sessions we provided a different story app on an *iPad* device to each parent-child dyad, and instructed them to read as they usually do at home (Fig. 3). Each reading session lasted around 20 min.

Fig. 3. The children and their parents interacting with the three different story apps.

3.4.3   Assessing Children's Preferences and Understanding of Hotspots

After each parent-child dyad reading session, we conducted a survey with the children to assess their preference and understanding of the different hotspots. For this, we used the Paper Ladder rating scale [19] combined with the Five Degrees of Happiness rating scale [20].

Paper Ladder is a method specially designed for carrying out research with children, it deploys a graphical and tangible version of a Likert scale [21]. Paper Ladder allows children to express their preferences by positioning printed cards with graphical representations of the items under evaluation on the printed ladder. The higher the rung on the ladder, the more the child likes it, on a scale from one to five. In order to make it more understandable for the children we incorporated the graphic emoticons proposed by the Five Degrees of Happiness tool [20] into the Paper Ladder. This also facilitated the positioning of the cards by the children, who placed the printed cards exactly on the emojis (see Fig. 4).

We asked each child to position the cards representing each hotspot on the Paper Ladder. First the researcher made sure that the child could identify the hotspots printed on each card, and then asked her/him to position each card on the Paper Ladder according to his/her opinion. E.g. to check metric one (understanding, locating & recognizing

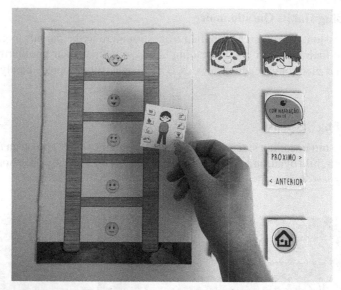

Fig. 4. The adapted Paper Ladder [19–21] and the printed cards representing the Hotspots present on the story app C.

hotspots), he asked the child to position a hotspot card on the ladder according to whether it was easy (top steps) or difficult (lower steps) to find on the app. According to the chosen position, the researcher then asked the child about his/her preferences. This procedure was carried out at the end of each session and lasted approximately 5–10 min.

3.4.4 Mediators

At the end of the reading sessions the parents were also invited to evaluate their experience with the hotspots during mediated reading, using a five-point Likert scale together with the printed cards that represented each hotspot. In total there were between six and nine different types of hotspots per application and five metrics (see Table 3, Sect. 3.2). Each mediator answered approximately 30 to 45 questions (see Fig. 5).

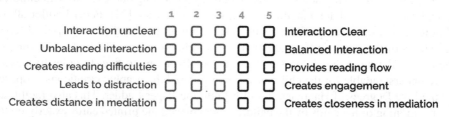

Fig. 5. Likert Scale with metrics for evaluating the mediators experience.

For each reading we also asked the parents how they considered in general their child's interactive experience with the application and about their own experience (see Fig. 6) during mediated reading.

Fig. 6. Likert Scale with metrics for evaluating the whole mediated reading experience.

3.4.5 Data Collection

The data was collected through observations, field notes, photographs and video recordings of the children and the mediators' interactions with the apps. Additionally, we created a check list to map and track the reader's interaction with the hotspots. In cases that the child and the mediator did not interact with some hotpots - even when we have requested them to carry out specific tasks at the end of the reading - we also took this into consideration for the data analyses.

3.4.6 Data Measurement

As mentioned above, the parental responses were assessed for each of the five metrics for each type of hotspot using a five-point Likert scale, where 5 and 4 corresponded to good, 3 and 2 corresponded to problematic and 1 represented a bad interaction experience. Some hotspots were present in all apps, therefore, they were evaluated in the eighteen reading sessions, while other hotspots were available in just one or in two apps (evaluated in six or twelve sessions respectively). In the following we present the hotspots with the most expressive results for each evaluated metric.

4 Observations and Results

All the six participant parents' had smartphones, tablets, computers or videogame devices at home and, with the exception of smartphones, most of them give their children access to these devices. The most used device was the tablet, in general the parents granted their children permission to use it for one hour daily.

Regarding the reading habits, three out of the six participating parents, read books daily with their children. One mother reads books once a week with her child and the remaining two do not have this habit. Only two parents had already read digital books with their children, the other had never used story apps.

During the reading sessions we observed that generally the children themselves assigned mediation roles to their parents, e.g. asking them for the meaning of words. The parents also guided the children helping them to focus on reading.

4.1 Children's Hotspots Preferences

According to the children's preferences, which were assessed using the Paper Ladder, their preferred hotspots were Games and Videos Hotspots. We speculate that this is because these areas provide a more playful interaction, enabling access to attractive multimedia content. In contrast, Navigation and Menus Hotspots were the ones that the children liked the least. Most probably because these hotspots are merely a functional feature. On the one side, it is appropriate that Menu and Navigation Hotspots are secondary during interactive reading in order to avoid casual interactions, on the other side, these hotspots may remain unnoticed by the readers or be underexplored as an interactive narrative resource.

4.2 Mediators' Hotspots Preferences

All the parents considered that the mediated reading experience with the apps was in general enjoyable, assigning it an average of 4.4 points. The parents considered it a very valuable experience for their children (4.5 average). When asked about what was missing for a complete enjoyable experience, most of the parents answered that the story apps should include more games with more levels. This aligns well with the children's preferences for the Game Hotspots.

By mapping the data obtained through the Likert scale with the observation notes we have realized that two recurring features may have impaired the mediators' experience: i) the Video Hotspots were usually controlled just by the children while the mediators, as viewers, often had to wait long and visualize the videos before they were able to continue reading; ii) the mediators that have identified Hyperlinks Hotspots in the apps avoided interacting with them and also prohibited their children to do it, since these interactive areas worked merely to direct the readers to e-commerce.

4.3 Understanding, Locating and Recognizing Hotspots

The icons for the Hyperlink Hotspots were the most difficult to locate and to understand. As these hotspots were available in all the three apps, they were evaluated in eighteen reading sessions. In four of the sessions the participating dyads considered that the Hyperlinks were easily identifiable (assigning a score of 4 and 5), in five of the sessions the participating dyads had some difficulties to identify these hotspots (assigning a score of 3 and 2) and in one session the participants did not identified the Hyperlink Hotspot (assigning a score of 1). In eight of the reading sessions the parent-child dyads did not find the Hyperlinks, although they were asked to perform a specific task that should lead them to find these hotspots on the apps.

Especially one of the story apps revealed a serious problem with the Navigation Hotspots due to the misleading representation of its icon. The Home icon (a symbol of an arrow pointing up) and the Navigation icon (to advance reading) were very similar. After reading the first page some children clicked to move to next page and continuing reading but instead she was redirected to the home page. Some of the children mistakenly clicked the Home icon to advance reading being redirected to home page instead of the next reading page as they have expected.

Overall, the analysis indicates that the first interaction problem faced by the users when reading a story app is the appearance and the location of the hotspots. In our analyses, we have identified three main aspects that need to be taken into consideration when designing hotspots for children's story apps: i) the design of the symbols has to be understandable for children, compatible with their visual cognitive repertoire and familiarity; ii) the design of each different type of hotspot should be different and graphically consistent with its function; iii) the hotspots' position on the screen or on the sections of the app needs to be carefully considered as this influences their identification.

4.4 Balanced Versus Unbalanced Number of Interactions

Concerning the Game Hotspots present in the three-story apps, in ten of eighteen reading sessions the parents of each participating dyad considered that the number of interactions was appropriate, assigning it a score of 4 and 5. The remaining eight participating dyads assigned it a score of 3 points. When asked the reason for their score the parents explained that they would like to have more game areas with more levels. We think that this is due to the fact that the game areas offer more possibilities for joint interaction between the children and their parents, in some cases the children prompt their parent to play together.

Overall, the Game or Ludic Activity areas promoted children's haptic interactions with the apps and higher levels of dialogue and body expressions between the children and their parents than the other interactive areas. However, this preference may pose difficulties. This is, it "may lure children's attention away from the narration and turn the activity into a game instead of a reading experience" [8:192]. Based on the results of this study, we provide two guidelines for the design of Game Hotspots: (i) provide short games that are only played once within the narrative and (ii) if available, design more complex games with more levels in a distinct area, apart from the reading pages. These games can be open to more than one player and used to reinforce the learning activity.

4.5 Reading Flow Versus Reading Difficulties During the Interaction

Regarding the Menu Hotspots - the interactive areas such as chapters or lists that enable accessing the app's activities - in ten out of eighteen reading sessions the parents considered that the interaction with these Hotspots provided a good reading flow (assigning a score of 4 and 5). However, in six reading sessions the participating dyads have attributed low rates to these hotspots (assigning a score of 3 and 2). This means that the interaction with the Menu Hotspots disturbed reading. In the other two sessions the readers have not found the Menu Hotspots, even after being requested to use them. This is mainly because none of the three apps contained Menu Hotspots in the inner pages. These were only displayed on the apps' Home Page. As a consequence, the readers always had to go to the Home Page or navigate page by page when they wanted to choose or return to a specific page. This interrupted the reading and frustrated the readers. Especially the parents have shown fatigue while guiding their child back to the reading activity. E.g., avoiding distraction caused by the child's attempt to access the games on the Home Page Menus'. To avoid this, we suggest that whenever possible, the story apps have main Menu Hotspots, especially chapter menus, in the inner pages. This allows the users to quickly and without distraction access menus that are relevant to the reading activity without leaving the page that they are reading.

4.6 Engagement Versus Distraction in Reading Caused by the Interactions

Regarding engagement, the Personalization Hotspots' were the most problematic. This hotspot was only available in one story app (C), as an interactive audio recording mechanism, which allowed the readers to record their own reading. Four out of the six parent-child dyads did not interact with this hotspot. The two other declined to rate it since they did not complete the recording of the first page. Apparently, this type of hotspot has not engaged the readers to interact with. However, this may be due to a lack of time of the parents, as they understood it as a complex activity or as an activity that would involve rereading the story.

4.7 Distance Versus Closeness in Mediation

Regarding the degree of closeness between the mediators and their children, during the interaction with the videos and animations, in ten out of eighteen reading sessions, the parents assigned it a score of 4 and 5. In two reading sessions, the parents have evaluated these hotspots as problematic (assigning a score of 3 and 2) and in four reading sessions the parents considered that the videos negatively impacted the reading activity and compromised the engagement between the children and their parents (assigning a score of 1), as both were merely spectators. In two of reading sessions the mediators have not even remembered app's video and animation areas, consequently, they have not evaluated these hotspots.

However, while the visualization of long videos turned the mediators into merely spectators, the Game Hotspots created closeness between the parents and their children. The children spontaneously prompted their parents to "play" with them and sometimes they started a competition. This probably explains why both the parents and the children wished to have more such interactive areas in the apps, as above-mentioned. The hotspots that promoted the highest interaction level between the parents and their children in mediated reading were those that provided the possibility to simultaneously interact with the app.

5 Conclusions

This paper presents the research process and the results of a user study, carried out with six parent-child dyads during mediated reading. Our goal was to identify positive and negative aspects of the readers' experience with different types of interactive areas - hotspots - on children's digital books to inform the design of such areas. The results indicate that:

1) it is fundamental that the users are able to easily identify the hotspots and their function, therefore it is important that the distinctive design of the hotpot icons' is aligned with children's visual repertoire and cognitive development, as well as the appropriate location on the app's interface;
2) contrary to previous studies that generally discourage the implementation of games in digital books, the children and the parents that have participated in this study

expressed the wish to have more Game Hotspots, providing that these promote more dynamic interaction moments between the parents and their children and engage them in the story. We conjecture that when such areas are well integrated into the story, they have the potential to provide additional opportunities for joint and mediated reading;

3) the reading flow can be improved when the most relevant Menu, Configuration and Navigation Hotspots are conveniently placed, especially on the reading pages that provide reading customizations and navigation between pages or sections;

4) interactive features that demand complex interactions, require a great amount of time to interact with or are perceived as an extra task will probably not engage the readers, may distract them or even lead to ending the reading activity;

5) the engagement between the child and the mediator is more intense when the app provides space for the children, who usually controls the device, to invite the adult to help them, e.g. explaining unknown words, or to "play". However, long videos and animations can fatigue the mediators, as they may feel that their presence is superfluous.

Overall, although story apps may offer highly interactive resources that may contribute to help and engage children in reading, they do not replace the presence of reading mediators. In this paper we have present some observations which may contribute to improve the design and integration of hotspots in children's digital books, and to facilitate mediated reading with these devices aimed at children that are learning to read and can benefit from assisted reading.

Acknowledgments. We thank the children from the school EB1 Gualtar, in Braga, Portugal, for their valuable contributions, the school principal Prof. Guilherme Barbosa, and the teachers for the permission to conduct this study. We also thank the reviewers for their valuable insights and suggestions, which contributed to improve the quality of this paper. The first author acknowledges the CNPq Brazil support (process 206788/2017-7). This study has been financed by the Portuguese Foundation for Science and Technology - FCT, and European Regional Development Funds through the Competitiveness and Internationalization Operational Program reference Mobeybou-POCI-01-0145-FEDER- 032580.

References

1. Salmon, L.G.: Factors that affect emergent literacy development when engaging with electronic books. Early Child. Educ. J. **42**(2), 85–92 (2014)
2. Homer, B.D., et al.: Moved to learn: the effects of interactivity in a Kinect-based literacy game for beginning readers. Comput. Educ. **74**, 37–49 (2014)
3. Morgan, H.: Multimodal children's e-books help young learners in reading. Early Child. Educ. J. **41**(6), 477–483 (2013). https://doi.org/10.1007/s10643-013-0575-8
4. Follmer, S., Ballagas, R., Raffle, H., Spasojevic, M., Ishii, H.: People in books: using a Flash-Cam to become part of an interactive book for connected reading. In: ACM 2012 Conference on Computer Supported Cooperative Work, CSCW 2012, pp. 685–694 (2012)

5. Timpany, C., Vanderschantz, N., Hinze, A., Cunningham, S.J., Wright, K.: Shared reading of children's interactive picture books. In: Tuamsuk, K., Jatowt, A., Rasmussen, E. (eds.) ICADL 2014. LNCS, vol. 8839, pp. 196–207. Springer, Cham (2014). https://doi.org/10.1007/978-3-319-12823-8_20

6. Kucirkova, N.: Digitalised early years. Where next? Psychologist **24**(12), 938–940 (2011)

7. Hoffman, J.L., Paciga, K.A.: Click, swipe, and read: sharing e-books withtoddlers and preschoolers. Early Child. Educ. J. **42**(6), 379–388 (2014)

8. Bus, A.G., Takacs, Z.K., Kegel, C.A.T.: Affordances and limitations of electronic storybooks for young children's emergent literacy. Dev. Rev. **35**, 79–97 (2015)

9. Sargeant, B.: What is an ebook? What is a book app? And Why should we care? An analysis of contemporary digital picture books. Child. Lit. Educ. **46**(4), 454–466 (2015)

10. Guernsey, L., Levine, M., Chiong, C., Severns, M.: Pioneering Literacy in the Digital Wild West: Empowering Parents and Educators. The Joan Ganz Cooney Center, New York (2012)

11. Knoche, H., Rasmussen, N.A., Boldreel, K., Olesen, J.L.O., Pedersen, A.E. .: Do interactions speak louder than words? dialogic reading of an interactive tablet-based e-book with children between 16 months and three years of age. In: 13th International Conference on Interaction Design and Children, IDC 2014, pp. 285–288 (2014)

12. Menegazzi, D., Sylla, C., Padovani, S.: Hotspots em livros infantis digitais: um estudo de classificação das funções. In: Proceedings of Digicom 2018 – 2nd International Conference on Design and Digital Communication, pp. 45–56 (2018)

13. Norman, D.: Emotional Design: Why We Love (or Hate) Everyday Things. Basic Books, New York (2003)

14. Hassenzahl, M., Platz, A., Burmester, M., Lehner, K.: Hedonic and ergonomic quality aspects determine a software's appeal. In: Proceedings of the SIGCHI conference on Human Factors in Computing Systems CHI 2000, vol. 2, no. 1, pp. 201–208 (2000)

15. Cahill, M., Mcgill-Franzen, A.: Selecting "app" ealing and "app" ropriate book apps for beginning readers. Read. Teach. **67**(1), 30–39 (2013)

16. Kao, G.Y.-M., Tsai, C.-C.C., Liu, C.-Y., Yang, C.-H.: The effects of high/low interactive electronic storybooks on elementary school students' reading motivation, story comprehension and chromatics concepts. Comput. Educ. **100**, 56–70 (2016)

17. Smeets, D.J.H., Bus, A.G.: The interactive animated e-book as a word learning device for kindergartners. Applie Psycholinguistics **36**(4), 1–22 (2012)

18. Kucirkova, N., Messer, D., Sheehy, K., Flewitt, R.: Sharing personalised stories on iPads: a close look at one parent-child interaction. Literacy **47**(3), 115–122 (2013)

19. Sylla, C., Segura, E.M., DeWitt, A., Arif, A.S., Brooks, E.I.: Fiddling, pointing, hovering, and sliding: embodied actions with three evaluation tools for children. In: Proceedings of the 2018 Annual Symposium on Computer-Human Interaction in Play (CHI PLAY 2019). ACM, New York (2019)

20. Hall, L., Hume, C., Tazzyman, S.: Five degrees of happiness: effective smiley face likert scales for evaluating with children. In: Proceedings of the 15th International Conference on Interaction Design and Children, pp. 311–321. ACM (2016)

21. Sylla, C., Arif, A.S., Segura, E.M., Brooks, E.I.: Paper ladder: a rating scale to collect children's opinion in user studies. In: Proceedings of the 19th International Conference on Human-Computer Interaction with Mobile Devices and Services, 96, Vienna, Austria, 04–07 September 2017 (2017)

Designing a Smart Toy Interactive Setting for Creating Stories
From Free Play to Story Structure and Reflection Support

Silke ter Stal[1,2], Alejandro Catala[3(✉)], Mariët Theune[4], and Dennis Reidsma[4]

[1] Roessingh Research and Development, Enschede, The Netherlands
s.terstal@rrd.nl
[2] Faculty of Electrical Engineering, Mathematics and Computer Science,
University of Twente, Enschede, The Netherlands
[3] Centro Singular de Investigación en Tecnoloxías Intelixentes (CiTIUS),
Universidade de Santiago de Compostela, Santiago de Compostela, Spain
alejandro.catala@usc.es
[4] Human Media Interaction, University of Twente, Enschede, The Netherlands
{m.theune,d.reidsma}@utwente.nl

Abstract. Smart and robotic toys introduce more possibilities than ever for building interactive settings for playful learning. Here we explore their use for supporting the development of storytelling skills in children. Previous research on interactive storytelling prototypes has already shown their potential to this end. However, the focus has often been set on technical implementation issues or using very specialized hardware that may limit their potential to go outside the lab. The lack of a general and integrated application with off-the-shelf affordable components has encouraged our research on how to combine a tablet application with an existing smart robotic toy, so that it supports the creation of structured stories and children's reflection on them. Thus, this paper reports on the design and development of a multimedia storytelling application that includes a smart robotic toy, adopting a user-centric approach with iterative design and user-testing cycles.

Keywords: Interactive digital storytelling · Smart toys and robots · Structured narrative support · Application for primary school children

1 Introduction

Nowadays toys enhanced with animated behavior are becoming more advanced and ubiquitous by including digital capacities and embedded electronics. Intelligent or smart toys exhibit autonomous believable responses to changes in their environment [1]. An emerging strand of smart toys are programmable robot toys [3], fueled by their increase in popularity and suitability to STEM[1] activities

---

[1] STEM stands for Science, Technology, Engineering and Mathematics.

© ICST Institute for Computer Sciences, Social Informatics and Telecommunications Engineering 2020
Published by Springer Nature Switzerland AG 2020. All Rights Reserved
A. Brooks and E. I. Brooks (Eds.): ArtsIT 2019/DLI 2019, LNICST 328, pp. 601–610, 2020.
https://doi.org/10.1007/978-3-030-53294-9_44

both at school and home. However, as largely discussed in [19], the range of skills expected to be developed by children far exceeds a strict interpretation of STEM education. Skills such as creativity, communication, and collaboration are consistent across frameworks for 21st century competence. When considering activities with smart toys that can be used for strengthening and supporting development of these skills, we focus on *storytelling* as it has been presented as a suitable new media approach for learning (see [5,16]-p. 300).

During primary school, children's narratives are expected to move from very linear and chronological to something more coherent and evaluative, by including a clearer resolution or conclusion, connectives (e.g., *so, then, next, finally*) and comments about thoughts, feelings and intentions based on memories and critical thinking. This transition, however, is not homogeneous in all children and is affected by individual differences [4] (p. 390). For this reason, having tools and activities supporting the construction of stories interactively can be beneficial, to learn by interacting in small groups and reflecting on the process. Our research aims to start filling this gap. As most interactive digital storytelling systems for children (see [9]) typically involve *ad hoc* or very specialized technical developments, which are not easily adopted outside the research lab, we used a commercially available smart robot and affordable toys to create an interactive story world. Our contribution lies in the iterative design of a tablet app that integrates interaction with the robot and guides children to create coherent narratives. Specifically we try to support children's inclusion of structurally important narrative elements such as causal links between actions, references to goals and to internal states of characters [18].

2   Related Work

Much of the existing related work combines a sort of display providing a visual story world representation with tangibles as input devices, which children can use to influence the on-going narrative [10,13]. Some projects have used a tabletop display, coupling in this way both input and output to provide a more direct manipulation [2,12]; tablets have also been used to represent the state of the story world [21]. Regardless of the underlying technology, tangibles are used to encode assets, behaviors for the characters and props that have an effect on the unfolding of the story.

Sometimes children are allowed to expand the available assets by creating drawings, either digital [12] or paper-based [20]. Some storytelling systems rely on pre-scripted stories, although variation is still possible by means of plot choices [2,11]. These systems restrict children in the stories that can be created, but in turn, they define relationships between story assets, which can be useful to develop higher quality stories by linking the assets together in the narrative.

Besides tangibles, more active devices have been incorporated, such as small robots. The work in [17] uses a turtle toy capable of moving, which is driven by means of handheld projectors. The system in [20] can record the movements of the robotic tangible to be played afterwards. The small robot in [12] can move by using tangible cards on a digital tabletop, whereas the robot in [6] can be tele-operated using a tablet app with digital assets and motion controls, as part of the narrative being created. A dinosaur robot is used for storytelling in [15], but it is more focused on programming sequences of behaviors linked to tangible cards than their narrative value. Advanced humanoid robots have also been used as storytellers with pre-recorded behavior [8] or fluffy robots as companions in supportive storytelling activities [21].

Overall, most systems focused on how innovative technology can be used to enable storytelling, but less attention has been paid to encouraging the development of narrative structure, besides organizing assets by scenes, episodes or programs. This observation motivated our research presented below.

3   Iterative Design: Rationale and Implementation

We followed an iterative approach, in which three design cycles were carried out with both implementation and testing stages. They are briefly summarized next.

3.1   First Design: Free-Play Setting with Emotions

Playing with toys is a common activity in childhood, but how children use them to create stories is complex, since it might involve a mix of pretend play, free play and some narrative. Similar to the approach in Davis et al. [7], we created a setting to observe children's free-play with a smart robot toy as shown in Fig. 1-Left. The toy we used was the Cozmo robot designed by Anki[2]. Its physical size and features, such as the possibility to change its speech and facial expressions, made it suitable for use as the main character in the storytelling activity.

A map of the story world was printed on an A0-sized play mat to be placed onto a table. We gave it a space theme, with the earth, the moon and a planet positioned in space. We added simple tangible figures to the setting, since related work suggested that these can help shaping the story world, giving context to the storytelling activity. For this we used Playmobil figures, which also fit the space theme and, besides, they are robust and match the size of the robot. Finally, a tablet was included. The first version of the tablet interface only displayed the robot's mood reactions visually. Depending on the character in front of the robot, or its location, the robot showed a different emotion as a way to introduce reactions and trigger a sort of meaning making process in children.

Evaluation. Ten children (4 female, 6 male; aged from 5 to 10 y/o) participated[3] in the evaluation in this stage. The children played in groups of two,

---

[2] https://www.anki.com/en-us/cozmo.

[3] Previous to their participation, ethical approval from the University was acquired and informed consent forms were signed by the legal tutors of every child participating in any design stage reported in this paper.

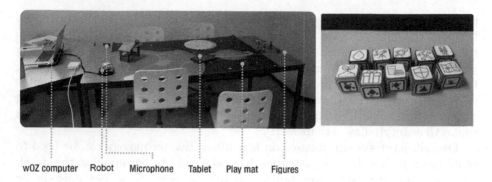

Fig. 1. (Left) Set up for the free play setting. (Right) Picture blocks used as prop in the revised assisted settings with autonomous functions in designs 2 and 3.

resulting in five trials. They were invited to freely play with the setting and tell a story within the space theme with the robot as the main character. The researcher used a Wizard-of-Oz (wOZ) computer interface, which at this stage of development showed the emotional responses of the robot to the children's play.

In all trials children played continuously without having pauses longer than twenty seconds. However, in most trials children mainly played to explore the robot behaviour. This can (at best) be seen as a primitive form of emergent storytelling rather than as creating a coherent narrative. Communication between children was mainly based on individual events, such as explanations of the robot's actions, e.g. "He needs to go into the farm" or "What about that?" while pointing at a figure to be placed in front of the robot. In all trials the children said aloud how they thought the robot was feeling. Sometimes they specifically referred to the character or location shown on the tablet or made exclamations representing the emotion being shown. The trial made clear that the children did see the robot as a character and recognized its emotions (except for disgust, which we left out in the following designs). However, the design did not invite them to create structured stories.

3.2   Second Design: Interaction Mediated by Tablet

In order to support the transition from free play to creating structured stories, we decided to constrain the storytelling task in a number of ways. First, we introduced a goal for the main character (wanting to go to the moon) to encourage the construction of goal-directed narratives [18]. Second, we provided a set of actions for the children to choose from, and changed the tablet app to mediate the interaction, making the storytelling process more controllable by forcing the children to take some necessary steps in order to progress in the construction of the story. Via the tablet, the children had to select an action from a predefined general set. After each action, the robot responded. Then, the children could again select an action. This sequence continued until the children believed the story to be finished (the robot could depart for the moon). A selection of the designed screens can be seen in Fig. 2.

Actions were displayed as verbs on the tablet screen. They are general actions that could be valid for many different themes, supported by the following action taxonomy: Social-entity [*meets, talks to*], Social-object [*gives, receives*], Location [*goes to, finds, brings*], and Generation [*makes, buys*]. These actions were chosen as they could be easily linked to each other and the robot's goal, and combined with many of the locations, objects and characters in the setting. General tangible objects in the shape of picture blocks were introduced as props that could be used in the actions, for example, a rocket, a telescope and a map. In short, the children were guided in the storytelling process by forcing them to select actions from a predefined set, but this set was still sufficiently open for the children to use their creativity.

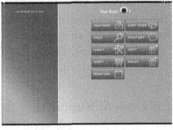

1. *Start screen.* Cozmo explains he would like to go to the moon and asks for help. Pressing the button in the bottom right starts the playing.

2. *Action selection screen.* This screen allows for selection of what Cozmo needs to do. At the left an overview of the story so far can be seen. At this point, no story is created yet.

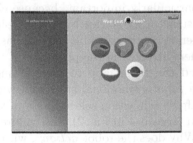

3. *Location selection screen.* The user can select where Cozmo travels in the story. Again, at the left the story overview is presented. The button in the top right can be pressed to return to the previous screen.

4. *Thought screen.* Cozmo provides the user with feedback by a thought bubble containing the recognised location. The next screen appears after a fixed period of time. In the E condition also a random emotion is generated, resulting in an emoticon shown on the tablet and the robot playing an animation.

Fig. 2. Selection of tablet screens used in the second and third design.

The features previously enacted through wOZ were now actually implemented, so that the computer software was handling the sensing and the corresponding autonomic responses of the robot. That required the inclusion of fiducial tags in objects, figures and flags placed in the locations that were recognized by the built-in robot camera (see Fig. 1-Right).

Evaluation. Thirty-three children (15 female, 18 male; aged 6 to 9 y/o) played in pairs with the second design (one child took part twice). In many trials, some story content was present. Children included causality by describing reasons for the occurrence of actions or emotions. They mentioned goal-directed arguments, such as: "he wants to make more friends", "he should wear his suit", "he needs food, otherwise he dies", and "he needs a rocket to go to the moon".

Nevertheless, we observed in the interviews we held afterwards with each pair that most children had difficulties with telling a summary of the story they had created. This indicates that the children still needed some extra scaffolding to structure their narratives and foster connection between story elements. Only a few children specifically mentioned connections between story actions, such as the robot wanting a shield to protect himself, arranging a rocket or map to go to moon, or meeting with an astronaut to get information about space.

3.3   Third Design: Supporting Story Structure and Reflection

In previous steps we learned that interaction in the physical setting could successfully be mediated through the tablet so that there is some order and sequence in the story actions. Giving the robot a goal, having a range of objects to be used in the actions and emotional responses can stimulate children to find links between story elements and make meaning of events that contribute to a certain narrative structure. There were still some issues such as a lack of explicit causal relationships between story elements. This is particularly important, because children at this stage need to develop skills in structuring stories by giving coherence and causal links and increase digital literacy (writing) skills, as emphasized in conversations with primary school teachers involved in the project.

For the final design step, we evolved the tablet app to include questions that would make children reflect on the robot's emotional state and why they selected certain actions in their story. After each action selection step (screen 2 in Fig. 2) and each robot thought screen (screen 4 in Fig. 2), the children were shown a new screen with the question "Why does the robot *action*", with *action* being the previously selected action for the robot. The children had to type their answers on the tablet. In the E condition of the user study (see below), the children were asked a similar question after each emotional response of the robot shown on the 'thought screen' (screen 4 in Fig. 2): "Why does the robot feel *emotion*?", with *emotion* emotion being the emotion shown by the robot. In the NE condition, they were asked "How does the robot feel?" instead. The purpose of the questions was to help the children to work with the concepts in the story world and make connections between them.

The second change we made was that at least three action sequences were required before the children could take the robot to the moon to finish the story. The rest of the tablet app functions and setting remained unchanged.[4]

Evaluation. Thirty children (15 females, 15 males; aged from 6 to 8 y/o) participated in testing the third design. They were all in the third and fourth grade of a Dutch elementary school that did not participate in any of the two previous design step evaluations.

We tested two conditions that differed on whether or not the robotic character showed emotional responses on the thought screen (Fig. 2, screen 4) and in its behavior. The condition with no emotions (NE) implied that the robot was mostly a regular toy, whereas the condition with emotional robot responses (E) implied a smarter toy with autonomous reactions. We focused on the emotional responses because they can be a source of feedback and introduce conflicts to the children's stories, with the potential to assess how such responsiveness might affect the storytelling process. The children were spread over fifteen trials, eight for the NE condition (n = 16) and seven (n = 14) for the E condition.

Based on the answers given by children during the storytelling activity, we assessed some aspects of story quality. Inspired by the story grammar scoring scheme of the Index of Narrative Complexity (INC) created by Petersen et al. [14], our criteria related to two aspects: Action reasoning and Emotion reasoning. For the first one, we assigned 0 points if there was no causal relation between motivation (answer to the 'why' question) and action, and 1 or 2 points depending on whether a local or a global causal relation was given, respectively. Unlike local causal relations, global causal relations link the action to the main goal of the robot (going to the moon), and thus they are signs of goal-directed storytelling. Examples are: "no breathing on the moon" as a reason for buying a space suit (global) and "to meet aliens" as a reason for going to the planet (local). An example lacking any causal relation (0 pt) is "saying woof" as a reason for talking to the dog. Emotion reasoning was scored similarly, but to prevent an unfair advantage for the E condition (where emotions were given by the system), the scoring system differentiated between the two conditions. In the E condition, 0 points were assigned if an emotion was mentioned but no reason for it; 1 point for a local reason (sad, because "there is no little space man") and 2 points for a global reason (angry, because "he does not want to wear a space suit"). In the NE condition, 1 point was assigned if an emotion was mentioned but no reason, and 2 points if also a reason was given (either local or global).

All stories were annotated by two annotators, leading to a substantial inter-rater agreement (Cohen's Weighted Kappa of 0.67). Differences between the annotators were resolved by discussion when giving the final score for stories. Table 1 presents the results of the annotations. It shows a slight trend in favour of the E condition. However, we must be cautious because larger samples would be needed as the scores largely varied across the different trials, ranging between two and eleven points with similar variability in both conditions. Children in the

---

[4] Video: https://www.youtube.com/watch?v=TfrfhNtuqHs.

Table 1. Story annotation scores.

	Condition NE		Condition E	
	M	SD	M	SD
Total score	5.83, median(5.5)	2.93	7, median(8)	2.94
Actions score	2.5	1.64	3.57	1.99
Emotions score	3.33	1.37	3.43	1.27

NE condition almost exclusively mentioned the happy emotion; they did so in all trials except one. In the E condition, emotions were more varied, as they were randomly generated by the system. The children mainly took the randomness of the robotý emotions for granted, but the 'why' questions did trigger them to come up with reasons to match the emotions with the story. They also included more emotions (happy, angry, sad, surprise) in their story summaries when retelling the story they had created. Also, their summaries more often centred around the robot as a protagonist, and explicitly referred to its goal.

It is worth mentioning that many children had problems with spelling and typing, which may have caused their answers to be more limited than if they could have provided them in some other way. Sometimes the question answering was a source of discussion because one child was telling the other that they were wrong or criticising their language skills. We also observed a child saying he was impressed by the reason the other child came up with, and a child laughing about what she had come up with herself. A child specifically mentioned the need to come up "with something logical" in order to go to the moon. This kind of reasoning and skills are to be trained and these reactions show that the structure of the task and app is supporting the process.

4   Conclusion and Future Work

In this paper, we have reported the iterative design of a multimedia application and tangible setting that includes a smart robotic toy in a storytelling activity. Giving the deserved importance to user-centred methods, the design process consisted of several steps, empirically evaluating the various prototypes involving seventy-three children in total.

To support children in moving from free play with toys to more coherent and structured story-based play, the final version of the app included additional why-questions to be completed during the storytelling, in order to let the children reflect and externalize links between elements in the story. The final prototype was tested in two versions, one in which the robotic toy expressed emotions in response to events (condition E), and another without such responses (condition NE). The results showed that introducing emotional responses by the robot led to differences in the way children incorporated emotions in their stories. The E version encouraged children to explore different emotions and reflect on them, linking them to possible causes and consequences. Children managed to create stories around the robot responses, suggesting that the tool can be evolved to support emotional development through stories in future work. We observed that typing the answers to the reflection questions was sometimes an issue. Hence, input can be improved by considering audio recording or using a speech recognizer specialized for children. This would also speed up the pace of interaction and story steps, hopefully leading to longer stories with more possibilities for children to explore different connections between elements in their story. As the prototype design evolved children's storytelling improved, but even in the final study the created stories were somewhat lacking in global coherence. Possibilities to improve the prototype to further encourage the creation of structured stories include extending the tablet app with a goal reminder, content specific questions from the main character's perspective, and story suggestions, to be tested in new follow-up studies with children.

Overall, the research indicates the designed prototype can be used as a starting point for an interactive storytelling system. It also raised many new issues, such as the relationship between play, creativity and storytelling, and how to measure the quality of stories produced. It is future work to research these issues and, in addition, perform brainstorm sessions with elementary school teachers, parents and caregivers on how the technology could best be used in practice.

Acknowledgements. Research partially funded by H2020 MSCA-IF grant No. 701991 coBOTnity, the Spanish Ministry of Science, Innovation and Universities (grants RTI2018-099646-B-I00,TIN2017-84796-C2-1-R) and the Galician Ministry of Education, University and Professional Training (grants ED431C 2018/29, "accreditation 2016–2019, ED431G/08"). Co-funded by the European Regional Development Fund (ERDF/FEDER program).

References

1. Ackermann, E.K.: Playthings that do things: a young kid's "incredibles"! In: Proceedings of the 2005 Conference on Interaction Design and Children, pp. 1–8. ACM, New York (2005)
2. Alofs, T., Theune, M., Swartjes, I.: A tabletop interactive storytelling system: designing for social interaction. Int. J. Arts Technol. **8**(3), 188–211 (2015)
3. Bellas, F., et al.: The Robobo project: bringing educational robotics closer to real-world applications. In: Lepuschitz, W., Merdan, M., Koppensteiner, G., Balogh, R., Obdržálek, D. (eds.) Robotics in Education, pp. 226–237. Springer, Cham (2018). https://doi.org/10.1007/978-3-319-62875-2_20
4. Berk, L.: Child Development. Allyn & Bacon/Pearson, London (2009)
5. Catala, A., Theune, M., Gijlers, H., Heylen, D.: Storytelling as a creative activity in the classroom. In: Proceedings of the 2017 ACM SIGCHI Conference on Creativity and Cognition, pp. 237–242 (2017)
6. Catala, A., Theune, M., Reidsma, D., ter Stal, S., Heylen, D.: Exploring children's use of a remotely controlled surfacebot character for storytelling. In: Chisik, Y., Holopainen, J., Khaled, R., Luis Silva, J., Alexandra Silva, P. (eds.) Intelligent Technologies for Interactive Entertainment, pp. 120–129. Springer, Cham (2018). https://doi.org/10.1007/978-3-319-73062-2

7. Davis, N., Comerford, M., Jacob, M., Hsiao, C.P., Magerko, B.: An enactive characterization of pretend play. In: Proceedings of the 2015 ACM SIGCHI Conference on Creativity and Cognition, pp. 275–284. ACM, New York (2015)

8. Fridin, M.: Storytelling by a kindergarten social assistive robot. Comput. Educ. **70**(C), 53–64 (2014)

9. Garzotto, F.: Interactive storytelling for children: a survey. Inte. J. Arts Technol. (IJART) **7**(1), 5–16 (2014)

10. Kara, N., Aydin, C.C., Cagiltay, K.: Design and development of a smart storytelling toy. Interact. Learn. Environ. **22**(3), 288–297 (2014)

11. Leite, I., et al.: Emotional storytelling in the classroom: individual versus group interaction between children and robots. In: Proceedings of the Tenth Annual ACM/IEEE International Conference on Human-Robot Interaction, pp. 75–82. ACM, New York (2015)

12. Leversund, A.H., Krzywinski, A., Chen, W.: Children's collaborative storytelling on a tangible multitouch tabletop. In: Streitz, N., Markopoulos, P. (eds.) DAPI 2014. LNCS, vol. 8530, pp. 142–153. Springer, Cham (2014). https://doi.org/10.1007/978-3-319-07788-8_14

13. Marco, J., Cerezo, E., Baldasarri, S., Mazzone, E., Read, J.C.: User-oriented design and tangible interaction for kindergarten children. In: Proceedings of the 8th International Conference on Interaction Design and Children, pp. 190–193. ACM, New York (2009)

14. Petersen, D.B., Gillam, S.L., Gillam, R.B.: Emerging procedures in narrative assessment: the index of narrative complexity. Top. Lang. Disord. **28**(2), 115–130 (2008)

15. Ryokai, K., Lee, M.J., Breitbart, J.M.: Children's storytelling and programming with robotic characters. In: Proceedings of the Seventh ACM Conference on Creativity and Cognition, pp. 19–28. ACM, New York (2009)

16. Çıralı Sarıca, H., Koçak Usluel, Y.: The effect of digital storytelling on visual memory and writing skills. Comput. Educ. **94**, 298–309 (2016)

17. Sugimoto, M.: A mobile mixed-reality environment for children's storytelling using a handheld projector and a robot. IEEE Trans. Learn. Technol. **4**(3), 249–260 (2011)

18. Trabasso, T., Stein, N.L., Rodkin, P.C., Munger, M.P., Baughn, C.R.: Knowledge of goals and plans in the on-line narration of events. Cogn. Dev. **7**, 133–170 (1992)

19. Voogt, J., Roblin, N.P.: A comparative analysis of international frameworks for 21st century competences: implications for national curriculum policies. J. Curriculum Stud. **44**(3), 299–321 (2012)

20. Wang, G., Tao, Y., Liu, E., Wang, Y., Yao, C., Ying, F.: Constructive play: designing for role play stories with interactive play objects. In: Proceedings of the Ninth International Conference on Tangible, Embedded, and Embodied Interaction, pp. 575–580. ACM, New York (2015)

21. Westlund, J.K., Breazeal, C.: The interplay of robot language level with children's language learning during storytelling. In: Proceedings of the Tenth Annual ACM/IEEE International Conference on Human-Robot Interaction (Extended Abstracts), pp. 65–66 (2015)

Our Little Secret: Design and User Study on an Electrochromic Ambient Display for Supporting Long-Distance Relationships

Hong Li[1(✉)], Heiko Müller[2], and Jonna Häkkilä[1]

[1] University of Lapland, Rovaniemi, Finland
{hong.li,jonna.hakkila}@ulapland.fi
[2] OFFIS - Institute for Information Technology, Oldenburg, Germany
heiko.mueller@offis.de

Abstract. In this paper, we present a non-light-emitting electrochromic ambient display, Our Little Secret, for supporting the communication in long-distance relationships (LDRs). The unobtrusive display technique was prototyped with an interactive picture frame, which was used as a probe to chart the possibilities of the technique in an interview-based user study (n = 12) and an in-the-wild deployment (one couple) of people living remotely from their partner. The salient findings showed positive response especially on the non-light-emitting nature of the display, and indicates that this type of solution has the potential to support LDR communication and relationship through a pair of private, meaningful, and always-on yet calm displays.

Keywords: Ambient displays · Electrochromic displays · Long-distance relationship · Ambient communication · Customisation · User experience

1 Introduction

Emotional communication and feelings connected with loved ones are a domain, where well-designed computing systems and user interfaces can offer support. Numerous unconventional form factors have been suggested to support long-distance emotional communication and connection [8,13]. In the connection with loved ones, often creating awareness for the other person, his/her context, activities, or presence is in the core of the concept [8]. For awareness, simple communication vocabulary may be enough, and the computing system mediating the communication does not have to be overly complex nor the communication channel excessively rich in expression. The design and aesthetics can however play an important role, as the user experience with such systems should be pleasant and support emotional connection with a loved one [6,21].

Ambient displays, placed in the periphery of the user's attention, offer possibilities for unobtrusive information delivery [15]. In a world, where multiple

A. Brooks and E. I. Brooks (Eds.): ArtsIT 2019/DLI 2019, LNICST 328, pp. 611–622, 2020.
https://doi.org/10.1007/978-3-030-53294-9_45

screens and devices compete for our attention, the ability to create communication and the feeling of connectedness in a subtle way is increasingly valuable. Electrochromism offers a way of creating non-light-emitting displays [10]. The display technique is interesting for its low cost, easy customisation and manufacturing processes. This makes it a candidate for creating ambient displays for emotional and peripheral communication.

In this paper, we explore the use of an electrochromic display, in the form of a picture frame, as an ambient display for computer-mediated communication for long-distance relationships (LDRs). We present the design and manufacturing of the picture frame, as well as a two-fold user study with interviews of people living in LDR (n = 12) and an in-the-wild part (one couple). To the best of our knowledge, we present the first user study of electrochromic displays as an ambient device implemented in-the-wild for connecting remote couples.

2   Related Work

Ambient displays have been employed as an aesthetically pleasing form of information visualisation in mediating emotions or creating the feeling of remote presence. Prior work has used a number of everyday objects as unconventional user interfaces to facilitate emotional communication [8], and, as specifically in our interests, to connect couples in LDRs [13]. Examples of unconventional interfaces to mediate connectedness and awareness of a distant loved one include connected chairs [19], slippers [3], and candle stands [6]. For a more comprehensive overview, Li et al. present an analysis of 52 unconventional interfaces for connecting distant loved ones [13].

Interactive picture frames have been showcased with different designs for creating a connection between people. LumiTouch consists of a pair of interactive picture frames that enhance emotional communication through the illumination of the paired picture frame when the local picture frame is being touched [2]. More recently, a pair of inflatable photo frames that create a feeling of connectedness by sharing the physical inflating movement of breathing on the surface of the paired user's photo frame [11]. Focusing on other aspects than LDR couples, interactive picture frames have been demonstrated for creating awareness for the daily activities of a remote elderly family member through a digital family portrait [20]. Dey and Guzman have presented Presence Displays, created through a co-design process, which were reported to create better awareness of and connectedness with a family member or friend than conventional online presence displays [5]. Uriu and Odom have studied interactive picture frames for the remembrance of deceased family members [22].

Electrochromism is the property of certain materials to reversibly change optical parameters such as colour, transmittance or opacity, when a voltage is applied [17]. Based on polymers or metal polymers, there is a wide range of electrochromic (EC) materials available. One of the most common applications is mirror tinting for rear-view mirrors in vehicles, or window-tinting in aviation or architectural applications. Different ink formulations allow for screen-printing or inkjet-printing of display designs [10].

Fig. 1. Our Little Secret in different modes (Color figure online)

EC displays are non-light-emitting, making them suitable for applications where luminescence is detrimental, such as deployment in the bedroom. Further, EC displays are transparent, free-form, and flexible. They are slow switching and of relatively low contrast, making them a promising candidate for ambient displays [4]. Unlike other non-light-emitting display technologies such as LCD or e-ink, they do not require complex driver electronics, making them suitable for rapid prototyping. EC displays exhibit temporary open circuit memory for periods up to a few hours, thus they are very energy efficient, as they only require an electric current when switching or refreshing the current state. EC displays are shape-based, rather than pixel-based [16]. EC displays have been demonstrated with different device form factors, including a bendable wristband [12], running shoe and household status display [4].

3 Our Little Secret - Design and Prototype

The design of Our Little Secret followed the framework derived from the work by Li et al. [14], which articulates different aspects for systems designed for computer-mediated emotional communication in LDRs. We started the design process by carrying out a number of semi-structured interviews with individuals (n = 10, M = 5, F = 5) who were involved in LDRs with time zone differences, in order to build empathy with them. The interviews were designed according to the key characteristics that had identified in the *user* and *LDR* dimension of the framework [14]. Each interview took approximately 30 min and was audio recorded. The interview participants came from different cultures (e.g., European, Asian, African) with an average age of 34 years.

The findings from these semi-structured interviews indicated that all of the participants preferred using mainstream lightweight communication media (e.g. instant messaging applications) that do not require much skill or effort. As mainstream communication media has enabled an easy, instant, low-cost, and convenient channel for many everyday aspects of LDR maintenance. On the other hand, mainstream communication media lacks the ability to enable the emotional connection for LDRs. The semi-structured interviews revealed the need for making the standardised communication tools symbolic and meaningful to the remote couples. Moreover, the importance of secrecy for intimate communication was highlighted. Several participants experienced an awkward moment when intimate messages sent by their remote partner were observable to bystanders from the screen previews. The participants who had large time zone differences with their remote partners had to schedule communication. Due to the asynchronous daily schedules, sending messages without disturbing their remote partners was said to be a challenge.

Based on the findings from the semi-structured interviews, we created a design for a connected picture frame, Our Little Secret. Our Little Secret (see Fig. 1) is a pair of ambient electrochromic displays that are designed to support emotional communication through secrecy, customisation, subtle cues, simpleness for couples in LDRs, particularly those with large time zone differences. Our prototype presents a city landscape and colourful spiral hearts (see Fig. 1), but the graphical contents can also be customised by the users. Our Little Secret comprised of three functions:

- The city landscape switches between day and night display according to the time of the paired user's location;
- The hearts switch colours when receiving a secret code from the paired user;
- The display stops switching when the interaction between the couple is low.

The centre-piece of the apparatus used in our study is an inkjet-printed electrochromic display built in vertical stack design using PET-ITO as combined substrate and electrode on both sides of the stack. The ITO layers have been partly removed across the display along the design to create two individually controllable areas in the same display, the city landscape and the hearts section (see Fig. 1). To enhance the effect of the hearts section, we added a printed background. A laser-cut frame and a fabric ornament hide the technical details from the users. In our prototype, we used an ink which two states are an almost transparent (to the human eye), blue and dark blue. It works at the switching voltage of 1.5 V, and switches from one state to another within seconds, depending on the size of the display. For the control, we used an ESP32 Huzzah microprocessor running Arduino code. The ESP32 is equipped with Bluetooth, which we used to connect to an Android app monitoring communication. When a message with certain content or from a certain sender was received, the hearts section was switched. The city landscape was switched according to the current day-time.

To embed Our Little Secret in context and help to communicate its usage in the user study, we envisioned a scenario of how it would be used in everyday life in an LDR:

A newly-married couple from Finland has to live apart since the husband has been relocated to work in the USA and often goes on business trips around the world. There are thousands of miles and time zone differences between them.

Fig. 2. The digital picture frame used in the study.

Communication has been a challenge for the couple as time zone difference leads to asynchronous life: it is early morning in the USA and the husband is about to go to work when the wife in Finland returns home from work and wants to have a chat about the day with her husband. What makes it harder to communicate with each other is that the wife always has to check the time zone difference when the husband goes on a business trip, so she knows if it is an appropriate time to call her husband without disturbing his work or sleep. With the help of Our Little Secret - a pair of customisable ambient displays - the couple discovered a new communication channel between them. The city landscape of the wife's picture frame on the table of the living room switches between day and night display according to the local time of the place where the husband is currently located. The hearts are a means to communicate that the couple is thinking of one another. Our Little Secret encourages the couple to engage in emotional communication, as it will stop switching if there is no communication between the couple for more than 24 h.

4   System Evaluation with User Studies

The evaluation of Our Little Secret consisted of two studies. We started from a Wizard-of-Oz study and conducted a one-week in-the-wild deployment. For both studies, we followed general qualitative coding principles for data analysis, in which we began by developing a number of codes based on the collected data, then organised emerging similarly coded data into categories.

4.1   Wizard-of-Oz Study

The Wizard-of-Oz study was conducted by a moderator who directly controlled the electrochromic and digital picture frames (Figs. 1 and 2) via the nRF UART app from Google's Play store. We took the Wizard-of-Oz approach to convince the participants the prototype was fully functional. The functions of the digital picture frame worked the same as the concept of Our Little Secret. The study consisted of the following phases, adding up to approximately 45 min per participant:

1. Signing a consent form and completing a background questionnaire.
2. Learning the usage scenario of Our Little Secret, and familiarising with the three functions, i.e., the switching between day and night display, the switching when getting a message from a paired user, and the neutral mode when the system stops working due to low interaction between the two users;
3. Selecting five terms from the Product Reaction Card (PRC) [1].
4. Learning and familiarising with the concept of the digital picture frame.
5. Selecting another five terms from the PRC [1].
6. Comparing the concept of Our Little Secret with the digital picture frame using the AttrakDiff^{TM}[7] seven-point scale.

We recruited twelve participants (M = 6, F = 6), the median age of 34 years, living in a steady LDR. Altogether, 10/12 had a partner living in another time zone (with 1–11 h difference), and 2/12 in the same time zone. Mainstream communication media, e.g. WhatsApp, Skype, Wechat, Messenger, were the most used computer-mediated communication tools used by the participants to communicate with their remote partners.

4.2 In-the-Wild Study

We recruited a couple involved in a commuter marriage for the in-the-wild study. The couple was heterosexual, married, and did not have children. They had been living apart from each other for two year due to the maintenance of dual-career, and reunited as often as every weekend. The couple used Our Little Secret for one week and filled out a daily logbook reporting their experience. We used the electrochromic picture frame with a custom made Android app that we uploaded to the participants' phones. This app monitored the communication and switched the display accordingly. To avoid any ethical issues and protect participants' privacy, the app did not track any conversation so the research moderator had no access to the couple's private conversations. The switching of colourful hearts was controlled by sending a digital number, i.e. 2, to the paired user's phone. The couple was asked to convey secret languages with which they could associate when the hearts were switching colours. Following the study, a separate interview was conducted with each participant. The interviews were audio-recorded and then transcribed for analysis.

5 Results

In this section, we report the results of our two-fold study, beginning with results from the Wizard-of-Oz study, and then continue with results for our In-the-Wild exploration.

5.1 Wizard-of-Oz Study

Specifically, on a scale of 1 (would strongly prefer the concept of the digital picture frame) to 5 (would strongly prefer the concept of Our Little Secret),

9/12 of the participants strongly preferred the concept of Our Little Secret. The most chosen terms that the participants selected from PRC to describe the concept of Our Little Secret for supporting LDRs were: *creative* (9), *customisable* (7), *meaningful* (7), *personal* (7), *calm* (5). User perceptions towards Our Little Secret were mostly positive. "*I felt intrigued by the switching, this is something new to me*" (P5). "*I like the idea that the graphics can be customised to my taste because these colourful hearts are too romantic and girly to me*" (P1). In total, 25 terms were selected to describe the concept, and there was only one negative term being selected, i.e. *slow* (2). As in these comments: "*It wasn't easy to tell the switching at first because the process took a little longer than I expected.*" (P11). "*The contrast was subtle at first and then took a bit of time to become stronger later.*" (P12).

The most chosen terms that the participants selected from PRC to describe the illuminating digital picture frame for supporting LDRs were: *distracting* (9), *ordinary* (8), *fast* (5), *rigid* (4). There were 21 terms selected to describe the concept of the digital picture frame while providing a clear contrast with the electrochromic prototype, user perceptions towards the concept of the digital picture frame were fairly negative. "*The screen* [of the digital picture frame] *glows all the time, so I'd easily get frustrated and annoyed because I can't sleep well unless my bedroom is totally dark.*" (P10). Another criticism of the concept of the digital picture frame was due to its lack of novelty, e.g., "*This* [the digital picture frame] *feels just like one more app in a tablet, nothing really special to me.*" (P2). Additionally, a concern of energy consumption of the concept of the digital picture frame was raised, e.g., "*It doesn't seem very sustainable to leave the screen* [of the digital picture frame] *always on.*" (P4).

Examining the participants' qualitative comments in regard to enhance the presented concept, 5/12 of the participants considered the switching of the display was too subtle, and hence would like to increase the contrast of the display or to enable more colours in the display. The feature of customisation was considered as beneficial, however, instead of a semi-fixed picture frame, 4/12 of the participants would like the concept to be smaller, portable or wearable, e.g., "*I'd have it* [Our Little Secret] *implemented on my phone case so it's with me all the time, and if he sends a message I can immediately notice it without disturbing anyone when I'm in a meeting*" (P12). "*The picture frame concept won't work for me, but if I can customise it* [the form factor of Our Little Secret] *and turn it to something smaller and more portable, like a water bottle or something wearable, so I can easily bring it with me ... But the digital picture frame is always just an iPad, I can't make any significant change on it* [the form factor of the digital picture frame]" (P9). Furthermore, 3/12 of the participants would like to enrich the display by customising more meanings to the display, e.g. enabling weather forecast of the remote partner's location.

Figure 3 outlines the participants' subjective ratings towards the concept of Our Little Secret and the digital picture frame across 28 pairs of opposite adjectives provided by AttrakDiff^{TM}. The analysis of the adjective-pairs can be further divided into four evaluation dimensions, i.e. pragmatic quality (PQ), hedonic quality - identity (HQ-I), hedonic quality - stimulation (HQ-S), and attractiveness (ATT). It can be seen from Fig. 3 that Our Little Secret performed better than the digital picture frame in general. Our Little Secret was scored highly positive over the digital picture frame in terms of *human, stylish, inventive, creative, innovative, captivating, novel, pleasant* areas. On the other hand, the digital picture frame was assessed comparatively better than Our Little Secret in regard to *predictable, professional, premium* areas.

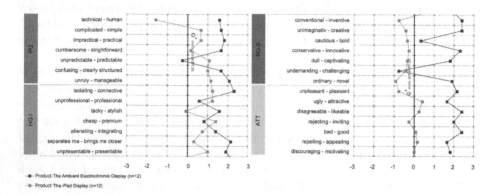

-■- Product: The Ambient Electrochromic Display (n=12)
-●- Product: The iPad Display (n=12)

Fig. 3. AttrakDiff^{TM} adjective-pair comparison of the electrochromic and digital picture frame

5.2   In-the-Wild Study

Our Little Secret was placed on the table of the female participant's living room as a decoration, while the male participant placed the paired one next to the computer where he spent most of the time. The frequency of checking the states of Our Little Secret was approximately 3–4 times per day in the case of the female participant, and about 2–3 times per day in the case of the male participant. The reason why the participants did not check the states more often was because the switching of the electrochromic displays was considered too subtle and did not have significant changes that could easily be spotted. The female participant conveyed *"I'm busy at work now, don't disturb!"* as the secret message in her husband's display, because she felt *"it was politer and more euphemistic to use it [Our Little Secret] to deliver the 'don't disturb!' message than literally texting it."* (P12). As for the male participant, he conveyed *"I am thinking of you now"* as the secret message in his wife's display, as he felt *"more comfortable to say it through the picture frame."* (P11). Most importantly, the participants found Our Little Secret helped to support their relationship as the pair of devices were *"something that could create better communication."* (P12): *"He isn't the most verbal guy, definitely not good at discussing his emotions, and maybe also a bit shy to express his affection... But I find him became a bit more romantic because I felt like he misses me all the time when I noticed the hearts were often switched on in the picture frame.*" (P12). "*I don't like texting because it gets very annoying when I'm still expecting her reply, and suddenly she just disappears... Using this* [Our Little Secret] *to communicate you don't really expect a reply... She doesn't have fixed work shifts, so I always have to figure out if she's at work before calling her...* [With the help of Our Little Secret], *it was easier for me to know if she's available for a call.*" (P11).

6 Discussion

Overall the concept of Our Little Secret was positively received, with all of the test participants preferred it over the conventional digital picture frame. This high level of positiveness was apparent not only in the positive adjective selected to describe the presented concept, but also in the wealth of ideas that the participants provided for iterating the concept. Given it has been pointed out that ambient displays are difficult to be evaluated in real-world settings [9], the aim of our in-the-wild study was not to evaluate or measure the awareness of significant changes in Our Little Secret, rather the focus was to investigate if the concept could work for a random remote couple and how they would use Our Little Secret in real life. The findings from the in-the-wild study highlighted that Our Little Secret added a new communication channel between the remote couple, which supported their communication and relationship at a distance through the form of a pair of private, meaningful, and always-on yet calm displays.

Although the results are encouraging, we acknowledge that our work is limited by the small sample size and a rather short duration of the in-the-wild study. Evaluating ambient displays can be challenging [9], and the user experience research in ubiquitous computing easily suffers from the challenges of organising in-the-wild studies [23]. It would have been valuable to be able to evaluate the concept with more LDR couples living in different time zones. It was impossible, and not our aim, to investigate how affective communication conventions could arise and evolve within a week, and if the communication mode provided by the electrochromic displays was sustainable for a longer period. Nevertheless, the remote couple who participated in the in-the-wild study had been involved in a typical distant relationship for a number of years. Moreover, we engaged this couple in multiple study sessions. Given the intensity of involvement, we believe this sample to be representative of the concept being used in LDRs in real-life use context. As future work, we are interested in exploring user cases further with a more diverse set of remote couples so as to enhance sample diversity, which would help to gain a deeper understanding of the applicability of the presented concept.

Our display could also be further evaluated from the public display point of view [18], as a picture frame is typically placed in the vicinity of others. Whilst there are numerous emotional communication mediated systems aiming to support LDRs, it has been pointed out that the availability of customisation is lacking in the design of many systems [13]. Electrochromic displays allow customisation of graphics, which can be printed with conventional techniques.

This would further enable the personalisation of the design and form factor to fit the user's preferences. The ability to customise the display graphics and the users' possibility to create their own designs should be explored more, and is one of our targets for future work. Also, the findings of our study indicate that digging deeper the possibilities of customisation would be an interesting direction for further exploration.

7   Conclusion

We have proposed an electrochromic display as an ambient display for connecting couples in a long-distance relationship, and conducted a user study with interviews as well as an in-the-wild deployment of one week to evaluate our concept and the design. The user study shows that the non-light-emitting electrochromic display was well-received for its calmness and pleasantness. The technology allows easy and cost-efficient manufacturing of customised displays, which could be placed on differently shaped surfaces.

Acknowledgements. This research has received funding from the European Union's Horizon 2020 research and innovation programme under Grant Agreement No. 760973, as well as the China Scholarship Council fellowship (201606150085).

References

1. Benedek, J., Miner, T.: Measuring desirability: new methods for evaluating desirability in a usability lab setting. Proc. Usability Professionals Assoc. **2003**(8–12), 57 (2002)
2. Chang, A., Resner, B., Koerner, B., Wang, X., Ishii, H.: Lumitouch: an emotional communication device. In: CHI 2001 Extended Abstracts on Human Factors in Computing Systems, CHI EA 2001, pp. 313–314. ACM, New York (2001). https://doi.org/10.1145/634067.634252
3. Chen, C.Y., Forlizzi, J., Jennings, P.: Comslipper: an expressive design to support awareness and availability. In: CHI 2006 Extended Abstracts on Human Factors in Computing Systems, CHI EA 2006, pp. 369–374. ACM, New York (2006). https://doi.org/10.1145/1125451.1125531
4. Colley, A., Hakala, L., Harjuniemi, E., Jarusriboonchai, P., Müller, H., Häkkilä, J.: Exploring the design space of electrochromic displays. In: Proceedings of the 8th ACM International Symposium on Pervasive Displays, PerDis 2019, pp. 38:1–38:2, ACM, New York (2019). https://doi.org/10.1145/3321335.3329687
5. Dey, A.K., de Guzman, E.: From awareness to connectedness: the design and deployment of presence displays. In: Proceedings of the SIGCHI Conference on Human Factors in Computing Systems, pp. 899–908. ACM (2006)
6. Häkkilä, J., Li, H., Koskinen, S., Colley, A.: Connected candles as peripheral emotional user interface. In: Proceedings of the 17th International Conference on Mobile and Ubiquitous Multimedia, MUM 2018, pp. 327–333. ACM, New York (2018). https://doi.org/10.1145/3282894.3282909

7. Hassenzahl, M., Burmester, M., Koller, F.: Attrakdiff: Ein fragebogen zur messung wahrgenommener hedonischer und pragmatischer qualität. In: Szwillus, G., Ziegler, J. (eds.) Mensch & Computer, pp. 187–196. Springer, Heidelberg (2003). https://doi.org/10.1007/978-3-322-80058-9_19

8. Hassenzahl, M., Heidecker, S., Eckoldt, K., Diefenbach, S., Hillmann, U.: All you need is love: current strategies of mediating intimate relationships through technology. ACM Trans. Comput. Hum. Interact. (TOCHI) **19**(4), 30 (2012)

9. Hazlewood, W.R., Stolterman, E., Connelly, K.: Issues in evaluating ambient displays in the wild: two case studies. In: Proceedings of the SIGCHI Conference on Human Factors in Computing Systems, CHI 2011, pp. 877–886. ACM, New York (2011). https://doi.org/10.1145/1978942.1979071

10. Jensen, W., Colley, A., Häkkilä, J., Pinheiro, C., Löchtefeld, M.: Transprint: a method for fabricating flexible transparent free-form displays. Adv. Hum. Comput. Interact. **2019**, 14 (2019)

11. Kim, J., Park, Y.W., Nam, T.J.: Breathingframe: an inflatable frame for remote breath signal sharing. In: Proceedings of the Ninth International Conference on Tangible, Embedded, and Embodied Interaction, TEI 2015, pp. 109–112. ACM, New York (2015). https://doi.org/10.1145/2677199.2680606

12. Kololuoma, T., et al.: Adopting hybrid integrated flexible electronics in products: case-personal activity meter. IEEE J. Electron Devices Soc. **7**, 761–768 (2019)

13. Li, H., Häkkilä, J., Väänänen, K.: Review of unconventional user interfaces for emotional communication between long-distance partners. In: Proceedings of the 20th International Conference on Human-Computer Interaction with Mobile Devices and Services, MobileHCI 2018, pp. 18:1–18:10. ACM, New York (2018). https://doi.org/10.1145/3229434.3229467

14. Li, H., Häkkilä, J., Väänänen, K.: Towards a conceptual design framework for emotional communication systems for long-distance relationships. In: Proceedings of the 8th EAI International Conference: ArtsIT, Interactivity & Game Creation, pp. 103–123. Springer (2019)

15. Mankoff, J., Dey, A.K., Hsieh, G., Kientz, J., Lederer, S., Ames, M.: Heuristic evaluation of ambient displays. In: Proceedings of the SIGCHI Conference on Human Factors in Computing Systems, pp. 169–176. ACM (2003)

16. Moere, A.V.: Beyond the tyranny of the pixel: Exploring the physicality of information visualization. In: 2008 12th International Conference Information Visualisation, pp. 469–474. IEEE (2008)

17. Monk, P.M., Mortimer, R.J., Rosseinsky, D.R.: Electrochromism: Fundamentals and Applications. Wiley, Weinheim (2008)

18. Müller, J., Alt, F., Michelis, D., Schmidt, A.: Requirements and design space for interactive public displays. In: Proceedings of the 18th ACM International Conference on Multimedia, pp. 1285–1294. ACM (2010)

19. Papanikolaou, D., Brush, A.B., Roseway, A.: Bodypods: designing posture sensing chairs for capturing and sharing implicit interactions. In: Proceedings of the Ninth International Conference on Tangible, Embedded, and Embodied Interaction, TEI 2015, pp. 375–382. ACM, New York (2015). https://doi.org/10.1145/2677199.2680591

20. Rowan, J., Mynatt, E.D.: Digital family portrait field trial: support for aging in place. In: Proceedings of the SIGCHI Conference on Human Factors in Computing Systems, pp. 521–530. ACM (2005)

21. Strong, R., Gaver, B., et al.: Feather, scent and shaker: supporting simple intimacy. In: Proceedings of CSCW, vol. 96, pp. 29–30 (1996)

22. Uriu, D., Odom, W.: Designing for domestic memorialization and remembrance: a field study of fenestra in Japan. In: Proceedings of the 2016 CHI Conference on Human Factors in Computing Systems, pp. 5945–5957. ACM (2016)

23. Väänänen-Vainio-Mattila, K., Olsson, T., Häkkilä, J.: Towards deeper understanding of user experience with ubiquitous computing systems: systematic literature review and design framework. In: Abascal, J., Barbosa, S., Fetter, M., Gross, T., Palanque, P., Winckler, M. (eds.) INTERACT 2015. LNCS, vol. 9298, pp. 384–401. Springer, Cham (2015). https://doi.org/10.1007/978-3-319-22698-9_26

Keeping Digital Libraries Alive: Designing an Interactive Scientific Publication to Drive Demands of Scholars Based on Participatory Design

Camila Wohlmuth[1]([⊠]) and Nuno Correia[2]

[1] FCT, Universidade Nova de Lisboa, Lisbon, Portugal
cw.silva@campus.fct.unl.pt
[2] NOVA-LINCS, FCT, Universidade Nova de Lisboa, Lisbon, Portugal

Abstract. Digital libraries are one of the primary sources of sharing scientific knowledge. Presently, an article is located on the main interface of a digital library, which contains information about the publication, authorship, references, abstract, along with the indexed full text in PDF. However, how do scholars imagine the ideal design of this interface to be? What's more, which features could the library provide to enhance the scholar's reading experience and, consequently, the acquisition of knowledge? Along these lines, this study sought participatory design approaches to discuss and find interesting possibilities for an interactive scientific publication interface. A contribution to this endeavor is included in three consecutive steps: a participatory design workshop, a follow-up exercise, and a prototype to demonstrate designing solutions. Finally, it presents lessons learned about the interface that the scholars conceptualize, suggesting demands to be incorporated into publications as well as a discussion to drive changes regarding how to present and communicate scientific results.

Keywords: Participatory design · Digital library · Scientific publications

1 Introduction

Publishers related to digital libraries are still independently consulting scholars (potential users) to create solutions for their interfaces and services, not giving the user an opportunity to participate in the entire process. The problem is not prioritizing the stakeholder's mental model, where ideas are being created and presented, but rather, the stakeholders themselves discussing social and political issues to identify problems and solutions. That is, space and relevance must be given to the scholar to debate and reach a solution for the present and future of digital libraries.

In this way, a case study previously presented solutions for the creation of interactive scientific publications interface, problematizing the lack of a closer and more participative relationship with the users to improve the achieved results [1]. Thus, the study

A. Brooks and E. I. Brooks (Eds.): ArtsIT 2019/DLI 2019, LNICST 328, pp. 623–632, 2020.
https://doi.org/10.1007/978-3-030-53294-9_46

has the goal of designing a novel interactive scientific publication interface to drive the scholars' demands based on participatory design, which is distinguished from other approaches in the field. The chosen methodology follows the notion that by engaging the scholar in the process, their knowledge is considered and applied to the design to identify the needs and find solid solutions.

The following section describes related work that goes through a quick contextualization and explores how participatory design can inform a series of insights and actions to achieve a design interface and discussion. We report our process in the development of a workshop and a follow-up exercise, resulting in a prototype; we detail the learning that took place through activities, observations through video recording as well as a discussion about solutions for interactive scientific publications.

2   Background and Related Work

Scientific content is evolving from a print-based format in the digital medium to a format that allows the possibilities offered by features from interactive interfaces, becoming available to digital libraries. In this way, the UI/UX design has a growing role in improving the interfaces of digital libraries. An example of related work is the ACM Digital Library [2], which has developed a set of projects to address immediate and future action for core functionality, content expansion, content organization/exposure, and customization. For this purpose, the ACM DL [2] in its methodology addresses workshops, and user feedback, demonstrating the importance of this study.

However, studies including advances in the creation of a novel interactive scientific publications do not usually incorporate the stakeholders into the designing process [1, 3–6]. There is a lapse in the importance of direct user involvement in the decision-making process, failing to include a deeper understanding of users' desires regarding the design of the imagined interface and its elements to increase engagement as well as improve the accessibility and consequently, the acquisition of scientific knowledge [1]. Nonetheless, digital libraries can benefit from the Participatory Design (PD) context to contribute directly to the needs and desires of the target audience.

We rely on previous work [7–17] to guide the design through changes to the scientific publication interface with a collection of design methods, including the user throughout the process. Therefore, the purpose of design is to engage researchers in activities in order to discover new ideas, priorities and flows for creating and redesigning interactive scientific publication interfaces in a more representative way. In this manner, we are inspired by the first two stages by Bødker et al. [16] and Steen [15] who describe and discuss tools and practices that support creativity and how they are part of design cooperation activities as in using the past to inform design and the curiosity that helps the researchers to empathize with others and their experiences.

Moreover, the participatory design approach employed by Ferati et al. [17] highlight the importance of creating the prototype with participants, dividing into two phases of creation, paper and digital, which provide enhancements regarding its look and feel. In addition, Ferati et al. [17] demonstrate the impact of the workshop of the future [10, 11] to engage participants in developing future plans, and we carry those thoughts to the possible future of scientific publications.

The methodology challenges the assumptions already made about feature improvements to be applied in publications [1, 3–6], as well as obtains various views of the dialogue among participants [7, 13]. According to Sanoff [8], an important point in the participatory process is learning through increased awareness of a problem and encouraging dialogue, debate, and collaboration. Thus, participation can be seen as the researcher´s shared decisions made for the scientific community that determine the quality and direction of scientific publication utilization.

3 Methods

There are three main steps of the study: (A) participatory design workshop, (B) follow-up exercise and (C) prototype development. The steps are integrated to infuse the concern of the participant into the design process (see Sect. 4). The workshop integrates steps adapted from the future workshop model [10, 11], which has multiple phases: preparation, critique, fantasy and implementation, each with its own practices. Through the execution of methodologies, such as the workshop of the future [10, 11] we are involving participants in multiple phases, raising political issues to scientific making and improving their communication as well as generating abundant ideas and emerging different suggestions. Consequently, the follow-up exercise collects the results of the sketches and the decisions from the implementation phase for a second decision stage with the participants. At this stage, the interface elements and their perceived functionalities are decided. Based on the previous steps, a prototype was developed.

4 Participant's Concern Infused into the Design Process

The participatory design that we seek derives from earlier concepts in which the user is not only included in the design, but mainly "intervenes in situations of conflict through developing more democratic processes" [9], providing both a theoretical logic and concrete methods to engage users. Therefore, we recognize PD as a process with many approaches and techniques. Thus, in the following subsections, we present the participatory design workshop, second-stage exercise, and finally, the prototype.

4.1 Workshop Conducted and Its Results

Preparation. The participants were recruited by a survey; the workshop methods, the schedule, and their rules were settled as well as the location and the materials used.

Recruitment. Fifteen participants were recruited, nine of whom attended the workshop. The participants (N = 55.6% female) learned the pre-requisites of the survey sent by email, they are researchers from different areas, ranging in age from 20 to 42, who frequently access scientific articles (more than 2 times a week). Moreover, all participants have read or browsed interactive publishing, of which 66.7% prefer interactive articles and 33.3% indicate that both (print-based or interactive) have their benefits.

Method. The method reliability was established using references [7–17]. Research questions were built to define the theme addressed during the dynamics: (a) What are the characteristics of the current interfaces of publications in different areas of knowledge experienced by scholars? (b) What characteristics should the interface provide to increase the engagement and accessibility of scientific information to the scholar? (c) What are the useful interactive multimedia resources and how should they be structured in the interface?

Flow and Agenda. A presentation was made for the participants to understand the flow of tasks and their contribution. The definition of the context covered understanding input materials and the intended outcomes, including the setup of the event agenda. The flow of tasks is related to the critique and fantasy phases in which the participants integrate the development of PD with their experiences and innovative ideas in a critical way to be discussed in a group. Following, we proposed video recording while the participants engaged in the workshop (the workshop lasted about 60 min).

Critique. In the second phase, we addressed the issuing brief. At first, publishing in digital libraries was contextualized in the current scenario to be critiqued and discussed by the group. Then, examples of different types of scientific publications were presented, as well as other types of rich publications to brainstorm ideas in a critical way. Participants took notes on goals they need to achieve with their design solutions.

Fantasy. In the third phase, we provided materials, such as a sheet of paper and colored felt pens, suggesting participants to draw the results of the brainstorm and encouraging creativity. Here, the participants were advised to sketch an interactive interface with features to enhance the reading experience, and the acquisition of knowledge. The imaginative warm-up was developed in this phase. We offered prompts to influence sketching with the perspective of future possibilities for the interface structure (Fig. 1).

Fig. 1. Different structures were presented: Newick tree, circular points and content blocks.

Sketching. Individually, participants sketched their interface mental model which functionalities that attended their demands as scholars who search, share, read, analyze, and understand data in scientific publications (Fig. 2). In groups of three, participants shared and discussed the promising ideas to be transformed as a possible and attainable core. Then, the participants were ready to share the viable ideas and the characteristics of their strengths with the whole group. The dynamic was performed through the participants' speech when they expressed the logic of the interface drawn. Hence, the desirable characteristics that the interface must assume in order to meet the user's needs are understood in a more complete and detailed way.

Implementation. In the fourth phase, the realizable ideas were checked, analyzed and evaluated by what concerns their practicability. The process occurred in an interactive way with mediation between designers and participants. Common features in the sketches were marked with the same colored stickers. The patterns were selected to be incorporated into the design decisions and implemented in the prototype. In this manner, markers in orange were related to the title and abstract with video/audio, the purple color was for grouped media, yellow for collapsible structure, and pink for the navigation map (Fig. 2). Additionally, green represented media icons and blue for visual references presented interactively. Patterns of the structure were evaluated and decided according to group consensus, e.g., a media preview at the top, percentage viewed with a checkbox per section, and connecting points of conclusion to other important parts.

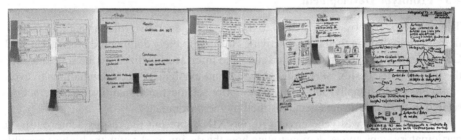

Fig. 2. Sketches made by participants being checked, analyzed and evaluated. (Color figure online)

4.2 Follow-Up Exercise

A follow-up exercise occurred as an activity related to the iconological outcomes and functionalities drawn and described in the sketches of the scholars with equal patterns observed in the implementation phase that generated ten icons presented in this phase (see Fig. 3). Thus, the study is justified by the participants' evaluation, perceiving the relevance of a more in-depth study related to the icons, their symbology, and functionalities that directly affect the user interaction with the scientific publication.

Participants' mental model [18] related to the features in a symbolic way with icons, visually simplifying the interface [19], especially for small screens as in mobile phones. The activity gave users the ability to express their decisions, allowing adjustments to the set of icons proposed in the design [17]. Dynamics of the exercise were made in two parts. The first part contained two options: participants could choose one of the three symbolic representations of the icon or draw a better representation. The second part included the participants writing a justification for the selection made and decided the functionality of the referenced symbol (Fig. 3). After data collection, an evaluation of the participants' inferences was administered, and the results were presented in a prototype to incite the possible solutions for the interactive publication interface.

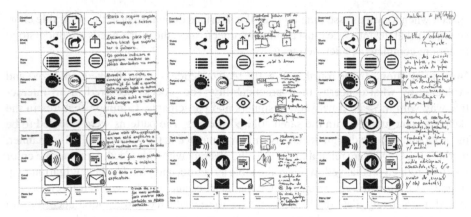

Fig. 3. Design decisions expressed in the exercises carried out by three participants.

4.3 Prototype Development

The prototype proposal was created to illustrate its generative role in enabling the participants to reflect on their design activities in a completely democratic process [11, 20]. Consequently, the prototype demonstrates the interface idealized by the scholars, after the problem discussion, sketching, analysis, and evaluation of commonalities to avoid ambiguity. Additionally, achieving assimilation of the functionalities and interactions related to the icons designed and justified by the participants.

The prototype was generated in Adobe XD to present the results achieved in the participatory steps above, demonstrating how the design works with the highest possible fidelity (Fig. 4). Providing enhancements regarding its visual quality, the prototype also explores the responsive design [21] as a solution for the mobile interface.

Fig. 4. Illustration of a few prototype screens.

Therefore, the prototype manifests design goals, building upon scholars' ideas to reveal important patterns in different aspects of novel interactive scientific publishing interfaces. For example, the screens shown in Fig. 4 illustrate the media preview in a slideshow, the dynamic images next to the text highlights the parts that are referenced, the drop-down menu simplifies the sections visually and provides intuitive interaction, among others. Likewise, the iconological solutions and their functions (text to speech, play audio abstract, percentage viewed and checkbox) from the follow-up exercise.

5 Lessons Learned

Following the requirement gathering phase using participatory design methods with a workshop and another follow-up exercise, we generated a prototype as a visualization of the results. Thus, we were ready to discuss the user interface design possibilities that the scholars idealize with interactive features. This section explores the ability of language-use to reveal user preferences [7, 13], allowing the lessons learned to drive demands to be incorporated into projects of interactive scientific publications interfaces.

5.1 Characteristics of the Interface to Provide Increased Engagement and Accessibility of Scientific Information to Scholars

A drop-down menu was an interesting concept thought of and sketched by participants, reflected in the organization of the publication structure to attend various screen sizes, as in mobile devices. Consequently, the reader has a view of the entire article, quickly checking the noteworthy sections. As summarized by [P4] and [P9] *"as the user is reading, it opens the content-related tab."*. The entire view of the article can be used for the responsive design solutions in any publication.

In order to create a media access mechanism, the participants reflected on a media preview in the over-part of the interface during the group discussion. The idea is that the media is always visible, so the reader could go directly to a graphic, image or video indexed in the article. In this way, the structure of interactive multimedia features is discussed to provide engagement and accessibility. In their sketches, participants indicated the desire for the integration and association of static and dynamic media in an interactive way with the entire article, as to be able to articulate the knowledge structure in a more engaging way, to make deeper visual connections to the results. Examples of this are *"topics being pulled from each result in the conclusions"* [P7], *"dynamic positioning/ free of media"* [P8], *"interactive visualization of the data"* [P6] and, *"Combine figures or graphics in a pop-up window animated by tabs to compare results"* [P1].

In such a way, by designing solutions for video and audio, participants entered into a consensus that an extended video/audio abstract containing parts of the introduction and conclusion would be extremely useful. A video "abstract" is valid in publications that can summarize the content in a schematic/illustrative way in a few minutes. At present, the audio "abstract" is more functional when the scholar does not necessarily need visual support to understand the issue of the article, as also clarified by [P2] *"... you can be doing something else while listening to the article..."*. Therefore, an audio is, in general, easier to make than video regarding media creation.

5.2 Icons as the Input of Interaction and Functionalities

The icons imagined and designed by the participants produce contributions directly for their interaction with the interface. The connection between symbol and functionality for the action should be intuitive and fast as well as summarize and highlight, explain actions and aid navigation [19]. Besides, the icons achieve the interactions between textual and media content, e.g., a text to speech icon was created to suppress the researchers' need for listening to the article sections independently by skipping irrelevant information (see Fig. 4). This symbol was the most laborious in order to find an appropriate metaphor, and in this way, the recommendations are labels and tutorials.

A percentage icon of the publication section view is created from an idea of a participant, shared in the group and discussed as reported by [P5] *"I think this part of checking the sections that I've read and seen, the percentage of what I have yet to read and what I have read is very useful, especially when we are looking at many papers at the same time."*. Thus, this functionality is given relevance to be incorporated into the user interface design of interactive scientific publications.

6 Discussion

At the beginning of the workshop, participants' main criticism was that there are few interactive publications, arriving at a consensus that PDF is still the format most seen in their research areas. Some publications are still heavily anchored to the printed format as discussed by [P7] *"... engineering articles rarely combine interactive tools or other features to make a publication more engaging."* But as [P6] argues, *"I have already seen some websites and journals that provide the PDF content in HTML with some enrichments such as a pop-up in the references."* For them, this is already considered a paradigm shift from the print format in the digital medium to an interactive one.

Reinforcing the arguments of the participants, as reported by Coper and Kalantzis, the information revolution did not produce a significant social or epistemic change in a publishing technology context [22]. This argument by the authors presents the PDF format as an example, which makes journal articles accessible. Nevertheless, they are only reproductions of the production processes and social relations of the printed journal [22], although PDF has been supporting the integration of three-dimensional (3D), audio and video content on-the-page since June 2008 [23].

The gradual evolution of electronic journals, the fourth phase described in 1995 by Lancaster [24], in which there would be the creation of an entirely new publication, based on the exploitation and use of multimodality and hypermedia, has not yet happened. The way information is structured still represents a paradigm for the understanding of the subject addressed and consequently, generation of knowledge. The participants, as researchers and article readers, comprehend that they are communicating complex results (difficult-to-illustrate and hard to record their mind's eye). Hence, the workshop sustained participants discussing mechanisms to make the publication more dynamic and interactive as well as support a quick content uptake (see in Sect. 4).

The absence of a policy for adding to submissions of audio or video abstract as a mechanism for a quick understanding of the article content is one matter discussed by participants. This type of media benefits not only the reader, but also the authors, as it can influence the visibility of the metrics of access, citation, and download of the article. Bringing the discussion to current reality, some publications suggest sending videos as in Plos One [25]. However, it is not mandatory, which is an issue according to the participants. Furthermore, the interactive multimedia features are not an integral part of the understanding process or tool to summarize the content within the publication.

The importance of dynamic content within the publications are also clarified to illustrate experiments as well as practical projects in different areas of knowledge. Taking as an example, [P3] reports *"I read many articles that relate to graphic design and they have publications with 3D images. I think it would be interesting … if we could also interact with this three-dimensional model … instead of just seeing a static image."*. Trying to close this gap, some scholars, as authors, add links to demonstrations in personal pages or platforms like *YouTube* in their articles. This fact occurs because of the lack of this capacity within the publication. Furthermore, the connection between text and illustrative material is broken by the separation of content on different interfaces, which can result in an overload of cognitive efforts by the user when trying to compare outcomes. As a consequence, users feel lost and frustrated.

7   Conclusions, Limitations and Further Work

Our experiences showed that designing a new interactive scientific publishing to address the scholars' demands based on participatory design pose a richness and variety of outcome lessons to improve the interface and critically discuss the need for changes in scientific communication. The search for an improved way to present research results in a digital and interactive age cannot happen without the direct interaction of scholars, as the continuous and interactive design process of dialogue involving stakeholders really demonstrates the needs of what the scientific publication will become.

One of the limitations of this study is that the evaluation of the prototype has not yet occurred, which will take place in the next stage. Thus, the stakeholders themselves are participating in important decisions about functionalities, and the visual aspects of the project should guarantee better results as the prototype will be tested. Future work will be based on the evaluation of the prototype according to satisfaction index and self-reported engagement. These improvements will be incorporated, and a new assessment will be generated to understand if there is greater cognitive engagement (assessment using eye tracking) and knowledge.

References

1. Wohlmuth, C., Correia, N.: User interface for interactive scientific publications: a design case study. In: Doucet, A., Isaac, A., Golub, K., Aalberg, T., Jatowt, A. (eds.) Digital Libraries for Open Knowledge, TPDL 2019, vol. 11799. Springer, Cham (2019)
2. ACM Digital Library. https://www.acm.org/articles/pubs-newsletter/2018/blue-diamond-nov-2018. Accessed 21 Feb 2019
3. Hodge, V., et al.: A digital repository and execution platform for interactive scholarly publications in neuroscience. Neuroinformatics 14(1), 23–40 (2015). https://doi.org/10.1007/s12021-015-9276-3

4. Shum, S.B., Sumner, T.: JIME: an interactive journal for interactive media. Learn. Publish. (14), 273–285 (2001). https://doi.org/10.1087/09531510175314137
5. Siegel, E.R., Lindberg, D.A.B., Campbell, G.P., Harless, W.G., Goodwin, C.R.: Defining the next generation journal: the NLM-Elsevier interactive publications experiment. Inf. Serv. Use **30**(1–2), 17–30 (2010)
6. Ackerman, M.J., Siegel, E., Wood, F.: Interactive science publishing: a joint OSA-NLM project. Inf. Serv. Use **30**(1–2), 39–50 (2010)
7. Luck, R.: Dialogue in participatory design. Des. Stud. **24**(6), 523–535 (2003)
8. Sanoff, H.: Community Participation Methods in Design and Planning. Wiley, New York (2000)
9. Bannon, L., Bardzell, J., Bødker, S.: Reimagining participatory design. Cover Story Interact. **26**(1), 27–32 (2019)
10. Vidal, R.V.V.: The Future Workshop: Democratic problem solving. Informatics and Mathematical Modelling, Technical University of Denmark, DTU. IMM-Technical report (2005)
11. van der Velden, M., Mörtberg, C.: Participatory design and design for values. In: van den Hoven, J., Vermaas, P., van de Poel, I. (eds.) Handbook of Ethics, Values, and Technological Design, pp. 1–22. Springer, Dordrecht (2014)
12. Spinuzzi, C.: The methodology of participatory design. Appl. Res. Tech. Commun. **52**(2), 163–174 (2005)
13. Iversen, O.S., Halskov, K., Leong, T.W.: Values-led participatory design. Co-Design **8**(2–3), 87–103 (2012)
14. Bødker, K., Kensing, F., Simonsen, J.: Participatory IT Design: Designing for Business and Workplace Realities. MIT Press Ltd., Cambridge (2004)
15. Steen, M.: Virtues in participatory design: cooperation, curiosity, creativity, empowerment and reflexivity. Sci. Eng. Ethics **19**(3), 945–962 (2013)
16. Bødker, S., Nielsen, C., Petersen, M.G.: Creativity, cooperation and interactive design. In: DIS 2000 Proceedings of the 3rd Conference on Designing Interactive Systems: Processes, Practices, Methods, and Techniques, pp. 252–261. ACM, New York (2000)
17. Ferati, M., Babar, A., Carine, K., Hamidi, A., Mörtberg, C.: Participatory design approach to internet of things: co-designing a smart shower for and with people with disabilities. In: Antona, M., Stephanidis, C. (eds.) UAHCI 2018. LNCS, vol. 10908, pp. 246–261. Springer, Cham (2018). https://doi.org/10.1007/978-3-319-92052-8_19
18. Nadin, M.: Interface design: a semiotic paradigma. Semiotica **69**(3–4), 269–302 (1988)
19. Lupton, E.: Type on Screen: A Critical Guide for Designers, Writers, Developers & Students, 1st edn. Princeton Architectural Press, New York (2014)
20. Lim, Y.-K., Stolterman, E., Tenenberg, J.: The anatomy of prototypes: prototypes as filters, prototypes as manifestations of design ideas. ACM Trans. Comput.-Hum. Interact. **15**(2), 7 (2008)
21. Wiener, L., Ekholm, T., Haller, P.: Modular responsive web design: an experience report. In: Proceedings of 1st International Workshop on Programming Technology for the Future Web, Brussels, Belgium, (ProWeb 2017), pp. 1–6. ACM, New York (2017)
22. Cope, B., Kalantzis, M.: Multiliteracies: Literacy Learning and the Design of Social Futures, 1st edn. Routledge, New York (2000)
23. Ziegler, A., Mietchen, D., Faber, C., et al.: Effectively incorporating selected multimedia content into medical publications. BMC Med. **9**, 17 (2011). https://doi.org/10.1186/1741-7015-9-17
24. Lancaster, F.W.: The evolution of electronic publishing. Ser. Rev. **21**(1), 518–527 (1995)
25. Plos One. https://journals.plos.org/plosone/s/supporting-information. Accessed 02 Apr 2019

Enabling Rural Women in India to Speculate Futures Through Games and Theatre: A Participatory Approach

Arjun Harish Rao$^{(\boxtimes)}$ (iD), Mahima Chandak(iD), and Shreya Mukta Gupta(iD)

Srishti Institute of Art, Design and Technology, Bangalore, India
arjunrao2709@gmail.com, mahimarameshchandak@gmail.com,
shreya.muktagupta@gmail.com

Abstract. The paper aims at reporting early findings from engaging in participatory and speculative design methods with rural women in Bihar, India. The research outlines a contextualized workshop that includes participants as equal contributors to the design of their futures. Many cultures like India are not naturally democratic and are comprised of politics and power structures within their setting. The paper highlights that in such contexts, participatory and speculative design methods can help give voices to the marginalized and uncover these complexities to gain a nuanced understanding. The findings of this paper are important for researchers, designers, and technologists who aim to uncover key factors that affect the functioning of complex systems to design sustainable interventions.

Keywords: Speculative design · Participatory design · Rural india · Games · Theatre · Women

1 Introduction

The paper explores new methods and tools to engage women in rural Bihar to speculate preferable futures. During our research, we learnt that the community in Bihar is deeply patriarchal. In such communities, women are often discouraged to express their opinions, argue or protest [12]. Enabling aspirations with such marginalised groups is a challenge due to their lack of agency and aspiration [1]. Our approach was to engage women in participatory activities, like games and theatre, to critique their existing realities and consequently imagine better futures.

A participatory approach was adopted, with an understanding that communities are experts in their local environment and needs, and no matter how experienced the designers are, what they perceive as being the best solution will inevitably be based on their world view [8]. Participatory design democratizes this process by giving communities more control in the design of their surroundings [11]. Some of the challenges we faced while conducting these sessions, was

© ICST Institute for Computer Sciences, Social Informatics and Telecommunications Engineering 2020
Published by Springer Nature Switzerland AG 2020. All Rights Reserved
A. Brooks and E. I. Brooks (Eds.): ArtsIT 2019/DLI 2019, LNICST 328, pp. 633–642, 2020.
https://doi.org/10.1007/978-3-030-53294-9_47

the participants' lack of aspiration and belief in their ability to change their condition. By creating spaces for collective imagination, through games and theatre, the workshop presented aims to create dialogue and allow women to critically reflect on their current conditions.

The paper presents the activities conducted over ten days in rural Bihar, the insights gained through contextual inquiries and how they informed the design of our game and participatory theatre. We then present our findings from the activities, both as a reflective critique of the methodology in the context and dialogues about preferable futures [3] with the women of the community. The studies were conducted in collaboration with a not for profit organization, Project Potential, who provided us with access to the community and local volunteers. The inclusion of local volunteers helped in bridging cultural differences and language barriers between the researchers and participants.

2   Background

2.1   The State of Bihar

Considering social and economic indicators, Bihar can be classified as one amongst the most rural and poor [9]. According to the latest census in 2011, Bihar is the least literate state in India, with an average literacy of 63.82%. The disparity between male and female literacy is also quite high, with 73.39% of males being literate as compared to only 53.3% females [2]. Most families living in the area fall below the poverty line.

2.2   Women and Patriarchy

Women within patriarchal settings have very little to no agency. They are strongly discouraged to speak in the presence of others, often resulting in men being the ones who speak for and make decisions for women and girls. It is not uncommon to see married women seek permission from their husbands and in-laws to leave the house premises or talk to other people [12].

3   Participatory and Speculative Design in Marginalized Communities

Through participatory design methods, we strengthen the capacity of the poor to exercise voice, to debate, contest, and oppose vital directions for collective social life as they wish, not only because this is virtually a definition of inclusion and participation in any democracy [13]. Projects in East Namibia on using participatory approaches to digitize indigenous knowledge have proved to be long term successes both from the view of the researchers and the community [7].

Games for speculative design create a playful subversive and irreverent space often described the 'magic circle'. During the design of the game, it is necessary to provide space for reflection while engaging in discussions about 'wicked problems' [10]. An exploratory design game framework supports participants in exploring aspects relevant in the projects collaboratively to gain new insights [4].

Participatory theatre technique as a sociological research methodology produces a specific kind of new knowledge whose main characteristics are embodied, dialogical and illustrative. [6] By bringing local knowledge and reactions into our frame for theorizing questions of social marginalization and exclusion, we encourage themes, discussions, and views that would otherwise tend to either fall out of sight or be diminished in our research [5].

4   Methods and Observations

The engagement with the community was conducted over a span of ten days, wherein the first four days were spent 'settling into' the context, followed by a five-day participatory and speculative workshop.

During the first four days, we took part in observation, conversation with the locals, and received input from the local not-for-profit organisations. One of the local women described her situation as *'My family wanted to avoid dowry, so they married me at the age of 12 to a partially blind alcoholic.'* These conversations served as starting points for our understanding of the women's lives and shaped the structure of our interviews with them.

We also identified other recreational activities the community engages in. This helped us recognize the cultural language through which appropriate props (such as games and theatre) would be later designed as research tools. The details of the activities conducted during the workshop are outlined below in the chronological order of events (Fig. 1):

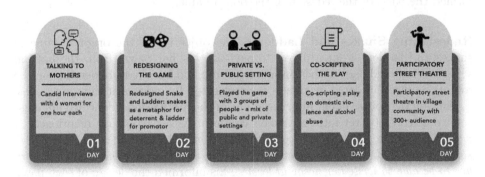

Fig. 1. Process outlined for a 5 day participatory workshop

4.1   Workshop Design

Interviews with Mothers: We conducted one-on-one semi-structured interviews with six participants, which helped us understand the prevalence of alcohol abuse, early marriage, lack of financial independence, to name a few. Each interview lasted for around an hour.

During our conversations, we experienced instances where members of the family tried different ways to cut our access to women. Our participants were either sent away to the kitchen or were regularly interrupted by visits and checks from the in-laws, which changed our participant's behaviour. In one case, the mother-in-law intentionally refused to take care of the woman's child, leaving our participant distracted during the conversation.

Such challenges led us to re-imagining how we could create a safe space to facilitate conversations with women. Identifying that engaging in recreational activities such as games and theatre was looked upon as harmless activities by the community, we were curious to see if we could model them as research tools. The board game 'Snakes and Ladders' was observed to be widespread and well-liked by the community. Street play or 'Nukkad Natak' was another common form of entertainment that we observed. We focused on how we could optimise these common forms of entertainment and its popularity to tackle the challenges faced.

The conversations from our interviews helped provide insights into the kind of topics that women would like to speculate about. On the topic of work and being independent, a participant mentioned *'I earned Rs. 100 a day but I have to give this to my husband'*. Another participant opened up about the domestic violence that takes place at her home, *'What is his contribution to the family? He only comes home and physically abuses me and my kids'*. A third participant highlights the early age at which women in the community get married *'We will get our daughter married immediately after her matriculation, at the age of 15'*.

Apart from these, we identified a total of nineteen social issues like alcoholism, dowry, lack of educational facilities, mother's health, to name a few. These issues formed the basis of the redesign of the board game.

Redesigning Snakes and Ladders: The objective of the original game of snakes and ladders is for a player to navigate his/her pawn, from the bottom square (numbered one) to the top square (numbered hundred), depending on the roll of the dice, hindered by snakes or accelerated by ladders at different nodes.

During the course of our interviews, one of the motivations identified amongst the women was better futures of their children. As a participant mentioned, *'I work hard in the fields to put together some money to educate my children. My son is bright and will go ahead and work in the city. As for my daughter, I want her to be able to write her name at least'*. This informed the design of each pawn as a male or a female child.

A prototype (Fig. 2) of the redesigned game was made where both snakes and ladders were placed on the same box. These boxes were made of paper cut-outs with the aforementioned issues written inside. If the player's pawn landed on such a square, she had to justify whether the given condition was a 'snake' (a metaphor for deterrent) or a 'ladder' (a metaphor for the promoter) for her child. To climb up the ladder, the participant had to speculate a better future and suggest the necessary steps that were needed to convert the 'snake' into a 'ladder'. If unable to do so, the condition would be considered a snake that brought her child down.

Fig. 2. Speculative Snakes and Ladders on field

Playing the Game in Public and Private Settings: The game was played in three different settings. The first one was a couple in a private home setting where the woman was the more vocal person on the topics discussed. The second group comprised of 7 women in the courtyard of one of the players, where the players were from the same neighbourhood and knew each other very well. The third group comprised of 25 women in 5 teams with a representative from each team rolling the dice. The setting had 30–40 onlookers as the game took place under a tree in the village square. The teams were divided based on age groups.

The game created a 'magic circle', a safe space within which women were able to explore an alternate world, detached from their existing realities. The rules of the game, wherein a player had to justify whether the mentioned situation was a deterrent or promoter, coerced women to critically reflect on their situations. Furthermore, the drive to 'win' stretched the women's imaginations and motivated them to propose various ways to improve their current situations. This game's setup also helped in regulating hierarchy because every player got a chance to talk at her turn. The game involves the principle of chance which could have led to some topics never being discussed at all. However, playing the game repeatedly with several groups of women helped us in covering a majority of the topics on the board.

Some of the conversations and debates that came about during the game threw light upon the rampant alcoholism amongst the men. Women shared instances such as, *'My neighbour's husband doesn't work at all, which results in her toiling in the farms. He comes back home in the nights to beat her up and take away her hard-earned money for more alcohol'* Another participant upon reaching the box exclaimed, *'This is the biggest 'snake' in our community!'*. One of the participants felt that *'Drinking occasionally is acceptable but as a habit, it can burn families.'*

Writing the Script in Collaboration with the Women: With these conversations around domestic abuse, alcoholism, and irresponsible husbands, a script titled, 'Haath Nahi Aawaz Utao' (roughly translating to raise your voice against domestic abuse) was co-written in collaboration with 7 women in a private setting. The group was accompanied by theatre artists from Project Potential and a team of design facilitators. The theatre approach was adopted to give voices to the otherwise unheard women. Co-scripting the play with a mixed group of literate and illiterate women meant finding a creative way to enable equal contribution. Writing dialogues using pen and paper was done away with and impromptu role-plays and dialogues were used.

Participatory Street Theatre with Community: The theatre artists from Project Potential along with design facilitators converted the audio recorded dialogues into a script of approximately 15 min. The intended actors were a mix of women who scripted the play, adolescents from the community and theatre artists from Project Potential. Although unintended, the dialogues were modified impromptu by the participants during their role-plays as the context and plot stemmed out of their realities (Fig. 3). We did multiple rehearsals with the intended group of actors in a private setting.

Co-scripting the play along with the women helped in arriving at relevant and contextual ideas, keeping in mind the relevant social structures within which the women operate. When one participant suggested, *'We women should have a helpline number where we can call the police for help'*, others protested saying, *'This will never work since this way the woman will only be saved for that time but when the husband is released, he will beat her up even more. Furthermore, this puts the name of the family at stake. These women will be looked down upon.'* A third arrived at a conclusion stating that, *'We should have a 'Mahila Sanghatan', a women's empowerment group run by women from the village, to address alcoholism, domestic violence and other such social evils. The group should take initiative in advising men against the ill-effects of alcoholism and attempt to solve problems internally, without bringing out these issues in public.'* All the women agreed on this idea.

The final street theatre or 'Nukkad Natak' took place in a public setting of 300+ villagers, but none of the women agreed to participate due to the apprehension of being seen by elders and male members of the family. Women shared that there would be consequences if they engaged in a powerful demonstration of feminism in front of the entire society. Their roles were replaced by design facilitators who staged their anonymous voices in front of the community.

Fig. 3. Rehearsals based on the co-scripted play

5   Findings and Insights

5.1   Capacity to Build Connections

The capacity to build connections between complex issues by the participants was the primary outcome of the snakes and ladders game as seen in Fig. 4. The players, during the gameplay, articulated and realized for themselves for the first time how many of the issues were interrelated and were quoted as saying so. For instance, one of the players saw more than three children in the family as a 'ladder' for her girl pawn. The same participant upon reaching the box of education negotiated it as well as a 'ladder'. This caused debate between the participants about the conflict in her decisions: if the girl had additional siblings, she would automatically take up the responsibilities of the younger ones at a tender age. This, owing to the busy nature of her parents, results in lesser focus and time spent on education. Instances like these helped the participants make connections between lack of family planning and increasing number dropouts in girls.

5.2   Enabling Imaginations of Plausible Futures Through Participatory Design

The games and participatory theatre enabled them to imagine and speculate preferable futures such as the existence of 'Mahila Sanghatan' bringing an end to domestic violence. Other preferred futures were women engaging in occupations apart from farm and fieldwork, toilets inside every home (as opposed to outside), quality education made accessible, hospital with free treatment located closer in terms of infrastructure, and factories and companies for better jobs and income.

5.3   Balancing Power Structures in the Community to Engage in Honest Conversations

In societies like India where subaltern power structures and hierarchy exists within the family/community, to engage in conversations with an individual of 'lower power' (women in this case), it is essential to create a safe space. The team faced instances where, in the presence of women of higher age groups,

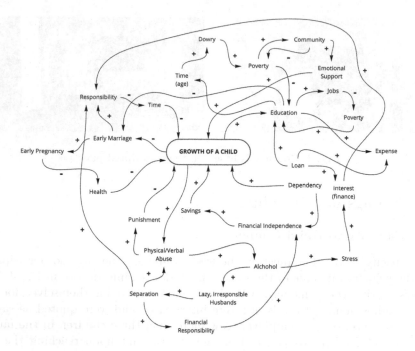

Fig. 4. A system feedback loop based on the community's perception

young mothers would not voice out their opinions as a result of hierarchy. In other instances, due to patriarchy, the presence of men resulted in them dominating the discussions and sometimes answering for the women. During the workshop when women of similar age group were gathered without male onlookers, the dialogues and debates that took place were honest, avoiding performative 'correct' answers.

6   Future Work and Discussion

6.1   The Workshop as a Toolkit to Uncover the Nuances of a Context

The workshop can be modelled as a toolkit and can work across different settings and demographics. The components of the toolkit would essentially comprise of the following:

1. Candid interviews to reveal issues of the stakeholders
2. Games or other social props (in this case snakes and ladder) as tools of provocation to generate dialogue and speculate around those issues
3. Providing the community with an interactive medium that is familiar to them (in this case a theatre performance)

The model can function by changing the stakeholders, or the social props or the final interactive medium or all three.

6.2   Potential of Snake and Ladders as a Research Tool

The simplicity and popularity of Snakes and Ladders make it applicable across genders, age groups and demographics to extract subdued opinions. A digital version of the game can also work across contexts where computers are accessible, urban children and women, elderly, corporate settings, to suggest a few. The tool can also help in fostering gender-related debates if played in mixed groups. It would then have the potential to come up with more sensitive and gender-balanced interventions.

7   Conclusion

The paper highlights the merits of participatory and speculative methods of research among rural communities in India to uncover complexities and hidden nuances of a context. The design of the workshop brings forward the value of contextualized activities such as indigenous games and street theatre as tools for enabling speculation. It was observed that participatory activities fostered the community to aspire and identify preferable futures. Suggested interventions for better futures came from the ground, birthed from the realities of people who understood their context better. These, not being top-down expert solutions, have higher chances of being sustainable within the community. Future work involves the application of workshop design in different contexts to understand its potential to scale as a toolkit for participatory and speculative design. Other future work discussed is the potential of using Snakes and Ladders as a tool for fostering gender-related debates.

Acknowledgement. We would like to thank Dr. Naveen Bagalkot, Kshama Nagaraja, Dr. Padmini Ray Murray and members of Project Potential for providing us with valuable support throughout the course of the project.

References

1. The capacity to aspire: Culture and the terms of recognition - GSDRC (2009). https://gsdrc.org/document-library/the-capacity-to-aspire-culture-and-the-terms-of-recognition/
2. Census of India 2011 (2011). http://censusindia.gov.in/2011-prov-results/data_files/bihar/Provisional%20Population%20Totals%202011-Bihar.pdf
3. Dunne, A., Raby, F.: Speculative Everything: Design, Fiction, and Social Dreaming. The MIT Press, Cambridge (2013)
4. Brandt, E.: Designing exploratory design games: A framework for participation in participatory design? In: Proceedings Participatory Design Conference (2006)
5. Tofteng, D., Husted, M.: Theatre and action research: How drama can empower action research processes in the field of unemployment. Action Res. **9**(1), 27–41 (2011)
6. Kaptani, E., Yuval-Davis, N.: Participatory theatre as a research methodology: Identity, performance and social action among refugees. Sociol. Res. Online (2008). https://journals.sagepub.com/doi/10.5153/sro.1789

7. Kapuire, G.K., Winschiers-Theophilus, H., Blake, E.: An insider perspective on community gains: A subjective account of a Namibian rural communities' perception of a long-term participatory design project. Int. J. Hum. Comput. Stud. **74**, 124–143 (2015)
8. Kate Ferguson, S.C.: Participatory Design Handbook. http://kateferguson.org/documents/Participatory-Design-Handbook.pdf
9. Harter, L., Sharma, D., Pant, S., Singhal, A., Sharma, Y.: Catalyzing social reform through participatory folk performances in rural India*. In: Communication Activism: Media and Performance Activism (2007)
10. Coulton, P., Burnett, D., Gradinar, A.: Games as speculative design: Allowing players to consider alternate presents and plausible futures. In: Proceedings of Design Research Society Conference (2016)
11. Spinuzzi, C.: The methodology of participatory design. Tech. Commun. **52**(2), 163–174 (2005)
12. Sultana, S., Guimbretière, F., Sengers, P., Dell, N.: Design within a patriarchal society. In: Proceedings of the 2018 CHI Conference on Human Factors in Computing Systems - CHI 2018 (2018). https://dl.acm.org/citation.cfm?id=3174110
13. Rao, V., Walton, M.: Culture and Public Action. Stanford Social Sciences. Stanford University Press, Stanford (2004)

Learning Designs and Participation Through Digital Technologies

Learning Designs and Participation Through Digital Technologies

Eva Brooks[1]([✉]) and Anthony L. Brooks[2]

[1] Department of Culture and Learning, Aalborg University, Kroghstræde 3,
9220 Aalborg, Denmark
eb@hum.aau.dk
[2] Department of Architecture, Design and Media Technology, Aalborg University,
Rendsburggade 14, 9000 Aalborg, Denmark

Abstract. This sixth part of the volume elaborates on questions related to how people can be prepared for as well as acting and learning in a digital world. In doing so, it contribute to defining effective and collaborative practices where stakeholders participate in technology-rich contexts as well as in environments that mix digital technologies with a 'making' or design approach.

Keywords: e-Learning resources · Inclusive educational technologies · Digital literacy · Digital game designs · Digital competence · Motivation and digital tools

1 Introduction

1.1 Scope

This part of the DLI 2019 proceedings focuses on how people can be prepared for as well as acting and learning in a digital world. How can technologies be designed to foster learning and participation in a digitised society and how can we develop learning designs that foster necessary future skills and competences by means digital technologies? Many technology-enhanced learning initiatives are influenced by demands from both users and politicians, e.g. the demands for 21st century skills/competences, launched for the school-system. The six chapters included here raise question about how such learning futures can be designed to encourage people to participate and shape their own learning processes.

> *The future is not a result of choices among alternative paths offered by the present, but a place that is created – created first in the mind and will, created next in activity. The future is not some place we are going to, but one we are creating. The paths to it are not found but made, and the activity of making them changes both the maker and destination. The place reached is rarely the place intended, and is often unrecognizable to the actor, who is himself altered by the activity [1, p. 321].*

A. Brooks and E. I. Brooks (Eds.): ArtsIT 2019/DLI 2019, LNICST 328, pp. 645–649, 2020.
https://doi.org/10.1007/978-3-030-53294-9_48

Even though considerable investment over the last decade into implementing digital technologies targeting learning in different contexts of use, recent research indicates that the relationship between learning and technology is not as simple as it first appears. The chapters in different ways contribute to defining effective and collaborative practices where stakeholders participate in technology-rich contexts as well as in environments that mix digital technologies with a 'making' or design approach.

The opening contribution in this sixth section investigates the impact of different e-learning resources in relation to their effectiveness and functionality in a classroom teaching process as well as in relation to curriculum requirements. The second contribution presents a study of innovative educational technology designs targeting students with disabilities, in particular addressing the concept of Universal Design for Learning (UDL) to bridge special needs education and regular classroom teaching. The third contribution includes an extensive literature review on digital literacy and organisational learning, where scenario-based exercises are put forward as safe end experiential learning environments enabling alternative problem-solving skills and innovative working techniques. The fourth contribution examines how collaboration between school children (9–10 years of age) is configured in problem-solving activities whilst developing digital game design. The fifth contribution addresses the question of how teachers can be supported in their professional learning and digital technology integration in a classroom context. Finally, the sixth contribution discusses whether people with Type 1 diabetes follow recommendations given to them and develop design guidelines for a digital tool to assist them in doing so.

The following text snippets elaborate from each contribution to further assist readership.

2 Teachers' Preferable Attributes of e-Learning Resources

The paper focuses on what king of e-Learning attributes that teachers prefer and is authored by *Valentina Terzieva, Elena Paunova-Hubenova, Katia Todorova, and Petia Kademova-Katzarova.* It is based on an online survey in the context of Bulgaria including 1652 replies from all regions of the country. The aim of the study was to investigate the impact of different e-learning resources in relation to their effectiveness and functionality in a classroom teaching process as well as in relation to curriculum requirements. The findings revealed that the majority of teachers considered content layout, non-text teaching aids, adaptability, and interactivity as the most important characteristics when being used in a classroom practice. Further, the results showed that teachers considered alteration and flexibility as a crucial issue for e-learning resources to be able to personalise their teaching according to students' level of performance.

3 Innovative Inclusive Educational Technology in Language Classrooms and Learner Perspectives: A Study of Nine Learner Narratives

This contribution by *Henrik Kasch*, presents a study of innovative educational technology designs targeting students with disabilities, in particular addressing the concept of

Universal Design for Learning (UDL) to bridge special needs education and regular classroom teaching. In a classroom-context, the author integrates Computer-Assisted Language Learning (CALL) and UDL using digital resources in the form of multimodal bilingual comprehensive; contiguous (words-in-context) and non-base-form glossing; text-to-speech with highlighting functionalities; bilingual retelling functionalities for individual e-book pages; and learner response functions. It is hypothesised that multimodal digital UDL resources can be integrated in language instruction materials and contribute to encouraging language acquisition in a diversity of learners. This assumption was investigated through semi-structured interviews with nine students from a lower-secondary school to explore the students' experiences of using a variety of digital UDL resources. Here, the focus was on functionalities of the technology, unintended or unexpected uses and experiences in the students' interaction with the technology. The outcomes of the study refer to students' sense of mastery and increased self-efficacy in using the digital UDL resources. However, the way of experiencing self-efficacy as well as the way of using the assistive functionalities and affordances differed among the students. For example, some students used text-to-speech functionality to facilitate the comprehension, while others used the same functionality for working on pronunciation. The author concludes that it thus makes sense to provide students with a variety of functionalities as diverse usages align the same assistive functionality with multiple student strategies.

4   GLOBE – Digital Literacy and Organizational Learning by Scenario-Driven Exercises

This contribution by *Sophia Willner*, presents an extensive literature review on digital literacy and organisational learning, where scenario-based exercises are put forward as safe end experiential learning environments enabling alternative problem-solving skills and innovative working techniques. Specifically, this refers to a concept of learning utilising collaborative learning methods where dialogues should contribute to individuals' up taking and revising their own perspectives. This, theoretical overview forms a foundation for the GLOBE conceptual design as a scenario-based management and leadership exercise supporting geographically distributed groups through virtual collaboration. The chapter includes the details of the conceptual GLOBE scenario based on cooperation between United Nations agencies in a humanitarian relief mission. The design targets enabling students to practice management and leadership skills in complex situations. Further, the chapter describes how students through practicing this kind of cooperation scenarios should achieve at a holistic and situational awareness related to aspects of organisational learning and quality management. In doing so, the design should invite the students to follow iterative cycles of information gathering and processing, prepare action recommendations, and apply certain collaborative actions. The author concludes that testing and experiencing such concepts in a safe digital environment enable participants to internalise principles crucial for a successful development and adaption of organisational change processes.

5 Problem-Solving and Collaboration When School Children Develop Game Designs

Reforms and policy documents cohere to changes in political, social, and educational practices that place increased pressure on institutions and organisations to improve quality of learning outcomes [2]. This evokes questions of how students can make sense of current complex demands on enhancing their digital competence to improve technological integration in learning settings. This contribution by *Eva Brooks and Jeanette Sjöberg* examines how collaboration between school children (9–10 years of age) is configured in problem-solving activities whilst developing digital game design. The authors put forward a 'making' design approach as motivator for collaboration and problem-solving as corresponding to a design process, where children can proceed through iterative design cycle and implementation of ideas. Based on this, the authors argue that developing game designs have potential to influence educational practices, in particular when it comes to inventing and exploring the tension between individuals' ideas and the evolving forms of social interactions. During the workshop, the children were provided with a wide range of creative material as well as with digital technology to create an idea for a game design and to make a short stop-motion film (with an iPad) to present their game design solution, as a prototype. The authors applied an interaction analysis and a quasi-content analysis approach to gathered video recordings and observation notes. This revealed patterns divided into either as *being* or as *doing*: the children were generally *being* task-oriented as well as other-oriented, and they were *doing* constant negotiations as well as taking leadership (or being led). Finally, the authors argue that developing digital game designs have potential to influence educational practices, in particular when it comes to inventing and exploring the tension between individuals' ideas and the evolving forms of social interactions.

6 To Become Digitally Competent: A Study of Educators' Participation in Professional Learning

Next contribution by *Eva Brooks, Marie Bengtsson, Malin Jartsell Gustafsson, Tony Roth, and Lena Tonnby*, addresses the question of how teachers can be supported in their professional learning and digital technology integration in a classroom context. The question emerges from recent updates of curriculums underlining that education should contribute to students' ability to act in an increased digitised society and develop their skills to use digital technology in their everyday lives. In this context, the chapter informs of a work-in-progress paper, which aims to shed light over how teachers in Swedish preschools and schools participated in professional learning to become digital competent. The study applies an action research approach focusing on the concepts of participation, involvement, and responsibility (the DIA-model). The study includes nine preschool units (including children 1–5 years of age) and two schools with 10 school units (including children between 6–11 years of age) in a municipality situated in the southwest of Sweden. In total, 21 preschool teachers and 16 primary school teachers participated in two baseline questionnaires. The analysis reveals three central themes: Shared comprehensive influence; Reconstitution of space and time for shared learning; and Providing tools to mediate professional learning. Based on this, the authors argue for the importance of a context-conscious leadership as well as promoting team learning and collaboration between teams to create dynamics between the teachers, when implementing professional learning in a school context.

7 Do People with Diabetes Follow the Recommendations? A Study of Motivational and Compliance Factors of People with Type 1 Diabetes

The last contribution in this part of the DLI 2019 proceedings is authored by *Anders Kalsgaard Møller and Marie Charlotte Lyngbye* and investigates whether people with type 1 diabetes are motivated to follow the recommendations given to them. This question is important from both an individual and a societal point of view. The chapter points to the increased number of people with diabetes, where currently more than 8.5% of the adult population has this diagnosis. This affect their everyday living as they must make significant changes to their life and habits and adjust it to the recommendations for diabetic treatment to avoid or delay complications related to the illness. The chapter presents empirical data from a survey, experience sampling data and interviews that addresses people with type 1 diabetes' adherence with the recommended blood sugar measurements, their physical activity level and motivational factors. The authors argue for the need of such information to understand and explain people with diabetes' adherence to follow the recommendations. To do so, the authors apply theories about self-efficacy and motivation. The findings form a foundation for recommendations regarding how digital solutions can be designed that can aid the users and motivate them to follow the recommendations and hereby potentially improve the quality of life for diabetes patients.

8 Epilogue and Acknowledgements

This sixth section introduces six contributions by to promote readership of each full paper that are presented in the following chapters. In doing so, the authors of this chapter acknowledge the contribution to this section/volume by each author whose original work was presented in the ArtsIT/DLI 2019 events in Aalborg, Denmark November 7–8, 2019.

References

1. Schaar, J.H.: Legitimacy in the Modern State. Transaction Publishers, Oxford (1989). Second printing
2. Chval, K.B., Reys, R., Reys, B.J., Tarr, J.E., Chávez, O.: Pressures to improve student performance: a context that both urges and impedes school-based research. J. Res. Math. Educ. **37**(3), 158–166 (2006)

Teachers' Preferable Attributes of E-Learning Resources

Valentina Terzieva(✉), Elena Paunova-Hubenova, Katia Todorova,
and Petia Kademova-Katzarova

Institute of Information and Communication Technologies, Bulgarian Academy of Sciences,
Acad. G. Bonchev St., Block 2, 1113 Sofia, Bulgaria
{valia,katia,petia}@isdip.bas.bg, eli_np@hsi.iccs.bas.bg

Abstract. The paper addresses some issues related to the preferable attributes of e-learning resources according to teachers' views. The first part introduces general requirements to educational materials, with emphasis on their relations to particular characteristics. The authors assert that the design of learning materials depends on a variety of factors such as educational goals, teaching approach, learners' profile, and subject matter. Further, they should meet teachers' needs of quality flexible resources that support an effective teaching process. The second part of the research presents the findings of the empirical survey conducted in Bulgaria in 2017–18. Teachers assess the attributes of e-learning resources in two directions: which are their essential characteristics so that to be easy to use and which of them they would like to be able to change. The results are analyzed both according to the school subject (STEM or Humanitarian) and educational level. A discussion on some of the essential research findings is provided.

Keywords: E-learning resources · Attributes of e-learning resources · Teachers' viewpoints · Survey

1 Introduction

In the past decades, progress in technology has radically changed most of the aspects of education. Computers and technological tools have improved the efficiency of the education process significantly – from altering the way teachers teach students to the way students learn. These tools allow faster applying of various pedagogical approaches and practices [2, 10]. Further, students positively benefit from many and different ways of knowledge acquisition through contemporary technological tools and e-learning resources. Reflecting these changes, the Bulgarian government has adopted a national strategy for the effective implementation of information and communication technologies (ICT) in educational domain [13]. It provides new frameworks for the curricula digitalization, but some questions concerning the design of e-learning resources arise. Might e-learning resources be able to offer a personalized experience based on the learning background, interests, preferences, and even learning style? How e-learning

A. Brooks and E. I. Brooks (Eds.): ArtsIT 2019/DLI 2019, LNICST 328, pp. 650–659, 2020.
https://doi.org/10.1007/978-3-030-53294-9_49

resources to be structured, which of their features to be flexible so they can be reused and fit different needs to engage students more in the learning process?

To answer these questions, the authors researched teachers' views about the preferable attributes of e-learning resources to be more useful and flexible. Often teachers use open educational resources (OER) that offer free educational materials, which can be adapted and reused with few or no restrictions. Such resources now are essential in technology-based support of teaching [2]. They give opportunities for teachers to provide students with personalized and flexible learning content enriched with online materials, audios, videos, etc. while ensuring the achievement of learning goals. Hence, teachers have to be able to choose and replace different attributes and components of used e-resources while still keep their essential basic features. Thus, in this research, the authors addressed the following issues: (1) Review of characteristics of e-learning resources that have the most considerable impact on their effectiveness and functionality in the teaching process. (2) Attributes that e-learning resources should have so that to be easy to use and reuse. (3) Characteristics of e-learning resources that teachers could change for better meet the needs of a particular student or group of students.

2 Literature Review

Plenty of research on e-learning practice outlines the characteristics of teaching materials such as technology, pedagogy, content organization, and creativity. These characteristics have the most considerable impact on the effectiveness of the educational process [2, 5, 7]. A survey identifies pragmatic and evidence-based key characteristics, which efficient learning resources have. It outlines usability and contextualization among the guiding principles to a good design of e-learning resources. Further, parameters like format and potential for adaptation or combination, cost, and intellectual property rights are recognized [5]. The selection of educational resources is affected by various factors such as educational goals, characteristics of learners, learning matter, design, and availability of educational materials, as asserted in [7]. Some criteria for the assessment of the didactic quality of e-learning resources are also discussed.

E-learning resources have some unique features and can provide students with interactive experiences that go beyond what a print version can offer. They are preferable for many students because of their convenience, remote access, flexibility, and searchability. Next, researchers point out that e-resources such as digital textbooks enable sharing content among students and thus can be more engaging for them than traditional ones [4]. E-books may also intensify the motivation of learners, as they provide a more exciting option, probably because of their different features [3]. Thus, students' learning improves when students are provided with e-book readers preloaded with learning resources. The pointed possible reasons are the adaptable presentation of study material, flexible timing, and the use of new reading strategies [3]. Additional, the provided feedback and students' learning styles also significantly affect learning outcomes. Thus, the quality of education considerably enhances when teachers modify teaching approaches to meet the learning styles of their students [6]. As students have different knowledge backgrounds, abilities, and preferences, teachers that include learning resources and activities with different attributes and use various instructional strategies for matching diverse learning styles, efficiently achieve the educational goals [11].

Empirical research shows that if all the attributes of paper-based and digital learning resources are equal (text structure, presentation, screen size, types of questions), overall reading performances (speed, comprehension) do not differ significantly [9]. Another research argues that the effects of the format of study materials depend on the students' prior knowledge and affect content recall [8]. An empirical study proves that e-learning resources rich in multimedia encourages critical and active learning and thus enhance the students' achievement [1].

3 Methodology

The methodology of this work combines the research of relevant surveys and the authors' views on the issues concerning the usability of e-learning resources, grouping them into factors to recognise and indicators to measure. The authors of present research consider characteristics of educational resources from three aspects – resources should respond to general, e-learning specific, and teachers' requirements. General requirements for e-learning resources – accessibility, usability, readability, and learnability, as described in [12], are mapped on the specific requirements for contemporary e-learning resources. The needs and preferences of the teachers regarding the parameters of learning resources are also taken into account. These preferences, based on experience gained in school practice, are the object of quantity and quality survey. The analysis of compliance of the general requirements with the specifics of ICT-based learning resources and the correlation of teachers' preferences to both aspects is performed.

The empirical study on preferable attributes of e-learning resources is part of the comprehensive survey on the use of ICT in Bulgarian schools [14]. Table 1 presents the distribution of the respondents according to the school stage and the subject they teach. In some cases, teachers educate students of various grades (especially in smaller settlements), and their opinion is reflected in the statistical analysis of each stage. For this reason, the overall quantity of teachers from all stages exceeds the total amount of respondents. The particular analysis of the opinions of teachers in STEM (science, technology, engineering, and mathematics) and Humanitarian subjects (languages, literature, history, geography, economics, and philosophy) is performed. Such separation is needed because e-learning resources in these subjects differ considerably therefore, the preferences to them are also different. This classification is not applied to Primary school teachers, because usually, they teach almost all lessons in class. So, when calculating the number of teachers in STEM and Humanitarian subjects, only those from secondary education are taken into account. More detailed information on the survey is presented in [15].

Table 1. Distribution of the teachers according to the a) degree and b) subject.

	Primary	Low sec.	High sec.	STEM	Humanitarian
Number	605	622	776	532	355
Percentage	36,6%	37,7%	47%	32,2%	21,5%

4   Essential Attributes of e-Learning Resources

Most of the schools use electronic platforms that create an integrated learning environment supporting classroom work. Currently, nearly a third of teachers (31.3%) actively use such tools, while about a half (48.8%) intend to use it. According to respondents, e-learning platforms provide "essential resources for continuing studying at and outside the classroom, maintaining the learning process as an activity in and out of school, which is very beneficial." In this way, teachers can easily share learning materials. Therefore, a question about the characteristics of e-resources that make them useful and efficient to reuse raises. With the ubiquitous spread of e-learning, a large number of e-learning materials in almost every subject are available. Hence, it can be difficult for teachers to select from a large set of resources those that best match their goals. The quality of e-learning resources is critical to the success of educational activities in both science and humanitarian subjects. Thus, the researchers investigate related issues in the abovementioned survey exploring teachers' views on the use of ICT in school education practice [14].

Figure 1 shows the authors' viewpoint on the interrelations between the requirements and the attributes of e-learning resources. *Modularity* is connected to the volume of learning units and the sequencing of the learning content. Small modules of learning material allow forming learning units in an appropriate size and sequencing of the study material, according to the specifics of a particular class or individual pupil. Thus, opportunities for multiple presentations of the content of learning units are possible. Different *layouts* of every single element of learning content are essential for high-quality teaching, for it allows the application of different learning methods. It is also necessary to have *non-text content* (e.g., visual, acoustic, multisensory illustrations) to reproduce appropriate effects that support the learning content. It is essential for learning materials to be *adaptable* to different learning contexts (e.g., school or home, individual or group tasks, projects). Appropriate adaptation can also effectuate different speeds in teaching, training, or testing, depending on learners' individual or group characteristics. The text layout also requires the availability of adaptive properties of the learning material, which is of paramount importance in the training of pupils with special educational needs (SEN). The features discussed (*content layout, demonstration resources, modularity, and adaptability*) build the basis for a good understanding of the essence of the material taught. Consequently, they have a direct influence on deep comprehension that is the goal of education, e.g., for the learnability of the resources. Teachers use different teaching methods where *interactive* learning materials provide substantial support for the engaging and varied planning of the learning process. Another essential quality of learning resources is their *platform independence* so that they can be used on different occasions and in different places. Hence, they must be accessible, have references, and enable connections to other learning and information materials. Connecting learning resources to additional information on the issue from different sources provides an in-depth understanding of the problem. Adding references to other subjects, disciplines, or arts links the learning material to other areas of human activity and leads to more conscious perception, understanding, and absorption of information.

Fig. 1. Requirements and preferences to attributes of e-learning resources.

5 Teachers' Opinions About Attributes of e-Learning Resources

5.1 Characteristics of e-Learning Resources

This paper outlines issues concerning features of e-learning resources, considered in the survey. Figure 2 presents the results from the question: "Which characteristics of the e-learning resources should be changeable to make them easier for usage?" Teachers also added other attributes they find significant as a comment.

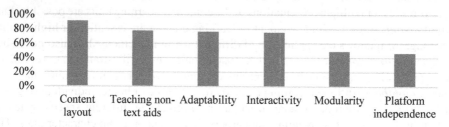

Fig. 2. Teacher's opinion about the characteristics of e-learning resources.

The most wanted characteristic is an appropriate *content layout* (91%), which includes design, format, font, color, images, and more attributes of the content presentation. The following comment of teachers is indicative: "The ability of the e-resources to be changeable and to support flexible learning while preserving its purposefulness is their most valuable quality."

An almost equal number of teachers assess the importance of the following three qualities: *non-text teaching aids* (such as visual, sound, multimedia effects) (77.5%), *adaptability* (76.3%), and *interactivity* (75.3%). The explanation can also be found in the comments: "Effects should be very moderate because they distract and burden small pupils."; "Diction! Actors should sound the learning resources."; "To be matched according to the students' age." and "To be able to change and upgrade."

Less than half of the respondents find *modularity* (49%) and *platform independence* (46.4%) essential characteristics. The last one is especially crucial for the schools without fast and stable Internet connection (about 49% of Bulgarian schools) [16] or sufficient technical equipment, as it becomes clear from the comments. "They should not require large technical resources, and can also be used offline."; "The Internet connection quite

often interrupts, and I need learning resources on compact discs or the lessons would fail."
Other recommendations by teachers concerning e-learning resources are summarized as
follows:

- to include various engaging content – "simulations and presentations";
- to enable active learning – "content to be presented in the form of games and tasks to
  stimulate competition";
- to be strongly related to the curriculum, because "in many cases, they are not, and
  thus are not suitable to be used in most of the school lessons";
- accessibility of content – "to be with open access, without a license and to allow
  offline use";
- to provide a lot of additional hands-on practice materials;
- to be modern and to involve innovative technology to be successful.

Authors investigate the differences between the opinions of teachers in STEM
and Humanitarian subjects. Figure 3 displays the results. For most of the characteristics, teachers' opinions practically coincide. The highest differences are for *modularity*
(61.3% and 44.2%) and *platform independence* (54.5% and 38.9%). For both, STEM
teachers have stronger preferences. Probably the reason is that they realize more clearly
the importance of these features for learning outcomes.

The differences in the opinions of teachers from the three stages in Bulgarian school
education are also an object of research (see Fig. 4). It makes the impression that the

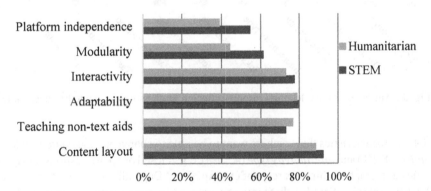

Fig. 3. Comparison of the opinions of STEM and Humanitarian teachers.

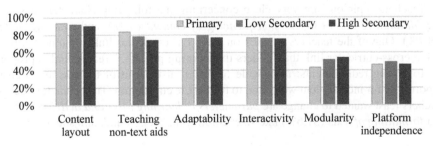

Fig. 4. Comparison of the opinions of teachers from the three school stages.

importance of *content layout* and the *teaching non-text aids* decrease with increasing the students' age. Unlike them, *modularity* matters more for students in secondary schools. The values for other characteristics are very close (within the statistical error).

5.2 Attributes of e-Learning Resources that Teachers Want to Change

This research also investigate the preference of teachers to be able to change some of the attributes of the e-learning resources. Figure 5 presents survey findings that reflect the answers of all respondents on the question: "Which characteristics of the e-learning resources would you like to be able to change, so that they suit better the needs of a particular student or group of students?" More than half (59%) of the teachers point out the *volume of learning units* and 52.5% – the *demonstration resources* like text, sound, illustrative materials, and multimedia. One of the teachers commented: "The biggest problem, at least in the History subject, remains the overwhelming depth of detail and the not-balanced content."

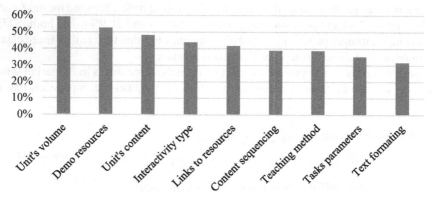

Fig. 5. Attributes of the e-learning resources, which teachers would like to be changeable

Other characteristics that teachers want to be able to change are the *content of learning units* (48.2%) and *interactivity type* (43.9%), e.g., closed or open questions, designing schemes and graphics, hints. A respondent explains: "Depending on the different levels of the different school grades, there must be appropriate complexity and volume of tasks and exercises."

Teachers' opinions are very close concerning the following characteristics: *links to additional resources* (41.7%), *sequencing of content* (39%), and *teaching method* (38.7%). One of the teachers stresses on the cross-curricular links: "Some textbooks lack a cross-curricular link that hinders the learning process." Teachers also proposed the following requirements: to provide feedback at the end of the lesson, to ensure opportunity for independent work, and to follow the curriculum. The characteristics that teachers least wanted to change are *parameters of learning tasks and activities* (35.2%) and *formatting of texts* (31.6%) like size, color, font, background, and sound.

Figure 6 presents the comparison of opinions of the STEM and Humanitarian teachers. A large amount of the available e-learning resources are related to STEM subjects. Thus, usually in STEM subjects, such means are more often used comparing to Humanitarian ones. Hence, STEM teachers have more experience and need to alter more resources' parameters to adapt them to the students' specifics and needs. According to the same survey, the average self-assessment of the competence of STEM teachers to apply ICT in the learning process is 3.6, while the mean value for all teachers is 2.7 referring to the 5-degree Likert scale. Substantial are differences for the content of learning units (50.8% and 44.8%), links to additional resources (45.1% and 39.2%), and parameters of learning tasks and activities (39.5% and 30.7%) for STEM and Humanitarian, respectively. Hence, more STEM teachers want to have control over these attributes, probably because of their importance for the comprehension of relatively more difficult subjects' matter. The values for the other parameters are very similar.

Figure 7 presents another comparison of teachers' opinions considering the three school stages in Bulgaria. The graph reveals that the differences are not significant.

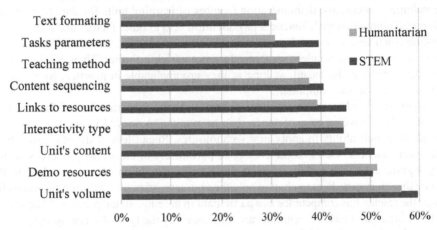

Fig. 6. Comparison of the opinions of STEM and Humanitarian teachers about the attributes of e-learning resources that they would change.

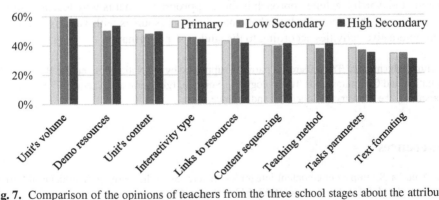

Fig. 7. Comparison of the opinions of teachers from the three school stages about the attributes of e-learning resources, which they would change.

However, it can be noted that *demonstration resources* are the most essential for primary teachers, and *text formatting* is the least important parameter, especially for high secondary school teachers.

6 Discussion and Conclusion

Research findings reveal that the majority of teachers consider the following characteristics of e-learning resources to be most significant for their classroom practice and curriculum needs: content layout, non-text teaching aids, adaptability, and interactivity. Further, when teachers evaluate available resources, they put special attention on the opportunity to alter some of the parameters. According to them, a well-designed educational resource can help students learn efficiently. Therefore, they consider the selection of the learning content to be an essential part of assembling an e-learning resource. It should be appropriate to the level and subject domain of the studied matter, to comply with the intended educational context and teaching methods, as well as the targeted students. More than half of the respondents outline this opportunity, especially as useful for the volume, content, and demonstration features of learning units for the clear presentation of learning material. Teachers pay attention also to other factors and attributes of learning resources, as one of the respondents commented: "The use of online resources unifies learning content unless someone does not enrich it further. Then, all the indicators mentioned are significant, as long as they are applicable in practice. Moreover, it depends on classroom equipment."

In general, STEM teachers are more willing to change the parameters of the resources they use. They have more experience than humanitarian ones [15], so they are more confident in their ability to apply new technologies. Regardless of the stage of school education, teachers' views on the change of parameters of electronic resources do not vary significantly. The authors support the expressed opinion of a respondent in the survey that "it is expedient to change only the characteristics of e-learning resources for which the teacher has competence as a participant in the educational process." The survey findings infer that teachers' opinions are influenced by the type of learning subject and students' understanding of the content of resources. In communication with students, the teachers are recognized not only as a source of knowledge and moderators but also as mentors. Further, during lessons, teachers estimate how students perceive learning content and which teaching approach is more appropriate. That is why teachers should personalize teaching practice by enhancing learning resources with various interactive or no interactive activities according to the students' performance.

Acknowledgements. The research is partially supported by the National Scientific Program "Information and Communication Technologies in Science, Education and Security" (ICT in SES) financed by the Ministry of Education and Science.

References

1. Amutha, S.: Impact of e-content integration in science on the learning of students at tertiary level. Int. J. Inf. Educ. Technol. **6**(8), 643–646 (2016)

2. Harnish, R.J., Bridges, K.R., Sattler, D.N., Signorella, M.L., Munson, M. (eds.): The use of technology in teaching and learning (2018). Retrieved from the Society for the Teaching of Psychology web site: http://teachpsych.org/ebooks/
3. Jang, D., Yi, P., Shin, I.: Examining the effectiveness of digital textbook use on students' learning outcomes in South Korea: a meta-analysis. Asia-Pacific Educ. Res. **25**(1), 57–68 (2016)
4. Lim, E., Hew, K.: Students' perceptions of the usefulness of an e-book with annotative and sharing capabilities as a tool for learning: a case study. Innov. Educ. Teach. Int. **51**(1), 34–45 (2014)
5. Littlejohn, A., Falconer, I., Mcgill, L.: Characterising effective eLearning resources. Comput. Educ. **50**, 757–771 (2008)
6. Markovic, S., Jovanovic, N.: Learning style as a factor which affects the quality of e-learning. Artif. Intel. Rev. **38**(4), 303–312 (2012)
7. Mazgon, J., Stefanc, D.: Importance of the various characteristics of educational materials: different opinions, different perspectives. TOJET **11**(3), 174–188 (2012)
8. O'Donnell, A.M., Dansereau, D.F.: Interactive effects of prior knowledge and material format on cooperative teaching. J. Exp. Educ. **68**(2), 101–118 (2000)
9. Porion, A., Aparicio, X., Megalakaki, O., Robert, A., Baccino, T.: The impact of paper-based versus computerized presentation on text comprehension and memorization. Comput. Hum. Behav. **54**(1), 569–576 (2016). https://doi.org/10.1016/j.chb.2015.08.002
10. Prensky, M. The role of technology. Educational Technology, 48(6) (2008)
11. Ren, Y., Dai, Z., Zhao, X., Fei, M., Gan, W.: Exploring an on-line course applicability assessment to assist learners in course selection and learning effectiveness improving in e-learning. Learn. Individ. Differ. **60**, 56–62 (2017)
12. Smythe, I.: Dyslexia in the Digital Age Making IT Work. Continuum, New York (2010)
13. Strategy for effective implementation of Information and Communication Technologies in education and science in the republic of Bulgaria (2014–2020). http://www.strategy.bg/
14. Survey: The use of ICT in Bulgarian schools. https://forms.gle/GHEEtbpfv5ydsHd69 (in Bulgarian). Accessed 17 Oct 2019
15. Terzieva, V., Paunova-Hubenova, E., Dimitrov, S., Boneva, Y.: ICT in STEM education in Bulgaria. In: Auer, M.E., Tsiatsos, T. (eds.) ICL 2018. AISC, vol. 916, pp. 801–812. Springer, Cham (2020). https://doi.org/10.1007/978-3-030-11932-4_74
16. Terzieva, V., Paunova-Hubenova, E., Dimitrov, S., Dobrinkova, N.: ICT in Bulgarian schools – changes in the last decade. In: Proceedings of International Conference EDULEARN18, pp. 6801–6810, Spain (2018). https://doi.org/10.21125/edulearn.2018.1612

Innovative Inclusive Educational Technology in Language Classrooms and Learner Perspectives: A Study of Nine Learner Narratives

Henrik Kasch[✉] [iD]

Aarhus University, Jens Christian Skousvej, 8200 Aarhus, Denmark
Henrik.kasch@edu.au.dk

Abstract. Emerging from studies of innovative educational-technology designs for disabled students, Universal Design for Learning (UDL) has established principles to bridge special needs education and regular classroom teaching. Although UDL has been around for some 40 years, apparently, only one empirical UDL study of language classrooms exists before Kasch, and no studies before him in lower-secondary language classrooms. Only Kasch has worked on integrating Computer-Assisted Language Learning and UDL in a pedagogically informed cross-pollinated Computer-Assisted Language Learning (CALL) and UDL design.

The present paper examines a sui-generis innovative language learning design and learners' interaction with it, affording the digital scaffolds: 1) multimodal bilingual comprehensive, 2) contiguous (words-in-context) and non-base-form glossing, 3) text-to-speech with highlighting functionalities as well as 4) bilingual retelling functionalities for individual Ebook pages and 5) learner response functions.

The hypothesis explored is that multimodal UDL digital scaffolds can be pedagogically integrated in language instruction materials and will help to bolster language acquisition in a variability of learners. The paper presents the findings from semi-structured interviews in a stratified sample ($n = 9$), appearing to offer support to the viability of the sui-generis CALL and UDL language learning design.

Keywords: Educational technology · Inclusive practice · Universal Design for Learning · Language teaching · Empirical study

1   Background

In recent understandings of educational technology for special-needs learners, researchers proffer inclusive rather than assistive uses of assistive or remedial technology in special education needs (SEN) pedagogy [9, 10] and in Universal Design for Learning (UDL) [12, 18]. In research on UDL in language classrooms, Strangman et al. [20, 23] have empirically explored the affordances of digitised texts and applicable

A. Brooks and E. I. Brooks (Eds.): ArtsIT 2019/DLI 2019, LNICST 328, pp. 660–670, 2020.
https://doi.org/10.1007/978-3-030-53294-9_50

general-purpose software for special-needs learners (like search engines and text-to-speech software, automatic translation engines as well as virtual animated "coaches" scaffolding learning/reading strategies). However, the authors apparently disregard the now well-studied limitations of pedagogically uninformed general-purpose software as well as general learning design criteria [5, 14].

Cross-pedagogically integrated understandings of assistive/inclusive educational technology in language classrooms have so far only been addressed by [15], who in 2018 investigated a cross-pollinated learning design hybridising computer-assisted language learning (CALL) and UDL in a pilot study [15]. Apparently, prior to Kasch [15] pedagogically integrated inclusive I(C)T designs in language classrooms have not been available[1].

CALL expands with technology [3] has of late moved into robot-tutoring [27] studying pre-schoolers' (social-) human-robot-interaction, the large-scale study finding, however, no increased learning gains over tablet-based instruction. The design of the study of the present paper, however, relies on the existing Bookbuilder platform for constructing Ebooks at cast.org. The scaffolds of the design comprise compendious clickable bilingual multimodal glossing (text, speech/sound, pictures) allowing learners to have access to help on all text and everywhere in the text and with chunks of contiguous text glossed, rather than lemma-/base-form glossing of words in isolation. Individual-word glossing is exceptionally used in 4–6 word cotext allowing word-for-word translation into Danish. Additional scaffolds offered by the design and examined in this study are audio files in English and Danish recapitulating the content of each page in the Ebook (prototype) and built-in text-to-speech functionalities. In addition, the built-in response field for each Ebook page was used, providing learners with a reflection question to scaffold learners' reading strategies. Figure 1 below shows the compendious multimodal glossary functionality from the Ebook prototype. At the bottom of the page, two clickable

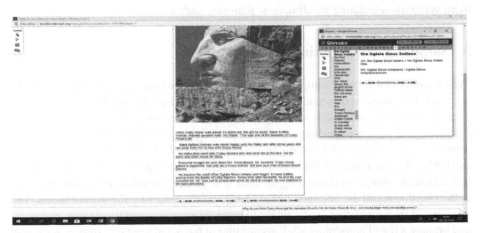

Fig. 1. Ebook functionalities (screen dump)

---

[1] Thus, a search of the entire ProQuest set of databases with the truncated search string "Universal Design for Learning (ab)" AND "empirical (ab)" for peer-reviewed publications only returned 34 hits on 29/03/2019. Of these, empirical studies - including review studies - examine only pedagogically neutral or general purpose ICT and UDL-guided applications.

audio files for having the page contents retold are accessible, as are the text-to-speech functionalities on the left-hand side of the graphic user interface.

To examine the viability of UDL-CALL design and the scaffolds, the paper sets out to examine learner experiences in classroom interventions. Using semi-structured interviews of learners drawing on Kvale and Brinkmann [4, 17] sampled from a four-point scoring range of (written) performance strata, the paper explores learner experiences of interacting with the design. The study is part of an ongoing parallel quantitative and qualitative research project with data integration [8, 11].

2 Qualitative Research Interviews: Research Questions and Interview Guide

The study of this paper carried out nine interviews in two days on the day of the last of three classroom interventions and on the following day. Based on Brinkmann and Kvale, [4, 16, 17] the author had designed an interview guide for a semi-structured interview, translating theory- and research-informed hypothesis-relevant research questions into quotidian parlance comprehensible for a Danish year-seven learner (13–14 years of age). The overall research question was "What does input channel augmentation and variability mean to foreign language learning processes?" The study hypothesises that assistive functionalities are helpful to learners in the whole classroom (and not just struggling learners) and that learners find other uses for functionalities than intended (remedial) ones [21]. This hypothesis was explored in questions asking interviewees to tell about usages and experiences of individual functionalities. The augmented scaffolding in the totality of functionalities were expected to produce a sense of "mastery experience" and "self-efficacy" [1, 2] in students. The interview guide also asked to the interviewee to give further relevant comments, if any. The author conducted interviews and transcribed them verbatim, annotating paralinguistic features, such as laughter.

3 Sampling, Interviewing and Narratives

The nine interviewees were sampled in conformity with the Danish national Code of Conduct and thus based on informed consent from parents and students alike. Accordingly, a sample reflecting multiple levels of performance at the five-point Danish nationwide Test in English-as-a-foreign-language (EFL) proficiency attained by the class was taken, representing the levels KUM (clearly below average), UM (below average), M (average) and OM (above average)[2]. A list of consenting students had been prepared by the collaborating teacher sample of consenting students was given to the interviewer, who was new to the classroom and did not know the students' levels until after the interventions. The teacher had been instructed by the author to conduct a national test prior to interventions and prepare a list of consenting students, aiming at having at least one student represent all performance strata. The original list contained 10 students, out of which, one student

---

[2] No student in the classroom had performed at KOM (clearly above average) level, but all other strata were represented.

regretted his/her consent. After this, the list of interviewees contained: one KUM student, one UM student, two M students and five OM students. The sample distribution does not quite match national performance averages of 2018 [26]: 5% KUM performers, 17% UM performers, 34% M performers, 37% OM performers, and 11% KOM performers. In other words, 3 OM (33.3% of the sample) and 3 M interviewees (33.3% of the sample) and 1 KOM (11.1% of the sample) might have provided the author with a more fine-tuned representative breadth. The additional M and OM informants gave the author, however, the opportunity to look into intra-level variability, if any, i.e. to see if students inside the same proficiency range would have different learning experiences and different narratives to tell.

No student, it turned out, had the exact same learning experiences or learning strategies: Hence, nine thematically different narratives. In conducting the interviews, the author strove to abide by the interview guide but also to make room for spontaneity and humour to reduce tension, if any, between him and the interviewee. The distillations performed aspired to represent the narratives of all interviewees and avoid biased representations. As transcriptions document, great care was taken to have the student's opinion and clarify their viewpoints by the use of follow-up questions.

Like Mark Turner's cognitive semantics [25], contemporary narrative inquiry [6] argues that human beings structure experiences as stories. In this light, Brinkman and Kvale's hermeneutico-phenomenological qualitative approach to research interviews translates into a co-constructed "story" or narrative structuring interviewee experiences [17], i.e. a collaborative effort on part of interviewer and interviewee to represent the interviewee's experiences. Transcribing the narratives (in itself an interpretation cf. [3]) then enabled a thematic meaning condensation by the author. In the narratives, gender-neutral reference is used ("they" for "s/he", "themselves" for "himself or herself", etc.) for anonymity.

3.1 Nine Narratives of Learning Experiences

The (transcribed) interview with KUM (clearly below average) is a narrative conveying the theme of pleasure, i.e. "intrinsic motivation" and "self-determination" [22] of having access to help: all functionalities helped KUM in learning as regards their recognition networks [12]. Functionalities helped KUM to "understand" the text and enabled them, KUM felt, to know how to explain the text in their native language. Thus, bilingual text glossing and pictorial glossing as well as bilingual sound glossing, retelling functionalities in Danish and English and text-to-speech with text highlighting functionality were used. The informant expressed "intrinsic motivation", saying it was very good to have them, and it was "actually rather fun"[3] to have such functionalities, as it was "something entirely new". KUM expressed that they would like to have such functionalities in their regular text-based instructional materials. KUM also explained how they felt that if you could not understand one meaning representation, you could just go on to the next and when asked of what individual functionalities offered, KUM told me that you got more "information". In summary, the student's narrative appears to depict an experience of

---

[3] All quotations were translated from Danish.

having the help to "self-regulate" their learning [19] – an experience alignable with Bandura's "mastery experience", which is a source of "self-efficacy" [2].

The narrative distilled from UM's interview pinpointed specific experiences with functionalities. The narrative saw no use in pictorial representation but great use in both bilingual glossing modalities (text and sound) as well the retelling functionality. The experiences, however, also pointed out that sometimes near-inaudibility of spoken glossing needed an increase in volume and that the text-to-speech function was not fast enough compared with that of a commercial assistive software package offered to dyslectics in Danish primaries and lower-secondaries, which UM used. The experience was, apart from easy access and a help for UM to understand "the meaning" of the word – to help the words to "sink in". The narrative also touched the themes of non-lemma-based and contiguous glossing, which were a pleasant alternative to confusing base-form dictionary entries (for non-base form look-ups) and multiple entries to keep track of with e.g. collocations or constructions abounding in low-frequency words. Information-retrieval from the standard lemma-based glossing in standard language teaching glossaries and online dictionaries made comprehension much more error-prone. The retelling function (in sound) was also experienced as useful and as something the interviewee used very much to make sure that they were "absolutely certain" "what the text was about", preventing them from relying on misunderstood guesses - but also something that helped them to communicate on the text, i.e. scaffolding both "self-regulated learning" and communication skills [19]. In addition, sound sources were also "nice" for having access to speech by a real human being to listen to as an alternative to built-in robotic software-based diction. The narrative may suggest that access to English spoken by (competent) humans is experienced as sparse in the classroom and that retelling augmentations can help to meet such needs in learners. On having the totality of functionalities at their disposal, the narrative expressed the interviewee's great satisfaction, saying it was "mega nice" without further ado, also expressing "intrinsic motivation". In summary, UM's narrative depicts a learner experience different from KUM's. Compendious glossary functionalities were felt to facilitate both vocabulary acquisition and communicating on the text and not just textual comprehension. The general theme of self-efficacy achieved via self-mastery is also represented here. Like KUM's narrative the functionalities involved "intrinsic motivation" [22], as suggested by the above "mega nice".

In M1's narrative, the experiences of using the glossary function were not as plentiful: only a few words had been looked up and sound glossing was not used at all, as M1 explained, because they had completely forgotten about the feature. However, both text glossing in English and Danish was used as it helped M1 to understand "what the text was about". M1 would read the glossing in English first and the Danish glossary entry. When explaining what the user experience was like, M1 stated that, "it felt easier to read (the text)". The informant's experience of using the highlighting text-to-speech function was one of listening while reading as, in M1's opinion, "it is easier reading the text and understanding it" when listening to the text-to-speech function, suggesting "super-additive" comprehension "effects" from bimodal learning integration [7]. M1 also used the retelling functions both in Danish and in English, which also M1 experienced as helpful for text comprehension and - especially helpful for a jigsaw task in intervention asking students to present part of the text. M1's narrative expressed concern about misaffordances. When asked about whether having all the functionalities at your disposal in other instructional materials would be of help, M1 expressed that it would only be the case if the functionalities were not too much help, as then, "we don't kind of learn things ourselves". On second thought, however, M1 expressed that it would not be too much help when having to communicate about the text in English. Like UM's and KUM's narratives, M1's pointed out that having the assistive functions meant that it "was much easier to learn English". Although M1's narrative also shares the theme of facilitated self-efficacy, it presents a special experience: listening to retelling function-alities in both EFL and Danish combined with listening to text-to-speech functionalities while reading apparently almost obviates the need for bilingual sound glossing and pos-sibly significantly reduces glossary look-ups, owing in part to bimodal integration [7]. This is a creative tack on functionality use: Bilingual retelling seems a near-substitute for compendious sound glossing. Astoundingly perhaps, the bilingual retelling func-tion originally meant to prepare dyslectic or struggling learners for reading the text, presents another learning opportunity, viz. use it for comprehension checks, scaffolding self-regulated learning [19] or cognitive executive functions [12].

M2's narrative depicts another learning experience of glossary function usage. M2 sometimes used pictorial glossing to see "what things looked like". As for textual gloss-ing, M2 only used the entry in Danish, not using the sound glosses at all. M2 did not need the sound glosses as they felt it was easier to just read the entry in Danish and since they felt they did not have literacy problems. M2 felt that textual glossary entries helped them learn the meaning of the individual glosses. When asked about the text-to-speech function, it turns out that M2 had mistaken this function for the retelling functions, of which they used both functions, listening to the Danish one before the English one. M2 explained that these functions helped them feel more certain about meaning comprehen-sion. In their narrative, M2 argued that the assistive functions would be of great help, if one were a "dyslectic or the like", but answered affirmatively when being asked if the functions could be of help to themselves. When asked about navigation in the graphical user interface, M2 expressed that they found it very easy. In summary, M2's narrative also speaks of self-efficacy with retelling functions in both Danish and English, as a help to self-efficacy and self-regulated learning [19], becoming certain about one's under-standing in addition to checking textual glossing in Danish. Moreover, despite their arguments that functions are most meaningful for "dyslectics and the like", retelling functions were found to be very useful to remove uncertainty. M2's narrative is inter-esting from the vantage point of language acquisition and cognition. According to e.g. usage-based theories of language acquisition [24] or general theories of cognition, it stands to reason that other learning is involved in M2's comprehension check in listen-ing to a paraphrase of the meaning content in two languages and comparing this with their own understanding(s). It seems to be rather a complex cognitive process calling for involving an integration of dense cognitive structures of possibly both monolingual and bilingual semantic networks. Unlike individual glosses, the comparison involves an entire Ebook page, i.e. M2 might very well have learned more than they themselves realize.

OM1's narrative shows us another combination of learner experiences. OM1 did not use pictorial glossing, as they did not find it helpful. OM1 used textual glossing in

English, though, and then textual glossing in Danish, if they did not comprehend the former. Glossing helped OM1, as they explained, to understand individual glosses and but also to understand the whole sentence and "constructing wholes". OM1's experiences portrayed a new version of the self-efficacy theme: the text-to-speech function, they said, helped them in acquiring pronunciation skills. OM1's narrative spoke of a preference for the auditory retelling scaffold in Danish, which was used for comprehension checks, but occasionally the retelling function in English was used first after reading to see if listening to the function made more sense than reading the text. Like the other narratives, the navigation was seen as easy, in fact "very easy" and seen as a good alternative to Google searches and Danish bilingual online dictionaries.

OM2's narrative is different. Saying that they are a relatively proficient EFL learner, OM2 argues that pictorial glossing was of little use to them and not used at all. Instead, OM2 used bilingual textual glossing, starting with the English entry and then consulting the entry in Danish. Sound glossing was not used by OM2 at all. Instead, apparently, OM2 used the text-to-speech function to find out about and hear the pronunciation of word highlighted. OM2 found it nice, however, that you could listen to somebody else read the text aloud if you were not sure that you understood. OM2 felt that glosses helped to acquire words, viz. glossary entries in English that OM2 felt that they might learn additional words from. In addition, OM2 used the response function, but unlike e.g. M1 who did not think it conducive to learning English, OM2 thought that it helped them to think about how to formulate answers, i.e. facilitated working on written proficiency and, therefore apparently, OM2 used the response function consistently. Again, we see a different variation on the theme of self-efficacy, namely a story of using the text-to-speech function for pronunciation practice rather than for auditory access to meaning construction. Similarly creative is the use of English glossing for extended vocabulary acquisition and using the response function to work on written proficiency, rather than the intended use of helping the learner with their "strategic networks" [13] regarding on-task behaviour.

OM3's narrative presented yet another learner experience. OM3 felt they did not need pictorial glossing and thought it a good idea to avoid the Danish retelling function, as it would make "things too easy". In fact, OM3 did not use retelling functions in general, as they felt they had no problems understanding the text, their only need being access to textual glossing occasionally. The glosses, they felt, helped them comprehend the individual entry as well as the whole text. However, OM3 mostly used the glossing in Danish, it being the most "convenient" access to meaning. However, like e.g. KUM, OM3 expressed "intrinsic motivation", saying that having all the functions was a "delightful experience", especially as, like UM, that the non-lemma-based glossing design gave them easy access to good explanations to help them understand the very "hard words". Unlike OM2, OM3 did not feel that the response field function helped them to acquire English. Here the themes of self-efficacy and "self-regulated learning" were expressed as having access to understanding the "very hard words", which sufficed for OM3 to move on, apparently, and to this end, the design was, as OM3 expressed, rather suitable.

OM4's narrative told of pictorial glossing as a help to envisage the meaning content but not as something helping them to acquire English. OM4 saw themselves as somebody who was good at English and found that they could learn more consulting textual glosses in English, which they found easy to understand, and not just Danish textual glosses. They felt that it was "cool" to use the textual glossing in English, and if they did not understand, they could just go to the entry in Danish. Like other OM informants, OM4 did not use sound glossing. However, they used the built-in text-to-speech function for working on pronunciation. OM4 liked having the retelling functions at their disposal although they did not use them: it helped them feel secure that if they needed help understanding the whole text, help could be offered. Moreover, OM4 found that the response field helped them to learn English in that it helped them "to dig deeper" - to think about if they had understood the text correctly and let the meaning content sink in, i.e., used the function to help them to keep track of the details of the meaning content. OM4 thought it "mega delightful" having access to all the assistive functions and using functions at their own discretion, and that navigation was easy and was, as in other narratives, a pleasant alternative to search engines and online dictionaries. OM4's narrative also expressed pleasure of participating in the "experiment". Also in OM4's narrative, we see a new variation on the themes of "self-efficacy" and "self-regulated learning" and "intrinsic motivation" [19, 22]. OM4 seems to use the English textual glosses for boosting their confidence to be motivated by a "mastery experience" - cf. [2]. It stands to reason that consulting the English glosses also helps the student to solidify their vocabulary and English proficiency in general in its capacity as interpretation practice and "usage-based" appropriation of the foreign language [24]. OM4's narrative of the learning experience expressed that consulting glossing in English may be a "cool" experience boosting confidence. OM4 liked to have the safety net provided by the mere access to retelling functions – though not used – to alleviate fears of misapprehension. Like OM2, OM4 presented a creative use of the text-to-speech function, viz. for practicing pronunciation skills.

Unlike the above OM narrative, OM5's narrative presented experiences with sound glossing. Like OM4, OM5 also used pictorial glossing to have an idea of what things were and like OM4, they used the textual glossing in English, and if not helped enough, the entry in Danish. OM5 expressed that they really liked the way glossing was "well-written". Unlike OM4, OM5 was not sure the response field was of any help to them regarding language acquisition, although they had used it almost consistently. Also here "self-regulation" was scaffolded: OM5 was very pleased with direct access to direct glossing and authoritative "well written" explanations and not having to rely on Google searches that they felt might not help them find the right answer. OM5 used sound glossing a few times because they found it pleasant to listen to as it they found it to be "good recordings" in English and Danish. They just wanted to listen to it (out of curiosity, apparently), as they felt they could easily under textual resources. OM5's narrative evaluated the assistive functionalities trying to take the point of view struggling learners and expressed that, in general, they felt that run-of-the mill instructional materials left struggling learners behind. When asked to clarify, OM5 told of a struggling learner they had as a friend, who they imagined could do well with such assistance, and that the assistive software their friend had was no good compared to the functions in the Ebook. Hypothetically, OM5 felt that they might use the retelling function in English but primarily understood it to be a very good helping hand to "struggling readers". Unlike OM4, as for whom retelling functionalities could inspire security and confidence,

OM5's narrative presented no such need, and their concern and empathy for struggling learners seem to convey a confident learner personality, for whom access to bilingual textual glossing apparently sufficed. OM5 preferred the Ebook prototype to course books because you had access to "all these explanatory resources", meaning that you could avoid situations when "you have to raise a hand to ask the teacher, 'What does it mean?'". Thus, thematically, OM5's narrative expresses a sense of assisted "self-efficacy" and "self-regulation". OM5's narrative concludes in the pleasurable experience - when asked for supplementary relevant remarks – it was very good to work with the Ebook and they felt that the Ebook was "hard to surpass" as an instructional material.

4 Findings and Conclusions

The sum of narratives conveys a variability of learner experiences and learning strategies/behaviours, presenting its answers to the research questions. A shared feature is one of facilitated learning processes by having access to the functionalities and ease of navigation, i.e., the hypothesis expecting a sense of increased self-efficacy was corroborated. Interestingly, the road to self-efficacy and self-regulation and the usage of assistive functionalities were both diverse and unpredictable. Learners found alternative uses aiding them in their language-learning process, using e.g. text-to-speech functionalities for pronunciation acquisition and retelling functions for comprehension checks. This lent support to the subhypothesis that different learners would experience and apply affordances differently. Apparently, only one learner applied the retelling functions for their originally intended use (KUM). The hypothesis that all functionalities would be of use to all learners in different ways was, however, only in part corroborated. Though they liked having access to all functionalities, most learners did not find all functionalities useful, but a variety of learner experience and usage concerning functionalities varied across performance strata and within strata of performance. For instance the narratives made clear that that some OM, M and UM learners might use the text-to-speech functionality to facilitate comprehension, while other M and OM learners might use text-to-speech functionalities for working on their pronunciation, but not the KUM and UM learners. It thus makes sense to provide all learners with all functionalities as diverse usages align the same assistive functionality with multiple learner strategies. Moreover, although there is trend in narratives for less usage to correlate with higher test performance, proficiency is in the narratives no good predictor for functionality use. Narratives rather show that assistive/remedial functionalities are of meaningful use to all strata of learners. Moreover, pedagogically informed assistive functionalities produced both a useful and delightful experiences. Since, however, only nine interviews have been conducted and individual variety abounds, further interviews are being conducted in current classroom interventions to reach a saturation point (cf. e.g. [17]) of the representative breadth. Moreover, there only being three Ebooks, which the author had to construct himself, aspiring to UDL principles compliance available precludes longitudinal studies, which could unravel further details on design viability. Even so, the narratives appear to corroborate the viability of all innovations of the instructional material design. In other words, pedagogically informed inclusive practices can be facilitated by a UDL-CALL learning design [15], i.e. time may be ripe for introducing pedagogically informed universal design to language classrooms.

References

1. Bandura, A.: Self-efficacy. In: Ramachaudran, V.S. (ed.) Encyclopedia of Human Behavior, pp. 71–81. Academic Press, New York (1994)
2. Bandura, A.: An agentic perspective on positive psychology. In: Lopez, S.J. (ed.) Posit Psychol Expecting best people, vol. 1, pp. 1–27 (2007)
3. Beatty, K.: Teaching & Researching: Computer-Assisted Language Learning. Routledge, Philadelphia (2013)
4. Brinkman, T., Kvale, S.: InterViews. Learning the craft of qualitative research interviewing, 3rd edn. Sage, London (2015)
5. Bundsgaard, J., Hansen, T.I.: Evaluation of Learning Materials: A Holististic Framework. J. Learn. Des. **4**, 31–44 (2011). https://doi.org/10.5204/jld.v4i4.87
6. Chase, S.E.: Narrative inquiry: Multiple lenses, approaches, voices. In: The Sage Handbook of Qualitative Research, pp. 651–679 (2005)
7. Cheetham, D.: Multi-modal language input: A learned superadditive effect. Appl. Linguist. Rev. **10**, 179–200 (2019). https://doi.org/10.1515/applirev-2017-0036
8. Creswell, J.W., Plano Clark, V.L., Gutmann, M.L., Hanson, W.E.: Advanced mixed methods research designs. In: Tashakkori, A., Teddlie, C. (eds.) Handbook of Mixed Methods in Social and Behavioral Research, pp. 209–240. Sage, Thousand Oaks (2003)
9. Emtoft, L.M.: Elevens deltagelse: IT, læring og inklusion. In: Quvang, C. (ed) Specialpædagogik: en introduktion, pp. 59–79. Hans Reitzels Forlag, Copenhagen (2016)
10. Emtoft, L.M.: Jeg har aldrig prøvet at være den første før: En undersøgelse af lærere og elevers praksis med IT og dennes betydning for deltagelse og inklusion. Roskilde Universitet, Roskilde, Denmark (2017)
11. Frederiksen, M.: Integration i 'mixed methods' forskning: Metode eller design? Forskningsdesign og Metod **1**, 17–40 (2013)
12. Gordon, D., Meyer, A., Rose, D.: Re-envisioning education through UDL. In: Universal Design for Learning: Theory and Practical, pp. 1–20 (2010). https://doi.org/10.1111/1744-7917.12072
13. Hall, T.E., Meyer, A., Rose, D.H. (eds.): Universal Design for Learning in the Classroom: Practical Applications. Guilford, Wakefield (2012)
14. Hansen, T.I., Skovmand, K.: Fælles mål og midler - Læremidler og læreplaner i teori og praksis. Klim (2011)
15. Kasch, H.: New Multimodal Designs for Foreign Language Learning, pp. 28–59 (2018). https://doi.org/10.7146/lt.v4i5.111561
16. Kvale, S.: The qualitative research interview: A phenomenological and a hermeneutical mode of understanding. J. Phenomenol. Psychol. **14**, 171–196 (1983)
17. Kvale, S., Brinkmann, S.: Interview: Det kvalitative forsksningsinterview som håndværk. (Transl: Interviews - The Qualitative Research Interview as a Craft). Hans Reitzels Forlag, Copenhagen (2015)
18. Leinenbach, M.T., Corey, M.L.: Universal design for learning: theory and practice. In: Proceedings of Society for Information Technology & Teacher Education International Conference (2004)
19. Pintrich, P.R., De Groot, E.V.: Motivational and self-regulated learning components of classroom academic performance. J. Educ. Psychol. **82**, 33–40 (1990). https://doi.org/10.1037/0022-0663.82.1.33
20. Proctor, C.P., Dalton, B., Grisham, D.L.: Scaffolding English language learners and struggling readers in a universal literacy environment with embedded strategy instruction and vocabulary support. J. Lit. Res. **39**, 71–93 (2007). https://doi.org/10.1080/10862960709336758

21. Rose, D.H.: Universal design for learning and the future of education. In: 2007 Federation for Children with Special Needs' Visions Community Conference (2007)
22. Ryan, R.M., Deci, E.L.: Overview of self-determination theory: an organismic and dialectal perspective. In: Handbook of Self-Determination Theory. Rochester University Press, Rochester, pp. 3–36 (2002)
23. Strangman, N., Meyer, A., Hall, T., Proctor, C.P.: New technologies and universal design for learning in the foreign language classroom. In: Worlds Apart? pp. 164–176 (2014)
24. Tomasello, M.: Constructing a Language: A Usage-Based Theory of Language Acquisition. Harvard University Press, Cambridge (2003)
25. Turner, M.: The Literary Mind: The Origins of Thought and Language. Oxford University Press, Oxford (1998)
26. Unge BU (2019) National Præstationsprofil (National Performance Profile)
27. Vogt, P., et al.: Second Language Tutoring Using Social Robots: L2TOR - The Movie, pp. 373 (2019). https://doi.org/10.1109/hri.2019.8673016

GLOBE - Digital Literacy and Organizational Learning by Scenario-Driven Exercises

Markus Bresinsky and Sophia Willner[✉]

Faculty of Applied Natural Sciences and Cultural Studies, Ostbayerische Technische Hochschule Regensburg (OTH-R), University of Applied Sciences, Galgenbergstraße 30, 93053 Regensburg, Germany
markus.bresinsky@oth-regensburg.de, sophia.willner@web.de

Abstract. Due to rapid technological development and fast-changing working environments, organizations active in such context find themselves facing internal change and adaption processes. Originally prominent among start-up or IT-companies, the use of management concepts to steer such change processes and to increase efficiency also spread among humanitarian organizations preoccupied with crisis management. In this regard, concepts retrieved from the domain of Organization Development offer a great potential to facilitate change processes and to enhance learning among practitioners. The notions of Learning Organization and Quality Management are combined with the theory of Argyris and Schön's Levels of Learning. This combination then serves as a theoretical decision-making base used in a simulation game at the University of Applied Sciences OTH Regensburg. Within this scenario-driven exercise, Quality Management, virtual collaboration and digital skills are trained. During the simulation game, participants are encouraged to think critically, to utilize new technologies and to apply their problem-solving skills to real-life examples, which ultimately aims at preparing students for a dynamic working environment within the era of digitization.

Keywords: Simulation games · Virtual collaboration · Organization development · Learning organization · Deming cycle · Situational awareness

1 Introduction

How can young professionals be prepared for a more than ever complex and fast-changing world and working environment? How can higher education institutions deliver digital competencies and skills needed to equip students to keep pace with the rapid technological change? And how can individuals ultimately contribute to successful development and change of organizations active in dynamic contexts?

Institutes of higher education bear the potential to incorporate innovation into the education received by young professionals, especially with regards to digital literacy and the capability of working in highly dynamic environments. Thus, as one of Germany's higher education institutes, a simulation game offered by the OTH Regensburg will be presented and analyzed with regards to organization development and the teaching of digital skills.

© ICST Institute for Computer Sciences, Social Informatics and Telecommunications Engineering 2020
Published by Springer Nature Switzerland AG 2020. All Rights Reserved
A. Brooks and E. I. Brooks (Eds.): ArtsIT 2019/DLI 2019, LNICST 328, pp. 671–682, 2020.
https://doi.org/10.1007/978-3-030-53294-9_51

2 Engaging in Turbulent Contexts

Typically, the public sector is well-equipped for dealing with routine problems and for delivering standard services, but when circumstances become exceptional, complex and more dynamic, public policy makers perceive effective problem-solving as increasingly challenging [1]. For instance, the governmental response to the natural disaster Hurricane Katrina was widely deemed as inadequate, and resulted in demands for novel, adaptive and networked approaches to meet such nonroutine challenges [2].

Not only the public sector but also non-governmental organizations (NGOs) and international organizations (IOs) find themselves facing complex challenges. Particularly in the field of development cooperation, peacebuilding and conflict transformation, practitioners operate in turbulent contexts where societies are either affected by direct forms of violence or are seemingly at peace but suffer from covert types of structural violence [3]. Since the 1990s, the characteristics of armed conflicts changed and shifted from conventional warfare to irregular tactics, internal civil conflict and the participation of non-state actors, making conflicts more and more protracted [4]. Furthermore, in response to the growing need for humanitarian relief, aid organizations increased their engagement in conflict-affected regions which ultimately placed more aid workers in precarious situations [5]. Consequently, aid workers find themselves immersed in complex and dynamic conflicts where it is increasingly challenging to develop a thorough understanding of the events occurring around them and the respective underlying causes [6].

2.1 Organization Development

Faced with the increasing number of seemingly intractable conflicts, the growing pace of change and the technological development, a rising number of internationally active organizations have adopted some kind of management concept as a tool to increase their efficiency and to make use of new technologies [7–10].

This increase of change and adaption within an organization has mostly been prominent in the private sector, particularly among start-up or IT companies [11]. The main external drivers for organizational change represent technological change and digitization, increasing dynamic and complexity [12]. Although technological change makes information and data more accessible and collectable, the vast amount of information and the speed with which information can change increases the difficulty to adequately process data [13]. These drivers lead to the creation of a multitude of managerial and organizational tools to facilitate concrete change strategies, many of which are discussed under the term 'agility'. For instance, start-up or IT companies perceive approaches such as 'Scrum' and 'Design Thinking' as particularly innovative frameworks for managing business processes [12].

However, scholars argue that the concept of 'agility' belongs to a long tradition of approaches to reduce organizational hierarchy [14, 15]. Thus, mentioned frameworks can be classified under the science of Organization Development (OD) [16].

Originated in the 1940s, OD applies social and behavioral science knowledge in a system-wide approach to the planned development, improvement, and reinforcement of strategies, structures, and process to help organizations change, improve and achieve greater effectiveness [17]. Several methods and concepts such as human resource management, social psychology, or Systems Theory are incorporated in OD, making the domain *"more of a confederation of subcultures trying to become a single occupational community rather than a profession in the more traditional sense"* [18].

One crucial commonality among all different kinds of approaches, methods or models within OD is a set of underlying normative and humanistic values that are reflected in the overall purpose of transforming tasks into more fulfilling activities that engage also a person's mind and motivation [19].

Thus, core functions of OD include generating and using data to:

- *"create a felt need for change through self-awareness and facilitated learning,*
- *develop a collaborative diagnosis of the prevailing and underlying issues,*
- *and determine and enact an intervention set with full organizational engagement intended to achieve a desired future state"* [19].

2.2 Organization Development in Volatile Contexts

When examining the literature on OD regarding organizations that engage in highly volatile contexts a recent development within the humanitarian aid and development sector has been the introduction of management concepts [21]. According to findings from sociology of work and industrial sociology, business managers establish and implement management concepts and rationalization strategies due to an augmented level of competition and the changing characteristics of markets associated with an increased burden of uncertainty [20, 23]. However, organizations working in humanitarian aid or development sector were traditionally reluctant to adopt management concepts from the business world as development organizations do not aim for economic profit and often view economization processes skeptically or even reject them for moral-political reasons [20]. In recent years however, this reluctance towards change management approaches originating from OD theories began to decline and the previous approach of 'muddling through' is more and more deemed as inadequate [21].

Astonishingly, the ideas, methods and instruments which originated from theories and practice in the business sector, such as the concept of Quality Management and Learning Organization, are primarily used to solve operational and structural problems of aid organizations [24]. Thus, no independent and own approaches specifically to enhance the efficiency of aid agencies are developed from scratch.

Hence, it can be followed that the prevalence of management concepts in different areas of society depends on their respective degree of abstraction [25]. The more abstract a concept and the problem-solving models it contains, the more compatible it is and the easier it is to apply to a wide variety of organizations.

Due to the general applicability of concepts originated from the corporate world and from OD, in the following the two concepts of Quality Management and Learning Organization are transferred to management in humanitarian aid missions [20, 26, 27].

2.3 Learning Organization and Quality Management

With regards to the term 'Learning Organization' in the context of complex peacebuilding, development or humanitarian aid concepts, the literature emphasizes the topics of enhancing performance and ensuring the quality of humanitarian aid [28]. However, the central issue that aid organizations face is that the conditions under which they operate are constantly altered and organizations are confronted with rapidly changing demands and challenges [29].

Senge (1996) postulates that in times of rapid change, only those organizations able to respond flexibly to change and to constantly evolve, learn and improve will be successful [30]. Flexibility is not only required of the members of the organization, but also of the organizational structures [20]. In this regard, Senge provides recommendations for managers on how to design organizations to suit the ideal of a learning organization. For instance, in order to transform an organization into a learning organization, it is indispensable to promote self-responsibility and independent thinking of its staff [30].

Incorporating processes and the atmosphere to allow for critical self-reflection proved expedient to foster flexibility and quick yet deliberate actions. Structural changes towards a learning organization thus contain decentralization and the formation of flexible work units responsible for changing or dynamic types of tasks [22].

The concept of organizational learning has also been coined by Argyris (1973) who argued that a core function fulfilled by practitioners of OD is the creation of data and knowledge. The goal of such generation is to reveal underlying structures that have an impact on the visible surface perceived by the members of an organization [31]. This step serves as a first dialogue-based examination ('diagnosis') before moving on to the correction of potential impediments for organizational effectiveness. Consequently, organizational change includes three different levels of learning [32]:

- Single-loop learning (correction of errors; superficial problem-solving)
- Double-loop learning (underlying structures and values are examined whether they need to be changed and the results feed into learning and decision-making)
- Meta-learning (enhancing single and double-loop learning to further develop organizational capabilities on how to learn, change and improve)

This classification of levels of learning offers a potential to be combined with the PDCA (plan–do–check–act) cycle (also referred to as Deming circle). The PDCA cycle represents an iterative tool to manage, control and continuously improve processes and outcomes [33].

The usual sequence of 'plan, do, check and act' involves the detailed development of an action plan, the implementation of such, controlling if intended outcomes or goals were reached, and, if necessary, the adaption of the previously created action plan [33]. Although this correction of errors can foster overall quality assurance and the achievement of the desired outcome, it mostly focuses on changing and adapting superficial elements embodied in the respective action plan. This would correspond to Argyris' & Schön's [32] single-loop learning as the mere implementation of a changed action plan would not target or question underlying values or structures. Incorporating double-loop learning in the PDCA-cycle would entail the analysis of those deeper structures leading to more substantial and sustainable quality management findings. The information generated from checking the course of action could lead to the revelation of systemic errors that would have otherwise remained unrecognized.

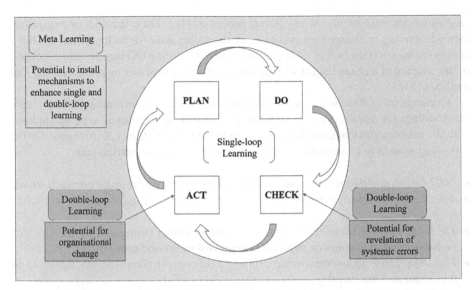

Fig. 1. Combination PDCA-Cycle [33] and three levels of learning [32] (own graphic)

Consequently, the revealing findings could feed into altering the quality management cycle or the respective decision-making process ultimately culminating in organizational change that fosters sustainable improvement of organizational processes and structures. Finally, the inclusion of meta-learning would eventually complete the ideal of organizational learning by enhancing single and double-loop learning mechanisms. For instance, this could be achieved by introducing specific structures to contribute to continuous learning and to promote the organization's capacity to learn about change and to improve. However, the present model relies on initiative and critical thinking by those involved in the process. Thus, a necessary requirement to benefit from such a model would be an atmosphere that encourages critical observations, and that allows voicing constructive criticism.

As it can be observed, organizational learning as a central theme of OD has the potential to enhance organizational change processes and to provide change management competencies through a learning-by-doing process [17]. Practicing OD therefore aims at facilitating continuous improvement [34]. Concerning the reoccurring critique towards the adoption of management concepts, OD offers a concept to compile approaches specifically for the needs and characteristics of humanitarian aid and development organizations [15]. Implementing concepts originated from OD benefits from viewing an organization as a living and adaptive system that can be used to generate fruitful insights on underlying dynamics and structures which result from the behavior and attitudes of members of an organization themselves [34]. Thus, according to OD researchers and pioneers, OD avoids being "*a mindless application of someone else's best practice*" [34].

However, a maximum and constant level of agility, flexibility and change of all organizations is neither necessary and nor effective [11]. The need to maintain effective management structures to perform routine tasks and deliver standard services will continue to exist for exact this purpose [11]. Furthermore, organizations still report high rates of failure when implementing change processes [16]. The difficulties organizations face when trying to change their processes or structures arise for multiple reasons, but a common concern is the lack of skills and knowledge regarding OD theories and concepts, or the absence of a change agent who facilitates change processes by implementing OD methods [34].

Consequently, OD scholars and practitioners advocate for incorporating OD concepts into trainings for managers and leaders and into academic institutions to equip students with the necessary managerial skills and knowledge [35]. Warrick (2016) argues for the following aspects to be included in academic and professional curriculums:

- *"OD models and theories for understanding, developing, and changing organizations.*
- *Action research and Systems Thinking as ways of approaching OD issues and change [...].*
- *The importance of knowing reality before treating reality (using assessment methods to discover what is going on before designing solutions and processes) [...].*
- *The importance of understanding process and content (how you do things is as important as what you do).*
- *How to change complex, global, virtual organizations"* [35].

With regards to the remaining high rates of failure when it comes to organizational change, incorporating principles of OD into curriculums of higher education and life-long learning becomes crucial. However, the lack of knowledge regarding organizational change is not the only risk that might jeopardize the success of organization development processes. Rapid technological change and digital illiteracy are determined as equally influential and must thus be incorporated in curriculums as well.

2.4 Digital Literacy and New Technologies in Dynamic Environments

In March 2016, the Federal Ministry for Economic Affairs and Energy of Germany set out its Digital Strategy 2025 program aiming at transforming Germany into a digital economy and combating digital illiteracy among its citizens [36]. One of ten steps towards future development comprises *"introducing digital education to all phases of life"*, placing institutions of higher education at the heart of digital innovation [36]. However, despite the effort to initiate digitization processes, in July 2019 the Organization for Economic Co-operation and Development (OECD) still called upon Germany to *"strengthen skills to cope with technological change"* [37]. Thus, whilst German policy makers agree on the vital need to translate the country's digital agenda into action, it becomes evident that the practical implementations must still unfold their full potential both in higher education, the private and the public sector [38].

For example, regarding the demand for innovation and change within the humanitarian sector, harnessing new technologies and cooperating with private businesses are cited as promising drivers in the amelioration of humanitarian aid [39]. Statements as *" [...] humanitarian aid organizations must adapt to work with new data sources"* and *"[...] must recognize, value and nurture the capacity to translate data into actionable information."* [40] further emphasize the need to implement new technology-based tools and to create the expertise to apply such tools.

How crucial it is to secure the promotion of digital literacy to future leaders and managers becomes apparent when examining the skills and competencies necessary to seize the opportunities that arise from a globalized and interconnected world (11). While novel technology applications and software such as the use of artificial intelligence and machine learning are already being used by numerous companies and organizations, synergy effects can only occur to a limited extent if the human element does not receive adequate training (42). Ultimately, the human factor in the interaction of human – technology – organization plays a decisive role even in the age of digitization.

Numerous studies have already been conducted on how the acquisition of digital skills can be integrated into school or university education (43). Prominent and proven examples include for instance blended learning, simulation games, or hackathons [43].

3 Transformational Learning by Simulation Games

A promising framework to implement and impart digital competencies and to test concepts as Learning Organization and Quality Management in a practical way is the use of simulation games and scenario-making [44]. Similar to the OD concept of action science and action learning where findings are established by applying knowledge and then feed into a learning process, scenario-making and simulation games can be designed in an equally stimulating way [45]. Learning on an individual level can be enhanced by actively involving participants in the process of acquiring information, developing courses of action and engaging them in a decision-making process all while countering problems that are designed based on real-life examples. Furthermore, individual learning is fostered by utilizing methods of collaborative learning where dialogue and cooperation contribute to revise one's own perspective [46]. Scenario-based exercises thus create a safe and experiential learning environment that enables students to test their cognitive abilities, to practice alternative problem-solving skills and to apply innovative working techniques.

3.1 GLOBE Exercises – a Scenario-Driven Simulation Exercise

A simulation game based on such premises has been introduced in the study program 'International Relations and Management' at the University of Applied Sciences OTH Regensburg in the field of International Politics [47]. The simulation called 'GLOBE exercise' represents a practically oriented project to teach competencies needed to fulfil complex collaborative tasks and to work in a digitized environment.

The GLOBE exercise is carried out in cooperation with international partner universities and other organizations (for instance the local fire brigade) and is designed as a multi-day event. In a scenario-based management and leadership exercise, students work together in international and geographically distributed groups by virtual collaboration. For this purpose, students practice the application of information and communication technologies (ICT) to communicate (e-mail, videoconferences, translation applications), information and knowledge management (data analysis and file organization) and project management (management tools). The content of the scenario is based on the cooperation between United Nations agencies in a humanitarian relief mission to enable students to practice management and leadership skills in complex situations. The scenario in the simulation reflects the ongoing conflict in Afghanistan with focus on the United Nations Assistance Mission in Afghanistan (UNAMA) and the NATO-led Resolute Support Mission (RSM), where students of the OTH Regensburg represent an agency of the UNAMA Mission (see Fig. 2). Based on the scenario, students are expected to develop a holistic situation picture (situational awareness) and to offer support for their locally distributed team members by providing reports, briefings and assessments and thereby perform effective crisis management.

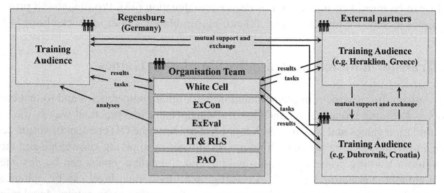

Fig. 2. Extended exercise structure GLOBE exercise (own graphic)

The structure of the exercises comprises a training audience, external partners and a team charged with the organization of the exercise. This organization team itself consist of multiple sub-teams responsible the overall steering and control (ExCon), the scenario-based scripting (Whit Cell), the observation, evaluation and feedback (ExEval), technical infrastructure and support (IT & RLS) and documentation and public relation (PAO).

The training audience (TA) consists of students from different fields of studies and academic backgrounds, ensuring a diverse and interdisciplinary working atmosphere. Participants receive information to introduce them to the thematic focus of the exercise beforehand and to ensure active involvement from the first day of the exercise.

During the exercise, participants collaborate based on the concept of holistic situational awareness. When developing a holistic situation analysis, participants inevitably follow processes and methods based on OD, such as learning organization and quality management. The learners follow an iterative cycle of information gathering and processing, the preparation of action recommendations, the application of actions, the control of whether goals have been achieved, and ultimately the correction of the recommended actions (see PDCA-cycle in Fig. 1).

Testing and experiencing such concepts in a safe environment enables participants to practice and to internalize principles crucial for the successful development and adaption of own organizational processes. Collaboration and feedback by their peers foster an atmosphere of critical reflection and independent thinking eventually attaining three levels of learning (see Fig. 1). Hence, learners are encouraged to change their mindset and cognitive processes sustainably, ultimately resulting better preparation for organizational change processes in a fast-changing working environment.

4   Discussion and Conclusion

The simulation game 'GLOBE Exercise' offers an opportunity to practice organizational management and digital skills based on a scenario-driven exercise, a first step towards Germany's goal of including digital education to all phases of life.

Furthermore, the implementation of problem-based training and learning can strengthen the participants' capabilities to think critically, and can enhance competencies concerning virtual collaboration, data and knowledge management, and situational awareness. With regards to crisis management, the concept of the 'GLOBE Exercise' allows for collaboration with external partners like rescue organizations and thus offers insights from first-line practitioners. Thereby, participants' ability to cope with crises can be improved, and learners can develop a wide set of skills in a collaborative learning environment.

Theories of organization development, quality management and levels of learning will be incorporated in future exercises. An own model combining the Deming cycle with the three levels of learning will serve as the base structure of decision-making processes in future the exercises. Therefore, a great potential regarding future research and future development of the exercise can be observed.

Nevertheless, technology in crisis management and humanitarian action must also be seen with caution although new technologies are often perceived as catalysts for innovation and change. However, humanitarian organizations must be aware of unintended consequences when employing technological tools in their mix of crisis management strategies.

Humanitarian technologies have already drastically changed the way humanitarian aid is delivered [48]. Thus, when further pursuing the potentials of new technologies and phenomena such as cyber-humanitarianism, the humanitarian sector must be prepared for a shift of paradigm, which then will be equally valid for the educational sector.

Therefore, when preparing young professionals for working in complex and fast changing contexts in the age of digitization, uncritically embracing new technologies should not be encouraged, which certainly poses a risk during simulation games.

References

1. Chapman, J.: System Failure. Why Governments Must Learn to Think Differently, 2nd edn. Demons, London (2004)
2. Kettl, D.: The Next Government of the United States. Why Our Institutions Fail us and How to Fix Them. W. W. Norton, New York (2008)
3. Galtung, J.: Violence, Peace and Peace Research. J. Peace Res. 6, 167–191 (1969)
4. Ricigliano, R.: Networks of effective action: implementing an integrated approach to peacebuilding. Secur. Dial. 34(4), 445–462 (2003)
5. Harris, A., Dombrowski, P.: Military collaboration with humanitarian organizations in complex emergencies. Glob. Gov. 8(2), 155–178 (2002)

6. Lederach, P.: The Little Book of Conflict Transformation. Clear Articulation of the Guiding Principles by a Pioneer in the Field. Good Books, Pennsylvania (2003)
7. Bowman, P., Chettleborough, J., Jeans, H., Rowlands, J., Whitehead, J.: Systems Thinking. An Introduction for Oxfam Staff. Oxfam GB, Oxford (2015)
8. Wils, O., Hopp, U., Ropers, N., Vimalarajah, L., Zunzer, W.: The Systemic Approach to Conflict Transformation. Concepts and Fields of Application. Berghof Foundation for Peace Support, Berlin (2006)
9. De Coning, C.: The United Nations and the comprehensive approach. Danish Institute for International Studies, Copenhagen (2008)
10. Allana, A., Sparkman, T.: Navigating complexity. A case study on adaptive management in Northern Uganda. Engineers without borders & Merci Corps (2014)
11. Häusling, A.: Agile Organisationen. Transformationen erfolgreich gestalten. Beispiele agiler Pioniere. Hauffe Gruppe, Freiburg (2018)
12. Finckler, P.: Transformationale Führung. Wegweiser für nachhaltigen Führungs- und Unternehmenserfolg. Springer, Heidelberg (2017). https://doi.org/10.1007/978-3-662-502 92-1
13. Bennet, N., Lemoine, J.: What VUCA really means for you. Harvard Bus. Rev. **92**, 1–24 (2014)
14. French, W.L., Bell, C.H.: Organization Development: Behavioral Science Interventions for Organization improvement. Prentice-Hall Inc, Englewood Cliffs (1978)
15. von Ameln, F., Brückner, F.: Agilität. Gruppe. Interaktion. Organisation. Zeitschrift für Angewandte Organisationspsychologie (GIO) **47**(4), 383–386 (2016)
16. Schiersmann, C., Thiel, H.U.: Organisationsentwicklung. Prinzipien und Strategien von Veränderungsprozessen, 5th edn. Springer, Wiesbaden (2018). https://doi.org/10.1007/978-3-658-03485-6
17. Cummings, T.G., Worley, C.G.: Organization Development and Change, 10th edn. Cengage Learning, Stanford (2015)
18. Schein, E.: Taking culture seriously in organization development. In: Rothwell, W.J., Stavros, J.M., Sullivan, R.L. (eds.) Practicing Organization Development. Leading transformation and change, pp. 233–245. John Wiley & Sons, New Jersey (2016)
19. Church, A.H., Shull, A.C., Burke, W.W.: The future of organization, development, transformation, and change. In: Rothwell, W.J., Stavros, J.M., Sullivan, R.L. (eds.) Practicing Organization Development. Leading Transformation and Change, pp. 419–429. John Wiley & Sons, New Jersey (2016)
20. Langhof, A.: Managementkonzepte in der humanitären Hilfe. Zum Verhältnis zu gesellschaftlicher Semantik und Organisationsstruktur. Springer, Wiesbaden (2018). https://doi.org/10.1007/978-3-658-21302-2
21. Lewis, D.: The Management of Non-Governmental Development Organizations, 2nd edn. Routledge, London/New York (2007)
22. Edwards, M., Fowler, A.: The Earthscan Reader on NGO Management. Earthscan Publications, London (2004)
23. Pohlmann, M.: Management, organisation und Sozialstruktur. Zu neuen Fragestellungen und Konturen der Managementsoziologie. In: Schmidt, R., Gergs, H.J., Pohlmann, M. (eds.) Managementsoziologie. Themen, Desiderate, Perspektiven, pp. 227–244. Rainer Hampp Verlag, München (2002)
24. Wallace, T.: Introductory Essay. Development management and the aid chain. The case of NGOs. In: Eade, D. (ed.) Development and Management, pp. 18–38. Oxfam, Oxford (2000)
25. Strang, D., Meyer, J.W.: Institutional conditions for diffusion. In: Theory and Society, vol. 22, pp. 487–511 (1993)

26. Edwards, M., Hulme, D.: Making a difference: scaling-up the development impact of NGOs: concepts and experiences. In: Edwards, M., Fowler, A. (eds.) NGO Management, pp. 53–73. Earthscan Publications, London (2004)
27. ICRC & HHI. Engaging with people affected by armed conflicts. Taking stock. Mapping trends. Looking ahead. Recommendations for humanitarian organizations and donors in the digital era. International Committee of the Red Cross (2018). https://www.icrc.org/en/dow nload/file/69676/engaging-with-people-in-armed-conflict-recommendationt.pdf
28. Roper, L., Pettit, J.: Development and the learning organisation. In: Roper, L., Pettit, J., Eade, D. (eds.) Development and the Learning Organisation. Essays from Development in Practice, pp. 1–21. Oxfam, Oxford (2003)
29. Garred, M., O'Reilly-Calthrop, S., Midgley, T., Scott, M.J.: Making Sense of Turbulent Contexts. Local Perspectives on Large-Scale Conflict. World Vision International, Uxbridge (2015)
30. Senge, P.: The Fifth Discipline. The Art and Practice of the Learning Organization, 2nd edn. Random House, Business Books, London (2006)
31. Argyris, C.: Intervention Theory and Method. A Behavioral Science View. Addison-Weasly, Reading (1973)
32. Argyris, C., Schön, D.A.: Organizational Learning: A Theory of Action Perspective. Addison-Wesley, Reading (1978)
33. Benes, G.M., Groh, P.E.: Grundlagen des Qualitätsmanagements, 4th edn. Carl Hanser Verlag GmbH & Co. KG, München (2017)
34. Rothwell, W.J., Stavros, J.M., Sullivan, R.L.: Practicing Organizational Development. Leading Transformation and Change. John Wiley & Sons, New Jersey (2016)
35. Warrick, D.D.: Authors' insights on important organization development issues. In: Rothwell, W.J., Stavros, J.M., Sullivan, R.L. (eds.) Practicing Organizational Development. Leading Transformation and Change, pp. 429–437. John Wiley & Sons, New Jersey (2016)
36. Federal Ministry for Economic Affairs and Energy (BMWi): Digital Strategy 2025. BMWi Public Relations: Berlin) (2016)
37. OECD. Economic Policy Reforms 2019. Going for Growth. OECD Publishing, Paris (2019). https://doi.org/10.1787/aec5b059-en
38. Bernhard-Skala, C.: Organisational perspectives on the digital transformation of adult and continuing education: A literature review from a German-speaking perspective. J. Adult Contin. Educ. (2019). https://doi.org/10.1177/1477971419850840
39. Sandvik, K.B., Jumbert, M.G., Karlsrud, J., Kaufmann, M.: Humanitarian technology: a critical research agenda. Int. Rev. Red Cross 96(893), 219–242 (2014)
40. UNOCHA: Humanitarianism in the Networked Age. Including World Humanitarian Data and Trends 2012. United Nations (2013)
41. Brynjolffson, E., McAfee, A.: The Second Machine Age. Work, Progress, and Prosperity in a Time of Brilliant Technologies. W.W. Norton & Company, New York (2014)
42. Pianfetti, E.: Focus on research: teachers and technology: digital literacy through professional development. Lang. Arts Texts Technol. Think. 78(3), 255–262 (2001)
43. Hochschulforum Digitalisierung: The Digital Turn – Hochschulbildung im digitalen Zeitalter. Arbeitspapier Nr. 27. Hochschulforum Digitalisierung: Berlin (2016)
44. Rappenglück, S.: Handbuch Planspiele in der politischen Bildung. Wochenschau Verlag, Schwalbach (2017)
45. Argyris, C., Putnam, R., Smith, D.: Action Science. Concepts, Methods, and Skills for Research and Intervention. Jossey-Bass, San Francisco (1985)
46. Hills, M.: Assuring organisational resilience with lean scenario-driven exercises. Int. J. Emerg. Serv. 4(1), 37–49 (2015)

47. Digital Learning Map. GLOBE - Praxisorientierte Kompetenzausbildung in der virtuellen Zusammenarbeit. e-teaching.org: https://www.e-teaching.org/community/digital-learning-map/globe-praxisorientiert-kompetenzausbildung-in-der-virtuellen-zusammenarbeit. Accessed 12 July 2018

48. Duffield, M.: Disaster-resilience in the network age access-denial and the rise of cyber-humanitarianism. DIIS **32**, 1–32 (2013)

Problem Solving and Collaboration When School Children Develop Game Designs

Jeanette Sjöberg[1]([⊠]) and Eva Brooks[2]

[1] Halmstad University, Kristian IVs väg 3, 301 18 Halmstad, Sweden
jeanette.sjoberg@hh.se
[2] Aalborg University, Kroghstæde 3, 9220 Aalborg, Denmark
eb@hum.aau.dk

Abstract. Digital technologies in combination with creative activities have been introduced in schools as a strategy for learning and teaching activities offering scaffolding opportunities. In recent years digital game-based learning (DGBL) activities also has been tried out in schools. In this paper, we examine how collaboration between school children is configured in problem solving activities whilst developing digital game designs. The study is based on a case of a creative workshop with school children (9–10 years of age) where game design activities were applied. Game design activities with the participating children, creative materials and technologies and children's actions as well as interactions are analysed by using interaction analysis and parts of content analysis. The research questions concern the patterns, features, and challenges that emerge among 9 to 10-year-old school children when collaboratively engaged in problem solving activities? The results of the study show that a sense of community emerged when the children worked on solving the problem of designing and producing a digital game. Hence, when designing for mutuality, the design should allow for the participants' experience acknowledging an affective awareness of a shared purpose.

Keywords: Collaboration · Digital Game-Based learning (DGBL) · Game-based design · Problem solving · School children

1 Introduction

Since research has started to support digital games as a means to enhance motivation and learning e.g. [1–3], the concept of digital game-based learning has emerged into the school context. The idea that technology can assist learning asks the question of how to design for learning activities where this technology can be used in a meaningful way. Research into learning potentials and affordances of digital technologies in designs for learning points to promising results in facilitating communication, and experiences of participation in learning processes [4–6]. In recent years, the issues of designing learning activities including digital technologies has become increasingly essential, in particular related to the question of what kind of skills and understanding children should have

A. Brooks and E. I. Brooks (Eds.): ArtsIT 2019/DLI 2019, LNICST 328, pp. 683–698, 2020.
https://doi.org/10.1007/978-3-030-53294-9_52

to become digital literate [e.g. 7, 8]. The European Commission has developed a conceptual reference model for digital competence, including communication and collaboration, digital content creation, and problem solving as crucial aspects of being digital competent [9]. Studies of social interactions within different educational settings are significant, not only considering that social development is a basic educational objective, but also because such interactions are essential building blocks of children's learning and development [e.g. 10, 11]. Interestingly, Lomangino et al. [12] underline the importance of identifying both positive and negative actions and discussions as accompanying aspects of children's collaborative interactions. In doing so, it is possible to provide a holistic understanding of the learning benefits and potentials of creative and digital materials and their suitability to foster collaborative problem solving actions among children. Webb [13] identified cognitive as well as socio-emotional influences on collaborative interactions, for example, resolving conflicts and motivation.

In this study we also address the attainment of collaborative processes as potentially mediated by intra- as well as interpersonal and environmental elements [see, 14, 15]. In this regard, digital technologies in combination with creative activities have been introduced in schools as a strategy for learning and teaching activities, encouraging engagement, productivity, and creativity as well as offering scaffolding opportunities [16–18]. Inspired by such an approach, we have applied 'making game designs' activities as motivators for collaboration and problem solving activities in a creative digital environment among children between 9–10 years of age from a primary school in southwest of Sweden. A 'making' approach corresponds to a design process where children can proceed through iterative cycles of design and implementation of ideas, where each implementation becomes an opportunity to promote problem solving in a collaborative way. Thus, we argue that developing game designs have potential to influence educational practices, in particular when it comes to inventing and exploring the tension between individuals' ideas and the evolving forms of social interactions. In other words, through developing game designs, participants can make their own choices and decisions and, thereby, find their ways of dealing with what they already know and their creative imagination; the given and the new. Eisner [19] states that this tension between the desire to invent and explore and the need to share with others, is a way for individuals to becoming social requiring learning of social conventions and working within their limits.

This paper examines how collaboration is configured in problem solving activities whilst developing digital game designs. The research questions posed are the following:

1. What are the patterns of collaborative interaction exhibited by 9 to 10-year-old school children when collaboratively engaged in problem solving activities?
2. What features facilitate collaborative interaction among 9 to 10-year-old school children when collaboratively engaged in problem solving activities?
3. What features challenge collaborative interaction among 9 to 10-year-old school children when collaboratively engaged in problem solving activities?

The following sections start with a description of the theoretical framework, which is grounded in a sociocultural perspective on learning. This is followed by an outline of the methods, which is characterised as an explorative study Then, a presentation of the study results and, finally, a discussion followed by conclusions end the paper.

2   Collaborative Interactions in Problem-Solving Activities

Collaborative activities in an educational setting is an approach to teaching and learning involving groups of learners working together to solve a problem, complete a task, or create a product [20]. Relative to the use of digital technology, the term collaboration is often associated with a social nature of interactions evolving from social demands of collaborative activities [5, 6, 21–23]. From a sociocultural perspective, negotiation and joint construction and understanding between children are considered as essential to collaboration and problem solving [10, 24, 25]. According to Vygotsky, social interaction becomes the means by which children develop new forms of thinking [26]. We will look more closely at children's collaborative interactions, and how they use the materials and technologies available to them, and at how they pursue their collaborative and problem solving engagement. All of these are important knowledge for this study. This stems from Vygotsky's and others' work on learning, in particular Rogoff's work on *communities of learners* [10, 27, 28] as well as Lave and Wenger's work on *participation in communities of practice* [29]. It follows that participating in social practices inevitably involves learning, where an action of participation should be understood as belonging to a community. Such processes, interactions, and experiences facilitate participants' sense of belonging.

Aligned is how Vygotsky as well as Rogoff believed children's interaction to be largely dependent on the degree and quality of *adult or peer mediation and engagement* [10, 26]. Rogoff elaborates on this by acknowledging guided participation as a means of access to a specific practice. Here, the participation is guided by more knowledgeable participants, who share goals and rules with novice participants helping them to develop an understanding of a situation and, thereby, enabling the novices to contribute to the activity. Hence, Rogoff proposes three planes of sociocultural activity: apprenticeship (referring to a novice participant), guided participation (referring to a knowledgeable other), and participatory appropriation referring to how individuals change through their involvement in an activity enabling them to become involved in related activities. This implies a consideration of the complex relationship between the individual, the activity, and the contextual environment as mutually integrated [29]. Furthermore, it implies that human action, social and individual, is mediated by tools and signs, which emphasises mediation of human action through cultural artefacts [30]. In this study, it was key to design the workshop to include opportunities for children to participate in collaborative problem solving activities.

Accordingly, mediation is a core concept in sociocultural theory [31, 32] in this study as it implies questionsm about how new digital technologies are introduced and implemented into problem solving scenarios changing the way children think and act [33]. To elaborate on this, mediation, in terms of Vygotsky [34], provides a link between the actions carried out by the individual, on the one hand, and the institutional context, on the other. Wertsch [35] expands upon this framework by focusing on artefacts as mediators and essential action shapers. Mediation is seen as a process involving the potential of artefacts to shape action, on the one hand, and the use of these artefacts, on the other. In this paper, we address the conceptual dimensions of mediation and children's participation and peer interaction in communities of learners.

3 Methodology

The present study is based on a creativity workshop case involving 22 Swedish third grade children, 16 boys and 6 girls, between 9–10 years old. The workshop was set up in a research laboratory environment and was designed to provide a playful and creative atmosphere inspiring the children to collaborate to create ideas for new digital games. During the workshop, the children were provided with a wide range of creative material (such as clay, paint, pencils, LEGO) as well as with digital technology (such as iPads and software applications). Their task for the workshop was to, in groups of four to five, create an idea for a game design. In addition, they were asked to make a short stop-motion film (with an iPad) to present their game design solution, as a prototype. The children's teacher, who also participated in the activity alongside another class teacher, decided the group constellations beforehand. There were six groups who were placed at one workstation per group, set up in two separate rooms. Each workstation had a table at the centre, chairs, workshop material and a fixed camera facing the table centre and recording the activities at the workstation. The workshop was introduced and led by a university teacher who presented the workshop, gave the instructions and kept track of time for the different sessions in the workshop. There were also three assistants who assisted when the children needed help, kept an eye on the cameras, and supplied the children with water and fruit during the workshop. This setup allowed the authors of this paper to observe the activities during the full duration of the workshop.

3.1 Procedure

The workshop sessions were outlined as described in Table 1 (below), starting with the introduction of the workshop in which the creativity framework and climate were established. This part was led by a university teacher.

Table 1. Overview of workshop sessions and timetable.

Time	Activities undertaken
09:00–09:15	Introduction. Establishing creativity framework and climate
09:15–10:45	Exploratory activity using analogue and digital tools
10:45–11:30	Transformative activity focusing on children's presentations of their narrative game design representations in digital form
11:30–12:00	Joint lunch and informal discussions about the workshop

In this initial phase of the workshop, each group was given a game context (e.g. the jungle, the ocean, the city) in which the games were supposed to be unfolded. All groups were also given a sheet of paper with four sections which they were instructed to fill in before starting developing the game design, that contained the following features: *game world/theme, characters, story, objects* (see Fig. 1a). Next, the children started the exploratory activities including the game design steps, using different materials, analogue as well as digital. In this part of the workshop, the ideas for the digital games were discussed and negotiated by the children in parallel with the construction of props for the stop-motion film. Entering the transformative phase of the workshop, the children started to produce their stop-motions films (see Fig. 1b), also in parallel of deciding on the final story of the games. This part of the workshop also included a session in the end where the children presented their final productions for each other and explained the major plot of their games while the stop-motion films were on display. Afterwards, and as a last activity, the whole group of participants (including children, teachers, researchers and assistants) had a joint lunch during discussion and evaluation of the workshop, again led by the university teacher.

Fig. 1. 1. a (left) and **1.** b (right). To the left: Instructional material provided in the initial phase of the workshop. To the right: one of the participants working on the production of a stop-motion film.

3.2 Data Collection

The study is characterised as an exploratory study [e.g. 36, 37], featuring a creative workshop with uncertain outcome due to the infinite number of opportunities for the children to work out their designs. The empirical data consist of video recordings from the six workshop stations (a total of 11 h), the children's final presentations, and observations and field notes by the two authors. All teachers and parents were informed about the study in writing and the parents agreed to let their child participate by signing informed consent forms. The children were informed that they could withdraw from participation in the game design workshop at any time if they e.g. felt uncomfortable in any way. In line with ethical guidelines, all the names of the children as well as of the school are anonymised and, thereby, no identifying information is provided.

3.3 Analysis

In the analysis we have adopted an interaction analysis as well as a quasi-content analysis approach. As described by Jordan and Henderson [38], an interaction analysis is an interdisciplinary method for the empirical investigation of human interaction, with each other as well as with their environment and the objects in it. This includes activities such as verbal and nonverbal interaction and the use of artefacts and technologies. This helps identifying routine practices and problems and the resources for solution [38]. In this approach, the video documentation is vital; the ability to play a series of events repeatedly is part of the analysis process. The content analysis, however, contains elements of more detailed frequencies that goes beyond the interaction analysis, such as the consideration of the context in a situation, hence we have added parts of content analysis in order to present a deeper analysis. Content analysis is a method that can be used with both quantitative and qualitative data, and it analyses written, verbal or visual communication messages (Cole, 1998).

The video recordings has been transcribed and analysed according to the principles of both interaction analysis [38] and content analysis [e.g. 39], referred to as "IA" and "CA" and presented step by step in Table 2.

Table 2. Analytical steps

Step 1 (IA)	Overall view of the material	Step 1 (CA)	Overall view of the material
Step 2 (IA)	Identifying patterns	Step 2 (CA)	Dividing the material into meaning-making units
Step 3 (IA)	Transcription of excerpts	Step 3 (CA)	Condensing of meaning-bearing units
Step 4 (IA)	Analyses of excerpts	Step 4 (CA)	Coding condensed material
		Step 5 (CA)	Categories & sub-categories out of coding process
		Step 6 (CA)	Formulating themes

4 Results

Aligned with the analytical steps presented in Table 2, the empirical data was reviewed by both authors (IA and CA, steps 1) to find patterns (IA, step 2) and dividing the material in more detailed meaning-bearing units (CA, step 2). Next, the transcription of chosen excerpts (IA, step 3), assisted in condensing the meaning-bearing units into fewer components (CA, step 3), which initiated the authors' coding of the condensed material (CA, step 4). Finally, the analyses of excerpts (IA, step 4) assisted in the process of categorising the condensed material (CA, step 5). This process resulted in the identification of three themes (CA, step 6), namely: (1) Patterns of collaborative interactions; (2) Features facilitating collaborative interactions; and (3) Features challenging collaborative interactions, which are presented in the following subsections.

4.1 Patterns of Collaborative Interaction

So, how did the collaboration unfold during the workshop? Recurring patterns in the material that were identified in the analysis can be divided into either as *being* or as *doing*: the children were generally *being* **task-oriented** as well as **other-oriented**, and they were *doing* constant **negotiations** as well as **taking leadership** (or being led). These patterns reveal crucial elements of the collaboration process during group work that included problem solving which influenced the outcome of the workshop, and that needs to be addressed when planning for group work.

Task-Orientation

All groups showed a strong sense of task- or goal-orientation (not least the fact that all groups finished their productions on time supports this claim) which most commonly was uttered by the children's ambitions to be finished within the given time frame. In one case, a group of four boys finalised their stop-motion film quickly, quite long before the time was up. While they were watching their film, they discussed their game-design as well as their working process, and they expressed relief amongst each other that they had finished in good time. Eventually, as they were studying some of the other groups ongoing work, they started to express a slight nervousness that their own production was not good enough, that the film was too short or too simple and that the idea behind their game was not thoughtful enough. This led to the assumption that even though their completion of the task was swift, perhaps it was not a very good representation of a task solution, as expressed in their group discussions. In the end, the group went back and made some additional work both on the stop-motion film and with their game design, resulting in a more qualitative final production. This example shows the dedication and the task-orientation that was displayed by the children during the workshop.

Other-Orientation

Another pattern amongst the participants were their general sensitivity for each other's views and ideas for their joint task; a so called other-orientation. This was especially noticeable in the initial phase of the workshop, when most of the groups were brain-storming around different game designs and what to include in their digital production (i.e. the stop-motion film). When a participant expressed an idea during this part of the workshop, it was usually received with enthusiasm and support from the others in the group and often generated new ideas from the others. An example of this is when in one of the groups one of the participants came up with the idea to create different obstacles in the game. This group had the desert as a specific theme and they had started to create a scenic reproduction of a desert: a large sheet of yellow paper on which they had painted some palm trees, an oasis and huts on. At this particular moment they were not yet quite clear on the story of their game. As they were talking about different objects of a desert, one of the participants then introduced the idea to include several obstacles in the game, starting with dangerous animals hiding in the water (in the oasis). The rest of the group quickly related to this and came up with several additional ideas to further this, including having to climb the palm trees and hide in the huts, and so on. This example shows that the other-orientation often supported creativity and development of ideas within the groups and facilitated the progression and completion of the task.

Negotiating

During the workshop, different negotiations of meaning regarding different aspects of the given task constantly went on between the participants. They were negotiating meaning about the game design, about the game itself and how to present it, about the content of the game and about numerous aspects regarding the production of the stop-motion films. At times, it almost seemed like they were in an argument or conflict with each other. However, the productive value of conflict that emerged when the children negotiated consensus is not to be relativised nor discarded. On the contrary, the negotiations often proved to be an important feature in progression with the task. While they were negotiating different aspects of the task, they were at the same time defining details concerning the task which kept the development in motion, moving forward. In the initial phase of the workshop, the negotiations were mostly characterised by an optimistic and constructive approach. As mentioned earlier, a sense of other-orientation were commonly shown among the participants, which also characterised the negotiations to adopt a more positive and allowing direction during this part of the workshop. The negotiations of a more crucial and critical kind usually took place during the final phase of the workshop, where the time-aspect became an issue to consider. During these negotiations less constructive solutions were expressed, and sometimes rather harsh decisions were made regarding, for example, what to be included and/or not to be included in the game designs or in the stop-motion productions, which led to some participants' wishes being completely cancelled or discarded.

Leadership

As in all group work, the participants took on (or imposed) different roles within the groups. Something that was evident in this particular workshop was the emergence of at least one or two leaders in each group, that took on themselves to lead the group work by taking command over the activities. This was most prominent during the initial stages of the first phase of the workshop, as well as during the duration of the final phase of the workshop. In the initial phase, the emergence of a leader/leaders within the group(s) were important for the work to get started. In one group, for instance, there was no immediate leader from the start. This group had problems getting started and would not seem to connect with the task initially. After some encouragement from the assistants, the group gradually started to engage with the task and after a while one of the participants emerged as a leader, dominating the origin of ideas within the group. One important thing while working within a group, is to make decisions that keep the work going and not letting the group getting stuck in details that will slow down the progression. During the workshop, leaders (either appointed by the group or by themselves) often made these decisions, and kept the groups work going. In the final phase of the workshop, the leadership became less inclusive and constructive, and decisions were made more promptly and sometimes single handled by the leader/leaders.

4.2 Features Facilitating Collaborative Interaction

The observations showed that the spatial design of the workshop area, the structure of the workshop as well as the materials available were crucial mediating factors with a powerful effect on children's collaborative interaction. The children picked up the materials available and explored them in many different ways to find out in what way a certain material could materialise their designs. For example, would a monkey jumping between trees in the jungle be best materialised in paper or in clay. The children did not need any explanations, they explored such matters solitary or jointly with their group members. In addition to spatial design and structure of the workshop activity, the game design focus and the digital technology in the form of iPads and a stop motion app forming the basis for their digital productions, directed the collaborative interaction. The below text elaborates on these aspects facilitating collaborative interaction: *spatial design and materials*, *step-by-step activity structure*, and *digital game design activity facilitating iterative learning processes and peer culture*.

Spatial Design and Materials Facilitating Fluid Interactions

The availability to a rich variation of materials enabled the children not only to express their ideas, but also to discuss and negotiate the meaning and thinking behind their ideas. It was notable that the setting facilitated a physical, energetic, and noisy collaborative interaction. The spatial design, i.e. how the room was furnished, influenced as well as directed the children's collaboration. The spatial design, where each group had their own workstation was set up with appropriate distance between the tables so that it was easy for the children to navigate between the work stations. Figure 2a shows how the back end table is situated with plenty of space to the foregrounded table. This encouraged the individual group members to interact not only in their own workstation area, but to become mobile resulting in that the children now and then visited other workstations to become inspired by others. In this way, the interaction became fluid, both within and between groups and workstations. The observations showed that the children were approaching the materials carefully although with engagement, absorption, and concentration. Figure 2b exemplifies both concentration and absorption at work as well as careful handling of materials to construct different features for this group's game design. These examples show how physical properties and spatial qualities created a 'living' space.

Step-By-Step Activity Structure Facilitating Collaboration

The workshop process followed concrete steps (see Table 1) and included instructional material provided in the initial phase of the workshop (see Fig. 1a) where the children, based on their given game theme, should elaborate on the narrative of the game world, which characters to include, the plot as well as other objects to include. This structure initiated the groups' negotiation and compromises in design decision-making. The observations showed that this kind of common structure in combination with an ready-made and assigned gameplay theme, facilitated the children's collaboration as well as shaped meaning for their activity as such. With this as a starting point, the children immediately jumped into idea generation without needing any discussions or negotiations about such initial matters, which clearly contributed to the collaboration. The children were

Fig. 2. 2. a (left) and **2.** b (right). To the left: Children cold move freely between the tables as they were situated with a great deal of distance between them. To the right: The children were absorbed and concentrated at work.

aware of the time constraint, i.e. that they did not have an unlimited amount of time. The groups effectively followed the time available for the idea generation as well as for producing the plot, and work on the digital production. Figure 3a shows how one of the groups had divided the work between themselves to document the details of their game design idea on the worksheet. One of the groups, however, had problems getting the idea generation going and to decide upon the plot, characters, and objects and they just sat at the table looking at each other without discussing or doing anything. The workshop assistant suggested that they should visit the station with the different creative materials to get inspiration from there. They did so and picked up crepe paper in different shades of blue and started to develop their scenic ideas of space which was their game design theme, and from there they continued with details of their game design (Fig. 3b). While the other groups started the idea generation by using the instructional sheet of paper to develop content for their game designs, this group reflected upon the mode of conveying their design rather than the content. This example shows that a step-by-step structure offered an openness and flexibility, which could facilitate hands-on collaboration, content creation as well as modes of conveying a specific message.

Digital Game Design Activity Facilitating Iterative Collaboration Processes and Peer Culture

At the workstation tables, the children shared materials as they advised each other on how to create characters and game objects. They divided the work between themselves to proceed effectively with the game designs. After working in a solitary mode with producing game features, they shared their creations and discussed how the different individually created details should come together in the stop motion video. This kind of process went on in iterative processes until the digital production (stop motion video) was finished. The children were concerned about what kind of material they used, how the colours conveyed a trustworthy message, and how the space was organised. They all had an intent to get characters, objects, and colours exactly right. Figure 4a shows how the group having the city as their game design theme jointly put together the different parts to construct the scenically elements as exact as possible. The result of this iterative cycles of collaborative work can be seen in Fig. 4b. By repeatedly trying out different

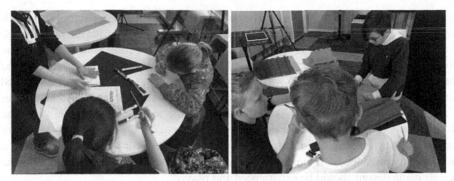

Fig. 3. 3. a (left) and **3.** b (right). To the left: The group members have divided tasks between them and are concentrated to detail the different parts of the game play. To the right: The group has found crepe paper and use this to identify how they can convey their game design idea the best way possible.

solutions and game details, they not only practised intense collaboration, they also found ways of dealing with what they individually had a desire to create and the need to share this with the other group members. This example that the digital game design activity with inherent iterative processes of collaboration fostered children's urge to contribute taking equal responsibility for the development of the game designs.

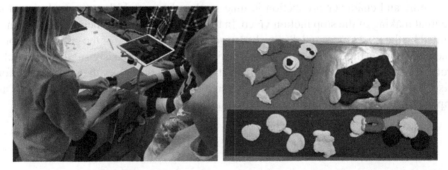

Fig. 4. 4. a (left) and **4.** b (right). To the left: To prepare for the stop motion video, two children are jointly putting together different parts of the game design. To the right: The game design idea is ready for the production of the stop motion video.

All groups finalised their game designs by producing a stop motion video. It was visible when the groups presented their stop motion videos for the other groups, that their productions enhanced the work, for example, making clear the design's perceptual properties, such as colour, texture, motion, and sound. Moreover, the group presentations assembled their operational experiences and ability to productively co-author game design proposals. This appeared to be a significant step in the game design process, where the groups' aspirations went beyond the game design itself drawing attention to the complexity of collaboration as well as knowledge about the culture of digital games as such. While all game design productions revealed signs of originality, they were influenced by the children's familiarity with the discourse of digital games. For example, the children's game designs included traditional game mechanics for the player or the game to follow, such as if the car in Fig. 4b was successful in collecting coins placed on the street, the coins were awarded to the player. Some of the game designs were level-based and in one of the designs, which was a multi-player design, the player who responded incorrectly to a challenge got immediate feedback in terms of "Game over, sorry Player 2". In this way, knowledge and skills related to game mechanics were built into the group's game design itself. This example shows that making digital game design is not just about using materials and technology to create content for a digital production, it involves acquaintance with the digital game discourse and ability to negotiate how the overall game design should be experienced and played.

4.3 Features Challenging Collaborative Interaction

At instances, the groups' collaboration and problem solving activities were challenged. Some of the group members got stuck in details, which created tensions between the group members individual ideas and the evolving forms of social interactions. For example, in one of the groups having the jungle as theme, a boy became skilled in making monkeys and when having done two of them, he expressed a desire to do more of them. However, the other three members of the group, strongly advised him that it was not a good idea as they would run out of time if he continued with making monkeys instead of helping with the overall production. The girls emphasised that it was important to finish the scenic and character production in time so that they would have enough time for the final making of the stop motion video. In this way, the space for negotiating became limited by the time aspect and the boy had to adapt to the majority of the group. Tensions emerged between the details in the game's design and the overall design as the boy would prefer to make his own monkeys, but the rest of the group realises there is no time for this. This example signifies a tension between a desire to invent and explore as well as impressing on others, and the need to share and negotiate with the group members.

5 Discussion

In this paper, we examine how collaboration between school children is configured in problem solving activities whilst developing digital game designs. Collaboration in this case refers to children's substantial perception of engagement and not merely to a formal problem solving abstraction. Thus, collaboration in learning situations should be understood with reference to an active creation of mutual engagement. and knowledge about the digital game discourse. In this regard, we argue that making digital game designs provides new possibilities for thinking about established pedagogical forms of teaching and learning, where collaboration in game design activities constitute substantially crucial features. When such activities are designed effectively for all participants, they enable efficient participation, the ability to negotiate not only how a game will be designed and played but promotes opportunity to learn from peers [10, 27, 28]. While co-construction can help clarifying the social dynamic of collaboration, it needs to be unfolded in regard to how the collaborators reveal a concern for achieving a mutual understanding of the task at hand of the construction to be made. What gets constructed constitutes a form of mutuality similar to what exists in a community of practice [29].

When designing for mutuality, the design should allow for the participants' experience acknowledging an affective awareness of a shared purpose. The results from this study exposed that a sense of community emerged when the children worked on solving the problem of designing and producing a digital game. Aligned with this is Vygotsky's concept of intersubjectivity [31, 34], emphasising that collaboration is not merely a set of joint experiences and understandings but depends on the child's awareness of that others know what (s)he knows. This kind of knowing has an affective dimension as well as a cognitive dimension related to solving a creative problem at hand. We could notice that within the instances when this happened, a collaborative encounter in the form of congruent togetherness emerged.

On creating a stop-motion video representing the group's game idea, was not a linear or easily task to do, but required intense negotiation. This, in turn, created an increased motivation as some of the group members realised that achieving this goal was dependent on not only themselves but also their peers. This seemed to influence how they provided both emotional and instructive support to each other. This kind of collaborative motivation seemed to increase the individuals' desire to be timely on the task. Here, the material and action-orientated aspects of emerging individual and social motivation should be adequately acknowledged [31, 32].

Identified recurring patterns in the material includes negotiation of meaning, task-orientation, other-orientation and taking leadership (in the group). It was obvious that the children had a sensitivity for the other group members, an other-orientation, as well as an insight into the importance of the social interaction and scaffolding for the progression of the collaborative group work. Likewise, the task-orientation among the participants was clear as well and the children were all eager to perform the task within the given time frame. Given the combination of other-orientation and task-orientation in the collaboration among the participants, there was a need for leaders to emerge within the group constellations, as well as the unfolding of negotiations taking place during the collaboration. Features that facilitated the collaborative interaction among the participants were closely linked to spatial design and materials of the workshop activities, the step-by-step structure of the workshop, and the focus on game design, including digital technology, supporting iterative learning processes and peer culture. Features that challenged the collaborative interaction includes participants getting stuck in details and the, at times, one sided negotiations that took place as a result of it, where individual group members had to give way to the majority of the group.

6 Conclusion

By means of a creativity workshop case performed with school children, this paper investigated how collaboration was configured in problem solving activities whilst developing digital game designs. An understanding of collaborative problem solving activities associated with digital making needs to move beyond approaches of knowledge-orientation to include actions and 'doings' in digital game making contexts. The implications for digital game making in educational settings are threefold.

First, the format and the material provided for the task requires explicit orchestration of the resources provided, where digital game making is simultaneously material, 'doing'-oriented, and discursive. The latter in the sense that the format is part of the children's culture as it fosters natural and intense collaboration, thereby, extending the problem solving activity to become not only a cognitive matter but also an affective. Studies of digital game design activities might provide ways forward for better understanding collaboration in terms of co-creation and materiality.

Second, the inclusion of digital activities (in this case the idea of a digital game design and the production of a stop motion film) serves as an enhanced progression of the collaboration and group work. For instance, as the participants had a shared experience of what a digital game is, they did not have to spend time on having to agree upon a mutual definition, thus they could immediately start on their joint task instead. This resulted in an affective and congruent sense of togetherness and the problem solving activity offered a clear sense of joint ownership of a common set of experiences. More research is needed to better understand digital game design activities and how they provide children with a safe and supportive space to develop agency.

Finally, we underline that developing digital game designs have potential to influence educational practices, in particular when it comes to inventing and exploring the tension between individuals' ideas and the evolving forms of social interactions. In other words, through developing game designs, participants can make their own choices and decisions and, thereby, find their ways of dealing with what they already know and their creative imagination; the given and the new. Eisner [19] states that this tension between the desire to invent and explore and the need to share with others, is a way for individuals to becoming social requiring learning of social conventions and working within their limits.

References

1. Squire, K.: Cultural framing of computer/video games. Game Stud. Int. J. Comput. Game Res. 2(1) (2002). http://www.gamestudies.org/0102/squire/. Accessed 20 Aug 2019
2. Squire, K.: Video game-based learning: an emerging paradigm for instruction. Perform. Improv. Q. 21(2), 7–36 (2008)
3. Peterson, M.: Computerized games and simulations in computer-assisted language learning: a meta-analysis of research. Simul. Gaming 41(1), 72–93 (2010)
4. Brooks, E., Sjöberg, J.: Evolving playful and creative activities when school children develop game-based designs. In: Brooks, Anthony L., Brooks, E., Sylla, C. (eds.) ArtsIT/DLI -2018. LNICST, vol. 265, pp. 485–495. Springer, Cham (2019). https://doi.org/10.1007/978-3-030-06134-0_51
5. Sorensen, E.K., Andersen, H.V.: Learning together apart – the impact on participation when using dialogic educational technologies for kids with attention and developmental deficits. In: Brooks, A.L., Brooks, E. (eds.) ArtsIT/DLI -2016. LNICST, vol. 196, pp. 264–271. Springer, Cham (2017). https://doi.org/10.1007/978-3-319-55834-9_31
6. Sorensen, E.K., Andersen, H.V.: Amplifying the process of inclusion through a genuine marriage between pedagogy and technology. In: Proceedings of the European Distance and E-Learning Network 2016 Annual Conference. EDEN, Budapest (2016)

7. Läroplan för Grundskolan samt för Förskoleklassen och Fritidshemmen (Lgr 11). Skolverket, Stockholm (2011). https://www.skolverket.se/undervisning/grundskolan/laroplan-och-kur splaner-for-grundskolan/laroplan-lgr11-for-grundskolan-samt-for-forskoleklassen-och-fritid shemmet. Accessed 14 Aug 2019
8. Nationell Digitaliseringsstrategi för Skolverket. Utbildningsdepartementet, Stockholm (2017). https://www.regeringen.se/4a9d9a/contentassets/00b3d9118b0144f6bb95302f3e0 8d11c/nationell-digitaliseringsstrategi-for-skolvasendet.pdf. Accessed 14 Aug 2019
9. DigiComp 2.0: The Digital Competence Framework for Citizens. JRC Science for Policy Report. European Commission (2016)
10. Rogoff, B.: Apprenticeship in Thinking: Cognitive Development in Social Context. Routledge, London (1990)
11. Clements, D.H., Nastasi, B.K.: Social and cognitive interactions in educational computer environments. Am. Educ. Res. J. 25(1), 87–106 (1988)
12. Lomangino, A.G., Nicholson, J., Sulzby, E.: The influence of power relations and social goals on children's collaborative interactions while composing on computer. Early Child. Res. Q. 14(2), 197–228 (1999)
13. Webb, N.M.: Student interaction and learning in small groups. Rev. Educ. Res. 52, 421–445 (1982)
14. Cohen, S.G., Bailey, D.E.: What makes teams work: group effectiveness research from the shop floor to the executive suite. J. Manag. 23, 239–290 (1997)
15. Wilkinson, I.A.G., Fung, I.Y.Y.: Small-group composition and peer effects. Int. J. Educ. Res. 37, 425–447 (2002)
16. Brooks, E.: Lekfull kreativitet. Fysiska användargränssnitt som erbjuder social och fysisk interaktion. PAIDEA 13, 55–65 (2017)
17. Sylla, C., Brooks, E., Tümmler, L.: Blocks as symbolic tools for children's playful collaboration. In: Brooks, A.L., Brooks, E., Vidakis, N. (eds.) ArtsIT/DLI -2017. LNICST, vol. 229, pp. 413–423. Springer, Cham (2018). https://doi.org/10.1007/978-3-319-76908-0_40
18. Resnick, M.: All I really need to know (about creative thinking) I learned (by studying how children learn) in kindergarten. In: Proceedings of the 6th SIGGCHI Conference on Creativity & Cognition, Washington, DC, US, 13–15 June 2007, pp. 1–6 (2007)
19. Eisner, W.E.: Discipline-based art education: conceptions and misconceptions. Educ. Theory 40(4), 423–440 (1990)
20. Dillenbourg, P.: Introduction: what do you mean by "collaborative learning"? In: Dillenbourt, P. (ed.) Collaborative Learning Cognitive and Computational Approaches. Elsevier-Pergamon, Oxford (1999)
21. Mercier, E., Vouloumi, G., Higgins, S.: Student interactions and the development of ideas in multi-touch and paper-based collaborative mathematical problem solving. Br. J. Educ. Technol. 48(1), 162–175 (2017)
22. Higgins, S., Mercier, E., Burd, L., Joyce-Gibbons, A.: Multi-touch tables and collaborative learning. Br. J. Educ. Technol. 43, 1041–1054 (2012)
23. Perlmutter, M., Behrend, S., Kuo, F., Muller, A.: Social influences on children's problem-solving. Dev. Psychol. 25(5), 744–754 (1989)
24. Littleton, K., Hakkinen, P.: Learning together: understanding the processes of computer-based collaborative learning. In: Dillenbourg, P. (ed.) Collaborative Learning: Cognitive and Computational Approaches. Elsevier-Perganon, Oxford (1999)
25. Mercer, N.: The quality of talk in children's joint activity at the computer. J. Comput.-Assist. Learn. 10, 24–32 (1994)
26. Bodrova, E.: Make-believe play versus academic skills: a Vygotskyan approach to today's dilemmas of early childhood education. Eur. Early Child. Educ. Res. J. 16(3), 357–369 (2008)
27. Rogoff, B.: Developing understanding of the idea of communities learners. Mind Cult. Act. 4(1), 75–91 (1994)

28. Rogoff, B.: The Cultural Nature of Human Development. Oxford University Press, Oxford (2003)
29. Lave, J., Wenger, E.: Situated Learning: Legitimate Peripheral Participation. Cambridge University Press, New York (1991)
30. Engeström, Y., Miettinen, R.: Introduction. In: Engeström, Y., Miettinen, R., Punamaki, R. (eds.) Perspectives on Activity Theory, pp. 1–16. Cambridge University Press, New York (1999)
31. Vygotsky, L.S.: Mind in Society: The Development of Higher Psychological Processes. Harvard University Press, Cambridge (1978)
32. Wertsch, J.V.: Mind as Action. Oxford University Press, New York (1998)
33. Vygotsky, L.S.: The problem of the cultural development of the child. In: van der Veer, R., Valsiner, J. (eds.) The Vygotsky Reader, pp. 57–72. Blackwell, Oxford (1994)
34. Vygotsky, L.S.: The genesis of higher mental functions. In: Wertsch, J.V. (ed.) The Concept of Activity in Soviet Psychology. Sharpe, New York (1981)
35. Wertsch, J.V.: Voices of the Mind: A Sociocultural Approach to Mediated Action. Harvard University Press, Cambridge (1993)
36. Denzin, N.K., Lincoln, Y.S.: The SAGE Handbook of Qualitative Research. Sage, Thousand Oaks (2011)
37. Merriam, S.B.: Qualitative Research: A Guide to Design and Implementation. Jossey-Bass, San Francisco (2009)
38. Jordan, B., Henderson, A.: Interaction analysis: foundations and practice. J. Learn. Sci. 4(1), 39–103 (1995)
39. Graneheim, U.H., Lundman, B.: Qualitative content analysis in nursing research: concepts, procedures and measures to achieve trustworthiness. Nurse Educ. Today 24(2), 105–112 (2004)

To Become Digitally Competent: A Study of Educators' Participation in Professional Learning

Eva Brooks[1]([⊠]), Marie Bengtsson[2], Malin Jartsell Gustafsson[2], Tony Roth[2], and Lena Tonnby[2]

[1] Aalborg University, Kroghstræde 3, 9220 Aalborg, Denmark
eb@hum.aau.dk
[2] Halmstad Municipality, Harplinge-Steninge Preschool and School District, Ekebergsvägen 2, 30560 Harplinge, Sweden
{marie.bengtsson,malin.j.gustafsson,tony.roth, lena.tonnby}@halmstad.se

Abstract. Digital competence has become a concept that gradually has been addressed in classroom practices as well as in policy documents. This is due to educational reforms regarding the digitisation of educational practices. How, then, can teachers make sense of these changes putting pressure on improved quality of their educational outcomes? The paper informs of a work-in-progress paper, which aims to shed light over how teachers in preschools and schools participated in professional learning to become digital competent. The overall research question addresses how teachers can be supported in their professional learning and digital technology integration through an action research approach, in particular inspired by Schön's perspective on designing and learning, focusing on the initial design process. We investigated teachers' tensions and sensemaking strategies regarding integration of digital technology in their educational practice through a model of participation, involvement, and responsibility (DIA model). Methodically, the paper is based on outcomes from two baseline questionnaires. The results unfold the importance of a context-conscious leadership as well as promoting team learning and collaboration between teams to create dynamics between the teachers.

Keywords: Digital competence · Teachers · Preschool · School · Professional learning · Participation · Involvement

1 Introduction

Digital competence has become a concept that gradually has been addressed in classroom practices as well as in policy documents: the term has also been subject for definition in the academic field. Recent updates to the curriculums of both preschools and schools in Sweden underline that education should contribute to students' ability to act in an

A. Brooks and E. I. Brooks (Eds.): ArtsIT 2019/DLI 2019, LNICST 328, pp. 699–713, 2020.
https://doi.org/10.1007/978-3-030-53294-9_53

increased digitised society and develop their skills to use digital technology in their everyday lives [1–3]. Aligned is how the European framework for the digital competence of educators, which acknowledges that teaching professions face rapidly changing demands, which requires a broader set of competences than previously. This framework provides guidelines for teachers at all curriculum levels including adult education. The framework highlights educator-specific digital competences organised in different areas. For example within professional interactions with colleagues, to managing the use of digital technologies in teaching and learning activities, and specific pedagogic competences required to facilitate students' digital competence [4]. This paper presents ongoing work attempting to address the overall question of how teachers in preschools and schools perceive their digital competence and how they consider their opportunities to improve their competences. An action research approach is taken inspired by Schön [9, 10].

2 Background

Reforms and policy documents cohere to changes in political, social, and educational practices that place increased pressure on preschools and schools to improve the quality of their educational outcomes [5]; in this case related to teachers' competence to integrate digital tools within teaching and learning activities. Researches underline that changes in educational practices highly depend on teachers' capacity to change their understandings and teaching repertoire [c.f. 6]. However, educational reforms are not simply a matter of teachers' willingness to apply new ways of acting or having access to digital tools, it is a multidimensional process of change including both a teacher's mindset as well as pedagogical dispositions informing new teaching strategies [c.f. 4]. This evokes questions of how teachers can make sense of current complex demands on enhancing their digital competence to improve technological integration in their classroom settings. As Phelps et al. [7] state, educational change should consider diverse needs of all teachers and avoid limiting approaches that often replicate existing historical and cultural practices in schools. The latter includes a risk of assimilating, or domesticating [8] traditional teaching approaches. Thus, it is crucial to apply a classroom-based authentic and contextualised approach to teachers' development of digital competence.

Schön [9, 10] emphasises that designing and learning are closely coupled forms of inquiry. From this point of view, a design process opens up possibilities for reflection as well as surprise that can trigger new ways of seeing things, and it demands commitments to choices revealing underlying values, assumptions, and models of phenomena.

The present study includes 21 preschool teachers and 16 primary school teachers in a school district in southwest of Sweden and is part of an ongoing project, Digi-DIA. The project focuses on developing students' and teachers' digital competence through participation, influence, and responsibility, conceptualised as the DIA-model[1]. Conceptually, this means that we do not apply top-down designed in-service training events to develop teachers' skills or other characteristics of a teacher [11]. Rather, the acts of professional learning can be explained as a bottom-up self-directed approach to professional needs or

---

[1] DIA stands for *Participation, Influence, Responsibility* and is a model developed by Tony Roth, Principal at Harplinge-Steninge Schools in Halmstad, Sweden.

interests, which are part of the pedagogical work that the participating teachers undertake daily in their classrooms. Raphael et al. [12] conceptualise professional learning as "ownership over compliance, conversation over transmission, deep understanding over enacting rules and routines, and goal-directed activity over content coverage" (p. 147). Thus, based on the above-mentioned overall question on how teachers in preschools and schools perceive their digital competence and how they consider their opportunities to improve their competences, this paper reports on a work-in-progress particularly focuses on the project's initial design process investigating teachers' tensions and sensemaking approaches regarding integration of digital technology in their educational practice.

3   Perspective on Professional Learning and Development

Designing a professional learning approach to developing digital competence can be compared to what Sanders and Stappers [13] conceptualise as a *complex and tangled nature of problem solving with a fuzzy front end*. Aligned is Rittel and Webber's [14] conceptualisation of a *wicked problem as a social phenomenon combining complexity, uncertainty and competing goals such that it challenges commitment*. The previous mentioned DIA model (Participation, Influence and Responsibility) gives both students and teachers a real influence on working methods and the content of teaching. It takes a holistic approach to the mission of preschools and schools to follow the intentions of the curriculum and at the same time secure quality of the education. While applying the DIA model, teachers systematically evaluate their own actions and leadership when interacting with the students. Through the DIA model, professional learning is considered as a synthesis of teachers' leadership in the classroom, their experiences, co-creation, and knowledge. All in all, this targets a development of the teacher profession as well as of the organisation.

The DIA model is anchored in the preschool and school organisation through a specific local organisational structure, the Council for Development and Innovative Thinking. This structure includes eight representatives from different parts of the organisation: the principal for the preschools, the principal for the schools, the school health representative, two representatives from the preschool, and three representatives from the school. This council is a crucial organisational entity ensuring transparency as well as a bottom-up perspective encapsulated and aligned with the model. The council meets every third week and is responsible for dealing with needs and thoughts from the co-workers, keeping an overview and monitoring pedagogical and policy issues, and, based on this, giving feedback to the co-worker teams. The organisation of the Digi-DIA project reflects the above-described model, where the project management includes the council's two principles as well as two representatives from the preschool and school context.

4   Sensemaking in a Problem Space

Participation in professional learning from a DIA perspective requires mutually constituting processes. Focusing on participation with other people, Dewey [15, p. 16] provides the following account:

"The social environment /.../is truly educative in its effects in the degree in which an individual shares or participates in some conjoint activity. By doing his share in the associated activity, the individual appropriates the purpose which actuates it, becomes familiar with its methods and subject matters, acquires needed skill, and is saturated with its emotional spirit."

Such conjoint processes can serve as mutual sensemaking between participants in a team or cross-over teams. In the case of Digi-DIA, the participants experienced tensions in not having enough space to jointly make sense of the issue of applying different digital tools in teaching and learning activities. These tensions between the teachers' attempts to make sense of a situation and at the same time experiencing frustrations could be analogised with Simon's [16] picture of designing as search within a problem space. In the context of this study, the problem space concerns a search between what is unfamiliar and what is already known.

4.1 Sensemaking as a Space for Professional Learning

Educational practices can be considered complex social systems, which as such includes uncertainty and instability [17, 18]. When individuals meet situations that are ambiguous, they engage in sensemaking trying to create meaning by, for example, trying out different ways of approaching a new situation [19]. In this way, sensemaking processes are social, intersubjective, and based on a context of norms, values, concepts, and habits [20, 21]. Rikkerink et al. [21] introduces a theoretical framework connecting domains involved in the practical use and making sense of digital learning technologies by teachers: Leadership, Context, Teacher characteristic, and Teacher learning. The authors state that when approaching professional learning it is necessary to assume that it is embedded in a complex and reciprocal interaction between these four domains.

In the present study, teachers were actively involved in such sensemaking processes, including iterative reflections on their teaching and learning practice [c.f. 10]. Howard et al. [22] point to how previous research regarding technology integration in educational practices primarily has focused on factors of teachers' practice. In particular, teachers' level of confidence with and knowledge of digital technologies. Furthermore, they posit how school leaders' guide teachers in their use of digital technology to improve technology integration. However, only minimal improvements in cultivating an integration of digital technology in teaching and learning have been noticed [c.f. 23]. So, how can these *complex and wicked problems* of technology integration be improved? Howard et al. [22] conceptualise processes of sensemaking as a space for teachers to identify where they may want or need support. To support this, school leaders should develop a culture of experimentation and learning to encourage teachers' use of digital technology in their teaching and learning activities [23]. Thus, an understanding of the contextual setting of teacher learning and technology integration is necessary. Drawing on the concept of sensemaking, we designed and performed a baseline questionnaire study by the start of the project and the same questionnaire was repeated 16 months afterwards. This paper reports on a work-in-progress and is based upon the outcomes of these questionnaires. The project as a whole also include interviews, workshops, casual conversations, and observations. As this data collection progresses, outcomes will be reported in later publications.

5 Method

The study includes nine preschool units (including children 1–5 years of age) and two schools with 10 school units (including children between 6–11 years of age) in a municipality situated in the southwest of Sweden. In total, 21 preschool teachers and 16 primary school teachers participated in the study.

The method used in this paper was two baseline questionnaires to investigate how teachers experienced their own competence regarding integration of digital technology in their educational practices. The questionnaires were distributed in February 2018 and the following one in June 2019. The first one intended to create a 'current state' of the teachers' use of digital technology in their teaching activities. The second questionnaire targeted a description of the 'new state' of the teachers' use of digital technology in their teaching activities. The teachers had designated time during their working hours to fill in the questionnaire. The questionnaire consisted of 33 questions, which on average took 20 min to complete. In the present paper, only the questions that concerned how the teachers in the preschools and schools perceived their digital competence and how they considered their opportunities to improve their competences are analysed. The questionnaire and the questions included are described in the next section.

5.1 The Questionnaire

The questionnaire consisted of 33 questions divided into seven themes:

1. Background information;
2. Teacher's experience of using digital tools together with the children;
3. The teacher's digital competence;
4. Digitisation and the DIA-perspective;
5. Digitisation and collaboration with parents;
6. Digitisation and the physical environment;
7. Digitisation and knowledge sharing with colleagues.

The themes included in the present study were: 2, 3, 7, and parts of theme 4. Theme 1 was only used to check how many teachers that responded and which school context they represented (preschool or primary school). Each theme included more than one question and with each having differing answers to select from, as in a Likert scale (e.g. "positive, negative, not used"; "very good; good; less good; not good at all" and "not at all; to a less degree; to some degree; to a great degree") [24]. For example, the question about the teacher's digital competence included questions about how the teacher estimated his/her current digital competence, what skills were needed to use digital tools, what motivation was needed to contribute to the digital development, and which support the teacher would need to become a competent user of digital tools in teaching activities.

When it comes to theme 4, we have only included one of the questions related to the open question about the teacher's experience of having or not having enough skills and competence to include the children in digital activities applying the DIA-perspective. Theme 7 included two questions where the teacher was asked to estimate time and space available for collegial knowledge sharing and whether the teacher experienced enough time for own digital competence development.

The teachers were informed that their answers were anonymous and that their names were coded and only identifiable by the researchers and, thereby, not accessible or trackable by their leaders.

6 Analysis

The collected quantitative data from the two questionnaires (carried out 2018 and 2019 respectively) underwent a simple statistical analysis visualising the material and identifying directional indicators to illustrate potential changes between the first and second questionnaire. The open answers were analysed qualitatively by a coding strategy where we carefully looked through the written and elaborated text answers, identified themes (e.g. in terms of opportunities and/or challenges). Next step was to code these themes, which then evolved through merging them into broader sets of themes [c.f. 25]. Through this quantitative and qualitative approach, we identified three overall themes: (1) Shared comprehensive influence; (2) Reconstitution of space and time for shared learning, and (3) Providing tools to mediate professional learning. These themes are elaborated in the below text.

6.1 Shared Comprehensive Influence

The teachers' experiences of using a number of digital tools together with the children in teaching activities changed between the first and second questionnaire. Teachers' experiences of using tools like digital camera, computer, digital microscope, TV screen, 3D printer, Chromebooks and mobile phone did not change. For example, while 3D printer and digital microscopes was still not used, mobile phones, Chromebook, and computers were experienced positively to the same extent between the first and second questionnaire. In the open writing parts of the questionnaires there were no negative responses. A teacher from one of the primary schools expresses her positive experience of using the computer for children's learning of writing as well as being able to not only use a pen when writing, but combining different modalities when using a computer.

[Computers are] increasing [pupils'] motivation, the pupils quickly understand, they are used to use digital tools from home, [the pupils] can use images and sound and other digital tools on the computer, [computers] can ease their writing acquisition (not necessary to all the time use pencils to write), [I] can adapt the teaching for pupils with difficulties.

To have an own Chromebook is a great inspiration for the pupils.

Preschool teachers emphasise that digital tools, such as computers, digital camera and mobile phones, enhance children's participation and engagement by, for example, enabling immediate finding of information on children's questions.

> [It is] positive to being able to catch moments in the children's everyday lives with, for example, the mobile phone. To document with mobile phones. It has a positive effect, children can participate [in the documentation].

The second questionnaire showed a slight increase (on average 6%) in teachers' use and documented positive experiences in regards to iPads, Cleverboards, and projectors. Also, in the open writing parts of the questionnaires there were no negative responses. In the open writing parts, projectors were in particular noted with several positive comments from the preschool teachers pointing towards specific engaging, participative, and pedagogical qualities.

> They [The children] think it is exciting to test new things and to learn more. They think it is fun with digital tools. Many of the digital tools are easy to use together with many children, for example by the projector where several children can watch at the same time. They can watch together and learn from each other.

> It is easy to show fairy tales and movies [with the projector]. This results in that the children directly can see a result of what is said, which is positive. The projector enables the children to, together with their friends, learn in a social context. We want to develop this further.

Regarding iPads, the teachers put forward their information finding qualities and how they contributed to more movements and reflection among the children.

> iPads can capture many children when using them for singing and movement from YouTube recordings of popular songs. The children do not need to sit still to concentrate, but can move to the music.

> Via pictures and videos documented with the iPad, the children can reflect upon their doings.

Cleverboards had more general comments, such as that they offer clarity when going through subject topics, which create a better overview, understanding and interplay among the pupils.

The biggest change in the experience of using digital technologies relates to programmable robots such as Beebots, Bluebots, and Ozobots. The second questionnaire showed an increased positive experience of using Beebots/Bluebots by 16% and an increased use of other programmable robots (which in this case relates to the Ozobot and Mindstorm robots) with 17%.

> The Beebots have really captured the children's attention, they are very curious and want to work with them.

> The children enjoy testing the Beebots and Bluebots.

Beside this increase, some teachers introduced new tools, such as Osmo in school classes and Tapioca in preschool units, between the first and second questionnaire.

```
I have positive experiences [of digital tools]. Osmo has
stimulated learning in math. It combines iPads with con-
crete material [e.g. wooden bricks].
```

These specific increases in some of the teachers' use of programmable robots and introduction of new tools to their digital teaching repertoire, can be related to their interest in sharing knowledge and experiences with the researchers. This led to that the researchers could contribute with framed input and suggestions related to the teachers' interests regarding the context of use, e.g. pedagogical goal, topic or subject of teaching, or children's age and experiences in programming.

We also noted a change in the kind of open answers/comments to this specific question between the two questionnaire investigations. Compared to the first questionnaire, the second one included more precise comments related to specific digital tools and their pedagogical qualities and values when applied in teaching and learning activities. In particular, the new tools (robots, Osmo, Tapioca) as well as the projector and Cleverboard were commented on. The comments concerned how they contributed to *concrete, collaborative,* and *participative* pedagogical qualities and values when integrated in teaching and learning activities.

```
I have mostly seen positive effects, for example when,
together with the children, working with Beebot, Ozobot,
or Tapioca, it becomes a collaborative learning activity
evoking children's curiosity as they can contribute with
and have different ideas about what the tool can be used
for.
```

```
[The children] try them out, explore different solutions,
present results in different ways, solve problems together
with others, argue, discuss and bring ideas forward, take
part of thoughts from others, questioning, become inter-
ested and joyfully learn.
```

To conclude this theme, the second questionnaire showed that the teachers' use of digital tools in their teaching activities was characterised by shared exploration together with the children. This created *comprehensive learning* experiences where both teachers and children contributed and could *influence* learning processes in the situation.

6.2 Reconstitution of Space and Time for Shared Learning

In the second questionnaire 73% of the teachers experienced a good or very good digital competence as well as skills in using digital tools and services in their teaching activities. This value was 10% higher compared to the first questionnaire study. However, while experiencing having a good or very good digital competence and skills in using digital tools, the teachers, in the open answering/commenting space, clearly asked for more time and opportunities for sharing knowledge with colleagues, or learning from each other. In line with Dewey [15], this was an expression not only to learn or to improve skills, but also to nurture and further develop their acquired skills and competences within an *educative social environment.*

> I wish support from a colleague that has more knowledge than I have.
>
> I am interested in and think it is fun to work with, for example, iPads, Beebots, and projectors as part of my teaching. This is motivating. However, it is very helpful to work together with colleagues who share the same or have more interest in digital tools. We would inspire each other.
>
> I do not have the time to develop or deepen my skills. [ ] miss colleagues to plan and discuss with.

While these quotes reveal the teachers' promotion of spaces for collegial support and sharing of knowledge, they also seem to state that there also is a lack of such interaction. In this space, the individual teacher could orientate towards a common object (improved digital skills and competence), which became a resource for the collective group of teachers (co-workers) to reflect on and learn from. In this regard, the 'doings' with different digital tools were emphasised. Several of the teachers emphasised that the collegial nature of knowledge sharing and support was crucial to bring about teachers as competent users of digital tools in teaching and learning activities, and for such tools to become an integral part of the work culture.

> I want to have more collaboration with my colleagues. To test and use [digital tools] is a good learning method, in particular while doing it together with colleagues.
>
> I need to learn more about the tools, how they work, if I shall use them among the children.

Regarding this theme, the second questionnaire also showed that teachers explored and learned qualities of digital tools together with the children. A number of the teachers noted a necessity to have courage to, as teacher, let the 'being in control' go away, when it comes to having time to develop digital skills and competence.

> It is good to have possibilities to lend digital tools (as we did at the X preschool) and together with the children test and challenge myself to use them during a longer time span.
>
> Increase my competence in additional ways of using iPads, where children and teachers jointly participate.

A clear difference between the first and second questionnaire related to the time the teachers experienced they had available for planning for inclusion of digital tools in their teaching activities as well as for individual professional learning. While the first questionnaire showed that the teachers considered that they had enough time for this, the second questionnaire showed that they considered that they did not have enough time for this. This can probably be explained by the teachers' increased knowledge about new digital tools and, at the same time, experienced that they did not have time enough to explore them.

In the first questionnaire, several teachers noted practical and technical problems with the digital tools, for example if an iPad was uncharged when it should be used in a teaching situation, led to loss of valuable time and as was stressful.

> I believe that I myself have to see the benefits with using digital tools and continuously transfer this to my practice together with the children and, then, evaluate what continuously can become better. I think that an uncharged iPad creates resistance to use them, limits the learning capacity. Updates and other issues should just work. If these components do not work, we will not use them. Time to keep up with problems creates stress and irritation.

In the second questionnaire, there were less comments like this, rather comments like the above-mentioned collegial and child-centred aspects were more frequently noted. Moreover, these collegial matters were related to notes about the importance of an individual investment of efforts and an acknowledgement from the leadership of getting time to explore and learn.

> One can never become too competent. Development happens all the time. For me it is about being curious and keep up with the development and getting some time to test and experiment.

> The fact is that when new tools or tasks are introduced, most often they come from 'above'. The leaders should give time to this; to get acquainted, to plan, and to learn.

When relating this quote to the teachers' professional learning to become digital competent, this is considered as taking place through relationships that enable or prevent professional learning. We argue for a need of reconstituting both space and time in order to promote both for teachers' shared learning, as well as for organisational learning. Here, the DIA-approach (participation, influence, responsibility, see Sect. 3) could be a vital factor.

6.3 Providing Tools to Mediate Professional Learning

> A red thread is necessary, a holistic view between colleagues regarding how and what [digital tools] we shall use. The overall goal with this digitisation needs to be clarified by the leadership as well as they need to make

time available and create practical and economic conditions for us to be able to work more digitally. More directions from the leadership and the leaders how we shall
work and to what goal. This has to be more conveniently
manageable in our everyday work.

Vygotsky [26] emphasises that learning by mediation happens when people use symbolic tools to regulate their activity. In the present context, it is significant that the teachers, by the second questionnaire, are ready for implementing digital tools and to professionally learn more about such tools and how to pedagogically use them. However, the teachers express a need for a clear and holistically considered direction from the leaders, including time, and space for the teachers to become professionally more competent. While some teachers find it complicated to develop their own and the children's digital skills and competence through the DIA approach, some teachers acknowledge it as a holistic tool, which, though complex, can assist a pedagogical dimension to implementing digital tools in teaching and learning activities.

The DIA-model as a tool is good as one gets a holistic
picture, one can catch up by looking at old DIA plans and
learn from them. However, the DIA tool is quite comprehensive with many parts. It [the DIA model] should be possible to make it easier to work with and to be able to work
with it more flexible, for example bringing in the digital
learning.

Other examples are:

I think the DIA model is an excellent tool to include children's participation, influence and responsibility in any
learning activity.

The DIA model could be complicated. Co-workers have difficulties in understanding how they should be done. We seldom
get feedback or help for development.

I experience that I have competence to use the DIA model.
We help each other within the working team. However, it is
never wrong to improve things now and then.

Vygotsky [26] clarifies that people engage in joint activity to pursue a goal. The ways people act and express themselves to the functions or limitations of a tool that they use. From this point of view, the transmission of knowledge among, for example, a team of teachers can be understood by socially constructed capacities and knowledge acquisition, which is an outcome of the interaction with tools. The concept of tools can be understood as the digital tools that teachers use, but here they refer to the overarching DIA model as a tool to support professional learning when it comes to professional use of digital tools in teaching and learning activities. As such the DIA model offers a pedagogical tool with practical qualities as it can act as a framework for the planning and documentation of teaching and learning activities. Designating a pedagogical tool like the DIA model implies that the users of it embrace a degree of direction and, at the same time a degree of discretion in the way of planning and documenting. It is, however, important to clarify that, according to Leont'ev [27] tools are not just physical artefacts as they incorporate a social utilisation structure. In the context of the present study, this means that the utilisation aspect of the DIA model explains an organisational culture rather than the physical artefact. This is revealed in the open answers/comments of both questionnaires, indicating that the DIA model, as a tool for professional learning, offers not only physical operations but also acts as a framework of a work culture characterised by a holistic view on collaborative learning and development.

> The model is very good as it starts from the children's perspective and puts participation, influence, and responsibility at the core. The children can contribute to the activities, discuss and share their experiences, experience participation.

> The model contributes to a sense of community. By starting from the children's interest and needs, it is also possible to create a greater engagement. To participate in the whole process [planning, performing and evaluating] is important to feel motivated. Motivation and possibility to participate creates engagement.

As previously noted though, this working culture needs the leadership's acknowledgement as well as space and time for such collaborative learning and development.

7 Conclusion

Professional learning in educational organisations can be a challenging issue. For an organisation to learn as an organisation, there has to be a common direction of its collective activity; *a sense of direction*. In the present work-in-progress study we investigated how teachers in preschools and schools perceived their digital competence and how they considered their opportunities to improve their competences. The study was based on two baseline questionnaire investigations including 21 preschool teachers and 16 primary school teachers. The first baseline questionnaire was distributed in February 2018 (by the start of the project) and formed a 'current-state' baseline. The second questionnaire was carried out in June 2019, where the outcomes formed a 'new-state' condition. The project as a whole includes several other kinds of data, but this work-in-progress paper only focuses on the quantitative data from these questionnaires and a simple statistical analysis. In addition, as some of the questions included space for open answers or comments, the analysis also included a qualitative coding of the written statements from the teachers.

In general, the teachers experienced that their digital competence increased between the first and second questionnaire; 74% of the teachers perceived themselves as being digitally competent after the second questionnaire. However, considering how they found their opportunities to cultivate or improve their competences, they expressed a concern of lacking adequate tools acknowledged by the leadership, in particular related to space and time for sharing knowledge as well as learning from each other as colleagues. This resonates with Rikkerink et al. [21] who states that sensemaking processes are intersubjective and involve complex interactions between the domains of leadership, context, teacher characteristics and teacher learning in the practical use and sensemaking of digital technologies. Hence, we argue that it is important for the continuation of the present project to focus on the cultivation of the integration of digital technology, rather than blindly focusing on the teachers' confidence with and knowledge of digital technologies in teaching ang learning situation [c.f. 23]. In other words, to become digital competent concerns a careful cultivation of a learning organisation, i.e. a holistic sense of direction.

The results from the questionnaires suggest that the DIA model, when adequately adjusted to the current digital landscape, can open up for a holistic view embedding organisational learning and promoting collaboration. Here, a relational practice [c.f. 28] constitutes recurring activities that embodies explicit values and norms, for example, making space and time for the cultivation of collaboration cross-over competences. This can generate a resourceful and socially integrative organisation. The implications of the findings of this study is that an organisation that wants to learn and develop as an organisation needs to bring about a culture change implied by the adoption of such constitutive practices. We identified three constitutive components that we argue can foster the cultivation of integrative activities and, accordingly, promote a learning organisation, namely: (1) shared comprehensive influence, (2) reconstitution of space and time for shared learning, and (3) tools to mediate professional learning. These components are closely aligned with the DIA model.

However, if these components should form a *sense of direction* and as such a context for strategic renewal considering the individual teacher and the team of teachers, the leadership practice should act as an engine for the organisational learning to create a dynamic balance between the teachers' experienced pressure [21]. Crossan et al. [29] explain this as flows of learning at every level of the organisation. The authors clarify this by placing processes of sensemaking at an individual level, which concern personal interpretations of experiences. This can lead to new ideas or new ways of approaching tasks. However, the effects of individual learning can only influence others when it is demonstrated and shared with colleagues who have had similar experiences. These exchanges of experiences are what Rikkerink et al. [21] characterise as *collective sensemaking* at a group level. This is where shared ideas can lead to mutually coordinated practice-based professional learning. The outcomes of this study have shown that this is not a straight-forward process, but rather turbulent, where feelings and knowledge (new and old) are mixed with each other and create tensions and worries. Thus, what the teachers ask for simply creates meaning: they want to try out for themselves new teaching and learning practices and then discuss their experiences (or lack of experiences) with their colleagues. When combined with the DIA model, including a distributed leadership, such repeating sensemaking processes could create a stability rather than worries and tensions, and as such create a pedagogy for professional learning.

References

1. Läroplan för Grundskolan samt för Förskoleklassen och Fritidshemmen (Lgr 11). Stockholm: Skolverket (2011). https://www.skolverket.se/undervisning/grundskolan/laroplan-och-kur splaner-for-grundskolan/laroplan-lgr11-for-grundskolan-samt-for-forskoleklassen-och-fritid shemmet. Accessed 14 Aug 2019
2. Läroplan för förskolan. Skolverket (2018). https://www.skolverket.se/download/18.6bfaca 41169863e6a65d5aa/1553968116077/pdf4001.pdf. Accessed 07 Aug 2019/
3. Nationell Digitaliseringsstrategi för Skolverket. Stockholm: Utbildningsdepartementet (2017). https://www.regeringen.se/4a9d9a/contentassets/00b3d9118b0144f6bb95302f3e0 8d11c/nationell-digitaliseringsstrategi-for-skolvasendet.pdf. Accessed 14 Aug 2019
4. Redecker, C.: European framework for the digital competence of educators: DigCompEdu. In: Punie, Y. (ed.) EUR 28775 EN. Publications Office of the European Union, Luxembourg (2017)
5. Chval, K.B., Reys, R., Reys, B.J., Tarr, J.E., Chávez, O.: Pressures to improve student performance: a context that both urges and impedes school-based research. J. Res. Math. Educ. **37**(3), 158–166 (2006)
6. März, M.B., Kelchtermans, G., Vanhoof, S., Onghena, P.: Sense-making and structure in teachers' reception of educational reform: a case study on statistics in the mathematic curriculum. Teach. Teach. Educ. **29**, 13–24 (2013)
7. Phelps, R., Graham, A., Watts, T.: Acknowledging the complexity and diversity of historical and cultural ICT professional learning practices in schools. Asia-Pac. J. Teach. Educ. **39**(1), 47–63 (2011)
8. Bigum, C.: Design sensibilities, schools and the new computing communication technologies. In: Snyder, I. (ed.) Silicon Literacies. Communication, Innovation and Education in the Electronic Age, pp. 130–140. Routledge, London (2002)
9. Schön, D.: The Reflective Practitioner: How Professionals Think in Action. Maurice Temple Smith, London (1983)
10. Schön, D.: Educating the Reflective Practitioner. Jossey-Bass, San Francisco (1987)
11. OECD (Organisation for Economic Cooperation & Development).: Creating effective teaching and learning environments: First results from TALIS (Teaching and Learning International Survey). OECD, Paris (2009)
12. Raphael, T., Vasquez, J., Fortune, A., Gavelek, J., Au, K.: Sociocultural approaches to professional development: Supporting sustainable school change. In: Martin, L., Kragler, S., Quatroche, D., Baserman, K. (eds.) Handbook of Professional development in education; Successful models and practices, pp. 145–173. Guilford Publications, New Yorg (2014)
13. Sanders, E.B.-N., Stappers, P.J.: Co-creation and the new landscapes of design. CoDesign **4**(1), 5–18 (2008)
14. Rittel, H.W.J., Webber, M.M.: Dilemmas in a general theory of planning. Policy Sci. **4**, 155–169 (1973)
15. Dewey, J.: Democracy and education. Simon & Brown (1916/2011)
16. Simon, H.: The sciences of the artificial. Massachusetts Institute of Technology Press, Cambridge Mass (1976)
17. Cvetek, S.: Applying chaos theory to lesson planning and delivery. Eur. J. Teach. Educ. **31**(3), 247–256 (2008)
18. Harjunen, E.: Patterns of control over the teaching-studying-learning process and classrooms as complex dynamic environments: a theoretical framework. Eur. J. Teach. Educ. **35**(2), 139–161 (2012)
19. Weick, K.E., Sutcliffe, K.M., Obstfeld, D.: Organizing and the process of sensemaking. Organ. Sci. **16**(4), 409–421 (2005)

20. Weick, K.E.: Sense-Making in Organizations. Sage, Thousand Oakds (1995)
21. Rikkerink, M., Verbeeten, H., Simons, R.-J., Ritzen, H.: A new model of educational inno-vation: exploring the nexus of organizational learning, distributed leadership, and digital technologies. J. Educ. Change **17**(2), 223–249 (2015). https://doi.org/10.1007/s10833-015-9253-5
22. Howard, S.K., Curwood, J.S., McGraw, K.: Leaders fostering teachers' learning environ-ments for technology integration. In: Voogt, J., Knezek, G., Christensen, R., Lai, K.W. (eds.) Second Handbook of Information Technology in Primary and Secondary Education, Springer International Handbooks of Education, pp. 1–19. Springer, Cham (2018)
23. Howard, S.K., Gigliotti, A.: Having a go: Looking at teachers' experience of risk-taking in technology integration. Educ. Inf. Technol. **21**(5), 1351–1366 (2015). https://doi.org/10.1007/s10639-015-9386-4
24. Field, A., Hole, G.: How to design and Report Experiments. Sage Publications, London (2003)
25. Graneheim, U.H., Lundman, B.: Qualitative content analysis in nursing research: concepts, procedures and measures to achieve trustworthiness. Nurse Educ. Today **24**(2), 105–112 (2004)
26. Vygotsky, L.S.: Mind in Society: The Development of Higher Psychological Functions. Harvard University Press, Cambridge (1978)
27. Leont'ev, A.N.: Activity, consciousness and personality. Prentice Hall, Englewood Cliffs (1978)
28. Edwards, A.: Relational agency: learning to be a resourceful practitioner. Int. J. Educ. Res. **43**, 168–182 (2005)
29. Crossan, M.M., Lane, H.W., White, R.E.: An organizational learning framework: Form intuition to institution. Acad. Manag. Rev. **24**(3), 533–537 (1999)

Do People with Diabetes Follow the Recommendations? A Study of Motivational and Compliance Factors of People with Type 1 Diabetes

Marie Charlotte Lyngbye[⊠] and Anders Kalsgaard Møller

Department of Culture and Learning, Aalborg University, Kroghstræde 3,
9220 Aalborg Ø, Denmark
{machly,ankm}@hum.aau.dk

Abstract. The number of people with diabetes is increasing and today more than 8.5% of the adult population is diagnosed with diabetes. People with diabetes must make significant changes to their life and habits and adjust it to the recommendations for diabetic treatment to avoid or delay complications related to the illness. In this paper, we present empirical data from a survey, experience sampling data and interviews that addresses people with type 1 diabetes' adherence with the recommended blood sugar measurements, their physical activity level and motivational factors. This information is used to understand and explain people with diabetes' adherence to follow the recommendations using theories about self-efficacy and motivation. Finally, we give recommendations for how digital solutions can be designed that can aid the users and motivate them to follow the recommendations and hereby potentially improve the quality of life for diabetes patients.

Keywords: Motivation · Diabetes · Persuasive technologies · Experience sampling method

1 Introduction

Diabetes is a disease where the body does not produce or use insulin very well. Insulin is a hormone used to help your body absorb glucose and turn it into energy. If the glucose is not absorbed it will stay in the blood which over time can cause severe health problems [1]. Type 1 diabetes mellitus is an autoimmune chronic disease where the pancreas does not produce insulin. As a result, people with type 1 diabetes must inject insulin themselves. The amount of insulin varies depending on food intake and activity level. People with diabetes must measure the blood sugar level daily to ensure the right level of insulin [1]. When physical active, people with diabetes need to know how the activity affect the blood sugar why health professionals recommend that the blood sugar is measured before, during and after the activity to adjust the insulin level [1]. Reports from healthcare professionals at Aalborg University Hospital South [13] and a qualitative

A. Brooks and E. I. Brooks (Eds.): ArtsIT 2019/DLI 2019, LNICST 328, pp. 714–722, 2020.
https://doi.org/10.1007/978-3-030-53294-9_54

survey (n = 138) conducted in 2018 [14] give the impression that people with diabetes rarely do the recommended blood sugar measurements.

In this paper, we present empirical data from surveys and interviews that addresses people with type 1 diabetes' adherence with the recommended blood sugar measurements and physical activities. To understand and explain people with diabetes' adherence to follow the recommendations we use a theoretical framework comprised of: Banduras' Self-efficacy [2], Decis' and Ryans' Extrinsic motivation [3]. Finally, we give recommendations for how digital solutions can be designed that can aid the users and motivate them to become more active and do the blood sugar measurements more regularly and hereby improve the quality of life for people with diabetes.

2   Background

The number of people with diabetes have increased from 108 million globally in 1980 to 422 million in 2014. This correspond to an increase in prevalence for adults over 18 from 4.7% (1980) to 8.5% in 2014 [6].

Diabetes can cause blindness, kidney failure, heart attacks, stroke and lower limb amputation; however, people with diabetes can delay or avoid the complications with the right diet, physical activity and the correct use of medication (insulin) [7]. People with diabetes must make significant changes to their life and habits and adjust it to the recommendations for diabetic treatment e.g. change their diet, activity level and monitor the blood glucose level daily [8]. Making behavioral changes and maintaining the new habits require the patient to have a high degree of health literacy which is defined by WHO as: *"The cognitive and social skills which determine the motivation and ability of individuals to gain access to, understand and use information in ways which promote and maintain good health"* [12].

In the specific case of diabetes - health literacy can be translated into people with diabetes' motivation to do blood sugar measurements, understand the measurements and use the information to adjust the amount of insulin along with other things such as how their activity level and food intake/type affect their health. Here we apply Deci and Ryan's definition of motivation who describes motivation as *"to be moved to do something"* [15]. Such motivation is linked with the feeling of wanting and doing something which leads to the question of why they are doing it? In the process of working with motivation, Deci & Ryan developed the 'Self- Determination theory' (SDT). SDT distinguishes between different types of motivation based on different reasons or goals that causes an action. *Intrinsic motivation* refers to doing something because one enjoys it or finds it interesting, such there are no expectation of a reward nor punishment, and *Extrinsic motivation* refers to doing something because it leads to a seconded outcome such focus is goal or reward oriented [3]. Not everyone possess the same level of intrinsic motivation because individuals are attracted to various things and subjects. Therefore Deci and Ryan focuses on humans native psychological needs for competence, autonomy, and relatedness as factors that, when fulfilled at the same time, enhances intrinsic motivation [15]. SDT takes the approach that external goals has a negative impact on an individuals' intrinsic motivation hence focus changes from wanting to do something into gaining a reward. If an individual is presented with a free choice of work, feels competent in doing so and experience cohesion Intrinsic motivation becomes stronger in the individual.

The feeling of competence is highly related to Self-efficacy defined by Bandura as *"... people's beliefs about their capabilities to produce designated levels of performance that exercise influence over events that affect their lives"* Self-efficacy beliefs determine how people feel, think, motivate themselves and behave [16].

A strong sense of efficacy enhances humans' well- being in many ways. Individuals with a high sense of efficacy approaches difficult task as a challenge to be mastered, rather than threats to avoid. When experiencing failure these individuals quickly recover, attributing the failure to insufficient effort, or lack of skills which are acquirable. Such an efficacious outlook fosters intrinsic interest and deep fascination in activities and pursuing personal goals. Individuals with a reduced sense of efficacy, avoid difficult tasks, which they think of as personal threats. When confronted with a difficult situation or task, they focus more on their lack of skills or the possible bad outcomes, rather than focusing on how to solve the task or situation successfully. To change the behavior of people with diabetes we therefore must understand what motivate people with diabetes to take the necessary actions and ensure that they can do so while maintaining a high level of self-efficacy. Knowing the motivational factors is the first steps in designing a digital tool that can aid the users and motivate them to follow the recommendations. Digital solutions with the purpose of motivating people to behavioral changes are known as persuasive technologies.

Persuasive technologies and design have increasingly been used within the area of health [9]. Captology is the study of Persuasive Technology and focuses specific on how people can be motivated or change attitude by interacting with technical products. J B Fogg has been doing research in Persuasive technology since the 90's and believes that the commissioning for behavior change depends on three variables (1) Motivation (2) Ability (3) Triggers. These three variables are dependent of each other and therefore needs to be activated simultaneously, which is why Fogg developed the equation B = MAT. Fogg believes that triggers should be recommending instead of instructional hence a behavior change is focused around the individuals own choice and intrinsic motivation [17].

One commonly strategy when using PT is tailoring the persuasive communication between the user and the system [18]. Tory Higgins developed two main motivational strategies when using PT. Promotion- Orientation which is a strategy that is focused on accomplishments and potential gains and Prevention-Orientation which is focused on safety, security and preventing potential losses [18]. Conducted a study on how individuals, who wanted to change behavior, perceived tailored health messages using Higgins' strategies. For the test they developed three types of messages one was promotion-oriented which highlighted the benefits of being physical active, and two was within the frame of prevention-orientation. Type 1 stressed the risks and consequences of not engaging in regular activity, and type 2 highlighted those health risks that can be avoided by performing regular activity. Their findings indicated that Promotion-messages are perceived to be the most effective, the second most persuasive message was Prevention-message type 1 and the least effective, prevention message type 2. They also did find a correlation between the level of motivation and the perceived persuasion from the messages.

Today continuous glucose monitoring solutions exists where blood glucose meters measure the glucose level in real time and insulin pumps can be adjusted to give the right amount of insulin [10]. According to the researchers, the information about how patients should use the data from the system in everyday life situations are lacking. This may lead to inefficient use and undesirable fluctuations in the blood glucose. Another shortcoming of the systems is that they are relatively big and hence not suitable to wear while doing physical activities. Only recently have the first activity trackers for diabetes started to emerge [11]. Activity trackers can potentially be useful for people with diabetes, but researchers report on several issues that prevent the optimal use of the information provided by the devices. Lack of access to the raw data, delays, synchronization problems and the devices overheating is among the reported problems. The preliminary results show potential for wearable solutions but how these systems can be utilized to support the patients and improve the treatment is relatively unexplored [10, 11].

3 Data Collection

The data collection methods consisted of a survey, an experience sampling survey and two qualitative interviews. The different methods and purposes will be presented in the following section.

3.1 Surveys

For data gathering, an electronic survey (survey 1) with a combination of qualitative and quantitative answering options were designed. Thus, investigating the people with diabetes' current behavior for adherence with their diabetes when being psychically active.

The survey was sent by email to a group of respondents (n = 105) whom the researchers had contacted in the early phase of the project. The survey was active for a period of two weeks, which resulted in 23 valid responses.

3.2 Experience Sampling

To compare respondents' responses of their experienced behavior with their actual behavior, we designed an electronic survey within the frame of Experienced Sampling Method (ESM survey). This is a diary-based method that allows researchers to explore the nature and quality of the respondents' experienced situation here and now [19]. A quantitative electronic survey, with the possibility of elaborating answers, containing six questions, was prepared. This was emailed once daily to the 23 respondents responding to the first survey. The emails were sent at varying times over a three-week period, with a total of 11 respondents contributing throughout the period.

3.3 Interview

Two qualitative unstructured interviews with two adult people with diabetes were conducted, such validating their preferred type of messaging when using PT. We had in advance designed 5 different types of messages within the frames of Promotion and Prevention-orientation and asked the people with diabetes to validate their preferences.

3.4 Analysis

Launsø et al's scheme [21] were used to classify data, which is a further development of Kvales' condensation method. Data was analyzed according to the principles of Grounded theory steps 1–3 [20]. 1) The analysis process was initiated by open coding, which creates an overview of data, thereby initiating a preliminary contextual classification. 2) The process continued with axial coding, where clarification of contexts was systematized in to main and subcategories 3) the process then continued with selective coding where we attempted a clarifying of contexts between the general categories, allowing us to focus on the contexts in a more abstract manner.

The quantitative data from survey 1 and the ESM survey where calculated and presented as percentage. A minor error occurred for some of the subjects answering the question in survey 1: 'have you been physically active today' two respondents experienced technical problems with the survey, when trying to answer NO. They have thus answered YES to the question and later elaborated in the open section of the survey that the reality was different. For example one wrote "I have answered yes, but my bicycletire ruptured, so I had to take the bus, I could not choose NO so I write here instead" As the researcher wanted data regarding activity level for a better understanding of the respondents behavior, these responses were adjusted from YES to NO according to the respondents statements, and the answers from the YES section regarding motivation etc. deleted.

4 Results and Analysis

4.1 Respondents

The respondents of this investigation were a heterogeneous group belonging to the upper- and middle-class society with education levels of a minimum 2-year higher education or longer. All respondents had Diabetes mellitus type 1 with various levels of duration and type of tools for diabetes care. 91% of the respondents from survey 1 informs that they are being physical active. The information about the subject is inconsistent when reading answers from survey 1 and the ESM survey where 79.2% of respondents informs that they are physical active in the 3-week period. The respondents expressed reasons as illness and problems with a deviating blood sugar as results of inactivity during the 3 weeks.

4.2 Registration and Measuring Blood Sugar Levels During Physical Activity

In general, the respondents express that they comply with the recommendations regarding registration of blood sugar, which is recommended for 4 times daily. Thus, consensus is identified in data from survey 1 and the ESM survey where measurement at least 4 times a day is stated to be 76% and 84%.

82% of the respondents inform that they do not register blood sugar levels during physical activity. They explain reasons for this as, them being disturbed in the activity they are performing because of the timeframe for measuring and registration of blood sugar, which they experience as being too long. They tend to forget measuring and registration, because their focus is on the activity and not the diabetes care, some do not feel the need to perform the measurements and registrations, and some express a need to avoid other peoples' awareness such thoughts about stigmatizing have emerged. Results from the preliminary survey from 2018, showed that people with diabetes felt stigmatized, and would prefer to use a smartphone or other fitness tool, for their diabetes care it would minimize the experience of stigma [13]. Of the 9% who measured and registered blood sugar both before, during and after physical activity, the percentages vary depending on the level of physical activity. Such the percentages are represented at High activity level = 18% moderate activity level = 36% and Low activity level = 9%.

72% of the respondents does not use a digital fitness tracker, like a watch or a bracelet, this is because of varies reasons like them experiencing that they have enough digital tools to attend to, they are not motivated by it, or it is too expensive. 46% of the 72% would use a fitness tracker if they had the possibility of measure and register blood sugar levels with it.

4.3 Motivation

The respondents' information about physical activity was distributed within Deci and Ryan's taxonomy. Some respondents felt externally regulated because of health specialists expecting physical activity as part of their adherence. The diabetic, in consultation with the hospital and own doctor, formulates goals for blood sugar levels, which should be adhered to in order to obtain a good self- management of the disease. The degree of motivation is thus identified as Adopted regulation.

The level of Integrated regulation are also identified by the respondents' indications of them being physically active, because they think that it is good for their health this being expressed of men 45% and woman = 36%. Intrinsic motivation is indicated by a higher percentage in men = a total of 63% versus 27% in women.

Of the qualitative data it is shown that woman are often physical active in a social setting together with people from their family or close friends. They also express intrinsic motivation for task they like to do in the household such being physical active at a low level. For example, polishing windows. The men express that type of behavior, knowledge of how to adhere and the possibility of attaining goals are motivating factors, such they are intrinsic motivated by being physical active alone or together with others. Both genders experience a high level of positive feelings and proudness when being physical active *"I get happy and the brain sends wonderful hormones into the bloodstream. I'm getting healthier"*.

They also experience a miner degree of negative feelings as sadness and failure when meeting obstacles which conflicts with their diabetes during their physical activity. *"I have struggled with high blood sugar levels today, they would by no means lower."* Such confirming Ryan and Decis' Intrinsic motivation theory.

4.4 Self Efficacy

The respondents inform that in general their self-management of their diabetes is good and therefore their diabetes is well regulated. Such they express possessing a high level of self-efficacy. This explains the level of 82% of the respondents not measuring blood sugar, hence they trust in experience instead of measuring when being physical active.

3 domains in which the respondents answer they tend to forget adhering with their diabetes was identified as: forgetting Dextrose, adjusting their insulin pump and forgetting blood sugar measurement during physical activity. *"Forget about measuring blood sugar, and lower the basal rate. Low blood sugar as a result. "Feeling defeat, frustration, waste of hard work when I have to eat" "By adjusting my pump. I get annoyed at myself*," this experience of failure could reduce people with diabetes' self-efficacy.

5 Discussion

The results from the study shows a difference between survey 1 and the ESM survey regarding if the respondents are physical active with 91% in survey 1 saying they are physically active while the data from the ESM survey showed that in the 3-week period only 79.2% was active. The difference here could be explained by the technical error we saw when answering survey 1 were some of the respondents could not select "NO" which affects the reliability of survey 1 and therefore the one could expect the number to be closer to 79.2% as reported in the ESM survey. In general, the results should be considered preliminary as 11 respondents in the ESM survey and 2 respondents' in the interview may not be considered a valid foundation for the creation of new knowledge. However, because of consensus in data from this survey and other research, further investigation in the subject is to be considered.

The study indicated that men possess an intrinsic type of motivation for being physical active, which they express as a personal desire whereas woman expresses physical activity as a job to be done hence, they are extrinsic motivated using adherence of their disease as a factor for being physically active. 73% of the respondents reports their diabetes as well regulated in general, whereas 9% of the respondents are compliant with blood sugar measurements when being physically active due to a high level of perceived self-efficacy, such the people with diabetes relay on experience instead of blood sugar measuring during physical activity.

Three primarily domains in which the respondents express having issues with adherence when physically active were identified as (forgetting Dextrose) (adjusting their insulin pump) (forgetting blood sugar measuring during physical activity). When repeatedly forgetting to adhere with ones' disease it may affect the level of a persons' self-efficacy. According to Bandura the experience of failure reduces a persons' self-efficacy, the respondents informs having experiences like, failures, sadness, frustrations, shame and self-blame. According to Banduras' theory of self-efficacy the experiences of positive outcomes increases a persons' level of self-efficacy, Such a latent need for a tool reminding the people with diabetes to adhere within the three domains was identified, thus contributing to a positive experience within these domains which must be assumed to enhance the people with diabetes' self-efficacy, and therefore contributing to an even better regulated diabetes.

Developing a digital tool that can aid the people with diabetes with remembering to adhere to their diabetes, may help enhance the people with diabetes' self-efficacy if an enhancement of self-efficacy is proven doable, an increase of the people with diabetes' motivation is to be expected, hence the experience of being competent, autonomous and relatedness enhances Intrinsic motivation. The informants from the interviews both express a reminding digital tool as a positive action for enhancing the people with diabetes' adherence with their disease. This correspond very well with Fogg's model of behavior change as the people with diabetes in general are very motivated and have the ability to test the blood sugar level, the only thing missing is the trigger. Contrary to suggested by [18] the respondents from the interview indicated that the wording of the trigger should be neutral in the expression but with an instructing message to measure blood sugar to create motivation to carry out the measurement. Both informants express that an image or symbol would be faster to decode than text, such the pictures or symbols need be within the diabetes discourse. The need for different types of modalities were also identified such as auditory, visual and vibration.

Results of the preliminary survey, and the interviews conducted in this investigation suggests that the respondents would prefer a digital wearable fitness tracker like a watch or a bracelet to manage their diabetes, such avoiding the feeling of stigma, and minimizing the risk of forgetting the tool, because one is wearing it on the wrist.

6 Conclusion and Recommendations

Based on data from this paper and other similar research it was concluded that most people with diabetes are being physical active. The study indicate that men in general are more intrinsic motivated to be physical active while woman a more extrinsic motivated. While the respondents express that they comply with the recommendations regarding registration of blood sugar, we found that many people with diabetes fail to adhere with recommendations for blood sugar measurements during physical activity, since only 9% of the respondents fulfilled the recommendations. Overall there is three domains in which people with diabetes tend to forget adhering with their diabetes: Forgetting Dextrose, adjusting their insulin pump and forgetting blood sugar measurement during physical activity.

Based on the findings we suggest a digital tool to remind the people with diabetes to measure their blood sugar. The digital tool should be based on the design of a fitness bracelet due to the wearability and because this is relative neutral and can worn without stigmatizing the people with diabetes. The wording of the trigger message should be neutral in the expression but with an instructing message to measure the blood sugar level. It is recommended that the digital tool has a display that can visualize text and pictures, such it is possible to decode a message by using a picture or a symbol, which sometimes are easier to interpret than a text message. It is necessary that the symbol relates to the diabetes discourse.

Multimodalities like vibration, auditory functions and visual effects are recommendable such providing the possibilities of personalizing the product.

In the attempt of enhancing the people with diabetes' self-efficacy and intrinsic motivation further investigation of what motivates men and woman are recommend hence men and woman are motivated by varies factors. The knowledge of knowing the motivational factors could be a helpful tool when designing the tailored message.

References

1. Diabetesforeningen. https://diabetes.dk/diabetes-1/fakta-om-diabetes-1.aspx. Accessed 07 Aug 2019
2. Bandura, A.: Self-efficacy mechanism in human agency. Am. Psychol. **37**(2), 122–147 (1982)
3. Deci, E.L., Ryan, R.M.: Intrinsic motivation and self-determination in human behavior, Perspectives in social psychology. Plenum Press, New York (1985)
4. Prochaska, J.O., DiClemente, C.C., Norcross, J.C.: In search of how people change: applications to addictive behaviors. Am. Psychol. **47**(9), 1102–1114 (1992)
5. Fogg, B.J.: Creating persuasive technologies: an eight-step design process. In: Proceedings of the 4th International Conference on Persuasive Technology. ACM (2009)
6. Emerging Risk Factors Collaboration.: Diabetes mellitus, fasting blood glucose concentration, and risk of vascular disease: a collaborative meta-analysis of 102 prospective studies. Lancet **375**(9733), 2215–2222 (2010)
7. WHO. https://www.who.int/news-room/fact-sheets/detail/diabetes. Accessed 07 Aug 2019
8. Heisler, M., et al.: The relative importance of physician communication, participatory decision making, and patient understanding in diabetes self-management. J. Gen. Intern. Med. **17**(4), 243–252 (2002)
9. Orji, R., Moffatt, K.: Persuasive technology for health and wellness: state-of-the-art and emerging trends. Health Inf. J. **24**(1), 66–91 (2018)
10. Pettus, J., Edelman, S.V.: Recommendations for using real-time continuous glucose monitoring (rtCGM) data for insulin adjustments in type 1 diabetes. J. Diab. Sci. Technol. **11**(1), 138–147 (2017)
11. Schwartz, F.L., Marling, C.R., Bunescu, R.C.: The promise and perils of wearable physiological sensors for diabetes management. J. Diab. Sci. Technol. **12**(3), 587–591 (2018)
12. Nutbeam, D.: Health promotion glossary. Health Promot. Int. **13**(4), 349–364 (1998)
13. Lyngbye, M.C.: En Forandringsproces i Endokrinologien på Aaalborg Universitetshospital Syd. Aalborg Universitet, Humanistisk Faktultet - Institut for læring. Semesterprojekt (2018a)
14. Lyngbye, M.C.: It, Læring og Organisatorisk omstilling -Eksamensopgave Interaktionsdesign. Aalborg Universitet, Humanistisk Faktultet - Institut for læring. Aalborg: Aalborg Universitet. Semesterprojekt (2018b)
15. Deci, E.L., Ryan, R.M.: Intrinsic and extrinsic motivations: classic definitions and new directions. Contemp. Educ. Psycol. **25**(1), 54–67 (2000)
16. Bandura, A.: Self-Efficacy in Changing Societies. Stanford University, Stanford (1995)
17. Fogg, B.J.: Persuasive Technology - Using Computers to Change What we Think and do. Morgan Kaufmann Publishers, San Francisco (2003)
18. Rezai, L.S., Chin, J., Bassett-Gunter, R., Burns, C.: Developing persuasive health messages for a behavior-change- support-system that promotes physical activity. In: Proceedings of the 2017 International Symposium on Human Factors and Ergonomics in Health Care, pp. 89–95. University of waterloo, Waterloo Canada, (2017)
19. Kubey, R., Larson, R., Csikszentmihalyi, M.: Experience sampling method applications to communication research questions. J. Commun. **46**(2), 99–120 (1996)
20. Brinkmann, S., Tangaard, L.: Kvalitative Metoder En Grundbog. København k: Hans Reitzels Forlag (2010)
21. Launsø, R.O.: Forskning om og med mennesker -Forskningstyper og forskningsmetoder i samfundsforskning. Munksgaard (2017)

Innovation, Inclusion and Emerging Technologies

Innovation, Inclusion and Emerging Technologies

Eva Brooks[1](✉) and Anthony L. Brooks[2]

[1] Department of Culture and Learning, Aalborg University, Kroghstræde 3, 9220 Aalborg, Denmark
eb@hum.aau.dk
[2] Department of Architecture, Design and Media Technology, Aalborg University, Rendsburggade 14, 9000 Aalborg, Denmark

Abstract. This section of the volume explores potentials in new technologies suggesting that this requires involvement of various disciplines across societies. Specifically, the society faces a considerable challenge in fostering new ecosystems of innovation to harness holistic agile development processes for new technologies targeting more inclusive societies, where solutions are tailored to users and their specific needs.

Keywords: VR · Simulations · ASD · Co-creation · Physio-therapists · VR-rehabilitation · VR games · Inclusive learning ecosystems · Social change · Entrepreneurship

1 Introduction

1.1 Scope

The seventh section of this volume is themed - "Innovation, Inclusion and Emerging Technologies" focuses on how technological advances are accelerating at such a pace to make current technologies obsolete. This is a challenge, as exploring potentials in new technologies require involvement of various disciplines across societies [1]. Specifically, the society faces a considerable challenge in fostering new ecosystems of innovation to harness holistic agile development processes for new technologies targeting more inclusive societies, where solutions are tailored to users and their specific needs. Thus, needs for innovative technologies is both determined by internal (organizational) needs and challenges, and external (political, technological and economic) expectations [1]. Researchers involved in innovative processes of technology development must therefore continuously consider their reasons and assure that the criteria for best practice and end-user needs are tailored to individual needs, not only political or economic interest. This part of the DLI 2019 proceedings takes an inclusive and innovative grip on aspects that allows for an inclusive mindset in design, learning, and training practices to increase ways for people to participate in such activities. It exemplifies different types of technological solutions and new practices and its possibilities and limitations.

A. Brooks and E. I. Brooks (Eds.): ArtsIT 2019/DLI 2019, LNICST 328, pp. 725–729, 2020.
https://doi.org/10.1007/978-3-030-53294-9_55

The first contribution discusses experiences from developing mediated learning situations in a VR-filmed context. The authors argue for how such productions requires approaches based on co-design and innovative team constellations including knowledge and skills from different areas to join forces for adequate VR solutions. The second contribution presents a study where the feasibility of using Virtual Reality (VR) to reduce disruptive classroom behaviour of a child diagnosed with Autism Spectrum Disorder (ASD). The third contribution presents an explorative case study investigating the declining use of a bespoke VR-based treatment tool for biking-based physical rehabilitation. The fourth contribution addresses the issue of an existing limited integration of Internet of Things (IoT) in K-12 education as well as current limited research on designing IoT projects in makerspaces or classrooms. The paper elaborates on these gaps through an investigation into an informal design process of IoT passion projects from a week-long maker-oriented March Break camp. The final and fifth contribution describes the ECAS framework (Entrepreneurial Cultural Affinity Spaces), which is an emergent instructional paradigm of heritage-led, local learning ecosystem approaches, to leverage on diverse assets of people in community settings.

The following text snippets elaborate directly from each contribution to further assist readership.

2   VR Situated Simulations

The paper is authored by *Michael Johansson, Thore Soneson, Kerstin Ahlqvist, Barbro Bruce, and Camilla Sotis Ekberg* and titled VR Situated Simulations. Here, the authors discusses experiences from developing mediated learning situations in a VR-filmed context. They argue for how such productions require approaches based on co-design and innovative team constellations including knowledge and skills from different areas to join forces for adequate VR solutions. In the chapter, the authors describe the process of developing VR learning situations by being inspired by related studies in the field of collaborative design, where various stakeholders were engaged in different parts of the production; from scriptwriting for interactive media, to creating and editing specific case studies in an interactive VR format, and, also, gathering students' experiences of the scripts and case studies. Based on this, the authors argue that 3D environments for reflection and discussion can be combined to form a common knowledge base in different fields of application, e.g. in the areas of education and Human Resources. Further, it is emphasised that simulations of authentic and real situations have an immersive potential to create pedagogical innovations.

3   Co-creating Virtual Reality Applications for Motor Rehabilitation with Physiotherapists

The paper on head-mounted display-based virtual reality to reduce disruptive behaviour in a student diagnosed with Autism Spectrum Disorder (ASD) by *Ali Adjorlu*, includes a study where the feasibility of using Virtual Reality (VR) to reduce disruptive classroom behaviour of a child diagnosed with ASD was investigated. The participant in the study is a ten years old male diagnosed with ASD as well as some other psychiatric diagnoses. The author explains that the participant shows great willingness to learn in school, wanting to be good at all of the subjects. However, whenever he has a hard time understanding a topic, he performs disruptive behaviours such as getting verbally abusive towards the teachers and other students, reducing the general level of the lectures for him and his classmates. The question addressed in this chapter concerns whether the participant's disruptive behaviour in learning situations would reduce if he received lectures in an immersive VR classroom instead of a real-life classroom. Based on learning design requirements from the teacher, the author describes how a VR application using Bigscreen VR was developed to run the study. This application was chosen as it works on a wide variety of different head-mounted displays and includes a virtual keyboard as well as pointing devices that can be controlled using VR input devices such as the Oculus touch or the HTC Vive wands. In this way, BigscreenVR enabled the teacher and the student to work on assignments created via different learning resources, e.g. book creator, in an immersive, interactive virtual environment. For a period of two months, the participant received math and Danish lectures in a HMD-based virtual environment, taught by a teacher who logged into the same virtual environment. During all of the VR lectures, the participant did not show any disruptive behaviour, which may be explained by the reduced amount of social information presented to the student during the virtual lectures in Bigscreen VR.

4 The Reality of Implementing Virtual Reality: A Case Study on the Challenges of Integrating VR-Based Rehabilitation

The paper addresses challenges related to implementing Virtual Reality (VR) in rehabilitation activities and is authored by *Emil Rosenlund, Christian Francis Reeves, Jon Ram Bruun-Pedersen, and Stefania Serafin*. This paper describes an explorative case study investigating the declining use of a bespoke VR-based treatment tool for biking-based physical rehabilitation. Based on a service-design approach, the data was collected through interviews with four physiotherapists and in-situ observations of patient-therapist interactions. The VR-equipment available to the therapists was Oculus Rift Consumer Version 1 (CV1), headsets, running on a high-end desktop gaming computer. The CV1 furthermore relied on external tracking from one or more motion trackers. The software provided a set of RVEs consisting of 4 different unique, digitally generated virtual landscapes. The authors applied thematic analysis to identify pain points and challenges related to the integration of VR in both hardware, software, and operation resources. The four identified themes were: VR service (user-experience and usability); Attitude and experiences of the therapist; Organizational culture; and Communication. Embedded are solutions proposed by the authors to increase the health workforce's acceptance and endorsement of VR-supplied service at a Danish outpatient municipality health centre. The authors conclude that therapists are important actors in intermediating the technology to the patients. If the therapists do not have incentive to use it, for example due to a steep learning curve, inadequate usability, or non-established workflow procedures, the technology will not reach a sufficient endorsement and will never consolidate. Thus, a VR system has to deliver simple and informative feedback, and work routines need to be clearly defined and visualized.

5 Co-designing a Head-Mounted Display Based Virtual Reality Game to Teach Street-Crossing Skills to Children Diagnosed with Autism Spectrum Disorder

Janette Hughes, Jennifer Anne Robb, and Margaret Samantha Lam authored the following paper addressing the question of how to design and learn with Internet of Things (IoT), in particular forcing on passion-based learning. Internet of Things (IoT) is a recent technological advancement. The concept is originally coined by Kevin Aston and involves a transformation of everyday objects into 'smart' objects which can transmit collected data through the Internet to IoT platforms. The advantages of IoT is said to include the ability to analyse in real-time and autonomous problem-solving and interactions. The authors point to that there currently exist over 8 billion smart objects, including cars, watches, appliances, and humans, that are connected through IoT, and this number is expected to surpass 50 billion by 2020. Considering this, a key aspect of understanding IoT is learning how to effectively design various components, including sensors, processors, actuators (motors, fans, etc.), and IoT platforms. Theoretically, the study applies a constructionism approach informed by aspects of design thinking and passion-based learning. The authors state a need for leveraging formal or informal design-based frameworks within creative and explorative environments, such as makerspaces, to help students learn and develop IoT working projects. Despite this impending need, the authors address a limited integration of IoT in K-12 education and minor research on designing IoT projects in makerspaces or classrooms. Thus, this chapter seeks to address these gaps through an investigation into an informal design process of IoT passion projects from a week-long maker-oriented March Break camp. Camp participants created their own IoT projects that were meant to solve a "real world" or relevant problem in their communities. During the camp, IoT concepts were explained, IoT technologies were discovered and informal design practices were encouraged, all to support learners as they developed their IoT digital artefacts. Method-wise the study applied self-reported online questionnaires, students' documentation of their own IoT passion project, online mapping, and images/videos and informal discussions, recorded field notes, and video-recorded work sessions. Finally so called exit interviews were carried out with the participants. The data was analysed through content analysis. The analysis showed that while guided inquiry can be an effective tool to drive passion-based maker projects, the amount of guidance needed to support design decisions can vary wildly. Based on this, the authors suggest that inclusion of more explicit workshop procedure explanation may have alleviated frustrations, promoted resiliency, and more effectively fostered emerging IoT designs. The authors conclude that engagement with IoT technologies in a constructionism-oriented environment, such as a community makerspace or a maker-oriented classroom, may facilitate a deeper conceptual understanding of IoT and its real-world applications.

6   Entrepreneurial Cultural Affinity Spaces (ECAS): Design of Inclusive Local Learning Ecosystems for Social Change, Innovation and Entrepreneurship

The final contribution in this part of the DLI 2019 section on innovation, inclusion, and emerging technologies is authored by *Stefania Savva, Nicos Souleles, and Ana Margarida Ferreira*. The paper focuses on the ECAS framework, which is an emergent instructional paradigm of heritage-led, local learning ecosystem approaches, to leverage on diverse assets of people in community settings. This targets a reconfiguration of design theory for social change as well as social collective mindset. The authors envisage that such transformations will create conditions for more dynamic and powerful collaborations that may stimulate and enable social innovation, entrepreneurship, and inclusion. This conceptual frame draws on concepts of affinity spaces and embodied learning, incorporated into local learning ecosystem ideas supporting viable, integrated, and participative urban regeneration. The chapter describes this conceptual framework, exploring how such ecosystems can be co-designed, implemented, and evaluated, to include disadvantaged and underrepresented groups (e.g. minorities, women, migrants, refugees, and asylum seekers) to empower them as lifelong learners and change-makers.

7   Epilogue and Acknowledgements

This seventh and final section introduces five contributions to promote readership of each full paper that are presented in the following chapters. In doing so, the authors of this chapter acknowledge the contribution to this section/volume by each author whose original work was presented in the ArtsIT/DLI 2019 events in Aalborg, Denmark November 7–8, 2019.

Reference

1. United Nations: Technology and Innovation Report 2018. Harnessing Frontier Technologies for Sustainable Development. United Nations, New York, Geneva (2018). https://unctad.org/en/PublicationsLibrary/tir2018_en.pdf

VR Situated Simulations

Thore Soneson[1]([✉]), Michael Johansson[1], Barbro Bruce[2], Kerstin Ahlqvist[2], and Camilla Siotis Ekberg[2]

[1] Digital Design, Kristianstad University, 29188 Kristianstad, Sweden
{thore.soneson,michael.johansson}@hkr.se
[2] Educational Sciences, Kristianstad University, 29188 Kristianstad, Sweden
{barbro.bruce,Kerstin.ahlqvist,camilla.siotis.ekberg}@hkr.se

Abstract. In this paper we discuss our experiences developing mediated learning situations in a VR-filmed context. This requires solutions where co-design and innovative teams with knowledge and skills from different areas join forces. Here we try to make use of previous projects in collaborative design to develop forms for mediated learning situations in a VR-based context. We design a process where stakeholders in different roles are engaged in all or some parts of the process in which learning occurs, from scriptwriting for interactive media to creating and editing the case studies in an interactive VR format to in the end having students experience, discuss and evaluate them. The cases we employ are developed from the need for more experience-based knowledge in the field of Work Integrated Learning (WIL).

Keywords: Work Integrated Learning · Digital Design · Virtual reality · Learning lab

1 Background

During the spring of 2019, Kristianstad University HKR established the Learning Lab 1.0 project, where a multidisciplinary team from the Faculty of Education and the Department of Design together explored and identified learning situations, technical platforms and software environments that could enable research-based development of pedagogy, methodology and learning experiences. The focus is on developing mediated learning situations in a VR-filmed context, a process that requires solutions where co-design and innovative teams with knowledge and skills from different areas join forces.

We made use of knowledge and experience from previous projects in collaborative spatial design [1], to develop formats for mediated learning situations in a VR-based context, see Fig. 1. Using this model, all members of the team were stakeholders with different roles in different phases of the process. In the initial Editor phase, the tasks were to write scripts, co-create, edit and test the filmed material and to make it interactive. In the second Player phase, the students were asked to work with the cases in an interactive VR format and, at the same time, document and analyze their experiences along with those of the teachers and researchers.

© ICST Institute for Computer Sciences, Social Informatics and Telecommunications Engineering 2020
Published by Springer Nature Switzerland AG 2020. All Rights Reserved
A. Brooks and E. I. Brooks (Eds.): ArtsIT 2019/DLI 2019, LNICST 328, pp. 730–738, 2020.
https://doi.org/10.1007/978-3-030-53294-9_56

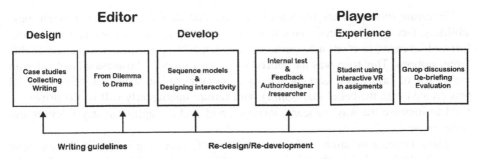

Fig. 1. Schematic model of our VR-simulation workprocess

It has long been considered problematic in professional education and training that students gain only limited insight into how their theoretical knowledge can be implemented in a real-life working context. On the other hand, what a student gains through experience in Work Integrated Learning (WIL) is at risk of including too little theoretical content. However, the connection between theoretical and practical knowledge is often only expressed in words without any direct connection to lived experiences, why there is a great need for more experience-based information to really understand [2, 3].

Work integrated learning (WIL) has the potential to meet this challenge, but there remains a problematic factor, namely that the individual student will encounter specific and random experiences that occur at the time and place where the WIL-period is set. This means that the student may well miss out on some types of relevant experiences, particularly those occurring less frequently or those that might be highly problematic. The diversity of students' experiences during WIL will also lead to a lack of common ground within the classroom, when experiences should be discussed and analysed together with other students and teachers. Our project aims to create common experiences in a VR setting to help establish common ground to support culture of discussion and theorizing and prepare for more constructive discussions of unique experiences which will always occur in real-life.

2   Research Issues

– Use VR-technology to simulate pedagogical challenges and dilemmas in life situations
– Achieve active learning through interactive, digital technologies

In our Learning Lab 1.0 project we conducted a workshop-based series in close collaboration with teachers and students and developed models supporting dilemma-based VR-movies. The aim here is to create an awareness of different situations and perspectives that students will encounter in their future professions.

The model for developing cases for simulation that we outline in Fig. 1 is implemented in two cases, based on actual situations and experience from work related programs at HKR. Together with lecturers from the Faculty of Health Sciences and Landscape Science Program, we designed and scripted dilemma-based scenarios. The specific aim here was to create VR material as a relevant case in an existing course and to use this as study material for an examination.

To create awareness and pre-knowledge the student will have to try different possibilities, face consequences, make mistakes and retry again; here we employ a "fail forward" scenario to create a deeper understanding of the possible consequences of different options. This term was introduced by Ashley Good, a business consultant who makes use of failure as a learning activity in workshops and scenarios: "Fail Forward was created with the belief that dealing with failure intelligently will be the driver we need to improve the way we learn, innovate, and find the agility to stay relevant and competitive."

These fictional situations and cases can be rarely occurring in real life for example during the WIL-period in education programs. However, in an educational "safe" model student can acquire knowledge of both the situation itself, and their own reactions and actions, in an ethically challenging and demanding situation.

Here we see a clear parallel with research being done in the field of interactive games. Game theorist and assistant professor Jesper Juul at The Department of Game Design at New York University NYU notes in the essay "The Art of Failure" [4] that we seek out failure to experience something we avoid in real life: "1. We generally avoid failure. 2. We experience failure when playing games. 3. We seek out games, although we will experience something that we normally avoid. This paradox of failure is parallel to the paradox of why we consume tragic theatre, novels, or cinema even though they make us feel sadness, fear, or even disgust."

In the workshops we emphasize that students during their studies in higher education must meet a variety of challenges some of which may not even occur during their WIL. This can lead them to feel better prepared to face ethical education challenges in real life. Preparing the students for a WIL can be positive and increase security [5, 6] (Fig. 2).

Fig. 2. Still from a scenario-based VR-case for training and preparing special teachers for a WIL period.

In a pilot case for Learning lab 1.0 made in 2017/2018, we produced a VR-case setup in a classroom situation were the teacher's ambition was to get the 9–12-year-old pupils to focus on the class and an upcoming exam. The film was shown for a group of WIL-teachers in special needs education who found it straightforward, relevant and close to reality. However, they also expressed that the teacher character had a too strong focus, whereas a wider perspective on the whole learning environment was hard to grasp. From this feedback we learned that the script for a VR-case setup must have an obvious focus on the expected learning outcome for the students.

The respondents in the pilot project reported that they had the perception of being present in the classroom and that they appreciated being able to rewind the film and the fact that all students could experience the same case. The two latter aspects are clearly not possible in the regular Work Experience parts of the education, so these are salient benefits that we see in using VR-film as a complement to WIL in vocational training. As one of our students put it "There is a great potential in simulating problematic situations that you cannot realistically experience under ordinary observing conditions". Another aspect is the potential for early preparation of students for challenging situations which cannot easily be planned out in other ways. As another student stated, "It can be an ethically important point to be prepared for encounters that occur in the reality of the work setting" [7].

Furthermore, the use of VR cases can improve the process around examinations and make them more legally secure. Students need to be invited to a more immersed and simulated activity to cope with the learning outcomes. Persson Aronsson [8] believes that it is important to use different forms of examination to be able to give a formative assessment, known as "feed forward". To use formative assessment can increase the efficiency of the teaching [9]. We see exciting opportunities for using VR-recorded film and providing formative assessment and feedback where the students are allowed to conduct a final examination with VR glasses.

2.1 VR - "Being There"

In a VR filmed scenario, it is possible for someone to assume a different identity, perhaps being immersed in a child's situation or one of a person´s with a disability. This addresses knowledge at an insight level, not necessarily vocalized, that could enhance empathic understanding. Virtual reality enables [10] immersion into a body of a person of a different social/ethnic/gender or another salient category. Such experiences have been shown to reduce stereotypes and prejudice toward those with different appearances, behaviour and reactions.

VR-systems today are supposed to deliver encompassing, immersive and vivid experiences where the user's interactions, movements and voice is matched to the system's "creation of a world where the users finds themselves, and thus entails psychological, and perceptual feeling of being present in the situation" [11], There are also symbolic aspects of VR-film, namely that the participants relate semantic and psychological factors to their own emotions, beliefs and value-systems [12].

One consideration when working with 360 video and cameras pointing in all directions at once is that this creates a spherical scene in which the user can look up, down and around using headsets. The 360 videos also place the user in a specific point in space. This underlines the importance of where to put the camera in a scene when it is being filmed, and to reflect upon who is watching and from where? There is also a need to find ways for a visitor to interact and experience these filmed VR scenarios, without too much prior knowledge of how to enter, navigate and perceive them, and in order to have the visitor feel both present and immersed by them. There is always a risk with new, technologies that have not been seen or experienced before that we will have the students exploring the technology itself rather than the topic of our attention.

2.2 Learning Lab 1.0

In our ongoing project Learning Lab 1.0 we construct and explore this immersive capacity. We do experiments with an initial repertoire of tools from game mechanics, using rhetorical and interactive models supporting our aim to develop dramaturgical tools and interactivity in Virtual Reality. VR engages multiple senses – sound/hearing, visuals/words/sight and space/body movement – to create immersion and presence. Creating active choices from multiple inputs demands a setup of affordances that are viable and realistic given the situation. A form of active learning is the notion of "failing forward" that we use as a learning element in its own right.

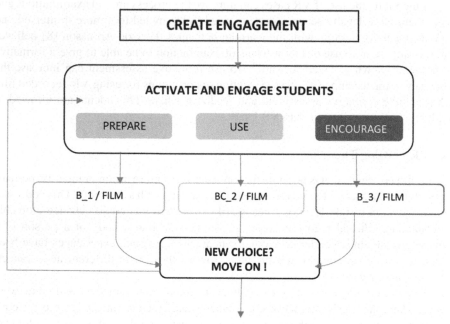

Fig. 3. Example of one of the sequence models used in developing script and dramatic dilemmas.

In the project, Learning Lab 1.0, we create a first generation of cases and examples. We emphasize development of an interactive technique, supporting exploration of how to take pedagogical advantage of dramaturgic strategies using dilemma-based situations. One important goal with this material will be to allow the students to develop a readiness to meet and integrate different perspectives and be confronted with new and unfamiliar situations. These capabilities are required in their future professions.

So far, we recorded and edited two cases with VR technologies and these interactive cases are tested out with students during the semester late 2019. The preliminary feedback supports our initial presumption that dilemma-based scenarios enacted with interactive VR technology can be used as part of the learning process. The overall response was positive regarding the possibility of experiencing work-related issues and situations before they encounter them in their professions. It appears that the interactive scenarios create an engaged experience, challenging them to respond and reflect.

Several questions among the test-students raised the possibility of creating good examples as a result of the dilemmas instead of scripting open-ended scenarios as were designed for the VR-cases. In our initial workshops and script design we discussed this at length. Our main argument against using good examples as a pedagogical tool were that we intended the interactive dilemma-based scenarios to be a method for active learning rather than creating a manual for good practice in their future profession. See Fig. 3 - flowchart for a dilemma-based script.

We have constantly throughout this project let the students give feedback on how feasible and usable the idea is. For example, we invited a group of special education teacher students to try out the pilot project's first VR-adapted film and then participate in a focus group interview. The feedback we got was that the fictional lesson based on authentic challenges was perceived as relevant, authentic and common. On the other hand, the students made us aware of the fact that the sound recording had a great focus on the teacher and that the ethical pedagogical challenge needed to be more clearly defined and portrayed. However, the interactive VR production felt realistic, almost like being "there" when you walked around in the classroom with VR glasses. They also thought it was good that everyone could see and discuss the same case. There are more opportunities for a different kind of discussion than there are if the students bring unique examples of challenges. We see the use of VR-recorded movies as a complement to practical WIL as an great opportunity.

3 Case Oriented Learning

To simulate, and engage the students in, these dilemmas we employ theories and knowledge from the interaction design field and game theory, using dramaturgical tools as described by Carolyn Miller in "Digital Storytelling" [13] – "Games provide an attractive solution because they involve competition, contain obstacles and a goal…" The interactor, in our case the student, is interacting with the scenarios in a "stimulus and response" manner, a classic game mechanic that forms a basis for digital interaction models used to create immersive involvement and engagement.

In a dilemma-based setup such as ours this interaction model can be used as a pedagogical tool; we construct cases with multiple choice scenarios for enacting possible real situations and outcomes. Using storytelling in active learning environments is not unique – on the contrary, scriptwriting in both analog and digital contexts is based on our common understanding and knowledge of how narratives are constructed. As Janet Murray writes in "Hamlet on Holodeck" [14] – "Once we understand simulations and interpretations of the world, the hand behind the multiform plot will feel as firmly present as the hand of the traditional author". Murray's classic takes on digital storytelling were formulated two decades ago and her assumptions are still a reality today; we accept and understand the relation between the real world and the interactive scenarios almost intuitively since they are constructed with classical storytelling tools.

In order to prepare the students for their working life, it is necessary that they can be offered opportunities to try out different approaches, and also to fail at times. Failing for learning is "failing forward" [15], but in training for professional life, such as being a special education teacher, it is not ethically acceptable to fail when there are actual and vulnerable children involved. Constructed as a VR-case, however, trial and error, risk-taking and failure, as well as success, is admissible and could be encouraged for the sake of learning.

4 Conclusion

Developing a digital learning environment that bridges over the current gap between theoretical and practical knowledge demands both competencies regarding the learning process in a broad sense, and competencies regarding VR production. This in turn presupposes a close-knit contact between research, distribution and educational sciences as applied in the classroom. To achieve these prerequisites, our findings suggest that it is necessary to involve students, lecturers and producers both in the initial phase and in evaluation to create educational VR-media. Otherwise the novelty and amazement of the technology in itself can hinder the actual learning benefits. This is similar to the way pilots during a training period use simulation of authentic and real situations [6]. Research and development of VR technology clearly shows that the experience differs fundamentally from that of 2D video, instead of watching from a distance you are in the center of events. Such a development of Work Integrated Learning (WIL) have the potential to create both pedagogical benefits and commercial profits in the learning sector.

Our experiences have directed us at possible implications in different educational contexts. For example, preservice special needs education students have been exposed to VR recordings of a dynamic assessment and trained in discussing the case with their peers. The benefits were twofold: first with respect to the ethical dilemma mentioned above, and second, a ground for future collaboration was established. That said, the experiences to date are already applicable at a general level for education. This could prove especially useful because the technology allows relational competencies to be targeted, which is broadly applicable, especially in health professions, where social factors and interpersonal meetings are central to the profession. Similar needs are also prevalent in professions of a more administrative or practical character, such as Human Resource professionals and Landscape scientists, where organizational matters or exercising authority can entail difficult meetings with concerned parties.

5 Future Work

In Learning Lab 2.0, we will continue to invite people early into the design process to broaden and deepening their understanding of what digital media is and how it can be used. They will then better understand, from their own expertise and experience, what kind of VR based tools and experiences they can build and put forward and use in their classrooms. As soon as next year, 2020, there will be a VR in the classroom course in the department of Higher Education Development at HKR based on the outcome of our pilots.

For the Digital Design program at HKR, we want to develop methods and environments to conduct better studio-based and online learning, and to further develop what we, since 2016, have done through introducing the Padlet platform [16] as our main platform for tutoring ongoing design work. The available VR environments that we tried out so far (Wonda spaces [17] and Oculus room [18]) are not yet open for collaborations using a variety of digital media. Further experiments using studio-based environment online are therefore necessary.

References

1. Fröst, P. Johansson, M., Warrén, P.: Computer games in architectural design. In: International ACM SIGGROUP Conference on Supporting Group Work (2001)
2. Samuelsson, M., Arvola, M., Nordvall, M., Stenliden, L.: Simuleringsbaserad undervisning som ett kompletterande inslag i lärarutbildningen vid Linköpings universitet, Sweden
3. Samuelsson, M.: Specialpedagogisk identifikation och problematisering av ett simulerat klassrumsledarskap, 1st edn. In: Eriksson Gustavsson, A.L., Frykedal, K.F., Samuelsson, M. (eds.) Specialpedagogik: i, om, för och med praktiken, pp. 116–134. Liber, Stockholm (2016)
4. Juul, J.: The Art of Failure: An Essay on the Pain of Playing Video Games. MIT Press, Cambridge (2013)
5. Gardesten, J.: Den nödvändiga grunden. Underkännanden och erkännanden under lärarutbildningens verksamhetsförlagda delar. (Doktorsavhandling). Linnéuniversitetet, Växjö (2016)
6. Lamb, R.: Virtual reality simulates classroom environment for aspiring teachers. http://www.buffalo.edu/news/releases/2017/06/038.html. Accessed 21 May 2019
7. Ahlqvist, K., Bruce, B.: Tekniken som svar på etiken i praktiken – virtuellt förberedd VFU. Högskolepedagogisk debatt **2**, 68–76 (2018)
8. Persson Aronsson, M.: Examinera att "uttrycka sig lekfullt musikaliskt" i förskollärarutbildningen men hur? I: I. Att förändra undervisning - mot studentcentrerat lärande och blended learning. Karlstads universitet Universitetspedagogiska enheten Karlstad, Sweden (2017)
9. Hattie, J., Timperley, H.: The power of feedback. Rev. Educ. Res. **77**(1), 81–112 (2007). University of Auckland, New Zealand
10. Herrera, F., Bailenson, J., Weisz, E., Ogle, E., Zaki, J.: Building long-term empathy: a largescale comparison of traditional and virtual reality perspective-taking (2018). https://doi.org/10.1371/journal.pone.0204494
11. Slater, M., Wilbur, S.: A framework for immersive virtual environments (FIVE): speculations on the role of presence in virtual environments. Teleoperators Virtual Environ. **6**(6), 603–616 (1997)
12. Dede, C.: Immersive interfaces for engagement and learning. Science **323**(5910), 66–69 (2009)
13. Miller, C.: Digital Storytelling. A Creator's Guide to Interactive Entertainment, p. 67. Routledge, London (2014)
14. Murray, J.: Hamlet on the Holodeck: The Future of Narrative in Cyberspace, p. 275. MIT press, Cambridge (1998)
15. Ashley Good, quoted from the company website: https://failforward.org/#home. Accessed 05 Jul 2019

16. Padlet Homepage. https://padlet.org. Accessed 05 Jul 2019
17. Wonda spaces. https://spaces.wondavr.com/lab. Accessed 05 Jul 2019
18. Oculus rooms Homepage. https://www.oculus.com/experiences/go/1101959559889232/?loc ale=sv_SE. Accessed 05 Jul 2019

Head-Mounted Display-Based Virtual Reality as a Tool to Reduce Disruptive Behavior in a Student Diagnosed with Autism Spectrum Disorder

Ali Adjorlu$^{(\boxtimes)}$ and Stefania Serafin

Aalborg University Copenhagen, Copenhagen, Denmark
{adj,sts}@create.aau.dk

Abstract. In this paper, we present a study investigating the feasibility of using Virtual Reality (VR) to reduce disruptive classroom behavior of a child diagnosed with Autism Spectrum Disorder (ASD). The child shows extensive, aggressive behavior in the classroom, making it hard for the teacher to teach him and his classmates. Even when receiving one-to-one lectures by a professional teacher, without the presence of other students, the child shows disruptive behavior. However, when receiving lectures in a virtual environment by a teacher, the child was calm, focused, and capable of working on his assignments without showing any disruptive behaviors. Even if the study has been applied to one single child, the promising results can be extended to more children showing similar behaviors.

Keywords: Virtual Reality · Autism Spectrum Disorder · Disruptive classroom behavior

1 Introduction

Disruptive behaviors in a classroom such as aggression, throwing and destroying objects or shouting, have a negative consequence on teachers' ability to disseminate knowledge to their students. Additionally, these negative behaviors can also have a far-reaching adverse effect on the learning motivations and classroom experience of both the students performing the disruptive behavior as well as their classmates [1].

Teachers employed in various special education programs face a difficult challenge dealing with disruptive behaviors with studies indicating that 14% to 38% of students with mental disabilities are engaging in disruptive and aggressive

The authors wish to thank the teacher Bo Jakobsen, the student from Skovmoseskolen and his parents for their participation, feedback and support during this study. Additionally, we would like to thank Sune Buch-Sloth from Rødovre municipality for putting us in touch with Skovmoseskolen.

A. Brooks and E. I. Brooks (Eds.): ArtsIT 2019/DLI 2019, LNICST 328, pp. 739–748, 2020.
https://doi.org/10.1007/978-3-030-53294-9_57

practices in the classroom [2]. Additionally, learning disabilities are pervasive among children diagnosed with Autism Spectrum Disorder (ASD), making the detrimental effects of disruptive classroom behavior even more prominent for the learning outcome of this specific target group [3]. Individuals diagnosed with ASD find it difficult to cope with unexpected changes in their environments [4], while they struggle with situations that require social skills such as a classroom environment. These difficulties can trigger negative classroom behavior by students diagnosed with ASD [5].

This emphasizes the importance of interventions that can help to reduce disruptive behavior in classrooms with students diagnosed with ASD, thereby increasing their learning outcome and helping them towards independent adulthood and positive participation in society.

Adults diagnosed with ASD are often dependent on parents or social agencies for support throughout their lives. A study conducted by Howling et al. indicate that only 8 out of 68 adults diagnosed with ASD were employed while only 3 out of the 68 participants did not live with their parents [6]. Another study measuring the adult outcome of individuals diagnosed with ASD shows that out of 48 participants, only one was employed while 44 lived with families or in a shared home with caretakers [7]. Studies indicate that school refusal behavior is observed in approximately 40% to 50% of students diagnosed with ASD, partially due to disruptive behavior [8].

Reducing disruptive behavior in the learning environments of children diagnosed with ASD might help to increase their motivation for going to school and improve their learning outcome which can results in employment upon adulthood and less dependent on parents and social agencies and generally better quality of life. Finally, a high prevalence rate of 1 out of every 50 children further emphasizes the importance of creating classroom environments with less disruptive behaviors for this target group [9].

Virtual Reality (VR) interventions have been used to help individuals with a variety of different mental disorders such as anxieties [10], anorexia [12], substance use disorders [11], and post-traumatic stress [13]. Using head-mounted displays, VR creates the opportunity to replace the users' real-world sensory information with digitally created sensory information designed to help with a variety of challenges. In this paper, we want to investigate whether VR technologies can be used to help a child diagnosed with ASD and who frequently show extensive disruptive in the classroom. A study conducted by Strickland et al. in 1996 illustrated that children diagnosed with ASD are capable of accepting, interact with and getting immersed in a head-mounted display (HMD) based VR intervention [14]. Since then, several studies indicate that HMD based VR environments have the potential to teach social and everyday living skills to children diagnosed with ASD. Adjorlu et al. created a VR supermarket training intervention within which, children diagnosed with ASD could practice shopping skills by navigating in the virtual supermarket and picking up items on their virtual shopping list [15]. Another study showed the potentials of HMD based VR to teach social skills to children diagnosed with ASD by placing the child inside a virtual classroom, within which one could practice how to share toys and take turn playing in a virtual school environment [16]. Another study illustrated the potentials of VR to practice basic math and purchasing skills for adolescents diagnosed with ASD [17]. In general, these studies have shown that VR interventions have the potential to be used as learning environments within which children and adolescents diagnosed with ASD can rehearse a variety of skills in a safe, interactive environment. Rebecca Adams et al. investigated whether a virtual reality classroom can be used to distinguish between children diagnosed with Attention Deficit Disorder and typically developing children [18]. The virtual classroom proved to be ecologically valid enough to be used as an assessment tool of the participants' mental diagnoses. In this study, we want to investigate whether an interactive virtual learning environment can reduce disruptive behavior compared to a traditional classroom environment.

2 Method

2.1 Participant

The participant is a nine years old student at Skovmoseskolen, a school for children with mental disorders located in Rødovre municipality in Denmark. He is a ten years old male diagnosed with ASD as well as some other psychiatric diagnoses. The teachers of the school are not allowed to share more information on the rest of his mental diagnoses due to personal data security policies in Denmark. However, they stated that the participant is on the high-functioning side of the autism spectrum. The participant shows great willingness to learn in school, wanting to be good at all of the subjects. However, whenever the participant has a hard time understanding a topic, he performs disruptive behaviors. These behaviors include getting verbally abusive towards the teachers and other students, reducing the general level of the lectures for him and his classmates. The teachers have to spend their energy trying to calm him down, making it hard for them to continue teaching. The participant's disruptive behavior gets further exaggerated when it is time to solve assignments in the classroom. The smallest challenge in his school assignments triggers actions such as throwing objects on the ground, towards the teachers or other students. He has also been observed hitting his fellow students and the teachers in the face. Once he initiates his disruptive actions, the teachers can't calm him down again. The only way the teachers can calm him down is by taking him out of the classroom into a different room until he calms down again. As an attempt to reduce the participant's disruptive behaviors, the teachers tried giving him one to one lectures. They hoped that without the presence of other students, his disruptive behavior might be reduced. Unfortunately, even during one to one sessions with a teacher, he still performed disruptive behaviors such as throwing objects and hitting the teacher.

2.2 The VR Intervention

In this paper, we present a study investigating whether the participant's disruptive behavior in learning situations would reduce if he received lectures in an immersive VR classroom instead of a real-life classroom. The teachers of Skovmoseskolen presented a set of requirements for a VR application to be used to teach their students:

- The teacher and the student should be able to log into the same virtual environment simultaneously.
- The virtual environment should contain a big screen that can be used as a blackboard by the teacher to present the course material to the student.
- Both the student and the teacher should be able to manipulate the content on the big screen via a pointing device or keyboard while wearing a head-mounted display. This function was needed for having the student solving assignments while in the virtual environment.

Bigscreen VR[1] was chosen as the VR application to run this study since it lives up to the teachers' requirements. BigScreen VR was released in 2016 by a California based start-up company as an immersive telepresence platform designed to bring people together using VR. Users can log in to virtual environments such as living rooms within which they can watch movies, play games, browse the web, or hang out together. The application works on a wide variety of different head-mounted displays such as The Oculus Rift or the HTC Vive. Bigscreen VR includes a virtual keyboard as well as pointing devices that can be controlled using VR input devices such as the Oculus touch or the HTC Vive wands. Using the VR input devices, the users can control a virtual hand with which they can type on the virtual keyboard and point on the virtual screen (see Fig. 1).

Using the virtual screen, the users can navigate their real desktop computer, enabling the users to run desktop applications while being in an immersive virtual environment. The ability to use desktop applications in Bigscreen VR allows the teachers to facilitate assignments in the virtual learning environment using some of the digital tools they already use in the real classroom environment such as skoltube[2] and bookcreator[3]. Skoletube is a teaching material production and distribution platform designed for teachers and students in the Danish elementary schools. Using skoltube, the teachers can create interactive assignments and share them with their students, who can then work on them using tablets and computers. Similarly, book creators another platform that allows the teachers to create and distribute interactive learning material by combining text, images, audio, and video. BigscreenVR enables the teacher and the student to work on assignment created via skoletube and book creator in an immersive, interactive virtual environment.

---

[1] https://bigscreenvr.com/.
[2] https://www.skoletube.dk/.
[3] https://bookcreator.com/.

Fig. 1. Screenshot from BigscreenVR application. The application enables the user to control windows desktop using a virtual keyboard and once finger as the pointing device

2.3   Results

Fig. 2. The participant logged in to the virtual environment in one room while the teacher is logged into the virtual environment from another room (buttom right). Screenshot from the teachers view (top right).

The participant received lectures by a teacher in a virtual environment using Bigscreen VR three times a week for a period of two months. The participant's parents signed a consent form, agreeing to him receiving lectures in a virtual environment using Bigscreen VR and participating in this study. Additionally, they also allowed him to be photographed during the first session. The participant logged into Bigscreen VR using the HTC Vive VR. The teacher also logged into Bigscreen VR using a HTC Vive as seen in Fig. 2. The teacher's computer was located in a room next to the room where the participant received his lectures in order to further immerse the participant into the virtual environment. Using Bigscreen VR, both the teacher and the participant entered a virtual living room with two big couches and a big virtual screen as seen in Fig. 1, 3 and 4. The teacher used the big screen in the virtual living room as a projector screen in a real-life classroom to give the participant lectures in math and Danish. Each session with a lecture lasted approximately 20 min, followed by a break. After the break, there would be another session in the virtual classroom where the child and the teacher would solve math and language assignments together. There was an employee from the IT department present in the room with the participant during the sessions. A camera filmed the participant during some but not all of the VR lectures. During all of the VR lecture sessions observed in this study, the participant did not showed any of the disruptive behaviors that he used to perform in the real-life classroom. He was calm during all of the lectures in VR, listening to the teacher, and asking appropriate questions when in doubt.

Fig. 3. The teacher's avatar seen from the participant's perspective in the virtual environment

In the real classroom environment, the participant's disruptive behaviors was the most aggressive when he was asked to solve assignments. This would usually result in him throwing objects, beating his classmates, and sometimes the teachers. However, when doing assignments in the virtual environment, he did not show any disruptive behavior during all of the sessions observed. He was however still verbally critical towards his level of skills and knowledge saying sentences such as "I am so bad at this", "Why will I never learn anything" and "I am so stupid". According to the teacher participating in the study, he was often capable of solving the assignment and illustrated improved skills in math and Danish compared to when he was doing the tasks in the real classroom environment. During the two months when he participated in lectures in the virtual environment, his disruptive behavior did not change when participating in the real-world classroom environment. Following the two months of this study, the teachers of the school agreed that this participant should continue receiving lectures in the virtual environment twice a week. Additionally, the school has decided to use the same approach for future students who illustrate the same level of disruptive behavior. Six months after the study, the authors of this paper contacted the school again to ask if there had been any changes in the participants' disruptive behavior in the real classroom and the virtual classroom. According to the teacher doing the lectures in the virtual classroom, the participant's disruptive behavior in the real-classroom remained unchanged. He still gets mad often, throwing stuff, shouts and beats the students and the teachers. He still receives lectures once or twice a week in Bigscreen VR where he still remains calm and focuses even after six months of exposure to VR.

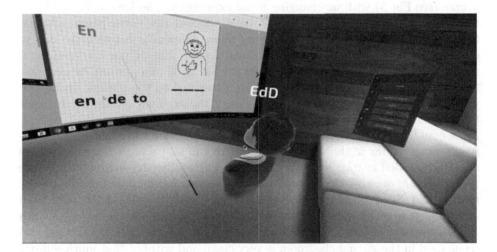

Fig. 4. The participant doing language assignments. Seen from the teacher's prospective in the virtual environment

2.4   Discussion and Conclusion

In this project, we presented an explorative study, investigating whether lectures in a virtual classroom environment can reduce disruptive behavior in a 9-year-old student diagnosed with ASD. For two months, the participant received math and Danish lectures in an HMD-based virtual environment, taught by a teacher who logged into the same virtual environment. During all of the VR lectures, the participant did not show any disruptive behavior. In general, children and adolescents diagnosed with ASD enjoy using computers and computer games due to their predictability and reduced requirements for social skills [20]. This can explain the reduced disruptive behavior in the participant while receiving lectures in a virtual environment. The participant learned how to use Bigscreen VR application, understanding what buttons to press to log in to the room in which he would meet his teacher. Additionally, the participant was capable of interacting with the big screen in the virtual environment. The system was predictable compare to the real classroom environment, where non-foreseen events often occur.

In the real-classroom, the participant showed disruptive behavior even when the teaching was done using learning applications on tablet computers. The tablets were used in the real classroom: an unpredictable environment requiring communication skills and the ability to analyze social cues. Even when receiving one to one lectures by one teacher without the presence of other students and with the help of tablet-computer based teaching tools, the participant showed disruptive behavior. Virtual reality enables the removal of all of the elements that are usually related to unpredictability and require social skills to navigate. Additionally, the teacher's avatar in the virtual environment was a low-fidelity avatar (see Fig. 3) with no changing facial expression. The low-fidelity and cartoonish looking teacher avatar might have affected the participant's attitude towards the social situation. One of the main differences between the one to one lecture in the real world and the virtual environment was the number of social cues communicated by the teacher via his facial and gestural expressions. The reduced amount of social information presented to the student during the virtual lectures in Bigscreen VR can be one of the explanations for his excellent behavior during these sessions.

It could be interesting for future studies to investigate whether a more realistic teacher avatar in the virtual environment can still achieve the same results as a low detailed avatar in Bigscreen VR. Additionally, the environment of the real classroom presents the student with a large amount of unpredictable sensory information. Studies indicate that individuals diagnosed with ASD suffer from abnormal sensory information processing, making it hard for them to cope with situations that presents them with a lot of sensory information [21]. The virtual scene used in the virtual classroom is very clean and without that much sensory information, as seen in Figs. 1, 2, 3, and 4, which can be another reason for the excellent behavior of the student.

Unfortunately, the positive behavior observed in the virtual environment was not transferred into the real-world environment, either after two or six months of exposure to the VR learning environment. In general, children and adolescents diagnosed with ASD have difficulties transferring knowledge gained in one context into another [22]. Future interventions could, by gradually increasing the level of social cues and avatar fidelities of the teacher in the virtual environment as well as sensory information in the virtual classroom, attempt to prepare the student for the real-life class that includes a variable amount of sensory information and social cues.

In this study, no attempts were made to measure the learning outcome of the lectures in VR directly. Future studies should investigate whether learning outcome in an HMD-based virtual environment is compatible with the learning outcome in a real-life classroom. Based on the teacher who ran the VR lectures, the participant seemed focused, solved assignments, and showed an increase in his knowledge when receiving lectures in Danish and math in the virtual environment. In general, the VR intervention showed great potential in reducing the participant's disruptive behavior while learning as well as showing potential in teaching academic skills. However, learning in a virtual environment only with another teacher will not help develop social skills, especially for individuals diagnosed with ASD who require learning how to behave in social contexts such as classrooms. One way to include social skills training in a virtual classroom application could be to allow for more than one student to login to the virtual classroom, making it more similar to a real class. By allowing more students to log in to the same virtual classroom can decrease the social isolation of the participant while providing the opportunity for him to learn social skills.

Additionally, further studies are required to understand the consequences of prolonged usage of head-mounted displays before implementing them as an everyday routine of school and learning establishments.

References

1. Scattone, D., Wilczynski, S.M., Edwards, R.P., Rabian, B.: Decreasing disruptive behaviors of children with autism using social stories. J. Autism Dev. Disord. **32**(6), 535–543 (2002)
2. Repp, A.C., Karsh, K.G.: A taxonomic approach to the nonaversive treatment of maladaptive behavior of persons with developmental disabilities. In: Perspectives on the Use of Nonaversive and Aversive Interventions for Persons with Developmental Disabilities, pp. 331–347 (1990)
3. O'Brien, G., Pearson, J.: Autism and learning disability. Autism **8**(2), 125–140 (2004)
4. DSM-5 American Psychiatric Association: Diagnostic and statistical manual of mental disorders. American Psychiatric Publishing, Arlington (2013)
5. Gerdtz, J.: Evaluating behavioral treatment of disruptive classroom behaviors of an adolescent with autism. Res. Soc. Work Pract. **10**(1), 98–110 (2000)
6. Howlin, P., et al.: Adult outcome for children with autism. J. Child Psychol. Psychiatry **45**(2), 212–229 (2004)
7. Eaves, L.C., Ho, H.H.: Young adult outcome of autism spectrum disorders. J. Autism Dev. Disord. **38**(4), 739–747 (2008)
8. Munkhaugen, E.K., Gjevik, E., Pripp, A.H., Sponheim, E., Diseth, T.H.: School refusal behaviour: are children and adolescents with autism spectrum disorder at a higher risk? Res. Autism Spectrum Disord. **41**, 31–38 (2017)
9. Xu, G., Strathearn, L., Liu, B., Bao, W.: Prevalence of autism spectrum disorder among US children and adolescents, 2014–2016. Jama **319**(1), 81–82 (2018)

10. Botella, C., Fernández-Álvarez, J., Guillén, V., García-Palacios, A., Baños, R.: Recent progress in virtual reality exposure therapy for phobias: a systematic review. Curr. Psychiatry Rep. **19**(7), 42 (2017)

11. Hone-Blanchet, A., Wensing, T., Fecteau, S.: The use of virtual reality in craving assessment and cue-exposure therapy in substance use disorders. Front. Hum. Neurosci. **8**, 844 (2014)

12. Mölbert, S.C., et al.: Assessing body image in anorexia nervosa using biometric self-avatars in virtual reality: attitudinal components rather than visual body size estimation are distorted. Psychol. Med. **48**(4), 642–653 (2018)

13. Rizzo, A.S., et al.: Development and early evaluation of the virtual Iraq/Afghanistan exposure therapy system for combat-related PTSD. Ann. N. Y. Acad. Sci. **1208**(1), 114–125 (2010)

14. Strickland, D., et al.: Brief report: two case studies using virtual reality as a learning tool for autistic children. J. Autism Dev. Disord. **26**(6), 651–659 (1996)

15. Adjorlu, A., Høeg, E.R., Mangano, L., Serafin, S.: Daily living skills training in virtual reality to help children with autism spectrum disorder in a real shopping scenario. In: 2017 IEEE International Symposium on Mixed and Augmented Reality (ISMAR-Adjunct), October 2017, pp. 294–302. IEEE (2017)

16. Adjorlu, A., Hussain, A., Mødekjær, C., Austad, N.W.: Head-mounted display-based virtual reality social story as a tool to teach social skills to children diagnosed with autism spectrum disorder. In: 2017 IEEE Virtual Reality Workshop on K-12 Embodied Learning through Virtual & Augmented Reality (KELVAR). IEEE (2018)

17. Adjorlu, A., Serafin, S.: Head-mounted display-based virtual reality as a tool to teach money skills to adolescents diagnosed with autism spectrum disorder. In: Brooks, A.L., Brooks, E., Sylla, C. (eds.) ArtsIT/DLI -2018. LNICSSITE, vol. 265, pp. 450–461. Springer, Cham (2019). https://doi.org/10.1007/978-3-030-06134-0_48

18. Adams, R., Finn, P., Moes, E., Flannery, K., Rizzo, A.S.: Distractibility in attention/deficit/hyperactivity disorder (ADHD): the virtual reality classroom. Child Neuropsychol. **15**(2), 120–135 (2009)

19. Farley, M.A., et al.: Twenty-year outcome for individuals with autism and average or near average cognitive abilities. Autism Res. **2**(2), 109–118 (2009)

20. Chen, J., Wang, G., Zhang, K., Wang, G., Liu, L.: A pilot study on evaluating children with autism spectrum disorder using computer games. Comput. Hum. Behav. **90**, 204–214 (2019)

21. Leekam, S.R., Nieto, C., Libby, S.J., Wing, L., Gould, J.: Describing the sensory abnormalities of children and adults with autism. J. Autism Dev. Disord. **37**(5), 894–910 (2007)

22. Arnold-Saritepe, A.M., et al.: Generalization and maintenance. In: Matson, J. (ed.) Applied Behavior Analysis for Children with Autism Spectrum Disorders, pp. 207–224. Springer, New York (2009). https://doi.org/10.1007/978-1-4419-0088-3_12

The Reality of Implementing Virtual Reality: A Case Study on the Challenges of Integrating VR-Based Rehabilitation

Emil R. Høeg(✉)[iD], Christian F. R. Scully, Jon R. Bruun-Pedersen[iD], and Stefania Serafin[iD]

Department of Architecture, Design and Media Technology, Aalborg University Copenhagen, A.C. Meyers Vænge 15, Copenhagen, SV, Denmark
{erh,jpe,sts}@create.aau.dk
christian.scully@gmail.com

Abstract. This paper describes an explorative case study that investigates the declining use of a bespoke VR-based treatment tool for biking-based rehabilitation, through interviews with four physiotherapists and in situ observations of patient-therapist interactions, in a Danish municipal outpatient health center. Thematic analysis was used to identify pain points and challenges related to the integration of VR in both hardware, software and operation resources. Prospective solutions are proposed to increase usability of the system. Moreover, site-specific proposals, including knowledge translation and co-production initiatives, are suggested to increase the health workforce's incentive to use the VR-supplied service, and endorse it to the patients who attend treatment in the health center.

Keywords: Virtual reality · Rehabilitation · Applied science · Human-centred design · Integrated health services · Service design

1 Introduction

Throughout the last decades advancements have been made in public health, medical breakthrough and improved quality of living, which have contributed to people living longer and healthier. According to the latest report from the United Nations Population Division, 2018 became the first time in recorded human history where the worldwide number of people over the age of 65 outnumbered children under 5 years of age [21]. This development is not expected to decline. In fact, the world population is expected to reach 9.7 billion in 2050, where people ≥65 will account for approximately one fifth (1.7 billion) [21].

Consequently, healthcare systems around the world are challenged by the rapidly growing older population, an increase of chronic diseases, and the rising cost for the quantity and the types of care being delivered. Recently the World Health Organization (WHO) called for a fundamental paradigm shift as to how health services are funded, managed and delivered to meet the current

© ICST Institute for Computer Sciences, Social Informatics and Telecommunications Engineering 2020
Published by Springer Nature Switzerland AG 2020. All Rights Reserved
A. Brooks and E. I. Brooks (Eds.): ArtsIT 2019/DLI 2019, LNICST 328, pp. 749–759, 2020.
https://doi.org/10.1007/978-3-030-53294-9_58

and prospective challenges of the diverse range of healthcare-related needs [23]. Central to their proposals is a move towards people-centred and integrated health services, with an emphasis on a continuous and active dialogue between patients and health service providers e.g. [24]. Furthermore, they note that emerging technologies can allow for new types of services that can bring efficient and innovative forms of care [23]. However, change is a necessity of innovation that frequently leads to new challenges that can disrupt existing practices and cause organization turbulence [6]. Moreover, the economic, political and peer-pressure of 'being innovative' can sometimes lead to the rapid adaptation of unproven innovations and poor implementation of new services. Another evolving field with a special focus on service organization and user-involvement is service design. Service design uses, among other methods, a human-centred approach, and strive to use participatory approaches in all stages of the design process or when identifying existing challenges of innovation. Organizational culture has a paramount role when facilitating change, and thus, the health work-force should always be considered when implementing new health services [5,24]. Despite numerous studies using participatory research approaches to understand contextual conditions of health service innovations, most studies focus on the views of the patients [10,18,19,22]. To our knowledge, very few studies deliver insights to the perspectives and views of the healthcare-providing workforce (such as physiotherapists and occupational therapists).

1.1 Context of the Case Study

The context of this study is framed by an ongoing PhD-project on virtual reality (VR) based rehabilitation in the Danish municipality of Frederiksberg. The project investigates how VR-based rehabilitation and immersive exertion gaming (exergaming) can cultivate intrinsic motivation, increase training intensity and deliver potential analgesic benefits. The municipality invested in the VR equipment, and implemented in 2016, following the supervision of Jon Ram Bruun-Pedersen in two municipality healthcare facilities, consisting of an inpatient care unit offering rehabilitation treatment during admission, and a health center offering outpatient ambulatory rehabilitation. After a period of acclimatization and preliminary testing, the immersive VR (VR-mode), delivered with a high-end Head-Mounted Display (HMD), saw a decline in usage. However, the TV-based version (TV-mode) of the virtual environment (VE) kept being used in the centers in individual therapy as well as for group-based rehabilitation and exercising.

In this paper we investigate the decreasing trend in usage, and evaluate the challenges faced with the integration of a VR-based treatment tool. Furthermore, we seek to identify critical situations which have a negative impact on the process of using the VR therapy. These will need to be prospectively solved in order to increase the health workforce's incentive to use the VR-supplied service, and endorse it to the patients, in the outpatient health center.

2   Related Work

2.1   VR-Based Rehabilitation

Repetition is a key component in most areas of motor rehabilitation. Paradoxically, repetitive activities are often what causes lackluster performances by patients in rehabilitation contexts due to a lack of motivation, which can lead to non-adherence with the therapy itself [13]. Therefore, the capacity to provide distractions that instill motivation to continually train the same underlying deficit is of major relevance. Furthermore, rehabilitation efficacy is more commonly achieved, when patients are inspired through intrinsically motivating factors. This can be driven by internal rewards, such as pleasure in doing the activity because it is self-rewarding [15]. For example: Zimmerli *et al.* increased patient engagement for motor rehabilitation through exploration of a virtual environment (VE) in augmented, low-immersive VR (desktop-based) [25]; Bruun-Pedersen *et al.* inspired intrinsic motivation in nursing home residents through exploration of restorative virtual environments (RVEs), using both high-immersive VR (head-mounted displays) and desktop variations [2]; Lewis *et al.* sought to motivate training-habits through a game-based rehabilitation intervention for people with stroke [12]; H.G. Hoffman *et al.* has conducted several studies on the non-pharmacological analgesic benefit of VR for the daily care of patients with severe burn injuries [8,20];

In a recent review, Keshner and colleagues examine literature on VR-based rehabilitation from 1996–2018, and conclude that "the community exists through interlinked networks rather than a single, cohesive field of study" [11]. Furthermore, in relation to development and implementation, it is noted that it may happen so quickly, that the evidence for an intervention's efficacy, and establishment of research and development priorities, are often more reactive than proactive [11]. Moremore, they note that interprofessional team-based approaches will likely strengthen the impact of the technology through the implementation process.

2.2   Service Design and Healthcare

Service design is an evolving field with a keen focus on human-centred approaches to understanding, improving and redefining the relationship between service supplier and receiver within fields such as finance, travel, manufacturing nonprofits, health, education and government [9,17]. Improvement of services and the developing new value proposition based on user needs, are examples of the benefit that service design can provide organizations [17]. Service design is increasingly being valued as an in-house capability for healthcare suppliers. The increasing complexity of an aging population, the need for integrated healthcare solutions and responsive service offers [24] emphasize the need for innovative problem-solving, and a higher inclusion of human-centred design of such services [14], to counter negative associations affiliated with an ongoing adoption, continuous development, and validation studies of a non-matured technology.

Service design also frequently deals with the concepts of touch points and pain points. Touch points are the points of contact between a service provider and the receiver [4]. However, the touch point can also refer to an interaction with an inanimate object such as a building, a website, or in this case, a VR-based treatment tool. A pain point or fail points refers to a specific problem that a receiver of a service may encounter [16]. In this context, we refer to pain points to describe critical situations, and situations generating friction, that e.g. the physiotherapists may encounter when using usual care, TV-mode or VR-mode.

3   Materials and Methods

The main purpose of the exploratory case study was to determine the circumstances in which physiotherapists and occupational therapists would decide to use VR as part of the therapy. Additionally, we evaluate the challenges faced with the implementation, including pain points related to the use of VR, through observations and interviews with physiotherapists in the outpatient health center.

3.1   Existing Materials and Apparatus

The VR-equipment available to the therapists contains two pairs of Oculus Rift Consumer Version 1 (CV1) headsets, running on a high-end desktop gaming computer. The CV1 furthermore relies on external tracking from one or more motion trackers. The software provided is a set of RVEs consisting of 4 different unique, digitally generated virtual landscapes [3]. These environments can be viewed either on a ultra high definition (UHD) TV screen, or with aforementioned VR equipment. A virtual on-rail locomotion system generates forward momentum, either with a fixed speed mode (i.e. pre-programmed constant speed) or a feedback controlled mode, measuring the angular velocity of the foot-pedals on the training bike, with a custom-build wireless tracker (called GIRO) connected to the computer via wi-fi [7].

3.2   Interview with Physiotherapists

A semi-structured interview method was used for the interview with the physiotherapists, but the scope of themes were focused primarily on their experiences of testing and running the VR. The purpose was to gain an understanding of their initial experiences with VR in therapy-sessions, their professional assessment using VR as a physiotherapy tool, the challenges of integrating the usage patterns, how they incorporated VR into their existing work patterns, and the experiences of operating a new type of unfamiliar system.

Four physiotherapists were interviewed separately. Two of them were professionally experienced, while the other two were relatively new to their profession. Each physiotherapist was considered a domain expert, and assigned to a specific specialized area, such as heart and circuit training, cancer rehabilitation, chronic obstructive pulmonary disease (COPD), and geriatric physical therapy. Furthermore, questions related to the specific details of how they approached procedures related to the VR therapy.

3.3   Observations

Specific points in the physiotherapist's journey were captured through observations. More specifically, using the observer as participant approach i.e. the observer played a neutral role, but the purpose of his presence was of an overt nature to the participants [1]. Observations were conducted through several visits to the health center, over the cause of three weeks. The expected outcome was to understand the context of the physiotherapist's work, including the interactions with their patients and the tasks they had to perform, in order to execute a patient rehabilitation session which included documenting the sequence of their routines. For one of the sessions, six patients with COPD were observed in the biking room, during a 30 min interval exercise warm-up session that was conducted by the physiotherapist specialized in the area. The observation included the preparations for running the VR experience including the entire sequence of attaching the sensor to the bike and fitting the HMD to the patient's head. Shorter observations were also performed (with a duration between 5 and 15 min) interspersed between interviews, in an attempt to determine the accuracy and rigor of the initial observation, as well as gaining an overall impression of the center's general rehabilitation services.

4   Results

Through the explorative case study, we identified several challenges and threads to the continuous use of the VR equipment, as well as probable reasons for why it has not been more successful, in terms of integration of the service. Furthermore, through thematic analysis we have identified four categories in which to organize the data:

1. VR service (user-experience and usability)
2. Attitude and experiences of the therapist
3. Organizational culture
4. Feedback and dissemination

4.1   VR-Service: User-Experience and Usability Issues

A full session with VR-mode adds additional steps for the physiotherapist to perform, as preparation and execution when selecting a VR-based or TV based treatment type. These are related to a combination of hardware and/or software tasks, that also account for the identified pain points. The first pain point experienced also relates to the category of organization culture and maintenance of the equipment. To function properly, the pedal-sensors have to be charged daily.

The assignment of charging the sensors, has previously been delegated to the closing shift, but it has not been routinely adhered to. Therefore, physiotherapists intending to use the VR-mode, frequently find that sensors have not been charged. The connection to the GIRO-sensor is crucial for running the virtual environments in feedback-controlled mode (either VR or TV), and a disconnected sensor or depleted battery will cause a system-crash. Therefore, the fixed speed mode is the most frequently used, as it introduces the VE on the TV-screens, with no significant pain points or challenges. This mode does not afford user-feedback in the form of changes in speed based on exertion, thus the fixed speed mode is conveniently left running across multiple sessions, in a comparable manner to that of a non-interactive screen saver.

An additional pain point is added in relation to the VR-mode. i.e. when assisting patients putting on the headset and fitting it for individual head-size, and calibrating it to match the patient's individual interpupillary distance (IPD). In group-based therapy, this results in a biased attention to the one patient trying VR, while other patients are not observed or supervised as the physiotherapist are busy tending to the one trying VR. By comparison, usual care requires only the pre-existing steps already familiar to the therapist (see Fig. 1).

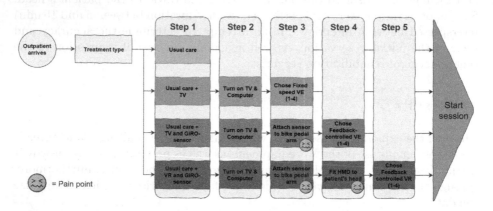

Fig. 1. Task dependency diagram showing the difference in amount of steps required to initiate a therapy with or without TV/VR-based therapy as well as identified pain points. The diagram presents a best-case scenario and does not include additional steps required in case of equipment malfunctions.

Moreover, Fig. 1 describes a best case-scenario, but physiotherapists have encountered issues in the form of a series of errors, occurring during the initializing process of the various interconnected components (headset, sensor, TV). This leads to additional steps and causes confusing situations for the physiotherapists, as these errors have been difficult to locate and solve on their own. The errors lead to delays of approximate 5 to 10 min, which subsequently cut into crucial patient-time. In relation to memorability, i.e. re-establish proficiency after a break in use, the sequence of the steps in the initializing process can be difficult for the physiotherapist to remember. Confusion can arise in situations when the set-up has altered since the last interaction, for instance how to strap the sensor to a new pedal arm, or to check the amount of potential reasons for equipment or system malfunctions. This could be anything from a depleted battery, accidental wi-fi IP-address reset, a disconnected cord, or Oculus Rift headset re-calibration requirements due to a shifted motion sensor.

4.2 Attitudes and Experience of the Therapist

The interviews with the physiotherapists revealed a certain skepticism about the benefits of applying VR to the therapy. This is further intensified by the fact that there is no systematic recording, reporting and evaluations of their collective experiences, related to the use of VR. Furthermore, no clear guidelines exist on the type of patients who could benefit from VR therapy. One physiotherapist suggested that enticement depends much on how the physiotherapist "sells it" to the group of patients in the waiting room. Positive reactions from patients have lead to surprising experience where patients have achieved a seemingly increased training efficacy, which have motivated another physiotherapist to keep recommending it to new patients. However, the use of VR is not at their priority list. The most common reasons given by physiotherapists are: frequently experienced reliability issues related to the technology or due to violations of the protocol (e.g. sensors have not been charged overnight); time pressure due to other strict timetabled tasks; and the extra steps required for setup and preparation of the VR-service.

One therapist uses a careful approach in order to reduce the patients nervousness, by ensuring that the patient can see the monitor first before starting the program, as opposed to having the patient sit with the goggles in pitch darkness, waiting for the physiotherapist to finish the last set-up tasks.

4.3 Organizational Culture

The interviews also clarified how the physiotherapists perceived the process of becoming acquainted with the technology. Showcasing of the VR technology has previously been organized by the management, but participation has been voluntary, and not everyone has had the opportunity to try VR themselves. One of therapists suggested that the use of VR eluded, due to a possible correlation between lack of endorsement and self-testing. Furthermore, a hands-on workshop was suggested for everyone, to get a chance to establish familiarity with the technology. New work routines connected to the VR therapy has been outlined and delegated by the center management; most notably, the previously mentioned task of recharging the sensors. However, an additional pain point may arise if the training room has been used for group therapy sessions. In that case therapists wanting to use VR may frequently find exercise bikes being turned away from the VR-setup and TV-monitor. Exercise bikes, weighing as much as 64 kg, then has to be rotated 180° before engaging in any other treatment type than usual care.

4.4   Feedback and Dissemination

According to the physiotherapists, the feedback they receive from the patients is mostly positive, and many patients find the experience fun and engaging. It is noted that some patients have experiences side-effects (such as nausea, oculomotor disturbances, and disorientation) during use, while others refuse to try it. One physiotherapist reported a near-fall experience which discouraged continuous use. However, overall the consensus was that the VR experiences tend to generate excitement among the patients, and has the capacity to add fun and motivating elements to the conventional therapy. However, currently there is no system in place to record and systematize the emerging collection of physiotherapist observations, experiences and anecdotes of patient-VR interactions (both positive and negative). Moreover, there are no official channels for reporting performance issues. At the moment if there is any handover information, it transports verbally between the therapists or to the functional leader.

5   Discussion

The case study gave valuable insights into specific challenges and helped concretize pain points related to both the functionality and usability of the VR tool, as well as organizational challenges which both needs to be rectified before the bespoke VR-based treatment can be properly integrated.

The current solution requires multiple steps when engaging with it, and each of these steps may be influenced by system errors. The first approach towards improving the system is to reprogram it, so the software itself troubleshoots and guides the user through. For example, through information visualization to indicate where the error might lie, through visualizing whether or not the sensor is detected by the system, or a battery voltage indicator. The lack of charging the sensors has to be embedded into existing work routines. However, from a technological viewpoint, sensors may be improved in relation to battery size and power consumption. The issues with fitting the headset will naturally be more manageable, as therapists become more accustomed with the technology. And future iterations of consumer-grade headsets will likely improve their ergonomics, leading to higher efficiency.

Physiotherapy is essentially a human-centred field, and therapists are motivated by working with patients. Using technology to achieve results is not in itself what drives their interest in the field, and if they use it, the technology has to be easily applicable, easy to learn and straightforward to maintain.

The introduction of VR essentially poses a two-fold challenge for the therapists: They have to familiarize themselves with a brand new technology, but they also need to learn how to integrate it into a specific treatment context which have already pre-established work routines, such as team training workouts. Furthermore, physiotherapy is an evidence-based practice, and there is no designated area where therapists are told that VR will lead to higher efficacy. Nor is there extended knowledge about validity or evidence. Moreover, although the use of clinical VR is on the rise within healthcare facilities around the world,

Denmark has yet to establish national clinical guidelines and recommendations on the use of VR-based rehabilitation.

In relation to communication, there is a need to establish official channels for reporting performance issues, as well as user experiences from patients and therapists alike. Right now, the health center lacks a consistent and periodic evaluation process about the technology. Additionally, some physiotherapists suggest that many of the other therapists are likely unaware of the purpose and goals of the ongoing project. And that many may be weary about using VR, because of 1) lack of knowledge on how to use it, and 2) fear and/or uncertainty about what it may do to the patient (and in what situations it may or may not be beneficial to use). Furthermore, the system has to be practically adapted into the existing interior without the need for heavy relocation of equipment.

VR offers a novel addition to the usual care provided by the health center. If the patients are to engage with the technology, the first step is to make the therapists comfortable with it and address skepticism. Therefore, the therapist is an essential collaborator to involve within all aspects of the design and development process. That can e.g. be approached through e.g. co-production initiatives or knowledge translation (KT) strategies (e.g. interdisciplinary journal clubs).

6   Conclusion

VR is a new world to therapists and patients alike. However, the therapist is an important actor in intermediating the technology to the patients. If the therapists do not have incentive to use it, for example due to a steep learning curve, inadequate usability, or non-established workflow procedures, the technology will not reach a sufficient endorsement and will never consolidate. The VR system has to deliver simple and informative feedback, and work routines need to be clearly defined and visualized. Furthermore, standardized channels for reporting performance issues and user-experiences need to be established and shared with all stakeholders, in order to create an open, transparent and sustained interest in VR-based rehabilitation. Moreover, KT strategies and co-production initiatives should be implemented more systematically to strengthen the impact of the VR-based rehabilitation systems.

References

1. Bjørner, T.: Qualitative Methods for Consumer Research: The value of the qualitative approach in theory and practice. Hans Reitzels Forlag, 1 edn. (2015)
2. Bruun-Pedersen, J.R., Pedersen, K.S., Serafin, S., Kofoed, L.B.: Augmented exercise biking with virtual environments for elderly users: a preliminary study for retirement home physical therapy. In: 2014 2nd Workshop on Virtual and Augmented Assistive Technology (VAAT), pp. 23–27. IEEE (2014)
3. Bruun-Pedersen, J.R., Serafin, S., Kofoed, L.B.: Restorative virtual environment design for augmenting nursing home rehabilitation. J. Virtual Worlds Res. 9(3), 1–24 (2016)

4. Clatworthy, S.: Service innovation through touch-points: development of an innovation toolkit for the first stages of new service development (2011)
5. Cresswell, K., Sheikh, A.: Organizational issues in the implementation and adoption of health information technology innovations: an interpretative review. Int. J. Med. Inf. **82**(5), 73–86 (2013)
6. Dixon-Woods, M., Amalberti, R., Goodman, S., Bergman, B., Glasziou, P.: Problems and promises of innovation: why healthcare needs to rethink its love/hate relationship with the new. BMJ Qual. Saf. **20**(Suppl 1), i47–i51 (2011)
7. Grani, F., Bruun-Pedersen, J.R.: Giro: better biking in virtual reality. In: 2017 IEEE 3rd Workshop on Everyday Virtual Reality (WEVR), pp. 1–5. IEEE (2017)
8. Hoffman, H.G., et al.: Virtual reality as an adjunctive non-pharmacologic analgesic for acute burn pain during medical procedures. Ann. Behav. Med. **41**(2), 183–191 (2011)
9. Holmlid, S., Evenson, S.: Bringing service design to service sciences, management and engineering. In: Hefley, B., Murphy, W. (eds.) Service Science, Management and Engineering Education for the 21st Century, pp. 341–345. Springer, Boston (2008). https://doi.org/10.1007/978-0-387-76578-5_50
10. Kangovi, S., et al.: The use of participatory action research to design a patient-centered community health worker care transitions intervention. Healthcare **2**(2), 136–144 (2014)
11. Keshner, E.A., Weiss, P.T., Geifman, D., Raban, D.: Tracking the evolution of virtual reality applications to rehabilitation as a field of study. J. NeuroEng. Rehabil. **16**(1), 76 (2019)
12. Lewis, G.N., Woods, C., Rosie, J.A., Mcpherson, K.M.: Virtual reality games for rehabilitation of people with stroke: perspectives from the users. Disabil. Rehabil. Assist. Technol. **6**(5), 453–463 (2011)
13. Lohse, K., Shirzad, N., Verster, A., Hodges, N., Van der Loos, H.M.: Video games and rehabilitation: using design principles to enhance engagement in physical therapy. J. Neurol. Phys. Ther. **37**(4), 166–175 (2013)
14. Mager, B., Nisbett, A., Siodmok, A., Katz, A., Mauldin, C., O'Sullivan, D., et al.: Service design impact report: public sector. Hundt Druck GmbH, Germany, Service Design Network (2016)
15. Ryan, R.M., Deci, E.L.: Self-determination theory and the facilitation of intrinsic motivation, social development, and well-being 55(1), 68–78 (2000)
16. Shostack, L.: Designing services that deliver. Harvard Bus. Rev. **62**(1), 133–139 (1984)
17. Stickdorn, M., Hormess, M.E., Lawrence, A., Schneider, J.: This is Service Design Doing: Applying Service Design Thinking in the Real World. O'Reilly Media Inc, Sebastopol (2018)
18. Stütz, T., et al.: An interactive 3D health app with multimodal information representation for frozen shoulder. In: Proceedings of the 19th International Conference on Human-Computer Interaction with Mobile Devices and Services - MobileHCI 2017, pp. 1–11 (2017)
19. Tochetto, J., Guimarães, C., Maranho, A.L., Tartari, A.L.: Design with me: i have special needs! the case for cerebral palsy. In: Antona, M., Stephanidis, C. (eds.) UAHCI 2016. LNCS, vol. 9737, pp. 214–222. Springer, Cham (2016). https://doi.org/10.1007/978-3-319-40250-5_21
20. Triberti, S., Repetto, C., Riva, G.: Psychological factors influencing the effectiveness of virtual reality-based analgesia: a systematic review. Cyberpsychology Behav. Soc. Networking **17**(6), 335–345 (2014)

21. United Nations, Department of Economic and Social Affairs, Population Division: World population prospects 2019: Highlights (st/csa/scr.a/423) (2019). https://population.un.org/wpp/Publications/Files/WPP2019_Highlights.pdf. Accessed 10 July 2019
22. Williamson, L.: Patient and citizen participation in health: the need for improved ethical support. Am. J. Bioeth. **14**(6), 4–16 (2014)
23. World Health Organization: Global strategy on people-centred and integrated health services: interim report (2015). https://apps.who.int/iris/bitstream/handle/10665/155002/WHO_HIS_SDS_2015.6_eng.pdf. Accessed 8 June 2019
24. World Health Organization: People-centred and integrated health services: an overview of the evidence: interim report (2015). https://apps.who.int/iris/bitstream/handle/10665/155004/WHO_HIS_SDS_2015.7_eng.pdf. Accessed 8 June 2019
25. Zimmerli, L., Jacky, M., Lünenburger, L., Riener, R., Bolliger, M.: Increasing patient engagement during virtual reality-based motor rehabilitation. Arch. Phys. Med. Rehabil. **94**(9), 1737–1746 (2013)

Designing and Learning with IoT in a Passion-Based Constructionist Context

Janette Hughes(✉), Jennifer Anne Robb, and Margaret Lam

Faculty of Education, Ontario Tech University,
11 Simcoe Street North, Oshawa, ON L1H 7L7, Canada
janette.hughes@ontariotechu.ca,
{jennifer.robb,margie.lam}@ontariotechu.net

Abstract. Internet of Things (IoT), one of the latest technological advancements, will transform our future in ways we can only imagine. The necessity for young people to understand and design with IoT technologies seems unequivocal; however, there is currently limited integration of IoT in K-12 education. To address these gaps in current research, we conducted a mixed methods, multiple-case study during a five-day "maker" camp focused on the informal design of IoT passion projects. Our research sought to understand what participants learned about IoT, as well as how they designed basic IoT artifacts within a constructionist context. Results indicated several factors contributing to a successful design, including guided inquiry, detailed planning documents, access to knowledgeable support in the form of peers or facilitators, and perseverance. Participants also experienced substantial gains in IoT knowledge and skills resulting from their experiences designing and creating IoT artifacts, which will be valuable as IoT becomes more prevalent in society. However, the inquiry-driven model also posed several challenges relevant to educators in formalized settings, including wide variability in the level of scaffolding and support required, progress paralysis resulting from a context with limited instruction and restrictions, and the impact of time constraints on students' learning and designs.

Keywords: Design thinking · Inquiry · Internet of Things (IoT) · Makerspaces · Constructionism · Passion-based learning

1 Introduction

The Internet of Things (IoT) is fast becoming one of the latest revolutionary technological advancements. Originally coined by technology pioneer Kevin Aston, IoT involves transforming everyday objects into "smart" objects which can transmit collected data through the internet to IoT platforms. The advantages of IoT include the ability to analyze real-time and varied data to better understand the world around us, enabling more efficient and autonomous problem-solving and interactions. Currently, there are over 8 billion smart objects, including cars, watches, toys, appliances, and even humans, that are all connected through IoT. Many people interact daily with smart devices with little

A. Brooks and E. I. Brooks (Eds.): ArtsIT 2019/DLI 2019, LNICST 328, pp. 760–771, 2020.
https://doi.org/10.1007/978-3-030-53294-9_59

appreciation for the inner workings of IoT or its security and privacy considerations. Children have enhanced play experiences through smart toys (i.e. Oslo the 'smart' bear) and smart gaming devices (i.e. Skylander IoToys) yet they can be compromised through collection of personal and play data [1]. Considering IoT objects are projected to surpass 50 billion by 2020 [2], we need to be cognizant of all the ramifications associated with interconnected smart infrastructures and devices.

A key aspect of understanding IoT is learning how to effectively design the various components, including sensors, processors, actuators (motors, fans, etc.), and IoT platforms. Leveraging formal or informal design-based frameworks within creative and explorative environments like makerspaces could help students learn and develop IoT working projects. Makerspaces and maker pedagogies are becoming commonplace in schools where passion-based, hands-on learning are often aligned to STEM or STEAM subject areas. These environments support inquiry-based, constructionist approaches which focus on discovery learning through social, active experiences while designing meaningful and relevant artifacts [3]. Furthermore, these contexts are enhanced with student choice and integration of the latest technologies, which could include IoT.

With over 50 billion IoT objects, our near future will be transformed in ways we can only imagine. Learning about IoT is integral for young people to help better understand and design this future world. Despite this impending need, there is limited integration of IoT in K-12 education and little research on designing IoT passion projects in makerspaces or classrooms. This paper seeks to address these gaps through an investigation into the informal design of IoT passion projects from a week-long maker-oriented March Break camp. Camp participants created their own IoT projects that were meant to solve a "real world" or relevant problem in their communities. During the camp, IoT concepts were explained, IoT technologies were discovered and informal design practices were encouraged, all to support learners as they developed their IoT digital artifacts. The research questions which guided our investigation are as follows:

- What happens when participants design an IoT passion project within a constructionist context?
- How does understanding of IoT develop in a constructionist learning environment?

2 Theoretical Framework

Our research is situated within a framework consisting of constructionism [4], design thinking [5–7], and passion-based learning [8, 9]. Each of these perspectives is a central component of the learning and activity that occurs within a makerspace and, taken together, form a cohesive lens through which to interpret our work.

2.1 Constructionism

The modern maker movement and its do-it-yourself (DIY) ethos evolved from Papert's [4] early work on constructionism [10], which postulated that students' engagement in the design, creation, and sharing of physical or digital artifacts promoted knowledge building and conceptual reinforcement [11]. He advocated for learning environments with "low floors and high ceilings," where little prior knowledge is required for participation, but students have ample opportunities to complexify their involvement and subsequent learning [4]. This interactive approach serves to make abstract concepts more concrete and personally relevant for students through the process of constructing tangible or digital representations of their knowledge [12, 13].

In makerspaces and classrooms that utilize maker pedagogies, learning occurs "through a range of activities that blend design and technology, including textile crafts, robotics, electronics, digital fabrication, mechanical repair or creation, tinkering with everyday appliances, digital storytelling, arts and crafts – in short, fabricating with new technologies to create almost anything" [14, p. 445]. These environments are student-centred and inquiry-driven, facilitating the development of scientific knowledge and process skills [15], critical thinking [13], perseverance [16], individual and collective agency [17, 18], and technological fluency [19], to name a few. Furthermore, an emphasis on critical maker literacies that encourage students to reflect on the purpose and impact of their designs, production processes, and sharing of completed projects can foster a sense of maker citizenship, linking students' making practices to real-world issues of rights, belonging, and social participation [17].

2.2 Design Thinking

Preparing students for the demands of a rapidly changing technological society necessitates the development of future-ready skills. Design thinking processes feature prominently in business and engineering and can act as a framework for interdisciplinary learning through making [7, 20], scaffolding the process from inspiration to completion. Although numerous models of the design process have been proposed (e.g., [5, 21]), each follows a similar pattern of identifying a problem, ideating solutions, and choosing one to prototype, test, and iterate upon until achieving a desired product [20].

Within the context of a makerspace, design thinking enables students to grapple with authentic, everyday problems, and create thoughtful solutions in response [4]. In doing so, they exercise positive risk-taking and creativity [20], the ability to direct and prioritize their own learning [5], as well as critical thinking, perseverance, and digital literacy skills [7].

2.3 Passion-Based Learning

Utilizing students' personal interests as a vehicle for learning is harmonious with the inquiry-driven nature of the makerspace [18]. Expanding upon Papert's [4] conceptualization of contexts with "low floors and high ceilings", Resnick and colleagues [8] recommended the addition of "wide walls" that would accommodate a variety of interests, recognizing the value of personally-relevant educational experiences. Not only are students more likely to remain engaged by an activity that integrates a topic of interest [22], they may also benefit from enhanced creativity [23] and other global competencies [16], and a deeper understanding of the concepts being learned [13].

Seely Brown and Adler [9] encapsulate the role of passion-based learning in modern education, asserting that finding something "that ignites a student's passion can set the stage for the student to acquire both deep knowledge about a subject ('learning about') and the ability to participate in the practice of a field through productive inquiry and peer-based learning ('learning to be')" (p. 28).

3 Methodology

3.1 Setting

This study was conducted during a March break camp at the STEAM-3D Maker Lab in the Faculty of Education at Ontario Tech University (formerly University of Ontario Institute of Technology). The camp lasted for five days, with four full days devoted to our research. Participants were selected on a first-registered basis. Three research assistants were actively involved in facilitating the maker camp activities and documenting ongoing field observations. Additionally, six teacher and teacher candidate volunteers were available to assist during various group activities and development of participants' IoT passion projects. The STEAM-3D Maker Lab at Ontario Tech University was established under Dr. Janette Hughes, Canada Research Chair in Technology and Pedagogy, to conduct educational research associated with maker pedagogies, digital literacies and the effective integration of technology and pedagogy.

3.2 Participants

The STEAM-3D maker camp involved 17 local participants aged 7 to 14 years with a mean age of 10 years. There was a maximum of 17 campers to ensure effective guidance and facilitation from the three research assistants. Participants had a nearly even distribution of genders: nine males and eight females. Ten participants were familiar with each other either as siblings, extended family members, classmates or friends. These participants tended to work together during early camp group activities however, only two of these familiar participants created their IoT passion project together. Previous experience with technology was not required, therefore participants varied in both experience and knowledge with different technologies and computing competencies.

3.3 Research Design

The maker camp was designed to accommodate two different research objectives: our IoT-themed passion projects and another related to girls in STEM. To answer our research questions, we used a constructionist, guided inquiry approach to introduce basic IoT concepts, technologies and designs with daily design themes and reflection prompts to guide participants' development of their IoT passion projects. Learning activities were structured to have participants focus on discovery and design with regular physical and mental technology breaks to avoid fatigue and over-exposure. Daily design themes were introduced with a "word of the day", group discussions, stories, videos and reinforced with daily reflective, online journals with prompting questions. Participants' IoT designs were encouraged to be socially conscious and problem-solving for either individual or community. Campers were given full freedom in their IoT designs, however, their prototypes and final models were limited by their four-day work period and the available

IoT technologies which included littleBits, micro:bit and Arduino Uno with some add-on sensors and actuators. Therefore, many designs were at a basic IoT level - exploring systems with sensors, interconnectivity, and possible extensions to data collection and management systems. Research assistants acted as camp facilitators, providing guidance on IoT technologies, concepts and designs on one-on-one or small group basis within the IoT passion project work periods.

4   Data Collection and Analysis

The study began with a self-reported online pre-study questionnaire featuring 23 open-ended questions. As the camp encompassed two distinct research goals, only 6 questions related to participants' understanding of IoT, their experience with IoT and other technologies, and thoughts on school subjects, STEM, and social justice were collected for this paper. The remaining questions asked about demographics (n = 4) or topics specific to the second research study (n = 13). An online application, Seesaw, was used to collect participants' project planning and process work, as well as reflective journals at the end of each day. Participants were prompted with questions aligned to design and/or IoT themes and their responses contained writing, images, videos, audio, or some combination of these. They also documented their IoT passion project brainstorming and design ideas using an online mind mapping application called Popplet. Finally, throughout the week, research assistants documented images/videos and informal discussions, recorded detailed field notes highlighting key insights and feedback, and video-recorded work sessions, group discussions and exit interviews which were all later transcribed.

The study was a subset of a larger, multilayered research project during the five-day school break in March. With only four days for participants to learn, design and build their IoT passion projects, it was not possible to collect complete data sets from all participants. In total, ten full participant data sets, which included pre-surveys, brainstorming designs, reflective journal posts, and final interviews, were collected. To analyze this data, directed content analysis was used with key themes pre-defined as the initial coding schemes [24]. These preliminary coding schemes were related to themes on IoT, design processes and skill sets, passion-based learning and constructionist approaches, with additional codes emerging through more thorough analysis. The collected data provided very rich and detailed descriptions of participants' conceptual models, prototype creations, and design-thinking processes. However, to effectively explore the first research question the authors narrowed their analysis to three distinct case studies. These three cases presented unique IoT passion projects with clear social significance and conceptual designs, while their IoT creations represented the full spectrum of success: fully, partially, and unsuccessful. Our second research question involved the analysis of all collected data using directed content analysis exclusively.

5   Findings

5.1   What Happens When Participants Design an IoT Passion Project Within a Constructionist Context?

Given the role of the design process in making, we were interested in participants' naturalistic tendencies towards design in a context with few requirements or constraints.

Although campers were provided with a copy of The Works Museum [25] Engineering Design Process in their digital design journals, they were encouraged to proceed however they felt most comfortable. They were given one hour and several prompting questions to begin designing their projects, after which they were free to direct their own process. For the purposes of scope, we outline three notable cases below.

Anisha & Derick's Home Security Monitoring System. Anisha[1] (age 10) and Derick (age 9) formed an organic partnership; as cousins, they had a pre-established level of comfort and rapport. They initially identified three potential passion projects before deciding upon a home security monitoring and alarm system with facial recognition. Later in the project, Derick explained that "it could help a lot of people that need a lot of security around their house," and Anisha cited issues with guns, violence, and the political climate as further inspiration. After selecting their passion project, they seemed unsure about how to continue until a facilitator encouraged them to think about the types of technologies they would need to accomplish their goal.

Despite being successful in identifying a problem and beginning to design a solution, Anisha and Derick had difficulty progressing with their project in the absence of dedicated guidance. Their ongoing challenges reinforce the notion that, despite literature supporting the role of passion-based learning and guided inquiry in promoting both learning and engagement [15, 22], one size does not necessarily fit all. Camp facilitators continued to assist them in refining their ideas and getting them started in the process of constructing their initial prototypes but were unable to provide the degree of support required to keep the pair moving towards their goal, as their focus was divided between other participants. Fortunately, another participant (Amalya, described below) had created similar components for her own passion project and was able to work closely with Anisha to create a 3D model she and Derick needed (Fig. 1).

Fig. 1. Amalya and Anisha working in TinkerCAD 3D modelling software.

At one point, another participant (also related to the pair) was excited to show Anisha and Derick the success she had achieved in coding her micro:bit, motivating Derick to

---

[1] All names are pseudonyms.

urgently say, "Anisha, we need to work on this!" However, this motivation was unable to sustain their momentum, as they were quick to disengage from their project and play games on the iPad whenever they experienced difficulty and support was unavailable.

This case illustrates the complex balance surrounding the type of inquiry employed within a makerspace. While giving young makers freedom and control over their design and making activities can sustain engagement and commitment to a task, facilitators must be conscious of their progress and offer timely support to avoid disengagement when learners are unsure how to proceed [17].

Emily's Endangered Species Tracker. Emily's (age 9) IoT passion project was inspired by a love of animals that she shared with her brother and a close friend. This informed her design of a robot that could track and report on the status of endangered animals to better inform conservation efforts. Her digital mind map deconstructed her project into several components, including a GPS tracker, a camera with pattern recognition, and motion sensors to guide the robot, reflecting the kinds of creative solutions that emerge when learners design projects in response to authentic, everyday problems [5]. This initial plan, as well as a conversation with one of the camp facilitators, guided her design and prototyping process.

Emily encountered numerous challenges with her design. After learning that the maker camp was unable to acquire a GPS tracker, she moved on to another element of her design without hesitation. Similarly, she had hoped to 3D print a small tiger to represent the endangered species her project was designed for, but each attempt failed due to issues with the model. Instead of becoming discouraged, she and one of the camp facilitators kept track of the failures, noting which print had made the most progress. The camera element of her project also posed a challenge, both to her and camp facilitators. Given a lack of standalone camera components in the lab, this feature required that a smartphone be connected to her micro:bit via Bluetooth wireless technology and then coded to take a photograph at certain intervals. However, the connection between the smartphone micro:bit app and the physical micro:bit board was tenuous, and after a full afternoon of troubleshooting with one of the camp facilitators, Emily was willing to abandon this aspect of her project as well (Fig. 2).

Fig. 2. Camp facilitator helping troubleshoot Emily's micro:bit.

To finalize her project, Emily had to assemble k8, a micro:bit-compatible robot [26]. Although she tried to complete this task independently, she had trouble locating the assembly instructions as well as physically fitting the pieces together. One of the facilitators was able to assist with the assembly process, modelling each step but ultimately encouraging Emily to complete the assembly. At one point, Emily says, "I don't like assembling k8, k8 is hard to put together." However, this did not seem to deter her from completing the build and successfully coding the robot's movement.

Amalya's Texting-and-Driving Deterrent. Amalya (age 13) was inspired by the social justice theme of the camp, saying, "for my passion project, I decided to help change the world." She chose to expand upon a school art assignment which illustrated the degree to which people were dependent on their phones. Explaining further, she wrote, "I found out that there are more people dying because of texting and driving than drinking and driving. And, for me, that was so crazy."

Amalya spent more time in the planning phase of her design than most other participants, using not only the mind mapping application provided, but also her digital design journal to make detailed notes (Fig. 3), and a digital painting application to create a rough sketch of her design. Her thorough, extended engagement in the design process enabled Amalya to exercise her creativity [20], as well as determine her priorities regarding the final product [5]. She decided to make a 3D-printed phone holder that utilized the micro:bit's onboard sensors to detect when a phone was removed from the cradle and activate an alarm that would remind the user not to look at their phone while driving.

Fig. 3. Examples of students' multimodal digital design journal entries.

While working on her 3D model, Amalya sought input on her design from camp facilitators and similarly-aged peers. She wanted to ensure that her measurements were correct, and that her model would hold an average-sized smartphone as well as the micro:bit and battery pack. She was comfortable with the process of learning to use new technologies as needed for her design, but often asked for feedback and validation on her project's specifications and usability. Given her growing comfort with tools that had not been explicitly taught during the camp's exploration sessions, Amalya also offered assistance to those in her immediate vicinity and was asked to assist other campers when facilitators were occupied. Echoing Marsh and colleagues' [17, 18] observations of makerspaces as sites of enhanced agency, this generated additional self-confidence in her abilities, which was evident when she realized that she had made a mistake in her project's dimensions and opted to start over.

After achieving success throughout various stages of her design process, such as finalizing her 3D model and achieving a working prototype, Amalya was excited to share her results with others. She reached out to camp facilitators and campers she had become friendly with to show them what she had achieved. Her pride was also evident upon the camp's completion, when she indicated that she would be interested in working with automotive engineers to integrate a similar design into cars currently on the road.

5.2 How Does Understanding of IoT Develop in a Constructionist Learning Environment?

While we did not expect participants to become IoT experts over the course of a five-day constructionist learning microcycle, our data suggest that there may be value in providing immersive, hands-on exposure to such advanced technological concepts.

On the first day of camp, the pre-study questionnaire asked participants whether they were familiar with IoT or smart homes and devices. Only three (18%) answered in the affirmative, while the remaining fourteen were either unsure (n = 10, 59%) or decidedly unfamiliar (n = 4, 23%). However, two of the three participants that had heard of IoT provided vague ("the internet is connected to every device") or incorrect ("Google") definitions, while an additional eleven campers (65%) indicated they did not know what IoT meant. Despite participants' lack of familiarity, opinions were mixed regarding their ability to use IoT to affect positive change in their lives, or the lives of others: six (35%) believed that they could, four (24%) said maybe, and seven (41%) did not think so.

As many participants were still working on their passion projects up to the last moment of camp, only 10 (59%) post-study interviews were able to be conducted. By this point, participants had developed a more comprehensive understanding of IoT, describing features such as the interconnectivity of devices to one another and to the Internet (n = 5), the use of a central device, typically a smartphone, to control connected devices (n = 6), the role of artificial intelligence in IoT (n = 3), as well as its ability to make your life more convenient (n = 2). Only one of the ten participants interviewed was unable to provide an accurate definition. Furthermore, participants identified numerous applications of IoT to improve their life or the lives of others, including driverless cars, reduced casualties of war due to unmanned planes and submarines, making homes more accessible for individuals with disabilities, increased home security and monitoring, and the automation of lights and appliances, resulting in money saved for consumers. They had also begun to form opinions on the use of IoT, describing it as cool (n = 3) or useful (n = 7), while emphasizing the need to protect data from hackers (n = 6) with added layers of security, such as encryption or firewalls (n = 2). While the scope of this study prevents any generalization of its results, the potential for passion-based learning [9] and makerspaces [11–13] to facilitate deeper learning, even with sophisticated concepts such as IoT, has inspired a shift to accommodate these elements in formal education [9, 10].

6 Discussion and Conclusions

This study explored the impact of a five-day learning microcycle, in the form of a constructionist March break camp, on participants' natural, informal design processes and their understanding of IoT. Our findings suggest that, while guided inquiry can be an effective tool to drive students' passion-based maker projects and explore new concepts (such as IoT), the amount of guidance needed to support design decisions can vary wildly, even within a small group. While many of our participants flourished with the ability to select and design their own projects with minimal constraints, others had difficulty progressing without a more well-defined plan. For these youth, a structured inquiry approach, featuring more explicit procedures and learning goals, may have alleviated their frustrations, promoted resiliency, and more effectively scaffolded their designs [15]. Furthermore, encouraging participants to design solutions for a problem they were personally invested in helped bolster their motivation in most cases, but the extent to which passion-based learning had a protective effect on their perseverance differed for each participant. Educators wishing to adopt an inquiry-based constructionist model in their own contexts will need to consider many factors, including time available for initial learning, exploration, and design, students' familiarity with the tools and technologies on hand, and the degree of structure required based on students' individual needs [17].

Several other factors were identified as affecting participants' informal design processes, including the comprehensiveness of their initial plans, the role of camp facilitators and peers in providing motivation, validation, or focused support as a "more knowledgeable other" [27], and the impact of perseverance and failure-positivity. Participants who were more detailed in their planning and set explicit goals for themselves in their reflective journals at the end of each day experienced fewer challenges in the process of making and were better prepared to navigate the issues that did arise. One limitation of our research design was that the limited timeframe prevented an in-depth overview of the design process, particularly the early planning stages. While iteration, failure positivity, and growth mindset were emphasized throughout the week, we failed to communicate the importance of setting a solid foundation for design work in the form of a plan, which resulted in several participants doing only as much as they felt was required by the facilitators. Despite the challenges faced by some of our participants, our results support Doppelt's [5] assertion that students need not follow any one specific design process in order to conceptualize, create, and share solutions in response to authentic problems.

Our research also suggests that engagement with low-floor IoT technologies in a constructionist environment, such as a community makerspace or a maker-oriented classroom, may facilitate a deeper conceptual understanding of IoT and its real-world applications. By the end of this short study, most of our participants were able to describe key features of IoT, including the interconnection of everyday devices, the need for management software to define interactions and set parameters, and the role that artificial intelligence plays in IoT. Participants were also able to offer suggestions for the use of IoT to benefit society, many of which were original ideas not covered in the group discussions or daily videos. While the scope of our March Break camp prevented an in-depth exploration of the more advanced connectivity, programming, and monitoring elements of IoT, these topics could easily be included in subsequent iterations with a longer timeframe and expanded in complexity as students get older.

These findings have compelling implications for educators of 21st century students. As IoT becomes a salient feature of society, future citizens must understand not only how it works, but also how to protect the personal data that sits at the core of these systems. Moreover, careers in IoT development are expected to increase as steadily as the number of connected devices [2], further elevating the value of IoT knowledge, as well as the design processes needed to effectively work with these technologies. As both the maker movement [15] and the integration of technologies for communication, coding, digital production, and more [28] continue to grow within formal education, multipurpose electronics kits like the ones used within this study can be used to introduce the basic concepts and concerns associated with IoT to K-12 students, better preparing them to live and work in a highly-connected society. Engaging students in critical making activities [13], whether at school or during visits to a local makerspace, can be another effective way to integrate IoT and other technologies into learning. Through a blend of traditional crafting and digital tools [14, 18], and an emphasis on low-floor, high-ceiling technologies [4, 8], makerspaces can offer a natural bridge into the digital landscape for learners of all ages.

References

1. Chaudron, S., Di Gioia, R., Gemo, M., Holloway, D., Marsh, J., Mascheroni, G.,..., & European Commission. Joint Research Centre: Kaleidoscope on the Internet of Toys: Safety, security, privacy and societal insights. Publications Office of the European Union (2017)
2. Ericsson Mobility Report. https://www.ericsson.com/assets/local/mobility-report/docume nts/2018/ericsson-mobility-report-november-2018.pdf. Accessed 06 May 2019
3. Cocciolo, A.: Situating student learning in rich contexts: a constructionist approach to digital archives education. Evid. Based Libr. Inf. Pract. 6(3), 4–15 (2011). https://doi.org/10.18438/B8DP6N
4. Papert, S.: Mindstorms: Children, Computers, and Powerful Ideas. Basic Books, New York (1980)
5. Doppelt, Y.: Assessing creative thinking in design-based learning. Int. J. Technol. Des. Educ. 19(1), 55–65 (2009). https://doi.org/10.1007/s10798-006-9008-y
6. Gobble, M.M.: Design thinking. Res. Technol. Manag. 57(3), 59–60 (2014)
7. Razzouk, R., Shute, V.: What is design thinking and why is it important? Rev. Educ. Res. 82(3), 330–348 (2012). https://doi.org/10.3102/0034654312457429
8. Resnick, M., et al.: Scratch programming for all. Commun. ACM 52(11), 60–67 (2009)
9. Seely Brown, J., Adler, R.P.: Open education, the long tail, and learning 2.0. Educause Rev. 43(1), 17–32 (2008)
10. Halverson, E.R., Sheridan, K.: The maker movement in education. Harvard Educ. Rev. 84(4), 495–504 (2014). https://doi.org/10.17763/haer.84.4.34j1g68140382063
11. Harel, I., Papert, S.: Situating constructionism. In: Constructionism, pp. 1–11. Ablex Publishing, Westport, CT (1991)
12. Noss, R., Clayson, J.: Reconstructing constructionism. Constructivist Found. 10(3), 285–288 (2015)
13. Ratto, M.: Critical making: conceptual and material studies in technology and social life. Inf. Soc. Int. J. 27(4), 252–260 (2011). https://doi.org/10.1080/01972243.2011.583819
14. Wohlwend, K.E., Peppler, K.A., Keune, A., Thompson, N.: Making sense and nonsense: comparing mediated discourse and agential realist approaches to materiality in a preschool makerspace. J. Early Child. Literacy 17(3), 444–462 (2017). https://doi.org/10.1177/146879 8417712066

15. Bunterm, T., Lee, K., Kong, J.N.L., Srikoon, S., Vangpoomyai, P., Rattanavongsa, J., Racha-hoon, G.: Do different levels of inquiry lead to different learning outcomes? a comparison between guided and structured inquiry. Int. J. Sci. Educ. **36**(12), 1937–1959 (2014). https://doi.org/10.1080/09500693.2014.886347

16. Hughes, J.M.: Digital making with "at-risk" youth. Int. J. Inf. Learn. Technol. **34**(2), 102–113 (2017)

17. Marsh, J., Arnseth, H.C., Kumpulainen, K.: Maker literacies and maker citizenship in the MakEY (Makerspaces in the Early Years) project. Multimod. Technol. Interact. **2**(3), 50 (2018). https://doi.org/10.3390/mti2030050

18. Marsh, J., Wood, E., Chesworth, L., Nisha, B., Nutbrown, B., Olney, B.: Makerspaces in early childhood education: principles of pedagogy and practice. Mind Culture Act. **26**(3), 221–233 (2019). https://doi.org/10.1080/10749039.2019.1655651

19. Kafai, Y.B.: Playing and making games for learning: instructionist and constructionist perspectives for game studies. Games Cult. **1**(1), 36–40 (2006). https://doi.org/10.1177/1555412005281767

20. Spencer, J., Juliani, A.J.: Launch: Using Design Thinking to Boost Creativity and Bring out the Maker in Every Student. Dave Burgess Consulting Inc, San Diego (2016)

21. Cahn, P.S., et al.: A design thinking approach to evaluating interprofessional education. J. Interprof. Care **30**(3), 378–380 (2016). https://doi.org/10.3109/13561820.2015.1122582

22. Hansen, A.K., Hansen, E.R., Hall, T., Fixler, M., Harlow, D.: Fidgeting with fabrication: students with ADHD making tools to focus. In: Proceedings of the 7th Annual Conference on Creativity and Making in Education (FabLearn 2017). ACM, New York (2017). https://doi.org/10.1145/3141798.3141812

23. Somanath, S., Morrison, L., Hughes, J., Sharlin, E., Sousa, M.C.: Engaging 'at-risk' students through maker culture activities. In: Proceedings of the 10th International Conference on Tangible, Embedded, and Embodied Interaction (TEI 2016), pp. 150–158. ACM, New York (2016)

24. Hsiu-Fang, H., Shannon, S.E.: Three approaches to qualitative content analysis. Qual. Health Res. **15**(9), 1277–1288 (2005)

25. The Works Museum. https://theworks.org/educators-and-groups/elementary-engineering-resources/engineering-design-process/. Accessed 05 July 2019

26. InkSmith. https://www.inksmith.co/k8-robotics-kit. Accessed 05 July 2019

27. Vygotsky, L.S.: Mind in Society: The Development of Higher Psychological Processes. Harvard University Press, Cambridge (1978)

28. Vega, V., Robb, M.B.: The Common Sense Census: Inside the 21st Century Classroom. Common Sense Media, San Francisco (2019)

Entrepreneurial Cultural Affinity Spaces (ECAS): Design of Inclusive Local Learning Ecosystems for Social Change, Innovation and Entrepreneurship

Stefania Savva[1]([✉]), Nicos Souleles[1], and Ana Margarida Ferreira[2]

[1] Art and Design: Elearning Lab, Cyprus University of Technology, Limassol, Cyprus
{stefania.savva,nicos.souleles}@cut.ac.cy
[2] UNIDCOM/IADE, Universidade Europeia, Laureate Universities, Lisbon, Portugal
ana.margarida.ferreira@universidadeeuropeia.pt

Abstract. The ECAS framework seeks to transform social design theory and practice through an emergent instructional paradigm of heritage-led, local learning ecosystem approaches, to leverage on diverse assets of people in community settings. This includes the cultural, social, sexual and religious diversity of locals. Such reconfiguration of design for social change, and our collective mindset, will create the conditions for more dynamic and powerful collaborations that stimulate and enable social innovation, entrepreneurship, and inclusion. The conceptual backdrop draws on the concepts of affinity spaces and embodied learning, incorporated into local learning ecosystem ideas that support viable, integrated and participative urban regeneration. This paper addresses the theoretical backdrop of how such ecosystems can be co-designed, implemented and evaluated, to include disadvantaged and underrepresented groups, such as minorities, women, migrants, refugees and asylum seekers, to empower them as lifelong learners and change-makers. We introduce the ECAS framework and how it can present an inclusive and open instructional paradigm that improves design for social change, innovation and entrepreneurship in practice through the framework, conditions, and support mechanisms developed.

Keywords: Urban regeneration · Local learning ecosystems · Embodiment · Entrepreneurship · Social innovation · Circular economy · Social design

1 Introduction

1.1 Design for Sustainable Urban Regeneration

Cultural heritage is considered a non-renewable identity resource and a catalyst for sustainable development through monetary and non-monetary values [1]. However, its preservation and utilization confront many binding barriers, resulting in profound abandonment and decay. As the Habitat III paper by UNESCO, Urban Culture and Heritage

© ICST Institute for Computer Sciences, Social Informatics and Telecommunications Engineering 2020
Published by Springer Nature Switzerland AG 2020. All Rights Reserved
A. Brooks and E. I. Brooks (Eds.): ArtsIT 2019/DLI 2019, LNICST 328, pp. 772–782, 2020.
https://doi.org/10.1007/978-3-030-53294-9_60

notes, the contemporary city calls for a new model of urban development, consistent with the Sustainable Development Goals (SDGs), particularly SDG 11 'Sustainable cities and communities' [2]. There is a need for a more systematic and comprehensive 'culturally sensitive' urban development approach, which recognizes that culture is a driving force in the development of cities. Social, creative and cultural entrepreneurship in community-led co-working spaces (CLCSs) [3] can boost heritage-led urban regeneration but needs specific support to grow.

The ECAS framework provides the groundwork for how to move from theory to practice in order to fulfill the Sustainable Development goals proposed for Agenda 2030. It is a research-based, open, innovation-driven infrastructure, which strategically responds to this challenge by developing the conditions for entrepreneurial solutions, products and services supporting viable, integrated and participative urban regeneration. The intention is to establish this heritage-led cultural entrepreneurship urban regeneration paradigm as a powerful tool to turn urban areas experiencing decay and abandonment into sustainable development hubs of entrepreneurship and social and cultural integration. Key domains to address include social innovation, cultural entrepreneurship, skill training, employability, well-being and the social and cultural integration issues. The proposed framework will be implemented as part of an Erasmus +, Adult Education-funded research project, entitled Cultural and Arts Entrepreneurship in Adult Education (CREATION). The project will run from November 2019 until October 2021 and seeks to address the gap in the field of theory, pedagogy and practice on cultural entrepreneurship, in particular with regards to the training of women entrepreneurs from diverse backgrounds.

1.2 Rationale

This research relates to significant local and global imperatives and challenges at the crossroads of lifelong learning and informal education for social design, innovation and entrepreneurship. Our fast-paced world requires reconsideration of the conditions to foster critical skills, such as problem-solving, reflection, creativity, critical thinking, learning to learn, risk-taking, collaboration, and entrepreneurship, essential to the adaptive capacity future job seekers need [4].

Education should be the means through which society overcomes the digital divide's challenges, gaps, and barriers, information flow imbalances, growing economic and social inequality, religious, ethnic and cultural divides, labor market disruption and ecological pressures [5]. While several initiatives address new ways of learning and new organizational forms work to transform education, including the OECD's Education 2030 project [6], formal education remains somewhat impervious to society's evolving challenges. The European Commission Overview of Employment and Social Developments in Europe in 2015 [7] revealed that "the lack of entrepreneurship education remains a significant bottleneck to stimulating self-employment and entrepreneurship in the EU". The 2016 EURYDICE report on entrepreneurship education concluded that the uptake of entrepreneurship education in the EU is still behind, and several sociocultural obstacles constrain the development of entrepreneurship and self-employment [8]. In America, immigrants are much more likely to start businesses than the U.S.-born [9];

however, 92% of venture capital-backed U.S companies have male founders, of which 87% are white [10].

Throughout Europe and the US, there have been numerous attempts at the adaptive development of tangible and intangible cultural heritage, viewed as a non-renewable resource and a catalyst for bottom-up, endogenous sustainable development through contribution to well-being, job creation and social cohesion [2, 11]. Still, certain socio-cultural groups are not sufficiently integrated in cultural heritage experiences [12].

As few people experience educational empowerment through conventional schooling alone [13], the concept of local learning ecosystems is gaining momentum worldwide in an attempt to radically transform education to enable all citizens to become future-ready. Katherine Prince from KnowledgeWorks [13] stresses the need "to design intentionally for a vibrant learning ecosystem, otherwise we risk creating a fractured landscape, in which only privileged learners have access to learning that adapts to and meets their needs."

Our standpoint is that informal education provides more promise to design for social change and sustainability through addressing the unexplored potential in local learning ecosystems that unfold in informal, community-led co-working spaces (CLCSs), usually not-for profit ventures/hubs that accommodate creatives. The ECAS framework will offer a concrete manifestation of transforming theory to practice to fulfil Agenda 2030's SDGs [6]. It is innovative as it bridges a gap between the conceptual framework and practical implementation to test its feasibility.

Despite substantial literature on the learning ecosystems concept, there has been neither a specific pedagogical framework for developing and evaluating local learning ecosystems nor an accessible online practice guide [13]. Furthermore, empirical research on real-world learning examples is lacking, especially in relation to the changes in and around ecosystems for learners and providers [13].

It is anticipated that social design for heritage-led regeneration will be advanced and improved in ECAS through empowering:

a) Adult educators and community facilitators

b) Disadvantaged/marginalised groups

c) Organisations that facilitate informal learning

This research addresses how such ecosystems can be co-designed, implemented, and evaluated to include disadvantaged and underrepresented groups, such as minorities, women, migrants, refugees and asylum seekers, to empower them as lifelong learners and change-makers. The research also addresses inclusive local learning ecosystems' barriers and enablers, as proposed in a recent WISE report (Hannon et al., 2019). We seek to demonstrate how real-world local learning ecosystems can present an inclusive and open instructional paradigm that improves design for social change, innovation and entrepreneurship in practice through the educational framework, conditions, and support mechanisms developed (see Fig. 1).

1.3 Research Objectives

The intention of the ECAS framework is to establish this new heritage-led cultural entrepreneurship urban regeneration paradigm as a powerful tool to turn urban areas experiencing decay and abandonment into sustainable development hubs of

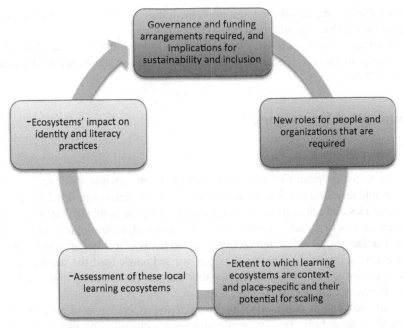

Fig. 1. Questions to explore local learning ecosystems' barriers and enablers. Adapted by Hannon et al. [13].

entrepreneurship and social and cultural integration, through targeting the areas of social innovation, cultural entrepreneurship, skill training, employability, well-being and social and cultural integration issues. The specific objectives to be pursued are:

- To provide evidence-based systematic evaluation of the economic, social, cultural and environmental impacts of integrated urban regeneration practices drawing on entrepreneurial solutions, stressing the significance of heritage-led solutions to sustainability and growth; (OBJ1)
- To provide EU-wide participatory policy guidelines to overcome existing cultural, social, economic, institutional, legal, regulatory and administrative barriers and bottlenecks for cultural heritage systemic urban regeneration entrepreneurial approaches, integrating local people's voices and respecting the identity of historic urban areas and cultural landscapes; (OBJ2)
- To develop, implement and evaluate innovative urban regeneration governance models and a set of evidence-based, participative, usable, scalable and replicable decision support evaluation intelligent system tools to improve policy and management options/choices on systemic urban regeneration through cultural entrepreneurship, in line with the circular economy; (OBJ3)
- To contribute to the creation of new jobs through capacity building and training in the circular economy through heritage-led solutions and services, targeting underrepresented groups in particular, such as women, migrants and refugees and ethnic minorities; (OBJ4)

- To contribute to the monitoring and implementation of SDGs, in particular SDG11 and the New Urban Agenda; (OBJ5)
- To consolidate the role of cultural heritage as the fourth pillar of sustainable development and contributor to economic growth, social inclusion and sustainability in urban areas. (OBJ6)

2 Conceptual Framework

2.1 Design Approach

According to a European Commission report [14], any attempt to design for social change should take into consideration the complexity of 'inter-connected ecosystems', such as attitudes and relevant cross-disciplinary knowledge domains. Factors identified include awareness of social, personal, economic, cultural, technological, physiological and political factors, as well as interaction with the areas of technology and behavioural and economic sciences. In a previous paper, we acknowledged the need to consider also the knowledge of tools and strategies that support participatory and collaborative solution-focused strategies [15].

Towards this end, it is important to consider the aspect of 'resilience' in relation to social innovation [16]. This 'systemic approach', identified by the Waterloo Institute for Social Innovation and Resilience [16], acknowledges how emergent needs are often adapted to existing systems [17]. The intention in ECAS is to develop a circular, design-led approach that incorporates understanding of a 'think like a system, act like an entrepreneur approach', following a design thinking logic akin to the double diamond proposed by Conway, Masters and Thorod [18]. In this conceptualization, the first diamond is about the problem discovery and understanding systemic conditions. The second diamond is about understanding how to act opportunistically like an entrepreneur to achieve change. Specific emphasis is put first on the stages of learning ecosystem development and second on the impact of learning ecosystems on existing learning provision [13]. The key principles of sustainability, namely environmental, social and economic, will be explored alongside pillars of knowledge-based urban sustainable development: socio-cultural development, urban development, economic development, sustainability capacity and organising capacity (see Fig. 2).

2.2 ECAS Theoretical Synergies

Central to the ECAS framework is the understanding of the importance to design for and with local learning ecosystems in mind. This local learning ecosystem approach allows connections across formal, informal and everyday learning [19]. Simply put, learning ecosystems comprise diverse provider combinations (schools, businesses, community organisations and government agencies), creating new learning opportunities and pathways to success [13]. Of essence are the cultural geographies of the place, the patterns and interactions of human culture, both material and non-material, in relation to the natural environment and the human organisation of space. The ECAS conceptual framework draws on sociocultural and holistic conceptualisations of pedagogy as cultural

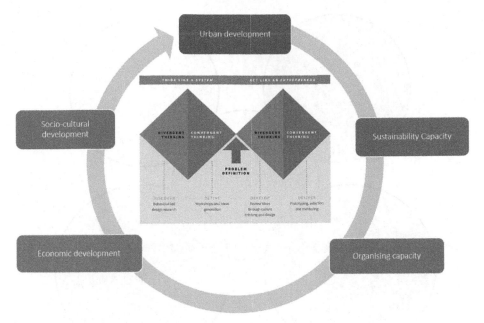

Fig. 2. ECAS development cycle

intervention in human development. In every community, different cultural factors and interactions act as cultural assets—material, immaterial, emotional or even spiritual—to form creative cultural clusters [20]. The aspiration is to establish an ecosystem framework that nurtures cultural entrepreneurship (CE) 3.0. The term CE 3.0 relates to 'cultural making' or the extent to which culture is both a medium (a 'deploying') and outcome (a 'making') of entrepreneurial action [19].

Interweaved in the ECAS ecosystem are the creative synergies of co-creation and capacity building through overlapping learning ecologies at place (see Fig. 3). The intention in the ECAS is to create hubs of entrepreneurship in community-led coworking spaces (hereafter CLCSs) as not-for profit ventures that accommodate different creatives in an informal and more community-driven type of coworking space.

These learning ecologies are brought to life in virtual or physical affinity spaces [21], acting as CLCSs. Affinity spaces are social learning spaces where people interact and share ideas based on common interests, endeavours, goals or practices, irrespective of race, gender, age, disability or social class [22]. To nurture learning that facilitates flexible, "multi-skilled profiles" and "multi-contextual learning practices" [23], we refer to multiliteracies and embodied learning theories. Multiliteracies' framework of thought [24, 25] acknowledges the complexities of practices, modes, technologies and languages that literate people need to engage in the contemporary world as they navigate changes every day [26].

Embodiment is often defined as "how culture gets under the skin" [27]. As noted by Csordas [28]: "If embodiment is an existential condition in which the body is the subjective source or inter-subjective ground of experience, then studies under the rubric of embodiment are not about the body per se. Instead they are about culture and experience

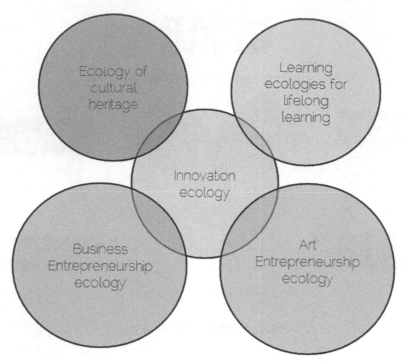

Fig. 3. Ecological synergies in the ECAS

insofar as these can be understood from the standpoint of bodily being-in-the-world. Also of interest here is enacted embodiment. The most successful projects place emphasis on the participants' development, the creative processes and the artistic outcomes" [29].

Embodied learning relates to multiliteracies discourse as a theory which emphasises the use of the whole body in educational practice [30]. This research explores in particular a novel concept, namely "embodied entrepreneurial identity", proposed by Kasperova and Kitching [31]. Entrepreneurial identity refers to a distinct set of meanings, attitudes and beliefs, attributes and subjective evaluations of behaviour, which define an entrepreneur [32]. We assert that to develop inclusive local learning ecosystems such as ECAS it is crucial to consider the whole body and embodied non-linguistic practices, such as movement, posture, gestures and facial expressions in the formation of identity [33]. Interestingly though, the entrepreneur in entrepreneurship education is in fact usually disembodied, as a result of gendered stereotypes [34]. Aspiring to empower individuals belonging to diverse communities as emergent entrepreneurs, we recognise how they potentially possess particular embodied properties and powers, crucial for understanding identity and action.

3   ECAS Infrastructure

The ambition of the ECAS framework is to go beyond the current state of the art and provide a transdisciplinary forum for knowledge sharing, promoting substantial coordinated and balanced research and innovation cooperation in relation to urban regeneration. To substantiate the ECAS framework, a particular infrastructure is essential. Some important directions include to:

a) Strengthen the literature on the added value of cultural heritage in sustainable urban development [35] with multidimensional indicators for the impact (ECAS Knowledge Repository)
b) Develop open innovation tools for heritage-led urban regeneration decision making, which could provide incentives to mobilise investments in the sector leading to the emergence of a global market for heritage-led innovative solutions and services (ECAS Decision Path)
c) Develop new business and governance models for a dedicated fast-track acceleration programme for start-uppers and individuals (ECAS Cycle)
d) Establish long-term cross-border collaborations and sharing of knowledge, formal and informal, on heritage-led integrated urban regeneration (ECAS Knowledge Society)
e) Bridge the gap on the characteristics of CLCSs through empirical research during the implementation of the ECAS framework.

The ECAS Repository, an online platform, will support the local learning ecosystems through an open access tool, the ECAS Path. Building on previous sectorial research, the ECAS Path is a Decision Support System (DSS), which makes use of predictive applications (Intelligent Analytics) to process large amounts of information in real-time that will run both in the Cloud and on the premises, using Agile Scrum Methodology that will integrate into a systemic tool a set of specific planning, design, economic and multi-criteria analysis indicators able to support decision-makers in urban regeneration management choices and design choices. The intention is to develop, implement and evaluate the ECAS Path in pilot areas and merge real-time analytical processing with on-the-spot decision making. Geographical Information System (GIS) and remote sensing techniques can supplement the software as a decision support tool for planning inclusive cultural management, research and practice (implementation of cultural equity plans).

The ECAS Repository will also feature:

a) Analysis of gaps and conflicts in nurturing local learning ecosystems through the ECAS Cycle, in particular for diverse audiences.

b) The ECAS Framework with real-time implementation examples (ongoing projects).

c) The ECAS Toolkit on the go; the design principles for implementing the ECAS framework and evaluating the programmes.

d) The ECAS Courses as practical guidelines and resources for community practitioners and educators.

e) An online network of ECAS-makers to enable virtual connection and cooperation.

4   Concluding Remarks

The aspiration of the ECAS framework is to go beyond the current state of the art and provide a transdisciplinary paradigm for knowledge sharing, promoting substantial coordinated and balanced research and innovation cooperation in relation to urban regeneration. The innovation potential lies in three pillars:

a) The evidence-based leveraging practices for integrated sustainable urban regeneration through predictive artificial intelligence systems, such as the ECAS Path. This will be continuously developed and updated, so it can lead to a new window of opportunities for market opportunities to promote a global market for heritage-led innovative solutions and services.

b) A common framework for Cultural and Creative Entrepreneurial Competences and the Indicators on Entrepreneurial Learning and Competence (ECAS Knowledge Society) to set the foundations for a new generation of entrepreneurs.

c) The introduction of innovative urban regeneration governance models (such as the ECAS CYCLE).

This paper aimed to introduce the ECAS framework as an ecological model of social design. In comparison to other frameworks such as Triple Helix for Creative Entrepreneurship (De Miranda et al., 2009) [36], ECAS is different in that it provides the theoretical backdrop to support practice. The implementation of ECAS will be pursued through the established Consortium of the CREATION project, consisting of seven partners from across Europe (Portugal, Italy, Greece, Cyprus, Ireland and Germany), including higher education institutions, NGOs and SMEs. The findings from the first implementation cycle will be discussed following the first year of the project, in November 2020. There is specific provision for transnational project meetings, intellectual outputs, learning activities and multiplier events to occur over the course of the two years of the project implementation.

References

1. Urban Culture and Heritage: UNESCO. Habitat III Issue Papers **4**, 1–8 (2015)
2. UNESCO Global Report: Culture: urban future; global report on culture for sustainable urban development (2016)
3. Avdikos, V., Iliopoulou, E.: Community-led coworking spaces: from colocation to collaboration and collectivization. In: Rosalind, G., Tarek, V., Pratt, A. (eds.) Creative Hubs in Question, Place, Space and Work in the Creative Economy, pp. 111–129. Dynamics of Virtual Work, Palgrave McMillan (2019)
4. Savva, S.: Multiliteracies Dynamic Affinity Spaces: Analysing the Potential of a New Framework to Educate for Knowmad Society. In: Moravec, J. (ed.) Emerging Education Futures. Education Futures, US (2019)
5. Center for Global Education: Investing in Knowledge Sharing to Advance SDG 4. Center for Global Education at Asia Society, Results for Development, Teach For All, The Boston Consulting Group, and World Innovation Summit for Education (2018). https://asiasociety.org/education/events/accelerating-progress-education-invest ing-knowledge-sharing-advance-sdg-4. Accessed 21 July 2019

6. OECD: The future of education and skills Education 2030. The future we want. OECD series (2018). https://www.oecd.org/education/2030/E2030%20Position%20Paper%20(05.04.2018).pdf. Accessed 1 June 2019

7. ESDE Report: Employment and Social Developments in Europe 2015. European Commission Directorate-General for Employment, Social Affairs and Inclusion (2015)

8. European Commission/EACEA/Eurydice. Entrepreneurship Education at School in Europe. Eurydice Report. Publications Office of the European Union, Luxembourg (2016)

9. Anderson, S.: NFAP Policy Brief: March 2016 Immigrants and Billion Dollar Startups. National Foundation for American Policy. http://nfap.com/wp-content/uploads/2016/03/Immigrants-and-Billion-Dollar-Startups.NFAP-Policy-Brief.March-2016.pdf. Accessed 16 June 2019

10. McCauley, A.: New Orleans trying to find its own startup identity at Entrepreneur Week. https://www.theadvocate.com/new_orleans/news/business/article_4209c73e-4cc7-11e9-9727-7b477bfb2188.html. Accessed 23 June 2019

11. Ilmonen, K.: The Role of Culture in Regional Develoment Work – changes and tensions. University of Jyvaskyla, Kokkola University Consortium Chydenius (2009)

12. Smith-Hunter, A.E., Boyd, L.R.: Applying theories of entrepreneurship to a comparative analysis of white and minority women business owners. Women Manag. Rev. **19**(1), 18–28 (2004)

13. Hannon, V., Thomas, L., Ward, S., Beresford, T.: Local Learning Ecosystems: Emerging Models. WISE report series in Partnership with Innovation Unit. https://drive.google.com/file/d/1Lp6q1iKTqKeLobwhsxKxGMBgNk8dhOyZ/view. Accessed 27 June 2019

14. Thomson, M., Koskinen, T.: Design for growth & prosperity. Report and Recommendations of the European Design Leadership Board, DG Enterprise and Industry of the European Commission (2012)

15. Souleles, N., Ferreira, A.M., Savva, S.: Threshold concepts and design for social change. In: Goossens R., Murata A. (eds.) Advances in Social and Occupational Ergonomics. AHFE 2019. Advances in Intelligent Systems and Computing, vol. 970, pp. 80–89. Springer, Cham (2020)

16. Murray, R., Caulier-Grice, J., Mulgan, G.: The Open Book of Social Innovation, Social Innovator Series: Ways to Design, Develop and Grow Social Innovation, NESTA & Young Foundation (2010)

17. Ferreira, A.M., Souleles, N., Savva, S.: Social design, innovation and ergonomics: reflections on education, transdisciplinarity and new blurred models for sustainable social change. In: Goossens, R., Murata, A. (eds) Advances in Social and Occupational Ergonomics. AHFE 2019. Advances in Intelligent Systems and Computing, vol 970. Springer, Cham (2020)

18. Conway, R., Masters, J., Thorod, J.: From Design Thinking to Systems Change. How to invest in innovation for social impact. RSA Action and Research Centre (2017)

19. Bevan, B.: STEM Learning: Ecologies Relevant, Responsive, and Connected. http://csl.nsta.org/2016/03/stem-learning-ecologies/. Accessed 23 June 2019

20. Lee, B.M.: Cultural Asset based Rehabitation and Regional Development. Paper presented at 2016 International Conference on "Innovation, Clusters & Economic Performance" 7th July 2016. https://www.academia.edu/32386132/Cultural_Asset_based_Rehabitation_and_Regional_Development. Accessed 08 Jan 2019

21. Gehman, J., Soublière, J.E.: Cultural entrepreneurship: from making culture to cultural making. Innovation **19**(1), 61–73. https://doi.org/10.1080/14479338.2016.1268521. Accessed 11 Aug 2019

22. Gee, J.P.: Situated Language and Learning: A Critique of Traditional Schooling. Routledge, London (2004)

23. Cobo, C.: Skills and competencies for knowmadic workers. In: Moravec, J. (ed.) Knowmad Society, pp. 57–88. Education Futures (2013)

24. New London Group, NLG.: A pedagogy of multiliteracies: designing social futures. Harvard Educ. Rev. **66**(1), 60–92 (1996). Massachusetts
25. New London Group, NLG.: A pedagogy of multiliteracies: designing social futures. In: Cope, B., Kalantzis, M. (eds) Multiliteracies: Literacy Learning and the Design of Social Futures, pp. 182–202. Macmillan, Melbourne (2000)
26. Clark, K.R.: Charting transformative practice: critical multiliteracies via informal learning design. UC San Diego Electronic Theses and Dissertations (2007)
27. Worthman, C.M., Costello, E.J.: Tracking biocultural pathways in population health: the value of biomarkers. Ann. Hum. Biol. **36**(3), 281–297. https://doi.org/10.1080/030144609 02832934. Accessed 19 June 2019
28. Csordas, T.J.: Embodiment and cultural phenomenology. In: Weiss, G., Haber, H. (eds.) Perspectives on Embodiment, pp. 143–162. Routledge, New York (1999)
29. Arts Victoria, Vic Health, Castanet Making: Art With Communities – A Work Guide, Victoria https://creative.vic.gov.au/__data/assets/word_doc/0019/57070/Community_Partne rships_Workguide_plaintext.docx. Accessed 14 Aug 2019
30. Skulmowski, A., Rey, G.D.: Embodied learning: introducing a taxonomy based on bodily engagement and task integration. Cognitive Research: Principles and Implications **3**(6), https://doi.org/10.1186/s41235-018-0092-9. Accessed 19 June 2019
31. Kašperová, E., Kitching, J.: Embodying entrepreneurial identity. Int. Journal of Entrepreneurial Behaviour and Research **20**(5), 438–452 (2014)
32. Hoang, H., Gimeno, J.: Entrepreneurial Identity. Wiley Encyclopedia of Management, pp. 1–6. https://doi.org/10.1002/9781118785317.weom030052. Accessed 29 May 2019
33. Shepherd, D.A., Patzelt, H.: Entrepreneurial Cognition. Exploring the Mindset of Entrepreneurs. Palgrave Macmillan, Cham. https://link.springer.com/content/pdf/10.1007% 2F978-3-319-71782-1.pdf. Accessed 22 June 2019
34. Myllyaho, A.H.: Provoking Entrepreneurial Thinking – Gendered Embodiment and Entrepreneurship Education. Presentation at YKTT 2017. https://www.oulu.fi/sites/default/ files/192/Esitys_yktt_Anu%20HarjuMyllyaho.pdf. Accessed 26 June 2019
35. Nocca, F.: The Role of Cultural Heritage in Sustainable Development: Multidimensional Indicators as Decision-Making Tool. Sustainability 2017 **9**(10), 1882, https://doi.org/10.3390/ su9101882. Accessed 29 June 2019
36. De Miranda, P.C, Alberto, J., Aranha, S., Zardo, J.: Creativity: people, environment and culture, the key elements in its understanding and interpretation. Sci. Public Policy **36**(7), 523–535 (2009). https://doi.org/10.3152/030234209x465552. Accessed 21 Oct 2019

Short Papers

The Deadly Gamification Challenge of #BlueWhale

Selcen Ozturkcan[✉] [iD]

Linnaeus University, Kalmar 391 82, Sweden
selcen.ozturkcan@lnu.se

Abstract. This manuscript reviews the past literature on the Blue Whale Challenge, which is known to be a dangerous gamification activity that spreads on social media to target vulnerable teenagers. It aims to nurture workshop discussion for collaborative future research directions on the matter.

Keywords: Bluewhale · Deadly gamification · Bluewhalechallenge · #bwc

1 Introduction

1.1 A Subsection Sample

Recently, the Blue Whale Challenge, also referred to as the Blue Whale Game, attracted public attention due to much unfortunate news about teenagers harming themselves as they engage with the so-called game all across the world [1, 2]. Even though known as a game, it is reported to involve a series of self-harming tasks [3] that often propagate via social media for completion in 50 days [4]. Amongst these tasks, the latest final task is to commit suicide [5, 6]. Victims of the disseminated challenge are frequently teenagers and young adults; therefore, concerned families demand the topic to treated as that of a severe public health issue [7]. To the author's awareness, the blue whale challenge is the only gamification, where completion demands its player to end his/her life [8]. This workshop proposal aims at providing a literature review of the past research on blue whale challenge in an attempt to develop a discussion of the topic for future research.

2 Literature Review

Initially spread on the Russian social networking website named VKontakte (VK), Blue Whale Challenge is reported to have spread to Twitter, Instagram, Facebook, Reddit as well as other social networks [5]. Philipp Budeikin, who was 21 years old when he got arrested in November 2016 with charges for inciting teenagers to suicide, is known as the creator of the Blue Whale Challenge told Russian media that "there are people, and then there is biodegradable waste. I was cleansing our society of such

A. Brooks and E. I. Brooks (Eds.): ArtsIT 2019/DLI 2019, LNICST 328, pp. 785–787, 2020.
https://doi.org/10.1007/978-3-030-53294-9

people. Sometimes I start to think that it is wrong, but in the end, I had the feeling I was doing the right thing" [9].

The pending question is, how is the 'game' still flourishing when the original curators are in jail. It appears that there are numerous misconceptions about the Blue Whale Challenge, where one of them is considering that it is only a game available on some website or an app. Blue Whale Challenge is not an application, but thrives on social media due to those involved in the hunting of vulnerable future victims to direct them with gamified self-harming 'tasks.' An analysis of social media data groups - the different types of users involved in the game as potential victims, propagators or pretentious curators, and hashtag hijackers [5].

Medical literature remains short in presenting the Blue Whale Challenge related cases that the media extensively covers [1]. In a recent article, a detailed report of the consultation provided in a health care institution with regards to an admitted boy that carried out Blue Whale Game resembling tasks that he accessed through a mobile phone application [1]. Accordingly, the boy received a link through his social media account. Upon clicking, an application with a big fish icon installed on this mobile phone. Early tasks included activities such as clapping twice and saying out loud that he was powerful. The following tasks, though, turned out demanding hurtful actions such as carving F57 on his forearm with a pointed object. The father, who was informed about the Blue Whale Challenge from cases appearing in media, realized the newly installed app in the boy's mobile phone, and immediately deleted it. Along the same lines, the father took the boy to a behavioral addiction clinic for diagnosis and treatment of any psychological conditions. The child was found healthy, with no unusual behavior. He was someone who prefers to be by himself as much as possible. Yet, there were no observed changes to his behavior during his involvement with the game. The boy revealed that it was his curiosity that kept him engaged with the tasks, though he was aware of the link of the Blue Whale Challenge with suicidal cases.

Another similar article reports a 17 years old boy admitted to the Gauhati Medical College Hospital in India when his class teacher noted a scar depicting a fish carved on his left forearm skin [3]. Along the same lines, other past research on the topic refers to an ultimate brainwash of the players' minds in order to lead them towards self-harm via tasks such as "*waking up at odd hours, listening to psychedelic music, watching scary videos and inflicting cuts, and wounds on their bodies*" [5].

3   Conclusion

Despite its importance to the public and families, and the widespread coverage of the unfortunate cases in media, Blue Whale Challenge has not yet attracted sufficient interest from scholars of digitalization. Though it is known as a game, it truly is gamification ran by curators, who can be just any individual with bad intentions against vulnerable teenagers. It appears that the societal impact of researching the topic could be beyond measurability as understanding its dynamics would provide both families and policymakers with opportunities to prevent its further dissemination, hence bears the possibility of saving future lives. Therefore, future research is needed.

References

1. Balhara, Y.P.S., Bhargava, R., Pakhre, A., Bhati, N.: The "Blue Whale Challenge": The first report on a consultation from a health care setting for carrying out "tasks" accessed through a mobile phone application. Asia Pac. Pyschiatry **10**(3), (2018)
2. Sousa, D.F.d., Filho, J.o.d.D.Q., Cavalcanti, R.d.C.P.B., Santos, A.B.d., Neto, M.L.R.: The impact of the 'Blue Whale' game in the rates of suicide: Short psychological analysis of the phenomenon. Int. J. Soc. Psychiatry **63**(8), 796–797 (2017)
3. Narayan, R., Das, B., Das, S., Bhandari, S.S.: The depressed boy who accepted "Blue Whale Challenge". Indian J. Psychiatry **61**(1), 105–106 (2019)
4. Yılmaz, M., Candan, F.: Oyun Sanal İntihar Gerçek: "The Blue Whale Challange/Mavi Balina" Oyunu Üzerinden Kurulan İletişimin Neden Olduğu İntiharlar Üzerine Kuramsal Bir Değerlendirme. Akdeniz Üniversitesi İletişim Fakültesi Dergisi **30**, 270–283 (2018)
5. Khattar, A., Dabas, K., Gupta, K., Chopra, S., Kumaraguru, P.: White or Blue, the Whale gets its Vengeance: A Social Media Analysis of the Blue Whale Challenge. arXiv:1801.05588 (2018)
6. Volkova, I., Kadyrova, S., Rastorgueva, N., Algavi, L.: From the silent house meme to the blue whale-game: the storyworld's transformation. In: 4th International Multidisciplinary Scientific Conference on Social Sciences and Arts SGEM, pp. 253–0260 (2017)
7. Kumar, A., Pandey, S.N., Pareek, V., Faiq, M.A., Khan, N.I., Sharma, V.: Psychobiological determinants of 'Blue Whale Suicide Challenge' victimization: A proposition for the agency mediated mental health risk in new media age. PsyArVix 1–20 (2017)
8. Mukhra, R., Baryah, N., Krishan, K., Kanchan, T.: Blue whale challenge: a game or crime? Sci. Eng. Ethics **25**(1), 285–291 (2019)
9. BBC News. https://www.bbc.com/news/blogs-trending-46505722. Accessed 8 Aug 2019

Author Index

Printed in the United States
By Bookmasters